COMBINED EDITION

THESE UNITED STATES

The Questions of Our Past

Sixth Edition

Irwin Unger

New York University

Historical Portraits and Documents by Debi Unger

Prentice Hall
Upper Saddle River, New Jersey 07458

Library of Congress Cataloging-in-Publication Data

Unger, Irwin,
    These United States: the questions of our past/Irwin Unger:
  historical portraits and documents by Debi Unger. —6th, combined ed.
    p.   cm.
  Includes bibliographical references and index.
  ISBN 0–13–174079-2
    1. United States—History.   I. Unger, Debi,   II. Title
E178.1.U54 1995 IN PROCESS
973—dc20   94–43671
                                                  CIP

Project manager: Virginia M. Livsey
Cover and interior design: Lisa Delgado
Acquisitions editor: Sally Constable
Editorial director: Charlyce Jones Owen
Editorial assistants: Tamara Mann and Wyzie-Yvonne Thrower
Copy editor: James Tully
Marketing manager: Alison Pendergast
Photo researchers: Joelle Burrows and Page Poore
Photo editor: Lorinda Morris-Nantz
Cover art: Jasper Johns, "Map" (1961)
         Oil on canvas, 6' 6" X 10' 3/8".
         The Museum of Modern Art, New York,
         Gift of Mr. and Mrs. Robert C. Scull.
         Photograph © 1994 The Museum of Modern Art,
         New York.

To Rita and Mickey, Libby and Arnie,
Phyllis and Jerry, and Norma and David—once more

©1995, 1992, 1989, 1986, 1982, 1978 by Prentice-Hall, Inc.
A Simon & Schuster Company
Upper Saddle River, New Jersey 07458

Printed in the United States of America
10 9 8 7 6 5 4

ISBN 0-13-174079-2

Prentice-Hall International (UK) Limited, *London*
Prentice-Hall of Australia Pty. Limited, *Sydney*
Prentice-Hall Canada Inc., *Toronto*
Prentice-Hall Hispanoamericana, S.A., *Mexico*
Prentice-Hall of India Private Limited, *New Delhi*
Prentice-Hall of Japan, Inc., *Tokyo*
Simon & Schuster Asia Pte. Ltd., *Singapore*
Editora Prentice-Hall do Brasil, Ltda., *Rio de Janeiro*

CONTENTS

23 PROGRESSIVISM

What Were Its Roots and What Were Its Accomplishments?   628

24 WORLD WAR I

Idealism, National Interest, or Neutral Rights?   660

25 THE TWENTIES

Happy Adolescence or Decade of Stress?   688

26 THE NEW DEAL

Too Far or Not Far Enough?   716

27 WORLD WAR II

Blunder or Decision in the National Interest?   **748**

28 POSTWAR AMERICA

Why So Security Conscious?   **780**

29 THE DISSENTING SIXTIES

Why Protest in the "Great Society"?   **816**

30 THE UNCERTAIN SEVENTIES

Why Did the Right Fail?   **850**

31   THE "REAGAN REVOLUTION"

32   A DIFFERENT AMERICA?

APPENDIX   959

PHOTO CREDITS   991

INDEX   993

MAPS

PREFACE

Each new edition of a text such as this represents a vote of confidence by readers and users of the previous one. It is also an opportunity for the author to improve his work.

These United States, Sixth Edition, reflects that opportunity. The book's basic plan remains the same. First, unlike most introductory texts, it still has a single author and speaks in a single voice. I hope readers will agree that there is an advantage to reading a book by a real, single person, rather than a committee. Second, the text is still organized around significant questions, one per chapter, each designed to challenge students to consider the complexity of the past. The plan, I believe, makes the learning of history a quest, an exploration, rather than the passive absorption of a fixed body of facts. Yet at the same time, as in the past, the facts are all there. *These United States* covers all the bases and provides all the "coverage" of the standard text.

The word "standard" here does not mean old-fashioned, however. Though *These United States* discusses political, diplomatic, and military events, it also covers—and extensively—social, cultural, and economic events and currents. It deals not only with events, moreover, but also with people. Each chapter has a "Historical Portrait" and a "Historical Document" in the words of some representative figure of the period discussed in the chapter. And these people are not only "great men." I recognize and applaud the expansion of the "canon" to include all the wonderful diversity of the American people. In these readings, as well as in the text itself, the reader will find women as well as men, people of color as well as whites, youths as well as adults, writers, artists, and musicians as well as politicians and diplomats. These people and these topics are not "tacked on"; they are integrated with the entire text.

The Sixth Edition therefore retains and expands on many of the features of its predecessors. But it contains significant changes as well. I have reviewed the entire manuscript line by line, correcting errors and smoothing stylistic bumps. I have added much new material. The last chapter of Volume II moves the story forward to include the early months of the Clinton administration. A new feature of several chapters focuses on "everyday life" in America. It describes how ordinary people got through their day, their week, their year. I have been strongly impressed with the environmental perspective on the past and have written, or rewritten, several sections to take into account the natural environment Americans encountered and their responses to it, good and bad. I have also expanded sections describing the environmental movement itself. The Sixth Edition, finally, has several new Historical Portraits by Debi Unger.

Here, then, is the Sixth Edition of *These United States*. I hope that, like its precursors, it meets with favor among faculty and students, serving both as a successful teaching instrument and an interesting and absorbing introduction to the American past.

Irwin Unger
Department of History
New York University

★ ACKNOWLEDGMENTS ★

Every author incurs debts in writing or revising a book. I have been the recipient of particularly generous help and advice and I should like to acknowledge it here.

First, I wish to thank a group of scholars and teachers who read and evaluated the fifth edition to help me correct mistakes in, and improve the quality of, the sixth. These include: James F. Hilgenburg, Jr., of Glenville State College; Johanna Hume of Alvin Community College; Robert G. Fricke of West Valley College; Steve Schuster of Brookhaven College; Kenny Brown of the University of Central Oklahoma; Paul Lucas of Indiana University; and last, but assuredly not least, Irving Katz, also of Indiana University. I did not always accept their thoughtful advice, but I always took it seriously.

At Prentice Hall I would like to thank Steve Dalphin for his continued faith in *These United States* and his efforts on its behalf. Virginia Livsey, of the College Book Editorial-Production Department, was a wonderfully efficient and cheerful editor and project manager. I also appreciate the keen eye and fine ear of James Tully, who read the entire manuscript and saved me from errors and infelicities.

Finally, I would like to thank Theresa McGrath of Howell, New Jersey, for expediting the taxing job of remounting text for revision and correction. Her help saved me much time and energy.

ABOUT THE AUTHOR

Pulitzer Prize winning historian Irwin Unger has been teaching American history for over twenty-five years on both coasts. Born and largely educated in New York, he has lived in California, Virginia, and Washington State. He is married to Debi Unger and they have five children, now all safely past their college years. Professor Unger formerly taught at California State University at Long Beach and the University of California at Davis. He now teaches at New York University, where he has been since 1966.

Professor Unger's professional interests have ranged widely within American history. He has written on Reconstruction, the Progressive Era, and on the 1960s. His first book, *The Greenback Era*, won a Pulitzer Prize in 1965. Since then he has written *The Movement* and (with Debi Unger) *The Vulnerable Years and Turning Point: 1968*. He is now completing a book on the Kennedy-Johnson Great Society. He also teaches a wide range of courses, including the introductory U.S. history survey, the Civil War and Reconstruction Era, the Gilded Age, U.S. economic history, and the United States during the 1960s.

Debi Unger is a former English teacher who is now a freelance writer. She often collaborates with her husband. Educated in New York, she has also lived in Indiana, Washington, Chicago, and California. She describes her professional relationship with her husband in classic business partnership terms: "He's the inside man; I'm the outside man."

THESE UNITED STATES

1 ★

THE NEW WORLD ENCOUNTERS THE OLD

Why 1492?

c. 38,000 B.C.	America's first settlers begin to cross a land bridge connecting Siberia and Alaska
986	Norwegian merchant Bjarni Herjulfsson becomes the first European to sight the mainland of North America
c. 1000	Leif Ericsson lands on "Vinland"
c. 1010–13	Thorfinn Karlsefni and others attempt to colonize Vinland
c. 1300	Venetian and Genoese merchants establish overland trade routes to the East
c. 1400	The invention of printing, advances in navigation and naval architecture, and the introduction of gunpowder increase possibilities for worldwide exploration by Europeans
1488	Bartolomeu Dias rounds Africa's Cape of Good Hope for the Portuguese crown
1492	Christopher Columbus lands on San Salvador in the Bahamas
1497	Henry VII of England sends John Cabot to find a short route to the Indies: Cabot reaches Newfoundland
1498	Vasco da Gama, Portuguese navigator, becomes the first European to reach India by sea around Africa
1519–22	Ferdinand Magellan's circumnavigation of the world proves that the Americas are new lands, not the Indies
1521	Hernando Cortés conquers the Aztec empire in Mexico for Spain
1523–28	France sends Giovanni da Verrazano to find a short route to the Indies; he explores the east coast of North America
1532	Francisco Pizarro conquers the Inca empire in Peru for Spain
1534	Jacques Cartier attempts to find a "northwest passage" to the Indies for France
1609	Henry Hudson establishes Dutch claim to the Hudson River region in his search for a northwest passage

Every schoolchild knows that Columbus "discovered" America in 1492. It is a "fact" firmly established in our national consciousness. Yet Columbus was not the discoverer of America, if by that statement we mean the first person to encounter the "New World," the two great continents that lie between Europe and Asia. At least two other groups stumbled on the Americas before Columbus. Sometime between 40,000 B.C. and 12,000 B.C. people from northeast Asia reached the New World from across the Pacific and settled the new lands. We call their descendants Indians, though many prefer to call them Native Americans. Then about A.D. 1000, Scandinavians from northern Europe called Norsemen touched North America coming from the east.

Given these earlier encounters, is there any special significance to that famous year 1492? Should we drop it from our list of crucial dates and substitute 40,000 B.C. or A.D. 1000? If we keep 1492, how do we justify it? Did Columbus's landing at San Salvador in the Caribbean have a greater impact on the world than the two earlier events, or does our traditional emphasis on it simply mark our Europe-centered biases? What did Columbus's discovery mean, both to those in the Old World of Europe, Asia, and Africa and to those already living in the Americas? To answer these questions let us look at the first discovery and its significance.

★ THE FIRST AMERICANS ★

The first Americans were migrants from eastern Siberia on the northern portion of the Asian mainland. Physically, they belonged to the same human stock as the modern Chinese, Japanese, and Koreans—a relationship suggested by the straight black hair, broad face, and high cheekbones of most modern American Indians. The migrants were a hunting, fishing, and food-gathering people who depended on roots, berries, seeds, fish, and game for food. As decreasing rainfall reduced these resources in Siberia, scholars conjecture, the native peoples gradually moved eastward seeking to keep alive. Today they would be stopped by the Bering Sea, but in that distant era we know that a land bridge joined Alaska in North America to Siberia. On the eastern side of this bridge the migrants probably found more abundant food supplies and a climate milder than in their homeland. Gradually they moved southward along various routes, and by the time Europeans arrived many thousands of years later, they had spread from just below the Arctic Ocean to Tierra del Fuego at the stormy southern tip of South America, and from the Atlantic to the Pacific. They had also increased enormously in numbers. From perhaps a few hundred or a few thousand original immigrants, by 1492 the Indian population of the Americas had swelled to over 50 million, a figure about equal to that of contemporary Europe. North of Mexico, in what is now present-day Canada and the United States, there were probably more than 9 million people.

The North American Setting. In North America the transplanted Asians encountered a magnificent expanse of territory. The continent stretched through about 70 degrees of latitude, from a few hundred miles below the North Pole almost to the equator. Excluding Alaska, the portion that would later become the United States was located in the most temperate part of the continent, from 49° to about 25° north latitude. This location did not preclude severe cold and heat at times but it did spare future Americans the extreme climates of many other countries. Few large nations of the world would enjoy the relatively mild temperatures and long growing seasons of the United States.

Though entirely within the temperate zone not all parts of the future United States were equally blessed by nature. The Atlantic and Gulf Coast regions were well watered and, influenced by the ocean, not subject to seasonal extremes of heat and cold. Beyond the 100th meridian, a line running through the middle of the Dakotas, Nebraska, Kansas, Oklahoma, and Texas, annual rainfall fell to under 20 inches a year, the amount needed for unaided agriculture. In this region, the Plains, the great north-south running Rocky Mountain chain created a "rain shadow" that partially blocked the moisture-bearing winds from the Pacific. The Plains consisted of a high plateau that became drier as the traveler moved westward. Still farther west, the intermountain region between the Rockies and the Sierras-Cascades—the Basin-Range—was an even drier zone that, at its southern edge, was true desert. Both Plains and Basin-Range, distant from the tempering oceans, experienced a more extreme climate than other regions of the continent. The variation between summer and winter was greater than on both coasts. Winters often brought blizzards and bitter cold; summers were often blazing hot.

Beyond the Sierra-Cascade chain was the mild Pacific Slope. In the north—the Pacific Northwest—winters were mild but rainy; summers dry and cool. Farther south, in California, the climate much resembled that of the Mediterranean, with hot dry summers and warm winters of moderate rainfall.

These major climatic features would profoundly influence the lives of all those who came to live in what would become the United States, whether from Asia, Europe, or Africa, whether they came early or late. Among the pre-1492 arrivals, climate and prevailing weather were especially important. Lacking the complex technology of modern societies, they were compelled to adapt to existing environmental realities that more technologically advanced groups could modify. Indians constructed a wide variety of dwellings to shelter themselves from the elements, but they also developed a greater personal tolerance to extremes of climate than peoples from the continents of Europe and Africa.

The natural resources of North America also molded the lives of the earliest arrivals. The eastern third of the continent was covered with dense forest. This was a mixture of evergreens—pine, spruce, fir, juniper, cedar—and broadleaf, deciduous trees—oak, beech, maple, ash, birch, hickory. The forests provided building materials and fuel for both those who came early and those who came late. Many of the deciduous trees also provided nuts and fruits.

The middle of the continent was dominated by grass, with trees confined primarily to river banks. The more humid eastern portion of this region, the Prairies, was covered with high grasses, like blue-stem. Farther west were low grasses, buffalo grass and the like. The vegetation of the Basin-Range region was drought-resistant sage, creosote, cactus, and grease wood. The Rocky Mountain region was forested, primarily with evergreens, as were the Sierras and Cascades of the Pacific Slope.

North America had some of the most fertile soil on earth. The forest soils of the East were relatively thin and soon lost their nutriments when used year after year to grow crops. But the soils that had developed beneath the grass, especially the prairie grass, were much deeper and richer and could stand greater abuse. In the Southwest, desert and near-desert soils were unfertile, but when water was applied by human intervention, these soils often proved capable of bearing good crops as well. Beneath the North American surface were minerals in great abundance. The Indians of the continent used no metal except for a little native copper found uncombined in ores. Their tools were made of stone and bone and abundant flint and quartz provided material for arrowheads, spear points, needles, knives, and hand axes. They also used various colored minerals for paints. But besides these, they left untapped the continent's vast deposits of coal, oil, gas, iron ore, copper, silver, lead, gold, zinc, and other minerals vital to an industrial society.

These early newcomers shared the continent with a multitude of other creatures. The forested Northeast sheltered fur-bearing animals: fox, wolves, bears, and beavers. Northeastern rivers ran with Atlantic salmon, sturgeon, and shad. Offshore were shallow regions—the Grand Banks and Georges Bank—where enormous schools of cod, flounder, whiting, and herring fed. It was said by some of the early Europeans that in the Newfoundland region the schools of cod were sometimes so thick in the waters that sailing vessels had difficulty making headway. The cold Atlantic waters also provided nutriment to lobsters and shellfish. The animal life of the warmer Southeast included millions of deer, opossums, wildcats, muskrats. The waters of the Chesapeake Bay provided a treasure-trove of shellfish.

The dominant animal of the Plains was the American bison, a large, shaggy, grass-eating hoofed creature that moved in giant herds across the interior continental grasslands. As late as 1830 observers estimated that 40 million "buffalo" grazed the interior Plains. The Plains were also home to a multitude of deer and, at the time of the first human inhabitants, herds of native wild horses. Fur-bearing animals also made the western mountains their home. Beaver built their dams along Rocky Mountain streams. Along the Pacific coast runs of silver salmon swelled the rivers each spring, while offshore, the playful sea otter feasted on shellfish and crabs. The bird population of the continent was abundant beyond belief. Eagles, hawks, vultures, turkeys, ducks, and every sort of songbird filled the air or scurried across the clearings. Passenger pigeons were so numerous—3 billion to 5 billion by one estimate—that their flight could darken the sky for hours at a time.

Ecologists today doubt that the environment of living things before humans arrived existed in a static, unchanging equilibrium. Many believe that the natural world is in constant flux. Climate shifts, earthquakes, lightning-set fires, floods, drought, and storms destroy plant and animal communities and constantly alter nature's balances. But most of these are slow acting and self-righting, they note. Humans are another case. They have done more to alter the natural environment of North America—and other continents—and in a shorter time, than any other agency.

What about the Indians? It used to be said that their hand rested very lightly on the physical environment. We are now not so sure. Some archaeologists and geographers believe the Indians distinctly modified the natural environment. In many places, especially in the upper Mississippi Valley, they set fires deliberately to clear land for crops and created many clearings in the forests. They were aggressive hunters who, some believe, killed off the native North American horse population. At least one Plains archaeological site, where hundreds of bison had been driven off a cliff by hunters, suggests that the Indians may have been just as potentially wasteful in their use of natural resources as the Europeans who came later. Still, when this is admitted, we must note that the Native American people in North America had neither the numbers nor the technology to exploit and change the continent's natural endowment as rigorously as their successors. Paleoecologists, students of the historical evolution of the environment, have recently shown that, while Indian occupation produced soil erosion and altered the existing forest cover of America, their impact was far exceeded by the Europeans who came later.

This then was the physical environment of the first Americans. As their numbers grew over the centuries the descendants of these Asian people diversified into many groups with distinct languages, cultures, and political and economic systems. By about 3000 B.C. some had begun to practice agriculture, with "maize" (corn), first developed from a grasslike native American plant, as their chief crop and the staple of their diet. They also grew tomatoes, squash, various kinds of beans, and, in South America, potatoes. Surpluses from agriculture transformed Indian life. Abundant food led to larger populations and also to more diverse societies. Not everyone was needed to produce food to sustain life, so classes of priests, warriors, artisans, and chiefs appeared. In the most fertile agricultural regions great civilizations arose with a command of technology, artistic sophistication, and political complexity comparable to the civilizations of Asia and Europe.

The Great Indian Civilizations. One of these Indian civilizations, that of the Mayas, built great ceremonial and administrative cities in the dense rain forests of Yucatán and Central America. The Mayas had neither a single ruler nor a unified state. Instead, each urban center was independent and governed by a group of priests. Mayan society was stratified, with sharp divisions of class and status among the people. It also possessed a culture of great sophistication: The Mayas alone among the American Indian peoples had a written language and books, and their mathematicians developed the idea of zero as a number place long before Europeans did. Mayan astronomers could calculate the cycles of the seasons and the times of eclipses as accurately as their Old World counterparts.

The Aztecs to the north, in central Mexico, borrowed much from their Mayan neighbors. But they were an even more warlike people and around A.D. 1300 established the core of a great and powerful empire on the site of what is now Mexico City. From there they extended their conquests over all of central Mexico, so that by the early 1500s the Aztec state ruled over 5 million inhabitants.

Aztec society, too, was stratified, but it was also centralized. At the head of the Aztec empire was a chief priest whose powerful authority enabled the Aztecs to conquer virtually all their enemies. In the course of many wars with their neighbors the Aztec rulers took thousands of prisoners and enormous quantities of feathered headdresses, jade jewelry, and beautiful gold and silver ornaments. The treasure went into the coffers of the chief priest and his nobles;

This is a reconstruction of what Cortés and his men saw when they arrived at "the great city of Mexico." The structure at the center of the plaza is the altar where prisoners were sacrificed to the Aztec gods.

the prisoners, by the thousands, were sacrificed by having their hearts cut out to appease the Aztec war god.

By the early 1500s Aztec wealth and power were at their height. When the Spaniards first entered the Valley of Mexico in 1519 after an overland march from the coast, they were awestruck by the splendors that the Aztec conquests—and the Aztecs' own ingenuity and skill—had produced:

> . . . When we saw so many cities and villages built in the water and other great towns on dry land and that straight level causeway going toward Mexico, we were amazed and said that it was like the enchantments they tell of in the legend of Amadis, on account of the great towers and pyramids and buildings rising from the water and all built of masonry. And some of our soldiers even asked whether the things that we saw were not a dream?

> Gazing on such wonderful sights we did not know what to say or whether what appeared before us was real; for on one side on the land, there were great cities and in the lake ever so many more, and the lake itself was crowded with canoes, and in the causeway there were many bridges at intervals, and in front of us stood the great City of Mexico, and we—we did not number four hundred soldiers.

The Incas of Peru, in the coastal mountains of South America, created an empire even larger than that of the Aztecs—including within its borders 7 million people at its height. Strong rulers like the Aztec priests to the north, the Inca emperors built fortresses on the Andes mountainsides and a network of roads that held their far-flung domain together. The Inca people were among the most skilled metallurgists of the time, making weapons, tools, and ornaments of gold, silver, copper, and bronze. The Inca privileged classes lived comfortably, but the sick and handicapped were also provided for by the government. Inca society has sometimes been compared to a modern social welfare state.

The Indians of North America. North of the great Indian civilizations were less complex, smaller scale cultures and societies. By 1492 there was a fairly substantial population in what is now the United States. In the past, scholars estimated that the Indian population only numbered about a million, but it now seems there may have been as many as 9 million. This population, however large, was anything but uniform. There were twelve different language groups in present-day United States, each embracing numerous in-

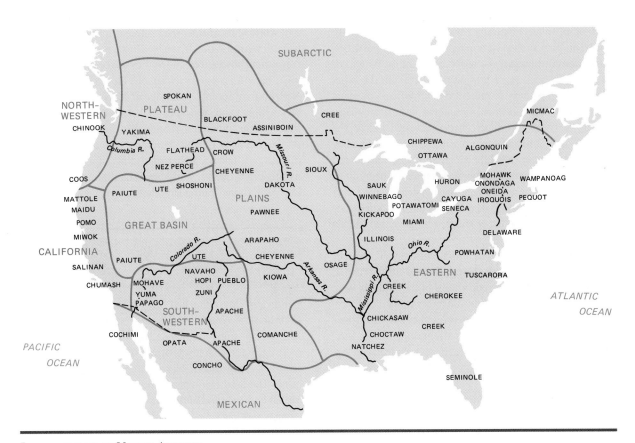

INDIAN TRIBES OF NORTH AMERICA

dividual tribes. The tribes also had differing economies. Some were hunters and food gatherers, others skillful cultivators of maize, beans, squash, melons, and tobacco. The Indians of the Iroquois Confederacy, or Six Nations, were warlike; the Delaware, who called themselves Leni-Lenape ("real person"), were peaceful. Indian dwellings ranged from tepees of skin-covered poles, the typical homes of the western Plains Indians, to the impressive lodges made of wooden beams covered with bark built by the Iroquois and other eastern peoples. Among the Hurons and many southeastern groups these structures were often grouped into towns surrounded by stockades. Although some Indian tribes were isolated and self-sufficient, others relied on traders who traveled long distances by canoe on the lakes and rivers to exchange goods with other tribes.

Many tribes were skilled in handicrafts, making beautiful pottery, light and swift birchbark canoes, and implements of copper. Some wove a kind of cloth from the inner bark of trees. Others, however, lived very simply, with few artifacts. The numerous peoples of California, for example, blessed with a mild climate and abundant food, made do with minimal clothing and crude houses. Only their beautiful basketwork revealed their skills with materials.

The first Indian contacts of the English settlers of North America were with the tribes of the Atlantic coast and the Mississippi Valley. Politically, these peoples varied greatly. The Iroquois Confederacy, originally comprising five tribes, was a powerful league, the terror of its Indian neighbors and the later scourge of European settlers. On the other hand, the Chippewas of present-day Ohio lived in many small bands that had little in common besides language. Among the tribes government structure varied widely. The Natchez of the lower Mississippi River Valley were ruled by an absolute despot called the Great Sun, who was chosen by the female Suns when his predecessor died. The Iroquois had a kind of representative political system. Female clan heads elected both the male delegates to the Confederacy council and the sachems, or chiefs, who governed the Six Nations.

Religion was important among virtually all Indians. Most believed in an ultimate being who had created nature, humankind, and all the good things of life. Indians were pantheists, who held that spiritual forces resided in all living things. Like other religious peoples, they expressed their feelings about the change of seasons, hunting, death, love, and war in elaborate ceremonies that included dancing, songs, feasting, and the wearing of vivid costumes and masks.

The Indians of North America held views of nature and property that differed from those of Europeans. Christianity assumed human primacy over other creatures not parity with them. Unlike all other living things, in the Judeo-

Christian cosmology, "man" was created in God's image and alone possessed an immortal soul. All of God's other creatures were there to serve human beings, to be bent to their use and exploited. Humans, said the Bible, should be "fruitful and multiply, and fill the earth and subdue it; and have dominion over the fish of the sea and over the birds of the air and over every living thing that moves upon the earth." The Judeo-Christian view of "man the master" was reinforced by the cultural theme of raw nature as dangerous, a "wilderness" of threatening animals, insects, poisonous plants, and human "savages," a place to be avoided or fundamentally altered. Even more powerful a force guiding Europeans in their relations to nature was avarice. Nature represented latent wealth and opportunity for personal riches. To stand in the way of exploiting nature's bounty not only hurt the enterprising individual but violated the laws of human progress. Associated with these attitudes were European views of property. The white settlers of America believed in exclusive individual possession of land, timber, minerals, and other natural resources and measured status by how much of these a person owned.

In many ways the Indian view of human relations with the natural world was the reverse of the European. Indians were not incapable of altering nature to meet their needs, as we saw, but they did not place themselves above the natural world and consider themselves in all ways superior to it. They were also not driven by a lust for limitless resource-consuming possessions and so they were not generally willing to sacrifice present satisfactions for remote future ones. Nor did they accept the European concept of private land ownership. Land, they believed, belonged to the whole tribe, not the individual, though they did recognize private property in fishing rights, hunting territories, and personal possessions. Taken together, these differing attitudes toward nature and property would have significant consequences for future Indian-European relations.

★ THE FIRST EUROPEAN "DISCOVERY" ★

Europeans first touched the Americas long before Columbus. According to the early Scandinavian sagas, in A.D. 986 a ship commanded by Bjarni Herjulfsson, a Norwegian merchant, was driven off course by a storm and narrowly escaped being dashed to pieces on an unfamiliar coast. The land Herjulfsson and his crew encountered—probably Newfoundland or Labrador—was covered with "forests and low hills." The Europeans, who were on their way to the Norse colony of Greenland when the mishap took place, were not interested in this new land and did not disembark. When they finally reached Greenland, however, they reported their discovery.

Ever on the lookout for new lands to settle, other Scandinavians soon followed up on Herjulfsson's lead. In the year 1000, Leif Ericsson, a founder of the Greenland colony, sailed westward to investigate reports of the new country. He and his party found it relatively warm, densely forested, with streams overflowing with salmon. It seemed a far fairer place than frigid Greenland, and the explorers settled down to spend the winter there. Finding what they later described as grapes, and hoping perhaps to encourage settlement, they dubbed the new country Vinland (Wineland) the Good.

Other Norsemen followed Leif Ericsson in an effort to colonize Vinland. In 1010 or thereabouts, three boatloads of Greenlanders set out to establish permanent communities in North America. Indian attacks drove the would-be settlers back home, but the Norse apparently made other efforts to colonize the new country. In 1960, archaeologists discovered the remains of a small Norse village at L'Anse aux Meadows in northern Newfoundland. The find confirmed for the first time the sagas of medieval Scandinavian exploration. But the simple structures and the primitive tools uncovered also suggest how feeble the Norse colonizing effort was. Whether because of insufficient resources or Indian attack, the little settlement had clearly lasted for only a brief time.

Some cursory knowledge of the Norse discoveries spread to other parts of Europe. Yet nothing happened. The first European contact with the Americas did not "take." Europe quickly forgot the eleventh-century Norse voyages to North America. It was as if they had never taken place.

★ THE RISE OF MODERN EUROPE ★

Of course the isolation of the Americas did not last. The Old World eventually intruded into the New, and within a few generations the collision of these two different worlds completely transformed both societies. To the people of Europe this contact with the Americas seemed a "discovery"; actually, it was a meeting. As one scholar has written: "Columbus did not discover a new world; he established contact between two worlds already old."

Medieval Europe. Why did Europe fail to follow up on the Norse voyages? And why did it respond differently in 1492? What had happened during the centuries separating Leif Ericsson from Columbus to change the way Europeans reacted to the momentous meeting of the two worlds?

In A.D. 1000, when the Norse stumbled on America, Europe was poor, politically divided, beset by local wars and civil disorder, its people largely illiterate and unfree. These conditions derived from the disintegration of the Roman-dominated Mediterranean political and social order. Eight hundred years before the Norse voyages a complex political entity, the Roman Empire, had joined all parts of the Western European world into a peaceful, prosperous, civilized whole. Then came the Germanic invasions, the Muslim conquest of the southern and eastern Mediterranean, and the devastating attacks on Europe by the Scandinavian Vikings. To prevent chaos there appeared a group of warlords, noblemen whose "keeps" and castles sheltered the common folk against raiders and brigands. Before long, however, the warlords became themselves the source of disorder as they battled one another for land and power. By the eighth or ninth century all long-range travel and trade within Europe and between Europe and other parts of the world had become unsafe. Goods, except for a few high-profit luxury items, ceased to move over the decaying Europeans roads or along pirate-infested sea routes.

Not surprisingly, Europe's economic cohesion declined. Outside of Italy, which retained its cities and trade, each small region of the continent was forced to become self-sufficient. By the year 1000, particularly north of the Alps, an atomized, localized economic system had replaced the large-scale complex organization of the Roman Empire. Each nobleman's estate or manor—with its manor-house, peasants' village, and surrounding fields—had to provide all the food, implements, and other commodities it needed. Because each manor supplied its own needs, there was little reason to produce a surplus or find new ways to increase the output of crops or other goods. Meanwhile, cities that had once been great centers of commerce and industry languished; many ancient cities disappeared entirely.

Most Europeans during this era were unfree peasants or serfs. Though not totally without rights, they could not leave the manor they were born on. Like farm animals, they went with the land when it was passed on from one nobleman to another through inheritance or conquest. In return for the right to till the soil, the peasant family gave the lord part of its crop plus various other payments in the form of work. Money seldom changed hands. Instead, exchanges and obligations were discharged through crops, animals, or services. Illiterate, superstitious, and often malnourished, as well as exploited, the serfs of Europe were a severe brake on economic change.

Even during the darkest of the "Dark Ages" Europe had a small merchant class. But traders did not count for much in the centuries from 700 to 1000. Doing business on a very small scale, they wielded little economic power. Moreover, their social status was low. Neither serfs nor priests nor feudal lords, they did not fit into the medieval social order, which presupposed a rural society composed of tilling peasants, praying clergymen, and fighting noblemen.

Nor did the Catholic Church, the ultimate repository of medieval values, find commerce congenial. The Church held that all economic relations must be subject to moral guidelines. Prices, for example, had to be "just," and were not to be determined by supply and demand or by what the traffic would bear. Charging interest was immoral; people borrowed money only when they were in desperate need, and to exploit them was un-Christian. The Church was suspicious of capitalists—those who risked their capital in trade or moneylending. They looked only to profits, the Church thinkers said, and as a result their occupations were morally suspect. These attitudes toward merchants and their activities reinforced the economic backwardness of Europe.

By the year 1000, Europe had disintegrated politically as well as economically. Kings reigned in France, England, Portugal, and other realms, but they were not like later monarchs. They did not have armies, navies, or corps of civil servants. Instead, they relied on their vassals—the feudal nobility—to supply them with men and arms in emergencies and to administer the customary law in their districts. Nor did the monarchs of this era have large financial resources. Nowhere in Europe were there national taxes. Although theoretically supreme, kings were often inferior in wealth and power to one or more of the feudal lords who supposedly were their vassals and owed them allegiance.

The one institution that held Europe together during the early Middle Ages was the Roman Catholic Church. Retaining many features of the Roman imperial government—the Latin language, a corps of literate officials, and a supreme head, the pope, residing in Rome—the Church preserved many of the values and much of the culture and organizational skill of the ancient world. Possessing a virtual monopoly on literacy, priests and other Church officials provided essential services to kings and nobles as scribes and officials. But the medieval church was no substitute for powerful secular rulers. In fact, many people disputed its right to exercise political power at all.

Nor was the Church's learning as useful for practical affairs as it might have been. Indeed, its attention to the salvation of the individual's soul focused Europeans' minds on the afterlife rather than on worldly matters. This emphasis probably discouraged the creative curiosity about nature and the physical world felt by men and women of ancient times.

In the year 1000, in short, Europe could not rise to the challenge of the newfound world to the west. It did not have the economic or technical resources, the political and social cohesion, or even the interest to do so. The disorganized, politically feeble, otherworldly, largely illiterate Europe of Leif Ericsson's time was incapable of responding to the Norse encounter with America.

★ EUROPEAN REVIVAL ★

The Lure of the East. Five hundred years later, when Columbus returned from the Caribbean to report the discovery of "the Indies," Europe reacted powerfully and overwhelmingly. Crucial to this change in Europe's response was the remarkable revival of trade and commerce in the half millennium between Leif Ericsson and Columbus. This revival, and the growth of capitalism, would eventually undermine feudalism and the self-sufficient manor-based economy on which it rested. But for trade and traders to flourish, Europeans had to change their attitudes and awaken to the opportunities of commercial relations with distant lands and cultures. Ironically, it was violent confrontation with an alien society that triggered the process of change.

From their first contact with the Islamic civilization that rimmed the eastern, southern, and western shores of the Mediterranean, Europeans had recognized the superior wealth and luxury of Christendom's major religious and cultural competitor. Compared with the rude commodities of France, England, and Germany, the silks, cotton, spices, cabinetwork, pottery, and weapons of the Muslims were marvels of delicacy and sophistication. Until the violent clashes with Islam that we call the Crusades, Western Christians were content with what they had. But then, at the very end of Leif Ericsson's eleventh century, thousands of Europeans set out for Palestine to recover the Holy Sepulcher, Jesus' tomb, from the Muslim "infidels." After the Crusaders captured Jerusalem in 1099, Europeans settled in the newly conquered Levant on the eastern edge of the Mediterranean. Though they generally disdained their Muslim foes as unbelievers, many came to appreciate the skills and artistry of Muslim craftsmen and developed a taste for sugar, silks, fine leatherwork, and other luxury goods of the Islamic world.

Even more intriguing, however, were the riches of the farthest Orient. By the eleventh century an extremely valuable trade had sprung up between Europe and China and India. Italian textiles, arms, and armor, along with north European copper, lead, and tin, moved eastward; silk, jewels, and spices moved the reverse way. The eastern end of the trade was in the hands of Asian traders—Chinese, East Indians, and Arabs. The western end was carried on largely by Italians from Venice and Genoa. Their immense profits soon made the Venetians and Genoese the envy of other European traders.

The spices displayed like jewels in this ornate box commanded high prices in Europe because merchants shipped them overland from the distant Orient. Emboldened by the profits a shorter, cheaper trade route would bring them, Europeans were encouraged to venture beyond the limits of the world they knew.

The most important portion of this East-West exchange was the spice trade. In the Middle Ages spices were more precious, relative to existing wealth, than oil and wheat are today. Spices seemed indispensable to civilized living. They retarded decay, relieved the blandness of daily fare, and disguised the poor quality of unrefrigerated meat. Of course, Europeans also used many locally grown herbs to flavor their food; but none of these could compare to pepper, cloves, nutmeg, and cinnamon, which came only from India, Ceylon, and the "Spice Islands" of present-day Indonesia.

Contact with Islam and the revival of long-distance trade were accompanied by a change in attitude toward money and the making of money. Monarchs and nobles could no longer afford to revile and oppress traders, for they were now rich capitalists whose wealth might be needed to pay royal debts or procure arms. New rules granted merchants privileges and provided them with protection. Before long the Church relaxed its ban against charging interest for lending money. Banking soon became both a respectable and a highly profitable enterprise.

The contact with the East also helped break down the self-sufficient manorial system. Before long the nobility had acquired a passion for the wondrous luxuries of Islam and the Orient. But to buy them they needed cash, and cash, in an era when almost all economic relations were based on payment in locally produced commodities or in services, was scarce. The need for cash soon changed these economic relations. Instead of paying their lord in labor or in crops, now serfs might be allowed to rent the land for money. Peasants who wanted to leave their manors might be permitted to buy their freedom. Lords might even allow serfs with cash to purchase some land and become peasant freeholders. Meanwhile, up-to-date nobles tried to improve their own cultivation methods to guarantee a surplus that they could sell for money in the growing towns. By the thirteenth or fourteenth century the revival of trade had led to the breakdown of the self-sufficient manorial system in many parts of Western Europe and the appearance of a small-landowner class.

Still another result of the revival of trade was the rapid growth of cities and the flowering of urban life. As trade returned, new cities sprang up and old ones expanded. Former serfs flocked to the trading centers with their markets, warehouses, docks, and shops to work for wages, as laborers, artisans, and craftsmen, and to enjoy the greater freedom and variety of city life. Increasingly, educated people made the growing urban centers their home. Besides the older cities of the Italian peninsula, newer towns arose along the Baltic and North seas to distribute the goods of the East and to serve the growing commerce of northern Europe. In southern Germany, merchants and bankers prospered by financing the shipping and distribution of eastern wares to central Europe.

The Nation-State. The merchant class of the growing cities was a powerful force for change in early modern Europe. The burghers, or bourgeoisie (from *burgh* or *bourg* meaning "town"), were natural foes of the feudal political system, which produced constant disorder and interfered with trade. What the merchants needed was peace and order that would allow goods and people to move safely and freely over long distances, protected and encouraged by a friendly and powerful central authority.

Inevitably the interests of the merchants made them the allies of feudal kings and helped revolutionize European political life as well. By borrowing money from the burghers, rulers could finance armies to impose internal order and put down disobedient vassals. They could free themselves from reliance on priests and bishops as administrators by employing the new literate middle class. The revival of trade by creating a money economy made it possible to impose national taxes. Before long, the modern nation-state, with its dedicated civil servants, its powerful armies and navies, and its capacity to mobilize resources to achieve national goals, had emerged in place of the chaotic, disjointed, hidebound feudal polities in Western Europe.

These political changes had immense implications for European relations with the rest of the world. The new national states were powerful instruments of European policy. The new rulers could marshal, organize, and focus vast forces to serve European ends and project these forces thousands of miles across the seas. In quest of wealth, the new centralized national states would finance exploration and conquest. Their early success would reinforce the process until it came to feed on itself.

Revolutions in Thought and Communication. Intellectual and cultural shifts also made 1492 different from A.D. 1000. People in the Middle Ages had little sense of historical change. To medieval Christians history was humanity's progress toward its final salvation. All that had preceded the birth of Jesus was a prelude to that great event; all that followed was a long epilogue that would culminate in Christ's return and the "end of days." Medieval people gave ancient times little credit for uniqueness. Nor did they see the distinctive qualities of their own era.

Then, in fourteenth-century Italy, scholars began to perceive that ancient times were different from their own. How and why this new realization occurred is not entirely clear. It was probably sparked by the interchange with Greek-speaking Constantinople and the Muslim Mediterranean world, which had preserved and translated many ancient Greek and Latin authors. Once under way, the new attitude toward the past was reinforced by the discovery of hundreds of ancient manuscripts hidden in monasteries, churches, and libraries for almost a thousand years.

The new contact with classical antiquity was a wonderfully stimulating experience. Encountering a new civilization, even one long dead, made European culture richer and more complex. Yet at the same time it gave Europeans a new confidence in their own society and in themselves. The ancients were great and creative people, surely, but their achievements were not beyond reach of the moderns. The new interest in history and literature—the new "humanism"—that this contact inspired also secularized the way people thought; that is, it directed their attention away from religion and salvation and toward the things of this world. The humanism of the era we call the Renaissance was not the irreligious, materialistic, and pleasure-obsessed set of attitudes people used to believe it was. But it did create new concern with the laws of physical nature and new appreciation of the beauties of form, color, and shape.

The new attitudes were immeasurably helped by the invention of printing. In ancient and medieval times books were rare and expensive because they had to be copied laboriously by hand. By the end of the Middle Ages the revival of trade had created a new class of literate men and women, but the high cost of recording people's thoughts inevitably checked the spread of ideas and knowledge. In the ninth century the Chinese had begun to print whole pages of text from single carved wooden blocks that were inked and pressed against paper. Then in the fifteenth century German craftsmen developed a way to print pages from movable type—individual, ready-made letters that could be assembled to form words and later disassembled for reuse again and again.

The system, probably perfected by Johann Gutenberg of Mainz, soon spread throughout Europe. By 1500, about 1,000 printers were working in the trade, and they had published 30,000 separate book titles in some 6 million copies. Many of these books were religious, but there were also scientific works, works on navigation and numerous accounts of discoveries in the Far East and West. Columbus's description of his first voyage to the "Indies" was quickly printed, widely circulated, and read. The new printed book marked another difference between the years 1000 and 1492. Cheap books encouraged literacy and helped create a communications revolution that guaranteed that Europeans would not forget America a second time.

New Technology. Advances in navigation and naval architecture also explain why Europe was better able to exploit its knowledge of the Americas after 1492. Between the times of Leif Ericsson and Columbus, marine engineering and the art of navigation had bounded ahead. In the year 1000 the Norse captains had been in the vanguard of navigation; half a millennium later their methods of locating their position on the open sea, by sighting the sun with the naked eye and guessing their speed, seemed primitive.

By 1492, Europeans had adopted the compass, a simple instrument consisting of a magnetized needle attached to a card marked with directions. Free to swing around a pivot, the needle was attracted to the north magnetic pole. Now, even when the pole star was obscured by clouds, a ship captain could calculate his direction. By the fifteenth century, as expanding trade made the need for establishing position on the featureless open ocean more pressing, European sailors were also beginning to calculate latitude with the quadrant and astrolabe.

Improvements in navigation were accompanied by advances in ship design. The typical merchant ship of medieval Europe was a high-sided tubby vessel with a rudder at the side and a single large square sail, useful only if the wind blew directly from behind. Gradually these ships were modified to carry adjustable sails and mount their rudders at the stern. Now, by "tacking"—following a zigzag course—vessels could sail without the wind directly astern. Faster, more maneuverable, and more stable ships expanded Europe's reach. As incorporated first into the Portuguese caravel and carrack during the fifteenth century, and then a little later in the Portuguese, Spanish, French, and English galleons, these changes gave Europeans the equipment needed to undertake long ocean voyages with relative confidence.

One more innovation was needed before Europeans were equipped to subdue the world: gunpowder. Discovered after A.D. 1000, probably by the Arabs, it was first used to propel missiles from cannons early in the fourteenth century. Employed initially for siege operations against walled cities, it was soon installed aboard ships as well. Artillery gradually became miniaturized so that by 1360 primitive small arms were being used. Within a century the arquebus, a hand-held weapon that looked like a modern rifle and was fired by a trigger, had become a common infantry weapon. These guns were heavy and inaccurate; but when combined with the horse, pike, metal armor, and steel sword, they would prove devastating against the native peoples of the Americas.

★ EUROPEAN EXPANSION ★

The invention of an easier way to produce books; the development of gunpowder, better ships, and navigational instruments; the rise of the strong nation-state; the growth of trade; the appearance of a sizable merchant class; the passing of feudalism and the self-sufficient economy of the manor—these are the events that made Europe in 1492 different from Europe in 1000. Even before Columbus they had produced their effects: By the 1400s, Europeans were launched on a campaign to explore the world and make contact with other lands and peoples.

A Portuguese galleon, of the sort that enabled Europeans to conquer the oceans and helped create the Portuguese empire in the sixteenth century. The gun ports on the sides and stern are realistic in this contemporary engraving, but the men on deck—and the fish—are exaggerated in size.

The "Indies" Described

While still aboard the *Niña*, Columbus composed a brief letter to his sovereigns describing his first voyage to America. This document was transmitted to Ferdinand and Isabella from Lisbon, where Columbus first made port after his return, and reached them at Barcelona sometime in March 1493. Called by different names, the letter is the first account in a European language of the New World, if we except the Norse sagas of 500 years earlier. The document was quickly printed in Latin and other languages and widely circulated in Europe.

Columbus's account gave Europeans their first glimpse of the New World. Unfortunately it played on their greed in a way that would have tragic consequences for the native peoples of the Americas. Note the simultaneous appeal to his sovereigns' piety and greed.

"SIR. Since I know you will take great pleasure at the great victory with which Our Lord has crowned my voyage, I write this to you, from which you will learn how in . . . [thirty-three] days I reached the Indies with the fleet which the most illustrious King and Queen, our lords, gave to me. And there I found very many islands filled with people without number, and of them all I have taken possession of for their Highnesses, by proclamation and with the royal standard displayed, and nobody objected.

"When I reached Juana [Cuba], I followed the coast westward, and I found it to be so long that I thought it must be the mainland, the province of Catayo [a part of China]. And since there were neither towns nor cities on the coast, but only small villages, with the people of which I could not have speech because they all fled forthwith, I went forward on the same course, thinking that I should not fail to find great cities and towns. . . . [Later] I sent two men upcountry to learn if there were a king or great cities. They traveled for three days and found an infinite number of small villages and people without number, but nothing of importance; hence they returned. . . .

". . . I saw toward the east another island . . . to which I at once gave the name *La Spanola* [Hispaniola, or Haiti]. And I went there and followed its northern part . . . to the eastward for 178 great leagues. . . . As Juana, so all the others are very fertile to an excessive degree, and this one especially. In it there are many harbors on the coast of the sea, incomparable to others I know in Christendom, and numerous rivers, good and large, which is marvelous. Its lands are lofty and in it are very many sierras and very high mountains. . . . All are most beautiful, of a thousand shapes, . . . and filled with trees of a thousand kinds and tall, and they seem to touch the sky; and I am told they never lose their foliage, which I can believe, for I saw them as green and beautiful as they are in Spain in May, and some of them were flowering, some with fruit. . . . And there were singing the nightingale and other little birds of a thousand kinds in the month of November. . . . Upcountry there are many mines of metals, and the population is innumerable. *La Spanola* is marvelous, . . . and the lands are so beautiful and fat for planting and sowing, and for livestock of every sort, and for building towns and cities. . . .

"The people of this island and of all other islands which I have found and seen . . . all go naked, men and women, as their mothers bore them, except that some women cover one

---

The quest began with the effort of Prince Henry of Portugal, later known as Henry the Navigator, to seek out new lands to the south and west. The third son of King John, Henry was not indifferent to gold, nor was he uninterested in filling the gaps in Europe's geographical knowledge. But he was not a fully modern man impelled primarily by curiosity or hope of profits. Rather, he was moved as much by medieval mystical and religious purposes as by modern practical ones. His chief concern, it seems, was to find the kingdom of Prester John (legendary ruler of a Christian land located in eastern Africa or central Asia) and reunite him and his people with the main body of Christendom.

To achieve these simultaneous purposes Henry sponsored a major exploration program along the west coast of Africa. Each year ships left Portugal to venture ever farther south, their captains spurred on by Henry's financial rewards for progress. By 1445, Dinis Dias had rounded Cape Verde and reached the humid, fertile part of the African coast below the Sahara. Ten years later Alvise da Cadamosto reached the Senegal and Gambia rivers and discovered the Cape Verde Islands. Meanwhile, the Portuguese had stumbled on the Atlantic islands of Madeira and the Azores, conquered their inhabitants, and settled them with Europeans.

After Henry's death his work was taken over by the kings of Portugal, who changed his goals. There was little thought now of Prester John; the sole purpose was to find the end of the African continent, sail around it, and head northeast for India, Cathay (China), and Xipangu (Japan).

place only with a leaf of a plant or with a net of cotton which they make for that. They have no iron or steel or weapons, nor are they capable of using them, although they are well-built people of handsome stature, because they are wonderfully timorous. They have no other arms than arms of canes . . . to the ends of which they fix a sharp little stick. . . . [O]ftentimes . . . I have sent ashore two or three men to some town to have speech, . . . and as soon as they saw them coming, they fled. . . . It is true that after they saw them coming, they have been reassured and have lost this fear, they are so artless and so free with all they possess, that no one would believe it without having seen it. Of anything they have, if you ask them for it, they never say no; rather they invite the person to share it; . . . and whether the thing be of value or of small price, at once they are content with whatever little thing of whatever kind may be given to them. I forbade that they should be given things so worthless as pieces of broken crockery and broken glass, and ends of straps, although when they were able to get them, they thought they had the best jewel in the world; thus it was ascertained that a sailor for a strap received gold to the weight of two and a half *castellanos* [worth today about $500], and others much more for other things which were worth much less. . . . I gave them a thousand good and pleasing things which I had brought, in order that they might be fond of us, and furthermore might be made Christians and be inclined to the love and service of their Highnesses and of the whole Castilian nation, and try to help us and to give us of the things which they have in abundance and which are necessary to us. And they know neither sect nor idolatry, with the exception that all believe that the source of all power and goodness is in the sky, and they believe very firmly that I, with these ships and people, come from the sky, and in this belief they everywhere received me, after they had overcome their fear. . . .

"In these islands I have so far found no human monstrosities, as many expected; on the contrary, among all these people good looks are esteemed; nor are they Negroes, as in Guinea, but with flowing hair. . . . Thus I have neither found monsters nor had report of any, except in an island . . . which is inhabited by a people who are regarded in all the islands as very ferocious and who eat human flesh [the Carib Indians, that is]; they have many canoes with which they range all the islands of India and pillage and take as much as they can. . . . In another island, which they assure me is larger than *Espanola*, the people have no hair.

In this there is countless gold, and from it and the other islands I bring with me Indios [that is, Indians] as evidence."

"In conclusion, to speak only of that which has been accomplished on this voyage, which was so hurried, their Highnesses can see that I shall give them as much gold as they want if their Highnesses will render me a little help, besides spice and cotton, as much as their Highnesses shall command; and gum mastic, as much as they shall order shipped; . . . and aloe wood, as much as they shall order shipped; and slaves, as many as they shall order, who will be idolators. And I believe that I have found rhubarb and cinnamon, and I shall find a thousand other things of value. . . .

"So, since our Redeemer has given this victory to our most illustrious King and Queen, and to their famous realms in so great a matter, for this all Christendom ought to feel joyful and make great celebrations and give solemn thanks to the Holy Trinity with many solemn prayers for the great exaltation which it will have in the turning of so many people to our holy faith, and afterwards for material benefits, since not only Spain but all Christendom and hence have refreshment and profit. . . ."

"At your service.

THE ADMIRAL"

For many years the spice trade had been monopolized by Genoese and Venetian merchants, and traders from the Levant. If the Portuguese could bypass the Italian and Muslim middlemen and go to the source itself, all the profits of Europe's Eastern trade would be theirs.

In 1488, Bartolomeu Dias finally rounded the southern tip of Africa. Unfortunately, Dias's timid crew forced him to turn back before he could penetrate into the Indian Ocean. Yet his achievement was enormously important. Encouraged by Dias's report, Vasco da Gama boldly set sail for India in July 1497. The following May his little fleet of four ships arrived at Calicut on the west coast of India. Da Gama collected a valuable cargo of pepper, ginger, cloves, and cinnamon and returned home safely in 1499, the first man to sail directly from Europe to India and back.

Once opened, the route around Africa became a busy thoroughfare. To expedite the trade in spices, silks, drugs, and other precious goods, the Portuguese established "factories" (trading posts) in Africa, along the Malabar coast of India, in Ceylon, and on the islands of the East Indies. In 1509, a Portuguese fleet of fast caravels armed with cannon defeated a Muslim fleet at Diu and established Portugal as the dominant power in India. The Portuguese commercial empire soon expanded to the western Pacific. By 1550 the small Atlantic nation had established a virtual monopoly of the world spice trade.

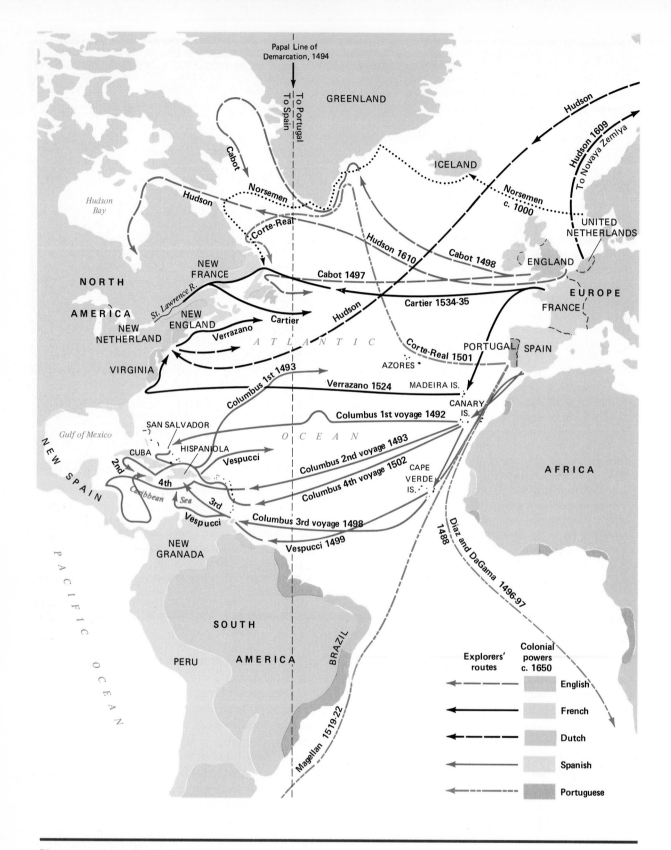

VOYAGES OF EXPLORATION

Columbus and the Spanish Explorations. The success of the Portuguese aroused the envy of the rulers of Europe's other nations. Eventually the Dutch, the French, and the English would challenge Portugal's stranglehold on the Eastern spice trade around Africa. But meanwhile, a Genoese adventurer and visionary named Cristoforo Colombo (Christopher Columbus) had arrived at an alternative that not only promised a shorter route but also seemed likely to avoid a direct confrontation with the Portuguese.

Columbus's scheme was simple—and based on false premises. The Earth, Columbus believed, was far smaller than it actually is and that Asia was immensely wide, extending much farther east than it actually does. Only water—and a rather narrow body at that—Columbus thought, lay between Europe and the Indies. The conclusion was clear: A ship sailing west, after only a few weeks, would reach Asia and its riches.

After unsuccessfully peddling his idea to every monarch of Western Europe, Columbus finally interested the rulers of Spain. These joint monarchs, Ferdinand of Aragon and Isabella of Castile, had just conquered the last Moslem stronghold in Iberia—concluding a centuries-long crusade against the infidel "Moors"—and were looking for new worlds to conquer. Pledging her jewels as security, Queen Isabella borrowed from a Spanish religious order some of the money Columbus needed. The rest came from the small city of Palos, whose burghers, as punishment for an infraction of Spanish law, were ordered to supply "the Admiral" with three small vessels. The total cost of the expedition was about 2 million maravedis (today about $14,000), a great fortune that could not have been marshalled for such a purpose 500 years earlier, in Norse times. With this sum Columbus fitted out three small vessels, manned them with Spanish seamen, and stocked them with supplies. On August 3, 1492, he and his crew of ninety left Palos. They arrived at the Caribbean island of San Salvador ten weeks later, almost exactly five centuries after the first European had sighted North America.

Columbus's first voyage was followed by three others, each better equipped than the first. The "Admiral of the Ocean Sea" explored the Caribbean, discovered its major islands, and touched the mainland of the Americas at several points. He also established the first permanent European communities in the New World. From these Caribbean island settlements Spanish commanders launched expeditions to the mainland. One of these under Vasco Nuñez de Balboa crossed the Isthmus of Panama in 1513, its members becoming the first Europeans to see the eastern shore of the Pacific Ocean.

But Spain's ambitions went beyond the Americas. In 1519 the Spanish crown sent the Portuguese navigator

Columbus's first voyage to the New World aroused intense interest all over Europe. This 1493 illustration accompanied an edition of Columbus's letter to his royal patrons printed in Switzerland. The landscape, with its European-style castles and houses, is imaginary, but the large ship does resemble the Admiral's flagship, the Santa Maria.

Ferdinand Magellan to finally do what Columbus had failed to accomplish: find an ocean route to the Far East by sailing west. In November 1520, Magellan discovered the strait at the tip of South America that bears his name, sailed through it, and launched his small fleet onto the vast Pacific. After harrowing experiences with hunger, scurvy, and thirst, he arrived in the Philippines, off the Asian mainland, months later. There he was killed in a skirmish with the natives. Eventually one of his vessels reached Spain by sailing westward around Africa. Though the route was far too long to be practical for the Europe-Asia trade, Magellan's voyage proved that the Americas were not part of the Indies. It was also the first circumnavigation of the globe, a milestone for humankind.

Spain Encounters the Indian Civilizations. Spain's Far Eastern empire never expanded much beyond the

Isabella of Castile

Isabella, queen of Castile, was called "the Catholic" by her subjects to honor her piety and deep devotion to her faith. Though married to Ferdinand, king of Aragon, she was not merely a royal consort, for in her own realm, Castile, she was sovereign. Like that other reigning early modern queen, Elizabeth I of England, Isabella was not "womanly" in the traditional passive sense. She was one of the most powerful and vigorous rulers of early modern times and she helped transform Spain into a strong, modern nation.

Isabella was already married to Ferdinand, the young heir apparent of neighboring Aragon, when she came to the throne of Castile in 1474. When Ferdinand became king of Aragon several years later, their alliance united the two realms that occupied the largest portion of the Iberian peninsula and ultimately formed the core of the modern Spanish state.

But Spain was anything but united religiously, culturally, or politically when the two young monarchs took up their joint reign. For centuries the Iberian peninsula had been a meeting ground—and a battlefield—of diverse peoples. Conquered in the eighth century by "the Moors" (Muslims), it had been reclaimed by the Christians bit by bit through fierce struggle. The process was incomplete, however, and until the

end of the fifteenth century the Moors continued to rule Grenada in the southeast. In addition, the peninsula was home to thousands of Jews, who formed a class of artisans, merchants, and professionals who contributed much-needed skills to Spanish society.

Few Spanish Christians believed religious or cultural tolerance to be a virtue. Non-Christians were infidels whose beliefs were wicked and dangerous. Though over the centuries there had been periods of relative harmony among the different Iberian communities, there had also been periods of fierce religious strife and intolerance. Such conflict had helped mold the passionate, valorous, and often ferocious temperament of the Spanish aristocracy. Isabella's accession to the throne of Castile ushered in the last stage of the Christian reconquest of the Iberian peninsula. By 1481 the Catholic monarchs were engaged in a final drive to conquer Grenada and thereby eliminate the last Muslim outpost in Western Europe.

Earlier Christian successes against the infidels had not led to internal order. Until Ferdinand and Isabella, Spain was a land wracked by turmoil and lawlessness, most of it inspired by the proud, warlike Spanish nobility. These men preyed on city folk and peasants alike, and their undisciplined

retainers ravaged the towns and the countryside, stealing, murdering, and raping. The previous rulers of Castile had been too weak to stop these unruly grandees, whose defiance effectively reduced the central government to an empty shell. Spain at the time of Isabella's accession exhibited the worst aspects of the feudalism that had characterized the Middle Ages and kept Europe too feeble to exploit the growing geographic knowledge of distant lands.

Isabella determined to smash the unruly aristocrats, reassert the authority of the crown, and put an end to lawlessness in the realm. Her methods were not gentle. In the province of Galicia her agent, Don Fernand de Acuna, razed forty-seven castles of the unruly nobility and hanged some of the worst offenders. Hordes of brigands and assassins fled the province.

The monarchs' chief instrument for imposing order was the Hermandad, or brotherhood, a league of city people disgusted with the lawless aristocrats. Under the crown's sponsorship, the Hermandad contributed men and money for an internal police force to suppress brigandage and violence in the towns and along the highways. Its militia exacted terrible penalties of the culprits they caught. "The executioners," in the words of one later historian,

---

Philippines. Meanwhile, in the Americas its conquests soon made it master of two continents. In 1519 the Spaniard Hernando Cortés set out from Cuba with 600 men, 17 horses, and 10 cannons, landed at Veracruz, and marched to the Aztec capital of Tenochtitlán (Mexico City). The Aztec ruler, Moctezuma II, was a bold and determined man, but his resolve to resist the invaders was undermined by his belief that they were the white gods that Aztec myths said would one day return to the world of men. His warriors, moreover, were startled and demoralized by the Spaniards' strange horses and firearms. Taking advantage of this com-

bination of trust and fear, the Spaniards seized Moctezuma and plundered the overflowing Aztec treasury. Soon after, Cortés left the capital briefly to deal with an expedition sent from Cuba to punish him for departing on his adventure without permission. During his absence the Aztecs at the capital turned on the remaining Spaniards, and Moctezuma was killed in the fighting. Cortés returned to the city with a larger force of Spaniards, as well as many Indian allies who deeply resented the harsh Aztec rule of Mexico. In the battle that followed, the Spaniards fought to kill, unlike the Aztec warriors, who usually fought primarily to take cap-

"cut off feet and hands, shoulders and heads, neither sparing nor veiling the rigor of justice."

In their drive to consolidate Spain under royal authority, Isabella and Ferdinand waged implacable war against all those elements within the Iberian peninsula who marred the kingdom's religious unity. These included many converts from Judaism and Islam who had changed their faith to Christianity out of expediency. In 1478 the royal monarchs established, under papal authority, a tribunal called the Inquisition to root out secret backsliders among the "New Christians" and punish them, by burning at the stake if necessary. But this was not all: The practicing Jews and Muslims remained, and these groups, too, had to be dealt with. They were.

In that momentous year of 1492, the Jews of Spain were ordered expelled from the kingdom. At the very same time, after a decade of war, the Moorish kingdom of Grenada fell to the Christian knights and soldiers. Faced with the alternative of exile, most of Grenada's Muslim inhabitants accepted baptism into the Catholic faith.

Columbus was a major beneficiary of Isabella's determination and strength of will. Spain was ready for new projects. The success of its joint rulers in suppressing the aristocracy and establishing their authority gave the crown the resources needed to support such speculative ventures as voyaging west to reach India and the Far East. With its internal enemies defeated as well, there were new energies for further conquest. If the plan of the Genoese mariner succeeded, the newly united Spain would steal the lead on Portugal's attempt to bypass the Italian middlemen in the fabulous spice trade with the Orient.

Columbus also enjoyed a special rapport with the queen. He and Isabella were as alike, physically, as brother and sister: Both were blue-eyed and auburn-haired, rarities in southern Europe. More important, they had similar personalities. Isabella, like the Genoese mariner, was a visionary who responded to Columbus's bold schemes. Columbus would later write of his patroness: "In all men there was disbelief, but to the Queen, my lady, God gave the spirit of understanding and great courage and made her heiress of all. . . ."

But the queen was no instant convert to the "Enterprise of the Indies." Columbus visited the Spanish court several times over a span of seven years before Isabella agreed to sponsor and finance his expedition. Finally, early in 1492 the monarchs authorized the expedition, pledged financial support, and furnished "the Admiral" with the necessary documents to set his enterprise in motion.

They joyously greeted Columbus in Barcelona when he returned from his first voyage in 1493, confirmed all the titles and privileges they had promised, and provided him with the ships and men he needed to return to "the Indies" as soon as possible. During the following years, while the discoverer collected enemies in Spain and in the new colonies, the queen remained his champion. But by the time he returned from his fourth voyage in 1504, she was old, sickly, and bowed with cares. A devoted mother, she had seen three of her children die while still young. Another child, Joanna, sole surviving heir to the Spanish throne, was insane, and the queen trembled at the prospect of the kingdom under her rule.

During the last months of her life Isabella, always pious, turned more and more to her devotions. On November 26, 1504, she died. Her will made no provision for Columbus, and when he passed away scarcely eighteen months later, he was a near pauper.

Invigorated by the treasure of the New World, Spain would become the most powerful nation in Europe. But having driven from the realm some of its most creative people and confirmed a tradition of intolerance, it ultimately failed to benefit from its good fortune. In the following centuries Spain, once past the first flush of prosperity, became an economic backwater and surrendered leadership in science and the arts to other nations. In the end Isabella had bequeathed to her beloved nation an ambiguous legacy.

tives. The Spaniards' ferocity, guns, and horses produced an astonishing European victory. In the next few months Moctezuma's successors sought to rally the Indians of Mexico against the invaders, but few tribes would cooperate. By 1521, resistance was over. The mighty Aztec empire had fallen to a few hundred Europeans.

The conquest of Mexico was soon followed by the fall of the Inca empire in Peru. The *conquistador* this time was Francisco Pizarro, a young man of lowly birth and overweening ambition, who, while in Panama, had heard of a great native empire full of wealth along the Pacific coast of South America. Wasting no time, Pizarro joined two other eager adventurers and set off to find the fabled land. For a while it eluded him, but in 1532, after a forty-five-day climb up the high wall of the Andes from the Pacific coast, Pizarro and his 102 men and 62 horses finally reached the frontier of Peru.

Through emissaries Pizarro assured the Inca ruler, Atahualpa, that he and his men intended to stay in the Inca realms for only a short time. Confident of his own strength, Atahualpa allowed them to advance. When he finally confronted the Europeans, they attacked, cut down 5,000

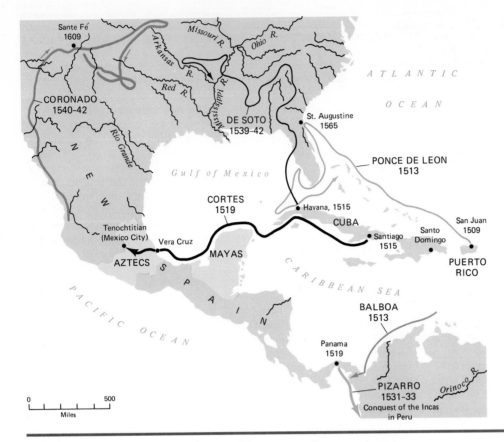

SPANISH EXPLORATIONS IN THE GULF OF MEXICO AND CENTRAL AMERICA

Indian warriors, and took the Inca emperor prisoner. The royal captive offered the Spaniards a roomful of silver and gold to buy his freedom. Pizarro accepted. Then, with the treasure safely in his hands, he had Atahualpa bound to a stake and strangled.

In the next few months the Spaniards found various puppets among the Inca royal family to aid them in their conquest; in addition, they had the advantage of guns and horses. Eventually the Indians cornered the Europeans in Cuzco, the Inca capital, and sought to starve them out. But the Spaniards held out long enough to force the Indian army to abandon the siege. This was the end of effective Inca resistance. Over the next few years the Europeans extended their control over the whole of the vast Inca domain, from modern Colombia to what is now central Chile.

The conquest of the Mayas was slower and less dramatic because there was no single Maya state to confront the invaders. In 1527, Spanish forces first entered Yucatán and encountered guerrilla resistance. Over the next twenty years the Spaniards advanced and retreated; not until about 1550 were the Mayas of Central America subjugated and placed firmly under the control of the Spanish king. The last great native civilization of the Americas was gone.

Spain's Rivals. By 1600 Spain had conquered virtually all of Central and South America except for Brazil, which was awarded to Portugal by the Treaty of Tordesillas in 1494. In 1580, Spain absorbed Portugal, adding that small country's rich empire for a time to her own.

The wealth of the New World proved immense. Gold and silver confiscated from the Indians poured into Spain. Additional streams of precious metals soon flowed from new mines in Peru and Mexico. From 1500 to 1650 Spain extracted almost 20,000 tons of silver and 200 tons of gold from its American colonies. In addition, cocoa, tobacco, dyes, and other American products found ready markets throughout Europe, providing another source of Spanish income. All this New World bounty helped make Spain the richest and most powerful nation in Europe.

At first Spain's rights in America were unchallenged. But the Spanish monopoly could not last indefinitely. To the monarchs of France and England and, somewhat later, the leading merchants and gentlemen of the Dutch Republic, Spain's example seemed irresistible. But what gave the Spaniards and Portuguese the right to divide the non-European world between them? As the French king Francis I remarked to the Spanish ambassador in 1540, "The

This illustration from a 1615 Spanish chronicle of life in the New World depicts a cultural difference between Europeans and Indians present from the beginning. The Inca asks, amazed by the European lust for precious metals, "Do you eat this gold?" The Spaniard replies, "Yes, we eat this gold."

France joined the quest for overseas wealth in 1524, when Francis I dispatched the Florentine mariner Giovanni da Verrazano to seek out the Far East by the still-elusive western route. Verrazano reached the Americas, probably somewhere along the Carolina coast, and sailed north, touching New York and Narragansett bays and then Nova Scotia. Later Francis sent better-financed expeditions under Jacques Cartier to the region farther north. Cartier explored the coasts of Newfoundland, Prince Edward Island, and the Gaspé Peninsula and, on a second voyage, sailed up the St. Lawrence River to the site of present-day Montreal. Cartier's voyages did not lead immediately to successful settlements, but they gave France a claim to part of North America.

The Dutch began exploring relatively late. By the beginning of the seventeenth century most of modern Holland had achieved autonomy from Spain and was developing into a prosperous country dominated by aggressive mer-

John White, who came with Sir Walter Raleigh to Carolina in 1585, did this watercolor of the Indian village of Secota. It is one of the earliest pictures of East Coast Indian life we have.

sun shone for him as for others," and where, he wondered, in "Adam's will" had the Americas been divided between Spain and its Iberian neighbor.

England was the first northern European country to join the scramble for a share in the New World. In 1496 Henry VII authorized John Cabot to sail west under the king's "banners and ensignes . . . to seeke out, discouer, and finde whatsoeuer isles, countryes, regions or prouinces of the heathens and infidels whatsoeuer they be. . . ." Cabot, a Venetian, made two voyages to North America. On the first he sighted either Nova Scotia or Newfoundland, and on the second he sailed down the Atlantic coast as far as Delaware or Chesapeake Bay. The English government did not follow up on these voyages, but Cabot's report of cod-fish in Newfoundland waters did attract many fishermen from France and England to the area. More important, his voyages became the basis for English claims to North American territory.

chants and bankers. In 1609 a group of these capitalists, joined as partners in the Dutch East India Company, hired Henry Hudson, an English sea captain, to find a water route to the Far East through North America. Hudson was no more successful than the other explorers who had sought this Northwest Passage, but he added to Europe's geographical knowledge and Holland's claim to part of North America by sailing down the Atlantic coast from Newfoundland to Virginia. During this trip Hudson explored Cape Cod and Delaware Bay and sailed partway up the broad river that now bears his name.

These expeditions were only a small part of the sixteenth- and early seventeenth-century exploration of the Americas. There were scores of other expeditions along every coast and into every accessible bay, inlet, and navigable river of the two western continents. At the same time Spanish captains like Hernando de Soto and Francisco Vásquez de Coronado, and the Frenchman Samuel de Champlain, pushed deep into the heartland of North America. By about 1650 Europeans knew the essential outlines of the New World continents and had even learned something of their remote interiors.

★ THE "COLUMBIAN EXCHANGE" ★

In 1552 the Spanish historian Francisco López de Gómara declared "the greatest event since the creation of the world (excluding the incarnation and the death of Him who created it) is the discovery of the Indies." If we discount the word *discovery* and allow for some exaggeration, López was correct: Few if any events have so changed the history of

Evidence like this contemporary picture suggests that the "Black Legend" of Spanish cruelty in the Americas was not entirely mythical. Here we see Spanish soldiers slowly roasting an Indian nobleman to death on the Caribbean island of Hispaniola.

the world as the encounter of Europeans and Native Americans at the end of the fifteenth century.

In Central and South America, except in the most remote interior regions, Europeans quickly swept away all traces of Indian self-rule. North of Mexico the process of conquest was slower but no less thorough. Vicious warfare against the Indians was part of the history of every European colonial power—not just Spain.

The European response was not consistent. At times the kings of Spain, France, and England sought to protect their new Indian subjects. Friars, priests, and ministers often denounced the cruel treatment of the native Americans. Yet these efforts seldom achieved their ends. Even when Europeans refrained from outright murder, they treated the native peoples harshly. In the Spanish colonies Indians were enslaved and sometimes worked to death. Where not enslaved in a strict legal sense, they were subjected to forced labor for European masters. Well into the nineteenth century Indians in Spanish-held lands remained "peons" whose lot resembled that of medieval serfs. In the English colonies the Indians generally escaped forced labor but less because of humane considerations than because the North American tribes were less settled than their southern counterparts and could easily escape their oppressors by slipping away into the forest.

Contact with Europeans injured the native peoples even when the whites intended no harm. Because of their long separation, humans of the Old and the New Worlds had developed immunities to different diseases. As a result, neither people could fend off the infections of the other. Europeans encountered a virulent form of syphilis in America, and it quickly spread over all of Europe. Thousands broke out in horrible sores and died before anyone knew how to deal with the malady. The Indians suffered far more. Even European childhood diseases like measles became killing scourges among populations without protective antibodies. Smallpox, too, along with tuberculosis and cholera, hit the native populations hard. In Mexico the 25 million Indians of 1519 were reduced to 2.5 million by 1600. Along the Atlantic coast of North America a similar grim process took place. In 1656 Adriaen Van der Donck reported that the Indians of New Netherland claimed "that before the arrival of the Christians, and before the small pox broke out amongst them, they were ten times as numerous as they now are. . . ." Indeed, the English and Dutch occupations of the eastern coast were greatly facilitated by the European diseases that had spread to North America from the south and decimated the native population even before the Europeans themselves appeared.

Disease was only part of the damage that Europeans inflicted on Indian societies. In many areas native agriculture was destroyed by the great herds of sheep and cattle introduced by the conquerors. European manufactures swamped native crafts and undermined native skills. Even efforts to implant the Christian faith often did harm. The European missionaries hoped to benefit the Indians by bringing them the blessings of Christianity. At times they won converts by their example of humility, kindness, and courage; however, some sought conversions by fierce assaults on the Indians' religion, including their temples and religious artifacts. Bishop Diego de Landa of Yucatán de-

Syphilis fell like a scourge on Europe shortly after Columbus returned from the New World. It was the real "Montezuma's Revenge." This picture of a victim was drawn by the German artist Albrecht Dürer in 1496.

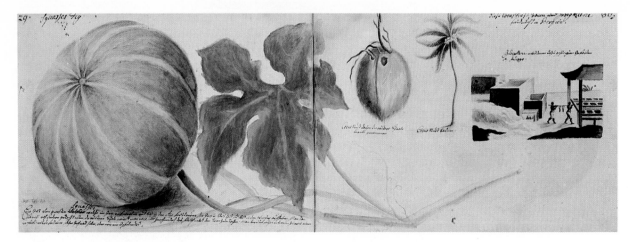

Europeans encountered many strange—and valuable—plants in America. This squash grew in the gardens of eighteenth-century German immigrants to New Ebenezer in Georgia.

stroyed thousands of Mayan books in his effort to stop idolatry, impoverishing both the Mayas themselves and our knowledge of their civilization and history.

Europe Benefits. The transatlantic encounter after 1492 was no less momentous for Europeans. But the effects were almost diametrically opposite. With few exceptions (such as the scourge of syphilis), the contact between the Americas and Europe benefited Europe dramatically. Its fabulous American treasure catapulted Spain into the first rank of European powers. Simultaneously, the deluge of American gold and silver stimulated European trade, commerce, and industry, though Spain benefited less from these advances than Germany, France, and the Netherlands, which were better prepared to take advantage of growing demand and rising commodity prices. These same rising prices helped further weaken the feudal system by accelerating the conversion of labor services into cash payments. The treasure also provided national rulers with enormous new incomes, giving them an additional edge over their unruly and disobedient vassals. Finally, the events following 1492 accelerated the rise to wealth and influence of the merchant-capitalists who entered the American trade. In short, the "discovery" of America speeded the modernization of Europe that was already well under way when Columbus sailed from Palos.

The transatlantic contact also provided Europeans with an enormously expanded and improved diet. Potatoes and Indian corn would eventually become staples consumed by millions of Europeans. Tomatoes, pumpkins, a wide assortment of beans, and many new fruits were also brought eastward to be widely grown in Europe. Rubber and chicle were other useful American borrowings. Not all the plant imports were blessings. Some would consider tobacco al-

most as serious a scourge as syphilis, and there are those who have their doubts about chewing gum, made from American chicle. Yet it is clear that America was a botanical, as well as a mineral, treasure trove.

The Old World's encounter with the New World also enriched Europe's intellectual life. In some ways it merely confirmed the European sense of superiority. After observing the Aztec sacrifices, the Spanish were certain that the native religions were bloodthirsty superstitions. The relative ease with which Europeans conquered the New World peoples also encouraged European arrogance—on the theory, apparently, that strength and ferocity equaled virtue. But not all Europeans found their prejudices reinforced. Some felt wonder at the variety of the world's cultures. Some saw native Americans as "noble savages" living in the same state of simplicity and grace Adam and Eve had enjoyed in the Garden of Eden. It is not surprising that the first modern utopia was conceived by Sir Thomas More in 1516, soon after the Spanish discoveries. This contact with new cultures widened Europe's horizons and produced new fields of knowledge and new intellectual disciplines, including the predecessors of anthropology and sociology.

★ CONCLUSIONS ★

We focus on 1492 as *the* date of America's discovery for several good reasons. One of these, no doubt, is that we tend to accept a Europe-centered view of the world. Still, from any cultural perspective, 1492 was a profound historical turning point. After Columbus's return from the New World, human history changed fundamentally. For the millions in the Americas, the change was a social disaster marked by disease, misery, bondage, and cultural disintegration. For Europe as a whole, 1492 marked the beginning of a new era of expansion—geographic, intellectual, and economic.

Columbus's landing at San Salvador in 1492 was an event that transformed two worlds. The encounter did not confer equal benefits on both populations, but that it was of transcendent importance for humanity cannot be doubted.

By 1500 Europeans were also about to embark on the greatest mass migration of all time, one that would eventually pull 100 million human beings across the Atlantic. We have seen something of the "forces" that led to this momentous occurrence. Let us now consider the personal motives that impelled countless ordinary, and not-so-ordinary, individuals to risk their lives and their fortunes creating new communities in the strange lands across the ocean.

✳✳✳✳✳✳✳ FOR FURTHER READING ✳✳✳✳✳✳✳

Alvin M. Josephy. *The Indian Heritage of America* (1968)
This is an overall survey of the Indian peoples of both American continents, region by region and era by era. Josephy recounts the story of each native American culture group and briefly describes Indian-white contacts and relations over the centuries. The book contains excellent picture portfolios.

Brian M. Fagan. *The Great Journey: The Peopling of Ancient America* (1987)
A fascinating book by an anthropologist about how Asian peoples first settled the Americas across "Baringia," the land bridge that once connected the Old World to the New World.

Francis Jennings. *The Invasion of America: Indians, Colonialism, and the Cant of Conquest* (1975)
Jennings has written an angry book about Indian-European relations. An "ethnohistorian" who deals with the evolution of cultures, Jennings seeks to redress the traditional story that makes the Indians into "savages" and the Europeans into the civilized party to the Old World–New World encounter after 1492. He is especially hard on the Puritan settlers of New England, whom he considers hypocrites. Jennings pushes his useful reinterpretation too far.

Alfred W. Crosby. *The Columbian Exchange: Biological and Cultural Consequences of 1492* (1972)
Crosby sees the contacts between Europeans and the native peoples of America as a two-way street—both for good and ill. He notes the exchanges between Old World and New World of animals and plants. A particularly fascinating section of the book describes the exchange of lethal diseases: European smallpox for American syphilis.

J. H. Parry. *The Age of Reconnaissance: Discovery, Exploration, and Settlement. 1450–1650* (1963)
An excellent review of the roots and course of late medieval–early modern European overseas expansion.

Samuel Eliot Morison. *The European Discovery of America: The Northern Voyages, 400–1600* (1971); and *The Southern Voyages, 1492–1616* (1974)
Both of these volumes are superb blends of lucid text, maps, and photographs by a sailor-historian who was a master of his craft. They deal with people, ships, and weather more than with "forces." You will learn how sailors spent the day at sea in the sixteenth and seventeenth centuries, what they ate, what songs they sang. You will also learn how a ship was navigated in this age of sail.

Samuel Eliot Morison. *Christopher Columbus, Mariner* (1955)
This is the condensed paperback edition of one of the great biographies in American historical literature, *Admiral of the Ocean Sea*. Morison demolishes most of the legendary nonsense and phony mystery that has grown up around the figure of Columbus. The author's preparations for writing this book included following Columbus's routes in ships comparable in size and rig to those the great explorer himself sailed.

Charles Gibson. *Spain in America* (1966)
An informative and tightly written analysis and interpretation of Spanish-American history from the earliest explorations to the nineteenth century. Gibson discusses the power and influence of the Roman Catholic Church, relations between Spaniards and Indians, and the social, economic, and labor patterns that developed in Spain's American colonies. Valuable for the contrast it reveals between Spanish-American and British-American history.

C. R. Boxer. *The Portuguese Seaborne Empire, 1415–1825* (1969)
This is by far the best modern account of that epic expansion.

Carlo M. Cipolla. *Before the Industrial Revolution: European Economy and Society, 1000–1700* (1980)
A first-rate survey of the economy of early modern Europe.

J. H. Parry. *The Spanish Seaborne Empire* (1966)
The best work on the subject. It complements Parry's broader *Age of Reconnaissance*.

G. V. Scammell. *The World Encompassed: The First European Maritime Empires, 800–1650* (1981)
The best, and most recent, treatment of European expansion in the Middle Ages and early modern period. Contains much material that is new to specialists as well as general readers. But too detailed, perhaps.

2★

THE OLD WORLD COMES TO AMERICA

What Brought Europeans and Africans to the New World?

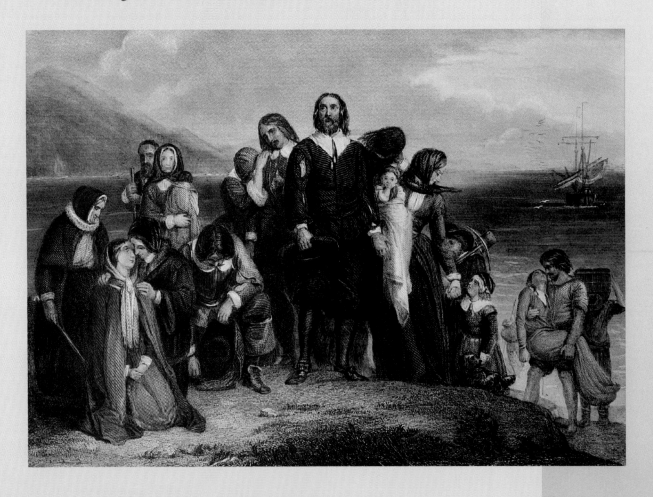

1517–21	Martin Luther launches the Protestant Reformation
1527–39	Henry VIII of England defies the pope and declares himself head of a new Church of England
1577	Elizabeth I of England privately begins to promote exploration and colonization in America
1587–88	Sir Walter Raleigh founds England's first American settlement on Roanoke Island
1607	The London Company establishes the first permanent English settlement at Jamestown
1619	The first Africans in British North America arrive at Jamestown • The House of Burgesses is established as Virginia's legislature
1620	The Pilgrims settle at Plymouth on Cape Cod Bay
1624	The Dutch establish New Netherland in the Hudson Valley
1629	Puritans receive a charter for Massachusetts Bay Colony
1632	Lord Baltimore is granted a charter to found Maryland
1635	Roger Williams establishes Rhode Island at Providence
1636	Bostonian Thomas Hooker founds colony at Hartford, Connecticut • Dissenter Anne Hutchinson is banished from Massachusetts
1664	New Netherland becomes the English colony of New York
1681	William Penn receives a charter to found the Quaker colony of Pennsylvania
1701	East Jersey and West Jersey are united as a single province
1701–03	Delaware is separated from Pennsylvania and becomes a separate colony
1732	James Oglethorpe founds Georgia as refuge for English debtors

As we have seen, America was not an empty continent when Columbus first stumbled on San Salvador in October 1492. Yet today the Indian population of the United States represents less than 1 percent of the total. The rest are descendants of men and women who crossed the oceans from some part of the Old World after 1492.

The process of emigration from the Old World to the New would last for hundreds of years. Indeed, it continues today. Immigration to America is one of the great sagas of world history and a central part of the American experience. We will have occasion to talk about it again, when it becomes relevant in later periods. Here, however, we will consider the first wave of Old World settlement, the one that began in the early seventeenth century and continued to independence in the 1770s.

Establishing a colony in the New World required both promoters and settlers. Someone had to conceive, organize, finance, and lead an expedition to the coast of North America and then guide it through its formative years. But besides promoters there had to be men and women who actually risked themselves, whose contribution to the new colony was their own lives.

The reasons some people promoted colonies, some people settled colonies—and a few did both—are not obvious. America may be a land of freedom, plenty, and stability compared to many other nations today, but it was surely not these things in the year 1600. Early explorers by sea claimed they had found an earthly paradise, a "fruitful and delightsome" land with "most sweet savours" wafting from its shores. But most Europeans took these descriptions with a large grain of salt. Europeans of the day were repelled by raw, untamed nature. America, with its vast gloomy forests, its wild beasts, and its painted "savages," seemed beset by "thorns and thistles." Besides, there was the ordeal of getting there. During the two to four months the average transatlantic passage took in the seventeenth and eighteenth centuries, crews and passengers were packed into tight quarters on tiny ships, confined below deck in bad weather, and fed on salt meat, worm-infested ship's biscuit, and foul water. "Ship fever," a form of typhus, frequently raged through these vessels, carrying off old and young alike. Shipwreck was common. During the age of sail, thousands went to watery graves without ever seeing their new homeland. Promoters, too, had reason to be skeptical of the new land. America might have great potential resources, but to find and develop them was certain to be risky and time-consuming. Why take a chance on the financial uncertainties of a distant, savage land when there were better alternatives at home?

Yet despite the fears, the discomforts, and the risks, both promoters and settlers staked their lives and their

This vision of plenty supported reports of Virginia's abundance. Many aristocratic Englishmen believed the New World a potential feudal paradise, and eagerly sought great estates there.

money on the gamble of America. What moved these people? Was their goal wealth? Did they crave adventure? Were they seeking prestige? Were they primarily in quest of religious or political freedom?

★ THE ARISTOCRATIC IMPULSE ★

Many early colony promoters were driven by the desire for glory, adventure, status, and power. England about the year 1600 was full of young gentlemen and aristocrats who found life at home uninteresting and confining. Under the English laws of primogeniture (derived from Latin words meaning "the first born"), the eldest son alone inherited his father's land and—if a nobleman—the family title. Younger sons had to make their own way in the world. Many turned to the professions; others swallowed the lofty disdain of "gentlemen" for trade and entered business. Still others sought out rich wives. None of these alternatives fully compensated for the accident of being born in the wrong order, and by the early years of the seventeenth century many had begun to look expectantly at America. Not understanding the realities of the American environment, they envisioned a New World version of England where they might live as feudal noblemen amidst the trappings of chivalry and privilege—a life already largely past in England itself.

The English gentleman of this period was not lazy, but he did not enjoy soiling his hands with physical labor. He also typically disdained the bourgeois virtues of prudence, patience, and frugality, and valued and cultivated boldness, passion, and openhanded hospitality. Such men saw exploration and colonization of the New World as a bold adventure. As one gentleman explained in verse:

> Who seeks the way to win renown
> Or flies with wings of high desire;
> Who seeks to wear the laurel crown,
> Or hath the mind that would aspire;
> Tell him his native soil eschew,
> Tell him go range and seek anew.

The Roanoke Attempts. Such attitudes were to be part of most early British attempts to plant settlements in the New World. The first of these, Sir Walter Raleigh's 1585 expedition, transported 100 men, most of them gentlemen determined to find glory and treasure, to Roanoke Island off the coast of North Carolina. Belligerence toward the Algonquian tribes and disdain for fishing, farming, and hard physical labor made the colonists' lot precarious. In 1586, after only a year, the small band returned home.

The noble promoters of English colonization in America did not learn easily that settlement in North America required more substantial virtues than aristocratic gallantry and courage. In 1587 Raleigh sent a second expedition to present-day North Carolina under the immediate command of John White. This time women and children went along, including White's daughter and son-in-law, whose child, Virginia Dare, was born soon thereafter. But again, there was also a sizable group of gentlemen with coats of arms to identify them and their descendants as members of the new feudal aristocracy they hoped to establish in America. The colonists arrived on Roanoke Island toward the end of July, too late to plant a crop, and had to rely on the Indians for food. In less than a year the settlement had disappeared, apparently destroyed by the local tribes, who no doubt quickly found the Europeans' dependence on them too great a burden to bear.

Aristocratic Entrepreneurs. The aristocratic yearning for adventure and disdain for work continued to handicap English colonists long after Raleigh's failures. The first permanent English settlement in North America, established at Jamestown in 1607, for instance, would also suffer from the idleness of gentlemen more interested in finding gold, carving out personal estates, or despoiling the Indians than in clearing the land, raising crops, and founding self-sustaining communities. Still, we must not dismiss the contribution of aristocratic impulses to settlement of the New World.

The strength of the aristocrats' yearning for the feudal past as a colonizing force can be seen in the case of the "proprietary" colonies. In the region from Pennsylvania southward most royal charters for new colonies conferred on a noble "proprietor" the powers of great feudal lords. The 1632 royal charter for Maryland, for example, gave George Calvert (Lord Baltimore) the right to create special titles of nobility and confer them on his friends and associates. These vassals of the proprietor in turn would rule over a population of tenants, the American equivalent of serfs. Disputes among these tenants, as in feudal England of the past, would be brought before manor courts where the lord would preside as chief magistrate. Calvert and his descendants were also allowed to levy "quit rents." These were taxes in place of medieval labor services to the lord of the manor. Maryland was not the only colony that sought to impose this kind of outdated feudal scheme. The Carolina colony, established in the 1660s, was to have "landgraves," a new kind of titled nobleman, ruling over rent-paying commoners. Even the Dutch, though more democratic than the English, tried a feudal plan in their colony along the Hudson River. Any Dutch gentleman who brought fifty settlers to New Netherland could claim a sixteen-mile stretch of land along any navigable river where he might reign as "patroon," or lord of the manor.

All these attempts to establish a feudal system in America eventually failed. The English proprietors and the Dutch patroons did succeed in inducing some men and women to come to their domains by paying their passage or by granting them certain privileges. But in general the aristocratic scheme was not successful as a colonizing approach. There were simply too many applicants for the position of manor lord and too few for the job of serf. The proprietors and would-be patroons quickly found that they could not compete with colonies where land was cheap and distinctions of rank not so sharp. In the end the schemes to re-create a feudal world in America had to be abandoned.

★ THE PROFIT MOTIVE ★

More important for colony promotion was the simple yen for wealth. Whether we consider the role of the state or of private promoters, the desire for profit and riches over-

Sir Walter Raleigh and his eldest son, both dressed in the sumptuous garb of sixteenth-century English gentlemen.

shadowed the desire for rank and titles in summoning forth colony-founding energies.

Mercantilism and the Nation-State.   No group of Europeans was more eager to exploit the riches of the New World than kings and princes. In part, the rulers were inspired by Spain's example. But they were also influenced by a group of thinkers called *mercantilists*, whose goal was to formulate policies to strengthen their nation and elevate it above all others. The key to political supremacy among nations, these publicists and writers held, was wealth—especially gold and silver. These were the "sinews of war" that enabled rulers to hire soldiers, buy weapons, build fleets, and conduct an ambitious and successful foreign policy. Such had been the experience of Spain and would be the experience of any state wise and lucky enough to imitate its example.

The English mercantilists hoped, of course, that their own nation, like Spain, would find fabulous mines of silver and gold in its overseas possessions. But even if England were not so lucky, colonies were still certain, they claimed, to bring it wealth. An overseas empire would provide the mother country with vital consumer goods for its own citizens plus surpluses to sell. Northern Europe, they noted, could no longer do without tropical products such as sugar, tobacco, dyewoods, and citrus fruit. England also lacked furs and adequate timber. Buying these commodities from foreign countries drained gold and silver from the kingdom. If England had colonies of its own, these losses would cease. In fact, like Spain, England would be able to sell surpluses of colonial goods for hard cash and so draw coin from other nations.

And this was not all. The colonies themselves might be markets for English goods. According to Richard Hakluyt the Younger, the native peoples of America were certain to be eager consumers of English manufacturers. In his *Discourse Concerning Westerne Planting* (1584) Hakluyt pictured the North American Indians clothed in English woolens, sleeping in English beds, and using English tools. These new customers would greatly stimulate English industry and overseas trade. Eventually, he wrote, hundreds of ships would criss-cross the ocean, carrying American products to Britain and British products to America. Employment in Britain would leap, turning the thousands of dangerous jobless "sturdy beggars" who roamed the English countryside into busy artisans and seamen.

Hakluyt addressed his *Discourse* directly to Elizabeth, England's shrewd and ambitious queen. But at first Elizabeth felt that England was not strong enough to challenge directly Spain's claim to sole possession of North America. She did encourage Raleigh's two attempts at settlement, but on the whole she preferred to work behind the

A Declaration for the certaine time of dravving the great ſtanding Lottery.

The Virginia Company sometimes ran lotteries when other means of raising funds to sustain its colony proved inadequate. This broadside announces a lottery held in London in 1615, a year when news from Jamestown was largely bad.

scenes, secretly investing her own money in exploratory missions and encouraging English sea captains, such as the "sea dogs" John Hawkins and Francis Drake, to attack and plunder Spanish ships and settlements in America. In 1577 she financed the half-exploratory, half-piratical around-the-world expedition of Drake, which established England's claim to present-day California and British Columbia and made Drake and the queen rich from the proceeds of a captured Spanish treasure galleon.

After Elizabeth's death in 1603, the English crown proved more willing to defy Spain. Yet none of the Stuart monarchs who followed sponsored a colonization project directly out of public funds. The colonizing role of the English government was indirect, though vital. Under James I and his successors the crown provided exclusive charters and grants to proprietors and commercial companies, thereby encouraging them to risk their funds. It suspended laws that restricted emigration from England to help colony promoters people their grants. As we shall see, it conferred various economic privileges on producers of colonial products needed in Britain. Finally, it provided military and naval protection to new settlements. All told, it is hard to see how British North America could have been created and successfully nurtured without the aid of the English nation-state.

Merchants and Profits. Even more directly moved by potential profit than English rulers were English merchants, the bourgeois businessmen with capital to invest who had become such a great force in postfeudal European society. These men hoped to get rich by trading in the furs, timber, metals, and tropical products that Britain needed and the

colonies could supply. They also anticipated making money transporting passengers to the new settlements. Some also looked forward to large windfalls from speculating in land.

Unfortunately, few individual merchants could afford the large sums needed in the early stages of exploration and settlement. Although almost no one foresaw how long it would take to make a colony a going concern and how uncertain the outcome, commercial investors did recognize that it would be wise to divide the risk with others by pooling their capital. Accordingly, merchants interested in colonial investment sold shares in joint-stock companies. These shares, like those of modern corporations, represented ownership in the company. They entitled investors to a part of the company's profits in proportion to their investment. Shareholders often had other privileges as well, such as a personal claim to a certain amount of land in the New World or the right to trade with the Indians on their individual account. If all the company's ventures failed, all alike suffered moderately; no one lost everything.

Jamestown: A Commercial Enterprise. The first of the commercially inspired colonies—and the first successful English "plantation" in the New World—was Jamestown in Virginia. Behind this enterprise were two groups of merchants, one from London and the other from the smaller ports in the west of England, including Plymouth and Bristol. In 1606 these two groups combined their interests and secured a dual charter from the crown that established two Virginia companies. ("Virginia" was the name Sir Walter Raleigh had given to the entire eastern coast of what is now the United States in honor of Elizabeth, the unmarried "Virgin Queen.") One of these, the Plymouth Company, under the merchants from the western ports, had the right to plant settlements anywhere between the Potomac and what is now Bangor, Maine. The second, the London Company, controlled by London-based investors, was given the right to settle between Cape Fear in present-day North Carolina and the site of what is now New York City. The overlapping strip was open to each. Governing their combined areas would be a royal council; ostensibly an arm of the English government, it was made up largely of company officials.

Each group got off to a quick start. In the summer of 1607 the Plymouth Company deposited forty-four men on a rocky projection of the Maine coast as the preliminary to a larger effort the following year. After one cruel winter the Maine settlers had had enough; when spring came, the survivors returned home, leaving behind the rotting timbers of Fort St. George. Discouraged by this disaster, the Plymouth group abandoned colonization.

The better-financed Londoners were more successful. In April 1607 three vessels under their sponsorship arrived off the Virginia coast with a complement of 105 passengers. After a month's search the colonists disembarked on a point of land jutting into the James River and set up tents and shacks. The promoters hoped that the new settlement—called Jamestown after James I—would be self-sustaining. When the vessels departed for home with a cargo of clapboards soon after, it seemed that all would go well.

It did not. Part of the problem was the colony's human material. Not a single one of the first settlers was a woman, a fatal flaw in what was meant to be a self-sustaining colony. Thirty-six, moreover, were gentlemen who could not be expected to dirty their hands with manual labor. Besides, the site of the town, which was chosen partly for defense against the Spaniards, was swampy and malarial. That first year, and for many years thereafter, the Jamestown settlers would suffer from dangerous fevers and "agues."

During the first summer the colonists, considered employees of the company, planted orange trees, cotton, and exotic melons, not the grain they needed for food. Meanwhile, despite the efforts of John Smith, head of the seven-man governing council, to get them to cooperate, they squabbled and fought. The winter was still worse. In January a company ship arrived from England, bringing 120 new settlers to reinforce the surviving 38, which further strained the settlement's limited resources. Soon after, a fire destroyed all the settlement's houses and storehouses. The colonists were now virtually without food, but instead of foraging for supplies, they threw themselves into a frantic search for gold.

Fortunately, Smith was able to keep the settlers alive. He stopped the gold hunt and put men to work building, planting, and producing pitch, tar, and wood ashes. To tide the settlers over until harvesttime, he negotiated with Powhatan, the local Indian chief, for food. The game, corn, fish, and other supplies Powhatan gave them cut the death toll to fewer than a dozen during the winter of 1608–1609.

Smith's successor as president of the council was not as able, and could not maintain good relations with the Indians. Powhatan's warriors attacked settlers on the colony's outskirts and drove them back to Jamestown proper, where overcrowding and bad sanitation killed many. The winter of 1609–1610 was Jamestown's tragic "starving time." Food was so scarce that some colonists resorted to cannibalism. In the spring, when another contingent of set-

A very early view of the fort at Jamestown by an artist rather indifferent to rules of perspective. Still, it captures the primitive nature of this first successful European settlement in British America.

tlers arrived, the supply situation became even more critical; at one point the colony's leaders decided to abandon the settlement altogether.

The following year, 1611, was the turning point. Under Sir Thomas Dale strong leadership was restored. When, in 1612, colonist John Rolfe learned that the native tobacco could be made palatable to Europeans, the colonists discovered their true vocation: tobacco growing. In a few years English smokers were paying premium prices for "Virginia leaf."

The new tobacco crop quickly made Jamestown into a boom town. Farmers abandoned food crops to plant tobacco. Seamen reaching the colony jumped ship and stayed to raise the "noxious weed." Before long, tobacco was growing in the very streets of the little town. Small fortunes were quickly made and quickly lost; gambling, drunkenness, and crime became rampant. Yet tobacco provided a solid base for growth even when tobacco prices came down after 1630. For the remainder of the colonial period Virginia and its neighbor, Maryland, provided most of the better tobacco Europeans consumed.

The London Company's wise policies also contributed to the colony's growth and stability after 1612. The Jamestown settlers had been company servants and their poor performance in part had derived from the absence of incentives for hard work. In 1616, however, the company began to grant some of its land to settlers as their own. Effort would now confer benefits on the worker himself. A year later the company started to hand out large tracts of land called "Hundreds" to enterprising people willing to buy stock in the company for the sake of establishing their own "particular plantations." In 1619 the company sought to further add to Virginia's attractions by establishing a legislative assembly consisting of a council appointed by the governor and an assemblage of elected "burgesses." The right to vote for the new House of Burgesses was highly restricted, but it was the first representative political body in the New World. To cap the campaign to build a permanent, self-sustaining colony, the company also began to pay for the shipment of young women from England to become wives of the planters.

In the midst of these gains Virginia was plunged into a devastating Indian war. Until 1622 the relations between Indians and whites in Virginia had been held in balance by mutual exploitation. Powhatan had used the Europeans as allies against his tribal enemies, and they in turn had counted on him for food during lean times. Neither side much liked the other. A few company officials believed in the possibility of an integrated community. They tried to establish a college where Indian youths might learn Christian ways and offered to settle Indian families in the white communities in houses donated by the company.

Though this plan obviously reflected the European sense of superiority, it was at least benevolent. Unfortunately, whatever the colony's leaders felt, most settlers despised the Indians. As a Jamestown official noted, "There is scarce a man amongst us that doth soe much as afforde them [the Indians] a good thought in his hart and most men with their mouthes give them nothinge but maledictions and bitter execrations."

For a while Powhatan's successor, Opechancanough, ignored the insults. But when the expanding white population pushed out along the banks of the James River, ignoring Indian claims, he decided to strike. In March 1622, Opechancanough's warriors attacked the unsuspecting Virginia settlers, killing 357 men, women, and children.

After lulling the Indians into a false sense of security, the English struck back with a war of extermination. They wiped out whole communities and resorted to such dirty tactics as setting out casks of poisoned wine for unsuspecting Indians to drink. When the smoke of the campaign had cleared, the English had virtually destroyed the tribes of coastal Virginia and ended the "Indian menace."

Although the colonists had eliminated their human foes and established a firm economic base, profits eluded the London Company. Between 1607 and 1624 it declared not a single dividend, and indeed kept calling for additional funds from its English stockholders to stave off bankruptcy. In 1624 the crown intervened, annulled the company's charter, and made Virginia a royal colony under a governor appointed by the king.

The Virginia experience was not unique. Few joint-stock colonizing ventures made money for their investors. The Plymouth Company effort along the Maine coast, as we saw, failed dismally. Dutch investors in the joint-stock Dutch West India Company established several settlements along the Hudson River from 1624 on, but the Dutch never considered their colony much of a commercial success. When the English captured New Netherland in 1664 (and renamed it New York), the Dutch did little to get it back. Few people made money, then, from these merchant-promoted settlements. Nevertheless, the joint-stock company proved to be an invaluable way to pool economic resources and harness the profit motive to the task of founding colonies in America.

★ "THE BEST POOR MAN'S COUNTRY" ★

However useful they were as promoters, aristocrats and rich merchants could scarcely populate the new settlements by themselves. Few chose to leave the wealth and comfort of

England, and in any case, there were not many of them to begin with. Immigrants in large numbers had to be drawn from the "common" people of Britain; America had to be made attractive to laborers, artisans, servants, shopkeepers, and farmers—both men and women—if the new settlements were to take root and prosper.

We do not know precisely how many Europeans crossed the Atlantic to the British North American colonies. In the seventeenth century about 155,000 came from England alone. In the eighteenth century the number of European arrivals increased. During the fifteen years preceding the American Revolution (1760–1775), 125,000 emigrants left the British Isles (England, Scotland, Wales, and Ireland) for mainland North America, while another 12,000 immigrants arrived from Germany and Switzerland. A majority of all immigrants were young. Youth, with its physical strength, adaptability, and sense of adventure, was required by the new land, and the infant settlements received them gladly.

Mixed Motives. Most immigrants to America during the seventeenth and eighteenth centuries came willingly, though not always wisely. Boredom sent some to America, as did flight from the law or from unpleasant jobs or family circumstances. In 1660 the mayor of Bristol, England, then a favorite point of departure for the New World, described the motives of some of the immigrants gathering in his city to leave England:

> Among those who repair to Bristol from all parts to be transported to his majesty's plantations beyond the seas, some are husbands who have forsaken their wives, other wives who have abandoned their husbands, some are children and apprentices run away from their parents and masters, . . . and many that have been pursued by hue-and-cry for robberies, burglaries or breaking prison, do thereby escape the prosecution of law and justice.

In 1732, debtors, who were then often jailed when they could not pay their creditors, joined the stream of people fleeing the heavy hand of English law. In that year a group of philanthropists led by James Oglethorpe founded Georgia as a haven for English debtors, a place where they could get a new start in life. Georgia was the last British colony to be established in North America, and would still be a sparsely settled community at the time of the Revolution.

Only a small number of immigrants were runaways, lawbreakers, or debtors, however. According to the surviving lists of seventeenth-century immigrants from London and Bristol, some were orphan boys sent to the colonies by the Anglican church to relieve British taxpayers of the burden of supporting them. The adult males emigrating through Bristol were mostly farmers; those departing through London mostly artisans and tradesmen—carpenters, weavers, shipbuilders, wheelwrights, barrelmakers, and cobblers. All in all, scholars believe, a disproportionate number of Europeans were craftspeople and artisans from the cities and towns. Propelling these people from their homeland were low wages, increasingly high rents, bad harvests, and severe depression in the woolen industry.

About a quarter of the immigrants on the London and Bristol lists are women. Most of these were in their early twenties, the usual age of marriage in Britain. There is reason to believe that many were fleeing an environment where husbands were scarce and few economic opportunities existed for unmarried women.

Going beyond the London and Bristol lists, the proportion of women immigrants to colonial America varied according to the stage of the community and the particular colony. There were more women immigrants when a community had passed beyond the pioneer stage. At the same time, some colonies—Massachusetts, Connecticut, and Pennsylvania, for example—were the destination of whole families, even in the early years, including of course, the women of the family—wives, mothers, daughters, and sisters.

High Wages and Cheap Land. In addition to the forces pushing people from Europe, we must consider the attractions pulling them to America. During the seventeenth and early eighteenth centuries colony promoters hired agents to travel through Britain and the European continent recruiting colonists. As these agents often received a fee for each immigrant they signed up, they were not always truthful about life in the New World. On the Continent, "Newlanders," wearing jewels and fancy clothes, circulated among the peasants, telling the ignorant that America's mountains were full of precious metals and that its springs gushed milk and honey.

It was not all humbug. Ordinary people could expect to make real gains by moving to America. The New World was not a paradise: No one could succeed there without hard work. But hard work paid richer dividends than in Europe. The reason was simple. North America was a vast continent bursting with resources that could be turned into wealth. The missing ingredient was labor, and those who could supply it were certain to receive a higher economic reward than at home.

For Europeans, then, colonial America promised high wages. Still better, it promised cheap land. This fact was well understood by seventeenth-century colony promoters, who soon began to offer a free "headright" of fifty or a hundred acres to settlers who paid their own way to the New World, and even more to those who financed additional settlers. Where land was not actually given away, it was sold cheaply. Proprietor William Penn, for example, sold 15,000 acres in Pennsylvania to a group of Germans for £300, less than 5 cents an acre.

One interesting variant of the land-pull pattern was the settlement of South Carolina. This region attracted its first settlers not from Europe but from English-settled Barbados off the coast of South America. By the 1670s, all the land in Barbados was divided up into sugar plantations, and the island could neither feed itself nor provide land for anyone but the richest gentlemen. Joining a desire for cheap land with the hope of supplying the Barbados plantations with food and raw materials, several thousand free white Barbadians crossed over to the lands south of Virginia granted shortly before by Charles II to a group of English aristocrats and named Carolina in his honor. Before long the settlers of this colony had carved out farms and were sending "provisions" and timber back to Barbados to supply the slaves' and the sugar planters' needs.

Indentured Servants. It is clear that the material advantages of America exerted a strong pull on the peasants and laborers of Europe. But how could these people move themselves to the new land? The Atlantic passage for a single person in the seventeenth century cost about the equivalent of $100 today—far more than any laborer or landless husbandman could afford. The solution for most would-be settlers was the *indenture*—a labor contract. In return for having the cost of the passage paid by a ship captain or prospective employer, immigrants agreed to work for a specified time at a certain wage or for a specified amount of food, clothing, and shelter.

There were several kinds of indentured servants. The most fortunate was the bondsman or bondswoman, who possessed a needed or uncommon skill and therefore could get favorable terms while still at home. The indenture for these "servants" was normally four years. Often their labor contract described the trade the servant would work at and defined acceptable working conditions; frequently it promised "freedom dues"—clothes, tools, and even land—when the indenture expired. A Maryland statute of 1640 spelled out that colony's freedom dues as "one good Cloth Suit of Keirsy or Broadcloth, a shift of white linen, one new pair of Stockins and Shoes, two hoes, one axe, 3 barrels of Corne, and fifty acres of land whereof at least to [two] be plantable."

"Redemptioners" were less fortunate than other servants. These were people who in the eighteenth century fled Germany and Switzerland in the wake of war and hard times. Unlike the typical single bondservant, redemptioners moved as families. They arranged for merchants to pay their fare and agreed to reimburse them when they arrived in America. If they could not find the passage money immediately, they had to allow the merchant or his agent to sell their services for a time sufficient to recover the debt. This arrangement sometimes led to the separation of families; children might be sold to one master, their parents to another.

Indentured servants often had a hard life. They usually worked from ten to fourteen hours a day, six days a week. Masters had the right to whip them for disobedience or failure to work. Normally, they could not marry, vote, or engage in trade. Their indenture and their persons could be transferred from one master to another. If they ran away, their terms of service could be extended. Many failed to survive the difficult indenture period and were buried in unmarked graves.

Yet a proportion, particularly in the earlier years, did achieve success in America, working off their contracts and establishing themselves as free farmers or craftspeople. In Maryland in the 1640s and 1650s, for example, a majority of indentured servants became prosperous small farmers; a small group even became leading figures in the colony. News of their achievements drifted back to Europe and inspired others to follow, thus ensuring the indenture system's survival despite its risks and uncertainties. Indentured servants were not spread evenly throughout the colonies. New England was peopled overwhelmingly by free families who either paid their own way or were sponsored by the community. But by 1750 a large part of the white population from Pennsylvania southward was composed of indentured servants or their descendants.

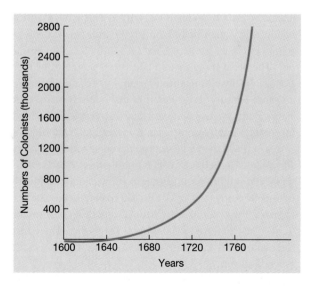

Population growth in the colonies, 1610–1780. Source: Historical Statistics of the United States, Colonial Times to 1957.

Thus far, in considering the reasons why people from the Old World came to America during the colonial era, we have assumed that men and women made a personal choice, that they came voluntarily. But there were many thousands who had no choice, who were brought across the Atlantic against their will. In describing their motives for coming to America we must say, in effect, they had none; or rather, that the motives that brought them were the motives of other people, not their own.

Involuntary immigration was an unadorned product of greed. The inducements colonial promoters offered to would-be settlers were often not enough to attract the laborers needed to clear the forests, plant the fields, and build the towns of the new settlements. In the southern colonies especially, following the introduction of commercial crops such as tobacco, rice, and indigo, labor shortages could be crippling. Unless they could find an abundant supply of labor, planters could not take advantage of cheap land and a ready market for their crops in Europe. Rather than forgo profits, they were willing to pay good prices for forced labor from whatever source they could find.

Involuntary European Immigrants. Some of the involuntary immigrants were Europeans. During the seventeenth and eighteenth centuries kidnappers operated in every English port, enticing the young, naive, or intemperate aboard ship and collecting a fee from the captain, who would then carry the victims across the Atlantic and sell them as indentured servants in the colonies. More numerous were "His Majesty's Seven Year Guests"—convicts given the choice of going to America as seven-year indentured servants or facing a hangman's noose at home. Those who accepted "transportation" were pardoned and turned over to merchants, who bore the expense of the transatlantic trip in exchange for the right to sell the convicts' labor to the colonists.

Every colonial legislature protested this dumping of England's "fellons and other desperate villaines" on America. Parliament remained unmoved, however, and the planters of Maryland and Virginia, where most felons were sent, were generally happy to have their labor. Historians estimate that some 20,000 convicts were sent to America during the eighteenth century alone.

Black Slaves. Indentured servants, convicted felons, and kidnapped youths notwithstanding, labor remained in short supply in America, especially in the regions south of Pennsylvania. Europe, it seemed, simply could not produce enough workers to satisfy the needs of the New World's profit-making enterprises.

But Africa could. Well before the first voyage of Columbus, Portuguese explorers were bringing back captured Africans to work in Europe and on the Portuguese islands in the Atlantic. When the Portuguese settled Brazil and began raising sugar, the market for black labor in the New World expanded enormously. Meanwhile, destruction of the Indian tribes in the Caribbean created a labor vacuum that Spanish planters quickly filled with African workers.

Unlike indentured servants, these black workers were not free in any sense. Though slavery no longer existed in Christian Europe, it survived in Islamic lands and existed in Africa itself among the native peoples. The Portuguese, the Spanish, and later the French, Dutch, and English responded to the lure of profits and readily adopted the system for their labor-short American colonies. Many Europeans rationalized slavery by arguing that the African peoples were "heathens" who worshiped idols, or "naked savages" who might benefit from contact with Christian, "civilized" people.

In reality, the Africans brought to the Americas were anything but savages. Slaves were plucked from many peoples and nations along Africa's Atlantic coast, largely between present-day Guinea and Angola, including the Asante, Fon, Yoruba, Beni, Pawpaw, Ibo, and Coromantin. These West Africans practiced a productive hoe agriculture that provided them with abundant food. They had also brought to a high level the arts of weaving, metalworking, pottery making, and wood and ivory carving. The bronze sculptures of Benin, the silver and gold jewelry of the Yoruba, and the rugs and carpets of the Asante were outstanding artistic achievements. In the arts of government, too, West Africans revealed great talent. Powerful states such as Benin, Congo, Dahomey, and Ghana brought order and prosperity to large areas of Africa, conducting foreign affairs in much the same way as contemporary European kingdoms did.

The slave trade that ripped these people from their homes was a well-organized system by the end of the seventeenth century. At first Europeans themselves captured slaves along the Guinea coast. But this proved dangerous, for whites could not withstand West Africa's tropical diseases. By 1700 the white slavers had come to rely on black African merchants and chiefs as middlemen to supply them with captured prisoners of war or with victims snatched by raiders from the interior of the African continent. Chained together, these unfortunate people were brought overland to the coast by the merchants or by war parties. There they were sold to the European traders for guns, powder, cloth, beads, and rum.

Once aboard ship, the next step in the African slave trade was the infamous "middle passage." The "slavers" that carried this human cargo across the Atlantic were about the

same size as the ships used for indentured servants, but they were far more crowded. Vessels as small as ninety tons—scarcely bigger than a fishing boat—sometimes packed in 400 slaves besides the crew and supplies. The captives were chained together to prevent rebellion. Wise captains attempted to keep them healthy, but they seldom succeeded. Slaves lived in filth below deck where temperatures rose into the nineties and higher. Inevitably the death rate was appalling. Some slave vessels arrived in the Americas with well over half their passengers dead from dysentery, smallpox, or some European disease to which Africans had little natural resistance.

The first slaves reached the English mainland colonies in 1619 when a Dutch vessel unexpectedly put in at Jamestown with a cargo of twenty Africans. The slave system was still unfamiliar to the English, and these people evidently were treated as indentured servants. Over the next thirty or forty years a small trickle of blacks were brought to the Chesapeake region and most, it seems, were kept as bondservants for a few years and then freed.

At first the market for slaves in the plantation colonies was limited despite the labor shortage. Africans were prob-

ably more resistant to the diseases of subtropical America than Europeans. But the mortality rates of all immigrants to the southern plantation colonies were extremely high

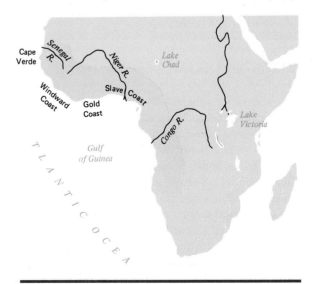

AFRICAN ORIGINS OF THE SLAVE TRADE

How Africans Came to America

The *Hannibal*, commanded by Captain Thomas Phillips, sailed to the west African coast in 1693–1694 to collect a cargo of slaves for the West Indies market. In the Caribbean many of these unfortunate people would be "seasoned" for later transport to the mainland colonies. Phillips was a merchant under contract to supply slaves to the Royal African Company, the firm which for many years possessed a monopoly on the slave trade to the English colonies.

Phillips was an unusual man. He kept a diary and also, despite his occupation, was capable of feeling some compassion for his victims. The portion of his account reproduced here tells of what followed the local king's sale of a slave parcel to the European slave traders.

"The negroes are so willful and loth to leave their own country, that they have often leap'd out of the canoes, boat and ship into the sea, and kept under water till they were drowned, to avoid being taken up and saved by our boats, which pursued them, they having a more dreadful apprehension of Barbados than we can have of hell. . . . [W]e have likewise seen divers [a number] of them eaten by the sharks, of which a prodigious number kept about the ships in this place. . . . We had about twelve negroes did willfully drown themselves, and others starved to death, for 'tis their belief that when they die they return home to their own country and friends again. . . .

". . . When our slaves are aboard we shackle the men two and two while we lie in port, and in sight of their country, for 'tis then that they attempt to make their escape, and mutiny, to prevent which we always keep sentinels upon the hatchways, and have a chest full of small arms, ready loaded and prim'd constantly lying at hand upon the quarter deck. . . . The men are all fed upon the main deck and forecastle, in case of any disturbance; the women eat upon the quarterdeck with us. . . . When we come to sea we let them all out of irons, they never attempting to rebel, considering that should they kill or master us, they could not tell how to manage the ship. . . . I never heard that they mutiny'd in any ships of consequence, . . . but in small [vessels] where they had but few men . . . then they surpriz'd and butchered them, cut the cables, and let the vessel drive ashore. . . . We often at sea in the evenings would let the slaves come up into the sun to air themselves, and made them jump and dance for an hour or two to our bag-pipes, harp and fiddle, by which exercize to preserve them in health; but notwithstanding all our endeavour, 'twas my hard fortune to have great sickness and mortality among them. . . .

"We spent in our passage from St. Thomas to Barbados two months eleven days. . . . [A]mong my poor men and negroes, that of the first we buried 14, and of the last 320, which was a great detriment to our voyage, the royal African company losing ten pounds by every slave that died, and the owners of the ship ten pounds ten shillings. . . .

"I deliver'd alive at Barbados to the company's factors [agents] 372, which being sold, came to about nineteen pounds per head one with another. . . ."

during the early years of settlement, and so the lifetime service of a black slave offered little advantage over short-term white servitude. And because few children could be counted on to survive, the fact that a slave's offspring became the property of the master meant little to the owner. By the 1660s or 1670s, however, life expectancies in the southern colonies rose as settlers learned how to deal with American diseases and as food supplies improved. At this point high-priced slaves for life began to promise an economic advantage over cheaper indentured servants for four years.

Racial attitudes as well as economics played a part in establishing slavery in North America. However harshly they were treated, white indentured servants were not without rights. As fellow Europeans, they could not be severely mistreated or abused with impunity by their masters. Women servants could not be exploited sexually. If the master of an indentured servant violated the custom of the country or the terms of the contract, he or she could be sued by the servant. Except in the earliest period, Africans enjoyed no such rights. The English were prejudiced against the physical characteristics of Africans and viewed them as lesser beings. Brutally torn away from all that was familiar, brought among strangers, surrounded by other captives who did not speak their language, and confronted with an alien landscape and an unfamiliar climate, blacks were in no position to protect themselves.

As the value of African workers increased they gradually ceased to be treated as indentured servants. First they became "servants for life," and then subject to ever more elaborate "slave codes" that defined their legal position in de-ways and placed severe restrictions on their movements and conduct. Under these codes they became "chattel property," to be bought, sold, inherited, and bequeathed like houses, horses, or plows. By the end of the seventeenth century the distinction between black slaves and white servants had become sharply defined: Servants were humans; slaves were things.

As slaves became more valuable as property, the planters sought to increase their number. Prices rose and each year more and more were imported from Africa or from the Caribbean islands. Some 300,000 Africans were landed at the docks of the mainland colonies during the seventeenth and eighteenth centuries. More than ten times as many slaves were brought to the Caribbean and Latin America during this period. There the high profits on the sugar plantations permitted the owners to bring in few women, work the males to death, and then replace them by importing new male slaves. The Virginia planters, who made smaller profits on tobacco, could not afford such an extravagant system, and from the beginning they imported female slaves as well. The relatively high proportion of women, plus the healthier conditions of the North American mainland, resulted in a rapid increase in the slave population through an excess of births over deaths. By 1759 more than a fifth of the inhabitants of mainland British America were black slaves, and many of these were native-born Americans.

★ AMERICA AS A RELIGIOUS HAVEN ★

Americans like to think of their country as a haven for the oppressed. We should be careful not to exaggerate this self-congratulatory view; in the end the yearning for land and a better living standard pulled more people from the Old World to the New than any other force. But America did serve as a refuge for thousands, and ultimately millions, of transatlantic migrants fleeing Old World oppression. In the seventeenth century most of these were refugees from religious intolerance and, although all the colonies received some, they came primarily to the settlements north of the Chesapeake, especially to New England and Pennsylvania, imprinting on these communities many of their values and characteristics.

Those settlers moved by religion came from every class of European society. At the top, serving as colony promoters, were rich merchants and landed gentlemen who sought to aid their poorer co-religionists. In the case of Massachusetts, many of the gentry actually joined the migration to America. Most of those who came to escape persecution at home, however, were ordinary laborers, artisans, farmers, housewives, servants, and shopkeepers,

much like those who came to escape poverty.

One point needs to be emphasized: Most of those fleeing religious oppression had no interest in freedom of worship for its own sake. They were often as intolerant as their persecutors. Their complaint was merely that the wrong people were dictating the religious rules. It is not surprising, then, that such people would often become persecutors in turn when they found themselves in a position to dictate religious beliefs and practices.

The Reformation. To understand what the refugees from persecution were fleeing, we must look at the religious scene in sixteenth- and seventeenth-century Europe. Until the 1520s all Western Europeans were Roman Catholic Christians except for a few thousand Jews. Christians gained salvation for their souls and avoided eternal damnation through participation in the Roman Catholic sacraments and acceptance of the Roman Catholic creed. Through its rituals, ceremonies, ministries, and confessionals, the all-embracing Catholic Church provided solace and hope for the multitude. It also provided cloistered refuge for those with a contemplative bent, succored the poor, and nursed the sick. Its spiritual authority was reinforced by its stewardship of the Bible, which was available only in Latin, the language of the Catholic clergy and a small lay elite. The supreme head of the Catholic Church, the pope, seated in Rome, not only served as the final authority in matters of faith and morals, but also sought at times to assert temporal power over the rulers of the European states.

By 1500 many Europeans had become critical of the Catholic Church. Some saw the richness of the Church's ceremonies as a reflection of a growing clerical taste for luxury and worldliness. Popes, bishops, and even ordinary priests now seemed obsessed with wealth and secular power. Even the monasteries and convents were no longer centers for the contemplative life, said the critics, but all too often were refuges for the idle and even the immoral. To the most skeptical it seemed that the Church had become hypocritical, venal, and corrupt and in need of fundamental reform.

In 1517 Martin Luther, an Augustinian friar, attacked the Church's sale of indulgences—papal letters remitting punishment for sin—that were being peddled in Germany to raise money for building St. Peter's basilica in Rome. From this assault on what he perceived as the Church's greed, Luther soon moved on to attack its claim to be the guardian of the gates of heaven. In its place he asserted the "priesthood of all believers"; that is, he said that salvation was a transaction between God and the individual, needing no priest as intermediary. Luther denounced the self-imposed isolation of monks and nuns and insisted that all Christians participate in the world's affairs. In theology he denied the

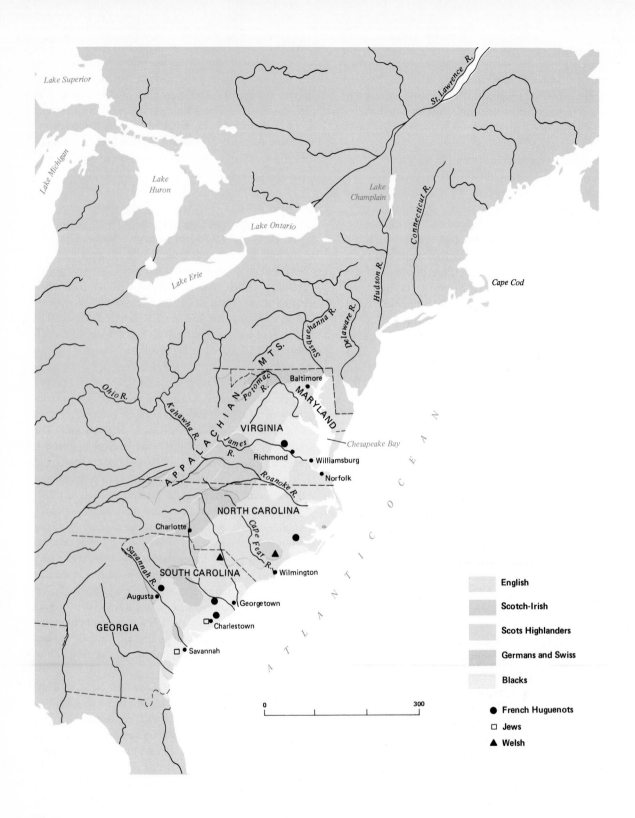

Lake Superior

Lake Michigan

Lake Huron

Lake Ontario

Lake Erie

Lake Champlain

St. Lawrence R.

Connecticut R.

Hudson R.

Cape Cod

Susquehanna R.

Delaware R.

Potomac R.

Ohio R.

APPALACHIAN MTS.

Kahawha R.

James R.

Baltimore

MARYLAND

VIRGINIA

Chesapeake Bay

Richmond

Williamsburg

Norfolk

Roanoke R.

NORTH CAROLINA

Charlotte

Cape Fear R.

Wilmington

SOUTH CAROLINA

Savannah R.

Augusta

Georgetown

Charlestown

GEORGIA

Savannah

ATLANTIC OCEAN

0   300

English

Scotch-Irish

Scots Highlanders

Germans and Swiss

Blacks

● French Huguenots

□ Jews

▲ Welsh

COLONIAL SETTLEMENT BY NATIONALITY IN THE SOUTH, 1770

This eighteenth-century French brig, at anchor in a West Indies port, is a "slaver," a vessel that carried Africans to America in the notorious "middle passage."

Catholic emphasis on "good works" as the road to salvation and substituted the idea of faith. Only those on whom God had conferred the capacity to believe would be spared damnation. One could not earn salvation by deeds, however pious or virtuous.

Luther's demands for change quickly spread through Europe. Before long the reform movement expanded into a thorough assault on Church ceremony, worldliness, papal power, and the belief that the sacraments of the Church were essential to salvation. The attack begun by Luther against the established religious order eventually touched many other aspects of life, producing the Continent-wide upheaval known as the Protestant Reformation.

For a while the Reformation scarcely affected England. King Henry VIII had no quarrel with the Catholic Church's doctrines or forms of worship. But when the pope refused to annul Henry's marriage to Catherine of Aragon and excommunicated him for setting her aside in 1533 to marry Anne Boleyn, the king declared himself supreme head of the Church of England. He also authorized an English translation of the Bible so that it might be read by all literate people, not just priests and a tiny elite, and he dissolved the monasteries, confiscating their vast property.

For the next century England became a battleground between the forces of Catholicism and Protestantism. Eventually, under Elizabeth I, a Protestant Church of England (the Anglican Church) emerged, controlled by the English crown but retaining many of the old religion's ceremonies and beliefs. This outcome did not please everyone. Some English people refused to accept Anglicanism and remained loyal Catholics. Others sought to go beyond Anglicanism to embrace the tenets of John Calvin, a French Protestant reformer, who had established his headquarters at Geneva. Calvinists, more loudly than Lutherans, insisted that humans, even the best of them, were sinful and wicked. As one English Calvinist expressed it, "every natural man and woman is born full of sin . . . as full as a toad of poison, as full as ever his skin can hold; mind, will, eyes, mouth, every limb of his body, and every piece of his soul is full of sin; their hearts are bundles of sin." Such beings obviously deserved damnation and could not ransom themselves through good works. But God, in his infinite mercy and regard for Christ's sacrifice, would save a few. But these few, these "elect," were *predestined* to be saved from hell, since God, who knew all, and determined all, had selected them, like all things to come, at the beginning of time.

English Calvinists demanded that the Church of England "purify" itself entirely of Catholic belief and ceremonies and abandon the episcopal church-governing structure that it still retained from the old religion. At first these "Puritans" were content to remain within the official Anglican Church as "dissenters" or "nonconformists,"

This print of a slaver's interior only hints at the misery for the Africans below decks in the middle passage to the Americas. Imagine also the heat, the noise, the stench.

working to change it from the inside. Eventually, after being harrassed and persecuted, many became "separatists" and renounced the Church of England entirely.

In the half century following Elizabeth's death in 1603, England experienced a religious ferment that threatened to tear the country apart. New sects rose to prominence, each, it seemed, more extreme and unusual than the one preceding. There were various kinds of Antinomians (literally, opponents of the law) who believed that those whom God had granted salvation were incapable of sin and therefore exempt from moral restraint. Groups like the Baptists (originally called Anabaptists) and the Quakers insisted that individual conscience was the sole source of moral values. Some of these "sectaries" were intensely hostile to the existing social system, despising and denouncing political absolutism, class deference, intellectual authority, and even private property.

It is not surprising that the English crown and its agents attacked the sectaries as subversives. But they also assailed the more moderate Nonconformists and the remaining Catholics. Merely by rejecting the Church of England, these people seemed to be undermining the authority of the crown and destroying the unity of the nation, besides endangering their own souls and infecting with error all who came in contact with them.

As noted, the victims of Anglican religious persecution generally did not advocate religious toleration. Only the Quakers insisted that all people be allowed to discover spiritual truth for themselves. Most of the others held that they alone were right and accepted the state's right to impose religious uniformity.

The Pilgrims of Plymouth. By the early 1600s several religious minorities had abandoned hope of change in England and had begun to consider emigration. The first to depart was a small body of radical Puritan Separatists, the Pilgrims. In 1608 this group moved to Leiden in the Netherlands, then a refuge for religious minorities from all over Europe. For a while they prospered, but as time passed the little congregation began to fear for its survival and its purity of belief in the face of the easygoing religious ways of the Dutch. In 1617 the Pilgrim leaders decided to move the congregation to "Virginia," where they could maintain their preferred mode of life and form of worship without distraction.

Unfortunately the community was poor and could not provide itself with ships or supplies. It also had no royal charter that would guarantee English protection from Spain or ensure the Pilgrims' right to exclude undesirables. At this point the Pilgrims turned to the London Company: In exchange for liberty of conscience, the settlers agreed to develop some of the company's otherwise worthless real estate in America.

After selling their possessions in Holland and securing loans from the company and from Thomas Weston, a London merchant, about thirty of the Pilgrims departed for England. At Southampton they joined a larger group of non-separatists hired to work in the colony by the profit-seeking Weston. On September 16, 1620, after many difficulties and much delay, the 180-ton *Mayflower*, with 149 passengers and crew, sailed from Plymouth harbor for America.

The Pilgrims' original destination was the region near the mouth of the Hudson River. Severe storms drove them to the north, however, and they decided to stay where they touched land. This was at Cape Cod Bay, at a place they called Plymouth, after their port of departure. Fearful that the nonseparatists ("strangers") among them might dominate the community, and worried that their charter might not have legal force because the region was outside the London Company's grant, the Pilgrims adopted the Mayflower Compact before leaving ship. This short document established a civil government with powers "to enact, constitute, and frame such just and equal Laws, Ordinances, Acts, Constitutions, and Offices, from time to time, as shall be thought most meet and convenient for the general Good of the Colony."

During the first winter the colonists suffered grievously from disease. Fortunately, the weather was relatively mild. In addition, since smallpox had swept the region shortly before the *Mayflower* arrived, they had few Indians to contend with. The Indians who had survived, moreover, proved helpful. One, Squanto, had been seized by a European trader years before and taken to England, where he had learned the language. He and Massasoit, the grand sachem of the local Wampanoags, befriended the colonists, teaching them how to plant maize and other native plants and showing them the best fishing streams. In spite of this aid the Pilgrim community, like almost all early white settlements, went through a "starving time" that first winter. By spring nearly half the colonists were dead. During the summer the survivors put the Indians' teachings to good use; by fall their storehouses were well stocked. In November 1621 they celebrated their success with a harvest festival that has come down to us, after many twists, as Thanksgiving.

The Plymouth colony expanded gradually, reaching a population of about 1,000 in 1640 and 3,000 in 1660.

Uncertainty over the charter persisted, however. There were financial problems, too. Successors to the London Company forced the Plymouth colonists to pay rent in addition to the sums they had borrowed to finance the settlement. To meet their debts the Pilgrims were forced to turn to fishing, trading with the Indians for furs, and commerce with the Dutch in New Amsterdam at the mouth of the Hudson. Although life was hard, William Bradford and the other Pilgrim leaders never forgot that their mission was to found a godly colony. Yet Plymouth religious orthodoxy was never intolerant or harsh. For seventy years the "Old Colony" modestly prospered. Then, in 1691, it was absorbed into the Massachusetts Bay community.

The Massachusetts Bay Puritans. The Puritans who settled the Massachusetts Bay Colony were also propelled by religion. The Puritan dissenters within the Church of England were more numerous, more prosperous, and socially more prominent than the Pilgrims and other separatists. Until the 1620s they had hoped that they could reform the established Church of England. By the middle of that decade, however, they, too, began to lose heart and to look to the New World as a promising refuge.

The Puritan concern was for the future of the godly in a nation ruled by Charles I and Anglican Archbishop William Laud. Considering Puritan doctrines wicked and erroneous, Laud, in cooperation with the king, suppressed Puritan books, forbade Puritans to preach, and attempted to impose Anglican practices and beliefs on all dissenters. Then in 1629 Charles dissolved Parliament, where the Puritans had many friends, and assumed personal rule of England. Clearly, now was the time to leave.

A few Puritans had already departed. In 1625 forty had emigrated to the fishing colony of Salem, north of present-day Boston. Now a number of prominent Puritan gentlemen procured a royal charter for a new colony. This document established the Massachusetts Bay Company, a corporation authorized to own and govern all land between the Merrimack and the Charles rivers, from the Atlantic to the Pacific. The charter also prescribed a structure for the new Massachusetts Bay Company that omitted the provision, common to such grants, that the governor, assistants, and freemen of the company had to remain in England to do business.

In the summer of 1629 the promoters of emigration persuaded John Winthrop, a Cambridge University-educated gentleman and attorney, to accept the governorship of the company. Winthrop agreed on condition that the settlers bring the company's charter to New England. There it would be out of easy reach of the English authorities, and the colonists would enjoy virtual autonomy in their political and religious affairs. Winthrop knew about the hard fate

John Winthrop

At fifteen Master John Winthrop, son of Squire Adam Winthrop of Groton Manor in Suffolk, went off to Cambridge University to acquire the polish and classical learning expected of a seventeenth-century gentleman. He returned two years later and married Mary Forth, as had been arranged between his father and hers. Ten months later while only seventeen, he became father of a son.

Life was usually short in seventeenth-century Europe, so it was necessary to cram a lot into a brief period. Yet the young man's course marked him as precocious even for his time. But it was not surprising that John would act quickly to take on the responsibilities of adulthood, for he had become a Puritan, and like others of the faith, was imbued with a new seriousness of purpose and a sense that he must follow the Lord's commandments.

The Puritan view of the Christian life placed an enormous strain on believers. They must avoid sin while living with the world's temptations. Yet they could not count on earning salvation merely by virtuous behavior. Salvation was God's gift alone and predestined from the beginning of time. The young Winthrop enjoyed hunting; he relished good food. Like most Puritans, he was not a dour killjoy. But he also feared excess and closely examined his conscience and conduct to see if his recreations and pleasures had "ensnared" his "heart so farre in worldly delights" that he had "cooled the graces of the spirit by them."

Despite his prudence, Winthrop's life had its share of tragedy. Mary died in 1615 after bearing him six children. He married his second wife six months later, and within the year she, too, died. But he had his portion of joys as well; in 1618 he married for a third time. He would later describe Margaret Tyndal as "a very gracious woman," and the relationship would be a long and happy one. Meanwhile, John became an attorney and in the late 1620s spent much time in London on cases heard before the royal courts.

During these years England, under Charles I, was a deeply troubled land. The king believed that he ruled by divine right and need not heed Parliament. He also despised the Puritans within the official Church of England and he and Archbishop Laud harassed and persecuted them. From his perch in London, Winthrop could see still another deplorable aspect of the existing regime: its extravagance and corruption.

For a time the Puritans hoped that their many friends in Parliament would help them, but in March 1629 the king disbanded that body and began to govern directly. To many Puritans the time now seemed ripe to "separate" from England and seek refuge in America.

Winthrop had misgivings about the move, and when approached by a group of other prominent Puritan leaders, men associated with the newly chartered Massachusetts Bay Company, he dithered. Should the virtuous depart, leaving behind their fellow Puritans to face the wrath of Laud and the king alone? Would the new colony

of the Virginia colonists and had terrible doubts about the new venture. He soon became its zealous promoter, however, and in a communication sent to leading Puritans argued that the tribulations of Jamestown should not deter others from going to America. The Virginia settlers had fallen into "great and fundamental errors," he stated, because, among other things, "their mayne end was Carnall and not religious." The new venture would avoid that mistake.

In addition to Winthrop's appeals and the desire to escape Laud's harassment, the depression in the English wool industry in the late 1620s helped push the Puritans to the New World. Men and women facing both persecution and hunger sold their property, paid their debts, and signed up for Massachusetts. In the early spring of 1630 four well-equipped, crowded vessels left for New England. They were soon followed by seven more, all of which arrived safely. Most of the settlers were from East Anglia, the bloc of English counties northeast of London. In a few months 1,000 settlers were building cabins, clearing fields, and planting crops in the Shawmut (Boston) area. Despite some sickness and a few untimely deaths the first year, settlers continued to arrive and the population grew fast. By 1640 Massachusetts had about 9,000 inhabitants, almost as many as Jamestown, founded thirty-three years earlier.

Offshoots of the Massachusetts Bay Colony. Religious oppression would operate as a colonizing force in America itself. Under John Winthrop and the other learned Puritan "magistrates," Massachusetts Bay functioned as a theocratic republic. All adult male family heads who were full-fledged members of the church were considered "freemen" and allowed to participate in political decisions. Women were denied all political rights, but so were many men who were not church members or who owned no property. Nor did

be able to achieve economic independence and attain some prosperity? Most of Winthrop's doubts were resolved by mid-1629, and that fall, while still in England, he was elected governor of the new enterprise.

The four small vessels that braved the rough north Atlantic in April and May 1630 carried 400 people, each of whom cost £50 to transport. Many paid their own way; others had their passage and outfitting paid for by richer Puritans like Winthrop or one of the other "gentlemen." Another 600 men, women, and children arrived in Massachusetts soon after.

As in all the early settlements, even one so well planned and financed as the Puritan colony, the first months were hard. During this difficult time Governor Winthrop was a rock of strength, though he had to cope with the personal tragedy of his son Henry's drowning shortly after arrival. He moved the settlers from their initial landing point near Salem to the east shore of Massachusetts Bay and eventually brought them to the site of what would be named Boston. Food was in short supply, and before the community became self-sustaining, he dispatched vessels to Cape Cod to collect corn for the winter and contacted the settlers' friends in England to raise money to buy provisions. Despite the sickness, hunger, hard work, discomfort, and danger, he did not lose heart. That September he wrote Margaret, still in England: "I like so well to be heer, as I doe not repent my comminge. . . ." He had, he added, "never slept better, never had more content of minde."

Two hundred settlers died that first winter and an equal number returned to England in the spring. Yet the colony survived and eventually prospered. Margaret and the rest of Winthrop's family arrived in the fall of 1631, to be greeted en masse by the whole colony and presented with gifts of "fat hogs, kids, venison, poultry, geese, partridges, etc., so as the like joy and manifestations of love had never been seen in New England."

During the next eighteen years Winthrop served his community well as governor, deputy governor, and assistant. At times he was accused of excessive leniency, though he was adamant in his prosecution of Anne Hutchinson and her followers. From our modern perspective, this was not admirable behavior, but few contemporaries anywhere believed that dangerous heretics and sowers of sedition like Hutchinson should be allowed to spread their poison. Winthrop was not a democrat, but rather held the view that a good magistrate must act as he thought best without regard for the opinions of his constituents. That he was popular nonetheless is proved by the fact that he was reelected to office time and time again.

In 1647 Margaret died. In his journal John called her a "woman of singular virtue, prudence, modesty, and piety. . . ." He soon married a fourth time, but he was sixty and ailing, and in March 1649 he too went to his reward. Though he was not a perfect man, his strength of character, resolve, and good common sense stood the Puritan colony in good stead. His descendants would make distinguished contributions to Massachusetts, and the community he helped to found and sustain would bear the imprint of his own conscientious personality. Ultimately, in the shape of the "New England conscience," a part of John Winthrop of Groton Manor would be incorporated into the essential character of America itself.

the leaders of the colony welcome those who did not accept Puritan religious views. As John Cotton, a prominent Puritan minister later noted, "the design of our first planters was not toleration, but [they] were professed enemies of it. . . . Their business was to settle, and (as much as in them lay) secure Religion to Posterity according to that way which they believed was of God." Before long political and religious intolerance had begun to drive independent-minded people out of the Bay Colony itself.

One of the first to go was the Reverend Thomas Hooker. Though himself a minister, Hooker demanded that Massachusetts church membership not be a requirement for voting. When the Massachusetts authorities refused to yield, Hooker joined with others who at this time were leaving the Bay Colony to find better land. In 1636 small groups of men and women seeking religious liberty trekked westward to the banks of the Connecticut River and settled in a region already claimed by both the Dutch and the Plymouth Pilgrims.

Hooker's group established a colony at Hartford and adopted the Fundamental Orders, a form of government that, though scarcely democratic, gave the magistrates less power than they had in the Bay Colony and imposed a more lenient religious test for full citizenship. Soon after, other former residents of Massachusetts established New Haven on the north shore of Long Island Sound. Still other communities, peopled from Plymouth, Massachusetts Bay, and the Connecticut River settlements themselves, sprang up nearby. In 1662 the river communities and those on the sound were merged as the self-governing colony of Connecticut.

The Connecticut settlements derived from a mixture of economic, political, and religious factors. Rhode Island's origins were almost entirely religious. The father of the

John Winthrop expected the Massachusetts Bay Colony to be an example of order, morality, and conformity for wayward humanity. "We shall be as a Citty upon a Hill, the eies of all people are uppon us."

colony was Roger Williams, another Puritan minister who came to Massachusetts in 1631 and promptly antagonized the Bay Colony's religious leaders. Williams quarrelled with the Massachusetts ministers and magistrates over whether the community had fully separated from the Church of England and whether its charter was legal. He further antagonized the Bay Colony's leaders by denouncing the practice of requiring church attendance and the payment of taxes to support the Puritan clergy. In 1635 the Massachusetts authorities ordered his arrest, and Williams fled to Narragansett Bay, just east of Connecticut. There he bought land from the Indians and established the community of Providence Plantation. The new colony's key principles were the complete separation of religion and government (separation of church and state), toleration of all religious beliefs, and the sovereignty of the people.

Other dissenters soon flocked to the Narragansett area. One of the most remarkable was Anne Hutchinson, "a woman of ready wit and bold spirit," who like Williams had tangled with the leading clergymen of the Bay Colony over religious doctrine. Hutchinson espoused the idea that only those infused with the Holy Spirit could preach the word of God and that only a few, herself included, could determine to whom the Holy Spirit had been revealed. Besides threatening the leadership of the Bay Colony ministers,

Hutchinson's outspokenness also defied the principle of female subordination. The church leaders summoned her to a hearing and demanded that she retract her views and cease to preach. She refused and in an unguarded moment warned her accusers that if they continued to persecute her, God would ruin them, their posterity, and "this whole State." When asked how she knew this would happen, she declared: "By an immediate revelation." Shocked by her boldness and presumption, the leaders expelled Hutchinson from the church and declared her a heretic. She and some of her followers soon moved to Aquidneck near Providence.

Other exiles and dissenters also came to the Narragansett region, enlarging the population of the little cluster of towns. In 1663 King Charles II granted Rhode Island and Providence Plantation a royal charter as a separate colony.

Penn's Woods.   Pennsylvania, too, was the offspring of religious persecution—in this case of the Quakers, as outsiders called those belonging to the Society of Friends. Quakers believed that to understand God's will people needed only to examine their own consciences, consult their "inner light"; an elaborate credo and a trained ministry were irrelevant. In the 1640s and 1650s, Quaker "enthusiasts" traveled through England passionately preaching their message of the "inner light," and advising their listeners to throw off the vanities of the world and renounce war and excessive respect for authorities. Plain in their speech and dress, they refused to tip their hats to their social betters and were unusually respectful of the rights of women and tender in the raising of children.

The Anglican clergy, and many orthodox English people, considered Quaker behavior and teachings even more offensive than those of the Puritans. One contemporary called them "a new fanatic sect, of dangerous principles, who show no respect to any man, magistrate, or other, and seem a melancholy, proud sort of people. . . ." The English government feared the Quakers' contempt for a "hireling ministry" and their refusal to take oaths or pay church tithes. In 1655 the government ordered the Quakers to desist from their disorderly practices and enforced the command by a flock of legal prosecutions.

During the 1650s Quaker missionaries fanned out from England, many going to the British colonies. Here, too, they were persecuted. Except in Rhode Island, their emotional preaching and breaches of religious decorum resulted in savage punishment. For refusing to desist from preaching, several Quakers were whipped and imprisoned in Massachusetts. Between 1659 and 1661, four were hanged.

In the 1670s a few Quaker families from England began to settle along the Delaware River in an area that in 1701 would join with Puritan-settled East Jersey to form the royal province

Four Quakers were hanged in Massachusetts between 1659 and 1661. This statue of Mary Dyer, one of the four, was erected three centuries later. It stands on the grounds of the Massachusetts State House, across the street from Boston Common, the place of execution.

of New Jersey. Then, in the 1680s, the trickle of Quakers crossing to America became a flood. The organizer of this migration was William Penn, the son of an influential English gentleman, who had become a "Friend" against his father's strong wishes. Despite his disapproval, when the elder Penn died, he left his son William a fortune that included as an asset a large financial claim against the crown. In 1681 Charles II repaid this debt by granting the younger Penn a giant block of American territory. In addition, the king's brother gave Penn three counties along the lower Delaware River, which would become the separate colony of Delaware in 1701.

In the 1670s, realizing his coreligionists had a dim future in England, Penn launched a scheme for a mass mi-

gration of Quakers to Pennsylvania (Penn's Woods). To prepare the way he constructed a "frame of government" for the colony and composed a set of laws. The result was one of the most enlightened political systems in the contemporary world. In Pennsylvania any male who owned or rented a small amount of land or who paid any taxes would be allowed to vote. No taxes would be imposed on anyone without the approval of the elected colonial legislature. All trials were to be before juries. In place of the long list of crimes punishable by death in England, in Pennsylvania there would be only two capital crimes: treason and murder. No atheists were to be admitted to the colony, but all who believed in God, regardless of their denomination, were welcome and would be allowed to worship in peace.

In 1682 Penn visited his new colony to observe the laying out of Philadelphia, one of the first modern planned cities. During this visit he also cemented cordial relations with the local Indians by paying generously for their land. Settlers soon began arriving in large numbers, drawn by Penn's policies of selling land at low prices and extending religious liberty to all Christians. Pennsylvania attracted not only thousands of British Quakers, but also French Protestants (Huguenots), who were in disfavor in Catholic France, and many German Pietists (radical Protestants), victims of persecution by German Catholics and Lutherans alike. By 1689, with 12,000 inhabitants, the colony was already a going concern.

The Limits of Religious Toleration. Seventeenth-century religious dissidents from Europe also settled in Maryland, the Carolinas, and New Netherland. Maryland was a particular refuge for George Calvert's Catholic co-religionists, though it also attracted Puritan and Anglican Protestants. In New Netherland the tolerant Dutch attracted religious minorities from almost every part of the Western world—Huguenots from France, Jews from the Portuguese colony of Brazil, and assorted religious refugees from Germany, England, Massachusetts, and elsewhere. By the end of Dutch rule in 1664, the small colony—and especially its chief town, New Amsterdam on Manhattan Island—had become a cosmopolitan community inhabited by a score of nationalities and a wide assortment of religious groups.

America, then, served as a refuge for religious dissenters from Europe. Pennsylvania, New Netherland, Rhode Island, and, for a while, Maryland, accorded the right to worship to a wide array of faiths. But religious toleration was far from universal even in the mainland British colonies. In few places were Catholics or Jews allowed to practice their religion openly. Toleration, if accorded at all, generally meant toleration only for Protestants of various kinds.

In many colonies, as we have seen, even Protestants who differed from the founding denomination suffered disabilities. In most of New England only Puritans were wel-

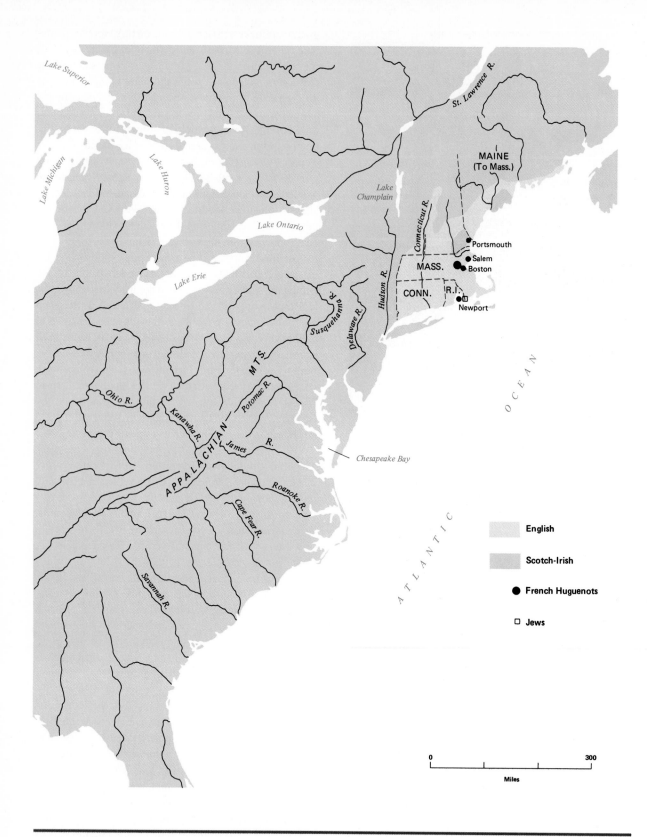

Legend:
- English
- Scotch-Irish
- ● French Huguenots
- □ Jews

Map labels: Lake Superior, Lake Michigan, Lake Huron, Lake Ontario, Lake Erie, St. Lawrence R., Lake Champlain, MAINE (To Mass.), Connecticut R., Portsmouth, Salem, Boston, MASS., CONN., R.I., Newport, Hudson R., Delaware R., Susquehanna R., APPALACHIAN MTS., Ohio R., Kanawha R., Potomac R., James R., Roanoke R., Cape Fear R., Savannah R., Chesapeake Bay, ATLANTIC OCEAN

0 — 300
Miles

COLONIAL SETTLEMENT BY NATIONALITY IN NEW ENGLAND, 1770

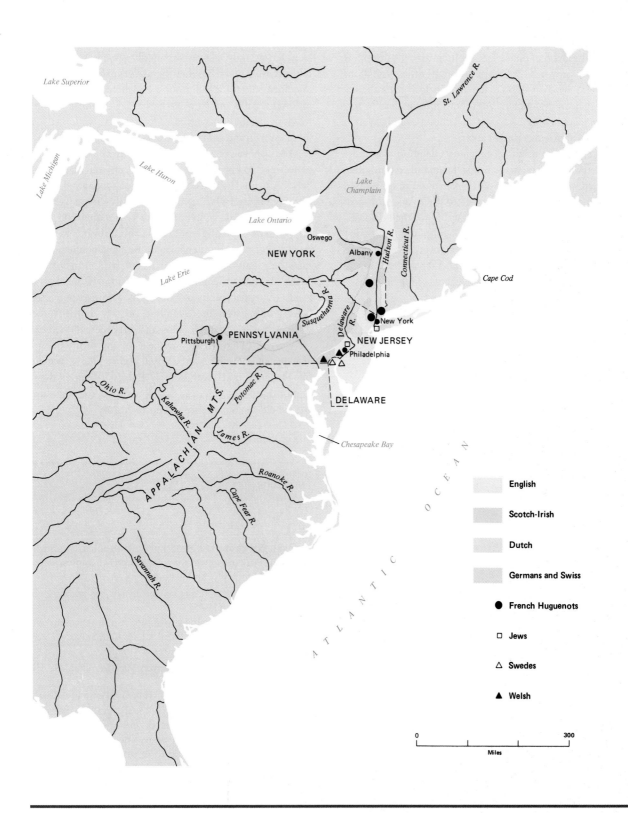

COLONIAL SETTLEMENT BY NATIONALITY IN THE MIDDLE COLONIES, 1770

come. In southern New York and most of the colonies south of Pennsylvania only Anglicans enjoyed full civil and religious rights. In both Calvinist and Anglican colonies ministers of the favored "established" churches received support from the provincial treasury through tithes—religious taxes—imposed on all residents of the colony regardless of their religious preferences. All other ministers had to rely on their parishioners to support their churches and pay their salaries, if allowed to preach at all.

Yet taken as a whole, religious toleration was more complete and general in the British mainland colonies than elsewhere in the Western world. Spain and France refused to allow religious dissenters to go to their American possessions, and this restriction seriously limited their colonies' growth. Much of the advantage in wealth and population eventually enjoyed by English America over New Spain and New France derived from the more liberal British approach, which preserved the energies and talents of religious dissidents for the benefit of the British Empire.

★ CONCLUSIONS ★

The motives, then, of those who promoted and those who settled the American colonies present a mixed picture. Americans may prefer to see their country as founded primarily on freedom, a refuge for those fleeing oppression and bigotry, but at best this view is only partly true. New England, Pennsylvania, and, to a lesser extent, Maryland, New Jersey, and Delaware assuredly served as havens for religious dissenters. But they themselves exhibited religious tolerance only for select groups. Nowhere, except perhaps in Rhode Island and New Netherland, were those of every religious persuasion welcome. Nor should we forget that for many men and women who crossed the Atlantic America was the opposite of a haven: It was a prison. For thousands of transported European felons and for an even larger number of Africans, America was a place of bondage.

For those who came voluntarily, moreover, the strongest lure was not freedom; it was economic and social opportunity. Capitalists could make profits from trade, land speculation, and commercial agriculture; gentlemen could raise their status and restore their shattered fortunes; rulers could enrich their realms and make themselves more powerful. The expectations of Europeans who had only their lives to invest were more modest, perhaps, but they, too, were primarily economic. Most ordinary men and women crossed the Atlantic to acquire the economic independence and decent comfort that the social and economic systems of England and continental Europe denied them. Opportunity was America's basic premise in the beginning and would remain so throughout its history.

★★★★★★★★ FOR FURTHER READING ★★★★★★★★

Thomas J. Wertenbaker. *The First Americans, 1607–1690* (1927)
Disregard the age of this book. It is still an excellent and well-written survey of the early settlement patterns of British America. Concentrates on Virginia and Massachusetts.

James Morton Smith, editor. *Seventeenth Century America: Essays in Colonial History* (1959)
The work of many authors, this book includes several important essays on early colonization as well as good chapters on early Indian-white relations in North America.

Carl Bridenbaugh. *Vexed and Troubled Englishmen, 1590–1642* (1974)
The author used manuscripts, printed plays, ballads, broadsides, letters, diaries, and court records to write this social history of ordinary English people during the early years of American colonization.

Edmund Morgan. *The Puritan Dilemma: The Story of John Winthrop* (1958)
A fine biography of the early Puritan leader of Massachusetts who did so much to make that colony a success. Deals with Winthrop in England and America and tells us much of the Puritan motives for colonization. An impressive fusion of biography and history.

Alden T. Vaughan. *American Genesis: Captain John Smith and the Founding of Virginia* (1975)
The early history of the Jamestown colony approached through the biography of the colorful soldier John Smith. A lively way to learn the early history of Virginia.

Edmund S. Morgan. *American Slavery, American Freedom: The Ordeal of Colonial Virginia* (1975)
Not only is this brilliant book an excellent account of the early years of the Virginia colony, but it also deals interestingly with the issues of race and labor relations between whites and Indians and between whites and black slaves in the first permanent British North American colony.

Abbot Emerson Smith. *Colonists in Bondage: White Servitude and Convict Labor in America, 1607–1776* (1947)
Tells how indentured servants and convicts were induced, seduced, kidnapped, and "spirited" to America. Some discussion of their fate once here.

Daniel Mannix and Malcolm Cowley. *Black Cargoes: A History of the Atlantic Slave Trade* (1962)

The best brief survey of the subject. An eye-opener for readers who have accepted the conventional wisdom about early black Africa and the international slave trade.

John Barth. *The Sot-Weed Factor* (1964)

This long historical novel spoofs the heroic accounts of early American settlement. A bawdy and irreverent version of the John Smith–Pocahontas legend and the story of tobacco, transplanted from its original Virginia setting to Maryland.

David Galenson. *White Servitude in Colonial America: An Economic Analysis* (1981)

In this work, Professor Galenson traces the shift in the colonial work force from indentured servitude to slavery and relates it to changing costs of both skilled and unskilled labor.

Barnard Bailyn. *Voyagers to the West: A Passage in the Peopling of America on the Eve of the Revolution* (1986)

Volume 1, dealing with immigration from Britain on the eve of the Revolution, of what will be a multivolume history of colonial immigration. Authoritative, lively, and detailed.

Philip D. Curtin. *The Atlantic Slave Trade: A Census* (1969)

This work is a detailed demographic examination of the Africa-America slave trade. It emphasizes the trade to the Caribbean and to Latin America, but it is also relevant to the mainland colonies.

3★

COLONIAL SOCIETY

How Did Old World Culture Change in the Wilderness?

1636	Harvard, in Massachusetts, is the first college to be founded in the colonies
1642, 1647	Massachusetts Bay Colony enacts compulsory school laws
1662	The "Half-Way Covenant" allows the children of Massachusetts Bay church members to join the congregation without a conversion experience
1675–78	Indian-white tensions erupt into King Philip's War in New England
1675	Bacon's Rebellion in Virginia
1692	Twenty-one men and one woman are executed in the Salem, Massachusetts, witch trials
1705	Virginia's legislature establishes a Propositions and Grievances Committee to receive public petitions proposing new laws
1732	Publication of the first issue of Benjamin Franklin's *Poor Richard's Almanack*
1734–37	Congregationalist minister Jonathan Edwards sparks a religious revival in New England
1739	Stono Rebellion of South Carolina slaves
1740	George Whitefield's "Methodism" leads to a "Great Awakening" throughout the colonies
1746–52	Benjamin Franklin's experiments with electricity earn him international fame

*I*n 1782, shortly before the Treaty of Paris ending the Revolutionary War, J. Hector St. John de Crèvecoeur, a French gentleman who had settled in the colonies, asked a question about America that would be posed in various forms again and again: "What, then, is the American, this new man?" Crèvecoeur's answer was that the American was a mixture of the old and the new. He was an individual

> who leaving behind all his ancient prejudices and manners, receives new ones from the mode of life he has embraced, the new government he obeys, and the new rank he holds. . . . Americans are the western pilgrims, who are carrying along with them that great mass of arts, sciences, vigour, and industry which began long since in the east; they will finish the great circle. . . .

Americans, then, were not simply transplanted Europeans, according to Crèvecoeur. They had carried with them to the new land many of the habits and much of the cultural heritage of the Old World. But they had also left behind a good deal, and much of what they had taken with them had been transformed in their new circumstances.

Were Crèvecoeur's conclusions correct? Had the human mixture of the colonies blended into a new type? Was there a distinctive American culture by the eve of the Revolution? Or were Americans merely transplanted Europeans with attitudes, values, and institutions directly traceable to the European continent? In what sense and in what ways were Americans "new," and if they were new, how had the change occurred?

★ A NEW MIXTURE IN A NEW LAND ★

It would have been very surprising if American values, ideas, artifacts, and institutions had not quickly diverged from those of Europe. Two powerful factors clearly worked in this direction: a different physical environment, and a different mixture of human beings.

A New Physical Environment. If Europe in the seventeenth and eighteenth centuries was a continent of ancient cities, well-tilled fields, vineyards, and orchards, America, as late as the Revolution, was still almost entirely a forested wilderness. Most of the population of the British colonies was confined to a narrow strip of coast between the Appalachian Mountains and the sea, stretching from present-day Nova Scotia to Spanish Florida. Beyond the coastal

tidewater region tongues of settlement extended along the rivers that rose in the Appalachian mountains, but much of the "West" was a vast expanse of forest dotted by a few clearings and threaded by Indian trails. Even the most densely settled coastal areas of the colonies differed from Europe. In 1775 only five American towns had more than 10,000 inhabitants. Four of these—Boston, Newport, New York, and Philadelphia—were in the North. South of Pennsylvania, only Charleston, South Carolina, could be considered a true city. Elsewhere in the southern plantation colonies, outside of two or three small provincial capitals, the rural county was the significant political and social unit. Nor did the countryside, even in the older regions, much resemble its European counterpart with its trim fields, neat fences and hedgerows, stone barns, and well-built farmhouses. Everywhere in colonial America there were more woods than cleared land and even established farms with their timber dwellings and scraggly wood fences seemed impermanent and ill-tended by European standards.

Travel in this great wilderness was slow and uncomfortable for transplanted Europeans. When Sarah Knight, a Boston schoolmistress, journeyed from her New England home to New York City in 1704, she described her trip as an ordeal. Roads were dirt tracks through the forest; bridges, where they existed at all, were logs laid across stones. Knight found few public inns and was forced to put up at farmhouses where the beds were infested with fleas and the food was skimpy and ill-cooked. Nor was her experience unique. So slow was colonial overland communication that the mounted riders of the continental postal service took three weeks to cover the 310 miles from Boston to Philadelphia. It is not surprising that people and freight moved by water wherever possible.

The difficult physical environment helped to shape the settlers' daily lives and ultimately their attitudes and culture. To subdue it and build the infrastructure of a European society required enormous outlays of time and energy. As the astronomer John Winthrop, descendant of the Bay Colony founder, explained in 1768:

> Plantations in their beginnings have work enough and find difficulties sufficient to settle a comfortable way of subsistence, there being buildings, fencings, clearing, and breaking up of ground, lands to be settled, orchards to be planted, highways and fortifications to be made, and all things to do as in the beginning of the world.

Not only was America wild and undeveloped compared to Europe but it also had a different climate. The East Coast of North America was warmer in the summer and colder in winter than Western Europe, where most white immigrants came from. This difference challenged Europeans to adapt their food, clothing, and shelter to suit the new environment. The adjustment was often slow. Until quite recent times, for example, American men continued to wear wool jackets and neck pieces (ties, cravats, etc.) even during the fierce heat of an American summer, at least on formal occasions.

Diversity among the Europeans. Crèvecoeur believed that in America "individuals of all nations are melted into a new race of men," but even white Europeans often refused to mingle, much less melt. True, Crèvecoeur's Protestant compatriots, the French Huguenots, had quietly merged with the majority when they reached America. In South Carolina, particularly, the Huguenot families of the seventeenth century joined the English elite and in a few years lost their original culture. Intermarriage among different groups did occur. Crèvecoeur told of one family in which each of four sons had married a woman of a different nationality. Yet such enthusiastic assimilation was not common. In the seventeenth century, as streams of French, Dutch, Swedes, and Germans joined the largely English population, the result was a lumpy demographic stew rather than a smooth blend. Most groups retained their characteristics generation after generation, practicing their own religion, speaking their own language, pursuing their own customs, and marrying within their own fold.

New streams of European immigrants converged on America soon after the Treaty of Utrecht in 1713 ended the War of the Spanish Succession and brought peace to Europe. Between 1700 and 1775 about 100,000 Germans crossed the Atlantic to the mainland British colonies. Many went to Pennsylvania, which had provided a haven for German Pietists in the previous century; many others settled in western Maryland and western Virginia.

Unlike the Huguenots, the Germans tended to hold onto their own ways rather than adopt those of the English-speaking majority. As Philadelphia scientist Benjamin Rush wrote in 1789, even their farms seemed different from those carved out by English settlers:

> A German farm may be distinguished from the farms of . . . other citizens . . . by the size of their barns, the plain but compact form of their houses, the height of their enclosures, the extent of their meadows, and the general appearance of plenty and neatness in everything that belongs to them.

Because they were numerous and slow to assimilate, the Germans aroused the suspicion of English-speaking Pennsylvanians. In 1727 the Pennsylvania legislature required the newcomers to take special oaths of fidelity to the king, the colonial proprietor, and the colony charter. Still, suspicions lingered. In the 1750s Benjamin Franklin, usually the most cosmopolitan of men, penned an exasperated outburst against the "Palatine boors" that expressed a widely held view among British Pennsylvanians of the dangers they posed:

> Advertisements intended to be general are now printed in Dutch [German] and English. The signs in our streets have inscriptions in both languages, in some places only German. They begin of late to make all their . . . legal instruments in their own language . . . which . . . are allowed in our courts, where the German business so increases that there is continued need of interpreters; and I suppose within a few years they will also be necessary in the Assembly, to tell one half of our legislators what the other half say. In short, unless the stream of importation can be turned from this to other colonies . . . they will so outnumber us that . . . we . . . will . . . not be able to preserve our language, and even our government will become precarious.

The Scotch-Irish were another group that poured into the North American colonies in the eighteenth century. These people were Presbyterians who had moved from the Scottish lowlands to the province of Ulster in northern Ireland in the early seventeenth century to settle on the lands of the Irish Catholics expelled by their English conquerors. They prospered in their new homes by raising cattle and weaving wool and linen cloth until the British government imposed duties on imports from Ulster, severely damaging the Scotch-Irish economy. Masses of Ulster Presbyterians soon flocked to America.

Some tried New England, where their fellow Calvinists, the Puritans, seemed likely to provide a haven. But the New Englanders saw the newcomers as more Irish than Calvinist and made them unwelcome. Thereafter most of the Scotch-Irish turned south, flooding into the Pennsylvania backcountry to the west of the older settled regions. Many also moved into western Virginia and then down through the Great Valley (the Shenandoah) and the frontier counties of the Carolinas as far as northern Georgia.

In Pennsylvania their appearance disturbed the provincial government. The Pennsylvania authorities feared that they would not pay for land. They were even more concerned that they would violate the rights of the Indians and set off a major Indian war. These fears were not unfounded. The newcomers were the very image of the frontiersmen of legend: tall, red-haired, quick to anger, hospitable, fiercely independent. Such hot-blooded people did not get along well with their neighbors and were constantly embroiled in disputes and quarrels with the Indians. Yet they made valu-

Georgia, like the other British colonies in mainland America, attracted many non-English Europeans. Here is a depiction of the Georgia colony founder, James Oglethorpe, greeting some of his settlers from the Scottish highlands.

able additions to the American population. Herdsmen and hunters rather than farmers, they filled in the colonial back-country, where their qualities made them useful, if sometimes troublesome, pioneers.

But even among the English there was considerable diversity. Recently, the historian David Hackett Fisher has suggested that distinctive British cultural patterns, derived from four different regions of Great Britain—East Anglia, the West country, the northern border, and London—were carried to America and persisted there through the entire colonial era. In matters of religion, people's relations to government and authority, the treatment of women, respect for learning, naming patterns, and in many other areas of attitudes and behavior, he says, these regional differences remained relatively intact for generations. To some extent, he claims, the social and cultural differences among New England, the middle colonies of Pennsylvania and New Jersey, the Chesapeake area, and the western frontier re-

gions observed by contemporaries can be explained by the origins of their populations from different areas of Great Britain itself.

Native Americans. From the beginning European-Indian contacts affected both sides in profound ways. Generally the two societies remained distinct although they interacted at many points where they touched.

Some of the interactions were clearly benign. The early settlers of New England had learned Indian farming techniques and borrowed from the Native Americans many food plants and dishes whose Indian names—*squash, hominy,* and *succotash,* for example—entered the English language. Some scholars believe that the powerful Iroquois Confederation helped inspire colonial attempts at continent-wide unity before 1776 and may even have influenced the drawing up of the U.S. Constitution. For their part, the Indians acquired the colonists' muskets, cloth, iron implements, and other goods through trade in beaver pelts and deerskins. In later years several tribes in the Carolinas and Georgia absorbed the best of white culture and created an interesting blend of native and European societies.

More commonly, however, the transfer from European to Indian proved damaging to the latter. The Indians were quickly entangled in the transplanted economy of the Europeans, especially the fur trade. Though not, as we saw, the perfect ecological heroes posited by sentimentalists, Indians did not normally place too heavy a burden on the animal life of the forest. But when whites appeared, ready to trade metal tools, guns, cloth, and "firewater" for animal pelts, many succumbed to temptation. The fur trade flourished on the northern frontier, particularly in New York and New England, and wherever it flourished it decimated the beaver and other animal populations. It also undermined the Indians' own economy and their self-reliance. Increasingly, they became dependent on trade with whites and less able to do without the white man's goods. And the firewater proved particularly harmful. Whether from the rum of the English or the brandy of the French, drunkenness and alcoholism became a corrosive part of Indian life, damaging the health of individuals and tearing at the very fabric of Indian society.

Strictly from a cultural perspective, however, the exchange between Indian and European was relatively superficial in the British colonies. Colonists of English and Scottish extraction did not mix as readily with the Indians as did the Spanish in Mexico and Florida and the French in Canada. In addition, people of northern European origins intermarried less often with the Indians than did whites of southern European extraction.

Nowhere is the isolation of the English from the Indians more apparent than in the religious sphere. In the Catholic colonies of France, Spain, and Portugal thousands of native souls were "saved" by conversion and baptism. In British America the impulse to "convert the heathen" was weaker. In the southern colonies, the few proselytizers accomplished little. In New England the effort was somewhat more effective. In 1649 the English Parliament in London, dominated at the time by the pious Puritan party, created the Society for the Propagation of the Gospel in New England. The society helped to establish an Indian college at Harvard and supported the Reverend John Eliot's mission to preach the gospel to local Massachusetts tribes. In the 1660s Eliot translated the Bible "into the Indian tongue." In all, Eliot established fourteen towns of "praying Indians" with over 1,000 Indian converts. By the mid-1670s there were perhaps 4,000 Christian Indians in New England.

But however concerned Eliot and his supporters were with the state of the Indians' souls, they had little respect for their culture. In the praying towns the converts were expected to follow the white people's ways, abandon their ancient customs and traditions, and become "civilized." A more admirable example, by modern lights, was the conversion effort among the Delawares by the Moravians,

German Protestant Pietists who settled in Pennsylvania in the 1740s. The Moravians, one scholar has noted, "did not make an assault upon the Indian's personality." Still, the total effort in Protestant America was relatively feeble. Protestants simply lacked the zeal for saving heathen souls that their Catholic rivals in Canada, Brazil, and New Spain displayed.

Indeed, rather than Christian love, Indian-white relations were generally marked by hostility and violence. Here the competing view of land ownership often led to troubles. Outside Pennsylvania, where the white Quaker officials respected Indian rights, Indian-white contacts produced constant warfare. We have already seen how, in 1622, tensions between the Jamestown settlers and the Virginia coastal tribes tripped off a massacre of white colonists and a war that destroyed the power of the Indians in the region. In the 1630s the Pequot War decimated the Indian population of eastern Connecticut. Most serious of all, during the first century of settlement, was King Philip's War, which erupted in New England in the mid-1670s.

The problems that led to this conflagration had long been brewing. Until grand sachem Massasoit's death, rela-

Not all the English despised the Indians. Puritan minister John Eliot was one of those who felt that they too were God's children. Inevitably, however, their salvation seemed to require that they abandon their "heathen" ways and adopt the religion of the Europeans. Many did, but in the end the conversion did not save them from the wrath of the whites.

This is a contemporary drawing of Metacomet, usually called King Philip. He looks rather gentle here, but he proved a formidable enemy of the New England settlers.

tions between the Wampanoag Indians and the Plymouth colonists had been cordial. Philip, Massasoit's son and successor, preserved the goodwill for a while, but when colony officials tried to impose tribute on the Wampanoags, he grew increasingly resentful. Meanwhile, other tribes in southern New England were also becoming restless in the face of steady encroachment by whites on their land and hunting grounds. Then, in 1675, Philip's warriors attacked the town of Swansea. Two tribes—the Narragansetts of Rhode Island and the Nipmucks of Connecticut—soon joined Philip's warriors in the struggle.

The Indian method of fighting was too much for the New Englanders at first. Accustomed to moving in massed formations against an enemy that stood fast and fired back, they found the Indians' ambushes and surprise raids exasperating. The Indians, for their part, saw the European method of fighting as stupid. Armed for the first time with guns, the Indians devastated the white settlements with their hit-and-run tactics.

Before long the colonists adopted Indian methods of warfare: surprise raids, ambushes, and even scalping. Eventually the war against the "savages" made the colonists savage. Soon they were torturing prisoners and using large dogs to tear the Indians apart. In the end the Europeans' superior numbers and organization prevailed. By 1676 the southern tribes were defeated and subdued. By 1678 the Indians of Maine and New Hampshire, who had taken up arms in support of their southern brothers, were also pacified.

King Philip's War exacted an enormous toll on both sides. According to one estimate, one-sixteenth of the white male population of New England died in the fighting. The monetary cost to Plymouth, Massachusetts, and Connecticut was crushing. On the Indians' side, one casualty of the war was Eliot's praying Indians. Although they had remained loyal to the whites, they were interned for three years on Deer Island, where they were forced to live on shellfish. Many died. Philip himself was captured and shot, and many of his followers were sold into slavery in the Caribbean or indentured as servants to whites. Indian lands were awarded to the victorious white troops. After 1678 the New England Indians ceased to be a challenge to the white population except on the most remote frontiers bordering French Canada.

Colonial Blacks. The cultural mix of the American colonies included not only diverse European and Indian groups but also Africans. In 1760 about 325,000 of the approximately 1.6 million people in British North America were black. Of these, 12,000 lived in New England, another 25,000 in the middle colonies (New York, New Jersey, and Pennsylvania), and the remainder in the southern colonies, with Virginia and South Carolina far in the lead. Almost all of these people were slaves; only a few hundred were "free people of color."

Black workers were a vital part of the laboring class in colonial America. In New England and the middle colonies black slaves were employed as day laborers, seamen, house servants, or craftsmen's assistants in the ports and towns. In only a few places in the North—Rhode Island and here and there in the Hudson Valley—were black slaves field-workers. In the Chesapeake region and the Carolinas, on the other hand, slaves formed the backbone of the labor force on the plantations and farms producing tobacco, rice, indigo, and grain. Even in the southern plantation colonies, however, many blacks worked as house servants and artisans.

This forced labor on colonial farms, plantations, and in towns transformed the culture of enslaved Africans. Slaves had to learn occupations that were not part of their African culture. For example, in South Carolina, Virginia, and elsewhere they quickly acquired trades such as bricklaying, "plaistering," wig making, silversmithing, and gun-

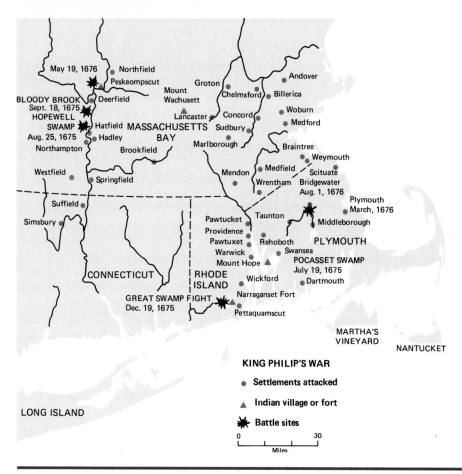

KING PHILIP'S WAR, 1675–1676

smithing. The cultural exchange was not all one way, however. Slaves brought skills and knowledge from Africa and used them in America. West Africans were familiar with boats and the sea; in South Carolina many of them worked as fishermen. They introduced the West African *perriauger*—a kind of canoe—for transportation along the Sea Islands and through the many rivers and streams of the Carolina coastal lowlands. Slaves also introduced West African agricultural products to South Carolina—including melons, gourds, and probably even rice, a crop that became one of the area's chief exports. Although black cooks learned the techniques of European cuisine, they contributed their own methods and ingredients; for example, sesame seeds and red pepper. In fact, much of the South's distinctive cooking is derived from the merger of African and European elements.

The African family and kinship systems also survived the transplant to America. In most of the slaves' original homelands each individual was tied to the community through elaborate kinship networks. These bound together parents, children, grandparents, cousins, uncles, aunts, nieces, and nephews, specifying the support and obligations each owed to the other. Through these complex attachments, the slave family was able to endure severe external pressure in the New World. In their new homes, husbands and wives, parents and children, were often separated against their will. But the inherited African kinship networks made it possible for slaves to remain in touch with distant relatives for many years, despite infrequent chances for face-to-face contact.

Little is known about the religion of the first generation or two of American slaves. Most West Africans worshiped the spirits of the dead, who were believed to remain close by, protecting their descendants. Priests—usually the oldest member of each family line—conducted the group's ceremonies. It seems likely that the first slaves tried to practice their religion much as they had at home, though far from the graves of their venerated ancestors. But there is evidence that transfer to America was destructive to the African religious *system* as a whole. It is also clear that many discrete practices—belief in amulets, conjurers, faith healing—survived the Atlantic leap and flourished on the new soil.

In most of the colonies few efforts were made at first to convert the Africans to Christianity, in part because Christians were not supposed to enslave their fellow Christians. Nonetheless, there is evidence that slaves absorbed the Europeans' faith to some degree in this early period, merely through contact. In the middle of the eighteenth century formal conversion of slaves became more common. By this time a new emotionalism had developed in Protestantism, and it made Christianity more attractive to many slaves.

The lot of the colonial American slave varied from place to place, time to time, and master to master. In New England slaves were relatively well treated because they often lived in close contact with whites in a family setting. In the South the slave system was harsher. By the standards of the day, slaves were usually well fed and given adequate medical care, but some masters abused their slaves cruelly. The Virginian Robert Carter, generally considered a decent man by his white neighbors, underfed his slaves and expected them to make up the deficiency by raising their own food in their spare time. The slaves' housing was often minimal. One eighteenth-century white Virginian, forced to take shelter one evening in a "Negro cabin" with six blacks, reported that the shack "was not lathed or plaistered, neither ceiled nor lofted above . . . one window, but no glass in it, not even a brick chimney, and as it stood on blocks about a foot above the ground, the hogs lay constantly under the floor, which made it swarm with flies."

Colonial slaves were harshly disciplined to ensure obedience. In seventeenth-century South Carolina, slaves judged guilty of offenses such as murder, striking a white person, or plotting an insurrection could be castrated, branded, and burned alive. In the eighteenth century whipping replaced most of the earlier sentences, but whipping too was a brutal and terrifying experience.

Slave control consisted of more than punishment, however. In South Carolina slaves who left their plantations were required to carry "tickets" indicating their owners' permission to be away. In Charleston professional constables were authorized to detain "suspicious" blacks and determine their business. In other parts of South Carolina mounted patrols stopped blacks on the roads, entered black homes for inspection, and confiscated black-owned firearms.

Despite all these efforts to impose discipline, colonial blacks found ways to express their hatred of the slave system. They fought back by deliberately breaking their master's tools, injuring cattle and horses, destroying crops, and running away. From South Carolina slaves often escaped to the Spanish settlements in Florida. Some slaves fled to the Indian frontier, though Indians and blacks were often enemies. Virginia slaves frequently destroyed property before they escaped. To discourage this behavior the colony "outlawed" runaways, allowing anyone who encountered such persons to kill them on sight without penalty.

The most serious slave protest was group rebellion. Nowhere in the mainland colonies did slaves mount a large-scale uprising or set up independent black communities, as slaves eventually did in Brazil, Surinam, and places in the Caribbean. But there were several organized rebellions during the colonial period. In New York City in 1712 twenty-five slaves armed with knives, axes, and guns set fire to a white man's outhouse. When whites rushed to save the burning building, the slaves attacked them, killing nine. The authorities called out the militia, who quickly rounded up the insurrectionists. Twenty-one were executed.

The Stono Rebellion in South Carolina, where slaves were far more numerous than in New York, was a much more serious threat to white rule. The uprising began near Charleston in September 1739 when a group of slaves broke into a storehouse and seized arms and supplies. The rebels intended to flee to Spanish Florida; as they marched south gathering recruits, they attacked any white who got in their way. After a few days the militia caught up with the fugitives and killed them. In all, thirty whites and forty-four blacks lost their lives.

The Stono Rebellion sent a shock wave through South Carolina. The colony tightened its patrols, initiated a program to inculcate submission, and tried to limit slave importation. It also sought to improve the lot of slaves by limiting their hours of work to fifteen per day between March and September and thirteen the rest of the year. Once fears had quieted, the planters relaxed somewhat; but white South Carolinians would never feel entirely safe again.

★ REGIONS ★

New England, Middle Colonies, the South. Diversity in colonial America also extended to patterns of settlement. Much of New England was divided into "towns," small communities of about 500, composed of families. Towns were formed by the political authorities, who established the first ones at the time of initial settlement and created new ones as required to meet a growing population. Under this system, Massachusetts, as well as the other New England colonies, grew by a sort of budding process.

The New England town was a relatively homogeneous community. All of its members belonged to the same Puritan faith; most came from the same part of east-central England. Most town residents were farmers, but each community also had a minister, a schoolmaster, artisans, and craftspeople of various kinds. The dwellings within the town were distributed around the perimeter of the "common," an open space where sheep and cattle grazed and where the community held its militia "musters" and conducted other collective activities. The village church, with its austere white exterior and tall steeple, usually bordered the common. Each family normally had a small plot of land to cultivate as a garden close to its dwelling and larger fields at a distance from the town center where their chief crops were grown.

Life in the typical New England town has been portrayed by many historians as placid and orderly. Community decisions were made through the monthly town meeting where, though women, minors, servants, and nonchurchgoers were disfranchised, a sizable proportion of the adult males voted. These towns, one scholar has said, were "peaceable kingdoms," where disputes were readily resolved and a wide consensus achieved by discussion. They were also ideal settings for community activities, whether educational or religious. Some of the edge that New England has enjoyed in science, the arts, and business enterprise has been ascribed to the compact settlement of the New England town, which made schools, for example, more practical than where settlement was more scattered. The gradual erosion of community feeling with the arrival of commerce by the end of the seventeenth century has long served as a theme for historians concerned with the corrosive effects of capitalism on traditional village life.

It is common to contrast the seventeenth-century New England pattern rather starkly with the typical community unit elsewhere in the colonies. And in fact the contrast is roughly valid. In the middle colonies (New York, New Jersey, and Pennsylvania), on the western border, and in the South, such tight-knit communities were rare, except in a few places, like Long Island, where New Englanders had settled. Instead, settlement patterns were open and scattered. People lived on detached family farms, often separated from their neighbors, especially on the western frontier, by large stretches of forest. In the middle colonies commerce helped create a sprinkling of small cities, but in the Chesapeake region (Maryland and Virginia) and the Carolinas, these were uncommon. Aside from a few provincial capitals like Williamsburg, Virginia, Annapolis, Maryland, and the port of Charleston, little approaching a true city could be found in the region south of Pennsylvania until almost the very end of the colonial era.

Given these patterns of land occupation, it is not surprising that historians have supposed that the life of the typical Pennsylvanian, say, or Virginian entailed far less intense community involvement than that of the contemporary New Englander. But did it? We know that there were penalties for the scattered settlement pattern outside of New England. As we shall see, religion and education were both impoverished by the absence of compact population centers. Yet the picture is not as simple as this implies. A study of Middlesex County, Virginia, in the period 1659–1750, by Darrett and Anita Rutman, demonstrates that communities in the Chesapeake region were not the chaotic, impersonal places often assumed. Although the county had been settled helter-skelter by individuals, in time, circles of kinship and friendship developed that served to create the same sense of community as prevailed in the New England towns. Though the people of Middlesex County did not come together each month in a formal legislative town meeting, as in New England, they had their equivalent social, if not political occasion, in the monthly county court day. On court days, not only were criminal and civil cases heard by the magistrates, but people without court business came for the horse racing, the liquid refreshment, the gossip, and for the chance to renew acquaintanceships and do business.

Studies such as the one by the Rutmans have narrowed the gap between New England and the colonial South. Moreover, there is reason to think that we have exaggerated the communal solidarity of many towns in New England. A recent study of Marblehead and Gloucester, both in Massachusetts, shows, for example, that community solidarity and homogeneity were often lacking even in the Bay Colony, especially in the ports and the fishing communities.

Thus, we can no longer draw such sharp contrasts between the social texture of New England and that of the South, yet it remains true that differences remained and affected the course of regional development.

East-West Differences. Among the regional divisions that marked colonial society, East-West differences were especially troublesome. Much of the sectional tension involved the Indians.

It was on the frontier that the white population pushed against Indian groups unwilling to surrender additional lands or permit Europeans to settle among them. In the clashes that ensued, the authorities in the older coastal areas, preferring to preserve the peace at all costs, sometimes sided with the Indians against the western frontiersmen. This response created deep resentment between East and West.

These East-West tensions first appeared in Virginia, where by the 1670s settlers had pushed beyond the Tidewater, the coastal region where the slow-flowing streams rose and fell daily with the ocean tides, and had moved into the Piedmont, the plateau region immediately to the west. Piedmont settlers soon came to feel that the Tidewater planters who controlled the provincial government were unconcerned with their problems. They especially resented their indifference to Indian attacks on the frontier.

In 1675 and 1676 Virginia's Piedmont-Tidewater tensions came to a head in Bacon's Rebellion. When Indian warfare broke out on the frontier, the Virginia governor, Sir William Berkeley, called for restraint. The frontiersmen, under the leadership of Piedmont planter Nathaniel Bacon, ignored him and attacked local Indian villages, almost wiping them out. Berkeley considered this attack mutiny and soon marched to the scene with 300 armed men determined to "call Mr. Bacon to accompt." By the time Berkeley arrived, Bacon and his followers had disappeared into the forest, where they mounted further attacks on the local tribes, friendly and hostile alike. Bacon, now a hero in the Piedmont, was elected to the Virginia assembly and went to Jamestown to take his seat accompanied by armed partisans to see that he was not arrested.

This session of the Virginia legislature was called "Bacon's Assembly" to mark its domination by the rebel planter and his supporters. The rebellious delegates passed a series of laws, long advocated by Piedmont planters, including measures to liberalize voting, open offices to small property holders, make taxes less burdensome for poorer colonists, and improve defenses against the Indians. Bacon himself played little role in this legislative program, but he soon asserted his power by demanding to be made commander of all the colony's armed forces. Berkeley refused, but the assembly, afraid of Bacon's armed supporters, yielded. Bacon soon departed with his men for the frontier intent on killing some more Indians. What followed was a series of maneuvers by militia loyal to the governor and Bacon's partisans that ended with the burning of Jamestown in September 1676. In this moment of triumph Bacon suddenly died of a "Bloody Flux," ending his cause. Berkeley was not forgiving and hanged thirty-seven of Bacon's followers.

Although Pennsylvania had long had a tradition of fair dealings with the Indians, it too began to experience Indian-white and East-West tensions as the western frontier was settled. The Scotch-Irish settlers in the western part of the colony had complained for years that the Quaker-dominated government in Philadelphia did not support them adequately against the Indians. In December 1763, a mob of frontiersmen from the towns of Paxton and Donegal, taking the law into their own hands, attacked a group of peaceful Conestoga Indians, killing six. When the horrified Pennsylvania assembly ordered the "Paxton Boys" arrested, the enraged westerners marched on Philadelphia, prepared to get "justice" at the point of a gun. For a while it looked as if the colony would be thrown into civil war. Fortunately, Benjamin Franklin intercepted the rebels and negotiated a solution. Though further violence was avoided, this near-rebellion left a legacy of sectional antagonisms within Pennsylvania that lasted to the end of the century.

★ FAMILIES ★

The mixture of peoples in British North America did not produce a smooth new combination. The blend remained full of undigested parts. Just as in our own era, the diverse ethnic and cultural ingredients continued to be separate. Yet more than today, the Anglo-Saxon heritage—itself diverse—dominated. But this does not mean that the New World environment did not affect transplanted Old World institutions, attitudes, and practices. On the contrary, the new setting profoundly modified the most basic Old World forms and in the process helped produce a society characteristically American.

Birth Rates, Death Rates, and Family Size.   Even the most fundamental institution of all, the family, was altered by the new American environment. Exposed to New World conditions, the European family became both larger and more egalitarian than it had been in the mother country.

Life generally was short in seventeenth-century Europe. Famines, plagues, and wars ravaged the land and cut down thousands of men, women, and children before their time. By itself this situation would have limited family size. But there were also social reasons why families were relatively small. Scholars used to believe that English families of the early modern era were *extended* families consisting not just of parents and children, but also of grandparents and other relatives, and even servants. We now know that except for the aristocracy, the *nuclear* family of parents and young children was typical; that once grown, children in England were expected to set out on their own to establish their own households. This custom, coupled with the high death rates in this period, made for relatively small families, not more than four or five people.

The new American environment created a different family pattern. In New England from the beginning, people lived longer. Historian John Demos estimates that during the seventeenth century the average life expectancy for men in Plymouth Colony came close to that of our own day. In Dedham, in the Bay Colony, death rates were half those of contemporary Europe. At the same time, in most of the New England towns birth rates were high, usually higher than in Europe. The net effect of these low death rates and high birth rates was to create larger families in New England than on the other side of the Atlantic.

The long life and large families of seventeenth-century New Englanders were made possible by the region's distinctive settlement pattern. The relative equality among town residents, their physical proximity to one another, their self-sufficiency, and their isolation from Europe and its dread diseases made the Puritan villages healthy places to live even without modern medicine and sanitation. At first the family history of the southern colonies was quite different. Most early immigrants to Maryland and Virginia were single men who came either as planters or servants. The authorities tried to attract women by paying their passage, but their success was limited. In 1704, for example, only about 7,200 of the 30,000 white people in Maryland were women. Most male Virginians and Marylanders were forced to remain bachelors.

The generally unhealthy state of the Chesapeake region also held down family formation. Malaria and dysentery killed many people in early colonial Virginia and Maryland and hit pregnant women particularly hard. In addition, European diseases were carried to the Chesapeake region by the tobacco-collecting vessels that came directly to each planter's dock. In South Carolina the rice-growing lowlands with their "agues" continued to be unhealthy well into the 1800s.

Still, as time passed, an ever-larger proportion of the Chesapeake and Carolina population consisted of the native-born, a development that equalized the numbers of males and females. This return to a normal sex ratio made more marriages possible, so that by the eighteenth century the family became the normal household unit even in the South. Meanwhile, because of closer commercial contact with other parts of the world, smallpox, malaria, and other illnesses invaded New England, increasing mortality rates. By the later years of the colonial period the disparity in size between the southern and northern colonial family had virtually disappeared.

As the decades passed, the difference between European and American demographic characteristics also began to narrow. Yet they never entirely vanished during the colonial period. As late as 1790 American families were larger than their European counterparts. Population grew faster too. Because land was cheaper and more abundant in America than in Europe, young people could afford to marry early. In the absence of birth control they usually had many children. Even without heavy immigration this would have made for a rapid population increase. But the flood of European immigrants magnified the effects.

Family Roles. In colonial America the family was the central social institution, one that served many functions. It was, for one thing, the center of education. Parents taught young children their first "letters" and their earliest religious precepts. Fathers taught their sons how to farm, repair tools, hunt, and fish. If the father was a craftsman, he taught his son his trade. Girls learned from their mothers how to perform the many household tasks expected of colonial women—cooking, baking, sewing, candlemaking, weaving, and spinning.

The family was also a "little commonwealth" within which people's lives were prescribed and regulated, an agent through which acceptable social behavior was taught and enforced. Fathers were the rulers in these small political units; the law in the Puritan colonies even allowed them the power of life and death over their children, though none as far as we know ever chose to exercise it. This patriarchal system was deeply entrenched in Europe and was carried to America. It was reinforced by the father's control over the family land and property. In the southern colonies, with their looser settlement patterns and their more abundant fertile land, this arrangement was probably not a serious problem for children. In early New England, however, where towns were limited in size and where fathers usually lived to old age, the patriarchal system could be galling. Grown sons were often forced to live in their parents' household, subject to continued patriarchal control, or to become tenants on their father's land. Fortunately, New England sons had an escape route. By the beginning of the eighteenth century an ever-larger number were leaving the crowded Massachusetts and Connecticut towns to move to cheap land in the Berkshire Hills, and Green Mountains, and to New Hampshire and Maine.

Within the colonial family the roles of fathers and mothers differed distinctly. Fathers typically carried on the family's public functions—such as casting its vote, serving in the militia, filling governmental positions—and its work outside the home. Mothers were responsible for private domestic matters and for acting as "helpmeets" to their husbands. Within this limited domain women had considerable power. Mothers were expected to supervise the children, particularly the youngest ones; fathers generally did not involve themselves in everyday child-rearing matters. But in addition to their household duties, many married women helped in the family business, supplemented family income by running their own businesses or by selling surplus produce or handmade goods, and helped organize church functions. Because women were considered subordinate to men, their tremendous behind-the-scenes contributions were sometimes credited to their husbands. An eighteenth-century newspaper article praised a Newport man for the 300 skeins of yarn and 369 1/2 yards of cloth "spun in his own house." In fact, it was the women of his family who had done the work.

However inferior their status to American men, American women had greater privileges than women in Europe. Colonial men recognized the value of women's work. In one Plymouth community a man was denied a license to run a tavern because he had no wife to help him in the business. Laws of the times granted American women higher legal status than their English sisters. Divorce was easier for wronged wives. Husbands who abused their

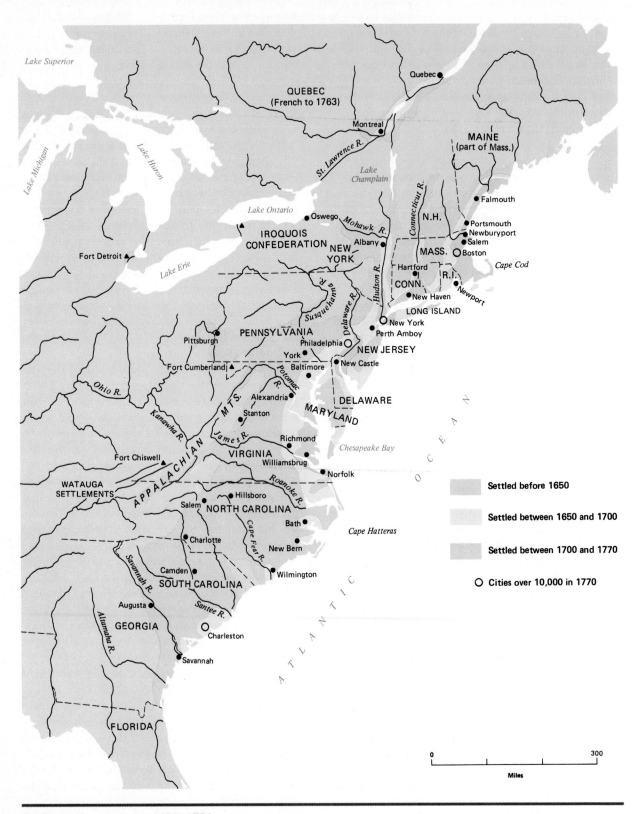

COLONIAL SETTLEMENT, 1650–1770

Lake Superior

Lake Michigan

Lake Huron

QUEBEC
(French to 1763)

Quebec

Montreal

St. Lawrence R.

Lake Champlain

MAINE
(part of Mass.)

Lake Ontario

Oswego

IROQUOIS
CONFEDERATION

Fort Detroit

Lake Erie

NEW YORK

Albany

Mohawk R.

Connecticut R.

N.H.

Falmouth

Portsmouth
Newburyport
Salem
Boston

MASS.

Cape Cod

Hartford

CONN.

R.I.

New Haven

Newport

Susquehanna R.

Hudson R.

Delaware R.

LONG ISLAND

New York

Perth Amboy

Pittsburgh

PENNSYLVANIA

Philadelphia

NEW JERSEY

York

Baltimore

New Castle

DELAWARE

Ohio R.

Fort Cumberland

Potomac R.

Alexandria

Stanton

MARYLAND

Chesapeake Bay

Kanawha R.

APPALACHIAN MTS.

James R.

Richmond

VIRGINIA

Williamsbrug

Norfolk

Fort Chiswell

Roanoke R.

WATAUGA
SETTLEMENTS

Hillsboro

Salem

NORTH CAROLINA

Bath

Cape Fear R.

Cape Hatteras

Charlotte

New Bern

Camden

Savannah R.

SOUTH CAROLINA

Wilmington

Augusta

Santee R.

GEORGIA

Altamaha R.

Charleston

Savannah

FLORIDA

ATLANTIC OCEAN

Settled before 1650

Settled between 1650 and 1700

Settled between 1700 and 1770

○ Cities over 10,000 in 1770

0   300

Miles

spouses, especially in New England, were often reprimanded by the authorities. And colonial widows were entitled to a larger fixed amount of their husbands' estates than was common in the mother country.

Professor Christine Heyrman describes one amusing case of colonial women's superior condition. In Marblehead, an important Massachusetts fishing port, women were relatively scarce. This situation, apparently, allowed them a degree of leeway in their relations with men not usual even for the rest of the colonies. There were numerous cases in the Marblehead court records for the late seventeenth century, for example, of women abusing their husbands, even physically. When Robert Laverance complained of his wife's dallying with one of the couple's boarders, she called him "a bald pated old rogue and struck him with her fist." Richard Rowland's wife came home drunk one evening and beat him. Rowland fled to his neighbor's house and begged to be taken in. He could not sleep at his own house, he exclaimed, "for the devil was at home."

Instances such as these notwithstanding, it remains true that the colonial woman's role and status were inferior to the man's. Marblehead's assertive women paid dearly for their bold behavior by abundant verbal abuse. Even their services as wives and mothers conferred little freedom or prestige on colonial women, and many felt keenly their subordination. Their response was more often resignation than rebellion, however. As one South Carolina woman noted, her "self-denying duties" were "a part of the curse pronounced upon Eve" and nothing could be done about it.

Beneath father and mother were children, and perhaps servants and slaves. All helped in the family's work. As in England, servants were treated as part of the family because typically, unlike domestic workers today, they did not return to their homes after their chores; they "lived in." Masters had the authority to discipline them and sometimes were obligated to provide them with an education. In the South slaves were in some ways members of the master's family, too. In law, slaves were treated as the children of their masters or mistresses, who, like parents, were expected to provide food, clothing, and shelter, and to mete out rewards and punishments.

The structure and power relations of colonial families were not static. They evolved over time, and by the eighteenth century a new pattern, according to historian Philip Greven, had begun to emerge, though the older, patriarchal one remained very much alive. This new "genteel" type flourished among richer, better-educated, and less pious Americans. It appeared late because wealth, comfort, and a secular outlook were relatively late developments in America.

Genteel families were bound together by affection rather than by authority and fear; they were more children-centered. Fathers were less insistent on their despotic rights and were more likely to accept the autonomy of their wives and children. One effect was the greater freedom of adult children to choose their spouses rather than have them selected for them by their parents. Scholars have theorized that the soaring rate of premarital pregnancy in the late eighteenth century may have reflected the desire of grown daughters and sons to force the consent of fathers to marriages they would otherwise have forbidden.

These genteel family qualities, says Greven, may have had far-reaching public effects. Children brought up in a genteel environment were assuredly more self-confident and independent-minded than the norm. As adults they were apt to be leaders and doers. Their egalitarian upbringing possibly reinforced their outrage at British policies and the British crown after 1763, for they were impatient with arbitrary authority of any sort. Admittedly, this view is speculative, but it could be more than accident that most of the "Patriot" leaders during the Revolutionary ferment after 1763 were men and women of genteel family origins.

★ EVERYDAY LIFE ★

How people lived day by day in earlier times is always a fascinating subject. The popularity today for visitors of "Plimoth Plantation," Colonial Williamsburg, and Greenfield Village—with their antique public buildings, barns, and private homes, their pre-modern workshops, furniture and artifacts—suggests how absorbing we find the everyday life of our predecessors. But to describe coherently how colonial Americans lived presents many problems. The colonial era was a long stretch of time—170 years by conventional measure. (From 1607 to 1776.) During that interval habits, customs, styles, and values changed. Daily life in the colonial era also differed among classes, races, and regions. To note the obvious, the rich did not live the same way as the poor. Nor did townsfolk live like farmers, nor Germans of eastern Pennsylvania like backcountry Scotch-Irish of North Carolina. Yet when this is all said, some roughly common qualities of daily life can be extracted from the immense diversity.

Housing among the earliest settlers was often primitive. The first Europeans to touch shore often dug caves in the hillsides, or put up lean-tos and canvas tents. Some built walls of sod and roofed them with branches and leaves. Some even adopted Indian wigwams of skins to provide shelter for the first weeks or months after arrival. But this improvised approach quickly ended and as soon as possible the settlers built in styles familiar at home. Until well into the eighteenth century, farmhouses in the northern colonies were made by driving posts into the ground, siding the structures with clapboard, and capping them with a wood-shingled roof. Many of these were no larger than twenty-by-twenty feet and rose a story-and-a-half, the "half" being a loft reached by an inside ladder. Each of these structures had a fireplace, preferably constructed of stone or brick, but often of logs partially protected from fire by clay plastering. They were usually unpainted since paint was imported and expensive. Glass was uncommon in such homes, and to exclude cold weather householders used wooden shutters. These kept out the rain and wind, all right, but they also excluded the daylight. Houses such as these were often dark, dank places inside. Travelers described rural housing in the southern colonies as ramshackle with substantial gaps between the boards. Southern farmhouses could afford to be less weather-tight than their northern equivalents in part because southern winters were milder and summers hotter.

Housing in the towns was generally better than in the countryside. Because fire in the close-packed urban centers was such a danger, town buildings were more often of brick or stone than farm structures. As dwelling places for the colonies' prosperous merchants, shopkeepers, and skilled artisans, the towns also had many of America's largest and most luxurious private houses, structures with two or three stories, many bedrooms, parlors, and multiple fireplaces. Some of these were designed by professional architects. In the South a few show plantation homes matched the luxury of the best town houses in Salem, Newport, Boston, and Philadelphia.

Ordinary houses, even of the eighteenth century, had few amenities. Rooms were seldom differentiated by function. There were no bedrooms, or living rooms, or bathrooms as such. People slept, washed, sat in whatever room was handy, though there were sleeping lofts in houses with more than one story. Sanitary facilities were primitive. People bathed—when they did bathe—outdoors. They used privies set some distance from the house to keep the flies away. There were no window screens in those days, and mosquitoes and flies often made life in summer an ordeal. Rooms lacked closets. Clothes were folded away in chests or hung on pegs on the wall. Furniture was sparse and crude. Meals were consumed on tables made of boards set on trestles. Benches and stools were more common than chairs. Beds were hard mattresses stuffed with grass or feathers laid over a rope "spring" attached to a wood frame. Tableware—bowls, plates, trenchers—consisted of hollowed-out wood at first and then later of pewter, a silver-gray alloy of copper and lead. Spoons were common but forks were rare until late in the colonial period.

Food was abundant but plain. The forests and waters provided game, fish, fowl, berries, fruits, and nuts in abun-

dance. The settlers planted European parsnips, turnips, carrots, cabbage, and onions in their kitchen gardens. They also sowed wheat where it would grow and raised hogs, sheep, cattle, and chickens. They borrowed maize and beans from the Indians. These ingredients they consumed roasted, stewed, or in the form of breads, and various sorts of mushes or porridges. Frying—with lard—was a common way to prepare meats, especially in the South. Breakfast often consisted of porridge of grain mixed with milk and flavored with molasses. The main meal was dinner served in the afternoon and often featuring a stew with meat and vegetables. Supper often repeated breakfast or was leftovers from dinner. In the towns, especially of New England, fish such as cod and herring was a common article of diet. Cuisine, generally, was not very flavorful, at least from our perspective. Most cooks used few spices and did little to preserve natural flavors. None of this was especially healthy. The fat content of colonial food was high; the vitamin content undoubtedly low. Still, its variety and abundance made it superior to the diet of contemporary Europeans. Americans, we know, were taller and heavier than were Western Europeans on average as early as the 1770s, a fact attesting to their superior nutrition.

Colonial Americans scorned water as a thirst quencher. At the outset milk was one of the few alternatives, but as soon as possible the colonists turned to beer, wine, hard cider, and distilled liquors, the latter mostly rum made from West Indies molasses. By the eighteenth century tea had become common, but through most of the colonial era beverages containing alcohol were the drink of choice. What this practice did to health over the years we can only guess at, but it cannot have contributed to longevity. We do know that drunkenness was a common colonial problem.

American dress was tied to class. The male farmer wore, on workdays, a linen shirt under a tight jacket called a "doublet." Below the waist he wore knee breeches, usually of wool but often of leather, ending in long cotton or linen stockings. His feet were shod either in moccasins or boots, depending on the season. The city artisan often supplemented this dress with a leather apron. Women of the farm or artisan class typically wore a three-piece outfit: a long skirt, a bodice, and sleeves that were attached to the bodice by ties at the armholes. Headgear for men consisted of woolen caps; for women, hoods or scarves.

Needless to say, among the richer colonists dress was fancier. Breeches and bodices were often velvet or satin and made of silk; leather shoes had silver buckles. Men wore three-cornered hats of beaver felt, at least by the eighteenth century. Wigs became the almost universal head covering among "gentlemen" during the early eighteenth century, though at times, in the towns, even slaves wore them. Heavy, hot, and expensive, when wigs lost popularity they were replaced by longish hair whitened with chalk and tied in a queue behind. Rich women wore slippers of satin or morocco leather, and donned long skirts over several layers of petticoats. In the eighteenth century they adopted the hoop-petticoat, an outside skirt stiffened with whalebone. Women often wore their bodices low-cut. Slim waists were prized and the middles of prosperous young women and matrons were confined by tight-lacing and corsets.

The typical colonial American had a different sense of time from ours. Mechanical clocks were few; watches nonexistent. Most colonists judged time by the sun and, though it was not very accurate, it was generally sufficient for their purposes since few daily activities required precise timing. They also lived largely by the sun. It was costly to turn night into day as we do. Homemade candles of tallow, bayberry, or beeswax were time-consuming to make. The best candles, of spermaceti from whales, were expensive and virtually reserved for the rich. All candles were used sparingly so that many colonials went to bed early and rose early.

The workweek was a six-day affair for most colonial people. Only on Sunday did work cease, and for the pious that did not mean leisure but church-going that took up long hours followed by sedate occupations such as visiting, reading, and conversation.

Life also revolved more around the seasons than is true today. Most men, after all, were farmers and their year was governed by the crop-growing cycle of spring plowing and planting, summer weeding, and fall harvesting. Winter, on the farm, was the slow season devoted to fence and house repair, handicrafts, and the like. Women's tasks were probably less affected by the season. Each week, whether summer or winter, brought the same routine of washing, cooking, nursing, house cleaning.

The colonists, except for the most devout, craved amusement for their leisure hours. In the South, especially, there were a number of spectator sports: horse racing, and the two cruel "blood sports," cockfighting and bull baiting. In the latter dogs were induced to attack a bull while the spectators watched the gore and mayhem. Children everywhere played games. In the winter northern children ice-skated and sledded; in the South—as well as the North—they hunted and fished. Colonial boys even played games with a ball and a bat that resembled modern baseball.

★ GOVERNMENT ★

Political institutions, too, were modified by the new American environment. In England, toward the end of the seventeenth century, power had already begun to shift from the crown to commoners; in British North America the process went further. Yet *democracy*—rule by popular majorities through freely elected representatives—was not highly regarded as a political system by the best minds of the day, even in the colonies. Indeed, many contemporaries considered democracy indistinguishable from mob rule. Still, the most enlightened thinkers of the day did not wish to exclude democracy entirely as an element of government since the "popular voice" could serve as a useful check on tyranny and corruption. In the end most political thinkers preferred a system of "mixed government" that combined democracy with elements of monarchy (government by a hereditary sovereign) and aristocracy (rule by a small, permanently privileged class).

The English Model. At the opening of the seventeenth century England was not far removed from the rule by despotic kings and princes that prevailed in France, Germany, and elsewhere on the European continent. Then, between about 1630 and 1690, when many of the American colonies were being founded, the Stuart kings clashed with Parliament over the powers of ruler and subject. Eventually the conflict produced two civil wars—the Puritan Revolution (1642–1646) and the Glorious Revolution (1689)—marked by the beheading of one king (Charles I) and the overthrow of another (James II).

By the end of the seventeenth century England had become a constitutional monarchy; that is, one in which the powers of the king were restricted by custom and law. Increasingly English sovereigns chose their ministers and advisers by the consent of Parliament, and increasingly these ministers, not the crown, conducted the day-to-day affairs of the realm. Furthermore Parliament, not the crown, imposed taxes and passed laws.

But England's government was not democratic. The monarch remained powerful, and Parliament itself was not a very democratic body. Membership in the upper chamber—the House of Lords—was largely hereditary; its members were Anglican bishops and noble peers with hereditary titles. Members of the lower chamber—the House of Commons—were elected, but the right to vote was strictly limited by property and religious requirements. In fact, only a small fraction of adult English males—about one in twenty-five—could vote. Even in the few districts where a greater proportion of men were enfranchised, the voters usually deferred to their "betters" and sent only "gentlemen" and rich merchants to Parliament. The House of Commons, accordingly, was composed of nontitled gentry, businessmen, and retainers of the nobility, not the common people. Even local government was in the hands of the elite. Most county and borough officials were appointed, not elected, and most of these officials were local landholding gentlemen or squires, as they were called.

As the clothes and bearing of David, Joanna, and Abigail Mason suggest in this 1670 portrait, colonial Americans considered children merely smaller versions of adults.

Although the gentry dominated English political life, the system had liberal features. English subjects had rights that French, Spanish, and German subjects did not. Their homes were their castles, and the law could not invade them except with a warrant issued by a judge. English subjects could also count on trial by jury if accused of a crime. Moreover, they were accorded equal protection under the law; there was one law for both lord and commoner. Nor was the average Englishman entirely without power in governing the realm. Even though few could vote, the English constitution recognized the representative principle that lawmakers derived their powers, if only indirectly, from those who were expected to obey the laws they imposed. To most English people, whether in Britain or America, this system seemed freer and more liberal than any other in Europe—as indeed it was—and they took pride in their political heritage.

Colonial Political Structure. British immigrants to America brought with them the political ideas, customs, and practices of the mother country. On the local level, for example, both the town in New England and the church

vestry in the South were political units transplanted from England. The colonial sheriff and justice of the peace resembled the same officials in England, and there was an obvious parallel between Parliament and the colonial legislatures. Beginning with Virginia in 1619, settlers were empowered one by one to set up legislatures in each of the British mainland colonies. These were given different names in different colonies (General Court, House of Burgesses, General Assembly), but they served the colonies much as Parliament served England. And like Parliament, most colonial legislatures had a lower and an upper house.

Each colony also had a chief executive, the equivalent of the crown. In royal colonies (in 1776, New Hampshire, Massachusetts, New York, New Jersey, Maryland, Virginia, North Carolina, South Carolina, and Georgia) the governor was appointed by the British sovereign. When the royal governor—or, more likely, his deputy, the lieutenant governor—came to America, he represented the British crown and ministry. In proprietary colonies (Pennsylvania and Delaware, and New York, Maryland, and the Carolinas before they became royal colonies) the governor represented the proprietor, the man who held the original charter. Only

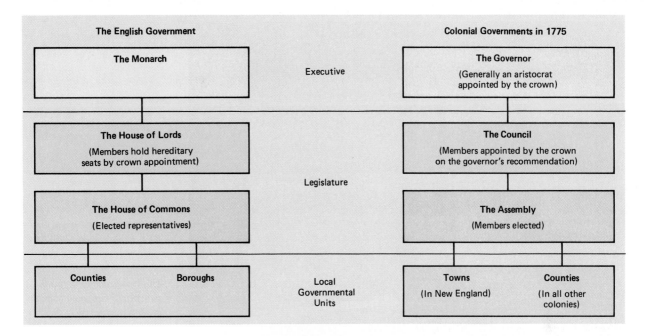

The English Government		Colonial Governments in 1775
The Monarch	Executive	**The Governor** (Generally an aristocrat appointed by the crown)
The House of Lords (Members hold hereditary seats by crown appointment)	Legislature	**The Council** (Members appointed by the crown on the governor's recommendation)
The House of Commons (Elected representatives)		**The Assembly** (Members elected)
Counties **Boroughs**	Local Governmental Units	**Towns** (In New England) **Counties** (In all other colonies)

Some similarities between colonial governments and their English model. (Note: The exceptions to this sample chart are many. In Connecticut and Rhode Island, for example, voters elected their governor. Pennsylvania's legislature was composed of only a single House.)

in Connecticut and Rhode Island was the governor elected by the local enfranchised citizens. No matter how he was chosen, the governor usually could veto acts by the colonial legislature, much as, in theory at least, the English sovereign could veto acts of Parliament.

As time went by, the governors were forced to give up some of their power to the assemblies. At first British authorities refused to consider these bodies true legislatures. One British official described them as only "so many Corporations at a distance, invested with an Ability to make Temporary By Laws for themselves." But in time, encouraged by the growing colonial population, the distance from England, the official British policy of ignoring restrictions on the colonies to allow them to prosper and thus enrich England, and by British inefficiency in administering colonial affairs, the colonial legislatures expanded their powers. Early in the eighteenth century the colonial lower houses forced the governors to allow them to debate freely without executive interference, to judge the qualifications of their own members, to exclude crown officials from their deliberations, and to meet when and for as long as they wished. Most important, they forced the governors to surrender to them "the power of the purse."

The right to control the purse strings required a long battle. When representative government was first established in the colonies, governors received an annual lump-sum appropriation from the legislature. The governors disbursed these funds as they saw fit. This system gave them the power to pursue policies without any check by the legislature. By the middle of the eighteenth century, however, the assemblies had stopped the lump-sum grants; instead they earmarked appropriations for specific periods. They also began to pay the governors' salaries for a single year— and only at the end of it—to guarantee their good behavior. In several colonies these efforts to control the governors touched off furious battles. By the 1750s most of these struggles had been decided in favor of the legislatures.

By the end of the colonial era the provincial assemblies were miniature parliaments exercising almost all the hard-won rights of their English model. These rights included control over taxation, expenditures, the salaries of officials, military and Indian affairs, and everything that affected religion, education, and what we today would call welfare. The legislatures' power was not unlimited, however. Governors continued to veto laws they opposed. And even if the governor approved a measure, it could be "disallowed" by the Privy Council in England. Especially during the early years of the eighteenth century, however, the English government did little to restrain the colonial assemblies, and during this period of "salutary neglect" much real political power slipped into the hands of the colonists.

Voters and Their Representatives. Although the framework of the colonial governments was similar to that of

This handsome Georgian structure is supposed to be an exact reproduction of the Virginia colonial capital at Williamsburg. The House of Burgesses met here during the eighteenth century.

Great Britain, political power was more widely diffused in the colonies than in Britain. The upper houses of the colonial legislatures, the councils, were appointed and were composed typically of landed gentlemen, prosperous lawyers, and rich merchants. On the other hand membership was not hereditary, as it was in the English House of Lords.

More significant was the relatively broad electorate that chose the colonial lower houses. By modern standards the colonial franchise was severely limited. Slaves, of course, could not vote, nor could indentured servants. At times some women exercised considerable public authority. For example, in the seventeenth century "Mistresse Margarett Brent, Spinster" ran her own plantation and, as executor of the estate of Leonard Calvert, proprietor of Maryland, virtually ruled that colony's affairs. But neither Margarett Brent nor any other colonial female had the right to vote. Even free white adult males had to own land or houses, or lease them for a long period, to qualify as voters. This was only one side of the picture, however. Property was so easily acquired and so widely held in America that the election laws disqualified relatively few free adult males from voting. Furthermore, traditional requirements linking church membership to voting privileges were undermined by the growing diversity of religions in America. The end result was a relatively broad franchise. In various Rhode Island towns in the mid-eighteenth century, for example, 60 per-

cent or more of the total adult male population was eligible to vote. In some New York districts up to 80 percent of all adult males had the vote. In Massachusetts, according to conservative Governor Thomas Hutchinson, "anything with the appearance of a man" was allowed to exercise the franchise.

Though many ordinary people could vote, colonial officials were not carbon copies of the colonial population. Members of the colonial assemblies were richer, better educated, and of higher status than their constitutents. Colonial voters generally preferred to send the local squire, a prosperous merchant, or a rising young lawyer to the House of Burgesses or House of Assembly rather than a farmer, craftsman, or small shopkeeper. Local officials were also members of the elite. Southern vestries appointed their own successors and were dominated by the "squirearchy" of rich planters, who resembled the county gentry of England. Nor was the town, the basic governmental unit in New England, entirely democratic. Virtually all adult males participated in the town meeting, but town leaders were generally men of high status. In a word, the political system of colonial America was not democratic.

On the other hand, political deference—submission to social superiors—was decidedly weaker in America than in England. When the local squire ran for office, he had to campaign hard and promise to abide by the wishes of the voters. Candidates were expected to act democratically and avoid aloofness. During election campaigns they made it a point to mingle with the electors and offer them "refreshment," liquid or otherwise. When Colonel George Washington of Fairfax County, Virginia, ran for the House of Burgesses in 1774, he provided the "Freeholders and Gentlemen" of Alexandria with a "hogshead of Toddy." After the returns were in, he threw a victory party for the voters that was "conducted with great harmony."

Nor did representatives, once elected, forget their constituents. Colonial legislatures and governments were surprisingly responsive to the will of the citizens. By 1705, for example, the Virginia legislature had acquired a Propositions and Grievances Committee that regularly received public petitions proposing new laws. The committee would pass along the worthiest suggestions to the House of Burgesses, which then could act as it saw fit. Historians Robert and Katherine Brown have declared that "nothing in our legislative system today approximates the direct influence which the people of colonial Virginia could exert on their legislature."

We must conclude that colonial government was neither predominantly democratic nor predominantly aristocratic; it displayed both tendencies. Democracy as we know it did not exist anywhere in the seventeenth- and eighteenth-century world. But as political institutions were transferred from England to America, they were changed in ways that allowed greater popular freedom and self-determination.

★ RELIGION ★

Organized religion was another institution that changed in the New World. White settlers brought with them a great variety of faiths—Presbyterian, Quaker, Baptist, Anglican, Jewish, Lutheran, Mennonite, Catholic, and others. Before long, under the special conditions in America, the practices of many of these groups began to diverge from their European norms.

Guarding the Flame in New England. Religious change in southern New England is particularly well documented and instructive. The Puritans who immigrated to Massachusetts did not come to found a separate church. Rather, they came to escape the harsh repression of a powerful state and the Anglican bishops. But once free of these restraints, they created the New England Way, a distinctive pattern that differed from both the Puritanism and the Anglicanism of Old England.

One of the differences involved church structure. In the Old World bishops or a council of church elders (pres-

byters) ruled the church. But in America the sparseness of the white population and the relative isolation of settlements encouraged church government by individual self-governing congregations. Each group of Christians, led by their ministers, developed, in the words of the Reverend John Cotton, "complete liberty to stand alone." This system was called Congregationalism.

The New England Way also changed Puritan doctrine. At the heart of the Puritan faith was the Calvinist notion that all people since Adam's fall were depraved and deserved damnation. Only a few—the "elect" or "saints"—would, through God's mercy, be saved from hell. European Puritans believed that this salvation was totally beyond the individual's control; the elect were chosen, or "predestined," long ago. But in New England the alternate idea of the "covenant" appeared: People could effect their salvation by entering into a kind of contract with God by which God would agree to guarantee them the faith needed for salvation. Thus saints were not predestined but "reborn," or converted.

These saints, the Puritans believed, would not only behave well outwardly, but would also avoid wicked thoughts. Their faith thus placed a tremendous moral and emotional burden on the New England Puritans. Some became tortured souls obsessed with a sense of their own sinfulness. Michael Wigglesworth, a Congregational minister at Malden, kept a diary between 1653 and 1670 in which he constantly lamented his depravity. A typical entry noted:

> Peevishness, vain thoughts, and especially pride still prevail in me. I cannot think one good thought; I cannot do anything for God but presently pride gets hold of me. . . . I find my heart prone to take secret pleasure in thinking how much I do for others' good: but Lord how little is done for thee. I fear there is much sensuality and doting upon the creature in my pursuit of the good of others.

New England Puritans were concerned with their neighbors' salvation as well as their own. In order to shape people's lives in accordance with God's will, they closely linked the church with the colony's government. Everyone was expected to attend services and pay taxes to support the Congregational ministry, regardless of their religious preference. But not all church attenders were church members: Only those who had experienced conversion could belong to the church. And only converted males could vote or hold office, although all were expected to obey the laws. Massachusetts was a community where God was considered the ruler and his will was expressed through the church leaders. Though clergymen did not hold office, they advised the secular rulers, and were consulted in all matters that pertained to public life and community policy. Questions that we today would consider matters of personal preference were treated as public issues subject to law. Sexual behavior in all its aspects fell under close public control; so did family concerns, such as children's disobedience. Blasphemy was a serious crime punishable by the authorities, as was breaking the Sabbath by game playing, drinking, or levity. Public education was intended not only to transmit skills and secular culture but also to imbue religious principles.

For a time it seemed possible to establish in Massachusetts a truly godly community—"a City upon a Hill"—where holiness might guide every aspect of life and people might avoid the corruptions of England. In the early days of settlement, when religious enthusiasm was high, young men and women could expect as a matter of course to have the required conversion experience, to demonstrate to the elders of the congregation "the worke of grace upon their soules," and to be admitted to the religious community as full equals. But as time passed, New Englanders increasingly turned to worldly affairs and shifted their attention from God to gain. By the middle of the seventeenth century the pious Puritan was already giving way to the get-ahead, enterprising Yankee. Before long many church members failed to experience conversion and so their children could not be admitted to church membership. This shrinking of the elect left many people without civil rights and threatened the churches with much-diminished membership.

In 1662 a group of ministers met in Boston to tackle the difficult problem. Their answer was the Half-Way Covenant, which provided that persons who had been baptized and who led virtuous lives could become "half-way" church members. No conversion experience was necessary. These people could not participate in the Lord's Supper, one of the few sacraments remaining in Calvinism, but they were no longer disqualified from normal civil rights. On the other hand *their* children could not even be baptized.

The new policy eased the crisis, but it did not check the erosion of orthodoxy in the Puritan colony. Some historians have connected the notorious Salem witchcraft trials of 1692, during which more than twenty persons were put to death for consorting with the Devil, with this Puritan decline. Although belief in witches was widespread, this particular outbreak was almost a community hysteria. The panic may have been fanned by the earnest efforts of the Puritan clergy, including the Reverend Cotton Mather, to raise a new fear of sin and thus revive the orthodox church.

The High Church in the Wilderness. The American environment affected other denominations as well. In the Anglican communities on the Chesapeake local circumstances wore down traditional religion even more than in New England. With its elaborate ceremonies and complex

This benign-looking man is Jonathan Edwards, the fire-and-brimstone preacher of the colonial Great Awakening.

organization, the Anglican Church was less suited to the wilderness than the Puritan Church. The distance between settlements and plantations in the Chesapeake area and the absence of cities and towns made it hard to practice Old World Anglicanism.

It was especially difficult to maintain the traditional governance of the church. In England bishops ruled the Anglican Church, but no bishop came to America during the colonial period. Low salaries, isolation from the amenities of civilization, and the absence of substantial towns made English Anglican ministers reluctant to accept duties in America. And with no bishop in the colonies, young Americans who desired to become clergymen had to travel to England for ordination. Because few were willing to make the voyage, many parishes were forced to do without an ordained spiritual leader or to accept an inferior one. The net effect was that in Virginia, Maryland, and elsewhere the Church of England moved toward a congregational system, placing control of religious matters in the hands of the vestry, the ruling lay group of the parish.

The lack of long-accumulated wealth and the scattered settlement pattern also made it hard for Anglicanism to reproduce the rituals and ceremonies of the homeland.

Sinners and an Angry God

Jonathan Edwards became his grandfather's assistant as minister at the Northampton Congregational Church in 1726. There he continued the Reverend Stoddard's vivid preaching and helped to launch the Great Awakening.

Edwards was a throwback to the early days of Calvinism when preachers proclaimed the infinite majesty of the Lord and the limitless sinfulness of humankind. Only by surrendering themselves to God's mercy and preparing to accept grace could men and women be saved, and even then few would attain the kingdom of heaven. Edwards's passion and vivid imagery, always impressive, were given a new intensity by his contact with the English preacher George Whitefield during his visit to America in the 1740s. Edwards's famous *Sinners in the Hands of an Angry God* (1741) is the classic expression of the "fire-and-brimstone" sermon, designed to put the fear of God into his congregation and make them seek conversion. It

helped confirm his reputation as the most powerful revivalist in the English colonies.

"The God that holds you over the pit of hell, much as one holds a spider, or some loathsome insect, over the fire, abhors you and is dreadfully provoked; His wrath towards you burns like fire; He looks upon you as worthy of nothing else, but to be cast into the fire; He is of purer eyes than to bear to have you in His sight; you are ten thousand times more abominable in His eyes, as the most hateful and venomous serpent is in ours. You have offended him infinitely more than ever a stubborn rebel did his prince. And yet, it is nothing but His hand that holds you from falling into the fire every moment. . . .

"O sinner! consider the fearful danger you are in: it is a great furnace of wrath, a wide and bottomless pit, full of the fire of wrath, that you are held over in the hand of that God, whose wrath is provoked and incensed as much against you, as against many

of the damned in hell. You hang by a slender thread, with the flames of divine wrath flashing about, and ready every moment to singe it, and burn it asunder; and you have no . . . Mediator, and nothing to lay hold of to save yourself, nothing to keep off the flames of wrath, nothing of your own, nothing you have ever done, nothing that you can do, to induce God to spare you one moment. . . .

"Thus it will be with you that are in an unconverted state, if you continue in it; the infinite might and majesty, and terribleness, of the omnipotent God shall be magnified upon you. . . . You shall be tormented in the presence of the holy angels, and in the presence of the Lamb; and when you shall be in the state of suffering, the glorious inhabitants of heaven shall go forth and look on the awful spectacle, that they may see what the wrath and the fierceness of the Almighty is; and when they have seen it, they will fall down and adore that great power and majesty. . . ."

Increasingly, the American Anglican Church simplified its forms and dogmas. A Virginia planter expressed the religious preferences of many colonial Anglicans in 1720: "The high-flown up-top notions and the great stress that is laid upon ceremonies . . . are what I cannot come into the reason of. Practical godliness is the substance—these are but the shell."

Though Puritans and Anglicans tacked to the changing winds of America, they both suffered losses. People drifted away from church membership and church attendance. Nor were they the only troubled religious bodies. By the beginning of the eighteenth century most of the transplanted European denominations were losing ground. On the frontiers of New York, New Jersey, and Pennsylvania the German Lutherans and Pietists and the Scotch-Irish Presbyterians were slow to form congregations. In eastern Pennsylvania, as the Quaker community grew richer, its members replaced piety with worldiness.

The Great Awakening. The general decline of orthodoxy created a vacuum in the lives of many people. Increasingly among farmers, craftspeople, and other ordinary men and women, religion seemed remote and unsatisfying. This attitude eventually triggered a religious resurgence that we call the Great Awakening.

The movement began in the 1720s as a series of revivals among the Presbyterians and Dutch Reformed groups in the middle colonies. During the next decade it was infused with new power by the Congregational minister Jonathan Edwards of Northampton, Massachusetts. Edwards, a Yale graduate, was appalled by the decline of orthodoxy that he observed all around him, and he resolved to do something about it. In 1729 he began to preach the old Calvinist doctrine of predestination, calling people back to God and threatening them with eternal damnation for their sins. Edwards's theology was old-fashioned, but his emotional preaching style was new, and his sermons shocked the traditionalists, who considered them unseemly. Ordinary people, however, flocked to hear him preach at his Northampton church. Before long clergymen throughout New England were emulating Edwards's hellfire-and-damnation sermons.

In 1738 the English preacher George Whitefield visited America and turned the Great Awakening into a religious event of continental proportions. Whitefield was a spellbinder who preached the traditional old-time Calvinism of predestination and damnation for all but an elect. Of one group of young women who came to hear him, Whitefield himself wrote: "A wonderful power was in the room, and with one accord they began to cry out and weep most bitterly for the space of half an hour. . . . Five of them seemed affected as those that are in fits. . . ." Benjamin Franklin, skeptical of organized religion in general and of Whitefield's appeals for money to found an American orphanage in particular, went to hear the preacher, but was resolved not to contribute to his cause. "I had in my pocket,

a handful of copper money, three or four silver dollars, and five pistoles in gold," Franklin later wrote. "As he proceeded I began to soften, and concluded to give the copper, another stroke of his oratory determined me to give the silver; and he finished so admirably that I emptied my pocket wholly into the collector's dish, gold and all."

The doctrines of the revivalists varied. Some were Calvinists who believed most souls damned. Others were Arminians who rejected predestination and assumed a forgiving God. But most of their followers embraced their passionate appeal for surrender to Jesus and a commitment to live an exemplary Christian life rather than their theology. Whitefield, Edwards, and the other revivalists presented these views so simply and with such emotional effect that thousands were brought back to religion. Attacked by educated people as "shouters," "enthusiasts," and disturbers of the peace, the revivalists of the Great Awakening were immensely successful among common people. Many joined, or rejoined, the older denominations. Within these

With religious centers across the sea and ministers in short supply, orthodox religion in America suffered. The Great Awakening—a spiritual revival led by George Whitefield—brought new fervor. Unstructured, emotional, and free from elaborate ceremony, revivalism fit America's simpler needs. The peculiar eyes of Whitefield depicted here do not reflect the painter's lack of skill. Whitefield was cross-eyed.

churches congregations and clergy soon divided between those who followed the decorous old way—the Old Lights—and those who followed the emotional new way—the New Lights. Many more people flocked to newer denominations such as the Baptists and later the Methodists. Thus, by producing new sects and dividing congregations and ministers, the Great Awakening further diversified religious expression in America.

The Enlightenment. The Great Awakening lured many ordinary people back into the traditional religious fold. But by the middle of the eighteenth century many educated people in America were turning not to religion but to a new set of secular beliefs known to us as the Enlightenment.

This major alteration in the way Western thinkers perceived the world was rooted in the scientific revolutions of the day, especially in the ideas of Sir Isaac Newton. In the new view the world appeared a rational, orderly place, operating not according to the immediate will of God but by changeless natural laws. Several important concepts followed from this view: First, that as members of this rational universe, human beings were good, not sinful; second, that by use of their reason, human beings could discover the natural laws of the universe; third, that knowledge of these laws would enable people to control their environment and society; and finally, that the inevitable result of this control would be progress over the course of human history. Science played a significant role in this world picture because it was by means of scientific method—observation and experiment—that natural laws could be discovered.

A few members of the "enlightened" elite rejected all religion and became agnostics or atheists. Most, however, chose deism. Deists continued to believe in God, but theirs was a god who operated through natural laws, not miracles. He showed himself through nature, not Christian revelation. God's role in the world was much like that of a clockmaker—a being who makes a clock, winds it up, and then leaves it to work by its own mechanical laws.

Deism developed late in the colonial period and affected only a small group of Americans. The deists, however, were an influential group—including Benjamin Franklin, Thomas Jefferson, Ethan Allen, and Thomas Paine—who would have influence in the world of ideas disproportionate to their numbers.

Established Churches. As Old Lights battled New Lights, Calvinists fought Arminians, and deists denounced the orthodox—and as many people simply slipped away from traditional religion—it became increasingly difficult to impose any sort of religious conformity on America. But it was not for want of trying. In most of New England and the South, and in part of New York, colonial legislatures gave special privileges to "established" denominations. In New England it was the Congregational; elsewhere it was the Anglican. By the mid-eighteenth century other sects were generally free to preach, pray, and proselytize but they did so without public support. The established churches, on the other hand, received public largesse. Taxes imposed on all, even nonbelievers, paid the salaries of Congregational and Anglican clergy. Some Americans had come to believe that religion and all its practices belonged in the private, not the public, domain. But "separation of church and state" was still a novel concept.

As the religious pot continued to boil and bring to the surface new sects the growing diversity would undermine the established churches and lead to ever greater toleration. Ultimately, Americans developed the most fluid, tolerant, and voluntary religious life of any people, not primarily through the power of noble principles, but because no one group could overwhelm the others.

★ Intellectual America ★

The conditions of colonial America that led to changes in the social, political, and religious institutions transplanted from Europe also molded science, education, and the professions that depended on them. For better or worse, intellectual development in America lagged behind or diverged from the Old World experience.

Science. The seventeenth century was an era of immense progress in the natural sciences. It was the time when Galileo first used the telescope to observe the solar system, William Harvey detected the circulation of the blood, Johannes Kepler formulated the laws governing the orbits of the planets, and Isaac Newton discovered the basic laws of motion and the role of gravity. These scientists were all Europeans, however; Americans made few contributions to basic scientific theory.

Neither the social nor the physical environment of colonial America encouraged theoretical science. Engaged in a day-to-day struggle to earn a living, the colonists tended to be interested in practical, not theoretical, matters. Moreover, even at the very end of the colonial era the scaffolding necessary for a flourishing scientific enterprise was absent. Theoretical science requires laboratories, patronage, centers of learning, and stimulating contact among thinkers. Colonial America—lacking large accumulations of wealth, inhabited by a sparse and scattered population, and far from the intellectual centers of the Western world—was not a likely birthplace for a Harvey, a Galileo, a Kepler,

This portrait of Benjamin Franklin, painted around 1746 when he was forty, shows a successful man of affairs who also had begun his famous experiments with electricity and already invented his "Pennsylvania Fireplace."

or a Newton. Twenty-five Americans were elected before 1776 to the prestigious British scientific body, the Royal Society of London, but they were honored for their acute observations of natural phenomena, not for grand theories or major intellectual breakthroughs.

Only one colonial scientist deserves comparison with the best of Europe: Benjamin Franklin. Franklin's experiments with electricity in the 1740s and 1750s contributed to an early understanding of that phenomenon and won him an honorary doctorate from a European university. Yet among the practical Americans "Doctor" Franklin was largely famous for his invention of the lightning rod to protect buildings from electrical storms and for the efficient parlor stove that bears his name.

Education.   In America, education also took on a distinctive cast. At the lower levels American education was advanced for its day. Primary schools, staffed by both men and women, existed in every colony, but educational opportunities varied greatly. More boys than girls attended schools, a fact reflected in the higher literacy rate of colonial men than women. Slaves received no formal education, though a few learned to read and write. There were also strong regional inequalities in access to education. Because of the scattered set-

tlement pattern in the southern colonies, it was hard to bring together a concentration of pupils sufficient to support a local school. Rich planters hired private tutors for their sons and daughters, and occasionally these tutors also instructed the sons and daughters of the planter's poorer neighbors. But educational opportunities in the southern colonies were generally limited, especially for the children of common farmers.

The more densely settled northern colonies, particularly New England, did better by their young people. The Dutch in New Netherland were quick to establish schools supported by the colonial treasury. Still more conscientious were the Massachusetts Puritans, who believed that it was essential to salvation for individuals to be able to read and understand the Scriptures for themselves. In 1647 the Massachusetts General Court required each town in the province with fifty families to establish a "petty" school to teach children to read and write. Any town with at least a hundred households was also required to establish a "grammar" school (high school) to prepare students for the university and the learned professions. The purpose of the law, the legislators noted, was to defeat "ye ould deluder, Satan"; but its most important effect was to create in New England a body of literate people probably unique among contemporary Western communities.

Educated Americans kept in touch with European thought through books and journals, and some tried to nurture higher education even in the crude early settlements. In 1636, just six years after the Puritans settled Massachusetts, Bay Colony authorities established Harvard College in Cambridge, to create the literate, educated ministry the Puritans considered vital to religion. At first the college curriculum consisted primarily of humanistic studies and theology, but gradually it expanded to include "natural philosophy" or, as we would say, science.

Massachusetts's example was soon followed by other colonies. By the time of the Revolution eight other institutions of higher learning had been established: the College of William and Mary (1693); Yale (1701); the College of New Jersey, later called Princeton (1746); Queen's College, later called Rutgers (1766); King's College, later called Columbia (1754); the College of Philadelphia, later called the University of Pennsylvania (1754); Rhode Island College, later called Brown University (1764); and Dartmouth (1769).

Like Harvard, most of these colleges were sponsored by religious denominations. They emphasized religion and the classics and turned out men with "liberal" educations who either became clergymen or, after further training, entered one of the other traditional learned professions—law or medicine. But at least one college took a different turn. Under the influence of Benjamin Franklin, Philadelphia's most prominent citizen, the College of Philadelphia devoted a third of its curriculum to mathematics and the natural sciences. Even this course of study differed greatly from the practical curriculum of a modern American university; but under Franklin's auspices, the College of Philadelphia took the first step toward higher education to advance the practical arts.

Law and Medicine.   Colonial conditions molded professional education, too. In England members of the legal profession endured a long and elaborate training process at the old and respected Inns of Court. English lawyers included barristers to plead cases, attorneys to start the legal machinery going, solicitors to offer legal advice, and notaries to prepare legal documents. The structure resembled England's class system: an elite at top with lesser folk beneath.

The struggling colonists could not support this elaborate and expensive system. At first there were no lawyers in the colonies except for a few who had been trained in England; when a legal profession did appear, its structure was much simpler than in England. In America there was only one all-purpose attorney, who drew up documents and briefs, advised clients, and pleaded cases before the courts. Instead of attending law schools like the English Inns of Court, lawyers

learned by working in law offices, reading standard law books, such as Sir William Blackstone's *Commentaries on the Laws of England* and Sir Edward Coke's *Reports*, attending court, and performing minor legal chores for senior attorneys.

Toward the end of the colonial period, however, the legal profession drew closer to its English model. Some Americans began to go to London for legal training. But despite America's growing exposure to English forms, the English legal structure remained too cumbersome for America, with its weaker system of higher education and its more open class structure.

A similar simplification took place in the colonial medical profession. Despite scientific advances in medicine in seventeenth-century Europe, medical men still enthusiastically embraced theories of disease expounded by ancient or medieval authorities. These theories usually ascribed disease to some imbalance in the four "humors"—choler, blood, bile, and phlegm. The physician's task was to diagnose the nature of the imbalance and restore equilibrium—often, as it happened, with harsh and ineffective remedies. Fortunately for Americans, the European physicians' learned

Harvard College in the mid-1700s, a century after its founding.

Benjamin Franklin

Benjamin Franklin was the first self-made American. When Ben was born in 1706, his father, Josiah, was a candlemaker and soap manufacturer with premises on Milk Street in Boston. Like most of his forebears, Ben was destined for a leather apron, not a silk waistcoat; at the age of twelve he was apprenticed to his older brother, James, who ran a print shop in the New England capital. Though he became an intellectual celebrity, a major political leader, and a favorite of royalty, Franklin never forgot his origins in the sober, hard-working American lower middle class.

Ben and his brother did not get along, yet the lad profited by his work in the print shop. James was not only a job printer, he was also publisher of one of America's earliest newspapers, *The New England Courant*. This was a single-sheet weekly, like the handful of other colonial newspapers, but it afforded abundant scope for young Ben's talents and energies. In the intervals between setting type, sweeping the floor, and running errands, he had time to make up for the deficiencies in his formal education. Ben read widely the ancient classics in translation, as well as in the best of contemporary English prose. He also learned to write with skill, and at sixteen composed a series of humorous articles for the *Courant* under a pseudonym. In later years he taught himself mathematics, Greek, Latin, and several modern languages, but he never lost the straightforward, unpretentious quality of the self-taught individual.

In 1723, following months of squabbling with James, Ben left Boston to seek his fortune as a printer elsewhere. He went first to New York, but unable to find work, he moved on to Philadelphia.

The young man of seventeen arrived in a town of 10,000, a community smaller than Boston, but one that was growing faster and was more open to the talented go-getter. During the remainder of his long life Franklin would spend extended periods abroad, in London and then in Paris, but practical, tolerant Philadelphia left an indelible impression on him and provided the base for all his later success. Here he established his own newspaper, *The Pennsylvania Gazette*, and made his fortune as editor, pamphlet and almanac publisher, bookseller, and paper maker. Here he achieved international fame as "Poor Richard," a fictional old man whose lips spouted wise maxims and proverbs recorded in *Poor Richard's Almanack*. Here he married Deborah Read Rogers, a young woman whose aid in the printshop-bookstore was an essential part of his financial success. Finally, the City of Brotherly Love provided the setting for Franklin's extraordinary and wide-ranging intellectual activities.

Franklin was a philosopher, a scientist, and an inventor. In London, while on a visit to buy a press and type for his paper, he picked up the fashionable deism of the day. He later wrote several pamphlets and articles defining the idea of a scientist-God who made "the glorious sun, with its attending worlds . . . and prescribed the wondrous laws, by which they move." But he gave him, characteristically, a practical twist. Franklin's God was not remote and aloof. He was a benevolent being who delighted in virtue and frowned on vice.

All knowledge interested Franklin. He was fascinated by the expanding world of contemporary science. He could not crack the mathematical complexities of Sir Isaac Newton's revolutionary work on gravity and planetary motion, but he was adept at empirical science. His famous kite experiments of 1752 proved that lightning was a form of the mysterious

ignorance could not be transplanted easily to North America. In Europe doctors trained at the universities. Few cared to surrender the high fees and status they enjoyed in Europe to come to the American wilderness, nor did American colleges teach medicine until the eve of the Revolution. Moreover, the exotic drugs and preparations used by European doctors were hard to duplicate in America.

The dilution of European practices in the colonies probably improved medical care. Colonial medical practitioners, like colonial legal practitioners, learned by apprenticeship and from day-to-day contact with patients. Without mistaken theories to lead them astray, doctors re-lied on experience, observation, and common sense. Instead of purges, poultices, bleeding, and the foul potions prescribed in Europe, they turned to local herbs, often ones recommended by the Indians, for cures. Even when these did no good, they generally did little serious harm.

American medicine was also structured more democratically than European medicine. The shortage of trained personnel created opportunities for people who could not have practiced in England. Many medical practitioners in the colonies were women, and a number of slaves and free blacks were respected for their medical knowledge. Cotton Mather, who became a crusader for smallpox vaccination over the ob-

"electrical fluid" and made Franklin a celebrity. Colleges and universities hastened to confer honorary degrees on the Philadelphian. Thereafter he was universally addressed as "Doctor Franklin."

Franklin's intellectual labors were characteristically American. Even his most theoretical scientific work had a practical side. One important outcome of the kite experiment was the lightning rod to protect buildings in electrical storms. Besides this useful device, Dr. Franklin invented a fuel-efficient stove and bifocal eyeglasses.

Franklin also carved out a distinguished career as a public servant. He served as a member of the Pennsylvania Assembly, as a delegate to the 1754 Albany Congress, as Pennsylvania's "agent" in London, and as joint deputy postmaster general in North America. As the strains between the American colonies and the British Empire grew during the 1760s and 1770s, he emerged as a leading "patriot" who supported increased autonomy for America and opposed Britain's drive to tighten imperial controls. Most of his work for his countrymen he performed abroad. Between 1766 and 1775 he served in effect as ambassador and chief lobbyist of the American colonies in London. Franklin returned to America in 1775 in time for the dramatic final crisis that led to independence and served on the committee of Congress that drafted the Declaration of Independence. In late 1776 he went to France as one of the three commissioners of the new United States to negotiate an alliance that would offset powerful Britain in the fierce struggle now under way.

His work in France proved invaluable. He was more than the official United States envoy. Franklin fulfilled a fantasy about the "natural man" then in vogue among Europe's educated classes, and the French saw him as the very essence of the new American man, simple in dress and manner, practical yet learned, tolerant and industrious, and free of the Old World's corruptions. In all but possibly the last they were correct. Though there was a conscious element of guile and self-advertisement in Franklin, he was a blunt, pragmatic, unpretentious man. But he was also a man of strong appetites. His marriage to Deborah, with its long separations, did not meet his romantic needs. In France the American ambassador was especially popular among the ladies, and Abigail Adams, on a visit to the Franklin residence at Passy near Paris, was shocked by the free manners and the frankness of speech she encountered there. Fortunately for Franklin and the United States, his gallantry only made him more popular with the French people.

Franklin, of course, had more important things to do in France than please the ladies. While there he negotiated the Franco-American Alliance of 1778 and the accompanying commercial treaty. In 1783 he, John Jay, and John Adams negotiated the peace treaty with Britain that ended the war and confirmed American independence.

In July 1785 Franklin left France for America, having been away from his native land for still another decade. He arrived in Philadelphia to be greeted by pealing bells and roaring cannon. Soon after, he was elected president of the Pennsylvania Executive Council under the state's novel new constitution.

The last important role of his career was as Pennsylvania delegate to the Constitutional Convention in Philadelphia. He had not been among those who deplored the country's state during the immediate postindependence period, but he approved the convention's results and wrote in favor of his state's ratification of the Constitution. His last public act, at the age of eighty-four, was to sign, as head of the Pennsylvania Society for Promoting the Abolition of Slavery, a petition to end human bondage in the United States. To the end Franklin remained enlisted in the party of humanity and enlightenment.

jections of European-trained physicians, first learned about the procedure from his black slave, a man named Onesimus.

★ THE ARTS ★

In the fine arts colonial American accomplishments generally fell well below the best of Europe. Early American writing was predominantly nonfiction with an emphasis on biography, travel descriptions, religious exposition, and history. Much of it is today of interest only to academic students of American literature. At times, however, these works achieved some distinction. William Bradford's *Of Plimmoth Plantation*, an account of the founding and early days of the Pilgrim colony, was a heartfelt and effective narrative, though it was not published until many years after its author's death. The work of another New Englander, Cotton Mather's *Magnalia Christi Americana* (1702), by the scion of a distinguished Bay Colony ministerial family, is a rich encyclopedic review of New England's early history, replete with biographies, descriptions of wondrous happenings, and defenses of the New England way. In the South, Robert Beverley, an American-born planter, wrote the epically proportioned

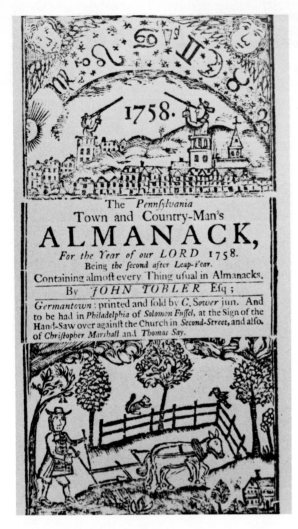

The History and Present State of Virginia (1705), a work that reveals the author's compassion for the Indians and his hope that Virginia would become a pastoral paradise.

Fiction was sparser. The first American novel did not appear until after independence, but there were several talented colonial poets. The best perhaps was Edward Taylor, an English-born minister educated at Harvard College. Taylor wrote more than 200 devotional poems full of rich imagery and subtle nuances. Unfortunately, almost none of his poetry was published until the 1930s. Anne Bradstreet of Andover, Massachusetts—a "Tenth Muse lately sprung up in America," her publisher called her—was more fortunate. Bradstreet had come to Massachusetts as a bride with

the first Puritan wave in 1630 at the age of eighteen. Like many pioneer women, she had been dismayed by the crude frontier environment. But, as was expected of colonial women, she accepted her fate. "I changed my condition and was married," she later wrote, "and came into this country, where I found a new world and new manners, at which my heart rose [that is, was stirred against it]. But after I was convinced it was the way of God, I submitted to it. . . ." During the next forty years, amid the cares and labors of raising eight children and attending to her busy husband, she wrote reams of verse. Her later work, with its unaffected language and faithful images of the American landscape, is the first authentic American poetry.

Although imaginative literature did not flourish in colonial America, newspapers, broadsides, pamphlets, instructional books, and almanacs were produced in abundance. The colonists read widely because they needed practical information. Newspapers were read by proportionately more Americans than Europeans; they contained vital information about colonial affairs. Almanacs were useful to farmers and merchants, who had to know about prices and the weather. In the hands of Benjamin Franklin, the famous *Poor Richard's Almanack* came close to being a form of creative literature. Besides the usual data on planting times, seasonal changes, tides, eclipses, and the like, *Poor Richard's* contained entertaining little word sketches by "Richard Saunders" (Franklin's pseudonym) and pithy maxims that have become part of America's folk heritage. Americans also wrote and imported practical handbooks on medicine, navigation, agriculture, architecture, brick making, and other skills that could help them conquer a continent.

Music did not fare as well in colonial America. Colonial churchgoers, especially Puritan ones, enthusiastically sang the psalms. But as the European traditions receded, the colonists' music became so dreary and unmelodious that Cotton Mather, no great aesthete, labeled it "an odd noise." Folk songs that we still know, such as "Greensleeves" and "Barbara Allen," began as Elizabethan English folk music and were modified by American singers. But there were two important American composers before 1776: William Billings, a self-taught musician who composed "fuguing-tunes" for several voices singing different parts; and Francis Hopkinson, a talented Philadelphia composer of songs and instrumental pieces. (Hopkinson also painted, wrote poetry, and—contrary to the myth about Betsy Ross—designed the first American national flag.)

Though Americans lagged badly behind Europeans in the fine arts, they excelled in the production of functional objects. This bent helps to explain the relatively high level of painting in the colonies. Colonial artists did not, like their European counterparts, paint romantic landscapes, or gamboling gods and goddesses, or heroic battle scenes. Instead,

Americans made little distinction between artists and craftsmen until late in the colonial period, when the wealthy began to have their portraits painted. Before portraying the most distinguished of the Revolutionary War generation, Charles Wilson Peale, who limned his large family here, was a saddler and signpainter. (Collection of the New York Historical Society)

they focused on portraits, the most practical genre of painting. Here they could count on a ready market for their efforts. In the absence of photography, wealthy merchants and planters, who had little interest in art for art's sake, turned to painters to glorify their affluence and preserve their likenesses and those of their family for posterity.

The earliest American artists were amateurish daubers who often paid the rent by doing sign painting. Then, toward the end of the colonial era, John Singleton Copley and Benjamin West, of Boston and Philadelphia, respectively, began to attract wealthy patrons. But even in the second century of settlement, America could not hold on to its most talented artists. In 1760 West left for Rome and soon after settled in England. In 1775 Copley too left for Britain, in part to escape attack as a Loyalist, but also to expand his artistic horizons.

American architecture was also primitive and limited at first. As we saw, the earliest settlers lived in lean-tos, dugouts, and tents. Later in the first century of settlement, they began to imitate European models. In New Amsterdam the Dutch settlers copied the architecture of contemporary urban Holland, buildings with high gabled ends and narrow sides abutting the street. Seventeenth-century houses in Massachusetts and Virginia resembled Tudor English structures, replete with gables and small-paned leaded windows. Even the log cabin was a European borrowing, brought to the Delaware Bay region in the seventeenth century by Swedes and Finns.

In time, American architecture became more original. The new style of the eighteenth century took its name—Queen Anne or Georgian—from the English monarchs of the day. With its regularly spaced rows of windows, white-trimmed brick, and fine detailing at doors and openings, Georgian architecture was not strictly speaking a native genre at all. But it was adapted to American needs and circumstances in ways that frequently transcended mere imitation. The best of eighteenth-century colonial architecture blended admirably with the American environment; to this day Independence Hall in Philadelphia and domestic buildings like William Byrd's Virginia mansion, Westover, convey a sense of a vigorous provincial society evolving a distinctive cultural tradition.

A similar progression from imitation to innovation can be observed in the minor arts and the crafts. In the seventeenth century there were few skilled craftsmen in the colonies, and the settlers either used English artifacts or made their own crude ones. But by the eighteenth century many talented workers in brass, pewter, glass, silver, clay, and wood had immigrated to America from England and the Continent. Meanwhile, the skills of both white and black Americans had matured to a high level. Paul Revere of Boston combined native inspiration with imported forms and designs to create exquisite bowls, trays, and tea services in silver. At his glassworks at Mannheim, Pennsylvania, the German entrepreneur Henry William Stiegel produced glassware that is still eagerly collected. Skill and creativity marked the approach of colonial women to functional crafts, such as recycling bits of material into boldly designed quilts. Their work is now being recognized and appreciated as the expression of artistic sensitivities that transcended the drudgeries of primitive life in the New World.

★ CONCLUSIONS ★

Crèvecoeur was right. By the eve of the Revolution America was no longer a carbon copy of Europe, and Americans were not simply transplanted Europeans.

Several factors had contributed to the change. British North America included a mixture of racial and ethnic components unknown in Europe; even the European ingredients of this mix were present in different proportions and existed in different relationships to each other than in the Old World. Americans were not Englishmen, though many were English immigrants or their descendants. In part, they were German, and exhibited a skill in agriculture still uncommon in Britain. They were also Scotch-Irish, and on the frontier revealed a sternness and militancy not typical of England. The Indian and African elements in the New World mixture were completely unknown to Europeans; yet they affected the military practice, technology, language, and customs of the new society.

In addition to the changes that accompanied the mingling of diverse cultures, there were those produced by the special physical and social environment of the New World. The abundance of land relative to the population made for better health, larger families, and ultimately a larger electorate and a more democratic political system. The relative scarcity of women allowed them some freedom to take on nontraditional roles and helped improve their legal status. A more scattered population and a less elitist social structure made it difficult to implant complex European institutions intact; as a result, the legal and medical professions were simplified and transformed. Meanwhile, the absence of a substantial leisure class, of great universities, and of private and government patronage altered the character of the arts and learning, pushing them toward greater practicality.

Nevertheless, we must qualify Crèvecoeur's announcement of a "new man" in America. Many of the distinctive national and cultural groups existed side by side without blending. In the case of blacks and Indians, their contributions were deliberately inhibited by the European majority. It would take generations before the blending process could produce a uniform new cultural mix, and the process is not complete today, nor will it ever be.

And there is another qualification to the Crèvecoeur formula. At the end of the colonial period, as wealth increased and transatlantic communication improved, the culture of the colonial elite began to move closer to Britain's. In many ways, by the eve of the Revolution, religion, the professions, the arts, and political life had begun to take on the characteristics of the mother country. In 1775 American society was becoming a provincial offshoot of Europe.

Yet the differences remained and the convergence would soon slow. By the mid-eighteenth century the actual interests of Americans and English people had begun to draw apart. British-American differences would soon produce a crisis that would sever the imperial connection and create a separate American nation and with it a still more distinctive culture.

★★★★★★★★ FOR FURTHER READING ★★★★★★★★

Daniel Boorstin. *The Americans: The Colonial Experience* (1958)
A bold attempt to demonstrate how the American environment altered transplanted Old World institutions and culture. Boorstin probably exaggerates the extent to which the transplants were changed by wilderness America, but along the way he makes many interesting points about colonial religion, language, the arts, and the professions.
John Demos. *A Little Commonwealth: Family Life in Plymouth Colony* (1970)
A fascinating study of family life in Plymouth Colony drawn from both the written records and the archeological evidence of surviving artifacts, houses, and utensils. Demos reconstructs the roles and relationships within the Pilgrim family and shows how the family influenced the individual development of its members.

Philip Greven. *Four Generations: Population, Land, and Family in Colonial Andover, Massachusetts* (1970); and *The Protestant Temperament* (1977)
The first of these two books is a demographic study of a seventeenth-century New England town that shows the remarkable longevity and prosperity of the early settlers and the gradual deterioration of both as population became excessive for the town's area. The second deals with child-rearing practices in America from 1600 to 1830. It makes the point that there were three types of families—pious, aristocratic, and in-between—largely associated with distinctive religious views. Difficult but interesting.
Kenneth Lockridge. *A New England Town, The First Hundred Years: Dedham, Massachusetts, 1636–1736* (1970)
This is a brilliant study of one New England town during its

first century. It deals with land, population, families, and social and political power. If you want to know how the early social unit of New England, the town, functioned, you must read this model study.

Carl Bridenbaugh. *Myths and Realities: Societies of the Colonial South* (1952)

Bridenbaugh maintains that the colonial South was not one but three distinct cultures: a Chesapeake society, a Carolina society, and the back settlements. A brief and readable treatment of the often neglected southern colonial heritage.

James R. Lemon. *The Best Poor Man's Country: A Geographical Study of Early Southwestern Pennsylvania* (1972)

Much broader than its title suggests, this is an interesting study of the interplay of the institutions and physical environment of early Pennsylvania. Written by a geographer, it is nonetheless an excellent social history. Makes the point about colonial Pennsylvania expressed in the title.

Peter Wood. *Black Majority* (1975)

This study of early South Carolina is by far the best treatment we have of colonial slavery. Wood believes that transplanted Africans contributed significantly to the culture and institutions of early southern society. In all likelihood, for example, it was they who introduced the canoe and the cultivation of rice.

Louis B. Wright, editor. *The Cultural Life of the American Colonies, 1607–1763* (1957)

This general survey of colonial cultural and intellectual history summarizes developments in religion, literature, education, science, architecture, theater, and music. Written with wit and admiration.

Henry F. May. *The Enlightenment in America* (1976)

Intellectual history at its best by a master of the field who left his usual period, the Gilded Age and Progressive Era, to take a new look at the eighteenth and early nineteenth centuries. May sees the American Enlightenment as a complex three-part development, with the phase described in this chapter (the defense of balance and order) as the most characteristically American.

Charles Sydnor. *Gentlemen Freeholders: Political Practices in Washington's Virginia* (1952)

A brief reinterpretation of Virginia's colonial political life that emphasizes its "popular" features by contrast with the aristocratic ones given prominence by earlier authors.

Robert E. Brown and B. Katherine Brown. *Virginia 1705–1786: Democracy or Aristocracy?* (1964)

The Browns' answer to the question that they raise in their title is clear: Colonial Virginia was a remarkably democratic society in a political sense. Some scholars believe the Browns' position is overstated.

Robert E. Brown. *Middle-Class Democracy and the Revolution in Massachusetts, 1691–1780* (1955)

Massachusetts, the author believes, was a middle-class democratic society by the eve of the Revolution and it was the threat to the liberty of a people used to freedom that tripped off the anti-British defiance of 1763–1775.

Jack P. Green. *The Quest for Power: The Lower Houses of Assembly in the Southern Royal Colonies, 1689–1763* (1963)

This scholarly study deals with the struggle of the southern provincial assemblies to become independent legislatures rather than rubber stamps of royal governors or Parliament. Green shows how much they had already achieved by the 1760s to make the American colonists a self-governing people.

Nathaniel Hawthorne. *The Scarlet Letter* (1850)

A classic of nineteenth-century American literature, *The Scarlet Letter* is an incomparable introduction to the gloomy, brooding, morbid side of Puritan New England. Hawthorne's great-grandfather, a judge at the Salem witch trials, was cursed by an old woman, one of those condemned to death.

Michael Zuckerman. *Peaceable Kingdoms: New England Towns in the Eighteenth Century* (1970)

This work, emphasizing the consensus aspect of New England towns, set off much of the 1980s research in the nature of colonial community ties and interactions.

Christine Leigh Heyrman. *Commerce and Culture: The Maritime Communities of Colonial Massachusetts, 1690–1750* (1984)

A fine description of colonial life in Marblehead and Gloucester, two major New England ports. Professor Heyrman concludes that "the conversion to a trading economy did not precipitate a sweeping, uniform set of changes in provincial seaports." She also finds an interesting anti-Quaker motive behind the witchcraft trials in Gloucester, a close-by neighbor of witchcraft-ridden Salem.

David Freeman Hawke. *Everyday Life in Early America* (1988)

An interesting depiction of daily life in colonial America. Brief but entertaining. Contains several good photo sections of colonial artifacts.

Darrett B. Rutman and Anita H. Rutman. *A Place in Time: Middlesex County, Virginia, 1650–1750* (1984)

In this work the Rutmans demonstrate that the colonial Chesapeake region was not the structureless, individualistic place that scholars had formerly believed. A wonderful evocation of what life was like to the several hundred families, black and white, rich and poor, who inhabited this tobacco-growing county on the western shore of Chesapeake Bay.

Gloria Main. *Tobacco Colony: Life in Early Maryland, 1650–1720* (1982)

A recent description of the other Chesapeake colony—Maryland. Professor Main deals with the social abstractions of colonial Maryland—demographic processes and the impact of market forces on development. She also deals with the concrete details of daily life—what people ate and drank, how they dressed, the kinds of beds they slept in, what their houses were like, what they read—if they read at all.

David Hackett Fischer. *Albion's Seed: Four British Folkways in America* (1989)

Fischer advances a fascinating hypothesis about the transmission from Britain to colonial America of four distinctive cultural patterns and their persistence, relatively intact and unblended, right through the colonial period—and beyond.

Jon Butler. *Awash in a Sea of Faith: The Christianization of the American People* (1990)

Butler is skeptical of any colonial "Great Awakening." He says the phenomenon has been greatly exaggerated.

4★

MOVING TOWARD INDEPENDENCE

Why Did the Colonists Revolt?

1651	England passes the first "navigation act" to prevent Dutch intrusion into the colonial trade
1688	The overthrow of James II begins the "Glorious Revolution" in England
1699	The Wool Act • France establishes the settlement of "Louisiana" on the Gulf of Mexico
1721–48	The period of "salutary neglect"
1732	The Hat Act
1733	The Molasses Act
1750	The Iron Act
1754	Benjamin Franklin proposes the Albany Plan of Union to the colonies, but it is never adopted
1754–63	The French and Indian War: Colonists disobey England's ban on all trade with France and its colonies • War with France ends with the Treaty of Paris • Colonial settlement west of Appalachians prohibited by the Proclamation of 1763
1764	The Sugar Act • The Currency Act
1765, 1766	The Quartering Acts
1765	The Stamp Act • The Intercolonial Stamp Act Congress resolves that colonists should be taxed only by a representative legislature
1765–66	New York and other cities respond to the Stamp Act by adopting nonimportation agreements
1766	Parliament repeals the Stamp Act, but reaffirms with the Declaratory Act its right to legislate for the colonies
1767	The Townshend (or Revenue) Acts provoke another boycott of British goods
1770	Parliament repeals Townshend duties, except those on tea • The Boston Massacre
1773	The Tea Act threatens to undercut the colonial smuggling trade • East India Company tea is destroyed in the Boston Tea Party
1774	Boston harbor is closed by the Coercive (or Intolerable) Acts • The First Continental Congress attacks Britain's restrictions on colonial trade
1775	Armed confrontation at Lexington and Concord

ew events in American history are as fundamental as the great struggle that ended with independence in 1783. Yet the causes of this crucial upheaval have long been controversial. Thomas Jefferson believed that Britain's "deliberate, systematical plan of reducing us to slavery" had spurred Americans to take the drastic step of declaring their freedom. Other participants in the events of 1763–76 blamed religion as much as politics for inciting the Revolution. John Adams recalled many years later that the British threat to establish Anglican bishops in America had "spread a universal alarm against the authority of Parliament." Yet a third group of contemporaries, as well as later scholars, have stressed economic oppression as the ultimate cause of strains in the imperial relationship. In 1766 British customs officials in Rhode Island complained bitterly that the interests of "the Mother Country & this Colony" were "deemed by the People almost altogether incompatible, in a commercial View. . . ." Any official who attempted to defend British trade policies had been "threatened as an Enemy to this Country. . . ." A hundred and seventy-five years later Louis Hacker declared that the "basic reason for the onset of crisis and the outbreak of revolutionary struggle" was the "economic vassalage" imposed on the colonies.

Which of these explanations is correct? Is each partly correct? Is one fundamental and the others secondary? Let us consider the economic one first.

★ THE COLONIAL ECONOMY ★

What was the colonial economy like, and what were its strengths and weaknesses? Did British policy hinder or help it? Did Americans have valid economic grievances against the mother country?

Agriculture. Agriculture was the foundation of the colonial economy. On the eve of the Revolution it employed 80 percent of the working population and created most of the wealth produced.

A majority of American cultivators were small farm owners, yeomen, engaged in mixed agriculture—growing corn, rye, wheat; raising cattle, sheep, horses, hogs; and planting fruit trees, potatoes, and vegetables. The farmer's own family consumed most of these products, but except on the frontier, where distances to markets and particularly poor transportation made it impossible, farmers sold a part of their output to townspeople or even to customers overseas. In most places the farmer's labor force consisted almost entirely of himself and his family.

American farmers were not especially efficient or innovative by the best European standards. Except for the German settlers of Pennsylvania, the colonists impressed foreign visitors as slovenly and wasteful cultivators who neglected both the fertility of the soil and the care and improvement of their livestock. As one American admitted, they "generally choose to continue in the old track of their forefathers." The critics were right, but there was a simple reason for their behavior: American farmers could rely on the sheer abundance of fresh, fertile land to carry them through. Besides, improved methods required more labor and more capital and labor and capital, unlike land itself, were scarce and expensive on this side of the Atlantic. As Thomas Jefferson remarked, "We can buy an acre of new land cheaper than we can manure an old one." In later years Americans would learn to regret this wasteful attitude, but in colonial America it suited the circumstances of the time and place.

Many regional differences existed in colonial agriculture. New England farmers faced such rocky soil almost everywhere except in the Connecticut Valley and a few other favored spots, that it was said they had to shoot the seed

A depiction of Martin van Bergen's eighteenth-century Hudson Valley farm. The Catskill Mountains are seen in the background.

into the ground with a gun. Yankee farmers could seldom do more than provide for the needs of their own families and the small group of neighboring town dwellers who did not till the soil. Connecticut produced some surplus livestock, grain, and dairy products for export, and Rhode Island raised horses for the Caribbean trade. But with these exceptions New England agriculture had mostly local importance.

In contrast, New York, New Jersey, and Pennsylvania were the "bread colonies," harvesting large surpluses of wheat from their fertile fields. They converted this grain to flour in the region's many gristmills and exported much of it to the Caribbean or southern Europe. In addition, the bread colonies exported potatoes, beef, pork, and other farm products.

The Chesapeake region, encompassed by the colonies of Virginia and Maryland, was British America's great tobacco-growing area. By the mid-eighteenth century tobacco cultivation had moved from the Tidewater region to the Piedmont plateau where the soils were fresher and more productive, leaving the remaining coastal farmers to switch to grain. The Piedmont planters faced more difficult transportation problems than their Tidewater predecessors. Located above the "fall line," where the eastward-flowing streams dropped sharply to the coastal plain, they could not put their crops directly aboard ships tied to their own dock. Instead, they sold their tobacco to local merchants who packed the leaf into huge hogsheads and rolled them to towns like Richmond or Petersburg, which lay along the fall line. There they could be loaded aboard seagoing vessels for shipment to foreign buyers.

Throughout the eighteenth century the output of Chesapeake tobacco increased at a fairly steady pace. By the 1770s Maryland and Virginia were shipping about 100 million pounds annually for the pipesmokers and snuff-takers of England, Scotland, and continental Europe—tobacco worth £1 million, or about $50 million in modern money. The Chesapeake region also became a major grain exporter, with the crop going largely to the south of Europe and the West Indies.

Rice was the major crop of the South Carolina lowlands, although some was also grown in North Carolina and Georgia. Requiring vast amounts of water, as well as a long growing season, rice was suited to the swampy coastal regions of the most southerly colonies and proved highly profitable there. In 1710 South Carolina exported 1.5 million pounds. By 1770 the rice-growing colonies, with South Carolina far in the lead, exported almost 84 million pounds. Most of it went to England, but the sugar plantations of the Caribbean, the other mainland colonies, southern Europe, and, through Britain, northern Europe as well, were also large consumers of American rice.

The lowland areas of South Carolina and Georgia also produced indigo, a blue dye widely used for coloring woolen cloth. The crop was introduced in the 1740s by Eliza Lucas Pinckney, an enterprising young woman newly arrived from the Caribbean island of Antigua. Helped by a British government bounty of six pence a pound, the production and export of indigo quickly leaped. Though never as important as rice, by 1770 almost 600,000 pounds of indigo, valued at over £130,000, were being shipped from the port of Charleston each year.

One other extractive product of the southern mainland deserves mention—naval stores. This term includes the tar, pitch, resin, and turpentine extracted from the pine trees of coastal Carolina (and also New Hampshire) and widely employed in the shipping and paint industries. Britain itself did not produce these products and was forced to turn to Scandinavia and the Baltic region for its supply, a circumstance that made it vulnerable to shortage, especially in time of war. To meet this danger, in 1704 British officials encouraged naval-store production within the empire by offering a bounty for pitch, tar, and resin. The industry soon took off. By 1770 North Carolina was exporting naval stores worth about £35,000 each year, almost all of it to Great Britain.

Fishing and Whaling. The sea was one of the earliest sources of food and wealth for New England. The first Massachusetts settlers caught hake, haddock, halibut, and mackerel in local waters for their own tables. By the mid-1630s they were beginning to sell the preserved catch to distant customers.

When fully developed, the New England fishing industry was based on cod. Each season hundreds of vessels sailed from the towns of Gloucester, Marblehead, Salem, and other ports to fish for cod at the Grand Banks off Newfoundland. These small craft were manned by crews who received between a sixth and a tenth of the season's catch as their share with the rest going to the boat owners.

The cod was an important item in the Massachusetts economy. Some of it was consumed at home of course; but when salted and dried, the best grades were sent to Catholic southern Europe and to the "Wine Islands" of Madeira and the Canaries off Africa, while the worst went to the West Indies to feed the sugar planters' slaves. The export trade in dried fish represented a large part of the Bay Colony's total exports.

Whaling was another profitable enterprise of the northern colonies. Begun as a local activity in small New England and Long Island ports in the eighteenth century, as the local whale supply declined, capitalists fitted out larger vessels for longer trips well out into the Atlantic. The whalers from Nantucket, New Bedford, and Sag Harbor were not interested in the flesh of the great mammals. Their goal was whale oil, the liquid rendered from whale blubber, which supplied much of the lighting fuel for colonial lamps, and spermaceti, a waxy substance from the heads of sperm whales, which was used to make fine candles. One Rhode Island firm, the Browns of Providence, shipped spermaceti candles all over the Western Hemisphere.

Colonial Industry. Besides the 80 percent who tilled the soil, perhaps 5 percent of the colonial work force were full-time craftsmen, "mechanicks," or artisans in the cities, towns, and villages. In addition, thousands of rural colonists produced finished or semi-finished goods at home for sale on a part-time basis.

Almost all colonial manufactured goods were produced by hand. In many colonial farm houses women spun wool and flax fiber into yarn and then wove it on hand looms into cloth. Farm women also molded candles from wax extracted from bayberries. They churned butter and made cheese from milk from the family cow, and pressed cider from apples and perry from pears. Rural men also used the home as a workshop. Farmers often devoted the long winter evenings to carving ax handles, gunstocks, and other wooden articles.

In the towns, full-time craftsmen using hand tools—hammers, chisels, augers, saws, and planes—manufactured items for customers in their workshops. Every colonial town of any size had a long list of craftsmen. Coopers made the barrels that packaged colonial flour, tobacco, sugar, rum, and other bulk goods. Wheelwrights turned out the wheels for carts, wagons, and coaches. Cordwainers produced shoes;

blacksmiths made nails, horseshoes, shovels, and edged tools; tanners produced the leather that others made into shoes, aprons, saddles, and other items. Every growing colonial village needed housing and the demand was met by carpenters, masons, bricklayers, and various laborers. As communities became richer and more populous, colonial craftspeople became ever more skilled. By the eve of the Revolution they were producing beautiful silverware and fine furniture. In addition, the small cities were full of barbers, wig makers, tailors, milliners, and other skilled providers of goods and services for the prosperous consumer.

Even in the cities the typical manufacturing establishment was a small workshop run by the owner with the help, perhaps, of a young apprentice and an older journeyman who had not yet set up shop for himself. The urban master craftsman generally lived above his shop, which was both a little manufacturing establishment and a retail store. Much of his work was done on direct order from a customer, but he usually made additional wares in slack times to have ready for people coming to the door. Sometimes he sold his surplus to traveling peddlers. Often the craftsman's wife handled the selling in the front while he and his helpers turned out the product in the back.

In only a very few colonial industries do we encounter something resembling the modern factory with hired labor, expensive machinery, and the separation of workplace from home. With water power widely available, mills with waterwheels and machinery, often made of wood, sprang up in every colony to do especially heavy work. There were few settled localities without sawmills to cut boards and gristmills to grind grain into flour. The millers of grain, par-

Black slaves producing blue dye from indigo, a cash crop in the coastal South. Roughly twenty percent of the population in 1775, slaves provided the basis for much of the prosperity enjoyed by the white population.

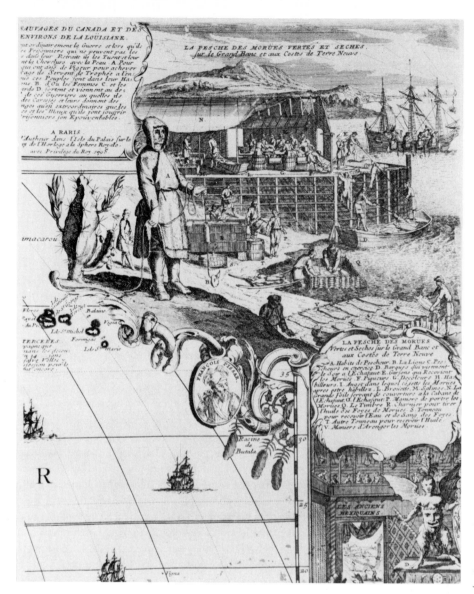

A French illustration of the colonial Grand Banks cod fishery. The racks in the background were used for drying the fish.

ticularly, were often the community's news center as well as its flourmakers. In many rural areas millers also ran general stores where they sold the produce they acquired from the farmers who paid them in "country pay" to grind their grain. A few of the most successful grain millers—"merchant millers"—established large-scale operations and overseas markets for their flour.

Shipbuilding was one of the largest-scale industries in colonial America. The first colonial-built ship was the thirty-ton *Blessing of the Bay*, launched in Boston in 1631. By 1670 Massachusetts had turned out 730 vessels, and between 1696 and 1713 the colony built more than 1,000 ships of almost 70,000 tons total displacement. Besides the shipyards along the Charles River, there were large ship-building establishments in Salem, Portsmouth, New

Hampshire, Newport, Rhode Island, and Philadelphia, each employing scores of workers. In addition to the shipyards themselves, the major ports acquired scores of sail-making establishments and rope-walks to provide rigging for the vessels.

Another relatively large-scale, factorylike colonial manufacturing enterprise was iron making. It too had its start in Massachusetts when, in 1644, Governor John Winthrop set up an iron foundry at Lynn. By the middle of the eighteenth century the center of the industry had moved to Pennsylvania, though New Jersey, Maryland, and Virginia also had large furnaces producing pig iron from ore. By 1700 the American colonies were producing about 2 percent of the world's total pig iron; by the 1770s they accounted for 15 percent. The two largest colonial iron foundries employed

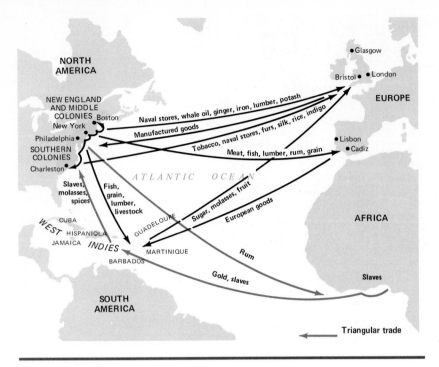

COLONIAL TRADE ROUTES

about 100 men each and represented capital investments of £100,000 and £250,000, respectively.

Commerce.   Commerce or trade was the final and, next to agriculture, the most important leg of the colonial economy. Ultimately, it was foreign markets that drove the colonial economy. Even though a fast-growing population at home consumed most of what local farmers and artisans produced, foreign buyers provided the means for raising the colonial economy above the subsistence level. Commerce sustained the bread colonies, which relied on the Caribbean market to absorb their surplus grain and provisions. Without markets in Britain and Europe the tobacco, rice, indigo, and naval-stores colonies would have been far poorer. Both overseas and intercolony trade supported the shipbuilding, sail-making, and rope-making industries and encouraged flour milling, lumbering, barrel-making, and iron manufacture.

Exports helped Americans pay for the sophisticated luxury goods they could not produce for themselves. The better grades of paper, hardware, pottery, and cloth, as well as wines, the latest books, fine furniture, and scientific instruments could only come from Britain, the Continent, or the Wine Islands. To pay for these goods, Americans needed coin or commercial credits from sales of their own goods abroad. Unfortunately, colonial trade relations were out of balance geographically. England needed the tobacco, rice,

indigo, and naval stores of the Chesapeake region and the Carolinas; these colonies, accordingly, easily earned the credits needed to pay for what they imported from the mother country. The English did buy some pig iron, lumber, furs, and ships from the northern colonies, but the major northern products—fish, grain, and cattle—were not wanted in Great Britain since it produced its own. Because each year the northern colonies bought more from Britain than they sold to it, they were forced to find other customers whose purchases would offset the British deficit.

The Caribbean served this role. In the West Indies thousands of black slaves, working for a few hundred rich European planters, concentrated all their energies on growing sugar cane for the European market. The islanders' almost total neglect of everything but sugar made them excellent customers for cheap food, horses, lumber, and barrels from the northern mainland colonies. By 1700, hundreds of vessels from northern ports sailed to the islands each year; the ships were laden with provisions, flour, and dried fish to feed the slaves and their masters, and with lumber, hoops, and staves to build structures and to package sugar, rum, and molasses.

Once he had found buyers for his miscellaneous cargo, the New England or middle-colony merchant accepted payment in several forms. One form was coin, and the colonies acquired a wide assortment of shillings, doubloons, guilders, and pieces of eight in the West Indies. But mo-

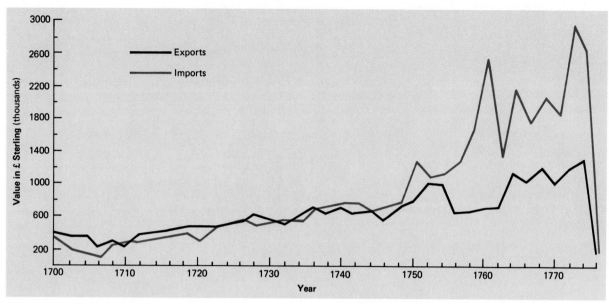

Value of trade between England and the colonies, 1700–1776. Note: The pound of colonial times is roughly equal to fifty modern dollars. *Source: Historical Statistics of the United States. Colonial Times to 1957.*

lasses and sugar were also acceptable. These products could be consumed directly at home, or the molasses could be converted into rum and, in that form, traded with the Indians for furs or exported overseas. The trader could also accept bills of exchange on England. These were receipts, in effect, that the planters received when they sold their sugar in England, and they represented credits that could be used like cash to pay for English goods or to pay debts to English creditors. With their holds full of molasses and perhaps a little West Indies cotton or citrus fruit, and the captain's strongbox stuffed with coin or bills of exchange, the ship sailed home to Boston, Providence, New York, or Philadelphia.

The transatlantic slave trade also helped make up the commercial deficit with the mother country. Most of the slaves carried from Africa to America in the eighteenth century were transported by the French, the British, or the Dutch. But some were carried by slavers out of Boston and Newport. The typical New England slave trader sent a small vessel to the west coast of Africa with a cargo of rum distilled from West Indies molasses. On the African coast the Yankee captain rendezvoused with a trader from London or Bristol and exchanged some rum for British goods, such as iron, cloth, gunpowder, cheap jewelry, and glass beads. With this mixed stock he bought slaves from an African middleman and loaded the human cargo aboard his vessel. He then returned to the Caribbean where he sold the captives for the same coin, molasses, or bills of exchange that

other cargo brought. Only a small proportion of the slaves stolen from Africa were transported directly to the Carolinas or the Chesapeake on the mainland. Many came first to the Caribbean.

Over the years the ingenious merchants of the northern colonies developed many other trading route patterns. As the eighteenth century advanced, merchants from New York and Philadelphia, especially, began to invade the direct carrying trade with Britain, a route that British merchants had previously monopolized. The intercolonial coastal trade was also profitable. Hundreds of sloops, schooners, brigs, and other small sailing ships plied the waters along the Atlantic bringing Philadelphia flour to Charleston or Salem, or Yankee codfish to Annapolis or Savannah. Ships from the northern colonies also traded with Spain, Portugal, and Italy—handling most of the rice, fish, flour, and other commodities that went to these countries, and the wine, salt, and cash that came back. Colonial merchants also made money insuring vessels embarking on long voyages, a business later taken over by marine insurance companies.

Wealth and Inequality. How did Americans fare, overall, under this evolving economic system? And did its benefits fall on each person equally?

By one measure, population growth, the American community prospered mightily. Benjamin Franklin would later claim that Americans doubled in numbers every

Surinam was a Dutch sugar-growing colony on South America's Atlantic coast. It was an important trading partner for British North America, and especially for Rhode Island. In this 1758 John Greenwood painting we see a group of Rhode Island sea captains—including a future governor of Rhode Island and a future commander in chief of the Continental Navy—rowdily enjoying their layover in Surinam before returning home with sugar, molasses, and rum. Note the black servants at lower right and upper left.

twenty-five years. And he was more or less right. In 1680 there were fewer than 80,000 settlers along the Atlantic coast. By 1700 there were about a quarter of a million. Fifty years later population had passed the million mark and by 1770 had soared above 2 million. This surge in part marked the heavy immigration to America, itself a sign of prosperity. But it also marked the abundance of land and food that encouraged early marriage and large families and prevented the malnutrition and famine that cruelly pruned population elsewhere in the contemporary world. It is in some ways the most convincing measure of sustained colonial prosperity.

And despite the explosion of people, during each decade average per capita income grew. Output, that is, expanded even faster than population. The best estimate that we have of the advance suggests that overall per person growth of output in colonial America ran about 0.6 percent a year. This does not seem spectacular, but it was unusually high for a preindustrial society and was fast enough to double the average colonial's income over the course of 120 years.

By the eve of the Revolution, Alice Hanson Jones has said, average income in colonial America had reached $800 in modern dollars, a figure far higher than that of almost every modern nonindustrial nation. Compared to other *contemporary* societies, the standard of living in British North America, according to Jones, was "probably the highest achieved for the great bulk of the population in any country up to that time."

But of course not everyone benefited equally from the overall growth trend. The group most obviously excluded from the benefits of a growing economy was the slaves. By 1770 there were about 460,000 black slaves in the mainland colonies out of a total population of some 2.1 million. Obviously they did not receive very much of the wealth that their labor produced, and there is no reason to believe that they were much better off at the end of the colonial period than at the beginning.

For free rural Americans, the location of land and how it was held and the size of landholdings determined individual levels of prosperity. Yeoman farmers who owned a hundred or so acres near a population center could grow surplus crops for sale. Such lucky cultivators were better off than tenant farmers who rented their land, or yeomen without nearby markets who grew crops only to supply their own family needs.

Commercial agriculture made for prosperity, but it also encouraged inequality. In towns close to the Boston market, such as Milton or Roxbury, for example, where farmers sold to urban consumers, there was a sharp division between rich and poor. In 1771 about a quarter of the taxpayers in the two communities were landless, while the wealthiest 10 percent owned 46 percent of the real estate. In general, both less wealth and greater equality were to be found in the frontier regions of each colony where land per person was abundant and major markets too distant to support commercial agriculture. Thus, Goshen, Connecticut, which was just then emerging from the frontier stage, had forty landowners in 1741 out of a population of fifty-seven adult males. In the South the picture was similar: Regions of subsistence farming, such as the Shenandoah Valley, had many landowners and a high degree of equality. By contrast, the commercial rice- and indigo-growing Carolina coast and the tobacco-growing Chesapeake tidewater were the realms of the great slaveholding gentry. White yeomen farmers of the middle rank were rare in these regions, though there were many poor folk living on infertile, marginal lands.

Colonial cities had a different economic hierarchy. In the towns marketable skills counted as much as real estate in determining an individual's prosperity. Apprentices, journeymen, laborers, and seamen—groups that had the fewest skills to sell—made up the urban lower class. Fully trained craftsmen and shopkeepers did better; at the top of the pyramid were the merchants and professionals. Those merchants who sold goods door to door in nearby rural areas were poor by comparison with the great overseas traders who sent their ships to Europe, Africa, or the West Indies. It was difficult to break into the ranks of the overseas traders, but the class was not completely closed to the energetic, ambitious, or lucky.

Obviously, economic inequalities existed in the American colonies. But were these inequalities growing or diminishing in the years before the Revolution? Were the rich getting richer and the poor getting poorer?

The most recent analyses seem to show that inequality was increasing in the larger cities and in rural parts of the older settled regions. The opening of new settlements, however, offset this trend to some extent, for the colonial frontier remained a region where there were few rich and few poor. And even in the older sections, we must not forget that the overall income trend was upward. Almost all free Americans were getting richer. The growing gap was not because the poor were getting poorer in absolute terms. It resulted from the fact that those at the top were increasing their wealth and incomes faster than those at the bottom.

But whatever trends modern historians may detect, colonial Americans thought themselves a people uniquely blessed with equality. A British nobleman visiting America in 1764 noted: "The leveling principle here, everywhere operates strongly and takes the lead, and everybody has property here, and everybody knows it." Lord Adam Gordon certainly exaggerated, but his statement reflected what many Americans believed to be true of their society. All in all, as Robert Beverley had written of Virginia early in the eighteenth century, America was "the best poor Man's Country in the World."

★ COSTS AND BENEFITS OF EMPIRE BEFORE 1763 ★

At least through the first half of the eighteenth century, then, the colonial economy was buoyant and fostered a fair amount of equality. But how did America's place in the British Empire affect its economic success? The colonial economy functioned within the framework of the empire, and it stands to reason that the colonists' success or failure within this relationship—or their perception of success or failure—was likely to influence how they felt about their political ties to Great Britain.

The Economic Balance Sheet. As we look at the colonial economy it is clear that there were both benefits and losses from the imperial relationship. The colonists were not free to trade where they pleased, but from the 1650s on were forced to accept a multitude of restrictions. Though frequently violated or circumvented, these restrictions limited their ability to work out their own economic destiny.

The system of commercial regulation was based on a theory of empire called *mercantilism* that harked back to Elizabethan times. As we saw in Chapter 2, colonies were supposed to enrich the mother country by supplying it with exotic commodities and hard-to-get raw materials and by consuming its surplus manufactures. Trade with the colonies, the mercantilists said, would give needed jobs to a host of people in the mother country and provide surplus products to sell abroad. It was these expectations that had led the mercantilists and the crown to support colonization at the outset.

With these potential benefits in mind, beginning in 1650, Parliament enacted a series of measures collectively called the Navigation Acts. Some of these laws were designed to keep the enterprising Dutch from profiting from the carrying trade within the empire and between the empire and other nations. Eventually they decreed that all ships engaged in such trade must be owned by either Britons or Americans, built in either Britain or America, captained by a subject of the British crown, and manned, predominantly, by such subjects. Other acts established lists of "enumerated articles" that had to be shipped to England first whatever their ultimate destination. The lists varied over time, but they always included the most valuable colonial exports such as sugar, tobacco, rice, naval stores, and indigo. Another law provided that, except for salt for the New England fisheries, wine from Madeira and the Azores, and servants and horses from Scotland and Ireland, all European commodities sent to the colonies had to be shipped from England, rather than from their place of origin, and in English-built ships. These measures, besides excluding foreigners from the imperial trade and encouraging shipping and shipbuilding, were intended to make England the distribution center (*entrepot*) for most of the goods entering or leaving the colonies. They would guarantee British merchants a key role in the colonial overseas trade and allow the British government to levy a tax on all goods passing through Great Britain. Over time the British government mandated a structure of naval officers and customs commissioners stationed in the colonial ports to enforce the Navigation Acts and collect duties imposed on overseas trade.

The British also sought to limit the manufactures of the mainland colonies to preserve them as markets for British producers and prevent colonial competition with home producers. The Wool Act of 1699 forbade the export of wool yarn or cloth from any American colony either to Europe or any other American colony. The Hat Act of 1732 prohibited the export of American hats from one colony to another and imposed strict limits on the number of workers in any hat-making shop. Finally, two Iron Acts, of 1750 and 1757, sought to encourage the production of American bar and pig iron, raw materials for the British iron and steel industry, but to restrict the colonial iron-finishing industry that the British wanted to keep for themselves. This measure forbade the construction in the colonies of rolling and slitting mills, of forges, and of steel furnaces.

Americans undoubtedly were penalized by these trade regulations. Enumeration hurt Maryland and Virginia especially. The enumerated tobacco sent to Europe had to be unloaded and then reloaded in England first. True, the tax paid in England was rebated, if it was then sent to the Continent, but the charges for this roundabout method of export to Europe were high, and the planters lost money because of it. Also on the debit side was the regulation that European goods must first be sent to England before crossing the Atlantic. This rule forced Americans to pay higher prices for French, German, Dutch, and Spanish goods.

Was the penalty imposed on the colonies by these regulations severe? To answer this question fairly, we should consider the overall benefits of the empire as well as the costs. The foremost benefit was that Britain assumed the expense of the empire's defense. During the seventeenth and eighteenth centuries, as we shall see, four great European wars placed the colonies in danger. The British army and navy often proved indispensable to colonial safety. Recognizing their stake in the outcome, the colonists contributed money and men themselves; but most of the cost by far was borne by the British. Without the mother country's contribution, the colonies would have been forced to lay out millions of pounds in extra taxes, a financial burden that would have lowered their incomes and retarded their economic growth.

And America received other economic benefits as part of the empire. The British paid bounties to encourage production of items that did not compete with English-made goods and for raw materials that were needed by English manufacturers; these brought thousands of pounds a year to American indigo growers, pig-iron manufacturers, and naval-stores producers. The merchants and shipbuilders of New England and the middle colonies gained by having their shipping enjoy the same protected status within the empire as those of their counterparts in Great Britain. This was the credit side of the ledger.

The measures to restrict colonial manufacturers do not fall either in the debit or credit columns. The Iron Act, aimed at finished iron products, did little to restrain the colonial iron industry because it was not rigorously enforced. As for the Woolen and Hat acts, they did not, as we might suppose, kill off promising industries. Many years after independence, when these measures were no longer in force, Americans continued to buy hats and woolen cloth from Great Britain and other foreign nations. The intention of these measures was clear: They were designed to limit future growth that might injure British producers. Still, in their day they probably had little effect.

It is also important to recognize that in restricting the imperial trade to subjects of the king, Parliament meant Americans as well as Britons. American-built ships, owned by American merchants, with American crews, were as much entitled under the Navigation Acts to protection against Dutch competition and the privileges of the imperial trade as their counterparts in England, Scotland, or Ireland. Under this arrangement American shipbuilding flourished so that by the 1763–75 period the thirteen continental colonies produced vessels worth £300,000 each year. About half this output was sold to British merchants. During these same years American ship owners earned an estimated £600,000 annually by carrying cargo and passengers to and from various points within the empire.

On the whole, the American experience within the mercantile system was positive. The colonial economy thrived. Rarely has an agricultural society advanced so fast or brought such benefits to its members. And Americans recognized, generally, how much they had gained economically from the imperial relationship. During the great controversy that led to the Revolution, the Navigation Acts as developed before 1763 were seldom mentioned by the colonists as a grievance. Only one economic measure caused serious friction. This was the Molasses Act of 1733, which imposed a high tax on molasses, sugar, and rum brought into the colonies from the Dutch, French, and Spanish West Indies. Intended to protect the British Caribbean sugar planters from the competition of lower-cost foreign producers, the act threatened the profitable trade between New England and the foreign West Indies. Yankee merchants responded by turning the smuggling of foreign sugar and molasses into a fine art. The law, never strictly enforced, became a virtual dead letter. Though it might have hurt, in actual practice, then, it did not.

The Political Ledger. When we measure the political debits and credits of the British-American relationship, we encounter a similar even balance through the 1760s. British rule in America before 1763 was generally considered "mild" by most colonists. There were periods of rather strict governance, however. During the reigns of Charles II (1660–85) and James II (1685–88), the British authorities had tried to tighten imperial control. In 1684 they revoked the Massachusetts Bay charter and soon after merged New England, New York, and New Jersey into the Dominion of New England. Especially under the stern rule of Governor Sir Edmund Andros, residents of the northern colonies were denied the right to tax themselves or to make laws regulating their day-to-day concerns. In the proprietary colonies farther south, the crown sought to impose direct royal control.

This effort at tight imperial regulation, while stirring deep fears among the colonists, proved short-lived. In 1689 a coalition of Whig noblemen, champions of Protestantism, and partisans of Parliament, inspired by the liberal political ideas of John Locke and other Whig thinkers, deposed the Catholic James II. They then invited the Protestant couple, William of Orange and Mary, James's Protestant daughter, to rule England in his place. Accompanying the offer was the Declaration of Rights, establishing Parliamentary supremacy in England and bolstering the rights of individuals as against the crown.

The Glorious Revolution produced a resounding echo in America. Led by the Puritan clergy, Massachusetts rebels arrested Governor Andros and his subordinates and shipped them all back to England. The Dominion of New England was dissolved and the individual colonies separated once more, though Massachusetts absorbed Plymouth colony and the sparsely settled region of Maine. The efforts to restore the former Bay Colony charter, allowing virtual self-rule, failed, however. Despite loud protest, in 1691 Massachusetts had to accept a new charter with a royal governor at the top, royal review of all legislation, and a property qualification for voting to replace the old religious test. There were changes in other colonies as well. In New York the Glorious Revolution led to a more powerful General Assembly with enhanced freedom to meet and power to make laws. In Pennsylvania there appeared a more independent representative provincial legislature with increased powers. In Virginia the high-handed royal governor, Lord Howard, was removed. The Massachusetts experience excepted, the thrust of the Glorious Revolution was to guarantee to the crown's subjects on both sides of the Atlantic a large measure of self-government through powerful representative legislatures and assemblies.

By the early eighteenth century, then, the colonists had achieved a large measure of political autonomy. The English Privy Council, a small group of the king's advisers, was still permitted to "disallow" measures passed by the colonial legislatures and approved by the colonial governors; but of some 8,500 colonial laws submitted to the council, only 469 were declared null. Nor was the Board of Trade, which shared colonial administration with the governors and the Privy Council, any more coercive. Particularly from 1721 to 1748, when Sir Robert Walpole and the Duke of Newcastle were the crown's chief advisers, the English government gave colonial economic growth higher priority than tight and tidy English rule. This era of "salutary neglect" helped encourage an even greater sense than before that the colonists were self-governing in all internal matters.

For several years during the 1750s this autonomy seemed threatened by the Earl of Halifax. Appointed head of the Board of Trade in 1748, he attempted to increase the board's power. At one point Halifax directly confronted the New York assembly for defying his instructions. But when Halifax left office in 1761, the Board of Trade once more lapsed into inactivity.

The Issue of Religion. Before 1763, then, Americans had little reason to complain of British political or economic coercion. But what about religious oppression?

By the middle of the eighteenth century a majority of colonists were Protestant nonconformists of some kind. Some feared that if the Anglicans had their way, they would establish "a tyranny over the bodies and souls of men," destroy the religious liberties of Americans, and restrict public office to Anglicans. Most of all they feared the British would create Anglican bishops for the colonies who would rule over American religious affairs as they did those of England.

In fact, the British government was not interested in establishing a Church of England episcopate in America. High British officials recognized that American religious dissenters were often firm supporters of the crown. Such people, in the words of one British official, "should not be provoked or alienated" by imposing bishops on them. The British government did occasionally interfere in colonial religious matters, but it was usually to insist that toleration be extended to some unpopular denomination, rather than to restrict religious expression. Though intolerant Americans sometimes were offended by such intrusion, few ever felt seriously threatened. In religion, as in politics and economics, the conflicts between mother country and colonies remained muted before 1763.

★ THE CRISIS OF EMPIRE ★

After 1763, many of the most influential and articulate people in the colonies would begin to find the system of imperial administration galling and the actions of the British government intolerable. Before long they would demand that they be changed. The dramatic change of heart would be linked to the end of the French threat to English America.

The English-French Confrontation. French Canada (New France) and English America had been planted at approximately the same time. Thereafter the two communities had evolved in different ways. The French did not permit their Protestant dissenters (the Huguenots) to emigrate to New France. French Catholics might have come in significant numbers; but the government at Paris favored aristocratic *seigneurs* over small farmers in granting land and allotting power, and few French peasants found the economic or political terms attractive. By the mid-eighteenth century Canada was a sparsely settled region with some 55,000 farmers cultivating the lands of the gentry, ruled autocratically by a royal governor. Pious and conservative, the French Canadians accepted the dominance of the *seigneurs*, the church, and the appointed royal officials without serious question.

Friction between English America and New France was almost inevitable. Both communities were political extensions of their respective mother countries and inevitably became enmeshed in the quarrels of the two European arch-rivals. Both were also religious antagonists. Before long Catholic New France and Protestant English America resumed the fierce political and religious conflicts that had beset the European world for two centuries.

Just as important as these transplanted European quarrels were the tensions native to America itself. New France and "new England" vied over control of the fishing trade in Newfoundland and over competing claims in the Caribbean. Even closer to home was rivalry over the fur trade with the Indians. For many years English traders based in Albany and French traders based in Montreal had competed for the beaver pelts that the Indians supplied from the interior. The British had the advantage of cheaper and better trade goods; the French, on the other hand, were more effective in winning the personal allegiance of the Indians. Canadian traders went to the Indians for furs rather than waiting for the Indians to deliver them to the European settlements. They lived with the Indians and often married Indian women. Their half-European, half-Indian children in turn forged bonds that the English could not match. French religious institutions also gave them an advantage with the Indians. Unlike the Protestants to the south, French Catholics were effective in converting Indians to Christianity.

Among the few native American groups that the French could not win to their side were the Iroquois, the powerful Indian confederation of western New York. The French incurred the hostility of the Five Nations early in the seventeenth century when they sided with the Iroquois' ancient enemy, the Hurons. Later, in the 1680s, egged on by Governor Thomas Dongan of New York, a royal official who hoped to seize the western fur trade for the English, the Iroquois attacked the French and drove them back to Montreal.

Soon afterward Britain and France clashed in the first of four major wars that would extend over several continents simultaneously. In the first (King William's War, 1689–97), Massachusetts colonial troops captured the French stronghold of Port Royal in modern Nova Scotia. The post was returned to France, however, by the Treaty of Ryswick (1697), which ended the conflict. Soon after the French decided to occupy the vast Mississippi Valley, a region also claimed by the American colonists under their provincial charters. In 1699 the French established an outpost at Cahokia, near present-day St. Louis; in 1703 they placed a fort at Kaskaskia in southern Illinois. They also planted settlements on the Gulf Coast and along the shores of the Great Lakes. When war broke out again in 1702 (Queen Anne's War, 1702–13), French troops and their Indian allies clashed with the Anglo-Americans in a vast arc from Maine to the outskirts of Louisiana, as the French called their new colony. By the Treaty of Utrecht (1713), which ended this conflict, England acquired Newfoundland, Acadia (renamed Nova Scotia), and the Hudson Bay region.

Following the Treaty of Utrecht, the French sought to consolidate their hold on Louisiana by establishing new posts and settlements in the disputed region. In 1718 they settled near the mouth of the Mississippi and called their new outpost New Orleans. The British countered by constructing Fort Oswego on Lake Ontario and fortifying the northern frontier against the pro-French Abenakis. When war between Britain and France broke out again (King

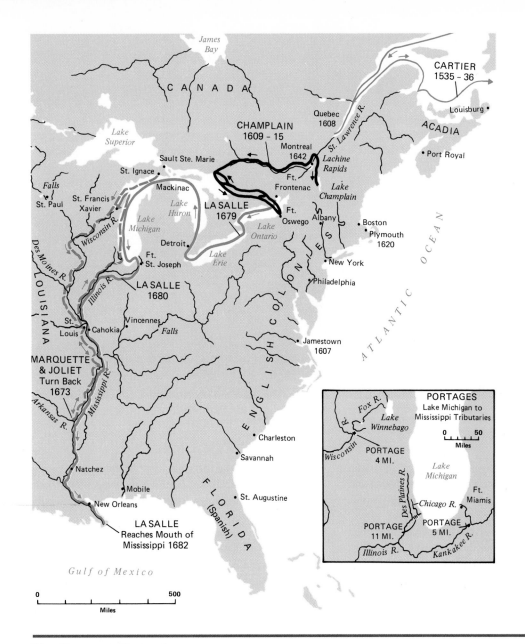

THE FRENCH IN NORTH AMERICA

George's War, 1740–48), both sides once more clashed in North America. New England troops captured the French strong point of Louisbourg in Nova Scotia, while in New York William Johnson, the province's commissary of Indian affairs, induced the Iroquois to attack the French. In retaliation the French and their Indian allies raided Albany and burned Saratoga.

The French and Indian War. These three wars were extensions of disputes that originated in Europe. The most destructive and momentous of all the colonial wars, how-

ever, started over an issue of immediate concern to many Americans.

To Americans with deep anti-Catholic prejudices, French expansion into the Mississippi Valley seemed to threaten the very existence of the British colonies as self-governing Protestant communities. Besides, a string of interior French colonies promised to block westward expansion and confine the eastern colonists within their existing boundaries. Colonial farmers looking to the west for fresh, fertile lands for themselves and their children would be walled off and confined to the dwindling acres east of

An "on-the-spot" depiction of Amherst's seizure of the French fortress of Louisbourg in 1758, drawn by Captain Ince of the 35th Regiment.

the mountains. Would-be speculators in western lands, who were especially prominent and vocal in Pennsylvania and Virginia, would be denied their expected windfall profits from land sales.

The crisis came in what is now western Pennsylvania and Ohio. Here, during and shortly following King George's War, Pennsylvania fur traders, led by George Croghan, had established a string of trading posts to collect pelts from the Indians. Hoping to head off further English encroachment, the French, under the Marquis Duquesne, determined to build a chain of forts from Lake Erie to the Forks of the Ohio at what is now Pittsburgh. In 1753 a construction party of several hundred Frenchmen and Indians established three stockades along Lake Erie and on French Creek. Still left to construct when winter came was the projected post at the strategic Forks, where the Allegheny and Monongahela join to form the Ohio River.

News of the French project alarmed Governor Robert Dinwiddie of Virginia, who not only feared Virginia's loss of the vast interior claimed under her early charter but also saw his own speculative profits evaporating. Dinwiddie responded by dispatching a tall, young Virginia planter, George Washington, with a force of armed men to warn the French to leave. He failed in his mission. The following year, after the French had completed Fort Duquesne at the Forks,

Washington returned to oust them by force. The young Virginian foolishly allowed himself to engage the French though outnumbered ten to one. At Fort Necessity, a hurriedly constructed American stockade, the French defeated the intruders and took them prisoner. When released from captivity, Washington and his little force returned to the Virginia capital, Williamsburg, carrying news that the French were on the verge of making good their claim to the great interior valley.

The confrontation of a few hundred men in western Pennsylvania triggered the French and Indian War, a struggle that lasted from 1754 to 1763. In 1756 the conflict spread to Europe itself when Britain and Prussia concluded an alliance against France, which in turn allied itself with Austria and then, in 1762, with Spain. Because Britain, France, and Spain were all great imperial nations, the struggle quickly turned into a "world war." Before it was over, armies and fleets had grappled in the Mediterranean, the Caribbean, the Far East, India, and on the European continent, as well as in the dense forests of North America. At first the war went badly for the English. But then, in 1757, William Pitt the Elder took over its management and brought Britain a series of brilliant victories that changed the course of history.

In America, as elsewhere, the war started badly for the Anglo-Americans when the British general, Edward Braddock, suffered a severe defeat in his effort to capture Fort Duquesne. Braddock's small force of 1,400 British redcoats, 450 Virginia militiamen under Washington, and 50 Indian scouts marched on the French from the Pennsylvania frontier, hacking their way through the tangled forest. On July 9, 1755, they encountered 600 French and 200 Indians seven miles from the French post. With flags flying and bagpipes skirling, the British advanced in a line in the approved European fashion. But matters did not go according to plan, and the battle quickly degenerated into a wild melee with the French and Indians pouring deadly fire into the advancing redcoats and Americans from concealed positions on either side. Wounded mortally, Braddock ordered a retreat. As the combined Anglo-American force limped back to their base, they were attacked by the enemy from behind every tree and rock. Only 500 of the 1,900 men who had set out arrived home safely.

Other British commanders were more successful. In the fall of 1758 General John Forbes, with a force of 6,000 men, cut his way through Pennsylvania toward the goal that had eluded Braddock. Seeing this powerful Anglo-American army approaching, the Indians of the Ohio country deserted the French. On November 24 the handful of French soldiers remaining at Fort Duquesne blew it up and fled, leaving it to the British, who reconstructed it as Fort Pitt. Impressed by this British victory, the Indians turned on their former French allies and virtually drove them out of the upper Mississippi Valley.

A still more brilliant British triumph came in the summer of 1759 when General James Wolfe and an army of 4,500 redcoats scaled the heights above the St. Lawrence River and debouched on the Plains of Abraham outside the walls of Quebec. The small city was the very soul of French Canada, seat of the governor and the bishop. Its commander was the able Marquis de Montcalm, but his force consisted only of ill-trained provincial troops. They bravely attacked the British, but in the face of the redcoats' deadly musket volleys, quickly fell back to the town and soon after surrendered. Both commanders died in the battle. With the fall of Quebec, followed later by the capture of Montreal, French power in Canada collapsed.

The war dragged on for many months following the fall of New France. In 1761 Pitt, despite his successes, resigned. The new king, George III, replaced him with Lord Bute and other "Tory" advisers who were more friendly to the idea of royal power than Pitt and his fellow Whigs. By this time the British people were weary of the war, which had cost them well over £100 million and had raised taxes to record levels. Soon after Pitt's departure the British, French, and Spanish opened peace negotiations and in February 1763 concluded the Treaty of Paris.

The treaty made sweeping changes in the political map of North America. By its terms France ceded Cape Breton Island and all of Canada to Great Britain and recognized the region from the Appalachians to the Mississippi and from the Great Lakes to Florida as British territory. Spain, France's ally, gave Florida, including much of the eastern Gulf Coast, to England. In return for this loss, Spain gained from the French what they had retained of Louisiana; that is, the portion west of the Mississippi. Other territory changed hands in India, Africa, and the Caribbean. To the Americans the crucial matter was that powerful France was now eliminated from the entire North American continent except for two tiny fishing islands off Newfoundland and several sugar colonies in the Caribbean.

The end of the French danger abruptly altered American attitudes toward the British Empire. As long as the French were nearby, the Americans clung to the protection of England. Now that the French menace was gone, the colonists could afford to consider the disadvantages of their subordinate relationship with the Empire. Moreover, the French and Indian War had created serious tensions between the British government and its American subjects that now clamored to be resolved.

British-American Relations During the War. From the British point of view, the Americans had not been the best of subjects during the war, or even the best of allies. When, for example, the British in 1756 had prohibited trade between the colonies and France (the Rule of 1756), the Americans had defied the regulations. American vessels had sailed to the French Caribbean islands, trading for sugar supplies that these islands could not obtain because of the British naval blockade. American merchants had also exchanged American flour and fish for French wines and gold at Hispaniola, initially a neutral Spanish port, despite Pitt's complaint that this trade enabled the enemy "to sustain and protect" the "long and expensive War."

The British government sought to stop the illegal commerce with France by issuing writs of assistance. These were general search warrants allowing customs officials to inspect private property—ships, warehouses, even homes—to determine whether smuggled goods were present. Though such writs had been issued before, during the French and Indian War they aroused fierce opposition among colonial merchants, who saw them not only as a threat to their lucrative new trade but also as a dangerous violation of the rights of private citizens. In 1760 several Boston traders hired attorney James Otis to argue against the legality of the writs. In a fiery address that John Adams later called the "first scene of the first act of opposition" to British authority in America, Otis denounced the writs as "against the fundamental principles of law" and the British constitution, and hence void. In the end the writs were upheld by the Massachusetts court and confirmed by the

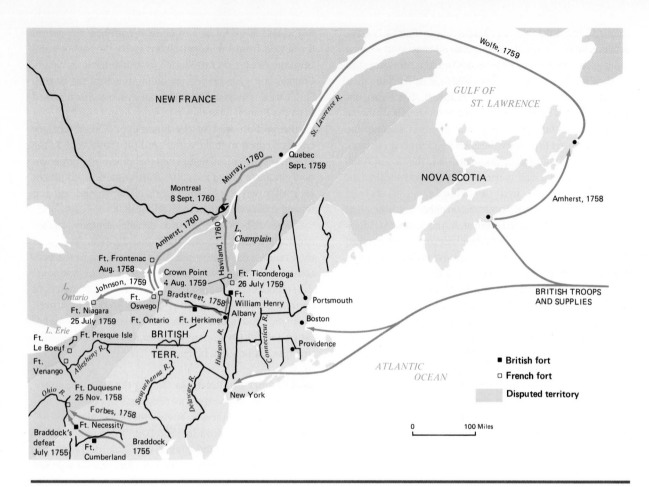

THE FRENCH AND INDIAN WAR

Townshend Acts, but they were never effectively used in the Bay Colony.

Nor, in British eyes, was the flouting of trade regulations the only American offense during the war. The colonists had also resisted paying their share of the war's costs. To help meet these, Pitt had imposed a "requisition" system whereby each colonial assembly would share with the British treasury the expense of recruiting and supplying troops. In addition, the British would reimburse the colonial legislatures for part of their initial outlays in the following year. This was an extremely generous scheme, British officials said, since the Americans were fighting the French as much for themselves as for the mother country. Yet time and again, it seemed to British officials, the Americans had failed to do their part. They had delayed voting money for defense or even refused outright to do so. According to Lord Loudon, British commander in chief in America, it had been "the constant study of every province . . . to throw every expense on the Crown and bear no part of the expense of this war themselves."

The Americans had also been unable to cooperate in a common policy toward the Indians. In 1754 the British Board of Trade, the advisory body for American affairs, had issued a call for a colonial congress to consider Indian-white relations generally and find a way to induce the tribes south of the Great Lakes to support the Anglo-American cause against the French. Only New England, New York, Pennsylvania, and Maryland had sent delegates to the meeting at Albany. The results were not impressive. The delegates took up Iroquois grievances against American fur traders and land speculators and considered charges that the British government had failed to protect them against the French. The congress recommended a number of measures to meet the Indians' complaints and adopted a proposal made by Benjamin Franklin for a political union of all the continental colonies to exercise jurisdiction over Indian affairs and deal with the overall problem of western development.

Yet the Albany Congress failed to achieve anything of permanent value. None of the separate colonies wished to surrender control over western policy; Virginia particularly, with its large western land claims, feared that such a supergovernment would thwart her plans for development in the region. The congress's recommendations were not adopted, and Indian-white relations remained chaotic.

Worse problems soon followed. In the wake of the British conquest of the West, hundreds of American traders crossed the Appalachian Mountains. Most were out for quick profits and did not care how they made them. They cheated the Indians and plied them with drink. At the same time scores of American, Scottish, and English speculators besieged Parliament, demanding land grants in the West that could be sold to eager would-be settlers. A flood of small farmers was already pouring into the Pittsburgh region, displacing the local Indians. British officials in the West were no more sensitive to Indian feelings than the Americans. Lord Jeffrey Amherst despised the "savages" and advised spreading smallpox among the tribes. In 1762 Amherst abruptly cut off the food and ammunition traditionally supplied to the Indians during the winter.

To the northern tribes Amherst's act seemed the final straw. By this time a major Indian renewal movement was under way, inspired by a religious leader called "the Prophet," who urged his people to abandon white ways and reassert their independence. One of the Prophet's disciples was the Ottawa chief Pontiac. In May 1763, shortly after the Treaty of Paris, Pontiac and his followers attacked Fort Detroit. The post held out, but the assault set off a fierce Indian uprising throughout the West that in two months drove virtually all the whites back over the mountains. The British struck back and by the summer of 1764 had put down Pontiac's rebellion. But the affair highlighted the chaos in Indian affairs and, more generally, Britain's problems in controlling its empire.

The Proclamation of 1763. With the French and Indian war over, British as well as American attitudes toward the empire changed. In general, the Whig leaders who had governed England during the period of salutary neglect had accepted the validity of colonial claims to autonomy in managing local affairs. Philosophically, they had opposed the assertion of royal power at home, and this attitude had carried over to their view of how to govern America. But the government of Lord Bute was dominated by men of a different temper. Bute and Chancellor of the Exchequer George Grenville were Tories who supported the crown against Parliament and had little use for colonial "pretensions" to self-rule. In addition, these men saw American behavior during the war and the problems with the Indians as proof of the dangers of lax imperial control. Tighter administration of the empire, they felt, was clearly needed.

The first move to tighten colonial control was the Proclamation of 1763 inspired by the Pontiac uprising. This measure prohibited colonists from settling west of the Appalachians and required all those already there "forthwith to remove themselves." East of the mountains, colonists were forbidden to purchase land directly from the Indians. The entire trans-Appalachian region was to be placed under the control of the British commander in chief and to remain an exclusive Indian preserve until further notice. Through the proclamation the British hoped to pacify the Indians and to give themselves time to contrive a rational policy for disposing of the crown's lands, especially in the West. Eventually colonists would be allowed to move across the mountains, but not before Indian claims had been dealt with and an orderly system of land transfer and settlement worked out.

Historians have argued that British western policy was very much like the one adopted by the American government itself after 1783, when it fell heir to the western lands. It was a rational attempt to avoid disorderly and expensive development of the public domain, and in any case it was temporary. Be that as it may, the proclamation dismayed many Americans. Those who had anticipated profits from land speculation, fur trading, and farming saw their hopes go up in smoke. Particularly in Virginia, which claimed much of the trans-Appalachian region, many influential men were dismayed by the new policy. The check on western settlement, they insisted, was designed to allow Englishmen to grab an unfair share of speculative profits in the American West. At the same time, the new western policy threatened to close an escape hatch for small farmers. Land was becoming scarce in the East, and delaying western settlement seemed sure to widen the gap between rich and poor.

Changes in British Tax Policy. Even more disturbing to most Americans, however, was Parliament's effort to raise revenue in America. Never before had this been attempted. The British government had imposed duties on certain imports through laws like the Molasses Act, but its primary purpose had been to regulate commerce, not to extract money from the Americans. Even during the recent war the requisition system had given the right to actually raise the money needed to the colonial assemblies, rather than Parliament. But now there were other considerations. Britain after 1763 labored under an immense debt that was costing it £4.5 million a year in interest alone. Military costs, too, were certain to continue. Though the French had been driven out of North America, Britain would have to maintain an expensive army to protect the colonists against the Indians. How could the British taxpayer be relieved of all these costs? The conclusion was obvious: Make the Americans help pay the bill.

NORTH AMERICA IN 1763

The first revenue measure of the Grenville ministry was the Sugar Act (1764). This law imposed import duties on non-English cloth, indigo, coffee, wine, sugar, and molasses. The tax on molasses was especially offensive. Even though the new duty was actually lower than the earlier Molasses Act rates, it remained too high to suit northern merchants. More important, the money was now really to be collected. To prevent the smuggling that had made the old law a sham, the new law forced American merchants to pass through a thicket of certificates, affidavits, oaths, and inspections. In addition, it added a new vice-admiralty court to those established earlier to enforce the Navigation Acts.

The new court could try suspected smugglers under rules that put more of the burden of proof than previously on the accused.

Most American merchants balked at this renewed effort to exclude them from the profitable foreign West Indies market. The Navigation Acts had pressed only lightly on the colonies thus far, largely because the Americans had offset their disadvantages through trade with the Caribbean. By cutting off trade with the foreign West Indies, the Sugar Act not only threatened profits but also endangered the northern colonists' elaborate adjustments to the requirements of the imperial economy.

The Stamp Act. The Proclamation of 1763 injured Virginians primarily; the Sugar Act promised to hurt New England and the middle colonies. The Grenville ministry next proposed a measure that angered powerful groups in every one of the colonies and threatened the political autonomy that Americans as a whole had gained over a century of effort.

During the summer of 1763 Grenville decided to impose a tax on legal documents and other items, to be paid with stamps purchased from the British treasury. The new law required that a revenue stamp be affixed to all licenses to practice the professions, to documents used in court, to papers concerning land transfers or exports or imports, to all private contracts, to newspapers, and even to college diplomas. These stamps were to be paid for in gold or silver, and the money collected was to be set aside for exclusive use in the colonies. Violations of the law would be tried in both the ordinary and the admiralty courts.

Before proceeding with the measure, Grenville had the foresight to consult the colonial governors and confer with agents of the colonial assemblies in London who informally represented colonial interests at the seat of empire. The Americans were dubious about such a tax, but the colonial legislatures, Grenville learned, would not accept the alternative of taxing themselves. Under the circumstances, he decided to push his scheme. In early 1765, after a brief debate, Parliament passed the momentous Stamp Act.

Two other measures supplemented Grenville's program of tightening imperial control. The Quartering Act (actually two separate measures of 1765 and 1766) required colonial authorities to provide barracks and supplies for British troops or, in lieu of barracks, to make provision for billeting troops in inns or unoccupied dwellings. The Currency Act (1764) forbade colonial legislatures to issue legal tender paper money. Previously applied only to New England, the prohibition was now extended to all the colonies.

The Quartering and Currency acts offended Americans. The first seemed a dangerous extension of British military power in America. The second hampered the colonial legislatures' efforts to provide currency that American business needed in place of scarce coin. Neither law, however, produced the wave of outrage that greeted the Stamp Act.

The Stamp Act touched almost every aspect of colonial social and economic life—the professions, commerce, the press, and education. It penalized two of the most articulate and influential groups in the colonies—lawyers and newspaper publishers. It also threatened the hard-won authority of colonial assemblies, which had previously exercised the power to levy taxes. Furthermore, the Stamp Act raised profound and disturbing constitutional issues. First, were the colonies subordinate to Great Britain, or equal

Although colonists could seldom cooperate in other ways, they did agree on their response to the direct taxes these innocent-looking stamps represented.

partners in the empire? Second, must American colonists pay taxes imposed by Parliament, where they were not formally represented? Few colonists expected their representatives to be seated in the English Parliament; rather, they wanted Parliament to recognize the authority of colonial assemblies, including their exclusive authority to tax Americans. Unlike most British measures during the imperial crisis that followed the French and Indian War, the Stamp Act jeopardized all the colonies equally. Thus it did more to create a common bond of opposition to British policies than the other measures. It was probably the most foolish and inexpedient bill passed by the British Parliament in its long history.

News that Parliament had passed the Stamp Act reached the colonies in mid-April 1765. In May the Virginia House of Burgesses, goaded by the young firebrand lawyer Patrick Henry, boldly resolved that Americans had all the rights of Englishmen and that only their own legislatures could tax them. Virginia's action electrified Americans everywhere. Newspapers all over the colonies praised the resolutions and denounced British policy. Other colonial assemblies quickly joined the House of Burgesses in attacking the act, and the Massachusetts General Court called for a colonial congress to meet in October to consider united action in the crisis.

But outraged citizens did not wait until the congress met. In almost every colony news of the act stirred up violence. Mobs of artisans, shopkeepers, sailors, and merchants, some organized as "Sons of Liberty," hanged and burned effigies of Grenville and royal officials in America and physically attacked tax collectors and supporters of the new tax. In Boston they burned the house of Lieutenant Governor Thomas Hutchinson. So effective was this intimidation that almost all the stamp distributors resigned their royal commissions.

By the time the Stamp Act Congress convened in New York (October 7–25, 1765), the act was a dead letter in every colony except Georgia, where an unusually firm governor succeeded in making the citizens comply with it. The congress adopted petitions addressed to the king, the House of Lords, and the House of Commons. Although mild in tone, they insisted once again that Americans could be taxed only by bodies that represented them directly.

The petitions did little to move the British government, and mob violence only angered English conservatives: Grenville, for one, was prepared to use troops to enforce the law. A few English leaders, such as Edmund Burke, supported the Americans on the grounds of justice, but in the end it was economic pressure that killed the tax. The merchants of England, skeptical of the Stamp Act from the outset, grew increasingly hostile to the measure when it became clear that the law was disastrous for trade with America. In some places in the colonies the courts were disrupted and the legal processes for enforcing commercial contracts stalled. Still more dismaying were the Nonimportation Agreements initiated by New Yorkers and widely adopted in the other colonies. Citizens pledged not to buy British goods, and merchants agreed not to import them. The resulting drop in transatlantic trade soon brought many British manufacturers and exporters to the brink of bankruptcy.

Parliament could not resist the complaints of the English merchants against the Stamp Act. On March 18, 1766, it repealed the detested measure but simultaneously adopted the Declaratory Act, affirming its right to legislate for the colonies "in all cases whatsoever." In effect, the English government was telling the Americans that it acknowledged the stamp tax as a mistake, but that it would not accept the principle of "no taxation without representation" that had been marshaled to oppose it.

The Townshend Acts. The rejoicing that followed news of the repeal of the Stamp Act was short-lived. In January 1766 the New York assembly refused to contribute support for British troops as required by the Quartering Act. Over the summer hostile feelings arose between New York citizens and British soldiers, and several Americans were injured in violent clashes between redcoats and Sons of Liberty, the secret organization formed to protest the Stamp Act. At the urging of Charles Townshend, Grenville's successor, Parliament suspended the New York legislature's powers in mid-1767.

During the debate over taxation Townshend had noticed that Americans had made a distinction between a tax for raising revenue and one intended to regulate commerce.

This is an unusual contemporary view of Gage's troops being disembarked at Boston in 1768.

The first, they had said, was a dangerous novelty; the second was traditional and acceptable. "Champagne Charlie"—a witty, charming, but shallow man—now seized on this distinction as a way around American resistance to revenue taxes. In May 1767 he proposed legislation that proved almost as foolish and inept as the Stamp Act: the Revenue Act of 1767.

Commonly referred to as the Townshend Acts, the law imposed new import duties on glass, red and white lead, painters' colors, paper, and tea. The imposts (taxes) were to be paid in coin and the money used to pay royal officials in the colonies, thereby ending their dependence on colonial legislatures for their salaries. The Townshend Acts also authorized the colonial higher courts to issue writs of assistance to help customs officers search private property for violations of the new law. A companion measure established a board of customs commissioners with headquarters in Boston and new vice-admiralty courts in Halifax, Philadelphia, and Charleston to enforce both old and new trade regulations.

Patriots again attacked British policy and once more demanded a boycott of British goods through Nonimportation Agreements. This time the colonial merchants were determined to keep the violence under control, and for a while they succeeded. Before long, however, the public began to defy the customs commissioners openly. In a number of places mobs rescued ships and cargoes held for suspected smuggling. In Rhode Island the courts were intimidated into acquitting accused smugglers.

The disorder never became as widespread as it had during the Stamp Act crisis, but it seemed sufficiently alarming to the royal governor of Massachusetts, Sir Francis Bernard, to require drastic action. Responding to Bernard's reports, the British government ordered the military commander in chief, Thomas Gage, to move troops from New York to Boston. At the same time the British ministry sent the governor two more regiments of redcoats from Britain. The troops were greeted with hostility and deep suspicion by Bostonians, who were convinced that the soldiers were there to intimidate the colony and arrest Patriot leaders. Actually their purpose was merely to keep order, but the people of the city remained apprehensive and skeptical.

Meanwhile, in Britain, pressure mounted to repeal the Townshend duties. They had brought relatively little revenue and by encouraging a second boycott had led to another drastic drop in American trade. Once more adopting an expedient course, Parliament canceled the duties in 1770, except for a three-penny tax on each pound of tea. By now, even such firm friends of America as William Pitt were beginning to fear that the colonists were determined to overturn the basic laws governing commercial relations between Britain and the colonies.

Fears for Colonial Religious Autonomy. The tightening of imperial bonds was not confined to the political and economic spheres. In religion, too, the advent of the crown's Tory advisers tripped off efforts to limit colonial autonomy. In March 1763 the archbishop of Canterbury, head of the Church of England, wrote that he and his fellow bishops finally intended to "try our utmost for bishops" at the next session of Parliament. The colonies did not have an episcopal structure; this void, the archbishop said, would have to be remedied.

The archbishop's scheme to attach the colonies more securely to Anglicanism eventually failed. Yet controversy over the religious issue continued to rage, constantly fed by rumors that the effort to establish Anglican bishops in America had not ended. Especially in New England where hostility to Anglicanism had always been intense, many colonists came to believe that there was a plot to impose upon them bishops, tithes for the Church of England, and even laws restricting public office to Anglicans. Inevitably the religious and political issues merged. The link between these issues seemed confirmed by the role of the Anglican clergy in America. Unlike the dissenting ministers, who were often the most vehement enemies of the Grenville and Townshend programs, clergy of the Church of England generally opposed active resistance to the stamp tax and Townshend duties, urging their flocks to obey the law and show respect for royal officials.

Patriot Insecurity. Before 1763 most Americans had been proud of their British heritage, and even those whose ancestors came from other lands had acknowledged their allegiance to Britain. Thereafter, they drifted away from this loyalty and eventually developed a rationale for autonomy that would carry them all the way to independence.

In part the process reflected American social insecurity. Yes, Americans were affluent and relatively free, but this condition, unusual among societies of the day, seemed precarious. As historian Gordon S. Wood has noted, "the people were acutely nervous about their prosperity and the liberty that made it possible." Wood sees special significance in the fears of the recently prosperous that British policy might undermine a shaky success and plunge them once more back into the mass of the undistinguished folk from which they had come. He also describes the resentment that many of these people felt against those who, owing to their connections with the British royal government, had special advantages in the scramble for wealth and "preferment," favors in the form of office or lucrative business arrangements. The patriot leaders were not democrats, but neither did they favor a system that conferred permanent privilege on a few. Above all they despised the hereditary principle entrenched in the British monarchy that birth to the right parents conferred, by right, permanent and unchallengeable advantages regardless of merit.

Patriot Ideology. During the imperial crisis of 1763–76 some of the best minds of America were devoted to the task of justifying colonial "rights." At various stages of the British-American conflict such men as John Dickinson, Thomas Jefferson, John Adams, and Benjamin Franklin published letters, pamphlets, and editorials that indicted British policies in the name of fundamental political principles. At times their writing was important largely for its immediate political utility. Dickinson's *Letters from a Farmer in Pennsylvania to the Inhabitants of the British Colonies*, for example, was an attack on the Townshend duties that emphasized the illegality of collecting internal taxes in America as opposed to merely regulating commerce. *Letters from a Farmer* helped rally support against those measures in 1767 and 1768. But there were also searching and thorough defenses of American freedom and the right to resist authority that, taken together, announced a new philosophy of government and a new perspective on the individual's relations to it.

Few of the pamphleteers and writers were entirely original thinkers. They borrowed widely from European, especially English, sources. Many of them turned for inspiration to the radical Whig publicists of the late 1680s and 1690s, who had sought to justify the Glorious Revolution against James II and later had worked out arguments to limit the power of the crown. John Locke's treatise *Of Civil Government* was an especially fertile source of ideas. Society, said Locke, was based on an agreement between ruler and ruled to preserve the natural rights of man inherent in the order of the universe. Although obedience to a just ruler was required by this "social contract," disobedience to tyranny was also an obligation.

Borrowing these and other ideas, Patriots almost always maintained that they were defending traditional rights guaranteed under the unwritten British constitution and endangered by either the king or his chief ministers. Far from demanding what was legitimate obedience from their subjects, they argued, the tyrants in Britain were attempting to subvert rights sanctioned both by history and by the laws of nature. Such arguments became vital weapons in the Patriot arsenal; as incorporated in the Declaration of Independence, they would be handed down to later Americans as part of their political heritage.

The Whig thinkers also provided Americans with a moral rationale for independence. In England political dissenters during the early eighteenth century had come to regard English society as corrupt. Compared with the past, royal officials were mere "placemen" who served royal power with no other aim but to grow rich. England itself had grown wealthy, its people a prey to luxury and vice.

Americans seized on this bleak picture enthusiastically, using it to support the Patriot position. In contrast to corrupt Britain, American society was pure and unspoiled. The colonists still lived honestly and simply. But would all this not end if Bute, Grenville, and the rest had their way? If Americans did not resist, surely a horde of locusts in the shape of royal officials would descend on America and consume its substance, meanwhile exposing the colonists to the dissipations and moral laxity that the young society had till now been spared. If for no other reason than to preserve American virtue, British policies must be resisted at all costs.

Massacre in Boston. Meanwhile, as the journalists, pamphleteers, and lawyers learnedly or passionately argued the extent of natural rights, ordinary men and women grew ever more hostile to British policy and restless at the visible symbols of British authority. Some outburst of violence was probably inevitable in Boston. The city was a hotbed of anti-British feeling and townspeople and redcoats had been trading insults ever since the soldiers had arrived from New York. To make matters worse, many Boston artisans deeply resented the fact that British soldiers were taking part-time jobs and so depriving them of scarce work. Then, one evening in March 1770, a mob attacked a British sentry at his post. The soldier called for help, and when the men dispatched to rescue him arrived, they encountered a rapidly growing, angry crowd. At some point someone gave the command for the redcoats to fire. When the smoke of the muskets cleared, three Americans lay dead and several were wounded, two of whom later died.

The incident threatened to touch off a major uprising. The townspeople, Governor Hutchinson reported, were in a perfect frenzy and might attempt to drive out all 600 redcoats stationed in Boston. If they attacked, it would plunge the colony into full-scale rebellion against the crown, the consequences of which would be too horrible to contemplate. Although unsure of his authority, Hutchinson quickly ordered the arrest of the soldiers involved in the "massacre" and directed that the British troops be removed from their barracks in town to Castle William in Boston harbor. From there they could continue to guard the city but would no longer be in direct contact with the irate citizens. Eventually seven of the redcoats were tried for the massacre. Ably defended by John Adams and Josiah Quincy, five were acquitted and two received light sentences.

The Gaspée Incident. Repeal of the Townshend duties in April 1770 cooled the argument between Britain and America. Yet the next two or three years were not without jarring incidents of American defiance and British reprisal.

The most serious of these was the *Gaspée* incident, involving a British revenue cutter operating out of Narragansett

These two pictures illustrate the radical change in colonial attitudes toward King George III after 1763. The first—a 1762 American engraving—celebrates George's recent coronation. The second—a later English cartoon—shows America ridding itself of tyranny, personified by the king carrying a whip composed of swords, bayonets, and a tomahawk to beat the stubborn American horse.

Bay. On June 9, 1772, while pursuing a suspected smuggler, the vessel ran aground on the Rhode Island coast near Providence, a hotbed of Patriot sentiment. That evening a group of the town's prominent citizens boarded the vessel, wounded its commander, disarmed the crew, and burned the ship to the keel. This was not only a crime against the king's property but also a blatant attack on a royal officer. Royal officials immediately posted a large reward for information leading to the conviction of the guilty parties and convened a commission of leading American Loyalists to investigate the affair. But no one chose, or dared, to come forward with information, and royal officials could only fume with frustration.

The Tea Act. The *Gaspée* affair notwithstanding, the period between 1771 and 1773 was one of relative calm. During these years the Patriot cause, without new outrages to feed on, went into eclipse. The militant Sons of Liberty

The Sons of Liberty

Sons of Liberty organizations first sprang up in many American towns in 1765 to oppose the Stamp Act. Often led by prosperous merchants and lawyers, these groups were responsible for much of the violence against Stamp Tax agents and citizens who complied with the detested act. In Boston the Sons of Liberty were responsible for burning the records of the vice-admiralty court and destroying the library and elegant home of Lieutenant Governor Thomas Hutchinson.

The Sons continued to be active through each confrontation with the English government over the next five years, but then, during the quieter years of the early 1770s, they became relatively dormant. The 1773 Tea Act revived the Patriot cause and reawakened the Sons of Liberty as a militant expression of that cause. The following resolution was adopted by the New York Sons of Liberty in late November 1773 to protest Parliament's apparent attempt to thrust East India Company tea on the colonists through favored agents, thus bypassing other merchants and creating a potential monopoly for British interests. The argument used, however, resembles the earlier protests against "taxation without representation."

". . . To prevent a calamity which, of all others, is the most to be dreaded—slavery, and its terrible concomitants—we subscribers, being influenced from a regard to liberty and disposed to use all lawful endeavors in our power to defeat the pernicious project, and to transmit to our posterity those blessings of freedom which our ancestors have handed down to us; and to contribute to the support of the common liberties of America which are in danger to be subverted, *do*, for these important purposes, agree to associate together . . . and faithfully to observe and perform the following *resolutions*, *viz*.

1st. *Resolved*, That whoever shall aid, or abet, or in any manner assist in the introduction of tea . . . into this colony, while it is subject . . . to payment of a duty, for the purpose of raising a revenue in America, he shall be deemed an enemy to the liberties of America.

"2d. *Resolved*. That whoever shall be aiding, or assisting, in the landing, or carting of such tea, from any ship or vessel, or shall hire any house, storehouse, or cellar . . . to deposit the tea . . . he shall be deemed an enemy to the liberties of America.

"3d. *Resolved*. That whoever shall sell or buy . . . tea, or shall aid . . . in transporting such tea . . . from this city, until the . . . revenue act shall be totally and clearly repealed, he shall be deemed an enemy to the liberties of America.

"4th. *Resolved*. That whether the duties on tea, imposed by this act, be paid in Great Britain, or in America, our liberties are equally affected.

"5th. *Resolved*. That whoever shall transgress any of these resolutions, we shall not deal with or employ, or have any connection with him."

---

were determined to compel the British government to rescind the remaining duty on tea and tried to force merchants to continue the Nonimportation Agreements. They were rebuffed. Instead, British-American trade revived—to the joy of the merchants, who no longer saw any purpose in boycotting English wares now that the other Townshend duties were dead. Meanwhile, Americans—then a tea-drinking people—evaded the duty by smuggling in their favorite beverage from Dutch sources.

Now the government in England blundered once more and set in motion the final phase of the British-American confrontation. The occasion for this misstep was the distress of the British East India Company. After decades of growing profit in trade with India and the Far East, the company had been brought to the edge of ruin by mismanagement and fraud. Its last remaining asset, 18 million pounds of tea, could not be sold because taxes in Britain and America made smuggled Dutch tea cheaper. To help the company

the British government, under the Tea Act of 1773, eliminated an export duty on British tea. Though the new law retained the existing three-pence-a-pound import duty on tea brought to America, this new arrangement would allow the East India Company to undersell American merchants who sold smuggled tea. But, in addition, the new law allowed the company to forgo the auction of its product in Britain and sell directly to various favored American consignees. Now it could bypass or undersell even the "fair traders," those American merchants who obeyed the law and bought only English tea. And the scheme, it seemed, might be the beginning of a new policy to favor those merchants in the colonies who supported British policies and penalize those who did not.

In each major port artisans, shopkeepers, and merchants gathered to condemn this latest threat to American liberty. Information was passed from cities to villages and from colony to colony through the Committees of

Sam Adams

Samuel Adams, a failure in business and law, was a resounding success in politics and propaganda. A man who could not manage his own family's financial affairs, he instigated the Boston Tea Party, the spark that ignited the American Revolution.

Samuel was a maverick member of the same Adams family that gave the nation two presidents, several distinguished historians, and a flock of business leaders. Born in Boston in September 1722, he was named after his father, "Deacon" Adams, a substantial brewer and merchant and a pillar of the Congregational church. His mother, Mary, was also a pious woman, a disciple of Jonathan Edwards, the fire-and-brimstone Calvinist preacher from Northampton. All his life the younger Samuel, though considered a political firebrand, would remain intensely loyal to his ancestral church and participate devoutly in its rites and affairs.

We have little information about Sam Adams's youth except the anecdotes he told in later years. Because his father was so busy, his mother raised the children and did so in a strict Puritan fashion. Mary Adams did not permit the products of the family brewery to be served in her prosperous home. Instead of lullabies, Samuel recounted, hymn tunes rocked him to sleep. The Bible was his first reading primer and deeply influenced his perceptions. Samuel played in the garden behind the house, but he was forbidden to eat the fruit that grew there. His plight made vivid to him the dilemma of Adam and Eve in the Garden of Eden.

Samuel was a lonely lad with few siblings or friends and, despite his mother's orders not to wander off, sought playmates among the sons of waterfront workers. At six, however,

he entered Boston Latin School where he drilled daily in the "dead languages" like other middle-class youths preparing for college. In 1736, at the age of fourteen, he entered Harvard and acquired a smattering of geography, geometry, physics, logic, "natural philosophy," as well as Latin and Greek.

College was a time of drastic change in Adams's life. In his junior year he lived off campus, a privilege accorded only to "delicate" students who could not eat college food or to the high-toned student who could afford better accommodations. Sam, apparently, qualified in the second category. But then his father lost his fortune in the Land Bank fiasco, forcing Sam not only to return to the college dining room but also to wait on tables to help pay his expenses.

The Land Bank crash damaged more than Sam Adams's social standing at Harvard. Founded in 1741 to issue paper money against real estate security, the Land Bank was designed to offset the chronic colonial money shortage and ease the burden of debtors in thrall to creditors at home and in Great Britain. Deacon Adams, though himself a merchant, was one of the Land Bank's founders and when, in 1741, the British government, goaded by Governor Jonathan Belcher, declared the Land Bank and its paper money illegal, Sam's father suffered severe financial losses. This debacle, it is said, taught Sam two critical lessons: First, he must not identify with the privileged classes and, second, British rule in America was both arbitrary and selfish.

Sam graduated from Harvard without a strong sense of vocation. For a time he tried reading law but did not like it. He studied for an advanced degree at Harvard and wrote a master's thesis on the subject "Whether It Be Lawful to

Resist the Supreme Magistrate if the Commonwealth Cannot Be Otherwise Preserved." The essay combined his reading of John Locke with his experiences during the Land Bank struggle. Its conclusion was "Yes."

By default Adams entered business, starting as a clerk with merchant Thomas Cushing, a family friend. Cushing quickly found that Sam was more interested in politics than the affairs of his counting house, and he asked him to leave. At this point the Deacon gave his son a thousand pounds to set up his own business. Sam lent half of it to a friend, who promptly absconded. In despair at his son's financial irresponsibility, the Deacon took him into his brewery where he could keep an eye on the feckless young man.

Sam spent as little time at the brewery as possible. He had no interest in making money, and somehow he could not pay attention to beer when there were so many exciting political issues in the air. In 1747 he and several friends founded a political discussion group, the Caucus Club, which soon issued a newspaper, the *Independent Advertiser*. This journal regularly attacked the governor and the aristocratic "prerogative party" with an "itch for riding the *Beasts of the People*," and demanded a return to an earlier day of Puritan simplicity. Adams was now well on his way to becoming a leader of the "country party" that would plague the royal governor and his pro-British associates until independence.

Meanwhile, Adams's financial circumstances continued to deteriorate. His father died in 1748, leaving Sam one-third of his property. But Adams quickly squandered this estate. In 1756 he became Boston's tax collector, but instead of profiting from this post he became personally responsible for

£8,000 in back taxes. During these years Adams married twice. His first wife died in 1757, leaving him with two small children. He married again in 1764 to Elizabeth Welles, a woman who raised his children, supported his political positions, and managed his household remarkably well on his small income.

Seventeen sixty-four was also the year that Adams began the political course that led to fame. By this time the war with France was over and Britain was determined to put the empire and its finances in order. In April 1764 Parliament passed the Sugar Act, which extended the duties on sugar and molasses imported from the non-British West Indies and imposed higher duties on a wide range of colonial imports. Accompanying this measure was a law that strengthened the British custom's service in America and drastically reduced the rights of accused violators of imperial trade laws.

Adams and his colleagues of the Caucus Club immediately denounced the new measures as tyrannical. In a statement authored by Adams, the Boston Town meeting instructed the Massachusetts legislature to work for repeal of the Sugar Act and join with other colonies in this effort. The statement also condemned the policy of allowing appointed officials to have seats in the Massachusetts General Court, the colonial legislature. This attack was aimed primarily at Thomas Hutchinson, the lieutenant governor and chief justice of Massachusetts, a man who himself opposed the new British measures, but, as a member of the Court Party, believed they must be obeyed.

The following March Parliament made an even graver mistake when it passed the Stamp Act, in effect placing a tax on legal documents, dice, playing cards, newspapers, almanacs, and many other American items. The outcry against this novel imposition came first in Virginia, where Patrick Henry denounced King George III and first raised the issue of taxation without representation. The "Patriot" party in Massachusetts responded more violently. During the summer of 1765, mobs of artisans, merchants, apprentices, and seamen, loosely organized as the Sons of Liberty, attacked the home of Andrew Oliver, one of the new stamp tax collectors and a relative of Hutchinson. Twelve days later another mob burned the home of Hutchinson himself and destroyed most of his papers.

Adams's role in this violence, if any, cannot be established. As yet he was merely a private citizen attacking the emerging Tory interest from within the Sons of Liberty, the Caucus Club, and other informal groups. But soon after, Adams was elected by Boston voters to the General Court and was in a position to take a more visible part in opposing the Tory loyalists. In fact, he soon became the unofficial leader in the legislature of the enemies of the new imperial policies.

Over the next eight years, until 1774, Adams served in the General Court as leader of the radical party, a group of men who resisted expanded British power and demanded ever greater American autonomy. He and his colleagues, including James Otis, Josiah Quincy, Joseph Warren, and his cousin, John Adams, helped to drive from power governor Francis Bernard, and when Hutchinson replaced Bernard in 1769, he helped make the new governor's life miserable as well. Meanwhile, Adams became the sparkplug of opposition to the Townshend duties, the measure that replaced the Stamp Act as a means to raise revenue in America when the opposition finally forced Parliament to rescind the earlier law. Adams authored the Circular Letter in February 1768, soliciting united action among the thirteen colonies to resist British encroachment on American liberties. He was also a vital force behind the second Nonimportation Association designed to pressure the British government into rescinding the detested Townshend duties, just as the first boycott had forced repeal of the Stamp Act.

Adams denied supporting violence, but his barrage of published attacks against the redcoats sent to Boston in 1768 incited the public to riot. According to Adams the British regulars were "bloody-backed rascals" who spread crime, vice, and impiety throughout the city. They violated the sabbath, caroused shamelessly, beat small boys, and raped matrons and young girls indiscriminately. Exposed to this flood of invective, crowds of angry young men, referred to as Adams's "Mohawks," were soon shadowing the soldiers wherever they went. On March 5, 1770, the antagonisms between them erupted as the famous Boston Massacre.

In April 1770 Parliament repealed the Townshend duties, removing a major incitement to anti-British feelings. That October a Boston jury acquitted the British soldiers of wrongdoing during the March 5 violence. During the next two years, the Patriot cause, supported by no new grievance, ebbed. But Adams would not let go—not while his detested enemy, Thomas Hutchinson, now governor, was assaulting the reputations of the Patriot leaders and denouncing their cause. During the next few years Adams engaged in a war of words against the Tories, which was designed to keep the struggle alive. In 1772 he induced the Boston Town Meeting to appoint a Committee of Correspondence to lay out the rights of the American colonists and established a network of communication with Patriot leaders all over British North America.

In May 1773 Parliament shocked the Patriot cause once more to life by passing the Tea Act. This new law retained the small tax originally placed on tea by the Townshend duties, but now permitted the East India Company to market its tea in America through its own agents and reducing its cost by rescinding an export tea tax. Americans would get cheaper tea, but American merchants—whether "fair traders" who had bought English tea legally or "free traders" who had smuggled tea in from Dutch colonies—would be undercut.

Adams and his firebrand friends had no intention of allowing this latest assault on American rights to go unanswered. The tea must not be landed and placed in warehouses, for once ashore it would certainly be distributed. And once the British had made good the process, they would feel free to impose taxes on all necessities purchased in Britain and even on the "land purchased and cultivated by our hard laboring ancestors." These revenues would then pay the salaries of corrupt officials "whose vileness ought to banish them from the Society of Men."

Adams might have accepted the scheme of Governor Hutchinson to refuse to allow the ships to actually enter the harbor. That would permit them to return to Britain without paying the cargo duties and so avoid a crisis. Adams would have none of this, however. Instead, he induced the ship captains to dock, though not unload, their tea. Now there was no way under the law that they could avoid paying the duties, but at the same time the Patriots would insist that the tea not be sold. Adams had created a deliberate crisis in order to revive the Patriot movement.

He and his friends now resolved it in a way designed to provoke maximum confrontation. As dusk fell on December 16, 1773, several hundred Sons of Liberty, fortified with rum and made up as Indians, headed for the Boston waterfront followed by a crowd of spectators. Many of the "Narragansett Indians" were Adams's followers from the city's North End—merchants, artisans, seamen. The painted, be-feathered men clambered aboard the tea ships and in a matter of minutes dumped 342 chests of prime Bohea tea into the harbor waters.

Adams and his fellow radicals got just what they wanted. The London government reacted violently to this criminal defiance of law and imposed a series of coercive measures that seemed to confirm every Patriot charge of British oppression. British truculence in turn created sympathy for Boston and Massachusetts everywhere in America. Adams and the other firebrands were overjoyed. The Boston Tea Party was "a perfect Jubilee," they announced. Step by step each side moved closer to armed confrontation.

During the next few years Adams was in the midst of the drive for independence. In September and October 1774 he served as Massachusetts delegate to the First Continental Congress that met at Philadelphia. Adams and his fellow Massachusetts delegates stayed in the background to avoid frightening the more conservative delegates and keeping them from taking a bold stand against Britain. Adams even supported the choice of the Anglican clergyman, Jacob Duché, to give the opening prayers, though in Puritan Massachusetts he had long baited the Church of England as an extension of Britain's power. In May 1775, after Concord and Lexington, Adams returned to Philadelphia for the Second Continental Congress. There he was one of the most ardent defenders of early separation from Britain and voted for, and signed, the Declaration of Independence, which created the United States of America.

During the Revolutionary War Adams served in the Confederation Congress and then in 1781 returned to Boston. During Shays's Rebellion he upheld the state authorities against the rebels. Though a radical opponent of Britain and her defenders at home, he was not an extreme social egalitarian. In 1768 he had denounced "utopian schemes of levelling and a community of goods. . . ." Yet he so hated England that, during the 1790s, with Britain and France at war, he would support the French Jacobins. In 1794–97 he served one term as Massachusetts governor. Though he had, rather reluctantly, endorsed the Constitution, Adams became a Jeffersonian, exchanging affectionate letters with the leader of the new victorious party. By now he was an old and feeble man, however, and no longer a figure to be reckoned with in the country's political life.

Sam Adams died October 2, 1803, at the age of eighty. He had requested a quiet burial, but his state and city refused to let him go gentle into that good night. The church bells of Boston tolled, the city's shops were closed, and soldiers fired off the harbor guns at sixty-second intervals. Adams was interred in the old graveyard where his Puritan predecessors, who had also smote the wicked, were buried. It was a fitting place.

Correspondence, building a broad and organized resistance. In New York radical leaders, inactive for three years, used the new outrage to reorganize the New York Sons of Liberty. In Philadelphia old Sons of Liberty resumed their defiant attacks on British policies and forced the merchants who had pledged to receive the tea to now refuse it. The radicals urged all Americans to abstain from drinking tea. Patriot women responded by turning to native concoctions that they loyally pronounced "vastly more agreeable" than anything out of India.

In Boston during the winter of 1773 the Tea Act produced an explosion that initiated the final steps to military confrontation. Leading the Boston radicals were the fiery Samuel Adams, who had organized the Massachusetts Sons of Liberty, and a prominent merchant, John Hancock. In late November the first tea-carrying vessels had arrived in Boston. On the evening of December 16 a group of Patriots dressed as Mohawk Indians boarded the ships and dumped the contents of 342 chests of tea—worth £10,000—into the harbor. Hundreds of people watched from the wharf as a thick layer of tea leaves spread over the water. They did not know it, but they were watching part of the British Empire sink beneath the waves.

The "Intolerable Acts".

Between March and May 1774, following other attacks on tea-carrying vessels, an angry Parliament passed the so-called Intolerable or Coercive Acts. The first of these measures was designed to punish Boston by closing the port to all commerce until the East India Company had been paid for its tea. The second, intended to prevent local juries from frustrating enforcement of imperial trade regulations, allowed royal officials accused of crimes while stopping a riot or collecting revenue to be sent to Britain for trial. The third modified the charter of Massachusetts by giving the royal governor enlarged appointive powers and limiting the authority of the town meetings, which had served as forums for anti-British radicals.

Patriots considered two other measures passed at this time, though not reprisals for the Boston Tea Party, equally "intolerable." The first extended the provisions of the Quartering Acts so that troops might be lodged in *private* dwellings. The second, the Quebec Act, established a highly centralized administration for the province of Quebec, Canada, won during the French and Indian War, and granted toleration for the Catholic religion that most of the French population embraced. The law also extended the boundaries of Quebec south to the Ohio River. Protestant Americans, revealing their age-old prejudices, objected to this acceptance of Catholicism. Citizens of Virginia, Connecticut, and Massachusetts denounced the extension of Canada into the area south of the Great Lakes as violating provincial claims to the region under founding charters.

The First Continental Congress.

It was now America's turn to be furious. In response to a widespread demand for a united colonial front against the Intolerable Acts, fifty-five delegates representing all the colonies except distant Georgia met at Philadelphia in early September 1774. This First Continental Congress was composed of men with widely differing views. There were radicals, who claimed that American rights were founded on natural law and that, accordingly, Parliament could not abridge them in any way. As one of them, Roger Sherman, expressed it, there were "no other legislatures over the colonies but their respective assemblies." There were also moderates who argued that American liberties came ultimately from the British constitution and that Parliament had the right to legislate at least on matters of imperial trade. Conservatives, led by Joseph Galloway of Pennsylvania, proposed a plan to establish a political union between Britain and America under a crown-appointed "president-general" and a kind of super Parliament. It was narrowly defeated.

During the debate a copy of the Suffolk Resolves, recently drafted in Massachusetts, arrived in Philadelphia. These condemned the Intolerable Acts and urged the people of Massachusetts to establish an armed militia, boycott British goods, and withhold taxes from the royal government. Presented to the delegates, the Suffolk Resolves were endorsed as the congress's own resolutions. In its own name the congress proved equally radical. Its Declaration of Rights and Grievances sharply attacked virtually all British trade legislation since 1763 and established a Continental Association, which forbade the importation or consumption of British goods and urged an embargo on colonial exports as well. The congress resolved to meet the following May if American grievances had not been redressed by then.

The First Continental Congress was a milestone on the road to American solidarity. Until this time provincial legislatures had acted independently to protest British actions; there had been no body that could claim to speak for Americans as a whole. This disunity reflected the entire thrust of colonial history, which had begun with individual settlements and had continued for over a century as a series of parallel but separate provincial developments. During the Anglo-French wars the colonies had cooperated with one another in a limited way. But the one serious effort at forming a voluntary union for limited purposes—the Albany Congress in 1754—proved a failure. Now, in 1774, another and greater crisis had finally broken through the selfish localism that had so often governed colonial relations. Americans would continue to resist surrendering local political autonomy to a collective government. But they had taken the first step toward political union.

Lexington and Concord.

In the next months the Patriot leaders prepared for the worst. In every colony men joined

Amos Doolittle recorded the Battle of Lexington for posterity, but he fiddled with the facts. The British were surprised and unprepared to fight the colonists. Here they appear as orderly, methodical killers.

militia units, collected arms and powder, and began to engage in military drill. In Massachusetts these groups were called Minute Men because they were expected to "Stand at a minute's warning in Case of alarm." In other provinces the assemblies voted to send money and supplies to the people of Massachusetts, who were suffering economically under the Intolerable Acts. Meanwhile, General Gage, now installed as governor of Massachusetts, prepared his forces for a Patriot attack. Gage particularly feared the Boston Committee of Safety, headed by John Hancock, which had been formed to coordinate Patriot military actions and to call out the Minute Men at the sign of further British provocation.

In mid-April Gage received orders to enforce the Intolerable Acts, by military action if necessary, and to stop Patriot preparations for armed defense. He immediately dispatched a force of 700 men to Concord to destroy Patriot arms caches. Learning of the redcoat destination, the Boston Committee of Safety sent Paul Revere and William Dawes to warn Hancock and Sam Adams, staying at nearby Lexington, to escape, and to alert the countryside. When the redcoats arrived at Lexington at dawn on April 19, 1775, they found seventy Minute Men ready for them. After repeated British commands to disperse, the outnumbered

Americans complied. At this point someone fired a shot. The British then let off several volleys, killing eight Americans. The Americans replied but got the worst of the exchange. At the end of the skirmish the British occupied Lexington Common.

The redcoats now marched to Concord, where they destroyed some Patriot supplies. By this time the countryside had been thoroughly aroused, and as the British troops marched back to Boston, they were attacked on every side by colonial militia. The twenty-one miles to Boston became a murderous gauntlet as Minute Men fired at the redcoats from behind walls, barns, and trees. By the time the British reached the safety of Charlestown, 250 had been killed or wounded. Also dead were almost 100 Americans.

★ CONCLUSIONS ★

Lexington and Concord turned a disagreement into a war. For the next eight years North America would be the arena for struggling armies and dying people. At the end there would be an independent United States.

In one sense this momentous result was the climax of the long process we observed in Chapter 3 that had helped to create a distinctive society and culture in America and a feeling among the colonists that they were not simply transplanted Europeans. It was also related to the growing economic and political maturity of British North America. Here, ironically, British policy was itself largely responsible. Unlike the other European colonial powers, Britain had done much to foster colonial political autonomy and economic prosperity. By 1763 British North America had the population, the material resources, and the political self-confidence to defy one of Europe's most powerful nations.

But cultural, political, and economic maturity by themselves were not enough for revolution. The ties to Britain remained too strong. The actual imperial crisis was precipitated by the special circumstances after 1763. One crucial matter was the French and Indian War. By relieving the colonists of a long-standing danger, it weakened American dependence on Britain. At the same time it loaded the British taxpayer with debt and demonstrated to Pitt's Tory successors that the Americans could not be counted on to bear the burdens of empire in an acceptable way.

However justified from the British perspective, the policies adopted after 1763 were foolishly conceived and executed. A few in Britain saw that the American colonies had become a mature society fast approaching England in wealth and numbers; but most Englishmen and, most crucially, King George's Tory ministers could see them only as disobedient children. Charging ahead blindly, they imposed measures that threatened many occupational and economic groups, deeply disturbed the elite merchants and planters, and aroused fears among many thousands of ordinary people that they were about to be enslaved and exploited by harpies in the shape of bishops and royal officials.

In short, we cannot separate the economic, religious, and political strands of causation. All these factors motivated the colonists, who eventually sought independence; and in each of these areas we find a common anxiety: fear of oppression. It was a fierce colonial attachment to self-determination in all spheres that was the ultimate source of the American Revolution.

✦✦✦✦✦✦✦✦ FOR FURTHER READING ✦✦✦✦✦✦✦✦

Gary M. Walton and James P. Shepherd. *The Economic Rise of Early America* (1979)

The best brief, overall view of the colonial economy. Also contains an interesting chapter on the economic impact of British imperial policies after 1763. Though written by two economists, the book is not difficult for students of history because the authors are careful to define all their technical terms.

Arthur M. Schlesinger. *The Colonial Merchants and the American Revolution, 1763–1776* (1917)

Examines the contribution of colonial traders to the origins of the Revolution. The author sees them largely as protective of their economic interests and opposed to the more radical revolutionaries, though at many points the interests of both overlapped. Very much in the tradition of Charles Beard and the "Progressive" historians.

James Henretta. *The Evolution of American Society, 1700–1815: An Interdisciplinary Analysis* (1973)

An interesting attempt by a social historian to integrate the social, economic, and political history of early America. Henretta takes a dimmer view of the equality of wealth and power in colonial America than I do.

Jackson T. Main. *The Social Structure of Revolutionary America* (1965)

Main studied the income, style, cost of living, and distribution of property in rural and urban society in mid-eighteenth century America. He depicts the colonists as prosperous and socially mobile. Colonial America, he says, was indeed "the best poor man's country in the world."

Edmund S. Morgan and Helen M. Morgan. *The Stamp Act Crisis: Prologue to Revolution* (1953)

The best short treatment of this crucial step along the road to independence. A balanced account of an unbalanced period in our history.

Bernard Bailyn. *The Ideological Origins of the American Revolution* (1967)

Bailyn takes ideas seriously as fundamental moving causes. In this examination of the pre-Revolutionary battle of words, he shows how the libertarian ideas forged in the seventeenth- and early-eighteenth-century English struggle with the crown helped mold the actions of American Patriots after 1763.

Robert A. Gross. *The Minutemen and Their World* (1976)

This study of the town of Concord, Massachusetts, before 1776 captures the hopes, frustrations, and fears of a small American community caught in the vortex of great imperial changes. Gross has a talent for combining the social scientist's hard facts with the humanist's sensitivity to ordinary people's feelings and responses.

Pauline Maier. *From Resistance to Revolution: Colonial Radicals and the Development of American Opposition to Great Britain, 1765–1776* (1972)

Professor Maier shows that the "radical" leaders of the American independence movement were really orderly and prudent men who opposed mob violence. Her book helps explain why the American Revolution seldom erupted into social excess.

Bernard Bailyn. *The Ordeal of Thomas Hutchinson* (1974)

This biography of the American-born royal governor of Massachusetts on the eve of the Revolution is a fine study of the mind and views of a leading American Tory. Bailyn makes it clear how difficult it is to find simple villains—and heroes—in history.

Merrill Jensen. *The Founding of a Nation: A History of the American Revolution, 1763–1776* (1968)

A long and well-written study of the whole sweep of events, from the French and Indian War onward, that culminated in the Declaration of Independence. Jensen gives attention to forces as well as human actors and deals with society as well as politics. He is convinced that the "history of the period is . . . one of extraordinary intricacy" and so he avoids simple answers to the problem of "causes."

John C. Miller. *Sam Adams: Pioneer in Propaganda* (1936)

A classic older study of a major Revolutionary radical. Still worth reading.

Dumas Malone. *Jefferson the Virginian* (1948)

By far the best treatment of Jefferson during the years he was intimately involved in the colonial struggle with Great Britain. This is volume I of a multivolume work, now completed, called *Jefferson and His Time*. Malone's monumental opus has been criticized as a eulogy of Jefferson.

Carl Van Doren. *Benjamin Franklin* (1941)

A classic of American biography by a brilliant stylist. Covers far more than Franklin's work as Patriot leader; deals also with his contributions to science and journalism. A work of literature as well as history.

Douglas Southall Freeman. *Washington: An Abridgment* (1968)

This is the one-volume condensation of Freeman's monumental seven-volume life of Washington. The abridgment has been skillfully done.

Alice H. Jones. *Wealth of a Nation to Be: The American Colonies on the Eve of the Revolution* (1980)

This is the definitive study of just how wealthy Americans were in the late eighteenth century and how their wealth was distributed among the various members of society. Theoretical and analytical rather than narrative.

John H. McCusker and Russell Menard. *The Economy of British America, 1607–1789: Needs and Opportunities* (1985)

This is an even more recent survey of the colonial economy. The book pulls together much of the newest research and suggests new directions and new areas of investigation for future scholars.

5★

THE REVOLUTION

How Did It Change America?

1775	The Second Continental Congress meets in Philadelphia; it declares war on Britain, organizes the Continental Army under George Washington, authorizes a navy, and appoints a Committee of Secret Correspondence • Ethan Allen captures Fort Ticonderoga • The Battle of Breed's (Bunker) Hill in Boston
1776–79	Main theater of war is in middle colonies; Philadelphia and Yorktown occupied by the British
1776	Paper money—"continentals"—printed • Thomas Paine's *Common Sense* • in Congress Richard Lee of Virginia introduces a resolution of independence from Britain • Congress approves the Declaration of Independence • Congress appoints a committee to plan for a permanent constitution
1777	Congress recommends that states sell Loyalist property • Horatio Gates defeats General Burgoyne at Saratoga, the turning point of the war • Congress approves a draft of the Articles of Confederation
1778	France and the American colonies establish a military alliance
1779	Spain declares war on Great Britain
1779–81	Main theater of war shifts to the southern colonies
1781	Final victory at Yorktown • Articles of Confederation ratified • The colonial monetary system collapses; Congress appoints Robert Morris to organize Bank of North America to strengthen public credit
1782	Americans and British agree on a preliminary peace treaty dealing with the states' western boundaries, fishing rights off Newfoundland, British garrisons in the West, colonial debts, and payment for Loyalist property
1783	The Treaty of Paris brings full independence • Massachusetts court interpretation of the state constitution prohibits slavery; thereafter slavery is illegal in the Bay State
1786	Virginia legislature adopts the principle of separation of church and state in an act drafted by Jefferson

riting in the summer of 1775, shortly after Lexington and Concord, John Adams described an encounter with a person he had defended in court as an attorney. The man—"a common Horse Jockey," Adams called him—greeted the Founding Father on the road. "Oh! Mr. Adams," he exclaimed, "what great Things have you and your Colleagues done for us! We can never be grateful enough to you. There are no Courts of Justice now in this Province, and I hope there will never be another!" Adams was appalled. Would the future of America be as the "common Horse Jockey" hoped? Would the colonies, in the course of changing governments, jettison all law to protect lives and property and have their entire social structure turned upside down? "If the Power of the Country should ever get into such hands," remarked Adams, "and there is great danger that it will, to what purpose have we sacrificed our Time, Health, and every Thing?"

Adams—and other conservative Americans—worried throughout the war about a takeover of power by the less respectable people of the colonies. Their concern was understandable. Eight years of bitter fighting followed the skirmishes at Lexington and Concord. During that time the American community expended vast amounts of energy and wealth and sacrificed thousands of lives. Surely a struggle of this magnitude—one, moreover, fought in the name of freedom from tyranny—could be expected to undermine conventional values, transform traditional relationships, and weaken long-standing institutions. Did it? The obvious and fundamental result of the American Revolution was independence. But how profoundly did the Revolution change American society? Did Adams's fears prove justified?

★ AMERICAN PROSPECTS ★

As Americans considered their prospects in the days following Lexington and Concord, they found it hard to predict what lay ahead. Ties of memory, habit, interest, and affection, and fears of the unknown, all acted as deterrents to a complete break with England. Few as yet wanted independence. Even among the most ardent Patriots the common hope was that Britain would see the light, abandon its punitive policies as expressed in the Intolerable Acts, and reconsider its fundamental relations with America. This hope was reflected in the Olive Branch Petition adopted by the Second Continental Congress in July 1775. Written by John Dickinson, the petition declared that the colonists remained loyal to King George and asked him to intervene to protect his American subjects against Parliament's tyranny.

Loyalists, needless to say, were even less willing to break with the past. Whether Loyalist or Patriot, virtually all Americans in the spring of 1775 recoiled at the thought of complete independence.

But whatever their ultimate goals, Americans recognized that resistance to the mighty British Empire was a chancy policy. Clearly there were strengths and weaknesses on both sides. Britain was probably the strongest nation on earth in 1775. Just twelve years earlier it had defeated France, its archrival in Europe, and now was dominant in North America, India, South Africa, and many other parts of the world. On the face of it, the British had an enormous advantage over the Americans in numbers, military experience, and political unity.

But the English also labored under great difficulties. British military and naval capacity had been formidable indeed at the end of the French and Indian War in 1763. Thereafter it had deteriorated. Meanwhile, France had rebuilt its military and naval forces and was in a position to challenge Britain again. More serious, Britain's victories in the late war had won it enemies and left it isolated. France, Spain, Holland, and Russia all feared British power and had grievances against England that they hoped to redress. These nations, especially France, were potential American allies in 1775. Their hostility to Great Britain would prove indispensable to the American cause.

Britain also faced enormous strategic problems in fighting a war in America. The British Isles were three thousand miles from the military scene, and troops and supplies sent to the battlefields would take two or three months to arrive. When they finally did, the troops would have to fight on unfamiliar terrain, often surrounded by a hostile populace. Americans were on their home ground, close to supplies and manpower, and able to apply the strength they had to the battle at hand.

Yet the "rebels," too, faced colossal difficulties. Several hundred thousand Americans were not only opposed to the Patriot cause but were willing to risk their lives and property to defeat it. The Loyalists would be a great source of strength to the British. Several regiments of Loyalists would be enlisted in the British army and would fight ferociously against their countrymen. Generally speaking, Loyalist troops were more enthusiastic than the British themselves and would be widely feared and detested by the Patriots for their zeal in the crown's cause.

Military Forces. Few Americans had military experience, let alone the knowledge required for raising, equipping, and leading a large army. A few colonials had served as officers during the French and Indian War, but none, not even George

The variety of uniforms in Baron Von Closen's watercolors of colonial troops suggests the fragmentation of Patriot forces during the Revolution. Note the black soldier at the far left.

Washington, had held a rank higher than colonel. And the professional foreign soldiers who flocked to America seeking military appointments were often incompetent. The Marquis de Lafayette, the Germans Johann Kalb (known as Baron de Kalb) and Baron Friedrich Wilhelm von Steuben, and the Pole Thaddeus Kosciusko were skilled soldiers. But there was no officer on the American side who had the experience of commanding large bodies of troops in the field or of planning military strategy for a whole continent.

The colonists were better off in ordinary military manpower. Americans believed then, and would continue to believe for most of their history, that a volunteer soldier was better than a hired mercenary. British redcoats, and still more the Hessians—German soldiers hired by the king to help put down the rebellion—were men who fought only for pay and supposedly lacked the spirit of those fighting for their homeland. By contrast, Continental troops, most Patriots insisted, were dedicated young men with freedom in their hearts.

In reality the situation was more complicated than this simple estimate. Colonial troops lacked the rigorous training of the redcoats and at times this difference strongly favored the British. On the other hand, most Americans knew how to use a rifle or musket, and many had experience in Indian warfare. In fact, their lack of traditional European military experience helped as much as it hurt. At the outset of a battle, British soldiers were trained to fire unaimed volleys at their opponents and trust to the sheer volume of lead to shock and disrupt the enemy. Then the ranks would charge the foe with bayonets. These tactics worked well enough on the open fields of Europe, where opposing armies faced each other in full view. They sometimes worked in the better-settled portions of America, too. But in the forests that covered so much of the colonies, where men could hide behind every tree and bush, they were unsuitable. Far more effective in the terrain of the New World was the American approach, in which troops equipped with accurate Kentucky rifles were deployed from behind cover. The British tried to modify their tactics to suit American conditions. Loyalist troops, moreover, were familiar with guerrilla fighting and were valuable auxiliaries to the British army. But on the whole, American commanders and enlisted men remained better adapted to war in America than the British.

Superior tactics might have helped improve the odds, but the Patriots could not count on a consistent and stable supply of manpower. It was one thing to turn out with your gun for a local skirmish or a few weeks of soldiering, and many young men did so willingly. It was another to enlist as a regular in the Continental Army, fight battles against professional soldiers, subject yourself to military discipline, and spend months or possibly years away from home and family. Under the circumstances it proved hard for the Continental Congress and the individual states to raise troops. At first patriotism was enough to bring in recruits; later, cash bounties and promises of land were necessary to induce men to enlist. And once they were in the army, the new recruits were hard to keep on the front lines fighting the British. Many served just a few months and then—with or without leave—returned to civilian life. Almost 400,000 men passed through the Continental armies during the war, but George Washington never had more than 20,000 troops under his command at one time.

Another American military problem was conflicting jurisdiction. In reality, there were fourteen Patriot armies: the Continental Army under Washington and thirteen state armies, called "lines." The men in each were paid differently and were enlisted for different periods. Often the armies acted at cross-purposes, and Continental and state officers frequently argued over who had the greater authority or higher status.

Supplying the army was also a problem for the Americans. There were many fine gunsmiths in the colonies, but they produced so many types and sizes of weapons that securing the proper ammunition was difficult. There was also a shortage of gunpowder and shot, and the dearth at times threatened to put the entire American army out of action. Artillery was in especially short supply, for the country was not yet capable of manufacturing big guns.

When it came to ships, the new nation was somewhat better off. American shipyards were not equipped to build large ships of the line, the battleships of the day. The Continental Navy, accordingly, could scarcely challenge the British fleet in direct battle. But Americans could and did produce excellent small craft that served effectively as privateers—armed private ships commissioned to attack the enemy. Privateers provided most of the American naval punch. Licensed by Congress with "letters of marque" to prey on British commerce, they attacked enemy merchant ships even within sight of the British coast. During the war privateers captured 3,200 British ships, at immense cost to Great Britain and its citizens. Privateering helped to balance the great losses suffered by northern shippers from the British blockade of American harbors and their seizure of hundreds of American merchant vessels on the high seas.

Creating a Government.   At the beginning, the Second Continental Congress was the country's only central political authority. This was a serious weakness. Although it regularly passed resolutions and proposed emergency measures, the Continental Congress was not an effective government. Sovereignty continued to reside in the indi-

vidual state governments; in fact, the assemblage in Philadelphia was more like a diplomatic meeting of sovereign states than a government. In the end, implementation of every proposal Congress made depended on the support of the thirteen state legislatures, and these as often ignored its wishes as observed them.

Despite its limitations, for many months the Second Continental Congress acted as the government for the American people. It created the Continental Army with George Washington as commander in chief. On May 29, 1775, it adopted an address to the people of Canada asking them to join in resisting British tyranny. In July it approved the Olive Branch Petition; and after that was rejected by the king, it disavowed American allegiance to Parliament. That same month Congress established a post office department and appointed commissioners to negotiate peace treaties with the Indians. In the fall of 1775 it authorized a navy for the "United Colonies," and soon after appointed a five-man Committee of Secret Correspondence to approach Britain's European enemies for aid.

Wartime Finance.   These moves were promising, but still the Americans lacked a strong, effective central government. One of Congress's chief weaknesses was that it had no power to tax. The state governments could impose taxes, but Americans were unused to heavy taxation, and the states found it hard to make their citizens bear the full burden of the war's cost. During the various colonial wars of the past the individual colonies had met this problem by issuing paper money. Now, once more, Congress and the states resorted to the printing press to pay military contractors, the army, and public officials. The paper money issued by Congress was called "continentals," and by 1780 notes with a face value of $200 million had been circulated. The states issued almost as much during the same period.

The American folk expression "not worth a continental" suggests the fate of this paper money. At first the continentals and state notes kept their face value surprisingly well. But as the volume of issues grew, their purchasing power fell. By 1780, $40 in continentals was worth less than $1 in gold and silver coin. Paper money prices soared so high that a bushel of corn that had sold for $1 in Massachusetts in the spring of 1777 sold for $80 by the summer of 1779. The governor of New Jersey, whose salary in continentals was $40,000 a year, estimated in 1780 that the purchasing power of this sum in prewar terms had declined to less than $1,000.

In a modern nation such hyperinflation is likely to produce social and economic disaster. Business ventures are jeopardized, for no one can count on the economic future. Creditors who are owed money and everyone with a fixed income are seriously hurt as the money unit declines in pur-

Backs and fronts of two Congressional "Continental" bills. These are worth far more now than a year or two after they were issued.

chasing power. And the inflation during the struggle for independence did harm some Americans. Patriots who bought Congress's bonds ("loan office certificates") or who accepted "commissary" or "quartermaster certificates"—government IOUs—in payment for supplies and services lost money when prices soared. Inflation also hurt officers and men of the Continental Army and the state forces whose pay plummeted in value. Still, the effects were limited. No one in those days had bank accounts or life insurance, and in this predominantly rural, agricultural economy relatively few worked for money wages or paid cash for the food they ate or the clothes they wore. Inflation, then, had far milder effects than it would today.

In effect, then, the paper money system of paying for the war worked moderately well. And in any event, neither Congress nor the state governments had any real alternative given the tax-avoidance traditions of America and Congress's inability to tax.

★ THE ROAD TO INDEPENDENCE ★

Early Battles. While the Second Continental Congress struggled to establish an independent government and to raise men and money for the war, important military events were taking place in the field. Following the skirmishes at Lexington and Concord, General Gage found himself besieged in Boston by several thousand New England troops.

In early June 1775 he prepared to dislodge the rebels from Dorchester Heights. The Americans countered by fortifying Breed's Hill (not Bunker Hill, as legend has it) in Charlestown, across the harbor from Boston. On June 17 British naval vessels began firing on the Americans, and at noon 2,400 redcoats landed on the Charlestown peninsula. Twice the heavily laden "lobster-backs" trudged up Breed's Hill into the murderous fire of the Americans entrenched on top; twice they retreated. The third time General William Howe ordered them to drop their packs and charge with fixed bayonets. The redcoats swept the Americans off their perch and off nearby Bunker Hill as well. At the end of the day the British held the field, but at the enormous cost of over a thousand dead. Though technically an American defeat, the Battle of Bunker Hill was a moral victory that helped convince Americans they could stand up to British regulars.

Bunker Hill had been preceded by Ethan Allen's daring capture of the small British garrison at Fort Ticonderoga on Lake Champlain. It was followed by a double American thrust, led by Benedict Arnold and Richard Montgomery, against Montreal and Quebec, designed to deprive Britain of a base of operations against the Americans. The Canadian expedition was dogged by bad luck and nearly led to disaster for the Americans. Montgomery took Montreal, but Quebec, defended by British regulars and Canadians who had rejected Congress's invitation to join the struggle against England, held out. In the battle to capture Quebec, Montgomery was killed, Arnold wounded, and several hundred Americans killed or captured.

The Revolution 121

In the South the early fighting went better for the Americans. There a force of Virginians and North Carolinians encountered the royal governor of Virginia, Lord Dunmore, and his army of white Loyalists and black slaves. The blacks had been promised their freedom if they supported the king. Lord Dunmore's small force fought enthusiastically but was overwhelmed by the Patriots.

The year 1776 began well for the Patriot cause. In a series of actions in the Carolinas between February and June, the Americans beat off the attacks of generals Sir Henry Clinton and Charles Cornwallis. In March, after Continental troops had dragged the big guns captured at Ticonderoga down to within range of Boston, General Howe evacuated the city. The British never seriously threatened New England again.

Turning Points. As the months of fighting passed, many of the remaining emotional ties to Britain snapped. The use of Hessian mercenaries, the king's contemptuous rejection of the Olive Branch Petition, the British proclamation in December 1775 declaring the colonies in open rebellion, and the closing off of all formal commerce with the rebellious Americans—these acts made it increasingly clear to Patriots that reconciliation was impossible. A critical event in the South was Lord Dunmore's arming of the slaves. This move violated one of the South's strongest racial taboos, and Chesapeake planters who had previously held back now rushed to support the Patriot cause.

With each passing day, then, Patriots found it easier to consider independence as their ultimate goal. Their need for allies provided an additional push toward independence. France viewed the British troubles in America with glee. Resentful of their defeat in the French and Indian War, the French hoped to see proud Britain humbled and France restored to an important place in North America. Both France and Spain considered Britain a threat to their Caribbean possessions and expected a weak, independent America to be easier to deal with than the mighty British Empire. Early in 1776 the French foreign minister, the Count de Vergennes, sounded out Spain on aid to the Americans. Soon both countries began to funnel secret money and supplies to the colonists. Americans welcomed the aid but realized that all-out French and Spanish support depended on their own willingness to fight for independence, for only independence would accomplish what the two continental powers wanted: a crippled Britain.

Yet something more was needed to convince most Patriots that they should take the final step. Even though they had become disillusioned with Parliament and the king's ministers, Americans still had a touching faith in the king himself and hoped that he would see the light. Then in early 1776 a recent immigrant from England, Thomas Paine, published a fifty-page pamphlet called *Common Sense* that destroyed their last illusions. It is hard to estimate the political influence of words, but if we can ever ascribe a major political event to mere eloquence, we can in this case. *Common Sense* was eloquent to a rare degree. In bold and ringing phrases Paine denounced King George and the British government and insisted that the time had come to sever completely the ties with Britain. Calling George the "royal brute," Paine helped to destroy the colonists' awe of the crown and respect for the king. Far from being a benevolent father to his people, George had unleashed the wrath of redcoats, Hessians, Indians, and desperate slaves on them. He was not worthy of their esteem. Furthermore, he represented a tyrannical system. Monarchy, Paine declared, was a form of government condemned by God; kings were "crowned ruffians." Concluded Paine: "The blood of the slain, the weeping voice of nature cries, 'TIS TIME TO DEPART.'"

Independence Declared. Paine's stirring polemic sold 120,000 copies in three months and was read throughout the colonies. Tories denounced it as treasonous and certain to encourage "republican" views—that is, ideas of popular government. *Common Sense* had an immense impact on Patriots. Washington found it "working a powerful change in the minds of many men." In April a convention of North Carolinians authorized the colony's delegates in Congress to support independence. Virginia, the most populous colony, did the same the following month. Then, on June 7, 1776, Virginia delegate Richard Henry Lee introduced a resolution in the Continental Congress that the United Colonies "are, and of right ought to be, free and independent States." In response to this motion, Congress appointed Thomas Jefferson, Benjamin Franklin, John Adams, Roger Sherman, and Robert Livingston to prepare a document declaring and justifying American independence. At the end of June a draft of the proposed statement, composed largely by Jefferson, was sent to Congress. On July 2, Congress voted for the principle of independence, and on July 4 it formally approved the revised Declaration of Independence.

The declaration had two aspects. One was a detailed indictment of King George for cruelties, crimes, and illegal political acts against humanity and America. George was made into a villain who personified British wrongdoing. The attack was unfair; the king was no worse than a host of parliamentary leaders. But it was an effective propaganda device. The second aspect was a statement of principles. The signers adopted Paine's radical antimonarchism and the views of the 1689 Whig publicists to justify the drastic action they proposed to take. The people's consent, not the divine right of kings, was the ultimate source of political authority, they declared. Governments were established to assure citizens of "certain unalienable rights," including the rights to "Life, Liberty and the pursuit of Happiness." These words were borrowed from Locke, but significantly changed. Locke had written "life, liberty, and property." Jefferson and his colleagues, though deeply respectful of property, shifted the emphasis to the dignity of individuals and their right to personal fulfillment. The declaration also asserted boldly and bluntly that "all men" were "created equal."

The words that followed these expressed the view, borrowed from the English Whigs, that the people had the right to overthrow a government not based on the "consent of the governed." Revolution should not be resorted to "for light and transient causes." But when, as in this case, "a long train of abuses and usurpations" had been committed, with the goal of an "absolute Despotism," then it was the people's right "to throw off such Government, and to provide new Guards for their future security." Though written in the heat of military and political crisis, the declaration was a moving defense of human freedom, and it would inspire millions around the globe for generations.

★ THE FIGHT FOR INDEPENDENCE ★

The Declaration of Independence was greeted throughout the nation with bonfires, toasts, fireworks, and bell ringing—the usual accompaniments of public celebration in those years. But there was still a long way to go before the reality of independence could be established. The British, certainly, did not take the declaration at face value. In September 1776 General Howe and his brother, Admiral Richard Howe, met on Staten Island with Benjamin Franklin, John Adams, and Edmund Rutledge, representing Congress, and offered the Americans reconciliation. But first they would have to rescind the Declaration of

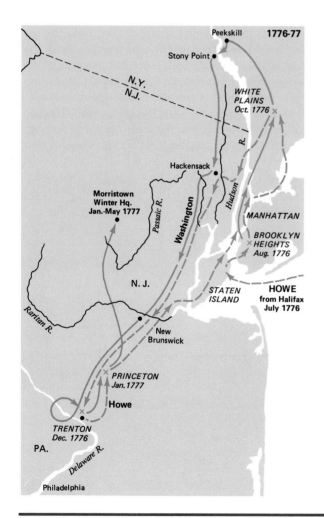

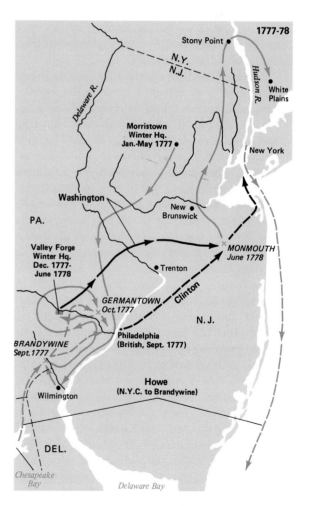

CENTRAL CAMPAIGNS, 1776–1778

Independence. The three Americans listened and then firmly rejected the terms. The fighting went on.

The War in the East, 1776–77. But the war was not going well for the Americans. Howe, in fact, had opened the September negotiations only after trouncing the Americans soundly. Foreseeing Howe's move to make New York the base for British operations in America, Washington had moved his victorious troops south from Boston soon after the British evacuated that city. In July of 1776 Howe landed his forces on Staten Island opposite New York City. At the end of August, with 20,000 men under his command, he attacked Washington's troops on Long Island (Brooklyn Heights), defeated them, and forced them to flee to Manhattan. When the British crossed the East River in pursuit, Washington retreated again, first to White Plains and then to New Jersey. Howe had won New York City, and the British kept it until the end of the war. At the very end of the year Washington partly redeemed his defeat in New York by attacking a force of Hessians at Trenton. The German troops, their vigilance impaired by too much Christmas cheer, were taken by surprise, and almost a thousand surrendered to the Americans.

The year 1777 held mixed fortunes for the rebels. Washington won an important victory at Princeton in January and cleared the British out of much of New Jersey. But in the summer Howe and Cornwallis routed the American general Anthony Wayne and occupied Philadelphia, forcing Congress to flee to avoid capture.

Still, 1777 brought the turning point of the war. During the summer, while Howe was moving on Philadelphia, British troops under General John Burgoyne were advancing south from Canada. The British plan was to split the colonies along the line of Lake Champlain and the Hudson River. As Burgoyne moved south, Howe was to advance up the Hudson. Howe's campaign to capture Philadelphia took too long, however, and he never launched his northward thrust. In late June Burgoyne's army of 8,000 British, Canadians, Indians, and Germans left Quebec and advanced on Fort Ticonderoga. They captured the fort but were soon struggling through the dense forests of northern New York, using up their supplies and getting farther and farther from their Canadian base. Near Lake George, Burgoyne's troops encountered stiff resistance from the troops of Horatio Gates. Gates's army consisted of Continental regulars and New England militia who had flocked to his ranks to avenge the brutal killings of civilians by Burgoyne's Indian allies. Burgoyne suffered serious losses and sought to retreat northward, but the move to escape was futile. He got as far as Saratoga and there was surrounded. On October 17, 1777, "Gentleman Johnnie" surrendered his remaining 6,000 men.

The French Alliance. The victory at Saratoga convinced the French that the Americans might very well make good their claim to independence. In September 1776 Congress had dispatched Silas Deane, Benjamin Franklin, and Arthur Lee to Europe to negotiate treaties with Britain's enemies. But at first progress was slow. In January 1778 the French minister of foreign affairs, Vergennes, convinced now that the Americans had a chance to win independence but fearing that British peace feelers might thwart that goal, told the American envoys that France was prepared to ally itself with the United States. Soon after he and the American representatives negotiated two important treaties. The first guaranteed each nation free trading rights with the other. The second was an alliance for joint military effort against Britain, to last until the United States had won its freedom. Each party promised not to conclude a peace with England without the other's consent.

In early May Congress ratified the French treaties. France was now in the war. Spain, although less certain of her strength and concerned that the rebellious Americans would set a bad example to her own New World colonies, declared war on Britain the following year. The Dutch, too, having clashed with the British over their smuggling of munitions to the rebels through their Caribbean possessions, broke relations with Britain in early 1781, though they never formally declared war. Soon French, Spanish, and later Dutch money—both gifts and loans—began to pour into America, enabling Congress to pay for much-needed arms,

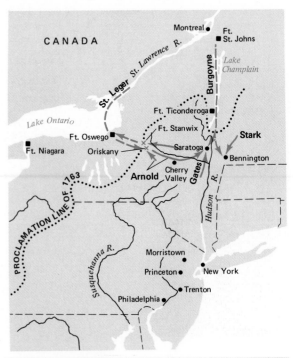

NORTHERN CAMPAIGNS, 1777

food, and equipment. Several other northern European nations, including Russia, Sweden, Prussia, and Denmark, organized the League of Armed Neutrality to keep their vessels supplying the Americans from being stopped by Britain. In all, by the end of the Revolution, Britain had been effectively isolated and placed on the diplomatic defensive. The European aid proved invaluable to America.

War in the West. The war that engulfed the older communities of the East also cast its lurid light across the West. On almost every colonial frontier Americans competed with the British for the friendship and aid of the Indians. In this struggle the British often had the advantage: They possessed the trade goods that the Indians wanted and, unlike the American settlers, posed no threat to the Indians' possession of ancestral lands.

During 1775 the settlers of western North Carolina fought off the Cherokees, who had proclaimed their allegiance to George III. More exposed to British-inspired Indian attack were the infant settlements in eastern Kentucky, just over the Appalachians, established by Richard Henderson and Daniel Boone only months before Lexington and Concord. In the summer of 1776 bands of Shawnee and Delaware, encouraged by the British, began to harass the Kentuckians and drove many in the outlying areas back to the settlement's three main villages. These managed to hold

British troops prepared to storm Breed's Hill after setting Charlestown ablaze. We call this event The Battle of Bunker Hill.

out and remained havens for many whites throughout the war, but away from the log walls of the village stockades, hostile Indians pounced on isolated travelers, stole livestock, and prevented farmers from planting crops.

On the New York frontier the plight of the Americans was even worse. There the British had the support of the powerful Iroquois and their leader, the Mohawk chief Joseph Brant. They also were aided by many Loyalists, organized as the Tory Rangers. The first clash in the region ended in a tie. In August 1777 American militia at Fort Stanwix stopped a British advance designed to reinforce Burgoyne. Soon afterward a supporting party of Americans under General Nicholas Herkimer was caught in an ambush at Oriskany, losing 200 men to a force of Indians, Loyalists, and Hessians under Colonel Barry St. Leger.

During 1778 Iroquois and Loyalists ravaged the New York and Pennsylvania frontiers. The Loyalists attacked the inhabitants of the Wyoming Valley in Pennsylvania and massacred hundreds. Meanwhile, the Iroquois spread panic throughout upper New York.

By this time it was clear that defensive policies in the West had not worked. In the summer of 1778 the Kentuckians, led by George Rogers Clark, determined on their own to go on the attack. On July 4 Clark and a small band of trained Indian fighters pounced on the British post at Kaskaskia, in present-day Illinois, and captured it. Clark and his men soon seized the other northwestern settlements established by the French a generation before. Clark's success inspired Congress to take the offensive, and in 1779 it sent several expeditions to nail down the West for the United States. Forays led by Clark himself and by Colonel Daniel Brodhead and General John Sullivan succeeded, but others failed and threatened to undo much of their work.

Throughout the frontier area the tide flowed back and forth through the remaining years of the Revolution. Both sides resorted to ambush and guerrilla war; and both at times spared neither women nor children. By the time the war ended, the Americans were in firm possession of the frontier in the South, but the British controlled the Northwest. The war in the West had ended in a draw.

A fanciful French view of the siege of Yorktown that ended the military phase of the Revolution. The ships offshore are the vessels of French admiral DeGrasse.

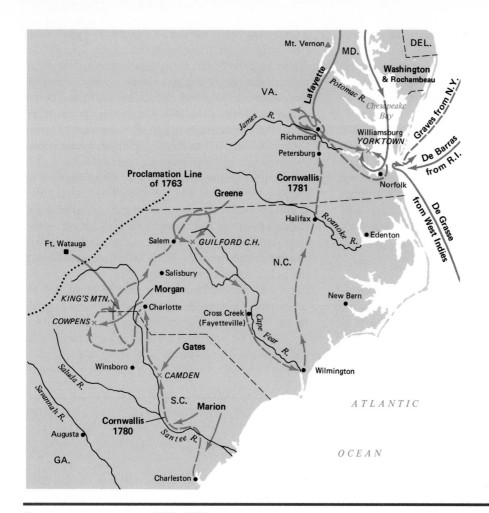

The following labels appear on the map:

Mt. Vernon, MD., DEL., Washington & Rochambeau, VA., Lafayette, Potomac R., Graves from N.Y., Chesapeake Bay, James R., Richmond, Williamsburg, YORKTOWN, De Barras from R.I., Petersburg, Proclamation Line of 1763, Cornwallis 1781, Norfolk, Greene, Halifax, Roanoke R., De Grasse from West Indies, Edenton, Ft. Watauga, Salem, GUILFORD C.H., N.C., Salisbury, Morgan, KING'S MTN., Charlotte, Cross Creek (Fayetteville), Cape Fear R., New Bern, COWPENS, Gates, Winsboro, CAMDEN, Saluda R., Savannah R., S.C., Marion, Cornwallis 1780, Santee R., Augusta, GA., Charleston, Wilmington, ATLANTIC OCEAN

SOUTHERN CAMPAIGNS, 1780–1781

Eastern Battles, 1778–80. It was in the older settlements that the war would be won. After their defeat at Saratoga in 1777, the British, though far from beaten, were weary. At news of the debacle, Lord North, now prime minister, expressed his heartfelt desire to get out of the "damned war." By now British taxpayers were complaining of the war's high costs, and British merchants, badly hurt by the loss of American trade, were in desperate straits. Hoping to avert the impending alliance between France and America, North dispatched a commission under the Earl of Carlisle to offer the Americans new terms for reconciliation. These included ending all efforts to impose revenue taxes on America and suspension of all parliamentary acts for America passed since 1763. When this effort failed, North offered to resign; but the king, who remained stubbornly and bitterly opposed to American independence, insisted that he remain. Out of loyalty he did.

The Americans, too, had their problems after Saratoga. In fact, the winter of 1777–78 is generally considered the low point for Washington's army. Worn down by sickness and losses, the Continental Army withdrew to winter quarters at Valley Forge, just twenty miles from Philadelphia, where the British were living in comfort. Valley Forge was a wretched place. Recent fighting had left the area denuded of supplies. Food and clothing might have been brought in, but a breakdown of supply services left the men cold, hungry, and ill-clothed. To make matters worse, discontent was rife among the officers, whose salaries were small and often unpaid. For a time the aggrieved officers threatened to resign en masse. Eventually Congress improved the pay situation, and a new quartermaster general, Nathanael Greene, established a more efficient supply service. Even so, the Continental Army barely survived the awful winter.

For the next three years the fighting went on intermittently and inconclusively. In the winter of 1778–79 the British won control of Georgia by taking Savannah and Augusta. In 1780 General Sir Henry Clinton captured Charleston, South Carolina, along with 5,000 American troops and 300 guns. Clinton's victory heartened southern Loyalists. In the interior of South Carolina the suppressed Tories now rushed to take up arms against their countrymen. Horatio Gates, the hero of Saratoga, attempted to retake the state for Congress, but was badly beaten by Cornwallis at Camden.

Fighting continued in the north as well. In August 1778 a joint Franco-American operation to capture Newport failed when a storm drove off the French fleet under Admiral d'Estaing. In New Jersey, New York, and the West the Americans were more successful. In July 1779 Anthony Wayne's troops captured a British garrison of 700 at Stony Point on the Hudson at the cost of only 15 American lives. In August Major Henry Lee drove the last British troops out of New Jersey.

Victory at Yorktown. The years 1780 and 1781 were full of confused advances and retreats, and American morale sank almost as low as during the Valley Forge winter. In May 1780 Washington's troops near Morristown, New Jersey, nearly mutinied. Restlessness among front-line regiments continued through the following year. In January 1781 troops on the Pennsylvania and New Jersey lines did rebel.

Disaffection was not limited to the lowest ranks of the army. In the fall of 1780 American militiamen captured Major John André of the British army near Tarrytown, New York. André carried papers that proved that General Benedict Arnold, now commanding the American troops at West Point, planned to surrender his vital post to the British. When Arnold learned of André's capture, he fled to the British lines and eventually became an officer in the king's forces.

Although initially discouraging, the year 1781 brought final victory at Yorktown. The Yorktown campaign opened in April 1781, when General Cornwallis left his base in North Carolina, hoping to crush the American forces in Virginia. He soon collided with troops under the young Frenchman, the Marquis de Lafayette. For four months Cornwallis and Lafayette danced around one another without reaching a showdown. When Wayne came to Lafayette's aid, the British commander retreated to the coast, hoping to establish a base where the Royal Navy could protect and supply him.

Washington heard of Cornwallis's move while he was besieging the British at New York. He quickly abandoned his effort to recapture the city and moved south. The moment was especially favorable because the French fleet under Count de Grasse could now join the attack. De Grasse soon stationed his ships off the Virginia coast, where Lafayette had pushed Cornwallis onto the narrow Yorktown peninsula. On September 14 Washington's troops and

5,000 French soldiers led by the Count de Rochambeau arrived at Yorktown. Immediately they besieged the smaller British force. Bit by bit, remorseless French and American pressure reduced the area under British control. Cornwallis had counted on help from the sea, but the French fleet—twenty-eight ships of the line—was too much for the British navy. Under relentless attack, Cornwallis notified Henry Clinton, his superior in New York: "If you cannot relieve me very soon, you must prepare to hear the worst."

General Clinton set out on his rescue mission on October 19. But he was too late. Three days earlier Cornwallis had made a desperate attempt to escape across the York River and had been frustrated by a storm. Seeing all hope for his army gone, the British general resolved to surrender. On October 19, 1781, 7,000 British and Hessian troops laid down their arms. Legend has it that as the defeated army marched out of its camp, the British military bands played a tune called "The World Turned Upside Down." The musicians' choice was prophetic. Yorktown was not only the last important battle of the war; it was also the end of the old British Empire.

★ THE ARTICLES OF CONFEDERATION ★

Victory had come not a moment too soon. By the fall of 1781 the United States was in serious financial trouble, its monetary system collapsing and prices and wages soaring out of sight. In the last months of the war Congress turned for help with its money problems to Robert Morris, a shrewd Philadelphia businessman. Morris was a former member of Congress who had already performed valuable financial services for the government. In February 1781 Congress appointed him superintendent of finance for the United States. He proceeded to reorganize the government's financial affairs, strengthened the public credit, and eliminated waste in the budget. Soon after taking office he also organized the Bank of North America, the first commercial bank in the United States.

The closing months of the war also saw the beginning of a new American government. It had taken the states almost five years to agree on a new political structure. In the meantime, as we have seen, the Continental Congress had acted as the American government. Little more than a convention of sovereign powers, it had not been effective, and since the beginning of the war it had been clear to most American leaders that the country needed a more formal and permanent government. In June 1776 Congress had appointed a committee to establish a constitution for the

United States that would end all doubt about congressional authority to conduct war and would provide the structure for a permanent union. The committee's proposal, composed largely by John Dickinson, called for a legislature in which each state would have one vote. The new congress would have fairly broad powers, but not the power to tax—Americans were still tax-shy. Instead, it might ask the states for contributions proportional to their population.

The Dickinson scheme immediately came under attack. Delegates from large states complained that small states would be overrepresented since each, regardless of population, would have one vote in the proposed congress. At the same time, states with large slave populations thought that basing financial contributions on total population was unfair. Slaves, they pointed out, were only property, not citizens, and so should not be counted.

The major stumbling block to adoption of the Dickinson plan, however, was its provision for ownership and management of western lands. It gave to the proposed congress the power to set westward limits to the states, to grant lands to private parties in regions beyond those limits, and to create new states in the West. This scheme stepped on many toes. Seven states claimed that their charters gave them boundaries that extended well into the trans-Appalachian region. Virginia alone claimed the region known as Kentucky and most of what would later be the states of Ohio, Indiana, Illinois, Michigan, and Wisconsin. Six states, on the other hand—New Hampshire, New Jersey, Rhode Island, Pennsylvania, Delaware, and Maryland—had no claims to western lands and generally favored their control by Congress. Why, they asked, should the common struggle to win independence lead to a few states grabbing the western domain that all had fought for? Marylanders and Pennsylvanians had an additional reason for favoring congressional control: Many were investors in northwestern lands bought from the Indians and worried that if Virginia's claims prevailed their purchases would be void.

The opponents of the Dickinson plan delayed its consideration until the fall of 1777. This time it passed, but with modifications. Each state would continue to have one vote in Congress. But Congress would not be allowed to set westward limits to the states, and state contributions to the central treasury would be based not on population but on the value of improved lands in each state.

This modified scheme won the support of twelve states by the end of 1778. Maryland, however, refused to go along with it because her big neighbor, Virginia, still retained title to the lion's share of the upper Mississippi Valley. Months of jockeying followed until finally the Virginia delegates agreed to accept congressional control of the western region. Soon afterward the Virginia legislature formally ceded its western lands to Congress. Finally, in March 1781, with Maryland's objections withdrawn, Congress announced the formal adoption of the Articles of Confederation.

The Articles were a clear improvement over the old arrangements. Most important, they formalized the union of the American states. In specific terms, they gave legal standing to several powers that the Continental Congress had exercised earlier. The Confederation Congress could conduct war and foreign affairs, make commercial treaties, and negotiate with the Indians. It could borrow and coin money and issue bills of credit. The Articles also gave Congress the new power to manage public lands in the West.

Yet many imperfections remained. The new government consisted of only a legislature; it had no separate executive or judicial branches. And not all of the new Congress's powers were exclusive. The states could continue to deal directly with foreign governments and engage in war with Congress's consent. And even without it, they could borrow, maintain mints, and issue bills of credit. The states also had the sole right to legislate in matters concerning debts, contracts, and family affairs. Most important of all, they alone could levy taxes. And if experience showed that changes in the Articles were desirable, they would be hard to make; amendments required the consent of every state.

Still, the Articles of Confederation were a substantial move toward American national unity. Until the middle of the eighteenth century the notion of a common national identity had been weak in America. Colonists often had closer contacts with residents of England or the West Indies than with their fellow "continentals." After 1763 their sense of common interests and needs had grown, and after 1775 the Revolution had reinforced continental ties and sentiments. Many young men serving in the Revolutionary forces saw more of America in a few months than their parents had in a lifetime. In Washington, Jefferson, Adams, and Franklin they found national heroes to praise and admire. The Continental Congress had not fully reflected these changes in attitudes. It had been a makeshift, a purely voluntary association entered into to deal with the imperial crisis. Now, with the Articles of Confederation, for the first time there was a permanent American government, one that would speak for the citizens of all the states.

The feeling of a common nationality remained incomplete, however, and in 1781 Americans continued to talk of Virginia, New York, or Massachusetts as "their country." The weaknesses of the Articles reflected Americans' still limited national allegiance. But they were an important milestone in a steady development that would not be completed until 1865.

The growing sense of a common nationality was only one of many changes that the war initiated. As Americans looked around them between 1775 and 1783, many were certain that they were also witnessing a social revolution. American Loyalists, particularly, detected radical change everywhere. The rebels, they believed, were more intent on overthrowing the social order than in righting the wrongs of imperial government. The Reverend Samuel Peters of Connecticut called the Patriots "ungovernable, righteous and high-handed moberenes." Another Yankee Loyalist saw Patriot control of Massachusetts after 1775 as the triumph of the rabble:

> 'Everything I see is laughable, cursable, and damnable; my pew in the church is converted into a pork tub; my house into a den of rebels, thieves and lice, my farm in possession of the very worst of all God's creatures; my few debts all gone to the devil with my debtors.'

The suffering these Tories had endured at the hands of their rebel fellow Americans doubtless colored their attitudes. But even Patriots felt uneasy about the class resentment and the "levelling spirit" that disorder and change had brought to the surface. Langdon Carter of Virginia worriedly reported to Washington that some Patriots in his neighborhood wanted "a form of government that, by being independent of rich men, every man would then be able to do as he pleased." John Adams, after recounting his meeting with the disrespectful "Horse Jockey," described earlier, exclaimed: "Surely we must guard against this Spirit and these Principles or We shall repent of all our Conduct. . . ."

Carter, Adams, and other moderates feared that what had begun as a dispute over the governing of the empire was turning into a social revolution. A number of modern historians, too, have seen the War of Independence as an internal revolution. As one, Carl Becker, expressed it, the war with Britain was as much over "who shall rule at home" as over "home-rule."

A Revolutionary Experience? The French Revolution of 1789 and the Russian Revolution of 1917 are prototypes of what most of us consider *social revolutions*. These events are abrupt and often violent overthrows of an elite that has monopolized power and enjoyed most of a society's wealth and privileges. Their successors, the new rulers, claiming to speak for the poor and the powerless, expel or exterminate the old "oppressors," seize their property, and distribute it among "the people." Ignoring the issue of whether such revolutions in fact ever precisely fit the prototype formula, let

Many Loyalists fled the colonies, but those who remained behind found the Revolution a trying time. Here a Virginia merchant signs a nonimportation agreement to escape being tarred and feathered.

us consider whether the model resembles the course of events in America between 1775 and 1783. Was the American struggle for independence a social revolution?

The term revolution *does* fit some of what took place during these years. The fate of the American Loyalists, about 20 percent of the population, resembles the fate of the French and Russian elites at the end of the eighteenth century and the beginning of the twentieth, respectively. During and immediately after the Revolutionary War, some 80,000 Loyalists fled the United States to settle in Upper Canada (present-day Ontario), the Canadian Maritime Provinces, England, and the West Indies. Often they left hurriedly, just before the Patriot mob intent on hanging or tar-and-feathering arrived. Many abandoned their property—which the Patriot state governments promptly confiscated—or sold it in a panic at knockdown prices. This exile and confiscation or forced sale of property looks very much like social revolution. By removing an elite of rich landowners, prosperous attorneys, and successful merchants and dividing their property among those, presumably poorer, Americans who remained, surely America became more democratic and more equal.

The facts only partially support such a conclusion, however. Loyalists were not all from the upper crust. They came from every sector of colonial society. Many of the leading Tories—De Lanceys, De Peysters, and Crugers in New York; Shippens, Penns, and Allens in Pennsylvania, for example—certainly were "high-toned" folk. Rich merchants and landlords, successful lawyers, royal officials, and many of the Anglican clergy supported the British cause. On the other hand, many poor people, especially in rural areas, also chose to fight for the king. In New York, the tenants of the Hudson Valley landlords were promised the lands of Patriot patroons if they remained loyal, and many did. In the back country of the Carolinas, where small farmers bitterly resented the political domination of the provinces by the rich Patriot leaders on the seaboard, there were yeoman Loyalists. Many of these people during the early 1770s had taken up arms against the coastal elite, and they did not forget their resentments when the War for Independence erupted. There were even black Tories. Lured by promises of freedom if they deserted their masters and fought the rebels, thousands of blacks joined the crown's forces. So alarming was this defection that, to counter it, Congress reversed Washington's policy of rejecting black enlistees in the Continental Army. Thereafter, black soldiers, both slaves and free men, fought in the American army. Nevertheless, many blacks continued to prefer the king. When the war ended, hundreds of them refused to remain in the land where they had been enslaved and departed for Canada or the Caribbean like other Loyalists.

Patriots, too, came from both the highest and lowest ends of colonial society. Slaves, as we noted, fought for the Patriot cause, as did seamen, apprentices, artisans, and journeymen of the port towns. But so did a large portion of the colonial elite, from the planters of the South to the great merchants of New England and the middle colonies. As for the middle class of small farmers and shopkeepers, it was they, or at least their sons, who formed the backbone of the Continental Army. In short, the Patriots were anything but "a rabble," as some Tories claimed. They were a cross section of the American people.

What this evidence points to is reasonably clear. There were only marginal differences between the social standing of those who supported independence and stayed in America and those who fought it and left. The Tory exodus did not deprive the country of a ruling class as did the departure of emigrés from France in the 1790's and "white Russians" from the land of the czars in 1917. The exodus, accordingly, lends little support to the idea of an American social revolution between 1775 and 1783.

And what of the redistribution of wealth, the second standard by which we may identify a social revolution? The property of many Loyalist grandees, especially those who fled to the British lines during the war, was indeed taken by state governments. Pennsylvania confiscated the Penn family's lands, reputed to be worth £1 million, and gave the

heirs only £130,000 as compensation. Maryland expropriated the property of Lord Baltimore's heirs, and the rebel government of Virginia seized the giant Fairfax estate. Declaring 117 persons guilty of disloyalty, Georgia confiscated their property. New York took over the valuable property of the De Lanceys in Manhattan.

Did these seizures revolutionize existing property-holding patterns? Probably not. Late eighteenth-century America was not, after all, a society of a few great landlords and a vast landless peasantry, like France in 1789 and Russia in 1917. Many people already owned land, and the amount confiscated from the Tories could not have affected the balance very much. Even if every acre seized had been handed over to the landless, it would not have done much to equalize land-holding. Besides, when the states sold the confiscated farm acres and town lots, they did not generally go to the poor or the "common folk." Much of it, it seems, was snapped up by Patriot landholders or speculators. Existing inequalities, if anything, were probably magnified by the resale of confiscated Tory real estate.

It seems clear, then, that the expulsion and expropriation of the Loyalists did little to change the nature of property-holding in America or drastically alter the social profile of the community. But this is not to say that the Revolution did not liberalize American life. Indeed, there is good evidence that it helped in many ways to make America a more democratic community.

Democratization. Even if the Tory exiles included the "lower orders" and the middle class, historian Gordon Wood believes that they included disproportionately the families at the very apex of colonial life. Though not numerous, they were particularly powerful and their departure broke the crust allowing new families to rise. Unlike the old, these depended more on merit and achievement and less on "connections" for their wealth and power.

More significant, perhaps, was the growing concern for equity and social justice that accompanied the Revolution.

Slavery, the most blatant social inequity in America, was weakened by the Revolution. In the South thousands of slaves won their freedom by cooperating with the British. Unfortunately, slavery did survive south of Pennsylvania, where slaves were numerous and where the institution was tightly woven into the social fabric. Though temporarily weakened, it eventually recovered its strength. In the North, however, it collapsed under the blows of war and revolution.

Although white Americans were mostly concerned with their own rights and freedoms, the dispute with Britain following 1763 forced them to ponder the issue of human liberty. Most Patriots found themselves able to protest colonial servitude to Britain and at the same time excuse or forget the slaves' bondage. But some could not. How can we

Benedict Arnold

Arnold was a respected name in colonial New England. The first American Arnold had been associated with Roger Williams in the founding of Rhode Island. His son, the first Benedict Arnold, was a rich merchant of Newport. Thereafter, though the family's fortunes fluctuated, Arnolds would remain prominent citizens of southern New England through four generations. The Benedict Arnold born in 1741 would make the family name synonymous with "traitor."

The fourth Benedict Arnold grew up in Norwich in southern Connecticut. As a child he was a leader, recognized by his neighbors as "bold, enterprising, ambitious, active as lightning." Though apprenticed to a merchant, his spirit of adventure led him to join the American forces during the French and Indian War. He served briefly during the French attack on Fort William at Lake George, returning soon after to complete his apprenticeship.

Despite his unauthorized flight to join the army, Arnold pleased his employers, the Lathrops, and in 1762, when he had completed his apprenticeship, they gave him £500 to establish an apothecary shop in New Haven. Arnold did well there. He not only sold medicines but he also invested in the West Indies trade and soon had a flourishing business selling horses and mules to the sugar planters of Antigua, St. Croix, and other Caribbean islands. In 1767 he married Peggy Mansfield,

daughter of one of New Haven's respected merchants, and entered into business partnership with his father-in-law.

Like many New England merchants, Arnold was a passionate opponent of British imperial measures after 1763. In 1764 he led a mob protesting the Sugar Act. In 1774 he denounced the Boston massacre as "the most cruel, wanton, and inhuman murders. . . ." When news of Lexington reached New Haven, Arnold left with sixty militiamen under his command to join George Washington's forces outside of Boston.

Arnold rose rapidly in the ranks of the Continental Army. He fought at Ticonderoga as a colonel and in December 1775 led a hopeless attack during a snowstorm against the British bastion of Quebec, garrisoned by a larger force than his own. The attack failed, and Arnold's co-commander, General Richard Montgomery, was killed. Arnold was forced to lift the siege, but despite this failure, Congress recognized his skill and gallantry by promoting him to brigadier general. The following year he further distinguished himself by helping to stop Guy Carleton's advance from Canada on New York City. In 1777 Arnold commanded American troops in the battles that led to the defeat of Burgoyne at Saratoga, the campaign often judged the turning point of the war.

At no time during these tumultuous months was there any outward sign that General Arnold was anything but a fiercely loyal Patriot. But his sense of grievance had begun to build. In February 1777 Congress passed him over for a promotion to major general. He eventually got the promotion, but the delay rankled. His real disaffection, however, dates from mid-1778, when he was appointed military commander at Philadelphia, then newly evacuated by the British.

The general's first wife had died three years before, and Arnold soon became enamored of Peggy Shippen, the beautiful eighteen-year-old daughter of Edward Shippen, a prominent Philadelphia lawyer and admiralty judge allied before the war with the colony's proprietors, the Penn family. Despite this connection and his role as an officer of the crown, Judge Shippen, a timid man, had tried to stay neutral in the evolving struggle between the Patriots and the British government. When the first Continental Congress met in Philadelphia, Shippen invited the delegates to dinner. Then, when the British occupied the town in September 1777, Judge Shippen was happy to welcome the young English officers to his house to pay court to his daughter. Among those who vied for a smile from the lovely Peggy was Lieutenant John André, the young, dashing aide-de-camp of the British general Charles Grey.

The British evacuated Philadelphia in June 1778. Arnold, as American military commander, moved into

---

"reconcile the exercise of SLAVERY with our *professions of freedom*," Richard Wells, a Philadelphia Patriot, asked pointedly. John Allen, a Baptist minister in Massachusetts, accused his fellow Americans of hypocrisy in refusing to admit the evil of slavery. "Blush . . . ye trifling patriots! who are making a vain parade of being advocates for the liberties of mankind, [and] . . . are . . . thus making a mockery

of your profession by trampling on the sacred and natural rights and privileges of Africans."

Happily, the attack on slavery went beyond words. In 1775, Quakers, who had always rejected human inequality, established the first antislavery society in Philadelphia. Five years later Pennsylvania passed the first law providing for the gradual freeing of slaves. In 1783 the Massachusetts

the mansion formerly owned by the Penns and was soon emulating General Howe's grand style with housekeeper, coachman, groom, seven other servants, and a fine coach-and-four. Such an establishment could not be supported on the salary of a Continental officer, and General Arnold entered into several morally dubious deals with merchants in New York and other British-occupied towns to trade in illegal goods. These shady schemes got him into trouble with the Pennsylvania authorities and with Congress. To clear his name Arnold demanded a court-martial. Though declared innocent of most charges, he earned a public reprimand from Washington. During this time he also began to associate with Philadelphians who favored a negotiated peace without independence.

Inevitably the middle-aged general was drawn to the young and vivacious Peggy Shippen, who belonged to the circle of near-Tories. Ambitious for social distinction and wealth, Peggy was attracted to Arnold in turn. In April 1779 they were married in a simple ceremony appropriate to the now strained pocketbook of Edward Shippen, and went to live in Arnold's newly purchased mansion, Mount Pleasant, on the banks of the Schuylkill.

It was while in Philadelphia that Arnold began to correspond with British General Sir Henry Clinton, commander in chief of his majesty's forces in America. Arnold's motives for betraying his country were clearly mixed. First, came money. The general found good living irresistible, and with a young, extravagant wife to please, he was desperate for cash. He was also angry at the mistreatment he felt he had received at the hands of Congress and the Pennsylvania authorities. He may also have had less ignoble motives than lucre and resentment. As a good New England Protestant, Arnold despised the alliance with Catholic France and believed it tainted the American cause irretrievably. Better to abandon independence and return to the British fold than to accept association with the despised French.

From mid-1779 through 1780 Arnold sold information to André, now Clinton's aide, concerning American and French naval and troop movements, the disposition of supplies, and the identities of French spies in the British camp. Peggy conducted her own spying operation and at one point was paid £350 for her services. The couple's value to the British leaped when, in the summer of 1780, Washington appointed Arnold commander of the vital American post at West Point on the Hudson. Here was a real prize indeed, and Arnold demanded £20,000 for its surrender to the British. Clinton sent André to negotiate. On the way back from the meeting, André was intercepted by American militia while in civilian clothes. When Arnold learned of the capture, he fled to a nearby British ship. André was tried as a spy and executed in October 1780.

During the remainder of the war Arnold served as brigadier general of Loyalist forces in the British army. In late 1780 he conducted a series of ruthless Tory raids in Virginia. Governor Thomas Jefferson offered a £5,000 reward for his capture. The following year Arnold led Tory attacks against the Americans in Connecticut. Soon after, he and Peggy sailed for England, where they remained permanently.

Like many Loyalist emigrés they found life away from their native land a grim trial. In their last years the Arnolds associated with the circle of Loyalist exiles in London. They found some comfort in these relationships, but it never consoled them for the self-inflicted wounds of betraying their native country. Arnold never received more than £5,000 or £6,000 for his treason, though he frequently petitioned the British government for a more generous reward. The best he could get was a land grant in Canada in 1797. He never visited his Canadian lands and never profited by them. Peggy's life in England was not happy. She kept in touch by letter with her family in Philadelphia, but missed her native city desperately. In late 1789 she visited Philadelphia, hoping to find a spirit of forgiveness. She was disappointed. Many of her old friends cut her and she went back to England after a few months, never to return. Toward the end of her life Peggy became a semi-invalid.

Arnold tried to get a military command from the British government during the Napoleonic Wars, but failed, though his grown sons were more fortunate. He turned to business once again, and for a time was active in the West Indies trade. His ventures did not restore his fortunes, however, and when he died in 1801, Peggy was left to pay off his many debts. Some would say he had paid the price for treason.

courts interpreted the state constitution as prohibiting slavery, and thereafter slavery was illegal in the Bay State. Other northern states soon followed these leaders, either ending slavery by judicial act or by adopting gradual emancipation laws. And even in the South slavery was affected by the Revolutionary ferment of egalitarianism. Prominent Patriots like Jefferson and Henry Laurens, imbued with the ideals of the Enlightenment, attacked the system. Several southern legislatures passed laws making it easier for masters to free (manumit) their own slaves and restricting the slave trade in various ways. By the end of the century, in every state from Pennsylvania northward, slavery was on the way to extinction, and it seemed to some Americans that even in the South it was in decline.

The reluctance of Americans to enlist slaves in the military did not extend to free blacks. This picture of a free black Continental sailor, painted in 1779, was discovered recently in Newport, Rhode Island.

The attack on slavery and its gradual disappearance in the North was only one sign of the revolutionary zeal for freedom. Another was the decline of indentured servitude, the system of unfree labor that had met the work needs of the colonies and helped facilitate the transfer of people across the Atlantic from Europe. In the new atmosphere of challenge to authority many Americans began to think that keeping people in near bondage, even if only for a period of years, was anachronistic. Believing that indenture was "contrary to . . . the idea of liberty" America had "so happily established," in 1784 a group in New York raised a public subscription for a shipload of servants so they would not have to accept the condition of indentured servitude.

Lawbreakers too benefited from the changes in attitudes awakened by the struggle for independence. Before the Revolution—and, in truth, for years after—men and women convicted of felonies were often subject to brutal penalties. Criminals were placed in stocks, branded,

whipped, and mutilated. The list of capital crimes with death as the penalty was appallingly long. After 1776, however, several states reduced the number of crimes punishable by hanging and replaced torture and the lash with imprisonment. In Pennsylvania, soon after independence, some effort was even made to replace harsh punishments with reformation of offenders. The purpose of sentencing, said the state legislature, should be "to reclaim rather than destroy. . . ." Years would pass before other states would imitate Pennsylvania—and the hope rings hollow today—but clearly in this area too the Revolution was a minor watershed.

Finally, there was the improvement in women's lot. During the war American women had sought to contribute to the Patriot cause in age-old ways. They made blankets and shirts for Washington's army and spun woolen cloth to offset restricted British imports. They took over jobs and businesses in the absence of fathers and husbands. "I find

Slavery Struck Down

Though it was not a deep-running social upheaval, the American Revolution wiped away vestiges of the past's privileged order. Yet none of the social changes it produced was more significant than the blow against slavery north of the Mason-Dixon line. In most of those northern states that took steps to end slavery during the Revolution and immediately thereafter, the process was accomplished by act of the legislature. In Massachusetts, however, slavery ended as the result of a judge's decision as to the meaning of a provision of the state constitution of 1781. The case before the Massachusetts court involved an assault by a white man on a black man. The white man was indicted, but pleaded not guilty on the grounds that the man he had struck was his slave. This plea induced the judge, Chief Justice William Cushing, to consider the question of whether slavery legally existed in the commonwealth. His decision, expressed briefly below, reflects the liberating spirit of the Revolutionary era.

"CUSHING, C. J. As to the doctrine of slavery and the right of Christians to hold Africans in perpetual servitude, and sell and treat them as we do our horses and cattle, [it is true that it] has been heretofore countenanced by the Province Laws . . . but nowhere is it expressly enacted or established. It has been a usage—a usage which took its origins from the practice of some of the European nations, and the regulations of British government respecting the then Colonies, for the benefit of trade and wealth. But whatever sentiments have formerly prevailed in this particular or slid in upon us by the example of others, a different idea has taken place with the people of America, more favorable to the natural rights of mankind, and to that natural, innate desire of Liberty, with which heaven (without regard to color, complexion, or shape of noses . . .) has inspired all the human race. And upon the ground our Constitution of Government, by which the people of this Commonwealth have solemnly bound themselves, sets out with declaring that all men are born free and equal—and that every subject is entitled to liberty and to have it guarded by the laws, as well as life and property—and in short is totally repugnant to the idea of being born slaves. This being the case, I think the idea of slavery is inconsistent with our own conduct and Constitution; and there can be no such thing as perpetual servitude of a rational creature, unless his liberty is forfeited by some criminal conduct or given up by personal consent or contract. . . . *Verdict Guilty*."

DISTRIBUTION OF ASSESSED TAXABLE WEALTH IN CHESTER COUNTY, PENNSYLVANIA, 1760–1802

Data on landholding and wealth before and after the Revolution are not available for all the colonies. Studies on a smaller scale suggest, however, that the resale of abandoned and confiscated Loyalist property did not redistribute wealth to the poorer classes. In Chester County, in fact, the rich as a class were better off after the Revolution than before it.

Taxpayers	PERCENTAGE OF TOTAL WEALTH HELD IN		
	1760	1782	1800–1802
Top 10%	29.9	33.6	38.3
Next 30%	43.3	44.5	44.2
Next 30%	20.5	17.3	13.7
Lowest 10%	6.3	4.7	3.9

James Lemon and Gary Nash, "The Distribution of Wealth in Eighteenth-Century America: A Century of Changes in Chester County, Pennsylvania, 1693–1802," Journal of Social History, vol. 2 (1968), pp. 1–24. Reprinted by permission.

it necessary to be directress of our husbandry," Abigail Adams wrote her husband John in 1776, and "I hope in time to have the reputation of being as good a farmer as my partner has of being a good statesman."

They also expanded their horizons. Some became active in fund-raising for the Continental Army or participated in other Patriot causes. Others developed interests in public issues they had neglected before and joined political discussion groups. A very few women actually engaged in combat. Mary Ludwig Hays McCauley, better known as Molly Pitcher, took her husband's place behind a cannon at the Battle of Monmouth when he was overcome by the heat.

Some women expected their sex to benefit as a group from the war. The spirited Abigail Adams wrote her husband in 1776 that "in the new code of laws" then being considered by Congress—that is, the Articles of Confederation—it was important for the legislators to "remember the ladies and be more generous and favorable to them" than their ancestors had been. "Do not," she urged, "put such unlimited powers in the hands of the husbands."

"A New Touch on the Times," by an anonymous Daughter of Liberty. So great was the temporary improvement in women's status that a very few fought in colonial armies as fully paid regulars. (Collection of the New York Historical Society)

changed charters to constitutions. In some the structural changes were relatively modest—not much more than the replacement of the appointed governor by one elected either by the voters or by the state legislature, and the replacement of the appointed upper house of the colonial legislature by an elected one. In other states there were more sweeping changes. Virginia, Pennsylvania, North Carolina, and Massachusetts ended or reduced the gross underrepresentation of their frontier counties. Pennsylvania, Delaware, North Carolina, Georgia, and Virginia liberalized their franchises so that almost any white male taxpayer, no matter how poor, could vote. Most states reduced the power of the executive branch, considered aristocratic, by taking away the governor's veto over laws passed by the assemblies. In Pennsylvania the shift of power to the legislature was carried the furthest. The Keystone State entirely eliminated the legislature's upper house, thereby concentrating all power in the lower one, and fragmented the executive branch by substituting for the governor an executive council of thirteen members. Virginia and several other states pioneered another important democratic advance: They adopted formal written bills of rights guaranteeing freedom of speech, conscience, assembly, petition, and privacy, as well as the right to trial by jury and other legal safeguards for the individual.

A final democratic innovation, widely adopted in these years, was the constitutional convention, a meeting called for the specific purpose of altering the fundamental frame of government. Only such a convention, it was believed, could validly express the wishes of the people. Its decisions, especially when confirmed by a direct vote of the electors (referendum), took precedence over actions of a mere legislature. First put in practice by Massachusetts during the Revolutionary era, the concept that a convention best expressed the will of the people governed the call for the federal Constitutional Convention in 1787. It was a major contribution to democratic theory and practice.

The use of conventions to frame instruments of fundamental law reflected the new idea that in some ultimate sense "the people" alone were the source of power. Republicanism was a related concept. Republicans wished to reduce the role of birth, breeding, rank, and family influence in political life. These seemed relics of colonial days and royal government when, despite the widespread franchise, Americans had acknowledged hereditary authority and had shown deference to officials. Such attributes, said republicans, should no longer count; only talent, virtue, and devotion to the common good should qualify a person for political advancement and high office.

We must qualify the view that the Revolution liberalized political ideology, however. The leaders of the Revolution were carried by the logic of their opposition to

Abigail Adams and those who thought like her would not fully realize their hopes. And yet the war and the forces it released did have some effect on women's circumstances. In New England the rhetoric of freedom led to liberalized divorce laws that placed women on virtually the same plane as men in seeking legal separation from a brutal or unfaithful spouse. In many states, the laws for the first time recognized the equal right of sons and daughters in inheritance and gave women greater control over their property. The years of debate over American rights also stimulated the first feminist questioning of existing female education. In the 1770s, for example, Judith Murray of Gloucester, Massachusetts, charged that traditional upbringing and education for girls trivialized their minds and forced them to rely excessively on their physical attractions. Most of the great battles for female "emancipation" lay in the future. Yet we must not dismiss the revolutionary impulse entirely as a force for female liberation.

New Politics. The political system also felt the liberalizing effects of the great upheaval. As they transformed themselves from provinces to "states," the former colonies

royal government to condemn hereditary privileges, but few of them ever got over their fear of pure democracy, in which numbers alone counted and everyone was politically equal. Though they acknowledged that "the people" were the source of power, they did not include women, blacks, Indians, and men without some property in the term. Moreover, except for a few "violent men"—or, as we would say, radicals—republicans did not believe that elected representatives should submit totally to the wishes of the voters. Instead, they favored a "mixed" government in which the popular voice representing "numbers" would be tempered by "talent" of superior leaders.

Privilege. In several areas of colonial life the law had upheld the privileged position of specific institutions and individuals; here, too, the Revolution had a liberalizing effect.

In those states with an established Anglican Church there was progress toward the complete religious toleration and separation of church and state that we have come to consider peculiarly American. It was inevitable that Anglicanism should lose standing after the Declaration of Independence. It was, after all, the denomination most closely associated with the English crown, and many Anglican clergymen were Loyalists. But the whole idea of an established church had become increasingly distasteful to Patriots. During the war, Jefferson, allied with the state's Baptists, Methodists, and other dissenters, fought to disestablish Anglicanism in Virginia. Afterwards, he and his allies secured passage of the Bill for Establishing Religious Freedom (1786). Other states also disestablished the Anglican church, and several of them removed the remaining restrictions on non-Protestant voting and officeholding.

The Congregationalists were a tougher nut to crack. Though many New Englanders had become Baptists, the religious outsiders at first made little progress toward ending the special status of the region's Congregational churches. Unlike the Anglicans, Congregationalism was not identified with the mother country. In fact, the Congregational clergy had been among the most ardent defenders of the Patriot cause. This close association with the fight against Britain gave the Congregational establishment an extended lease on life. Connecticut did not disestablish the Congregational church until 1818. In Massachusetts its privileged position lasted until 1838. It took more than half a century, then, before New England finally achieved the separation of church and state that came elsewhere during the 1780s and 1790s. Yet on the whole, in religious matters too, the Revolution was a major liberalizing force in American life.

The Revolution also ended *entail* and *primogeniture*, two practices that reinforced economic inequality and privilege. Entailing was a legal procedure that allowed a property holder to forbid his heirs to sell their inheritances. Primogeniture was the practice of favoring the firstborn son in inheritances in the absence of a will providing for a more equal property distribution. Together these two practices were designed to preserve large landholdings and buttress the power and wealth of aristocratic families.

Although both procedures had fallen into partial disuse in the colonies, to men like Jefferson they seemed decrepit relics of feudalism and offensive to a free society. In 1776, Jefferson drafted a law that abolished entail in Virginia. Similar laws were soon adopted in other states. In 1777, the Georgia legislature prohibited primogeniture, and by 1800 the practice was dead everywhere in America.

★ MAKING THE PEACE ★

Much of this liberating change took place against the background of war; peace would bring other challenges and changes to the new nation. But first the terms of peace had to be settled. After Yorktown, American officials wrestled simultaneously with tangled domestic problems and complicated negotiations for peace in Paris.

France and the United States had agreed not to negotiate a separate peace with Great Britain, but both countries found it hard to resist working out their own arrangements. By 1781 the French were tired of the war and beset by financial problems, problems so serious that they would soon threaten the monarchy's survival. Having achieved their prime goal of humbling the arrogant British Empire, they saw little reason to continue the fighting. The Americans too, if conceded their independence, had little reason to fight on. However, there was stubborn Spain. The 1778 treaty with France that brought Spain into the war promised that it be given Gibraltar—the great British fortress guarding the Atlantic entrance of the Mediterranean—if Spanish troops could capture it. But month after month the British defenders held out against the Spanish siege, depriving the Madrid government of its goal. If France stuck by its European ally, it looked as if peace—and American independence—depended on the transfer of a pile of rock.

Fortunately, the American diplomats into whose hands the peace negotiations fell proved adept. In early 1782 Lord North, discredited by the defeat at Yorktown, finally resigned and his successor, the Marquis of Rockingham, prepared to concede independence to America. Rockingham soon died and negotiations with the Americans were taken over by Lord Shelburne, a man willing to accept American independence only as a last resort. But Shelburne miscalculated. He sent to Paris as British negotiator, Richard

Oswald, a philosophical Scottish gentleman, an old friend of Benjamin Franklin from the Philadelphian's London days. Oswald proved to be exceptionally accommodating. When Franklin proposed a settlement that included as "necessary" terms independence "full and complete in every sense," the total evacuation of all British troops from American soil, boundaries that extended to the Mississippi in the west and the Great Lakes to the north, and free access for American fishermen to the Grand Banks off Newfoundland, Oswald saw no objections. Nor did he even balk at one of Franklin's secondary, but "desirable," terms: the concession of Canada to the new American nation!

But difficulties with France soon intervened. Franklin trusted Vergennes, the French foreign minister, but Franklin's colleague, John Jay, who had joined in the Paris negotiations, did not. Jay correctly believed that the French did not intend to make peace until Spain, France's other ally, got what it wanted from the war. But beyond its obligations

to its ally, France wanted different things from the peace than the United States. Seeking to protect their own rights on the Grand Banks, the French were unwilling to stand behind American claims to fishing rights off Newfoundland. Vergennes even seemed ready to accept boundaries for the United States that surrendered much of the lower Mississippi Valley to Spain and conceded the northwest region, the area between the Great Lakes and the Ohio, to Great Britain. As Franklin later stated, such a treaty would have "cooped us up within the Allegheny Mountains."

Hoping to divide its enemies and save Gibraltar, Britain pushed its separate negotiations with the United States. On October 5, 1782, Jay and Oswald, without France, agreed on a draft for preliminary articles of peace, not to go into effect, however, until France and Britain had entered into a similar preliminary agreement. The terms at their core included all of Franklin's earlier demands. In London the British ministry insisted that compensation for Loyalist

At Versailles a lady offers Benjamin Franklin a laurel wreath, perhaps to replace the fur cap he often wore to charm the French court. Franklin, a marvelous diplomat, secured formal recognition of the United States and a military and commercial alliance with France; later he helped negotiate the Treaty of Paris, which brought the war to a close.

North America, 1783

property confiscated during the war and repayment in British money for all debts owed by Americans to British creditors be added to these terms. John Adams, now in Paris to join the negotiations, urged acceptance of these features, and they were included in the final draft.

As finalized, the peace articles acknowledged American independence. The new nation's boundaries would be generous. In the west they would reach the Mississippi; to the south they would extend to Spanish Florida. To the north, in the western portion, its border would touch the Great Lakes, and in the northeast it would run along an ill-defined line roughly corresponding to the present Canadian-American boundary. The British agreed to allow Americans to fish off Canadian territorial waters and promised to evacuate American territory still under British occupation "with all convenient speed." In return, the United States promised to place "no lawful impediment" in the way of repayment by Americans of debts owed British creditors and agreed to recommend that the states restore to the Loyalists their civil rights and their confiscated property.

Before signing, the American negotiators considered whether to first inform the French of the peace terms and ask their permission to proceed. Besides the moral obligation enjoined by the 1778 Franco-American treaty, Congress had so instructed them. But they decided against it for fear that France, with its own agenda, would scuttle the agreement. Yet they could not cut France out entirely. After the treaty was initialled, Franklin went to tell Vergennes of their action. Sheepishly admitting some "impropriety" to the French Foreign Minister, he urged him strongly to accept the agreement. The French by now were thoroughly tired of the war, and Vergennes chose not to be offended. Instead, he approached the Spanish ambassador in Paris and told him that American perfidy had left France unable to support Spain's claims to Gibraltar any longer. The Count de Aranda saw the light. With this hurdle pushed aside, Spain and France concluded a peace with Great Britain. On September 3, 1783, all these preliminary negotiations, including the Anglo-American articles of agreement, were incorporated into the Treaty of Paris. The great struggle for independence was over.

★ CONCLUSIONS ★

At news of the peace, a wave of elation and thanksgiving surged through the country. So intense was the joy in Philadelphia that prudent citizens urged the city fathers to restrain the celebration to keep it from getting out of hand.

The jubilant mood could not last. The infant nation now confronted the problems of repairing the damage of seven long years of war and learning how to function as an independent state. The difficulties would be formidable. The war had caused extensive physical destruction to both the cities and the countryside. In the South the British had carried off thousands of slaves and destroyed dikes and dams. New Jersey, "cockpit of the Revolution," where so many battles had been fought, had been ravaged by advancing and retreating armies. All this damage would have to be repaired.

There would be social mending to do as well. Loyalists—those who had not fled for good—would have to be reconciled to the new regime. Several thousand free blacks in the North would have to be absorbed into the larger society. But on the whole, these adjustments would be minor. American society had not undergone a true social revolution. The war had accelerated processes that had long been moving the American community toward greater democracy, legal equality, and religious toleration. Between

1776 and 1783, religious establishments had been severely undercut, slavery had been eroded, the treatment of women and prisoners had improved, and the few surviving vestiges of feudalism had been swept away. Yet compared with the fundamental upheaval that marked the great French Revolution of 1789 and the Russian and Chinese revolutions of our own century, these were relatively small changes.

But if America did not experience a major social revolution, it did undergo a political one. From a colony it became an independent nation. The Revolutionary War was primarily a colonial war of independence. If it resembles any upheaval of recent times, it is the decolonization struggles of African and Asian peoples after World War II. And the problems that the new nation would face belonged largely in the same realm: the political. Though the war had advanced the unity of English-speaking America and helped create a sense of shared nationality, it had not forged a cohesive nation. Previous republics had always been small, homogeneous city-states. Never had one been so huge in extent. Could this unusual creation called the United States, with its 900,000 square miles and 3 million people, survive and prosper as an independent republic? In the next few years the issue would be put to the test.

******** **FOR FURTHER READING** ********

Howard H. Peckham. *The War for Independence: A Military History* (1958)
A brief narrative of the military aspects of the Revolution. Peckham takes note of the weaknesses of both sides.

Samuel Eliot Morison. *John Paul Jones: A Sailor's Biography* (1959)
This portrait of the Revolutionary War sea captain also describes the growing pains of the tiny American navy. The fight between Jones's *Bonhomme Richard* and the superior *Serapis* is splendidly rendered—as are the inventory of Jones's ship and his adventures ashore with women.

Henry S. Commager and Richard B. Morris, editors. *The Spirit of '76: The Story of the American Revolution as Told by Participants* (1958)
This is history straight from the sources. It is a vast miscellany of letters, diaries, journals, diplomatic correspondence, parliamentary debates, and more. The editors provide a long introduction.

Alfred F. Young, editor. *The American Revolution* (1976)
A volume of essays emphasizing class conflict in several states during the Revolution. Several contributors detect a "popular" ideology, opposed to government by the rich, and see this as a potent source of Revolutionary zeal.

James Franklin Jameson. *The American Revolution Considered as a Social Movement* (1925)
The classic statement of the social dimensions of the American Revolution. Jameson sees the Revolution as a powerful engine of social as well as political change. In many ways the book is dated, but it is still the takeoff point for any discussion of the issue it deals with.

Richard B. Morris. *The American Revolution Reconsidered* (1967)
This work, originally a series of lectures, is an attempt to update Jameson. On the whole, it suggests that the Revolution was less revolutionary than Jameson claimed.

Mary Beth Norton. *Liberty's Daughters: The Revolutionary Experience of American Women, 1750–1800* (1980)
An important and interesting book that supports the view that the Revolution—like other wars—helped to improve the lot and increase the freedom of women. Professor Norton does not emphasize new laws so much as new attitudes.

Arthur Zilversmit. *The First Emancipation: The Abolition of Slavery in the North* (1967)
The best study of the process, extending well beyond the years of the Revolution, by which the northern states excluded slavery from their borders.

Jack Sosin. *The Revolutionary Frontier, 1763–1783* (1967)
Tells the important story of the West in both the origins and the course of the Revolution.

Gordon Wood. *The Creation of the American Republic, 1776–1787* (1968)
An important reinterpretation of the Revolutionary period as well as the Confederation era that emphasizes the rise of a republican ideology. Difficult, somewhat disorganized, but rewarding to the serious student.

Kenneth Roberts. *Arundel* (1930) and *Rabble in Arms* (1933)
Benedict Arnold is a principal character in these two entertaining historical novels. Most of *Arundel* deals with Arnold's heroic Canadian expedition to capture Quebec. *Rabble in Arms* ends with the Battle of Saratoga. The work is sympathetic to the Loyalists and Arnold, though he was to become the archtraitor of American history.

John R. Alden. *A History of the American Revolution* (1969)
This is probably the best single-volume history of the Revolution.

Richard Morris. *The Peacemakers: The Great Powers and American Independence* (1965)
Deals with the diplomacy of the Revolution.

Arthur Bowler. *Logistics and the Failure of British Arms in America, 1775–1783* (1975)
A specialized study of the military aspects of the Revolution that points the finger at supply problems as the reason for British defeat.

Gordon S. Wood. *The Radicalism of the American Revolution* (1992)
In this more recent book by Gordon Wood the thesis of a real revolution in 1775–1783 is restated in a sophisticated way that meets some of the skepticism of critics in the past.

6★

THE ORIGINS
OF THE CONSTITUTION

By Popular Demand?

1781	Articles of Confederation ratified • Congress proposes a duty on imports to raise revenue, but it is defeated by Rhode Island
1783	Congress proposes another import duty; it is defeated by New York • Fearing attack by unpaid American troops, Congress flees Philadelphia • Robert Morris sends *Empress of China* to open trade with China
1784	Spain refuses to allow Americans to transship their goods from New Orleans
1785	Congress adopts the Land Ordinance of 1785, a model for future federal land policy • Maryland and Virginia sign an agreement about navigation rights on the Potomac and in the Chesapeake Bay
1785–87	Shays's Rebellion in Massachusetts
1787	The Ordinance of 1787 prohibits slavery in the Northwest Territory and establishes that new states carved from it will be fully equal to the original states • Constitutional Convention meets at Philadelphia; state delegations approve the completed draft of the Constitution
1788	Delaware, Pennsylvania, New Jersey, Georgia, and Connecticut ratify the Constitution • Massachusetts ratifies with a request for a Bill of Rights • Rhode Island rejects • Maryland, South Carolina, and New Hampshire ratify • Congress certifies adoption of the Constitution • Virginia ratifies with a request for a Bill of Rights • New York ratifies • Congress adopts the first ten amendments to the Constitution (the Bill of Rights) • Rhode Island and North Carolina ratify
1789	George Washington becomes president; John Adams, vice president

The great nineteenth-century English statesman William Gladstone once described the American federal Constitution as "the most remarkable work—in modern times—to have been produced by the human intellect at a single stroke in its application to political affairs." Clearly not every American has agreed with this estimate or we would not have fought the Civil War or amended the document twenty-six times. But few Americans today would deny that our unique frame of government has served the nation extraordinarily well over more than two centuries.

From a modern vantage, then, it does not seem remarkable that Americans gathered at Philadelphia in 1787 to compose the Constitution. Yet it required a tremendous act of faith and will to abandon the Articles of Confederation and replace them with a new political framework for the federal union. Six years earlier the states had ratified the Articles. Although by no means perfect, they had established the sort of political union most Americans wanted—indeed, to the end of the Confederation period, the Articles would have loyal supporters. Obviously many Americans must have had a change of heart. Who were these people and what caused them to alter their views?

The origins of the federal Constitution have interested historians for many years. In the nineteenth century it was usually held that the failings and inadequacies of the Articles were so obvious that all could see them. John Fiske called the Confederation period—the time between the British surrender at Yorktown in 1781 and the establishment in 1788 of the new federal government under the Constitution—the "Critical Period." He believed that during these years the nation was "rapidly drifting toward anarchy." Because the Articles were unable to provide the political and social glue to hold the country together, the calling of the Constitutional Convention and the adoption of the document it produced were merely the logical and valid results of broad public concern. The Constitution, in effect, carried to its natural conclusion the nationalistic trend of the Revolution itself.

Fiske's view reflected the self-congratulation that was common among nineteenth-century Americans. In our own century this gave way to greater skepticism. Just before World War I Charles A. Beard attacked Fiske's interpretation. The Critical Period, he said, was not so critical. The United States was "in many respects steadily recovering order and prosperity," and "the economic condition of the country seemed to be improving." Ultimately, he wrote, only one important group had suffered under the Articles: those who held the wartime securities of the Continental and state governments. These individuals—few in number but pow-

erful—wanted the public debts fully repaid. They feared that the state governments and the Confederation Congress would not be able to withstand pressure from taxpayers to scale the debts down. Taxpayers had the advantage of numbers over creditors, and a democratic system in which each man's vote counted would favor their cause. The only way for the creditors to protect their interests was to establish a strong central government that would limit the power of numbers and have sufficient taxing power to collect the public debts. The net effect of a new constitution would be to check what the merchant-creditor class considered an excess of democracy following the Revolution. The American federal Constitution of 1787, Beard and his disciples insisted, was a reactionary document intended to restore to an elite the power they had lost during the Revolution. It was not called for by wide popular demand or justified by broad national need; instead, it was intended to protect the economic interests of the powerful.

Let us examine the state of the nation in the 1780s to see which of these interpretations is more convincing, to see how and why the Constitution replaced the Articles of Confederation and became the fundamental law under which Americans have lived for more than two centuries.

★ AMERICA IN THE 1780s ★

Agriculture. Peace brought economic troubles to American farmers. During the war years armies had swept across the countryside, destroying fences and barns, burning crops and farmhouses. On the frontier Indian raids had pushed back the line of settled farming. In the Carolinas the dikes that controlled the tidal streams in the rice country had been damaged by hostile troops and by neglect. In Virginia the flight of Loyalist slaves and the removal of others by the British had seriously depleted the labor force on the plantations. In 1783 America faced a major repair job.

In time the physical damage and the labor disruption were mended, but political changes continued to cause difficulties for American agriculture. The severing of imperial ties had unforeseen consequences for farmers. Once the war ended, the British government removed the bounty that it had paid indigo planters, and indigo virtually disappeared as a crop from the Carolina coast. The bounty on naval stores also ceased. At the same time Britain imposed a high tax on American tobacco. Still more damaging was British commercial retaliation. Before independence American agricultural commodities had found a ready market in the British West Indies. But then Americans had been subjects of King

This fan is reputed to have been manufactured in China in 1784 to the specifications of Captain John Greene of the Empress of China. Note the picture of the vessel left of center. (Collection of the New York Historical Society)

George. Now they were foreigners, and they no longer could expect special rights in British-controlled markets. Shortly before the war ended, the English government clamped down on the export of many mainland commodities to their Caribbean possessions. Products such as horses, cattle, hogs, poultry, beans, potatoes, flour, rice, and oats could be sent from the mainland only in "British built ships owned by His Majesty's subjects"; cured meats, fish, and dairy products were excluded totally. Farmers of Massachusetts, the Connecticut and Hudson valleys, eastern Pennsylvania, and the grain-growing areas of the Chesapeake were thus deprived of markets for their surpluses. Unsold crops piled up; farm prices fell.

Frontier farmers beyond the Appalachians also faced difficult times after the war. By the middle of the 1780s thousands of settlers lived across the mountains in what is now Kentucky and Tennessee. These people needed salt, guns, powder, shot, plows, cloth, notions, and small luxuries, all produced in the East or in Europe. To pay for these they grew extra grain, raised extra livestock, or gathered furs and cut lumber from the surrounding forests. But how could they get these goods to market? As the crow flies, the farmers of eastern Kentucky and Tennessee were not very far from their customers on the seaboard. Unfortunately the trip by pack animals across the Allegheny and Blue Ridge mountains was hard, slow, and expensive.

The Mississippi River and its tributaries were the natural links between the western farmers and the outside world. The westerners could load their products on rafts or flatboats, float them south with the current, and land them at New Orleans to be shipped to the east coast or the Caribbean by oceangoing vessels. But under the 1763 treaty ending the French and Indian War, Spain controlled the mouth of the Mississippi; and Spain was unwilling to allow Americans to land their wares at New Orleans for such a purpose except on payment of a stiff tax. Although the Spanish had supported the Americans during the Revolution, they considered the revolt a dangerous example to their own discontented colonies and also feared that the Americans would one day seize the loosely held Spanish lands in the West. Why help them prosper? The potentially busy Mississippi waterway remained closed, while surplus crops went unsold and western farmers complained bitterly.

Commerce. Overseas commerce, too, was depressed in these years. Independence did bring some commercial gains. The imperial Navigation Acts had restricted direct American trade with many parts of the world. Americans, for example, could not export directly to northern Europe, and most European imports had to come by way of Britain. Enumerated articles had to go to Britain on the way to their ultimate destination. Though there had been no legal impediments to colonial voyages to the distant East, English merchants had been so dominant in the trade with China, India, and the East Indies that Americans had, in effect, been excluded. With the Navigation Acts gone and newly independent Americans more confident of their prowess, enterprising men jumped at the chance to develop trade with new customers and to open new trading routes. For the first time American ships visited places like Copenhagen, Rotterdam, Stockholm, Bremen, and even ports in faraway Russian North America. In 1783 Robert Morris opened direct trade with China when he and his associates sent the *Empress of China* on a voyage to Canton that brought extraordinary returns to the promoters. Thereafter, American vessels from Boston, Salem, New York, Philadelphia, and other East Coast ports regularly rounded "the Horn" or "the Cape" on the way to the East Indies and China, the "Celestial Empire." Trade with France, much restricted before 1776, swelled under the treaty of

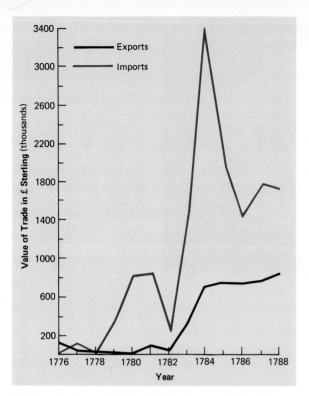

American foreign trade during the Revolution and Critical Period.

1778, which gave Americans special privileges in French dominions. American commerce with the French, Dutch, and Danish West Indies also grew.

Yet the new trade routes did not compensate for the loss of British imperial customers. Not only were Americans excluded from the trade with the British West Indies but they also could no longer trade with the Newfoundland and Nova Scotia fisheries. Nor could New England and middle states shipbuilders count on a protected market for their vessels in the empire. American-built ships were now "foreign" and no longer accorded a privileged position in the imperial trade. Britain also placed a high duty on American whale oil. The results of all these changes were damaging. By the end of the 1780s American foreign commerce had partly recovered from wartime and immediate postwar disruption. By 1790 Americans exported more than they had in 1772. But when measured on a *per capita* basis, American exports were 30 percent lower in 1790 than in the average year just before the war.

And other problems beset the country's commercial interests. After 1783 the agents of British firms set up offices and warehouses in every American port and began to push Americans out of the large transatlantic trade in British goods. Before long British vessels were even carrying British products from port to port along the Atlantic coast at the expense of American coastal traders. American merchants demanded that the United States favor imports carried by American ships and exclude foreigners from the coastal trade. Such laws—in effect, American "navigation acts"— would be no different from the British mercantile restrictions that Americans had been subjected to. Few Americans saw the irony; self-interest was enough to overcome a foolish consistency.

Industry. The livelihoods of city artisans, mechanics, and craftspeople—the "manufacturers" of the day—were also uncertain in the immediate postwar era. During the war consumers in many areas had been forced to turn to domestic artisans and craftspeople for goods formerly imported from Great Britain. American manufacturers had flourished until, with the return of peace, consumers went on a spending spree for British wares. Suddenly the American cabinetmakers, weavers, hat makers, tailors, silversmiths, and cobblers found their shops empty of customers.

The "manufacturers" appealed to the state legislatures for help. One Massachusetts petition sought relief for "persons out of employ who have wives and children asking for bread." Several states came to the rescue. They exempted some industries from taxes, lent money to others, and offered premiums to investors and inventors. What the artisans really wanted, however, was tariff protection—high duties that would make foreign imports expensive and thus force American consumers to buy the home product. Massachusetts, Rhode Island, New Hampshire, Connecticut, Pennsylvania, New York, and several southern states did impose taxes on imports. Where importing merchants opposed these, they generally lost to the artisans.

Unfortunately for the new nation's industries and those who earned their livings by manufacture, the system of duties was piecemeal and ineffective. The states tried to avoid conflicts with one another by exempting goods imported from other states. This practice simply nullified the duties. Importers in states without tariffs sent foreign goods into neighboring states disguised as American-made commodities. New York engaged in a preposterous trade war against New Jersey and Connecticut over this evasion. In 1787 the New York legislature decreed that foreign goods coming through the two nearby states must pay four times the duties of American goods. New Jersey retaliated by making New York pay £30 a month for the privilege of maintaining the Sandy Hook lighthouse on New Jersey property. Connecticut imposed duties on goods coming from New York.

The economic warfare among the states never went very far, but it could have led to a system of commercially insulated, competing states that would have thrown away the blessings of continent-wide free trade. Before long, alert citizens were asking how the country could avoid such an

A 1790 view of Mississippi commerce in New Orleans. In the center of the picture is a keelboat; to the right a flatboat. The river's width is greatly reduced.

outcome and still protect itself against the superior industry of Great Britain.

Creditors and Debtors.   Creditors, too, found the Confederation period a trying time. Unable to impose taxes, Congress ceased paying the interest and principal of the national debt. Thereafter, the value of government securities—Congress's promises to pay back money it had borrowed during the Revolution—dropped sharply. Speculators willing to take the chance that Congress might eventually pay its obligations bought up government IOUs at a fraction of their face value and soon held a large part of the total amount. The original holders of the securities thus got something for their money, but many felt cheated. Many state creditors felt the same way. After the war some states taxed themselves heavily and paid their debts. Others did not, and their depreciated securities, like Congress's, soon passed into the hands of speculators.

Nor were private creditors much better off. The postwar years brought a sharp drop in general prices. Imports, as we have just seen, had boomed briefly after 1783 as

American consumers, starved for British goods during the war, snapped up every cargo from Bristol, London, and Liverpool. To pay for this merchandise merchants and customers shipped overseas the gold and silver coin left behind by the French army or lent to Congress during the war by Dutch bankers. But there was a limit to the available cash, and the country soon reverted to its normal condition of currency dearth.

When money is scarce, it becomes more valuable relative to the things it buys. Thus prices for domestic goods now fell sharply and painfully. This *deflation* hurt farmers and artisans, who produced goods for sale. It also hurt debtors, who found it hard to get money to pay their creditors. To relieve their distress, debtors demanded paper money, and in several states the legislatures passed measures to oblige them.

In most states the paper currency caused few problems because the authorities printed only moderate amounts and did not make it "legal tender" that creditors had to accept even if they did not want to. New York and Pennsylvania businessmen actually supported their state's paper money issues to help end the currency famine and make business easier to conduct.

The situation was very different in Rhode Island. In that turbulent state the debtors were in complete control and seemed determined to cheat their creditors. In 1786 the legislature, acting under debtor pressure, issued £100,000 of legal tender paper money and declared that everyone had to accept it at face value even if it lost purchasing power. A creditor who resisted was breaking the law, and the debt would be canceled. Soon debtors were pursuing their creditors and paying them without mercy. Creditors complained bitterly, but to no avail.

The evidence thus confirms the economic difficulties of the Confederation period. And it also shows that the distress was widespread, not confined just to creditors, as Charles Beard argued. Merchants, farmers, and craftspeople, as well as creditors, had good reason to complain in these early postwar years.

The general distress had important political repercussions. Who was to blame for the problems? Why had prices dropped? Why had the British refused to make trade concessions to Americans? Why could Spain close the port of New Orleans without retaliation? Why were American craftspeople not protected against cheap foreign goods? Why could Rhode Island debtors arbitrarily scale down their debts? Why must national creditors sell their government securities to speculators at a fraction of their face value? The fault in every case, many Americans would soon come to believe, was the weak national government established by the Articles of Confederation. Something had to be done to strengthen it if the country was to prosper and fulfill its economic promise.

Confederation Finances. Congress had not paid Revolutionary soldiers, security holders, or any of its other creditors—and could not deal with many of its other pressing problems—because it lacked financial resources. Under the Articles of Confederation the central government had no power to tax and could do no more than assign revenue quotas to the states. Raising these funds then became the responsibility of the thirteen state legislatures. Under this scheme money came in very slowly because the states had their own expenses and were reluctant to fulfill their national obligations.

To meet its needs Congress offered large blocks of western land for sale to speculators. Under one such arrangement, 1.5 million acres of land were sold for less than eight cents an acre in hard money to a group of Boston businessmen and promoters. Congress also resorted to borrowing money from abroad as well as from Americans. But these loans were a mere stopgap, since the government could not expect bankers to continue to lend to it when it

had no means to repay them. Meanwhile, Washington's restless army remained unpaid and undischarged in its camp at Newburgh, New York.

Hoping to solve the government's revenue problems, in 1781 some members of Congress proposed an amendment to the Articles allowing Congress to levy a duty of 5 percent on all goods entering the country. The revenue from this "impost" would be used to pay the defaulted debt. Amending the Articles, however, required the unanimous consent of the states. Twelve states quickly ratified the amendment, but Rhode Island held out. In November 1782 it rejected the proposal. Another impost amendment, put forward in 1783, failed when New York ratified it with such crippling conditions that the other states would not accept it.

These failures had serious consequences. As we have seen, many people were forced to sell their government securities to speculators for whatever they would bring. Veterans were denied the cash bonuses Congress had promised them. Continental officers, who believed they were entitled to half-pay for life, were especially angry and were soon muttering of rebellion in the army's camp at Newburgh.

Nationalism. Besides economic distress, another important source of political change in this period was nationalism. This feeling links individual happiness to the interests and welfare of the nation as a whole; it is the emotional bond that joins citizens of a country to one another. Nationalism is a powerful binding force that can overwhelm individual and group interest and at times inspire sacrifice of life itself.

The active nationalists of the period were mostly young men who had served in the Continental Army or in Congress. They had fought and sacrificed for the United States. They had seen many parts of the country, had met men like themselves from every region, and had shared with them their hopes for a new national future. Their experiences had broadened their perspectives into a "continental" view and had made them aware of the inadequacies of localism.

The heightened continental consciousness could be seen in many areas in the immediate postwar period. Before 1776 Americans had looked to Britain and Europe for religious, cultural, and intellectual leadership. In the first years of independence they sought to end this inferiority. In these years Americans established religious autonomy from Europe. American Anglicans (who took the name Episcopalians), led hitherto by distant church superiors, now acquired their own bishops and a separate church government. In 1784 the Methodists left the British-controlled Methodist Conference and organized an independent

American Methodist Episcopal Church. In 1789 the pope selected the first resident American Catholic bishop, a move that recognized American independent nationhood.

Americans also declared their cultural independence of the Old World. In 1780 a group of Bostonians formed the American Academy of Arts and Sciences to encourage "every art and science" that might add to "the interest, honor, dignity, and happiness of a free, independent, and virtuous people." Five years later a reinvigorated American Philosophical Society issued its first volume of scientific transactions. A leader of the new movement for cultural independence was Noah Webster, a Connecticut-born Yale graduate. Soon after Yorktown Webster set out to create a distinctive intellectual life for "the confederated republics of America." In 1783 he published his *Blue-Backed Speller*, a volume, he proclaimed, that would help make America "as independent in *literature* as she is in *politics*." In the next few years he also published a grammar and a reader that used stories and examples drawn from American life as exercises for children learning their letters. Another sign of the new cultural nationalism—a dubious one perhaps—was the publication in 1787 of the first American history textbook.

To the growing body of nationalists the Confederation's political feebleness seemed humiliating. Everywhere they looked they found distressing signs of their country's plight. In June 1783 Congress had made itself look ridiculous by fleeing Philadelphia in fear of attack by unpaid and mutinous Continental troops. During the next months it wandered from town to town trying to find a decent resting place. When the new Dutch minister to the United States arrived to present his credentials, Congress was ensconced in Princeton, a small college town without proper facilities for state occasions. The embarrassed president of Congress, Elias Boudinot, wrote the representative of the nation's former ally to apologize for the inadequacy: "We feel ourselves greatly mortified that our present circumstances in a small Country village prevent us giving you a reception more agreeable to our wishes. But I hope these unavoidable deficiencies will be compensated by the sincere Joy on this occasion." In the end the ceremony went off creditably, but few who observed Boudinot's plight were proud of their country's government.

Though alert enough when threatened by physical attack, Congress seemed indifferent to everything else. In the six weeks following ratification of the 1783 peace treaty so few members attended sessions that it was difficult to gather a quorum to do business. In mid-February 1784 James Tilton of Delaware wrote a fellow member that "the situation of Congress is truly alarming; the most important business pending and not states enough to take it up. . . ." Another member declared: "The Congress is abused, laughed at and cursed in every company." Is it any wonder that sincere patriots feared for their country's future?

★ FOREIGN AFFAIRS ★

Even more disturbing to patriotic nationalists than the domestic weakness of the Confederation was its feebleness in foreign affairs. Almost everywhere the United States was treated with contempt. France remained friendly and honored the trade privileges specified by the treaty of 1778; but Spain and Britain were antagonistic, and even minor powers felt they could disregard American interests. As Jefferson, serving as American minister in Paris, wrote in 1784: "All respect for our government is annihilated on this side of the water from an idea of its want of energy."

The British, in particular, took advantage of American weakness. Besides excluding Americans from the profitable West Indies trade, they refused to evacuate a flock of forts and trading posts on American soil. They had good commercial reasons for thus violating the 1783 peace treaty. With British troops garrisoned at Michilimackinac, Detroit, Niagara, Oswego, and other posts, American fur traders were forced to surrender the trade of the Northwest to their Canadian rivals from Montreal. But the continued occupation was also a political response. The Americans had failed to live up to two provisions of the Treaty of Paris: They had not fully compensated Loyalists for their property losses, and they had not paid all prewar debts owed British merchants. Although Congress earnestly recommended that the states encourage both actions, the plea had been largely ignored. Loyalist groups and British creditors complained bitterly, but it did little good. The American government could not force its own citizens to comply with its treaty agreements.

The American minister to London, John Adams, pleaded with the British to adopt a more generous policy toward American trade and to evacuate the northwestern posts. Royal officials treated the American envoy with a "dry decency" and cold "civility," but refused to budge. Britain might have dealt more generously with the United States if Congress had been able to impose duties on British imports. As Jefferson noted, the United States "must show" the English that "we are capable of foregoing commerce with them, before they will be capable of consenting to equal commerce." But of course Congress lacked the power to exclude foreign goods, and the British knew it. As Lord Sheffield, a defender of British shipping interests, remarked, it would "not be any easy matter to bring the American states to act as a nation. They are not to be feared as such by us."

American relations with Spain during the Confederation era also revealed Congress's weakness. Besides restricting American Mississippi trade, Spain refused to allow American ships to trade with their colonies in Latin America, thus cutting off a profitable relationship that had developed during the war. These blows to American interests finally goaded even the sleepy Congress to act. In 1785 it authorized John Jay, the secretary for foreign affairs, to open negotiations with Spain over these issues.

Once more the American government proved incapable of achieving results. The Spanish minister, the lady-pleasing Don Diego de Gardoqui, was willing to make concessions on trade with Spanish-American ports, since these did not threaten his nation's control over territory. He refused, however, to yield on the right of tax-free deposit at New Orleans. His position suited some influential easterners, who feared that a too-rapid growth of the West would draw off population from the older states and eventually lead to western secession from the United States. It also coincided with the interests of northeastern merchants, who stood to gain by enlarged trade opportunities with Spanish America but saw little advantage in the right of deposit. Yet it was just this right to unload their cargo at New Orleans and transfer it to oceangoing ships that was the crucial matter to westerners.

Despite this disunity in American goals, a stronger government might have forced each group to accept a compromise for the national good. As it was, the treaty finally negotiated with Spain outraged the West. In exchange for Latin-American trade concessions, the United States agreed to forgo the right of deposit for twenty-five years. Unrepresented as yet in Congress, the westerners received the support of southern congressmen, who saw little gain for their section in the trade provisions and so could afford to take a nationalist position. Voting solidly against adoption, the southern representatives defeated the treaty. No one got anything. Once again, American weakness had betrayed American interests.

In the Mediterranean, too, the feeble American government was humiliated. For centuries the Barbary states in North Africa—Morocco, Algiers, Tunis, and Tripoli—had lived by preying on the commerce of Europe. Swift Barbary corsairs would swoop down on merchant ships and seize their cargoes; the pirates would then remove passengers and crews and hold them for ransom. Most European powers either paid tribute to the Barbary beys and bashaws in return for safe passage or provided their citizens with naval protection. Before 1776, English men-of-war had protected American commerce against the corsairs. Now that Americans were independent, they could no longer rely on the Royal Navy, and their merchant ships soon became fair game for the Barbary corsairs in the Mediterranean and off the coasts of Spain and Portugal. In 1787 the United States signed a treaty in which Morocco agreed to respect American rights. But negotiations with the other Barbary states failed because they insisted on bribes, which Congress could not pay. Unable either to pay tribute or provide naval protection for its shipping, the United States suffered continuing harassment from the North African pirates.

★ THE PUBLIC DOMAIN ★

In one important area of national concern—the administration of the public domain—the Confederation government can at least be given a mixed review. When Virginia finally surrendered its claims to the Northwest in 1784, Congress found itself in possession of almost a quarter of a billion acres of some of the finest land on earth. What should be done with this princely realm? How should it be disposed of? Who should get it? Should it be considered primarily a source of revenue for the federal government, or as an opportunity to shape American society in some desirable way? And how should the communities carved out of this land be governed? Should they be equal politically to the original states? Or should they be kept in leading strings to the East? If the problems were immense, so were the stakes, for the course chosen would profoundly affect the nation's future.

One issue never in doubt was whether the "West" should be subjected to the needs of white Americans. As part of the revolution in sensibility called "Romanticism," which swept Europe and America toward the end of the eighteenth century, a few sensitive souls came to appreciate untamed nature. During the 1780s Philip Freneau, a Patriot poet, sang of the "wild genius of the forest" and contrasted it with the corruption of civilization. The prominent Philadelphia doctor Benjamin Rush noted about this time that "man is naturally a wild animal, and . . . taken from the woods, he is never happy." But few others in this era questioned the goals of clearing the forests and plowing the prairies of the region beyond the Appalachians and converting them into farms and towns. And even if such skeptical views had been stronger and more widespread they could not have overcome the demands for cheap land and the ethic that equated resource exploitation with human "progress."

The Land Ordinance of 1785. The first issue Congress tackled was how to transfer land from public to private hands. As yet no one seriously considered giving the land away, if for no other reason than Congress needed some source of revenue. But there remained many other unanswered questions. Should the price be high or low? Should the land be sold in large blocks to speculators, or in small

WESTERN LANDS CEDED BY THE STATES, 1782–1802

parcels to farmers? One crucial question was whether to adopt the New England system of first surveying the land and then selling it in compact blocks, or the scheme used more commonly in the South of selling a receipt for a particular number of acres and then allowing the buyer to choose his land more or less where he pleased with the survey to follow. The New England plan had the advantages of encouraging orderly and compact settlement and of avoiding overlapping land claims. But it was likely to slow the pace of settlement by forcing people to buy bad land along with good and by requiring that each section opened be filled before others became available. The New England pattern also promised to avoid the sort of pell-mell rush to the West that was certain to disturb the Indians. On the whole, however, westerners favored the southern scheme, for all its potential for trouble, because it promised faster settlement.

The Land Ordinance of 1785 was Congress's attempt to choose a course among these conflicting alternatives. It provided that all government lands be surveyed and divided into square townships of six miles on an edge. Each township in turn would be cut into thirty-six sections, each of a square mile, or 640 acres. Half the townships would be sold as complete units of over 23,000 acres each. The other half would be sold in 640-acre sections. Some land was reserved for Revolutionary veterans after the land was surveyed; all the rest would be sold at auction at a minimum price of a dollar an acre.

The Land Ordinance followed more closely the New England than the southern tradition. As in New England, it mandated orderly surveying and compact tracts. Southerners, however, preferred relatively small tracts, so they got part of what they wanted in the provision for sale of single sections. On the other hand, the measure also allowed for the large block sales that speculators preferred. All in all, the scheme favored the principles endorsed by northeasterners over those desired by the rest of the country. Westerners, in particular, would not find it satisfactory. Over the next century they would agitate to alter the public land laws to favor the small farmer and the family farm over the land speculator and the large holding.

Congress's Indian Policy. Congress was no more successful in dealing with the Indian tribes than with foreign powers. In 1784 it dispatched a group of commissioners to the Northwest to get the local tribes to surrender a major portion of their lands to white settlers. At Fort Stanwix the commissioners induced the Iroquois to give up all claims to the region for a few presents. Soon after, at Fort McIntosh, they persuaded the Chippewa, Ottawa, Delaware, and Wyandot Indians to make a similar concession. But these two treaties did not accomplish their aim. The Indians of

Ohio charged that the Iroquois had no right to dispose of their lands at all. And the Shawnee objected to the Fort McIntosh agreement and refused to join the other tribes in signing it. The two treaties also provided an excuse to bands of renegade whites from Kentucky, Virginia, and Pennsylvania to cross the Ohio River and stake out claims on Indian lands still in dispute. By the spring of 1786 it looked as if a major Indian war was about to erupt in the Northwest.

At this point the western settlers, in a pattern that would be repeated many times in later years, decided to take matters into their own hands. Their first step was to call on the Indian fighter George Rogers Clark to come to their aid. Though old and in ill health, Clark rose to the challenge and launched an offensive of white settlers against the Ohio Indians. It failed when the western volunteers mutinied. Much encouraged, the Indians now repudiated the two treaties and declared that white settlers would be excluded from the whole Northwest. The "line now cutting Pennsylvania," they announced, "shall bounde them on the sunrising, and the Ohio shall be the boundary between them and the Big Knives." Congress was dismayed by this Indian barrier, but in its usual feeble way it could do nothing to prevent it.

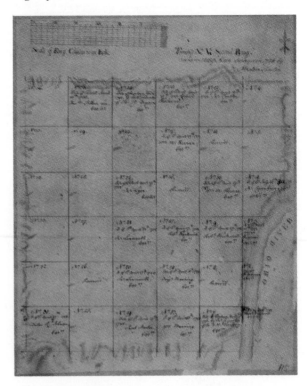

A contemporary map of the first land surveyed in the Northwest under the Land Ordinance of 1785. Note the square grid of parcels, a pattern imposed on virtually all the American public domain.

Clearly, then, there were many reasons for economic dissatisfaction with the Articles of Confederation during the postwar years, not just one. Charles Beard and his followers were wrong to focus on the state and national creditors as the sole malcontents. But the facts of the Confederation period also support a nationalist interpretation of the origins of the Constitution. Even if the years immediately following the Treaty of Paris had brought general prosperity, the failure of the Confederation government to assert America's international rights effectively and to deal vigorously with the Indian tribes would have stirred discontents. By 1785 many citizens felt that Congress had dwindled to little more than a shadow, unable to protect American in-terests abroad or solve major problems at home. Was it for this, patriots asked, that Americans had fought and died?

The Ordinance of 1787. Despite its weakness, the Confederation Congress could claim one major political ac-complishment: the Northwest Ordinance that provided a government for the region north of the Ohio River and west of Pennsylvania.

In 1784, following Thomas Jefferson's suggestion, Congress had adopted an ordinance providing for ten com-munities in the trans-Appalachian region. When the pop-ulation of any of these reached 20,000, the inhabitants could adopt a constitution and apply for admission to the

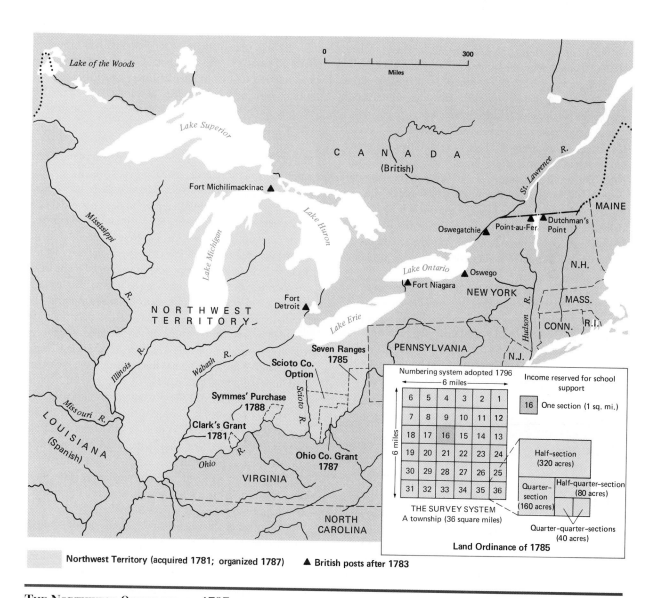

THE NORTHWEST ORDINANCE OF 1787

Union as a state equal in status to the states already comprising the Confederation. Although it was never put into effect, this measure served as the model for the Northwest Ordinance adopted three years later.

Section one of the 1787 Northwest Ordinance mandated that no fewer than three nor more than five states be formed out of the Northwest Territory. In its political provisions it was less liberal than Jefferson's plan. Section two, instead of allowing the people of a new territory self-rule from the outset, required a three-stage process toward autonomy. At the outset the territory would be governed by a governor, a territorial secretary, and three judges appointed by Congress. Then, when the adult male population had reached 5,000, it could elect a legislature to share power with a council of five chosen by the governor and Congress. It could also elect a territorial delegate to Congress though he could not vote. Finally, when the territory's total population had reached 60,000, it could apply for admission to the Union as a self-governing state equal to all the others. Section three of the Ordinance prohibited slavery in the new communities and provided a bill of rights for their inhabitants.

The Northwest Ordinance was a momentous piece of legislation. Its exclusion of slavery ensured that the entire North would be free territory. Equally important, the ordinance determined the future of the West and the Union by establishing the principle that new states would be equal to the original thirteen. If we consider the possible alternative of holding new territories in colonial thralldom, we can see how beneficial a precedent the ordinance was. Ray Billington, a historian of the American West, has declared:

> The Ordinance of 1787 did more to perpetuate the Union than any document save the Constitution. Men could now leave the older states assured that they were not surrendering their political privileges. [By enacting the Ordinance] Congress not only saved the Republic, but had removed one great obstacle to the westward movement.

★ THE CONSTITUTIONAL CONVENTION ★

The Confederation government, then, was not without accomplishments. But they were outweighed by its failures. By 1785 it seemed clear to many Americans, not just a small elite, that the nation needed a more powerful and effective central government to serve its material interests and embody its patriotic yearnings.

The road to the Constitutional Convention was not direct, however. The process of revising or replacing the Articles began in 1785 when Maryland and Virginia signed

an agreement over navigation rights on the Potomac River and Chesapeake Bay. The success of this pact induced Maryland to call for a broader arrangement that would include Pennsylvania and Delaware and cover disputes over import duties, currency, and other commercial matters. Nationalists in the Virginia legislature quickly proposed that *all* states meet in September 1786 at Annapolis to consider common commercial problems. Only five states attended the conference, but the nationalists—led by Alexander Hamilton of New York, James Madison of Virginia, and John Dickinson of Delaware—took advantage of the situation. Because a majority of states were not present, they convinced the delegates to petition Congress for a full-scale convention to meet at Philadelphia in May 1787 to discuss not only economic problems but fundamental political changes as well.

By this time, Congress's long decline had brought it close to paralysis. The Annapolis Convention's resolution was referred to a committee of three, which proposed to submit it to another committee of thirteen, which the legislators never got around to appointing. Congress, it seemed, intended to let the proposal die.

Shays's Rebellion. Then events in Massachusetts, a center of political turbulence since the 1760s, jolted the country and Congress into action. Massachusetts was one of those states that had obligated itself to pay its war debt. To meet this commitment the Bay State legislature had imposed on its citizens the heaviest taxes in New England. To farmers already suffering from low crop prices, the taxes were a disaster. Debts and bankruptcies soon mounted in the western counties, and many yeomen fell behind in their tax payments. As if this were not enough, Massachusetts law required that the pettiest commercial transactions be recorded by a court, necessitating the payment of high fees to lawyers and court officials. The large volume of legal business resulting from hard times thus added to the heavy tax load imposed on the state's citizens.

By the summer of 1786 discontent among farmers in the western counties had reached the flash point. In late August they convened in Worcester and condemned the taxes and heavy legal fees. Shortly afterward, an armed mob of 1,500 men, eager to end foreclosures for tax delinquency and debt default, stopped the convening of the Hampshire County Court. In early September three more county courts were kept from sitting by groups of angry men.

Although the Massachusetts legislature made some effort to ease the burden of debtors, disaffected westerners began to arm and drill as if they expected to take on King George's redcoats once more. Led by Daniel Shays, a former Continental Army officer, they formed a committee to resist what they considered intolerable conditions.

Annapolis Convention

Many steps intervened between first perceptions that the Articles of Confederation were inadequate and the actual meeting of the Constitutional Convention at Philadelphia during the summer of 1787. One of the more important was the Annapolis Convention, called originally by Virginia as a commercial meeting to discuss the chaotic trade relations among the states. Nine states accepted the invitation, but only five actually sent delegates. The poor turnout made it impossible for the twelve delegates present in the Maryland capital to proceed with their business. But the nationalists were not to be deterred from their purposes. Under the leadership of New York's Alexander Hamilton, they drafted a "call" for a new convention to meet in Philadelphia in May. This meeting would discuss not only trade disunity, but all the weaknesses of the government under the Articles. The following is a shortened version of that call.

"To the Honorable, the legislatures of Virginia, Delaware, Pennsylvania, New Jersey, and New York—

"The Commissioners from the said States, respectively assembled in Annapolis, humbly beg leave to report . . .

"That the express terms of the powers of your Commissioners supposing a deputation from all the States, and having for object the Trade and Commerce of the United States, your Commissioners did not conceive it advisable to proceed on the business of their mission,

under the Circumstances of so partial and defective a representation.

"Deeply impressed, however, with the magnitude and importance of the object confided in them on this occasion, your Commissioners cannot forbear to indulge an expression of their earnest and unanimous wish that speedy measures be taken, to effect a general meeting of the States, in a future Convention, for the same, and other purposes, as the situation of public affairs may be found to require. . . .

"That there are important defects in the system of the Federal Government is acknowledged by the Acts of all those States which have concurred in the present Meeting; that the defects, upon a closer examination, may be found greater and more numerous, than even these acts imply, is at least so far probable, from the embarrassments which characterise the present state of our national affairs, foreign and domestic, as may reasonably be supposed to merit a deliberate and candid discussion, in some mode, which will unite the Sentiments and Councils of all the States. In the choice of the mode, your Commissioners are of the opinion that a Convention of Deputies from the different States, for the special and sole purpose of entering into this investigation, and digesting a plan for supplying such defects as may be discovered to exist, will be entitled to a preference from considerations which will occur without being particularised.

"Your Commissioners decline an

enumeration of those national circumstances on which their opinion respecting the propriety of a future Convention, with more enlarged powers, is founded; as it would be a useless intrusion of facts and observations, most of which have been frequently the subject of public discussion, and none of which can have escaped the penetration of those to whom they would in this instance be addressed. They are, however, of a nature so serious, as, in the view of your Commissioners, to render the situation of the United States delicate and critical, calling for an exertion of the united virtue and wisdom of all the members of the Confederacy.

"Under this impression, your Commissioners . . . beg leave to suggest their unanimous conviction that it . . . may advance the interests of the union if the States. . . would themselves concur, and use their endeavours to procure the concurrence of the other States, in the appointment of Commissioners to meet at Philadelphia on the second Monday of May next, to take into consideration the situation of the United States, to devise such further provisions as shall appear to them necessary to render the constitution of the Federal Government adequate to the exigencies of the Union, and to report such an Act for that purpose to the United States in Congress assembled, as when agreed to by them, and afterwards confirmed by the Legislatures of every State, will effectively provide for the same."

Meanwhile, in the eastern part of the state, people had begun to panic. In Boston Governor James Bowdoin decided to raise a military force to suppress the disorders. Rather than impose new taxes to support this small army, Bowdoin appealed to the city's rich men, who, in their fright, promptly came up with $25,000. In January 1787 a rebel

force of 1,200 met the smaller group of Bowdoin's militia at Springfield. The state troops fired a single artillery volley, and the rebels fled in panic. The uprising was over by spring.

Shay's Rebellion was actually not much of a threat to the social order, yet it frightened many people. One citizen later insisted that if the rebels had won, there would have been "an abolition of all public and private debts" followed by "an equal distribution of property." The rebellion also dismayed the country's nationalists. Washington wrote that he was "mortified beyond expression" by the disorders. For the country "to be more exposed in the eyes of the world and more contemptible" than it already was seemed "hardly possible." Congress at last took heed of the restless mood of many citizens, and on February 21 it voted to ask the states to send delegates to a constitutional convention at Philadelphia. All except Rhode Island complied.

The Challenge. The convention in stately Independence Hall opened on May 14, 1787. It was an assembly of giants. Leading the rest in prestige were George Washington, Benjamin Franklin, James Madison, Robert Morris, James Wilson, John Dickinson, and Alexander Hamilton. There was also a large contingent of less famous but able men: George Mason, George Wythe, and Edmund Randolph, all of Virginia; John Rutledge and Charles Pinckney of South Carolina; William Paterson of New Jersey; Roger Sherman and Oliver Ellsworth of Connecticut; and Rufus King of Massachusetts. The rest of the fifty-five delegates made lesser contributions to the convention's work, though most enjoyed high standing in their states and had played important roles in national events.

Seldom has any group taken on so momentous a task. Civilized governments have usually been the products of historical accident and the gradual evolution of tradition and experience. The idea of a written frame of government, of a structure of fundamental law put down in precise words at one time, is an American invention. The practice began, as we saw in Chapter 5, with the making of state constitutions after 1775. Its finest expression is the federal Constitution of 1787.

A crude but vigorous portrait of the rebels Daniel Shays and Jacob Shattucks. Both of these leaders of Shay's Rebellion had been army officers during the Revolution.

The "Founding Fathers" did, of course, draw on the traditions of the colonies and Great Britain; the English experience is imprinted on every legal and governmental institution of the United States. They also relied on their understanding of the ancient world, especially Rome, and on the views of the great political and legal thinkers of modern times including Locke and Montesquieu. But in the end they were guided primarily by their own practical experience of government.

A number of the men at Philadelphia owned substantial amounts of unpaid Continental and state debt certificates. But although most were rich men, their wealth was largely in the form of land. A more important bond among the delegates than their status as creditors was the nationalism, or continentalism, that we noted earlier. The period from 1781 to 1787, they would have agreed, was indeed critical: America had been treated with contempt abroad while mob rule had threatened at home. There were some defenders of states' rights at Philadelphia—Robert Yates of New York, George Mason of Virginia, and Luther Martin of Maryland, for example—but most delegates believed that the Articles of Confederation had failed as an instrument of government and that the United States needed a stronger central authority.

Few of the delegates, however, wished to strengthen the government at the expense of freedom. The goal of the majority was balance, an end much harder to achieve. They wished to establish a "mixed" government, combining popular and aristocratic elements, that would protect private property, but also personal liberty. They intended to construct a strong central government, but one that would preserve local autonomy and local rights. In a nation of continental proportions the diversity of interests, opinions, and philosophies made the task formidable. During the deliberations small states would clash with large states, slave states with free states, commercial interests with agrarian interests, democrats with aristocrats, champions of local rights with nationalists. In the end, compromise would be unavoidable.

The Debate on Representation*. Following some preliminary skirmishing over procedural rules, the convention began its real work when Edmund Randolph, acting for James Madison, submitted a proposal that has come to be known as the Virginia Plan. Randolph advocated, not merely a revision of the Articles of Confederation, but a completely new government, with separate legislative, executive, and judicial departments. Congress would have two houses, and the states would be represented in each in proportion to their population. In each house the elected

*The text of the completed Constitution may be found in the Appendix.

The small room in Independence Hall, Philadelphia, where the debates on the Constitution were held in 1787.

members would vote as individuals, not as part of a single state unit, as they did under the Articles. They would, in effect, represent themselves or their constituents, not their states. The legislature would choose the persons to fill positions in the executive and judicial branches of government.

The Madison-Randolph proposal emphasized the central government as opposed to the states. Randolph hoped to establish a "strong *consolidated* union, in which the idea of states would be nearly annihilated." The Articles had created a league of virtually independent states; the new plan would confer broad powers on the central government, which would "legislate in all cases to which the separate States are incompetent"—that is, in every area where it chose to assert its power. But Randolph's proposal did not spell out precisely the new government's powers.

The Virginia Plan was countered by the New Jersey Plan, submitted by William Paterson. Paterson recommended that the Articles be revised, not replaced. His new government was to be a "federal," not a truly centralized one; that is, there would be a central government, but the states would retain independent authority in some spheres. The New Jerseyite, speaking for a smaller state than Randolph, endorsed the one-house legislature of the Articles, in which each state was represented equally, regardless of its wealth or population. States would continue to vote as units in Congress, so that the states, rather than the people, would be represented in the new government. But the New Jersey Plan did improve on the Articles by granting the national government the power to tax and regulate foreign and interstate commerce. It also made federal laws and treaties superior to all state laws, another advance over the Articles.

It is easy to see that the New Jersey Plan would benefit states with small populations more than the Virginia Plan. If Paterson's proposal was adopted, the less populous states would have representation in Congress equal to that of the more populous ones. If, on the other hand, the Virginia Plan prevailed, the small states' voices would be drowned out by those of their larger neighbors. For this reason it is often said that the two plans represented a conflict between large and small states. But the disagreement was just as much between the strong centralists and their more locally oriented colleagues.

The two plans became the basis for debate, and both were modified in the discussions. On the whole, the centralizers came out ahead. The new government would have greatly enlarged powers, but they would be specified and not left to Congress to decide. It would also be a true central government. Congress would represent the citizens of the United States, not the states as entities. Members of Congress would therefore vote as individuals, and not merely to decide the vote of their state. On the other issues of representation, a compromise was adopted. In one house, the Senate, each state would have equal representation regardless of population; in the other, the House of Representatives, population would determine the size of state delegations.

At this point the delegates had to consider the issue of what constituted "population." Were slaves only property, or were they people? If the former, they might, like other forms of property, be the basis for levying taxes, but could not be considered in calculating a state's representation in the lower house of Congress. If they *were* people, they should be counted for determining representation. However, because slaves were not free and could not vote, treating them

Daniel Shays

The people of Massachusetts found the peace after Yorktown a dubious blessing. In the coastal regions of the state the end of hostilities brought nothing but difficulties. The Barbary pirates cut off trade with the Mediterranean. The English vengefully excluded American vessels from the West Indies. Hardship for the merchants also meant hardship for the sailors, the sailmakers, the ship carpenters, and all the other "mechanics" who worked in the port towns and earned their living from overseas commerce.

The difficulties soon spread to the farmers of the interior. The people of Massachusetts had gone on a buying spree when British goods became available soon after Yorktown. Unable to ship goods to the English West Indies colonies in exchange, they had to pay for these British goods in specie—gold and silver. The import deluge quickly drained the community of all hard money and compelled hard-pressed import merchants to demand quick repayment of all outstanding debts. Soon they were dunning their customers among the retail shopkeepers of the interior market towns. The retail merchants in turn had no alternative but to pressure *their* customers—the local farmers and mechanics—to immedi-

ately pay all outstanding debts, and in coin, not farm produce as in the past. By this chain reaction, before many months the cash shortage of the coastal port towns had been transmitted to the entire state.

The cash dearth proved a bonanza to local lawyers, for when their farm customers refused to pay, the besieged storekeepers turned to the courts. Between August 1784 and August 1786 the Hampshire County Court of Common Pleas prosecuted almost 3,000 debt cases, a 260 percent increase over 1770–72. Matters were made worse by the state's tax system. Land bore two-thirds of the total Massachusetts tax burden, while the personal property of the business and professional classes escaped taxation. The result of this combination was that many farmers in the interior and western counties faced not only suits for debts but also the forced sale of their property for nonpayment of state taxes.

Into this picture of severe rural distress intruded the figure of Daniel Shays of Pelham in Hampshire County. Shays was seen as Robin Hood by his supporters; his foes considered him a dangerous social leveler. He was really neither. A former captain in Washing-

ton's army, Shays had fought gallantly at Bunker Hill, Saratoga, and Stony Point. But Captain Shays had none of the "nobler" qualities expected of a hero. In 1780 he sold for cash a sword that the Marquis de Lafayette had presented to him as a mark of esteem. The act scandalized many of his fellow officers. Soon after this event Shays resigned his commission and returned to his native state.

Shays was not the chief mover of the events that have been given his name. The "rebellion" started as a wave of peaceful petitions to the state legislature for relief in the form of paper money and the closing of the courts where creditors had brought suit against the farmers. Patience soon wore thin, however, and during the late summer, fall, and winter of 1786 spontaneous bands of "regulators," attempting to stop the lawsuits and the forced sales, shut the courts in western Massachusetts. Captain Daniel Shays played little part in the earliest of these attacks. But when in late September the rebels tried to stop the sitting of the court in Springfield, he was abruptly catapulted into leadership. Wearing his old buff-and-blue Continental officer's uniform, Shays rode up and took charge of the protesters in front of the courthouse. He talked General Shepard, commander of the

---

as people would give the southern states a voice in Congress disproportionate to the actual number of their voters. Each voter in the South, where slaves were numerous, in effect would have more power than each voter in the North, where they were few. Northerners naturally objected to such a scheme. Southerners, noting that their wealth in slaves would force them to pay a heavy tax bill, insisted on some political compensation for the burden they would bear.

The issue was very sensitive, for it touched on the continued existence and prosperity of slavery in the South. And slavery, the South's "peculiar"—that is, special or unique—institution, was entangled in every aspect of southern life.

True, ever since the Revolution had proclaimed that "all men are created equal," the supporters of slavery had been on the defensive. But slaves still tilled the South's fields, built its fences, and performed its household chores. Though slavery was fast disappearing in the North, only a handful of enlightened southerners were willing to contemplate its abolition in their own section.

The men at Philadelphia would deal with slavery at several other points; this time they elected to compromise. Taxes and representation in the lower house of Congress would be based on "the whole number of free Persons," excluding Indians but including indentured servants and

militia, into allowing the regulators to parade around the town square without interference to express their grievances. He was now a marked man.

During the remainder of 1786 Shays was in the thick of the growing disorders. In late November, following the violent capture of two rebel leaders by the loyal militia, Shays signed a manifesto proclaiming that "the seeds of war are now sown. . . ." He was soon busy planning an attack on the court scheduled to meet in Worcester in early December.

A thousand insurgents assembled in Worcester to stop the meeting of the court, prepared if necessary to die for their cause. The sacrifice proved unnecessary. A winter storm descended on central Massachusetts the evening before the court session, completely blocking the roads and preventing the judges from getting to the town. The insurgents, cold, wet, and miserable, soon drifted off for home. Shays and a number of other disappointed leaders had to settle for another proclamation detailing the sufferings of the farmers and demanding the release of rebel prisoners and the suspension until spring of the courts in three western counties.

By this time the conservative citizens of the commonwealth were in a state of panic and demanding "condign punishment" of the rebels. The state legislature responded with a barrage of measures punishing rioting, suspending the writ of habeas corpus, and making "the spreading of false reports to the prejudice of government" an indictable crime. It also passed an Act of Indemnity pardoning all rebels who would take an oath of allegiance. Meanwhile, an alarmed Confederation Congress in New York, at the behest of the Massachusetts authorities, voted to raise a force of federal troops to put down the rebellion, the money to be supplied by a requisition on the states of $530,000.

As usual, nothing came of Congress's good intentions. The states refused to appropriate the money and the Massachusetts authorities were forced to suppress the rebellion by themselves. In January 1787 Governor James Bowdoin began to organize a small army of volunteers, financed by private contributions, to put down the rebels. Money and recruits poured in, and by the end of the month five companies of troops under General Benjamin Lincoln were on their way to the scene of the disorders. Before they arrived, Shays and his associates, in quest of arms and ammunition, attacked the federal arsenal at Springfield. The attack was met by the militia, who opened fire with artillery loaded with grapeshot. The third volley smashed into the charging rebels, killing three. Shays tried to rally the men, but most had never faced gunfire before. Crying "Murder!", they broke and ran for cover.

During the next few weeks Shays and his little army retreated before the approaching forces of General Lincoln. At Petersham, Lincoln and his men caught up with the Shaysites and surprised them at breakfast. Fortunately there were few casualties. The rebels once again panicked and ran from the field. Most escaped and over the next few months continued a sort of guerrilla war against the authorities. But the Petersham defeat broke the back of the rebellion.

Shays himself fled to Vermont with a price on his head. In 1788, with order restored in the commonwealth, the Massachusetts legislature pardoned the rebel leaders. Shays returned home and for a while lived quietly in Pelham. Then he joined the trek of many rural Yankees to western New York, where he spent his remaining years as a Revolutionary War pensioner.

Occasional visitors came to see the notorious rebel. They were generally disappointed. The firebrand was just a genial old man, a little too fond of the bottle. Shays died in Sparta, New York, in 1825 at the age of 84. By this time few remembered the man who had inspired terror among the rich and mighty of the commonwealth of Massachusetts and, by giving a final push to the nationalists' demand for a stronger federal union, helped alter the course of American history.

"three-fifths of all other Persons." Thus, with the "three-fifths compromise," America's Founding Fathers managed the neat trick of simultaneously treating a slave as property and as three-fifths of a human being.

Freedom or Order? Not only did the Founding Fathers compromise conflicting interests; they also compromised conflicting principles. As we have noted, the delegates desired both the representative principle on the one hand, and order and rule by the "best men," a kind of elitism, on the other. Some leaned strongly to one side, some to the other; most were in the middle.

The give-and-take among these approaches resulted in several important features of the Constitution, particularly the principle of separation of powers. Borrowing from Montesquieu, the delegates assigned to each branch of government—executive, legislative, and judicial—distinct powers and directed that members of each be selected in a distinct way. This separation would ensure the independence of each branch. In addition, the Founders adopted the idea that each branch must be able to "check and balance" the others. By such an arrangement the greatest freedom would be ensured, for if one branch grew too powerful and sought to dominate the others, it could be constitutionally stopped.

This 1790 engraving of the Pennsylvania State House (later renamed Independence Hall) shows a rear view of the structure where, three years earlier, the Founding Fathers had hammered out the Constitution.

Checks and balances were a defense of freedom in one way, but they could also be a brake on excessive freedom—say of a Daniel Shays. During the years when the states were writing their own constitutions, extreme democrats generally favored weak governors and strong legislatures. At Philadelphia the principle of checks and balances seemed like a fine way to accomplish both things at once: Check "the mob" and also check the executive.

To this end, the chief executive was to have a veto over acts of Congress, the most democratic part of the new government. But the president was not to be all-powerful. His veto could be overridden by a two-thirds vote of Congress. The chief executive could make treaties with foreign powers, but they would have to be confirmed by a two-thirds vote of the Senate. He was to be commander in chief of the army and navy, but only Congress could declare war. Finally, he could appoint a host of officials, but these appointments would have to be confirmed by the Senate. As a final check on the president—and his appointees—the House of Representatives could bring impeachment charges against federal officials. If impeached officials were then found guilty of "high crimes and misdemeanors" by the Senate, they would be removed from office.

Standing guard against the excesses and abuses of Congress and the president was to be the third branch, the federal judiciary, capped by a Supreme Court. Although it is nowhere stated in the Constitution, legal scholars believe that the delegates at Philadelphia assumed the right of the federal courts to declare acts of Congress contrary to the Constitution and hence invalid. To free the judges of political influence, they gave them lifetime tenure and declared that during their terms of office Congress could not reduce their salaries.

Checks and balances offered one way to combine strong and stable government with a popular voice. The mixture of democratic and aristocratic methods of choosing the officers of each branch was another. The president would be selected not by the direct vote of the people but by an electoral college chosen by the states as they saw fit. The number of electors from each state would be equal to the number of representatives and senators it sent to Congress. State law would determine how they would be chosen, but it was assumed that they would not be elected directly by the people. Nor was the Senate, the upper house of Congress, conceived of as a stronghold of democracy. Senators would be selected by their state legislatures. To limit popular control of Congress further, senators were to have long terms of six years; only one-third would be seeking reelection in each congressional election held every two years. Finally, the federal judiciary, including the Supreme Court, was to be appointed by the president and confirmed by the Senate, and thus far removed from popular pressure. To temper these aristocratic features, the House of Representatives would be directly controlled by "the people." Representatives would be elected for two-year terms by the same liberal rules that governed the selection of members of the lower houses of the state legislatures.

Powers of the New Government. Besides establishing a new structure, the Constitution greatly enlarged the powers and scope of the national government. The new government, as we have seen, would impose its authority on the people directly, not through the states. It would also fuse the nation into a single legal whole. Under the new charter each state was required to give "full faith and credit" to all laws and court decisions of the others and to surrender to the others all criminals who fled across state lines to avoid prosecution. To protect property rights, states were forbidden to pass laws "impairing the Obligation of Contracts." The new government could also do many specific things its predecessor could not do. It could impose and collect taxes from citizens, though by the Constitution's original terms these taxes had to be proportionate to each state's population. It could regulate foreign and interstate commerce, although at the urging of the southern states that shipped large amounts of rice and tobacco abroad, it was forbidden to tax exports. The new government had sole control over the coinage of money and could establish a postal system, build post roads, and pass laws of naturalization. It was also endowed with the power to establish a system of uniform weights and measures, a uniform bankruptcy law and to encourage invention and the arts and sciences, a patent and copyright system. Finally, the Constitution declared that the new government could "make all laws which shall be necessary and proper for carrying into Execution the foregoing Powers, and all other Powers vested by this Constitution in the Government of the United States." This provision, which is known as the elastic clause, later became the justification for greatly expanded federal authority. In sum, a strengthened national government was to exercise broad authority over economic and political affairs, and over a single economic and legal unit.

Still, the Constitution created not a unitary but a federal government; it left the states with independent authority in some spheres. Crime and breaches of the peace were in the states' jurisdiction, except when a state legislature or governor specifically requested federal help to put down local violence. Social relations, including marriage, divorce, and education, were also left to the states, as were laws regarding purely local commercial relations and most business affairs.

Although slavery was considered a "domestic" institution much like the family, it could not be left solely to the states' jurisdiction. Conflict over representation had resulted in the three-fifths compromise, and the problems of slaves escaping to free states as well as the foreign slave trade also had to be considered. After much debate the Philadelphia delegates agreed that Congress could not forbid the foreign slave trade until 1808, but thereafter it might

do so if a majority wished. Congress could, however, pass laws to deal with runaway slaves who crossed state lines and guarantee slaveholders the right to recover such fugitives regardless of local antislavery laws.

All through the summer and into September the delegates debated every issue. The discussion, like the weather, was often heated. To quiet ruffled tempers and encourage goodwill among the delegates, Franklin at one point proposed that a chaplain be invited to open each morning session with a prayer. Washington, the presiding officer, also worked to maintain peace; and although he said little, his dignity and calm demeanor helped to keep the delegates' differences from getting out of hand.

Nothing could prevent disagreement. A number of the delegates considered the completed draft of the Constitution far too centralizing. New York's Robert Yates and John Lansing, George Mason of Virginia, Luther Martin and John Mercer of Maryland, and Elbridge Gerry of Massachusetts denounced the work of the convention. Lansing, Yates, and Mercer went so far as to quit Philadelphia in protest. On the other hand, the most extreme centralizers believed the proposed constitution did not go far enough. Alexander Hamilton wanted the states abolished outright in favor of a strong, unitary government. The views that ultimately prevailed were those of James Madison, Oliver Ellsworth, and Roger Sherman, who succeeded in mobilizing the majority around the compromise proposals.

On September 8 the convention sent the completed draft to the Committee of Style and Arrangement. This group of five polished the convention's paragraphs and rearranged them in logical order. One of its members, Gouverneur Morris of Pennsylvania, wrote a preamble that described the promotion of "the general welfare" as one of the purposes of the new framework of government. On September 17, 1787, each of the state delegations voted its approval, and the convention adjourned.

★ RATIFICATION ★

Now the Constitution's friends faced the problem of securing its adoption, and it seemed likely that the battle would prove difficult. The Confederation Congress had authorized the Philadelphia convention only to "revise" and "amend" the Articles of Confederation—not to propose a new form of government. Would Congress reject the convention's work? On September 29 the new Constitution was presented to Congress. That body was almost dead and had no heart for resistance. After some minor debate it recommended the plan to the separate states for consideration by convention. The more difficult task was winning state-by-state ratification. The opposition fought hard against it. Certain groups of debtors, aware that state-issued paper money would be illegal under the new government, were naturally opposed to it. So were taxpayers in states that had paid their debts and feared that through new federal taxes they would pay someone else's as well, and those who considered strengthened national government a retreat from "true republicanism." Finally, there were the temperamentally cautious people, inclined to stick to the ills they had rather than fly to others they knew not of.

At one time scholars emphasized the formidable opposition to the Constitution and described the battle to get it adopted as a fierce struggle. In part, this view projects back into the adoption period attitudes that gelled in the years following. It also reflects the fact that in a few states the adoption issue was indeed hard fought. Because it would have been difficult to achieve a successful Union without them, the debates that took place in these states *were* important. Still, it is clear that the "federalists"—those who favored the new federal government—won with relative ease.

The delegates at Philadelphia had decided that the new government would go into operation when nine states had ratified the Constitution. Delaware, Pennsylvania, and New Jersey were won over almost immediately, the first and third by unanimous votes in their conventions. Early in 1788 Georgia's convention also ratified unanimously. Connecticut soon followed with a heavy federalist major-

ity. In Massachusetts the friends of the Constitution encountered their first serious opposition. By early estimates the state convention had a solid antifederalist majority. Among the initial opponents were the influential Sam Adams and John Hancock, for years leaders of the state's popular party. If these men could be converted, enough delegates would follow them to carry ratification. Fortunately for the Constitution, Adams was induced to change his mind by a mass meeting of Constitution supporters staged by Paul Revere. Convinced that the rally expressed the views of the state's common folk, Adams agreed to support the Constitution. Hancock, now the state's governor, was coaxed and flattered by federalists into believing he was in line for high federal office under the new Constitution.

One of the federalists' problems in Massachusetts and a number of other states was that the Constitution lacked a bill of rights to protect citizens against federal tyranny and to guarantee civil liberties. Some opponents of the Constitution used this lack primarily to delay or defeat adoption. But others, such as Hancock, were sincere in their concern. When Hancock agreed to endorse ratification, he proposed simultaneously that nine amendments be added to protect the citizen against federal oppression. With this request tacked on to its motion, the Massachusetts convention voted 187 to 168 for adoption.

In March the federalists suffered their first actual setback when maverick Rhode Island overwhelmingly rejected the Constitution by a popular vote. The state, as we saw,

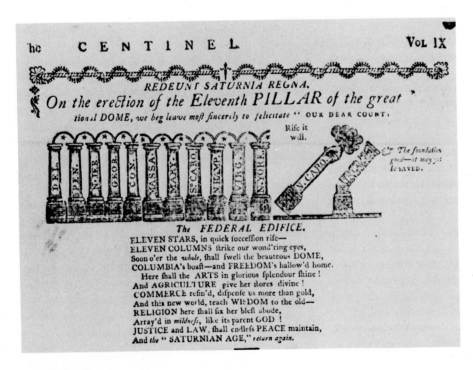

Cartoon from the Massachusetts Centinel of July 26, 1788, expressing hope that the two holdout states, North Carolina and Rhode Island, would ratify the Constitution and join the new Union.

True to his revolutionary principles, nine-term Massachusetts Governor John Hancock refused to support the proposed Constitution without amendments guaranteeing the rights of citizens.

had been the center of debtor-imposed paper money schemes and had not sent a delegation to Philadelphia. During the ratification battle the federalists did not stand a chance, so they boycotted the vote. The results were as expected: The supporters of the Constitution received only 10 percent of the votes cast.

Rhode Island's rejection did not stop the federalists' forward momentum, however. In April and May, Maryland and South Carolina joined the parade of adoptions, and by large convention majorities. Then, by a close vote on June 21, New Hampshire became the ninth state to ratify the Constitution. Under the rules that the convention had prescribed, the Constitution was now officially in force. But New York and Virginia had not acted. If these two large states voted no, it would be impossible to maintain a workable federal system.

Federalist forces in Virginia were strong and well organized. Among them were some of the most prestigious men in the state, including James Madison, George Wythe,

Edmund Randolph, and John Marshall. Also working in the federalists' favor was the general assumption that the first president under the Constitution would almost certainly be the state's greatest son, George Washington. Not yet the "father of his country," he was nevertheless a commanding figure in the new nation and seemed to embody the finest type of patriotism.

On the antifederalist side, however, there was an impressive array of talent, too, including Patrick Henry, Richard Henry Lee, James Monroe, and George Mason. Henry was the spearhead of the antifederalist attack. In an impassioned speech to the state convention he portrayed the new Constitution as dangerous to liberty. Under it the citizen would be abused, insulted, tyrannized. Henry also appealed to localism and the self-love of his listeners. "The Constitution reflects in the most degrading and mortifying manner on the virtue, integrity, and wisdom of the state legislatures," he declared. It assumed "that the chosen few who go to Congress will have more upright hearts, and more en-

Claimed by
Great Britain

BRITISH   CANADA

Lake Superior

Mississippi R.

Lake Michigan

Lake Huron

St. *Lawrence R.*

MAINE
(To Mass.)

Lake Ontario

NEW YORK
July 1788

N.H.
June 1788

MASS.
Feb. 1788

Lake Erie

PENNSYLVANIA
Dec. 1787

R.I.
May 1790

CONN.
Jan. 1788

NEW JERSEY
Dec. 1787

Ohio R.

DELAWARE
Dec. 1787

LOUISIANA
(Spanish)

Claimed by Virginia

MARYLAND
April 1788

VIRGINIA
June 1788

O
C
E
A
N

Mississippi R.

Claimed by North Carolina

NORTH CAROLINA
Nov. 1788

A
T
L
A
N
T
I
C

SOUTH CAROLINA
May 1788

GEORGIA
Jan. 1788

SPANISH

FLORIDA

Gulf of Mexico

Federalist majority (for)

Antifederalist majority
(against)

Evenly divided

0   300
        Miles

RATIFICATION OF THE CONSTITUTION. 1787–1790

Washington taking the oath of office as first president. The event was every bit as dignified as the picture indicates. (Collection of the New York Historical Society)

lightened minds, than those who are members of individual legislatures." Many in his audience believed it was the finest address of his distinguished career as an orator. In the end, though, Henry's eloquence was not enough. The convention voted to ratify narrowly with the proviso that a bill of rights be added to the new frame of government.

The battle now shifted to New York. Without New York the Union would be physically split in half; with it, the Union would be complete in all essentials. For weeks the federalists had been bombarding the state's newspaper readers with articles written by Hamilton, Madison, and Jay. These *Federalist Papers*, explaining, defending, and praising the new Constitution, were, of course, partisan expositions of the federalist position. But they were more than propaganda; they were also brilliant analyses by unsentimental men of the way politics was practiced in the real world. Ordinary men were not equipped to govern the country directly, they stated. They did not have the necessary knowledge or understanding. The country would be well ruled only by those who recognized that government was a "complicated science" requiring "abilities and knowledge of a variety of other subjects, to understand it." Every just and successful government must respect the wishes of ordinary people, but wisdom must temper the decisions of majorities. Majorities were frequently temporary and more often moved by passion than by mature judgment. In the future, moreover, when social inequalities had become greater than at present, they were certain to attack property rights. Government must be strong enough to guard against the natural but mistaken leveling tendencies of democracy.

The persuasiveness of the *Federalist Papers* and Hamilton's impassioned presentation of the federalist posi-

tion at the state convention gave the adoption drive a great boost. But the pro-Constitution people had more than eloquence on their side. If New York State did not join the Union, New York City might choose to join anyway to avoid losing the lucrative commerce that flowed through it to New Jersey and southern New England. What would the state do then? In the end the logic of circumstances prevailed. On July 26, 1788, the New York convention voted 30 to 27 to adopt the Constitution.

The new Union was now secure. Early in 1789 national elections were held for the first time under the Constitution, and federalist candidates won a majority in the new Congress. In January the electoral college voted unanimously for Washington as president and settled on John Adams as his vice president. Rhode Island and North Carolina were still outside the Union, and their citizens did not participate in the election.

Soon after the elections the new government, as promised, adopted the first ten amendments to the Constitution that are commonly called the Bill of Rights. The first nine guaranteed the rights of free speech, press, and assembly, and forbade the federal government to make any law "respecting the establishment of religion or prohibiting the free exercise thereof." They affirmed the right of the people "to bear and keep arms," protected citizens against "unreasonable searches and seizures," required jury trials in criminal and major civil cases, and forbade "excessive" bail or fines and "cruel and unusual punishments." The tenth amendment "reserved" to the states all powers not given the United States by the Constitution.

Note that these amendments placed limits on Congress and the federal government; they did not apply to the state governments. As most states already had similar restraints in their own constitutions, it was considered at this time unnecessary to rein in the state governments in the same way.

With their last objections gone, and fearful of being treated as foreign nations if they did not join the Union, North Carolina and Rhode Island reversed their earlier stands and ratified the Constitution in 1789 and 1790, respectively. The United States was now a nation; it had ceased to be a league of petty states.

★ CONCLUSIONS ★

Between Yorktown in 1781 and Washington's inauguration in 1789 the country underwent a constitutional transformation of startling dimensions. The end of fighting did not bring the blessings of peace and freedom to the American people. Instead, it ushered in a period of declining trade, falling prices, and unemployment. It also brought national humiliation. In foreign affairs the United States was treated with contempt; even minor powers felt free to disregard American rights.

Thousands of citizens found the period deeply disappointing. Farmers, planters, craftspeople, creditors, and merchants—easterners as well as westerners, northerners as well as southerners—looked on in dismay as material conditions worsened; they longed for a way to protect their interests and improve their circumstances. Patriots, who saw their dreams of a glorious national future fading, felt despair, and demanded a more effective government to assert their country's position in the world community.

All of these groups turned to constitutional revision as their solution, and the great convention at Philadelphia was the result. Predictably, the Constitution that emerged from the deliberations reflected the feelings of the nationalists and all those who blamed weak central government for their plight. One can almost deduce the political and economic problems of the "Critical Period" from the specific grants of power to the new federal government. No doubt, that government was supported by the country's elite and the defenders of strong restraints on debtors and social levelers. But it was also endorsed by thoughtful and politically active citizens of every social persuasion. We will never be able to say for certain whether a majority of adult Americans in 1788 supported the Constitution. For more than a generation, however, scholars have been convinced that the federal Constitution was indeed written and adopted "by popular demand."

★★★★★★★ FOR FURTHER READING ★★★★★★★

Merrill Jensen. *The New Nation: A History of the United States During the Confederation, 1781–1787* (1948)
This work seeks to refute the notion that the Confederation era was a critical period. Jensen stresses the successes of the Articles of Confederation, which he understands as the true embodiment of the Declaration of Independence, and brands those who wanted them changed as antidemocratic.

Marion Starkey. *A Little Rebellion* (1955)
In this entertaining account of Shays's Rebellion, Starkey captures the bitterness of western Massachusetts farmers and the fear and hatred they aroused in the seaboard merchants.

Jackson Turner Main. *The Anti-Federalists: Critics of the Constitution, 1781–1788* (1961)
Main sees the opponents of a stronger central government in the 1780s as largely isolated farmers who were not tied to the sale of commercial crops and so had little interest in foreign trade.

Irving Brant. *James Madison: The Nationalist, 1780–1787* (1948)
The second volume of a three-volume biography of Madison describes government under the Articles of Confederation and Madison's concern with reforming the courts of Virginia, establishing free public schools, and ensuring religious liberty for his native state. Most important, however, is the story of Madison's dismay at the weaknesses of his country during the 1780s and his efforts that culminated in the federal Constitution.

Charles A. Beard. *An Economic Interpretation of the Constitution of the United States* (1913)
The classic "Progressive" interpretation of the Constitution's origins that all later historians have had to reckon with. Beard's thesis is that the fathers of the Constitution—most of whom, he insists, were wealthy merchants and government creditors—constructed a frame of government that was designed to serve the economic needs of their class. In Beard's view, the Constitution was a counterrevolutionary retreat from the democratic and egalitarian spirit of the Declaration of Independence.

Robert E. Brown. *Charles Beard and the Constitution* (1956)
A reexamination of Beard's thesis that finds it seriously wanting. Brown reveals how even great scholars can commit errors and distort facts if they are too intent on making a point.

Forrest McDonald. *We the People: The Economic Origins of the Constitution* (1958); and *E Pluribus Unum: The Formation of the American Republic, 1776–1790* (1965)

The first of these two books challenges as oversimplified Beard's description of the economic factors and groups behind a stronger central government in the 1780s. The second is an interesting if sometimes highly personal discussion of the drive toward the Constitution and the formation of a new national government.

Benjamin F. Wright, editor. *The Federalist* (1961)

The *Federalist Papers*, written by Madison, Hamilton, and John Jay, are essential to understanding the thinking of the Constitution's supporters. Wright has converted the language of the essays into modern usage to make them easier to follow, and he introduces them with a helpful essay.

Robert A. Rutland. *The Ordeal of the Constitution: The Anti-Federalists and the Ratification Struggle of 1787–88* (1966)

Sympathetic to the antifederalists who opposed ratification of the Constitution, Rutland explains the strategy of the two opposing groups and the reasons for antifederalist defeat. He concentrates on the important Virginia debates.

Irving Brant. *The Bill of Rights: Its Origin and Meaning* (1965)

This full treatment (515 pages), by a leading biographer of Madison, of the first ten amendments to the Constitution deals with the Bill of Rights' roots in both English and American experience, its creation early in the new republic, and its application over the many years that have ensued. The book goes well beyond the period covered in this chapter, but this should not deter the serious student.

7 ★

THE FIRST PARTY SYSTEM

What Issues Divided the New Nation?

1789	The French Revolution • Congress adopts the Tariff and Tonnage acts to raise the first federal revenues • Congress establishes the State, Treasury, and War departments, and prescribes the structure of the Supreme Court and the federal courts in the Federal Judiciary Act
1790–91	Hamilton presents his financial program to Congress
1790	Congress enacts Hamilton's plan for public credit in the Funding Act
1791	Congress charters the Bank of the United States
1793	War breaks out between France and Britain, Spain and Holland • France sends "Citizen" Genêt as minister to the United States • Jefferson resigns as secretary of state and is replaced by Federalist Edmund Randolph
1794	Britain authorizes the seizure of neutral ships trading between the French West Indies and Europe • The United States and Britain sign the Jay Treaty • General Anthony Wayne crushes the Indians at Fallen Timbers; rapid settlement of the Northwest Territory follows • The Whiskey Rebellion in Pennsylvania
1795	The Pinckney Treaty concluded between United States and Spain • With the Treaty of Greenville the Indians cede territory in what will later be Ohio
1796	Washington's Farewell Address; Adams elected president
1797	The French order American ships carrying British goods confiscated
1797–98	The "XYZ Affair"
1798	Congress votes to triple the size of the army and enlarge the navy • The Federalist Congress passes the Alien and Sedition Acts; Secretary of State Timothy Pickering prosecutes opposition leaders under the laws • Kentucky and Virginia declare their right to nullify acts of the national government
1800	The Convention of 1800 between France and the United States nullifies the Treaty of 1778 • Jefferson elected president

Americans had every reason to expect the government under the newly adopted Constitution to be stronger and more effective than its predecessor. The nation finally had the political machinery needed to deal with its public business. Or did it?

Today every representative government operates through a political party system. Political parties are durable organizations of people with roughly similar views on political issues who collectively select platforms, choose candidates for office, and formulate legislative programs. They are essential attributes of modern democratic nations in which free elections are held.

The delegates at Philadelphia in the summer of 1787 did not see things this way. They had established offices for the new federal government with defined powers and modes of selection, but they had supposed that these positions would be filled by men whose only concern would be disinterested public service, not the furthering of a particular political group or viewpoint. Public officials, moreover, would be chosen by citizens who placed the common good above their own special needs. Each issue would be decided on its own merits, not on the basis of ideology or preconceived positions. When the Philadelphia delegates considered political parties, the word they commonly used was *factions*, by which they meant groupings around particular political chieftains for purely selfish reasons, such as the rewards of political office or the favor of the leader. Factions or parties, they believed, would divide citizens into hostile camps. They were not part of the legitimate machinery of government; they were cancers on it. Government by party, then, seemed a disruptive, selfish, and often dishonest way to conduct a nation's political affairs.

And yet within a decade after the adoption of the Constitution two great national parties had emerged in the United States. Many thoughtful citizens were horrified that the country should so quickly fall from political virtue. But this first party system, which lasted until about 1815, became an essential part of the young republic's political life. Without it, Americans learned, it was difficult to get anything accomplished; indeed, free government itself was endangered.

What produced this momentous change of heart? Were the new parties the result of differences over ideology? Did opposing views of the Constitution create the party divisions? Were the parties deliberately planned to meet administrative or political needs? Were they the outgrowth of personality clashes among magnetic individuals driven by opposing ambitions? Let us look at the circumstances under which the parties emerged, for events generally determine the shape of evolving institutions.

But first one confusing matter should be clarified. One of the two parties that appeared during the 1790s was called Federalist; the other was often referred to as Anti-Federalist, though it was also called Republican or Democratic-Republican, or sometimes Jeffersonian. These two groups must not be confused with the federalist and antifederalist partisans of the period when the Constitution was being debated. It is true that many of the federalists who endorsed and fought for the Constitution later became members of the Federalist party. But Madison and Jefferson were both federalists in the first sense; yet they became the organizers of the Democratic-Republic party. And Patrick Henry was an antifederalist who opposed adoption of the Constitution, yet he later became a strong Federalist. There was an overlap between the positions of federalists and Federalists and between those of antifederalists and Anti-Federalists, but it was not complete. The issues that divided the two political parties of the "first party system" went beyond the disputes of 1787–89.

★ THE NEW GOVERNMENT LAUNCHED ★

National Finances. When Congress convened in New York early in 1789, the atmosphere reflected a common determination to solve the country's major problems. Clearly the new government needed revenue, and early in the first session the legislators adopted two important tax measures: the Tariff Act of 1789, which placed duties on a wide range of imported articles, and the Tonnage Act, which taxed foreign vessels entering American ports. Congress also established three executive departments—State, Treasury, and War—and, in the Federal Judiciary Act, prescribed the structure of the Supreme Court and the federal court system. The Tonnage Act debate revealed some important sectional seams. Northerners, who did the nation's shipping, sought advantages for American merchants. Southerners, who exported tobacco and rice, wanted cheap shipping, whether provided by Americans or foreigners. Representatives from the two sections squabbled a bit over the Tonnage Act, but generally debate was calm and disagreements were muted. It is the measure of the relative political peace of these early months that Washington could appoint Jefferson, soon to be the leading Republican, and Hamilton, soon to be the leading Federalist, as his first secretary of state and secretary of the treasury, respectively.

Yet even in this first session of the First Congress there were signs of trouble to come. One hint was the farcical dispute over how the president should be addressed. Was Washington to be called "His Elective Majesty," "His Highness the President," "His Excellency," or merely "Mr. President"? The first three titles had overtones of British monarchy; the last suggested American republicanism. The argument seems trivial, but it divided people into temperamental aristocrats and temperamental democrats, and foreshadowed later party differences.

Relative harmony became loud discord when, in its second session, the First Congress confronted the pressing issue of the unpaid war debts. Millions of dollars of state and national obligations were long overdue. Some money was owed abroad, and failure to pay it had hurt the international prestige of the United States and made it impossible for the American government to borrow from foreign bankers. Most of the debt, however, was owed to American citizens, including war veterans, former army suppliers, and those who had lent money to Congress or the states. The public creditors also included many businessmen and speculators who had bought up securities and debt certificates in the hope that they would rise in value

when the government was finally able to repay them. How were all these people to be paid? And were they to be paid fully and equally?

Hamilton's Plan for America. The man who had to answer these questions in practice was the new secretary of the treasury, Alexander Hamilton of New York. Hamilton was one of the most intriguing and controversial men who ever occupied high office in the United States. Born illegitimate in the West Indies, he lacked the advantages of "good birth" and family wealth so useful in getting ahead in eighteenth-century America. But he made up for this by exhibiting at an early age enormous charm, drive, and intelligence. The young man so impressed prominent men on the island of St. Croix that they sent him to be educated on the mainland. In 1773 he entered Kings College (now Columbia University) in New York City.

At eighteen Hamilton arrived in New York in the midst of the imperial crisis and promptly joined the Patriots. In 1774 he enrolled in a New York militia unit and soon saw action against the British. Before long his skill as an artillery

Alexander Hamilton at about the time of his leadership of the Treasury Department.

officer brought him to Washington's attention, and he was appointed aide-de-camp to the American commander in chief. After Yorktown he returned to his adopted city and set up as a lawyer. His rise might have been slow despite his war record and his legal brilliance; there were many bright and ambitious young veterans in the city anxious to make their mark. But in 1780 he married Elizabeth Schuyler, daughter of the rich and prominent Philip Schuyler. This connection gave him the social standing and influence that his foreign birth and dubious parentage had denied him. His career was soon flourishing.

Hamilton was an excellent choice for Washington's cabinet. Skeptical of human nature and convinced that people must be firmly restrained, he believed in strong government and had been instrumental in getting New York to adopt the Constitution. He thought the new Union was still too weak, but at least, he reasoned, it was better than the old Confederation. When he was offered the job of secretary of the treasury, Hamilton leaped at the chance. In that office he could help forge a strong national government and transform the United States into a unified and prosperous nation.

Whatever we may think of Hamilton's ambition and distrust of human nature, he was a political innovator with an expansive vision of America's future. The United States of 1790 was a nation of 4 million people, most of them farmers or farm workers. The first national census recorded that only about 3 percent of the population lived in cities with more than 8,000 people. The country was more than self-sufficient in food, fiber, and raw materials; but it continued to import most manufactured goods just as it had in colonial days. Exported grain, rice, tobacco, lumber, beef and pork, and other "primary" products of its fields and forests paid for the imports.

Hamilton hoped to change this society. He recognized the importance of agriculture in America and understood that it would remain the country's economic mainstay for many years to come. Yet he believed that the United States must turn to manufacturing for its future prosperity. Industry would free the nation from foreign dependence. It would also transform it. Looking at England, then fast becoming the workshop of the world, Hamilton perceived the wealth and power that might lie in store for America.

In 1791 Hamilton had joined a group of friends in supporting the Society for Establishing Useful Manufactures to develop as a manufacturing center the water power site on the Passaic River in New Jersey. As a public servant, he hoped to do more than just straighten out the country's tangled finances. In many ways the first secretary of the treasury was the first great national planner. Like more recent leaders of developing nations, he sought to encourage economic growth and social modernization. Although today

we can see some of the drawbacks of unrestrained industrialization, for its time Hamilton's was a progressive vision.

Hamilton incorporated these goals into three major reports submitted to Congress between January 1790 and December 1791. The *First Report on the Public Credit* proposed a plan for putting national finances on a sound basis. Now that the government had a guaranteed revenue from taxes and duties, let it pay its own creditors. It should also take over ("assume") the remaining state debts. Hamilton knew that even with its newly acquired taxing power the government could not simply pay off these debts in one lump sum. There was a way around this difficulty. The government would issue new securities that would bear an attractive interest rate, and holders of the old, defaulted debt could exchange it for the new "funded debt."

Hamilton's motives here were in part political. He hoped to strengthen the national government by attaching to it the interests of the rich and powerful, the country's chief creditors. But he also had larger purposes. Defying conventional thinking, the secretary believed that a public debt was a "blessing," not a "curse." The new funded debt would be a form of property, and like any other property—land and houses, for example—it could be used as security for raising money. An abundance of money or credit—which amounted to the same thing—would in turn stimulate commerce and provide investment capital for a capital-poor nation. The new funded debt would be "an engine of business, an instrument of industry and commerce."

The secretary spelled out the way this process might operate in the second of his major reports, the *Report on a National Bank*. In this document he recommended that Congress charter a bank. Besides providing a convenient agency for handling federal tax collections and disbursements and for aiding private business transactions, a federally chartered bank would provide money for circulation and credit for investment. Only part of the bank's capital, he explained, needed to be silver and gold, commodities in short supply in America. The rest could consist of the funded debt—that is, the new government bonds—which would-be investors in the bank could use instead of specie to buy bank stock. These bonds would now be used as the backing for an issue of paper money—"bank notes"—that could then be lent out to investors and used as the normal cash of the country. By such means, Hamilton theorized, banks in general and the federal bank in particular could become "nurseries of national wealth."

In his final important state paper, the *Report on Manufactures*, Hamilton urged Congress to support industry with subsidies, a tariff, and a system of roads, canals, and other "internal improvements." Pointing out that America's high labor costs and its shortage of investment capital put it at a disadvantage against the better-developed

European countries, he declared that these handicaps could be overcome only by government action. So long as certain industries were weak, the government should nurture them. When they grew strong, they could compete independently in the world marketplace and government aid would become unnecessary. The benefits of supporting "infant industries," Hamilton was sure, would be felt not only by promoters of industry and the laboring classes but also by farmers, who would find new markets for their products in the manufacturing cities and towns that the government's protective policies would encourage. Of Hamilton's three major reports, only this one on manufactures resulted in no immediate action by Congress. But as a glimpse of the future and an arsenal of arguments for government protection of American industry, it, too, was a landmark.

Enacting the Hamiltonian Program. The Funding Act of 1790 sought to enact the first part of Hamilton's program. The bill had two sections. Part one authorized all present holders of national securities to convert them into federal bonds at face value, though at varying rates of interest. Part two empowered the federal government to assume the outstanding state debts. State creditors, too, could convert their securities into the new funded debt.

The measure aroused the ire of James Madison, now a leader in the House of Representatives, where the Hamiltonian program had to begin its legislative course.

The Hamiltonians, Madison said, were showing excessive consideration for speculators and not enough for the "original holders," who had paid cash or provided valuable goods or services in exchange for Continental or state securities during the war. These people had expressed their faith in the Patriot cause, but many had been forced to sell their securities at large discounts to speculators. Why should these original holders not receive some part of the gain that would come when the debt was funded? Why should all the profit go to the gamblers?

Though he talked much about the ethical aspects of the issue, Madison was also concerned about the interests of his section—the South—just as his opponents were about theirs. Assumption was offensive to many southerners. The southern states had already paid most of their debts. Now burdened southern taxpayers would be asked to pay federal taxes to redeem the debts of delinquent northern states.

Though it took a sectional form, the debate also reflected social differences. To Madison and his supporters the North represented trade and commerce, the South, agriculture. The Funding Act, accordingly, seemed designed to benefit the commercial interests at the expense of the agricultural interests. After all, they declared, most of the speculators who would gain from the act lived in the port towns of New England, New York, and Pennsylvania.

The first section of the Funding Act passed after a bitter battle. But the second, which authorized assumption of

The building that housed the first Bank of the United States helped set the fashion in Greco-Roman bank structures that has continued until recently. The architect clearly intended to inspire confidence in the durability of the building and the institution.

Report on Manufactures

A critical issue separating the two political parties during the 1790s was whether the country's future lay with agriculture or with industry and commerce. The apostle of the second course, one that required major changes in America's economy and social system, was the first secretary of the treasury, Alexander Hamilton. In his *Report on Manufactures* of 1791 Hamilton argued for government policies that would transform America from a land of farms into one of workshops, mills, and busy cities as well. This document, the last of four major reports, did not lead to immediate congressional action, but like the others it helped define the coherent political philosophy that we associate with the Federalist party. By its challenge to those who wished to keep America as it was, it also helped to clarify the position of the Jeffersonian Anti-Federalists.

"There . . . are . . . respectable patrons of opinions unfriendly to the encouragement of manufactures. The following are . . . the arguments by which these opinions are defended.

"In every country (say those who entertain them) Agriculture is the most beneficial and *productive* object of human industry. This position . . . applies with peculiar emphasis to the United States on account of their immense tracts of fertile territory, uninhabited and unimproved. Nothing can afford so advantageous an employ-ment for capital and labor, as the conversion of this extensive wilderness into cultivated farms. . . .

"To endeavor, by the extraordinary patronage of Government, to accelerate the growth of manufactures, is, in fact, to endeavor, by force and art, to transfer the natural current of industry from a more, to a less beneficial channel. Whatever has such tendency must necessarily be unwise. . . . To leave industry to itself, therefore, is . . . the soundest as well as the simplest policy.

"This policy is not only recommended to the United States by considerations which affect all nations . . . it is [also] dictated to them . . . by the smallness of their population compared with their territory. . . . [This fact] conspires to produce . . . a scarcity of hands for manufacturing occupations, and dearness of labor generally. . . .

"If contrary to the natural course of things, an unseasonable and premature spring can be given to certain fabrics, by heavy duties, prohibitions, bounties, or by other forced expedients, this will only be to sacrifice the interests of the community to those of particular classes. Besides the misdirection of labor, a virtual monopoly will be given to the persons employed on such fabrics; and an enhancement of price, the inevitable consequence of every monopoly, must be defrayed at the expense of the other part of society. . . .

"[In reply to these arguments] . . . it ought readily to be conceded that the cultivation of the earth . . . has *intrin-sically a strong claim to pre-eminence over every other kind of industry. . . .* But, that it has a title to anything like an exclusive predilection in any country, ought to be admitted with great caution. . . .

". . . [M]anufacturing establishments not only occasion a positive augmentation of the Produce and Revenue of the Society, but . . . they contribute essentially to rendering them greater than they could possibly be, without such establishments. These circumstances are—

1. The division of labor.

2. An extension of the use of Machinery.

3. Additional employment to classes of the community not ordinarily engaged in the business.

4. The promoting of emigration from foreign Countries.

5. The furnishing of greater scope for the diversity of talents and dispositions which discriminate from each other.

6. The affording a more ample and various field for enterprise.

7. The creating in some instances a new, and securing in all, a more certain and steady demand for the surplus produce of the soil.

"Each of these circumstances has a considerable influence upon the total mass of industrious effort in a community. Together, they add to it a degree of energy and effect, which are not easily conceived. . . ."

state debts, seemed certain to go down to defeat. Hamilton appealed to Madison not to cripple his plan. With Jefferson's approval the two arranged a deal. In exchange for yielding on assumption, the South would get the new national capital. After first moving to Philadelphia, in the North, for ten years, the seat of the federal government would be established in 1800 at a site on the Potomac between Maryland and Virginia. Thus sugarcoated, the Funding Act, with both sections intact, passed. In the end principle had yielded to sectional pride.

Early in 1791 Congress received Hamilton's bank bill. Madison attacked this measure, too. His objections were probably based on an agrarian suspicion of banks and, once again, on a reluctance to advance commerce and industry at the expense of agriculture. But preferring to appeal to higher principles, he based his arguments on the Constitution. Though he had been a strong nationalist in the 1780s, Madison now expressed the fear that the central government might become too powerful. Where in the Constitution, the astute Virginian asked, was Congress authorized to incorporate such a bank? He refused to accept Hamilton's answer that certain powers were "implied" in the Constitution.

Despite Madison's resistance, Congress established the Bank of the United States with a twenty-year federal charter. The new institution would function in part as a privately owned commercial bank does today. It would accept deposits, make loans, and perform other familiar banking services. In addition, it would do several things normally done in the twentieth century by the Treasury Department or by the Federal Reserve System. It would, for example, handle the government's financial business, including its tax collections and disbursements. More important, it would issue up to $10 million in paper money, backed partly by gold but largely by the funded debt. In this way, as Hamilton intended, the federal debt would become the basis for a money circulation and a source of credit for a capital-poor land. In structure the bank would combine public and private features. Five of the twenty-five directors of the bank were to be appointed by the government, the rest by the private stockholders.

When the bank bill came before Washington for his signature, the president was frankly puzzled about what he should do. Washington would eventually become the Federalists' hero, but at this point he was not yet a strong political partisan. He understood his symbolic role as a wise, dispassionate, and just father who must rise above the fray. To take an obviously partisan stand without very good reason might destroy the image. In his dilemma he turned to his cabinet—Hamilton, Jefferson, and Attorney General Edmund Randolph—for advice. Two written statements resulted, presenting the classic arguments for "loose construction" and "strict construction" of the Constitution. Hamilton defended the bank with his doctrine of implied powers. Jefferson and Randolph argued that powers not explicitly granted Congress by the Constitution were beyond its authority. In a decision that foreshadowed his later shift to Federalism, Washington accepted Hamilton's views and approved the bill.

★ THE BEGINNINGS OF PARTIES ★

The Economic Division. The Hamiltonian program drove a wedge through the nation, dividing Americans into opposing political camps. On one side were the emerging Federalists. They included speculators in government securities, merchants, manufacturers, and would-be manufacturers. Those they employed—merchant seamen, artisans, clerks, bookkeepers, and all who worked in trade—also tended to support Hamilton's program. On the emerging Republican side were many small farmers and southern planters, especially those of middle rank.

The division along occupational lines transcended geography. The "commercial" classes were particularly numerous in New England and the Middle Atlantic states; southerners mostly belonged to the "cultivator" class. This situation largely accounts for the sectional split in Congress over the bank and funding. But in the South, wherever there were large pockets of people engaged in finance, trade, and industry, Federalists established secure footholds. In Charleston, Baltimore, Norfolk, and Savannah Federalism spoke in a southern drawl. On the other hand, there were many Republicans in the North. In places like the valleys of the Susquehanna, Delaware, Connecticut, and Hudson rivers, where surplus crops were produced for export, the farmers were Federalists. In more isolated farm areas cultivators expressed Republican sentiments in the "Dutch" accents of New York and Pennsylvania, the twang of New England, and the rough, direct speech of the frontier.

The Ideological Division. Economic interest, however, was not the only element that separated Hamiltonians from Jeffersonians, Federalists from Republicans. There were ideological and philosophical differences as well—differences in attitudes toward freedom, toward human nature, toward majority rule, and toward the role of government.

Republicans like Jefferson, Madison, and John Taylor regarded the Hamiltonian-Federalist dream as dangerous. Committed libertarians, they deplored paternalistic government. Individuals were far better judges, in general, of their own interest, they felt, than any set of government officials. Tyranny was more to be feared than chaos. Unless checked, government would grow excessively powerful and end by destroying freedom. However unfair, they saw their opponents as disguised monarchists who were scarcely different from King George III and his ministers. Also, as much as possible, power must be dispersed from the center to the periphery. Strictly limit the power of the national government, they exhorted, and assign as many functions as possible to the states. By contrast, the Federalists supported a strong activist federal government that could manage or alter the economy in ways that seemed desirable.

Recent scholarship has made it clear that the Jeffersonian Republicans were not naive anticapitalists. Joyce Appleby has described them, rather, as believers in free markets, as laissez-faire followers of the Scottish philosopher-economist Adam Smith. Yet they were also

Rembrandt Peale, a famous American artist, painted this portrait of Jefferson in 1805. It was completed in time to be displayed at the president's second inauguration. (Collection of the New York Historical Society)

"agrarians," people who especially cherished the ideal of a society composed of small freeholders. According to Jefferson, the nation's farmers were "the chosen people of God, if he ever had a chosen people." John Taylor proclaimed that "divine intelligence" had "selected an agricultural state as a paradise." At times the Jeffersonians admitted artisans, journeymen, and laborers into their charmed circle of the virtuous classes. But they were also suspicious of the urban masses. City "artificers," wrote Jefferson, were often "the panders of vice & the instruments by which the liberties of a country are generally overturned."

The fear of the urban "mob" was the fear of the propertyless. Those without property had no stake in society and could easily be corrupted and used by demagogues. It also reflected the Jeffersonian disdain for cities. Virtue inhered in fields and flocks, not in factories, shipyards, and offices. Even more dubious were those shadowy forms of urban wealth, stocks and bonds. Drawing on views deeply embedded in Western consciousness, the agrarians attached a moral stigma to money lending and "stockjobbing." In fact, many of the wealthy planters who led the Republican party were deeply entangled in real estate speculation, but they failed to see that there was little moral difference between gambling in land and "speculating" in paper securities.

Republican prejudices logically extended to homegrown industry. Though he later modified his position, in 1781 Jefferson would declaim: "While we have land to labour, then, let us never wish to see our citizens occupied at a work-bench or twirling a distaff. Carpenters, masons, smiths, are wanting in husbandry; but, for the general operations of manufacture, let our work-shops remain in Europe." The preference for "husbandry" did not preclude commerce; obviously American farmers would want to trade their surpluses for foreign manufactures. Yet it was primarily as an adjunct to agriculture that commerce deserved favor.

Whatever their economic preferences, the Jeffersonians were not backward-looking social reactionaries. They were optimists who believed in the ability of human intelligence to improve people's lot. Jefferson himself was a creative, inventive man who designed his home, Monticello, invented an improved form of moldboard for the plow, and kept in touch with the most recent scientific developments throughout the Atlantic world. On the other hand, in the original sense of the word the Jeffersonians were conservatives—they wished to conserve what already existed. America must remain a nation of farms and forests. Their motto could have been "Keep America Green!" By contrast, for all their social caution, the Federalists sought to alter the economic status quo in fundamental ways.

Federalists and Republicans disagreed, too, over the workability of majority rule. Federalists were elitists. They distrusted human nature and feared the rule of mere numbers. Such a regime took power from the trained and the able, the "wellborn," and gave it to their inferiors. To Hamilton, the people were "a great beast." Other Federalist leaders were equally blunt in expressing contempt for the people and "their rabble rousing" leaders. Harrison Gray Otis of Boston called the voters a "duped and deluded mob." John Jay of New York, first chief justice of the Supreme Court, reflected that "the mass of men are neither wise nor good, and virtue . . . can only be drawn to a point and executed by . . . a strong government ably administered." Even John Adams, though never one of the extreme or "High" Federalists, feared the end of all "decorum, discipline, and subordination" if rule by majorities was not restrained.

Republicans, by contrast, proclaimed human nature to be inherently good. That human vices "are part of man's original constitution," announced one New York Jeffersonian, had been shown to be false. The evil deeds that people at times committed should be traced rather "to the errors and abuses that have at every period existed in political establishments." Jefferson himself regarded the people as eminently trustworthy. "I am," he announced, "not among those who fear the people; they, and not the rich, are our dependence for continued freedom." At moments Jefferson even sounded like a radical. In letters to friends and associates he wrote that "the tree of Liberty must be watered periodically with the blood of tyrants" and "a little revolution every twenty years is an excellent thing." These

He was not the best of farmers, but Thomas Jefferson did worship the plow. Unlike Hamilton, he placed his trust in the common people and dreamed of a nation of farmers. The class divisions that grew out of Hamilton's industrial economy threatened to destroy Jefferson's ideal of a virtuous agrarian republic.

statements show the Sage of Monticello playing with ideas—today he would be called an intellectual. In his public statements and acts he was far more reserved. We should also remember that he and his political allies tended to limit the "people" to the white tillers of the soil. Of the "mobs of great cities" they were far more suspicious. It is clear, nevertheless, that philosophically the Republicans were more democratic than their opponents.

We must not draw the distinctions between Federalist aristocracy and Republican democracy too sharply, however. Many southern Jeffersonians were slaveholders. Many deplored slavery in the abstract, but considered it unavoidable. Jefferson himself did not believe in absolute human equality but in "natural aristocracy." This was an elite based on talent and ability, rather than birth, but it was an elite nonetheless. Nor should we assume that Hamilton and his followers were unqualified aristocrats or "monocrats," as their enemies called them. Generally they accepted representative government as unavoidable in America and never seriously intended to establish a monarchy.

Yet when all these qualifications are noted, it remains true that Federalists had less faith in majority rule than their opponents. The Republicans, in turn, had less confidence in persons of wealth and position than in "the people."

The Role of Religion. We have seen how the Federalists won their battle with the Republicans over Hamilton's financial program. Over the next decade they would win a

fair share of both state and national elections and enact additional parts of their program. Their success is puzzling. Young America was largely a nation of farmers, and farmers as a whole, surely, admired Jefferson's principles and disliked Hamilton's. Why, then, were the elite Federalists, with their commercial biases and antidemocratic rhetoric, so successful in the nation's first decade under the Constitution?

Momentum from the Confederation period is part of the answer. In a sense, the Federalists had a mandate in the early 1790s to create a strong, sound government and economy. Before the mandate ran out, they had enacted much of their program. They were also helped by the prestige of George Washington. Although above the battle at first, he eventually drifted into the Federalist camp. As long as he was alive, his incomparable standing among Americans bolstered the Federalist position regardless of material or ideological factors. Another element of Federalist successes is that for reasons that we do not fully understand, not more than a quarter of the eligible voters went to the polls in the 1790s. A large proportion of the people who did vote were educated, and they were more inclined to support the "high-toned" Federalists than their "rabble-rousing" opponents.

But these factors are only part of the answer. Religion, too, helped the Federalist cause. In the 1790s the Federalists attracted Congregationalists in New England and Episcopalians in the Middle Atlantic states and the South. The Republicans won the support of a hodgepodge of Baptists, Methodists, Roman Catholics, nonbelievers, and deists. These groupings may not appear to make much sense—Roman Catholics and nonbelievers do not seem to have much in common. If we take a second look, however, we can see the pattern: Members of established churches—those that received financial support from state governments and so had privileged positions—or formerly established churches, voted Federalist, whereas the others tended to prefer the Jeffersonians.

The Republican appeal to nonbelievers is easy to understand. Jefferson himself was a deist whose religious creed rejected many orthodox Christian elements. Conversely, leading Federalists were often outspoken defenders of traditional Christian beliefs. The Republican appeal to Catholics and evangelical Protestants, such as Baptists and Methodists, requires a little more probing. These groups had long been victims of legal discrimination. By the 1790s they were still disqualified from holding office in some areas, and in parts of New England where Congregationalism was still the established church, they remained second-class citizens. The role of Jefferson and Madison in securing the Virginia Statute for Religious Freedom earned the Republican leaders the gratitude of all those outside the established religious order everywhere. In Connecticut and

THE TIMES, A POLITICAL PORTRAIT

The Cannibals are landing

Triumph Government, perish all its enemies—
Traitors be warned, justice though slow is sure

A Federalist cartoon showing Washington leading American troops against French "cannibals" while Gallatin, Citizen Genêt, and Jefferson try to halt his chariot. (Collection of the New York Historical Society)

Massachusetts the Republicans confirmed this attachment by leading the fight to end the preferred status conferred on Congregationalism. It is not surprising, then, that people who thought of themselves as religious outsiders should find Republicanism more congenial than Federalism.

Here, then, is another explanation for Federalist successes: Although far more Americans belonged to occupational groups that benefited from Republican positions than to those that the Federalists endorsed, religion served to counteract economic interest as a decisive factor. A Congregational farmer in Massachusetts, for example, might well vote Federalist, though the Republicans represented the agrarian interests. On the other hand, a Baptist merchant from Connecticut or a rich Catholic lawyer from New York—people we would normally expect to vote for the Federalists on the basis of occupation—might well support the Republicans for religious reasons. On the whole the religious factor seemed to help the Federalists more than their opponents.

★ RELATIONS WITH EUROPE ★

The first party system was not only a response to domestic events and attitudes. It was also the offspring of America's complex relations with the rest of the Atlantic world.

America's foreign relations were in disarray in 1790. Many problems remained from the previous decade. Spain controlled the mouth of the Mississippi and still denied

Americans the right of deposit at New Orleans. The British continued to restrict American trade with their empire and refused to abandon the military posts they occupied in the Northwest. And even France had begun to limit American trade with its colonies, despite the commercial treaty of 1778.

Revolution in France. The outbreak of the French Revolution of 1789 would make these problems infinitely worse. The greatest political convulsion of modern times aroused strong passions in America. At first most Americans rejoiced at the overthrow of the corrupt, aristocratic, and worn-out Old Regime in the most powerful nation on the European continent. The fall of the Bastille, a hated symbol of tyranny, and the release of its prisoners seemed a triumph of the principles of freedom and equality that Americans had recently fought for. One enthusiastic Yankee orator saw the event as a "spark from the altar flame of liberty on this side of the Atlantic, which alighted in the pinnacle of despotism in France and reduced the immense fabric to ashes in the twinkling of an eye." The *Gazette of the United States* called it "one of the most glorious objects that *can arrest the attention of Mankind.*" In Boston, streets were renamed for revolutionary ideals—Royal Exchange Alley became Equality Lane. Some Americans replaced *mister* with the revolutionary *citizen* and Mrs. with the awkward *citess*. At first even men of conservative temper welcomed the change. President Washington graciously received from Lafayette the key to the Bastille as a link between the American and French struggles against tyranny.

But bipartisan support for the revolt quickly waned. The fall of the Bastille was followed by the overthrow of the French monarchy, the execution of King Louis XVI, the Reign of Terror against the Revolution's enemies, confiscation of the property of French nobles, and ever more violent attacks on the church and traditional Christianity. American public opinion quickly split. Federalists were shocked and frightened by the events in France. Fisher Ames, a Massachusetts Federalist, denounced revolutionary France as "an open hell, still ringing with agonies and blasphemies, still smoking with sufferings and crimes, in which we see . . . perhaps our future state." Other Federalists warned that the French "moral influenza" was to be more dreaded than a "thousand yellow fevers." If Americans were not careful, it might spread to their shores. Jefferson, Madison, and their allies, however, continued to admire the revolutionaries, cheering the end of "superstition" and applauding the "rule of reason." Many approved of the execution of Louis XVI and even saw virtue in the Reign of Terror.

The party split became wider when in 1793 war broke out between the new French Republic and England, Spain, and Holland. How should the United States respond? France was America's ally, and although it had not lately taken the friendship seriously, the French Republic needed American support now that it was fighting for its life. The United States could be a source of food and supplies for France and the French colonies in the Western Hemisphere. It might even become a base of operations against British and Spanish possessions in North America.

Citizen Genêt.   Hoping to gain American aid, the French government sent "Citizen" Edmond Genêt to the United States as its minister. Genêt immediately became a magnet for controversy. Secretary Hamilton opposed receiving him for fear that it would involve the nation in the war. Secretary Jefferson claimed that if we refused, we would be repudiating our alliance with France. Neither man wished to see the United States enter the war, but they differed over how and when to assert neutrality. Hamilton believed that it was the president's task to proclaim neutrality and that he should do so at once. Jefferson held that Congress should make the announcement, but only after the United States had squeezed concessions out of both the British and the French.

Washington took his treasury secretary's advice and in April 1793 issued a proclamation of neutrality. The president asked Americans to be "impartial" toward the belligerents and forbade engaging in actions favorable to either side. Republicans found the proclamation offensive. It was too neutral. "The cause of France is the cause of man," declared one protesting Jeffersonian. Madison and Hamilton

were soon engaged in a shouting match in which they loudly set forth their clashing positions in the press on the momentous events in Europe.

Meanwhile, Genêt was making plans. Hoping to make the United States a base for operations against Britain and Spain, he hired George Rogers Clark, the Indian fighter and hero of the Revolution, to lead an expedition against the Spanish in Louisiana and Florida. At the same time he passed out commissions in the proposed army and authorized privateers to sail from American ports to attack British and Spanish shipping. Finally, in midsummer of 1793, Genêt demanded that Washington call Congress into special session to decide what the United States would do to aid the French Republic. If the president refused, Genêt arrogantly declared, he would take his case to the American people over Washington's head.

Genêt's activities further polarized American opinion. The Republicans at first befriended him, and Jefferson filled the Frenchman's ears with the misdeeds of his Federalist opponents. The Federalists despised him and used his activities as a stick with which to beat their opponents. The English-born Federalist journalist William Cobbett labeled the Republicans the "bastard offspring of Genêt, spawned in hell, to which they will presently return."

Before long Genêt's activities had so embarrassed the American government that even Jefferson agreed he must be sent home. France, however, was now in the hands of the radical Jacobins, who despised the moderates who had sent Genêt to America. Rather than send the amiable but foolish emissary to certain execution, Washington granted him asylum in the United States.

The Partisan Press.   The controversy over Genêt propelled party conflict to new heights. By now Federalists were being sneered at as pro-British "Anglomen" by their enemies and were in turn calling their Republican opponents "Gallomen"—partisans of France. Differences over foreign policy, combined with the disagreements over the Hamiltonian program, had produced a combative party press that further aggravated the political rivalry. Americans today are used to partisan journalism. Most newspapers support one or other of the major parties and are not always generous to their political opponents. Compared with the party press of the 1790s, however, they are models of decorum, objectivity, and tolerance.

Federalist and Republican newspapers published scathing criticisms of their opponents. John Fenno's *Gazette of the United States* made Hamilton into a demigod and spewed out insults against his enemies. These Jacobins—as the French revolutionary extremists were called—were working to corrupt the nation's youth and "make them imbibe, with their very milk . . . the poison of atheism and disaffection." The *General Advertiser*, edited by Franklin's grandson, Benjamin Franklin Bache, and Philip Freneau's *National Gazette* denounced the Federalists as outright monarchists and dupes of British policy. Bache even maligned Washington as the "scourge of all the misfortunes of our country," a man who had given currency "to political iniquity and to legalized corruption."

Within Washington's cabinet the relations between Jefferson and Hamilton became so bad that at the end of 1793 Jefferson resigned as secretary of state and was replaced by Edmund Randolph, a Virginia Federalist. But Jefferson's departure did not end his leadership of the Republicans. From Monticello, his hilltop home in Virginia, the former secretary continued to put out a flood of political advice, remaining in close touch with Madison, the party's chief tactician in Congress.

Relations with England. Just before Jefferson's retirement, European affairs once more reached a crisis. This time the United States found itself pitted against the world's greatest naval power, England. The difficulty concerned neutral rights on the high seas in time of war; it would not be settled for twenty years.

Basically the two nations disagreed over whether the United States could trade freely with France, England's enemy. The French, unable to protect their shipping against the British navy, had opened their imperial trade, normally restricted to French vessels, to neutral commerce. The British, rightly, saw this as a damaging maneuver and invoked the Rule of 1756, which had been used against Americans trading with the French colonies during the French and Indian War. This rule declared that trade forbidden in time of peace could not be legally pursued in time of war. In effect, a weak naval power could not protect itself by hiding behind a neutral. Britain and the United States also argued over contraband. International law recognized the right of one nation to blockade its wartime enemy's ports and prevent neutral nations from delivering certain war goods—contraband—through the blockade. But contraband was not clearly defined, nor was the legal status of neutral trade in other goods.

Soon after Anglo-French hostilities began, Britain proclaimed a blockade of France and its colonies and deployed its navy to destroy French shipping and commerce. The French immediately lifted all restrictions on foreign imports and opened their ports to foreign ships. Neutral America seized the opportunity to supply French shipping needs. For the next two decades, as Britain and France struggled to dominate Europe, French demand stimulated American trade beyond all previous measure. Hundreds of new vessels, manned by thousands of newly recruited seamen, scudded across the Atlantic and the Caribbean carrying car-

goes to Europe and the West Indies. Salem, Boston, Providence, New York, and Philadelphia boomed as the value of foreign trade leaped from $46 million in 1790 to $140 million by 1796.

The British found this new American prosperity doubly offensive. The Americans were profiting from Britain's troubles and at the same time helping to make them worse by supplying its chief enemy. Even more annoying, England was unintentionally supplying many of the seamen for the bloated American merchant fleet. Some of these were deserters from the Royal Navy who preferred the lenient treatment and good pay of American merchant seamen to the harsh discipline, bad food, and physical dangers of the British navy. When a British man-of-war docked beside an American merchant ship in any harbor in the world, it was certain to lose part of its crew to the Yankees, who were always happy to get experienced mariners. British merchant seamen, too, jumped ship for the higher pay and better working conditions of the American merchant marine.

To deal with the loss of sailors, the British began to stop American vessels to inspect the crews for deserters, "impressing" both those deemed guilty and those who merely looked like apt recruits for the depleted Royal Navy. Americans were outraged by impressment, but their anger was tempered by fear that worsening relations with Britain would destroy entirely the lucrative trade with France. To New Englanders and residents of the middle states' ports—the chief beneficiaries of this trade—it seemed wiser to submit to British practices, however arbitrary, than to defy Britain, provoke war, and see the new trade completely shut down. Expediency was reinforced by political sympathy. The port cities were also the centers of Federalism, and many of their inhabitants were reluctant to denounce Britain, the embattled bulwark against the Jacobins, no matter how ruthlessly it violated American rights.

The British and the Indians. In one area of Anglo-American relations, however, almost all Americans agreed that British policies were deplorable. In the Northwest, a decade after the treaty ending the War for Independence, British garrisons still occupied American soil and British fur traders still monopolized business with the Indians. Besides these affronts to national pride and American commercial interests, Americans were also certain that the British were encouraging the Indians south of the Great Lakes in their policy of harassing American settlers. In 1790 General Josiah Harmar set out with a band of ill-trained militia to teach the Indians a lesson. At the Maumee River his men were ambushed and 183 killed. The following year Arthur St. Clair, governor of the Northwest Territory, walked into a similar trap. St. Clair and part of his force escaped, but they left behind 630 dead.

Jubilant over their successes, during the winter of 1791–92, the Indians drove the Ohio settlers back to the region's two well-defended villages. Meanwhile, seeing an opportunity to check the American westward advance, the British sent agents from Canada to urge the tribes to demand an Indian state north of the Ohio where no white man could settle. In the summer of 1792 Canadian officials and their Indian allies agreed to propose such a buffer state to the Americans at a meeting scheduled at Sandusky the following spring.

The Sandusky meeting never took place. Learning in advance of the Indian demands, the Americans called off the conference. President Washington now decided to settle the conflict by force and dispatched a new army under Anthony Wayne to the Ohio region. Wayne, an abler strategist than his predecessors, trained and seasoned his troops through the winter and spring of 1793–94. In August 1794 he encountered the Indians at Fallen Timbers and decisively defeated them.

The Jay Treaty. In the fall of 1793 the crisis between England and the United States came to a head when a British order in council—an executive proclamation—authorized English naval commanders to seize neutral vessels trading

BURNING JAY'S EFFIGY.

They called John Jay "that damned arch-traitor Sir John Jay" when he returned from England with the treaty that seemed a sell-out to Britain. Here they are burning him at the stake—in effigy.

with the French Caribbean islands. In short order 250 American ships were boarded by British naval parties, escorted to British ports, and confiscated. The seizures infuriated Americans, and it soon seemed like 1775 all over again. Mobs roved the streets of seaport towns, denouncing Britain and insulting and threatening Englishmen, including the British minister to the United States. British tempers were equally hot. The commander of the British forces in the Northwest declared that he looked forward to meeting Washington "with adequate force and on a just occasion—face to face." War appeared imminent. To avoid a military showdown, for which the United States was ill prepared, Washington decided to send a mission to England headed by Chief Justice John Jay.

Jay's instructions, drafted by Secretary of State Randolph, were conciliatory. But in late 1794 the British were not inclined to be overly generous with the upstart Americans, especially when they learned that they did not intend to join with other neutrals to defy British naval policy. In the end they drove a hard bargain. They agreed to surrender the western posts and pay for American ships recently confiscated. They also yielded slightly on the long-festering issue of trade with the British Empire. The United States would be allowed to trade with British India, and small American vessels would be permitted to enter British West Indies ports. But in most other matters they refused to budge. They rejected American demands for full commercial equality with British subjects. They denied liability for the slaves they had removed from the South during the Revolution. They refused Jay's claim that American ships could legally carry a wide range of French goods. The final agreement contained a broad definition of contraband that made many American goods liable to seizure as well as a proviso that the United States must close its ports to French privateers. To satisfy long-standing English complaints, the United States also agreed to refer all unpaid American private debts owed English creditors to a joint commission for settlement. On western problems, too, the United States made concessions. In return for surrendering the Northwest posts, Britain would be allowed to exploit the resources of the region south of the Canadian border as in the past.

The Jay Treaty brought down the wrath of the Republicans on Federalist heads. To France's friends and England's enemies the treaty seemed a sellout. Jay was denounced as an "archtraitor" and hanged in effigy by irate crowds all over the country. The agreement itself was referred to widely as "that damned treaty." For a while there was doubt that the Senate would confirm it or the president sign it. But the Senate's strong Federalist majority passed the treaty after striking out one of the more unfavorable trade provisions. Washington hesitated but approved it when he realized that the alternative might well be war with England. Even after adoption the treaty continued to rankle, and Washington was reviled for endorsing it. Jefferson claimed that he had "undone the country," and a bitterly partisan Virginian ventured the shocking toast: "A speedy death to General Washington."

Hostility to the Jay Treaty powerfully reinforced party formation. According to one historian of the Massachusetts Republicans, "More than any other act, the Jay Treaty influenced the development of party" in the Bay State. In the House of Representatives—the body that would have to appropriate money to carry out several provisions of the pact—Republicans organized the first congressional party caucus ever held to consider ways to defeat the treaty. In the end their attempt failed, but the close House vote revealed the new strength of the opposition and the extent to which foreign affairs had polarized Congress along party lines.

The Whiskey Rebellion; The Pinckney Treaty. The major disputes with Great Britain now settled, however badly, the Washington administration turned to differences with Spain. In the Northwest, Britain's surrender of the military posts meant the abandonment of their Indian allies. Chastened by their defeat at Fallen Timbers, the Indians signed the Treaty of Greenville in 1795, surrendering all of Ohio except for a small strip along Lake Erie. Before many months a mass movement of white pioneer farmers into the Northwest was under way. In the Southwest, where Indian resistance to the whites was weaker, by 1796 there were already two new states—Kentucky and Tennessee—carved out of a region that had had no permanent white inhabitants twenty years earlier.

The westerners were a restless and unruly lot. For years frontier farmers had been angry over federal tax policy. Unable to sell their grain to distant urban customers because of high transportation costs, they had found an ingenious alternative. To make their grain portable, they made it potable, distilling it into whiskey, which could be easily carried to market in barrels. When the government imposed a tax on distilled liquors in 1791 to raise money for Hamilton's funding plan, westerners defied the authorities and threatened tax collectors with physical harm.

In 1794 the farmers of western Pennsylvania carried defiance to the point of open rebellion. The "Whiskey Rebels" closed down federal courts and robbed the mails. They attacked federal troops guarding the tax collector for the Pittsburgh district. Seven years before, when Daniel Shays's men had defied the tax collectors in the same way, the central government had been helpless to act. Now Washington quickly ordered out the militia, which, with the militant Hamilton as second in command, marched on the rebels. To Hamilton's dismay the insurgents surrendered

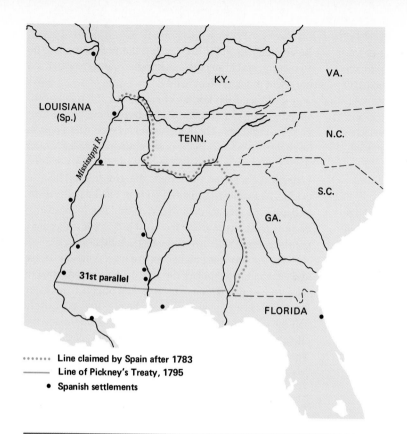

.... **Line claimed by Spain after 1783**
——— **Line of Pickney's Treaty, 1795**
• **Spanish settlements**

PINCKNEY'S TREATY, 1795

without a shot. The government proved lenient. Some twenty woebegone Whiskey Rebel prisoners were paraded down Market Street in Philadelphia; two were convicted of high treason and then pardoned.

No lives were lost in the incident, but it confirmed western disgust at the trigger-happy Federalists. At the same time it showed the government that westerners were not to be trifled with. Now they were demanding that the federal government do something about Spain's refusal to allow the right of deposit at New Orleans. If the United States government did not give them what they wanted, they threatened to take matters into their own hands and negotiate directly with Spain.

To prevent such an outcome, Washington ordered Thomas Pinckney to Spain to arbitrate the differences between the two nations. Fortunately for the United States, Spain was ready to negotiate. In short order Pinckney and the Spanish foreign minister concluded a treaty granting the United States free navigation of the Mississippi and the right of tax-free deposit at New Orleans for three years, subject to renewal. The treaty also set the boundary between the United States and Florida at the thirty-first parallel, conceding the Yazoo Strip of southern Georgia and Mississippi to the Americans. The Jay Treaty had left many issues unresolved. The Pinckney Treaty, for the moment at least, settled the nagging problem of Mississippi navigation at virtually no cost to the United States, and was immensely popular.

Washington's Farewell. In 1796 Washington decided that two terms as president were quite enough; he would retire to his plantation home at Mount Vernon on the Potomac. Before leaving, however, he delivered a formal farewell to his fellow Americans in the form of a letter published in the newspapers. This "Farewell Address" has always been considered a foreign policy statement, but it was concerned largely with domestic matters. The departing president cautioned against "permanent alliances with any portion of the foreign world." But most of his message, even the part dealing with foreign relations, was a warning against the "spirit of party" and a tribute to the virtues of "fraternal affection" and national unity. Toward the end of his administration Washington had been drawn into the ranks of the Federalists. Still, he did not believe in the party system, and he told the American people that factionalism served to "distract the public councils and enfeeble the public administration."

Despite the president's warning, the spirit of party marked his very departure. To the Federalists, who had borrowed his prestige to bolster their policies, his retirement was a blow. To the Republicans, it was a blessing. Benjamin

Franklin Bache's paper rejoiced that a new era was dawning. With Washington gone, public measures would have to stand on their own merits. "The name of WASHINGTON from this day," it crowed, "ceases to give currency to political iniquity." Bache was right: The Federalists were now deprived of an immense political asset. In the election of 1796 they would not have the nation's greatest popular hero at the head of their ticket. This time there would be a real contest for the presidency.

The Election of 1796. No one was quite sure how the presidential candidates would be selected in 1796 and how, once chosen, one would be elected to office. Washington had faced no opposition as nominee or candidate and had not campaigned. Now things were different. How could matters be arranged? In a few states, notably Pennsylvania, there were already permanent party organizations and a formal nominating procedure. In others, and at the national level, party machinery was primitive. The Republicans had an informal party chairman in the clerk of the House of Representatives, John Beckley, but the Federalists had no equivalent; and in any case, an informal party chairman did not wield much power.

In the end the leaders of each party informally consulted with one another and decided who to support as their party's candidates. The Republicans' choice was never in doubt: Jefferson was their most commanding figure, and there was no one to challenge his candidacy. Among the Federalists, however, the leaders disagreed. The High, or extreme, Federalists supported Thomas Pinckney, the treaty negotiator. Moderates preferred Vice President John Adams. Because the party leaders were unable to settle on a single nominee, there were two Federalist candidates.

The contest was fought over the unpopular Jay Treaty and general foreign policy, though the Republicans tried to make the supposed monarchism of their opponents a major issue. Official electors were chosen by popular vote in only half the states; in the others the state legislatures made the choice. The Federalists won a majority in the electoral college, carrying most of the states from New Jersey north. But

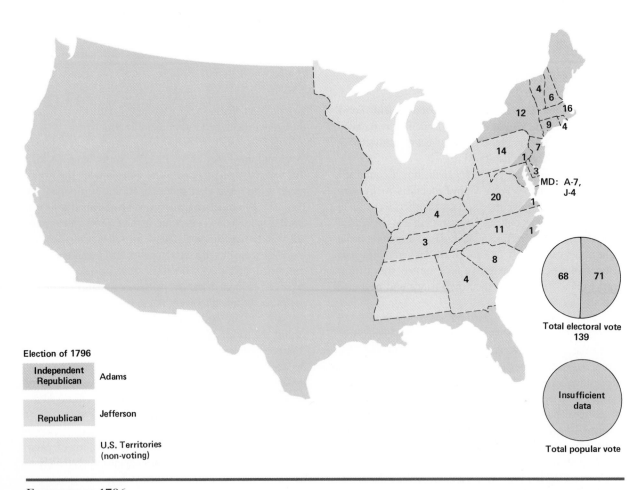

Election of 1796

Independent Republican — Adams

Republican — Jefferson

U.S. Territories (non-voting)

MD: A-7, J-4

Total electoral vote 139

Insufficient data

Total popular vote

ELECTION OF 1796

since they were divided between High Federalists and Adams men, the Federalist electors could not coordinate their votes. Adams received the highest number of votes and became president. Enough Federalists refused to support Pinckney, however, to give Jefferson the second highest number of votes, thereby making him vice president under the existing terms of the Constitution. To us today it seems curious to have a president and vice president of opposing parties but of course the Founding Fathers had not anticipated a party system.

The XYZ Affair.   John Adams no sooner took office than the United States found itself in an undeclared war with its recent ally, France. The French government, now in the hands of the Directory, a new ruling group, considered the Jay Treaty a virtual Anglo-American alliance. The election of Adams, the candidate of the pro-British Federalists, seemed to confirm American sympathies for England, and French policy toward America quickly became more hostile. In 1797 the French authorities ordered that impressed American sailors captured from the British be hanged and that any intercepted American ship carrying British goods be confiscated. They also refused to receive the American minister, Charles Cotesworth Pinckney.

Adams might have used these insults to break relations with France. But unlike the High Federalists, who were more inflexible and more strongly prejudiced against the French, he chose to negotiate. As commissioners to settle with the French, he appointed the rejected Charles C. Pinckney; John Marshall, a Virginia Federalist; and Elbridge Gerry, a Massachusetts man with Republican leanings. At the same time, as a precaution, the administration asked Congress to provide funds to expand the army and navy.

When the American commissioners arrived in France, they were received by Charles Talleyrand, the French foreign minister. A wily and corrupt man, Talleyrand made them cool their heels and then turned them over to three of his agents. These men—mentioned in the diplomatic dispatches as X, Y, and Z—promised to speed up negotiations. But first the Americans were to pay Talleyrand and the Directors of the French Republic $250,000, lend France $12 million, and apologize publicly for some harsh words President Adams had recently hurled their way. The commissioners refused to accept the French proposals. They had not been instructed to pay a bribe, they said, and such a large loan to France would seriously damage relations with England. Besides, how could they know whether, after paying, the United States would gain a favorable treaty?

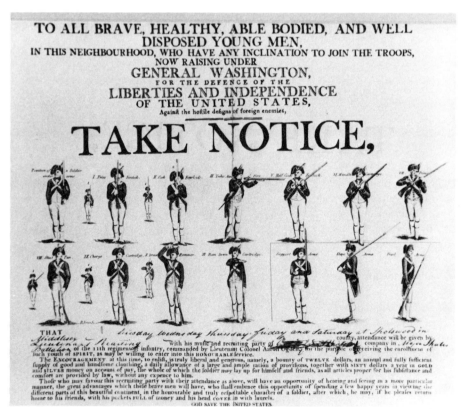

After the XYZ Affair it looked as if the United States would go to war with France. This appeal to "all brave, healthy, able bodied, and well disposed young men" was designed to meet the expected French threat.

Timothy Pickering

Timothy Pickering came by his reputation for self-righteousness honestly. His father, a prosperous farmer and businessman of Salem, Massachu-setts, and deacon of the Third Congregational Church, was the town scold, constantly embroiled in public battles with those whose views on political and religious issues he considered wicked. The elder Pickering's appearance betrayed his personality. John Adams noted of the man that "he has an hypocritical demure on his face . . . ; his mouth makes a semicircle when he puts on that devout face."

Timothy attended Harvard, graduating in 1763 at the age of eighteen with almost nothing good to say about his four years in Cambridge. Back in Salem, he studied law and became an attorney, but he was never interested in legal practice. By this time the American colonies were embroiled in the struggle with Britain for autonomy, and Pickering, like his father before him, found public controversy more compelling than the humdrum pursuit of a legal career.

Salem, though more conservative than Boston, was a Patriot town, and

Pickering joined the ranks of those opposed to the British attempt to tighten control over their American empire. During the War for Independence he served as adjutant general and quartermaster general in the army. In these posts he became a close associate of Washington and many of the leading politicians of the new republic. During the months following Yorktown Pickering was one of those army officers who despaired at the feebleness of Congress, especially its inability to meet its back-pay obligations to the Continental soldiers. During the Critical Period he moved his family to Philadelphia and established himself as a commission merchant. But the postwar deluge of British imports soon drained the country of cash and badly hurt the firm of Pickering and Hodgdon.

Unable to make the private fortune he craved, in 1790 Pickering accepted appointment as federal agent to treat with the Iroquois Indians. He proved to be remarkably generous and fair and was rewarded for his success by appointment as postmaster general in Washington's cabinet.

Pickering at first stayed clear of the factional disputes that divided Washington's cabinet and shaped the first political parties. Not until he became secretary of state in 1795 did he become an ardent Federalist, and his conversion derived from his attitudes toward France rather than his views on domestic issues. Retained in Adam's cabinet, the secretary became a member of the "war party," who held that nothing would "satisfy the ambitious and rapacious" French Directory except "universal dominion." England, he told the British minister, was "the last bulwark against the usurper of civilization." Following the revelations of French contempt for the United States in the XYZ Affair, Pickering urged an actual military alliance with Britain. His fear of France led him to support the Alien and Sedition Acts, which were designed to purge the nation of all "Gallomen" who might subvert the government. President Adams, though shocked by the XYZ revelations, rejected war and eventually resumed talks with the French. The president's conciliatory attitude placed him on a

When news of the negotiations reached the United States, it produced a tremendous uproar. Americans considered the French demands an unforgivable insult to their nation. The Federalists attacked the French and their Republican friends with renewed fury and made Pinckney and Marshall, the two Federalist commissioners, into heroes. One Federalist journalist proudly boasted that when the French had asked to be bribed, Pinckney had retorted: "Millions for defense, but not one cent for tribute!" What he actually said was far less eloquent: "No, no, not a sixpence!" Pinckney tried to set the record straight, but the story would not die. The phrase was engraved on his tombstone.

The bad feeling following the XYZ Affair ignited a naval war between the former allies. French raiders from the

Caribbean began attacking American vessels in United States coastal waters. Congress responded by voting money, over the opposition of the Republicans, to triple the size of the army and build forty new ships for the navy. In May 1798 it created the Navy Department with a secretary of cabinet rank to head it. Washington was recalled to public service and placed in command of the army, with Hamilton, yearning, as always, for military glory, second in command. In July Congress nullified the French alliance of 1778, ending the pretense of special friendship for that country. For the next few years American and French ships attacked one another in the Caribbean. The Americans also helped the British and their ally, the black patriot Toussaint L'Ouverture, overthrow the French regime on the island of

collision course with his warlike secretary of state, and in May 1800 he dismissed Pickering.

After a brief professional detour while he tried pioneer farming and land development in western Pennsylvania, Pickering and his family returned to Salem. Here he resumed his political career as a High Federalist, and in 1803 the Massachusetts legislature elected him to the United States Senate. Pickering arrived in Washington when that raw capital was in the hands of the Jeffersonians. He might have assumed leadership of the Federalist opposition, but many of his party colleagues considered him an extremist and consigned him to the obscure party backbench. Out of touch with the give-and-take of everyday politics, Pickering indulged his imagination and constructed a conspiracy theory that depicted his Republican opponents as subverters of the nation's institutions. Jefferson, he convinced himself, was plotting to make himself president for life. The Republicans would not let the Constitution get in their way, he believed. Their sponsorship of the Louisiana Purchase, an act not authorized by the Constitution, made that clear. Pickering's penchant for controversy and extremist statements made him a favorite target of the Jeffersonians, who cited his intemperate remarks as a way of stigmatizing the entire Federalist party.

During the crisis with Britain that culminated in the War of 1812, Pickering predictably opposed the Republican administration's foreign policy. In 1813, after he had been rejected for a second Senate term, he returned to Washington as Representative from the Essex County district of eastern Massachusetts. As early as 1803 Pickering had conceived the idea of an independent confederacy of New England and other northeastern states opposed to the policies of the Jeffersonians. Now, in the midst of war, he once again entertained the scheme of New England secession from the Union and heartily endorsed the Hartford Convention called in late 1814 to consider regional grievances against the Madison government. When the convention adjourned without proposing secession, Pickering was bitterly disappointed.

During most of his political career Pickering's views had coincided with those of his eastern Massachusetts constituents, though he often expressed them in exaggerated ways. After the war, however, a gap opened between him and the Essex County voters. Eastern Massachusetts by 1815 had begun to turn away from the sea and foreign trade and to take up manufacturing. Pickering's constituents supported the tariff bill of 1816, and when he opposed it, they were angry enough to repudiate him at the polls.

At the age of 72, Pickering left Washington to spend his remaining twelve years in Salem battling with everyone in sight. Fittingly for this son of the old deacon, he would embroil himself in religious controversy—but not as a defender of the old order. Pickering was a rationalist in religion and took the side of the Unitarians when they challenged the old Congregational establishment. The final irony of his career was his support of Andrew Jackson in 1824 over John Quincy Adams. But perhaps it was not so surprising after all. Resentment had always been a prime motivating force in his life, and he could never forget that the younger Adams's father had dismissed him from office a quarter century before. Pickering died in January 1829, still defending his actions and denouncing his enemies.

Hispaniola and establish Haiti as the first black nation in the New World.

The pressure on Adams formally to declare war on France was immense; but the president, aware of American unpreparedness, refused. In 1799 the French government, fearful that the United States might be a formidable adversary, began to show a more conciliatory attitude. Late in the year Adams sent three new emissaries to Paris to reopen negotiations. The president wanted the French to compensate Americans for their recent "spoliations" of American commerce, and he insisted that France formally accept nullification of the 1778 treaty. Now led by Napoleon, the French refused the first condition but accepted the second. On that basis the two countries signed the Convention of 1800. The United States had again avoided war.

The crisis with France stirred up American military ardor, improved Anglo-American relations, and made the Federalists more popular. It also set in motion a train of events that ultimately led to the emergence of the Republicans as the majority party.

As yet, few Americans understood the role of a "loyal opposition." Equating active political opposition with disloyalty, if not treason, they could not see the value of a second party in keeping the first honest. Neither side pulled its punches and partisan hostility often went beyond the bounds of decency. In the *General Advertiser*, Benjamin Franklin Bache called the president the "old, querulous, bald, blind, crippled, toothless Adams." Vermont Congressman Matthew Lyon was almost expelled from Congress for spitting in a Federalist member's eye and wrestling with him on the floor of the House.

The Alien and Sedition Acts. Bitter partisanship, deep ideological differences, a sense that they were the custodians of the nation's virtue and its bulwark against foreign evil, and finally the surge of patriotism in the face of French danger—all these things explain (though they do not excuse) the extreme actions that the Federalists took against their enemies. In 1798 the Federalist Congress, claiming national security as justification, passed four laws known collectively as the Alien and Sedition Acts. The Naturalization Act extended the residence requirement for naturalization as a citizen from five to fourteen years. In effect, it kept the vote from recent Irish and French immigrants, many of whom were pro-French Republicans. The Alien Act gave the president power to expel from the country any alien considered dangerous or suspected of treasonable acts. He was also authorized, under the Alien Enemies Act, to arrest, imprison, or expel enemy aliens in the event of war. The Sedition Act affected the rights of citizens as well as aliens by making it illegal to (1) impede the execution of federal laws; (2) bring the federal government, Congress, or the president into disrepute; (3) instigate or abet any riot, insurrection, or unlawful assembly; or (4) prevent a federal officer from performing his duties.

Under the Sedition Act Secretary of State Timothy Pickering prosecuted four leading Republican newspapers and several individuals, including Bache, Congressman Lyon, and Dr. Thomas Cooper, a prominent Republican scientist and pamphleteer. Ten of the indictments resulted in convictions, and a flock of foreign political activists fled the country rather than face almost certain prosecution. Despite these "successes," the Alien and Sedition Acts were a tremendous political blunder. The Federalists had their opponents on the run until the passage of these laws. Unable to support the France of the XYZ Affair and the undeclared naval war, many moderate Republicans had defected to the side of the administration. Now the government's vindictiveness and disregard of free speech propelled the waverers back to the Republican side.

Jefferson and Madison considered the Federalist measures a serious threat to civil liberties and a dangerous expansion of federal power relative to the states. To meet this challenge the two Republican leaders induced the legislatures of Kentucky and Virginia to denounce the recent Federalist measures on constitutional grounds. The Virginia and Kentucky Resolutions relied on the "compact theory" of the Constitution. That is, they held that the Constitution was a compact, or agreement, among the states to confer limited powers on the national government. Whenever it

Timothy Pickering as Secretary of State. Note the pursed mouth—apparently a family trait.

exceeded these powers—as it had outrageously with the Alien and Sedition Acts—the states, the statements proclaimed, had the right to oppose it. To clarify how this was to be done, the Kentucky legislature later asserted the right of states to resort to "nullification . . . of all unauthorized acts" by the national government.

Both states called on their fellow commonwealths to join their protest. Few did. Where the Federalists were in control, the legislatures rejected the idea that the states were the proper judges of constitutionality. Even Republican legislatures were reluctant to approve the nullification doctrine. Nevertheless, the Virginia and Kentucky resolutions gave effective voice to widespread rank-and-file Republican outrage at the administration's disregard of civil liberties. They were also significant precedents for the later southern position on states' rights.

The Transfer of Power. By the time Congress ratified the Convention of 1800, Adams was out of office and Thomas Jefferson had become the third president of the United States. The 1800 presidential contest that ended in Republican victory was one of the most critical events in the evolution of American political institutions. It was the first time that one modern political party peacefully sur-

LOOK ON THIS PICTURE,   AND ON THIS.

—— *As what a grace was seated on this brow——*
—— *An eye like Mars to threaten and command——*
—— *A combination and a form, indeed,*
Where every God did seem to set his seal.
To give the world assurance of a man——

THIS WAS——

HERE IS——

—— *like a mildew'd ear.*
Blasting his wholesome brother——

Vide H'amlet.

New-York. June. 1807.

The nation's newspapers reflected and fostered the development of partisan politics. By 1804 Jeffersonian-Republicans were calling on their fellow citizens to save the country from Thomas C. Pinckney, and the Federalists were maintaining that Jefferson was a vile wretch compared to the immortal Washington.

rendered power to another, and was a milestone in the development of modern democratic party government. The magnitude of this achievement becomes all the clearer when we recall how bitter the political and ideological passions of the day were and how few Americans had confidence in party government.

The Federalists seemed to be ahead when the 1800 campaign opened. Adams's peace policy was popular with the moderate public, and Federalists, despite the Alien and Sedition Acts, had made gains in the state elections of 1799. But the party was actually in trouble. Washington's death at the end of the year deprived it of a powerful unifying force. Soon the personal rivalry and temperamental differences between Adams and Hamilton became an open scandal. Moreover, Republican efforts to woo northern business interests and town laborers had begun to produce results. Few contemporaries as yet saw these weak spots.

In May 1800 a caucus of Federalist congressmen chose Adams and Charles Cotesworth Pinckney of the XYZ Affair as their candidates. The Republicans nominated Jefferson and Aaron Burr of New York by the same congressional caucus system. Both caucuses pledged to support each candidate equally, even though this commitment created the risk that the House of Representatives, under the existing constitutional proviso, would have to choose between them for president and vice president if there should be a tie in the electoral college. This in fact was what happened.

The campaign was another step toward modern political parties. Federalists and Republicans employed, either for the first time or to a much greater extent than previously, such modern tactics as printed party tickets, appeals to party loyalty, and public speechmaking. When it was over, Adams and Pinckney had only 65 electoral votes, and Jefferson and Burr were tied with 73 votes each.

Who would be president and who second in command? No one doubted that the Republicans had intended Jefferson to be their candidate for the top office; but as things stood, the House of Representatives would have to decide the question, with each state casting one vote, and the Federalists would be in a position to veto whichever candidate they wished. Here was irony indeed. The party that had savagely attacked the Sage of Monticello as an atheist, a two-faced intriguer, and the libertine father of several mulatto children now had the power to deny him his fondest goal.

But would it? To some Federalists it seemed that if Jefferson was bad, Burr was even worse. Hamilton admitted that Jefferson "had some pretentions to character," but Burr was a complete rogue, a man "bankrupt beyond redemption." When Jefferson's friends gave the Federalist congressman from Delaware, James Bayard, assurances that the Virginian would leave Hamilton's financial system intact, maintain the armed forces at full strength, allow most Federalist civil servants to keep their jobs, and continue to steer the nation on a neutral course in foreign affairs, Bayard

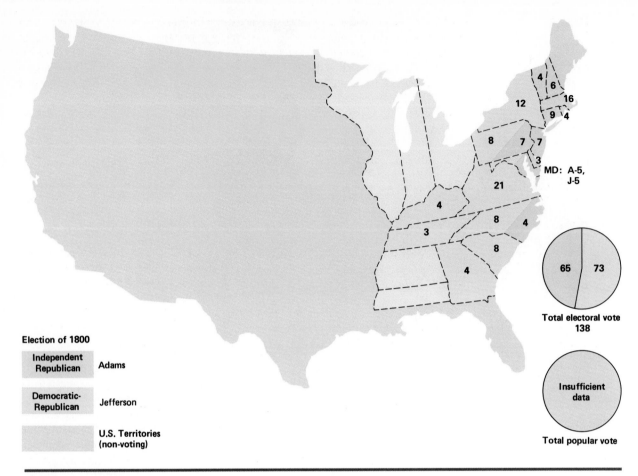

Election of 1800

Independent Republican	Adams
Democratic-Republican	Jefferson
	U.S. Territories (non-voting)

4
6
12   16
9 4
8   7 7
3
MD: A-5, J-5
21
4
8   4
3   8
4

65 | 73

Total electoral vote
138

Insufficient data

Total popular vote

ELECTION OF 1800

threw his state's vote to the Virginian. This shift of one state decided the election. The transfer of power was now complete. Jefferson, the arch-Republican, would be the third president of the United States.

★ CONCLUSIONS ★

In a little more than a decade Americans had laid the foundation of a modern political party system. They had discovered that the machinery of government that the Constitution provided had to be supplemented by voluntary political institutions called parties. But Americans had not made a deliberate, considered decision; parties had been forced on them by the circumstances of the day. The need to put America's economic house in order and deal with its unsettled finances had created passionate disagreements between people with commitments to agriculture and those engaged in trade, banking, and manufacture. Differences over the French Revolution had divided the country between those who felt the exhilaration of a freer,

more democratic, and more secular Europe, and those who saw revolutionary France as a dangerous enemy of religion and social order and Britain as a bastion of stability.

Constitutional biases also divided Americans. During the years of Washington's and Adams's administrations, the Federalists had, understandably, favored a broad interpretation of national powers; and they had stretched these to the limit to achieve their legislative ends. The Jeffersonians, by contrast, had fought centralized, concentrated national power and favored protection of the states' authority. Time would show that much of this difference depended on which party was "in" and which was "out." After 1800, with Jefferson and his successors in office, the Republicans would talk far less about states' rights than before; the Federalists would reverse the process. And yet we must not be too cynical about the parties' professions of constitutional principles. What started as rationalization often ended as sincere conviction. In the end the Jeffersonians and their successors would express a persistent bias toward local power and against central power, while the Federalists and their successors would reverse this position.

However it came about, by 1800 the country had acquired two great national parties. Neither had a monopoly of virtue or wisdom. The Republicans had shown greater sensitivity to personal rights and freedom; ideologically, they would point the way to a more open and democratic society. But their vision of the nation's social and economic future was naive. The Federalists had seen that America's greatness could not be limited by the past. They had recognized that the United States was fated to become a land of busy workshops as well as fertile farms and pastures. Yet they had failed to understand the average person's yearning for equality and the immense value of personal liberty and free expression in a progressive society. It remained to be seen now if the party of Jefferson could avoid the excesses of its opponents and find a workable balance for the nation.

✦✦✦✦✦✦✦✦ FOR FURTHER READING ✦✦✦✦✦✦✦✦

John C. Miller. *The Federalist Era, 1789–1801* (1960)
One of the best short political histories of the administrations of Washington and Adams. Miller carefully distinguishes between Adams Federalists and Hamiltonian Federalists.

Lance Banning. *The Jeffersonian Persuasion: Evolution of a Party Ideology* (1978)
Banning sees the Jeffersonian Republicans as men whose view of the political world was largely a product of "real Whig" ideology—as was the thought of those who led the Revolution. He takes ideology too seriously, probably, in explaining the rise of the first party system. Nevertheless, the book well repays reading.

Richard Hofstadter. *The Idea of a Party System, 1780–1840* (1969)
Like everything else Hofstadter wrote, this book is illuminating and graceful. It deals with the emergence of parties in the United States as a part of our intellectual history.

Joseph E. Charles. *The Origins of the American Party System* (1956)
The first modern interpretation of the first party system by a promising scholar who died young.

John C. Miller. *Alexander Hamilton: Portrait in Paradox* (1959)
Miller considers Hamilton's preoccupation with the creation and maintenance of a strong Union the key to all his ideas and policies. The paradox is that his efforts to cement the Union contributed to a distinct cleavage between the North and the South.

Paul A. Varg. *Foreign Policies of the Founding Fathers* (1963)
An analysis of the economic and ideological factors in early foreign policy, the conflict between moralism and realism in policy-making, and the contribution of foreign-policy disagreements to the early formation of national political parties.

Harry Ammon. *The Genêt Mission* (1973)
A brief, pro-Jefferson account of Edmond Genêt's mission to enlist American support for republican France against England.

Leland Baldwin. *The Whiskey Rebels: The Story of a Frontier Uprising* (1939)
The Whiskey Rebellion and its background treated with special attention to the feelings of those involved.

Manning J. Dauer. *The Adams Federalists* (1953); and Stephen

G. Kurtz. *The Presidency of John Adams: The Collapse of Federalism, 1795–1800* (1957)
These are two essential monographs on the Federalist party after the departure of Washington from the political scene. Important, though somewhat dry, accounts.

Paul Goodman. *The Democratic Republicans of Massachusetts: Politics in a Young Republic* (1964)
This is a superior state study of the Jeffersonians in a commonwealth where it was an uphill fight for the followers of the Sage of Monticello.

James T. Flexner. *George Washington and the New Nation, 1783–1793* (1969); and *George Washington: Anguish and Farewell, 1793–1799* (1972)
These two volumes cover Washington's presidency and last years as completely as the student could wish. Despite their length, they make interesting reading.

Reginald Horsman. *The Frontier in the Formative Years, 1783–1815* (1970)
Tells the important story of the West during the early years of the republic, when Britons, Spaniards, and Americans all fished in troubled waters and all took advantage of the Indians.

James M. Smith. *Freedom's Fetters: The Alien and Sedition Laws and American Civil Liberties* (1956)
Jefferson termed the period 1798–1800 a "reign of witches." Externally threatened by France, the Adams administration encouraged national chauvinism and fear of internal subversion. Take note of when Smith wrote this book.

Joyce Appleby. *Capitalism and a New Social Order: The Republican Vision of the 1790s* (1984)
In this slim volume, Appleby seeks to depict the Jeffersonians as forward-looking democratic innovators rather than nostalgic agrarians. The source of their ideas was not the radical Whig publicists of the late seventeenth century, as others have said, but the new forces of commerce that also influenced Adam Smith and helped to produce modern individualism.

Stanley Elkins and Eric McKitrick, *The Age of Federalism: The Early American Republic, 1788–1800* (1993)
A long, but well written and insightful review of the years of Federalist ascendancy by two brilliant historians. Considering the overall pro-Republican biases of scholars, this work is remarkably pro-Hamilton.

8★

THE JEFFERSONIANS IN OFFICE

How Did Power Affect Republican Ideology?

GENERAL JACKSON'S VICTORY AT NEW ORLEANS.

D. M. CARTER PINX'T.

1800	Jefferson elected president • Washington, D.C., becomes the national capital
1801	President Adams appoints "midnight judges" to tighten Federalist control of the courts
1802	The federal government sells its shares in the Bank of the United States • The Republican Congress repeals the Judiciary Act of 1801
1803–06	Lewis and Clark explore the West
1803	*Marbury* v. *Madison* • The Louisiana Purchase
1805	The Essex decision: Congress retaliates with the Nonimportation Act
1805–06	The Wilkinson-Burr conspiracy
1806–07	England and France issue decrees limiting neutral trade in Europe
1807	The *Chesapeake-Leopard* affair • Jefferson activates the Nonimportation Act of 1806 • The Embargo Act
1808	James Madison elected president
1809	The Nonintercourse Act
1810	Macon's Bill Number Two
1811	Southern and western "War Hawks" dominate the House of Representatives • American naval ship *President* attacks English navy's *Little Belt* • Congress defeats an attempt to recharter the Bank of the United States • Battle of Tippecanoe
1812	Congress provides for a 35,000-man regular army, gives Madison the power to call up state militias, and declares war on England
1814	Napoleon defeated in Europe; British troops are transferred to America and move on Washington • The Hartford Convention • The Peace of Ghent provides settlement of minor disputes between United States and Britain, leaves major issues of war untouched
1815	Andrew Jackson's victory over the British at New Orleans
1817	Rush-Bagot Agreement provides for demilitarizing United States–Canada border

*I*n December 1815 James Madison sent his seventh annual message to Congress. The president reported Captain Stephen Decatur's defeat of the dey of Algiers, a victory that finally forced the Barbary pirates to cease their attacks on American ships and their demands for tribute. He also reported progress in concluding peace with the Indian tribes in the West and described the still-disturbed state of the country's finances in the wake of the recent war. But the most arresting portion of the message was its last paragraphs. In these Madison recommended a protective tariff to encourage domestic industry, a program for building roads and canals, and "a national seminary of learning" within the District of Columbia, to be financed by the federal government. This national university would serve as "a central resort for youth and genius from every part of the country, diffusing on their return [to their homes] those national feelings, those liberal sentiments, and those congenial manners which contribute cement to our Union and strength to the great political fabric of which it is the foundation."

These proposals were startling. Madison was the man who had fought Hamilton's scheme to fund the debt and establish a national bank. He had drafted the Virginia Resolution of 1798, which proclaimed the limited power of the federal government under the Constitution. His party was the party of states' rights and strict construction. Jefferson, the Republican sage, had warned Madison in 1796 against federal support of post roads, "a source," he declared, "of boundless patronage to the executive, jobbing [graft] to members of Congress and their friends, and a bottomless abyss of public money."

Now the leader of the Republican party, Jefferson's friend and long-time colleague was asking Congress for some of these very things! What had produced this about-face? Only fourteen years had elapsed between the disputed election of 1800, which made Thomas Jefferson president, and Madison's seventh annual message. What had taken place in this decade and a half to cause such a drastic change of direction among Republicans?

★ PRESIDENT JEFFERSON ★

Part of the answer is Republican adaptability. Once in office, Jefferson proved to be less strongly partisan and dogmatic than many of his opponents had feared. Instead of delivering a fighting, partisan inaugural speech or a crow of triumph, Jefferson sought to quiet fears and disarm his enemies. The recent political campaign had been bitter, he noted in his inaugural address. Now that it was over, the country must unite. His party would respect the funded debt established by the Federalists. It would also respect the rights of political minorities. Though the two parties called themselves by different names, their members were "brethren of the same principle," Jefferson declared. "We are all Republicans, we are all Federalists." Nor would the victorious Republicans return the country to its feeble state before the Constitution. It was important, he said, to support "the State governments in all their rights"; but it was also necessary to preserve "the General Government in its whole constitutional vigor, as the sheet anchor of our peace at home and safety abroad."

A New, Republican Spirit. Despite Jefferson's conciliatory spirit, he sought to introduce "republican" principles

Thomas Jefferson first broke with tradition by walking to the Capitol on Inauguration Day. Although Jefferson disregarded etiquette in dress, as we see here, a French chef cooked White House dinners, and one year's wine bill was $2,800.

into the conduct of the government. The new president reduced the formalities that had surrounded Washington and Adams. In place of his predecessors' regal ceremonial visits to Congress to express their wishes on new legislation or policy, Jefferson sent written messages. Instead of "levees," stiff, formal occasions at which members of the government and resplendent diplomats paid court to the president in strict order of rank, Jefferson gave state dinners at which guests took whatever seat they could find. Many affairs at the executive mansion, moreover, were open to the public; and ordinary people took advantage of the opportunity to rub shoulders with the great, much to the chagrin of the less democratic worthies. Still more characteristic of Jefferson were his small dinners, with guests seated at a round table where no one could claim precedence over anyone else. For these informal gatherings the red-haired president often dressed in carpet slippers and a threadbare scarlet vest, his shirt not always perfectly clean. The guests discussed philosophy, the arts, literature, and science while eating food prepared by an excellent French chef, though often served by the president himself. Besides their use in conveying a new spirit of simplicity, these dinners had political value. Political guests, including congressmen and foreign envoys, were flattered and dazzled by the chief executive and found themselves unable to deny him the favors he asked. Some of Jefferson's legislative and diplomatic successes can be attributed to his talents as a host.

Federalist Legislation Repealed. Jefferson tried to break with the Federalist past in more fundamental ways as well. At first he labored to reduce the role of the national government, and he was partially successful. The Seventh and Eighth Congresses, which spanned his first administration, passed only 173 bills, most of them unimportant. Meanwhile, the Swiss-born secretary of the treasury, Albert Gallatin of Pennsylvania, reduced the detested national debt by cutting down appropriations for the army and the navy, which the Republicans neither liked nor considered essential. At the same time the new administration was able to do away with several unpopular internal taxes imposed by the Federalists. This feat of simultaneously cutting taxes and reducing the debt was made possible by the large revenues from import duties during the foreign trade boom that lasted through 1809.

The Republicans attacked or eliminated other Federalist policies or programs. They repealed some of the Alien and Sedition Acts, allowed others to expire, and pardoned all those the Federalists had imprisoned for sedition. They also whittled away at the Bank of the United States and eventually disposed of it. Because it had a twenty-year charter, the bank could not be dismantled until 1811, but

in 1802 the federal government sold its shares of bank stock at a profit and got out of the banking business.

A Strong Executive. The initial Republican attack on "big government" soon gave way to a more pragmatic approach. The third president, whatever his theoretical position, was by temperament a vigorous leader who did whatever was needed to advance the national interest as he saw it. He was also able to learn from experience. Although he had earlier condemned a powerful central government, after 1801, when he passed from opposition to power, he shifted ground. As president he decided that he could not be overburdened with constitutional scruples if he was to get things done. His critics charged him with hypocrisy, but we can see the inconsistencies in Jefferson's behavior as growth. Jefferson learned that power was not necessarily bad if used for good ends, and he developed great skill in using the authority of his office.

Though willing to reassure his opponents, Jefferson had no intention of allowing them to dominate the national government or tie his hands. As yet, the politicians had not raised to a lofty democratic principle the "spoils system" of replacing government personnel of the defeated party with members of the victorious one. Jefferson himself believed that the measure of fitness to hold appointive office should be merit. But he had to reckon with a number of realities. First, not all the Federalist officeholders could be counted on to administer fairly the laws passed by a Republican Congress and approved by a Republican president. Second, some of them were corrupt or incompetent. Finally, he could not disregard the fact that many Republicans lusted after the jobs of Federalists and could see no reason why they should not get them as rewards for loyal service to the president and the party. Jefferson would have preferred to allow positions to become available by retirement or death. Unfortunately, he noted, the vacancies "by death are few; by resignation none."

In any case, Jefferson did not have the opportunity for the wide-ranging appointments that later presidents had. In 1801, in the new, raw "Federal City" on the banks of the Potomac, there were fewer than 300 federal employees. In the rest of the country there were an additional 2,500. These 2,800 clerks, postmasters, marshals, and lighthouse keepers equaled less than one-thousandth of the federal civil service in 1990. During Jefferson's first two years in office he replaced almost 200 Federalists with members of his own party. Federalist leaders, who believed that the new president had promised to leave all positions below cabinet rank alone, protested, but to no avail.

The Attack on the Judiciary. A particularly thorny problem for the incoming president was the national judiciary. United States judges were virtually all Federalists, and these

Jefferson in Office

Once elected, Thomas Jefferson, like most other victorious presidential candidates, sought to make peace with his opponents. His inaugural address of March 1801 was intended as an overture to the more moderate Federalists. The new president hoped to cool the heated feelings aroused by the election campaign. His goal was to make governing the nation a less difficult task. But the address also expressed some of Jefferson's most characteristic ideas: the rights of minorities, frugal and limited government, assured civil and religious liberties, the dangers of militarism, and the primacy of agriculture. Unfortunately he was not always as good as his words, but the inaugural address is an eloquent statement of traditional liberal principles.

"During the contest of opinion through which we have passed the animation of discussions and of exertions has sometimes worn an aspect which might impose on strangers unused to think freely and to speak and to write what they think; but this being now de-

cided by the voice of the nation, . . . all will, of course, arrange themselves under the will of the law, and unite in common efforts for the common good. All, too, will bear in mind this sacred principle, that though the will of the majority is in all cases to prevail, that will to be rightful must be reasonable; that the minority possess their equal rights, which equal law must protect, and to violate would be oppression. Let us, then, fellow citizens, unite with one heart and one mind. Let us restore to social intercourse that harmony and affection without which liberty and even life itself are but dreary things. . . .

". . . [E]very difference of opinion is not a difference of principle. We have called by different names brethren of the same principle. We are all Republicans, we are all Federalists. If there be any among us who would wish to dissolve this Union or to change its republican form, let them stand undisturbed as monuments of the safety with which error of opinion may be tolerated where reason is left free to combat it. I know, indeed, that some honest

men fear that a Republican government cannot be strong, that this Government is not strong enough; but would the honest patriot . . . abandon a government which has so far kept us free and firm on the theoretic and visionary fear that this Government, the world's best hope, may by possibility want energy to preserve itself? I believe this, on the contrary, the strongest Government on earth. I believe it is the only one where every man, at the call of the law, would fly to the standard of the law, and would meet invasions of the public order as his own personal concern. Sometimes it is said that man cannot be trusted with the government of himself. Can he then, be trusted with the government of others? Or have we found angels in the forms of kings to govern him? Let history answer this question.

"Let us, then, with courage and confidence pursue our own Republican and Federal principles, our attachment to union and representative government. Kindly separated by nature and a wide ocean from the ex-

men were not impartial or disinterested. Supreme Court Justice Samuel Chase, for instance, the presiding judge at several sedition trials, had actively supported the Federalist prosecution and had insulted the defendants and their lawyers. Because United States judges were appointed for life, the president could not remove Chase or others like him. Matters were made particularly acute, from the Republican point of view, by the Judiciary Act of 1801, passed during the final days of the Adams administration. The act relieved Supreme Court justices of the burden of having to travel from place to place to hear lower court cases; it gave that job to sixteen new circuit judges. As a whole, the law improved national legal enforcement. But it also gave the Federalist party even tighter control over the United States court system. On the evening of March 3, 1801, the day before Jefferson's inauguration, Adams signed the commissions of the new circuit judges along with those of a flock of new federal marshals, attor-

neys, and justices of the peace. All the "midnight appointees" were Federalist party members, and it now looked as if the opposition party had locked up control of at least one branch of the government for decades to come, despite the Republican victory of 1800.

The Republicans were outraged by Adams's action. Jefferson noted that the Federalists had "retired to the judiciary . . . and from that battery all the works of Republicanism are to be beaten down and destroyed." To keep the new appointees from assuming office, Secretary of State James Madison refused to deliver their commissions. As far as the new administration was concerned, the appointments were void. Soon after, the Republican Congress repealed the 1801 Judiciary Act and replaced it with one of its own, the Judiciary Act of 1802.

At this point the commanding figure of John Marshall, chief justice of the Supreme Court, enters the picture. A

termininating havoc of one quarter of the globe; too high-minded to endure the degradation of the others; possessing a chosen country, with room for our descendants to the hundredth and thousandth generation; entertaining a due sense of our equal right to the use of our own faculties, to the acquisitions of our own industry, to honor and confidence from our own fellow-citizens, resulting not from birth, but from our own actions and their sense of them; enlightened by a benign religion, professed, indeed, and practiced in various forms, yet all of them inculcating honesty, truth, temperance, gratitude, and the love of man; acknowledging and adoring an overriding Providence, which by all its dispensations proves that it delights in the happiness of man here and his greater happiness hereafter—with all these blessings, what more is necessary to make us a happy and prosperous people? Still one more thing, fellow-citizen—a wise and frugal Government, which shall restrain men from injuring one another, shall leave them otherwise free to regulate their own pursuits of industry and improvement, and shall not take from the mouth of labor the bread it has earned. This is the sum of good government,

and this is necessary to close the circle of our felicities.

"About to enter, fellow-citizens, on the exercize of duties which comprehend every thing dear and valuable to you, it is proper you should understand what I deem the essential principles of our Government, and consequently those which ought to shape its Administration. I will compress them within the narrowest compass they will bear. . . . Equal and exact justice to all men of whatever state or persuasion, religious or political; peace, commerce, and honest friendship with all nations, entangling alliances with none; the support of the State governments in all their rights, as the most competent administrations for our domestic concerns and the surest bulwarks against antirepublican tendencies; the preservation of the General Government in its whole constitutional vigor, as the sheet anchor of our peace at home and safety abroad; a jealous care of the right of election by the people—a mild and safe corrective of abuses which are lopped by the sword of revolution where peaceable remedies are unprovided; absolute acquiescence in the decisions of the majority, the vital principles of republics,

from which is no appeal but to force, the vital principle and immediate parent of despotism; a well-disciplined militia, our best reliance in peace and for the first moments of war, till regulars may relieve them; the supremacy of the civil over the military authority; economy in the public expense, that labor may be lightly burthened; the honest payments of our debts and sacred preservation of the public faith; encouragement of agriculture, and of commerce as its handmaid; the diffusion of information and arraignment of all abuses at the bar of the public reason; freedom of religion; freedom of the press, and freedom of person under the protection of the habeas corpus, and trial by juries impartially selected. . . .

"Relying, then, on the patronage of your good will, I advance with obedience to the work, ready to retire from it whenever you become sensible how much better choice it is in your power to make. And may that Infinite Power which rules the destinies of the universe lead our councils to what is best, and give them a favorable issue for your peace and prosperity."

dignified Virginian of strong Federalist views, Marshall insisted that the Supreme Court had the right to check the fickle and headstrong representatives of the people by declaring acts of Congress unconstitutional. Judicial review, as this process is called, had been talked about earlier, but it had never been conclusively established. Republicans considered it unrepublican and claimed that the power to judge constitutionality belonged to either the executive or the legislative branch or both. In any event, they noted, judicial review at this point would just further strengthen the Federalist party.

Early in 1803 Marshall saw his chance. He would assert his precious principle, but do so in a way the Republicans would find difficult to oppose. His opportunity came in the case of *Marbury* v. *Madison* in which William Marbury, who had been nominated justice of the peace for the District of Columbia by Adams and refused his com-

mission by Madison, sued to have the commission delivered by the secretary of state. In 1803 Marshall, speaking for the Court, denied Marbury's claim by declaring the federal law under which he had sued to be unconstitutional. In effect, Madison and the government had won on the question of Marbury's appointment, but their victory depended on accepting the right of the Supreme Court to decide whether a law passed by Congress was in conflict with the Constitution and therefore void. An important claim held by many Federalists had been established: The Supreme Court, whose members were beyond easy reach of popular opinion, was to be the final judge of constitutionality.

Marbury v. *Madison* did not end Jefferson's attack on the existing Federalist-dominated court system. In 1803 the administration turned to impeachment to remove the most ardent Federalist partisans from the federal bench and re-

In 1800, Washington, D.C., was a city of "magnificent distances," as this picture attests. In the background you can see the President's House; it was not called the White House until after the War of 1812, when it was white-washed to cover scorch marks left by fires the invading British had set.

Chief Justice John Marshall's ruling in Marbury v. Madison helped entrench Federalist principles in American law. Marshall had fought at Valley Forge; his experience there, he wrote later, had confirmed him "in the habit of considering America as my country and Congress as my government."

place them with Republicans. To launch their attack, they selected two targets: John Pickering, a federal district judge in New Hampshire, and the notorious Judge Chase of the Supreme Court. Both men were outrageously partisan Federalists; Pickering, besides being an alcoholic, was clearly insane. He was impeached by the House of Representatives and removed by the Senate with little difficulty. But Chase—however ill-tempered and unfair—convinced enough senators that he had not committed the "high crimes and misdemeanors" that were the specified constitutional grounds for removal from office. The government's case, pleaded by the unpredictable and eccentric John Randolph of Roanoke, was based on the claim that only unbecoming and unfair conduct need be proved for a federal official's dismissal. Randolph bungled the prosecution and failed to convince the Senate. Chase's acquittal virtually ended the Republican assault on the Federalist judiciary.

★ INTERNATIONAL POLITICS AND REPUBLICAN POLICY ★

It was the need to deal effectively with foreign powers more than any other single factor that pushed Jefferson and his successor toward Federalist principles of strong central government. Jefferson had always recognized the need for executive leadership in foreign affairs. He might delegate authority to his secretary of state, James Madison; but ultimately, he knew, the responsibility for foreign relations rested with him.

Jefferson Buys Louisiana. In 1801 the United States was still entangled in the complicated issues that had grown out of the French Revolution. Britain and France were briefly at peace following the Treaty of Amiens in 1802. But then in May 1803 hostilities between Napoleon and his enemies erupted once more and darkened the Atlantic world for another dozen years.

Once again America was sucked into the conflict. The first warning came in 1800 when Spain and France signed the Treaty of San Ildefonso. This agreement allowed France to resume control of Louisiana, which it had lost to Spain in 1763 as a result of the French and Indian War. News of the deal caused great alarm in the United States. Jefferson, skeptical of French policy and motives ever since the rise of Napoleon, feared France's effort to reestablish an empire in North America. It was not that the president had ceased to dislike the British, but for the moment his suspicions of the French were stronger. It was one thing for a weak Spain to occupy New Orleans. It was far worse for a powerful and arrogant France to control the mouth of the Mississippi, and be in a position to choke off American commerce from the great river and its tributaries.

This 1805 painting shows the city of New Orleans shortly after the United States acquired it from France. Its harbor was already crowded with American seagoing vessels prepared to lead river freight for shipment to Europe and the Atlantic coast.

Even more than in the previous decade the United States had vital interests in the Mississippi Valley. Hundreds of thousands of Americans now lived beyond the Appalachians. Ohio alone in 1800 had over 45,000 people, Tennessee had 105,000 settlers, and Kentucky 220,000 more. Over 150 vessels regularly plied the great central river, carrying over 20,000 tons of freight annually. As Jefferson was painfully aware, whoever controlled the Mississippi wielded enormous power over the United States.

> There is on the globe one single spot [he declared] the possessor of which is our natural and habitual enemy. It is New Orleans, through which the produce of three-eighths of our territory must pass to market, and from its fertility it will ere long yield more than half of our whole produce, and contain more than half our habitants.

If France gained control of the region, "from that moment we must marry ourselves to the British fleet and nation."

When rumors of the French agreement with Spain reached the United States, Jefferson dispatched Robert R. Livingston to Paris. Not knowing that West Florida was unaffected by the French-Spanish deal, Jefferson directed the American emissary to buy both that province and New Orleans from Napoleon. From the outset Livingston encountered difficulties. Talleyrand, the French foreign minister, would not let him see Napoleon. The devious Frenchman was waiting to see what would happen in Santo Domingo, where a French army was struggling to put down the slave revolt led by Toussaint L'Ouverture. If Toussaint was destroyed, France could protect Louisiana and once more establish itself as a North American power. The scheme did not work. The black liberator was eventually captured by trickery, but the Haitians refused to surrender. Black guerrillas slipped out of the mountains and mercilessly attacked the French troops. Even more dangerous was the yellow fever mosquito. Before many months had passed, the French commanding general in Haiti was dead of fever along with two-thirds of his army.

News of the growing French disaster trickled back to Paris slowly. Meanwhile, American anxiety increased when the Spaniards, who had not yet officially turned over Louisiana to the French, suspended the precious right of deposit at New Orleans allowed by the Pinckney Treaty of 1795. Spain's unfriendly act, Livingston's lack of progress, and the westerners' growing outcry against Spain goaded Jefferson to new action. In January 1803 he named James Monroe as joint negotiator with Livingston and arranged with Congress for a $2 million appropriation for the purchase of New Orleans and part of West Florida.

By this time the mood in Paris had changed. It was now clear that the Santo Domingo campaign was a costly disaster and that France must forgo all thought of a new North American empire. Besides, it looked as if hostilities were about to break out again in Europe. War, Napoleon realized, would expose Louisiana to British attack from Canada or military conquest by the Americans. Louisiana, then, was virtually worthless to France—unless the great, rich province could be converted into cash, in which case it could contribute handsomely to French ambitions in Europe. On April 11, 1803, the First Consul told his minister of finance, François de Barbé-Marbois: "I renounce Louisiana. It is not only New Orleans that I will cede, it is the whole colony without reservation. . . ."

Napoleon's new attitude completely altered the picture. No sooner had Monroe arrived in Paris than he and Livingston were confronted with a remarkable and totally unexpected proposition. Instead of only New Orleans, Barbé-Marbois asked, why not take all of the immense Louisiana territory? Another 20 million francs would pay for outstanding claims of American citizens against France dating back to the naval war of the 1790s. This offer exceeded the expectations and instructions of the American emissaries, but they eagerly grabbed it. On May 2, 1803, they signed the treaty transferring Louisiana to the United States for $15 million.

The treaty was a wonderful piece of good luck. But it left many questions unanswered and many problems unsolved. Spain had never formally surrendered the province to France and was chagrined at getting little or nothing of what Napoleon was due to receive. It could be expected to cause trouble. There was also great uncertainty about the territory's precise boundaries. When Livingston questioned Talleyrand on the colony's limits, the Frenchman had remarked cynically that the Americans had "made a noble bargain" for themselves and would no doubt "make the most of it." They would indeed; but in the meantime the uncertainty was sure to rile Spain and Great Britain, whose colonies of Mexico and Canada bordered Louisiana.

Most difficult of all, however, were the constitutional problems raised by the purchase. Fifty thousand French and Spanish Creoles—descendants of the original European settlers—and French-speaking exiles from Acadia ("Cajuns"), inhabited the colony. Under the treaty they were to become American citizens. Did the United States have the constitutional right to incorporate these people without their consent? And what about the process of acquiring new territory by treaty? Nowhere did the Constitution confer authority on anyone to buy new territory for the nation. Federalists, who objected to almost anything the administration did, denounced these assumptions of powers. Each side called the other hypocritical for reversing its usual position on implied powers under the Constitution.

Jefferson himself was troubled by constitutional scruples, and for a while hesitated. But not for long. It seemed certain that the Louisiana Territory would support millions of small land-holding farmers, and that prospect was dear to the president's heart. Trying to get a bargain and preserve his principles at the same time, Jefferson proposed that Congress should simultaneously confirm the treaty and adopt a constitutional amendment expressly authorizing such territorial acquisitions. But Napoleon would not wait for the president to overcome his philosophical misgivings. Warned that the First Consul was becoming restless, Jefferson abandoned the idea of a constitutional amendment and pushed the treaty through the Senate. On December 20, 1803, in a simple ceremony at New Orleans, the French flag was lowered and the Stars and Stripes raised in its place. Louisiana, a region almost equal in extent to the original United States after the 1783 peace treaty with Britain, was now American.

The Lewis and Clark Expedition. Even before Napoleon had made his startling offer to sell the Louisiana Territory, Jefferson had recruited his private secretary, Meriwether Lewis, and a former soldier, William Clark, younger brother of George Rogers Clark, to lead an expedition to explore the vast region. Jefferson's motives were a mixture of the political and the commercial. Initially, he had sought to establish an American claim to the region through exploration. More important, he saw Louisiana as vital to his Indian policy. The president hoped to gather the eastern Indian tribes into reservations where they could be induced to abandon their "savage" ways and settle down as "civilized" farmers.

Jefferson conceived of this change as advantageous to the Indians themselves, and it was certainly far better than the extermination policies advocated by some American officials. But it also had the advantage of freeing vast tracts of land for white settlers. To carry out this policy, the president believed, the Indian traders who encouraged the Indians' roaming ways must be attracted to regions farther west. Lewis and Clark, accordingly, were asked to investigate the fur resources of the new region and also to establish commercial relations with the western tribes. News of the Louisiana Purchase added to these goals an intense curiosity about what exactly the United States had bought for $15 million. The expedition, the president directed, must make careful observations of the flora, animal life, minerals, soils, and geography of the regions they crossed.

Lewis and Clark's small party of fifty spent the winter of 1803–1804 in the St. Louis area; in the spring they set off up the Missouri River in small boats. By fall they had reached the villages of the Mandan Indians in what is now the Dakotas and settled down in winter camp. The group that set out for the Pacific the following April consisted of thirty-seven men and a woman, Sacajawea. A Shoshone captive of the Dakota tribes, she was given her freedom in exchange for guiding the expedition across the Rockies. Sacajawea took them as far as the Lemhi Pass on the Continental Divide, where they were met by Shoshone tribesmen. Grateful for the return of their kinswoman, the Indians provided the expedition with horses and guides for the next stage of the journey, over the remaining ranges of

A reconstructed scene of the Lewis and Clark expedition. York, Clark's slave, is at left shouldering the rifle. To his left is Lewis; then Clark; then Sacajawea, their Indian guide.

the Rockies to the valley of the Clearwater River. There they were given food and shelter by the friendly Flathead Indians, who also supplied a new flotilla of canoes. By mid-November, after traversing the rapids of the Clearwater and the Columbia, the weary explorers arrived at the shores of the Pacific.

When the explorers returned to St. Louis in September 1806, they were received with wild enthusiasm. At the cost of only a single life and some $50,000, they had established relations with several important Indian nations; discovered usable passes through the Rockies; and provided important botanical, zoological, geological, and anthropological data about a vast stretch of western North America. Their expe-

dition helped to open the trans-Mississippi region, and was soon followed by others that laid the groundwork for the wave of settlement that would carry millions of Americans across the continent.

The Wilkinson-Burr Conspiracy. Acquisition of Louisiana had finally ended one source of western troubles: It was no longer a political problem for western farmers to send their goods to market through New Orleans. But the Louisiana Purchase had not laid to rest all the westerners' complaints by any means. The West was still not sure that it could entrust its future to the government in Washington. Many easterners, the people of the trans-Appalachian

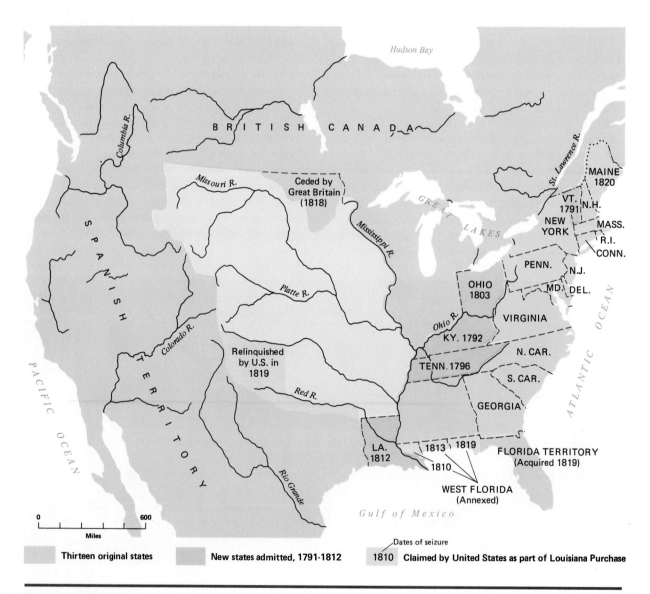

THE LOUISIANA PURCHASE AND NEW STATES, 1791–1812

region knew, were suspicious of growing western power and numbers. In Massachusetts, for example, extreme Federalists, members of the so-called Essex Junto, were talking of detaching New England, New York, and New Jersey from the Union and forming a new confederation of states. This new nation would insulate the commercial Northeast from the attacks of the allied agricultural South and West.

Western resentments and suspicions offered opportunities for ambitious and unscrupulous men to carve careers for themselves as champions of the trans-Appalachian region. Two of the most dangerous of these adventurers were General James Wilkinson, commander of United States troops in the West and governor of the Louisiana Territory, and Vice President Aaron Burr of New York. Wilkinson was one of the most disreputable characters in American history. Though a trusted lieutenant of every American president from Washington through Madison, the handsome, hard-drinking officer was in the pay of the Spanish government as Agent Number 13.

Aaron Burr was a far more talented man. Intelligent and cultivated, he exerted a strong fascination on men and women alike. Though descended from a long line of Puritan ministers, Burr was a compulsive womanizer, a reckless pleasure seeker, and a cynic, driven by ambition and the desire to win fame and glory. Despite these serious flaws, he still might have attained the presidency if he had not made a fatal misstep. In 1804, angered by Hamilton's role in defeating him when he ran for governor of New York, Burr challenged the former treasury secretary to a duel. The two men met on the Hudson Palisades opposite New York. Hamilton deliberately held his fire; Burr shot to kill and succeeded. People called Burr's action murder. From that point on, a conventional course to power was closed to Burr, and he turned to intrigue and conspiracy to achieve his ends.

Burr looked to the West for a way to restore his shattered fortunes. Though the exact truth is still in dispute, it appears that he and Wilkinson sought British and Spanish support for a scheme to detach the West from the United States, combine it with parts of Spanish Mexico, and then set up an independent nation with themselves as rulers. To raise money Burr connived with the British minister in Washington, who seemed interested in any plan that promised to diminish American strength.

For a time Wilkinson was prepared to sell out his Spanish employers in order to further the scheme. But eventually the general decided to continue his profitable relationship with the Spanish authorities. Posing as an American patriot anxious to defend his country's interests, he betrayed Burr to Jefferson. Tried before Chief Justice Marshall, Burr was acquitted of treason but rather than face various state charges against him fled to Europe. He re-

turned to America and practiced law in New York for over two decades. At the age of 77 he married a widow 20 years younger than himself. His divorce was finalized the day he died.

Neutral Rights Once More.   The acquisition and exploration of Louisiana reveal Jefferson at his most energetic. Clearly the third president was capable of vigorous action in pursuing the national interest. But besides creating opportunities, European antagonisms caused serious difficulties for the United States that Jefferson found harder to handle.

After 1803 almost all the disputes between the United States and the major European belligerents, England and France, repeated those of the 1790s. Impressment, blockades, neutral rights, contraband, and Indian incitements continued to disturb America's relations with the two leading European powers. The country's foreign involvements during 1803–1812 seem like a replay of 1793–1800 with the volume turned up.

Soon after the outbreak of hostilities between France and England in 1803, the British resumed their impressment policy. Before long, British ships were hovering off East Coast ports, ready to swoop down on American ships and remove seamen from their decks for the Royal Navy. In July 1805, in the *Essex* decision, a British admiralty court declared illegal the American practice of carrying French West Indian produce to American ports and then shipping it to France. These commodities were not neutral goods, the court said, they were really French, and under the Rule of 1756 could be confiscated like other enemy goods if intercepted by the British navy.

The American government protested this ruling, but to little effect, and Congress retaliated in April 1806 by passing the Nonimportation Act, a measure designed, like the colonial trade boycotts of the 1760s, to force the British into a more acceptable response through economic pressure. This measure forbade the importation of many goods that Americans normally bought from Britain but could, if necessary, produce at home. The operation of the law, however, was to be delayed until mid-November pending an acceptable agreement with His Majesty's government on neutral trade and impressment. Jefferson held the law in abeyance while British and American negotiators tried to hammer out an accommodation. These talks in fact produced an agreement but, embarrassed by how little it conceded to the United States, Jefferson refused to submit it to the Senate for confirmation.

Meanwhile, American commerce and pride continued to suffer under a barrage of measures and countermeasures by Napoleon and his chief European adversary. In May 1806 Britain announced a blockade of the European continent

Albert Gallatin

One of the most prominent leaders of the party established by Thomas Jefferson was not even American-born. Not until 1780, when he was nineteen, did Albert Gallatin come to the United States, the country where he was to achieve such great political distinction.

Gallatin was born in Geneva, an independent city-republic in what is now Switzerland, of a distinguished French-speaking Protestant family. Given a classical education in the local schools, he reached his teens discontented with the limited economic opportunity and conservatism of his community. In school he had become acquainted with the writings of the Enlightenment philosopher Jean-Jacques Rousseau, himself a native of Geneva, and belonged to a circle of young men who yearned for a better political and social order than existed in Europe under the Old Regime. By now all of "enlightened" Europe knew of the brave cause of the Americans fighting against British tyranny, and in 1780 Gallatin and a friend left Geneva to cast in their lot with America.

Gallatin spent his first few years in the United States in quest of a vocation. By the time he arrived, the war was virtually over, so a military career was precluded. For a while he taught French at Harvard, but he was drawn to the West and western opportunities. For a number of years he tried to make money as a speculator in western lands. Though these schemes did not work out, he came to know western Pennsylvania and, in

1785, established his permanent home there.

Fayette County in the 1780s was frontier, with all the frontier openness to newcomers. Even a foreigner like Gallatin who spoke heavily accented English could make his mark. In 1788 his fellow citizens sent the young man to represent them at a convention in Harrisburg called to change the recently adopted federal Constitution. There Gallatin met other men like himself who feared the centralizing tendencies of the new frame of government. This concern would remain an important part of Gallatin's political ideology and a major bond with the Jeffersonians.

Gallatin's career following this debut was meteoric. In 1790 he was elected to the Pennsylvania state legislature and served there for three terms. As a legislator he sponsored bills for a statewide system of public education, the abolition of slavery, and reform of the penal code. His program closely echoed the work that the great Jefferson had accomplished in Virginia as governor during the war. Yet at the same time, Gallatin was no enemy of banks or "fiscal responsibility." He helped rid Pennsylvania of its depreciated paper money, got the state to pay its public debt in specie, and sponsored a state-controlled bank. In many ways this program resembled Hamil-ton's almost simultaneous efforts at the federal level. But there was one crucial difference: Hamilton believed a permanent

federal debt was a useful political and economic device; Gallatin, like all Republicans, believed public debt undesirable. The state must always follow the principle of pay-as-you-go for all its expenses.

In 1793 the legislature elected Gallatin to the United States Senate and he went to Philadelphia to take his seat. In the nation's temporary capital he met and married Hannah Nicholson, member of a New York family with close ties to the emerging Republican or Anti-Federalist party. Soon after, Gallatin was disqualified for his Senate seat on the grounds that he had not met the constitutional requirement of citizenship for nine years. He returned to his farm on the Monongahela with his new bride and a total fortune of £600 in cash.

He arrived in Fayette County just in time to become embroiled in the uprising against the federal authorities over the 1793 excise tax that we call the Whiskey Rebellion. Though a Republican and man of the West, Gallatin played a moderating role and succeeded in preventing a civil war. By the time the federalized militia appeared, the rebellion was over and nothing remained to be done but arrest a few holdouts and drag them to Philadelphia to be tried.

In 1794 Gallatin was elected to the federal House of Representatives. Here, during the three terms he served, he became a major Republican leader, second only to Madison, and a prime

from the Elbe River in Germany to the port of Brest in France. Napoleon responded with the Berlin Decree, placing Britain under blockade and forbidding all British commerce with France. The British then issued two orders in council threatening to confiscate all ships engaged in French coastal trade or entering those European continental ports still not off limits. Only if they first stopped in Britain, paid

duties, and secured British clearance would neutrals be allowed to trade with any part of Europe. Napoleon replied with the Milan Decree, which declared that all vessels that obeyed the orders in council would be subject to French seizure.

The British-French war of regulations seemed designed to produce maximum irritation in America. If American

target for Federalists, who derided his accent and foreign birth and accused him of being a ringleader of the Whiskey Rebels. He quickly became known as an expert in finance who could argue with the Federalists on their own ground and show where their much-vaunted financial measures had been costly and unnecessary to the economic health of the nation. He also succeeded in establishing the House Ways and Means Committee as Congress's permanent watchdog over treasury affairs.

Because he was one of the few Republicans who understood the intricacies of national finance, it was inevitable that Gallatin would become Jefferson's secretary of the treasury. He would serve in that office for almost thirteen years, until well into Madison's second term.

As secretary, Gallatin's first priority was debt reduction. His second, related to the first, was reduction of taxes. This in turn required cutting the budget drastically, especially the outlays for the army and the navy. Finally, he believed that Congress must be more careful in overseeing the finances of the country than it had been under the Federalists. All told, it was a good Jeffersonian program of frugality, simplicity, and limits on the operations and ambitions of government.

Yet Gallatin was also a man of vision. He did not oppose the Louisiana Purchase, though paying Napoleon's price required going many millions of dollars further into debt. Unlike his chief, Gallatin was not an inveterate enemy of the Bank of the United States. When the president demanded that the treasury transfer a large part of its deposits to various state banks, Gallatin resisted. Also at odds with the president was his support of "internal improvements" legislation to tie the country together with a network of roads and canals. In 1808 he issued a report laying out a grand design, estimated to cost $10 million, that would rectify all the deficiencies of nature's own plan for connecting the various parts of the Union. Congress, dominated by more conventional Jeffersonians, refused to fund this proposal. Not until the War of 1812 had demonstrated the dangers of a fragmented nation did party leaders reconsider their position.

Gallatin was skeptical of the War Hawks' zeal for war in 1811 and 1812, especially after the votes of many of these same men helped defeat a bill to recharter the Bank of the United States. Without the bank to help, the treasury would have trouble raising money for the government during the war. Fortunately for the secretary, he would not have to face all the difficulties of financing the war, for in May 1813 he left the treasury and went to Europe as American peace envoy. Eventually he helped negotiate the Treaty of Ghent, bringing peace between Britain and America.

Gallatin was never again active in American domestic politics. From 1816 to 1823 he served as American envoy to France. When he returned to the United States, he was disappointed at the low level of politics in his adopted homeland. He soon went off to England as American envoy, but returned again after a single year.

In 1830 Gallatin moved his family to New York, where he accepted the offer of tycoon John Jacob Astor to become president of a bank. The move to the country's commercial metropolis enabled Gallatin to help his two sons establish themselves financially and allowed him to be close to his married daughter, Frances, and his seven grandchildren. Gallatin continued to be active in public affairs, however. In 1830 he was approached by a group of New York business and civic leaders to lend his name and influence to establishing a modern university in the city. Gallatin joined the enterprise as a strong advocate of a new, more commercially and scientifically oriented institution of higher education. His help proved vital to the formation of what would later become New York University.

During his last years the alert old gentleman took an active interest in the city's intellectual life. He served as president of the New York Historical Society and helped found the discipline of "ethnology," the forerunner of modern anthropology. He also continued to pronounce on financial and political questions. When sectional issues came to the fore during the 1840s, he endorsed excluding slavery from the newly acquired regions in the West. In May 1849 Gallatin's wife of fifty-five years died. Six months later, at the age of eighty-eight, Gallatin himself died quietly at his daughter's summer house on Long Island.

Though a creator of one of the two great parties that have dominated American political life, Albert Gallatin was a voice for moderation and reason, a man who could see the best in the other side.

merchants bowed to the British, they would offend the French, and vice versa. To make matters worse, the regulations contained large loopholes in both their provisions and their enforcement. These continued to entice Americans into the lucrative trade with Europe and the West Indies, but made it hazardous and uncertain. Americans might have been less aggrieved if they had known from the onset that they could trade with Europe only by engaging in outright smuggling.

The Chesapeake-Leopard Affair.   While the barrage of decrees and orders in council flew through the air, the impressment issue became acute. Vice-admiral Sir George Berkeley, commander in chief of his majesty's naval forces at Halifax, Nova Scotia, was particularly irked by the supposed connivance of American officials in the desertion of British seamen. The situation was especially bad in the Chesapeake Bay region, where many deserters from the Royal Navy had taken refuge and a number had enlisted in the American navy. One of these deserters, Jenkin Ratford, now a sailor on the U.S.S. *Chesapeake*, was reported to be swaggering through the town insulting British officers on leave.

This was the last straw. On June 1, 1807, Berkeley directed his subordinates to stop the *Chesapeake* if they should encounter it beyond American territorial waters and search it for deserters. Not long afterward H.M.S. *Leopard* overtook the American frigate as it left Norfolk bound for the Mediterranean on a shakedown cruise. The American captain, Commodore James Barron, suspecting nothing—for the British had never attempted to impress from an American *naval* vessel before—allowed a British officer to come aboard. Barron was presented with Berkeley's order and a note from the British captain demanding that the deserters be surrendered. Barron refused. The *Leopard's* response was to fire three broadsides into the American ship, killing three Americans and wounding eighteen. Not yet fully outfitted for combat, the *Chesapeake* was able to fire back only a single token shot before it surrendered. A British search party then boarded the vessel, lined up its crew, and removed Ratford and three other deserters. Ratford was later hanged.

The attack on the *Chesapeake* outraged Americans. Never before had the British so blatantly violated American sovereignty. Indignation swept the country, and protesters organized mass meetings in dozens of cities to condemn British high-handedness. In Virginia the governor called out the militia to keep supplies from reaching the Royal naval squadron cruising off the coast. The British consul in New York had to be given police protection, and a mob attacked and almost demolished a British vessel at its pier in the harbor. Many Americans expected war or hoped for it. The Washington *Federalist* declared:

> We have never . . . witnessed the spirit of the people excited to so great a degree of indignation, or such a thirst for revenge, as on hearing of the late unexampled outrage on the *Chesapeake*. All parties, ranks, and professions were unanimous in their detestation of the dastardly deed, and all cried aloud for vengeance. . . . The Administration may implicitly rely on the cordial support of every American citizen, in whatever manly and dignified steps that they may take, to . . . obtain reparation for the injury.

The Embargo. Jefferson could easily have brought a united nation into war at this point, but he chose instead to dampen the public outcry. The president issued a proclamation closing American waters to the Royal Navy and then, rather than initiate hostile actions, sent an emissary to negotiate the impressment issue with the British. Unfortunately the American representative accomplished little. Not until 1811 did the British make acceptable reparation for the *Chesapeake-Leopard* affair. Meanwhile, the clamor abated and war enthusiasm cooled.

This Federalist cartoon shows public discontent with Jefferson's Embargo of 1807. Not only were farmers and merchants angered by the closing of America's ports, but Jefferson's fellow Republicans worried about the act's legality and feared the federal government's growing power.

Jefferson had mixed motives for taking a moderate course in the *Chesapeake* affair. War, he thought, was not necessary to solve the impressment problem. The president also realized American military weakness. Jefferson and the Republicans were themselves responsible for this condition. Ever since the undeclared naval war with France in 1798–1800—which many Republicans believed a pro-British, Federalist venture—they had denounced standing armies and a strong navy as "dangerous to liberty" and conducive to "the spirit which leads to war." Militarism was Federalist, not Republican, they said, for it went along with Federalist faith in centralized political power. Jefferson was not indifferent to American defense, but he thought it could be provided largely by the citizen militia and by small, lightly armed coastal vessels using oars and sails. Under this system the country would be spared a large and expensive military establishment.

Jefferson was also moved by other considerations. The United States had a better weapon against British and French high-handedness than an army and navy: the power to withhold its goods from the warring nations and close American markets to their exports. Americans had practiced such economic warfare effectively against Britain during the great imperial crisis before independence. Now, in December 1807, the president activated the first Nonimportation Act and soon after asked Congress to go far beyond this measure by placing an embargo on all exports from the United States. Congress responded with the 1807 Embargo Act, which forbade American vessels to sail to foreign ports without special permission and forbade foreign vessels to carry off American goods. American ships could continue to engage in the coastal trade between domestic ports, but the owners of such vessels had to post bonds twice the value of the ships and their cargoes to guarantee that they would not violate the embargo by sailing off to foreign ports once out to sea. The law did not explicitly prohibit imports in foreign ships; but if foreign ship owners could not carry American cargo on their return trips, they had little incentive to trade with the United States. The law also restricted overland trade to British colonies. In effect, Congress had sealed off the country from foreign trade on the theory that Europe needed America more than America needed Europe.

Theory was one thing; reality was another. The law was impossible to enforce. Some state governors took advantage of its loopholes to peddle exemptions to merchants for cash or political support. Merchants, too, found ways to get around the law. Many risked the loss of their bond by directing their ships to sail for Europe or the Caribbean once out of sight of land. Others conducted illegal commerce with British Canada across the Great Lakes. Defiance was greatest in New England, where Jefferson was denounced

as a tyrant executing an unconstitutional law. The embargo was also unpopular in the middle states, where the merchants of New York and Philadelphia suffered under it as much as their New England counterparts.

For a while, wholesale evasion made the law tolerable. But the Giles Enforcement Act of 1809 closed the loopholes, and foreign trade virtually ceased. Farmers—especially those who sold grain, cotton, and tobacco for European markets—saw the prices of their crops plunge dramatically. Even more seriously hurt were the traders of the port towns and all who depended on them. New York in 1809, one contemporary reported, "looked like a town ravaged by pestilence." The city's waterfront streets were deserted, its ships dismantled, and its countinghouses closed and boarded up. Boston and seaboard New England were hardest hit of all, with thousands of seamen, dock laborers, sail makers, and rope makers idle. One Yankee expressed the region's suffering in verse:

> Our ships all in motion once whitened the ocean
> They sailed and returned with a cargo;
> Now doomed to decay, they have fallen a prey
> To Jefferson—worms—and embargo.

And to top it all, the law failed to achieve its ends. It hurt some British manufacturers, but it was English wage earners and Caribbean planters and slaves who suffered the most, and none of these groups carried much political weight in Parliament. Even when the embargo finally began to pinch important commercial interests in Britain, sheer stubbornness kept the British government from yielding to American pressure.

For a year and a half the administration sought to enforce its policy, using militia and regulars to halt the overland trade with Canada and the navy to stop violations by sea. Driven by frustration, the president, a great defender of liberty while in the opposition, proposed to declare whole communities in rebellion and subject to prosecution for treason. At one point he told a Republican congressman that in times of emergency "the universal recourse is a dictator."

Popular opposition to the infamous embargo soon reached a crescendo. Town meetings throughout New England condemned the administration, and the Massachusetts and Connecticut legislatures proposed what amounted to nullification of the Embargo Act. Even Republicans, in the shipping states, pleaded that the policy be abandoned. In Congress the Federalists and a group of rebellious Republicans called the Quids, led by John Randolph, fought to have the embargo policy changed. Faced by this overwhelming pressure and the obvious failure of its policy to alter British and French behavior, the administration finally yielded. In March 1809, as one of his last official acts, Jefferson signed the Nonintercourse Act, repealing the embargo and reopening foreign trade except with Britain and France, but allowing the president to restore trade with either country, or both, if they ceased violating American rights.

Madison Takes the Helm. Soon after, Jefferson left Washington for Monticello. Never again would he serve in high political office. The remainder of his long life was devoted to creating a university in his home state, completing his mansion near Charlottesville, playing his violin, and generally cultivating the arts and sciences.

Jefferson was not proud of his presidency, but he underestimated it. True, he had not solved the nation's major international problems; nor had he brought the country the prosperity he had sought. Nevertheless, he had successfully guided the United States through a major transition from the rule of one party to the rule of another; had doubled the physical size of the country; and had brought a new, more democratic tone to the nation's political culture. These were accomplishments that few presidents would match.

His successor, James Madison, was a man in the Jeffersonian mold. Co-founder of the Republican party, Jefferson's secretary of state, and one of the chief architects of the Constitution, Madison had earned the right to be his party's choice. His nomination was contested by the Quids, but Madison was the clear choice of the Republican congressional caucus and went on to defeat Federalist Charles Cotesworth Pinckney in the 1808 election.

Historians have generally considered Madison's presidency a failure. Although a profound student of government, an effective legislative leader, and a charming conversationalist, he lacked executive ability. In peace and war he would prove irresolute; and when he did bring himself to act, he would often do the wrong thing.

Madison's first blunder came in the second month of his presidency, when he arranged with David M. Erskine, the British minister in Washington, to suspend the Nonintercourse Act in exchange for British withdrawal of the 1807 orders in council. Erskine, however, had exceeded his instructions, and the British foreign secretary in London repudiated the agreement when he heard of it. Madison, now believed by many to be the dupe of the British, felt compelled to restore the prohibition on British-American trade.

The Nonintercourse Act having put too great an economic strain on the country, Congress in 1810 replaced it with Macon's Bill Number Two. This was a curious measure. The United States, the bill stated, would immediately reopen commerce with both Britain and France. If either country, however, should cease to violate American commercial rights, the president could then reimpose trade prohibitions on the other, after a three-month wait to give the slower-acting power a chance to rescind its trade restrictions. In effect, as an inducement to cease attacks on

"A withered little applejohn" is what Washington Irving called James Madison. He looked even less like a president than his loose-jointed predecessor.

James Madison fell short in personal charms, but his wife, Dolley, was one of the liveliest and most delightful of the nation's first ladies. (Collection of the New York Historical Society)

American trade, the United States promised to support against its enemy the first nation to act.

This tricky law was too clever by half. The wily Bonaparte saw that he might trap America into becoming his unwitting ally against England. The Duc de Cadore, the French foreign minister, quickly informed the American minister in Paris that the Berlin and Milan decrees had been revoked. Napoleon, however, did not intend to alter his policy toward American traders; in fact, on the very day Cadore told the American ambassador of the supposed French change of heart, Napoleon signed the Decree of Trianon, which ordered the confiscation and sale of all American vessels that had called at French ports after May 20, 1809. Friends warned Madison that Napoleon was shamming, but the optimistic president swallowed the bait. On November 2 he announced that trade restrictions against Great Britain would be reimposed early in 1811. Without surrendering a thing, Napoleon had gotten the United States to strike a blow against France's archenemy.

Further Western Troubles. The British were understandably irked by Madison's actions, and Anglo-American tensions were further aggravated by events in the West. Though the British had finally removed their troops from the Northwest, western settlers and their spokesmen remained convinced that England was stirring up troubles with the Indians. In fact, the British were innocent of wrongdoing. They wanted to keep the western tribes friendly and, if possible, detach them from allegiance to the Americans, but they had not incited them to attack American settlers. Yet Americans were certain that British agents were behind the disorders. The continued presence of British-Canadian fur traders in the Northwest, as allowed under the Jay Treaty, created further antagonisms and suspicion of British intrigue.

Actually, Americans themselves were responsible for the Indian troubles. At the behest of land speculators, frontier officials, many of them Jefferson's appointees, had for years extracted vast tracts of land from the native Americans, giving them little in return. In 1802 Governor William Henry Harrison of the Indiana Territory had called the Kickapoo, Wea, and Delaware tribes together and demanded that they cede to the United States several million acres in what is now southern Indiana. When the chiefs refused, he threatened to use force. The Indian leaders backed down. The resulting Treaty of Vincennes became the evil precedent for a rash of coerced agreements that compelled the northwestern and southwestern tribes to surrender millions of acres of choice lands for a few thousand dollars and a few baubles.

Harrison's provocative actions notwithstanding, by 1810–1811 settlers throughout the West were certain that

This determined man is Tecumseh, the great Shawnee leader. He tried to stop white encroachment on Indian land by welding all Indians into a defensive confederation. When this union failed, he joined the British and died fighting the Americans.

"British gold" was being used to encourage Indian militancy. Many of the fears and complaints centered on the activities of the Shawnee chief Tecumseh and his brother, "the Prophet," a chieftain believed to possess supernatural powers. These two remarkable men recognized that Harrison's success at land grabbing depended to a large extent on the disunity of the Indian tribes. To defeat Harrison and his kind, they proposed creating a tribal confederation that would present a united front to white officials. But their ultimate goals were far more ambitious. Tecumseh proposed nothing less than the old dream of Pontiac: to expel the whites and free the Mississippi Valley for the Indians. The white men, the Shawnee chief told his people, must be driven "back whence they came, upon a trail of blood, they must be driven." Despite such threats, Tecumseh at first urged his followers to exercise restraint as long as Harrison did not try to take possession of the Indian lands that the Americans had inveigled. Then, after Harrison indicated that he intended to proceed, he pulled out the stops and urged all-out war against the American settlers. "Burn their dwellings," he urged a meeting of Creeks, Cherokees, and Choctaws. "Destroy their stock. The red people own the country. . . . War now. War forever. War upon the living. War upon the dead; dig up their corpses from the grave; our country must give no rest to the white man's bones."

In September 1811 Harrison and a thousand troops set out to punish the Indian leaders. The small army reached Prophetstown in early November and camped outside it. Just before daylight on November 7 the Indians attacked while the Americans still slept and almost overwhelmed them. Harrison's seasoned troops held, however, and when the American cavalry charged the Indians broke and fled.

Though the Battle of Tippecanoe would help make Harrison's reputation as an Indian fighter, it was actually a kind of defeat. The vanquished Indian warriors abandoned their capital and scattered throughout the West. Wherever they went, they carried their hatred of the white man and their pan-Indian vision. Before long the whole West, north as well as south, was in flames.

Westerners had other grievances against the British. They were responsible for the hard times that followed the orders in council. British policies, it was said, had cut off the European market for western grain and created large unsold surpluses. Prices had dropped, causing distress to many western farmers. Though the American embargo had only made matters worse, westerners hoped it would eventually force Britain to back down, and western representatives in Congress were among the law's staunchest supporters.

Western attitudes would have been an important element in the decision to go to war in any case. But western views were given added weight by the skillful maneuvering of the War Hawks—some forty western and southern representatives elected to the Twelfth Congress that met in 1811. Led by Henry Clay, the group included such notable men as John C. Calhoun, William Lowndes, and Langdon Cheves of South Carolina; Felix Grundy of Tennessee; Richard M. Johnson of Kentucky; and Peter Porter of western New York. Marked off from other members of the Twelfth Congress by their aggressive nationalism and their resolve to shake the nation loose from subservience to Great Britain come what may, the War Hawks succeeded in electing Clay speaker of the House and packing the important foreign relations and naval committees with their members. Thereafter every move to condemn Britain or to appropriate money for the army and navy received their enthusiastic support.

Congress Votes for War. No single dramatic event finally pushed the country into war. All through 1811 relations with Britain deteriorated. The British government did not take kindly to Madison's proclamation reimposing the embargo on Anglo-American trade. British cruisers were soon gathering in increasing numbers off the Atlantic coast, stopping more American vessels than ever and removing suspected British deserters in droves. Once more, impressment set off a major naval incident. In May Commodore John Rodgers, commanding the frigate *President*, stumbled on the British corvette *Little Belt* off Virginia. Rodgers chased the British vessel, overtook it, and attacked, inflicting severe damage. The *President* did not sink the smaller British ship, but most Americans felt satisfied that the disgrace of the *Chesapeake* defeat had finally been avenged.

Matters moved swiftly to a head. In April 1812 Congress gave President Madison power to call up the state militias for six months' service. On the same day British Foreign Secretary Lord Castlereagh rejected the American demand that the 1807 orders in council be withdrawn. But the British economy was now finally beginning to feel the pinch of the embargo, and continued pressure would probably have forced the British to back down if fate had not unexpectedly intervened. On May 11, 1812, a madman shot Prime Minister Spencer Perceval, throwing the British government into turmoil. By the time it began to function again, Castlereagh was ready to suspend the orders in council. But his announcement, like other European news, took weeks to reach America and arrived too late to influence events. Two days after Castlereagh's concession to the United States, Congress declared war on England.

Who Wanted War. The declaration of war against Britain on June 18 was not unanimous. Of 128 representatives voting, 49 voted no. In the Senate 13 out of 32 members refused to support the war declaration. Historians have tried to determine the motives for war by analyzing the war vote, but the picture remains murky. Representatives of coastal New England clearly opposed war, but those from interior New England favored it. New York, too, opposed the war, but Pennsylvania, including the port of Philadelphia, voted to fight. The South, especially the Carolinas and Georgia, was almost solidly in support of the war, as was the West beyond the Appalachians.

More important perhaps than whether a congressman lived in the North, the South, or the West was whether his constituents exported farm products—in which case he tended to support the war—or engaged in ocean commerce—in which case he was likely to vote against it. In other words, pocketbook considerations seem to have been more important than geography in determining the way individual representatives voted. Sectional factors in this view seem significant mostly because many westerners and southerners were certain that their prosperity depended on teaching the British that they must not interfere with American export trade, whereas many New Englanders feared that war with Great Britain would lead to the complete destruction of American commerce by the powerful British navy.

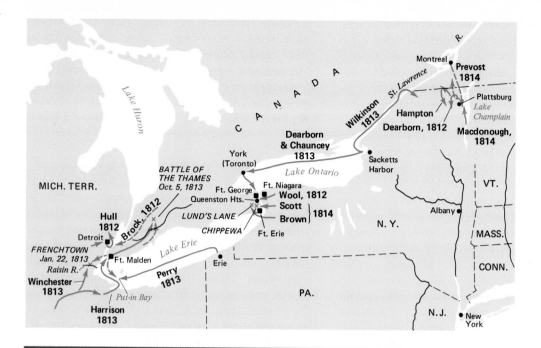

NORTHERN CAMPAIGNS, 1812–1814

Perhaps the most workable analysis, however, connects the war vote to politics and party. Generally speaking, John Randolph's dissenting Quid Republicans and the Federalists voted against the war; and administration Republicans, including, of course, the War Hawks, favored it. Professor Bradford Perkins estimates that fully 90 percent "of the real, available Republican membership [of the House of Representatives] backed the bill" to declare war. It is true that some administration Republicans had misgivings. Indeed, the president himself was not eager to fight. But the strong anti-British stand of the party ever since the 1790s, and particularly since Jefferson's embargo, committed them to taking this step.

If we look behind the war vote in Congress, we can identify something more fundamental than economic interest and party, however. The War of 1812 was the result of an upsurge of nationalism among Americans. By 1812 many citizens were determined to avenge the humiliations the United States had suffered at British hands for almost a generation. Though their country had won its formal independence in 1783, it still seemed to be under Britain's thumb. Impressment, orders in council, incitement of Indians, confiscation of American ships—all contributed to the anger and hurt pride that these Americans felt. Many Federalists and New Englanders might have preferred to ignore the incidents, believing it better to suffer these ills for the sake of profit and safety. Some westerners, as John Randolph charged, might have supported the war out of lust for British Canada to add to western land and wealth.

But for many Americans, the prospect of continued submission to haughty Britain seemed ample reason for military resistance.

★ THE WAR OF 1812 ★

The eminent amateur historian Harry S Truman would call the War of 1812 "the silliest damn war we ever had." On the whole he was right; the war was badly bungled. Yet we must remember that Commander in Chief Madison had a difficult task before him. Owing at least in part to Republican hostility to peacetime armies, American military and naval forces were feeble at the outbreak of hostilities. Congress had provided for a 35,000-man regular army in January 1812, but at the beginning of June it consisted of only 6,700 officers and men. Worse, the troops were not stationed close to Canada, the most accessible part of the British Empire, but were scattered all over the country. Although he was authorized to bring 100,000 militia into federal service, the president was effectively deprived of the best-trained state troops by New England's virtual neutrality during the war. Facing the motley American army would be an uncertain number of equally nondescript Canadian militia plus 7,000 British and Canadian regulars. Many of the British regular troops had fought the French in Europe, and behind them—once Napoleon was defeated—was potential reinforcement by many thousands of tough veterans of the Duke of Wellington's Spanish campaign.

The Americans were even worse off on the high seas. In June 1812 the American navy consisted of sixteen regular vessels, only seven of which were substantial seaworthy frigates, and over a hundred almost worthless gunboats. By contrast, Britain had over two hundred frigates and ships of the line—most with twice the firepower of the largest American vessels. Americans could and would add to their navy, and they would send out scores of privateers against British ocean commerce. The American naval effort during the war, nevertheless, would resemble a scrappy minnow nipping at a shark's tail.

In financial matters, too, the United States was handicapped. In 1811 Congress had defeated by a close vote an attempt to recharter the Bank of the United States. The bank, as Hamilton had predicted, had helped the government manage its financial operations and had provided businessmen with much-needed credit and capital. Although hostile at first, Albert Gallatin and other Republicans eventually came to favor it. But the bank had not converted all its opponents, and it had made new enemies among some business groups. These forces had defeated it. Now, without a central bank to make loans to meet the government's extraordinary wartime needs, the treasury found itself in difficulties. The situation was made worse by New England's reluctance to lend to the treasury from its large reserves of available capital.

Still another problem the president faced was poor communications. Although transportation up and down the Atlantic coast by ship was relatively swift and easy, communication with the interior, especially across the mountains, was slow and difficult. Roads were few throughout the nation; those crossing the Appalachians were no more than Indian trails. The Great Lakes were potentially useful, but nowhere on American territory were they connected by water to the country's major population centers. Bad communications imposed serious handicaps on military commanders, who were forced to move supplies and men along crude trails hacked out of the forest.

The Hartford Convention. New England's financial tight-fistedness suggests some of the political difficulties in Madison's way. Almost the whole area north and east of the Hudson sat out the war. Many Yankees regarded Great Britain not as America's enemy, but as the world's last hope against the tyrant Napoleon, and they condemned Madison for having made the United States Bonaparte's ally. Antiwar sentiment was especially strong in the Connecticut River Valley. In 1814, after seeing their commerce virtually swept off the seas by the British navy, antiwar Yankees forced the calling of a convention at Hartford, Connecticut. There they intended to discuss how to deal with the war and to consider whether the discontented states should secede from the Union. Fortunately, the extremists at Hartford were outmaneuvered by the moderates, and the convention took no action beyond endorsing state nullification of federal acts and proposing constitutional amendments limiting the power of the president and Congress over foreign relations. New England disaffection stopped short of outright disloyalty, yet the hostility to the war in the Northeast would be a dead weight around Madison's neck.

The Early Years of the War. After we acknowledge all of these difficulties, however, Madison still must bear much of the blame for the failures of the American war effort. As commander in chief, he appointed the generals, and his first choices were abysmal. Major General William Hull was sent to attack the British in Upper Canada (Ontario), but was forced to surrender to the British commander, Isaac Brock, near Detroit. William Henry Harrison, ordered to retake Detroit, gave up much of the Northwest to the British and their Indian allies. An American invasion of the Niagara peninsula under Generals Stephen Van Rensselaer and Alexander Smyth was turned into a tragic farce by the incompetence and cowardice of the New York militia. When ordered to cross into Canada to fight the enemy, they refused on the grounds that they had no obligation to fight outside their home state, and stood idly by watching the regulars across the Niagara River being slaughtered by Brock's troops. Only the famous victories of the frigates *Constitution* and *United States* in single-ship combat with the *Guerrière* and *Macedonian* kept up American spirits in the first year of war.

Despite the disasters in the field, Madison was reelected for a second term in 1812 over De Witt Clinton of New York, the Federalist candidate. During the election a group of younger Federalists tried to make their party and candidates more popular by adopting such Republican tactics as canvassing from door to door, treating the voters to food and drink, and putting on spectacular political rallies. They increased their party's vote in some areas; but despite Madison's spotty war record, they could not push their candidate to victory. The president's 128 electoral votes represented the prowar sections, largely in the South and West; Clinton's 89 represented the antiwar regions of New England, with New York, New Jersey, and part of Maryland thrown in.

The second year of the war went only a little better than the first. Under Harrison's overall command American troops continued to battle in the Northwest. In January 1815, Harrison's subordinates were defeated in a series of battles south of the Great Lakes. Because the British seemed likely to be successful so long as they could move freely on Lake Erie, the government ordered Captain Oliver Hazard Perry to build a small navy on the south shore of the lake.

On September 1, Perry's fleet met a somewhat smaller flotilla under Captain Robert Barclay. In a fierce exchange Perry sank or captured the entire British force. "We have met the enemy and they are ours," read Perry's succinct dispatch to Harrison.

With Lake Erie under American control, Harrison moved against the British in Upper Canada. In the Battle of the Thames in early October he and his Kentucky militia encountered a small force of British regulars, Canadian militia, and some 1,500 Indians, these last led by Tecumseh. The shock of the first volley scattered the British and Canadians. The Indians held out longer, but they, too, soon turned and ran. Tecumseh was presumed dead, though his body was never found. This defeat led to the collapse of the Shawnee chief's confederation and the desertion of many tribes from the British cause.

The year 1813 also saw the outbreak of Indian troubles in the Southwest. The Creek War brought on the grim ambushes, scalpings, and indiscriminate murder of women and children invariably perpetrated by both sides in Indian-white wars. In August a Creek force of 1,000 killed 250 white settlers jammed for safety into Fort Mims in southern Alabama. Later that year the Tennessee militia avenged the deed by slaughtering 186 Indians near Jacksonville, Alabama.

The fighting during the Indian war marked the rise to prominence of Andrew Jackson, a Tennessee planter-politician who commanded the government's forces as major general of the state militia. Early in 1814 Jackson marched on the Creeks in what is now Alabama. At Horseshoe Bend he attacked and overran the Indians, massacring 800. This blow smashed the power of the southwestern tribes. The surviving Creeks were forced to sign a peace treaty at Fort Jackson surrendering a giant slice of territory in southern Georgia and central Alabama. For his services Jackson was made a major general in the regular army.

The Last Campaigns. Meanwhile, in Europe Napoleon had finally been defeated by a coalition of British, Austrians, Russians, and Prussians at the Battle of Leipzig, and in April

The battle of the U.S.S. Constitution and H.M.S. Guerrière as depicted in a contemporary painting. Single encounters like this one were among the few naval victories the United States could claim in the War of 1812. They scarcely affected the outcome of the war, but they did help American morale.

1814 he was sent into exile on the Mediterranean island of Elba. Bonaparte's surrender freed thousands of seasoned British troops for the American war, and in late summer 1814, some 11,000 of these veterans set out from Canada under George Prevost for New York City. But all hopes of cutting the United States in two along the old Champlain-Hudson route ended when American gunboats under Captain Thomas McDonough defeated an English fleet at Plattsburgh on Lake Champlain. With the Americans in control of the lake, Prevost hurriedly retreated, leaving behind a mountain of supplies and hundreds of deserters.

The second prong of the British knockout campaign, aimed at Chesapeake Bay, proved more successful. In June the British navy transported 4,000 troops directly from France to the Patuxent River. From there they advanced on the national capital. At Bladensburg, Maryland, a hastily gathered force of militia, sailors, and a few regulars tried to stop them. The British veterans routed the motley American army and then marched into Washington unopposed. Shortly before, Congress and the president had fled the city, leaving behind the spirited first lady, Dolley Madison, to save Gilbert Stuart's portrait of Washington. Mrs. Madison could not save other national treasures, however. The British burned the Capitol, the presidential mansion, and all the city's public buildings except the Patent Office.

The redcoats now turned north to Baltimore, the country's third-largest city. Here they were checked. Fort McHenry and the fortifications quickly thrown up around the city were manned by thousands of militia, sailors, and some regulars. The British fleet bombarded the fort for two days, but it held out. To commemorate the heroic defense, Francis Scott Key wrote the "Star-Spangled Banner" to the tune of an old British drinking song. It is appropriate that the only serious literary work evoked by this mismanaged war is associated with befuddlement.

The third prong of the British campaign was an attack on New Orleans. In late November a British army of 7,500 under Sir Edward Pakenham left the island of Jamaica and landed at Lake Borgne, forty miles from New Orleans. Andrew Jackson sped south from Baton Rouge and engaged the enemy in skirmishes east of the city, slowing the British advance. On New Year's Day Jackson's skilled artillerymen severely punished the British troops, compelling Pakenham to wait for reinforcements.

On January 8, 1815, the British resumed their advance against Jackson's force of U.S. regulars, Kentucky and Tennessee riflemen, and New Orleans and Louisiana militiamen composed of Bayou pirates, free blacks, and young bluebloods from New Orleans. In a dense morning fog the British regulars moved forward against the Americans, lined up behind a low wall. Before the red-clad troops had gone very far, the fog began to lift, and at 500 yards the American artillery opened fire with devastating effect. Still the disciplined redcoats trudged on. When the British came within rifle range, Jackson ordered some of the big guns to cease their fire so that their smoke would not obscure the riflemen's targets. He then ordered his men to blaze away.

The combination of rifle and artillery fire was too much for even experienced troops to bear. In less than an hour one-third of the British force was cut down, and three of

An unusually incompetent American high command allowed the British to capture Bladensburg, Maryland, and march on the capital unopposed. In retaliation for the destruction of Toronto, the British burned Washington's government buildings, including the "Yankee Palace."

the highest-ranking British officers, including Pakenham, were dead. Another third of Pakenham's original force was in complete disarray. Faced with the reality of defeat, General John Lambert ordered retreat. On January 27 the surviving British troops sailed for home.

The Peace of Ghent. The Battle of New Orleans cost the British over 2,000 lives. It would never have taken place if transatlantic communications had been swifter in these years. On December 24, British and American negotiators had concluded a peace at Ghent in what is now Belgium. The peace treaty, signed before Jackson's stunning victory, was an ambiguous and tentative document that brought the United States few gains. It said nothing about impressment, ignored the neutral rights and Indian issues that had bedeviled British-American relations for years, and left the Canadian-American boundary where it had been before the war. None of the goals that had prompted Americans to action were realized by the treaty.

It did not satisfy the British either. For them the war had begun as a defensive struggle, but their early military successes had led the English leaders to hope for territorial concessions from the Americans and perhaps an Indian buffer state between the United States and Canada. War

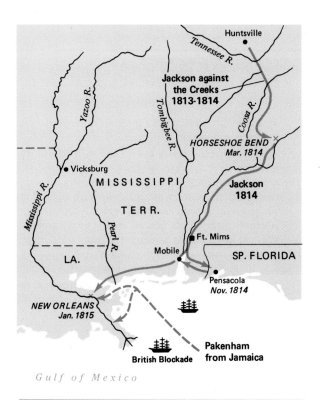

SOUTHWEST CAMPAIGNS, 1813–1815

weariness and fear that fighting might shortly resume in Europe led the British to abandon these goals at Ghent.

Little was accomplished by the treaty, except for the restoration of peace. It provided for a commission to settle the disputed boundary with Canada in the far northeast and mentioned future settlement of differences over navigation of the Great Lakes and the Newfoundland fisheries. In 1817, to implement the agreement at Ghent, Britain and the United States signed the Rush-Bagot Agreement by which both nations accepted almost total disarmament along the Canadian-American border. Applied at first solely to the Great Lakes region, it eventually converted the whole of the Canadian-American boundary into the longest unarmed frontier in the world.

Yet the fact remains that the document ending the war was less significant than the victory at New Orleans. Weeks after the Ghent negotiations had ended, the British government ordered reinforcements to Pakenham—a move that suggests that if their army had defeated Jackson, they would have refused to confirm the treaty. Great Britain had never recognized the legality of the Louisiana Purchase, and it is likely that if Pakenham had taken New Orleans, Britain would have carved out a sphere of influence along the lower Mississippi. Jackson's triumph ended the possibility of a new British Empire at the expense of the United States.

More important, however, were the profound psychological results of Jackson's victory. New Orleans left Americans with a sense that they had defeated British tyranny a second time. It created a new national hero in the person of testy, rough-hewn Andy Jackson, and a proud new national mythology. Unspoiled, sturdy, and independent American frontiersmen, so the myth went, had taken on Europe's best and defeated them decisively. Jackson's triumph produced a surge of patriotism that all but obliterated the disunity that had afflicted the country at the beginning of the war. However it had begun, by its glorious ending the war reaffirmed American self-respect and pride. "The war," Albert Gallatin would write a colleague, "has renewed and reinstated the national feelings and character which the Revolution had given, and which were daily lessened. The people have now more general objects of attachment. . . . They are more American; they feel and act more as a nation."

Gallatin's view is confirmed by the facts. President Madison's 1815 message to Congress expressed the new spirit that had captured the nation: Even the party of states' rights must now devote its energies to forging closer national bonds and stronger national institutions. Republicans had learned their lesson. The country had been severely handicapped by poor communications and the absence of a central bank. Perhaps Hamilton and his friends had been right after all. Why not give their ideas a try at least?

Ironically, although the war made the Republicans into nationalists, it destroyed the party that formerly had had a virtual copyright on the nationalist label. If the war had ended on a sour note, the Federalists might have come out of it with enhanced prestige. As it was, New Orleans made the party of Washington and Hamilton seem unpatriotic and treasonous. After 1815 the Federalists would never again be a serious threat to the Republicans on the national level.

★ CONCLUSIONS ★

Between the 1800 presidential campaign and James Madison's seventh annual message to Congress, American political attitudes had taken a 180-degree turn. Jefferson's election had been a repudiation of Federalist excesses and a mandate for the party that represented local as opposed to national power. The public had exaggerated Jefferson's differences from his opponents. Nevertheless, the Republican victory of 1800 represented an endorsement of a less activist national government and a repudiation of the strong centralizing bent of the Federalists.

The American people could not have foreseen that they and their leaders would do an about-face. Events would overtake everyone's theories. In the decade and a half that followed Jefferson's inauguration, the growing confrontation with France and England required an ever more active and effective central authority. The clash also created a new sense of national priorities, especially among southerners and westerners, whose agricultural interests, as opposed to the commercial interests of New Englanders, did not conflict with a strong stand against the country's foreign enemies. The war itself made clear to many former opponents of Federalist "follies" that to function, the country must accept much that Hamilton and his allies had proposed. Finally, with the splendid climax at New Orleans, the country experienced a new sense of unity and a self-confidence that would last until immense new issues once again reactivated the divisive forces of localism.

New Orleans and the Treaty of Ghent closed one chapter of American history. For fifty years the United States had been embroiled in Europe's remote affairs. Now, with Napoleon gone, Europe settled down to a long period of relative international calm. For almost a century the United States would be spared the clash of empires that had unsettled it for so long. And with peace, Americans could go about the business of exploiting their bounteous human and natural resources and converting them into tangible wealth.

★★★★★★★ FOR FURTHER READING ★★★★★★★

Merrill Peterson. *Thomas Jefferson and the New Nation: A Biography* (1970)
Peterson relates Jefferson's private life and his thought to his public role, and is lucid on the political issues of the day. A fine fusion of biography and history.

Fawn Brodie. *Thomas Jefferson: An Intimate History* (1973)
Here is a fascinating portrait of Jefferson the man—husband, father, slaveowner, and friend—as well as the political leader and social philosopher. Though criticized by some scholars for suggesting an intimate relationship between Jefferson and his female slave, Sally Hemmings, this work is a superior psychobiography of our third president.

Forrest McDonald. *The Presidency of Thomas Jefferson* (1976)
This brief, well-written volume is like several other works by McDonald: It has a strong point of view that not every scholar can accept. Well worth reading, however.

Bernard De Voto, editor. *Journals of Lewis and Clark* (1953)
The chronicle of a great adventure: the twenty-eight-month-long search for an overland route to the Pacific. De Voto's long introduction establishes the historical context of the explorers' expedition.

Leonard Levy. *Thomas Jefferson and Civil Liberties: The Darker Side* (1963)
This is a revisionist study of the Jefferson presidency that depicts the third president as a man who often violated his own precepts in matters of civil liberties. A necessary antidote to the many Jefferson eulogies, yet Levy probably goes too far in seeking to redress the balance.

Henry Adams. *History of the United States During the Administrations of Jefferson and Madison* (1881–91)
This nine-volume work is a classic of American historical literature. It is written in a grand manner by a scion of the Massachusetts Adamses.

Reginald Horseman. *The War of 1812* (1969)
The best one-volume history of the war. The emphasis is on military events.

Bernard Sheehan. *Seeds of Extinction: Jeffersonian Philanthropy and the American Indian* (1973)
Sheehan describes how the Indian reformers of Jefferson's day,

hoping to lead the tribes from "savagery" to "civilization," only managed to drive them brutally into the interior, thereby making way for white speculators and settlers.

Bernard Mayo. *Henry Clay: Spokesman of the New West* (1937)
Mayo tells the story of Clay's life to 1812, when he was the thirty-five-year-old Speaker of the House of Representatives and leader of the War Hawks. He writes well about Clay's social background and political career.

Bradford Perkins. *Prologue to War: England and the United States, 1805–1812* (1961)
Perkins ascribes the drift of Britain and America toward war to the unyielding and condescending attitude of the English on the one hand and to American insistence on neutral trade in a world beset by war on the other. He emphasizes the maritime factors behind the war more than the others that have been suggested in this chapter.

Julius Pratt. *Expansionists of 1812* (1925)
Emphasizes how American interest in acquiring Canada, Florida, and possibly Mexico influenced the decision for war in 1812. Not all scholars agree.

Gore Vidal. *Burr* (1973)
A historical novel about Aaron Burr in the form of a memoir. Vidal is very much biased toward Burr, and Washington, Jefferson, and Hamilton all emerge as narrow-minded, comical wheeler-dealers with much weaker characters than Burr himself. Good fun, if not too reliable.

9★

THE AMERICAN ECONOMIC MIRACLE

What Made It Possible?

1793	Eli Whitney invents the cotton gin
1794	The Philadelphia-Lancaster Turnpike opens
1802	West Point established
1803	The Louisiana Purchase
1807	Robert Fulton's steamboat *Clermont* makes a round trip between Albany and New York
1811	The federal government begins work on the National Road at Cumberland, Maryland • Fulton-Livingston interests awarded an exclusive charter from the Louisiana territorial legislature to operate steamboats on the Mississippi
1815	Entrepreneur Francis Cabot Lowell's Boston Manufacturing Company produces cotton cloth on a new power loom
1816	The Second Bank of the United States chartered
1817	New York's legislature approves funds for the Erie Canal
1818	The National Road reaches the Ohio River
1819	Financial panic and economic depression
1825	Completion of the Erie Canal: Shipping rates between Buffalo and New York fall more than 75 percent • Rensselaer Polytechnic Institute founded
1827	Mechanics Union of Trade Associates founded in Philadelphia
1828	The Baltimore and Ohio Railroad chartered
1830	Congress passes Pre-emption Act for the public domain
1837	Financial panic and economic depression
1844	Samuel F. B. Morse transmits the first intercity telegraph message
1847	Lawrence Scientific School established at Harvard
1853	The Gadsden Purchase secures an important southwestern railroad pass for the United States
1857	Financial panic and economic depression
1859	Edwin Drake drills the first successful oil well at Titusville, Pennsylvania

In 1833 Michael Chevalier, a French mining engineer, crossed the Atlantic to study the young American republic's canals and railroads. A keen student of the industrialization process then well underway in such European centers as Birmingham, Manchester, and Lille, Chevalier was amazed at what the Americans had accomplished. One of the most arresting sights was the city of Pittsburgh, where eighty years earlier the French had established Fort Duquesne amid the solitude of the unbroken forest. Now, Chevalier wrote, Pittsburgh was

> a manufacturing town which will one day become the Birmingham of America. . . . It is surrounded . . . with a dense black smoke which, bursting forth in volume from the foundries, forges, glasshouses, and the chimneys of all the factories and houses, falls in flakes of soot upon the dwellings and persons of the inhabitants. It is, therefore, the dirtiest town in the United States. . . . Nowhere in the world is everybody so regularly and continually busy as in Pittsburgh. I do not believe there is on the face of the earth a single town in which the idea of amusement so seldom enters the heads of the inhabitants.

The rest of the country, Chevalier found, had not changed as much from its eighteenth-century condition. Great expanses remained forested. Most cities were small. The majority of Americans were still farmers, and almost all the rest were employed in petty trade and handicrafts. But as Pittsburgh demonstrated, immense changes were taking place. By 1860 the United States would have a dozen Pittsburghs, beehives of industry belching smoke into the air. It would also have clusters of cleaner factories humming with the sound of looms and spindles. Meanwhile, crisscrossing the fields and woods, chugging "iron horses" would carry the products of the new mills and factories, along with great quantities of grain, livestock, cotton, and other commodities created by a surging agriculture. On the eve of the Civil War the United States would be one of the world's economic giants, ahead of all but Britain, its people enjoying one of the highest per capita living standards in the world.

How did this "economic miracle" come to pass?

★ FACTORS OF PRODUCTION ★

True economic growth requires not only the expansion of a nation's total output; it requires total output to expand faster than population. If population and output only increase at the same rate, no one on average is better off at the end of the process than at the beginning. The nation as a whole may be richer and its greater wealth may increase its overall power relative to other nations. But if we are interested in the material well-being of individual Americans, then it is per capita expansion that we must consider.

Historians and economists disagree over the causes of economic growth. Some emphasize the investment side of the process. They focus, that is, on the various "factors of production"—the inputs of labor, natural resources, skills, capital, and technology—that must be added to the economic mix to increase output. Other experts give special weight to the consumption side of growth. They assume that the dynamic element in economic expansion is the swelling demand for goods and services that comes with increases in population, changing consumption patterns, and government tax and spending policies. A third school, though not inconsistent with the others, is especially impressed by the cultural elements that encourage societies to alter both their investment and consumption patterns. In reality, to understand how the United States increased its output enough to create relative abundance for its people, we must look at all sides of the equation.

Resources.   From the outset the United States was richly endowed by nature. Its agricultural resources were enormous. The nation in 1815 consisted of over a billion acres. No other country in the world possessed so much level, well-watered, fertile land in the earth's temperate zone, where the growing season is long.

Few countries had timber reserves to equal America's. The forests, although they initially impeded farming, were a unique resource, for virtually everything in the nineteenth century was made of wood—houses, fences, wagons, even clocks and machinery. Wood, moreover, was a major source of fuel, used by steamboats, locomotives, factory steam engines, and by most householders to cook their food and heat their homes, even in the cities.

America was also rich in minerals. The ores of the Appalachian region from central Vermont to the Carolinas formed an "iron belt" that as early as 1800 was dotted with forges, smelters, and mines. Copper and lead deposits were found in Michigan and Missouri. Pennsylvania and Ohio had excellent coal and—though as yet unused—the country possessed vast petroleum reserves.

In waterpower, too, the United States was blessed. The Appalachian chain, extending from Maine to Georgia, hindered westward movement, but it was also the source of many rivers that emptied into the Atlantic. Along the fall line, where the Piedmont plateau drops abruptly to the Atlantic coast plain, scores of swift cascading streams offered a vast reserve of water power to turn mill wheels.

Pittsburgh in 1796 and 1857. Located at the junction of three navigable rivers, the village thrived before 1800. In 1799 businessmen set up a nail factory there, and by the 1850s Pittsburgh's population worked in coal mines, steel mills, and glass factories under an ever-present cloud of industrial soot.

In 1815 relatively little of the country's land was being farmed. In the West dense settlement by white farmers was found only in the regions adjacent to the Ohio Valley and a few pockets elsewhere. Everything else remained Indian land or, although officially transferred to the government in Washington, was still unsettled by whites. Almost all of it was forest except tracts of present-day Indiana, Illinois, and Iowa, which were covered with tall prairie grass. Even in the Atlantic coast states forests and unused farm woodlots covered the landscape, especially in northern New England, New York, western Pennsylvania, and the mountain regions of the southern states.

Nor were the nation's power resources much used. Aside from some gristmills for grinding wheat and corn into flour and meal, and sawmills for slicing logs into boards,

the waterpower of the fall line went largely to waste. Also neglected was the coal of eastern Pennsylvania; as long as wood was cheap, people had no incentive to exploit the unfamiliar black stone for fuel. As for petroleum, though people knew "rock oil" would burn, they did not know how to guarantee a steady supply, so it remained a curiosity sold by quacks and hucksters as medicine.

In the forty-five years following the War of 1812 the accessible and usable resources within the country's 1803 boundaries were greatly expanded. Growing population and easier access to consumers induced farmers to cut the woodlots and expand their cultivated acreage. Increasingly, similar incentives moved businessmen to build water-powered mills and exploit coal deposits. In 1859 Edwin L. Drake, backed by New Haven capitalists, found that by

POPULATION DENSITY, 1820

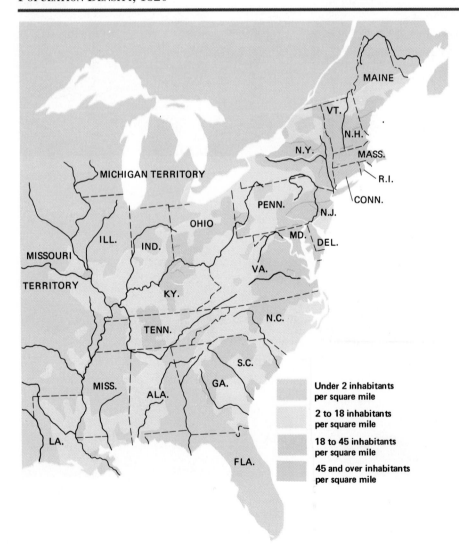

Under 2 inhabitants per square mile

2 to 18 inhabitants per square mile

18 to 45 inhabitants per square mile

45 and over inhabitants per square mile

drilling into the ground, an abundant supply of petroleum could be assured. Drake's well at Titusville, Pennsylvania, set off a "rush" to the oil regions that resembled the earlier gold rush to California.

But besides learning to exploit its existing resources, the country added to them by enlarging its boundaries. Between the Louisiana Purchase in 1803 and the Gadsden Purchase fifty years later, the United States grew by 830 million acres. A large part of the new territory was arid, but it also included great stretches of fertile land in the Central Valley of California, in east Texas, and in Gulf Coast Florida; vast deposits of copper, silver, gold, lead, and zinc in the Rocky Mountain area; and unique timber resources along the coasts of California and Oregon.

Labor. The increasing availability of the nation's natural resources was one reason for America's extraordinary economic growth, but without men and women to utilize these resources, they would have remained merely "potential" forever. The United States was a sparsely populated country in 1815. With 8.5 million people spread over 1.7 million square miles, it had under 5 inhabitants for every square mile (640 acres) of land, compared with about 80 per square mile today. In 1820 the population reached 9.6 million, including some 1.8 million blacks. Though legal importation of slaves had ceased in 1808 (when Congress implemented

the constitutional provision allowing it to end the Atlantic slave trade), blacks remained about 19 percent of the country's population.

With so few people spread over so much land, the United States suffered from a chronic labor shortage. Before 1815 the shortage was alleviated somewhat by the unusually high birthrate. The country's population was youthful: In 1817 the median age was 17. In an era when people began to work at 13 or 14, such a young population was a distinct economic asset. Offsetting this advantage, however, was the problem of disease and ill health. There were major cholera epidemics in 1832 and again in 1849/1850 that killed thousands and disrupted economic life. In low-lying, swampy areas many people suffered each summer from "fevers" or "agues," mosquito-borne malaria. William Dean Howells, the writer, recalled that during his boyhood in southwestern Ohio during the 1840s "there were few houses where [malaria] was not a familiar guest. . . . If the family was large, there was usually a chill every day; one had it one day and another the next. . . ." In addition, typhus, typhoid, whooping cough, and tuberculosis killed or disabled vast numbers of working people every year. After 1815 the potential labor force was further depleted by individual efforts to limit family size. The American birthrate dropped sharply, so that by 1850 it was below that of many countries in Europe.

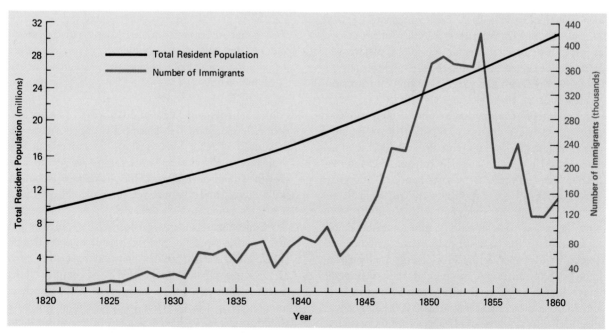

Population and Immigration to the United States, 1820–1860. *Source: Historical Statistics of the United States, Colonial Times to 1957.*

Steamships began crossing the Atlantic in the 1830s, but most immigrants—such as these arriving in New York in 1855—traveled in sailing packets. Of that year's 200,000 immigrants, almost half were destitute Irish peasants.

The Old World helped to offset the New World's labor shortage as in the past. Between independence and 1808 the South's labor force was swelled by an unusually large number of slave imports. Then, on January 1, 1808, the foreign slave trade became illegal. Some smuggling of captive Africans continued, but as a result of British-American naval cooperation in the South Atlantic, the number of slaves who arrived in the United States from abroad was drastically cut. Thereafter the South had to rely primarily on natural increase for the growth of its black labor force.

But Europe's contribution to America grew with each passing year. The period from 1776 to 1815 was a time of slack immigration, with no more than 10,000 Europeans entering the United States annually. Between 1815 and 1840 the number of European arrivals rose to over 30,000 a year. Then came the deluge of the 1840s and 1850s. Economic dislocations in Germany and Scandinavia and the potato blight in Ireland made life hard, in some cases intolerable, for hundreds of thousands of Europeans. Combined with quicker and cheaper transatlantic passage and spreading knowledge of America's opportunities, these disruptions and disasters brought on a flood of people. During the 1840s and 1850s a staggering average of 200,000 Europeans arrived each year at American Atlantic and Gulf Coast ports. Most of these immigrants were in their most productive early adult years. Europe had nurtured them through their dependent years, and they added their brawn and their skill to the American labor pool at scarcely any cost to their adopted nation. Almost all of these additions accrued to the North. European newcomers perceived the South as an alien place where slaves competed with free labor and the chances of economic success were limited. They avoided Dixie. All told, by 1860, the nation's labor force, as a result of natural increase and transatlantic immigration, had grown to over 11 million people.

Public Schools and Economic Growth. Modern economic development has depended as much on the improvement of labor force quality—the enhancement of "human capital," as economists call it—as on the sheer growth of numbers. In America the upgrading of labor force skills, literacy, and discipline was the work of the system of public education.

Educational standards had been relatively high in colonial America, especially in New England, but they had declined during the half century following the Revolution. In 1835 Professor Francis Bowen of Harvard complained that New England's celebrated school system "had degenerated into routine . . . [and] was starved by parsimony. Any hovel would answer for a school house, any primer would do for a textbook, any farmer's apprentice was competent to 'keep school.'" In the West, if we can believe the students of one small rural school, the teaching level was still lower. At the end of the academic year these pupils inscribed this verse on the wall of their schoolhouse:

Lord of love, look from above
And pity the poor scholars.
They hired a fool to teach this school
And paid him fifty dollars.

But even as Bowen—and the "scholars"—wrote, labor leaders, philanthropists, businessmen, and concerned citizens were struggling to upgrade the country's educational system. The most effective worker for improved schools after 1835 was Horace Mann, a self-made man of remarkable charm and great persuasive powers. A lawyer who gave up a successful legal practice to become secretary of the Massachusetts Board of Education in 1837, Mann believed that an educated body of citizens was essential for a healthy democratic society, but he and his disciples also linked education to economic growth. As one of Mann's successors on the Massachusetts Board of Education noted: "The prosperity of the mills and shops is based quite as much upon the intellectual vigor as the physical power of the laborers." During Mann's twelve years as secretary of the board, Massachusetts doubled teachers' salaries, built and repaired scores of school buildings, opened fifty high schools, and established a minimum school year of six months. Other states, especially in the North, soon followed the lead of the Bay State.

The new school systems taught useful values as well as useful skills. Not only did children attain literacy but they also learned punctuality, good hygiene, industriousness, sobriety, and honesty—all valuable qualities for an emerging industrial society. Lucy Larcom remembered in later years her experiences in New England schools during the 1830s. "I was," she wrote, "penetrated through every fiber of thought with the idea that idleness is a disgrace. It was taught with the alphabet and the spelling-book; it was enforced by precept and example." Other boys and girls remembered how the schoolmaster or schoolmistress told stories of success achieved through hard work and a willingness to sacrifice present pleasures for future gains. Even before the Civil War the rags-to-riches myth had become a powerful reinforcement for the industrial virtues. It would be a mistake to see this indoctrination as the central goal of pre–Civil War educational reformers, but there can be no question that the new public schools encouraged the qualities the nation needed in its labor force.

Many large gaps remained in the country's educational system even after the advent of the state-supported primary school. Secondary education, except in Massachusetts, remained the privilege of the rich who could afford the tu-

ition of private "academies" for their children. One of the most serious deficiencies was in the education of girls and young women.

At the elementary level young girls were treated the same as boys. Beyond the first few grades, however, women's education was often inferior. American women did not attend colleges until Oberlin admitted its first female student in 1833. The typical secondary school or academy for women around 1815 was a "finishing school" where the daughters of businessmen, professionals, and wealthy farmers or planters were taught French, music, drawing, dancing, and a little "polite" literature. Then, in the period of 1820–40, educational reformers, both men and women, began to conceive of a new sort of secondary schooling for women.

These reformers attacked the idea that women should be mere playthings and ornaments. In a bustling progressive society, they said, women had a vital role to play as mothers and teachers, educating the leaders of the nation in all areas of life. This "cult of domesticity" propagated by Catharine Beecher and Sarah Josepha Hale, editor of the widely circulated magazine *Godey's Lady's Book*, did not assert women's equality with men. But it did insist that in their

This unusual photograph of one of the new female academies—The Emerson School for Young Ladies in Boston—dates from the early 1850s. The poses seem stiff, especially that of the schoolmaster; but that may be as much the result of slow lenses and photographic emulsions that required long exposures as of the social rigidity of the antebellum classroom.

own "spheres" women were an immense but seriously neglected resource and that this waste must not continue.

The new idea of the importance of the female role transformed women's education, especially in the Northeast. Under the leadership of Emma Willard, Mary Lyon, Joseph Emerson, and Catharine Beecher, female "seminaries" were established throughout the region. Schools such as Willard's Troy Female Seminary (1821) and Lyon's Mount Holyoke Female Seminary (1836), unlike the earlier finishing schools, taught algebra, geometry, history, geography, and several of the sciences. These more "muscular" subjects were thought appropriate for the mothers-to-be of statesmen, soldiers, and captains of industry. The most important role of these schools, however, was to provide a flood of trained women to fill the ranks of the burgeoning teaching profession. Without the female seminaries it is hard to see how the new public school movement could have succeeded.

Though the educational system had its failings, by 1860 the United States had a highly skilled and literate labor force. It was ahead of every nation in the world except Denmark in the ratio of students to total population, and New England was even ahead of the advanced Danes. Literacy made it possible for workers to read plans and make reports and gave them access to new ideas and new ways of doing things. It is no accident that the ingenious Yankee tinkerer became a legendary figure or that New England became a beehive of shops, mills, and factories, producing cloth, clocks, shoes, hardware, and machinery for the rest of the nation.

Technology.   Americans have long had the reputation of being an inventive people. They had to be, for through most of their history they were pioneers, forced by their isolation to be self-reliant. During the colonial era the improvements in kitchen equipment and metal- and wood-working tools that emerged from ordinary household practices were supplemented by larger advances such as Benjamin Franklin's heat-conserving stove and his lightning rod to protect homes during electrical storms. After the Revolution the new patent laws of the federal government, along with labor scarcity, added to the incentives for mechanical improvements.

One man who rose to the challenge was Oliver Evans of Philadelphia. In the 1780s Evans developed an ingenious system of milling flour that eventually revolutionized the industry. In Evans's new mill the grain was carried in buckets attached to a water-powered moving belt to the top of the structure and allowed to descend to the bottom while being automatically cleaned, ground, cooled, sifted, and barreled. In his mill along the Brandywine in Delaware, six men could convert 100,000 bushels of wheat into flour a year, a 60 percent saving on labor. Nor was Evans an iso-

lated case. Eli Whitney of Connecticut invented a machine to make nails to offset the shortage during the Revolution. In the 1790s, as we shall see, he went on to perfect the "gin," a machine that revolutionized cotton growing in the South. He also helped introduce the idea of interchangeable parts to speed the manufacture, and lower the cost, of rifles for the government.

The nation's vast size and poor roads also encouraged inventiveness in transportation and communication. Evans was interested in linking the steam engine to transport and designed a steam-powered vehicle that could be used on both roads and waterways. In 1787 John Fitch launched a boat using steam-powered oars. This vessel proved impractical, but twenty years later Robert Fulton, a New Yorker, assembled the first commercially feasible steamboat, using steam-driven paddle wheels. In August 1807 his vessel, the *Clermont*, made the trip up the Hudson from New York to Albany in thirty-two hours, proving the practicality of steam nagivation and setting off a national steamboat boom. Some years later another Connecticut Yankee, Samuel F. B. Morse, invented the dot-and-dash code used in telegraphy and made improvements in the primitive telegraph instruments then being developed by others. In 1844 Morse transmitted the first intercity telegraph message—between Baltimore and Washington.

All these men, and the many others who advanced technology in these years, were self-educated or had acquired their training on the job. Whitney learned about machinery at his father's farm in rural Massachusetts. Evans started as an apprentice to a wagon maker. Morse was a talented portrait painter who took up electrical experiments out of curiosity. Fulton was an artist and draftsman who taught himself the rudiments of marine engineering. Most of the country's first civil engineers learned their trade by working on the early turnpikes and canals.

Gradually, however, more formal means to train technicians and scientists were developed. West Point (founded in 1802), Norwich University (1820), Rensselaer Polytechnic Institute (1825), and the Lawrence Scientific School at Harvard (1847) eventually provided civil engineering courses for planning the canals, designing the bridges, and surveying the railroads that would knit the country together.

Growing Markets.   We can treat the growing and ever-more skillful population of the country as an addition to the supply side of the economic growth equation. It was also a factor on the demand side. As population increased, so did the market for everything from babies' cribs to old folks' canes. Both young families and new immigrants needed housing. Their needs stimulated construction in the towns and the countryside. Americans were already well

"Buy American" was the cry of American manufacturers after the War of 1812. By the 1840s they were making goods previously imported and inventing all sorts of baubles to tempt domestic consumers. Here, in 1845, they exhibited their products at an all-American trade fair.

supplied with food, clothing, and shelter, and each addition of family income provided money for modest luxuries. Before the Civil War the finer industrial goods were commonly obtained from Britain or France, but with each passing year American industry expanded to meet the growing home market for jewelry, furniture, carriages, carpets, writing paper, clocks, fine cloth, and a thousand other sophisticated manufactured articles.

Capital. The growing labor force of the United States was matched by a growing supply of capital. *Capital*, as economists use the term, is not just money, but money invested in machines, barns, factories, railroads, mines—that is, money invested in "tools" that produce other commodities. (Today, as we saw, the term *capital* is also applied to the skills people acquire that improve their ability to produce.) When employed, capital becomes the basis for increasing the rate of economic growth.

Where did the capital come from that helped produce America's "economic miracle"? During the colonial period much of it came from abroad in the form of implements, credits, and cash brought by immigrants or lent to Americans by European promoters and merchants. After independence the United States continued to rely on foreign sources of capital. As the number of immigrants increased, so did the amount of money they brought to America. After 1840 this amounted to millions of dollars annually. Larger than this source of foreign capital were the loans extended by British, French, Dutch, and German bankers and business people. The total amount of the nation's outstanding foreign loans went from under $100 million in 1815 to $400 million by the eve of the Civil War.

Foreign trade was yet another source of capital. The United States in this period exported vast quantities of raw materials and farm products to foreign nations. They, in turn, bought our tobacco, wheat, lumber, beef and pork. Cotton from the South alone represented almost half the value of the country's total annual exports in the mid-1850s. Profits from these sales enabled the country to buy not only European consumer goods like French wines and British

Samuel F. B. Morse

The career of Samuel Finley Breese Morse refutes the conventional view that artists are quixotic dreamers. One of America's foremost pre–Civil War painters, Morse was also the inventor of a practical system of transmitting messages by electricity and the creator of the telegraph industry, precursor of the vast telecommunications enterprise of today.

Born in Massachusetts in 1791, Morse came of distinguished New England forebears who included famous preachers, scholars, judges, and a colonel in the Continental Army. His father, Jedidiah, was a prominent Congregational minister, Federalist leader, and one of America's first geographers. Samuel (called Finley by his family after one of his middle names) grew up near Boston, in a household where people prized learning and knowledge.

Though his family was well equipped to educate him at home, he was sent away to school at Phillips Academy in Andover when he was just eight. The young Finley disliked boarding school and did not do well, but he found consolation in drawing. His father preferred books to pictures, but he did not at first discourage the lad and in fact proudly sent a specimen of his work to Finley's grandfather with the comment: "[H]e is self taught—has had no instructions."

In 1805, at the age of 14, Morse entered Yale. The college was scarcely an intellectual feast in the early nineteenth century. It had only three professors and its curriculum was almost exclusively devoted to the classical languages. Yet at Yale, Morse first learned about electricity. Equally important, to earn pocket money, he began to paint miniature portraits on ivory, a genre much admired in that day. The acclaim of his peers convinced him that his future lay in art, and on graduation he told his father that he wished to study with Washington Allston, an American painter then passing through Boston. The Reverend Morse put his foot down. His oldest child, he said, would become a bookstore clerk in Boston while considering a proper career.

Though bitterly disappointed, Morse obeyed his father. But while working at Mallory's bookstore he continued to paint. The work he did in his spare time so impressed influential people that his father relented and agreed to send him to England in the company of Allston to perfect his talents and learn from the masters of Europe.

Morse spent the next four years in London, studying with Allston and painting a number of important canvasses. He returned to Boston in 1815 and opened his own studio, full of hope that he could make a living from his painting and at the same time launch an artistic renaissance in America. He was disappointed. People admired his pictures and liked the young man personally, but they did not give him commissions. No one wanted the landscapes and historical paintings that Morse preferred to paint. He did manage to make a little money doing portraits, but this required him to move from place to place to accommodate patrons. In the next eight years Morse wandered from Concord, New Hampshire, to Charleston, South Carolina, finally settling in New York in 1823.

During this period his talent matured, but it did not lead to the fame and recognition he craved. These were not good years for Morse. His wife, Lucretia, died in 1825, leaving him with four young children. His father and mother died soon after. In 1829 he returned for a while to Europe, where he believed that art and artists were better appreciated. When he came home in 1832, he was appointed pro-

woolens but also machinery, iron rails, locomotives, and other capital goods. At the same time the American merchant marine, whose swift clipper ships were the nation's pride, earned income carrying European goods to Australia, South America, and the Far East. Finally, after 1849, gold from California helped pay for capital goods imported from the advanced industrial nations of Europe. In personal terms, foreign trade created fortunes for merchants, particularly in the middle states and New England—fortunes often reinvested in domestic industry.

Personal savings, whether of one's own citizens or foreigners, are always the source of funds for additions to a so-

ciety's plant and equipment. But a person who has surplus money may not know what to do with it. Institutions such as savings banks and mortgage and insurance companies provide an investment outlet for personal savings. These institutions offer the depositor of personal savings a profit in the form of interest or dividends, while in turn lending the money to business people and promoters who convert it into capital. Another effective device for converting savings into real capital is the corporation. Like the seventeenth-century joint-stock company, corporations enable many individuals to pool their funds in a single firm, but they have the additional advantage of limited liability. That is, in-

fessor of painting and sculpture at New York University, but the position was purely honorific, without salary. During these disappointing years his frustrations led him into nativist, anti-Catholic politics, a position he later came to regret.

During the 1830s Morse also drifted away from painting. On a return voyage from Europe he had first conceived the idea that electricity could be used to transmit messages over a wire. By 1832 he had set down in his notebook the plan for a device that would send signals by the opening and closing of a circuit, a receiving apparatus that would record the signals as dots and spaces on a paper strip moved by clockwork, and a code to translate the dots and spaces into the letters of the alphabet. Over the next few years Morse perfected his device, relying heavily on the scientific knowledge of Joseph Henry, a science professor at Princeton, and the financial backing of Alfred Vail, a rich young man whom he had taught at the university.

Morse filed his "electric telegraph" patent in 1837, but for the next seven years he could not secure enough financial support to demonstrate his invention's practical value. During this period, rather than go into debt, Morse actually went hungry at times. Finally, in 1843, Congress appropriated $30,000 to build an experimental telegraph line between Washington and Baltimore. On May 24, 1844, surrounded by friends and associates in the Supreme Court chamber of the Capitol, Morse tapped out the biblical phrase: "What hath God wrought!" In Baltimore Vail received the message and responded. The effect of this demonstration was strongly reinforced when the telegraph was used immediately after to transmit news of the Democratic national convention meeting in Baltimore. Vail sent news from the scene of the convention; Morse tacked up the messages on a board in the Capitol rotunda. It was the beginning of the new "information age" that is still evolving in our day.

Despite these successes, neither Morse nor the telegraph experienced clear sailing thereafter. Morse would have been happy to accept a government award and return to his art. But Congress refused his request for $100,000, and he was forced to seek commercial support for his invention. He was not a businessman, but fortunately he had Vail and a former postmaster general, Amos Kendall, to handle his business affairs. Morse and his partners beat off numerous lawsuits by other claimants to the invention and competed energetically with other companies offering telegraph services to newspapers and private users. Together the Morse associates and their competitors helped to wire the nation into a network of instantaneous communication. In 1858 Morse and his friends formed the Magnetic Telegraph Company in a deal that finally made the inventor a rich man after twenty years of struggle.

Morse lived until 1872, long enough to see a functioning Atlantic cable tie Europe to America. His last years were marked by contentment. He lived with his second wife and second family at an estate on the Hudson, while enjoying a townhouse in New York City. Colleges showered him with honorary degrees and governments awarded him medals and decorations. In 1871 the telegraph operators of America commissioned a bronze statute of the man who had created their industry, to be mounted in New York's Central Park. Morse did suffer one major disappointment in this period of his life, otherwise marked by comfort and acclaim. In 1864, when he tried to resume painting, he discovered that his talent had ebbed and he gave up the attempt.

Morse's death was marked by memorial services all over the nation. It was the inventor whom the country honored; little was noted of the artist. Posterity has been kinder to the artistic side of his career, however. He is now regarded as one of the nation's greatest painters. Morse now seems, in the words of his chief biographer, the "American Leonardo"—like the great da Vinci, a genius in art as well as technology.

vestors in a corporation buy as much stock as they wish or can afford; this is their total financial commitment. If the firm they have invested in goes bankrupt, the stockholders' liabilities are limited to the extent of their investment. No matter how large the debt of the corporation, the investors' other property or wealth is not endangered. Such an arrangement can encourage timid investors to risk their precious savings on chancy new enterprises.

Changes in law were necessary to popularize the corporation. At the beginning of the nineteenth century many people were suspicious of limited liability, which seemed a way by which bankrupts could escape paying their creditors. But gradually state legislatures, beginning with Massachusetts in 1830, permitted limited liability provisions in corporate charters. After 1837 they also passed general incorporation laws that allowed businessmen and investors to get charters by applying to a state official rather than by a special act of the lawmakers as before.

These early corporations seldom sold stock to a broad anonymous public as their counterparts do today. That development would not come until the end of the century. Rather, in most cases the stockholders consisted of a few score or a few hundred friends, associates, or family members. Still, the corporation form allowed the investment net to be spread much wider than in the old-fashioned firm consisting of one owner or a few partners. By 1860 the corporation was used more widely by Americans than by Europeans as a way to pool the savings of many people.

Banks and Banking. We have seen how certain sorts of banks act as catch basins for savings and convey these funds to investors. The country's commercial banking system also made an important contribution to the growth of private capital between 1815 and 1860 by creating money or credit—which amounts to the same thing—and lending it to business borrowers.

At first glance, the role of commercial banks in creating money seems a puzzling thing. Isn't money either coined or printed by the government? It is, but banks also play a vital role in the money-manufacturing process. The key to this function is the fact that, taken as a whole, the commercial banking system keeps only a small reserve of money against the debts it owes to its depositors and the loans it makes to borrowers. This reserve is enough to meet normal withdrawal requests, cash checks, pay employees, and so forth. This means that on a small amount of paid-in capital or deposited savings, it can lend a large amount to investors. In effect, the commercial banks are money machines, geared to advance the cash or credit they create to business people who want it to buy new equipment, embark on new enterprises, or develop new products or services.

This system depended on balance to work successfully. If bankers were not careful and lent to unreliable borrowers or if, carried away by a spirit of speculation, they made loans far beyond what a cautious reserve policy required, they jeopardized their firms and often the economy as a whole. Depositors, or other creditors, fearing for the safety of their savings, might demand immediate repayment. If enough of a bank's creditors simultaneously demanded their money back, a "run" on the bank developed, and it would often be forced to "suspend payments"—that is, close its doors.

Such suspensions often occurred in waves. If the bank that failed was especially large or prominent, and if others were also overextended and on shaky ground, the individual run might turn into a general money panic, where everyone demanded cash and sought to make their creditors pay up their due debts. Under these circumstances, interest rates would soar and thousands would go bankrupt. Serious panics occurred in 1819, 1837, and 1857, and each ushered in a long-lasting economic downturn. For a time business people would not invest and consumers would not buy. Economic activity slowed, and workers lost their jobs.

One important service that banks performed in the pre–Civil War period was to provide the paper money that people used in their daily buying and selling. A person who borrowed from a bank usually took the loan in the form of a packet of the bank's notes. The treasury also issued a coinage of gold, silver, and copper, but this was not enough to do the people's business. Instead, in all but minor transactions the "bank note," issued by some banking corporation, served the public as money. These notes were legally backed by a reserve of gold that the banks kept on hand, but the enforcement of the requirement that banks pay out gold for each note presented for redemption was often lax. The Second Bank of the United States, chartered in 1816, had little trouble keeping its circulation of paper notes "as good as gold." Many of the state-chartered banks, however, issued excessive amounts, given their reserves, because each paper dollar lent to a borrower earned interest and made a profit. When a bank could not redeem its notes, it was forced to suspend operations in the same fashion as when it could not repay depositors. When this happened, those who held the bank's notes found themselves with worthless paper, much as depositors in defaulted banks found themselves with worthless bank accounts.

Growth of the Banking System. Despite these failings, the country's banking system aided the investment plans of aggressive business people and promoters, accelerating the

This five-dollar note of the Second Bank of the United States dates back to 1819, when William Jones, the bank's incompetent first president, was still in charge. BUS notes such as these were redeemable in gold on demand and provided a sound and secure currency for the country until 1836.

growth of the nation's pool of capital. In the years before the Civil War the American banking system expanded exuberantly. The first modern American commercial bank was the Bank of North America, chartered by Congress in 1781 and located in Philadelphia. In 1784 New York and Massachusetts chartered two additional banks. Another was added by New York in 1799 under the name the Manhattan Company.

Meanwhile, as we have seen, Congress, acting on Hamilton's financial program, chartered the first Bank of the United States (or BUS). Like any other commercial bank, the BUS lent money, but it also served as the government's financial agent, holding the treasury's deposits, transferring government money from one part of the country to another, and even collecting United States customs duties. It also issued much of the country's paper money. Finally, before its demise in 1811, it took on some of the functions of a central bank. That is, it tried to control and stabilize the entire economy by providing extra funds to state bank lenders when credit was scarce and by seeking to limit the loans of the state banks when the BUS directors believed that credit was excessive.

The Second Bank of the United States, chartered in 1816, was even larger than its predecessor; it had $35 million in capital compared with the first BUS's $10 million. It, too, sought to provide a balance wheel for the economy. At times, however, it blundered badly. Under its first president, the Second BUS initially followed an easy-credit policy, lending freely to businessmen and speculators and failing to curb similar practices by the state banks. It was this policy that helped fuel a western land boom after 1815. When the second president came to office in 1819, he tightened credit by reducing the BUS's own loans and demanding that the state banks reduce theirs. This contraction was necessary and perhaps overdue, but it was too abrupt and helped set off the Panic of 1819.

Meanwhile, a state banking system was growing up alongside the federally chartered institutions. In 1820 there were 300 state banks; in 1834, 500; and in 1860, almost 1,600. At first most state banks were established by charters granted individually by state legislatures. By the 1840s, however, banks could use the same general incorporation system used by other businesses: securing charters by applying to designated state officials and meeting general legal requirements. In some states these requirements were strict. New York, for example, insisted that each state bank contribute a certain sum annually to a "safety fund" to be used to pay the bank's creditors in the event it failed. The provision helped ensure public confidence and financial stability and contributed to New York's growing preeminence as the nation's financial center.

Strict banking laws were most common in the Northeast, the region where savings were most abundant.

In the newer parts of the country there were fewer people with money to invest; yet it was precisely there that the need for capital to clear land, build barns, construct railroads, and lay out towns was most acute. Interest rates—the price of money—accordingly were higher in the West than in the East. Under the circumstances, it is not surprising that many western states were lax in their banking laws and still laxer in enforcing them. Western banks often ignored requirements that each dollar issued and lent to borrowers have a partial gold reserve to back it. This led to large issues of "wildcats," paper money backed by hope and faith rather than "specie," that is, gold. Local western banks also often lent on such security as land, which they could not quickly convert into cash in case of need. As a result, they encouraged a boom-and-bust pattern in the western economy, but their free-and-easy practices also helped meet a vital need for rapid increases in capital in the emerging parts of the country. All told, economic historians conclude, the banking system of this period, for all its faults, met the expansive needs of the economy well, providing for rapid capital growth without serious inflation.

Government Actions. Not all Americans believed the government should have a major role in the area of economic growth. Old-line Jeffersonians continued to fear federal and state intrusion into the economy as a danger to freedom. Other citizens, influenced by the laissez-faire ideas of the English economists Adam Smith and David Ricardo, believed that government intervention would only hamper economic progress. The nation must rely solely on private enterprise, they said; the profit motive alone would lead to growth and prosperity.

These opponents of government intervention won some battles, but government in fact played a vital role in the country's growth. Through laws favorable to the easy chartering of banks and corporations, it encouraged private capitalists to pool their savings for investment purposes. The federal tariff system, proposed by Hamilton and implemented by the Republicans in 1816, by making imports more expensive, protected American manufacturers against foreign competition and so encouraged capitalists to risk their money in factories and mills. There was also the tax system. Everywhere in pre–Civil War America taxes were low. No matter how much profit a businessman made, he kept almost all of it. The effect of this profit retention was to make large accumulations of private capital available for investment.

The legal system, buffered by lawyers, contributed to the growth surge that marked these years. Never far removed from the commercial realm, lawyers came to identify ever more closely with the entrepreneurial spirit. Increasingly, judges and lawyer-dominated legislatures made the right to earn a profit superior to traditional rights under the common law to be unmolested. A Kentucky court decision of 1839, for example, allowed a railroad to build its track right through the heart of Louisville despite the nuisance the smoke-belching engines might cause. The "agents of transportation" were so essential "in a populous and prospering country," the court said, that "private injury and personal damage . . . must be expected." Another manifestation of this new attitude was the growing use of "eminent domain" principles to allow government takeover of property for public purposes, provided just compensation was paid.

Governments also contributed to capital formation more directly. Many investments, such as canals, required so much money and posed so many risks that private investors hesitated to undertake them. Some projects seemed unlikely to reward the individual investor, though they might confer economic benefits on many people or whole regions. Railroads through sparsely settled wilderness areas, for example, might take years before they produced returns, though they promised to stimulate settlement enormously. To encourage growth in these instances, state and local governments in the years before 1860 joined with private promoters to build roads, canals, and railroads. The state of Pennsylvania even invested in manufacturing concerns. Sometimes the states lent money to private capitalists; in the case of the canals, they often financed projects directly. New York put up the $7 million for the Erie Canal after efforts to secure federal funds failed. The states' funds came either from taxes imposed on the public or, more often, from borrowed funds raised by selling bonds to investors in the United States or Europe. The federal government, too, contributed, especially to transportation. Federal taxes built the National Road, begun in 1811 and completed in 1850, from Cumberland, Maryland, to Vandalia, Illinois, a distance of 700 miles. The federal government also financed the St. Mary's Falls ship canal linking Lake Huron and Lake Superior, built coastal lighthouses, dredged rivers and harbors, and, in the 1850s, contributed millions of acres of land to promoters of the Illinois Central Railroad connecting the Great Lakes with the Gulf of Mexico.

States and localities also funded projects that encouraged growth by improving the health of the community or raising its educational level. All told, the government contribution to pre–Civil War investment was enormous. One scholar has estimated that by 1860, states, counties, and municipalities had spent about $400 million toward building the country's transportation network alone. If we add to this sum the federal government's contribution and the millions spent for schools, hospitals, and other vital public facilities, we can see that laissez faire was more a myth than a reality in pre–Civil War America.

★ THE COURSE OF AMERICAN ECONOMIC GROWTH ★

America, then, was endowed with stupendous natural resources, a skilled, acquisitive, and disciplined population, and values and institutions conducive to hard work, saving, and capital growth. How did these elements combine to produce an economic miracle?

The Birth of King Cotton. Most people associate nineteenth-century economic growth with factories, forges, and mines. But agricultural advance was another vital part of the process. The nation's fields also became more productive in these years, and their food and fiber supplied the growing armies of labor in the towns and cities. They also provided surpluses of grain and cotton for export abroad to pay for capital equipment imported from Europe.

The major economic advance in agriculture before the Civil War was the opening of the "cotton kingdom." Cotton cloth had been known for centuries as a light, easily washed fabric. East Indian calicoes, made from cotton yarn, were much prized in Europe, but hand-woven cloth from Asia was relatively expensive. Toward the end of the eighteenth century several ingenious Englishmen developed machines to spin cotton yarn and weave it into fabric. By the 1790s the mills of Lancashire in northwest England were producing cheap cotton cloth for an ever-expanding market.

But where was the raw cotton to come from for the hungry mills? India could not produce enough. A small amount of cotton was grown on the Sea Islands off the South Carolina and Georgia coasts and on the immediately adjacent mainland. Sea island cotton is silky and has long fibers; laborers could easily remove its seeds from the fiber by hand. But the region where it flourished was limited, so the output remained small. Cotton with a shorter fiber would grow throughout the South's vast upland interior, but upland cotton had burrlike green seeds that clung tightly to the fibers and required much hand labor and time to remove. If the United States had had the teeming millions of India to draw on for labor, this quality of upland cotton might have been unimportant. But even in the slave South, labor was relatively expensive. As long as short-staple cotton had to be cleaned by hand, it was not economical to grow. American cotton culture remained confined to the narrow Carolina-Georgia coast.

Yet the South badly needed a new crop. Its three major staples from colonial times—tobacco, rice, and indigo—had all suffered declining markets after independence. Wheat and corn remained, but neither could produce the cash income of the major colonial crops. What could be

By mid-century, Americans made the world's best farm machinery. Eli Whitney's gin, shown in a mid-century-version, cleaned cotton fifty times faster than a hand laborer, and incidentally increased the demand for slaves.

Shrewd Cyrus McCormick, whose reaper sped the harvest of midwestern wheat, was one of the first businessmen to guarantee his products.

done to make short-fiber cotton a practical replacement for rice, tobacco, and indigo?

The answer was provided by the Yankee Eli Whitney. In 1793, while visiting the Georgia plantation of Mrs. Nathanael Greene (widow of the Revolutionary War general), Whitney learned about the problem confronting southern planters. As a gesture of gratitude to his gracious hostess, he put together a simple machine that would efficiently remove the sticky seeds from the upland cotton boll. Now a single laborer using Whitney's new "gin" (from *engine*) could do the work of fifty hand cleaners.

The gin, and cotton culture, quickly spread throughout the lower South. Thousands of planters, white farmers, and slaves migrated into western Georgia, Florida, Alabama, Mississippi, Louisiana, Arkansas, and east Texas to clear fields and plant cotton. From about 2 million pounds in 1793, short-fiber cotton output shot up to 80 million pounds by 1811. In 1859 the United States produced 5 million bales of 400 pounds each and had become the world's major supplier of raw cotton. On the eve of the Civil War cotton was "king," and its realm spanned the region from North Carolina on the Atlantic coast 1,300 miles westward to central Texas and from the Gulf of Mexico to Tennessee.

The North and West. If cotton was king in the South, wheat was king in the agricultural North, although its reign was not so absolute. Like cotton, wheat was a major cash crop, produced in vast amounts by farmers for sale. Some American wheat went abroad, but before the Civil War most was consumed at home. In the form of bread, it provided the chief item in the diet of the growing army of urban people.

Grown since colonial times in almost every part of North America except New England and the deep South, wheat continued to be important in the Middle Atlantic states and the upper South after 1815. As late as 1839 Pennsylvania, New York, and Virginia each produced between 12 and 16 percent of the total American wheat crop. Thereafter, as canals and railroads made the prairies accessible, wheat growing moved westward. By 1859 Illinois, Indiana, Ohio, and Wisconsin had become the chief wheat-producing states.

The soils of the new wheat region were especially fertile. Besides, the prairies that covered large parts of several northwestern states were practically treeless; farmers did not have to clear forest, an occupation that consumed much of their time in the middle states. The shift of wheat growing to the Midwest accordingly increased the output per

COTTON-GROWING AREAS

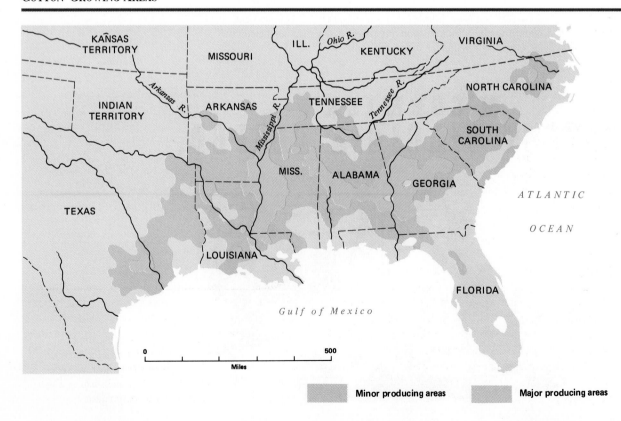

Minor producing areas   Major producing areas

capita of American agriculture and helped to supply expanding national markets at ever-lower costs.

Farm labor still remained a problem. There was generally enough for plowing, planting, and cultivating. But at harvest time, when the crop had to be gathered quickly, there was not enough help to go around. In the 1830s Obed Hussey and Cyrus McCormick invented machines to speed the harvesting process. Both the McCormick and Hussey horse-drawn reapers had long metal blades mounted on a horizontal cylinder that turned as the horse pulled it along. The new machines added immensely to the productivity of harvest labor. A man with a hand-operated "cradle" could cut from three to four acres of ripe wheat a day; with the new reaper he could harvest more than four times as much. The cost of harvesting wheat dropped by 50 cents an acre, a considerable saving.

The labor shortage was not all that encouraged farm mechanization in America. The size of the American farm also played a part. In 1850 the average American farmer owned about 200 acres of land. The 200-acre family grain farm was large enough to employ reapers efficiently and encourage their rapid spread. By 1860 there were some 80,000 harvesting machines at work on the fields of the North and West—more than in the rest of the world. By that date the implements and machinery found on American farms were worth $246 million.

Land Policy. The size of the American farm was not accidental. It was encouraged by deliberate government policies pursued after 1800. Congress was under constant pressure to accelerate the conversion of public lands to family-size farms. In the West, particularly, the public demanded land policies that would provide the ever-growing population with family farms at low cost. In 1800 Congress allowed settlers to buy land at a minimum of $2 an acre in tracts of 320 acres, or half the smallest parcel previously permitted. The same law also gave the buyer four years to pay and provided a discount of 8 percent for cash. The Land Act of 1804 lowered the minimum price to $1.64 an acre and reduced the smallest amount purchasable to 160 acres.

Federal land policies, however, were not consistent. The states and the federal government occasionally sold public land in large blocks, some of 100,000 acres or more. But these large tracts were not worked as great estates. Rather, they were bought by speculators, often on credit, and resold in small parcels to settlers. The system allowed free-wheeling business people to make large profits; yet in the end it did not prevent widespread ownership of land by people of small and middling means.

Low land prices and easy credit combined to set off periodic waves of speculation in the West. Buyers with little capital placed claims to much larger amounts of land than they could ever expect to farm themselves in hopes of selling most of it for profit later. Meanwhile, they met their payments to the government by borrowing from the banks. To prevent widespread default Congress passed periodic relief acts that delayed collection of overdue payments. Such measures did not always help, however. When speculation got out of hand in 1819, the country experienced a major depression set off by panicky speculators trying to unload their land at a time when no one wanted to buy. In 1820, Congress rescinded the easy-credit feature of the 1800 land law, but to offset this move, it reduced the minimum price to $1.25 an acre and lowered the minimum purchase to 80 acres. The Panic of 1837 also stemmed in part from western land speculation.

Not every would-be farmer waited for land to be surveyed and put up for sale. Many jumped the gun and descended on unsurveyed lands, cleared some acres, erected a log cabin, and in effect farmed illegally. Such "squatters" stood to lose everything—fences, barns, houses, and the land itself—when the tract they had settled and "improved" was finally offered for sale by the government. In 1830 champions of the squatters, led by Senator Thomas Hart Benton of Missouri, convinced Congress to pass the Preemption Act to allow those who had illegally occupied portions of the public domain on or before 1829 to buy up to 160 acres of land at the minimum price of $1.25 an acre before others were allowed to bid. In 1841 the time restrictions on the Pre-emption Act were removed.

The 1820 land law and the measures benefiting squatters remained the basis for land policy until the Civil War. Benton and his colleagues, joined at times by labor leaders, continued to fight for a "homestead act" that would give land free to all bona fide settlers. But many easterners feared that free western lands would drain off eastern labor; southerners feared it would give the government an excuse to raise the tariff to offset the loss of land-sale revenues and also that it would encourage the growth of free states. In 1854 an emerging alliance of the Northwest and Northeast permitted passage of the Graduation Act, which allowed land that had remained unsold for a given number of years to be sold at sharply reduced prices. But the continued opposition of the South blocked a homestead law until 1862.

Farm Productivity. It is customary to associate economic growth in these years with the advent of railroads and factories. And of course, as we shall see, they contributed powerfully to the economic surge. But agriculture was still the largest sector of the American economy as late as 1860, and overall growth would not have been possible had it remained unproductive. It did not. The beginnings of mechanization helped push the productivity of farm labor higher. But in the end it was the opening of new lands, previously forested or

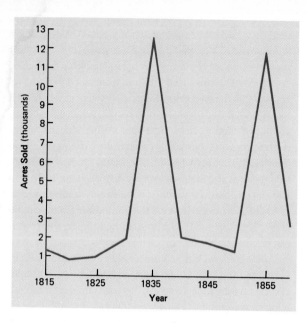

Public land sales, 1815–1860. Source: Historical Statistics of the United States, Colonial Times to 1957.

grass-covered, that explains much of the spurt. The new "virgin" lands simply yielded far more for each outlay of labor and capital than the older lands of the East. We know today there was a serious downside to this phenomenon: It mined centuries-long accumulations of top-soil nutriments wastefully. But it also churned out ever cheaper wheat, pork, beef, fruits, vegetables, and fiber in a profusion seldom attained anywhere, anytime. Without this development there would not have been an "economic miracle."

Steamboats and Roads. In some ways American geography favored efficient, cheap transportation. The Mississippi River system combined with the Great Lakes made it possible for ships to penetrate deep into the vital interior of North America. But neither the rivers nor the lakes were ideal for navigation. At two points—between Lakes Huron and Superior, and between Ontario and Erie—the Great Lakes were connected only by unnavigable rapids. They also lacked lighthouses and port facilities. The drawbacks of the Mississippi system were still greater. Flatboats and rafts carrying mountains of heavy freight could easily be floated down to New Orleans, propelled by the current. But the trip upstream by poled keelboats required backbreaking labor and took far longer.

For some time capitalists and inventors had been working on schemes to apply steam power to river navigation, but as we have seen, not until Robert Fulton took up the quest, backed by the powerful Livingston family, did it become economically feasible. Soon steamboats were operating on schedule up and down the Hudson. In 1811 the

Fulton-Livingston interests, having already secured a legal monopoly of steamboat traffic in New York State waters, received an exclusive charter from the Louisiana territorial legislature to operate steamboats on the lower Mississippi. If unchecked, the Fulton group might have monopolized steamboat navigation on all the inland waters. However, the Supreme Court struck down these monopoly privileges in the case of *Gibbons* v. *Ogden* and opened up steamboat navigation to all investors. Entrepreneurs were not long in seizing the opportunity. By 1855 there were 727 steamboats on the western rivers with a combined capacity of 170,000 tons; many more plied the Great Lakes as well as the streams and coastal waters of the Gulf and the Atlantic.

The steamboat revolutionized the schedules and costs of inland travel and transport. Where once it had taken four months to pole a keelboat upstream from New Orleans to Louisville, by 1819 the steamboat had cut the travel time to seventeen days; by 1853 it was under four and a half days. Freight rates on the same route fell from an average of $5 a hundred pounds to under 15 cents.

Despite this drop in price, promoters' profits remained high, attracting millions of dollars of private capital. Yet even where the incentives to private investment were adequate, the government made an important contribution. Although there was little government investment in steamboats themselves, the state and federal governments laid out large amounts to deepen river channels, remove snags, construct canals around river obstructions, and erect lighthouses on the Great Lakes.

Impressive as the advances in inland navigation were, there still remained the problem of transportation where there were no natural waterways. The obvious solution was to replace the muddy or dusty trails in use since the colonial period with all-weather, surfaced roads for horses, carriages, and wagons. To pay for these roads, tolls would be charged to users. The first major "turnpike" in the country was the Philadelphia-Lancaster Road in Pennsylvania, built with private capital and opened in 1794. Soon the entire country caught the road-building fever. In the Northeast private capital built most of the turnpikes; in the South and West state governments built the roads directly or bought stock in private turnpike companies. By 1861 Virginia had contributed almost $5 million for roads and turnpikes, and other states had contributed lesser, but still substantial, amounts. The federal government also joined in the rush, investing $7 million in the construction of the National Road.

Canals. Turnpikes considerably lowered the cost and time of transporting people and goods, but land transportation remained more expensive than water. Where there were no navigable streams or lakes, the solution was canals. A few miles of artificial waterway were constructed in the Northeast just before the War of 1812. The real boom got under way after the war, in 1817, when the New York State legislature, on the urging of Mayor DeWitt Clinton of New York City, appropriated funds for constructing an enormously long canal between the Hudson River and Lake Erie. This bold venture would connect the Great Lakes with the Atlantic Ocean, bypassing the Appalachian barrier by a more direct route than down the Mississippi to New Orleans and around to the Atlantic coast by sea.

The New York engineers were favored by geography: The Appalachian barrier to east-west travel dipped to only a few hundred feet in the central part of the state. Still, the project was an impressive achievement. The state authorities sent an observer to England to see how the British had built canals, but even the English had never tried to construct a project of such dimensions. The New York engineers learned on the job and improvised a score of new tools and techniques. In the end they moved millions of

cubic yards of earth, constructed 83 locks, scores of stone aqueducts, and 363 miles of "ditch" 4 feet deep and 40 feet wide.

The completed canal, opened by a colorful ceremony in 1825, was an engineering marvel that astounded the world. Power for the canal boats was provided by horses and mules that treaded towpaths on either side of the waterway. Leading the animals was a man or boy; another man at the tiller kept the boat in mid-channel and signaled passengers sitting on top of the cabin to duck by blowing a horn when the vessel approached a low bridge.

The canal was also an immense economic success. In 1817, before its completion, the cost of shipping freight between New York City and Buffalo on Lake Erie was 19.2 cents a ton. By 1830 it was down to 3.4 cents. Freight rates to and from the upper Mississippi Valley also plummeted. By 1832 the canal was earning the state well over a million dollars yearly in tolls and was providing enough revenue to pay the bondholders for the money the state had

Locks such as these on the Erie Canal near Albany made it possible for canal boats to ascend and descend from one level to another. The motive force for the boats was provided by mules walking a towpath and attached by ropes, as seen at right. (Collection of the New York Historical Society)

MINN.
TERR.

CANADA

Lake Superior

MAINE

WISCONSIN

Mississippi R.

MICHIGAN

Lake Huron

Eastport

St. Lawrence R.

NEW
YORK

VT.

N.H.

IOWA

Lake Michigan

Portland

Lake Ontario

Syracuse   Erie Canal   Troy   Lowell

Buffalo   Genesee Turnpike   Albany   MASS.   Boston

Detroit

Lake Erie

Chicago

La Salle

Toledo   Cleveland

PENNSYLVANIA

CONN.   Providence

R.I.

New Haven

Hudson R.

Connecticut R.

ILLINOIS

Illinois R.

Fort
Wayne   Akron

Pittsburgh   Harrisburg   Lancaster
Turnpike   N.J.

INDIANA   OHIO

National Road   Wheeling   Forbes Road   Philadelphia

Vandalia

Missouri R.

Terre Haute   Columbus   Cumberland   Lancaster   MD.

Wabash R.   Cincinnati   Baltimore
Turnpike   Baltimore

St. Louis   Frankfort   *Ohio R.*   Portsmouth   Washington   DEL.

MISSOURI   Louisville   Valley
Turnpike   VIRGINIA   *Potomac R.*

Evansville   Bonnesborough   *James R.*   Richmond

KENTUCKY   Wilderness
Road   Lynchburg

Cumberland R.   Portsmouth

Nashville   Cumberland
Gap

ARKANSAS   *Cumberland R.*

Memphis   *Tennessee R.*   NORTH
CAROLINA

TENNESSEE   *APPALACHIAN MTS.*   Raleigh

Natchez Trace

Mississippi R.   *Cape Fear R.*

MISSISSIPPI   SOUTH
CAROLINA

ALABAMA   Augusta   *Savannah R.*

Jackson   *Tombigbee R.*   *Alabama R.*   GEORGIA   Charleston

Natchez   Savannah

LOUISIANA   *Apalachicola R.*

St. Augustine

New Orleans

Gulf of Mexico   FLORIDA

ATLANTIC OCEAN

	Roads
	Canals
	Navigable rivers

0   300

Miles

CANALS AND ROADS, 1820–1850

borrowed and still leave a large surplus to construct new canals and extensions on the Erie. Best of all, from the perspective of New York City merchants, the canal drew off much of the trade that had gone down the Mississippi and its tributaries and redirected it eastward to the Atlantic metropolis, confirming its growing economic advantage over all the nation's other business centers.

New York's experience inevitably aroused the envy of merchants in the other Atlantic ports. Baltimore, Boston, Philadelphia, and Charleston businessmen now demanded that their respective states follow New York's lead. At the same time, promoters, speculators, farmers, and merchants in the Northwest saw that their region's prosperity depended on constructing canals to link up with the waterways built or proposed. The pressure on state governments soon got results. By the 1830s the dirt was flying all over the Northeast and Northwest as construction crews raced to create a great network of canals. In 1816 there were 100 miles of canals in the United States; by 1840 over 3,300 miles of artificial waterways criss-crossed the Middle Atlantic states, southern New England, and the Old Northwest.

Few canals built after 1825 were as successful as the Erie. Some such as Pennsylvania's "mainline" never overcame difficult engineering problems; others never attracted sufficient business to collect tolls large enough to repay investors. Still others were built too late and were overtaken by the railroads, which provided quicker and less easily interrupted service.

Nevertheless, canals and steamboats conferred immense benefits on the United States. The sharp decline in freight and passenger rates was a great boon to interregional trade. Farmers in the West, whose surplus crops had often sold for a song or piled up for want of buyers, now found new outlets in the East for their wheat, corn, pork, beef, and other commodities. With transportation costs lower, the price of manufactured goods in the West fell, enabling eastern manufacturers to sell more to western customers. By the 1850s manufactured goods were cheaper in the West and raw materials and foodstuffs cheaper in the East than ever before. Everyone benefited.

The Railroads Arrive. The railroads, too, helped knit the country together. First developed in England to haul coal from mines to riverside, they quickly attracted the attention of Americans. For cities such as Boston, Baltimore, Philadelphia, and Charleston, which faced greater engineering challenges than New York in constructing a canal to the West, railroads provided a way to compete with the city on the Hudson.

The early steam railroads were plagued by technical problems. Engines frequently broke down or even

THE RAILROAD NETWORK, 1850–1860

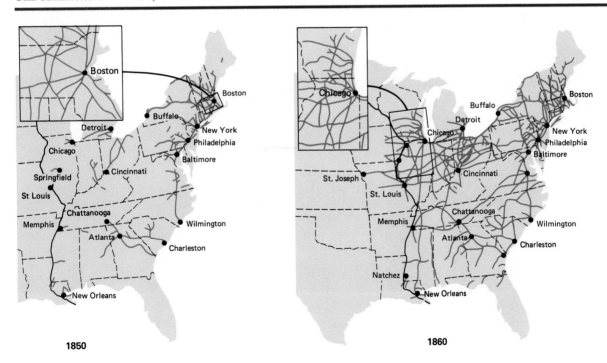

1850

1860

exploded. And even on a normal trip, passengers emerged from the cars nearly suffocated by smoke or with holes burned in their clothes from flying sparks. Rails were at first flat iron straps nailed to wooden beams. When these came loose, they sometimes curled up through the floors of passenger cars, maiming or killing the occupants. Cattle that got in the way of trains caused derailments. Some of these problems were inevitable in so new a system, but accidents were also the result of makeshift construction imposed by the shortage of capital and the desire to build quickly. Trains moving rapidly over lightly ballasted rails and around sharp curves did not always stay on the track.

Gradually railroad technology improved. The strap rail on wood was abandoned for the all-iron rail. Passenger cars became more substantial. The cow catcher was added to the front of the locomotive to push aside all but the most immovable obstructions. Boilers were improved and made more dependable; smokestacks were enlarged to contain the hot sparks. Finally, to deal with the hairpin curves characteristic of American railroads, engineers developed loose-jointed engines and cars with wheels that swiveled to guide trains around turns.

The first major American railroad was the Baltimore and Ohio, chartered in 1828. In 1830 the first 13 miles of B & O track were in operation. Three years later the Charleston and Hamburg in South Carolina reached its terminus 136 miles from its starting point, making it the longest railroad in the world. By 1860 the country boasted some 30,000 miles of track, and passengers and freight could travel by rail from the Atlantic coast as far west as St. Joseph, Missouri, and from Portland, Maine, to New Orleans. The system was far from complete, and many communities remained without rail connections. The Great Plains and the Pacific coast had few if any railroads. Even in the East and Midwest track gauges (distances between the rails) varied from line to line, making frequent changes necessary for "through" passengers and freight. Nevertheless, the accomplishment was impressive.

Surprisingly, the economic impact of the railroads was not as great as we might assume. Economic historians now conclude that the sharpest drop in pre–Civil War freight costs came before the railroads were built and was the result of canals and steamboats. Still, we must not dismiss the "iron horse" as a negligible contributor to American economic growth. The railroads, unlike the waterways, provided all-weather routes. When the canals, rivers, and lakes froze over, the railroads continued to run. They could also serve arid or mountainous regions, where canals could not

This view of Lowell, Massachusetts, dates from the 1840s. It catches the campuslike quality of the town. The long building with many chimneys and the building with the cupola are the Merrimack mills. The two smaller buildings, left foreground, are boardinghouses for the mill girls.

penetrate, and areas where streams were nonexistent or too swift for navigation. Moreover, for fast freight like mail, parcels, or perishables, and for impatient freight like people, the speed of the train was a distinct advantage.

But whatever the economic historians believe, contemporaries saw the railroads as the inception of a new era. As an elequent minister wrote in 1859:

> We hear no more of the clanging hoof,
> And the stage-coach rattling by,
> For the steam-king rules the traveled world,
> And the old pike's left to die.
>
> We have circled the earth with an iron rail,
> And the steam-king rules us now.

The Factory System. Advances in agriculture and transportation contributed immensely to the pre–Civil War economic surge. But the most dynamic development of the antebellum economy was the rise of the factory system initially in southern New England.

There had been large workshops here and there in the colonial period, but none of these had brought together hundreds of "operatives" and expensive power-driven machinery under one roof to produce a single uniform product. Based on the mechanical ingenuity and organizing skill of a group of early eighteenth-century English inventors and entrepreneurs in cotton textile manufacture, the modern factory only arrived in the United States after independence and at first in a rudimentary form. The first mill using water power to spin cotton yarn was probably the Beverly Cotton Manufactory of Massachusetts incorporated in 1789. In 1790 an English mechanic, Samuel Slater, arrived in the United States attracted by offers of a bonus for bringing to America knowledge of British technology. Slater soon linked up with Almy and Brown, a concern descended from colonial candle-makers and West Indies traders. Almy and Brown supplied the capital, and in 1790–1791 the firm opened the first cotton spinning mill at Pawtucket, Rhode Island. Before long, the small state was home to a vigorous yarn-making industry of small spinning mills employing whole families, including women and young children, tending the banks of water-powered spindles.

The Rhode Island mills only produced a part of the final product. The cotton yarn was still peddled to skilled hand loom weavers for conversion to cloth. The first true modern textile factory arrived about twenty years later in Massachusetts. Much of the entrepreneurial leadership of the Massachusetts cotton mills came from Francis Cabot Lowell, a Boston merchant hard hit by Jefferson's embargo. In 1810, while his ships were idle, Lowell visited Lancashire, the center of the flourishing British textile industry, and took careful note of the latest machines that wove yarn into cloth. When he returned home he carried the plans in his head and with the help of a skilled mechanic was able to build a power loom superior to the original.

Lowell now pooled his resources with a group of other merchants, and together they secured a corporate charter for the Boston Manufacturing Company. With their combined capital they built a mill at a water power site in Waltham on the Charles River where the new power looms could be linked with spinning machines to make the entire product. The first cotton cloth came from the company looms in 1815 and proved superior to British imports. Between 1816 and 1826 the Boston Manufacturing Company averaged almost 19 percent profit a year.

Before long the promoters found they could not produce enough cloth at the limited Waltham power site to satisfy the demand, and they made plans for a complete textile community to be established along the swift-flowing Merrimack. For this purpose they raised $600,000 by selling corporation shares to a select group of Boston investors.

The new mills at Lowell, Massachusetts, were much larger than either the Waltham factory or the earlier spinning mills in Rhode Island. Attracting enough labor for the new mills and keeping it housed in good physical and moral health were major problems. The promoters solved their labor difficulties by hiring Yankee farm girls, a resource hitherto untapped. These young women were attracted to Lowell by promises of good wages and cheap, attractive dormitory housing built at company expense. The company also provided a lyceum, where the literate and pious young women who worked in the mills could hear edifying lectures, and paid for a church and a minister. By the mid-1830s Lowell was a town of 18,000 people with schools, libraries, paved streets, churches, and health facilities. The mills themselves numbered some half dozen, each separately incorporated, arranged in quadrangles surrounded by the semidetached houses of the townsfolk and the dormitories of the female workers.

So attractive did the Lowell scheme seem to contemporaries that its fame spread even across the Atlantic. Distinguished foreign visitors to the United States commonly made pilgrimages to Lowell and were invariably impressed by what they saw. The British novelist Charles Dickens, who had encountered at home the worst evils of industrialism, noted that the girls at Lowell wore "serviceable bonnets, good warm cloaks and shawls . . . , [were] healthy in appearance, many of them remarkably so . . . , [and had] the manners and deportment of young women, not of degraded brutes."

During the "hungry forties," when the nation's business pace slowed, conditions in the mills worsened. The girls' wages were cut, and when they protested, they were

The Lowell Girls

Not all the workers at the Lowell Mills were content with their lot. As early as 1834 angry factory girls at Lowell "turned out" to protest wage cuts and other acts of the corporation "agents" that they considered arbitrary and unjust. Yet life at Lowell was a mixture of good and bad, and many of the farm girls found it a welcome relief for a few years from the boredom and narrowness of life in the declining New England countryside.

Harriet Hanson Robinson, whose account of her Lowell experience in the mid-1830s is excerpted below, was not entirely typical of the Lowell "operatives." She was born in Boston and moved to Lowell with her mother shortly after her father's death. There Mrs. Robinson ran a boardinghouse for girls who worked in the Tremount mill. Harriet herself, along with her three siblings, entered the mill at the age of ten and remained there until her mid-teens. She later married a newspaper editor and became an active women's suffrage leader. Below, from the perspective of over half a century, she tells what it was like to be a "doffer" in the mill.

"I had been to school constantly until I was about ten years of age, when my mother, feeling obliged to have help in her work besides what I could give, and also needing the money which I could earn, allowed me, at my urgent request (for I wanted to earn *money* like the other little girls), to go to work in the mills. I worked first in the spinning-room as a 'doffer.' The doffers were the very youngest girls, whose work was to doff, or take off, the full bobbins, and replace them with the empty ones.

"I can see myself now, racing down the alley, between the spinning frames, carrying in front of me a bobbin-box bigger than I was. These mites had to be very swift in their movements, so as not to keep the spinning-frames stopped long, and they worked only about fifteen minutes in every hour. The rest of the time was their own, and when the overseer was kind they were allowed to read, knit, or even to go outside the mill-yard to play.

"Some of us learned to embroider in crewels, and I still have a lamb worked on cloth, a relic of those early days, when I was first taught to improve my time in the good old New England fashion. When not doffing, we were often allowed to go home, for a time, and thus were able to help our mothers in their housework. We were paid two dollars a week; and proud I was when my turn came to stand up on the bobbin-box, and write my name in the paymaster's book, and how indignant I was when he asked me if I would 'write.' 'Of course I can,' said I and he smiled as he looked down on me.

"The working hours of all the girls extended from five o'clock in the morning until seven in the evening, with one-half hour for breakfast and for dinner. Even the doffers were forced to be on duty nearly fourteen hours a day, and this was the greatest hardship in the lives of these children. For it was not until 1842 that the hours of labor for children under twelve years of age were limited to ten per day; but the 'ten-hour law' itself was not passed until long after some of these little doffers were old enough to appear before the legislative committee on the subject, and plead, by their presence, for a reduction of the hours of labor.

"I do not recall any particular hardship connected with this life, except getting up so early in the morning, and to this habit I never was, and never shall be, reconciled, for it has taken nearly a lifetime for me to make up the sleep lost at that early age. But in every other respect it was a pleasant life. We were not hurried any more than was for our good, and no more work was required of us than we were able easily to do."

---

replaced with newly arrived Irish immigrants who would accept lower wages. But for a time the Lowell system served as a showcase for the benefits of industrialization.

★ INDUSTRIAL WORKERS ★

In 1815, well before Lowell, the Erie Canal, and the Baltimore and Ohio Railroad, Americans were already a rich people by the standards of the day. Few European travelers failed to note the prosperity they encountered in the United States. One visitor to the Ohio Valley in 1818 wrote:

> I believe I saw more peaches and apples rotting on the ground than would sink the British fleet. I was at plantations in Ohio where they no more knew the number of their hogs than myself. . . . And they have such flocks of turkies, geese, ducks, and hens, as would surprise you. . . . The poorest family has a cow or two and some sheep . . . and adorns the table three times a day like a wedding dinner—tea, coffee, beef, fowls, pigs, eggs, pickles, good bread; and their favorite beverage is whiskey, or peach brandy.

Unequal Gains. During the next thirty-five years the wealth and income of the American people increased enormously. One scholar believes that between the mid-1830s and the Civil War alone annual GNP (gross national product, a dollar measure of all goods and services produced) more than doubled. Growth in per capita GNP was also high, as much as 2.5 percent a year in the 1825–1837 period, for example, though it was not as great as the total GNP increase.

Yet it is clear that all Americans did not gain equally from the economic changes taking place. The economic surge enlarged the urban middle class. In the early 1800s this group had consisted of merchants, shopkeepers, schoolteachers, lawyers, doctors, and ministers. As the mills, mines, and railroads spread across the nation, they created jobs not only for laborers and factory operatives but also for engineers, clerks, bookkeepers, factory managers, and others. Most of these were native-born Americans whose familiarity with the English language and American ways gave them the pick of the new jobs. The new salaried "white-collar" class enjoyed less prestige than those who made up the older middle class, but they had higher incomes and social standing than the wage-earning "blue-collar" workers employed in the new industries.

The industrial leap also created a new class of rich manufacturers, bankers, and railroad promoters. Many of these were former merchants who already were wealthy. But others were "new" men who used the industrial transformation to lift themselves out of poverty. Slater, for one, had come to America in 1790 with almost nothing; he was worth $700,000 by 1829. In fact, the economic growth of the 1815–1860 period was accompanied by growing inequality of economic condition. Studies of wealth ownership between the end of the colonial era and 1860 show a considerable increase in the proportion of property—houses, land, slaves, bank accounts, ships, equipment, factories, and other kinds of property—owned by both the richest 1 percent and the richest 10 percent of the American people, compared with everyone else.

Wages and Working Conditions. Do these growing inequalities mean that the working class, who did the hard physical labor of the nation, failed to benefit from the overall progress of the period? In the past some scholars claimed that the changes accompanying the industrialization process degraded the wage-earner class. They are probably wrong. Leaving aside the South's slaves (see Chapter 13), we have reason to believe that, taken as a whole, American wage earners made real advances during the generation preceding 1860.

But individual circumstances varied. Women workers were a low-wage group. Relatively few married women worked for wages, but those who did were badly paid. When women teachers flocked to the new public schools, teachers' overall wage levels fell. For traditional "women's work" the situation was similar. Wages for household servants were low (in the case of the housewife they were nonexistent). In 1850 they received, typically, a little over a dollar a week plus their room and board. Manufacturers of straw hats, ready-made clothes, and shoes relied on a large pool of poorly paid female workers, many employed part-time at home and paid by the "piece." These women

Young women formed the bulk of the labor force in the early textile mills. There were male workers, too— usually foremen or skilled mechanics who, needless to say, earned more than the women. Power for the looms came from overhead shafts and belts that were driven by waterwheels.

often earned no more than 25 cents a day. The Lowell girls were relatively affluent at $2.50 to $3 a week.

Many men were paid not much better. Common laborers, who dug ditches and foundations, carted, stevedored, and the like, in 1850 received 61 cents a day with board, or 87 cents without board. Skilled labor was in shorter supply and so better rewarded. Blacksmiths earned on the average about $1.10 a day in 1852. In 1847 a skilled iron founder in Pennsylvania could make as much as $30 per week. The Boston Manufacturing Company paid department superintendents $12 a week and machinists up to $11.

What did these wages mean? Today such money incomes would scarcely support a single individual, much less whole families. But money went much further in those times; there were many fewer consumer goods to buy, and those that were available cost much less. The *New York Tribune* estimated in 1851 that a minimum budget of about $10 a week was needed to support a family of five in expensive New York City. This meant that an unskilled worker needed help from other family members. And, apparently, they usually got it. In many families children were put to work at ten or twelve and earned enough to push total family incomes past the bare subsistence point. One scholar estimates that just after the Civil War family heads in Massachusetts earned just 57 percent of total family income; the rest came from the children.

On the other hand, even individual wage earners were better off in the United States than in Europe. During his American visit Michel Chevalier encountered an Irish railroad construction worker. The man told him that he received wages of 75 cents a day plus board, which included meat three times a day. When he wrote home to his family in Ireland he told them he ate meat three times a *week*. Why, Chevalier asked, did he not tell them the truth? Because, the man replied, "if I told them that, they'd never believe me." In fact, the abundance of cheap food, especially items seldom part of working-class diet in Europe, invariably astonished people accustomed to foreign practice. Virtually no American worker ate dark rye or oat bread. In the United States the staff of life was white "wheaten" bread, a luxury in much of Europe. One immigrant expressed amazement at what his New York boardinghouse offered its patrons. Breakfast included "beef steaks, fish, hash, ginger cakes, buckwheat cakes etc such a profusion as I never saw before at the breakfast tables." And at dinner there was even "a greater profusion than breakfast."

But good wages and the abundance they bought were not the whole story. Wage earners' lives were not easy. Work hours were long. The Lowell girls spent twelve hours a day, six days a week, at their machines. Outdoor workers averaged eleven hours a day, fewer in winter, more in summer. Foreigners, seeking to explain superior American wages, believed that Americans worked harder than their own compatriots. And they probably did. Though the pace of factory labor was more leisurely than today, it was difficult for people used to the slow rhythms of the nineteenth-century farm to adjust to the remorseless pace of the factory machines.

Pre–Civil War workers and their families also experienced great insecurity. Work accidents were common, and when workers were injured, they lost their income and often their job. When men were killed in the mines or factories, there was frequently no one to take care of their families. Besides industrial disaster, there was the uncertainty of employment. People's economic fortunes were at the mercy of the weather. A bad harvest or a particularly hard winter often left agricultural workers destitute. They were also victims of the business cycle. Severe periodic depressions produced acute hardship among laborers and factory workers. During the hard times that began in 1819, an English traveler through the East and Northwest noted that he had "seen upwards of 1,500 men in quest of work within 11 months past." Again, following the 1837 and 1857 panics, unemployment forced many wage earners to ask for government relief for themselves and their families. In 1857 there were food riots in several northern cities. One young New York mechanic, Asa Shipman, the only support of six brothers and sisters and a widowed mother, later recalled events during the months following the Panic of 1837:

> After a short time work with me began to get short. First I had only half of the time and finally I was told that there was no work. Imagine my situation if you can. We had food enough in the house to last perhaps a week and my last wages lasted perhaps another week. In the meantime I spent every day in search of some kind of employment but all in vain. Nothing could be got. . . . We often went with one meal a day and that of the plainest kind. How we ever lived for 6 weeks that way I cannot now imagine.

City and county authorities and various private charities provided some help for the unemployed, but not very much. Soup kitchens, emergency free bread, and the "poorhouse" or the county "poor farm"—gloomy institutions like asylums where paupers went to keep from starving—were about all the jobless and their dependents could expect. In what was still a largely agricultural society unemployment was treated as a freak event or an act of God. No clear distinction was made between the chronically poor and those impoverished because they were thrown out of work during a depression. Poverty, social opinion leaders said, was the result of improvidence or sloth. The community could not let people starve, of course, but it had little responsibility for finding jobs for them.

The limited concern of public authorities for the unemployed can be explained in part by the common belief

THE AMERICAN ECONOMIC MIRACLE, 1815–1860

	1815		1860	
Total land area, in square miles	1,716,003		3,022,387	
Total population	8,419,000		31,513,000	
Rural	93%	(1820)	80%	
Urban	7%	(1820)	20%	
Population by region				
Northeast	50.4%	(1820)	36.5%	
South	30.4%	(1820)	25.6%	
West	19.2%	(1820)	37.8%	
Immigrants arriving annually	8,385	(1820)	153,640	
Labor force, ten years and older				
Free	2,185,000	(1820)	8,770,000	
Slave	950,000	(1820)	2,340,000	
Per capita GNP (1840 = 100)	67.6	(1820)	137.0	
Average monthly earnings with board for farm labor	$9.45	(1818)	$13.86	
Government investment in canals (cumulative)	under $50,000		$1,200,000,000	
Miles of railroad in operation	23		30,626	
State-chartered banks	208		1,562	
Currency in circulation	$67,100,000		$435,407,000	
Patents issued	173		4,589	
Value of exports	$52,557,753		$333,576,000	
Value of imports	$85,356,680		$367,760,000	
Cotton exports	$17,529,000		$191,806,555	
Gross farm output, in current dollars	$338,000,000		$1,579,000,000	
Value of produce received in New Orleans from interior	$9,749,253	(1815–16)	$155,863,564	
Cotton production, in bales	209,000		3,841,000	
Lumber production, in board feet	600,000,000	(1819)	8,000,000,000	(1859)
Coal Production				
Soft, in tons	253,000		9,057,000	
Pennsylvania anthracite, in short tons	2,000		10,984,000	
Pig-iron shipments, in long tons	20,000	(1820)	821,000	

Sources: Historical Statistics of the United States, Colonial Times to 1957; D. C. North, The Economic Growth of the United States, 1790–1860; and Paul A. David, "The Growth of Real Product in the United States Before 1840," Journal of Economic History XXVII (1967).

that all who wished to work could find jobs in the West. But the West was a refuge for the out-of-work in only a limited way. Western cities, all growing very rapidly, were chronically short of mechanics and laborers, and even during business downturns they probably offered more job opportunities than the older communities of the East. But few unemployed eastern wage earners had the means to move west and reestablish themselves in their accustomed trades, much less take up farming.

Still another source of distress was the downgrading of skills and the loss of independence that sometimes accompanied mechanization and the factory system. The fate of the Massachusetts shoemakers is a case in point. In the opening years of the nineteenth century they had been skilled, semi-independent craftsmen. Merchants brought them cut leather and paid them a given sum for each pair of shoes they sewed and finished in their "tenfooters," the ten-by-ten sheds they worked in behind their homes. These skilled craftsmen owned their own tools and often employed their wives and grown children to help with the work. Not only were they well paid; they also enjoyed a sense of independence that came from their relation to the merchant as a kind of subcontractor and from the fact that they were the heads of their households, not only in a social and legal sense, but also in a direct economic way.

Gradually, as the market for ready-made shoes, especially for southern slaves, expanded, the shoemakers' independence and incomes declined. Merchants broke up the shoemaking process into smaller and simpler parts and "put out" the work to unmarried young women in New England country villages. Eventually power-driven machines that sewed heavy leather were invented, enabling the merchants to establish factories where wage workers could use the expensive, capitalist-owned machines. By the eve of the Civil War the independent master craftsman working in his ten-footer had been replaced with semiskilled labor working for weekly wages in factories.

The Labor Movement. Clearly many wage earners were unhappy with the new aggressive capitalism and the new factory system. In 1836 the young women at Lowell went on strike to protest a wage cut. Three thousand gathered on one of the city's open places to hear one of their leaders give a passionate speech, one of the first labor addresses ever delivered by a woman. In the end the factory owners won and the wage cut stuck. In 1860 the shoemakers of Lynn, Massachusetts, "turned out" to protest declining wages; before the strike ended, some 20,000 Massachusetts shoemakers had left their places at the machines.

All through the antebellum period workers struck for higher wages or better working conditions. Most of the strikes were unplanned uprisings in response to some unexpected blow such as a wage cut. But some grew out of long-standing grievances such as the sheer drudgery of factory life or the loss of worker independence. These grievances created a labor movement of considerable dimensions. The small community craft societies organized in the early 1800s expanded over the next thirty years into citywide labor unions, each representing a whole trade. Later local unions joined together into national organizations to improve working conditions and wages. Their strikes achieved some gains; but after the Panic of 1837, when the depression forced many workers out of their jobs, employers usually defeated the strikers by threatening to hire the many unemployed. Strikes failed and trade unions declined. In the next two decades labor discontent generally was diverted from labor unions to political action and various reform movements.

We must not exaggerate the extent of labor discontent during these years, however. The school system, as well as the churches, worked hard to instill the "work ethic" into the labor force, and on the whole, they were successful. By and large the American work force cooperated with economic growth. As one pre-1860 observer noted, in New England "every workman seems to be continually devising some new thing to assist him in his work, and there [is] a strong desire both with masters and workman . . . to be 'posted up' [that is, kept informed] in every improvement." Skilled English workingmen who came to American machine shops in the 1830s and 1840s were often startled to find that their American counterparts, rather than fighting the shop owners, were "fire eaters" whose "ravenous appetites for labor" made their own performance look bad. Several eminent students of American economic development are convinced that this enthusiastic cooperation was one of the most important elements in creating the pre–Civil War economic miracle.

★ CONCLUSIONS ★

Many things contributed to the nation's impressive economic performance during the antebellum period. Nature had endowed the United States with uniquely rich resources. History had given it a vigorous, frugal, hard-working people. After 1815 Americans vastly improved on what they had inherited from nature and their own colonial past. During the succeeding decades European immigrants added their brains and brawn to the working population and its accumulated skills. Foreign investors, seeing the United States as a land of opportunity, sent their capital across the Atlantic. Government encouraged enterprise by passing general incorporation laws and tariffs, constructing schools, and investing directly in canals and roads. Skillful entrepreneurs, benefiting from low wages and low taxes, threw themselves into the task of making their communities—and themselves—rich. The country's values and ideals also contributed to material progress by creating a work ethic that made wage earners feel they had a share in the nation's economic progress.

Whatever the causes, economic growth was not an unrelieved blessing. Though most Americans benefited, the contrast between rich and poor became more pronounced. A by-product of America's spectacular economic surge, these inequalities would assume greater importance in the generations ahead.

★★★★★★★★ FOR FURTHER READING ★★★★★★★★

George R. Taylor. *The Transportation Revolution, 1815–1860* (1951)

The best single-volume treatment of economic growth during the period covered by this chapter. As the title suggests, Taylor believes that improved transportation is the crucial item in pre–Civil War American growth.

Stuart Bruchey. *The Roots of American Economic Growth, 1607–1861: An Essay in Social Causation* (1965)

This book takes a much longer running start than Taylor's. It is also more up-to-date in its reliance on modern economists' growth theory, though Bruchey also stresses the importance of national values and political, scientific, and technological developments.

Alan Dawley. *Class and Community: The Industrial Revolution of Lynn* (1976)

Professor Dawley's book disagrees with one important part of the industrialization process as described in *These United States*. His interesting study of the mid-nineteenth-century Lynn, Massachusetts, shoemakers describes them as strongly opposed to the emerging industrial values and practices of the age and—borrowing from the English socialist scholar E. P. Thompson—he depicts them as determined to preserve a preindustrial working-class ethic even if that meant resisting "progress."

H. J. Habakkuk. *American and British Technology in the Nineteenth Century* (1962)

Habakkuk, an English economic historian, compares English and American technology during the early industrial revolution. He finds American technology superior, in large part because American skilled workers were better educated and more willing to cooperate with their employers in furthering change than were their English counterparts.

Ronald Shaw. *Erie Water West: A History of the Erie Canal, 1792–1854* (1966)

The social and political history of the great canal. Includes the story of its sponsors and opponents, its construction and operation, and its social and cultural consequences.

Mark Twain. *Life on the Mississippi* (1883)

Not a novel, but a beautifully written narrative of Twain's experiences as apprentice to a Mississippi River steamboat pilot before the Civil War. "Mark Twain," the pen name Samuel Clemens adopted, was the chant steamboaters sang out to the pilot to tell him that the river was two fathoms (twelve feet) deep and so safe for the boat to proceed.

Norman Ware. *The Industrial Worker, 1840–1860: The Reaction of American Industrial Society to the Advance of the Industrial Revolution* (1924)

An older work that examines the roots of the American labor movement and sees it as a reaction to the loss of skill and autonomy ushered in by the factory system.

Hannah Josephson. *Golden Threads: New England Mill Girls and Magnates* (1949)

A well-written social and economic history of the early New England textile industry. Deals with the mill workers as well as their bosses.

Anthony Wallace. *Rockdale: The Growth of an American Village in the Early Industrial Revolution* (1978)

A fascinating study of an early textile community near Philadelphia. Written by an anthropologist, it is full of interesting details concerning how early textile mills worked and how those connected with them—both workers and owners—lived and thought.

Paul E. Johnson. *A Shopkeeper's Millennium: Society and Revivals in Rochester, New York, 1815–1837* (1979)

This book describes the religious roots of the pre–Civil War work ethic. An interesting marriage of intellectual and social history.

Merritt Roe Smith. *Harpers Ferry Armory and the New Technology: The Challenge of Change* (1977)

Smith shows how the cultural milieu of a community affected its industrial performance.

Sean Wilentz. *Chants Democratic: New York City and the Rise of the American Working Class, 1788–1850* (1984)

An interesting account of what the author considers a class-conscious labor movement in pre–Civil War New York.

10★

JACKSONIAN DEMOCRACY

What Was It and How Did It Change Political Life?

1810	The United States claims the region as part of the Louisiana Purchase • *Fletcher* v. *Peck*
1812	James Madison reelected president
1816	Congress incorporates the Second Bank of the United States (BUS) • Tariff Act for the first time protects American industry from foreign competition • James Monroe elected president
1818	Andrew Jackson's raid on Spanish Florida
1819	*Dartmouth College* v. *Woodward* • *McCulloch* v. *Maryland* • The Adams-Oni's Treaty with Spain
1821	*Cohens* v. *Virginia*
1823	The Monroe Doctrine announced
1824	Henry Clay's "American System" becomes the Whig platform • John Quincy Adams is elected president by the House and Jackson's supporters suspect a "corrupt bargain"
1828	Congress passes "Tariff of Abominations"; John Calhoun writes *Exposition and Protest* • Andrew Jackson elected president
1830	Indian Removal Act
1832	Tariff Act lowers 1828 duties only slightly; South Carolina declares the new tariff null and void • *Worcester* v. *Georgia* upholds Cherokee land claims • Jackson vetoes the bill renewing the BUS charter • Jackson removes government deposits from the BUS
1832–34	Biddle reduces and calls in BUS loans
1833	Congress passes the Force Bill; South Carolina agrees to a compromise tariff, but nullifies the Force Bill
1835–42	Florida Seminoles forcibly resist removal west
1836	Jackson issues Specie Circular • Martin Van Buren elected president
1838	Cherokees leave Georgia for Oklahoma on the "Trail of Tears"
1840	Whig William H. Harrison elected president

arch 4, 1829, was moving day in Washington. Andrew Jackson was to be inaugurated seventh president of the United States, and for weeks many of the city's oldest inhabitants had been packing their possessions and preparing to leave for new residences. To Margaret Bayard Smith, the elegant hostess who had presided over Washington society for twenty-five years, the change was a tragedy. "Never before did the city seem . . . so gloomy," she wrote. "Drawing rooms in which I have so often mixed with gay crowds, distinguished by rank, fashion, beauty, talent, . . . now empty, silent, dank, dismantled. Oh! 'tis melancholy!"

While some were leaving the still-raw capital on the Potomac, others were moving in. The city had filled with visitors, and the hotels overflowed. Washington endured a flood of new people every four years, of course, but this time there were more of them and they were different. Besides the usual frock-coated dignitaries and bureaucrats, rough-looking men in leather shirts and coonskin caps and equally unfamiliar types with Irish lilts to their voices strolled the capital's streets. The crowd was playful and good-humored, but also fiercely determined. Every face, according to Mrs. Smith, bore "defiance on its brow." "I never saw anything like it before," wrote the new senator from Massachusetts, Daniel Webster. "They really seem to think the country is rescued from some dreadful danger."

The determined mood of the newcomers was understandable. For fourteen years—ever since his great victory at New Orleans—Andy Jackson's admirers had fought to make their hero president. The general was the most magnetic political leader since Washington; to many his personal qualities of bluntness, courtliness, and charm, combined with his stature as a military leader, would always be his chief political assets. But was hero worship the only reason for the excitement? Or was there more than personal loyalty behind the defiant brows? Was something important taking place? Would Old Hickory's election make a difference in the way the country was run? Would it bring new groups to power with new ideas and new programs? Obviously Webster and Mrs. Smith believed they were witnessing some sort of revolution. So did the rough-hewn men who wandered the streets of the capital that week in March 1829. Were they right? Was a major political change in the air? And if so, what was it? To answer these questions we must look first at the era before Jackson's election.

★ THE ERA OF GOOD FEELINGS ★

By 1817, when James Monroe was inaugurated as fifth president, the "first party system" had run its course. The bad judgment that had led the Federalists to bet on the wrong horse in the War of 1812, along with the limited appeal of their aristocratic ideology, virtually destroyed them as a significant political force. Though the Federalists continued to be important in New England, Delaware, and a few other places, the party of Washington, Hamilton, and John Adams never recovered to challenge the Republicans in a national election again.

Federalist principles lived on, however. In the War of 1812, as we saw in Chapter 8, the Republicans learned the value of banks, roads, and national self-sufficiency; in 1815 President Madison had asked for a new national bank, a protective tariff, and a system of internal improvements. In Congress Henry Clay, John C. Calhoun of South Carolina, and other "new Republicans" who had taken instruction from Hamilton, supported the president. Madison got most of what he had asked for without serious opposition. In April 1816 Congress passed a measure to incorporate a second Bank of the United States with a larger capitalization than its predecessor. A few weeks later it approved the Tariff Act of 1816, which for the first time protected American manufacturers against the lower costs and greater efficiency of European industry. Early the following year Congress approved the president's third recommendation by enacting a major internal improvements bill. The old Federalist Gouverneur Morris watched this Republican turnaround with amazement. "The Party now in power," he mused, "seems disposed to do all that Federal men ever wished. . . ."

With the Federalists gone, ideological tensions declined. For a while it looked as if Jefferson had spoken prophetically when he said in 1801: "We are all Republicans, we are all Federalists." Certainly the Republicans' adoption of Hamiltonian principles ended the bitter political disagreements of the 1790–1815 period.

Historians have called the decade following the War of 1812 the Era of Good Feelings. This is a useful label if we consider only the placid presidential elections, contests without clashes of parties with distinct ideologies. It is a misnomer if it is intended to mean that political conflict had ceased. Political disagreements continued during these years, but they took the form of intraparty squabbling and personal rivalry, as in colonial times. Within the states there were frequent battles between one Jeffersonian Republican faction and another. In New York the followers of De Witt Clinton, sponsor of the Erie Canal, and Martin Van Buren, leader of the so-called Albany Regency, fought constantly over who should run the state government. In Ohio competing groups, both calling themselves Republican, organized around James Gazlay and General William Henry Harrison. Nationally, the differing political factions looked to Calhoun, Clay, John Quincy Adams, or Senator William H. Crawford of Georgia for leadership. But none of these men was as yet capable of evoking great enthusiasm among the voters. Moreover, the issues debated were obscure—if there were issues at all. Public indifference was widespread and the voter turnouts in elections were small.

National elections continued, of course, but they merely confirmed the choices of Republican leaders. At the highest level "King Caucus" decided who should be president. Every four years the Republican leaders in Congress "caucused"—got together in closed session—and nominated the party's candidate, and in the fall their choices were duly ratified by the voters. Making matters even more cut and dried, the caucus leaders invariably chose either the incumbent or, if he had served two full terms, his secretary of state. Thus Secretary of State Madison succeeded Jefferson, Secretary of State Monroe succeeded Madison, and Secretary of State John Quincy Adams would succeed Monroe. To top off the whole cozy arrangement—and turn off the voters—four of the first six presidents were Virginians, and the other two were from Massachusetts. With so little real choice, it was no wonder that voter participation in elections declined so sharply.

The Virginia Dynasty. The presidents from Jefferson to Monroe (1800–1825) were part of what is known as the Virginia dynasty. (John Quincy Adams, who followed Monroe in office, belonged to this group in spite of his Massachusetts origins.) Jefferson excepted, none of these men was a dynamic leader. They were cultivated gentlemen, but they were also colorless and withdrawn. And they proved surprisingly timid in domestic affairs. Although Madison had recommended a major internal improvements program to Congress, he vetoed the measure that did pass, the so-called Bonus Bill establishing a fund to be used for roads and canals. Five years later President Monroe vetoed a measure to repair the lagging Cumberland Road and provide it with toll-collecting facilities.

John Quincy Adams was the boldest thinker of all these men, again excepting Jefferson. The sixth president was a man of intelligence and learning who sought to make the federal government a patron of science and the arts as well as a sponsor of economic progress. His first annual message to Congress recommended federal support for a national university and a national observatory, a system of uniform weights and measures, a new Department of the Interior, reformed patent laws, and a massive program of internal improvements. But Adams, too, lacked leadership ability. However intelligent and able, he was also aloof and humorless. One associate said of him: "It is a question whether he ever laughed in his life." It is not surprising that he found the normal roughhouse of national politics dis-

John Quincy Adams, shown in this early portrait, was typical of the presidents during the "Era of Good Feelings." Aloof and aristocratic, he lacked the personal warmth needed to attract voters. Still, he was a man of broad learning and rigorous character who swam daily in the Potomac, even in the coldest weather, wearing only a skullcap and goggles.

tasteful. Congress, controlled by his political enemies, ignored his recommendations, and the president, too fastidious to use his influence or the power of patronage to gain its support, accomplished little.

John Marshall's Court. Domestic political achievements might have remained meager during the Era of Good Feelings if not for Chief Justice John Marshall. Marshall was a throwback to the earlier, confident Federalism of Hamilton. Unlike the new Republicans, he did not waiver in the cause of strengthening federal power and encouraging a climate attractive to business and enterprise. In 1810, in *Fletcher* v. *Peck*, he had struck down a state law as unconstitutional—the first time the Supreme Court had done so—on the grounds that it violated a state contract with private parties. Nine years later, in the *Dartmouth College* case, he again upheld the inviolability of a private contract when he forbade the state of New Hampshire to amend the royal charter of Dartmouth College. A public charter to a private corporation, he pronounced, was equivalent to a contract and so protected by the Constitution. As Justice Joseph Story, one of Marshall's colleagues, remarked, the decision would protect "private rights" against "any undue encroachment . . . which the passions of the popular doctrines of the day may stimulate any State Legislature to adopt." Clearly, so long as John Marshall had his way, government would not ride roughshod over private property rights.

Marshall also fought to expand the authority of the federal government over the states. In 1819, the same year as the *Dartmouth College* case, the state of Maryland placed a tax on the paper money issues of the Second Bank of the United States. The action was not designed to raise revenue but to restrict the BUS, an institution highly unpopular with many local state bankers. In a classic statement of the "loose construction" view of the federal Constitution, Marshall declared the Maryland law unconstitutional and hence void. The issue he announced in *McCulloch* v. *Maryland* was twofold: Did Congress have power to charter a federal bank in the absence of a specific provision to that effect in the Constitution, and could states tax federal property? His decision was yes on the first question and no on the second. The right of Congress to charter a bank could be readily deduced from the Constitution's clause authorizing it to make all laws "necessary and proper" for "carrying into execution" the powers actually specified. "Let the end be legitimate," he declared, "let it be within the scope of the Constitution, and all means which are appropriate, which are plainly adapted to that end, which are not prohibited, but consist with the letter and spirit of the Constitution, are constitutional." As for state taxation of federal agencies, the "power to tax" involved "the power to destroy." No state could destroy a legal creation of Congress, and so the Maryland law was unconstitutional. In *Cohens* v. *Virginia* (1821) Marshall asserted that state court decisions were subject to review by the federal courts when they involved violation of federal law.

Foreign Affairs. The Virginia dynasty presidents may have been indifferent leaders in domestic affairs, but they were vigorous and successful champions of American international and diplomatic interests. The years following the final defeat of Napoleon at Waterloo (1815) presented the United States with thorny problems and challenges. Spain had been seriously weakened by the international turmoil between 1793 and Waterloo. In 1810, while both Spain and England were preoccupied with Napoleon, the United States took possession of the western spur of Spanish West Florida from the Pearl River to the Iberville on the dubious grounds that

this strip of territory had been included in the Louisiana Purchase. Spain protested vigorously, but could do little. In May 1812 the United States occupied another strip from the Pearl to the Perdido.

This serving of West Florida did not satisfy the American appetite, however. A sizable strip of the Florida Gulf Coast panhandle still remained in Spanish hands, but still more enticing was the great southern loop of the peninsula itself. Acquiring this would not only round out the southeastern corner of the nation; it would settle the problem of escaped slaves, hostile Indians, and white renegades who periodically staged raids from Florida into Georgia and then fled back across the border into Spanish jurisdiction, where the American authorities could not touch them.

Secretary of State John Quincy Adams urged Spain to sell Florida to the United States and at the same time settle the uncertain boundary between the Louisiana Purchase territory and the Spanish provinces in Mexico. Spain was not interested. In 1818 Andrew Jackson's impetuous behavior brought the situation to an unexpected head. As commander of American forces patrolling the Florida-Georgia border, Jackson was authorized by his superiors to cross into Spanish territory to suppress the raiders, but told to avoid attacking Spanish posts and settlements in the colony. The general had little patience with such a namby-pamby policy. Claiming that he had received instructions from the government to conquer Florida, Jackson crossed the border, captured the Spanish fort of St. Marks, executed two British subjects—Alexander Arbuthnot and Robert Ambrister—whom he considered troublemakers, and went on to occupy Pensacola, deposing the Spanish governor in the process.

Ordinary Americans cheered Jackson's bold acts; in Washington, London, and Madrid there was consternation. The only cool head was that of Secretary of State Adams, who saw that the general's rash behavior could be turned to America's advantage. Rather than apologize to Spain, Adams took the offensive. He dismissed Spain's loud protest, charged the Spaniards with failure to protect their own possessions, and enlarged United States claims to Spanish territory in the Far West under the Louisiana Purchase treaty.

Adams's brazen tactics worked. The Spanish minister in Washington, Luis de Onís y Gonzales, blustered and complained, but his government recognized that it could no longer hold Florida and came to terms with the United States. In February 1819, in the Adams-Onís Treaty, Spain ceded Florida to the United States and surrendered its claim to Oregon. In return, the United States assumed the payment of $5 million in debts owed by Spain to American citizens and agreed to accept the southwestern boundary of Louisiana as the Sabine River, thereby excluding the Mexican province of Texas.

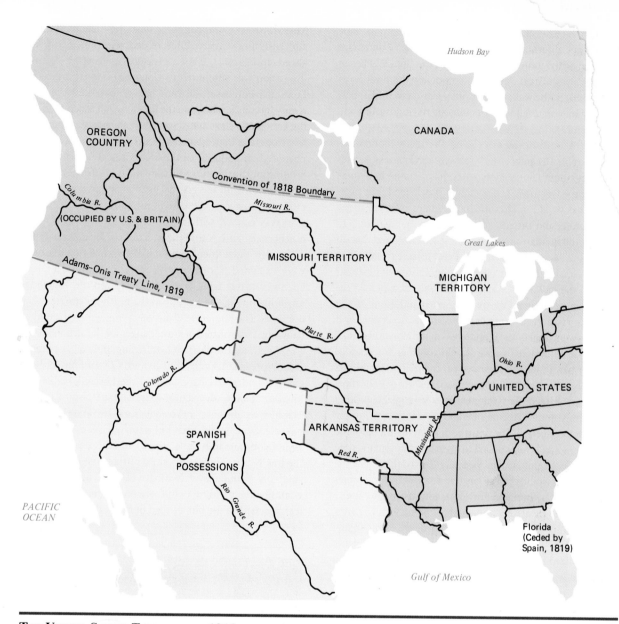

THE UNITED STATES TERRITORIES, 1819

Spain's weakness created hazards as well as opportunities for the United States. By 1820 all of Spanish America, except several Caribbean islands, had won independence. But Spain still hoped to regain control of its former possessions. These hopes were encouraged by France, Prussia, Austria, and Russia, whose monarchs in 1815 had established the Holy Alliance to resist the forces of democracy and liberalism wherever they appeared. Among the European powers, only Great Britain opposed the Alliance. If the Alliance came to Spain's help in America, the British feared, France would regain her lost influence in the Western Hemisphere. A revived Spanish-American empire

would also probably exclude Great Britain and other nations from the profitable trade that had developed with Latin America since its independence. With both these possibilities in mind, the British foreign secretary, George Canning, proposed that his nation and the United States work together to prevent Spain from regaining control of her former colonies.

The Americans, like the British, were dismayed at the prospect of Spanish restoration and the intervention of the great European powers in the Americas. They were also disturbed by Russia's recent expansion from its far northern Alaskan settlements down the west coast of North America.

In 1816 the Russians had established a trading post, Fort Ross, near California's Bodega Bay. But Secretary Adams was skeptical of any joint arrangement. For the United States to cooperate with Great Britain would put it in the position of "a cockboat in the wake of the British man-of-war." Far better for America to go it alone without relying on Britain's uncertain backing.

On Adams's recommendation President Monroe included in his December 1823 message to Congress a statement regarding Latin America that has become known as the Monroe Doctrine. The president proclaimed four principles that would guide the United States in its relations with Europe and the rest of the Western Hemisphere. To counter the Russian advance, Monroe first declared that no part of the American continents were "to be considered as subjects for future colonization by any European powers." Second, the new Latin American nations must remain independent republics. "We owe it . . . to candor and to the amicable relations existing between the United States and those powers [that is, the monarchies of the Holy Alliance]," he noted, "to declare that we should consider any attempt on their part to extend their system to any portion of this hemisphere as dangerous to our peace and safety." The third principle pledged the United States to respect existing European colonies in America and to stay out of purely European concerns. The fourth element in the Monroe Doctrine, actually announced in a separate diplomatic note to the Russian minister in Washington, asserted that the United States would oppose any transfer of existing colonies in the Americas from one European country to another.

Monroe's principles appeared to the nations of continental Europe to be "blustering," "arrogant," and "monstrous." They were. The United States was asserting rights unrecognized by international law or treaty—rights it also could not yet defend. The pretensions of the puny American nation seemed ludicrous. "Mr. Monroe, who is not a sovereign," scoffed the French foreign minister, "has assumed in his message the tone of a powerful monarch whose armies and fleets are ready to march at the first signal. . . . Mr. Monroe is the temporary President of a Republic situated on the east coast of North America. . . . Its independence was only recognized forty years ago; by what right then would the two Americas today be under its immediate sway from Hudson's Bay to Cape Horn?"

The United States was counting on Great Britain to stand behind it in case of challenge. Without Britain's support the new policy would be an empty gesture. Nevertheless, it took courage for a nation of scarcely 10 million to defy the powers of Europe. It also took idealism. No matter how the United States might later twist the Monroe Doctrine to serve its own interests, it was originally a generous statement in defense of international freedom and republican institutions.

The Missouri Compromise.   One event late in Monroe's administration carried hints of serious political troubles ahead. In February 1819 a measure to admit Missouri to the Union was submitted to Congress. Carved out of the Louisiana Purchase, Missouri had been settled predominantly by southerners, and the Enabling Act accepted it into the Union as a slave state. Soon after the measure came before Congress, Representative James Tallmadge of New York proposed an addition to the Missouri statehood bill prohibiting any further introduction of slaves into the new state and providing for the gradual emancipation of all children of slaves born after the date of its admission. The halls of Congress echoed with angry debate for two sessions as northerners and southerners attacked or defended the Tallmadge amendment. Southerners warned that if slavery were excluded from Missouri, the Union would be torn apart. Even the aging Jefferson considered the Tallmadge amendment and the attitude of the northern congressmen ominous. The Missouri debate was a "fire bell in the night," he wrote, that warned of grave danger for the Union ahead.

After months of heated wrangling, the voices of moderation prevailed. Under the Missouri Compromise of 1820 Congress admitted two states to the Union—Maine and Missouri. Maine, carved from Massachusetts, would be free; Missouri would be slave. The balance of free and slave states in the Union would thus be preserved. The slave South would continue to have as many United States senators as the free North. The compromise further provided that the southern boundary of Missouri (36°30′ north latitude) would be the dividing point between future slave and free territory within the remaining Louisiana Purchase.

★ JACKSON RISES TO POWER ★

By this time the politicians were hard at work considering Monroe's successor. If precedent had remained a guide, there would have been little dispute. As secretary of state, John Quincy Adams would be the choice in 1824. But the precedents followed during the Era of Good Feelings were ceasing to exert much influence on American politics. The voters were tired of being King Caucus's rubber stamp. A people on the move across a continent, growing in self-confidence and national pride, Americans were less willing than in the past to have decisions made for them by gentlemen, however liberal, learned, and decent they might be.

Democratic Reforms in the States.   The new attitude created a quiet political revolution. For some time a trend toward eliminating the last vestiges of state property qualifications for voting had been gaining strength. In some older seaboard states the impetus came from Republicans as they displaced their aristocratic Federalist opponents. In New York the arrival of great numbers of New England Yankees with liberal views was the crucial element in advancing democratic change. In a number of the more laggard eastern states, the suffrage reformers used the argument that the older states must emulate the newer western states or lose population to them. Whatever the reason, an already broad electorate became still broader.

Other changes also advanced the trend toward a more democratic political process. Several states in this period ended "stand-up" voting, which required citizens to acknowledge their candidate publicly on election day and face the possible wrath of influential men; instead, there would be printed ballots to protect the privacy and independence of the voter. Most states eliminated the remaining property qualifications for officeholding and reapportioned their legislatures to give underrepresented areas the political weight they deserved. By 1832 every state except South Carolina had also taken away the legislatures' power to choose pres-

idential electors and given it to the voters. The electoral college remained, but its members would be selected by voting citizens. Many states changed appointive offices into elective ones. The convention system, in which the party rank and file had a voice, soon replaced the elitist caucus as a method of nominating candidates for office. First adopted on the state level in New Jersey and Delaware early in the century, it spread to other Middle Atlantic states during the 1820s and to New England at the end of the decade. In 1831 the small Anti-Masonic party first used it to choose a presidential candidate, and the system soon became the norm in national as well as local politics.

It used to be said that these changes originated in the West and only later spread to the East. The evidence shows that it was often the other way around. In political affairs, at least, the East was the pioneer and eastern practices were carried west by emigrants. It was also at one time commonly held that Andrew Jackson and his supporters were responsible for many of the changes. In fact, most of the changes preceded rather than followed the Jackson movement.

Politics became more democratic as states eliminated property requirements and "stand-up" voting. With greater public involvement, candidates wooed the masses with parades, barbecues, and rallies, as shown here. Voters enjoyed this attention and appreciated the privacy of casting paper ballots in boxes.

The Election of 1824. Although he was not responsible for these new trends, Jackson was clearly their beneficiary. The general alone among the contenders in 1824 was a genuine popular hero. Adams was a man of great ability, but his reserve and close association with the old Virginia dynasty hurt him with the voters. William Crawford of Georgia had supporters in the lower South but failed to strike sparks elsewhere. Even the formal endorsement of the dying congressional caucus would do him little good. Clay and Calhoun were endorsed as candidates by local groups in Kentucky and South Carolina, respectively; but despite their prominent roles as national leaders during and immediately following the War of 1812, neither had national support. Calhoun soon dropped out of the race. There was no opposition party in 1824. Except for the small group of Anti-Masons, everyone called himself a Republican, and in the end the campaign turned out to be primarily a popularity contest.

If the campaign was uneventful, its aftermath was not. No candidate won a majority of the electoral college vote. Jackson was first in both electoral and popular vote; Adams was second; and Crawford and Clay trailed well behind both. The Constitution, as provided in the Twelfth Amendment, declared that in the event no candidate received an electoral vote majority, the selection of a president would rest with the House of Representatives, where each state would cast a single vote for one of the top three candidates. It did not require that individual representatives vote for the man with the largest electoral or popular vote; if it had, there would have been no point to the procedure. Still, Jackson's supporters believed that the House had a moral obligation to endorse their candidate as the man who had won the most popular votes. When thirteen state delegations—more than half—gave Adams a majority and the victory, they denounced the result as a denial of the people's will. Clay, they charged, had used his influence in the House to throw the election to Adams. Ignoring the general ideological agreement between Clay and Adams, Jackson's supporters charged that the two had struck a "corrupt bargain" when the new president appointed Henry Clay as his secretary of state.

Adams's administration was dogged by that charge and by the rancor of Jackson's supporters. The country had seen nothing like this for ten years, and the effects were unfortunate. As we have noted, almost nothing in President Adams's domestic program passed Congress. Even in foreign affairs, where his great experience should have been an advantage, he accomplished little. Typical of his experience in diplomacy was the farce of the Panama Conference of 1826. When he and Secretary Clay recommended two men as delegates to this meeting of Western Hemisphere nations in Panama, their political foes in Congress tied up

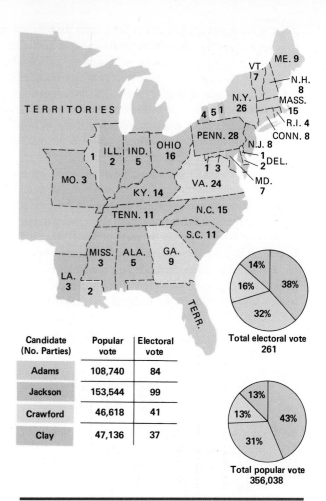

Candidate (No. Parties)	Popular vote	Electoral vote
Adams	108,740	84
Jackson	153,544	99
Crawford	46,618	41
Clay	47,136	37

Total electoral vote 261

Total popular vote 356,038

ELECTION OF 1824

the appointments by months of angry debate. When Congress finally approved delegates, it was too late. One of them died on the way and the other set out so late that the conference had adjourned before he reached Panama.

The Tariff of Abominations. All through his administration Adams fought Jackson and his supporters. A major focus of their battle was the tariff.

By 1828 the last important tariff revision was already twelve years old. Now the modest protectionist provisions of the tariff of 1816 no longer suited many groups. Increasing numbers of wool growers, textile manufacturers, and ironmasters—and even many farmers—demanded higher duties on imports to protect them from foreign competition. The "protectionists" were concentrated in the Northeast and to a lesser extent in the Old Northwest. Southerners of virtually all economic classes opposed any increase in duties because they had little industry to protect. Indeed, they were happy to rely on Great Britain, the cheapest producer of manufactured goods, for their imports. In 1816, when the South's economic future was still in doubt, many southerners had endorsed the tariff. In 1828, after it had become clear that the region's fate was to be supplier of raw materials for a world market, its leading spokesmen saw the protective tariff as an instrument for increasing northern profits at the South's expense.

The issue was highly charged, and most politicians would have preferred to avoid it. But Martin Van Buren of New York's Albany Regency believed that a major tariff revision would help get his friend Jackson elected president by winning him support in the North and West. The tariff bill he sponsored, when it finally emerged from the pro-Jackson Congress, injured the manufacturers of New England by raising the rates on raw materials that they needed to produce their goods. At the same time, southerners faced the prospect of higher prices for many English imports. Only Middle Atlantic industrialists and the producers of hemp, raw wool, and a few other farm products got anything positive out of the bill. So objectionable was the measure that puzzled contemporaries assumed that the foxy Van Buren had intended to raise the political stock of the Jackson men by giving them a universally unpopular bill that they could then loudly denounce.

Most scholars now agree that Van Buren honestly favored the tariff of 1828 because his New York constituents wanted it and because he believed a higher tariff would win support for Jackson in the North and West, where its major benefits would be felt. Because the South would not vote for Adams in any case, this northern and western support would ensure the general's election. Van Buren did not intend the bill to offend northerners; that was the doing of Congress, which in the give-and-take of tariff making had twisted the measure out of its original shape.

Whatever its purpose, this "Tariff of Abominations" particularly outraged the South. Everything southerners now bought would cost more, and this at a time when world cotton prices had taken a sharp drop. The southern outcry was general and emphatic, but it was John C. Calhoun who took it upon himself to make a constitutional case for his section's interests. Published anonymously by the South Carolina legislature, Calhoun's *Exposition and Protest* denied that Congress had the right to levy a tariff so high that it would exclude imports. The Founding Fathers had intended to impose only moderate duties on imported goods as a means to raise revenue. The 1828 law, he stated, was obviously discriminatory, favoring the manufacturing states and hurting those sections that relied on imports and had little industry to protect. Calhoun went beyond those familiar low-tariff arguments to insist that if Congress persisted in taking such an unconstitutional course, it was the right of any state to call a convention and declare such a measure null and void. *Exposition and Protest* revealed that

its author, once a confirmed nationalist, was well on his way to becoming the great southern sectional champion.

The Election of 1828.   Despite Van Buren's hopes, the 1828 presidential election revolved around personalities rather than issues. Adams, with Richard Rush of Pennsylvania as his running mate, was nominated by the "National Republican" convention at Harrisburg, the first major-party presidential convention. Jackson and Calhoun were selected by the Tennessee legislature and then placed on the ballot by their supporters in the various states. Although President Adams alone had the endorsement of the new, more democratic convention procedure, he was actually the weaker candidate. His partisans were numerous only in New England and other areas settled by New Englanders.

The contest was one of the dirtiest on record. The Jackson men, who had long been brooding over their defeat in 1824, revived the corrupt bargain charge to discredit Adams and resorted to scandalmongering. In Pennsylvania

ELECTION OF 1828

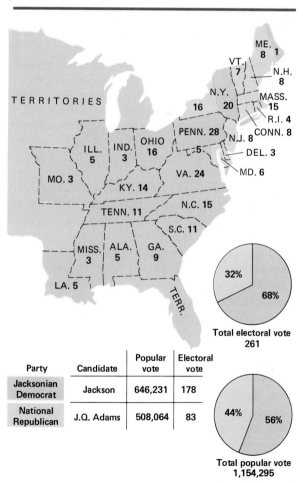

Party	Candidate	Popular vote	Electoral vote
Jacksonian Democrat	Jackson	646,231	178
National Republican	J.Q. Adams	508,064	83

Total electoral vote 261
32%
68%

Total popular vote 1,154,295
44%
56%

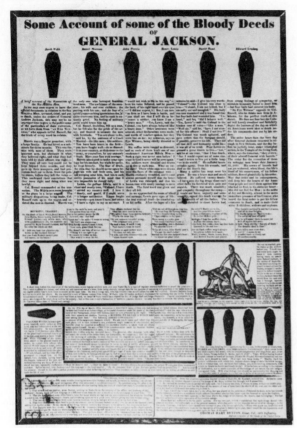

The election of 1828 was an especially negative campaign. The candidates' personalities became campaign issues. In this broadside, the so-called Coffin Handbill, Adams's supporters portray Jackson as a hot-tempered frontier brawler with a penchant for dueling and a harsh disciplinarian who had six militiamen court-martialed and shot.

the Jackson press claimed that Adams's wife, Louisa, had been born out of wedlock. A pro-Jackson Missouri editor charged that Adams had lived in sin with his wife before they were married. Equally scandalous stories were spread by the other side. Rachel Jackson, the Adams people said, had not been divorced from her first husband when she married the general. As for Jackson himself, he was a brutal man who had ordered the execution of six innocent militiamen during the campaign against the Creek Indians a decade before.

There was almost no discussion of issues. Though we conventionally date the rise of the second party system from this era, few principles seemed to separate the candidates. One contemporary noted that no one in the New York State convention that confirmed Jackson's nomination for president knew the candidate's views on public matters. A Pennsylvanian observed that "the great mystery of the case" was that "the South should support General Jackson avowedly for the purpose of preventing tariffs and internal

improvements and that we should support him for a directly opposite purpose." Adams's positions were a little easier to discern. He stood for an active and paternalistic national government, if he stood for anything, and in New England the surviving Federalists clearly found him the more congenial candidate. Yet he also received the support of many Yankee Republicans, who saw him as the spiritual descendant of Jefferson.

Only the Anti-Masons seemed to have a clear program. This curious group had appeared in New York following the mysterious disappearance of William Morgan, a former Mason who in 1826 had written a book exposing the Masonic order's rituals and other "secrets." Morgan was presumed murdered by the Masons, and the public indignation that followed led to the formation of a political organization dedicated to reducing the power of secret

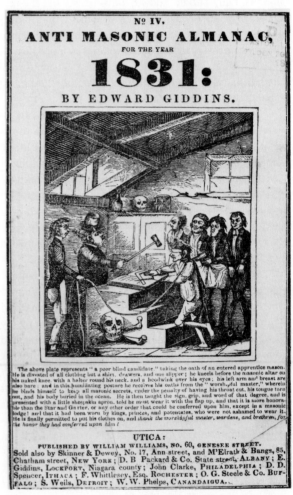

The Anti-Masons were certain that the order they opposed was a dangerous conspiracy against the liberties of a free people. As this cartoon from the Anti-Masonic Almanac of 1831 shows, they also believed that the Masons were determined to humiliate any person so foolish as to join their ranks.

groups in national affairs. In 1828 the new party generally supported Adams, but in later years the Anti-Masons would nominate their own candidates and mount an attack on privilege in government and the economy that would be far more wide-ranging than anything undertaken by the reputedly radical Jackson party.

The 1828 contest, if we ignore the Anti-Masons, did not contribute very much to establishing—or reestablishing—well-defined and competing party ideologies. On the other hand, in several states, especially in the Middle Atlantic region, the Jackson-Adams contest aroused political instincts dormant for over a decade. A two-sided contest, particularly one that included the colorful Jackson, was more gripping than either the rubber stamps of 1816 and 1820 or the four-sided competition of 1824. In much larger numbers than four years before, voters came out to cast their ballots. Jackson won decisively, receiving 178 electoral and 646,000 popular votes to Adams's 83 electoral and 509,000 popular votes.

★ KING ANDREW ★

The Spoils System. Jackson's first order of business was distributing the political loaves and fishes. The new president did not eject his political opponents from office wholesale, as scholars used to believe. In his first year and a half he removed 900 of over 10,000 federal employees, only 9 percent of the total. Yet Jackson's policy was something new on the political stage. The Virginia dynasty presidents had favored members of their own party in filling vacancies, but they had seldom fired officeholders who opposed their policies primarily to create new openings. Jackson and his friends were fierce partisans and took no such moderate view of the federal civil service. Loyalty to the president, they quickly made clear, would be the prime consideration in retaining office. If the number of those actually dismissed was small, it was only because so many bureaucrats were already Jackson supporters or quickly became supporters to avoid losing their jobs.

Nor had Jackson's predecessors elevated the "spoils system" into a noble principle. At times the Jacksonians frankly admitted the narrow political reasons for removing long-time civil servants from office. "To the victor belong the spoils of the enemy," declared Senator William L. Marcy in 1832. Generally, however, they tried to pass it off as a political reform. "Rotation in office" was a democratic policy, they said, that ended the previous monopoly of officeholding by privileged gentlemen and provided many more citizens with the opportunity to exercise power. Since, in Jackson's words, "the duties of all public officers are . . . so

plain and simple that men of intelligence may readily qualify for their performance," no group need be excluded from serving the nation. Scholars, accepting the Jacksonians at their own word, have often treated the spoils system as a democratization of the political process.

In fact, rotation in office was not particularly democratic. It did not replace gentlemen with common folk; the Jackson appointees' social backgrounds differed little from those of their predecessors. Nor were the Jacksonians primarily interested in spreading power. Their chief purpose was to provide political muscle to the party system. The lure of office would be a powerful incentive to ambitious men to work for party causes, while officeholders could be assessed for contributions out of their government salaries to party coffers. The spoils system would be a useful and important component of the emerging second party system, but it should not be taken as evidence that Jackson and his party were more democratic than their predecessors.

The new policy damaged civil service morale, and at times the effects of job uncertainty were tragic. "A clerk in the War Office, named Henshaw," exPresident Adams recorded in his diary, "three days since cut his throat from ear to ear, from the mere terror of being dismissed. Linneus Smith, of the Department of State, has gone raving distracted and others are said to be threatened with the same calamity." Besides reducing efficiency, the spoils system encouraged corruption. In the New York customhouse, where dishonesty reached a nadir, the collector Samuel Swartwout embezzled over a million dollars and escaped to England before he could be arrested.

Jackson's penchant for favoring friends and acquaintances over disinterested public servants is apparent in his choice of close advisers. Generally he ignored the official cabinet and instead relied on his so-called Kitchen Cabinet, drawn from early supporters of his presidential bid. These men were given undemanding government posts to support them while they devoted their time to politics and political service to Jackson.

Whatever the deficiencies of the Virginia dynasty presidents, they had maintained a high level of honesty and efficiency in the public service. The Jackson men—and their successors—undoubtedly lowered the moral and intellectual tone of American political life. At the same time, however, they did make it possible for the ordinary man to feel a sense of participation. This new mood was not at first reflected in the voting statistics, except in the 1828 presidential election. Larger election turnouts would have to wait until real two-party contests had appeared in all the states and the voters had been caught up in the rivalries of close elections. But the Jackson party did infuse a new, more open spirit into political life—a spirit essential to the success of the second party system.

Jacksonian Democracy

Mrs. Margaret Bayard Smith, wife of a Washington banker, editor, and Jeffersonian politician, witnessed the transition from the Virginia dynasty to the age of Jackson. A keen observer of politics as it was played out in the nation's capital early in the nineteenth century, she recorded her impressions in letters to friends and family, later collected as *The First Forty Years of Washington Society*. The following excerpt from that work describes Inauguration Day, 1829, when the "people's" hero, Andy Jackson, became president of the United States, ushering in a new, more democratic age. It was an age that clearly did not fully please Mrs. Smith, who was unused to the unruly exuberance of the masses come to celebrate their day in the sun.

"A national salute was fired early in the morning, and ushered in the 4th of March. By ten o'clock the Avenue was crowded with carriages of every description, from the splendid Barronet and coach, down to waggons and carts, filled with women and children, some in finery and some in rags, for it was the people's President, and all would see him. . . . Some one came and informed us [that] the crowd before the President's house, was so far lessen'd, that they thought that we might enter. This time we effected our purpose. But what a scene did we witness! *The Majesty of the People* had disappeared and a rabble, a mob, of boys, negros, women, children, scrambling, fighting, romping. What a pity, what a pity! No arrangements had been made; no police officers placed on duty, and the whole house had been inundated by the rabble mob. We came too late. The President, after having been *literally* nearly pressed to death and almost suffocated, and torn to pieces by the people in their eagerness to shake hands with Old Hickory, had retreated through the back way or south front and had escaped to his lodgings at Gadsby's. Cut glass and china to the amount of several thousand dollars had been broken in the struggle to get the refreshments. . . . [P]unch and other articles had been carried out in tubs and buckets, but had it been in hogs-heads it would have been insufficient. . . . [They supplied] ice-creams, and cake, and lemonade, for 20,000 people, for it is said that [that] number were there tho' I think the estimate exaggerated. Ladies fainted, men were seen with bloody noses and such a scene of confusion took place as is impossible to describe,— those who got in could not get out by the door again, but had to scramble out of windows. At one time, the President, who had retreated and retreated until he was pressed against the wall, could only be secured by a number of gentlemen forming around him and making a kind of barrier of their own bodies, and the pressure was so great that Col Bomford who was one said that at one time he was afraid they should have been pushed down, or on the President. It was then the windows were thrown open, and the torrent found an outlet, which otherwise might have proved fatal.

"This concourse had not been anticipated and therefor not provided against. Ladies and gentlemen only had been expected at this Levee, not the people en masse. But it was the People's day, and the People's President and the People would rule. God grant that one day or other, the People do not put down all rule and rulers. . . ."

Jackson's Style. The spoils system was one Jacksonian contribution to the political revival of these years, though obviously one with mixed results. Another was a strong president. Jackson was a military man, used to command and unwilling to brook defiance by Congress, state legislatures, or the chief justice of the Supreme Court. A vivid personality who inspired intense feelings of either hatred or affection among the voters, he was not a learned man or even a clear and consistent thinker. The general acted on the prejudices he had acquired as a young man and never abandoned. A southerner and slaveholder, he had few objections to slavery and despised abolitionists. A man from the frontier state of Tennessee and a leader in the Indian wars, he had little love for the Indians. Having been almost ruined in 1819 by the tight credit policies of the Bank of the United States, he hated banks in general and the Bank of the United States in particular. Jackson personalized almost all his political attitudes, turning political opponents into enemies who had to be destroyed lest they destroy him. Many Americans thought Old Hickory principled and spirited, but his opponents condemned his irascibility and high-handedness and called him King Andrew. Their adoption of the name *Whigs* was intended to identify them as opponents of arbitrary power, just as the English Whigs had opposed royal absolutism in the late seventeenth century.

The Nullification Crisis. Jackson's intolerance of opposition surfaced during the tariff controversy that marked his first term. Though he had criticized the Tariff of Abominations during the election campaign, he disap-

Jackson's use of the veto, his tightening of executive control, and his personal approach to the presidency led Republicans to dub him "King Andrew." As proper for the enemies of kings, they called themselves "Whigs."

pointed the South by refusing to sponsor a substantial reduction in import duties. When, in 1832, Congress passed its own measure reducing the 1828 rates only slightly, South Carolinians, led by Vice President Calhoun, precipitated a political crisis by calling a convention and declaring the tariff void in the Palmetto State.

The South Carolina Ordinance of Nullification reflected more than southern economic discontent. By 1832,

as we shall see in Chapter 12, slavery had become a major social and political issue in the nation. Just two years before, firebrand Massachusetts editor and reformer William Lloyd Garrison had begun to demand "immediate and complete emancipation" of southern slaves and had used angry language to denounce slaveholding and slaveholders. Garrison's attack had ushered in a new, more aggressive phase of the antislavery movement and had frightened and offended the South Carolina planter elite. These men now saw in the antislavery attack a serious threat to the stability and profitability of their slave-linked society. Nullification, they believed, was an appropriate weapon by which to defend the South's interests against a militant North that, for all they knew, had begun to rally around the new antisouthern movement.

South Carolina's action was a direct threat to the Union. Jackson, however, characteristically took it as a personal affront as well. The president declared that the state's action was "without parallel in the history of the world," and called Calhoun a madman. Yet this time, at least, he sought to avoid a direct confrontation. In his December 1832 message to Congress he pointed to imminent changes in the tariff duties and told South Carolinians that their reaction was exaggerated. Soon after, he issued a proclamation warning the people of the state that nullification endangered the nation's political integrity. At the same time, Jackson asked Congress for additional powers to enforce the customs laws—a request that Congress granted in the Force Bill. In 1833 Clay arranged a compromise tariff bill that saved protection for nine years, until 1842, in exchange for dropping protection thereafter.

Finding no support in other states, the South Carolina planter elite backed down. The state legislature rescinded the Ordinance of Nullification against the 1832 Tariff Act, but at the same time, as a gesture of defiance, it nullified the Force Bill. In the relief at getting past the crisis, few complained about the state's refusal to abandon the principle of nullification.

Indian Policy.   Jackson's position on nullification seems to confirm his strong nationalism. But he was perfectly willing to see the federal government's power disregarded when it suited his purposes or accorded with one of his fundamental prejudices. A blatant instance of this was his defiance of John Marshall over Indian policy.

The peace treaty with England in 1815 had removed the plug blocking western settlement. Settlers had poured into the Great Lakes Plain, the Ohio Valley, and the Gulf Plain by the thousands to establish farms, plantations, and towns. The remaining Indian tribes, both north and south of the Ohio River, threatened to stop the rush of white civilization, and increasingly the government decided that the best way to deal with them was to remove them beyond the Mississippi. In 1817 Jackson, as agent for the War Department, had coerced a treaty out of the Cherokees of Georgia, by which they agreed to exchange their tribal lands for an equal amount of land in the West. Those Indians who did not want to go might remain and settle down as farmers. Though the Georgia lands would have to be surrendered as tribal holdings, each Indian family might have 640

acres as an individual holding. To Jackson's disgust, virtually every Cherokee chose to remain in Georgia; indeed, many bought slaves and began to raise cotton on their new 640-acre plantations.

This failure at Indian removal in the South was offset by successes in the North. In 1818 and 1819 the Wyandot, Chippewa, and Delaware tribes were removed by treaties from enormous areas in Indiana and Illinois. But such piecemeal progress seemed too slow, so in 1825 President Monroe announced that henceforth all the tribes of the eastern portion of the nation would be removed beyond the ninety-fifth meridian to a "permanent Indian frontier." There they could live in peace, the president declared, unmolested by whites and able to preserve their ancestral ways. No longer would the government attempt to turn the Indians into copper-skinned Europeans.

Under the direction of Secretary of War Calhoun, Congress set about removing the remaining tribes of the Northwest and South. The Indians resisted, and the new policy could only be carried out by unsavory tactics. Government agents bribed chiefs to sign treaties that committed their whole tribes to move, then claimed that the move was the collective will of the Indian people. Unwilling tribes were "persuaded" by military threats and force. In 1825 the Osage and Kansas tribes surrendered to the government all of Kansas and northern Oklahoma except for two reservations. Over the next fifteen years all the Northwest Indians were similarly moved—the Shawnee, Kickapoo, Sauk, Fox, Potawatomi, Ottawa, Iowa, Miami, and Peoria tribes.

But the tribes of the Southeast proved more stubborn. In Georgia, the Carolinas, Alabama, and Mississippi the Five Civilized Nations—the Cherokees, Creeks, Choctaws, Chickasaws, and Seminoles—owned some 33 million acres of valuable land. These Indians had become a settled agricultural people with a sophisticated political and social system and a high level of literacy. They had conformed to the white man's ways, and by all the professed principles of contemporary white Americans, they should have been left alone to enjoy their unusual blend of European and Indian cultures. But their holdings aroused the greed and envy of their white neighbors. In 1827, hoping to head off Georgia's effort to oust them from their lands, the Cherokee wrote a constitution at New Echota establishing an independent republic. The outraged Georgians called this a violation of the federal Constitution and demanded that Washington evict the Cherokees as punishment. Congress responded by offering a bribe. The tribe would receive lands in the West and each Cherokee family that agreed to leave would get $50 in cash as well as a blanket, rifle, five pounds of tobacco, and other supplies. During the summer of 1828 federal agents pressured the Cherokees to accept this offer. There were few takers.

Jackson's election, and the discovery of gold on Cherokee lands, encouraged the Georgians to harsher action. A new state measure provided that beginning in 1830 the tribe would be under the jurisdiction of state rather than federal law. Indians, moreover, would no longer be allowed to bear witness in court against whites or be parties to any suit involving whites. The Indians now had little or no protection against unprincipled whites coveting their land. The Cherokee protested to the federal government, which responded sternly with the Removal Bill allowing the president to send any eastern tribe beyond the Mississippi if he wished, using force if needed. The Indians, meanwhile, asked the U.S. Supreme Court for an injunction to stop Georgia from enforcing its repressive laws but the Court refused on the grounds the Cherokee were not, as they claimed, a foreign nation and so could not sue before the Supreme Court.

Now followed an ugly orgy of greed and brutality at the Cherokees' expense. The Georgia government cancelled debts owed the Indians, stopped payment of subsidies, and seized their property. State agents sought to stir up ani-mosities within the tribe to break the Cherokees' morale. Christian missionaries who protested this ill-treatment were clapped in jail. A renewed appeal to the U.S. Supreme Court this time produced a favorable opinion from Chief Justice Marshall in *Worcester* v. *Georgia* (1832). The Indians did possess the status of a "domestic dependent nation," he declared, and were therefore entitled to federal protection against the state. But Jackson refused to enforce the chief justice's opinion, supposedly retorting: "John Marshall has made his decision, now let him enforce it!"

During the months that followed federal agents, determined to get rid of the Cherokee, found a turncoat leader who, in late 1835, agreed to abandon all the tribal lands for $5.6 million and free transportation to the West. A majority of Cherokee denounced the agreement but realized they could no longer resist. For the next three years thousands of Indian families, grieving for their ancestral homes, set out on the "Trail of Tears" for what is now Oklahoma. The last holdouts were driven away by federal troops in the dead of winter. Many died on the way west.

The Trail of Tears, the forced relocation of 15,000 Cherokees. Although Andrew Jackson apparently supported a strong federal government, he so hated Indians that he disregarded the Supreme Court's ruling that they had a right to their land. Such inconsistencies made Jackson's personality one of the divisive issues of his presidency.

Similar grim fates awaited the Choctaw and Creeks, but the Seminoles of Florida were more resolute. Under Chief Osceola they took up arms against the federal government and were subdued only after a brutal war. The Second Seminole War began in 1835 and dragged on for seven years, costing the federal government between $40 million and $60 million. In 1842 the last resisters were sent off to the West or forced into the most inaccessible depths of the Everglades.

Humane Americans, especially easterners, denounced Jacksonian Indian policies. The New England press labeled it "an abhorrent business." But it continued unabated. Few instances of white-Indian relations in North America exhibit the total callousness of the removal of the Civilized Tribes by Jackson and his successors.

The Attack on the Bank.   Andrew Jackson hated banks—especially "The Bank"—even more than he hated Indians. After its inauspicious start when it helped trip off the Panic of 1819, the Second Bank of the United States had settled down to a useful existence under its third president, Nicholas Biddle. The bank lent money to merchants, helped expedite foreign trade, handled checking accounts, issued paper money backed by gold, held the deposits of the federal government, and transferred government funds from one part of the country to the other. Most important of all, it served as an informal central bank and the economy's balance wheel. As the nation's largest commercial bank, it could force the state banks to limit their credit when it felt the economy was too active or encourage them to lend readily when the economy was in the doldrums.

These operations made many friends for the bank. Many state bankers, especially in the capital-poor South and West, supported it, as did nationalist politicians and business interests who often borrowed from it or used its foreign-trade services. This support was not always disinterested, however. Newspaper editors and some of the most prominent men in government—including Daniel Webster, Henry Clay, and some Jacksonians—were in the bank's pay. The "God-like Daniel," who was frequently in debt, was a particularly shameless dependent of the bank, constantly asking that his "retainer" be "renewed or refreshed."

The bank also made many fierce enemies. Some aggressive and speculative businessmen found its generally conservative credit policies a hindrance. Its most important opponents, however, were agrarians like Senator Thomas Hart Benton of Missouri, who deplored all banks. Mostly southerners and westerners, these men favored "hard money" and believed that the paper money that banks issued was unwise and immoral. It provided a select few with profits based not on gold and silver—God's own money—but on doubtful promises to pay. An Alabama legislator noted: "Banking and paper money [are] in conflict with justice, morality and religion." Agrarians also held that banks in general, and the Bank of the United States in particular, endangered free government. With its $35 million in capital, Biddle's "monster bank" was the largest corporation in the country by far. Such size by itself gave it a potential power over the economy that was frightening. Add to this Biddle's sense of its regulatory responsibilities, and its influence on politicians, and it seemed obvious to many that the bank had to be destroyed or it would destroy the country.

The bank's twenty-year charter was due to expire in 1836. Fearful of the opposition beginning to form among Jacksonians and wishing to ensure the bank's continuity, Biddle applied for renewal in 1832. The measure passed Congress, but Jackson vetoed it. In a stinging attack the president explained his motives in terms that appealed to old Jeffersonian values. He ignored the hard-money argument, but denounced the bank as a privileged monopoly controlled by foreign investors. Jackson warned that it would wield its great powers to punish its enemies if it became entrenched. The president undoubtedly believed that the Bank of the United States was a dangerous institution in a nation composed of many small economic units, but he also had a strong personal motive. "The Bank is trying to kill me," he told Van Buren, "but I will kill it."

Sequoyah, a brilliant Cherokee who invented an alphabet for the Indian language.

The bank veto unleashed a storm of protest. Biddle called Jackson's veto message a "manifesto of anarchy." Webster, of course, also denounced it, as did two-thirds of the nation's press, much of the business community, and many state bankers. The veto immediately became the chief party issue during the 1832 presidential election, with Jackson's supporters treating it as an attack on monopoly and privilege and his foes condemning it as an example of King Andrew's tyrannical temperament.

Whigs and Democrats.   By this time the second party system was rapidly taking shape. The Jackson party, now beginning to be called the Democrats, was a heterogeneous group that differed in its programs and principles from one part of the country to another. Most Democrats tended to favor low tariffs, hard money, antimonopoly, and a government hands-off policy toward the economy. Jackson himself in 1830 had vetoed a federal appropriation for the Maysville Road in Kentucky on the grounds that the Constitution did not confer on the national government the power to finance internal improvements located entirely within a single state. But in some places—New York, New England, and Pennsylvania, for example—the Jackson men favored banks, protective tariffs, and government aid for internal improvements. On this last matter, Jackson himself was inconsistent. Though he vetoed the Maysville Road bill—some said mostly because it benefited Henry Clay's home state—he approved other federal outlays for roads.

The Whigs were less divided in their economic principles. Their "American System" called for protective tariffs, federal aid for internal improvements, and a strong national bank. First announced by Clay in 1824, the American System projected a paternalistic national government that would nurture business, protect industrial workers from cheap foreign competition, and provide a secure market for farmers in America's growing cities.

The Whigs and the Democrats also differed somewhat in their political ideologies. The Democrats claimed to be the party of the "common man," and there was some truth to their claim. James Silk Buckingham, an aristocratic English visitor, constantly heard the Democrats attacked by their opponents as "agrarians, incendiaries, men who . . . desire to . . . seize the property of the rich and divide it among the poor." The Jackson men, wrote William Seward, a New York anti-Jackson leader, considered the parties distinctly different in their class orientation: "It's with them the poor against the rich." These were the views of their enemies, but where there was smoke there was some real fire.

Nicholas Biddle, the powerful head of the Second Bank of the United States. Under his direction, the bank loaned business money prudently and helped smaller banks survive temporary setbacks.

Yet the differences between the parties must not be exaggerated. In New York the regular Democratic party often attacked the "Locofocos," a radical "equal rights" wing of their own party, as "infidels," "agrarians," and the "scum of politics." Moreover, the Jackson Democrats, as well as the Whigs, were led in these years by successful and prosperous lawyers, businessmen, and gentlemen, though the Jacksonians were probably somewhat less aristocratic than the Whigs. It is true that the Whigs had a "silk-stocking" element that had no real equivalent among the Democrats. These high and mighty folk often expressed contempt for the "rabble" that supposedly made up the political opposition. But they generally did so in private. The leading Whigs—Clay, Webster, and Seward—were popular figures who cultivated the voters and flattered them as effectively as Jackson, Van Buren, Marcy, and the other leading Democrats. And the Whigs' disdain for the ordinary voter did not color the party so intensely that a young ambitious Illinois politician like Abe Lincoln found any difficulty reconciling his obscure origins and sympathies for the common man with his affection for Henry Clay and his Whig political beliefs.

The differences between the parties' ideologies and class orientations, then, were not sharp, and each attracted voters from various classes, sections, and occupations. Clearly, if all farmers and wage earners had voted for Jackson and his Democratic successors—the supposed party of the common man—the opposition could never have won; farmers and wage earners, after all, were the great majority in the nation. But Jackson's opponents were not invariably defeated. Many husbandmen and workers withheld their votes from the Democrats. In the cities màny "mechanics" voted for the Whigs or for various "workingmen's parties," which advocated "radical" measures such as laws limiting the workday to ten hours and abolishing the inconvenient militia service required of male voters. Farmers, too, were

It is easy to see from this portrait of Henry Clay why he was so admired, especially by the "high–toned" folks of the day.

Peggy Eaton

Peggy Eaton was a beautiful woman who loved not wisely but too well. Her sex denied her an official role in politics, but for a time during the Jackson administration, her vivacity and charm made her a force in the political life of her nation.

Born Margaret O'Neale in 1796, Peggy learned early the skills that would make her a political presence. Her father, William, was Scotch-Irish, and his brick house on I Street in Washington was one of the first in the new federal district. William O'Neale offered board and lodging for members of Congress and the executive branch who came to the raw, new capital for only a few months each year, leaving their wives and families at home. The congressmen and government officials, deprived of their own children, spoiled the pretty little girl shamelessly. She in turn learned early how to please men, even those busy ones deeply immersed in high affairs of state.

Her father's boarding house cum tavern, which he called the Franklin House, was the source of still another sort of education for Peggy. Women were totally excluded from politics in this era, and the few who tried to influence the course of political events indirectly were scorned. As one contemporary publication described it, "a female politician is only less disgusting than a female infidel." Yet it was difficult for Peggy to avoid absorbing political ideas or learning political strategy with so many argumentative and brilliant politicians dining each day at the family table or puffing their pipes around the Franklin House tavern fire.

Though her father was only a "tavernkeeper," Peggy went to the best school for young ladies that the capital afforded. There she was exposed to the standard curriculum of the day for girls: reading and writing, penman-

ship, French, drawing and painting, and twenty-five different kinds of needlework. Her favorite subjects, however, were music and dancing. In 1812 Peggy's dancing skill impressed President Madison's wife, Dolley, when she served as judge for the ball that Mr. Generes, the capital's most prestigious dancing master, gave each year for his pupils. Mrs. Madison awarded Peggy the prize as Carnival Queen, a triumph that reinforced her romantic streak and magnified her yearnings for fame and fortune.

That same year, when she was still not yet sixteen, Peggy tried to elope with a handsome army officer stationed in Washington. She was caught by her father wriggling down a rope from her second-floor bedroom window and sent off to a finishing school in New York where she would be far from the dashing captain. But William O'Neale, like most other men, found it difficult to deny Peggy her wishes and he soon allowed her to return home.

For the next year or two Peggy, now the object of much tongue-wagging among Washington's respectable matrons, served as hostess in her father's tavern. In June 1816 she met John B. Timberlake, a purser in the U.S. Navy. Impressed by his blond good looks she accepted his proposal of marriage. At twenty, Peggy became a wife.

The marriage was not happy. Timberlake was a rolling stone who refused to settle down. He also drank too much. He and Peggy had three children, but the marriage never really jelled. Timberlake was away on duty much of the time, and Peggy and the children generally stayed at the O'Neale boarding house where she, though now a young matron herself, continued to charm the politician boarders.

One of these was the young senator from Tennessee, Major John

Eaton, a good friend of Andy Jackson, the hero of New Orleans. In 1823 Jackson himself was elected to the Senate and came to reside at the O'Neale house with his young, though politically senior, colleague. Both men were enchanted with Peggy Timberlake. Jackson wrote home to his wife, Rachel, of the "amiable" O'Neale family and particularly of Mrs. Timberlake, who "plays the Piano Delightfully & every Sunday evening entertains her pious mother with Sacred music to which we are invited."

Andrew Jackson would always retain the image of Peggy playing "Sacred music" for the pious Mrs. O'Neale. John Eaton apparently found her person more attractive than her accomplishments, and rumors were soon circulating that his attentions to Mrs. Timberlake were more than old-fashioned gallantry. One congressman who served in Washington during this period wrote that Peggy Timberlake "was considered as a lady who would be willing to dispense her favors wherever she took a fancy." Peggy became so notorious that Eliza Monroe, the president's proper wife, excluded her from White House receptions.

In 1828, while on duty with the Mediterranean squadron, John Timberlake died and was buried in Spain. Major Eaton quickly resolved to marry the young widow, but before acting he consulted his friend Jackson, now president-elect. Jackson was a generous and loyal man who, moreover, remembered how the gossips had tried to besmirch the reputation of his own beloved Rachel, claiming that she had lived in sin with him before they were legally married. He told Eaton to go ahead. "[I]f you love the woman, and she will have you, marry her by all means." In January 1829 Eaton and Peggy were married by the chaplain of the Senate at Franklin

House. Hours before, Congressman Churchill C. Cambreleng of New York wrote his friend, Governor Martin Van Buren, in Albany: "Poor Eaton is to be married tonight to Mrs. T. . . ! There is a vulgar saying of some vulgar man . . . on such unions—about using a certain household [item] and then putting it on one's head."

The marriage might have become a minor footnote to the social history of Jacksonian Washington if the president had not asked Senator Eaton to join his cabinet as secretary of war. Eaton at first refused the bid, probably because he feared to embarrass his friend, but Jackson insisted and Eaton "very reluctantly" agreed.

Eaton's doubts proved sound. At the inaugural ball the wives of the politicians ignored Peggy, though their husbands flocked around the witty and vivacious young matron and the president himself singled her out for "marked attention." Worse was to follow. Enemies of Eaton were soon circulating rumors that he and Peggy had taken trips and registered in hotels together while she was still Mrs. Timberlake and that she had conceived a child a year after her husband had departed for overseas duty. The gossips were to be found in the president's own household. Rachel Jackson had died shortly before Jackson's first term began, and the president's young niece, Emily Donelson, served as his official hostess. Mrs. Donelson quickly made it clear that she would not "receive" or call on Mrs. Eaton.

Nor were the other cabinet wives any more cordial. Leading the anti-Peggy pack was Floride Calhoun, the wife of Vice President John C. Calhoun and a very proper southern lady. With their wives so adamant, it proved difficult for other administration officials to accept Peggy Eaton socially. They avoided invitations to affairs that included the Eatons. They excluded the secretary of war and his wife from their balls and dinners. One exception was Martin Van Buren, now secretary of state. A widower whose own father had been a tavernkeeper, Van Buren saw no reason to snub Peggy Eaton. Indeed, the canny New Yorker recognized that Peggy's ostracism was causing the president pain, and he went out of his way to be chivalrous to his cabinet colleague's wife.

But Van Buren's generosity was not enough for Jackson. On September 10, 1829, he called his official family together to lay to rest the stories concerning the Eatons' premarital relations. With Eaton himself absent, the president denounced gossip in general and defended both his Tennessee friend and his friend's wife. John Eaton was innocent. As for Mrs. Eaton, she was "as chaste as a virgin."

Jackson's effort to lay down an official line on Peggy to his subordinates did not work. The president's colleagues and advisers split in two, one group willing to abide by his desire that Peggy be treated with respect, the other strongly opposed. The division disrupted his household. In mid-1830 Jackson exiled Emily and his nephew, Andrew Jackson Donelson, from the White House for refusing to socialize with the Eatons. It also had political consequences. Jackson was a fierce partisan. Those who did not agree with him were his sworn enemies and he would not cease until he had destroyed them.

The president's commitment to the Eatons helped split the Jackson party, contributing to the emerging Whig–Democratic rivalry that would soon enliven the political scene. It affected the political fortunes of Van Buren and Calhoun, both of whom nursed presidential ambitions and, even this early, sought the endorsement of the popular hero.

Jackson had other reasons to dislike Vice President Calhoun besides his disdain for Peggy Eaton. Back in 1818, when Calhoun was secretary of war under Monroe, he had harshly criticized General Jackson's "unauthorized" incursion into Florida, the bold stroke that had led to the hanging of Arbuthnot and Ambrister. In 1832 Jackson would clash again with the South Carolinian over the right of a state to nullify an act of Congress. But clearly the vice president's attitude toward Mrs. Eaton contributed to the antagonism. Meanwhile, Van Buren had become the general's favorite. In 1840, after Jackson stepped down, Van Buren would win the Democratic nomination; Calhoun had by this time become the champion of the South's special interests.

Peggy at first had stubbornly sought vindication, though even some of John Eaton's friends felt the president was risking too much for her cause. But finally even she lost heart and began to withdraw from possibly embarrassing social occasions. Having lost the battle for the rights she believed she deserved, she had no objection when her husband agreed to

split, with many rural voters, especially in New England and the Yankee-settled areas of the Old Northwest, voting for the Democrats' opponents. The Whigs were strongest in New England and those places where New Englanders had settled, but they had supporters in every part of the country. In the South small farmers voted Democratic; but large planters—despite their hostility to the tariff favored by Whigs—voted Whig largely because they needed cheap bank credit to market their cotton. Farmers in the West, eager for internal improvements, were also attracted to the Whigs. And in the cities the Whigs' American System attracted manufacturers and many industrial wage earners.

According to some scholars, however, what truly set Whigs and Democrats apart were distinctive cultural and

resign his post in 1831 in a general cabinet reorganization. Peggy hoped to remain in Washington where she had lived all her life and where, the prudes aside, she had made friends. But Eaton preferred to return to Tennessee and soon after they took up residence in the Eaton family house near Nashville.

But the major found private life dull. In 1832 he decided to run for the Senate. Though beaten, he continued to seek office, and in 1834 Jackson appointed him governor of Florida Territory. There, in Tallahassee, Peggy's health, not good since leaving Washington, improved. Yet she was not happy. The shabby little territorial capital seemed dull after Washington. Fortunately, in 1836 Eaton was sent as ambassador to Spain, and Peggy had a new, and far more cosmopolitan, social world to conquer.

Peggy liked Madrid. She, her husband, and her two surviving children by Timberlake—Margaret and Virginia—lived in the beautiful former home of the Duke St. Lorenzo. She adored the Spanish people. The common folk were joyous yet respectful. The men of the upper class were courtly—much like President Jackson—and their wives, daughters, and sisters showed none of the priggishness of American women. Especially gratifying was the friendly attitude of Maria Cristina, the queen, a woman who, like Peggy, had had her share of flirtations and amorous escapades. Peggy would describe the four years in Spain as the happiest in her life, a time full of balls, bullfights, fiestas, and other lively distractions.

The idyll was disrupted in 1840 when Jackson's successor as president,

none other than Martin Van Buren, recalled Eaton so that he could replace him with the famous New York author Washington Irving. The Eatons returned to America and settled once again in Washington where the major, perhaps disgruntled by Van Buren's recall, became a Whig. The change of party did not lead to preferment. Bored with inactivity, Eaton drank too much. In 1856 he died, leaving Peggy, now a 60-year-old grandmother, a rich woman.

Peggy Eaton did not settle down to respectable old age. In 1859, the elderly widow startled Washington, and revived all the lurid old stories, by marrying Antonio Buchignani, a dancing instructor of nineteen, one-third her age! Despite the scandal, the marriage was happy for a time. The couple were even accepted by Washington's respectables. Then "Tonio" began to show his true colors, stealing silver from his wealthy wife and playing on the affections of Emily, Peggy's sixteen-year-old granddaughter.

In 1866, after seven years of marriage, Tonio ran off to Europe with Emily and most of Peggy's fortune. The errant couple set up as husband and wife in Leghorn, Italy, had a child, and quickly squandered their ill-gotten wealth. They returned to America in September 1868, and Peggy had Tonio arrested as a swindler and seducer.

Peggy divorced Buchignani soon after and resumed use of her former name. She lived in New York for a time and then returned to her beloved Washington. In 1874 a Washington newspaper reporter interviewed her for a feature story for his paper. She

was, he wrote, "a hale, vigorous, well-preserved lady," in whose "form and face" could be detected "many of the lines and lineaments of that queenly beauty which once held captive so many men." This story launched a flock of others, and for a time Peggy once again became a celebrity. Mathew Brady, the famous photographer, asked to take her portrait. The picture is the only photograph we have of her and, notwithstanding the newspaper reporter's chivalrous remarks just a few years before, it shows an old lady dressed in black with only the faintest traces of the charm and beauty she once possessed.

On a gray day in November 1879, Margaret O'Neale Timberlake Eaton Buchignani died. The president's wife, Lucy Hayes, sent a large wreath of white roses to the funeral, and the Washington chief of police was the head pallbearer. Once again Peggy made the headlines. One paper called her a "One-Time Society Queen." The New York Times reviewed her life and marveled at its strange twists. Another daily, the New York Tribune, was ungallant. She had "created a noise quite out of proportion to her importance," Horace Greeley's old paper concluded. The judgment is unfair. Peggy Eaton was only a minor mover and shaker in politics, it is true. As a woman in her day she could not be more. But for a time in the 1820s, she demonstrated the power of elemental human drives to mold a nation's public life even in a repressed era.

religious emphases. There is evidence that in some states, such as Michigan and New York, the Democrats were the party of laissez faire in religion and morals as well as in economic affairs, whereas the Whigs were determined to police the public's personal habits and behavior. Thus the Whigs often endorsed Sunday closing laws for businesses and insisted that the government not deliver the mail on

the Christian Sabbath. They also favored laws outlawing alcohol or encouraging temperance. By contrast, Democrats generally believed that drinking and doing business on Sundays were private, not public, matters. These divergent attitudes also made the Whigs in the North more hostile to slavery than northern Democrats. Northern Whig voters often saw slavery as sinful and, like other sinful practices, within reach of government control; most northern Democrats believed that, however deplorable slavery was, it was none of the government's business what southerners did with their local institutions.

These outlooks in turn appealed to different cultural and religious groups. Whig policies attracted evangelical Protestants, who considered politics a valid arena for moral reform. Democratic laissez faire appealed to Catholics, Episcopalians, and free thinkers—all groups that preferred government to pursue a hands-off policy toward personal behavior and rejected politics based on morality. Because many New Englanders belonged to evangelical denominations, areas with a New England stamp voted Whig. Many of the recent immigrants were Catholics, and they generally joined the party of Jackson.

But as the election of 1832 approached, many of these distinctions were only beginning to emerge. Jackson's opponents, meeting in convention at Baltimore, nominated Clay. The Jackson supporters in turn renominated their hero, but selected Martin Van Buren as his running mate in place of Calhoun. The vice president by now was in Jackson's bad graces. His wife, the snobbish Floride Calhoun, had snubbed Peggy Eaton, wife of Secretary of War John Eaton, who she believed was a loose woman. The president liked Peggy, and besides, remembering his own beloved Rachel's suffering under the false gossip of his enemies, he sympathized with her plight. He was also angry at the vice president for defending South Carolina's nullification position. Besides the two major parties, the Anti-Masons were in the field with William Wirt of Maryland as their candidate.

The chief issue in the campaign was ostensibly the Bank of the United States and the Jackson veto of the recharter bill. Actually, personalities were still vital to the voters. They were either utterly charmed by Clay—"Old Coon," "Harry of the West," "The Mill Boy of the Slashes"—or repelled by his easygoing ways, his drinking, and his card playing. Jackson was to some voters a great national hero; to others, the imperious and impetuous King Andrew. In the end the president won a decisive victory, with Clay second and Wirt a poor third.

Economic Ups and Downs.   The outstanding political event of Jackson's second term was the slow, agonizing death of the Bank of the United States. The president interpreted his election victory as a mandate to proceed immediately against the bank, even though its charter left it four more years of life. Disregarding the advice of two successive secretaries of the treasury, he ordered the removal of government deposits from the bank. These funds he then placed in twenty-three state-chartered banks especially favored by the Democrats, which the Whigs promptly labeled "pet banks."

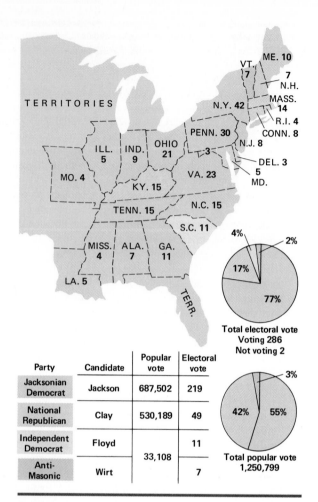

Party	Candidate	Popular vote	Electoral vote
Jacksonian Democrat	Jackson	687,502	219
National Republican	Clay	530,189	49
Independent Democrat	Floyd	33,108	11
Anti-Masonic	Wirt		7

Election of 1832

Nicholas Biddle considered the administration's actions vindictive and determined to fight back no matter what the cost. "My own course is decided," he wrote a friend. "All the other Banks and all the merchants may break, but the bank of the United States shall not break." In the next months the BUS reduced its loans and called in those already outstanding, creating a credit squeeze that caused businessmen severe hardship. Actually, Biddle had few alternatives. With the treasury's $10 million removed from its reserves, the bank had to contract. But Biddle's determination to demonstrate the bank's importance to the country's prosperity made him forget his former principles of responsible and public-spirited financial management, and he contracted faster and further than strictly necessary.

Worse was soon to come. The Biddle contraction did not last long enough to set off a major financial crisis. But with the Bank of the United States no longer regulating the country's credit and money supply, a major source of financial restraint was gone. The pet banks, with millions in government money in their reserves, began to lend extrav-

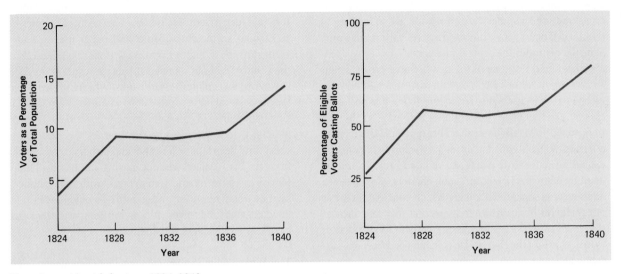

Voters in presidential elections, 1824–1840

Note: The graph on the left reflects the widening franchise. The graph on the right suggests increased voter interest: of those who had the right to vote, a larger portion actually exercised it.

Source: Historical Statistics of the United States, Colonial Times to 1957.

agantly. Businessmen and speculators promptly invested their borrowed money in western lands, while states initiated ambitious canal-building schemes. The nation experienced a runaway boom that drove all prices, especially those of land, to record heights.

Jackson was dismayed. He had not struck down Biddle's "monster" only to see it replaced by a state bank system that was even more irresponsible and dangerous. Nor did Jackson wish to see the notes of the Bank of the United States, which were backed by gold, replaced by "wildcats" of a hundred banks that were little more than vague promises to pay. To halt the unhealthy boom, the president issued the Specie Circular in July 1836. Henceforth, he announced, the federal government would accept only gold and silver in payment for public lands.

The Specie Circular pricked the bubble. The public abruptly lost confidence in the notes issued by the state banks and fought to convert them into specie. Hoping to hold on to their gold, the banks in turn tried to call in their loans. Other creditors, fearful of the future, refused to lend further and clamped down on debtors. The result was a severe panic that halted business and brought down prices with a resounding crash. A decade of hard times followed.

Recent scholarship has absolved the Specie Circular of some of the blame for the panic and ensuing economic depression and has pointed to the collapse of international cotton prices as a major culprit. Jackson's supporters blamed the panic on "overbanking and overtrading." But many contemporaries condemned the president and criticized his hard-money and antibank policies. Fortunately

for the Democrats, the full force of the economic collapse did not make itself felt until 1837, and so did not affect the 1836 presidential election.

★ POLITICS AFTER JACKSON ★

The Van Buren Administration. The 1836 contest was a confused affair. The Whigs, not yet a solid party, selected several regional candidates, including Webster of Massachusetts and Hugh Lawson White of Tennessee. Their strategy, masterminded by Biddle, was to run local candidates strong in a particular area, with the hope that (as in 1824) the election would be thrown into the House of Representatives. William Henry Harrison, the former governor of the Indiana Territory, received the Anti-Mason endorsement. The better-organized Democrats, required by the two-term tradition to pass over their leader, nominated Vice President Martin Van Buren. Their convention did not adopt a formal platform, but Van Buren pledged to follow in Jackson's footsteps. On this basis he won a comfortable victory in the fall.

Scarcely was the new president installed in office when the full force of the economic storm broke. Van Buren called Congress into special session to deal with the emergency, but he proposed little beyond a scheme to end all government connection with banks, central and pet alike. In a classic statement of the laissez-faire, let-alone position, he noted that government was "not intended to confer special favors on individuals or on any classes of them to create systems of agriculture, manufacturers, or trade, or to engage in them. . . . The less government interferes with private pursuits the better for the general prosperity."

The timid response of the new Democratic president lends support to the label "laissez-fairist" that had been attached to the Jacksonians. But as if to refute this neat conclusion, Jacksonians in the states ignored Van Buren's philosophy. In Massachusetts and Pennsylvania Democratic administrations stepped in to rescue the local economy by extending state aid to canal and railroad projects and by handing out many new corporation charters. Most western and southern states did not initiate such policies; but it was not solely for philosophical reasons that they failed to aid distressed business groups. As one witty scholar has said, in many parts of the country Jackson men had "feet of Clay" and had few scruples against supporting business enterprise. The deterrents were practical. Already deep in debt for the canal and road projects they had sponsored during the boom, western and southern states were finding it hard to pay the interest. By the end of 1842 nine states had defaulted on their bonds.

For the rest of Van Buren's ill-starred term the politicians remained preoccupied with the economy and economic legislation. To aid the treasury during the crisis, Congress ended the government's recently adopted policy of distributing to the states federal surpluses derived from excise taxes, the tariff, and land sales. In 1837 Van Buren proposed a scheme for a separate federal financial depository not dependent on banks. The proposal expressed Jacksonian suspicion of banks and paper money, and it seemed to the Whigs a primitive system that would leave the country without a financial balance wheel or an effective means to regulate the state banks. Whigs and Democrats fought over the issue until 1840, when the Democrats in Congress managed to establish the Independent Treasury System. Under this measure the treasury was required to collect and keep federal revenues and disburse them at need from its own vaults without relying on private banks. Moreover, government transactions with the public— salaries, taxes, bounties, and so forth—would now be confined to gold and silver. It was a primitive system that handicapped business and commerce.

The Whigs Take Power. As the 1840 presidential election approached, the usual maneuvering for position began. Van Buren, despite his spotty record and the bad times, had few opponents among the Democrats. On the Whig side the logical choice was Henry Clay, but the Whigs were wary of selecting a man too closely identified with the political battles of the past and with well-defined views. At the Whigs' first national convention, in December 1839, the delegates passed over Clay. Instead, as has frequently been the case with the weaker party, they turned to a nonpolitician without strong political commitments: William Henry Harrison.

The mass political rally, such as this one held in Cincinnati shortly before election day, was a central part of Whig strategy in the 1840 campaign. An arch was erected across Main Street for the event, and Harrison flags and banners were widely evident.

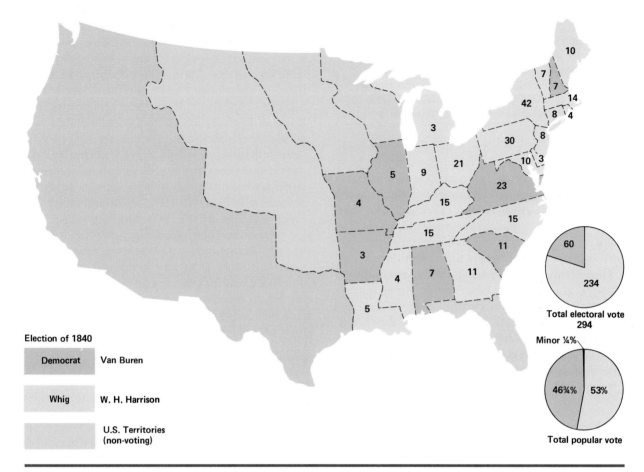

Election of 1840

Democrat	Van Buren
Whig	W. H. Harrison
U.S. Territories (non-voting)	

Total electoral vote
294

Minor ¼%

Total popular vote

ELECTION OF 1840

Harrison, though now sixty-seven, had a number of distinct advantages. He was the first "most available" man. A southerner by birth, he was sure to win many votes in the South that might otherwise go to the Democrats. He was also a military hero—having defeated Tecumseh's forces at Tippecanoe in 1811—and after Jackson, the Whigs had good reason to recognize the advantages of military renown. Most important of all, Harrison had no known political principles. For a party that had lost once by running its most representative figure, the obscurity of his views was a distinct asset.

The campaign revealed how well the Whigs had adapted to the sharp political partisanship that had appeared since 1828. The candidate, the party leaders concluded, would be kept from expressing his ideas on any controversial issue. Let Harrison "say not one single word about his principles or his creed," advised Nicholas Biddle. "Let no committee, no convention, no town meeting ever extract from him a single word about what he thinks or will do hereafter." The Whigs' major problem, besides their candidate, was their aristocratic image. Fortunately, a careless remark by a prominent Democrat—that if Harrison were given a pension, a barrel of hard cider, and a log cabin to live in, he would never run for president—bailed them out. The Whigs immediately seized on the snobbery implied by the characterization. Picturing the wealthy Harrison as a simple man and a true democrat, they painted Van Buren as an aristocrat who lived in lordly style on his estate in Kinderhook, New York. According to a Whig campaign song:

> Tippecanoe has no chariot to ride in,
> No palace of marble has he to reside in,
> No bags of gold eagles, no lots of fine clothes—
> But he has a wealth far better than those;
> The love of a nation, free, happy, and true
> Are the riches and portion of Tippecanoe.

On the other hand:

> Proud Martin rides forth in his splendor and pride,
> And broad are his lands upon Kinderhook side,
> The roof of a palace is over his head,
> And his table with plate and with dainties is spread;
> But a log cabin shelters a patriot true,
> 'Tis the home of our hero, bold Tippecanoe!

The "Log Cabin and Hard Cider" campaign was the first time a political party successfully marshaled the powerful forces of ballyhoo and propaganda to sell a presidential candidate to the American people. The Whigs dressed up supporters as Indians to advertise Harrison's victory over Tecumseh. They distributed vast quantities of cider to thirsty voters. Whig party workers organized enormous parades with bands, giant banners, flaming torches, and flags.

The vote was huge—almost 60 percent greater than in 1836—and it was strongly Whig. Harrison and his running mate, John Tyler of Virginia, carried nineteen of the twenty-six states and received 53 percent of the popular vote, an unusually high proportion for this period. The opposition had succeeded in the difficult task of turning an incumbent president out of office and had demonstrated the vitality of the newly revived party system.

★ CONCLUSIONS ★

By 1840 two new political parties had come into being. After a long gap that saw government become the preserve of public-spirited gentlemen, the people once more insisted on being heard. The change was not Jackson's doing: It had begun years before, in the states. Jackson was its beneficiary, not its author.

The two new parties seemed to parallel those of Hamilton's and Jefferson's time. Whigs and Democrats superficially resembled Federalists and Jeffersonian Republicans, respectively—without the powdered hair and velvet knee breeches. But on closer examination we see that the reality was different. Neither party was as closely associated with a single class as their predecessors. There was a difference in the parties' social focus: Democrats probably won the support of more small farmers than the Whigs, and because small farmers were a majority of Americans, this made them in some sense the party of the common people. But we should not make too much of this tendency. In an age that professed to be democratic, both parties had to accept—or appear to accept—the voice of the "sovereign people."

The two new party organizations were not as clearly different in ideology as the old parties were, either. They disagreed over banks, tariffs, and internal improvements; but their leaders were apt to be more practical and accommodating than the Federalists and Jeffersonians. The emergence of the second party system marked the development of a pragmatic political consensus: Both parties would avoid extreme ideological positions and try to stand close to the political center. This tendency continues in the politics of our own day.

The arrivals and departures in Washington on March 4, 1829, indeed betokened something momentous, but not what Mrs. Smith and Senator Webster believed: Jackson's victory did not set off a revolution in the social and political order. But it did loosen the rigid political framework of the day. By refusing to accept the gentlemanly procedures of the Virginia dynasty, the Jacksonians revitalized American political life. After 1828 the country would once more have a lively and effective two-party system, and the change would make the nation's government more responsive to public needs and public wants. What Mrs. Smith and Senator Webster were seeing was the return of two-party government to American political life.

★★★★★★★ FOR FURTHER READING ★★★★★★★

George Dangerfield. *The Era of Good Feelings* (1952)
An elegantly written narrative history of the years between the War of 1812 and the rise of Jackson as a major political figure. Dangerfield gives the foreign affairs of this crucial period considerable attention.

Robert Remini. *Andrew Jackson* (1966)
Andrew Jackson was an ardent office-seeker from his early twenties onward. This biography concentrates on his role in strengthening the presidency, his deft handling of the Calhounites, the nullification crisis, and his battle with the BUS.

Thomas Govan. *Nicholas Biddle, Nationalist and Public Banker* (1959)
The public life of the BUS president during the years when the "Monster Bank" was locked in combat with "King" Andrew. Govan is pro-Bank and anti-Jackson, depicting Biddle as a public-spirited citizen and Jackson as a demagogue.

John William Ward. *Andrew Jackson: Symbol for an Age* (1955)
Ward's book deals with Jackson's popular image as a folk hero. By describing Fourth of July orations, popular songs, campaign speeches, and political cartoons, Ward shows us

how Jackson and Jacksonianism became an important cultural myth.

Arthur M. Schlesinger, Jr. *The Age of Jackson* (1945)

This is now the classic defense of Jacksonian democracy by a master of historical prose. It concludes that Jacksonianism was genuinely democratic and forward-looking, and that its source was the industrial East rather than the frontier West.

Marvin Meyers. *The Jacksonian Persuasion: Politics and Belief* (1957)

After considering the views of a host of representative Jacksonians, Meyers, in this subtle study, concludes that they were moralistic rather than materialistic, a conservative set of men who pined for an America long past.

Richard P. McCormick. *The Second American Party System: Party Formation in the Jacksonian Era* (1966)

It has often been said that the Jackson era saw an upsurge of voter participation in elections. McCormick uses actual election data to prove this assumption. He describes how the second party system actually came together during the 1820s and 1830s.

Lee Benson. *The Concept of Jacksonian Democracy: New York as a Test Case* (1961)

Written by one of the fathers of the ethnocultural school of political history. Benson claims that religion, culture, and ethnicity were more important determinants of party affiliation in New York during the second party system than class or occupation.

Ronald Formisano. *The Birth of Mass Political Parties: Michigan, 1827–1861* (1971)

A study of the second party system in a state where the ethnocultural interpretation of party choice works exceptionally well. By a student of Benson.

William W. Freehling. *Prelude to Civil War: The Nullification Controversy in South Carolina, 1816–1836* (1966)

Blending biography with economic, social, and political history, Freehling treats nullification primarily as a frightened reaction of the South Carolina planter class to abolitionism, which threatened to overthrow slave society.

Richard N. Current. *John C. Calhoun* (1963)

A short, well-written biography of the 1812 "War Hawk" who eventually became secretary of war, vice president, and ardent defender of southern minority "rights." Current devotes most of his book to Calhoun's political thought and its influence on his time.

Grant Foreman. *Indian Removal: The Emigration of the Five Civilized Tribes of Indians* (1932)

Foreman tells the story of the forced migration of the Choctaws, Creeks, Chickasaws, Cherokees, and Seminoles from their homes in the Southeast to Oklahoma. His sympathies lie with the Indians, who were terrorized and defrauded by state governments and white settlers. Includes maps and illustrations.

Marvin E. Gettleman. *The Dorr Rebellion: A Study in American Radicalism, 1833–1849* (1973)

In Jacksonian Rhode Island democratic political change came in a violent way. This is a study of a group of political reformers far more radical than the Jacksonians as a whole—in Gettleman's view. A sympathetic attempt to find native American radical roots, but not uncritical of the Dorr rebels.

Edward Pessen. *Jacksonian America: Society, Personality, and Politics* (1978)

A highly critical view of Jackson and the Jacksonians. Pessen denies most of the egalitarian virtues usually ascribed to both.

Charles Sellers. *The Market Revolution: Jacksonian America, 1815–1846* (1991)

A brilliant and original reinterpretation of Jacksonianism and of America in the Jackson era. Restores Jackson as the champion of the masses in an effort to hold back the forces of imperialistic capitalism.

11 ★

THE MEXICAN WAR AND EXPANSIONISM

Greed, Manifest Destiny, or Inevitability?

1803–06	Lewis and Clark Expedition to Pacific
1812	Astor establishes fur-trading post on Pacific in Oregon
1818	A treaty between Great Britain and the United States provides for joint occupation of Oregon Territory
1819	Adams-Onís Treaty establishes the western boundaries of the Louisiana Purchase
1823	Mexico grants Stephen Austin the right to settle in Texas with 300 American families
1836	Texas declares its independence from Mexico • Texans force captured Mexican leader Santa Anna to recognize the Texas Republic
1841	President Harrison dies and John Tyler becomes president
1842	Webster-Ashburton Treaty signed by Great Britain and the United States
1844	James K. Polk elected president
1845	Congress admits Texas into the Union • Anticipating war, Polk sends General Zachary Taylor and 4,000 troops to occupy Mexican territory on north bank of Rio Grande • Polk secretly authorizes American consul Thomas Larkin to encourage the secessionist movement in California • The Slidell Mission discusses Texas's southern boundary and offers to buy New Mexico and California for $30 million
1846	Mexico declares defensive war on the United States; Congress votes for war • The Oregon dispute with Great Britain is settled by treaty
1847	Polk authorizes General Winfield Scott to attack Vera Cruz and Mexico City
1848	The Mexican-American War ends with the Treaty of Guadalupe Hidalgo • Mexican Cession adds 339 million acres to U.S.
1850	Congress admits California into the Union

On May 11, 1846, the clerk of the House of Representatives read the war message of President James K. Polk to a solemn joint session of Congress. The message was expected. Rumors had been circulating for weeks that a break with Mexico was imminent. Just two days before, people in Washington had learned that Mexican troops had crossed the Rio Grande del Norte and attacked American army units on its northern bank. Several Americans had been killed, and others injured.

"The cup of forebearance had been exhausted before the recent information from the frontier of the Del Norte," the president declared. "But now, after reiterated menaces, Mexico has passed the boundary of the United States, has invaded our territory and shed American blood upon American soil. She has proclaimed that hostilities have commenced, and that the two nations are now at war." "By every consideration of duty and patriotism," the president concluded, Americans must "vindicate with decision the honor, the rights, and the interests of their country."

Congress voted for war by an overwhelming majority, yet many representatives and senators were uneasy with the decision. During the next weeks and months, United States forces would go from triumph to triumph in a crescent of territory that stretched 2,000 miles from the Gulf of Mexico to the Oregon boundary; but many Americans would denounce the war. In Congress, Senator Thomas Corwin of Ohio would describe it as blatant aggression, unjustified by anything except greed. "If I were a Mexican I would tell you," he trumpeted to his Senate colleagues, "'Have you not room in your own country to bury your dead men? If you come into mine we will greet you with bloody hands, and welcome you to hospitable graves.'" In the House a young Illinois Whig, Abraham Lincoln, would call the president "a bewildered, confounded, and miserably perplexed man" with a "painful" conscience. Lincoln would spend much of his single term in Congress demanding that Polk prove his allegations that the Mexicans had provoked the war by attacking Americans on their own soil.

Outside Congress other critics were quite as negative. New Englander James Russell Lowell's fictional Yankee spokesman, Hosea Biglow, called the attack on Mexico "a national crime committed on behoof of slavery." An ardent enemy of slavery, Lowell was certain that the "slave power" was determined to seize Mexican territory "so's to lug new slave states in." Henry Thoreau, who valued Mexico as a refuge for escaped slaves, considered the American invasion justification for "honest men to rebel and revolutionize."

Different theories of the war's origins are implied by these charges. In Lincoln and Corwin's view the conflict was an instance of naked United States aggression against a weaker neighbor. Thoreau and Lowell's Hosea Biglow saw the war as the result of a southern slaveholders' plot. Modern scholars, too, have advanced competing theories of causation. One recent supporter of the slavepower position is Eugene Genovese, who perceives the cotton South as forced to expand territorially or suffer from declining profits as its soils lost their fertility and cotton ceased to produce abundant wealth. Another modern economic interpretation of the Mexican War emphasizes American interest in acquiring Pacific ports in order to establish commercial connections with the Far East. In this view it is the business classes of the North that provided much of the impetus to expansion.

Other historians are more inclined to see Americans as inspired in 1846 by the ideological attitude of continentalism, or Manifest Destiny, which justified United States dominion over the continent—indeed, made it seem inevitable—on grounds of supposed American cultural, political, or even racial superiority. Mexican scholars agree in ascribing the war to America's sense of superiority, though they also blame it on Yankee greed. In either case, they insist, the United States was a blatant aggressor.

A final school of interpretation seeks to avoid simple praise or blame. In this view the pre–Civil War expansionist impulse was the expression of what was almost a physical law. To the west of the growing, vibrant United States, it says, lay a sparsely populated and loosely governed expanse of territory. It was almost an empty region in a political and social sense, and American expansion into it resembled the rush of air to fill a vacuum. The war, in this view, was an inevitable event arising out of the unavoidable circumstances of history and geography.

The Mexican War marked the last phase of continental expansion that carried the American people to the Pacific. The war itself added 530,000 square miles of territory to the United States, and the related settlement of the Oregon boundary dispute with Great Britain added another 258,000. The total addition was truly imperial in extent, but was it also imperialist in origin? Was it greed—for ports or more cotton lands—that led President Polk to send his war message to Congress that day in early May? Was it misperceived idealism? Or was it the working out of some sort of geopolitical law?

★ THE OREGON COUNTRY ★

In 1830 the line marking the western edge of dense agricultural settlement in the United States did not extend much beyond the bottomlands of the Mississippi River. Farmers had already moved out along the banks of the Missouri, Arkansas, and Red rivers well into the states of Missouri, Arkansas, and Louisiana. But with the exception of these projections of white settlement, almost all of the trans-Mississippi West remained the domain of the Indian tribes. Beyond the western boundary of the Louisiana Purchase was a vast region of mountain, desert, plateau, and rocky ocean coast still barely touched by European culture and institutions.

Political title to much of this region was uncertain. In 1819 the Adams-Onís Treaty had settled the boundary between American and Spanish possessions and surrendered Spanish claims in the Oregon country to the Americans. But title to Oregon—a vast expanse including present-day Oregon, Washington, Idaho, British Columbia, and parts of Montana and Wyoming—remained in dispute between Great Britain and the United States. British claims rested on the voyages of Captains James Cook in the 1770s and George Vancouver in the 1790s, and on the activities of Canadian and British fur companies. American claims had a similar basis in discovery. For years before Vancouver's voyage, American merchant vessels had periodically visited the northern Pacific coast. In April 1792 Captain Robert

Gray had discovered the Columbia River, which was named after his vessel. Then, in 1805–1806 Lewis and Clark had wintered at the mouth of the Columbia.

Until the 1840s, however, the region called Oregon had no more than a handful of white inhabitants. A vast territory extending from the northern boundary of California to the southern boundary of Russian America (Alaska) at 54° 40′ north latitude, it was the home of many Indian tribes belonging to diverse cultures. Along the coast were the salmon-fishing, wood-working tribes, the Tlingits, Haida, Kwakiutl, and Salish. In the interior plateau the Flatheads and Nez Perces fished along the streams and gathered roots and berries. Some of these tribes would cooperate with the whites; others would resist. In the end, as on so many other frontiers, all would be pushed aside.

Despite the presence of no more than a few hundred Americans, the United States guarded its claim to the Oregon region jealously. In 1818 Secretary of State John Quincy Adams negotiated a convention with the British providing for joint occupation of Oregon for ten years. In 1827 the Anglo-American occupation was extended for an indefinite period, subject to termination by either party on a year's notice.

Lieutenant Henry Warre came to Oregon in 1845 with an expedition of the Hudson's Bay company intended to protect British claims and bolster British defenses. Sketches made by Warre on his journey—like this view of the settlement at Oregon City—give a fascinating glimpse of frontier life.

The Far Western Fur Trade. Ultimately the dispute over Oregon was resolved not by diplomacy but by actual white settlement. But as on so many other frontiers, before the settlers—and preparing the way for them—came the fur traders. Ever since the beginnings of English North American colonization in the seventeenth century, the quest for animal pelts had spurred geographical expansion. As early as the 1780s the fur trade had reached the Pacific Northwest after leaping over much arid intervening terrain. For the next thirty years the beautiful skins of the Pacific sea otter attracted American merchants, who made the Oregon coast a stopping place on their way to China, where the pelts were highly prized.

Several groups of businessmen were involved in the far northwestern fur trade. In Oregon the impresario was John Jacob Astor, a German-born entrepreneur who had come to the United States in 1783. Starting as a clerk in a New York City store, Astor soon became a successful fur merchant and entered the Oregon trade shortly after the United States acquired the Louisiana Territory. In 1811 he established a trading post at the mouth of the Columbia, which he named—in his characteristically modest way—Astoria. The post flourished briefly until the threat of British attack during the War of 1812 forced its sale to a Canadian firm. Thereafter Astor confined his fur-trading operations to the Great Lakes region.

After the war two fur-trading companies, the British-owned Hudson's Bay Company and the American-owned North West Company, entered the Oregon country. The English company built European-type forts where white employees lived apart and refused to adapt to the Indian way of life. The North Westers accepted the necessity of providing the Indians with gifts, of feasting with them, and of avoiding any hint of force or coercion. After competing bitterly for a while, the two companies merged in 1821. Soon afterward the new Hudson Bay Company established Fort Vancouver on the north bank of the Columbia River in what is now Washington State. Placed in charge of the new settlement was Dr. John McLoughlin, a man of intelligence and strong personality. McLoughlin soon set about the task of nailing down Britain's claim to the Oregon region and excluding the Americans.

Meanwhile, farther east, in the Rocky Mountain region, another group of Americans, under Missourian William Ashley, was uncovering new fur-bearing regions in what is now southwestern Wyoming. Ashley saw that to make a profit he needed not only a new source of furs but also a new method of collecting them. In the past, Indians had been the trappers, trading the furs to white agents. But beginning in the spring of 1825, Ashley sent his own employees to roam the newly opened region for furs. Under Ashley's successors in the Rocky Mountain Fur Company,

as many as 600 "mountain men" of American, French, Mexican, black, and mixed Indian-European backgrounds spent the year in the mountain wilds, many of them with their Indian wives and children. In the spring the trappers hunted the beaver along streams. In July they gathered at a "rendezvous," where they exchanged their "hairy bank notes" for cloth, rifles and shot, trinkets, food, liquor, and other commodities brought west by the company. Cut off from others for months at a time by the deep snows and fiercely cold winters, the mountain men turned the July meetings into wild debauches. After a week or two of heavy drinking, gambling, fighting, and general hell-raising, the trappers and their families staggered off to rest for the coming hard year. The company agents returned east with furs worth twenty times their cost.

The Way West. The western fur trade helped open the trans-Missouri region for white settlement. Agents and officials of the fur companies—Kit Carson, Jim Bridger, Milton and William Sublette, and others—ranged widely through the Great Plains, Rocky Mountain, and Great Basin regions, marking convenient routes, exploring rivers, and discovering new passes through the mountains. In 1823 one of Ashley's agents, Jedediah Smith, found South Pass, a major break in the towering mountains that blocked the overland route west. The following year Peter Ogden, of the Hudson's Bay Company, was the first white man to view the Great Salt Lake. The fur traders opened the country in still another way. By bringing to the Indians the whites' ways, their superior technology, their vices, and their diseases, they helped erode the Indians' customs and institutions, and reduced their ability to resist the intruders.

Not all the explorations of the trans-Missouri region facilitated settlement. In 1806 Zebulon Pike returned from a government-authorized expedition through the High Plains and called the area too dry for cultivation. After a trip to the same region in 1820, Stephen Long, of the United States Topographical Engineers, named it the Great American Desert. The land was "wholly unfit for cultivation, and . . . uninhabitable by a people depending upon agriculture for their subsistence," Long wrote. His account of a Great American Desert just to the east of the mountains helped delay settlement for decades and turned people's eyes to the well-watered, forested lands of Oregon farther west.

The first Americans to make permanent homes in the Oregon country were Methodist missionaries who came in the 1830s to the Willamette Valley, south of the Columbia, to bring the Christian God and European notions of morality to the Indians. During the hard times of the 1840s, when farm prices were low, reports of cheap Oregon land and of insatiable markets for agricultural produce in Asia created an "Oregon fever" throughout the West. By 1845 there were over 5,000 Americans living in Oregon.

The journey of these Oregon pioneers was a rugged overland trek across hundreds of miles of dangerous, inhospitable country. Typically, the trip was made by families. By one estimate half the emigrants on the Oregon Trail were women and children. Each spring, beginning in 1841, eager Oregon-bound families assembled in Independence, Missouri, the jumpoff point for the trip west. The settlers traveled in canvas covered farm wagons, which had served Americans since colonial days. Into these vehicles they crammed supplies and as much equipment as they could carry. Oxen in teams of six drew the wagons, while women and older children—at least in good weather—walked. The men either drove or rode saddle horses to scout for game and potential danger.

Each party, moving in a broad train several wagons wide, was commanded by a captain elected by the men. Some of these men were skilled guides who had made the trip before or were natural leaders. Others, however, were incompetents who had to be replaced in mid-journey. The going at first was easy. The lush green lands of the eastern portion of the Oregon Trail were level and pleasant to cross. Three hundred miles from Independence, however, the pioneers reached the Platte River, in present-day Nebraska, a shallow stream "too thick to drink and too thin to plow." Full of quicksand, it was dangerous to ford. After 500 miles of rolling grass-covered plain, the travelers encountered the Rocky Mountains. Here the real challenges began. At times the wagons bounced over terrain so rocky that the trail was covered with blood from the oxen's lacerated hooves. At many spots the men were forced to put their own shoulders to the wagons and push them along by brute strength. At this point, over the side would generally go all heavy gear—plows, stoves, tables, sofas, even pianos—that optimistic emigrants had stowed in hopes of making their new lives more comfortable. Finally, at the Dalles in what is now central Oregon, the travelers reached the Columbia River. After caulking the wagons' seams to make them watertight, they floated down the great river to their destination, the fertile and well-watered valley of the Willamette River.

Women found the trip particularly hard. To many the most difficult part was leaving behind familiar places and loved ones. "Nothing can atone for the loss of society of friends," wrote Anne Booth in her trail journal. Women tried to recreate the familiar by arranging their family wagons as small mobile homes. Nonetheless, the long trip was a trial for eastern women, who normally led sheltered lives. But it did have its compensations. The trail community was a foretaste of the new pioneer society that the emigrants were about to create, and like that society it lacked many of the rigid gender distinctions of the East. Women on the trail were essential for survival on a day-to-day basis. They often had to take on what were normally male responsibilities, such as hunting or scouting or using a rifle to protect the wagon train. Such roles were especially unavoidable when, as all too frequently happened, husbands or fathers died of disease or accident along the way.

The British in Oregon watched this American influx uneasily at first. The settlers were clearly reinforcing the American claim to the Oregon country. The British were virtually all employees of the Hudson's Bay Company; nowhere could they match the Americans in numbers. It soon became clear that the British had lost the competition

THE SUMMER RENDEZVOUS.

The yearly rendezvous between mountain men and fur company agents quickly turned into debauchery, since the trappers received whiskey as payment for their furs. Although wild and solitary, these men helped open the Oregon country to traders, missionaries, and settlers.

Severe hardships awaited those who took the way west. Many emigrants lost their possessions in turbulent rivers or quicksand. Others succumbed to the harsh weather and fierce terrain of the Rocky Mountains.

south of the Columbia, where in any case the beaver had been trapped out. At this point McLoughlin generously helped the settlers in the Willamette region by providing jobs and other aid. In effect, the company surrendered what is now the state of Oregon to the Americans, though it continued for a while to oppose American entry into the region further north.

Before long, excluding Americans from that area began to seem hopeless, too. In 1845 the Hudson's Bay director, fearing for the safety of his valuable stores across the river from the American settlements, moved the firm's chief base to Vancouver Island in what is now British Columbia. The British had virtually conceded that the Americans would control the whole block of territory between Puget Sound and the California boundary.

★ THE MEXICAN BORDERLAND ★

For a generation preceding the migration to Oregon a few Americans had been drawn to the Southwest, where Mexico, formerly a Spanish colony, loosely held a million square miles of territory. Hundreds of miles distant from the capital city in the south, the Mexican borderland from Texas to California was a generally arid region. But within its limits there were tracts, such as east Texas and the great Central Valley of California, where the land was well watered and enterprising farmers could raise lush crops.

The Native People. At the time it began to arouse American interest, most of the borderland had few American inhabitants. About half the population was Indian. In Texas the Comanche, Apache, Kiowa, and other tribes were nomadic peoples who for centuries had hunted buffalo on foot with bow and arrow. During the late seventeenth century they had acquired horses from Spanish Mexico, and then rifles. These new possessions improved their prowess as hunters; they also made them formidable foes of both their Indian neighbors and the Spaniards who began to push up from Mexico after 1700.

Farther to the west, in what is now New Mexico and Arizona, were the Zuñis, Acomas, Hopis, and several other tribes grouped under the name Pueblo Indians. Dependent on agriculture, they lived in densely populated, settled communities (pueblos) with mud-brick (adobe) structures that resembled modern apartment houses. These dwellings sometimes rose to four stories and were often grouped around central plazas used for ceremonies and communal events. The Pueblo tribes were generally peaceful people; they seldom waged offensive war against their neighbors, though they were capable of fighting fiercely for their homes and rights.

Still farther west, along the Pacific in what is now California, was an Indian population composed of many tribal groups. When the whites arrived in the eighteenth century, as many as 350,000 California Indians were spread through the narrow Pacific coastal plain, in the interior valleys, and along the lower reaches of the region's rivers. The

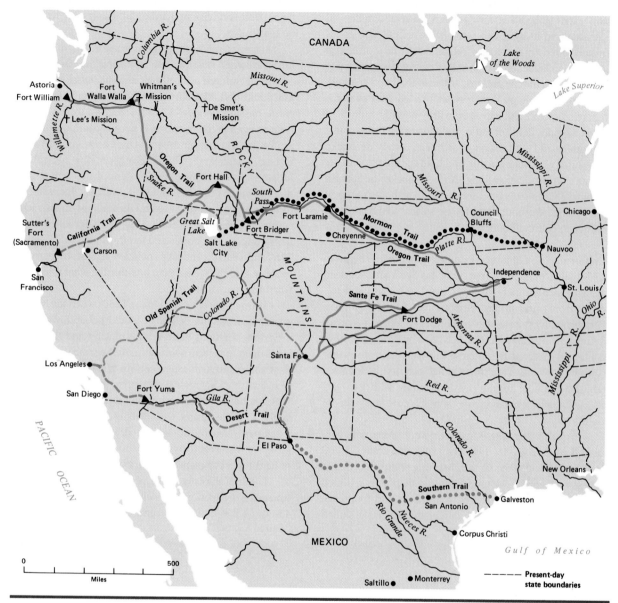

TRAILS TO THE WEST

California tribes had a simple economy and technology, though they were expert basket-weavers. The abundant acorns, from which nutritious flour could be prepared, and the warm climate simplified living and made agriculture and elaborate clothing and shelter unnecessary. Though their material possessions were meager, the California Indians had developed a complex religious and ceremonial life, and a rich oral literature of songs, stories, and myths passed on from generation to generation.

Spanish Penetration. The remainder of the region's population consisted of people of Spanish background or mixed Spanish-Indian ancestry. The earliest Spanish settlers had come to the interior of the Southwest around 1600, when parties of soldiers from Mexico established Santa Fe in what is now central New Mexico. Soon afterward, a different kind of Spanish penetration took over. On every previous Spanish frontier soldiers had led the way and missionaries had followed. Now missionaries preceded the military, pushing into every corner of the present-day American Southwest.

The pattern soon became standardized. A Spanish friar of the Dominican, Franciscan, or Jesuit order would set off with a few Indian dependents for an unsettled region. When he had located a favorable spot, he went back to "civilization" and gathered a few soldiers, several families of Christianized Indians, and some fellow friars. He then returned with them to the new frontier, where he rounded up local Indian labor and constructed a community consisting of an adobe church, gardens, blacksmith shop, gristmill, and other workshops. If all went well, in a decade or so the friars had established a mission with vineyards, cultivated fields of grain, herds of cattle, and clusters of Indian huts, all dominated by a mission church, elaborately decorated to beautify Christian worship and hold the attention of the Indian converts. Before long this new pocket of Spanish colonial civilization would send out other shoots to repeat the process and contribute to the steady advance of the European cultural frontier.

California. In California the missionary process began in 1769 when Franciscan friar Junípero Serra and fourteen brown-robed brothers led a party of 126 Indians and soldiers from present-day Arizona to San Diego Bay. Dispatched by the Spanish authorities to forestall Russian designs on the California coast claimed by Spain, the move combined imperial self-interest with the desire to gather souls for the Lord. Over the next half century the friars established another twenty missions, along with two garrisoned towns (*presidios*), in what is now the state of California.

In many ways these missions were immensely successful enterprises. By 1800 they sheltered some 13,000 Indians and had taken on the charming physical form that tourists see today: whitewashed churches with red-tiled roofs, courtyards with arched colonnades and fountains, and ingenious workshops containing the artifacts of skilled Indian artisans. It is also easy to imagine the vineyards, grain fields, fruit and olive orchards, and vast grazing herds that no longer exist.

But there was another, grimmer side. Infant mortality in the crowded missions was appalling. In 1820, 86 percent of all children born at the California missions died before adulthood. Mortality as a whole was high. During the entire mission period—1769 to 1833—a total of 82,000 Indians lived in the missions. A normal death rate for such a population in this period would have been around 40,000. Instead, there were 62,000 deaths among the mission Indians. Nor was this the full extent of the demographic disaster visited on the California Indians. The whites as usual brought their diseases and their almost equally lethal culture. The former killed directly; the latter killed by undermining Indian morale and family life. All told, between 1769 and 1846 the Indian population of California dropped to about 100,000—less than one-third of what it had been when the friars first arrived.

The mission era ended in the 1830s when the Mexican government, at the behest of would-be landowners, deprived the missions of thousands of acres and threw their lands open to private ownership. At the same time it ended the friars' paternal but stern control over the Indians. In the next few years aggressive entrepreneurs established some 700 ranchos, each covering thousands of acres. Devoted largely to cattle raising, each giant estate was controlled by a *ranchero*, usually of Spanish descent, who supervised groups of *vaqueros* (cowboys), who did the common labor of herding, fence mending, branding, and slaughtering.

Life in California in the years immediately preceding American occupation was colorful and, for the *rancheros*, almost idyllic. Little news came from the outside world to

San Francisco at the time of the Gold Rush. No cable cars, no Fisherman's Wharf— but the magnificent Bay is the same.

disturb the few thousand Spanish-Mexicans in their pursuit of pleasure amid the abundance provided by their lands and the delights of the region's climate. Government in Mexico City was remote, and its hand rested lightly on the inhabitants. If we can believe the accounts of visitors, the life of the small Spanish elite was a round of fiestas, races, dancing, and courtship rituals.

Americans in small numbers began to drift into California in the 1830s, attracted by the climate and the carefree life. Some, such as Thomas Larkin and the part-black William Leidesdorf, came by sea and established themselves as merchants in Monterey, San Diego, and other towns. Others came overland by way of the California Trail and became successful ranchers. Europeans came, too. The Swiss John Augustus Sutter arrived in Monterey in 1839 and talked the Spanish governor into granting him a vast domain near present-day Sacramento, which he named New Helvetia in honor of his homeland. Many of the newcomers converted to Catholicism and married into prosperous Spanish families.

The affluence of the *rancheros*, whether Spanish or American, was not matched by that of the majority of Californians. For the former mission Indians, life was scarcely better than before. Freed from bondage to the friars, they were recruited by the *rancheros* as laborers and spent long days purifying tallow, tanning hides, and loading skins onto ships for markets in the United States and Europe. They were paid nothing for their labor beyond their food, clothing, and shelter. If they left the ranch, they were hunted down like runaway slaves. It is not surprising that the California Indian population continued to fall at an appalling rate.

New Mexico. California's political and cultural isolation was matched by that of another Mexican borderland, New Mexico. This region—bounded by the Louisiana Purchase on the north, the Mojave Desert on the west, and Texas on the east—was separated from the nearest settlements of northern Mexico by 600 miles of barren plains and rugged mountains. Like California, though a century and a half earlier, the region had been settled by friars who planted missions as centers of Christian civilization and incidentally as outposts to protect New Spain against the French in Louisiana.

Three hundred years before the Spanish arrived in New Mexico, the Zuñi Indians lived in adobe apartment houses, some four stories high with as many as 500 rooms. Their culture had a distinct identity and resisted the influence of Catholic missionaries. Tradition seems to live on in this 1873 photograph. (Collection of the New York Historical Society)

Unlike the indigenous peoples of California, the Indians of the New Mexico region were not easy to dominate. The mission system put down only shallow roots. The Pueblo Indians had no need of the friars. Though they acquired sheep and goats from the Spaniards, they kept their tight-knit agricultural communities intact, and to this day preserve a distinctive and strongly defined culture. Several Hopi pueblos are the oldest continuously occupied settlements in what is now the United States.

Whereas the Pueblo peoples managed to fend off the Spaniards by their cohesion, the nomadic Apache, Navaho, and Comanche tribes in the New Mexico–Arizona–west Texas region repelled the Europeans by their warlike qualities. Before the Spaniards came, these tribes preyed on the Pueblo Indians, stealing slaves and booty. When the Spaniards arrived about 1700, they too came under attack. Enmity between the Europeans and these fierce warriors was perpetuated by the Spaniards, who enslaved captured Indians and offered bounties for their scalps. At first, the Indians fought on foot; once they acquired horses from their enemies, they became formidable mounted warriors whose swift raids and quick retreats made them difficult to subdue. Indeed, not until the advent of the repeating revolver in the mid-nineteenth century would the European become the military equal of the Apache or Comanche horseman.

Despite these difficulties, the Spaniards succeeded in establishing several permanent communities in the New Mexico–Arizona region. By the 1820s New Mexico had about 40,000 settled inhabitants, many of them clustered around the provincial capital, Santa Fe. Like the Californians, these people (mixed Indian-Mexican-Spanish) were self-sufficient in food, but they were starved for manufactured goods that distant and economically undeveloped Mexico could not supply. American traders were happy to fill these needs in exchange for the gold, silver, and furs of the region. In the early 1820s a Missouri merchant, William Becknell, launched a lucrative trade in textiles, rifles, tools, and other goods between St. Louis and New Mexico by way of the Santa Fe Trail. By 1824 parties of as many as eighty men with a score of wagons and over a hundred pack animals were using the trail blazed by Becknell to carry goods to and from New Mexico.

Texas. The growing American influence in New Mexico and California was minor compared with the American impact in Texas, then an ill-defined region between Louisiana and the northern desert of Mexico. Like the other outlying Mexican provinces, Texas was sprinkled with a few missions and garrisons. Early in the nineteenth century Americans in small numbers began to cross the Sabine River into Spanish-held territory. In 1823 the Mexican Republic, newly independent from Spain, granted Stephen F. Austin

the right to bring in 300 American families as permanent settlers to help develop the region. The newcomers were required to be of high moral character and were to adopt the Catholic faith. In return, the Mexicans promised each family a free square league (about 4,000 acres) for farming and raising cattle. Austin's settlement was followed by others under various *empersarios*. Individuals also were attracted by the region's fertile land. Some brought slaves. Fearful of the flood of Americans, in 1830 the Mexican government prohibited further United States immigration. The law was not enforced, however, and by 1835 there were about 20,000 transplanted Americans living in Texas.

★ THE ANNEXATION OF TEXAS ★

Texas might have remained a contented province of Mexico but for difficulties that were not solely of the Texans' making. Religious and cultural differences between the American settlers and the Mexican officials played a part. The Americans were Protestant and resented efforts to convert them and to suppress Protestant worship. Most were southerners determined to grow cotton with slave labor, and they disliked Mexico's laws forbidding slavery. Moreover, most transplanted Americans disdained Mexicans as culturally or racially inferior. Yet despite these points of friction, the American settlers proved remarkably loyal to their adopted country. When, in 1826, a small band of dissident Americans led by Haden Edwards revolted against the central government, the main body of settlers under Austin helped the Mexican authorities put down the insurrection.

The Texas Revolution. Unfortunately, neither the citizens of the United States nor the Mexican government could let the Texan-Americans alone. In the United States many people regretted the surrender of Texas to Spain in the Adams-Onís Treaty of 1819. Six years later, as president, John Quincy Adams tried to undo his own work by offering Mexico $1 million for Texas. His successor, Andrew Jackson, raised the price to $5 million and sent Anthony Butler to Mexico City to pressure the Mexican government into accepting it. Butler tried to bribe Mexican officials; failing to do so, he urged Jackson to take Texas by force.

The Mexican government, too, could not let the Texans be. Its policies, including those regarding immigration, were infuriatingly inconsistent. Mexican officials, holding two competing philosophies of government, continually battled among themselves. "Federalists" advocated local autonomy for the individual Mexican states and weak control from Mexico City. This circle of politicians favored policies to encourage immigration. "Centralists," on the other hand, demanded tight, centralized government to hold the unwieldy country together. Centralists were generally unfriendly to immigration. When they held power, they revoked the provincial autonomy that made immigration attractive and feasible to Americans. These two groups—and innumerable other factions organized on ideological lines or around particular leaders—constantly squabbled. The country was frequently plunged into civil war; almost never was there a peaceful succession of administrations, and the government was seldom able to maintain any policy for very long.

The bewildering shifts of factions and leaders within the Mexican government had serious effects on the relations between Mexico and her newest citizens, the Texans. In 1834 Antonio Lopez de Santa Anna, who had first won and then lost power in the 1820s, became the nation's leader for the second time. Possessing an exceptional talent for detecting the latest political currents and riding them to

power, Santa Anna would be the leading figure in Mexican political life during the 1830s and 1840s. His return was bad for the Texans. Though originally a Federalist, he soon became a Centralist and a tyrant. In 1834 he rescinded the autonomy the Federalists had allowed the Mexican states and established a harsh dictatorship in Mexico City.

His rise to power worsened an already uncomfortable situation for the Texans. For some time the American settlers had been unhappy with their limited self-rule. Texas was part of the Mexican state of Coahuila with its capital at Satillo, 300 miles to the west, a great inconvenience to those subject to its authority in the distant northern region. Under the Federalists the Texans had hoped to achieve separate statehood for themselves, but now these hopes were dashed, and in fact there seemed a distinct possibility that the Mexican government might try to expel all Americans from Texas. When Santa Anna sent troops to garrison several points within Texas, these fears seemed vindicated.

THE TEXAS REVOLUTION

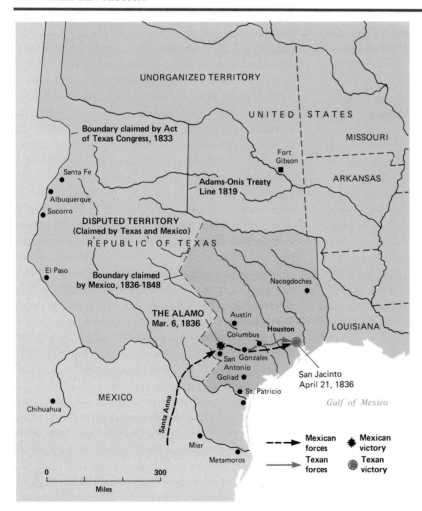

Sporadic fighting soon broke out between Texans and Mexican troops. Though there were special reasons for Mexican–Texan tensions, hostility to the Santa Anna government was widespread in Mexico generally, and other outlying parts of the republic were in revolt against the dictator as well.

In 1835 Santa Anna marched north with an army to punish the Texans and confiscate their arms. Waiting to stop him were 187 Texans commanded by William B. Travis, holed up in the Alamo, an adobe-walled former mission in San Antonio. In late February 1836 Santa Anna and 6,000 troops arrived at San Antonio and surrounded the small American force. The Americans held out for two weeks, but on March 6 they were overwhelmed by the Mexicans. Every defender, including Travis and the frontier heroes Jim Bowie and Davy Crockett, died in the siege. So did 1,500 Centralista troops. Just before the defeat, fifty-nine delegates, meeting in the little village of Washington, adopted a declaration of Texas independence, named Sam Houston (a former U.S. army officer and governor of Tennessee) commander in chief of the Texas army, and created a constitution that recognized slavery and granted each citizen a square league of land. All that remained was to transform these intentions into reality in the face of an apparently vastly superior Mexican military force.

In the next few weeks Houston and his men retreated before Santa Anna's army. Though the Texans were buoyed by their new rallying cry, "Remember the Alamo!" matters seemed discouraging. Actually, they were better than Houston and his lieutenants could know. Santa Anna's forces, composed of reluctant conscripts, old men, convicts, and Indians who could not speak Spanish, were racked by disease and close to exhaustion. As they chased the Texans eastward their fighting effectiveness dwindled. As Mexican strength declined, Texan strength grew, helped by American volunteers who crossed the border to join Houston's small army. At San Jacinto, Houston finally turned to face the enemy. At noon on April 21, 1836, his small band of 800 seasoned campaigners, shouting "Remember the Alamo," attacked the Mexicans and defeated them. Six hundred Mexicans were killed in the fighting and 730, including Santa Anna himself, were captured.

San Jacinto brought Texas its independence. Houston forced the Mexican leader to sign treaties ending the war and accepting the independence of Texas. When news of Santa Anna's defeat and capture reached Mexico City, the Mexican Congress promptly repudiated the agreements on the firm ground that they had been coerced. Little attention was given to the question of the boundaries of Texas. The Mexicans claimed it stopped at the Nueces; the Texans insisted that it reached to the Rio Grande, farther west. From the Mexican standpoint, Texas was still part of Mexico and the whole issue was irrelevant. Despite its renunciation of the treaties, however, Mexico was in no position to resume the war, and Texas settled down uneasily to a brief existence as an independent nation.

★ EXPANSIONISM: ADVOCATES AND OPPONENTS ★

The knotty problems of Oregon, of the Mexican borderland, and indeed of virtually all the boundaries of the United States fell into the lap of President John Tyler when he assumed office in April 1841. A dour and rigid Virginian and a former Democrat who had broken with Jackson over King Andrew's dictatorial ways, Tyler became president when William Henry Harrison contracted pneumonia and died a month after his inauguration. This was the first time a president had died in office, and it was not clear whether "His Accidency," as his opponents called Tyler, should exercise the full powers of a duly elected chief executive. The skepticism of Whigs was magnified by their knowledge that Tyler was really a Democrat who had been placed on the Whig ticket to win southern Democratic votes. Tyler refused to accept an inferior status and stubbornly and successfully asserted his full presidential prerogatives.

But in domestic matters Tyler's doggedness and vigor accomplished little. With Harrison in office, the Whigs had looked forward to rechartering a federal bank, raising the tariff, and carrying out other nationalistic measures. Congress was under Whig control and it seemed a rare opportunity to dismantle the Jackson program and enact their own. Congress did pass a new federal bank bill, but Tyler, true to his Jeffersonian states' rights principles, promptly vetoed it. In short order his entire cabinet, except Secretary of State Daniel Webster, who still had important diplomatic business to complete, resigned in protest. Thereafter, Tyler and the Whig leaders in Congress remained at loggerheads. The president vetoed two Whig efforts to raise the tariff and signed the Tariff Act of 1842 only after Henry Clay's pet scheme to distribute surplus federal revenues to the states had been eliminated from the bill. Having gotten the ball and their chance at making their domestic goals, the Whigs had fumbled.

In foreign affairs, where the Constitution allows the chief executive a freer hand, Tyler was more effective. The president was a moderate expansionist. As a southerner, he craved new territory within slavery's supposed "natural limits"—the region where cotton, sugar, rice, and other warm-climate, slave-grown crops could flourish. Such a place was Texas, where the American settlers were already using slave labor to produce bumper cotton crops. Tyler was indifferent to expansion elsewhere.

The president's attitude affected the course of negotiations with Britain over the disputed boundary between Canada and the states of Maine, New York, Vermont, and New Hampshire. In 1838 this disagreement had produced a violent clash when Maine tried to eject British subjects from parts of the Aroostook district claimed by the Canadian province of New Brunswick. For a while an undeclared Aroostook War raged between American and Canadian lumbermen and trappers in the dense forest along the boundary. Fortunately, more serious fighting was avoided when the Maine and New Brunswick authorities agreed to desist temporarily from further settlement.

The boundary dispute continued to fester, however, while other arguments with Britain accumulated. The unwillingness of the United States to join the British in suppressing the illegal Atlantic slave trade deeply offended British antislavery opinion. There was also the affair of the *Caroline*, an American-owned steamship hired by Canadian rebels to aid them in an uprising against British rule. Pro-British Canadian volunteers had crossed the border and destroyed the *Caroline* near Niagara Falls and, in the process, had killed one American citizen on American soil.

Rather than challenge the British in these matters, Tyler and Secretary of State Daniel Webster chose to be conciliatory. The British, too, preferred compromise, and the envoy they sent to negotiate with Webster, Lord Alexander Ashburton, was a pro-American banker married to an American woman. In a few short weeks the two men worked out a compromise in the Webster-Ashburton Treaty (1842). Under its terms the United States would keep about 4.5 million acres of the 7.7 million in dispute along the Canadian-American boundary; the province of New Brunswick would get the rest. In addition, the United States government agreed to join Britain in supporting a naval squadron stationed off the African coast to capture slave ships attempting to bring Africans to the Americas. In a supplementary exchange of notes Ashburton in effect also apologized for the *Caroline* incident.

Before the treaty could be adopted, however, Maine had to be satisfied. Webster accomplished this by showing the state authorities a long-lost map, supposedly drawn at the time of the 1783 peace treaty with Great Britain, that depicted the Canadian border as dipping far south into Maine. The United States, Webster observed, had made a better bargain than it deserved. Confronted by this information, Maine authorities withdrew their objections and the treaty was confirmed. Still, many northerners felt that the administration had been too weak, and they were right. A map discovered in 1933 clearly demonstrated that Maine's original claim was valid and that the United States had unnecessarily given away over 3 million acres of the national domain.

Tyler's rather tepid interest in northern real estate also applied to Oregon. Many Americans, especially northern Democrats, insisted that the United States rightfully owned all the Oregon country from the northern boundary of California at 42° north latitude to the southern boundary of Russian America at 54° 40′ north latitude. Tyler proposed to the British that Oregon be divided at the forty-ninth parallel. He would accept even less territory, he told them, if they would pressure Mexico to give the United States the excellent Pacific port of San Francisco. The British were unwilling to accept this arrangement, and the Oregon dispute remained unsettled.

Victory for Tyler. Tyler's major diplomatic success came in Texas. No sooner had they achieved independence than the Texans sought admission to the Union. Many Americans, especially Whigs, fervently opposed the annexation of Texas. Eager to centralize national power within the existing limits of the United States, the Whigs resisted any dispersion of that power over a broader area. Many northerners, including some Democrats, feared that Texas, which would surely enter the Union as a slave state or even a number of slave states, would reinforce the "slave power" in the national government. A group of antislavery congressmen, led by former President John Quincy Adams, called the effort to annex Texas a "slavocracy" plot to add to southern strength in Congress. Still other citizens feared war. The Mexican government had refused to recognize the independence of Texas and had even tried unsuccessfully to reconquer its former province. Annexation might well goad the Mexicans into attacking the United States.

With so many Americans hostile to slavery, skeptical of expansion, or fearful of war, the Texas annexation issue was a political hot potato, and for most of a decade the American government gingerly avoided it. In early 1837, just before leaving office, Jackson granted official diplomatic recognition to the Texas Republic, and during the next few years Americans established trade relations with the young nation. Annexation, however, remained stalled.

Various forces soon goaded the United States to action. Discouraged by American indifference, the Texans began to dicker with England and France for recognition and loans in exchange for free trade in cotton and generous land grants to French and British subjects. This flirtation with the major European powers, intended to force Congress's hand, disturbed many Americans. Slaveholders feared that Britain, which had abolished slavery in its colonies in the 1830s, might acquire Texas and end slavery there, exposing the South's western flank to abolitionist influence. Other Americans, although reluctant to incorporate Texas into the Union, objected even more to allowing her to become part of the British Empire. Proannexation sentiment was further reinforced by an influential group of capitalists who owned Texas bonds and Texas lands and believed that annexation would guarantee the safety and profits of these investments.

Tyler cleverly played on the interests of all these groups to secure annexation. To the proslavery southerners he pointed out the dangers of British abolitionism in Texas. To Anglophobes and patriots he suggested that British interest in Texas was part of a plot to encircle the United States. Through a personal friend, Senator Robert J. Walker of Mississippi, he promised Pacific ports to the commercial men of the Northeast interested in the China trade.

Despite Tyler's and Walker's efforts, the Senate defeated an annexation treaty in 1844, and Texas remained outside the Union almost to the end of Tyler's term. Annexation and Oregon became major issues in the 1844 presidential contest. By this time Tyler had completely lost the support of his nominal party and was not seriously considered for renomination. Instead, the Whigs turned to Henry Clay, who opposed annexation on the grounds that it would mean war with Mexico. Rather than repudiate their candidate's stated principles, the Whigs avoided any mention of Oregon or Texas in their platform and thus maintained party harmony. The Democrats, as usual, became embroiled in a lengthy battle over men and policies. Martin Van Buren considered himself the party's titular leader despite his defeat in 1840, but he was opposed to annexation, and most of the party favored it. Annexationists successfully blocked his nomination, but they deadlocked the convention in the

THE OREGON CONTROVERSY, 1818–1846

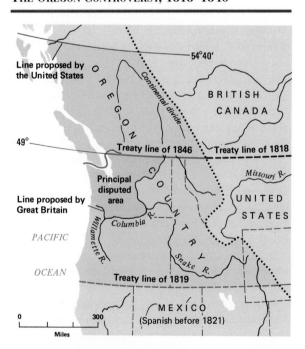

process. Maneuvering went on for days until, on the ninth ballot, James K. Polk of Tennessee, former speaker of the House of Representatives, received the prize. The Democratic platform, written by Senator Walker, called for the "reoccupation of Oregon and the reannexation of Texas at the earliest practicable period." The suggestion in this wording—that the United States was merely exerting clear existing rights in these regions—was dubious history, but it accurately expressed the expansionists' convictions.

The Democrats went on to victory, but just barely. The tariff and Texas were the major campaign issues, and on both, the candidates wavered and waffled—to the public's general disgust. In the end Polk won, but only because James Birney, candidate of the tiny Liberty party, drew enough antislavery voters from Clay to give Polk New York by 5,000 votes and a paper-thin electoral majority.

Polk's election was not, then, a strong mandate for annexation. Nevertheless, many formerly undecided citizens, now concluding that annexation was inevitable, gave it their support. To Tyler this was a cue to renewed efforts. Rather than submit yet another annexation treaty, which would require the approval of two-thirds of the Senate, he asked Congress for a joint annexation resolution, which would need only a bare majority of both houses for adoption. This approach worked. By heavily Democratic votes in both houses, Congress approved the resolution. On March 1, 1845, in the closing hours of his administration, Tyler signed the joint resolution. Texas entered the Union as a slave state in December 1845, but only after another heated debate in Congress with Adams and other antislavery Whigs leading the opposition.

★ MOVING TOWARD WAR ★

For many months the Mexican government had been threatening retaliation if the United States absorbed Texas. Now, in the wake of the joint resolution, the Mexican minister to Washington asked for his passport and returned to Mexico City eager to tell his superiors that the Americans had no stomach for war and could be easily intimidated.

The minister had not taken the correct measure of James K. Polk. A slight man of forty-nine with cool gray eyes and thin-lipped mouth, the new president was not impressive physically. Nor did he loom much larger intellectually. Polk's talents and mind were both mediocre. But he was a remarkably strong-willed man, in his aggressive spirit and willfulness resembling his hero and patron, Andrew Jackson. Determined to make his mark, Polk mastered the details of government through sheer energy. He soon became so adept at department routines that at one point he

Manifest Destiny

Every nation with expansionist designs has found a rationale for its urges. The United States was no exception. Its justification was called Manifest Destiny, and it was the creation largely of a New York lawyer-journalist named John Louis O'Sullivan, who probably first used the phrase in 1845.

In the July-August 1845 issue of his paper, *The United States Magazine and Democratic Review*, O'Sullivan argued in favor of Texas annexation against those who attacked it as either a "slave power" scheme or an act of pure greed against a weaker neighbor. The excerpt of this editorial included here carries the argument beyond Texas to justify all of American continental expansion. Note O'Sullivan's emphasis on demography and his prediction of America's population a century ahead. He was not too far off the mark.

". . . Texas has been absorbed into the Union in the inevitable fulfillment of the general law which is rolling our population westward; the connexion of which with that ratio of growth in population which is destined within a hundred years to swell our numbers to the enormous population of *two hundred and fifty millions* (if not more), is too evident to leave us in doubt of the manifest design of Providence in regard to the occupation of this continent. It was disintegrated from Mexico in the natural course of events, by a process perfectly legitimate on its own part, blameless on ours; and in which all the censures due to wrong, perfidy, and folly, rest on Mexico alone. And possessed as it was by a population which was in truth but a colonial detachment from our own, . . . their in-corporation into the Union was not only inevitable, but the most natural, right and proper thing in the world—and it is only astonishing that there should be any among ourselves to say it nay. . . .

"California will, probably, next fall away from the loose affiliation which, in such a country like Mexico, holds a remote province in a slight equivocal kind of dependence on the metropolis. Imbecile and distracted, Mexico can never exert any real governmental authority over such a country. The impotence of the one and the distance of the other, must make the relation one of virtual independence, unless, by stunting the province of all natural growth, and forbidding that immigration which alone can develop its capabilities and fulfill the purposes of its creation, tyranny may retain a military dominion which is no government in the legitimate sense of the term. In the case of California this is now impossible. The Anglo-Saxon foot is already on its borders. Already the advance guard of the irresistible army of the Anglo-Saxon emigration has begun to pour down upon it, armed with the plough and the rifle, and making its trail with schools and colleges, courts and representative halls, mills and meeting-houses. A population will soon be in actual occupation of California, over which it will be idle for Mexico to dream of dominion. They will necessarily become independent. All this without agency of our government, without responsibility of our people—in the natural flow of events, the spontaneous working of principles, and the adaptation of the tendencies and wants of the human race to the elemental circumstances in the midst of which they find themselves placed. . . .

"Whether they will then attach themselves to our Union or not, is not to be predicted with any certainty. Unless the projected railroad across the continent to the Pacific be carried into effect, perhaps they may not; though even in that case, the day is not far distant when the Empires of the Atlantic and the Pacific would again flow together into one. . . . But that great work . . . cannot remain long unbuilt. Its necessity for this very purpose of binding and holding together in its iron clasp our fast settling Pacific region with that of the Mississippi valley . . . gives assurance that the day cannot be distant which shall witness the conveyance of the representatives from Oregon and California to Washington within less time than a few years ago was devoted to a similar journey by those from Ohio. . . .

"Away, then, with all idle French talk of *balances of power* on the American Continent. There is no growth in Spanish America! Whatever progress of population there may be in the British Canadas, is only for their own early severance of their present colonial relation to the little island three thousand miles across the Atlantic; soon to be followed by Annexation, and destined to swell the still accumulating momentum of our progress. And whatsoever may hold the balance, though they should cast into the opposite scale all the bayonets and cannon, not only of France and England, but of Europe entire, how would it kick the beam against the simple solid weight of two hundred and fifty or three hundred millions . . . destined to gather beneath the flutter of the stripes and stars, in the fast hastening year of the Lord 1945?"

bet his secretary of state, James Buchanan, several bottles of champagne that the latter had made a mistake in a diplomatic note. Polk won the wager. It is the measure of the man's humorless personality that he refused to collect his prize.

Manifest Destiny.   Like many Americans of his day, Polk was imbued with the mystique of Manifest Destiny. First given this name by John L. O'Sullivan, a New York magazine editor, the doctrine proclaimed that the American people had the God-given right to "overspread and to possess the whole of the continent which Providence has given us for the great experiment of liberty and federated self-government." This process could not be stopped until the nation reached from the Atlantic to the Pacific, its "natural boundaries," for it was ordained and irreversible. "Make Way for the Young American Buffalo," declaimed a bombastic New Jersey defender of American destiny:

> He has not got land enough. . . . I tell you we will give him Oregon for his summer shade, and the region of Texas as his summer pasture. Like others of his race, he wants salt, too. Well, he shall have the use of two oceans—the mighty Pacific and the turbulent Atlantic shall be his.

Manifest Destiny was not a new doctrine. As a sense of special "mission," it can be traced back as far as the Puritans of Massachusetts Bay. Reinforced by the tremendous national energies unleashed following independence and by the aggressive economic opportunism and buoyant confidence that accompanied pre–Civil War economic growth, Manifest Destiny reached a climax in the 1840s. It was a self-serving ideology. Like the French, British, German, and Japanese rationalizations of territorial ambitions at other times, it sought to justify policies that were based on selfish national interest. Certainly the peoples and nations who stood in the path of America's expansionist urge found it difficult to see it as divinely inspired and benevolent. Their skepticism was not misplaced. All too often Manifest Destiny would serve to excuse the most brutal disregard of the rights of others. It also contained a large element of cultural and racial arrogance. Its implicit theme was that American civilization and "Anglo-Saxon" stock were superior to any other; at times it revealed explicit contempt for the nonwhite and Hispanic peoples of North America.

Yet American expansionism differed from its Old World equivalent in at least one important way. Americans have never been comfortable with colonies. The Northwest Ordinance of 1787 had established the precedent that all new territory acquired by the United States would eventually be organized into self-governing states to be incorporated into the Union as equals of the others. This principle

served as a check on American expansionism. Whether out of prejudice against other cultures and races or merely in recognition of cultural disparities, Americans have been reluctant to annex densely populated regions of peoples with different traditions, customs, and beliefs. In 1846 this attitude would help put a damper on the "All Mexico!" movement that followed the war that was about to begin.

Polk and his cabinet endorsed the premises of Manifest Destiny. In Oregon the president seconded his followers' cry of "Fifty-four forty or fight." He also believed that Britain coveted the rich province of California and was planning a takeover. We now know that England had no such plan, but the weakness of Mexico's hold on California and the intrigues of local British diplomatic agents made Polk and his advisers understandably uneasy and anxious to beat England to the punch. Polk's expansionism also led him to support the Texas claim to territory reaching southwest to the Rio Grande. The Mexican government insisted that the province extended only to the Nueces River many miles to the northeast, and the precedents for this position were strong ones. Polk never questioned the Texans' claims, however, and was willing to use force to make them good.

Debate on Expansionism.   Not all Americans accepted Polk's ambitious territorial goals. In New England and parts of the Northeast where antislavery sentiment was strong, there were few expansionists. Southerners, though eager for Texas and the Southwest, cared little about Oregon. Americans as a whole felt that California and the Southwest, with their mixed races and large stretches of barren desert and craggy mountains, were probably more trouble than they were worth.

Expansionist feelings were strongest in the Mississippi Valley and among the business classes of the Northeast. In Pennsylvania and New York commercial men and industrialists looked forward to continental markets and the access to the Far East that Pacific ports might bring. The business community was small, but its views counted politically. In the Mississippi Valley land hunger was the fuel for expansionism. Many people in this vast, lightly settled region already feared the disappearance of cheap land and looked to the Far West as a reserve for future generations.

Still, politics probably affected attitudes toward expansion more than sectional and occupational interests. Whig voters tended to see politics as an extension of morality: Because expansion favored slavery, it was unethical. Democrats were less inclined to treat politics as a moral arena: They either considered the expansion of slavery an irrelevant issue or, in the South, actually welcomed it. Moreover, the two parties had different traditions regarding territorial growth. The Democrats were largely the heirs of the Jeffersonian Republicans, who had acquired

Columbia brings a new day to North America, laying railroad tracks, plowing fields, and stringing telegraph wire, as Indians, buffalo, and other wild animals flee before her advance. Americans believed they were ordained by God to farm Oregon and Texas, mine California, and build ports on the Pacific coast. A telling symbolic depiction of the "development" ethic that prevailed.

Louisiana and Florida. On the other hand, the Whigs, as a party, were largely descended from the Federalists, who had resisted geographical expansion.

Age, too, affected how Americans thought about extending the nation's boundaries. Expansionists were generally youthful. Democrats associated with the "Young America" group led the movement for a totally American continent. Made up largely of political leaders like the thirty-two-year-old Stephen A. Douglas of Illinois and such youthful journalists as twenty-six-year-old Walt Whitman, Young America exhibited all the enthusiasm for great, bold deeds traditionally associated with vigorous young people. President Polk, who at forty-nine was the youngest man to hold presidential office until then, was temperamentally a member of this group.

Compromise with England. Although he coveted new territory, Polk was not anxious to fight a war for it. In his inaugural address he repeated the claim of the 1844 Democratic platform that the American title to Oregon was "clear and unquestionable." But in later months he blew hot and cold on Oregon, alternately threatening and appeasing Britain. Soon after his inauguration he proposed settling the Oregon dispute by extending the existing Canadian-American boundary, the forty-ninth parallel, all the way to the Pacific. When the British minister haughtily rejected this proposal, the angry Polk withdrew it. Several months later, in his first message to Congress, the president again demanded all of Oregon to the 54° 40′ line and asked

Congress to give the required one-year notice to Britain ending joint occupation of the region.

The threat of a direct confrontation with the United States startled the British, and they asked the American government to renew its forty-ninth parallel offer. The touchy president refused, but allowed Secretary of State Buchanan to tell the British that if *they* initiated a compromise, the American government would reconsider. In early June 1846 the London government proposed extending the boundary along the forty-ninth parallel to the Pacific, but reserving all of Vancouver Island for Britain. Polk now submitted the plan to the Senate. The bellicose Young Americans denounced it as a betrayal of American interests, but by a vote of 41 to 14, the Senate adopted it. The Oregon question, which had dragged on since the days of John Quincy Adams a generation before, had finally been settled by good sense and compromise.

And not a moment too soon. Polk had not expected war with Mexico when he first proposed a settlement to the British; but by the time the Senate approved the Oregon treaty, Americans and Mexicans were killing one another along the entire border from Texas to California.

The Slidell Mission. Polk blundered into war. He coveted Mexican territory; but as in the case of Oregon, he was reluctant to fight for it. In the fall of 1845 he had dispatched John Slidell to Mexico to see if the United States could get what it wanted by negotiation. Mexico had broken diplomatic relations with the United States at the time of the

Texas annexation, and Mexican patriots were still outraged at what they considered the theft of one of their country's choice provinces. Anti-American Mexicans refused to accept negotiations and demanded war against the United States. Nevertheless, Polk remained hopeful of a peaceful settlement. Slidell was to say that if Mexico recognized the Rio Grande as the southern boundary of Texas, the United States would pay the $3.25 million that Mexico owed to American citizens as a result of disorders and defaults in that chaotic country. He was also to offer $5 million for the province of New Mexico and $25 million more for California. He did not expect these negotiations to fail, Polk informed his envoy; but if they did, he would ask Congress "to provide proper remedies." Historians have interpreted this phrase as a threat of war, and it probably was. But Polk was convinced that the negotiations would be successful, and he made it clear that he considered the use of force highly unlikely.

The Slidell mission went wrong from the very beginning. Mexican patriots, having gotten wind of Slidell's purpose, demanded that the Mexican people overthrow their own rulers lest they sell the entire country to the United States. At first the Mexican government of José Herrera was inclined to negotiate, but the pressures of public opinion made it hesitate and pursue a confusing policy. Although Slidell was permitted to enter Mexico, he was held at arm's length and not allowed to present his proposals.

Soon after Slidell reached Mexico City, the Federalist Herrera government fell. The new Centralist administration under Mariano Paredes attacked its predecessor for "seeking to avoid a necessary and glorious war" and began to negotiate with Great Britain for support against the United States if war should come. Disgusted with what he considered Mexican bad faith, Polk ordered General Zachary Taylor to move his troops to the north bank of the Rio Grande to occupy the disputed Texas border region and protect Texas against possible attack. The Mexican government soon gave Slidell his walking papers.

Hope for a negotiated settlement faded with Slidell's dismissal. By the spring of 1846 Polk had concluded that war was inevitable. So had the Mexicans. Confident that they would have the support of Britain, that the American war effort would be shackled by New England and abolitionist opposition, and that Mexicans, man-for-man, were better soldiers than Americans, they were not averse to conflict. On April 23 Paredes announced that Mexico had declared "defensive war" on the United States.

News soon reached Washington that the Mexicans were preparing to attack Taylor's army. Early in May, Polk discussed a war declaration with his cabinet. All of his advisers except Secretary of the Navy George Bancroft agreed that a declaration was justified. But before Secretary of State Buchanan could prepare a statement of grievances against Mexico, news reached the capital that Mexican troops had crossed the Rio Grande and attacked a unit of Taylor's troops in the disputed region. Two days later Polk's war message was read to Congress. War was declared by a vote of 40 to 2 in the Senate and 174 to 14 in the House.

★ WAR WITH MEXICO ★

The war lasted almost two years, cost 13,000 American lives, and $100 million. It was a remarkable triumph for American arms. This time, the combination of a small regular army and a mass of volunteers worked well. Young men flocked to the recruiting offices. Many enlistees came from the Mississippi Valley and especially the south-central slave states, where the spirit of Manifest Destiny was at its most fervent. To lead these spirited troops the country had a cadre of well-trained officers, graduates of the military academy at West Point. Although few West Pointers had yet commanded large military units, their professionalism and overall competence made them quick and able learners. Besides skilled military leadership, the country also enjoyed excellent morale. Many Whigs remained skeptical of the war, and antislavery people strongly opposed it. But it was a short and relatively popular war. Most Americans enthusiastically supported the armies in the field and cheered each victory.

Taking the Borderland. Never before, and not again until World War II, would American soldiers march and fight over so wide an area. In the north the Army of the West under Stephen Watts Kearny—with all of 1,658 men and sixteen cannons—marched from the Missouri River in June for Santa Fe the capital of New Mexico and the major commercial town of the Southwest. On August 18, 1846, they took the city without a fight. A month later, with a tiny force of dragoons, Kearny set out for California, reaching San Pascual near San Diego with 100 half-naked, half-starved and exhausted men in December.

By this time major battles had been fought in northern Mexico where the main American force under "Old Rough-and-Ready," Zachary Taylor, confronted a Mexican army of poorly trained conscripts and convict soldiers under General Mariano Arista. Earlier at Palo Alto, on May 8, 1846, the two armies had collided. American artillery blew great holes in the Mexican ranks, though the Mexican troops held fast. Arista then launched his mounted lancers against the American infantry but the horsemen were repulsed with heavy losses. Once more the Mexicans attacked, this time throwing infantry against the Americans, who replied with devastating fire from their eighteen-pounder cannon. The fighting stopped at darkness, and the next morning Taylor awoke to discover the Mexicans had disengaged. But they remained full of fight. At Resaca de la Palma, the next day (May 9, 1846), the two armies clashed once again. This time the Mexican defeat was decisive. Arista and his army retreated across the Rio Grande. On May 17 the American troops occupied Matamoros, the major Mexican port at the mouth of the Rio Grande.

Zachary Taylor's two victories made him an instant hero at home. Congress voted him two gold medals, and war enthusiasm soared. A recruiting poster of these early months caught the mood of the nation: "Here's to Old Zach! Glorious Times! Roast Beef, Ice Cream, and Three Months' Advance!" Volunteers poured into the recruiting offices. A call by the Tennessee authorities for 2,800 men brought a response of 30,000. By August Taylor's army on the border had swelled to 20,000 troops.

On August 19 Taylor began his advance on Monterrey, capital of Nuevo León. Once more the American artillery proved devastating. After several days of fighting in and around the city, the Mexicans agreed to withdraw after extracting an armistice from the Americans that allowed them to keep their sidearms and remain unmolested for eight weeks. On September 25, 1846, Taylor raised the Stars and Stripes over Monterrey. He had lost 800 killed and wounded.

Although another American victory, Monterrey damaged Taylor's reputation. Critics charged that he should not have allowed the Mexicans such generous terms. President Polk's skepticism was reinforced by his fear that the Whig general would be a political rival in 1848. In January 1847 he ordered Taylor to remain at Monterrey while four-fifths of his troops were transferred to General Winfield Scott for an invasion of the Mexican heartland by way of Vera Cruz, the port on the Gulf of Mexico east of Mexico City.

Meanwhile, events were rapidly taking place in California. Even before the outbreak of formal hostilities, the province had become a hotbed of American-master-

This fierce-looking man is Zachary Taylor, "Old Rough-and-Ready," the American commander in northern Mexico. Though a soldier, unskilled in politics, he proved to be a competent president during the two years he served in office before his death.

John Charles Frémont

Whether John Charles Frémont was a pathfinder, a pathmaker, or merely a pathfollower is open to question, but there is no doubt that he is one of the most romantic figures in America's history.

Frémont's mother was Anne Beverly Whiting, a descendant of one of the Founding Fathers and member of a distinguished but impoverished family. His father was John Charles Frémont, a French royalist who had fled from Napoleonic France on a ship bound to Santo Domingo and ended up in Richmond, Virginia, in 1808.

It was in Richmond that the dashing French émigré met Anne, the childless and unhappily married wife of Major John Pryor, a tyrannical and wealthy man forty-five years her senior, and began a romantic relationship. After a showdown with the angry husband, the couple eloped and, without benefit of legal ceremony, settled in Savannah where Anne took in boarders and John Charles taught dancing and French. On January 21, 1813, their first child, John Charles Frémont, Jr., was born.

The family moved to Nashville soon after and then to Norfolk. There Anne and John, Sr., were married after Major Pryor's death. John, Sr., died of pneumonia in 1818 when his eldest son was only five. Gossip about the family continued to haunt Mrs. Frémont, so she moved to the more cosmopolitan, less puritanical city of Charleston, where she supported her three children on a small inheritance, supplemented by paying guests at her house.

Young John was brilliant, handsome, and charming, and although his social credentials were not impeccable by class-conscious southern standards, he made many friends among Charleston's best families. He also at-

tracted powerful patrons, a talent he would retain all his life. The first of these was John W. Mitchell, a lawyer who gave him a clerkship in his office and sent him to be educated at a fancy preparatory school. At sixteen he was able to enter Charleston College where he excelled in mathematics and natural science. Mitchell continued to help him financially as did the rector of St. Philip's, Charleston's most socially prominent Episcopal church. Unfortunately, John fell in love, neglected his studies, and cut classes. After several warnings he was expelled, just three months short of his graduation, for "habitual irregularity and incorrigible negligence."

Frémont was now forced to earn money to help support himself, his mother, and his siblings. Luckily his intellectual reputation won him a teaching position at a private secondary school in Charleston. Through his teaching he continued to meet and charm distinguished Charlestonians who were happy to help the talented and personable young man. One of these newest patrons was Joel Roberts Poinsett, Jacksonian politician, member of the St. Philip's congregation, first U.S. minister to Mexico, and the man who introduced the red tropical flower, the poinsettia, to the United States. Poinsett got John a job as mathematics teacher to navy midshipmen on the U.S.S. *Natchez*, then about to undertake a training cruise down the coast of South America. Two years later, when the *Natchez* returned, Frémont passed the examination for professor of mathematics in the navy. While he was debating whether to accept this position, Poinsett secured his appointment to the United States Topographic Corps as assistant engineer to survey the route of a projected railroad to run from Louisville to Charleston. When

Poinsett became secretary of war in 1837, he commissioned his protegé second lieutenant in the army and appointed him assistant to Joseph Nicolett, a famous French scientist, on two government-sponsored surveys of the territory between the upper Missouri and Mississippi rivers. The two expeditions took lieutenant Frémont all through present-day Minnesota and the Dakotas. Here Frémont saw for the first time the vast sea of buffalo that then covered the Great Plains. When he returned to Washington in 1839, he and Nicolett collaborated on a series of maps and scientific reports.

In Washington, the ever-obliging Poinsett introduced the twenty-six-year-old Frémont to Democratic Senator Thomas Hart Benton, a leader of the expansionists in Congress and a strong supporter of government-sponsored exploration of the West. The young officer was soon dining regularly at the Benton home and paying court to his host's beautiful and intelligent teenage daughter, Jessie. However much they liked Frémont, the Bentons were opposed to the match. Jessie was too young and the handsome lieutenant's prospects were not very good. When their lecturing failed to deter the young couple, Senator Benton prevailed on Poinsett to send John Charles off on another expedition.

With Nicolett ill, Frémont was put in charge of the trip, a survey of the Des Moines River and Iowa Territory, a region rapidly being settled by farmers. Frémont spent the spring and summer of 1841 exploring and mapping Iowa Territory and by August was back in Washington ready to resume his courtship. Unable to overcome the Bentons' objections, the couple were secretly married in

October. In November they informed the senator, who finally accepted the situation when his daughter clutched her husband's arm tightly and quoted the words of Ruth in the Bible: "Whither thou goest, I will go." Frémont had won himself not only a rich and beautiful wife but another powerful patron.

Through Benton's influence Frémont was chosen to head a succession of major western expeditions. In 1842, with Christopher (Kit) Carson as his guide, he explored the Plains as far as South Pass in Wyoming. This trip produced a scientific map of the Oregon Trail and a report that confirmed the fertility of the adjacent lands and furnished practical advice to would-be emigrants. The following year Benton induced Congress to sponsor the second American expedition to the mouth of the Columbia. This trip was almost canceled when Frémont decided to take with him a portable howitzer cannon. The War Department feared that this would tag the expedition as a military venture against Mexico and dispatched an order asking Frémont, then collecting supplies in St. Louis, to return to Washington. Jessie Frémont, ascribing it to jealousy of her beloved husband, intercepted the order, and wrote her husband urging him to speed up his departure. Fortunately, when the defiance was discovered, the senator deflected blame from his daughter. But his son-in-law was branded within the professional army as an officer who would not obey orders.

The expedition took Frémont to California, a place with which his name would always be connected. But first he visited the Great Salt Lake and wrote a glowing report of its surroundings that would attract the attention of Mormon leader Brigham Young four years later when he was looking for a refuge for his persecuted people. When he reached the Dalles in Oregon in October 1843, prudence suggested

that Frémont turn back before winter struck. Instead, he turned south to explore the forbidding Great Basin. In February, after struggling through deep snows, the Frémont party crossed the Sierras into California and arrived in the warm Sacramento Valley. Soon after, they reached Fort Sutter, not far from the present California capital. Here they were treated hospitably by Captain John Augustus Sutter, the Swiss entrepreneur who had arrived in California six years before and established a combination ranch–farm–fort on 50,000 acres granted by the Mexican government. Sutter filled in the American officer on the volatile politics of the province and the restlessness of the many American settlers under Mexican rule.

From Fort Sutter Frémont continued to move southeast, exploring parts of Nevada and Utah before finally returning to Washington at the end of the year. During the winter of 1844–1845 he and Jessie together drafted the report on this second trip to the far West, emphasizing the fertility and beauty of the region and the practicality of the Oregon Trail. Congress received this report with enthusiasm and ordered the printing of 100,000 copies at government expense.

In March 1845 the fiery expansionist James K. Polk took the oath of office as president. Manifest Destiny was in the air. Soon after, Benton and Frémont induced Congress to authorize another western reconnaissance. Like the others, the ostensible purpose of this trip was scientific, but Frémont later admitted in his *Memoirs* that "in arranging this expedition the eventualities of war were taken into consideration." Secretary of the Navy George Bancroft, he explained, expected him to convert his party of sixty-two into a military force if he found that war had begun by the time he reached California.

Blazing a new trail through Nevada, Frémont reached Sutter's Fort

on December 9, 1845. From there he and his men proceeded to Monterey on the pretext of collecting additional supplies and contacted Thomas Larkin, the American consul, who told the young officer about the confused state of affairs in the province and described the American settlers' movement for secession from Mexico. Under orders from the suspicious Mexican authorities to leave, Frémont set off for Oregon. Though Frémont did not yet know it, by this time Mexico and the United States were at war.

In early May, while camped at Klamath Lake, Frémont and his men received dispatches sent originally to Larkin from Washington directing the consul to seek peaceably to detach California from Mexico with the ultimate goal of annexation to the United States. Though he did not know that Mexican and American armies were already fighting along the Rio Grande, Frémont turned south and prepared to enter into the struggle for California's fate.

By this time the American settlers in the province were chafing under the repressive hand of the Mexican authorities; many feared massacre by the Indians. Frémont's arrival in Sonoma helped to precipitate a revolt. Inspired by the presence of the soldiers, on June 14 a tiny party of American settlers attacked the Mexican military post in the seedy town and raised the banner of the "Republic of California," inscribed with a grizzly bear. When the Mexican officials sent troops, Frémont dropped all pretense that his was purely an exploring expedition and intercepted them. Still without official knowledge of events in the East, he had personally declared war on Mexico.

When official news of hostilities finally reached the West Coast, Commodore Robert Stockton appointed Frémont major of the California Battalion, a force composed of his own small military unit, plus volunteers among the American settlers.

After the American capture of Los Angeles, Stockton made him military governor of the province. This put Frémont on a collision course with General Stephen W. Kearny, who claimed to have official sanction to set up a government in the captured province. With Stockton's support, Frémont ignored Kearny's claims. When Kearny's orders were confirmed, Frémont was arrested, court-martialed, and found guilty of mutiny and conduct prejudicial to military discipline. President Polk eventually remitted his sentence of dismissal from the army, but let the guilty verdict stand. Hurt and indignant, Frémont resigned from the military.

Shortly after, Senator Benton and some wealthy St. Louis friends financed a fourth Frémont expedition to survey routes for a Pacific railroad.

Frémont arrived in California in time for the great gold discovery at Sutter's Fort. Providentially, before he had left California in disgrace two years before, he had bought for $3,000 the large Las Mariposas tract in the Sierra foothills as a future home. In 1849 Mexican laborers discovered rich veins of gold ore on this property. Overnight Frémont became a millionaire. He soon abandoned his survey work, acquired real estate in San Francisco, develped his foothill property, and for a brief time lived an affluent life in Monterey with Jessie and their three children.

When California became a state in 1850 Frémont was elected ad interim United States senator, but failed to win the regular election in 1851. By this time the Frémonts, their land claims in dispute and their financial prospects in doubt, left California for

the East. Frémont made another exploratory trip west, this one again to survey a Pacific railroad route. The expedition was not especially fruitful.

By this time the nation was in the throes of the sectional struggle over slavery extension. Though southern bred, Frémont was a free soiler, and in 1856, as a glamorous popular hero, won the presidential nomination of the newly formed Republican party. He lost to James Buchanan by an electoral vote of 174 to 114 and half a million fewer popular votes than his Democratic rival. When the Civil War broke out Lincoln appointed him major general and commander of the Western Department headquartered at St. Louis. Frémont's problems in his new post were almost insurmountable. Missouri was strongly secessionist and full of angry men determined to defy

minded, anti-Mexican intrigue. In 1845 Polk had secretly authorized Thomas O. Larkin, the American consul in the California capital, to help stir up a secessionist movement among the several thousand American residents. Before Larkin's plans could mature, however, a group of Americans jumped the gun. In early June they proclaimed the "Republic of California" and adopted a national flag emblazoned with a star, a stripe, and a crudely drawn grizzly bear. At this point Captain John C. Frémont arrived in California with a contingent of American troops supposedly sent for exploring purposes. The hotheaded young officer took over leadership of the Bear Flag Revolt, and he and his men soon clashed with a force led by Jose Castro, the province's Mexican governor, and routed it. On July 1 Frémont occupied the Mexican fort at San Francisco and spiked its antique guns while Castro fled south to Los Angeles.

By this time the United States was officially at war with Mexico and prepared to seize the province. At news of the war declaration, a naval squadron under Commodore John D. Sloat, already on the Pacific Coast, sailed for California. Sloat arrived in Monterey in early July and on the seventh he raised the U.S. flag over the Mexican custom house. The next day he read a proclamation stating that "henceforth California will be a portion of the United States." In illhealth, Sloat was soon replaced by Robert Stockton who

joined with Frémont to impose American authority on the province.

The task proved more difficult than expected. Mexican troops drove the Americans out of Los Angeles, Santa Barbara, and San Diego. Virtually the whole of southern California was in Mexican hands when Stephen Kearny arrived outside of San Diego with his small force. Kearny attacked the Mexican troops defending the town and suffered a minor defeat. Fortunately, the enemy did not follow up this success and Kearny was rescued by Stockton. Together the two leaders, with larger forces, retook the towns previously lost, occupying Los Angeles on January 10. As Stockton and Kearny moved north, the California Battalion under Fremont moved south from Sacramento. On January 13 the remaining Mexican forces in California signed the Capitulation of Cahuenga. The beautiful province was now firmly in American hands by right of conquest.

Victory in Mexico. The United States now controlled all the Mexican borderlands—Texas, New Mexico, California—from the Gulf of Mexico to the Pacific Ocean. But the war was far from over. By this time Santa Anna was once more back in the picture, having inveigled the *Norteamericanos* into allowing him safe conduct through the naval blockade by promising to make peace on their terms. Once back home he reneged and took command of the

the Union authorities. Surrounded by enemies, the general had few arms and insufficient supplies and manpower to impose loyal government on the state. But he made matters still worse by declaring martial law and issuing his own, premature emancipation proclamation for the state's slaves. Lincoln might have retained him if he had proven an effective military leader. He was not, and his defeats in three minor battles prompted Lincoln to remove him from command. As usual, if Frémont had made enemies, he had also made friends. The radical antislavery Republicans protested his removal, and Lincoln reappointed him head of the Mountain Department with headquarters at Wheeling.

Having proven ineffective against Confederate general Stonewall Jackson, he once more lost his command.

Senator Benton had died in 1858, but Frémont still did not lack for powerful friends and patrons. In 1864 a radical faction within the Republican party pushed him as an alternate to Lincoln in the presidential election. Though he was skeptical of Lincoln, he withdrew for the sake of party unity.

Frémont's life went downhill from this point on. During the war dishonest business associates cheated him of his Mariposa estate. Then, after the war, he invested his remaining capital in an unprofitable Pacific railroad enterprise. When this scheme failed, he lost his mansion in Manhattan and his estate in Westchester, and he and Jessie were forced to give up their extensive travels in Europe. Jessie sought to keep the poorhouse at bay by writing newspaper articles, children's stories, and travel accounts. Frémont himself

wrote his *Memoirs*, a 650-page tome published in 1886. It was not a financial success, and his labors on it exhausted him. In 1887 he and Jessie went once more to California, this time for health reasons. Two years later John returned East to look after his remaining business affairs leaving Jessie behind in Los Angeles. In July 1890, while staying with one of his sons, he died of peritonitis at the age of 77. Jessie was not at his bedside.

Although his life ended in failure, Frémont had helped conquer a western empire for his country. His name, conferred on over twenty geographic sites scattered across the western third of the nation, marks his achievements.

Army of Liberation. By February the erratic strong man was leading an army of 20,000 troops against Taylor still holed up in Monterrey with an army one quarter the size. The two forces met at Buena Vista, and once again American artillery proved decisive. After three days of fighting, the badly bloodied, hungry Mexican army retreated southward to meet a new American threat, this time coming from the east.

Winfield Scott ("Old Fuss and Feathers"), commanding 12,000 men, arrived off Vera Cruz in early March, hoping to take the tropical city quickly to avoid the summer yellow-fever scourge. Putting his troops ashore on the beach, he surrounded the city and began a bombardment with big guns manned by naval crews. On March 29 the city surrendered and Scott quickly turned it into his base of operation for the advance on the Mexican capital high on the country's cool central plateau.

The first American troops headed for the "Halls of Montezuma" on April 8, 1847. At Cerro Gordo, fifty miles inland, they encountered Santa Anna prepared to catch and destroy the American forces in a narrow defile on the road to the capital. The scheme did not work. Scott's 9,000 men routed the larger Mexican army in hand-to-hand fighting with bayonets and muskets used as clubs at a cost of 63 killed and 337 wounded. As the Americans climbed farther into the mountains the fierce heat of the lowlands gave way to the cold of the highlands. But by this time many of the

men had thrown away their blankets and warm clothing and they now suffered severely. They were also harassed by Mexican guerrillas who picked off stragglers, couriers, and isolated detachments. To deal with the irregulars Polk despatched a contingent of Texas Rangers, each of whom carried a rifle, four pistols, a knife, and assorted ropes to deal with the enemy. The Rangers took few prisoners.

In mid-May Scott occupied Puebla, eighty miles from the capital, and remained there until reinforcements, under command of Franklin Pierce, arrived from the United States in August. Fighting soon resumed with the Americans defeating Santa Anna once more at both Contreras and Churubusco.

Santa Anna now withdrew to Mexico City and requested an armistice while he and the U.S. peace commissioner, Nicholas Trist, attached to Scott's army, conducted negotiations. Meanwhile, the Americans camped outside the capital waiting for Mexican surrender. Negotiations soon broke down, and the fighting resumed. The final American assault on the capital took place in early September with a series of battles culminating in the American attack on the fortified hill of Chapultepec, bravely defended by a thousand Mexican troops including the young cadets of the Mexican military academy. The Americans took the rocky hill by scaling it with ropes and ladders and on the evening and early morning of September

13–14 fought their way into the capital. The formal capture of Mexico City was marked by the raising of the American flag over the "Halls of Montezuma" by the U.S. marine battalion.

But Santa Anna refused to capitulate. As the Americans were entering the capital, he and a force of 8,000 men attacked the small American garrison left behind at Puebla. When this operation failed Santa Anna fled the country leaving the unavoidable surrender and peace negotiations to the ad interim president, Pedro Anaya.

The Peace. As wars go, the Mexican conflict was brief; the fighting lasted less than a year and a half. The peace negotiations, however, dragged on for months. With Santa Anna gone neither President Anaya nor any other Mexican leader could at first muster the will and authority to accept defeat and the inevitable loss of territory. In the United States, indecision about American territorial goals further impeded a settlement. At the outset of fighting the ambitions of

Americans had been relatively modest: California and New Mexico. But with each new dazzling victory the national appetite grew until the cry "All Mexico" became a powerful slogan and movement. As Lowell's skeptical Hosea Biglow phrased it: "Our Destiny higher an' higher kep' mountin'."

For a while the "All Mexico" surge seemed unstoppable. Besides its appeal as the logical culmination of Manifest Destiny, it was attractive to the country's commercial interests. Ports on the Pacific at San Francisco or on Puget Sound were all very well, but overland transportation between the West Coast and the manufacturing and commercial centers of the East was time-consuming and expensive. For generations Americans had talked of building a canal across the narrowest part of the North American continent in Central America. With Mexico in its possession, the United States could build such a canal on its own territory at the Isthmus of Tehuantepec. By absorbing all of the defeated nation, American enterprise, progress, glory, and greatness might all be furthered simultaneously.

THE MEXICAN WAR, 1846–1848

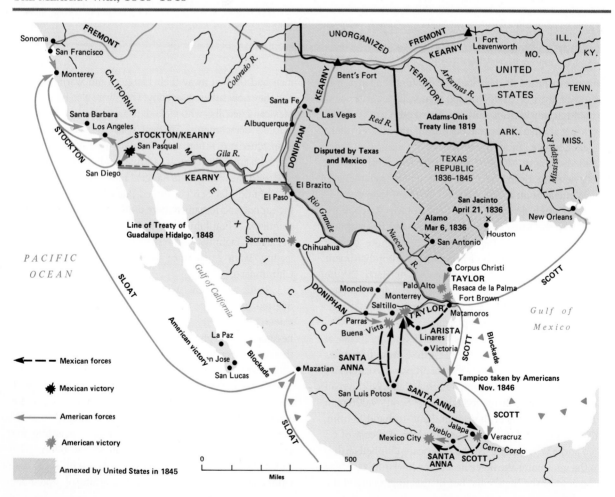

300 Chapter 11

STORMING OF THE CASTLE OF CHAPULTEPEC, BY THE AMERICAN ARMY UNDER GENERAL SCOTT, SEPT. 13, 1847.

In the midst of the Mexican War an American editor proclaimed it "our destiny to civilize that beautiful country and enable its inhabitants to appreciate some of the many blessings and advantages they enjoy." Here General Scott's forces storm Chapultepec, killing all of its defenders— including unseasoned teenage cadets. (Collection of the New York Historical Society)

But the "All Mexico" advocates did not reckon with the Mexicans themselves. In New Mexico and California, and in the Mexican heartland, the occupying American troops were soon facing attacks by Mexican irregulars. At Taos, New Mexico, Mexican and Indian guerrillas killed the American governor, Charles Bent, and had to be put down by soldiers hastily brought in from Santa Fe. If the United States insisted on all of Mexico, it could expect more of this resistance. Who knew how long the fighting might last?

The "All Mexico" issue was ultimately decided by the reluctance of most Americans to take on the responsibility of governing a large non–English-speaking population with different institutions and traditions. Meanwhile, peace negotiations proceeded slowly. In October 1847 Polk recalled Trist, but the headstrong, ambitious Virginian, on the advice of General Scott, refused to return and continued to negotiate with Mexican officials. Fortunately for Trist, Santa Anna's successors, faced with the prospect of renewed fighting, finally concluded that they could not avoid concessions. On February 2, 1848, they signed an agreement with Trist at Guadalupe Hidalgo.

The Treaty of Guadalupe Hidalgo gave the United States the provinces of California and New Mexico and confirmed the Rio Grande as the southern boundary of Texas. The Mexican Cession would include the present states of California, Nevada, and Utah, and parts of Arizona, New Mexico, Wyoming, and Colorado. In return, the United States agreed to pay Mexico $15 million and to assume the $3.5 million of American citizens' claims against the Mexican government.

These terms differed only marginally from those Slidell had been authorized to propose before the war, and some Americans favored rejecting them. After a costly and total military victory, why take only as much as you had asked for in the first place? President Polk himself disliked the treaty because it had originated with Trist, whom he had relieved of his commission. But most Americans were inclined to accept it. "Admit all [the treaty's] faults," wrote one newspaper editor, "and say if an aimless and endless foreign war is not far worse. . . . *We are glad to get out of the scrape even upon these terms.*" This accommodating spirit prevailed when the treaty came before the Senate, and it was ratified by 38 votes to 14.

★ CONCLUSIONS ★

And so the war ended on a relatively moderate and conciliatory note. The Mexican government could consider the $15 million an acknowledgment of American guilt; Americans could see themselves as forbearing and generous.

But what were the causes? The war was part of a process of territorial expansion over which Americans—and even more clearly their government—had relatively little control. Greed—or acquisitiveness, if one prefers—was part of the American character and could not easily have been checked by laws or moral exhortation, even if the United States government had wanted to. No agency could have kept American citizens from moving into the loosely held Mexican borderland. Whatever Washington had done, it is likely that New Mexico and California would have taken the same course as Texas. American migration would have been followed by secession, demands for annexation, and eventual incorporation into the United States. No doubt war would have been part of the process.

The Mexican War, then, was in some ways almost inevitable. Had Mexico been a strong and stable country, Mexican-American relations would undoubtedly have taken a different turn. We cannot blame the victim for his misfortunes, but it is hard not to conclude that Mexico's history, which found it after independence a poor, disorganized nation, racked periodically by violence, with a powerful, dynamic, and materialistic neighbor, was a crucial factor in its fate. A wise Mexican has observed: "Poor Mexico, so far from God, so near the United States!"

The joke, however, was on the Americans. At the war's start Ralph Waldo Emerson predicted that the United States would conquer Mexico, but that the victory would "poison us." As we shall see in Chapter 14, it almost did.

★★★★★★★ FOR FURTHER READING ★★★★★★★

Bernard De Voto. *Across the Wide Missouri* (1947)

De Voto delightfully chronicles the Rocky Mountain fur trade that flourished in the 1820s and 1830s. He describes company rivalries, the carousals of the annual "rendezvous," and relations between fur trappers and Indians. Contains interesting sketches made on the scene in 1837–1838 by the artist Alfred Jacob Miller.

Francis Parkman. *The Oregon Trail* (1849). Edited and introduced by Harry Sinclair Drago (1964)

Parkman was only twenty-three years old and fresh out of Harvard when he and a cousin set forth in 1846 from St. Louis to live among the fur trappers and the nomadic Sioux. The title of this book—the creation of an enthusiastic publisher—is misleading because Parkman never came within 500 miles of the Oregon Trail. This is a fascinating contemporary depiction of the trans-Mississippi West.

John David Unruh. *The Plains Across: The Overland Emigrants and the Trans-Mississippi West, 1840–1860* (1978)

The best overall treatment of emigration by way of the various overland "trails" from the settled areas of the East to the West Coast before the Civil War. Written by a young scholar who died just before the book appeared.

Henry Nash Smith. *Virgin Land: The American West as Symbol and Myth* (1950)

The westward drive of empire, the Wild West hero, and the West as "garden of the world" were common images in the American mind during the era of westward expansion. Smith examines how the nineteenth-century West influenced the life and helped to shape the character of American society as a whole.

George R. Stewart. *Ordeal by Hunger: The Story of the Donner Party* (1936)

Stewart records the history of eighty-nine people on their way to California who were stranded in the High Sierra during the winter of 1846–1847. All experienced terrible hardships; forty-four died, and some of the others survived only by resorting to cannibalism.

Ray Allen Billington. *The Far Western Frontier, 1830–1860* (1956)

Here is a colorful survey of the Far West in the generation before the Civil War. Billington deals with all of the important aspects of the trans-Missouri westward movement—political, social, and economic.

Frederick Merk. *Manifest Destiny and Mission in American History* (1963)

The best discussion of this important topic by one of the deans of western history. Covers more than just the period of this chapter.

David M. Pletcher. *The Diplomacy of Annexation: Texas, Oregon, and the Mexican War* (1973)

Treats the background of the Mexican War and the economic and political interests of the United States, Mexico, Britain, and France during the 1830s and 1840s. Pletcher avoids the easy moralizing that others often bring to the subject.

Norman A. Graebner. *Empire on the Pacific: A Study in American Continental Expansion* (1955)

Graebner hunts for the reasons behind the acquisition of

Oregon and California. He concludes that it was not Manifest Destiny or the "pioneering spirit," but rather the desire of eastern commercial interests for ports on the Pacific.

Eugene Genovese. *The Political Economy of Slavery: Studies in the Economy and Society of the Slave South* (1965)

Most of this book deals with the profitability of slavery and so is relevant to Chapter 13. But it also deals with expansion. Genovese depicts expansionism as the effort of a southern planter elite to save slavery from a trap of soil exhaustion and declining profitability. When the North said no to any additional expansionism after 1848, the South seceded.

Otis Singletary. *The Mexican War* (1960)

A good, brief treatment of the war against Mexico.

Julie Roy Jeffrey. *Frontier Women: The Trans-Mississippi West, 1840–1880* (1979)

A fresh, entertaining discussion of women along the way to, and in, the Far West, from Oregon onward.

Oakah Jones, Jr. *Santa Anna* (1968)

This is an interesting revisionist biography of the Mexican leader. It depicts him as an honest patriot rather than the rank opportunist of other portraits.

12 ★

AMERICANS BEFORE THE CIVIL WAR

What Were They Really Like?

1790	The geographic center of American population is east of Baltimore
1793	Congress adopts first fugitive slave law
1794	Black preacher Richard Allen establishes the congregation that becomes the first African Methodist Episcopal Church
1821	Emma Willard founds the Troy Female Seminary (the Emma Willard School) in New York
1825	Robert Owen founds New Harmony (Indiana)
1831	First issue of William Lloyd Garrison's *The Liberator* • Nat Turner's Rebellion in Virginia: 57 whites and about 100 slaves die
1833	American Antislavery Society organize • Oberlin becomes the first college to admit women as full degree candidates
1837	Abolitionist editor Elijah Lovejoy, defending his printing press against a mob, is murdered in Illinois • Mary Lyon founds a women's academy, now Mount Holyoke College, in Massachusetts
1838	Sarah Grimké publishes *Letters on the Equality of the Sexes*
1840s	"Potato famine" sends hundreds of thousands of Irish to the United States
1844	Protestants riot against Irish Catholics in Philadelphia
1848	John Humphrey Noyes founds Oneida Community (New York) • Lucretia Mott and Elizabeth Cady Stanton organize the first Women's Rights Convention at Seneca Falls, New York
1849	Elizabeth Blackwell receives a medical degree from Geneva College
1850	Hawthorne's *The Scarlet Letter* published
1851	Maine passes the first state prohibition law • Melville's *Moby Dick* published
1855	First edition of Walt Whitman's *Leaves of Grass*
1865	The first all-women's college, Vassar, is established

In the decades before the Civil War, America and Americans fascinated people of other nations. Hundreds of educated Europeans visited the new country to see for themselves what manner of society was emerging on the North American continent.

Most European travelers were impressed by the social and economic democracy they encountered here. Harriet Martineau, an English intellectual, observed after her 1834 visit that few in America were "very wealthy; few are poor; and every man has a fair chance of being rich." Alexis de Tocqueville, in his famous *Democracy in America* (1835), wrote that in the United States people were "more nearly equally powerful, than in any other country of the world or in any other age of recorded history." Frances Trollope, who spent the years 1827–1830 in Cincinnati, noted that in America maids and other domestics refused to consider themselves inferior to their employers, referring to themselves as "help" rather than "servants." Sir Charles Lyell remarked that in the United States "the spirit of social equality . . . left no other signification to the terms 'gentleman' and 'lady' but that of male and female individual."

Not every visitor agreed that Americans were democratic. Some detected a deep streak of snobbery in the United States. Isidor Löwenstern, a Viennese scholar who traveled through the country in 1837, observed that "distinctions of rank have their defenders in America as zealous as in the Old World. . . ." Women, he wrote, were especially snobbish. The ladies of Philadelphia, for example, took "infinite pains and all their cleverness to differentiate themselves, and as much as possible to avoid contact with inferior classes."

Foreign observers also argued over the much-touted American individualism. The Swedish novelist Fredrika Bremer considered it a prominent American characteristic that "every human being must be strictly true to his own individuality—must stand alone with God, and from this innermost point of view must act alone according to his own conscientious convictions." On the other hand, Martineau complained that Americans suffered from a "fear of singularity"; and Tocqueville believed that public pressure to conform constituted a "tyranny of the majority" in America almost as stifling as European despotism.

Still another disagreement among the foreign observers of pre–Civil War America was whether Americans were practical, hardheaded, and materialistic—or romantic, sentimental, and idealistic. Trollope, no slouch herself at seeking wealth, wrote that she never met an American who was not trying to increase his fortune. "Every bee in the hive is actively employed in search of that honey . . . vulgarly called money; neither art, science, learning, nor pleasure can se-

duce them from its pursuit." Yet Bremer noted that Americans respected books and learning, and she was surprised by how much social and charitable work they did. Individual Americans were often anything but hardheaded and practical, she remarked. Nor did all observers believe that Americans worshiped money above all other things. Of all the cities of the world, wrote the Hungarian politician Ferencz Pulszky and his wife, Theresa, after their 1852 visit, Boston was "the only one where knowledge and scholarship" had "the lead of society." There a "distinguished author, an eminent professor, an eloquent preacher, are socially equals of the monied aristocracy."

What a confusing set of contrasts! Visitors saw equality; they saw snobbery. Americans were individualists; they were also conformists. A practical, materialistic people, they also seemed to be dreamers, poets, and philanthropists. How can we reconcile these conflicting views of antebellum Americans? Let us examine American culture, institutions, social structure, and values between 1815 and 1860. In this chapter we shall focus primarily on the pre–Civil War North and the West, saving the South for separate attention in Chapter 13.

★ THE MOVING FRONTIER ★

Generations of scholars have seen the West, the area where the older society and culture of the East touched the primitive frontier, as the key to American character and institutions. In the generation preceding 1860 the West was the fastest-growing part of the nation. Population increased rapidly in the Middle Atlantic states and parts of New England, too, but trans-Appalachian growth far outstripped the pace elsewhere. In the forty-five years following 1815 the West became home to 15 million Americans. By 1860, eleven years after the great Gold Rush, even distant California had almost 380,000 people. The country had over 31 million inhabitants when the first shots of the Civil War were fired, and half of them lived in states and territories where settled white communities had not existed at the time of Washington's inauguration.

Americans generally moved west along lines of latitude. Thus the heavy migration from New England first crossed the Berkshire Hills to central New York, then swept through the Mohawk Valley into northern Ohio, northern Illinois, and southern Michigan. One branch of the Yankee exodus reached out to distant Oregon. New Yorkers and Pennsylvanians tended to settle the middle portions of the trans-Appalachian region. Most southerners moved to the lower parts of the Old Northwest and to the newer slave states of Kentucky, Tennessee, and the Gulf region. Southern blacks as well as whites moved westward. Most blacks accompanied their masters to the cotton fields of the interior; others, however, were transported by slave dealers and sold to cotton planters in the new region. Meanwhile, the Indians were continually pushed westward, ahead of the powerful flood of white and black settlers.

The Migrants' Motives.   Leaving aside the involuntary slave migrants, what induced easterners to abandon familiar places, jobs, and families to expose themselves to the uncertainties of a new environment? Reasons for moving westward of course varied from person to person, group to group, and region to region. Some western pioneers were the "loners" of traditional romantic accounts who could not stay put once they had seen the smoke of a neighbor's hearth fire on the horizon. Americans generally were a restless people. They suffered, one observer wrote, from a serious "disease of locomotion" that disrupted families and separated neighbor from neighbor. This physical restlessness infected not only rural people heading for the frontier but also city folk. In many mid-nineteenth-century cities and towns May 1 was "moving day," when almost all house and apartment leases expired and people changed their residences en masse. On the day or two preceding the deadline, city streets were jammed with people, horses, carts, and wagons piled high with furniture, kitchen equipment, and personal belongings. "Move—move—keep moving—straw—soot—dust and ashes at every step—all confusion," wrote one disgusted pre–Civil War resident of Kingston, New York. "Everyone has his or her hands and arms full—all are in a trot—it is like the sacking of a city. . . ."

But restlessness was not the only reason why people "lit out for the territories." Some were refugees—people fleeing the law, their creditors, their spouses, or their own pasts. Married women and children went west without much choice because their husbands or fathers did. On the other hand, many single women regarded the West as a land of opportunity. Western farmers needed wives, and unmarried women could easily find husbands in the West's open spaces and the security and social status that only marriage and a family of one's own could then confer.

Economic considerations, however, probably outweighed personal and social motives. New England's first emigrants streamed to the cheap lands of the Genesee country of western New York in the 1790s following the rapid rise in land prices at home. In the 1820s there was another New England exodus as tenants and agricultural laborers, dislodged by conversion of arable land to sheep pasture,

In 1858 the raw town of Omaha on the Missouri River was an important jumping-off place for travelers crossing the Great Plains. In this contemporary watercolor two wagons, one bound for California and one for the new gold fields at Pike's Peak, are stocking up on provisions at Pundt & Koenig's "Outfitting house" and general store.

THE GEOGRAPHIC CENTER OF POPULATION, 1790–1860

moved west. In the next few decades further waves of New England migrants were induced by competition from western grain and meat. Unable to undersell the cheap commodities of the fertile Mississippi Valley, many Yankee farmers from Massachusetts or Connecticut simply gave up and joined the westward exodus.

The people of the Middle Atlantic region, where soils were good, had less reason to move than their Yankee neighbors. By the 1840s and 1850s, however, many former New Englanders who had settled in central and western New York, or their children, began a second migration to Wisconsin and Iowa, responding once again to the lure of cheap, fertile land.

The older South also felt the economic attraction of the West. Declining soil fertility pushed people out of the Chesapeake region and the older cotton areas of South Carolina and Georgia, while the more fertile cotton lands across the mountains exerted a simultaneous pull. Whenever cotton prices rose, Virginia, Maryland, Carolina, and Georgia yeomen and planters sold their land and their buildings, put their families and household wares on wagons, and, with their slaves trudging behind, departed for the beckoning Southwest.

The Frontier Type.   During the colonial period, as we have seen, the physical environment of the New World altered the Old World heritage of the earliest European immigrants. Did the West have similar effects on the eastern pioneers of the nineteenth century? Most scholars think it did. According to Frederick Jackson Turner, the nineteenth-century historian of the frontier, the West made pioneers

from the East into new people—individualistic, egalitarian, and idealistic. The West, Turner declared, was "productive of individualism" because the frontier reduced society to its essentials and forced people to rely on their own unaided resources. "Complex society was precipitated by the wilderness into a kind of primitive organization based on the family. The tendency is antisocial. It produced antipathy to control, and particularly any direct control." The West was also egalitarian, Turner felt. Among the pioneers, "one man is as good as another. . . . An optimistic and buoyant faith in the worth of the plain people, a devout faith in man prevailed in the West." Idealism was another characteristic that emerged from the westward movement. "From the beginning of that long westward march of the American people America has never been the home of mere contented materialism. It has continually sought new ways and dreamed of a new perfected social type."

Turner's interpretation of the West has left an indelible mark on Americans' perceptions of their past. The rugged-individualist hero—usually a sheriff, rancher, or gunfighter—with only his wits and his Colt .45 to defend himself and his cause, is a central figure of national mythology. He is not only self-reliant; he is also democratic and makes no distinction between ranch hands and ranch owners. By contrast, there is the "dude" from Boston or Philadelphia who has to learn the hard way that in the West clothes and manners do not make the man. And there is the posse or vigilante group to demonstrate the importance of spontaneous democratic social action.

The truth is more complex than this western myth. Western individualism was not unqualified. Community cooperation and social control existed on the frontier. Westerners joined in social activities and mutual-aid efforts like barn raising, fence building, cooperative harvesting, quilting bees, and assisting in childbirth. In politics westerners, like other Americans, rejected unqualified laissez faire and seldom hesitated to pass laws to control the economic and social practices of their neighbors when regulation suited their purposes.

Turner also exaggerated the extent to which the movement westward involved individuals and isolated families. New Englanders often settled in groups, creating compact communities modeled on the traditional "towns" of Massachusetts and Connecticut. Villages like Kent and Ashtabula in Ohio's Western Reserve were physical replicas of colonial communities in southern New England. At times entire eastern communities pulled up stakes as an entity and headed west. The migration of the Latter-day Saints (Mormons) from upstate New York to Ohio, Missouri, then back to Illinois, and finally to the high plain near the Great Salt Lake is a particularly striking instance of group migration. The new Mormon "Zion," moreover, scarcely con-

A REGULAR ROW IN THE BACKWOODS.

The pre–Civil War West was a violent place. This picture is a bit exaggerated, though there were moments when scenes like this one did indeed occur. Note the bottles and jugs on the ground. The artist was clearly making a statement about the source of much western mayhem and disorder.

formed to the stereotype of a community dominated by rugged individualists. Water shortages, the costs of sponsoring new waves of immigrants, the memories of recent persecutions by the "gentiles"—all created in Utah a tight-knit, closely regulated community in which decisions were made by elders and by Brigham Young, the charismatic Mormon leader.

Still, westerners were probably more individualistic than easterners. Spread more thinly over the land, without the steady support of close neighbors, they faced an unsubdued physical environment and had to be self-reliant or perish. The great distances between families also made it easier to be tolerant of differences. How your neighbors conducted their personal affairs was not very important when they lived a mile or more away.

Self-reliance and mutual toleration were the positive aspects of frontier individualism. Another, less attractive side was lawlessness. Westerners were much given to brawling and violent behavior. During the 1840s Iowans' use of the bowie knife made them world-famous for bloodthirstiness. Cutting, eye gouging, and nose biting were common ways of settling disagreements in the antebellum West. Although the use of vigilantes was an effort to impose law on lawless communities, it also expressed westerners' penchant for taking the law into their own hands.

In general, western compliance with social norms was rather poor by eastern or European standards. "I have rarely seen so many people drunk," wrote a traveler in the West in the 1830s. Tobacco chewing, spitting, and swearing were almost universal. Charles Dickens concluded after his American visit in the 1840s that westerners could scarcely speak without "many oaths . . . as necessary . . . words."

Turner's assertions about western egalitarianism and lack of concern for materialism must also be qualified. It is true that outside the Southwest, where the slave system made its strong impression, the rural West achieved a rough equality of material condition. As we saw in Chapter 9, abundant land and a democratic, if imperfect, system of land distribution created a large body of farm owners of middle rank by 1860. Even more significant, however, is the fact that western *attitudes* were egalitarian. One westerner did not regard another as superior merely because he possessed a better education or a more impressive pedigree. One high-born English lady was surprised that people in the California mining camps of the 1850s considered themselves as good as she was. A westerner who dismissed distinguished ancestors as grounds for respect remarked: "It's what's above ground, not what's under, that we think on."

But communities in the Southwest were also full of "cotton snobs" and newly minted gentlemen. In the fast-growing western cities class distinctions developed very quickly. Richard Wade asserts that social "lines sharpened, class divisions deepened, and the sense of neighborliness and intimacy weakened" in the new western cities between 1815 and 1830. And no matter how indifferent they were to ancestry, westerners were generally impressed by money. Pioneer farmers had come west to achieve modest independence at least, and to get rich if they could.

Turner's agreeable, positive picture, then, is an overstatement. Real westerners were cruder, more materialistic, and less egalitarian and individualistic in their behavior than he claimed. But their values were indeed individualistic and egalitarian, and values affect actions.

What about the rest of the country? Did the West's qualities mark Americans elsewhere as well? Frederick Jackson Turner claimed that they did. The West, he said, was the ultimate source of the democratic values of the nation as a whole. Attitudes and institutions developed on the frontier were carried back east, helping to make the entire country an open, democratic society.

Such an interpretation, however, leaves many things out of account. In the pre–Civil War years the Northeast was engulfed in a rush of economic changes that turned farm people into factory wage earners and brought to America's shores thousands of newcomers from Europe. These changes had vital effects unrelated to the frontier experience of the West.

Problems of Urbanization.   One social force that Turner ignored was urbanization. In 1800 the nation had only five towns with over 10,000 inhabitants: New York, Philadelphia, Boston, Charleston, and Baltimore. Although crowded with skilled artisans producing a wide range of manufactured goods, these small cities were primarily centers of foreign trade, shipping American grain, cotton, furs, lumber, tobacco, and other products of the land to distant places around the world and receiving manufactured goods from Europe and tropical products from Latin America. And even inland urban communities were mostly distribution centers for buyers and sellers.

As the economy changed and grew, the new factories and mills attracted a wave of people to the older towns and created new ones such as Lowell, Fall River, Chicopee, and Nashua in the Northeast. Cities also sprouted or expanded in the West. By the 1850s substantial towns such as Louisville, Cincinnati, St. Louis, Chicago, Cleveland, and Lexington had grown up in the trans-Appalachian region.

Wherever located, cities brought people together in schools, concert halls, theaters, clubs, churches, libraries, political parties, and other associations, creating a sense of community and shared interests and values. But cities were also troubled places with many disruptive social problems. One was the lack of transportation. At first cities were so small that people could get around on foot. By the eve of the Civil War, however, Baltimore, Boston, Chicago, Cincinnati, St. Louis, and New Orleans all had over 100,000 people; Philadelphia had over 500,000; and New York–Brooklyn, over a million. Such metropolises required public transportation systems. Omnibuses—elongated wheeled carriages pulled by horses—arrived in the 1830s.

But not until the appearance two decades later of the horse-drawn streetcar running on rails did the major towns acquire reasonably good transit systems.

Housing was another major urban problem—and it was never adequately solved. As middle-class people abandoned the city centers to move to newer districts, their dwellings were cut up into small apartments; many working-class newcomers were forced to accept this housing. Sometimes landlords built shacks in the gardens and backyards of older middle-class houses for the newcomers. By the 1850s most large cities had acquired the latest urban development: the slum.

The poor housing was matched by poor water supply, poor waste disposal, and poor health services. Early in the nineteenth century, Philadelphia, Cincinnati, and Pittsburgh built aqueducts to bring pure country water into their cities, but it was mid-century before New York, Boston, and other towns abandoned use of polluted wells and streams. Waste disposal in most American cities was almost primitive. Slop water from baths (infrequently taken), sinks, and "necessary houses" was often merely dumped into the streets. Where sewers existed, they were often connected to the same stream that supplied the community's drinking water. Scavenging pigs took care of much of the cities' garbage disposal. In the 1840s Dickens was amazed to see "gentlemen hogs . . . ugly brutes" trotting up New York's Broadway behind his carriage. Although the pigs performed a civic service by consuming some of the garbage, their droppings, along with those of horses by the thousands, were a major source of urban pollution. On a sweltering August day in 1852, one New Yorker noted, "the streets smell like a solution of bad eggs in ammonia."

It is not surprising that health was poor in antebellum cities. Typhoid fever and typhus were common. The devastating cholera epidemics of 1832 and 1849–1850 came from the infected water supplies. Smallpox, yellow fever, and malaria were other common urban afflictions. Not all these diseases were actually water-borne, but doctors thought they were, and the alarm they caused moved public-spirited citizens to improve water supplies and establish boards of health.

Crime and Violence.   The traditional social restraints of America often broke down in the antebellum cities. Cities became catch basins for the antisocial with weak social ties to families and other groups. Newcomers who succeeded in getting ahead could avoid the cities' corrosive effects, but those who failed or found only marginal places in the urban economy often succumbed to temptations or turned to antisocial occupations. Inevitably cities were full of burglars, footpads, pickpockets, and ruffians who preyed on law-abiding citizens. One 1858 estimate claimed that there was one prostitute for every fifty men in American cities.

This 1835 illustration of the Cincinnati riverfront suggests how important steamboats and rivers were to western urban development. At this time, the "Queen City of the West" was not only an important river port but also a town that boasted a medical college, an academy of fine arts, many libraries, and other cultural attractions.

The general violence and disorder of antebellum American life was magnified in the cities. But even small communities were not exempt. No Fourth of July or election day passed without broken heads and blood in the streets of America's country villages and hamlets. The metropolises were worse, of course. City slums, like New York's notorious Five Points, fostered gangs that conducted full-scale wars with one another and with the police. Crammed with the poor and outcast, districts of urban immigrants were especially violence-prone, a fact that led many native Americans to conclude that the foreign-born were a danger to society. Riots were frequent in antebellum cities. In 1837, Boston volunteer firemen and Irish mourners clashed violently at a funeral procession on Broad Street and state militia had to be called out to quell the mayhem. Still worse was the Astor Place Riot in New York in 1849. In this brawl

twenty-two people lost their lives and the new, luxurious Astor Place Opera House was severely damaged by a working-class mob that resented the British actor William Charles Macready and the high standards of taste and decorum that the city's cultural elite sought to impose on audiences.

At first, American cities had few means to deal with disorder. Until the 1840s the law was enforced by elected constables by day and a part-time "watch" at night. The increasing violence and rioting that marked these years of tensions between the native- and foreign-born and the urban erosion of rural-derived social controls made this antique system inadequate. In 1838, Boston established a professional daytime police force to supplement the night watch. In the following decade New York gave up the night watch entirely and established a twenty-four-hour-a-day police

This New York City intersection—the "Five Points"—was reportedly the most notorious neighborhood in the antebellum United States. This picture was painted in 1829; when Charles Dickens observed the neighborhood in 1842, it was still "reeking everywhere with dirt and filth." Note the numerous "Groceries"; at the time, groceries sold liquor to customers, who brought their own bottles to be filled. (Collection of the New York Historical Society)

force. Before long most other large eastern cities had taken the same road to a modern city police system.

Surging Immigration. Although Turner described America as an egalitarian society, increasing tensions between native-born Americans and recent immigrants clearly challenged the principle of equality. Immigration from Europe, as we saw, had been light during the half century following the Revolution. Then in the 1830s the number of new arrivals grew to almost 600,000; in the 1840s, to 1.7 million; and in the 1850s, to 2.3 million. The immigrants included Swiss, Netherlanders, Poles, Norwegians, Swedes, French, Russians, and Italians. Most, however, came from Britain, Germany, and the south of Ireland.

The two largest groups, the Irish and the Germans, did not fare equally well in America. The Irish came from a poorer land and brought less capital to America. For centuries the Catholic Irish peasants had suffered for their religion at the hands of the Protestant English. Denied economic and political rights, they lived as impoverished tenants on lands owned by rich Protestant landlords. In the late eighteenth and early nineteenth centuries the introduction of the potato permitted peasant families to raise more food on their small plots of ground, and Ireland's population soared. When the potato crop failed during the mid-1840s, hundreds of thousands of Irish fled to escape starvation. Some went to England. With their paltry possessions, many more crossed the Atlantic to America.

Unable to buy land or pay the fare to the West once they arrived, Irish families usually stayed in the eastern cities, where they took the lowest paying jobs—as construction workers, day laborers, factory hands, porters, handymen, and teamsters. To help make ends meet, many Irish women and girls worked part-time as laundresses or garment workers. Thousands became maids, cooks, and charwomen in the homes of middle-class native-born Americans. Eventually "Bridget" became almost a synonym for a female "domestic servant" in America.

The Germans were more fortunate. Most early nineteenth-century German immigrants were farmers who, like the Irish, were seeking better lives in America. But the pressures on them to leave their homeland were not so severe.

Many had owned their own land, and they brought with them to their new country the money they received from its sale. They were also, on the whole, more skilled than the Irish; a larger portion were craftspeople, mechanics, printers, and the like. Some were even members of the middle class—lawyers, doctors, musicians, soldiers, college professors, and business people—who were fleeing the antiliberal persecutions that followed the failure of the German Revolution of 1848. (The educated German immigrants of this period are often referred to as "Forty-eighters.")

With more money for travel fares and land, many of the German arrivals could leave the crowded labor markets of the large port cities for the cheap lands of Illinois and Wisconsin. Those who stayed in the East were often able to do better for themselves than the Irish. Every American city had German mechanics, printers, and craftsmen. Many Forty-eighters made their mark in business, medicine, academic life, and even politics. Carl Schurz, Gustav Koerner, and other German political refugees rose to prominent positions in nineteenth-century American public life.

Discrimination. Most immigrants found America a mixed blessing. True, there were jobs, and for some, land. No one starved. Immigrant children could go to school. The more fortunate and enterprising could pull themselves up from unskilled laborers to the level of small businesspeople, often providing services for their compatriots or selling them the imported old-country goods they craved.

Still, the social environment of their adopted land was not ideal. Americans talked about equality and took pride in the openness of their borders, but they disliked the immigrants and often treated them harshly. During the fifty-year period of slack immigration following the Revolution, white Americans had become a relatively homogeneous group. Unused to large blocks of aliens in their midst, native-born Americans were overwhelmed by the deluge of newcomers after 1830. Many viewed the immigrants as law-breakers, tipplers, and clannish people who refused to adopt the customs of their new country. Also, the newcomers were often poor. Confusing causes with consequences, native-born Americans frequently held the immigrants responsible for their squalid housing, their raggedness, their bad health, and the unsanitary conditions in which they lived.

Native-born Americans also reacted negatively to the immigrants' religion. Thousands of new arrivals, including virtually all the Irish, were Catholic. Protestant Americans had a long tradition of anti-Catholicism derived from the religious conflicts of the English Reformation. Although there were Catholics in the United States before 1830, the Catholic community had been small, unobtrusive, and assimilated. It was generally accepted by its neighbors. With the deluge of the 1830–1860 period, however, there suddenly appeared in every town and city Catholic churches, schools, convents, hospitals, and seminaries. A central Catholic hierarchy soon took shape. For the first time Americans encountered on their streets the unfamiliar sight of priests and nuns in black garments. They also experienced the newcomers' "Continental Sunday," which turned the sober Protestant Sabbath into an exuberant day of visiting, picnicking, athletics, and imbibing.

Troops in Philadelphia attempt to stop a riot between Catholics and bitterly anti-Catholic "nativists" in 1844. Fierce nationalists, the nativists objected to the Catholics' tie to a foreign authority: "the bloody hand of the Pope."

Latent anti-Catholicism soon became active anti-Catholicism. Protestant laymen and ministers, used to their own loose congregational system of church government, accused the highly centralized Catholic Church of antidemocratic tendencies. Catholics, moreover, were undermining the public school system, they said, by establishing parochial schools and demanding that the state support them. A few bigoted extremists even revived the time-worn accusations of rampant vice and immorality among Catholic priests and nuns.

Encouraged by such propaganda, antiforeign feeling surged dramatically, and between 1830 and 1860 the nation's cities witnessed violent confrontations between immigrant Catholics and militant native Protestants. More common, however, was the day-to-day discrimination that immigrants encountered. Landlords often would not rent to foreigners, especially the Irish. During the 1850s newspaper help-wanted ads frequently carried the warning "Irish Need Not Apply." If more of the immigrants did not find economic life intolerable, it was because the acute American labor shortage often gave employers little alternative to offering them jobs.

In the 1850s, when immigration was at its height, antiforeign, anti-Catholic feelings spawned a political movement based on bigotry. During the 1840s antiforeign, "nativist" societies had acted as pressure groups seeking to exclude foreigners from America or reduce their influence in American life. Most were strongly anti-Catholic. About 1850 one of these, the secret Order of the Star-Spangled Banner, began to be called Know-Nothings from the response of its members when asked to describe the organization. In the next few years the Know-Nothings abandoned their secrecy and, as the American party, became a force in American political life. The new party fell as quickly as it rose, splitting into factions and losing members when it was unable to deal with the overriding issue of slavery in the territories (see Chapter 14). By 1858 it was all but dead, but it left behind a harsh legacy of political nativism that has not completely disappeared.

Free Blacks. Even more than religion and nationality, race tested American egalitarian ideals. Two hundred thousand free blacks, largely the descendants of slaves freed after the Revolution, lived in the northern and western states in 1850. The free black community of the North included many talented men and women. Starting as an errand boy in Philadelphia, James Forten amassed a fortune as a sail maker. His granddaughter, Charlotte Forten, was a teacher, diarist, and prominent abolitionist. Some of the most stylish restaurants, barbershops, and catering establishments in northern cities were run by blacks. The larger cities also sheltered able black ministers and journalists. But these people were exceptional. The great majority of northern free blacks were unskilled laborers at the bottom of the social pyramid.

Bigotry harshly affected the life of almost every free black. Both north and south, white Americans often treated them with disdain, seldom questioning assertions of their inherent moral and intellectual inferiority. The one notable exception were northern abolitionists, especially the followers of William Lloyd Garrison, many of whom truly embraced an ethic of human equality. Denied admission to white schools, refused jobs they were qualified to perform, free blacks were also without elementary civil rights in most northern states. In many northern communities, Jim Crow laws (the name derived from the popular "blackface" minstrel show) mandated separate public facilities for blacks and whites. Prejudice against them was harshest in the Northwest, where state "black laws" disqualified them from serving on juries, testifying against whites in court, or joining the militia. Pandering to white wage earners' fears of job competition, these states also excluded blacks from taking up residence within their borders. Even in liberal New England, where most states allowed free blacks to vote, they were surrounded by a sea of prejudice in their daily lives and routines.

Their exclusion from many spheres of the larger community's life inspired some free blacks to creative solutions. When, for example, the white officials of St. George Methodist Church of Philadelphia tried to segregate the many blacks who came to hear the popular black preacher Richard Allen, Allen organized the Free African Society. In 1794 he established the African Methodist Episcopal Church, which eventually had thousands of communicants all through the North and South. Free black Christians of other denominations likewise established separate churches rather than accept inferior status within white ones. Blacks also founded separate Masonic, Odd Fellows, and other fraternal lodges when they were not admitted to full equality in existing white associations.

As the years passed, things got worse rather than better for free black Americans. Before the 1830s there had been a place, if a lowly one, for blacks in the northern economy. With the influx of immigrants, their lot deteriorated. Employers preferred native Americans above all, but would hire newly arrived Germans and Irish before free blacks. The immigrants themselves, especially the Irish, were hostile to blacks, seeing them as competitors in the labor market. At times immigrants made blacks scapegoats for their own frustrations and disappointments. Tensions between blacks and Irish sometimes erupted into savage riots in which scores of people were injured.

Women. Not only was American equality marred by racial, religious, and ethnic discrimination; it was also qualified

Elizabeth Freeman was a black Massachusetts woman who successfully sued for her freedom in 1783. Her victory, under Massachusetts constitution that declared "all men are born free and equal," established a precedent. Thereafter slavery ceased to exist in the commonwealth. Freeman lived to a ripe old age, residing in a house she bought with the wages she earned.

by discrimination based on sex. Antebellum America, like every other Western society, was male-dominated. Especially in the early years of the century women's legal status was inferior to men's. It was difficult for any woman, except perhaps a strong-willed and self-sufficient widow, to live independently of a man, whether father, husband, or brother. Under the law women were treated as minors. The earnings and property of married women belonged to their husbands. They could not sign legal papers. Their husbands could beat them without the law's intervention except in aggravated cases. Their children were not their own in a strict legal sense, and in a divorce they usually lost all claim to their offspring. Nor were matters much better in public realms. Women could not hold office or vote. Virtually all the professions were closed to them except schoolteaching, and as we have seen, women schoolteachers were paid

lower salaries than men. Indeed, most women's work outside the home tended to be unskilled or poorly paid or both.

Few married women worked for wages in this era. Working women usually were either young, unmarried girls waiting for husbands and families, or older spinsters or widows who had no choice but to support themselves. This meant that the life of a typical American woman was conditioned largely by her role and function in her family household. Here matters were improving somewhat in these pre–Civil War years, especially for middle-class women. For the wives of businessmen, professionals, and highly skilled workers, there were servants, usually young immigrant women, to help with the heavy chores of the typical household in the pre-electric, pre-running water, pre-telephone era. In addition, the burden of raising children began to lift as birthrates fell. Although birth-control methods were crude, by the eve of the Civil War, the numbers of children born each year per family had dropped about 40 percent from the 1800 levels.

This portrait, painted in Maryland in about 1830 by Elizabeth Glaser, epitomizes the contemporary "cult of true womanhood." The doll-like woman seems unsuited for anything more demanding than watering flowers. The painting attests to another pursuit allowed young ladies—painting itself, especially in a delicate medium like watercolors.

Other improvements came for middle-class women as new working conditions took men out of the household. In former years, when over 90 percent of all Americans lived on farms, entire families worked together. In many of the early textile mills, especially those of Rhode Island, work continued to be a concern of the entire family. But increasingly among middle-class city people, fathers went to work in the morning, leaving wives and children at home. This emerging pattern encouraged acceptance of a distinct women's "sphere"—the family circle—where their role was supreme. Reinforced by the idea that in a free republic women educated the sons who led the nation, the concept of a distinct women's sphere raised the status of women within the family. Women were still their husband's inferiors, but in the nursery and the kitchen they were supreme.

Despite some advances in status, women continued to suffer from male condescension. Male-dominated society claimed to honor women but often treated them as emotional and physical invalids. Women were thought to be frail creatures, dominated by their wombs, which made them nervous and sickly and not competent to bear the full burdens of adulthood. As protection, society surrounded them with a wall of stifling conventions and expectations, epitomized in the "cult of true womanhood." A true woman was sweet and gentle, modest and nurturing, pious and reverent, and irreproachably chaste. Even within the bonds of marriage, women were expected to be "pure" and dampen their "animal" urges.

There were perhaps some advantages to these misconceptions and myths. Some women, especially those of the middle class, were spared heavy physical chores and the pressures of making a living. Some scholars have recently argued that women used prudery as a way of retaliating against male superiority. But no matter how intended or used, the practice of treating women like children diminished their lives and deprived society of their talents.

★ EVERYDAY LIFE IN ANTEBELLUM AMERICA ★

Propelled by a flourishing agriculture and surging industry, Americans on average were getting richer by the decade. By 1860 per capita income in the United States was probably the second highest in the world, just behind Britain, the pioneer of the Industrial Revolution. But we must not exaggerate this prosperity. The lives of most Americans remained pinched and uncomfortable by our measure.

Housing standards, for example, were surprisingly poor. We have a snapshot of the nation's housing stock in 1798, at the opening of this period, from a federal government housing survey made to assess taxes to pay for national defense. The picture is not impressive.

According to the survey, most American homes were meager and shoddy, far more primitive than the few structures from that period—generally the show places of the day—that survive. In the West the log cabin was common. Nostalgia has transformed these buildings into glamorous abodes, but they were usually squalid shacks. And even in the long-settled East many people still lived in two- or three-room houses, usually of one story. By now windows usually had glass, and chimneys were of brick or stone, but the advance over the colonial period was not spectacular. One striking conclusion that emerges from the 1798 survey is that housing standards were very unequal, far more so than today. As social historian Jack Larkin notes, only one white American family in ten lived in a house valued at $700 or more, a sum equal to about double the yearly wage for unskilled labor. That amount would buy a two-story, seven-room New England farm house. At $3,000—affordable by only one in a hundred Americans—one could enjoy a ten-room Federal style house with paired chimneys at either end and a central hallway entrance. Not all the shanty housing was in the countryside. The back alleys and side streets of many towns and cities were crammed with cellarless wooden shacks often no larger than fourteen-by-seventeen feet in dimensions. Here day laborers and poor widows lived, sometimes more than one family to a structure! Nor were typical American homes well landscaped. A British traveler noted that the surroundings of the standard American farm house were "a sort of out-of-door slovenliness. . . . You see bits of wood, timber, boards, chips, lying about here and there, and pigs tramping about in a sort of confusion."

Dirt and foul smells were an unavoidable part of everyday life. Unpaved roads and streets produced clouds of dust. Open fireplaces threw off smoke and soot. For rural Americans, and even urban Americans, domestic animals were the source of stench, organic filth, and clouds of flies. In the towns and cities "necessary houses," ensconced in backyards, often overflowed spreading their effluvia over a wide area. It was not always much better on the farm. In some rural areas the general outdoors still served for indiscriminate disposal of human waste.

This environment made personal cleanliness difficult, and many housewives apparently accepted the inevitable. Not that they did not fight dirt as well as they could. On washdays women did prodigious amounts of laundry by hand, their arms plunged into giant tubs of hot water and dirty clothes. They often emerged at the end of the arduous day with "bleached, par-boiled fingers." Still, they could not keep the filth at bay. Visitors often commented on the dirty and littered floors of American homes. According to archaeologists, in the countryside, farm folk often tossed broken crockery, trash, and food scraps outside the nearest window.

As time passed and incomes rose, housing and sanitation improved. By the Civil War era, many middle-class householders had even begun to surround their dwellings with lawns, gardens, and white picket fences. But even in 1860 a majority of free Americans obviously lived in houses under conditions that we today would consider shabby and uncomfortable.

Nor at first was personal hygiene any better. Without indoor plumbing and hot water heaters Americans found bathing daunting. Imagine how often you would wash all over if you had to use cold water—especially in winter! Under the circumstances, most Americans kept grime off only their hands and faces. And what personal washing they did was usually without soap, a commodity reserved for dirty clothes. Day laborers and slaves, engaged in hard physical labor and even more poorly supplied with washing facilities than the affluent, were certainly dirtier than most. But virtually all Americans of the day must have been fragrant by our standards.

Sanitary standards began to improve by the 1840s, especially among the prosperous. More and more homes began to have washstands, basins, and pitchers available in bedrooms so the fastidious could wash all over. Chamber pots with covers also became more common. Big-city hotels led the change in personal hygiene. In 1829 the Tremont in Boston boasted indoor plumbing including eight bathtubs and eight "water closets." The affluent soon imitated the commercial pace-setters.

Ever since the colonial era, the diet of Americans had become more diverse, and food preparation more refined. By the middle of the nineteenth century, vegetables were more common in the average household with several new ones, like "Irish" potatoes in the North and sweet potatoes in the South, especially prominent. The improvement in transportation also made available in groceries and general stores a wider variety of spices, condiments, sugar, tea, and coffee. Between 1800 and 1840 consumption of coffee multiplied five times in the United States. Much of this growth was at the expense of beer, hard cider, rum and whiskey, beverages under ferocious fire from the temperance movement. After 1828, when New York's Delmonico restaurant introduced French cooking, affluent urbanites began to adopt new standards of culinary excellence. Cooks employed by the middle class soon learned to prepare food for their employers in the "Parisian" fashion. One important diet development was the advent of the "ice box," an insulated container, cooled by block ice, that made it possible to keep milk, fresh vegetables, and meat from spoiling in warm weather. The ice itself was cut by entrepreneurs from northern lakes in mid-winter and kept in insulated warehouses for summer use by those who could afford it.

Americans of this period used tobacco in large amounts. A cheap home-grown product, it was consumed, as in the past, in pipes and as snuff, but now also in the forms of "segars" and chewing tobacco. Chewing, especially, and the spitting that accompanied it, stirred the anger of the fastidious. Margaret Hall, writing in 1827, remarked that the floor of the Virginia House of Burgesses in Richmond was "flooded with their horrible spitting" and even church aisles were discolored with the "ejection after ejection" from the mouths of men singing in the choir. Mrs Hall was herself the victim of chewers. At a ball in Washington her partner let go a stream of tobacco juice as she and he were walking up the stairs and splattered the flounce of her party dress. Men were the chief users of tobacco products. But rural and working-class urban women smoked pipes and "dipped" snuff, particularly early in the period.

About the year 1800 there was a major change in clothing styles for both men and women. Men stopped wearing three-cornered hats, knee breeches, and broad-tailed coats and adopted pantaloons, short coats, and "stove-pipe" hats. Women at first gave up the full skirts of the past and began to wear trimmer, more revealing clothing. This trend soon reversed; by mid-century, hoops and flounces were back again. But men's attire never returned to the styles of the past. Men also changed the way they wore their hair. By about 1800 wigs, queues, and powder were completely out, replaced by relatively short hair. Until 1850 men were clean-shaven, but then beards began to come in. The Civil War confirmed the trend, for shaving in the field was difficult. Army veterans passed the custom on to the remainder of the nineteenth century.

★ THE ARTS IN ANTEBELLUM AMERICA ★

Just as the egalitarian sentiments Frederick Turner found in America were limited by biases, the idealism he praised was not universal. Materialism was rampant in antebellum America, especially in the North. Foreign travelers invariably commented that American men seemed capable of talking about nothing but prices, business, and get-rich-quick schemes. Southerners, too, often attacked Yankee materialism and contrasted it unfavorably with the supposed easy graciousness of their own region's life. Yet there was another side to the nation's values. Americans were an artistic, imaginative, and creative people who would make major contributions to the arts in the antebellum years. By 1860 American literature, architecture, and painting were beginning to catch up with the best that contemporary Europe could offer.

An American Literature. "Who reads an American book?" sneered the English critic Sydney Smith in 1820. By the time he uttered his famous insult, many educated Europeans were doing that very thing.

Americans themselves had always been readers. During the colonial period they read practical manuals, almanacs, and religious works. In the half century following the French and Indian War, while the British Empire was being torn apart and the young nation was struggling for survival, Americans devoured newspapers, pamphlets, and books dealing with political themes. Only after 1815, however, when Americans turned to matters besides politics, did the audience for "polite letters" expand sufficiently to encourage talented men and women to make careers as novelists and poets.

At the beginning of the nineteenth century Americans were apologetic about their lack of literary distinction. During the earliest years of the Republic the air resounded with voices clamoring for a national literature that would use American themes and avoid slavish imitation of Europe. Energy and enthusiasm were not enough to produce such a literature, however; genius was required. Abruptly, in the opening years of the new century, two New Yorkers—Washington Irving and James Fenimore Cooper—provided it.

Both men were deeply affected by the romantic revolution that had swept the entire Western cultural world toward the end of the eighteenth century. In the arts, romanticism brought the rediscovery of emotion after the long reign of reason and intellect. Whether in words, paint, sound, or stone, romantic artists celebrated feeling, especially their own. They probed individual personality, and were fascinated by eccentricity and extreme situations and emotions. Death, ecstasy, horror, and crime seemed proper subjects for their talents. So, too, did the quaint and the "picturesque." Romantic artists were especially sensitive to the beauties of nature.

Within the larger embrace of the romantic mood of the day, the mandate of American writers was to find in native materials the stuff of literature. The process was slow. Washington Irving's first important work was his contribution to the *Salmagundi Papers* (1807), a set of charming, graceful essays in an eighteenth-century style that delighted polite society. He leaped to international fame in 1819 with publication of a set of assorted short pieces, *The Sketch Book of Geoffrey Crayon, Gent.* These were written in England primarily on English themes. Indeed, several English reviewers called Irving the best British writer that America had yet produced. But included in *The Sketch Book* were two brilliant stories, "The Legend of Sleepy Hollow" and "Rip Van Winkle," that had as their setting the picturesque Hudson Valley with its stolid Dutch burghers and the misty green Catskill Mountains with their myths and legends. Though in reality based on German sources, this seemed to be authentic American material that answered the call for a native literature.

More authentically "American" than Irving's short stories were the novels of James Fenimore Cooper. Cooper was not the only pre–Civil War novelist to use the frontier as raw material. William Gilmore Simms's novel *The Yamassee* (1835) depicted the dramatic struggle between whites and Indians for control of colonial South Carolina. Yet Simms, an urbane Charlestonian, was never really at home in describing the raw frontier. It was Cooper, a New Yorker, who converted the battles of Europeans, white Americans, and Indians against one another and against the wilderness into a frontier epic in a series of novels called collectively *The Leatherstocking Tales*.

The first of these novels, *The Pioneers* (1823), set in the rapidly changing upstate New York of Cooper's childhood, recounted the struggles to impose "civilization" and the forces of "progress" on the pristine wilderness. Its cast of characters includes the untutored but wilderness-wise Natty Bumppo (Leatherstocking), his noble Indian friend, Uncas, and the symbol of change, Judge Marmaduke Temple. Cooper's own sympathies are divided. One part of him yearns for the past of the unspoiled forest and favors those, like the Indians and the American frontiersmen, who know how to live within it; the other part of Cooper is committed to civilization-building and those like Temple and others who are its apostles.

Bumppo is the hero of four other Leatherstocking Tales, including *The Last of the Mohicans* (1826). In these he personifies the "natural" man pitting his skills and sinews against the dangers of wild nature and wild men as well as the corrosive effects of civilization. Cooper's many other novels, including *The Pilot* (1824), *Lionel Lincoln* (1825), and *The Oak Openings* (1848), utilize elements of the American historical experience ranging from the early colonial Indian wars to the struggles against the British on land and sea between 1775 and 1815. In his early works Cooper is a celebrator of his country and its institutions. After returning in 1833 from a stay in Europe, he was appalled by the leveling tendencies of Jacksonian democracy and thereafter chided his compatriots on their vulgarity, lack of decorum, and unrestrained materialism.

The New England Renaissance. Irving and Cooper made New York the nation's first literary capital. By the following decade there were major writers elsewhere as well. The South would produce a cluster of minor interesting figures. Besides Simms there were the poets Paul Hamilton Hayne and Henry Timrod, both southern nationalists who sought to carve out a specific southern poetic genre. There were also a number of practitioners of the plantation novel, ancestral to Margaret Mitchell's *Gone with the Wind*, that glorified the planter class and their opulent way of life. The one southern writer of undisputed stature was Edgar Allen Poe, born in Boston but raised in Virginia.

Poe began his writing career as a poet, imitating Byron, Shelley, and the other great English romantics. We remember from his poetic output little more than "The Raven" and "Annabelle Lee." But his short stories—including "The Gold Bug," "The Fall of the House of Usher," "The Murders in the Rue Morgue," "The Cask of Amontillado," and "The Pit and the Pendulum"—have fascinated and moved generations of readers in Europe and America. To us, the somber Poe often seems less "American" than sunnier or less introspective writers like Irving and Cooper. Yet in his fondness for hoaxes, mysteries, and violence, he was very much in the national mood. His great talent notwithstanding, few Americans of the day considered this tortured, morbid alcoholic an adornment of the country's cultural life. Far more consistent with American pride were the literary giants who

Ralph Waldo Emerson looking the part of the sensitive, clear-headed, optimistic philosopher.

burst forth in New England, especially in and around Boston.

In the generation before the Civil War the Massachusetts capital was the ideal seedbed for a literary flowering. A relatively small community of under 100,000 in 1840, Boston was a "walking city." People could attend to their affairs on foot, and face-to-face contact among those of like mind and taste was easily achieved. Boston, moreover, had a tradition of learning based on the proximity of Harvard College and the heritage of a scholarly and intellectual New England clergy. The city and its suburbs also had an educated elite with money and leisure to patronize and encourage authors.

Boston's literary renaissance owed much to transcendentalism—an approach to God, humanity, and nature compounded of diverse elements of European romanticism, German philosophy, and oriental mysticism. Transcendentalists were philosophical "idealists" who believed the human mind, rather than nature, the senses, or divine revelation, the ultimate source of moral knowledge. Although they borrowed from foreign sources, they were distinctly American. Transcendentalism was optimistic: Humans were perfectible and God was forgiving. It was individualistic: Each person must follow his or her own inspiration. And it was democratic: All men and women had within them part of the divine spark. High-minded and humane, the transcendentalists rejected mere material gain.

The transcendental mood was best expressed in the essays—actually sermons in print—of Ralph Waldo Emerson. Emerson's calm optimism, reasonable and humane views, social generosity, pure motives, and high-mindedness seemed noble and reassuring. He respected American practicality and praised self-reliance, but at the same time he deplored excessive concern with material progress. The "invasion of Nature by Trade with its Money, its Credit, its Steam, its Railroad," he wrote, "threatens to upset the balance of man, and establish a new, universal Monarchy more tyrannical than Babylon or Rome."

In Concord, the semirural community outside Boston where he made his home, Emerson was surrounded by a group of talented and idealistic men and women, including Bronson Alcott, Henry David Thoreau, George Ripley, William Ellery Channing, Margaret Fuller, Elizabeth Peabody, and—for a time—Nathaniel Hawthorne. At Emerson's Tuesday evenings these bright people discussed their host's ideas and those of congenial European writers and thinkers. Their thoughts reached the cultured public through a small magazine, *The Dial*, first published in 1840. In the early 1840s Ripley and a few others of the Emerson circle established Brook Farm, a cooperative experimental community at West Roxbury, Massachusetts, a venture that tested their utopian belief in human perfectibility and innate goodness.

WALDEN;

OR,

LIFE IN THE WOODS.

By HENRY D. THOREAU,

AUTHOR OF "A WEEK ON THE CONCORD AND MERRIMACK RIVERS."

I do not propose to write an ode to dejection, but to brag as lustily as chanticleer in the morning, standing on his roost, if only to wake my neighbors up. — Page 92.

BOSTON:
TICKNOR AND FIELDS.
M DCCC LIV.

The title page of the first edition of Thoreau's Walden. *Our modern image of Thoreau is of a solitary, plainspoken man, but he wrote and revised his work with extreme care, and during his stay in the woods he visited or had visitors from Concord almost every day.*

Emerson was the theorist of transcendentalism, but Thoreau acted on it. Thoreau was living refutation of the charges that Americans were materialists and conformists. A native of Concord, he loved nature, disdained material values, and possessed a social conscience unusually sensitive to injustice even in this age of reform. Thoreau was far more sensitive than his contemporaries to the primacy of nature. "In Wildness is the preservation of the World," he told an audience in Concord. In 1845 he put his own precepts to the test by going to live in the woods at Walden Pond. There he discovered the essentials of existence and concluded that human beings needed very little to be happy. Thoreau was also a courageous individualist, defying the authorities during the Mexican War by refusing to pay his taxes to support what he felt was an unjust attack on America's weaker neighbor.

Nathaniel Hawthorne, the most creative of the Boston group, rejected many of its teachings. In fact, he was a conservative Democrat. But he, too, refused to accept the materialistic values of commercial-industrial America. Hawthorne's spirit harked back to the dour, pessimistic mood of early Puritanism when New Englanders were certain that all men and women were sinful and most were damned. Unlike his Concord acquaintants, he was a sardonic, skeptical man with a strong sense of the human capacity for evil. These qualities and perceptions he incorporated into many memorable short tales, and into the longer works *The Scarlet Letter* (1850) and *The House of the Seven Gables* (1851). Hawthorne's disagreements with some members of Emerson's group prompted him to satirize the impracticality of their social experiments in *The Blithedale Romance* (1852), a novel about Brook Farm.

Melville and Whitman. Emerson's transcendentalism was even less acceptable to another great American writer: New Yorker Herman Melville. Melville began his writing career after seven years at sea. His first novels—*Typee* (1846), *Omoo* (1847), and *Mardi* (1849)—related his adventures among the natives of the South Seas. In 1850 he began *Moby Dick*, in outward form a sea adventure, but actually a far more profound book. In his study of Captain Ahab and Ahab's single-minded determination to destroy the white whale, Melville created a powerful allegory of human obsession. *Moby Dick*, with its dark and complex themes, was not as enthusiastically received by antebellum American readers as Melville's earlier work, but today it is thought to be one of America's greatest novels.

Like Melville, Walt Whitman was not fully appreciated until this century. A writer of distinctly American character, Whitman carried individualism to the point of egotism. His "Song of Myself" begins with the lines:

> I celebrate myself and sing myself,
> And what I assume you shall assume,
> For every atom belonging to me as good belongs to you.

In this mood he reveals the boastfulness that we associate with the American frontier, although he himself spent much of his life in Brooklyn and Camden, New Jersey. Whitman was also a sensualist; whatever Americans of this generation did in private, few if any ever publicly proclaimed their lustiness, their admiration of personal beauty, and their delight in physical love as he did. Much of his poetry, incorporated into successively enlarged editions of *Leaves of Grass* (1855–1892), shocked its readers both for its arrogance and for its sexual explicitness. In his prose, most notably *Democratic Vistas* (1871), Whitman was the advocate of a vigorous and vital democracy that would enable people to fulfill themselves spiritually in spite of material abundance.

Thomas Eakins, the American artist, painted this portrait of Walt Whitman in 1887 when the poet was sixty-eight and had suffered a serious stroke.

The Fireside Poets.   In an excessive drive to find a native literary voice, Americans of this period often exaggerated the achievements of their writers. Four pre–Civil War poets—William Cullen Bryant, Oliver Wendell Holmes, James Russell Lowell, and Henry Wadsworth Longfellow—stand out as instances. Each of these "Fireside Poets" enjoyed major reputations in the nineteenth century. All were learned, successful men, Bryant a lawyer and long-time editor of the *New York Evening Post*, Longfellow and Lowell professors of literature at Harvard, and Holmes a prominent Boston physician. Much of their poetry, whether narrative or lyrical, was patriotic in theme. Works such as Longfellow's "Evangeline," "Paul Revere's Ride," "The Courtship of Miles Standish," and "The Song of Hiawatha," Holmes's "Old Ironsides," and Lowell's "Commemoration Day Ode" helped to create the nineteenth-century national consciousness. With good reason, today they are usually dismissed as naive and banal. But in their day these poems were widely read, recited, and declaimed at commencements, school assemblies, and around the family hearth.

Their appeal derived from their facile rhyme and easy meter, but they also validated distinctive middle-class American values and aspirations and convinced literate citizens of the still-young Republic that theirs too was a poetic land.

The People's Literature.   The Boston and New York writers appealed primarily to the educated middle class. The best were skeptical of American materialism and several exhibited a streak of pessimism that ran against America's postcolonial tendency to envision a bright future. They were the first group of American intellectuals at odds with the dominant values of their society. The literature of the masses, however, was unapologetically upbeat and frankly endorsed get-ahead materialism and conformity. During the antebellum period presses poured out a flood of inexpensive novels that reinforced positive American folk attitudes. Patriotism was one profitable theme. Joseph Holt Ingraham's *The Pirate of the Gulf* (1836) was a blood-and-thunder thriller about the pirate Jean Lafitte, who had aided Jackson at the Battle of New Orleans. Ingraham's success with patriotic adventure novels was matched by that of George Lippard and "Ned Buntline" (Edward Zane Carroll Judson), authors of crime and punishment tales. Another successful type was the religious novel of faith challenged and ultimately preserved.

Much of the audience for literature of any sort in these years was female; American men were too busy with practical matters to read books. Convinced that only women writers could tap this audience successfully, publishers sought out women skilled with words. A genteel occupation that could be practiced at home, writing presented one of the few opportunities besides teaching for middle-class women to earn their living in a respectable way, and they quickly took advantage of it.

Much of the output was potboiler literature. Mary Agnes Fleming, Catharine Maria Sedgwick, Susan Warner, Sarah Payson Willis, and other women churned out countless novels praising domesticity, chastity, true love, and assorted household virtues. These were often cloyingly sentimental. To sustain interest the authors included such melodramatic stock types as the "other woman," the weak husband, and the martyred wife. In the end justice triumphed, and no one but the villain—or villainess—got hurt. Meanwhile, on the way to the denouement, the reader was exposed only to the sweetest, noblest, and most conventional sentiments. But not always. Susan Warner's *The*

Wide, Wide World (1850), a story about how an orphan girl survived difficult circumstances and achieved maturity, contained vivid descriptions of rural America and brilliantly caught the language and style of country people. Sedgwick's books take up the themes of religious bigotry and national identity. Some contemporaries consider her superior to Cooper as a stylist.

The reading public snapped up these works. Warner's *Wide, Wide World* earned her the then-remarkable sum of $35,000 in royalties. In 1853 Willis's *Fern Leaves from Fanny Fern's Portfolio* sold 70,000 copies; during the same period Hawthorne's *Mosses from an Old Manse* (1846) brought him only $144. Not surprisingly, Hawthorne was bitter. "America," he wrote, "is now wholly given over to a damned mob of scribbling women." The great novelist was being unfair in singling out women, for men also contributed prodigiously to the mass of hack writing that affirmed the popular values of the day.

The literature of antebellum America thus expressed many of the contradictions of the nation. Most of the better writers were skeptical of commercial values. They celebrated the individualism of the nonconformist who resisted the dominant teachings of the day or defied nature. In Melville, Poe, and Hawthorne we also detect despair and pessimism, attitudes scarcely approved by Americans or ascribed to them by most foreign observers. Popular litera-

William Sydney Mount was the Norman Rockwell of his day. His America was the happy republic where everyone and everything wore a smile.

322   Chapter 12

ture, on the other hand, sang the praises of family, country, and traditional virtue and refused to carp at darker American characteristics.

Painting. The other arts are equally suggestive of the nation's inner contradictions. American artists achieved a high level of technical proficiency and produced much excellent work during these years. But many American painters disliked their country and considered their fellow citizens unappreciative materialists with philistine attitudes toward art. John Vanderlyn, a painter of elegant nudes, insisted that "no one but an artistic quack would paint in America." Washington Allston, like Vanderlyn trained in Europe, returned to the United States to experience the frustration that eventually led to his emotional breakdown and the collapse of his promising career. Later critics of the United States would cite Allston as a victim of the blighting effect of American materialism and lack of true appreciation for "culture" and the fine arts.

None of these dissenters, however, made dissent the subject of his art, and on the whole they were outnumbered by the celebrators of America. Thomas Cole, Asher B. Durand, and the lesser artists of the Hudson River school chose as their subjects the American countryside, especially the scenery of the Northeast. Their work was idyllic and romantic rather than realistic, but it avoided the artificiality of Allston and Vanderlyn. Still closer to the popular taste were painters like William Sidney Mount and George Caleb Bingham, whose scenes of rural life and homey anecdotes in paint resembled the sentimental popular novels but ex-

celled them in quality. George Catlin and John Audubon were less mannered and less sentimental about the American environment. Catlin's superb pictures of American Indians have enough accuracy and detail to delight an anthropologist. Audubon, of course, was a great naturalist as well as an excellent draftsman, and his watercolor and crayon sketches of American birds are scientific documents as well as objects of great beauty.

The Romantic and the Practical in Architecture. Americans between 1815 and 1860 were both practical house builders and romantic artists in stone, brick, and wood. The practical side was to be found in the innovative "balloon frame" house. Taking advantage of mass-produced nails and standardized cut boards, American home builders abandoned the heavy joined timbers that had made earlier house construction resemble fine cabinetmaking, and put up a light skeleton of uprights and cross pieces attached by nails. Over it they hammered siding of boards or shingles and a roof. The resulting structure was well suited to a fast-growing society that needed enormous amounts of new housing, had abundant timber, and was willing to sacrifice individuality and permanence for speed and cheapness.

Of course, there were people in both town and country who wanted more than a box with a roof in which to live. In this era they commissioned workers in the Greek-revival style to build gracious mansions. The traditional white-pillared Old South plantation house is representative of the Greek-revival style. Greek-revival also became the

American architecture ranged from Egyptian, Greek, Gothic, and even Chinese forms to the purely practical, shown here. Derisively called "balloon frames" because of their lightness, such houses were cheap and required "about as much mechanical skill as it does to build a board fence."

idiom for public buildings. Americans felt indebted to Rome and Athens for their institutions and found the new architecture so congenial that they used it for the Capitol in Washington.

Competing with the Greek-revival style for the affection of the prosperous and sophisticated was the nostalgic romanticism of the Gothic style. Gothic was better suited to churches and homes than to public buildings, though James Renwick's Smithsonian Institution is a distinguished exception. For churches Gothic was a natural style, and the traditions of the great European cathedrals and English parish churches were continued beautifully in such structures as Richard Upjohn's Trinity Church and Renwick's Grace Church in New York. It was in private homes, however, that the Gothic style flourished best. It lent itself not only to mansions; in some ways it was even more suitable for wooden cottages.

Greek-revival and Gothic were the romantic sides of American architecture during these years; the balloon-frame house shows the practical, materialist one. The romantic side searched for an American past that never was, whether in the austere dignity of the classical age or in the mystery, myth, and chivalry of the Middle Ages. The practical side sought a solution to the era's housing problem. Together they neatly bracketed the extremes of American national character before the Civil War.

★ THE PERFECT SOCIETY ★

The social scene of the pre–Civil War North, like the cultural flowering, contained elements that contradicted the charges of American materialism and conformity. Northern society exhibited a degree of dissent, a willingness to confront established social institutions and a zeal for tearing them down and replacing them with new ones, that could be found almost nowhere else in the world. This was a time, according to Emerson, when "madmen, madwomen, men with beards, Dunkers, Muggletonians, Comeouters, Groaners, Agrarians, Seventh Day Baptists, Unitarians and Philosophers—all came successively to the top, and seized their moment, if not their hour, wherein to chide, or pray, or preach, or protest."

Emerson was making fun of the more extreme reformers, but it is true that the reform impulse produced a confusion of voices and actions. Reformers worked at upgrading prisons, improving treatment of the mentally disturbed, enforcing temperance, carrying Christianity to the "heathen," ending warfare, preventing prostitution, extending women's rights, abolishing slavery, and creating utopian communities. Indeed, wherever sensitive and com-

passionate antebellum Americans encountered misery, vice, and injustice, they seemed determined to end them through innovative collective effort.

Religious Roots of Reform. The reform movements of the years preceding 1860 drew some of their energy and substance from the new religious spirit that swept the nation. At the beginning of the nineteenth century American Protestantism was languishing. Most Americans considered themselves Christians, and many attended services at one of the numerous Protestant churches on Sunday. But compared with the past, or so believers held, piety had declined drastically both on the frontier and in the East. In some Connecticut towns in the 1790s Congregational churches added only four or five new members a year. In New England and in those parts of upstate New York and the Great Lakes states where Yankees had immigrated, ministers worried that "the Sabbath would be lost, and every appearance of religion vanish."

Before long, the religious pendulum swung back to renewed religious fervor. During the first half century of the Republic, a second Great Awakening, led by traveling bands of Methodist, Baptist, and Presbyterian evangelists, induced thousands of Americans to consider their sins, contemplate a new life, affirm or reaffirm their faith, and join the church. Vast outdoor revivals drew great numbers of rural citizens to marathon preaching sessions, where eloquent evangelists like Charles Grandison Finney, Francis Asbury, and Peter Cartwright exhorted sinners to abandon their evil ways and find salvation in God's everlasting love. The most memorable revival meeting of all took place at Cane Ridge, Kentucky, where for almost a week between 20,000 and 40,000 participants listened to forty ministers. At one time more than 100 exhausted, repentant sinners lay prostrate amid the "solemn hymns, the empassioned exhortation, the earnest prayers, and the sobs, shrieks, or shouts bursting from persons under intense agitation."

The revivals were welcomed by many good Christians. In the wake of each visting evangelist, new members poured into the Methodist, Presbyterian, and Baptist churches. Many of the "saved" joined new denominations. Western New York, called the "burnt-over" district for the wave after wave of revivalism that swept across it, became a religious hothouse that fostered a score of new sects, among them the Latter-day Saints (Mormons), Adventists, and Shakers.

On the other hand, leaders of the more sedate groups like the Episcopalians and Congregationalists often attacked the new preachers as ranters and dangerous inciters of undignified emotional display. Orthodox Calvinists deplored their rejection of predestination. But orthodox Calvinism was also at war during these years with Unitarianism, an offshoot of Congregationalism that had divested itself of Calvinist pessimism along with the orthodox Christian belief in the Trinity. Unitarians were heirs of Enlightenment rationality who accepted a general Christian benevolence but rejected what they considered the supernatural and irrational in traditional Christian belief.

Unitarianism and evangelicalism attracted different sorts of individuals. The first appealed to educated merchants and professional people, especially in the Boston area; the second made greater headway among farmers and lower-middle-class artisans and tradespeople. For all their social differences, however, Unitarians and evangelicals agreed that men and women could effect their own salvation and perfect both themselves and their society. The converted, proclaimed the evangelist Finney, "should aim at being holy and not rest till they are as perfect as God." Sin was selfishness; virtue, selflessness and benevolence toward others. Sin, said the new breed of religious leaders, was vol-

untary; humanity could reject it; and collective sin—what we call social evils—could be rooted out by human will, education, and cooperative public action.

This "Perfectionist" doctrine quickly penetrated organizations already involved in efforts to improve society. By 1820 these groups were in close contact with one another and constituted an informal "benevolent empire" that devoted its attention to world peace, temperance, foreign missions, antislavery, and other good causes. The benevolent societies usually had limited, practical goals. The most zealous of the new reformers, inspired by the evangelists, believed that evil must be ripped out root and branch, as soon as possible. Not all reformers were so ambitious. Nevertheless, Perfectionism gave to the wave of humanitarian reform that swept the North and the West a passion, and at times a fanaticism, that it had lacked before.

The second Great Awakening fostered reform movements such as abolitionism, women's rights, and prohibition. After revivalist preachers "knocked out the (cork) and let nature caper," their flock "got religion" and rolled in the aisles, jerking about, even barking in ecstasy. Many worldly people had nothing but contempt for the revivals and revivalists.

The Desire for Social Control.   Other impulses besides Perfectionism inspired the reformers' zeal to change the world. Many believed that society in this era of emerging industrialization and urbanization was experiencing a severe breakdown, and feared that social chaos would result if something were not done to check the collapse. Reformers of this sort often blamed society's plight on family failure. According to the Boston Prison Discipline Society, it was the "confession of many convicts . . . that the course of vice, which brought them to prison, commenced in disobedience to their parents, or their parents' neglect." Insanity and alcoholism were also thought to stem from families' increasing inability, in an industrializing society, to discipline and train their members. To men and women who held such views, "asylums," where victims of their family's failings could find havens from the harsh new world and learn to cope with their difficulties, seemed the solutions.

Penitentiaries were one form of asylum that reformers of this kind sought to establish. Clearly, existing jails and prisons were deplorable. They were unsanitary places with wretched food, where first offenders were mixed with hardened criminals. They did nothing to rehabilitate lawbreakers. The reformed system of penitentiaries endorsed by Louis Dwight, Elam Lynds, and others separated first offenders from repeaters, provided better sanitation, and allowed prisoners some privacy. But as a would-be substitute for family discipline, it also imposed solitary confinement, hard physical labor, and regimentation. In the Auburn system of New York, established in 1816, prisoners were strictly regimented, marched to and from work in tight lockstep, and flogged for violating prison rules. It is not easy today to detect the humanitarianism of the penitentiary system, and in the end it failed in its primary aim of rehabilitating criminals. Yet the changes were considered models of enlightenment in their day, and dozens of European observers came to view the American system and learn from it.

Dorothea Dix's efforts to improve the treatment of the insane also called for asylums. The plight of the insane in antebellum America was clearly serious. In an earlier era "lunatics" had been kept at home in the care of their families. They were seldom cured, but at least they were usually well treated. Increasingly, however, the physical mobility of American families and their growing reluctance to carry the burden of unproductive relatives forced the community to care for the mentally disturbed. Unfortunately, there were few mental hospitals, and the insane were often treated like animals. When the passionately idealistic young Massachusetts reformer first observed how the insane fared in her home state, she was shocked. Mental patients, Dix reported, were kept in "cages, closets, cellars, stalls, pens!" They were "chained, naked, beaten with rods, and lashed into obedience." Dix demanded that Mas-

sachusetts establish asylums to provide the insane with humane treatment. With the aid of Samuel Gridley Howe, Horace Mann, and Dr. Luther Bell, by 1860 she had induced almost every state to provide improved facilities for mental defectives and the insane.

Alcoholism also aroused the reformers, though they seldom considered asylums the proper method of dealing with it. There can be no question that antebellum America had an alcohol problem. Captain Basil Hall, an English visitor of the 1820s, noted the "universal practice of sipping a little at a time, but frequently . . . during the whole day." Americans themselves worried about their countrymen's drinking habits. Ministers asserted that drunkenness and "lewdness" went hand in hand. The guardians of public morals believed that alcoholism was especially prevalent among the working class and immigrants; but in fact, all classes had their share of drunkards who squandered their wages, beat their wives, neglected their children, and committed vicious crimes while under the influence of "demon rum."

This is an idealized portrait of Dorothea Dix, the advocate of better treatment for the insane. Yet it captures the strong will and determination that made Dix so effective in persuading legislators to vote for the establishment of asylums.

The temperance reform movement developed two wings. The moderates wished to educate society on the evils of alcohol in order to reduce excessive drinking. The "total abstainers" condemned all drinking as a sin and demanded state prohibition laws to outlaw the production, transport, and consumption of alcoholic beverages. The battles between these two factions split the American Society for the Promotion of Temperance during the 1830s, and for several years the movement languished. Then, in the following decade, the prohibitionists, under the leadership of Neal Dow, gained control. Dow's first success came in 1851 when Maine, his native state, passed the first statewide prohibition law. In the next few years a dozen states, mostly in the North and West, adopted the "Maine Law."

Growing Female Assertiveness. Many of the reformers were women. At one time scholars ascribed their large numbers within the reform movements to the "natural tenderness" or the intrinsic nurturing quality of women. Today we are more likely to seek an explanation in the social setting of the day, especially in the experience of middle-class women. The cult of domesticity had given mothers higher prestige and sanctioned better education for women than previously. Yet society still believed that women's proper

Though she looks like a prim and proper Victorian lady, Elizabeth Cady Stanton was a fierce warrior for women's rights. Born in 1815, she died in 1902, less than twenty years before the Nineteenth Amendment gave women the vote.

sphere was the home and family. To the young women pouring out of the new seminaries, or otherwise affected by the new partial liberation, the countless remaining restraints on women's public role seemed increasingly galling.

At first women activists found it very difficult to assert their own rights. Striving for the betterment of others seemed more acceptable, for these efforts were related to women's traditional helping role. Dorothea Dix's work for the insane may be seen as an instance of such displacement. Many reform-minded middle-class women also turned to the problems of working girls forced into prostitution in order to eke out a living in the cities. Hundreds of middle-class women during these years also joined missionary societies to bring the message of Christ to the benighted frontier and to the heathen Chinese, Hawaiians, Burmese, and Africans overseas.

Women also participated in record numbers in the ranks of the American Peace Society, which opposed recourse to war as a means of settling disputes among nations. Although it attacked all wars, the society especially denounced offensive wars. This approach did not please true pacifists, who believed defensive as well as offensive wars evil. Led by William Lloyd Garrison, Angelina Grimké, Abby Kelly, Bronson Alcott, and others, the radicals seceded and formed the Non-Resistance Society, which rejected all submission to national interests that required violence. "We allow no appeal to patriotism, to revenge any national insult or injury," declared its Declaration of Principles. "We conceive that a nation has no right to defend itself against foreign enemies, or . . . punish invaders. . . ."

The antislavery movement also attracted women reformers, and their experience in the momentous attack on black bondage was a key catalyst in overcoming their reluctance to aid themselves. Within the antislavery movement few objected to women helping to raise money through such activities as bazaars or cake sales, for example. But at least a few bolder women wanted to take more active roles as speakers and organizers. The first woman to put such urges into practice was Angelina Grimké, who left the South in 1829 with her more retiring sister, Sarah, when they could no longer stand the scourge of slavery. In 1837, after becoming Quakers, the sisters began to give antislavery talks to small groups of women who came to hear about the "peculiar institution" from those who knew it firsthand. Men soon began to attend, and before long Angelina was addressing large gatherings of both men and women in New York and New England.

For women to speak before mixed male-female audiences was a shocking break with tradition and serious breech of decorum. Many moderate antislavery leaders, sensitive to conservative attack, decried Grimké's speeches and deplored the growing participation of women in the movement. But not abolitionist radicals. Frederick Douglass, a black antislavery leader who felt discrimination based on biology with special poignancy, praised Grimké and endorsed female activism. So did the firebrand William Lloyd Garrison. "As our object is *universal* emancipation," wrote Garrison, "to redeem women as well as men from a servile to an equal condition—we shall go for the rights of women to their utmost extent."

Despite—or perhaps because of—her opponents, Angelina Grimké evolved into one of the earliest feminists. In 1838 she published *Letters on the Equality of the Sexes*, in which she denounced the traditional education and indoctrination of women as designed to keep them in an inferior status. Women should be treated as full human beings. "Whatsoever it is morally right for a man to do," she announced, "it is morally right for a woman to do."

Other women, too, were propelled by the antislavery movement into grappling with their own social and political inferiority. When the 1840 World's Antislavery Convention in London excluded nine American female delegates from its sessions, two of these, Lucretia Mott and Elizabeth Cady Stanton, resolved to launch a new movement dedicated to improving the status of American women.

During the next few years various women's groups succeeded in getting a number of state legislatures to pass laws allowing married women to retain ownership of property and income they had inherited or acquired by themselves and to have joint guardianship of their children. But these gains were insufficient. In the summer of 1848 Mott and Stanton brought together 250 people in a women's rights convention at Seneca Falls, New York. Most of the delegates were women, but there were also a few male Quakers and reformers, including Frederick Douglass. Seneca Falls marked the true beginning of the women's rights movement. The delegates issued a Declaration of Sentiments modeled after the Declaration of Independence that replaced King George III with "man" as the oppressor. It demanded a series of changes to reduce women's legal inferiority and denounced male efforts to diminish women's "confidence in [their] own power" and lessen their "self-respect." The most radical demand, one that clearly violated the notion that women's "proper sphere" was domestic life, was for the "elective franchise"—votes for women!

Seneca Falls did not create a national women's rights organization. Instead, it energized a flock of local and state groups, often informal and temporary, and produced several rounds of state and national conventions where the Seneca Falls Declaration was refined and augmented. The informal networks of women's rights advocates during the 1850s continued to fight for state laws to eliminate gross legal discrimination against women and scored some further successes. They also succeeded in securing new recruits for feminism. They made no impression on resistance to female voting, however. Even women reformers doubted the wisdom of the drive for female suffrage. It seemed so extreme as to stigmatize the entire movement. Meanwhile, the going was often hard. Feminists were jeered at and mocked. Unlike the abolitionists, they were spared physical attack, but that was virtually all they escaped.

In addition to organized group efforts to defeat male domination of society, many middle-class women strove individually to improve their position. The first barrier to achievement, the inaccessibility of higher education to women, was breached when Oberlin in 1833, and then other colleges, admitted women as full degree candidates. In 1865 the first all-women's college, Vassar, was established.

With degrees in hand, women could now take on the professions. In 1850 Antoinette Brown took a theology degree at Oberlin and became the first ordained woman minister. The female breakthrough in medicine came with the Blackwell sisters, who earned their degrees at Geneva College, the only school that would admit them for medical training. Other women began to take law courses and set up practices as attorneys. In almost every case women professionals encountered resistance and ridicule in these years. But by the Civil War women had at least broken the crust of male domination of the public sphere, and it was apparent that more advances would follow.

Antislavery Sentiments. The antislavery movement was a momentous and controversial focus for reform in its own right. We have already seen how the Revolution undermined slavery north of the Mason-Dixon line. In succeeding decades the Quakers continued to oppose slavery, although they avoided harsh attacks on slaveholders. Antislavery groups remained active in many places for a time after 1783, even in the South itself.

One expression of antislavery sentiment in this early period was the colonization movement dedicated to returning free blacks to Africa. Some members of the American Colonization Society (founded in 1817), especially southerners, saw their movement primarily as a means of getting rid of a dangerous group that threatened the survival of slavery. Recognizing white southerners' fears that if slavery were abolished, the South would have an enormous problem adjusting to a vastly expanded free black population, others believed that returning blacks to Africa could serve as a first step in eventually freeing all the slaves. Whatever their motives, promoters of colonization did not take into account the costs of transporting millions of blacks to Africa, southern resistance to surrendering hundreds of millions of dollars' worth of property, or the feelings of black

Women's Rights

Lucy Stone was a founder of the pre–Civil War women's rights movement. Determined to get an education at a time when women were considered incapable of exercising the higher mental faculties, she was fortunate when Oberlin College in Ohio opened its doors to women and blacks. In 1847, soon after earning her degree, she joined the abolitionist movement and for several years worked for the American Antislavery Society. For Lucy Stone, as for other women, abolitionism served as a bridge to the women's rights movement. In 1850 she helped to organize the first national women's rights convention at Worcester, Massachusetts, and eventually became a leader of the women's suffrage movement as well. During her lifetime she was notorious for keeping her maiden name after marriage to Henry B. Blackwell. Other feminists who imitated her came to be called "Lucy Stoners."

The selection below is part of a speech Lucy Stone delivered extemporaneously at a women's rights convention in Cincinnati in 1855. It is a remarkable capsule summary of women's grievances and aspirations during the antebellum era as perceived by the feminists of the day.

"The last speaker alluded to this movement as being that of a few disappointed women. From the first years to which my memory stretches, I have been a disappointed woman. When, with my brothers, I reached forth after the sources of knowledge, I was reproved with 'It isn't fit for you; it doesn't belong to women.' Then there was but one college in the world where women were admitted, and that was in Brazil. I would have found my way there, but by the time I was prepared to go, one was opened in the young State of Ohio—the first in the United States where women and Negroes could enjoy opportunities with white men. I was disappointed when I came to seek a profession worthy an immortal human being—every employment was closed to me, except those of the teacher, the seamstress, and the housekeeper. In education, in marriage, in religion, in everything, disappointment is the lot of women. It shall be the business of my life to deepen this disappointment in every woman's heart until she bows down to it no longer. I wish that women, instead of being walking show-cases, instead of begging of their fathers and brothers the latest and gayest new bonnet, would ask of them their rights.

"The question of Women's Rights is a practical one. The notion has prevailed that it was only an ephemeral idea, it was but women claiming the right to smoke cigars in the streets, and to frequent barrooms. Others have supposed it is a question of comparative intellect; others still, of sphere. Too much has already been said and written about woman's sphere. Trace all the doctrines to their source and they will be found to have no basis except in the usages and prejudices of the age. This is seen in the fact that what is tolerated in women in one country is not tolerated in another. . . .

"I have confidence in the Father to believe that when He gives us the capacity to do anything He does not make a blunder. Leave women, then, to find their sphere. And do not tell us . . . that our province is to cook dinners, darn stockings, and sew on buttons. We are told woman has all the rights she wants; and even women, I am ashamed to say, tell us so. They mistake the politeness of men for rights—seats while men stand in this hall tonight, and their adulations; but these are mere courtesies. We want rights. The flour-merchant, the house-builder, and the postman charge us no less on account of our sex; but when we endeavor to earn money to pay all these, then, indeed, we find the difference. Man, if he has energy, may hew out for himself a path where no mortal has ever trod, held back by nothing but what is in himself; the world is all before him, there to choose; and we are glad for you, brothers, men, that it is so. But the same society that drives forth the young man, keeps woman at home—a dependent—working little cats on worsted, and little dogs on punctured paper; but if she goes heartily and bravely to give herself to some worthy purpose, she is out of her sphere and she loses caste. Women working in tailorshops are paid one-third as much as men. Someone in Philadelphia has stated that women make fine shirts for twelve and a half cents apiece; that no woman can make more than nine a week, and the sum thus earned, after deducting rent, fuel, etc., leaves her just three and a half cents a day for bread. Is it any wonder that women are driven to prostitution? Female teachers in New York are paid fifty dollars a year, and for every such situation there are five hundred applicants. I know not what you believe of God, but I believe He gave yearnings and longings to be filled, and that He did not mean all our time should be devoted to feeding and clothing the body. The present condition of woman causes a horrible perversion of the marriage relation. It is said of a lady, 'Has she married well?' 'Oh, yes, her husband is rich.' Woman must marry for a home, and you men are the sufferers by this; for a woman who loathes you may marry you because you have the means to get money which she cannot have. But when woman can enter the lists with you and make money for herself, she will marry you only for deep and earnest affection. . . ."

Americans themselves. This was their native land, most blacks said; Africa was not their country. Under the auspices of the Colonization Society, a few thousand free blacks, former slaves, and Africans taken from illegal slave ships were sent to Liberia, a new black republic founded on the West African coast. But as a serious solution to the slavery problem, colonization remained not only mistaken, but unworkable.

During the late 1820s the antislavery movement took on a new dimension when it linked up with religious Perfectionism and was converted into a crusade for immediate and total abolition. The instigator of the change was William Lloyd Garrison, a pious young printer from Newburyport, Massachusetts. After editing the *National Philanthropist*, the first temperance newspaper, and turning it into a journal of general moral reform, Garrison developed a white-hot determination to drive slavery from the land. Garrison's "immediatism" rejected the quiet tone and step-by-step approach of the Quakers as dealing too gently with sin. Now was the time to demand abolition—if necessary, in a way that did not spare people's feelings.

On January 1, 1831, the first issue of Garrison's *Liberator* appeared. It rang with the fervor for liberty and the righteous determination to end the evil of slavery that would make its editor the hope of the oppressed and the despair of moderates. In words that still inspire, Garrison wrote:

> *I will be* as harsh as truth, and as uncompromising as justice. On this subject, I do not wish to think, to speak, or write with moderation. . . . I am in earnest—I will not equivocate—I will not excuse—and I will not retreat a single inch—AND I WILL BE HEARD.

Despite its militant tone the *Liberator* at first attracted little attention. Then in August 1831 Nat Turner, a slave preacher, instigated a slave uprising in the Virginia tidewater that led to 57 white and 100 slave deaths. A wave of horror rolled across the South. Though Garrison had had nothing to do with the revolt, southerners were certain that he had inspired Turner. They demanded that he and his fellow abolitionists be stopped by every means possible. Garrison was not deterred. As the years passed, he became even more uncompromising and intransigent. A thorough Perfectionist, he became convinced that the criminal code, war, and government itself were all efforts to coerce human beings and were equally evil. By condoning slavery, the federal Constitution seemed particularly wicked, and in 1843 Garrison began to place at the head of his editorial column the words:

> Resolved, that the compact which exists between the North and South is a "Covenant with Death, and an Agreement with Hell,"—involving both parties in atrocious criminality,—and should be immediately annulled.

Not all abolitionists were as militant as Garrison. In the West, antislavery leaders spoke in more moderate voices. In Ohio, Oberlin College quickly became a center of antislavery sentiment and its students active missionaries in the antislavery cause. Led by the dynamic Theodore Weld, the Oberlin abolitionists refused to adopt the extreme positions and language of the Garrisonians. They were also not as certain as Garrison that women's rights and other reforms were the proper concern of abolitionists. In 1840 the Weld-Tappan group split from the Garrisonians to form the American and Foreign Antislavery Society with headquarters in New York, leaving the Garrisonians in possession of the American Antislavery Society with headquarters in Boston.

In addition to facing conflicts within their own ranks, abolitionists were often assailed by conservatives even in the North, who saw them as dangerous to social and political order. Mobs attacked Garrison in Boston, and murdered antislavery leader Elijah Lovejoy in Alton, Illinois when he refused to shut down his antislavery press. When not subject to physical violence, abolitionists were denounced as fanatics, dangerous agitators, and heretics. They were frequently denied basic constitutional rights. When Prudence Crandall attempted to admit a black girl to her Connecticut school in 1833, local whites broke her windows and poisoned her well. Eventually, despite abolitionists' efforts to defend her legal rights, she was driven from the state. Antiabolitionist feeling penetrated to the highest levels of public life. President Andrew Jackson attacked the antislavery advocates as extremists bent on instigating slave insurrections; his postmaster general denied abolitionists the use of the mails to distribute their newspapers, books, and pamphlets. In 1836, the House of Representatives adopted the "gag rule" placing all antislavery petitions of abolitionists "on the table," where they were simply ignored.

The physical, verbal, and legal assaults did not keep men and women from joining the antislavery movement. In fact, by converting abolitionism into an issue of free speech, the attacks may have created sympathy and attracted recruits. Hundreds of men and women—many of New England ancestry, though there were occasional southerners like the Grimké sisters and Alabama planter James G. Birney—flocked to the antislavery organizations. A majority of prominent abolitionists were white, but many free blacks also joined the movement. Unfortunately, blacks within the antislavery societies were often snubbed by white abolitionists who defended human equality in the abstract but could not overcome their actual prejudice against black people. Yet, despite the prejudice of whites, Frederick

Racism in action in the free North. This 1839 woodcut from The Anti-Slavery Almanac *probably depicts the attack by white bigots on Prudence Crandall's school for black girls at Canterbury,*

Douglass, the brilliant black editor of the antislavery *North Star*; Henry Highland Garnet, an eloquent black preacher; and Sojourner Truth, an illiterate former slave who spoke with effective simplicity for the cause of freedom—all became prominent members of abolitionist societies.

Utopian Socialism. Each of these movements—prison reform, improved treatment of the insane, temperance, women's rights, abolitionism—was an attempt to cure some perceived ill of American society while leaving the main structure untouched. There were Americans in these years, however, who rejected the very foundations of their society and chose to withdraw from it almost entirely or to demand drastic change from the bottom up.

These militants deeply deplored the social and moral climate of their country: America was too competitive and individualistic, too over to the pursuit of wealth, and too severely marred by inequality and exploitation. Yearning for a society closer to human scale where men and women could deal with one another face to face, eager to erase the distinctions between rich and poor, hopeful of replacing competition with cooperation, and determined to eliminate human drudgery, they went off to the woods or the frontier to found communities based on some idealistic economic, social, or religious philosophy.

Several of the new utopian communities were inspired by the writings of Charles Fourier, a French thinker who opposed capitalism as inhumane and competitive. Fourier proposed in its place a system of small cooperative communities scattered about the countryside where men and women could work at farming and industry while living in a communal structure—a "phalanx." No one would own the community's capital and collect its dividends. All would share both the labor and the profit. Government of each phalanx would consist of a Council of Seven, five of whom would be women.

Brook Farm, established near Boston by George Ripley, eventually adopted a Fourierist mode. The community was a place of intellect and warmth where New England intellectuals taught, farmed, and played. Everyone who visited found it lively, charming, and pleasant. But, alas, the New England literary folk were far better at words than at farming. "Never," remarked one skeptic, were there "such witty potato-patches and such sparkling cornfields before or since." But, he added, there was a "lack of method," and that explained the community's eventual failure. In 1847, realizing that the enterprise was losing money, the founders closed their doors.

A communitarian experiment that owed as much to religious as to political principles was Oneida, a community led by John Humphrey Noyes, a Yale-educated minister who settled with his followers in western New York in 1847. At Oneida, Noyes preached against what he called "the Sin system, the Marriage system, the Work system, and the Death system," combining religious evangelism and socialist economics. All work was reduced to what seemed essential and unavoidable. Women, particularly, were freed of drudgery by simplified methods of housekeeping. Men and women joined in the essential work of digging, building, and farming. To make this labor more comfortable, women cut their hair short and wore baggy trousers.

Noyes's most radical experiment was "complex marriage." He and his followers believed that monogamy (a single spouse) was selfish and interfered with a true sense of community. Instead, every man at Oneida was considered the husband of every woman and vice versa. Outsiders called this "free love" and condemned it as an utter breakdown of morality. But the Oneidaites responded that no one in the community was forced to accept sexual relations he

The sharp line between men's and women's spheres did not exist at the Oneida community, as this photo of a pea-shelling bee in the 1850s shows. At the far right, a woman wears the short (for the day) skirt over pantaloons typical of Oneida women. This outfit preserved female modesty while allowing women to work at "masculine" jobs.

or she did not desire. Though Oneida members practiced birth control, some children were born into the community; they were treated in an unusually permissive way, being allowed, for example, to sleep until awakened by the natural rhythms of their bodies. Unlike the typical schools of the time, which used memorization and rewards and punishments to prompt learning, Oneida schools sought to arouse curiosity and make learning pleasurable.

The Oneida community was an unusual success. It avoided the bickering that destroyed so many other communitarian experiments by a scheme of self-criticism whereby members could air their grievances before the whole group and work them out. Oneida also developed a firm economic foundation. Noyes, recognizing that industry was better suited to a community such as Oneida than agriculture, trained members in embroidery and silk making and mobilized their ingenuity in developing manufactures. The community basked in prosperity for many decades, becoming, ironically, the basis for a major commercial cutlery firm that is still in business.

There were many other experimental communities in this era. During the nineteenth century, it is estimated, more than 100 such institutions with 100,000 members were formed in the United States, most of them between 1820 and 1860. As Emerson wrote an English friend in 1840: "We are all a little wild here with numberless projects of social reform. Not a reading man but has a draft of a new community in his waistcoat pocket."

Most communities founded on some sort of political or philosophical plan were short-lived. New Harmony, a socialist experiment on the banks of the Wabash sponsored by the British philanthropist Robert Owen, lasted two years and then disbanded when internal bickering destroyed all chance of harmony. Icaria, designed as an experiment in communal ownership and use of capital, attracted a small group of French people to the new state of Texas in 1847. A year later it was defunct. The longest-lived of the Fourierist communities—at Red Bank, New Jersey—lasted only a dozen years.

Communities with a religious base were generally more successful than ones founded on a political ideal. Among

Frederick Douglass

The expression "a credit to his race" used to be applied to a certain kind of well-educated black man who conformed to white expectations. Such people had acquired an education, taken on the white man's speech, and dressed in a white-middle-class way. Above all, they accepted the racial status quo and did not seek to change it. Frederick Douglass was "a credit to his race" by all but the last criterion. He did not accept the way blacks were treated in the United States. Indeed, he was one of the boldest, most resolute enemies of the cruel racial regime that, whether in slavery or "freedom," white America imposed on his people.

Douglass was born in 1818 in Maryland, son of a slave mother and an unidentified white father. Like all North American blacks, he followed his mother's condition, and like her was the property of Aaron Anthony, a Maryland planter with thirty slaves and three farms.

Frederick's mother died while he was still a young child and he went to live on a distant plantation owned by Anthony. Here he observed floggings for the first time and learned that the violence done to blacks by their white masters sometimes made them cruel to one another. Fortunately his stay on the Anthony plantation was brief. In 1825 Frederick was sent to Baltimore to be the companion of the son of Hugh and Sophia Auld. Mrs. Auld was a kind woman and taught the boy to read and write. Her husband, however, was mean-spirited and disapproved of her act. Literacy, he shouted, would "spoil the best nigger in the world." Mrs. Auld never again taught the bright slave boy anything.

Yet Frederick never gave up his quest for learning. When he left the Aulds' household to work in a Baltimore shipyard, he continued to read. The white South was right to forbid slave literacy. At the age of thirteen Frederick bought a book of rhetoric that contained model speeches by the great orators declaiming the principles of freedom and even of slave emancipation. From this work he learned many of the skills and eloquent arguments he would later use with devastating effect against the "peculiar institution."

Following Hugh Auld's death, Frederick was shunted around from one heir to another and employed as a field hand far from the stimulating life of the city. His resentment of his new condition finally induced his latest master to return him to Baltimore, to be apprenticed to a trade and freed when he reached twenty-one.

But Douglass could not wait till then. In September 1838, dressed as a seaman, he hopped a train northward and arrived in New York soon after. In New York he was befriended by the black abolitionist Charles Ruggles, who gave him shelter. Ruggles also helped him resume contact with Anna Murray, a free-born black woman Douglass had met in Baltimore, and it was in Ruggles's house that Frederick and Anna were married.

Soon after, at Ruggles's urging, the young couple left for New Bedford, Massachusetts, a community where they believed Frederick was less likely to be betrayed as a fugitive slave than in New York. It was in New Bedford that Frederick abandoned his slave name and took "Douglass" as a further disguise.

A new life began for Douglass in New England. He soon came to the attention of the prominent abolitionist leader William Lloyd Garrison, and in August 1841 he was invited to speak at an antislavery convention. Douglass created a sensation. Even abolitionists seldom knew educated blacks and at times they, too, exhibited race prejudice and condescension. But no one could doubt that this imposing, eloquent black man was a superior being and a living reproach to slavery. The lesson must be spread. Douglass was immediately hired at $450 a year as speaker for the Massachusetts Antislavery Society.

During the next three years Douglass toured the North, denouncing slavery at dozens of abolitionist meetings. His effect on his audiences was powerful but, like many abolitionists, he was also heckled and even attacked physically. In 1845 Douglass published the first of three autobiographies recounting his life as a slave and harshly condemning slavery. Soon after, he took ship for England under the sponsorship of the American Antislavery Society to bring his message to the many friends of black emancipation in Europe.

Like many black Americans during slavery days—and after—Douglass found his contact with Europe liberating. Europeans had little of the color prejudice of white Americans. Douglass could go anywhere in Europe, speak to anyone, and never be treated as an inferior.

Despite this exhilarating experience, in 1847 Douglass concluded that he must return to his native land. Recognizing the danger that he would be recaptured as a fugitive when he set foot on American soil, his English friends purchased his freedom from his legal owner. Douglass arrived back in the United States in April 1847 at the age of thirty, a free man for the first time in his life.

Back home, Douglass decided to establish a newspaper to expound his views. His friends in the abolitionist movement tried to dissuade him, arguing that there were already too many abolitionist papers and that if he failed, it would reflect on the capabilities of his race. But Douglass was now unwilling to accept white direction; blacks, he believed, must have an independent voice in the movement. His persistence led to a break with Garrison, though not with the less doctrinaire white abolitionists. With their help Douglass began publishing the *North Star* out of Rochester, New York, in 1847.

He soon discovered how hard it was to run a newspaper, and there would be many times in the next dozen years when he would consider abandoning the enterprise. But the paper afforded a far better outlet for Douglass's views than the lecture platform. The *North Star*'s columns and editorial pages covered not only the antislavery movement but also temperance, discrimination against free blacks, and national politics. Douglass

and his paper were particular friends of women's rights. He was one of the sixty-seven men who attended the historic Seneca Falls Convention in 1848, which effectively launched the women's rights movement, and throughout his career he remained a strong supporter of Susan B. Anthony and Elizabeth Cady Stanton, the women's rights leaders.

As the country approached the final sectional crisis, Douglas became increasingly critical of Garrison's antipolitics position. He supported the Liberty party and its successor, the Republican party. In 1860 he endorsed Lincoln, though he had no illusions that the roughhewn man from Illinois would attack slavery head-on. Douglass considered the war that followed Lincoln's election providential. Here was the opportunity to finally strike slavery a mortal blow. But this result could not be left to chance.

Through the early months of the war Douglass hammered away in print and from the platform at the necessity of destroying slavery in order to put down the rebellion. He was jubilant when the president announced in September 1862 his intention to issue the Emancipation Proclamation.

On the night of December 31, 1863, Douglass and 3,000 other antislavery men and women gathered in Boston's Tremont Temple to await word from Washington that the Proclamation was finally in force. At 10 P.M. a man came running through the crowd shouting: "It is coming! It is on the wires!" The crowd burst into spontaneous cheers. Prayers were offered up and joyous speeches continued until dawn. After two and a half centuries the evil institution was dead in America.

Douglass would live for thirty more years. During the Reconstruction era he would demand "immediate, un-

the most enduring "utopian" communities were those established by the English Quaker Mother Ann Lee, who came to America in 1774 and organized her first small "Shaker" settlement soon after. At first the Shakers expanded slowly from this core, but then, during the 1830–1850 period, stimulated by the second Great Awakening, Shakerism experienced a great burst of energy. By the late 1840s there were about 6,000 Shakers living in a score or more communities scattered across the northern states.

In their trim, spare, simple villages the Shakers followed a life that combined economic cooperation with a pursuit of spiritual perfection that precluded sexual relations. Though their celibacy obviously limited expansion, the Shaker communities overcame this natural barrier to continuity by recruiting a steady stream of men and women who disliked the competitive, individualistic life of the larger society. Shakers prospered collectively by selling seeds, medicinal herbs, bonnets, cloaks, and cabinet-

work, and lasted as a group well into the twentieth century.

There were many other long-lived religious communities. The various Rappite villages founded by German Pietists around 1805 continued until 1900. The Pietist Amana Society, also German in origin, established its first villages in western New York in the 1840s. It, too, survived into the twentieth century, growing prosperous on weaving and blanket making. It still exists today, though it is now a successful manufacturer of electrical appliances.

The commercial success of the religious communities illustrates the paradoxes of antebellum America. Secular faiths were unable to deal with the craving for brotherhood and cooperation. During the pre–Civil War era no political or economic philosophy could overcome the acquisitiveness and individualism of the larger society. A religious perspective was more effective. But to survive, the religious communities found it necessary to become successful economic enterprises.

conditional, and universal enfranchisement of the black man in every State in the Union." He was one of the black leaders who visited Andrew Johnson in the White House in February 1866 to ask the president's support for giving freedmen the vote. The outspoken Douglass offended Johnson, who later told one of his private secretaries that he was "just like any nigger, and he would sooner cut a white man's throat than not." The suffrage issue put strains on the alliance of blacks and women. Susan B. Anthony and Elizabeth Cady Stanton wanted Douglass to support the simultaneous enfranchisement of women and blacks, but Douglass refused on the grounds that such linkage would jeopardize votes for blacks. Now, he said, "was the Negro's hour."

In 1872 Douglass and his family moved to Washington, where, during the administrations of Hayes and Garfield, he held minor but well-paying patronage jobs with the federal government. Republican preferment, plus the added years, cooled Douglass's ardor for change and curbed his critical pen and tongue. So much had been accomplished since slavery days for black people; it was hard to carp at the many inequalities that remained. Fortunately, successive versions of his autobiography sold well and provided the income he needed to live comfortably in the capital.

In 1882 Anna, Douglass's wife of forty-four years, died. Theirs had not been a happy relationship; Frederick was too public a man and had too many admirers, many of them female. He was a doting father to his three children and helped them whenever he could, but none of them achieved independence or conventional success. In 1884 Douglass scandalized blacks and whites alike by marrying a white woman. Yet despite the uproar, in 1889, when Douglass was seventy-one, President Benjamin Harrison appointed him minister to the black republic of Haiti. But Douglass disliked the climate and soon resigned.

He lived until February 1895, and in his last years regained some of his zeal for the black cause. Among his last writings was a series of attacks on the new epidemic of lynching that was sweeping the South. Seven months after he died another black leader would rise to speak at the Atlanta Cotton States Exposition. Booker T. Washington would make a pact with white America that would freeze the racial status quo for fifty years. A later generation of black leaders would condemn the Atlanta Compromise, but in all likelihood, his latest biographer believes, Frederick Douglass, who had waited so long to see even a flawed freedom, would have approved.

★ CONCLUSIONS ★

What were pre–Civil War Americans in the North and West truly like, then? Americans were competitive and individualistic; they were crude, bad-mannered, violent, and bigoted. They were also humane, romantic, creative, and socially speculative. It seems fitting to call them, as one historian has, a "people of paradox."

These inconsistencies can be traced to the special circumstances of the northern part of the nation in these years. The whole region north of Dixie was in a state of extraordinary flux. Still agricultural and rural, it was rapidly becoming industrial and urban. Still largely composed of native-born Protestants whose forebears had arrived in the colonial era, it was experiencing a deluge of newcomers from Europe, many of whom were Catholic. Besides the tensions these changes created, there were antagonisms between East and West. Easterners often disliked western manners and practices, yet they themselves were moving west in vast numbers and learning to adjust to western economic competition. These transplanted easterners were undoubtedly influenced by the western practices they deplored.

One important fact should be kept in mind as we consider the country's evolution: Virtually all the changes we have described in this chapter followed lines of latitude. In shifts of people, institutions, values, and problems, Northeast mixed with Northwest. This is not to say that the two sections did not retain many distinctive features, but by 1860 Northeast and Northwest were far more alike than either was to the South. This development of distinctive North-South sectional identities would have momentous consequences for the nation.

★★★★★★★★ FOR FURTHER READING ★★★★★★★★

Roger Brown. *Modernization: The Transformation of American Life, 1600–1865* (1976)

This book is an attempt to place social change in America within the framework of "modernization." A modern society is one in which custom and personal, face-to-face relations among people are replaced by impersonal, contractual relations. A modern society is subject to rapid and continuous change; traditional society is static. The North, in effect, modernized by 1865; the South did not.

Keith Melder. *The Beginnings of Sisterhood* (1977)

A fine, brief treatment of the social background and early course of the women's rights movement. Deals with the changes in women's status during the antebellum period and how they affected women's public roles in America.

Nancy Cott. *The Bonds of Womanhood: "Women's Sphere" in New England, 1780–1835* (1977)

Sees women's lives being transformed by the growing separation of family and work during the early years of the Republic. An important book, but one that perhaps exaggerates the extent to which the social change characteristic of our own day can actually be found in this earlier period.

Linda Gordon. *Woman's Body, Woman's Right: A Social History of Birth Control in America* (1976)

A book with a strong thesis: "Birth control represented the single most important factor in the material basis of woman's emancipation in the course of the last century." Professor Gordon describes the often gruesome measures used by nineteenth-century women to limit their families, including makeshift abortion and infanticide.

Russel B. Nye. *Society and Culture in America, 1830–1860* (1974)

A superior intellectual and cultural history by a scholar who has made every aspect of American cultural life, from high to low, his life's study.

Oscar Handlin, editor. *This Was America* (1949)

Contains excerpts from many of the accounts by foreign travelers that scholars have used to paint antebellum America's portrait.

John Kasson. *Rudeness and Civility: Manners in Nineteenth-Century Urban America* (1990)

An interesting discussion of the role of the arbiters of manners, especially the authors of etiquette books, on standards of behavior in nineteenth-century American cities.

Ray Allen Billington. *America's Frontier Heritage* (1966)

Billington is the outstanding historian of the frontier and the author of a major biography of Frederick Jackson Turner. In this book he examines Turner's frontier thesis and revises it in light of recent scholarship.

Oscar Handlin. *Boston's Immigrants, 1790–1880* (1968)

This study of Boston's "old immigrants" catches the essence of the urban immigrant experience in microcosm. Handlin has brought the story up to 1880 in this revised edition, but the emphasis remains on the years before the Civil War.

Ray Billington. *The Protestant Crusade, 1800–1860: A Study of the Origins of American Nativism* (1938)

This case study of mass reaction describes the development of anti-Catholic and antiforeign feeling that reached its peak in the 1850s. An older book that is still valuable and readable.

Leon F. Litwack. *North of Slavery: The Negro in the Free States, 1790–1860* (1961)

Litwack's thesis is that by 1860 most blacks in the states where slavery was forbidden were segregated from whites, economically oppressed, and without civil rights. Topics of special interest include black-Irish relations, the role of black religious leaders, and the efforts of black leaders and white abolitionists to improve conditions.

Alice Felt Tyler. *Freedom's Ferment: Phases of American Social History to 1860* (1944)

Still the best narrative history of the antebellum reform impulse. Covers everything from socialism to women's rights.

David Rothman. *The Discovery of the Asylum: Social Order and Disorder in the New Republic* (1971)

Rothman sees the origin of much of the antebellum reform impulse in the attempt by society to make up for the deficiencies of the American family. In his view, the penitentiaries, the poorhouses, and the institutions for the insane were established largely to prevent disorder and impose social control; the humanitarian element was secondary. An important book but one that exaggerates one side of the pre–Civil War reform movement.

Richard Wade. *The Urban Frontier: The Rise of Western Cities, 1790–1830* (1959)

Wade makes the point in this study of a group of Mississippi Valley cities during their pioneer phase that the antebellum West was not only a region of farms. It also consisted of fast-growing urban centers.

Milton Brown, Sam Hunter, John Jacobus, Naomi Rosenblum, and David Sokol. *American Art: Painting, Sculpture, Architecture, Decorative Arts, Photography* (1979)

This large, beautiful, and expensive volume covers all the visual arts from the beginning of colonial settlement through the 1960s. A stunning book.

Leonard Arrington. *Great Basin Kingdom: An Economic History of the Latter-Day Saints, 1830–1900* (1958)
An economic history of the Mormons from their beginnings in upstate New York to the twentieth century. Emphasizes their economic theories and practices as they were put into effect in Utah after 1846.

Jack Larkin. *The Reshaping of Everyday Life, 1790–1840* (1988)
Deals with how Americans of all classes, all occupations, and both races and genders lived before the Civil War. A lively and entertaining description of everyday life.

13★

THE OLD SOUTH

What Is Myth and What Was Real?

1807	Congress prohibits the slave trade with Africa, but illegal importation of black slaves continues
1822	Denmark Vesey and thirty-five slaves are hanged for planning a slave rebellion in South Carolina
1831	Nat Turner leads an unsuccessful slave rebellion in Virginia • Tariff of Abominations precipitates nullification crisis in South Carolina
1832	In response to Turner's rebellion the Virginia legislature debates the abolition of slavery
1836	Under pressure from southern congressmen, the House of Representatives adopts a "gag rule" prohibiting discussion of all abolitionist petitions
1849	John Calhoun writes *Disquisition on Government*: He states his theory of the "concurrent majority" in the Senate the following year
1852	Harriet Beecher Stowe's *Uncle Tom's Cabin* is published
1857	Hinton R. Helper's *The Impending Crisis of the South* is published
1858	James Hammond in a famous speech declares there has to be a "mud sill" upon which to erect a civilized cultured life
1860	Abraham Lincoln elected president • Slaves in the South number about 4 million, sixteen times the number of free blacks • South Carolina secedes from the Union

Magnolias and moonlight; white mansions with tall colonnades; beautiful hoop-skirted ladies and handsome, dignified gentlemen; thoroughbred horses; rich laughter and song drifting up from the slave quarters; waltzes and entrancing talk in the big plantation house. This was the Old South—a society that achieved for a brief moment a brilliance and happy harmony based on the mutual respect of classes and races, an idea of excellence, and good prices for cotton.

Or was it? There is another picture that is almost the complete opposite. In this view the Old South—the slave states in the half century before 1860—was a benighted region where a privileged white minority lorded it over millions of black slaves and "poor white trash." The typical elite planter was a newly rich "cotton snob," who abused his black chattels and showed contempt for the nonslaveholding class he himself had so recently left behind. The poor whites, in turn, were shiftless, dirty, violent, and ignorant people who lived by a little desultory farming and by hunting, fishing, and trading whiskey with the slaves for stolen plantation goods. Beneath the poor whites were the oppressed and exploited blacks. Subjected to a regime of terror and physical violence, they lived in fear and fought their oppressors by contrived laziness, deceptiveness, flight, or violence.

What was the Old South really like? Are both descriptions essentially fables? Is one fable truer than the other? Or is there some truth in both?

★ AN UNEXPECTED DIVERSITY ★

One myth about the Old South is that it was utterly distinct in its climate and geography. The Deep South indeed was warmer than the rest of the nation, and this made a difference economically. Short-fiber cotton and sugarcane need a long growing season—at least 200 days—and such a frost-free period could be found only in the region from North Carolina south through Florida and then west in a wide band through Georgia, Alabama, and Mississippi, as far as Texas. Much of the Deep South was too warm for wheat; its chief grain crop was corn. It had poor pasturage and so the corn-eating hog, rather than the grass-eating cow, was the basis of its animal husbandry. Thus, climate helped distinguish part of the South from most of the North.

But the climatic distinction must not be exaggerated. There was little difference between the climate of Kentucky and Virginia and, say, that of Ohio and Pennsylvania—and yet the first two states were parts of the Old South, the sec-

ond two of the North. Nor was the South's topography unique. The Appalachian plateau, the Atlantic coastal plain, and the Mississippi Valley were geographical features shared by the two sections. In short, it was not primarily the natural environment that defined the Old South.

Southern Agriculture. Another myth is that the Old South was a single agricultural unit. When we think of Dixie in this period, we imagine a gigantic cotton field. Yet cotton was only one of the region's many crops, and not even the most valuable. Corn, which grew everywhere, fattened the region's farm animals and, in the form of "pone," "hominy," and "roasting ears," fed most of its people. The southern corn crop was valued at $209 million in 1855; the cotton crop, at only $136 million.

Although cotton was second in total value, it was the great cash crop. Unlike corn, it was exported to the North and to Europe in vast quantities—almost a million bales in 1860—and it paid for the South's manufactures. It also made the South's fortunes. No one became rich by growing corn, but cotton was white gold that brought wealth to the efficient and lucky planter. On the eve of the Civil War the newer cotton-growing region of the Gulf states, the lower Mississippi delta, and eastern Texas was the richest part of the slave states.

Other staple crops brought in cash. Kentucky hemp, Louisiana sugar, Carolina rice, and Virginia, North Carolina, and Kentucky tobacco were important in their regions. Although none even came close to cotton as a source of income, they contributed to the region's remarkable diversity.

Industry. Another myth about the Old South is that it was economically backward. Until recently historians said that cotton growing was actually an unproductive enterprise. It exhausted the soil, so that by the eve of the Civil War large sections of the older South consisted of worn-out lands. Only by constant expansion into virgin soil could the planter ensure himself a decent profit. And cotton supposedly deflected capital from more productive enterprise. Planters poured their capital into new land and slaves rather than into machines and factories.

And even if southerners had been willing to invest in industry, the older view went, the slave system would have prevented it. Slaves lacked the necessary skills, incentives, and education for industrial work. Moreover, to set up successful industrial enterprises where the labor force itself was property was too great a burden for would-be investors. In addition to buildings and machines, they would have to purchase their workers. Finally, a slave society inevitably encouraged aristocratic values and contempt for hard phys-

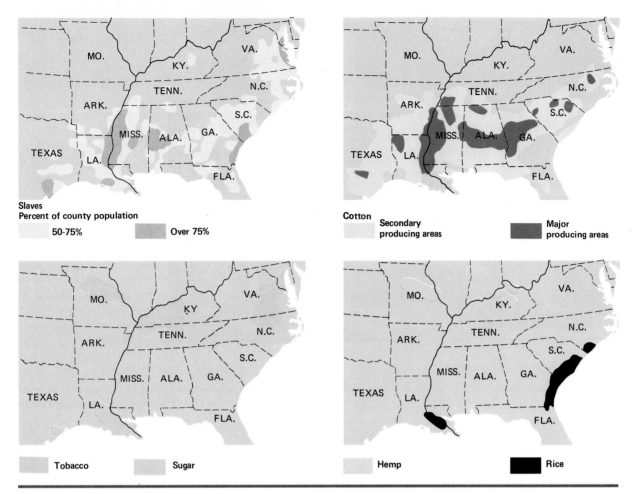

Slaves
Percent of county population
50-75%   Over 75%

Cotton   Secondary   Major
producing areas   producing areas

Tobacco   Sugar

Hemp   Rice

SLAVERY AND AGRICULTURAL PRODUCTION

ical work—attitudes at odds with successful industrialization. Given all these qualities of a slave society, historians once declared, it was not surprising that the South remained bound to agriculture and achieved a slower rate of economic growth than the rest of the nation.

Few scholars today accept these ideas without serious qualifications. It is true that the Old South developed its manufacturing potential more slowly than the Northeast and a few of the most advanced European countries. But the reasons have little to do with slavery. Most slaves were field hands, performing jobs that did not require much skill. Yet even among the slaves who worked in the fields, some who showed managerial talent served as "drivers" or even overseers supervising large work gangs. Moreover, many slaves were skilled craftspeople. Plantations needed coopers, masons, carpenters, brick makers, gardeners, and the like. Slaves filled these jobs effectively, which was one reason European immigrants generally avoided the Old South. On the sugar plantations of Louisiana black experts supervised most of the delicate operations of sugar refining. Slave

women were often skilled seamstresses, weavers, cooks, and midwives. Some even practiced medicine, on white as well as black patients. Clearly slaves could have supplied the work force for an industrial economy.

Nor did prospective factory owners in the South have to buy their employees. Many planters, unable to employ all their slaves full-time, hired them out at prevailing wage rates. Hired slaves worked as municipal workers in southern cities; they worked by the day for southern householders. They also worked in southern factories and industries. In the pine forests of the Carolinas several thousand blacks labored in the lumber and turpentine industries. Hired slaves were miners in Virginia, Kentucky, and Missouri. Deck hands on the river steamers of the Old South were generally black bondsmen, as were the construction workers on railroads and canals. Cotton mills in South Carolina, Alabama, and Florida used slave "operatives," and in Virginia slaves worked in tobacco factories. The Tredegar iron mills of Richmond, which would produce most of the Confederacy's artillery, were manned exclusively by hired slaves after 1847.

We think of slaves as toiling in fields of cotton, but some 400,000 were part of the South's urban industrial work force. Virginian tobacco factories such as this one relied almost exclusively on hired slaves, whose wages went to their masters.

Clearly, then, the slave-labor system did not exclude industry and business from the Old South. Neither did southern values. Dixie planters were not a collection of feckless romantics. Most were practical men who studied agriculture as a business, encouraged experimentation in crops and animal breeding, and organized their labor force efficiently. In fact, according to some historians, the "gang" system they developed on the cotton and sugar plantations was one of the most efficient work patterns for agriculture ever devised. The slaves were pushed hard by whip-wielding "drivers," themselves slaves. While the hours were not excessive by the standards of the day, the intensity of the effort was high and the output of their labor impressive. One scholar calls the pre–Civil War southern plantation "a modern business organization, and possibly even a leading business organization of its time."

A final proof of plantation slavery's efficiency was the actual overall economic performance of the antebellum South. The Old South was a remarkably productive community. Its industrial development was ahead of all but a very few European countries in cloth output and railroad mileage—important measures of economic development. In 1860 there were almost 200 textile mills scattered through the region, plus hundreds of tobacco factories, flour and lumber mills, and other manufacturing establishments that, primarily, processed the section's agricultural products.

Most interesting are the comparative figures of sectional income. In 1860 the average per person income for the entire United States was $128 (in 1860 dollars). For the North as a whole* it was $141. For the South**, if we include both slave and free, it was only $103, less than either. But if we only include the *free* population, the South's per capita income rises to $150, a figure higher than both the North and the national average. Of course slaves were people, and we are morally obliged to consider total population in these comparisons. But on the other hand, from the perspective of southern whites, including their political leaders, the southern economy was remarkably productive and advanced. And it was also growing at a faster rate than the country's economy as a whole. Between 1840 and 1860 the economy of the entire United States grew at the average yearly rate of 1.4 percent for each man, woman, and child. The North's average per capita growth rate in this same period was only 1.3 percent. The Old South's, on the other hand, was 1.7 percent.

Taken together, it is clear that the gap between the Old South and the North in the matter of industrialization did not arise from any aristocratic disdain for "trade"—though at times southerners did profess contempt for commerce and industry. Rather, it resulted from a rational estimate of profits on investment that induced planters to put their capital into agriculture rather than manufacturing.

---

*In this case the term "North" includes the industrial-commercial Northeast and the agricultural north-central region.
**The term "South" here includes the South Atlantic, east-south-central, and west-south-central regions.

Social Diversity. The Old South's social system has also been misperceived. In the past, few scholars questioned the existence of a three-tiered society of great planters, poor whites, and black slaves. But that scheme does not correspond very closely to reality. Each layer was far more complex than this view suggests.

The top layer was very thin indeed. In 1860 only 2,200 southerners owned 100 or more slaves, and these 2,200 made up less than 1 percent of the 383,000 slaveholding families in that year. The lordly domain—and the equally lordly planter aristocrat—was a rarity in the Old South.

The typical slaveholder was a member of the middle class. Seventy-one percent of slaveholders in 1860—almost 200,000—had fewer than 10 slaves. These small farmers could scarcely maintain the style and pace of the planter elite. They ate plain food and lived in houses that were little more than enlarged balloon-frame structures or even modified log cabins. They were often rough in their speech and in their ways. Although aspiring to wealth and gentility, they generally had far to go before they could claim either.

Even more numerous was the nonslaveholding yeomanry, consisting of white farmers who worked their acres themselves, helped by their grown sons and some occasional hired labor. Professor Frank Owsley and his students at Vanderbilt University have painted a picture of the Old South's yeoman class that resembles a sentimental Currier and Ives print. Sturdy, independent, democratic, they lived comfortably but simply. Their daily rounds were punctuated by hoedowns, camp meetings, cabin raising, corn shucking, and other assorted happy social activities. They were also politically influential, and like their counterparts in the North were often deferred to by the elite at election time.

Owsley's effort to redress the picture of the nonslaveholding whites is long overdue. The white yeomanry was indeed a substantial group and was particularly numerous in hilly upland regions and the "pine belts," away from the river bottomland. The soil of the river edges was extraordinarily fertile and, when drained and cleared, ideally suited to cotton culture. It was therefore in the Mississippi delta and the valleys of the Tombigbee, Pearl, and Suwannee rivers that the great plantations flourished. But since the bottomland was both malarial and expensive, the yeomen gave it a wide berth. Yet even in the delta regions of Mississippi and Alabama, small farmers could be found.

The yeoman class also wielded considerable political power. Voting rights in many parts of the Old South were as broad as elsewhere in the country, and southern politicians had to heed the yeomen's wishes. Moreover, in some areas the yeoman–small planter class was able to manipulate election districts so that countries where the white population was proportionately greatest—where the small farmers predominated—could control the state legislatures.

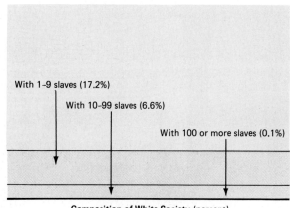

With 1–9 slaves (17.2%)

With 10–99 slaves (6.6%)

With 100 or more slaves (0.1%)

Composition of White Society (percent)

Nonslaveholders (78.1%)

Slaveholders (23.9%)

White society in the Old South, 1860. (Note: The Old South is here assumed to be all states in which slavery was legal in 1860. Slaveholders are defined as members of families owning slaves.) *Source: Eighth Census of the United States, 1860: Population by Age, Sex, Race, and Agriculture of the United States.*

But in revising the traditional view, we must not go too far. Wealth in the South was more concentrated than in the North. In part this was because few northern farms equaled the thousands of acres of some cotton plantations. It is also explained by the absence of slaves in the North. With a "prime" male fieldhand selling for about a thousand dollars, any owner of a half dozen slaves was a relatively wealthy person. If we include only nonslaveholders, southern yeomen were poorer than their northern counterparts. Besides the data that modern scholars have collected, we have the reports of contemporaries to confirm this impression. Travelers in the antebellum South often emphasized the yeoman's primitive existence. Frederick Law Olmstead, a northern gentleman farmer and well-known landscape architect, described his encounter with one central Mississippi white farm family in 1854 as follows:

> The house was all comprised in a single room, twenty-eight by twenty-five feet in area, and open to the roof above. There was a large fireplace at one end and a door on each side—no windows at all. Two bedsteads, a spinning-wheel, a packing-case, which served as a bureau, a cupboard, made of rough hewn slabs, two or three deerskin seated chairs, a Connecticut clock, and a large poster of Jayne's patent medicines, constituted all the visible furniture. . . . A little girl, immediately, without having had any direction to do so, got a frying-pan and a chunk of bacon from the cupboard, and cutting slices from the latter, set it frying for my supper. The woman of the house sat sulkily in a chair tilted back and leaning against the

A southern yeoman farmer and his family. Such people often eked out a living on the South's hilly lands, and without the help of slaves. Note the log cabin.

logs, spitting occasionally at the fire, but took no notice of me, barely nodding when I saluted her. A baby lay crying on the floor. I quieted it and amused it with my watch till the little girl, having made "coffee" and put a piece of cornbread on the table with the bacon, took charge of it.

Central Mississippi was still almost a frontier when Olmsted visited it; nevertheless, it seems clear that the level of comfort among the southern yeomanry was inferior to that of their northern counterparts. Nor is there any point in denying that there was a southern white lower class. Particularly in the pine barrens and in the hill country, where poor soils and steep terrain made farming difficult, small groups of white families made a precarious living by growing corn, raising hogs, and hunting. These rural poor were often despised. Fanny Kemble, a visiting English actress, called them "the most degraded race of human beings claiming an Anglo-Saxon origin that can be found on the face of the earth." Kemble was not an impartial observer: She hated slavery and sought to demonstrate that it degraded whites as well as blacks. But it is clear that whether explained by slavery, isolation, nutritional diseases like pellagra, or natural selection, there was indeed a group of wretched whites who inhabited the rural nooks and crannies of pre–Civil War southern society.

Nor can we fully accept Owsley's view of the Old South's middle-class democracy. Although the South's yeomen had to be heeded politically, they did not wield most of the region's political power. In the older parts of the South—the Carolinas, Georgia, Maryland, and Virginia—voting was rigged in favor of the plantation areas. In the newer states slaveholders often enjoyed special advantages such as relatively low property taxes. And even where the yeomen made their numbers felt, they often deferred to the planters. In many parts of the Old South, as in colonial times, the aristocracy occupied positions of influence far beyond their formal power. Talented sons of the yeomanry with political ambitions had to acquire land and slaves to succeed in public life. Jefferson Davis, whose father was an unsuccessful small slaveholder, had to marry into the planter class to become a United States senator, secretary of war, and finally president of the Confederate States of America. John C. Calhoun, whose father was a farmer with no slaves, married a Carolina rice heiress whose fortune freed him to pursue politics. Andrew Jackson, too, became important enough to be considered for Congress only after he became a prosperous planter.

Not everyone in the South admired the planter elite. Some of the South's white, nonslaveholding yeomen resented slavery and planter leadership. The spokesman for this generally inarticulate group was Hinton R. Helper of Heidelberg in western North Carolina. His book, *The Impending Crisis of the South* (1857), is a blistering attack on the planter class. These men, he claimed, had retarded the South's growth and oppressed its yeomen. As a group, they were "so depraved that there . . . [was] scarcely a spark of honor or magnanimity to be found among them." Helper, like many whites of his class, also despised blacks, but he was willing to use fire to fight fire. To destroy the power of the planters, he proposed to rally the nonslaveholders against them—with the help, if need be, of the slaves.

Helper's was a minority voice in a minority section. Most of the South's small farmers would wait fifty years before they would consider challenging the leadership of their "betters." Still, his *Impending Crisis* is an interesting glimpse beneath the prevailing myths of antebellum southern society.

★ LIFE UNDER SLAVERY ★

Like the white South, the black South has long been covered by a thick crust of myths. The older legend depicts "happy darkies" singing in the fields. Lovable but childlike creatures, they did not feel the oppression of slavery the way white people would. Of course slavery deprived black people of a fundamental right, these apologists admitted, but on a day-to-day basis it was a rather benign institution, and masters and slaves found it possible to develop mutual respect and to live comfortably with the inequality. There is a newer picture that is the diametric opposite. Slavery, it says, was a system of organized terror that either broke the spirit of black people or drove them to blind fury against their oppressors. Slaves were often whipped or maimed and were consigned to an incessant round of brutal, degrading labor. Worst of all, masters broke up the slaves' families and violated black women.

The truth is far more complex than either description allows. Slave life was very diverse. Like most white southerners, most blacks were employed in agriculture. Only a small portion of the southern population in 1860 was urban, and only about 17 percent of the total city population of the slave states was black. Yet black urbanites provided the black community with much-needed leaders and were an important element in the general cultural life of cities like New Orleans and Charleston.

Most southern blacks were slaves; but on the eve of the Civil War about 250,000—the same number as in the North—were free. Free blacks lived predominantly in the upper South, especially in Maryland, Kentucky, Delaware, Missouri, and Virginia, many in cities. In 1860 Baltimore's free black population outnumbered its slaves ten to one; Washington, D.C., had over 9,000 free blacks and fewer than 1,800 slaves.

Wherever free blacks lived in the South, their lot, as in the North, was not enviable. A few were successful in business, the skilled trades, the professions, or agriculture. Some free blacks even owned slaves of their own, and a tiny number were planters with considerable property, including slaves. Most, however, were unskilled laborers who huddled in the slums of the large southern towns, worked at menial tasks, suffered the contempt of whites, and were denied fundamental civil rights.

The South's slaves numbered about 4 million in 1860, sixteen times the number of free blacks. The great majority worked the soil. Whereas whites were mostly associated with small farm units, almost three-fourths of the South's slaves were found on relatively large plantations.

Working on a large plantation had some advantages. Where there were many slaves, there were many different jobs. On the large plantations slave women found employment as seamstresses, cooks, nurses, or maids in the master's house; slave men worked as butlers, coachmen, and valets. Black house servants were not free, but they were the envy of other slaves. Their jobs kept them out of the fields and brought them into contact with the more interesting world of the "big house." It also enabled them to control their working conditions to some degree. Few white masters or mistresses wanted to offend a good cook or laundress: It might ruin dinner or make it impossible to get a clean shirt. And on large plantations even slaves who were not house servants still enjoyed some advantages. Besides working in the field, they might serve as drivers, skilled mechanics, or craftsmen. Because skilled workers were often hired out in towns and were sometimes allowed to negotiate their own terms of hire, these slaves were unusually free—for slaves, that is.

Even the field hands on the large plantations were better off than those on smaller establishments. It is true that the labor was often intense. Worked in gangs under close supervision, the slaves were expected to be productive, and they were. The output per worker on large plantations was consistently higher than on small ones. But force was not the most effective means to encourage hard work; gen-

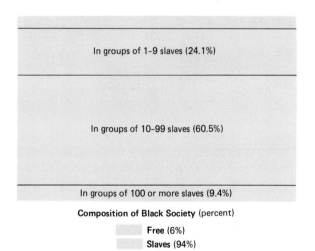

In groups of 1–9 slaves (24.1%)

In groups of 10–99 slaves (60.5%)

In groups of 100 or more slaves (9.4%)

Composition of Black Society (percent)

Free (6%)

Slaves (94%)

Black social structure in the Old South, 1860. (Note: The Old South is here assumed to be all states in which slavery was legal in 1860.) *Source: Eighth Census of the United States, 1860. Population by Age, Sex, Race* and Lewis C. Gray, *History of Agriculture in the Southern United States* (1933).

This sketch by the English-born architect Benjamin Latrobe shows Virginia slaves working under the eye of an overseer. We are repelled by the arrogant and indolent pose of the overseer, a response that the artist, who hated slavery, was probably trying to encourage.

erosity was sometimes a better method. Planters usually perceived this and acted accordingly. Where an absentee master employed a white overseer to manage his plantation, the slaves were sometimes treated more severely. Still, the overall estimate that the workload was seldom excessive on large plantations remains valid.

The physical comfort of slaves on large plantations was better than on small ones. Every slaveholder was interested in making money and understood that profits depended in part on maintaining a healthy, contented, well-nourished labor force. But only large plantations could provide medical services, weather-tight cabins, and the varied diet needed to maximize the efficiency of slave workers.

The one out of four slaves living on farms or small plantations no doubt had closer contact with the white owner and his family. They often ate at the same table with the master and sometimes even slept in the same cabin. But slaves who lived in such close quarters with their owners were constantly subject to white scrutiny, always made aware of their inferior social status, and had less opportunity to meet other blacks. In addition, small farmers were more likely to run into financial problems and be forced to sell their slaves. Blacks then faced the grim prospect that their families would be broken up. An earlier generation of historians assumed that slaves benefited from the close association with whites that was possible on the smaller farm. But this conclusion ignores the cultural and physical poverty of small-plantation life and assumes the superiority of white to black culture.

Slave Culture.   We now know that slavery did not prevent the development of a black American culture. This culture achieved a remarkable flowering in music and oral literature, particularly. Slaves sang about God and salvation, about their work, about love and passion, and about their daily lives. They composed humorous songs, bitter songs, and even rebellious songs that explicitly called for freedom. They also composed entertaining stories and poems. Talented black storytellers drew on the West African tradition of oral history, fable, and legend, combined it with Bible stories, and filled their tales with the animals and people of the southern environment. The stories, like the songs, often expressed the slaves' true feelings about their condition. One of the best-known group of tales featured Brer Rabbit, who manages to outwit stronger animals with his resourcefulness and trickery.

Music and oral literature comforted the slaves and helped them create a group identity. Religion played much the same role. West Africans accepted a supreme God, though they did not think of him as a jealous, exclusive deity. This belief enabled transplanted slaves to accept the Christian faith of their European masters. Blacks found the enthusiastic Protestantism of the Baptists and Methodists especially congenial, though they never fully accepted the Protestant emphasis on guilt.

Observers of the Old South never failed to comment on the deep religious commitments of black men and women and often noted that their piety put their "betters" to shame. Southern whites generally welcomed these religious feelings, and many planters employed white ministers to preach to their slaves, who seized the chance to attend religious services on the plantation. In the towns they often

A central component of slave culture was music. This slave boy's improvised "fiddle" suggests how strong the musical impulse was and how ingeniously some slaves were able to satisfy it.

The Slaves Speak Out

We have many surviving accounts of slavery from the inside, but virtually all of these were written by unusual people—literate black men and women who escaped from bondage and went north or to Canada. An exception is the collection of Slave Narratives made by the New Deal Works Progress Administration (WPA) during the 1930s. The WPA workers interviewed several hundred elderly southern blacks who had lived under the slave regime before 1863, and recorded their descriptions of personal experiences. The following selection is excerpted from the account of Mingo White of Burleson, Alabama, who at the time of the interview was between eighty-five and ninety years old.

"I was born in Chester, South Carolina, but I was mostly raised in Alabama. When I was about four or five years old, I was loaded in a wagon with a lot more people in it. Where I was bound I don't know. Whatever became of my mammy and pappy I don't know for a long time. I was told dere was a lot of slave speculators in Chester to buy some slaves for some folks in Alabama. I 'members dat I was took up on a stand and a lot of people came round and felt my arms and legs and chest, and ask me a lot of questions. Before we slaves was took to de tradin' post Old Marsa Crawford told us to tell everybody what asked us if we'd ever been sick dat us'd never been sick in our life. Us had to tell 'em all sorts of lies for our marsa or else take a beatin'.

"I was just a li'l thing, tooked away from my mammy and pappy, just when I needed 'em most. . . . My pappy and mammy was sold from each other, too, de same time I was sold. I used to wonder if I had any brothers or sisters, as I had always wanted some. . . .

"I weren't nothin' but a child endurin' slavery, but I had to work de same as any man. I went to de field and hoed cotton, pulled fodder and picked cotton with de rest of de hands. I kept up, too, to keep from gettin' any lashes dat night when us got home. In de winter I went to de woods with de menfolks to help to get wood or to get sap from de trees to make turpentine and tar. Iffen us didn't do dat we made charcoal to run de blacksmith shop with.

"De white folks was hard on us. Dey would whip us about de least li'l thing. It wouldn'ta been so bad iffen us had comforts, but to live like us did was 'nough to make anybody soon as be dead. De white folks told us dat us born to work for 'em and dat us was doin' fine at dat. . . .

"De white folks didn't learn us to do nothin' but work. Dey said dat us weren't supposed to know how to read and write. Dere was one feller name E. C. White what learned to read and write even durin' slavery. He had to carry de chillen's books to school for 'em and go back after dem. His young marsa taught him to read and write unbeknownst to his father and de rest of de slaves.

"After de day's work was done dere weren't anything for de slaves to do but go to bed. Wednesday night they went to prayer meetin'. We had to be in de bed by nine o'clock. Every night de drivers come around to make sure dat we was in de bed. . . .

"On Saturday de hands worked till noon. Dey had de rest of de time to work dey gardens. Every family had a garden of deir own. On Saturday nights de slaves could frolic for a while. Dey would have parties sometimes and whiskey and homebrew for de servants. On Sundays we didn't do anything but lay round and sleep, 'cause we didn't like to go to church. On Christmas we didn't have to do no work, no more'n feed the stock and do de li'l work round de house. When we got through with dat we had de rest of de day to run round wherever we wanted to do. 'Course we had to get permission from de marsa. . . .

"[After the war] I married Kizi Drumgoole. Reverend W. C. Northcross perform de ceremony. Dere weren't nobody dere but de witness and me and Kizi. I had three sons, but all of 'em is dead 'ceptin' one and dat's Hugh. He got seven chillens."

went to white churches, though they had to sit in separate places in the back or in the gallery. But blacks preferred religious autonomy. Throughout the antebellum period black preachers, many of them self-taught and unordained, ministered to the needs of blacks, sometimes in secret. During slave days, as in more recent years, black clergymen frequently served as the social and political leaders of their people.

Masters hoped that blacks would learn from Christianity the message of submission, obedience, sobri-ety, and what nineteenth-century white Americans considered seemly behavior. Black Christianity actually had very different consequences. Like black music and literature, it helped preserve a sense of black independence. Blacks took pride in their piety, which seemed to them more sincere and heartfelt than that of whites. They also found in their version of Christianity a message of hope and freedom. The popularity of spirituals like "Go Down Moses" suggests how closely the slaves identified with the Children of Israel and how eagerly they awaited liberation from bondage. Perceptive whites understood the subversive quality of black Christianity, and during times of slave unrest slaveowners often forbade religious meetings on the plantation.

Slavery as a Coercive System. Masters frequently accommodated the religious needs of their slaves and provided them with medical attention, decent food, and adequate housing. They also generally preferred to control behavior and encourage effort by rewards rather than punishments. Slaves were given time off to cultivate garden patches, to visit friends and relatives, and to hold parties. One of the most effective ways to guarantee obedience and hard work was to allow a slave to learn a craft or trade and so achieve the freedom of movement that came with "hiring out." In some cases owners conferred the ultimate privilege on skilled slaves: the right to buy their own freedom with the proceeds of their labor.

But slavery, however lenient in some places and at certain times, remained grounded on coercion. Slaves were punished by having privileges withdrawn or extra work piled on. They were flogged for stealing, for disobeying orders, for running away, for fighting and drinking. Young males—the most rebellious members of any population—were more likely to be lashed than other slaves, but no group was exempt from physical punishment. At times slaves were whipped without apparent cause. Mary Boykin Chesnut, wife of a South Carolina planter-politician, admitted that "men and women are punished when their masters and mistresses are brutes, not when they do wrong." Even slaves who were not themselves physically chastised were deeply affected by it; to witness grown men or women being flogged was an intimidating experience that drove home the lesson that the white owner was indisputable master.

Slavery and the Family. One of the most affecting parts of Harriet Beecher Stowe's best-selling antislavery novel, *Uncle Tom's Cabin* (1852), is the account of how Arthur Shelby, a kindly Kentucky master, is forced to sell the little slave boy Harry to a crude and brutal slavetrader in order to pay his debts. Harry's mother, Eliza, flees with him before the sale and—in a scene that became one of the most famous in all sentimental literature—mother and child escape to free territory across the ice-choked Ohio River. *American Slavery as It Is*, an important abolitionist tract, not only depicted the physical abuse of slaves in nauseating detail but also denounced slavery's disregard of black family life, its encouragement of moral laxity, and the opportunity it afforded for the sexual exploitation of black women.

Everything recorded in the antislavery tracts took place. Slave families were indeed broken up by sale; the experience of Eliza and Harry was not unique. Though no one re-

ally knows how often wives were separated from husbands and children from parents, the threat of separation was always a powerful weapon of social discipline. Slavery was at war with black family life in other ways. Nowhere in the Old South did the law recognize the sanctity of slave marriages; to have done so would have limited the power of slaveholders to dispose of slaves as they wished. On the other hand, the picture is not totally bleak. Masters often found it advantageous to encourage strong marriage ties among their slaves because they reduced rivalries and made for a more efficient work force. Generally speaking, slaves themselves preferred the married to the single state. But whether the initiative came from the master or from the slaves themselves, the result was a surprisingly large number of strong, loving, and permanent slave unions and stable slave families.

One of the most lurid charges leveled by abolitionists against the slave system is that it allowed white men to exploit black women sexually. There is truth to this accusation. Some slaveowners and white overseers had virtual harems. Less sensational, but more telling, the 1860 census records that 10 percent of the slave population had partly white ancestry. We must assume, given the disparity in power between white men and slave women, that the relationships that produced racially mixed offspring were frequently imposed on black women. Yet as Professor Eugene Genovese remarks: "Many white men who began by taking a black girl in an act of sexual exploitation ended by loving her and the children she bore. They were not supposed to, but they did. . . ."

Miscegenation—mating across racial lines—was rare on the well-run plantation, though less unusual in cities and towns. Wherever it took place, it was considered scandalous. Even a beloved black partner could never expect to be recognized and respected by the white community. Harmful to slave discipline and deeply resented by both slave men and women, it was also condemned by white society, which held that all sexual relations outside marriage were deplorable. Slave families, whose solidarity was formidable considering the trying conditions, were disrupted by the practice. White women, particularly, considered it a threat to their families, which explains why southern white women were often hostile to slavery. But miscegenation did take place, and it must be considered another count in the indictment of slavery.

The "Bottom Line" of Slavery. The most recent data on slavery seem to refute the grimmest assertions of its critics. Physical cruelty was not the universal experience of the average slave. The slave family survived. Slaves were able to express themselves in music, religion, and literature. Within the slave system there was some opportunity for the enterprising and the able to improve their economic well-being. Nevertheless, slaves were not the "happy darkies" of myth.

John Antrobus, Plantation Burial *(c. 1860). Slaves preferred to bury their dead at night, and they took the opportunity to socialize as well as to mourn and pray.*

The most obvious evil of slavery was its denial of individual freedom. Ultimately, the slaves' lives were not their own. Slaves were not free to move. They could not withhold their labor or maximize the benefit from it. They could not express their personalities fully. The peculiar institution also directly repudiated those sacred rights of life, liberty, and the pursuit of happiness that all Americans professed to cherish. Slaves knew of white America's professions, and the disparity between principles and performance undoubtedly made the pain of bondage all the greater.

And there was much else. Slavery provided no effective remedy for cruelty. There were laws against sadistic torture and mutilation of slaves; but the laws could not be easily enforced because the slave was a legal nullity who could not testify against whites in court. Masters might prefer to preserve slave families; but because nothing required them to do so, they did not when keeping families intact

conflicted with their pressing financial interests. Slavery also denied black people the full use of their abilities. Opportunities to become drivers or to acquire some skill were no substitute for the ability to reach the highest levels of business or the professions. In addition, it was illegal to teach slaves to read and write. Some masters ignored the law and themselves instructed their slaves to read or permitted literate blacks to teach their fellow bondsmen. Yet in 1860 more than nine out of ten slaves could not read, a condition that severely limited their access to many areas of knowledge and experience. When talented slaves like Josiah Henson, Solomon Northrup, and Frederick Douglass were free to tell their stories, they utterly condemned the system that denied them their humanity. Slavery, wrote Frederick Douglass in his *Autobiography*, "could and did develop all its malign and shocking characteristics." It was "indecent without shame, cruel without shuddering, and murderous without apprehension or fear of exposure, or punishment."

Finally, slavery reinforced racism. It was a mark of inferiority that affected all black men and women and did not disappear even when black people secured their freedom. Slavery accordingly amplified the original racial antipathies of white Americans and made black skin a stigma strong enough to survive even the destruction of the peculiar institution itself.

★ THE SOUTHERN MIND ★

Perhaps the most beguiling myth about the Old South is that it was a genial, cultivated society. There is some truth in the picture. Among the planters there were kindly and charming ladies and gentlemen who read the classics, appreciated music, and kept in touch with the best thought of England and Europe. Samuel Walker, a Louisiana sugar planter, was an avid reader of Charles Lamb and Jeremy Taylor and named his plantation Elia, the pen name of his favorite English essayist. Walker had literary talent and devoted his time to writing a novel. He valued education and sent his children to good schools rather than rely, like many of his neighbors, on tutors. The region also had many literate, upright yeomen whose natural dignity, independence, and generous hospitality would have warmed the heart of Jefferson. Nor were all southern whites hostile to change. The South, for example, joined the crusade against demon rum and against mistreatment of convicted felons. It was even a little ahead of the North in showing concern for the insane. During the 1820–50 period, moreover, many southern states adopted the principle of universal white-male suffrage. Yet by 1860 the white South had also become a land of fear and suspicion where dissent seemed treason and those who denied the region's superiority over all other societies were cruelly ostracized or brutally driven out. In such an atmosphere culture languished or became the servant of self-defense, and all chance of reform ended.

Slave Revolts. The South's fears were directly related to slavery. Although most southerners refused to acknowledge that slavery was a cruel and exploitative system, many recognized that the slaves resented their bondage and would end it if they could. Slaves revealed their hatred of the system by the day-to-day resistance of ignoring directions, engaging in slowdowns, abusing equipment and running away. Occasionally a male slave would attack his master or overseer.

The most feared of all forms of slave resistance was the slave revolt, eruptions of collective racial violence that sent shock waves through white society. Several of these occurred in the Old South era. In 1800 a slave named Gabriel Prosser was foiled in his attempt to capture the city of Richmond. A decade later, approximately 500 slaves began a march on New Orleans and had to be dispersed by troops. In 1822 Denmark Vesey, a free black from Charleston, organized a slave insurrection that was betrayed by a fellow slave. Vesey and thirty-four other blacks were hanged. Most

Historians long believed that slavery left blacks with little sense of family. But plantation slaves usually lived with their families and had strong ties to them. Here, three generations pose for a family portrait.

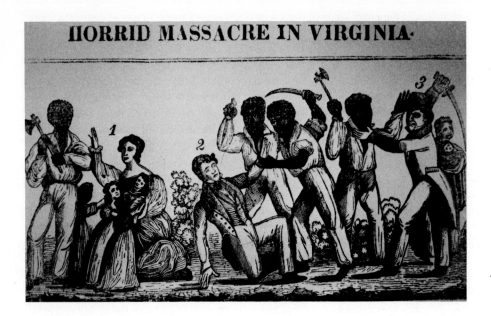

HORRID MASSACRE IN VIRGINIA.

This 1831 woodcut was inspired by Nat Turner's rebellion. The uprising alarmed white southerners because it was directed against slavery itself, not against a particularly brutal master. That meant that even the gentlest, fairest slaveholder might be murdered in his bed one night.

frightening of all, however, was the Nat Turner uprising in the Virginia Tidewater in 1831. Turner, a slave foreman and preacher inspired by the Bible, decided to strike a blow for freedom. On August 27, aided by a few other slaves, Turner killed his master and his master's family. Then, with seventy fellow bondsmen gathered along the way, he marched through the countryside, killing and burning. Before the rebellion was put down by state and federal troops, over fifty whites had lost their lives. Most of Turner's band were either captured or killed in skirmishes with the soldiers during the first forty-eight hours, and thirteen slaves and three free blacks were later hanged. It took an additional two months to capture the resourceful Turner, who then was tried, convicted, and executed.

Though slave revolts were far less common in the American South than in other New World slave societies, they revealed the true feelings of blacks in a particularly dramatic way and sent a chill through the hearts of white southerners. There were times when southerners seemed positively obsessed with the fear of a "servile insurrection" that might result in the mass destruction of white lives and property. This nervousness fed on itself; for each instance of actual slave unrest in the antebellum South, there were a hundred rumors of slave plots.

Quieting the Opposition. Occasionally southern fears led to honest soul-searching. Soon after the suppression of Nat Turner's insurrection, when slavery had not yet become sacred and untouchable, the Virginia legislature conducted a frank debate on the possible abolition of slavery in the state. Some representatives, primarily from the state's western, nonslaveholding districts, attacked the peculiar insti-

tution as "offensive to the moral feelings of a large portion of the community," "ruinous to the whites," degrading to labor, and a danger to the social order of the South. In the end, unfortunately, the debate led nowhere; slavery in Virginia, as elsewhere, was by now so intertwined with the culture and economy of the community that to a majority of whites abolition seemed a cure worse than the disease.

This 1832 debate was the last serious public discussion of abolition in the South. Thereafter the response to slave unrest was unqualified repression. Laws requiring slaves to carry passes when they were away from their masters were more carefully enforced. The patrol system, requiring groups of men to travel about checking on slaves off the plantation, was tightened. After 1832, in scores of southern communities innocent slaves were jailed or even executed in panicky reaction to anticipated slave uprisings.

These fears cast a pall over the political and intellectual life of the South. Many southerners became convinced that the restlessness of the slaves was the work of outside agitators: free blacks, black merchant seamen, and—above all—northern abolitionists. To deal with the problem southern legislatures passed laws that made manumission—the freeing of slaves by their owners—increasingly difficult and restricted the rights and movements of free blacks. Several states even sought to expel free blacks from their limits. In Maryland and Missouri the state legislatures appropriated sums for the purpose of returning ("colonizing") free blacks to Africa. South Carolina tried to prevent slaves from being "contaminated" by black merchant seamen working for northern and foreign firms by forbidding black sailors to set foot on the state's soil.

The fiercest southern response was reserved for the abolitionists. Of all the outside groups that endangered the peace and safety of the South, they seemed the worst. Governor John Floyd of Virginia accused the abolitionists of fomenting the Nat Turner revolt and labeled them "unrestrained fanatics." To other southerners they were "a pestilent sect," "ignorant and infatuated barbarians." Even though they were federal employees, postmasters throughout the South refused to deliver abolitionist newspapers and books. When antislavery activists denounced this as censorship of the mails, Postmaster General Amos Kendall, a Kentuckian by adoption, refused to intervene. "We owe an obligation to the laws," he conceded, but "we owe a higher one to the communities in which we live."

Censorship of the mails was the mildest of the South's efforts to preserve its system by cutting off the free exchange of ideas. After the Virginia debate of 1832 the subject of abolition was considered closed. Almost everywhere in the slave states toleration for social and intellectual dissent weakened. White southerners who refused to go along with the majority view, like James G. Birney of Alabama, the Grimké sisters of South Carolina, and Cassius M. Clay of Kentucky, were denounced, threatened, and eventually driven from the South. Southern leaders sought to suppress abolitionist agitation elsewhere as well. In 1836, as we have seen, the southern delegation in Congress, annoyed at the barrage of petitions asking for abolition of slavery in the District of Columbia, induced the House of Representatives to adopt a rule automatically laying such petitions "on the table" without action. This "gag rule" remained in force for eight years despite attacks by antislavery advocates and civil liberties champions, who assailed it as a denial of free speech and a violation of the constitutional right of petition.

Arguments in Favor of Slavery. The South also mounted a counterattack against its critics that produced some interesting—and generally deplorable—results. In the eighteenth century, southerners seldom defended slavery in the abstract. Though they were quick to defend the agricultural interests that depended on it, they often conceded that, ideally speaking, slavery was a violation of human rights. Its ultimate justification was necessity: The South could not survive without black laborers, and as it was unthinkable that blacks could be anything but social and economic subordinates, they must remain slaves. Still, however unavoidable, slavery seemed clearly wrong to many thinking southerners during these years.

After about 1800, however, southern leaders and publicists ceased to question the institution of slavery; indeed, they began to defend it. Slavery, they said, was sanctioned by the Bible and the Christian faith. In the Old Testament God made Ham, the second son of Noah, a servant of his two brothers. Ham's descendants, the dark races, must therefore serve the light-skinned progeny of Shem and Japheth. The New Testament supported the peculiar institution by enjoining "servants" to be obedient and dutiful to their masters. It is difficult to tell how seriously white southerners took the biblical defense of slavery. It was possible to extract other meanings from the Bible, as both black and white abolitionists had reason to know. For those already disposed to defend the peculiar institution on more practical grounds, it was nevertheless comforting to have the Lord's reinforcement.

In the thirty years before the Civil War, apologists for slavery also constructed a "scientific" defense. Blacks, they maintained, were biologically inferior to whites. They had smaller cranial capacities and a more limited intelligence. They were also closer to "brute creation" than the more intellectual and spiritual white race, as evidenced by the supposedly greater physical endurance and sexual prowess of Africans.

The most sophisticated proslavery argument, however, was sociological. In the writings of the brilliant but bigoted Virginian George Fitzhugh, slavery was converted from a necessary evil to a "positive good." Fitzhugh considered the North's vaunted freedom a failure. It had not brought comfort and security to the white masses: It had brought them slums, social dislocations, and grinding "wage slavery." By rejecting egalitarianism and individualism and accepting the idea of social hierarchy, the South had avoided the cruelty of a competitive society. Slaves, unlike free white laborers, were not tossed on the human rubbish heap after they had ceased being useful to their employers. The South, moreover, was free of such intellectual and moral taints as Mormonism, Perfectionism, Fourierism, trade unionism, and other disgusting and deplorable consequences of freedom. "In the whole South," Fitzhugh asserted, "there is not one Socialist, not one man rich or poor, proposing to subvert and reconstruct society."

Fitzhugh's attack on northern society and its democracy quickly became a commonplace of southern opinion. It was repeated by Calhoun on the floor of the Senate. It filled the pages of newspapers, books, and pamphlets, and was heard from pulpits throughout Dixie. Senator James Hammond of South Carolina gave it classic form in his famous speech of 1858, in which he declared that there had to be "mud sill" upon which to erect a civilized, cultured life. This mud sill was a class "to do the menial duties, to perform the drudgery of life . . . a class requiring but a low order of intellect and but little skill." Far better, said Hammond, that these people be black, as in the South, than white, as in the North.

Romance and Culture. The need to justify the South's way of life profoundly affected southern culture and social values. Influenced by the novels of Sir Walter Scott, liter-

William Gilmore Simms

It is ironic that William Gilmore Simms failed to gain from Charleston, South Carolina, his beloved birthplace, the appreciation and recognition that his achievements deserved. In the years between 1833 and the outbreak of the Civil War, Simms published more than thirty works of fiction. Most of these dealt with the South's heroic exploits during the colonial period or the nobility of the settlers on the frontier of the lower South. They helped create the mythology by which the Old South explained itself to the world. And yet, though honored elsewhere and by posterity, during his lifetime he never won the approval he wanted from his native city.

William Gilmore Simms was born in April 1806. Two years later his father, a Scotch-Irish immigrant, depressed by his wife's death and humiliated by his recent bankruptcy, left little William in the care of his maternal grandmother and went off to rebuild his life. Mrs. Gates, a "proper" Charlestonian, brought William up, sending him first to public schools and then, at the age of ten, to the College of Charleston.

His formal schooling, however, was not as important in molding his literary imagination as was his family history. Grandmother Gates captivated him with tales of his great-grandfather, who had battled the British invaders of Charleston during the Revolutionary War and fought alongside Francis Marion, the "Swamp Fox," to liberate the city. His father's exploits, transmitted through long letters from distant places, also stimulated his mind. After leaving Charleston, the elder Simms had become a friend of Andrew Jackson and had been with Old Hickory at the battles of Tallahatchie and New Orleans.

The port of Charleston was still another source of material for Simms's

tales and novels. After school, William sat on the docks, enthralled by visiting sailors' accounts of escapades in faraway places. When he was somewhat older he took advantage of Charleston's cultural and intellectual life, attending performances at the Broad Street Theater and joining the discussion at the Charleston Library Society.

While in his early teens his grandmother apprenticed him to a druggist, hoping it would eventually lead to a career in medicine. Simms found pharmacology boring, however, and compensated himself for the dull work by reading all night. He soon abandoned medical studies and went to serve an apprenticeship with an attorney who also loved literature. By this time, his father had become a plantation owner in Georgeville, Mississippi. He invited his son to visit, in hopes that he would come to live with him permanently. William traveled through the backroads and backwoods of the frontier, enjoying the time spent with his father and using his experiences as material for his Border Romances. But in the end he decided to return to Charleston, possibly because he had fallen in love with Anna Malcolm Giles, a local belle. His father advised him that he would be able to do more with his life if he stayed in Mississippi, that without connections and wealth he would never make a mark in Charleston. "I know it," he told his son, "only as a place of tombs." In later years his son bitterly regretted this choice, feeling it had done him "irretrievable injury." "All that I have," he wrote, "has been poured to waste in Charleston, which has never smiled on any of my labors, which has steadily ignored my claims, which has disparaged me to the last. . . ." The entire South, and particularly his home city, recognized only narrow avenues of success and were in-

different or hostile to those whose talents lay off the beaten track.

When he was nineteen and still studying law, Simms's first published poem appeared, a work commemorating the death of Charleston native Charles Cotesworth Pinckney, soldier, Federalist leader, and diplomat. In 1825 also, Simms brought out his first volume of poetry and worked as editor of the *Album*, a short-lived literary and political magazine. The next year, having completed his law studies, he married Anna, the daughter of a city clerk. It was thought to be a love match, for many felt that Simms might have improved his standing in the community by choosing a girl from a "better" family.

He could not practice law until he was twenty-one. While he waited for admission to the bar, he continued to write poetry, publishing two more volumes, which were reviewed admiringly by critics and readers. His literary progress convinced him that he might make a career out of writing rather than law. Although he passed the bar in 1827 and practiced law successfully for a while, Simms was truly seduced by *belles lettres*. In 1830 he invested what was left of his maternal inheritance in the *Charleston City Gazette*, a daily newspaper, which he conceived of as a forum for the free exchange of important ideas.

The position he took in the nullification controversy bankrupted his paper and temporarily ruined him. Simms loved his nation as well as his state, and he hoped that they could resolve their difficulties without resorting to extreme measures. Although he believed that the federal government was treading on the constitutional rights of South Carolina, he thought that the state's loyalty to the Union should triumph over its disagreements. "There are some . . . ," he declared, "who would destroy the body, to preserve a member—we are not of the class." He was viciously attacked by prominent politicians throughout the state. The mayor of Charleston suggested that he "confine himself to witticisms, poetry (good luck!) and literature for ladies (girls?). . . ." Eventually Simms lost most of his subscribers and all of his money. In 1832 he was forced to sell the *Gazette* at a loss.

The sale of his journal was not the only tragedy that befell Simms that year. Anna died, leaving him with a young daughter. By this time his father and grandmother had died as well. He had no desire to return to law, and with the Nullifiers in control of Charleston, he decided to go north. There he met the poet and journalist William Cullen Bryant, who introduced him to the New York literary scene. These writers, publishers, and editors were members of "Young America," a group that favored a cultural declaration of independence from Europe and the creation of a distinctive American literature.

In New York Simms published a long poem, "Atalantis," and a maritime adventure; wrote for the *American Quarterly Review*; and worked on his first novel, *Martin Faber*, a Gothic romance about a young frontiersman whose lust for status and money results in murder. Readers liked it, buying all but one of the printed copies. He soon followed with *Guy Rivers*, a "tale of Georgia . . . of a frontier and wild people, and the events [that] . . . may occur among a people & in a region of that character." Critics, who praised it, remarked on the uniqueness of the locale and urged the author to write more about those "untrodden paths" of fiction.

In 1835 Simms published *The Yemassee*, a fictional biography of a colonial governor of South Carolina and an account of the British conquest of the Yemassee Indians. The book also contains the first in a long series of upright, brave, imaginative, and ambitious southern heroes and virtuous, virginal (but physically alluring), intelligent southern women, the future mothers of a "Noble Race." In this book, which is the best known of all Simms's works and still in print, he praised slavery as a necessary and beneficial system and argued that slaves were content with their lot. In the same year he also brought out a romantic history of the Revolutionary era called *The Partisan*. The critical and commercial successes of these volumes finally convinced Simms that his destiny was to be a professional writer.

Although he had made friends and found success in New York, he longed to return to South Carolina. On a visit in 1836 he met and married Chevillette Roach, daughter of a rich plantation owner. His marriage enabled him to stay in his home for much of the year. For the next quarter-century Simms and his wife spent the months from October through May at Woodlands, an estate of 3,000 acres near Charleston. In the summer the Simmses went to Charleston or to New York and New England. While at Woodlands, Simms spent his mornings in the library writing, his afternoons managing the plantation, and his evening hours entertaining guests at dinner. A visitor described Simms's new life: "For a whole morning have I sat in that pleasant library . . . watching . . . the tall, erect figure at the desk, and quick steady passage for hours of the indomitable pen across page after page—a pen that rarely paused to erase, correct, or modify. . . . At dinner he talked a great deal, joked, jested, and punned, . . . or, if a graver theme arose, he would often declaim. . . ."

Now that he was a member of the planter class, Simms's sectional sympathies became more pronounced. He wrote a review for the *Southern Literary Messenger* attacking *Society in America* by Harriet Martineau, a British social observer. In Simms's view, Martineau had not only ignored the North's social problems while criticizing slavery, but she had also failed to note that the southern system was in fact ethically superior. The slaveholder actually bettered the lives of his slaves by improving their morals and intelligence. Someday, Simms promised, when blacks had been elevated to the proper level, they would be freed. Martineau had claimed that since the manufacturing North dominated the country's finances, the South was totally dependent on the North for its economic well-being. Not so, Simms declared. Northern industry could not operate without the South's cotton; therefore, slavery was the financial backbone of the whole nation. This article was acclaimed throughout the South. A version of what came to be called the "King Cotton" argument, it was widely reprinted and became a leading apology for slavery.

Pleased by his success, Simms continued to defend slavery and publicize the South's unique image. He compiled a history and geography of South Carolina. He wrote biographies of representative southern figures. He edited the *Southern Quarterly Review* and established *Simms Magazine*. Between 1844 and 1846 he was a member of the South Carolina legislature, and in the 1850s he actively advocated secession. But he did not give up on fiction. In these years before the Civil War he wrote nine novels, each in its own way glorifying his section and its people.

The era of the Civil War was a tragic one for Simms. The year before the war started, two of his sons died of yellow fever. Then his oldest son and namesake was wounded in battle. In 1863 his wife died at the age of forty-seven, having given birth the year before to her thirteenth child. Simms himself became mentally and physically ill for many weeks. In 1865 General William Sherman's men torched Woodlands and destroyed his art gallery and 10,000-volume library. Two weeks later he was an eyewitness to the burning and pillaging of Columbia, South Carolina, which affected him violently. At the end of the war he wrote to a friend: "Of all that I had . . . I have nothing left. . . ."

Yet he persisted in writing and turned out many poems, articles, and stories, earning money to rebuild his house and support his children. He wrote "Sack and Destruction of the City of Columbia, S.C.," describing vividly his experiences on "Black Friday," the day the beautiful old town went up in flames. In addition, he composed three more book-length southern romances. A month before his death he delivered the opening speech at the Charleston County Floral Fair.

Simms died on Saturday, June 11, 1870. Charleston appreciated him more in death than in life. The bells of St. Michael's tolled in his honor, and all sectors of the Charleston community sent condolences to his family. The *Charleston Courier* printed an apprecia-

tive editorial on Monday, the day of his funeral, when throngs of mourners came in a driving rain to pay their respects. But his best tribute had been written a decade earlier in *Debow's Review* of New Orleans: Simms, this article declared, "reflects . . . the spirit and temper of Southern civilization; announces its opinions, illustrates its ideas, embodies its passions and prejudices, and portrays those delicate shades of thought, feelings, and conduct, that go to form the character and stamp the individuality of a people. . . ."

ate southerners came to equate their society with the rigidly ordered and conservative social systems of medieval and early modern Europe. Southerners of the best sort, they asserted, were true gentlemen whose forebears were the cavaliers who fled England after the defeat of Charles I by Cromwell. They were, claimed one Alabaman, "directly descended from the Norman Barons of William the Conqueror, a race distinguished . . . for its warlike and fearless character, a race at all times . . . renowned for its gallantry, chivalry, honor, gentleness and intellect. . . ." Northerners, by contrast, were descended from Cromwell's Puritan Roundheads, people without breeding or gentility who, to top it all, exhibited the "severe traits of religious fanaticism."

This fantasy permeated upper-class southern life. In the Old South's cultural imagination, plantations became feudal manors, planters became chivalrous knights, slaves became respectful serfs. Southerners came to idealize the warrior virtues. They esteemed horsemanship and adopted fox hunting as a plantation sport. They held tournaments where young gallants jousted for prizes while lovely belles showered them with roses from the sidelines. In time only a military career could compete with planting as a proper calling for a gentleman.

Upper-class southern women were an essential part of the cult of chivalry. Southern "ladies" were placed on pedestals and treated with elaborate gallantry and outward deference. The reality of the southern white woman's life was often quite different, however. Most were not plantation mistresses, but the wives and daughters of common farmers. There was little pampering or chivalry in the lives of these women. And even the mistress of a great plantation often worked hard. Managing a large household and many house slaves was a complex and demanding job full of emotional turmoil. The house slaves were often "part of the family" and the tension between women's familial feelings for their servants and their need to exploit them for their own comfort was evident in the diaries of southern ladies. Meanwhile, the myth of female helplessness and need for protection limited the freedom and autonomy of southern women even more than "women's sphere" restricted their contemporary northern sisters.

It is not surprising that the forces that encouraged the flowering of this social mythology tended to stifle artistic growth in the antebellum period. William Gilmore Simms and Edgar Allan Poe aside, few southern writers rose above mediocrity. After Thomas Jefferson's death in 1826 there were few creative southern architects. All the important American painters of the antebellum years either were northerners or lived in the North or Europe. Although many popular songs—like Stephen Foster's "Swanee River," "My Old Kentucky Home," "Old Black Joe," and "De Camptown Races"—had southern themes, the composers, including Foster himself, were mostly northerners. Even the minstrel show, which fused theater, comedy, and music into a unique form of entertainment, was basically a northern white commercialization of southern black folk culture and owed little to the white South.

Southern defensiveness also affected intellectual life. On the whole, the colleges and universities of the Old South were not great centers of learning, though for a while, in

A classic Old South plantation house. This one is in Thomasville, Georgia.

the 1830s, the best university in the country was Jefferson's University of Virginia, and South Carolina College had the most distinguished social science faculty. Nevertheless, many young southerners went to Harvard, Yale, or Princeton. By the 1850s the growing fear of dissent had brought hundreds of southern students back home. The increasing restrictions on free inquiry meanwhile drove such interesting social thinkers as Francis Lieber of South Carolina College and Henry Harrisse of the University of North Carolina to move north. Harrisse, before his departure, trenchantly attacked the intellectual intolerance he saw all around him.

> You may eliminate all the suspicious men from your institutions of learning, you may establish any number of new colleges which will relieve you of sending your sons to free institutions. But as long as people study, and read, and think among you, the absurdity of your system will be discovered and there will always be found some courageous intelligence to protest against your hateful tyranny.

By contrast with the fertile, innovative contemporary North, the South, then, was a cultural backwater. It was a region turned inward and intent on building up a false self-image and a false self-confidence.

Southern Ideology. Although it may not be enough to fuel a creative revolution, defensiveness has its uses. Southerners were able to detect the flaws in the individualistic, liberal capitalism that had appeared in the North and raise questions about democratic political assumptions. Like so much else in the Old South, this conservative critique was a defense mechanism, but it called attention to some important issues.

The southern critique of northern political ideology was primarily an attack on majoritarian democracy.

Although most southern states had established universal white-male suffrage, some of the most articulate southerners continued to doubt the wisdom of majorities. Pure and simple majority rule was obviously a disadvantage to the South. If mere numbers were considered in making national political decisions, the South would have been consigned to certain defeat. Well before 1860 it had fallen behind the North in population and hence in congressional representation. Until the 1850s a sectional parity had been maintained in the United States Senate, if not in the House, by admitting into the Union one slave state for each free one. But almost certainly more free than slave states would eventually be carved out of the western territories; and when this took place, the South would lose its fragile political equality with the North in Congress.

Southerners worried about their section's decline and sought to discover its causes. A number—including J.D.B. De Bow, William Gregg, and Edmund Ruffin—concluded, contrary to fact, that the cause was slow economic growth owing to the South's vassalage to the North. During the late 1830s, when southern political victory had removed the tariff from center stage, the attack shifted to the North's commercial dominance. Virtually every aspect of the South's economy except the raising of crops, the apostles of commercial independence claimed, was dominated by northern business interests. Much of the South's shipping was done in northern vessels. Almost all imports came through New York, and until the 1850s even the cotton crop generally went to New York before being shipped to Europe. Northern capitalists and their agents also controlled most of the South's banking. Northern cotton "factors" (agents) residing in the South dominated agriculture, extending credit to planters and farmers, sending crops to market, and buying supplies their customers wanted. They were useful to the southern economy, but the price they exacted for their services, southerners insisted, was excessive.

The picture of northern dominance painted by the critics was exaggerated. Not all the South's business was handled by outsiders; the section produced a substantial crop of home-grown merchants, bankers, and manufacturers

Prized, pampered, and put on a pedestal—the southern belle. Whatever she was in fact, the southern woman (here, Sarah Knox Taylor, daughter of president Zachary Taylor and first wife of Jefferson Davis) was mythologized as the incarnation of the aristocratic virtues of plantation life.

who often combined town business with plantation ownership. Yet most southerners assumed northern dominance, chafed under it, and periodically determined to end it. Gregg, a successful textile magnate, constantly urged his fellow southerners to invest their capital in manufactures to make their section independent of the North and Europe. The publicist and editor De Bow used his *Review* to call for southern economic independence. "Action, Action, Action!!!" the *Review* demanded. "Not in the rhetoric of Congress, but in the busy hum of mechanism, and the thrifty operators of the hammers and anvil." Ruffin condemned southern farming practices and advocated improved agricultural methods to stem the flow of yeomen from the South and to help equalize free- and slave-state populations.

Beginning in 1837, southern merchants and publicists convened in various cities to consider ways to liberate their section from its supposed economic bondage to the North. These conventions proclaimed the need for the South to do its own importing and exporting as well as its own banking. Delegates discussed at great length how to end "the abject state of colonial vassalage" to the North by such devices as direct shipping of cotton to Europe from southern ports. The conventions achieved few concrete results, but they were effective forums for the display of antinorthern feelings. Toward the end of the 1850s, when sectional antagonisms reached their peak, the conventions went on record against northern books, magazines, and teachers and passed resolutions, demanding the reopening of the transatlantic slave trade, which had been closed since 1808.

The growing imbalance of population and potential power between the two sections of the country was an unpleasant fact of life that southerners had to face. How could the South remain a part of the Union and, as the weaker partner, defend its unique and controversial interests?

This problem obsessed John C. Calhoun in his later years. During the tariff crisis of 1831–1832 Calhoun had resurrected the theory of nullification first raised in the 1790s as part of the Kentucky Resolution. But nullification seemed more and more inadequate. Between the 1830s and his death in 1850, the South Carolinian sought a new formula to protect his section's minority interests. In a succession of treatises, speeches, and letters, Calhoun's solution slowly evolved into a critique of the democratic concepts of the age. People were not all equal, he declared. The Declaration of Independence expressed a noble theory, but an invalid one. The best societies, like those of classical Greece and Rome, recognized the inherent inequality of human beings and exploited the inferior groups to construct great civilizations. If people were unequal, it stood to reason that some should lead and others follow; otherwise the inferior many would impose their will on the superior few and the result would be a tyranny of the ignorant. In the United States, a despotism of numbers would result in sectional oppression: The North with its greater population would trample on the rights of the South.

How could those rights be protected? A "concurrent majority" was Calhoun's solution. Before any law that vitally concerned the interests of either section went into effect, let it be ratified by both sections of the country. This arrangement could be guaranteed by a dual presidency, with one president selected by the North and the other by the South. Both would have to approve any important measure passed by Congress before it became law. In this way the South could exercise a veto over a domineering North and check the normal tendency of a majority to ride roughshod over the rights of a minority.

John C. Calhoun died before the inner logic of his theories was expressed in deeds. He had not wished to see the Union destroyed; he hoped to preserve it by finding an accommodation with which the South could live. It is fitting, however, that when the people of Charleston received news of South Carolina's secession from the Union in 1860, they unfurled a banner bearing Calhoun's image.

★ CONCLUSIONS ★

The Old South was not a moonlight and magnolias society; it was too diverse for that. The happy harmony of that fabled state was marred by regional, class, and economic divisions. The South was not all multiacred Delta estates. It consisted of small farms in the back country and the mountain regions and poor whites living from hand to mouth by grazing, hunting, and foraging. Though upper-class southerners sought to create a fantasy land of modern chivalry, they were at best marginally successful. The Old South was ruled by a planter elite, but only with the consent of a substantial yeomanry and through the mechanism of universal white-male suffrage. And even the life of the planter was not what the South's spokesmen and writers sought to make it. Under the veneer of an aristocratic indifference to money was the firm reality of hard striving and profit maximizing. And it was just as well. The system was able to generate the high income that made the chivalrous pose possible.

The Old South, despite its economic success, was not a relaxed and confident society. Even if it was not solely the land of "the whip and the lash" as depicted by its opponents, it was a region that lived on the coerced labor of millions of black men, women, and children. Most of these slaves were able to accommodate to the system. They managed to snatch some satisfactions from the life of bondage and maintain a degree of personal and cultural autonomy.

Yet with some reason white southerns feared that they lived on the edge of a social volcano that could erupt at any time. The fear begat a degree of defensiveness that imposed conformity and intolerance of change and dissent.

To the very end southerners would continue to share with other Americans memories, political values, and cultural attributes. Yet with each passing year the South diverged more and more from the liberal mainstream of the United States and the liberal values of the Atlantic world. Before long many southerners would consider themselves people with distinct interests and a separate destiny. The consequences would be tragic.

★★★★★★★★ FOR FURTHER READING ★★★★★★★★

William R. Taylor. *Cavalier and Yankee: The Old South and American National Character* (1961)
The author examines the myth of the southern cavalier—a symbol of the agrarian South and the opposite, supposedly, of the money-minded, unchivalrous Yankee. In the popular fiction of the time, Taylor finds evidence that the planter's confidence gradually eroded into self-doubt as 1860 approached.

Frederick Law Olmsted. *The Cotton Kingdom: A Traveler's Observations on Cotton and Slavery in the American Slave States* (1861). Edited and introduced by Arthur M. Schlesinger, Sr. (1953)
Inspired by a discussion with William Lloyd Garrison, the planner of New York's Central Park went south in 1853 to write on the slave economy for the *New York Times*. In his colorful report, long a source of information for scholars and historical novelists, Olmsted demonstrates, to his own satisfaction at least, that dependence on slave-grown cotton fostered "lazy poverty" and was a barrier to the South's broad economic progress.

Grady McWhiney. *Cracker Culture: Celtic Ways in the Old South* (1988)
McWhiney seeks in this volume to explain the yeoman culture of the white Old South by tying it to the origins of much of its population to the Irish, Scottish, and Welsh areas of the United Kingdom rather than the English-speaking parts. An interesting attempt to account for conflicting depictions of the Old South.

Benjamin A. Botkin, editor. *Lay My Burden Down: A Folk History of Slavery* (1945)
This one-volume oral history was compiled from the Slave Narrative Collection made during the 1930s. Former slaves—75 to 105 years old when interviewed—describe slavery and their feelings about emancipation.

John W. Blassingame. *The Slave Community: Plantation Life in the Ante-Bellum South* (1972)
This is a compact, readable study of Old South slavery as seen from inside the system. The author demonstrates the extent to which slaves were able to create islands of freedom in which to conduct their personal lives.

Robert W. Fogel and Stanley L. Engerman. *Time on the Cross: The Economics of Negro Slavery* (1974)
An econometric study of Old South slavery that has drawn a lot of criticism both for its methods and for its conclusions. Using statistical data, the authors try to show that slavery was profitable and relatively benign. An interesting book, but one that must be read with care.

Herbert Gutman. *The Black Family in Slavery and Freedom, 1750–1925* (1976)
An important study of the evolving black family from the colonial era until well after emancipation. Gutman supports the view that black slave families were strong units.

Eugene Genovese. *Roll Jordan Roll: The World the Slaves Made* (1974)
Makes some of the same points as Gutman and Blassingame. According to Genovese, American slaves did more than merely survive; they formed a "black nation" in the South based on religion and strong family ties. The writer is a leading Marxist scholar.

Clement Eaton. *Freedom of Thought in the Old South* (1940)
This older but still useful work presents a critical view of antebellum southern intellectual life. Eaton traces a progressive retreat from free inquiry and tolerance in the Jeffersonian period to conformity and repression in the years immediately before 1860.

Ulrich B. Phillips. *Life and Labor in the Old South* (1929)
This work, now sixty years old, is the nearest thing we have to a scholarly version of the moonlight and magnolias view of the Old South. A Georgian, Phillips loved his native region and expressed his love well here.

Robert Fogel. *Without Consent or Contract: The Rise and Fall of American Slavery* (1989)
This is Fogel's "second thoughts" about the institution he and Stanley Engerman wrote about in 1974. It refines the economic conclusions and seeks to alter the slavery-was-not-so-bad impression of the earlier work.

Frank Owsley. *Plain Folk of the Old South* (1949)
The best summation of the Owsley-Vanderbilt school of southern history, which emphasizes the small farmers rather than the slaves and large planters. Written with great af-

fection for its subjects, it is a lively, readable—and short—book.

Ann F. Scott. *The Southern Lady from Pedestal to Politics, 1830–1930* (1970)
A brief survey of that social phenomenon, the southern lady. Written from diaries, letters, and memoirs, Scott's book makes the point that in the Old South white middle-class women were indeed pampered and patronized.

William Styron. *Confessions of Nat Turner* (1967)
Nat Turner, the black preacher who instigated the 1831 Virginia slave uprising, tells his own story in this widely acclaimed, though flawed, historical novel.

14★

THE COMING
OF THE CIVIL WAR

What Caused the Division?

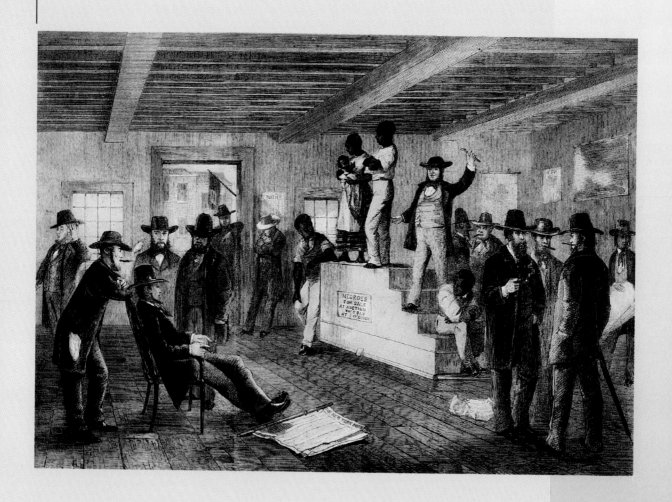

1780	Pennsylvania becomes the first state to prohibit slavery
1787	The Northwest Ordinance prohibits slavery north of the Ohio River and west of Pennsylvania
1812	Louisiana is admitted into the Union as a slave state
1820	The Missouri Compromise
1832–34	The South Carolina nullification crisis
1839	Antislavery leaders found the Liberty party
1846	Congressional debate on the Wilmot Proviso worsens sectional controversy
1848	The California Gold Rush • Formation of the Free-Soil party • Zachary Taylor elected president
1850	The Compromise of 1850, including passage of the Fugitive Slave Act
1852	Harriet Beecher Stowe's *Uncle Tom's Cabin* published • Franklin Pierce elected president
1854	The Kansas-Nebraska Act • The Republican party is formed by antislavery Whigs and Democrats
1856	John Brown murders five proslavery settlers in Kansas • James Buchanan elected president
1857	*Dred Scott* decision • Buchanan accepts Kansas's fraudulent constitution
1858	The Lincoln-Douglas debates focus national attention on the Illinois election for United States Senator
1859	John Brown's raid on Harpers Ferry
1860	The Democratic party breaks up at its national convention • Abraham Lincoln is nominated by the Republican national convention; he is elected president
1860–61	South Carolina, Georgia, Louisiana, Mississippi, Florida, Alabama, and Texas secede from the Union
1861	Delegates of six seceded states adopt a constitution and elect Jefferson Davis president • Lincoln says the federal government will hold its property in the South; Confederates fire on Union-held Fort Sumter • Arkansas, North Carolina, Virginia, and Tennessee secede

*T*he Civil War was the greatest crisis that ever befell the United States—the only one that threatened its very survival. No sooner had the fighting broken out than thoughtful citizens on both sides urgently asked: Why? Why had a union so promising, so prosperous, so self-confident, so triumphant, come to this terrible state? Students of American history still ponder the question today.

★ A HOUSE DIVIDING ★

On the eve of the American Revolution an outspoken Massachusetts citizen would not have felt seriously out of place in the social or intellectual environment of South Carolina. Similarly, southerners visiting the North could speak their minds without shocking or offending their hosts. North and South in, say, 1770 were not so far apart in their economic or labor systems. Agriculture was the chief occupation of all Americans from New Hampshire to Georgia by a wide margin. Slavery existed in every colony. There were more slaves in the South, but a considerable part of the work force north of the Mason-Dixon Line were half-free indentured servants. By 1800 even the religious differences that had separated Puritan New England from the Anglican South had receded as both regions felt the effects of evangelical revivalism and the breakdown of established churches.

Then, in the generation and a half following the War of 1812, differences between North and South multiplied. As we saw in Chapters 9 and 12, the North began to industrialize and evolve into an open, culturally diverse society. The South, meanwhile, confirmed its stake in plantation agriculture and embraced the social conformity and defensiveness described in Chapter 13.

Ideological Differences. We must not exaggerate the sectional contrasts. Both North and South were complex societies with a variety of dissenters from the prevailing orthodoxies. Only a minority of northerners were abolitionists, transcendentalists, or Perfectionists; many considered such people meddlers or fanatics. And the North was full of "doughfaces"—"northern men with southern principles"— who supported southern positions in the emerging sectional debates. And even the conformist South was not homogeneous. Southerners like J. B. D. De Bow and William Gregg urged their section to emulate the North's success in commerce and manufacturing, while among the small farmers in the upland regions and the back country there were those who despised both slavery and the slaveholding class.

Such internal divisions survived to the very end of the antebellum era. Yet there gradually emerged two distinct sectional outlooks which each year grew further apart and more militant and antagonistic. In the South, as we saw in Chapter 13, political and intellectual leaders came to glorify an agricultural society based on slavery. They condemned dissent, rejected commercial values, endorsed inequality, and fought social change. It became ever more difficult as the years passed for dissenters to speak out against the overwhelming weight of majority opinion. Part of the emerging southern ideology included a passionate attack on free society. Declared a Georgia newspaper: "Free Society! we sicken at the name. What is it but a conglomeration of greasy mechanics, filthy operatives, small-fisted farmers, and moon-struck theorists . . . hardly fit for association with a southern gentleman's body servant." When the time came, the mechanics, operatives, farmers, and theorists would remember the southern insults at the polls.

The North also adopted distinctive guiding beliefs in these years, though they evolved more slowly and never became so universal as the South's. The heart of the emerging northern ethos was the very quality that the Georgia editor attacked: freedom. This term meant different things to different people. To northern reformers it meant freedom to engage in social experiment. To northern intellectuals it meant freedom to speculate and criticize. To northern manufacturers it meant freedom from government control— though not exemption from government aid. To northern farmers it meant freedom to move west and take up cheap land. To northern wage earners it meant freedom to move wherever opportunity offered and to advance in life. Northern opinion leaders and officials never attempted to impose these sentiments on the people. Nevertheless, the whole thrust of northern society created an increasing agreement on the importance of "free" values and attitudes, especially in contrast to the South and what it represented.

Economic Conflict. The widening gap between the predominant northern and southern value systems has been seen as a reflection of fundamentally competing economies: northern commerce and industry versus southern agriculture. There is no question that the differing economic interests of the antebellum North and South pushed them into political conflict along a wide front. We saw in Chapter 10 how, during Jackson's presidency, the northern-sponsored tariff provoked the South into angry reaction and threatened the Union. During the 1840s southern political leaders, working through the predominant Democratic party, were able to secure constantly lower tariffs. The 1846 Walker Tariff lowered duties on imported manufactured

The young John C. Calhoun at about the time he served as President Monroe's Secretary of War and was still a nationalist.

goods. The tariff of 1857 reduced rates still further. By the eve of the Civil War duties on imports afforded little protection to northern industry. By the end of the 1850s, the tariff had become a hot political issue in Pennsylvania and New England; this time it was northern groups that felt aggrieved.

Nor was the tariff the only economic issue dividing the sections. Northern commercial interests favored federal subsidies to the American merchant marine to enable it to compete with foreign carriers; southerners saw little benefit to themselves in such measures and opposed paying the taxes required. Northern merchants and manufacturers favored federal appropriations for dredging rivers and harbors to improve navigation; southerners, believing that they would benefit from such measures less than northerners, fought the appropriations.

The two most important economic issues that roiled the sectional waters during the generation preceding 1860, were a Pacific railroad and a homestead act. By the 1850s most public-spirited Americans, northern and southern,

endorsed a railroad to connect the settled and developed portions of the United States with the newly acquired Mexican Cession and the Pacific Coast. Such a transcontinental road would facilitate commerce and travel and bind the country together. It was recognized, moreover, that building a railroad across hundreds of miles of empty country would require a large federal subsidy. Yet the location of the road triggered sharp sectional controversy. Southerners wanted to link New Orleans with San Diego or Memphis with San Francisco. Northerners demanded a route farther north that would connect the Great Lakes at Chicago or Milwaukee with either San Francisco or Puget Sound.

The sectional bickering produced an impasse. In 1853, Mississippian Jefferson Davis, secretary of war in the pro-southern administration of Franklin Pierce, arranged to buy a 30,000-square-mile slice of northern Mexico. The move was in part fueled by southern yearning for more territory. But the Gadsden Purchase (named for the American commissioner who negotiated it) also contained within its limits one of the better passes through the Rocky Mountains and was intended to improve the chances of a southern route for a Pacific railroad. The scheme did not work as intended. After the United States acquired the real estate, northern congressmen vetoed the route. Southerners, in turn, were able to frustrate the choice of a central or northern connection.

The two sections also battled over a homestead bill. Many ordinary southerners were interested in acquiring free farms in the West, and many southern political leaders favored it. Still, a substantial portion of southern opinion feared that free land in the West would draw off small farmers from the South to regions where slavery could not take root. In the end, then, homestead legislation would favor the North over the South. In the 1854 debate over a homestead bill, one southern congressman insisted bluntly that the proposed legislation was "tinctured with Abolitionism." Eventually, in 1860, a coalition of northeastern and northwestern congressmen passed a homestead measure over the opposition of a virtually united South. President James Buchanan, a "northern man with southern principles," vetoed it.

The Role of Slavery. These clashes over economic policies are not sufficient, however, to explain why the sections eventually resorted to war. Not all the battling over tariffs, railroad subsidies, and internal improvements pitted the sections against one another. Often the divisions were within each section, not between them. If most southern leaders opposed tariffs, the sugar planters of Louisiana favored them on the cheaper sugar of the Caribbean to improve their competitive position. If most southern politicians had become skeptical of homestead legislation by 1860, the most ardent proponent of a homestead act to the very end was the Democratic Senator from Tennessee, Andrew Johnson. Furthermore, sectional conflict over economic policy had raged before 1840 and would continue after 1865; yet only after 1848 did divisive forces actually threaten the Union. In the nullification crisis of 1832, the Tariff of Abominations failed to arouse strong disunionist sentiment outside of South Carolina. A generation later eleven states left the Union when confronted with a similar threat to the South's "rights." Clearly, during the years following 1832, the bonds among the slave states grew stronger while those attaching them to the Union as a whole weakened.

The economic and ideological differences between the sections that had emerged in the preceding half century or more no doubt contributed to the North-South split of 1860–1861. But these conflicts were not sufficient by themselves to explain the South's bold strike for independence. It was only in the decade following the Mexican War that grievances were converted to outrage and outrage to secession. What were the events and the forces that reinforced southern cohesion and loosened the South's ties to the rest of the nation?

★ THE DILEMMA OF TERRITORIAL GROWTH ★

A critical element in the snowballing North-South struggle was the country's geographical expansion and the sectional issues it raised. If, after 1846, the nation had not confronted the question of slavery extension, the sections might have remained at peace. But such was not to be. In the past, as new territory was added to the nation it became necessary to redraw the boundary between slavery and freedom first established in the early republic by state emancipation acts and by federal measures, the Northwest Ordinance of 1787 (slavery excluded from the Northwest), and the Southwest Ordinance of 1790 (slavery allowed in the Southwest).

Slavery already existed in parts of the Louisiana Purchase when the United States bought it in 1803, and Congress let it remain. In 1812 the most southerly portion of the new region entered the Union as the slave state of Louisiana. Then, in 1819–1820, as we saw, another part of the Louisiana Purchase, Missouri Territory, was admitted to the Union as a slave state, while the remainder of the purchase was divided by Congress along the line of 36°30′ north latitude into slave and free regions.

The Wilmot Proviso. As of 1820 the whole of the existing United States had been assigned to one labor system or the other either by Congress or by the states themselves. For the next fifteen years the territorial limits of slavery ceased to trouble Americans. Then, in 1835, Texas revived the issue. Many opponents of annexation feared that admitting Texas to the Union would tip the balance in favor of slavery. Southerners, on the other hand, as one Virginian wrote, considered admission of Texas "as indispensable to their security." As we saw, despite much northern opposition, Texas was admitted to the Union in 1845. Northerners only acquiesced because they expected President Polk to push hard to acquire all of distant Oregon, a region of fog, forests, and furs, from which several free states would certainly be carved in time.

The events of 1846–1848 reopened the slavery extension issue with a vengeance. Besides Oregon, the United States acquired the vast Mexican Cession in the Southwest. Many political leaders considered the far Southwest as uncongenial as Oregon to slavery. Not all southerners agreed.

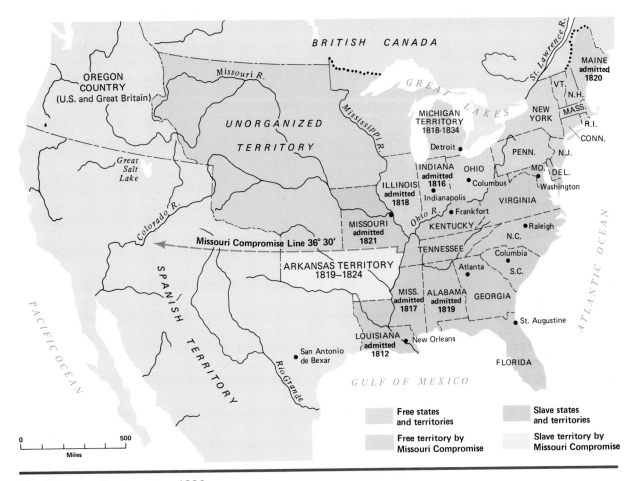

THE MISSOURI COMPROMISE, 1820

In any case, they insisted, why should slavery be legally and arbitrarily excluded from the region, especially when it had been won by the exertions of a southern president—Polk—two southern generals—Scott and Taylor—and an army two-thirds of whose volunteers came from slave states? When, in August 1846, only three months into the Mexican War, Democratic Congressman David Wilmot of Pennsylvania submitted a resolution requiring that a "fundamental condition" of acquiring "any territory from the Republic of Mexico" be that "neither slavery nor involuntary servitude shall ever exist in any part of said territory," he set off a political explosion.

Wilmot belonged to a group of northern Democrats hostile to the Polk administration for favoring the South. The president had sacrificed northern interests, they felt, by supporting tariff reduction, surrendering half of the Oregon region to the British, and vetoing rivers and harbors improvement legislation. The South, they feared, totally controlled the Democratic party, treating its northern members as outcasts. Some of this same group were aggrieved supporters of Martin Van Buren, the former president. The New York leader, they felt, had deserved the party presidential nomination in 1844, and they resented the desertion of their hero by southern Democrats in favor of Polk.

For months following the introduction of the Wilmot Proviso, the country remained in a fever of excitement. The aging Calhoun, once a strong unionist but long since the great champion of southern interests, countered the proviso with resolutions denying that Congress had the power to exclude slavery from the territories. Southerners, though slow to catch fire, were soon denouncing the North. The "madmen of the North and the Northwest have . . . cast the die," proclaimed the Richmond *Enquirer*, "and numbered the days of the glorious Union." On the other side, every northern legislature but one endorsed the proviso. Northern votes, both Whig and Democrat, carried the proviso's adoption in the House, but it was kept from coming to a vote in the Senate. In February 1847 the House once more passed it, but then, under administration pressure, a contingent of northern Democrats reconsidered, and the bill was defeated.

Though now placed on hold, the issue of slavery or freedom in the Mexican Cession territory remained very much alive with public opinion divided into several distinct positions. Many northerners continued to favor total exclusion of slavery from the newly acquired region. Northern and southern moderates endorsed extending the Missouri Compromise 30°30′ line to the Pacific Coast. Calhoun and his supporters would have neither of these solutions. Slaveholders must have equal access with their slave property to all the territories, they insisted. The southern elder statesman considered it a matter of life or death for the South. "If we flinch we are gone," he wrote a friend. "But if we stand fast on it, we shall triumph either by compelling the North to yield to our terms, or by declaring our independence of them."

Another position soon emerged that would provide a formula for compromise that middle-of-the-road politicians would rush to support. First advanced by Michigan Democrat Lewis Cass in 1847, "popular sovereignty" proposed "leaving to the people of the territory to be acquired the business of settling the matter for themselves." The scheme appealed to many Americans as an expression of grass-roots democracy: Let the people of the local community, rather than Congress, decide. But when would the people decide? When the territory entered as a state? During the territorial stage by vote of the territorial legislature? It was not clear. And did popular sovereignty supersede Congressional enactment regarding slavery in the territories entirely? But its very ambiguity was the beauty of popular sovereignty: It could please many people simultaneously and give the appearance of agreement when there really was none.

Free Soil. The slavery extension discussion inevitably colored the 1848 presidential campaign. Within both the Whig and Democratic parties there was a range of views from pro-Wilmot Proviso, through popular sovereignty, to the Calhounite position. The Whigs papered over the potentially disruptive conflict at their nominating convention by choosing as their candidate "Old Rough and Ready," Zachary Taylor, the hero of Buena Vista, and eschewing a party platform entirely. Their evasion enraged the antislavery "conscience Whig" faction, which denounced the choice of Taylor, a slaveholder, as an alliance between the "lords of the lash" (the southern planters) and the "lords of the loom" (the New England textile manufacturers).

The Democrats were even less successful in avoiding conflict. Democratic differences over slavery extension were amplified by the split in the powerful New York delegation between the Barnburners and the Hunkers. The first opposed southern dominance in the party; the second favored conciliating the South. The Barnburners were also loyal followers of Van Buren; the Hunkers his enemy. When the presidential nominating convention refused to exclude their Hunker opponents, the Barnburners left in a huff and nominated Van Buren in a separate convention. Meanwhile, led by southern and western moderates, the regular Democratic convention chose Cass on a vague plank regarding slavery that satisfied virtually no one. When the convention voted down by six to one William Lowndes Yancey's proposal endorsing southern rights in the territories, Yancey too walked out.

A third political group soon began to coalesce out of the discontented pro-Wilmot Proviso elements of both parties, joined with the minuscule antislavery Liberty party. Formed in 1839 by abolitionists who had turned away from propaganda and moral suasion to politics, the Liberty party had done poorly at the polls. Yet it survived and in late 1847 had nominated Senator John P. Hale of New Hampshire on a platform that demanded prohibition of slavery wherever federal power over the institution extended. Before long, the Liberty party leaders and the Van Burenites were negotiating a coalition that would combine Van Buren's vote-getting power with a strong platform against slavery extension. Meeting at Buffalo in August 1848, the rebels nominated Van Buren for president with Charles Francis Adams, son of the sixth president, as his running mate. The new Free-Soil party adopted a platform calling for "free soil, free speech, free labor, and free men."

The new party covered a spectrum of positions. A minority were outright abolitionists who hoped to see slavery ended throughout the United States. A larger group was more interested in preserving the territories for free labor than destroying slavery in the South. Their position was summarized by Senator Preston King of New York: "If slavery is not excluded by law" from the national territories, he declared, "the presence of the slave will exclude the laboring white man." Yet many delegates at Buffalo saw the free soil position as the first step toward ending slavery and left Buffalo convinced that the new party's showing in the fall would mark the start of slavery's downfall.

Unfortunately, the slaves' deliverance would have to wait until a later day. Taylor achieved an electoral as well as a popular majority, doing particularly well in the South. Van Buren won only a meager 300,000 votes, 14 percent of the northern popular vote. But the Free-Soil campaign was a portent. Van Buren's support came mostly from upstate New York, the Western Reserve of Ohio, northern Illinois, and southern Wisconsin. Along with New England itself, these were regions inhabited by people of New England descent and were, accordingly, unusually susceptible to the antislavery appeal. The new organization elected ten members to Congress who would be outspoken antislavery advocates in the bitter debates just ahead. The new party also broke new political ground. As yet most northern voters were still not ready for a single-issue, purely sectional, party, but the outlines of such an organization were coming into view.

Gold in California. Though a southerner and a slaveholder, as president, Zachary Taylor proved to be a bulwark of the Union. His strong nationalism was fortunate, for it would be needed in the months ahead.

The immediate problem was California. In January 1848 a laborer working for John Augustus Sutter, a Swiss businessman long settled in the Mexican province, found gold while constructing a water mill channel near Sacramento. Sutter tried to keep the discovery a secret, but the news soon leaked out. In December, after California was safely American, President Polk confirmed the lucky strike in his annual message to Congress, setting off a stampede to the gold fields. By the early months of 1849 over sixty ships packed with gold seekers were on their way to the Pacific Coast by way of Cape Horn. In the spring thousands of others set out overland on the California Trail established by settlers earlier in the decade. By the summer, wherever Americans gathered—on the front porches, in the parlors, at the saloons, and around the cast-iron stoves at the general store—the talk was largely about California and gold. The whole country was soon singing a new version of Stephen Foster's popular song:

Oh Susanna, don't you cry for me,
I'm off to California with my washbowl on my knee.

The fate of the forty-niners was often harsh. Hundreds sickened and died aboard ship or along the trail. By the fall, the route across the plains was lined by the skeletons of horses and cattle and the graves of gold seekers. Among those who reached the diggings, few struck it rich. Some gave up and straggled home. Others settled down in the new country to farm, work, keep store, or practice professions. By mid-1849 thousands of people from every state,

CALIFORNIA GOLD DIGGERS—A SCENE FROM ACTUAL LIFE AT THE MINES

This contemporary sketch of the California gold country shows why it was called the "diggings." As you can see, the miners often cooperated in a common enterprise— and shared the profits, if any.

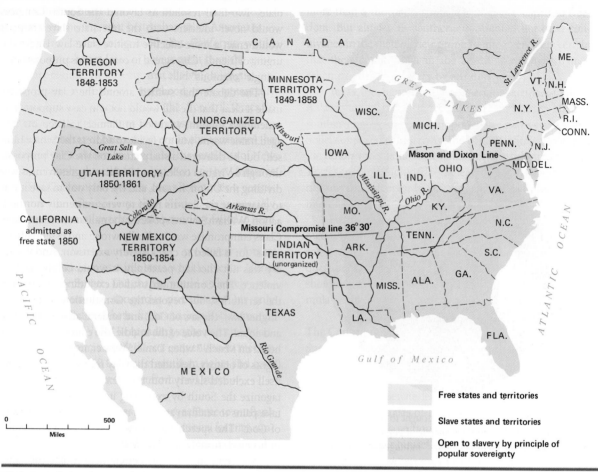

Free states and territories

Slave states and territories

Open to slavery by principle of popular sovereignty

THE COMPROMISE OF 1850

ished in the District of Columbia; there would be a new, far stricter, fugitive slave law. With the help of Fillmore, Douglas convinced a group of northern Democrats and upper-South Whigs to support all the measures. When combined with southern or northern partisans who would support those particular measures that favored their section, these moderate center votes were enough to pass the whole package of bills. What Clay could not achieve with a single measure had now been accomplished with five.

The Compromise of 1850 heartened unionists all over the country. Profoundly relieved at having escaped disunion, Congress celebrated the end of the unruly session with an enthusiasm that left many members with hangovers the next day. Jubilant crowds surged through the streets of Washington toasting Clay, Douglas, and Webster. In the country at large moderates gained confidence; many citizens agreed with Cass that the slavery question was finally "settled in the public mind." Soon after, the Nashville convention finally adjourned without taking a disunionist position.

The 1850 Fugitive Slave Act. The Union had been saved—or so it seemed. But both southern fire-eaters and militant antislavery advocates denounced the compromise, and as the months passed, it became clear that it would not put an end to sectional discord. Indeed, one of its components, the Fugitive Slave Act, seemed only to inflame sectional antagonism.

The provisions of the new fugitive slave law were hard for many northerners to swallow. It deprived suspected runaway slaves of virtually every right normally granted in American jurisprudence to those accused of violating the law. By merely submitting an affidavit to a federal commissioner, a person could claim ownership of an avowed black runaway. The commissioner might, on investigation, reject the affidavit, but if he did, he received a fee of only $5; if he ordered the suspect's return, he pocketed $10. During the investigation, the accused could not testify on his or her behalf. Still worse, the law required that any free citizen could be forced to join in the pursuit of any fugitive on pain

CAUTION!!

COLORED PEOPLE

OF BOSTON, ONE & ALL,

You are hereby respectfully CAUTIONED and advised, to avoid conversing with the

Watchmen and Police Officers of Boston,

For since the recent ORDER OF THE MAYOR & ALDERMEN, they are empowered to act as

KIDNAPPERS

AND

Slave Catchers,

And they have already been actually employed in KIDNAPPING, CATCHING, AND KEEPING SLAVES. Therefore, if you value your LIBERTY, and the *Welfare of the Fugitives* among you, *Shun* them in every possible manner, as so many *HOUNDS* on the track of the most unfortunate of your race.

Keep a Sharp Look Out for KIDNAPPERS, and have TOP EYE open.

APRIL 24, 1851.

The Fugitive Slave Act, part of the Compromise of 1850, led to bitter sectional antagonism. Shocked into active disobedience of the law, many northerners did what they could to warn and protect freedmen and fugitive slaves. This obstructionism was a prime cause of the South's grievances.

of stiff fines and jail sentences. In effect, the law made every American a potential slave catcher.

Anger at the law's disregard of civil liberties was amplified by its enforcement. The sight of black men and women, many long-time residents of the North, being dragged off to jail in chains and taken south to bondage by federal authorities, made hundreds of indifferent northerners antislavery converts overnight. In many northern communities citizens actively resisted efforts to enforce the law. In Syracuse, Boston, Oberlin (Ohio), New York City, and even Baltimore, the commercial capital of a slave state, people hid escapees, attacked slave-catching officials, rescued fugitives from jail, and whisked them away to Canada. In Lancaster County, Pennsylvania, irate citizens murdered one slaveholder pursuing an escapee from bondage.

Public outrage prompted nine northern states to enact new personal liberty laws providing state attorneys to defend fugitives, appropriating funds to pay their defense

costs, and denying the use of public buildings to detain accused escapees. It was an ironic outcome: The North, the time-honored champion of federal supremacy, was proclaiming local will superior to federal law. The fugitive slave issue also impelled the South to reverse its traditional constitutional position. At the South's behest, the federal government challenged the personal liberty laws, and in *Ableman* v. *Booth* (1859) the Supreme Court declared the laws unconstitutional. Obviously, in the heat of sectional rivalry, both sections were sacrificing venerable constitutional scruples.

One northerner appalled by the Fugitive Slave Act was Harriet Beecher Stowe. Stowe had little personal contact with slavery, but she was certain she knew evil when she saw it. As a little girl she had wept when her father, the Reverend Lyman Beecher, prayed for "poor, oppressed, bleeding Africa," and as a young woman she had been shocked at the sight of escaped slaves being plucked off the streets of Cincinnati by slave-catchers. In 1851 she wrote a series of slave-life sketches for the *National Era*, an abolitionist journal. She soon expanded these into a novel that appeared in 1852 as *Uncle Tom's Cabin.* The book was a huge success. In the sentimental style of the day, it recounted the story of a lively and vivid cast of characters, black and white, enmeshed in the tragic web of slavery, and victimized by its inherent cruelty. By the end of its first year the book had sold 300,000 copies, and eight presses were running day and night to keep up with the demand.

Southerners denounced *Uncle Tom's Cabin* as inaccurate and biased. Stowe, they said, was an ignorant and dangerous woman. But in Europe and the North the book was acclaimed a masterpiece. It aroused such strong sympathy for slaves and such utter detestation of slavery that it could not help but heighten sectional antagonism. Legend has it that when President Lincoln met Harriet Beecher Stowe during the Civil War, he remarked: "So this is the little lady who wrote the book that made this big war!"

But it would be a mistake to equate disdain for slavery with respect for black people. Many abolitionists, especially Garrisonians, believed in the true equality of the races. But there was a deep pool of racism in the northern, free states that affected almost everyone. In few places north of Dixie were blacks accorded equal treatment in education, voting rights, and access to public facilities. At the very time northern mobs were trying to rescue fugitive slaves from federal commissioners, at least four free states in the Northwest—Iowa, Illinois, Indiana, and Oregon—adopted "black laws" that forbade free blacks from taking up residency within their borders. Northern Democrats in particular were apt to be hostile to blacks. At times Democratic politicians made blatant race hatred an instrument to consolidate their hold on urban wage earners, especially Irish

Harriet Beecher Stowe

Harriet Beecher Stowe came from a family of high achievers. Her father was the Reverend Lyman Beecher, the most famous clergyman in America. Her younger brother was Henry Ward Beecher, a man who would be called "the archbishop of American Protestantism." Older sister Catherine was a well-known pioneer of women's education. Another brother, Edward, founded Illinois College; another sister, Isabella, was a leading woman suffragist. And there were other successful Beechers as well. Yet Harriet is undoubtedly the most renowned member of this prominent American clan. Today, we know her as author of *Uncle Tom's Cabin*, one of those rare books that influenced the course of history.

Harriet Beecher Stowe was born in Litchfield, Connecticut, in 1811, a time when many village men still wore three-cornered hats, knee breeches, and powdered wigs. Her father, Lyman, was a Congregational minister, not yet well known beyond his small community, but a man of great learning and strong opinions. Her mother, Roxana, was a warm, loving woman who died young in 1817. Roxana's children would remember her as a saint, but perhaps that was because her successor as their father's wife, Harriet Porter, was a reserved woman who seemed overwhelmed by her ready-made family of small children and adolescents.

Harriet was a cheerful little girl despite the loss of her beloved mother. Litchfield was only a village, and she enjoyed the unconfined life of the accessible countryside. She possessed few manufactured toys, but willow-bark whistles, barnyard animals and pets, and the horses in the stable were all diversions and sources of delight. Yet Harriet was no country bumpkin. The Beecher parsonage was an island of high culture and the source of its res-

idents' lifelong interest in literature and ideas. Lyman Beecher made it a point to immerse his children, even the youngest, in books and issues. And not only the dour literature and theology of Puritanism. Harriet read the *Arabian Nights*, the novels of Sir Walter Scott, and even the poetry of that dangerous heathen, Lord Byron. The Reverend Beecher, was no dour kill-joy and he delighted the children by playing lively old tunes like *Auld Lang Syne, Bonnie Doon*, and *Mary's Dream* on his fiddle.

At thirteen Harriet left Litchfield to attend the new Hartford Female Academy just founded by her older sister Catherine. The experience was maturing. With 6,000 people, Hartford was the largest city that Harriet had ever known, and it introduced her to more cosmopolitan sights and ways. Harriet was not an extraordinary student, but at the academy she acquired a good grounding in literature, languages, and even the sciences. After graduation she remained in the academy as a teacher of rhetoric and composition. But in her eight years in the Connecticut capital she did not attract a suitor. Harriet was not a beautiful young woman. Tiny, barely over five feet tall, her face was marred by the large prowlike nose of all the Beechers. It looked as if she were destined to become another spinster schoolteacher living with her father or older brother and making do with the leavings of his life.

Her fate changed abruptly when, in 1832, Lyman Beecher accepted the call to head Lane Seminary, a new school for training ministers, in the fast-growing Queen City of the West, Cincinnati. Harriet and most of the younger children, including several half-siblings, accompanied their father west and for the next eighteen years Harriet would make the thriving city of 30,000 her home.

Cincinnati would provide many of the crucial experiences she would later draw on for her novels and stories. There she would meet Calvin Stowe, professor of biblical literature at Lane, and marry him in 1836, two years after his first wife died of cholera. There she would be exposed for the first time to slavery and its human costs.

Just across the Ohio River from the slave state of Kentucky, Cincinnati was a way station for runaways from the "peculiar institution" of slavery. Cincinnatians themselves were divided on slavery. The city had an elite of transplanted Yankees who were susceptible to the new appeal of the "immediate abolitionists" who demanded that freeing the South's slaves be commenced right away. But the city's white working class often disliked blacks, and many of its merchants had close business connections with the South. Both groups despised the antislavery agitators, and in 1836 angry mobs attacked abolitionists and destroyed an antislavery press established by James Birney. Lane Seminary itself soon became a battlefield between moderates like Calvin Stowe and Lyman Beecher and a circle of immediate abolitionist students led by Theodore Weld, a firebrand inspired by the writings of William Lloyd Garrison. No radical herself, Harriet and other moderates were shocked by the widespread antiabolitionist vigilantism, and soon after the attack on Birney she published an anonymous article defending law and order and the right of abolitionists to express their views freely.

The years in Cincinnati were financially hard for the Stowes and their growing family. Calvin Stowe was an impecunious professor at an institution that had trouble recruiting students, especially after Weld and his followers left for the more congenial new seminary at Oberlin. All the

Beechers, in fact, found the years after the Panic of 1837 financially difficult. The Lane trustees were frequently slow in paying Lyman's salary. Older sister Catherine too was sorely pressed. She had joined the family hegira to Cincinnati and, after selling her Hartford school, had founded, jointly with Harriet, the Western Female Institute. In 1838 it closed, dashing Catherine's hopes to repeat in the growing West her Hartford success as an educator. Harriet earned a few dollars by writing sentimental sketches for magazines and New Year's annuals. The money enabled her to employ household help but made little further dent in the family's genteel poverty. And there were worse times as well. In 1849 the dreaded Asiatic cholera struck the city, killing over 4,400 Cincinnatians. One of the victims was little Samuel (Charley) Stowe, Harriet's youngest child.

In 1850 Bowdoin College, Calvin's alma mater, offered him the Collins Professorship, and the family left for Brunswick, Maine, with few regrets. Their first experiences confirmed the wisdom of the change. The Bowdoin faculty wives took pity on the shabby and pregnant little Mrs. Stowe and her brood of ill-dressed but well-mannered children, and they helped them get settled in a spacious frame house where Henry Wadsworth Longfellow had lived as a student years before. Calvin Stowe would soon get a still better academic offer, and in 1852 the Stowes would leave for Andover, Massachusetts. But it was in Brunswick that Harriet Beecher Stowe would write a novel that would resound through the nation's history and catapult her to fame.

By 1851 the nation was in a furor over the recently adopted Fugitive Slave Law. Part of the Compromise of 1850, the measure tightened the rules for recovering slaves who fled the South to free territory and ignited a fierce northern reaction to federal ef-forts to recapture accused fugitives and remand them to slavery. Soon after passage of the bill, antislavery mobs in Syracuse, New York, and Boston expressed northern indignation by storming the jails where fugitives were confined and threatening federal marshals attempting to return them to their southern masters.

Among the Beechers, Harriet and her younger brother, Henry Ward Beecher, now a prominent pastor at Brooklyn's Plymouth Church, were the most deeply offended by the brutal "man-catchers." Both decided to attack slavery and the harsh new law. Henry's method was to dramatize the plight of runaways by staging before his congregation an "auction" of a beautiful slave girl whose master had agreed to free her if she could raise enough money. The prosperous Brooklyn congregation rose to the challenge and more than met the shortfall. Henry's little dramas no doubt made converts among his congregation for the antislavery cause, but Harriet's assault electrified the nation.

For some time Harriet had been writing articles for a Washington, D.C., antislavery weekly, the *National Era*, published by an old Cincinnati friend, Dr. Gamaliel Bailey. In March 1851 she wrote Bailey to tell him of a new project she had in mind. It would be a series of sketches that would "give the lights and shadows of the 'patriarchal institution,' written either from observation . . . or in the knowledge of my friends." "I shall," she said, "show the *best side* of the thing, and something *faintly approaching the worst.*" Bailey liked her description and offered her $300 for a series of three or four installments. On June 5, at the top of the first column of page one of the *National Era*, appeared the heading:

UNCLE TOM'S CABIN
or
LIFE AMONG THE LOWLY
By Mrs. H. B. Stowe

There followed three and a half columns of text, the first words of a story set in Kentucky and Louisiana and describing the evils of slavery through a series of brilliant scenes involving the brutal slave overseer Simon Legree; the saintly "old darky," Uncle Tom; the courageous slave mother Eliza; the well-intentioned but weak slave owner, Augustine St. Clair, and a large cast of vivid characters caught in the toils of the "patriarchal institution."

Once begun the words poured from her with little delay for revision. She later ascribed her fluency to God. It "all came to me in visions, one after another, and I put them down in words," she explained. At first the public response was muted, but as episode followed episode—far beyond the anticipated three or four—reader enthusiasm grew. Before many weeks thousands of northerners were borrowing copies of the obscure antislavery paper to read the weekly installments to their families. By the time the last episode appeared in early 1852 Harriet had procured a book contract for the entire series from a Boston publisher. In early March the first advertisements for the novel *Uncle Tom's Cabin* appeared in New York and Boston newspapers, and bookstores all over the North were soon announcing that they intended to stock the new book in quantity.

Their optimism was fulfilled beyond anyone's dream. The novel became an instant best-seller. The public snapped up 10,000 copies in the first week. In a year 300,000 had been sold. Sales were even greater in Europe and especially Britain. Royalties rolled in and the Stowe's immediate financial troubles were over. Yet they never became rich. Harriet got a 10 percent royalty on American sales, but all the foreign editions were pirated—sold without royalty to the author—a system that flourished in the absence of international copyright laws.

Few copies of *Uncle Tom's Cabin* were sold in the South. By 1852 most southerners had lost patience with any attack on the peculiar institution, and they turned angrily on the Yankee authoress. The *Southern Literary Messenger* called the book a "criminal prostitution of the high functions of the imagination." Other southern critics charged her with ignorance of slavery and blind prejudice against it. Harriet replied in 1853 with *A Key to Uncle Tom's Cabin*, a book that was in effect a long footnote, providing the documentation to *Uncle Tom's Cabin*. It changed few southern minds.

But *Uncle Tom's Cabin* did change minds elsewhere. Inevitably, wherever people deplored slavery, the novel made a deep impression. And it also made converts to antislavery among thousands of complacent people who had accepted slavery as a necessary evil. The book made Harriet famous. When she visited England in 1853 she was treated as a celebrity. Everywhere in the British Isles people gathered to see or grasp the hand of the famous writer who had so touched their hearts. She met Charles Dickens, Lord Palmerston, the Lord Mayor of London, the Duchess of Sutherland,

and other grandees. She even met the young queen, Victoria, though the meeting was unofficial lest it offend the American government, then firmly dominated by proslavery northerners and the powerful southern bloc. The Stowes would make several trips to Britain and the European continent during the 1850s and would make many prominent European friends.

Uncle Tom's Cabin was the start of a long and successful literary career. Her second novel, *Dred, A Tale of the Great Dismal Swamp*, published in 1856, was another commercial success. Some of her later works—*The Minister's Wooing, The Pearl of Orr's Island*, and *Oldtown Folks*—were also critically acclaimed and widely read. For almost thirty years, Harriet Stowe would churn out almost a book a year. Not all of this flood was choice. Mrs. Stowe was a slapdash stylist, often sentimental and trite. As one later critic would note harshly, "the creative instinct was strong in her but the critical was wholly lacking." Yet she always remained popular with the reading public.

The Civil War affected the Stowes deeply. Fred Stowe, their second son,

joined a Massachusetts regiment in 1861 and went off to fight the rebels. He was wounded in action at Gettysburg and mustered out on disability before the war ended. The Beechers were fierce defenders of the Union cause. Harriet sought to use her influence in Britain to deflect the British upper classes from their pro-Confederate views. She made the abolition of slavery her fondest dream. She, Henry, and indeed the whole Beecher clan cheered Lincoln's preliminary Emancipation Proclamation. But they worried that the president would not come through with the definitive proclamation as promised. In the fall of 1862, on a visit to Washington to see First Lieutenant Fred Stowe, Harriet spent an hour with Lincoln at the White House. She told him of her efforts to influence British opinion and he, apparently, assured her that he would indeed make the Emancipation Proclamation official. It was on this occasion that, according to Stowe family lore, Lincoln exclaimed: "So this is the little lady who wrote the book that made this big war!"

The postwar years were not kind to the Beechers. Fred never readjusted

immigrants. But Free-Soilers too, and even some abolitionists, often could not overcome their prejudice against people "of color." As we have seen, most free-soil politicians appealed not to liberal racial values, but to the widespread northern desire to keep slaves out of the territories to preserve them for free white labor. It was one thing, then, to disdain the South and its peculiar institution or even sympathize with slaves cruelly treated; it was another to accept the equality of black and white.

★ WORSENING TENSIONS ★

If it seemed in 1850 that Clay, Webster, and Douglas had finally checked the mounting sectional antagonism, appearances were deceiving. Within three years the two older men would be dead. Douglas would remain, but events

would show that he lacked the political skill that had enabled his seniors to hold the nation together.

Meanwhile, there was a new occupant of the White House. In 1852 the Democrats nominated Franklin Pierce, a former U.S. senator from New Hampshire and a doughface Democrat who had long supported the South. The Whigs, badly divided on the slavery issue, chose as their candidate another Mexican War hero, Winfield Scott. With the Barnburners now back in the Democratic fold, Pierce won a resounding victory in both sections. The Whigs carried only two southern states. They had been reduced to a northern party almost entirely.

Southern Dreams of Empire. For four years, the Fugitive Slave Act notwithstanding, the nation avoided further sectional crisis. The Compromise of 1850 had put to rest the slavery expansion issue in the Mexican Cession, the only part of the country where the legality of slavery had been

to civilian life and eventually became an alcoholic. In 1870 he disappeared while on a visit to San Francisco and was never heard from again. The Beecher finances remained shaky. Though she earned much from her pen, she also spent much. Harriet poured thousands of dollars into building a large house in Hartford that was never comfortable to live in. She also invested money in an ill-conceived postwar scheme to grow cotton in Florida. After that failed, she retained an expensive winter home, Mandarin, near Jacksonville. Calvin, in retirement from Andover Seminary, surprised everyone with a tome on the origin of the books of the Bible that sold well. But still Stowe expenses constantly threatened to exceed Stowe income, and Harriet was forced to grind out stories, articles, and novels for the market.

In 1869 Harriet wrote an article for *Atlantic Monthly*, followed by a full-scale book, defending an English friend, Lady Anne Isabella Byron, Lord George Byron's widow, against charges of cruelty toward her famous deceased husband. In absolving her friend of blame for the early breakup of the Byron marriage, Harriet accused the dead poet of having committed incest with his half-sister. The charge created a sensation. In this mid-Victorian era the mere mention of incest was itself a scandal, and Harriet was blasted as a pornographer and a sensation-monger. *Atlantic Monthly* lost thousands of subscribers and almost went under.

Harriet and *Atlantic* both survived, but then in 1875 Theodore Tilton, editor of the influential weekly the *Independent*, publicly accused Henry Ward Beecher, his pastor at Plymouth Church, of having seduced his wife, Elizabeth Tilton, another of Henry's parishioners. During the sensational trial for alienation of affections that followed, Harriet rushed to the defense of her favorite brother. Henry was acquitted, but forever after the suspicion of hypocrisy and adultery clung to him.

Harriet's last years were marred by family and personal ill-health. In 1883 Calvin, whose voluminous white beard made him resemble the Old Testament prophets he wrote about, developed a serious kidney ailment. He died three years later. Henry too died in 1886. Harriet lingered on, living in the house in Hartford while her spinster twin daughters, Eliza and Hatty, took care of her needs and ran the household efficiently. In 1889, at the age of 78, she suffered a stroke. She recovered physically, but her mind was impaired. In 1893, during a lucid moment, she wrote her old friend Oliver Wendell Holmes that while *his* "lamp burns as brightly as ever," *hers* was "but a feeble gleam." Her mental condition, she said, had become "nomadic." There were few good times after that, and she died on July 1, 1896, two weeks after her eighty-fifth birthday.

She was buried at Andover cemetary between Calvin and little Charley, who had died so long before in Cincinnati. Harriet Beecher Stowe had outlived many of her contemporaries, and the funeral party gathered by the grave was small. Yet she had not been forgotten. On her casket was a wreath sent by the black community of Boston. The card was signed: "The Children of Uncle Tom."

uncertain. After 1850 the entire country appeared again to be staked out once and for all as either slave or free. The slavery expansion issue in existing U.S. territory seemed solved.

But there remained the destabilizing possibility of further geographical expansion. Southerners had never abandoned the yearning for new territorial acquisitions, especially to the south. There, rimming the Caribbean, could be found the weak republics carved out of the former Spanish empire. The United States had already wrenched immense chunks out of Mexico; why not more from that chaotic country? Also tempting were the Central American republics and the rich island of Cuba, the latter still feebly held by Spain. Through most of the 1850s southern political leaders and southern-dominated Democratic administrations continued to lust for more territory to extend the nation's imperial reach and, mayhap, provide more slave states to balance off the growing North. Mississippi Senator Jefferson Davis expressed the feelings of many of his colleagues. "We of the South," he declared, "are an agricultural people, and we require an extended territory. Slave labor is wasteful labor, and it therefore requires a still more extended territory than would the same pursuits if they could be prosecuted by the more economic labor of white men." Davis's evaluation of the slave economy was faulty, but he was expressing a common southern perception.

This latter-day Manifest Destiny sometimes took private forms. In 1854 a group of southern expansionists formed the Knights of the Golden Circle, an organization dedicated to creating a "golden circle" of slave states enclosing the Caribbean. During the 1850s a number of American "filibusterers" launched military raids into Mexico, often for private gain, but also for the purpose of carving out new slave states to the south. Others cast covetous eyes at Central America. The most famous of these adventurers was Tennessean William Walker. In 1856 this

THE FAMOUS JARRETT & PALMER LONDON COMPY · SLAVINS ORIGINAL AMERICAN TROUPE

CONSOLIDATED WITH

UNCLE TOM'S CABIN.

In the most sensational scene from the most sensational book of the 1850s, Eliza, pursued by bloodhounds, crosses the Ohio River to freedom. This picture is from the 1880s and was used to advertise one of the many traveling companies that put on performances of Uncle Tom's Cabin.

"grey-eyed man of destiny," backed by southerners who cherished the goal of new slave states, invaded Nicaragua with a small army and overthrew its government. Walker and his regime were soon ousted by a coalition of Central American states. Rescued by an American naval vessel, he was greeted as a hero in the South when he arrived home. Walker tried twice more to conquer Nicaragua but was finally captured by the Nicaraguans and executed by a firing squad.

In these years, strongly influenced by southern attitudes and values, the American government too went hunting after loose real estate to the south. Mexico was an obvious target, and the Gadsden Purchase had been part of a more ambitious scheme to acquire Mexican land that had been drastically scaled down by skeptical northern senators. But successive American administrations coveted Cuba even more. The "Pearl of the Antilles" already possessed a flourishing slave-plantation economy based on sugar and would be a congenial addition to the South. It was owned by Spain, but Spain was weak and perhaps could be induced to sur-

render its distant island colony. The Pierce administration made acquiring Cuba its major foreign policy goal and in 1854 dispatched Pierre Soulé, a flamboyant Louisianan, to Madrid as minister to try to buy the island. Soulé was to offer the Spanish government $130 million for Cuba. If the offer was rejected, Secretary of State William Marcy instructed, Soulé should direct his "efforts to the next desirable object, which is to detach that island from Spanish dominion."

When Spain refused to sell, Marcy ordered Soulé to meet with the other major American diplomats in Europe, John Mason and James Buchanan, to consider what to do. The three Americans conferred at Ostend, Belgium, in October 1854 and composed a memo to Marcy that bristled with arrogant self-assertiveness. Cuba was "as necessary to the North American republic as any of its present . . . family of states," they wrote. If Spain refused to sell the island to the United States, then "by every law, human and Divine, we shall be justified in wresting it from Spain."

When it became public, the Ostend Manifesto created an uproar. Antislavery groups attacked it as a "manifesto of Brigands." Many northerners considered it an outrageous assertion of American power. Embarrassed by the incident, Pierce recalled Soulé and abandoned the attempt to acquire Cuba.

The Kansas-Nebraska Act. One of the great ironies of our history is that the most damaging blow to sectional harmony during the 1850s was the work of Stephen Douglas, a strong unionist. The Little Giant had done much to cool sectional anger in 1850, but he undid most of his labor in January 1854 when he introduced a bill to establish a territorial government in the Nebraska country, a part of the Louisiana Purchase.

Douglas was moved by several considerations. An ardent expansionist, he hoped to accelerate western settlement by fostering community building on the frontier. Organizing the territories along the settlement routes westward was an essential part of the process. Related to this goal was his interest in a transcontinental railroad that would link Chicago to the Pacific Coast and bring prosperity to his home city and, incidently, himself.

The 1820 Missouri Compromise had excluded slavery from the Nebraska country. Douglas's new bill, as originally submitted, declared, as had the Utah and New Mexico territorial acts of 1850, that at the point of admission to statehood the people of the region could accept or reject slavery. Though this was a concession to the South, it was not enough for a group of southern senators including David Atchison of Missouri, James Mason and Robert M. T. Hunter of Virginia, and Andrew Butler of South Carolina, who roomed and ate their meals together in Washington on F Street and formed a tight-knit proslavery group. It was clear to these southern partisans that if slaves were excluded from a region during the territorial stage the new communities would probably enter as free states. Douglas sought to placate the "F Street Mess" by agreeing to allow the people of the territory to deal "with all questions relating to slavery" before the point of statehood. This was popular sovereignty, a position Douglas shared with Cass and other northern Democrats, and it opened the possibility of at least one new slave state in the Louisiana Purchase region despite the prohibition of the Missouri Compromise.

But this concession was not enough for the powerful southern bloc, and they insisted that the new measure include a specific repeal of the Missouri Compromise. Knowing that his bill could not pass without southern support, Douglas complied, and even induced President Pierce to use his influence and patronage to push the change through Congress. The revised bill explicitly repealed that part of the Missouri Compromise that forbade slavery in the Louisiana Purchase north of 36°30′. It also divided the region into two territories: Kansas to the south, Nebraska to the north. One of these, it seemed possible, would enter as a slave state. In effect, Douglas had opened a door once closed to slavery in a large slab of the unsettled west.

For four raucous months Congress debated the Kansas-Nebraska bill. Douglas defended the repeal provision by the specious claim that the 1850 Utah and New Mexico territorial bills had implicitly repealed the 36°30′ provision. Moreover, he said, echoing Daniel Webster in 1850, there was little likelihood that geography and climate would allow slavery to take root in the Nebraska country. Southerners supported the bill as an overdue recognition of their rights to the common territory of all the American people paid for by common sacrifice and taxes. Northerners exploded with anger. According to the *Appeal of the Independent Democrats*, a manifesto authored by two Ohio Free-Soilers, Senator Salmon Chase and Congressman Joshua Giddings, the Kansas-Nebraska bill was "a gross violation of a sacred pledge," a "criminal betrayal" and "part and parcel of an atrocious plot" to make the Nebraska country "a dreary region of despotism inhabited by slaves and masters." At one point feelings ran so high that northern and southern partisans came close to blows in the House.

Douglas's clever management and the president's support jammed the bill through Congress. But it was an ominous victory. President Pierce's support notwithstanding, the bill split the northern Democrats in half; it was passed by a solid South plus those northern Democrats who stayed with the administration. Disaffected was a large bloc of antiadministration northerners. The new law was clearly a victory for the South, but one that reopened wounds thought closed, if not fully healed.

National Parties Break Up. The Kansas-Nebraska Act put unbearable strains on an already weakened party system. The *Appeal of the Independent Democrats* triggered a resounding echo in the North. From Maine to California Democratic newspapers screamed with outrage at the actions of Douglas and Pierce. The Kansas-Nebraska bill, announced one, was "a triumph of Slavery [and] Aristocracy over Liberty and Republicanism." Democratic party loyalists defended Douglas and the administration, but many northern Democrats worried that their constituents would repudiate them at the polls.

Whig divisions went even deeper. The Whigs had lost most of their southern support; the South had already become almost solidly Democratic. They were also in trouble in the free states. The deaths in 1852 of Clay and Webster left the party without forceful leaders. Now, Kansas-Nebraska further divided the party's two wings. The pro-Nebraska stand of the southern Whigs in Congress had profoundly disillusioned such men as Horace Greeley, editor of the influential *New York Tribune*, and he proclaimed the North's "indignant resistance" to the measure.

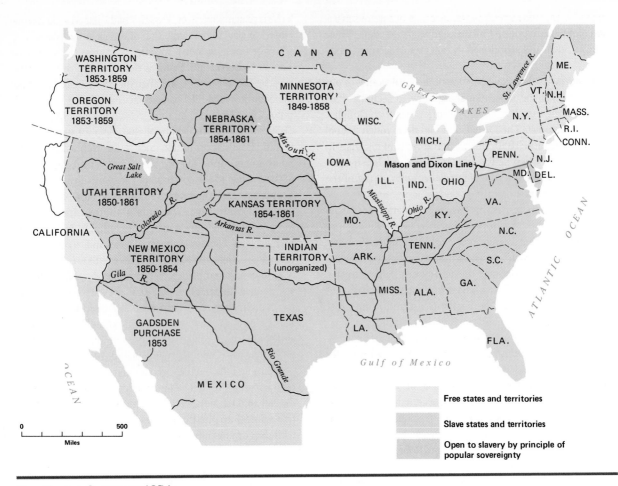

	Free states and territories
	Slave states and territories
	Open to slavery by principle of popular sovereignty

THE UNITED STATES IN 1854

For a time in 1854–1855, when they startled the nation with a string of spectacular electoral victories, it looked as if the Know-Nothings (the American party) might become formidable players on the political stage. The times seemed ripe for a new party that could shift attention to alien and Catholic plots and away from slaves. With a platform calling for extending the time required for naturalization from five to fourteen years, permitting only citizens to vote, and restricting officeholding to native-born Americans, the Know-Nothings expressed the rampant xenophobia and anti-Catholic feelings of the decade. But they also expressed the disenchantment with the existing party system.

Many contemporaries expected the Know-Nothings to replace the Whigs as the other major party. And indeed Whigs, north and south, many of whom shared its nativist and anti-Catholic prejudices, joined the new organization in large numbers further draining Whig strength. Some Free-Soilers too found their anti-Catholic and antiforeign positions congenial. But many antislavery and Free-Soil voters despised their bigotry. The Illinois "Conscience Whig"

Abraham Lincoln pilloried the nativist attitudes the new party represented. "Our progress in degeneracy appears to me to be pretty rapid," he declared. "As a nation, we begin by declaring that '*all men are created equal.*' We now practically read 'all men are created equal, *except negroes.*' When the Know-Nothings get control, it will read 'All men are created equal except negroes, *and foreigners, and Catholics.*'"

Happily for those stranded northern Whigs like Lincoln who could not stomach the nativists, an alternative soon appeared. In 1854–1855 anti-Nebraska political organizations sprang up all through the North in the wake of Douglas's ill-advised bill. At a meeting at Ripon, Wisconsin, in February 1854, one of these groups adopted the name *Republican.* Several months later another anti-Nebraska group met at Jackson, Michigan, and gave the Republicans their new platform: no slavery in the territories, repeal of the Kansas-Nebraska and Fugitive Slave Acts, and abolition of slavery itself in the District of Columbia. The new party grew rapidly in strength, recruiting many northern Whigs and a portion of northern Democrats. After 1856, many erstwhile northern Know-Nothings, seeing their party losing strength, also joined the Republicans convinced that it was more reliably Protestant and native American than its Democratic rival.

"Bleeding Kansas". The Republican surge was accelerated by the outbreak of a vicious guerilla war in Kansas. From the outset leaders of the two sections recognized that once the legislative smoke cleared, settlers would pour into Kansas, the more accessible of the two territories, to establish farms and towns. The political outcome of process would depend on numbers. Both sides threw down the gauntlet. "We will engage in competition for the virgin soil of Kansas," Seward told his Senate colleagues, "and God give the victory to the side which is stronger in numbers as it is in right." Senator Atchison, from Missouri, the slave state adjacent to Kansas, responded in kind: "We are playing for a mighty stake; if we win we carry slavery to the Pacific Ocean, if we lose we lose Missouri, Arkansas, and Texas and all the territories; the game must be played boldly."

In fact, a majority of Kansas-bound settlers were relatively indifferent to the sectional confrontation. Most free-staters were from the Midwest and were more interested in free farms than free soil. The contingent of Yankees financed by Eli Thayer's New England Emigrant Aid Society was exceptional in its antislavery zeal. The other side too consisted largely of men and women seeking better lives rather than

a particular social system. Most of the slave-state people came from Missouri; a few brought their slaves with them. Their opponents called them "border ruffians," but most were conventional southern farmers.

Yet within weeks of passage of the Kansas-Nebraska Act friends and foes of slavery in the territory were at each other's throats: Ambushes, arson, and murder quickly became the order of the day in "Bleeding Kansas." The struggle over Kansas was not over slavery alone. The government's failure to properly extinguish Indian claims or make essential land surveys created confusion and conflict. Inevitably, as in all frontier communities, there were disputes over water rights, town-site locations, and other issues connected with establishing new communities. There would have been some conflict and disorder even without the slave issue. But obviously differences in social philosophy made things worse. Men who disagreed over claims to a particular piece of real estate were all the more prone to fight when they also held irreconcilable views on slavery. In any case, Americans elsewhere, north and south, perceived the struggle as a bitter confrontation of the nation's two social systems and responded accordingly.

The early struggles favored the South. In late 1854 and early 1855, territorial governor Andrew Reeder called elections for territorial representative to Congress and the territorial legislature. The results were rigged. Though

Beginning with the Missouri Compromise in 1820, United States expansion was irrevocably linked with the conflict over slavery expansion. The Kansas-Nebraska Act, in Charles Sumner's words, put "slavery and freedom face-to-face, and bids them grapple." These Kansas antislavery supporters are ready for the confrontation.

free-state residents by this time probably outnumbered their opponents, several thousand Missourians crossed the river to vote illegally, giving the slave-state forces majorities. Though Governor Reeder recognized the fraud, he refused to authorize new elections. In short order, the proslavery legislature passed a harsh slave code and disqualified from office citizens who did not support slavery. In response, the free-state forces fortified the town of Lawrence and organized their own free-state party. Soon after, at a convention held in Topeka, they drew up a constitution prohibiting slavery in Kansas and convened a free-state legislature in opposition to the one recognized by Reeder. In time, Governor Reeder declared his sympathy for the free-state group. President Pierce, responding to southern pressure, replaced him with William Shannon, a more reliable proslavery man.

The maneuvering soon took a more dangerous turn. In the spring of 1856 a small army of proslavery men descended on Lawrence, destroyed the free-state printing press, tore down the hotel, burned several private homes, and ransacked the town. Southern newspapers depicted the raiders as gallant knights battling for a holy cause. Northern Free-Soilers denounced the "border ruffians." In New Haven, Connecticut, the popular Brooklyn minister, Henry Ward Beecher, urged an antislavery congregation to send more settlers to Kansas equipped with Sharps rifles. Thereafter many Kansas-bound northerners carried the deadly repeater rifles, now dubbed "Beecher's Bibles."

Among those who turned to violence in Kansas was one John Brown of Osawatomie, a stern, latter-day Old Testament partriarch sworn to free Kansas from the sin of slavery. Born in Connecticut, Brown spent most of his life wandering with his large family from place to place, trying to make a living and establish a home. He failed in virtually everything he attempted and became an embittered man. Brown identified his own suffering with that of the slaves and had come to see himself as an instrument of an avenging God to smite the slaveholders. In Kansas, Brown and his sons joined the free-state forces. Angered by the attack on Lawrence, in May 1856, the Browns and a small band of followers took revenge by hacking to death in cold blood five slave-state settlers at Pottawatomie Creek.

Extremism begat further extremism. The Pottawatomie massacre set off a virtual war in Kansas. Spring planting was neglected while bands of southern "border ruffians" and northern "bushwhackers" roamed the territory pillaging, burning, and killing. Scores died and millions of dollars of property was destroyed in the disorders. The events in Kansas raised sectional tensions in the rest of the country. As atrocity succeeded atrocity, even moderate citizens found it difficult to check mounting resentments of people from the other section.

A learned and courageous but often intemperate man, Charles Sumner represented the new breed of antislavery men the North began to send to Congress in the 1850s.

The Sumner-Brooks Incident. In this overheated atmosphere, outrageous things happened wherever the slavery issue was debated. One of the more militant antislavery leaders in Congress was the junior senator from Massachusetts, Charles Sumner. Sumner felt a zealot's need to right wrongs. No one in Congress was a more courageous and consistent defender of blacks. At the same time, few men in public life were as dogmatic, as certain of the unfailing rectitude of their positions, or as unwilling to give their opponents credit for honesty or good intentions as he. Like many northern free-state partisans, Sumner had watched the struggle over Kansas with growing dismay. On May 19, 1856, he rose in the Senate to deliver a blistering two-day denunciation of the South in a speech he called "The Crime against Kansas."

Elaborately prepared, sonorous, full of learned allusions, the address descended to crude personal attack, pillorying Douglas, the president, Senator Atchison, and others. But Sumner reserved his sharpest barbs for Andrew Butler, the venerable senator from South Carolina, calling him a Don Quixote, a foolish blunderer, and a liar, and cruelly alluding to his physical infirmities. Two days later, Butler's young kinsman, South Carolina Congressman Preston Brooks, entered the Senate chamber as Sumner was sitting at his desk writing letters and struck Sumner on the head repeatedly with a cane. Brooks stopped only when other senators forcibly intervened. By that time Sumner was bloody and unconscious.

The South considered Brooks's attack the just chastisement of a blackguard. The *Richmond Whig* called the caning "elegant and effectual." "The only regret we feel," remarked the editor, "is that Mr. Brooks did not employ a horsewhip upon his slanderous back instead of a cane." Several southern communities presented Brooks with replacements for his shattered walking stick. The assault and the South's response shocked most northerners. Free-Soil partisans called mass meetings to condemn the brutal caning, and the Massachusetts legislature, which had sent Sumner to the Senate, denounced it as "a gross breach of Parliamentary privilege—a ruthless attack upon the liberty of speech—an outrage of the decencies of civilized life, and an indignity to the Commonwealth of Massachusetts." Northerners who prized free speech noted that, having sup-

pressed dissent everywhere on their home ground, southerners were now trying to squelch it in the sacred halls of Congress itself. A small incident in itself, the Brooks-Sumner affair confirmed many northerners' skepticism of southern "chivalry" and convinced them that it was time to curb "the arrogant and aggressive" demands of the "slave power."

★ REPUBLICANISM AND THE WORSENING CRISIS ★

Bleeding Kansas, the Brooks-Sumner affair, and *Uncle Tom's Cabin* all garnered recruits for the Republican party. The new organization was a frankly sectional party. Pledged to contain slavery, it had virtually no support in the lower South and little in the border slave states. Its heartland was the "upper North" where the population was predominantly Yankee- or New England-derived. In the "lower North"— southern New York, Pennsylvania, New Jersey, and the

Clearly, "negative campaigning" did not begin in the 1980s. This 1856 Republican poster blames the Democrats for: (1) the caning of Charles Sumner, (2) the burning of Lawrence, Kansas, by southern "border ruffians," (3) filibustering expeditions in Central America, and (4) the mistreatment of southern slaves.

southern parts of the Old Northwest—Republicanism competed with strong attachments to the old Democratic party.

Only a small minority of Republicans were out-and-out abolitionists. All believed that the federal government could and should prevent slavery from expanding. Many agreed with Lincoln that slavery, if contained, would retreat and eventually die. Others were indifferent to the eventual fate of slavery; it was sufficient that the western territories be kept accessible for free labor. The new party at first attracted few business people. Most merchants, bankers, and manufacturers saw it as a divisive influence and feared that its success would upset the country's economic life along with its politics. Those with ties to the South were especially skeptical. Those merchants or manufacturers who joined the new party were putting ideology ahead of economic advantage.

The Republicans ran their first presidential candidate in 1856 when they nominated the California hero John C. Frémont. That year their platform demanded a free Kansas and congressional prohibition of "those twin relics of barbarism—Polygamy,* and Slavery." As an afterthought, it also endorsed government aid for a Pacific railroad and for internal improvements. The Democrats chose former Pennsylvania Senator James Buchanan of Ostend Manifesto fame, largely because, alone among prominent Democrats, he had been serving as U.S. minister to London and was one of the few prominent Democratic politicians free of "bleeding Kansas" taint. A third candidate, ex-President Fillmore, ran on the flagging Know-Nothing ticket and received the support of surviving Whigs.

The Republicans depicted Frémont as the champion of the "laboring classes" against the slaveholders. The Democrats appealed to white fears of black equality and of political disunity if Frémont and the "black Republicans" won. In the end, Buchanan carried the entire lower North, plus California, and fourteen of the fifteen slave states (Maryland supported Fillmore). Frémont won the rest of the North, a showing that alarmed southerners and filled them with foreboding.

Buchanan's Policies. Buchanan was not the man to guide the country through the four difficult years that followed. A well-meaning but indecisive leader, his talents lay in the traditional maneuvering of American politics as usual. Republicans sized him up as just another doughface Democrat, subservient to the South, and his choice of many southerners and proslavery northerners as advisers confirmed their judgment.

---

*The reference was to the Mormon practice in Utah territory of plural marriage, a custom most other Americans deplored.

Even before his inauguration, Buchanan set out to undermine the Free-Soil position by intruding into the pending case of a Missouri slave, Dred Scott, then before the Supreme Court. Through the auspices of antislavery activists, Scott was suing for his freedom on the grounds that his former owner had taken him to free territory, including a portion that had been closed to slavery by the Missouri Compromise. The case was that long-awaited opportunity to settle the question of whether the people of a territory or of Congress—as opposed to the people of a fully sovereign state—could exclude slavery from part of the United States. For almost a decade the issue had wrenched at the political system and threatened the Union. The politicians, including the president-elect, now saw the opportunity to duck the loaded issue and have the federal courts settle it once and for all.

Southerners were especially eager for a court decision since the chief justice, old Jacksonian, Roger Taney, was a proslavery Marylander, and four of the associate justices were also southerners. But the southern forces wanted at least one free-state judge to support their side to give it credibility. President-elect Buchanan now approached his fellow Pennsylvanian, justice Robert Grier, to urge him to side with the proslavery majority. Buchanan's plea succeeded. Knowing the now certain outcome, on March 4, in his inaugural address, Buchanan noted that whatever the court decision, "in common with all good citizens" he would "cheerfully submit" to it.

The actual decision two days later was a bombshell. Taney's opinion covered a number of issues that did not seem necessary to decide in connection with Scott's suit for his freedom. First, said the chief justice, Scott was still a slave. His freedom was denied. Second, as a black and a slave Scott was not a citizen and therefore had "no rights which the white man was bound to respect." Third, his stay in Wisconsin territory did not make him free since Congress did not have the power to exclude slavery from a territory and the law that had supposedly permitted it, the Missouri Compromise, was unconstitutional. Because Congress could not exclude slavery from a territory, neither could a territorial legislature, which was merely a creation of Congress. Most scholars today agree with the dissenting opinion of Justice Benjamin Curtis of Massachusetts, noting that some blacks had been legal citizens of the United States in past periods and that in no way did a congressional prohibition of slavery in the territories violate the Constitution. But the Supreme Court had spoken: Only the people of a state could keep slavery out of any part of the United States; the hands of Congress and a territorial legislature were tied. And, some antislavery partisans believed, the *Dred Scott* decision even called into question whether a state could exclude any citizen from bringing slave property into its border if he or she wished.

Republicans were especially appalled by the *Dred Scott* ruling. If it stood, it annulled the core principle of their party—the right and the duty of Congress to ban slavery from the territories. It also appeared to nullify the Douglas popular-sovereignty principle that conferred on the local populace the right to exclude slavery from an organized territory.

Buchanan soon gave the Republicans and the popular-sovereignty, Douglas wing of his own party further grounds for dismay when he approved the Kansas state constitution adopted by a proslavery convention at Lecompton in late 1857. This document was to be submitted to the Kansas voters with a choice of two clauses regarding slavery. One recognized the full rights of slaveholders and, in effect, made Kansas a slave state. The other stated that "slavery shall no longer exist" in Kansas, but "the right of property in slaves now in this Territory shall in no manner be interfered with." The voters could choose one or the other; they could not reject the constitution entirely. In effect, there was no way of excluding slavery from Kansas totally, and the rule banning future slave imports, should it prevail, was likely to be unenforceable. Similar efforts had been ineffective in several other states.

Republicans denounced the Lecompton proposal as "the Great Swindle." Stephen Douglas charged it was a perversion of true popular sovereignty. Even Robert Walker, Buchanan's choice as Kansas's territorial governor, called it "a vile fraud, a bare counterfeit." In Kansas most free-state partisans boycotted the referendum and, not surprisingly, the more extreme proslavery version passed overwhelmingly. Meanwhile, a free-state convention met and scheduled a referendum that would allow a vote on the entire constitution. When held, it was boycotted by the proslavery group, and the Kansas constitution as a whole went down to decisive defeat.

When the Lecompton constitution came before Congress for approval as part of the Kansas statehood bill the Buchanan administration rallied behind it as did virtually the entire southern House and Senate delegations. The president was frank about the status of the new state to be admitted under its provisions. In his message transmitting the bill to Congress, Buchanan noted that Kansas "is at this moment as much a slave state as Georgia or South Carolina."

The debate that followed was as bitter as any in Congress during the tumultuous 1850s. Stephen Douglas and most northern Democrats fought the bill as a travesty of popular sovereignty and a measure that would sink them and their party generally in the upcoming elections. Douglas told his Senate colleagues that he could never vote to "force this constitution down the throats of the people of Kansas." At one point a free-wheeling fistfight broke out on the floor of the House with "fifty middle-aged and elderly gentlemen pitching into each other like so many . . . savages." Wielding his patronage, President Buchanan managed to eke out a Lecompton victory in the House, but in the Senate Douglas Democrats joined the Republicans to defeat the bill by a narrow vote. A compromise bill, including a generous federal land grant to the state and a provision allowing acceptance or rejection of the entire constitution, was soon resubmitted to the Kansas voters. In August 1858 they rejected it by a vote of 11,300 to 1,788. Kansas would not enter the Union until 1861, after secession of the southern states.

The Emergence of Lincoln. The troubles of the Buchanan presidency were compounded by the Panic of 1857 and the economic slump that followed. Although the downturn was probably to be expected after ten years of booming economic growth and speculation, the North blamed it on southerners in Congress for lowering their tariff. Southerners, on the other hand, largely unaffected by a falling stock market and urban unemployment, saw the panic as a vindication of the slave economy. Buoyed by high world prices for cotton, they gloated at the misfortunes of northern commerce and industry.

Midway through Buchanan's term, the politicians were already looking ahead to 1860. Douglas was the obvious presidential front-runner for the Democrats. But the Little Giant had hurt his chances with proslavery Democrats by his disapproval of the Lecompton constitution. He also had antagonized the South by his formula to get around the *Dred Scott* decision and preserve popular sovereignty. Although slaveholders might have the right constitutionally to take their slaves into the territories, he noted, it would be a "barren and worthless right" unless the people of the territory provided a slave code and the other supportive laws the peculiar institution needed to flourish. In effect, by refusing to act on slavery at all, the people of a territory could exclude it. Such inaction did not conflict with the Supreme Court ruling. The formula dismayed states' rights defenders. Before long, southern Democrats were demanding a *federal* slave code to get around the Douglas position.

Among the Republicans there was no lack of political talent or ambition as 1860 approached. But more and more people were beginning to hear the name of Abraham Lincoln of Illinois.

We who recognize Lincoln's greatness may find it difficult to see him as he was in the 1850s. The lanky prairie lawyer was pithy, shrewd, and folksy, and combined keen realism with an idealistic strain. But as yet he gave little sign that he was capable of leading a great nation through trying times. Eastern men of wealth and refinement heard his plain speech and rustic stories and put him down as a crude frontier politician.

Abe Lincoln was a very young man when this portrait was painted. He became better looking!

Only gradually did he become politically "available." Following his single term in the House of Representatives (1847–1849), Lincoln had returned to Springfield, Illinois, and private law practice. For the next few years he devoted his professional life to defending slanderers, petty thieves, and the Illinois Central Railroad in the courts. All the while, however, he kept up his connections with the Illinois Whigs and shared their doubts and anxieties when their party began to disintegrate. He did not formally become a Republican until his law partner, without authorization, signed his name to a call for a local Republican convention. In 1856 Lincoln campaigned for Frémont.

In 1858 the Illinois Republicans gave Lincoln the party's official nomination for U.S. Senate. The move was unusual. Senators were then chosen by the state legislators and there was no reason to campaign among the voters and no need for a formal nomination. This time, however—in hopes of defeating Douglas—the state Republican leaders decided to make the state election hinge on the victory or defeat of their senatorial choice. The voters would be casting their ballots, actually, for individual legislators, with the senatorial candidates, in effect, representing the party.

The campaign format too was unusual. At first the two candidates went their separate ways, speaking to individual audiences. Lincoln opened with an acceptance speech, known to us as the "House-Divided" address. In it he sought to distinguish his own concern over slavery as a moral issue with Douglas's primary focus on the *process* of deciding on slavery in the territories. The country, he announced, could not remain permanently half slave and half free. "A house divided against itself cannot stand." Under the Democrats it would become all slave; under the Republicans all free, for the Republicans intended to "arrest the further spread of [slavery], and place it where the public mind shall rest in the belief that it is in the course of ultimate extinction."

Before long the candidates agreed to direct debate. Beginning in late August 1858 in the northern Illinois city of Ottawa, they would meet on the same platform in seven towns, ending in Alton in mid-October. In each they would fire questions at one another while the public watched. The contest attracted national attention because it had national implications. To remain in the 1860 presidential race, Douglas, one of the front-runners, had to overcome his opponent. Should he be defeated for a Senate seat, he was unlikely to win the Democratic presidential nomination. People from all over the country followed the debates in the newspapers, and their interest gave Lincoln invaluable national exposure.

Although the face-to-face format was unusual, the open-air political rally had long been a midwestern diversion, and thousands came to watch and listen to the speakers. The banners, the marching cadets, the glee clubs, and the general holiday atmosphere encouraged the candidates to banter and name-calling, but generally the level of discourse and discussion was high.

The debates zeroed in on race and slavery in the territories. Douglas at times appealed to crude white racism and fear of a mass invasion of Illinois by blacks if slavery were abolished. If, in the House-Divided speech, Lincoln sounded a bit like an abolitionist, at other points, especially in the southern part of the state where many of the voters were of southern descent, he pandered to the anti-black prejudices of his audience. When Douglas accused the "Black Republican party" of favoring racial equality and full civil rights for blacks, Lincoln said he did not believe that black people were the equal of whites, and as long as there were differences he expected the white race to have the superior position. Nevertheless, Lincoln's moral revulsion toward slavery came through clearly. At Alton, in the last debate, he announced that "the sentiment that contemplates the institution of slavery . . . as a wrong is the sentiment of the Republican party. . . ." Slavery was "a moral, social, and political wrong."

The *Dred Scott* decision inevitably engaged the debaters. At Freeport, Illinois, Lincoln tried to embarrass his opponent by asking him to reconcile his popular sovereignty doctrine with Chief Justice Taney's decision in *Dred Scott*. Douglas repeated the formula he had already advanced: All a territorial legislature need do was refuse to enact a slave code and slavery was effectively excluded from the territory. Though not new, this Freeport Doctrine publicized Douglas's differences with his southern colleagues and increased the tension between him and the party's southern wing.

On election day the voters of Illinois gave the Republican candidates for the legislature more total popular votes than they gave to the Democrats. But the Douglas supporters won more counties than their opponents, and the legislature reelected the Little Giant to the Senate. Having survived the challenge, Douglas was now clearly the front-runner for the Democratic presidential nomination in 1860. Lincoln, though he had lost, was now a national figure. In February 1860 he traveled to New York to speak before the city's wealthy and influential Republicans. His address impressed his distinguished audience. Old Abe would now be a presidential contender, too, on the other side.

Harpers Ferry. But first the country would have to undergo another ordeal of violence over slavery, and once again John Brown would be the instigator. Though many people knew of his role in the Pottawatomie massacre, Brown was never indicted and remained free to concoct other schemes to scourge the slaveholders. Between 1856 and 1859 he worked out a mad plan to foment a slave revolt that would bring down the institution of slavery. Starting with a nucleus of armed escapees in the inaccessible Virginia Blue Ridge, he and his band would advance south along the Appalachians attracting runaways and spreading slave insurrection all through the slave country of the East Coast. Brown recruited a group of New England abolitionists to solicit money for the scheme from antislavery philanthropists. Not every antislavery leader approved. Frederick Douglass, for one, believed that invading Virginia with two dozen men was harebrained and told Brown as much.

Warnings did no good. In the fall of 1859 Brown, his sons, and a small band of black and white supporters bought guns and drew up plans for an assault on the federal armory at Harpers Ferry in what is now West Virginia. The armory would provide the weapons for his insurrection, and its seizure would be the spark that would ignite the slave revolt. On the night of October 16 the rebels seized the armory and all its rifles and ammunition. But the slaves did not rise at the news. Instead, Brown and his small band remained holed up in the armory building not knowing what to do next. On the eighteenth a detachment of U.S. marines led by Colonel Robert E. Lee stormed the building and captured the surviving members of the implausible revolt.

Two views of John Brown: an 1856 photograph, and an idealized painting of him on the way to the gallows three years later. The first picture suggests Brown's fanaticism and capacity for cruelty; the second, by an abolitionist artist, suggests his love for the suffering slave. Brown was both of these at once.

Brown's raid raised sectional antagonisms to fever pitch. To southerners it was proof that the North would stop at nothing to undermine slavery including setting off a dreaded servile insurrection. Hundreds of southern students at northern colleges packed their bags and returned home in protest. Georgians attacked the crew of a northern ship at Savannah and a New Yorker, newly installed as president of an Alabama college, was forced to flee for his life.

Brown was tried for treason, convicted, and sentenced to hang. During the trial and in the weeks between sentencing and execution, he conducted himself with great dignity. Many northerners had initially condemned the attack, and even Lincoln and *New York Tribune* editor Horace Greeley believed Brown tragically misguided. But Brown's bearing and words after his capture made him a hero to many in the North. Henry David Thoreau compared him to Jesus, and novelist Louisa May Alcott named Brown "Saint John the Just." When he was hanged on December 2, he became, in the eyes of antislavery advocates, a martyr to the cause of human freedom. In two short years Union soldiers, advancing against the slave South, would be singing the words: "John Brown's body lies a-moldering in the grave but his truth is marching on."

The Party Conventions of 1860. Harpers Ferry kept the country in an uproar well into 1860, and by that time the nation was in the throes of the most fateful presidential campaign of its history.

As the Democratic convention assembled in April 1860 at Charleston, South Carolina, the handsome seaside city was already sweltering in summer heat. Charleston was the heart of "Secessia," and the city's usually charming and hospitable hostesses were notably unfriendly to the northern, Douglas delegates. So, too, were most of the southern delegates. Led by the fiery William Yancey of Alabama, these men demanded a federal slave code plank in the party's platform or else, they threatened, they would walk out of the convention.

The Douglas majority, certain that a federal slave code platform would ensure Democratic defeat in November, refused to yield to southern demands. When the Douglasites won the platform fight, Yancey and forty-nine other southern rights' delegates marched out of the convention hall. Meeting elsewhere in town, the minority adopted a federal slave code platform and waited to see what their adversaries would do. The majority continued to meet, but when the chair ruled that two-thirds of the delegates originally chosen, not merely two-thirds still present, were needed for nomination, they were unable to give Douglas the prize despite fifty-seven ballots. Frustrated, they adjourned, promising to convene again at Baltimore six weeks later to try again.

They were no more successful in Baltimore. The southern rights' bolters, some now back, as well as some newly chosen southern delegates, once again walked out. This time they held their own convention and nominated Vice President John C. Breckinridge of Kentucky on a federal slave code platform. Meanwhile, the remaining Baltimore delegates chose Douglas on a popular sovereignty platform.

The old Whigs also ran a ticket. On May 9 the remaining Whigs organized the Constitutional Union party with a fuzzy platform that endorsed the Union and "the enforcement of the laws." They chose as their candidates John Bell of Tennessee and Edward Everett of Massachusetts.

On May 16 the Republicans met in Chicago confident of victory. As the delegates crowded into the get-ahead young metropolis on the lake, the Republican front-runner seemed to be Senator William Seward of New York. But Seward was the author of "the higher law" doctrine, and in 1858 had made another provocative speech declaring that the two sections of the country were doomed to an "irrepressible conflict." Many Republicans considered him too radical to carry the lower North. Nor did Salmon Chase, the antislavery senator from Ohio, appear much better. At the other end of the Republican scale was Edward Bates of Missouri. But Bates was *too* moderate, and colorless besides. Simon Cameron of Pennsylvania, another possible nominee, was weighed down with a reputation for both party inconsistency and shady financial dealing.

The Lincoln forces made much of their rivals' weaknesses and pictured their candidate as the perfect balance between moderation and radicalism. He was also from the Midwest, they emphasized, a region the Republicans had to carry to win in November. Skilled maneuverers, the Lincoln managers packed the galleries with enthusiastic, leather-lunged Lincoln supporters. They effectively excluded Seward partisans by printing up extra tickets to the convention hall and having their own partisans come early to occupy all the remaining seats. Old Abe won the nomination on the third ballot. His running mate was Hannibal Hamlin of Maine.

The party platform, like the candidate, represented the more moderate Republican position. It demanded the exclusion of slavery from the territories, but endorsed the right of each state to "order and control its own domestic institutions." It also condemned the John Brown raid. The Republicans proved more sensitive to the economic interests of the North and West in 1860 than four years before. As Horace Greeley had written before the convention: "An Anti-Slavery man *per se* cannot be elected, but a Tariff, River-and-Harbor, Pacific Railroad, Free-Homestead man *may* succeed *although* he is Anti-Slavery." True to these Whiggish-Hamiltonian principles, the 1860 party platform endorsed a homestead law, a protective tariff, a northern-route Pacific railroad, and federal aid for internal improvements.

The Union Dissolves.   None of the candidates favored disunion. Douglas, of course, was a passionate unionist, and the platform of John Bell's party was little more than an assertion of national unity. The Republicans too tried to avoid stirring sectional resentments. During the campaign Lincoln and his colleagues soft-pedaled the slavery extension issue, especially in the lower North, to avoid frightening off moderate and timid voters. Even John Breckinridge decried secession, though, as Douglas correctly noted, every secessionist voter was also a Breckinridge supporter.

The Republican campaign, buoyed by confidence in victory, was marked by an outpouring of marches, banners, parades, and rallies. The young party emphasized the "free labor" theme, with Lincoln, the humble "rail-splitter," the perfect exemplar of its message. All of Lincoln's opponents recognized that they could not win against the united Republicans, and they sought various fusion arrangements that might deny the Republicans a victory by carrying the entire South plus a few crucial northern states. These fusion efforts failed except in a few localities, and it was soon

clear that the nation faced the probability of a Republican president representing an exclusively northern constituency.

Weeks before the results were in, the *Charleston Mercury* predicted that if Lincoln won, "thousands of slaveholders will despair of the institution." People in the border states would rush to sell their slaves while it was still possible, forcing down their price disastrously in the rest of the South. Other southern journals and politicians warned that the Republican administration would appoint abolitionist federal officials in the South who would work to undermine slavery. If slavery collapsed, white farmers and wage earners would be forced to compete with the cheap labor of freed blacks. The prospect of a Black Republican victory seemed intolerable. One Atlanta editor announced: "Let the consequences be what they may, whether the Potomac is crimsoned in human gore, and Pennsylvania Avenue is paved ten fathoms deep with mangled bodies . . . the South will never submit to such humiliation and degradation as the inauguration of Abraham Lincoln."

THE PRESIDENTIAL ELECTION OF 1860

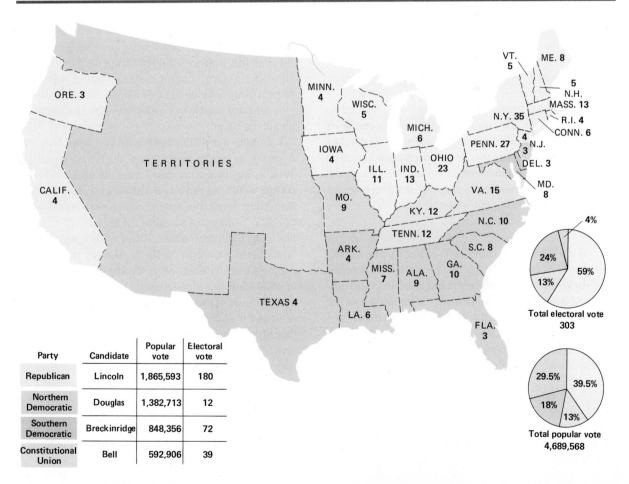

Party	Candidate	Popular vote	Electoral vote
Republican	Lincoln	1,865,593	180
Northern Democratic	Douglas	1,382,713	12
Southern Democratic	Breckinridge	848,356	72
Constitutional Union	Bell	592,906	39

Total electoral vote 303

Total popular vote 4,689,568

The election results did not endorse extremism of either sort. Lincoln won a clear electoral college majority over his combined opponents, carrying every free state except New Jersey, where he split the electoral vote with Douglas. But even if we consider his party extremist—and it was not—it won only 39 percent of the popular vote, virtually all from the free states. Douglas was second in popular votes with 29 percent, but in every state but Missouri he was second to someone else, and so could only claim 12 electoral votes. Together, the Little Giant and Bell, both strong unionists, won more popular votes in the slave states than Breckinridge. Even if we consider Breckinridge's support mainly secessionist, the 1860 election was scarcely a mandate for disunion.

Yet fearful and angry, the South moved quickly when Lincoln's election was confirmed. News of the result found the South Carolina legislature in session. Brushing aside the demand of moderates that the state wait for unified southern action, the majority voted for a secession convention. On December 20, 1860, by a unanimous vote, this convention declared that the "union now subsisting between South Carolina and other States . . . is hereby dissolved." In the next few weeks six more states—Alabama, Mississippi, Florida, Georgia, Louisiana, and Texas—joined the rush to leave the Union. Few outright opponents of secession were to be found at the secession conventions of the lower South. In each, however, there was a contingent of "cooperationists," people who favored waiting until the South as a whole decided to leave the Union. A certain proportion of this group were "conditional unionists" who wanted to delay action until the Lincoln administration committed some overt hostile act. The largest fraction of all consisted of "immediate secessionists," who demanded secession without delay and without qualifications. All through the lower South the immediate secessionist group represented the counties that were richer, more closely tied to slavery and cotton, and traditionally more Democratic than Whig.

Secession Winter. People who lived through the months between the election and Lincoln's inauguration remembered it vividly as a time of acute public anxiety. Southerners hovered between hope and despair, not knowing how the federal government would respond to secession and fearful that the confusion of the time would encourage slave revolt. Officials of the seceded states seized federal customs houses, post offices, mints, arsenals, and forts. Meanwhile, army officers, members of Congress, and other federal officials of southern birth declared their allegiances to their native states.

In early February six of the seceded states sent delegates to Montgomery, Alabama, and organized the Confederate States of America, a new federation to replace the old. Choosing Jefferson Davis of Mississippi and Alexander Stephens of Georgia as provisional president and vice president, respectively, they adopted a frame of government that in most ways resembled the old federal Constitution. The Confederate constitution, however, declared slavery everywhere protected by law, forbade protective tariffs, gave the president the right to veto specific portions of bills passed by congress, and confined the president to a single six-year term of office.

Northerners, too, felt confused and apprehensive in those secession winter months. In Washington rumors circulated that southern sympathizers intended to seize the capital. In New York City, where merchants and bankers had close business ties with the South, and where many of the white working class despised the Black Republicans, there was disturbing talk from the Democratic mayor, Fernando Wood, about taking the city out of the Union. Many northern moderates supported compromise to close the sectional breech before it became irreparable.

The lame-duck Buchanan administration, with four months still to go before leaving office, seemed paralyzed by the crisis. Buchanan did not approve of secession, but neither did he believe that the federal government had the right to take coercive steps to save the Union. As Seward would express it, his position seemed to be that "no state has a right to secede unless it wishes to." Buchanan hoped above all that violence would not erupt during his remaining weeks in office; thereafter secession would be his sucessor's problem. Surrounded at first by southern advisers, the president was unable to check the progressive disintegration of the Union.

Republicans themselves were divided and indecisive. A few strong antislavery partisans, like Horace Greeley, advised letting "the erring sisters depart in peace." Their departure would free the Union of the stigma of slavery. Some Republican moderates favored compromise on the territorial issue, perhaps by extending the Missouri Compromise line to the California border. Other Republicans, confusing "conditional Unionism" in the South with the much less common true Unionism, advised going slow until the forces of unity reasserted themselves in Dixie.

The core of the party, however, took a tougher stand: resistance to secession by every means necessary. Secession, they insisted, was wrong and dangerous. If the lower South could leave the Union, why not the other slave states, and then perhaps the West? Once allowed, could anything stop total dissolution of the Union? And for what purpose? The South had lost a political contest by the rules; could it now cry foul? Secession was not rebellion against tyranny, as in 1776, but an attack on the most benign, most liberal government the world had ever known. And how could the separation be effected without serious harm? The new

Confederacy would control the mouth of the Mississippi, on which the whole Northwest depended for its export trade. Could that vital spot be allowed to fall into unfriendly hands? And the territories—who would get them? No, resistance to secession was the only option.

The eyes of the country during these tense months inevitably turned on the president-elect. Many sincere unionists urged Lincoln to make some major conciliatory gesture on the slavery extension issue. Lincoln was unwilling to do so. He would support a constitutional amendment forbidding the federal government to meddle in slavery in the states. He would even agree to enforce the Fugitive Slave Act if it were made fairer. But he would not surrender the heart of his party's platform: the exclusion of slavery from the territories. If he did, the issue would only have to be fought all over again in the future. As he told a fellow Republican: "The tug has to come, and better now than any time hereafter."

Meanwhile, desperate efforts were under way in Congress and the states to patch together another sectional compromise. The most promising proposal was the scheme of Kentucky Senator John J. Crittenden to extend the Missouri Compromise line through the remaining federal territory. But along with several others it failed. All required that the Republicans surrender their platform. The Crittenden plan also opened the door for slavery to be extended to territories "hereafter acquired," an open invitation for further territorial expansion southward. Republicans in Congress rejected the Crittenden compromise as well as the others.

Major Anderson's Ordeal.   With each passing day the crisis deepened. Increasingly, the attention of the country focused on the two southern military posts still in federal hands—Fort Sumter in Charleston harbor, and Fort Pickens at Pensacola, Florida. Their status, like so many issues of the preceding decade, had become charged with tremendous emotional and symbolic importance. Even Buchanan was unwilling to give up the forts, though he had done little to prevent other southern seizures of federal property. In January, reinvigorated by new pro-Union cabinet advisers, he had despatched the merchant steamer *Star of the West* with munitions and 200 armed troops to reinforce the beleaguered Union army commander at Sumter, Major Robert Anderson. The South Carolina militia had fired on the vessel and forced it to turn back leaving Anderson's garrison as desperate as ever. But for a time the Sumter crisis eased.

By inauguration day, March 4, 1861, the issue of the forts had still not been settled. Lincoln's inauguration address adopted a conciliatory tone. The Union was "perpetual"; secession the "essence of anarchy." The government would "hold, occupy, and possess" federal property and "collect the duties and imposts." On the other hand, the new president declared, he would not insist on delivering the federal mails if such service were "repelled," nor would he appoint "obnoxious strangers" to federal offices in the South. Ultimately, the "momentous issue of civil war" was in the hands of the South. The federal government would not assail the South, but at the same time he, as president, was sworn to "preserve, protect, and defend" the government. Lincoln ended with an appeal to "the mystic chords of memory" that joined the North and South in a common history and heritage.

Once in charge, Lincoln was compelled to grapple with the question of the forts. Fort Pickens, located in remote Florida and more accessible by sea, could be reinforced without difficulty. Fort Sumter, in the heart of "Secessia" itself and under the direct guns of Confederate forces on shore, continued to fester. William Seward, now secretary of state, advised that the fort be evacuated and let Confederate commissioners in Washington believe that it would be done. Most of the other cabinet officers agreed that it would be better to surrender Fort Sumter than trigger a war. But Lincoln was under great pressure from Republicans around the country to save Sumter. And if he was going to do it, it would have to be soon. Major Anderson reported in early March that his supplies were running low and he could not hold out much longer.

On March 20 the president ordered the mounting of an expedition to reinforce Anderson. Seward still objected, and composed a memorandum advising abandonment of Sumter. Hoping to take charge of the nation's affairs from a man he considered weak and vacillating, he went beyond this suggestion, however, and made the preposterous proposal that the United States provoke Britain and France into a diplomatic crisis. Confronted by danger from the European powers, southerners, presumably, would rush to defend the Union. Lincoln quickly and firmly put Seward in his place. *He* alone, he told his puffed-up subordinate, must execute the nation's policies.

Lincoln proceeded with the Sumter relief expedition but took care to notify southern officials of his intentions. As a further precaution against provoking the South, he divided the expedition into two parts. One would only be for resupplying Major Anderson. The federal government would hold troop reinforcements in reserve to be used only if the supply ships were fired on. If the southern authorities did, the onus of war would be on the South's head. The upper South, he hoped, would not see the expedition as an attack.

Confederate officials could not accept this scheme. To Jefferson Davis and his colleagues the continued presence of U.S. property in the middle of Charleston harbor was a reproach to the very idea of Confederate independence and sovereignty. On April 9 Davis ordered the Confederate gen-

A reconstruction by the lithography firm of Currier and Ives of the bombardment of Fort Sumter in Charleston Harbor, the attack that launched the Civil War.

eral in command at Charleston, Pierre Gustave Beauregard, to demand Anderson's surrender before the relief expedition arrived. If he refused, the Confederate batteries should open fire. Anderson rejected the ultimatum, but told the Confederates frankly that his supplies were low and he would have to surrender soon in any case. Beauregard decided that this reply was unsatisfactory.

At 4:30 A.M., on April 12, 1861, the first cannon shot arced over Charleston harbor to land on Fort Sumter. For thirty-four hours the bombardment continued, breaching the fort's walls and starting some fires. True to his pledge to hold his post, Major Anderson returned the fire. On the afternoon of April 13, his ammunition exhausted, he lowered the Stars and Stripes and surrendered.

★ CONCLUSIONS ★

And so the war came. For the next four years the nation would suffer the agonies of fratricidal strife and skirt the edge of dissolution. What had brought the United States to this disastrous result?

Slavery comes closest to explaining the origins of the Civil War. But it was not moral outrage over the peculiar institution primarily that set northern armies on the march to crush the Confederacy. At the outset, only a small minority of northerners saw the war as a crusade against a fundamental social evil.

The actual role of slavery was more subtle and indirect. Southerners had developed a deep stake in the peculiar institution and feared both social and economic cataclysm if it failed. And that failure seemed the goal of the "Black Republican" party and the northern majority that brought it to power in 1860. Southerners were also infuriated by the evident intent of their northern fellow citizens to deny them their "rights" in the common territory of the nation. Northerners, for their part, had come to fear and despise an aggressive and demanding "slave power" that sought to ride roughshod over the rights of free men.

Slavery defined the South and set it off against the North. Deeply woven into the fabric of southern life, it helped to create a southern sense of distinctiveness. This sense took the form of a combined sectional aggressiveness and defensiveness, and these, in turn, made the clash of economic interests more bitter than it need have been. Slavery also converted the Mexican Cession—a national boon—into a constant and escalating source of friction that could not be contained by the existing party system or the other institutions that transcended section.

We must not blame the tragic schism on slavery alone, however; we must allow for the role of individuals and of accident. Sectional conflict might have been restrained if this generation of Americans had possessed the statesmanship necessary for compromise. Douglas, who might have filled the role played by Webster and Clay in the past, badly miscalculated in 1854 and helped wreck the Union. The other leaders of the decade, many of them talented men, were far too closely tied to sectional interests to bridge the chasm opening between the sections.

By whatever route reached, now began the nation's greatest ordeal.

Michael Holt. *The Political Crisis of the 1850s* (1978)

Holt's thesis is that the breakup of the Union can be ascribed to the need of the two parties to define themselves in different and opposed ways. To make the distinctions, unfortunately, they then polarized the nation along sectional lines.

Holman Hamilton. *Prologue to Conflict: The Crisis and Compromise of 1850* (1964)

Hamilton provides a dramatic and incisive analysis of the strategy of the factions that drew up the Compromise of 1850.

David Potter. *The Impending Crisis, 1848–1861* (1976)

A masterful analysis of the political turmoil that ended with the secession of the South. This is the last book by one of the most acute and judicious minds devoted to the scholarship of the Civil War era.

Robert E. May. *The Southern Dream of a Caribbean Empire, 1854–1861* (1973)

May concludes that sectional conflict increased when the Republican-controlled Congress refused to support southern expansion into Central America and the Caribbean. He details the exploits of southerner William Walker, who actually ruled Nicaragua for a time, and describes various attempts to obtain Cuba for the United States and slavery.

Eugene Berwanger. *The Frontier Against Slavery: Western Anti-Negro Prejudice and the Slavery Extension Controversy* (1967)

Many opponents of slavery expansion, especially in the West, fought it because of race prejudice: Blacks, whether slave or free, must not be allowed in the new lands. The author weighs the effects of this bigotry on the laws and politics of the old Northwest, as well as Iowa, Kansas, Nebraska, Oregon, and California.

James A. Rawley. *Race and Politics: "Bleeding Kansas" and the Coming of the Civil War* (1969)

The role of the Kansas-Nebraska question in national politics. In this analysis of the free-soilers' motives, Rawley—like Berwanger—emphasizes their race prejudice.

Eric Foner. *Free Soil, Free Labor, Free Men: The Ideology of the Republican Party Before the Civil War* (1970)

Ideology, Foner says, played a major role in bringing on the Civil War. The Republican leadership, less bigoted and more idealistic in its antislavery views than some scholars have claimed, viewed the North-South conflict as one between two very different societies. Foner believes that secession was the logical response to the election of Lincoln because he and his party were real threats to slaveholders.

Stephen B. Oates. *To Purge This Land with Blood: A Biography of John Brown* (1970)

Oates depicts Brown as a nineteenth-century Calvinist in a time made violent and fanatic by the slavery controversy.

David H. Donald. *Charles Sumner and the Coming of the Civil War* (1960)

An excellent, perceptive biography of a major figure in the rise of political antislavery. It is critical of Sumner as intolerant, ambitious, and at times self-deceived.

Harriet Beecher Stowe. *Uncle Tom's Cabin* (1852)

This enormously popular novel about slavery sold a million copies in the United States by the Civil War. Stowe's major theme is not—as many believe—the day-to-day brutality of slavery, but its more indirect consequences in the breakup of black families and the corruption of slaveholders themselves. The book has the reputation—undeservedly—of being naive and foolishly sentimental.

J. Mills Thornton III. *Politics and Power in a Slave Society: Alabama, 1800–1860* (1978)

This work is broader in its significance than its title suggests. Thornton believes that Alabama's secession in 1860 ultimately derived from its white citizens' fear that the North's actions endangered equality and freedom for the South's white people. A difficult but rewarding book.

William L. Barney. *The Secessionist Impulse: Alabama and Mississippi in 1860* (1974)

Barney ties the secession of two key slave states to fear of abolitionist plots, racial anxieties, the work of firebrands, and uneasiness over severe food shortages during the months of crisis.

Kenneth Stampp. *And the War Came* (1950)

A close analysis, by an outstanding Civil War scholar, of the final secession crisis and Lincoln's part in it.

Don E. Fehrenbacher. *The Dred Scott Case: Its Significance in American Law and Politics* (1978)

The best and most up-to-date treatment of the *Dred Scott* decision.

Kenneth Stampp. *America in 1857: A Nation on the Brink* (1990)

A dean of Civil War History examines the state of the American Union in a single year, "probably the year when the North and South reached the political point of no return." A brilliant, readable book.

William E. Gienapp. *The Origins of the Republican Party, 1852–1856* (1987)

The best recent study of this important subject.

15★

THE CIVIL WAR

How Did the War Change the Nation?

1861	Confederates fire on Fort Sumter • President Lincoln calls up 75,000 state militia • Lincoln suspends *habeas corpus* for the first time and endorses severe penalties for treason • The First Battle of Bull Run • Congress grants Lincoln power to take over railroads and telegraphs, imposes internal revenue taxes on manufactures, and passes an income tax law • The Second Confiscation Act
1862	The Union treasury begins to issue $450 million of "greenbacks" • Ironclads *Monitor* and *Merrimac* battle • Albert S. Johnston stops Grant's advance in the West at the battle of Shiloh Church, Tennessee • Union forces capture New Orleans • The Confederate States of America institute a draft • The Homestead Act • George McClellan's peninsular campaign is checked by Robert E. Lee • The Morrill Land Grant College Act • The first black Union regiments are authorized • Congress passes the first of two Pacific Railway Acts • The Second Battle of Bull Run • McClellan stops Lee's advance at Antietam Creek, Maryland • Lincoln issues the Emancipation Proclamation
1863	The Emancipation Proclamation goes into effect • Congress adopts a draft for the Union army • Joseph Hooker is defeated by Lee and "Stonewall" Jackson at Chancellorsville, Virginia • Democratic Congressman Clement Vallandigham is arrested and eventually banished to the South • Fifty pro-Union counties in Virginia are admitted into the Union as West Virginia • Battle of Gettysburg, Pennsylvania, the turning point of the war • Grant captures Vicksburg, Mississippi, and ensures Union control of the Mississippi River • The New York draft riots
1863, 1864	National Banking Acts establish uniform banking and currency practices
1864	Sherman captures Atlanta, Georgia, and marches to the sea • Second Pacific Railway Act passed by Congress • Lincoln re-elected
1865	Lee asks Grant for terms of surrender; they conclude a peace at Appomattox Court House • Lincoln is assassinated by John Wilkes Booth, and Andrew Johnson becomes president

Few Americans who lived through the Civil War doubted that it had made an enormous difference in the life of their nation. The two warring governments had spent billions of dollars on arms, supplies, and services. Vast armies had been mobilized and millions of men exposed to danger and death. The war had destroyed slavery and decisively shifted power to the North. It also seemed to mark a great divide between a sleepier agrarian America and a bustling America of great factories and giant cities. As they looked back on the events of 1861–1865, both ex-Yankees and ex-Confederates were certain that they had witnessed a profound transformation of the nation.

More recently some scholars have begun to have doubts about the extent of this change. The Civil War, they say, may have formally destroyed slavery, but it did not really free the nation's black people. Blacks had to wait until almost our own day for anything resembling real freedom and equality. Furthermore, the war, in this view, did not promote the economic growth of the United States nor represent the great watershed between an agrarian and an urban-industrial world. In fact, some historians believe it retarded economic development and slowed the shift from agriculture to industry, from country to city.

How *did* the war affect the nation? As we discuss the awesome "brothers' war," we must, if we are to answer the question, consider not just the battles and campaigns but also the social, political, and economic changes that accompanied the strife and carnage.

★ North and South ★

The Civil War was a military contest, a confrontation of two economies, an ideological battle, and a war between two state departments, two congresses, and two chief executives. With the advantages of hindsight, we might assume that in each of these the Union had the advantage. But few Americans living in 1861 perceived it this way, and the fact that the war lasted so long and cost the Union so much suggests that contemporary perceptions were not completely wrong.

The Balance of Forces.   An objective, neutral observer making up a Confederate-Union balance sheet at the beginning in April 1861 might well have bet on the South. True, with 9 million people, the seceded states had less than half the population of the North. Furthermore, 3.5 million southerners were blacks, whom the Confederacy was unwilling to arm. The South also seemed outclassed econom-

ically. In 1860 the whole of what became the Confederate States of America had only 18,000 manufacturing establishments, employing 110,000 workers. The North had over 100,000 factories and shops, with 1.3 million employees. New York, Massachusetts, and Pennsylvania each produced industrial goods worth more each year than the output of the entire South. In the means to transport goods and men, the North was also far ahead of the South, with more than 70 percent of the nation's railroad track and twice as many horses and mules as the Confederacy.

Yet many factors seemed to favor the Confederacy. The southern economy had its strengths. One was an abundance of food to feed its citizens, its draft animals, and its armies. Another was cotton. Cotton was useful for cloth and uniforms; but more important, it promised to be the keystone of Confederate diplomacy. Without cotton, southerners thought, Europe's great textile industry, particularly Britain's, would shut down. To restore a dependable supply of American cotton and save itself from industrial ruin, England would have to intervene on the South's behalf. To guarantee that Britain would feel the pinch, early in the war southern states embargoed cotton, and patriotic Confederate citizens pressured planters to limit the amount of cotton they planted. Some cotton was even burned. The campaign cut the South's 1862 cotton output to a third of its prewar volume.

The Confederacy also appeared to have important strategic advantages. For the South to win, it only had to survive. For the North to win, it had to conquer. The Confederacy, therefore, could use the normally less demanding and costly strategy of defense. This position also offered advantages of supply and maneuver. The defensive South would enjoy "interior" lines of communication; retreat from its borders would only shorten the distance between the South's core and its armies in the field, making it easier to supply and deploy Confederate troops. The North faced the opposite situation. As its attacking armies advanced further and further into enemy territory, they would experience the growing breakdown of supply and communication of constantly lengthening lines of communication. In the end, if only the price of the North's victory could be made high enough, southern independence seemed assured.

The success of this strategy depended on the North's will to fight cracking under the strain. Many Europeans were certain that here, too, the Confederacy had the edge. In their view the South had the better cause, fighting as it was for its rights, its freedom. Southerners clearly agreed. Mississippi, proclaimed Jefferson Davis in his farewell speech to the United States Senate, had left the Union only "from the high and solemn motive of defending and protecting the rights we inherited, and which it is our duty to transmit unshorn to our children." By contrast, he declared, only the North's desire to dominate, to achieve selfish economic and political ends, lay behind its refusal to grant the South its due. A better cause in turn guaranteed better morale. A society bent on conquest surely lacked the fortitude and determination of one struggling for its freedom.

The South also possessed superior military talent. Secession deprived the United States Army of a third of its officers, and the best third at that. Men like Joseph E. Johnston, Edmund Kirby-Smith, and—above all—Robert E. Lee took commissions in the Confederate armed forces only after great personal anguish. Their choice made, however, they supported the southern cause with dedication and skill; especially in the early months, before the Union discovered its own talented military leaders, they contributed immeasurably to Confederate successes.

At the level of the common soldier, too, it seemed that the Confederacy had the advantage. Southerners were an outdoor people, accustomed to hunting and fishing. They knew how to use rifles, and they were better adapted to physical hardship. Confederate sympathizers, certainly, had little doubt that young southern farm boys would make far better soldiers than the hollow-chested Yankee clerks from the counting-houses and shops of New York, Philadelphia, Cincinnati, and Chicago.

Leadership. Despite these appearances, we can now see that almost all the real advantages lay with the North. The man who led the Union during these trying years was, without question, the Union's greatest single asset. Abraham Lincoln was a consummate politician. For four of the most dangerous years the nation ever faced, he managed to make the right political decisions. The mobilization of Union resources to fight a great—and in many quarters unpopular—war required prodigious political juggling. State governors, even Republicans, were jealous of their powers; they often clashed with the federal authorities, especially over military recruiting. Within his own party Lincoln had to deal with both radicals and conservatives. At times he felt compelled to limit civil liberties to preserve order and to prevent "agitators" from discouraging enlistment. He also faced the problem of the border states, which remained in

During the weeks following Fort Sumter, the martial spirit affected everyone: Notice the enthusiasm as New York's Seventh Regiment leaves for the front. So many northerners tried to enlist that the United States turned down thousands.

the Union only precariously and had to be dealt with deftly to avoid pushing them into the Confederate camp. Finally, there was slavery: Emancipation was the North's moral trump card, but should it be played? And if so, when?

The president also had sound military instincts, often better ones than those of the generals. His chief claim to military leadership, however, was his choice of men. He was not always right, but he was capable of learning. Eventually he recognized the military genius of Ulysses S. Grant and William T. Sherman and gave them a free hand in managing the Union armies. The combination of their talents was an important step toward victory.

Lincoln's selection of civilian subordinates was also, on the whole, wise and successful. As secretary of state, William Seward was ultimately an excellent choice. Once he recognized he was not the prime minister in the administration, he served admirably. The secretary of the treasury was the high-principled, aloof, ambitious, and humorless Salmon Chase. Although he had no significant experience in finance, Chase guided the government through some of the most difficult financial shoals it would ever encounter. Lincoln's choice of Simon Cameron, the powerful Republican leader of Pennsylvania, as secretary of war was a mistake. Cameron was both corrupt and incompetent. Fortunately, Lincoln quickly discovered his error, sent Cameron to Russia as American minister, and chose Ohio Democrat Edwin Stanton for the post. Although Stanton was often caustic and intolerant, he was a prodigious worker and a passionate and skilled defender of the Union cause.

Lincoln's preeminent success, however, was as a symbol of the Union's will to survive and an articulator of goals beyond mere survival. He was a master of English prose, and his major state papers and speeches rank among the most inspiring evocations of the democratic spirit. Taking what could easily be interpreted as a war of conquest similar to the British effort to suppress the American colonists eighty years before, Lincoln transformed it into a struggle for the finest aspirations of the American people. The war was a "people's contest," a "struggle . . . to elevate the condition of men—to lift artificial weights from all shoulders—to clear the paths of laudable pursuit for all—to afford all an unfettered start and a fair chance in the race of life." The Union's survival, Lincoln told his fellow citizens, was humanity's "last, best hope." If it should be defeated, democracy would fail, and the forces of darkness and tyranny triumph. If, however, the Union prevailed, government "of the people, by the people, for the people" would "not perish from the earth."

And what of the Confederacy's leader, Jefferson Davis? A West Point graduate, commander of the Mississippi Rifles in the Mexican War, Franklin Pierce's secretary of war, and former United States senator from Mississippi, Davis

Jefferson Davis in 1849. He looked the part of a president, far more so than his homely antagonist, Abe Lincoln, but he did not have his counterpart's capacity to lead.

seemed eminently suited to guide the besieged Confederacy. He was honest, courageous, and intelligent; and his sharply etched lean features and dignified bearing gave him the look of a national leader. Davis's performance, however, was not as impressive as his credentials and appearance. He had to have his hand in everything, both civilian and military, and often he botched the job. According to Stephen R. Mallory, Davis's secretary of the navy, the Confederate president "neither labored with method or celerity himself, nor permitted others to do so for him." He was also argumentative and, unlike his northern counterpart, insensitive to public opinion. Although many Confederate setbacks were the fault of others or were inherent in the South's situation, Davis's weaknesses clearly contributed to the South's defeat.

★ THE WAR BEGINS ★

The first responsibility of each president was to raise an army. Immediately after the attack on Fort Sumter, Lincoln had called for 75,000 state militia to join the small regular army for three months' service. The war, he expected, would be brief, and the troops would be home for late spring plant-

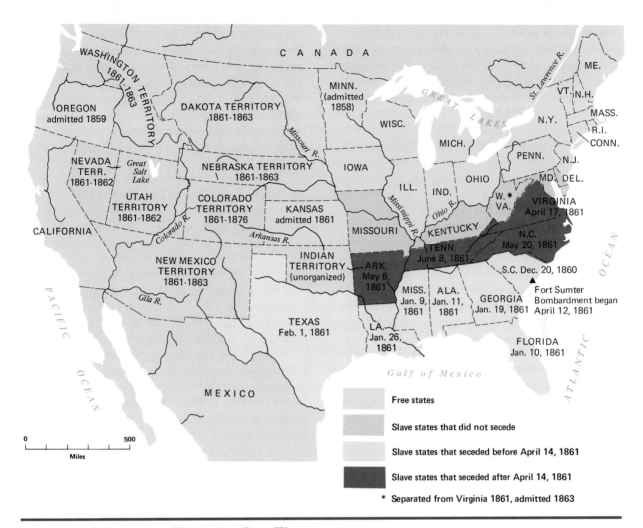

THE UNITED STATES ON THE EVE OF THE CIVIL WAR

ing. Patriotic fervor swept the North. "It seems as if we never were alive till now; never had a country till now," exclaimed an exhilarated New Yorker. Except in those slave states still in the Union, the response was quick and enthusiastic. Young northerners regarded the war as a glorious lark, and they flocked to recruiting offices. State quotas were quickly oversubscribed; and militia regiments, many composed of untrained men without rifles or proper uniforms, rushed off for Washington to meet their country's call.

Lincoln's move to put down the rebellion tripped off a furious reaction in the uncommitted slave states. Between April 17 and May 20 four more states—Virginia, Arkansas, Tennessee, and North Carolina—seceded and joined the Confederacy, bringing with them much of the South's manpower and agricultural and industrial capacity. War fever also seized the South and propelled thousands of southerners into the army to defend southern rights. The

Confederacy had the opportunity to make a formidable force out of this raw material, but it let the chance slip. President Davis, now residing with his government in the Confederate capital of Richmond, expected a long and difficult war, but his voice went unheeded. Like Lincoln, the Confederate Congress believed the war would end by winter, and it accepted many short-term volunteers who soon had to be replaced.

Bull Run. In this case Davis was right and Lincoln was wrong. The fighting would be bloody, bitter, and seemingly interminable. Skirmishing between Union and Confederate forces began in mid-April, shortly after Sumter. Many of these early clashes took place in the strategically important border regions—Kentucky, Missouri, eastern Tennessee, and western Virginia—where the two sections touched one another and where the people were deeply divided in their allegiances. The first major military confrontation occurred in July 1861 at Bull Run, a small tributary of the Potomac twenty miles west of Washington. There 30,000 men under Union General Irvin McDowell met a smaller force commanded by Confederate General Beauregard. The Confederates were outgunned and outnumbered, but better led and better coordinated. For a time the Union forces held the upper hand, but the green Yankee troops gave way when the Confederates, screaming their shrill "rebel yell," counterattacked. The federals soon panicked, discarding their weapons and abandoning their artillery, and fleeing pell-mell to the safety of Washington. Accompanying them in their headlong retreat was an array of civilians, including several congressmen and many ladies, who had come out from the Union capital on a summer's day to watch the expected rebel rout.

The defeat at Bull Run (called the battle of Manassas by Confederates) was in some ways a powerful blow to northern morale. It seemed to confirm Confederate claims that southerners were superior fighters and perhaps gave southern troops an early edge in self-confidence. On the other hand it provided a healthy antidote to northern overoptimism. Republican governors from all over the North telegraphed the War Department offering new state regiments to protect the capital and prepare for resuming the march south. These men, moreover, would be enlisted for three years. Patriotism, the glamor of a uniform, and the love of adventure and danger were still potent stimulants to enlistment; another 75,000 volunteers streamed into training camps near Washington prepared to put down the "rebellion."

Lincoln's Early Commanders. The man who took charge of this force was George B. McClellan, a small, wiry man with a bristling black moustache and a Napoleonic complex. As a young officer, "Little Mac" had served in the Mexican War; but he had spent most of his military career in the Corps of Engineers, and when the war broke out he was a civilian railroad director. His training and experience as an organizer and administrator helped him pull the army together. McClellan drilled his troops rigorously, welding the new arrivals and the ragged, dispirited mob that had fled to Washington into a confident, spit-and-polish army. He was soon being hailed as a savior.

Organizing abilities, however, are not enough for a successful military leader. Despite the early minor victories in western Virginia that had brought him to the administration's attention, McClellan was not a good field commander. He lacked the daring and drive needed. As a Democrat, he was also suspicious of the president and his party. He took months to equip and train his men before resuming the attack. Finally, after insistent urging by Lincoln, in

March 1862 McClellan's magnificent army of 130,000 set out for Richmond from Hampton Roads where they had arrived by sea. At Williamsburg, in early May, McClellan first encountered the enemy. The engagement was indecisive. For the next two months McClellan fought a series of battles—the Peninsular Campaign—against two of the South's ablest military leaders, Robert E. Lee and Thomas J. ("Stonewall") Jackson. He managed to avert defeat; but his army returned to Washington in June bruised and badly battered. Nothing had been achieved.

In the West Union forces under the Virginian George H. Thomas and the shaggy, hard-drinking Ulysses S. Grant were having better luck. In late January Thomas defeated the Confederates at the Battle of Mill Springs in Kentucky. Several weeks later Grant captured Fort Donelson on the Cumberland River, taking 14,000 Confederate prisoners. Soon Nashville fell to Union forces. Grant believed that he was now in a position to crush the Confederate army in the West decisively, but he underestimated the recuperative powers of his foe. On April 6, 1862, Albert Sidney Johnston attacked the exposed Union position near Shiloh Church (a meetinghouse near Pittsburg Landing, Tennessee) and pushed back the federal troops commanded by William Tecumseh Sherman. A confused two-day battle brought heavy casualties to both sides, including the death of the Confederate commander. Ultimately, the Confederate attack was repulsed, but Grant's men were exhausted and hungry and could not muster the energy to pursue the beaten Confederates.

McClellan's lack of offensive zeal disturbed Lincoln. In addition, the general was becoming a political liability. A moderate Democrat, he was thoroughly detested by the "Radicals" in the Republican party, who advocated abolition of slavery and a more aggressive war policy to defeat the South. In July 1862 the president replaced McClellan as field commander in the eastern theater with General John Pope, simultaneously elevating Henry W. Halleck to general in chief of the Union armies.

For the next year the tide of war swept back and forth, with Lincoln unable to find a field commander to match Lee. After Pope's drubbing at the hands of Lee and Jackson in the Second Battle of Bull Run (August 29–30, 1862), Lincoln turned once again to McClellan, who once again disappointed him. Cocky and arrogant in manner and speech but timid in action, McClellan stopped Lee's advance into Maryland at Antietam (September 17, 1862) but lost the opportunity of decisively defeating the far smaller Confederate force. In November Lincoln decided to replace McClellan with Ambrose E. Burnside. The choice was unwise. In December 1862 at Fredericksburg, Virginia, the new Union commander sent massed infantry against entrenched Confederate troops whose rifles and artillery

The Civil War was not all battles and bullets. At times it wore a festive aspect, and civilians often came out to the camps and battlefields to see the sights. The woman here with the parasol is Kate Chase Sprague, daughter of treasury secretary Salmon P. Chase and wife of Rhode Island's millionaire senator, William Sprague.

slaughtered the charging blue-clad federals. Lincoln replaced Burnside with Joseph Hooker, who quickly demonstrated that he was no better. At Chancellorsville, Virginia (May 2–4, 1863), Lee and Jackson severely mauled Hooker's Army of the Potomac. The only consolation for the Union forces was that Jackson was accidentally killed by his own men.

Union Strategy. The Union was not only slow in finding a competent military leader; it also had difficulty evolving a clear, overall military strategy. To many northerners "On to Richmond!" seemed at first enough of a plan. To others this appeared simple-minded, though in fact, to the end of the war the Union concentrated excessively on taking the Confederate capital. Early in the war the aged commander in chief, Winfield Scott, proposed that the North, like the great Anaconda snake, should seize its victim in its coils and squeeze it tightly. Union armies would contain the South along its borders while the northern navy cordoned off the Confederacy from the rest of the world. Simultaneously, other Union forces would cut the South in half along the Mississippi River. Seeing that its cause was hopeless the South would surrender. The Anaconda Plan relied too much on the belief that southern unionism, given time, would bring the South to its senses. It was greeted with derision by the northern press and never adopted as such.

Yet several features of the Anaconda were in fact incorporated into Union strategy. Early in 1862 the Union armies launched an offensive to divide the Confederacy along the Mississippi. In April, Union land and naval forces under the Massachusetts political general Benjamin F. Butler took New Orleans, the South's largest city and control point for sea access to the river. Bit by bit the Union forces advanced up and down the banks of the Mississippi. In the summer of 1863 the final Confederate positions on the river fell when Grant, aided by David Porter's river gunboats, took Vicksburg, Mississippi, and Port Hudson, Louisiana. The Confederacy was now cut in two by a Union north-south corridor.

The Naval War. The squeeze tactics were especially effective at sea, where each month the northern naval blockade grew tighter. In early 1862 the *Merrimac*, a Confederate ironclad converted from a scuttled United States naval vessel, threatened to break the Union blockade of Hampton Roads, Virginia. The federal navy rushed its own brand new ironclad, the *Monitor*, to the scene. The two vessels battled to a draw, and the southern ship retired, never again to challenge Union naval supremacy.

Its naval advantage was to stand the North in good stead. In the western theater federal gunboats on the Mississippi and its tributaries supported Union military operations with their canon and kept river supply lines open. Along the Atlantic and Gulf coasts the seagoing Union fleet made possible successful amphibious attacks against southern ports like New Orleans, Mobile, Savannah, and Port Royal. The most useful naval action, however, was the coastal blockade. Each month, as the number of available ships grew, the sea noose around the South drew tighter. In 1861 the federal navy captured one Confederate vessel in ten that tried to escape to the open sea; by 1865 its record had improved to one in two, and growing Confederate shortages of many products hitherto imported from Europe attested to the mounting effectiveness of the blockade.

The Confederates also had their moments of glory at sea. Many Confederate blockade-runners—swift, shallow-draft vessels—successfully evaded Union ships and dashed to Bermuda or some other British-American port. There they loaded Enfield rifles, medicines, and lead, as well as scarce luxury items; if they were lucky, they brought their cargoes back safely to the besieged Confederacy. On the high seas the *Alabama* and other Confederate raiders destroyed millions of dollars' worth of Union shipping. To protect themselves against disastrous loss, northern ship owners transferred their vessels to foreign registry or were forced to pay high insurance rates. Despite these successes, the Confederates were never able to challenge the Union navy on the waters, and each month saw the northern advantage grow as its shipyards turned out scores of new vessels to augment Union naval strength. In June 1864 the United States Navy's *Kearsarge* finally caught up with Captain Raphael Semmes of the *Alabama* off Cherbourg, France, and put an end to his spectacular raiding career.

The Diplomatic War. Europe's need for cotton had promised the Confederacy a chance to secure diplomatic recognition and possibly military help from Britain and France. The South could also count on Europe's upper classes, who felt they had more in common with the southern planter elite than with the crude, money-mad Yankees. Besides, nothing would suit British policy better than cutting the bumptious United States down to size by helping divide it in half. The French, for the most part, followed Britain's anti-Union lead. But, after establishing a puppet regime in Mexico that challenged the Monroe Doctrine, they had their own reasons for favoring a Yankee defeat and an enfeebled United States.

In the end King Cotton diplomacy proved to be a disappointment. Britain was overstocked with cotton in 1861 and for a time felt no pinch. Thereafter, the British imported cotton from Egypt and India to replace some of the lost southern supply. And northern wheat, which England needed, gave the Union a similar, though less powerful, lever on British policy. The North also had one high card

that its enemy lacked: the prospect of emancipation. Though they might not be averse to southern independence, the British middle and working classes could not morally support the slave system. If the North could convince the British people of its antislavery intentions, the London government would find it difficult to throw its weight against the Union.

For three years, however, the Union and the Confederacy fought desperately to curry favor with the British. The South won the early diplomatic rounds. Late in 1861 the Confederate commissioners to France (John Slidell) and England (James M. Mason) ran the Union blockade and reached Havana, where they boarded the *Trent*, a British merchant vessel, for passage to Europe. On November 7, Captain Charles Wilkes of the U.S.S. *San Jacinto* intercepted the *Trent*, arrested Slidell and Mason, and took them to Boston. The British, furious at this violation of their high seas rights, demanded their release, as well as reparations and an apology. With Union sentiment hostile to Britain, Lincoln and his secretary of state, William Seward, sat on the situation for a time, then quietly returned the commissioners with an apology. But the *Trent* affair gave the Confederates a diplomatic edge. Early in 1862 the British government permitted the Confederates to use British shipyards to build and outfit the *Alabama* and other sea raiders, and soon after allowed the Confederate navy to contract with the Laird shipbuilding firm in Scotland for several powerful, ironclad "rams." For a while, too, English investors were receptive to lending money to the Confederacy.

The tide turned, however, when British friends of the United States, led by Richard Cobden and John Bright, appealed to British antislavery opinion and succeeded in creating a strong pro-Union current. The efforts of these sympathetic Britons, the tireless maneuvering of Lincoln's minister to England, Charles Francis Adams, and, above all, Union victories on the battlefield, combined to shift British opinion in favor of the North. In October 1863 the British government seized the Laird rams before the Confederates could take delivery, ending their threat to the Union blockade. Though the North's worst diplomatic fears were allayed by the end of 1862, the possibility of a falling-out between Britain and the Union threatened Lincoln's war effort and gave hope to the South almost to the end of the war.

★ WAR AND SOCIETY ★

The titanic military, naval, and diplomatic drives of North and South were sustained by equally stupendous efforts of their respective home fronts. The raising of troops, the mar-

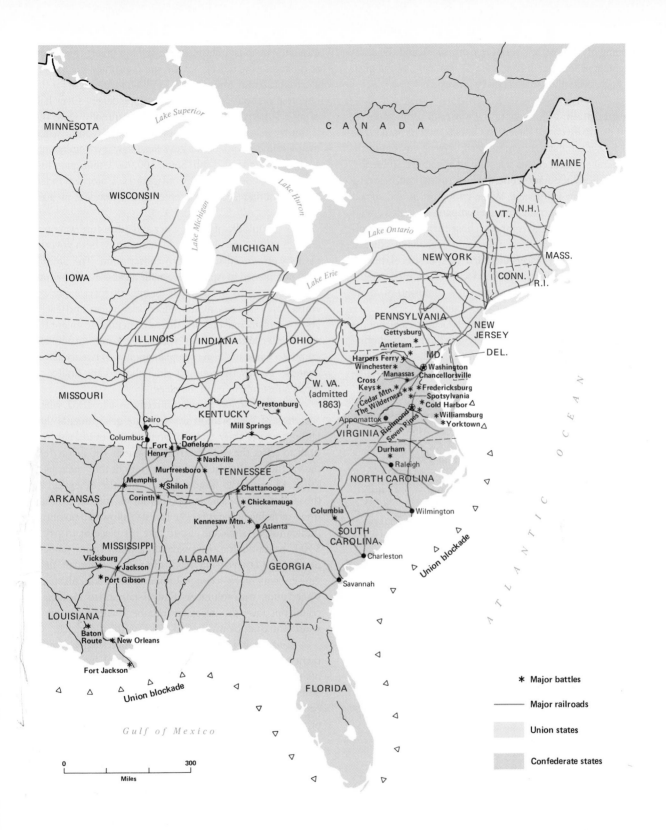

MAJOR BATTLES OF THE CIVIL WAR, 1861–1865

shaling of financial and economic resources, and the management of internal dissent were all vital parts of the great struggle on both sides to achieve victory.

Conscription. Throughout the war both combatants relied primarily on volunteers to fill their military ranks. For the first year the system worked well. Typically, in the North, a prominent local citizen who craved adventure, influence, or a military reputation opened a recruiting office and issued a call for volunteers. When enough men had signed up they formed a company; ten companies equaled a regiment. The men of the company chose their own junior officers, who in turn chose the senior regimental officers. Usually the senior officers included the sponsors of the regiment. In the early months the local communities or the states supplied uniforms, leading to a confusion of colors until the federal government settled on blue.

The pure volunteer system could not last. A few months of bitter fighting, growing casualty lists, and news filtering back to the home front of the danger, the discomfort, and the hard work of soldiering dampened youthful enthusiasm and patriotism; fewer and fewer volunteers turned up at the recruiting offices. Yet the war consumed manpower at a frightful rate. More than 2.1 million men fought for the Union and about 800,000 for the Confederacy. Over half of all northern men of military age eventually wore the Union blue; over four-fifths of the South's young white males donned Confederate gray. Relatively few combatants escaped wounds or death. Some 360,000 Union men lost their lives; about 260,000 Confederates. Union wounded totaled another 275,000; Confederate wounded, at least 100,000.

By the middle of 1862, glory and adventure were not enough to fill Confederate and Union ranks; both governments were forced to resort to conscription. The South's draft law, passed in April 1862, made all able-bodied white males between 18 and 35 liable for military service, but exempted civil servants, militia officers, clergymen, and teachers. A supplemental measure that fall, intended to guarantee racial order and encourage vital agricultural output, exempted a white male on each plantation with twenty slaves or more. Finally, the southern draft allowed any draftee to hire a substitute to go in his place.

Union coercion began indirectly in late 1862 when Secretary of War Stanton warned state governments that failure to meet their quota of volunteers would lead to a draft to offset the state shortfall. In March 1863 Congress passed the Enrollment Act making every healthy male aged 20 to 45 subject to a federal draft with the exception of those who were the sole support of widows, motherless children, or indigent parents. The law also allowed a potential draftee to pay someone else to take his place or to pay a $300 commutation fee exempting him from service. Because the law was intended primarily to stimulate flagging enlistment, each congressional district could fill an assigned quota with volunteers. Only if state and local officials could not raise the necessary numbers within fifty days would the draft be invoked to make up the difference.

Conscription in both sections produced anger, resentment, and a multitude of abuses. In the North local officials offered large bounties to avoid the drafting of local citizens. Some men—"bounty jumpers"—made it a business to accept hundreds of dollars from several districts, one after the other, and then fail to report for service. In both sections, critics charged that the draft benefited the rich. The "twenty-slave clause" in the Confederate draft supposedly favored the planter class over the small farmers. The provision for buying substitutes in both draft systems, though intended primarily to soften the harsh law, also seemed tilted toward those with ready cash. Under the North's Enrollment Act, moreover, rich districts were able to outbid poorer ones for able-bodied substitutes and so spare more of their citizens from military duty. These provisions led to charges in both

WAR IN THE WEST, 1862

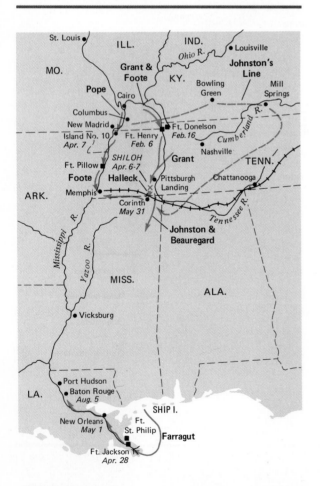

The wounded near Fredericksburg. The emptiness and despair on these soldiers' faces contrast with the confidence and optimism of the early volunteers. With inadequate food, shelter, and sanitation, the ideals of glory and victory gave way to the realities of pain and death.

North and South that it was "a rich man's war and a poor man's fight."

Recent research into the social makeup of Union and Confederate armies casts doubt on the common charge of class bias in Civil War military recruitment. Allowing for the youth of most soldiers, the occupations and class affiliations of the boys in blue and the boys in gray resembled those of their society's as a whole. In both sections the sons of the rich as well as the sons of the poor risked their lives in proportionate numbers. Both armies had many foreign-born soldiers. In the Union the foreign-born troops reached 26 percent of the total.

Still, the draft acts aroused resentments and led to resistance in both sections. In the southern highland regions, where the war had never been very popular, young men escaped to the remotest mountains and often joined with deserters from the Confederate army to defy the authorities. Union draft resistance took an especially violent form in New York City. There the Irish working class, Democratic in its politics and often resentful of blacks, considered the draft emblematic of the despised Republican administration. Beginning on July 13, soon after federal officials began to draw the names of New York draftees, mobs of whites attacked the symbols of the Union cause, looting the homes of prominent Republicans, destroying the offices of the *New York Tribune*, and burning down the Colored Orphan Asylum. The crazed rioters also lynched a half-dozen innocent black people. The federal government rushed troops from the Gettysburg battlefield to end the anarchy, and General George Meade's veterans fired volleys into the mob. When, after four days, the ghastly riots finally ended, more than a hundred people had died.

Conscription did not raise many soldiers directly. In the North only 46,000 men were actually drafted into service. But many thousands more volunteered rather than accept the stigma of forced recruitment. All told, a recent student of the draft system concludes, it worked moderately well to get the job done.

Conscription, whatever its failings or virtue, was a novel exercise of central government power. The three previous American wars had been fought by volunteers. Now, under the goad of necessity, both Union and Confederate governments had asserted a right never claimed before, the right to compel men to risk their lives for the nation. But this innovation was only one of many, all pointing to enhanced national over local power and all increasing the physical and institutional integration of the country.

The Beginnings of Modern National Finance. Paying for the war was a major challenge for both governments. In 1861, after three generations of independence, Americans were still not used to heavy taxes. But the war cost both governments enormous sums. At one point the Union treasury was paying out $2 million a day for munitions, supplies, military pay, and other war-related expenses.

The Confederacy initially tried to meet most of its costs with money borrowed from foreign and domestic sources. This approach yielded little, for few capitalists at home or abroad would lend money to the South except at outrageous interest rates. A "produce" loan of cotton and other crops was equally disappointing. As early as 1861, following the precedent of the Revolution, the Confederate treasury turned to paper money. Because there was little gold in the South, this was "fiat" money, mere IOUs.

Though the Confederate printing presses spewed out over $1.5 billion in paper money during the war, even that sum proved inadequate for the Confederacy's needs. Before many months the value of Confederate currency had fallen so low that the government was forced to adopt other means for paying its bills. In early 1863 the Confederate Congress authorized the impressment of slaves for the building of fortifications and for other government work. It also empowered the government to detail soldiers for work in vital war factories. And in April 1863 it assumed the authority

As enthusiasm for the war waned, both Confederate and Union governments went to greater lengths to attract new men, as this poster illustrates. In 1862 a northerner could receive $300 or more for enlisting; the same sum could buy his exemption from the draft.

to take from each farmer a tenth of all the major crops he produced. The levy on crops, though unwieldy, was the best expedient a desperate Confederate government could design to meet its needs.

In the North the need to supply the military forces led to a parallel, though less drastic, inflation of national power, and because it was the Union government that survived, that growth was momentous for the nation's future. With access to the markets of Europe, the gold of the West, and most of the country's banking capital, Union Secretary of the Treasury Salmon Chase was better able than his Confederate counterpart to tax and borrow. By 1865 Congress had imposed internal revenue taxes on hundreds of manufactured items, created a Bureau of Internal Revenue to administer the tax laws, and established America's first income tax. Using the excuse that heavily taxed American manufactures must be protected against cheaper foreign wares, the Republican Congress also raised tariff rates to levels never before reached, drastically reversing the prewar trend under the Democrats.

Internal taxes and import duties were not enough, however, and the Union, too, resorted to borrowing. Under Chase's prompting, Congress authorized the sale of several hundred million dollars of bonds, paying 6 percent interest in gold. The treasury's chief agent, Philadelphia banker Jay Cooke, advertised this issue in every northern newspaper and sent his subagents all over the country to peddle the securities from door to door. Eventually he sold $362 million in bonds. By the war's end these bond sales and other loans had pushed the Union debt to the immense figure of $2.5 billion.

The treasury's financial needs produced a major revolution in the country's banking system. The state banks that had supplied the country's currency and credit since the demise of the Second Bank of the United States in 1836 proved inadequate to meet the country's political emergency. Matters were brought to a crisis in December 1861, when public hoarding of gold and excessive treasury borrowing forced the banks to cease redeeming their notes in specie. With the need to keep a gold reserve no longer imposing a limit on their paper money issues, the banks were free to turn on the printing presses. The country now faced the prospect of a deluge of worthless paper bank notes to meet its day-to-day currency needs.

To end this chaotic situation and at the same time tap the banks for funds, Chase proposed a national currency backed by government bonds and issued by a new system of federally chartered banks. Under the National Banking Acts of 1863 and 1864, business people who bought a specified amount of federal bonds could organize new banks and issue bank notes backed by the government securities. Now, instead of a multitude of privately issued bank notes unsecured by gold, the country would have a uniform paper money system under strict federal control. And after the war these notes would be doubly safe, for then, it was assumed, gold would once more return to normal circulation and the government and the banks would be able to redeem their obligations in "specie" on demand. The measure also sought to put the state banks out of business or force them to convert to national banks by taxing their note issues.

The national banking system would prove less of an economic boon than its sponsors had hoped, but it did help the treasury finance the war. By June 1863 there were 450 national banks in existence, with millions of dollars' worth of federal bonds in their reserves, representing large revenues to the federal government. More important, however, the national crisis had broken the stiff resistance to a federal banking system. For the first time in a generation Washington was back in the business of regulating the country's banking affairs.

The national banking system helped ease the Union's financial problems and at the same time provided a new sort of paper money for the nation's commercial needs. Still, this was not enough. Long before the bond sales and the new taxes produced results, the treasury was empty. There seemed no alternative to the intolerable situation but treasury-issued paper money, as had been done in the South, with its value shored up by a vague promise to rdeem the "greenbacks" in gold after the war. The Union's superior resources, however, allowed it to limit the issue of greenbacks to $450 million and prevented their severe depreciation. By late 1864 northern prices were about two and a half times those of 1860. In the South price levels had risen fiftyfold.

The Spreading Rail System. The expansion of the government's role in finance was matched by its growing involvement in transportation. In 1861 the Union had 22,000 miles of railroad track. This was already the most extensive railroad network in the world, but it was not an integrated system. Many smaller communities had no railroad connections, and different track gauges prevented rapid through-traffic on many routes. The most glaring defect of all was the lack of rail connections to the West Coast.

The war reduced each of these deficiencies. After 1860, with the South out of the Union, Congress passed a measure to subsidize a transcontinental railroad. The Pacific Railway Act of 1862, as supplemented in 1864, gave the private promoters of the Central Pacific, building east from Sacramento, and those of the Union Pacific, building west from Omaha, 20 million acres of public land and a federal loan of $60 million in bonds. Little actual trackage was laid down during the war, but soon after Appomattox construction crews were pushing iron rails across the plains and mountains at a furious pace.

Meanwhile, the Lincoln administration pursued a vigorous and successful policy of controlling and coordinating existing railroads to meet war needs. In January 1862 Congress granted the president power to take over telegraph and rail lines. After May 1862 the railroads operated under overall government direction. In addition, the military superintendent of railroads arranged the construction of 650 miles of new track to link existing routes, encouraged the standardizing of track gauges, the building of new central terminals, and double-tracking along heavily used routes. The government's expanded role in transportation enabled the railroads to perform marvels in moving Union troops and guaranteeing that they always had what they needed to fight and live.

The Richmond government, in contrast, failed to mobilize southern railroads. Jefferson Davis and his subordinates, though handicapped by the blockade and the South's inferior industry, did less than they might have to prevent locomotives and rolling stock from breaking down and tracks from wearing out. Scores of small private companies continued to set rail rates and make other decisions affecting the southern economy and war effort. Generally, troops arrived where they were needed, but goods moved slowly and at high cost. Because of railroad breakdowns, toward the end of the war southern troops were often shoeless, hungry, and ragged, while Confederate warehouses bulged with supplies and clothing.

Government Becomes Big Business. The demands of war enormously swelled the size of the Union government. Disbursements and tax collections brought an army of clerks to the stately Treasury Building across from the White House, while in the field hundreds of treasury agents fanned out to regulate the illegal cotton trade between northern buyers eager for scarce fiber and southerners eager for scarce goods. The War Department's scale of operation became even greater than the treasury's. Under Quartermaster General Montgomery Meigs, it performed prodigious labors in supplying the army. During the year ending June 30, 1865, alone, the Quartermaster Department purchased 3.4 million trousers, 3.7 million pairs of drawers, and 3.2 million flannel shirts, laying out for these and countless other articles over $431 million. To procure these items armies of government clerks and purchasing agents negotiated thousands of contracts with manufacturers and wholesalers. In 1861 the federal civil service had employed 40,000 people; by 1865 there were 195,000, a fivefold increase.

Government orders invigorated the North's economy. The gigantic War Department procurement did much to lower costs in private armories. It also stimulated production in a wide array of businesses directly connected to the war effort. In the boot and shoe industry, for example, it was reported in 1863 that "operatives are pouring in [to Lynn, Massachusetts, a major shoe center] as fast as room can be made for them; buildings for shoe factories are going up in every direction; the hum of machinery is heard on every hand." By 1864 production of coal, iron, copper, and leather was greater than before the war. Frequently the scale of government orders encouraged standardization and mechanization of production, establishing a model for postwar development. The canning industry was stimulated by government orders: When Gail Borden's condensed milk factory opened in early 1861, its entire output was "immediately commandeered" for the army. All told, the index of manufacturing for the North alone by 1864 was 13 percent higher than for the whole nation in 1860.

Organizing Agriculture. In the South invading armies, the breakdown of transportation, and the erosion of the slave labor system led to agricultural decline. In the North agriculture burgeoned under wartime need. The process of mechanizing the American farm was already under way in 1860. The departure of thousands of young men from the farms precisely when the demand for farm products reached an all-time peak accelerated the acceptance of horse-drawn harvesters and mowers. During the entire decade of the 1850s American farmers had bought 100,000 of these machines; in 1864 manufacturers were turning out that many each year.

The expansion of northern farm output during the war was only obliquely a consequence of government action. But the government had an important direct impact on the social side of American agriculture. For years various northern and western farming groups had demanded favors of the federal government, only to see them blocked by Democratic and southern opponents. Now, with the South out of the Union and the Republicans in control of the government, the walls came down. In 1861 Congress authorized a department of agriculture within the Patent Office to be headed by a commissioner. In 1862 it enacted the Morrill Land Grant College Act, setting aside several million acres of federal land for support of agricultural and industrial higher education. The 1862 Homestead Act provided that any citizen or any alien who declared his intention of becoming a citizen and who was also head of a family and over 21 might claim 160 acres of land on specified surveyed portions of the public domain. After residing on this land, adding improvements, and paying a small registration fee, he would become its owner, with no further strings except the usual local taxes. The law would be less than perfect in the way it was administered, yet it represented a triumph of the ideal of a free family farm and a fulfillment of Republican promises to western farm groups.

The War and Economic Growth. The war undoubtedly stimulated the northern economy in many ways. At one time scholars believed that it accelerated overall American economic growth and marked the basic shift of the American economy from an agricultural to an industrial base. It is now clear, as we saw in Chapter 9, that the structural transformation from rural-agricultural to urban-industrial was already well under way by 1860. It did not require the trigger of the Civil War. But the issue of the war's stimulating effect on the economy is less clear. Figures that lump together data for both sections show a slowing down of the American economy during the 1860s, the war period. Total commodity output in the United States was growing at the average rate of 4.6 percent a year in 1840–1859; during the period 1870–1899 it would increase annually by an average of 4.4 percent. In 1860–1869, however, it was only 2.0 percent, less than half these rates.

Given the economic surge in so many wartime northern industries, this is puzzling. But several matters must be kept in mind. First, these figures add South to North. During the war the South's economy suffered devastating blows from northern invasion and from the failure to repair and replace factories, railroads, barns, livestock, and other items that make up a nation's capital stock. Any gains in northern output, then, must be set against large declines in the South. But there is also good reason to believe that the spurt in northern war-stimulated industries was also offset. If some enterprises surged, others declined. With a million or so young men in the army, the Union lost a vast amount of productive labor, and total output inevitably suffered. But what about expenditures by the Union government? Government spending on a vast scale when an economy has unused labor and capital often stimulates economic growth. But these conditions did not obtain in 1861 when the war began. Rather, resources were already rather fully employed, and government outlays for war were mostly at the expense of the private sector with no real addition to the net output of the economy.

There is a related question to consider here. Did the *political* effects of the war have significant economic consequences? With the South out of the Union, as we saw, it proved possible to get on with the building of a Pacific railroad, to pass a protective tariff, and to restructure the nation's banking system. Clearly, the Union government under the Republicans was more friendly and helpful to economic "progress" than its southern and Democratic-dominated predecessor. And this shift of power and ideology would persist for years beyond 1865 with significant effects on the country's future economic development. It is difficult to avoid the conclusion that although the war may not have been *caused* by sectional economic competition, *its consequences* may well have favored the predominant interests of the business-industrial classes over the agrarian classes.

New Bonds Between Citizens. The war emergency that enhanced the role of government in many areas also strengthened the nation's private voluntary institutions. Before 1861 the United States was anything but united in the spheres of life that affected ordinary citizens. In fact, the growing sectional confrontation during the 1850s had torn apart what little connective tissue existed. The war made the North-South split still deeper, of course, but within the Union itself it stimulated the growth of new civic bonds and attachments.

Everywhere patriotic people came together to help with those tasks that were still not considered the legitimate responsibility of the government. The United States Sanitary Commission, raising money through numerous "sanitary fairs," assisted the army's medical department. The Christian Commission of the Young Men's Christian Association supplied Bibles to the troops, provided them with other reading matter, and helped them send money to their families.

Voluntary associations also boosted civilian morale. The Loyal Publication Societies of New York and New England churned out pamphlets explaining and defending the Union cause. Many leading intellectuals, including Charles Eliot Norton, Ralph Waldo Emerson, and Professor Francis Lieber of Columbia University, joined the societies and lent their names and their writing skills to their work. The Union League, active in eighteen northern states by 1862, brought prominent northern businessmen, professionals, intellectuals, and politicians together to propagandize for the Union and promote policies to help defeat the South. After 1865 the Union League became a permanent network of clubs that united an urban elite for the support of nationalist Republican policies.

The participation of northern intellectuals in organizations like these, along with the moral support of the Union demonstrated by writers and intellectuals, marked a reversal of the critical attitudes of America's thinkers toward their country's leading institutions and values. The revolution in attitudes went beyond the cultural leaders. Northern youth, too, apparently developed a new faith in their society. President Julian Sturtevant of Illinois College noted at midpoint in the struggle: "We were evidently in need of some vigorous discipline. The element of reverence for rightful authority was slipping out of the national mind. Our young men were beginning to feel all authority is despotism, all government tyranny, and all submission an obedience servility." The war, he wrote, had ended these signs of rebelliousness among the young and forged a more cohesive society.

This new faith of intellectuals and educated young people would have long-lasting effects. Before 1860 their views had tempered the materialistic attitudes of Americans and supplied a critical ingredient to the northern ethos. For a generation after 1865 few voices would be raised to challenge the values of a commercial-industrial society. Only in the South would some people demur; but their skepticism, associated as it was with disloyalty, defeat, and poverty, would go unheeded. Meanwhile, the brashness and thrust of Yankee businessmen and promoters would come to epitomize the nation. The Civil War, then, would mark not only the triumph of northern arms but also the victory of the practical, go-ahead, and materialistic side of the prewar northern personality.

Dissent. Despite the war-kindled patriotism, dissent flourished in both the Union and the Confederacy. In each it would create serious difficulties for the government. Ironically, repression would be stronger in the North, which prided itself on its intellectual freedom, than in the South, with its tradition of intolerance.

Dissent in the North ranged from mild disagreement with Republican policies to violent opposition that bordered on treason. The so-called War Democrats often differed with Lincoln and the Republicans over the best ways of achieving victory, but they followed the lead of Stephen Douglas in offering their whole-hearted support to the Union. The Little Giant died in June 1861, depriving the War Democrats of their outstanding leader; but to the end of the struggle, they were among the Union's staunchest supporters. More critical of the administration's positions were the Peace Democrats. Though they initially supported the war effort, as the months passed they became more and more convinced that only a negotiated peace that would restore the prewar sectional balance would do. At the depths of Union fortunes a substantial fringe of Peace Democrats talked of letting the Confederacy go, in effect conceding victory to the South.

Called Copperheads by their enemies, the Peace Democrats were especially numerous among Catholic immigrants in the urban centers and among the southerners who had settled in the free states of the Midwest before 1860. Ideologically they were opponents of the centralizing tendencies of the Republicans and of the new powers of the federal government. Men such as Clement Vallandigham, S.S. Cox, George Pendleton, and Daniel Voorhees regarded the Lincoln administration as the agent of "revived Whiggery." They, along with most other Democrats, also denounced the administration's efforts to make slavery's abolition a part of the Union cause and to abridge freedom of speech and of press. They were dissenters as well against the cultural values that the Republicans represented. The Lincoln party, they held, was the embodiment of moralistic New England puritanism. Congressman Cox blamed the war on the New England "tendency to make government a moral reform association."

The Copperheads were not the only opponents of administration policies. In the slave states that remained in the Union—Delaware, Maryland, Kentucky, and Missouri—anti-Union sentiment was often intense. During the war several border states became battlegrounds between pro-Union and pro-Confederate groups. Neighbor fought neighbor with a viciousness that sometimes went beyond anything found on the battlefields. In Missouri full-scale guerrilla war broke out between Union and Confederate sympathizers. The state soon resembled "Bleeding Kansas" during the 1850s as roving bands of irregulars attacked innocent—and not-so-innocent—citizens of the opposite persuasion. In suppressing the disorders in Missouri and elsewhere in the border region, Union commanders frequently alienated the prosouthern populace and stirred up even greater dissatisfaction.

Inevitably, Lincoln had to consider how much dissent was permissible in a nation threatened with dissolution. The president was strongly committed to free speech. But his first responsibility, he felt, was to preserve the Union.

To head off his opponents and those he considered dangerous to the Union cause, Lincoln employed a combination of guile, persuasion, and coercion. Within his own party he had to contend with the Radicals, Republicans who fervently opposed slavery and believed that the president was not moving fast enough or firmly enough against the South. They particularly deplored his unwillingness to use the war as an opportunity to destroy slavery and his reluctance to employ blacks in the armed forces. Republican conservatives pulled the other way, saying that the war to restore the Union must not be "abolitionized." To attack slavery would only drive the border states out and confirm southern determination to resist. Lincoln dealt with the opposing wings of his party, as he explained at one point, by carrying "a pumpkin in each end of the bag." In his cabinet this meant balancing Seward against Chase and seeing to it that neither prevailed. In Congress this meant listening to all Republican voices, keeping his options open, and moving only when it helped the Union cause.

Dealing with dissenters outside the party was more difficult. The remaining Democrats in Congress were often a thorn in the president's side. Historians James A. Rawley and Eric McKitrick have suggested that the presence of a functioning two-party system in the Union during the war was a significant northern advantage over the South. It kept opposition to the administration within the bounds of party

The war experience transformed a people accustomed to improvising into a disciplined nation concerned with planning and control. Volunteer nursing and individual acts of kindness yielded to the large, impersonal United States Sanitary Commission staffed by paid workers.

conflict, they say, and prevented it from becoming destructive and irresponsible. In the South, on the other hand, attacks on the Davis administration quickly turned into destructive personal assaults on the president, which seriously undermined his authority. Their observations, however valid, are hindsight. To Lincoln, Democratic opposition at times seemed indistinguishable from disloyalty, and it was hard for him to resist wielding his authority as commander in chief to suppress his critics.

Civil Liberties During Crisis. Lincoln's first response to the dangers of disloyalty came in mid-1861 when, in several districts of the country, he suspended the writ of *habeas corpus*, a fundamental protection against unlawful legal imprisonment. In September 1862 he expanded the area in which the suspension applied and authorized the arrest by military commanders of all "Rebels and Insurgents, their aiders and abettors within the United States, and all persons discouraging volunteer enlistments, resisting militia drafts, or guilty of any disloyal practice." All told, the Union government arrested about 15,000 civilians during the war for disloyal activities, espionage, sabotage, or some other action detrimental to the Union cause. A number of times it also interfered with freedom of the press by excluding "disloyal" papers from the mail and on a few occasions shut down papers accused of hurting the Union cause. None of this was admirable behavior for a democratic government. Yet, all told, given the serious danger to the nation's survival, the government and the military used moderation in suppressing dissent.

The most famous, or infamous, breech of civil liberties by the Lincoln administration involved Clement Vallandigham. In May 1863 the former congressman, campaigning for the Democratic nomination for governor of Ohio, deliberately provoked the administration by denouncing the war as a failure, demanding repudiation of the Emancipation Proclamation, and calling for a negotiated peace with the Confederacy. General Burnside, then military commander in Ohio, promptly arrested Vallandigham and a military commission sentenced him to prison for the duration of the war.

The affair embarrassed Lincoln. The Ohioan was a prominent Democratic leader, and the arrest made the administration seem despotic while at the same time converting the ex-congressman into a free-speech martyr. On the other hand, the president did not see how he could ignore those people who threatened Union survival. "Must I shoot a simple minded soldier boy who deserts," he wrote a group of Democrats who protested the Vallandigham arrest, "while I must not touch the hair of a wily agitator who induces him to desert?" Lincoln solved the problem by banishing the Ohio Democrat to the Confederacy. Vallandigham soon escaped to Canada and resumed his campaign for governor long-distance. But he was no longer an embarrassment to the administration.

The Emancipation Proclamation. The Lincoln administration's willingness to invade civil liberties and limit the rights of free speech are still further instances of war-inflated government power. Fortunately, the repressive policy proved a temporary lapse that did not outlast the war. But in another area, race relations, the use of government war powers worked a profound, permanent, and beneficent change.

Lincoln and the Radicals differed on the question of slavery. As part of a Union-first policy, the president initially tried to steer clear of the issue. As long as there was any danger that the border slave states might still join the South, Lincoln believed that he must focus the public mind on reuniting the nation rather than on ending the peculiar institution. When General John Frémont, the former Republican presidential candidate, proclaimed in late 1861 that all slaves held by rebels within his Missouri command were free, Lincoln overruled him. The president also refused to use a feature of the Second Confiscation Act of 1861 that provided that captured slaves employed by the Confederacy against the Union be freed. When Horace Greeley publicly criticized him for his inaction against slavery, Lincoln replied that his "paramount object" in the struggle was "to save the Union, . . . not either to save or destroy slavery."

But Lincoln and the Radicals were not free agents: Both were at the mercy of circumstances. Blacks were not pas-

sive observers of emancipation. In the North black abolitionists joined their white colleagues in asserting that the war was a struggle over slavery and that to win it the Union must destroy the hateful institution. Slavery, Frederick Douglass proclaimed, was "a tower of strength" to the Confederacy. "The very stomach of this rebellion is the negro in the condition of a slave. Arrest that hoe in the hands of the negro and you smite the rebellion in the very seat of its life."

Even more compelling than the words of northern blacks were the deeds of southern blacks. Despite the absence from the farms and plantations of thousands of young white men, the black population of the South did not seize the opportunity to rebel and liberate itself. Generally, slaves continued to work at their accustomed tasks: They did indeed serve as "the very stomach" of the rebellion.

The slaves failed to rebel because they saw that resistance in the heavily armed and militarized wartime South would have been suicidal. This did not mean that they acquiesced, however. When Union armies drew near, the odds changed dramatically, and blacks showed their real feelings. According to the outraged *Richmond Enquirer*, one black coachman, when told by federal troops in 1862 that he was free, "went straight to his master's chamber, dressed himself in his best clothes, put on his best watch and chain, took his [walking] stick, and returning to the parlor where his master was, insolently informed him that he might for the future drive his own coach."

Black men and women generally voted against slavery with their feet. As Union armies advanced into the Confederacy, black refugees flocked to their lines. At first Union officials did not know what to do with these homeless and destitute people. The government initially had no clear legal mandate to free them. Slavery was still legal and they were still the property of white owners. General Benjamin F. Butler shrewdly called them "contraband of war" and paid them to work as free laborers on military fortifications. Other military commanders, following Butler's lead, employed thousands of "contrabands" at military jobs. Other refugees were set to work growing cotton for northern mills or took jobs with private employers for money wages. Long before the end of the war a substantial part of the South's slaves had, in effect, liberated themselves from bondage.

More than self-liberation was required to demolish the pernicious institution, however: The country needed a national policy. Lincoln originally hoped that compensated emancipation and colonization in either Africa or Central America would finish slavery. At one point he pushed a measure through Congress appropriating a half million dollars to settle freed slaves on an island off Haiti. But blacks were hostile to colonization, and in the border states slave-

Lincoln on Slavery

Lincoln despised slavery, but he loved the Union even more. For months following Fort Sumter his primary concern, perforce, was to keep more states from joining the Confederacy and to bring back into the Union, by force if necessary, those that had left. Slavery could wait. Other Americans—the abolitionists and other strong antislavery people—reversed the priorities. On August 19, 1862, Horace Greeley, the editor of the prominent antislavery newspaper the *New York Tribune*, published an editorial, "The Prayer of 20,000,000 People," demanding that the president attack slavery head on, without worrying about the political consequences. Lincoln replied in the letter below three days later. It is the statement of a man with little doubt about where his first loyalty lay, and suggests to what extent the abolition of the "peculiar institution" was a by-product of the war.

"Executive Mansion. Washington
      "August 22, 1862
"Hon. Horace Greeley.

Dear Sir: I have just read yours of the 19th, addressed to myself though the New York *Tribune*. If there be in it any statements or assumptions of fact which I may know to be erroneous, I do not, now and here, controvert them. If there be in it any inferences which I may believe to be falsely drawn, I do not, now and here, argue against them. If there be perceptible in it an impatient and dictatorial tone, I waive it in deference to an old friend whose heart I have always supposed to be right.

"As to the policy I 'seem to be pursuing,' as you say, I have not meant to leave any one in doubt.

"I would save the Union. I would save it the shortest way under the Constitution. The sooner the national authority can be restored, the nearer the Union will be 'the Union as it was.' If there be those who would not save the Union unless they could at the same time save slavery, I do not agree with them. My paramount object in this struggle is to save the Union, and it is not either to save or to destroy slavery. If I could save the Union without

freeing any slave, I would do it; and if I could save it by freeing all the slaves, I would do it; and if I could save it by freeing some and leaving others alone, I would also do that. What I do about slavery and the coloured race, I do because I believe it helps to save the Union; and what I forbear, I forbear because I do not believe it would help save the Union. I shall do less whenever I shall believe what I am doing hurts the cause, and I shall do more whenever I shall believe doing more will help the cause. I shall try to correct errors when shown to be errors, and I shall adopt new views so fast as they shall appear to be true views.

"I have here stated my purpose according to my view of official duty, and I intend no modification of my oft-expressed personal wish that all men everywhere could be free.

Yours, A. Lincoln"

---

holders proved unwilling to consider freeing their slaves even if paid. Lincoln now faced the prospect of simply ending slavery—an institution deeply embedded in American life and representing $4 billion worth of private property—by direct action under the presidential war powers. It was a momentous step to take, and he was reluctant to act.

The hope that the destruction of slavery would shorten the war finally tipped the balance in favor of abolition by federal proclamation. Three considerations worked powerfully on the president. One was Frederick Douglass's point: the reliance of the Confederacy on slave labor. If the blacks of the South knew that the federal government intended to set them free, they would cease to be a source of strength for the Confederacy. Another consideration was the potential value of black soldiers. If the North could tap this human reservoir, it could offset the immense losses on the battlefields and the declining zeal of white volunteers. Multitudes

of slave refugees might join the Union armies if they were offered their freedom in exchange for military service. A final factor was the moral advantage of turning the war for the Union into a war for human freedom. If the Union cause were identified with the destruction of slavery, it would be difficult for any European power to aid the Confederacy.

By July 1862 Lincoln had concluded that a proclamation of emancipation was "absolutely essential for the salvation of the Union." He postponed making his intentions known, however, fearing that if the news came at a time of military difficulties, it would be taken as an act of desperation. On September 22, following Lee's defeat at Antietam, he issued a preliminary emancipation proclamation declaring that on January 1, 1863, in every part of the South then still in rebellion, all slaves would be "thenceforward and forever free." As scheduled, on New Year's Day, 1863, the final Emancipation Proclamation took effect.

Technically, it affected only those places where federal law could not be enforced—the Confederacy. It said nothing about slavery in the border states, and had the Union lost the war, it would have become a symbol of futility. But the Union won, and the proclamation in the end effectively sounded the death knell for slavery all over the United States.

It also affected the Union's standing abroad. Henry Adams, serving as his father's secretary at the American legation in London, wrote home after news of the proclamation reached Britain: "The Emancipation Proclamation has done more for us here than all our former victories and all our diplomacy."

The Home Fronts. Behind the lines the war caused dramatic changes in civilian life. In the South it produced great hardship for virtually every citizen. As prices rose, as transport broke down, as the blockade took effect, southern living standards deteriorated. In Richmond a clerk in the Confederate War Department complained bitterly in 1863 that the inhabitants of the city were "almost in a state of starvation" though there was abundant food in the Confederacy as a whole. In Mobile, food riots, led by women carrying banners reading "Bread or Blood" and "Bread and Peace," broke out in 1863. All through the South tea and coffee, both imported items, became scarce; and southern consumers turned to parched wheat, corn, peanuts, and even acorns as substitutes. When commodities were available, they often sold at prices far beyond the means of the average consumer. Another Confederate War Department official noted in 1863 that his yearly salary of $3,000 would "go about as far as $700 would in 1860. Flour $28 against $4 then, tea $15 against $1.25, bacon $1.25 against 20 cents, and other things in proportion."

As living conditions deteriorated in the South, they improved in the North. "Secession winter" and the first months of the war had been a time of economic uncertainty and

THE RECRUITING QUESTION—A HINT TO RAILCAR COMPANIES.

Fascinating Conductress of City Car (to surprised Passenger)—"Yes! you see my good man has gone to the war, and as the Company continue half his wages, I've come along to earn the other half—hurry up, sir, if you please."

The Civil War created labor shortages in both sections, opening new opportunities to women, especially in the less conservative North. This cartoon, however, expresses a hope more than a reality. Women moved into government work and nursing; few, if any, became "fascinating conductresses" on the street cars.

fear for northern businessmen. But then war orders began to pour in. By 1863 the North as a whole wore an air of bustling prosperity. In the cities the stores were jammed with shoppers, many of them buying silks and expensive imported luxuries from France and England. City theaters were thronged with avid pleasure-seekers. In eastern Pennsylvania the newly opened oil regions experienced a boom comparable only to northern California during the Gold Rush of a decade earlier. On the farms of the West, too, prosperity prevailed. Unprecedented high farm prices stimulated output, and thousands of new prairie acres were plowed up to meet the urgent demands of civilian and military markets. But the wartime economic surge did not benefit all. Wage workers often found that they could buy less with the amount in their pay envelopes than before. Prices rose faster than money wages, reducing the average worker's *real* income by about 20 percent and causing some labor unrest behind northern lines.

Northern women were significant beneficiaries of the war. Before 1861 employment opportunities for women had been strictly limited. With thousands of able-bodied men now in the Union armies, traditional sex barriers weakened. Many women joined the vastly expanded War and Treasury departments as secretaries, copyists, and clerks. In the private sector the number of women factory operatives, schoolteachers, and clerical workers also increased. Unfortunately, unskilled women workers were among those most seriously hurt by rising prices.

One of the most important breakthroughs for women was the creation of a female nursing profession. Florence Nightingale, an Englishwoman, had already proved the competence of women as military nurses during the Crimean War; but men in authority resisted the use of women in Union military hospitals. They did not count on the determination and patriotism of strong-willed women like Clara Barton and Dorothea Dix, who insisted on sharing the work and sacrifices of the war effort.

Though women on both sides organized societies to aid the war effort, only in the North were they carried beyond the local level. The most powerful of these societies was the Women's Central Association of New York City. Organized by Dr. Elizabeth Blackwell, the association eventually founded the American Sanitary Commission in 1861. Through several thousand local ladies' aid societies in the North, the commission organized the diet, cooking, clothing distribution, medical transport, military hospital, medical supply, and relief services for soldiers and their families. Dorothea Dix was appointed superintendent of women nurses for the Union army. Some 10,000 white women served as nurses, receiving $12 a month in the North. About 4,000 black women worked for the Union as practical nurses, cooks, laundresses, and orderlies at $10 a month.

Many of the gains in paid employment for women were temporary. After 1865, as government departments contracted and men returned to civilian life, women were forced back into their drawing rooms or kitchens. But not all the advances were lost. The Civil War did much to establish nursing as a profession for women and to develop formal training and certification in that field. Clara Barton, who founded the American Red Cross twenty years after the Civil War, noted that by the time the war ended, "woman was at least fifty years in advance of the normal position which continued peace . . . would have assigned her."

The land of "chivalry" did not accord women as much opportunity to contribute to the war as the North. The Confederacy, for example, had no central association of women's organizations to coordinate women's participation in the war effort. The South also had no place for women nurses. Yet southern women were able to do their part in fighting the Yankees. They took on clerical and schoolteaching jobs, and even performed field labor on the South's farms to help meet the labor shortage. Legend has it that no one in the South so ardently defended the Confederate cause as "the ladies." The expression is patronizing, but it is nevertheless true that southern women were especially effective in spurring the patriotic ardor and enlistment rates of southern men.

★ THE LAST YEARS OF BATTLE ★

Lee's defeat of Hooker at Chancellorsville in May 1863—though it led to the accidental death of Stonewall Jackson, one of the South's most gifted generals—lifted the spirits of the entire Confederacy. Yet the South's situation, taken as a whole, did not seem encouraging. In the West, Grant was advancing on Vicksburg and would soon place that strategically important Mississippi city under Yankee siege. Along the Atlantic coast the Union was preparing to attack Charleston. All through the Confederacy, prices were soaring; the blockade's noose was growing tighter. Something must be done to prevent the South's collapse.

With some misgivings, the Confederate government decided to adopt Lee's plan to invade the North. This tack might relieve the pressure in the West, skim much-needed supplies from the prosperous northern countryside, encourage the peace forces in the North, and even lead to the capture of Washington or Philadelphia. On June 15 General Robert Ewell's corps, under Lee's overall command, forded the Potomac. The remainder of the Army of Northern Virginia soon joined it and together the combined Confederate force swept across the Mason-Dixon Line into Pennsylvania. As the Confederates advanced they levied tribute on local Yankee storekeepers, farmers, and bankers, and destroyed railroad property and Congressman Thaddeus Stevens's iron works. Lee's advance alarmed the entire Union. Having lost faith in Hooker, Lincoln placed General George G. Meade in command of the Army of the Potomac to face the threat.

Gettysburg. The choice was a good one. Though neither colorful nor aggressive, Meade was competent. Moving north parallel and to the east of Lee he converged on the Confederates at Gettysburg, a small town fifty miles from the Pennsylvania state capital at Harrisburg. Meade's men dug in on ridges both to the south and to the north of town and prepared to repulse the Confederate attack. The 88,000 federals not only outnumbered Lee's 75,000 but also had superior artillery.

The battle was a seesaw affair lasting three full days (July 1–3, 1863). Lee's forces came close to sweeping the federals off their perches several times. The fighting was exceptionally bloody, some of it hand to hand. Union artillery was devastating and so were union rifles. The replacement of the smooth-bore musket by the far more accurate rifle as the standard infantry weapon gave the defense a tremendous advantage. Masses of infantry charging an entrenched enemy were ripped to pieces by the minié balls (lead bullets that expanded to fit the rifled barrel) of the defenders. It was the misfortune of the Confederates that Lee believed in the concept of the offensive-defensive—fighting what was basically a defensive war by aggressive attack on the enemy. In the new era of the rifle this approach produced ferocious casualties. And so it was at Gettysburg. Each brave charge of the gray-clad Confederates was sent hurtling back after fearful carnage.

On the last day of battle the Confederates launched forty-seven regiments, 15,000 men, under General George Pickett against the Union center on ominously named Cemetery Hill. The men in gray advanced across the open field against murderous artillery fire and swept to the top of the Union emplacement. Then, their momentum exhausted, they reeled back, leaving behind several thousand dead and wounded.

Pickett's charge was the last spurt of Confederate strength. Lee expected Meade to counterattack, but the federals were almost as exhausted as the Confederates and sat tight. Seizing this opportunity to disengage safely, Lee ordered a general retreat. Soon he and his ragged army were safely back in Virginia.

Lee's defeat at Gettysburg coincided with Grant's capture of Vicksburg following a long campaign and costly siege. Then, in the fall of 1863, Grant and General George H. Thomas won the battles of Lookout Mountain and Missionary Ridge and finally pushed the Confederates out

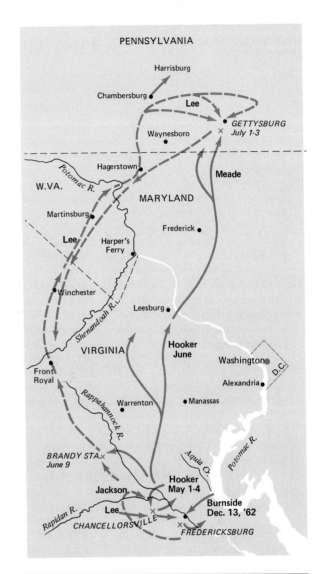

FREDERICKSBURG TO GETTYSBURG, 1862–1863

of ravaged Tennessee. Called to command all the Union forces, Grant came east in March 1864 to take over the Virginia front. In the next months he aimed massive sledgehammer blows at Lee and his lieutenants in the forested country between Washington and Richmond. The gains in ground were negligible, and the losses on both sides were appalling. Yet Grant realized that the attrition was easier for the Union to bear than for the enemy. Southern manpower was by now all but exhausted; the North, though weary, still had human reserves.

"Johnny Reb" and "Billy Yank." Although Gettysburg had been the war's turning point, many dismal months of fighting remained. The chief sufferers toward the end, as in the beginning, were the common soldiers of the Union and

Mary Boykin Chesnut

Mary Boykin Chesnut's fame rests on her Civil War diary. She kept it locked up and out of her husband's sight, but won renown in later years for the journal she worked on in secret. When *Diary from Dixie* was finally published, it was favorably compared to the famous diaries of Cotton Mather and John Quincy Adams.

Mrs. Chesnut's life was that of a privileged southern belle. Her family was prominent in South Carolina. At the time of her birth in March 1823, her father, Stephen Decatur Miller, was a state senator who, five years later, became governor and then United States senator. Mary was a precocious, intelligent child who responded to the politically active environment around her. In a letter written before her ninth birthday she told her father she was looking forward to reading his Senate speech on the tariff.

In 1833 Miller resigned his Senate seat and moved with his family to his cotton plantation in Mississippi. When Mary was twelve, she was sent back to Charleston to acquire a "finishing school" education at Madame Talvande's French School for Young Ladies. In addition to the "accomplishments" expected of every well-bred antebellum southern woman, she learned history, rhetoric, natural sciences, literature, and German, and became particularly fluent in French. She was an excellent student and a popular classmate, as well as a boisterous social leader who occasionally had to pay the price for her pranks. Her training at Madame Talvande's resulted in a life-long attraction to intellectual pursuits and literary conversation, and a love of music, novels, the theater, and French culture.

Charleston, one of America's most gracious cities, became the scene of Mary's lifetime love affair. When she was a thirteen-year-old schoolgirl, she went for moonlight strolls on the Battery, the walk skirting the harbor, with James Chesnut, Jr., of Mulberry° Plantation, a twenty-one-year-old Princeton graduate. Mary was brought back to Mississippi to cool her romance, but her parents soon returned her to Madame Talvande's to finish her education. Following her father's death in 1838, she became formally engaged to Chesnut. Soon after, her fiancé went to Europe to study and travel. He wrote Mary from Paris that he would try to "become worthy of the girl I love and honor." He had "no hopes that stir my soul, no visions bright . . . which amuse my fancy that are not colored with thoughts of you. . . ."

On June 23, 1840, when Mary was seventeen and Chesnut twenty-five, they married and went to live at Mulberry Plantation, where her husband's parents, a couple in their mid-sixties, still lived. Although Mary assumed she would soon become mistress of Mulberry, her in-laws, both physically and mentally energetic, lived into their eighties and continued to direct the operations of house and lands. While his parents ran the plantation, James practiced law in neighboring Camden and served in the state legislature as representative, senator, and president until 1858, when, like his father-in-law, he was elected to the United States Senate.

During these years, with her in-laws in charge of her home, her husband involved in politics, and unable to have children, Mary often felt rest-less and useless. She occupied her time by reading, taking care of her young nieces and nephews, and visiting Charleston, Columbia, and the northern spas at Saratoga and Newport. She also acted as her husband's hostess and secretary and maintained her interest in politics. In 1845 she persuaded James to take her to London on a literary pilgrimage to the homes of Dickens and Thackeray, hoping that the sea journey would help her health and the mental stimulation of travel would lift her spirits. But these activities did not really fill the time or energies of this bright, vivacious woman, and her years at Mulberry Plantation were troubled by depression and poor health.

Her husband's election to the United States Senate in 1858 provided Mary with the opportunity to live in Washington. She was extremely happy during these next two years. She made friends easily with both the politicians and their wives, and charmed everyone she met with her intelligence, sense of humor, and conversational skill. She was soon invited to all the capital's important social functions and became a close friend of Varina Davis, wife of Jefferson Davis, the distinguished senator from Mississippi.

Her Washington years came to an end, however, after Lincoln's election in 1860. James resigned from the Senate to help draft the South Carolina Ordinance of Secession and organize the Southern Confederacy. In 1861 Mary accompanied her husband to Montgomery, Alabama, seat of the new Confederate government, and ran a lively salon where the men politicked and planned the strategy of the new nation, and their wives, excluded from such weighty matters, gossiped and intrigued.

Mary began her diary at this time. She was in Charleston in April 1861 when Fort Sumter was attacked, and watched the proceedings from a rooftop. In her original account she wrote: "At half past four we heard the booming of the cannon—I started up—dress & rush to my sisters in misery—we go on the housetop & see the shells bursting. . . ." When the smoke had cleared hours later, the Union had surrendered the fort to the Confederates and it was revealed, to Mary's relief, that no lives had been lost. Mary joined the celebration of the victory.

The Chesnuts returned to Montgomery for the second session of the Provisional Confederate Congress and in June 1861 went to Richmond, the new Confederate capital. Dreading to return to isolated Mulberry where her tyrannical father-in-law still presided, Mary hoped her husband would be appointed minister to France when he lost his bid for reelection to the Confederate Senate. No such foreign appointment saved her, and she was forced to spend a half year in Camden, where she frequently complained in her diary of her husband's lack of interest in the war. "If I had been a man in this great revolution—I should have either been killed at once or made a name & done some good for my country. Lord Nelson's motto would be mine—Victory or Westminster Abbey."

She was rescued from the plantation in January 1862 when her husband accepted the chairmanship of the South Carolina Executive Council in Columbia. In the fall Chesnut became an aide to Jefferson Davis, a position that brought the couple back to

Richmond. In the Confederate capital Mary involved herself in both serious and frivolous things. The Chesnut's quarters at the Arlington Hotel was the scene of dinners, parties, and amateur theatricals. They had frequent house guests, including family and friends from all over the South. The Chesnuts and the Davises were devoted friends and visited each other constantly. Mary and her circle often chatted about personal affairs as well as news of the war and sometimes enjoyed a touch of scandal. "We discussed," read a diary entry for June 1862, "clever women who help their husbands politically. . . . These lady politicians—if they are young and pretty—always get themselves a 'little bit' talked about."

Behind the lively and gracious social screen, however, were more somber thoughts. Mary's diary for these war years reveals her underlying despair at the numbers of brave young men killed or maimed, the beautiful plantations destroyed, and the growing hardship of life in Richmond as the Yankee noose tightened. As early as March 1862 she would note that her "world, the only world we cared for," was being "kicked to pieces. . . ." In January 1865, with James away on military business, she was frightened. "Yesterday, I broke down—" she admitted, "gave way to abject terror. The news of Sherman's advance—and no news of my husband."

After Appomattox the Chesnuts moved back to Camden, living temporarily in one of her father-in-law's plantation houses that had been spared destruction. Mulberry itself had been sacked by Union soldiers and its cotton burned, but it survived, and was eventually restored. Mary continued her diary until July 1865. During the first months of Reconstruction she was ill with a heart condition and de-

pressed by both the South's defeat and her own isolation. But her natural vivacity reasserted itself and she took over the management of the household, kept financial records, helped oversee the affairs of the plantation and the farm, and ran a butter-and-egg business with her maid, Molly. In 1873 the Chesnuts moved into a new home, Sarsfield, built with bricks from the old kitchen buildings at Mulberry.

During the 1870s and early 1880s, Mary wrote fiction to make additional money. In 1881 she began to work on a book based on her wartime diaries. James became ill in 1884 and Mary took time off to nurse him. He died at the end of the year, and then a week later her mother died as well. James had so many debts that Mary lost most of the land to his creditors, keeping only Sarsfield and a small dairy business. She continued to work on *Diary from Dixie*, but died on November 22, 1886, of a heart attack before the book was published.

Mary Chesnut was a perceptive reporter who vividly documented southern society during the Civil War. She had a sharp eye for the foibles of human nature and a keen understanding of life's contradictions. Her presence in the Confederate capital during the important years of the Civil War and her ability to record her observations of events and personalities make her *Diary from Dixie* an invaluable historical document. It is also a lively personal portrait that reveals Mary Boykin Chesnut as an outstanding woman of her time and, in the words of Lyman Butterfield, editor of the Adams Papers, "a great lady."

the Confederacy. Of the two, "Billy Yank" had the easier time, especially after the North's factories began to operate at high gear. The resources of the Union assured him enough food and clothing to keep the inner and outer man reasonably content. But his life was no picnic. Being a Union soldier involved long periods of hard foot-slogging over rough roads in every sort of weather, days of boredom in bivouac, followed, finally, by terrifying exposure to flying lead and iron. If wounded, his chances for survival were poor. Thousands of the injured died of shock, gangrene, or loss of blood. Many others were swept away by diseases picked up in unsanitary camps or as a result of exposure and exhaustion.

"Johnny Reb" experienced all these afflictions and several others besides. The southern soldier often lacked adequate shoes, clothing, and food. Despite Confederate ingenuity in manufacture and supply, much of his equipment, including his rifle and ammunition, was captured from the Yankees. There was seldom enough to go around.

The men of both armies had their good moments. Many lifelong friendships were forged in the heat of battle. But however warmly veterans later recalled their fighting days, soldiering was not an occupation that many men cared to stay at indefinitely, and in both armies the desertion rates were stupendous. In all, 200,000 Union men and 104,000 Confederates deserted, almost 10 percent of all Yankees and 13 percent of all "Rebs."

Black Soldiers. One source of northern strength denied the South was the manpower of black Americans. Partisans of black equality strongly favored the use of black troops. As Frederick Douglass declared: "Once let the black man get upon his person the brass letters, U.S.; let him get an eagle on his button, and a musket on his shoulder, and bullets in his pocket, and there is no power on earth which can deny that he has earned the right to citizenship." But opposition to the use of black soldiers and sailors was formidable. Many white Americans were immovable bigots who feared the very consequences that Douglass prized. In February 1863 forty-three Democratic congressmen signed a statement condemning Republican plans to enlist black soldiers as a plot to establish "the equality of the black and white races."

As it became more and more difficult to fill the depleted ranks of the Union Army, however, much of the opposition faded. Why not share the burden of dying for the Union with one of the chief beneficiaries of the war, many whites began to ask. By early 1863, with Lincoln's enthusi-

The Civil War has been called "the war of brothers." On rare occasions brothers did fight on opposing sides. More common was the situation depicted here: The Union officer on the right is George A. Custer, of later Indian-fighting fame; the other man is a Confederate prisoner, James Washington, who was Custer's classmate at West Point.

astic support, the War Department began to authorize the creation of black regiments composed of northern free blacks and, in larger numbers, ex-slaves freed by the Emancipation Proclamation. At first the Confederate government had threatened that any captured member of a black regiment, whether white officer or black private, would be severely punished. But when Lincoln threatened to retaliate against captured Confederates, the Richmond government backtracked.

These troops fought magnificently in many battles. Placed almost invariably under white officers and treated initially as second-class troops in matters of pay, bounties for service, and other benefits, black soldiers nevertheless established a record for bravery and enterprise equal to any group in the Union army. In March 1863 Lincoln called black troops "very important, if not indispensable" to the Union war effort. By the end of the fighting the Union armed forces had enrolled 179,000 black soldiers and another 20,000 black sailors.

The valor of foreign-born and black troops had favorable effects on ethnic and racial attitudes in the North. Antiforeign sentiment declined. Racial bigotry continued, but the legal and social positions of northern blacks improved. Midwestern legislatures repealed state laws discriminating against free blacks or denying them the right to reside within state borders. Several cities ended the common practice of segregating blacks on streetcars and in schools. America scarcely became a racial paradise, but the shining record of black troops fighting for the Union made many white citizens reconsider their prejudices.

The Election of 1864. The lessening of ethnic conflict was not matched by a decline in political strife. Eighteen sixty-four was a presidential election year and nobody suggested passing over the campaign in the interest of national harmony. At Baltimore the Republicans renominated Lincoln and chose Andrew Johnson, the Tennessee Unionist Democrat, as his running mate. Johnson's selection was intended to reach out to non-Republicans, and to reinforce this strategy the delegates renamed their party the National Union Party. The Democrats turned to General McClellan as their presidential candidate. McClellan was a war Democrat, but his running mate, George Pendleton of Ohio, supported a negotiated peace with the South as did the

Black Union troops, the Fifty-fifth Massachusetts Regiment, enter Richmond in 1865, at the war's close. Richmond's black residents, at least, appear happy.

Democratic platform. During the campaign the Republicans charged their opponents with disloyalty, and they were not completely wrong. The Richmond government yearned for Democratic victory, and southern agents secretly poured money into the campaigns of midwestern Democrats. For a time the Democrats believed they could ride to victory on the wave of discouraging northern defeats during the late spring—the Wilderness, Spotsylvania, Petersburg, and the Crater. Lincoln himself was pessimistic and thought it "exceedingly probable that this Administration will not be re-elected."

But then the military picture abruptly changed. In early May a Union army of 100,000 men led by William T. Sherman cut south from Tennessee and advanced on Atlanta, Georgia, a major rail junction and manufacturing center. Through much of July and all of August Sherman halted before the city while he and his Confederate foe, John B. Hood, maneuvered for advantage. Then on September 2, Union troops marched into the city. Sherman telegraphed the president: "Atlanta is ours, and fairly won." And there were other Union victories to cheer the Republicans and bolster their campaign. On August 23 the Union navy under admiral David G. Farragut captured Mobile Bay, shutting down a major port for Confederate blockade runners. In the Shenandoah Valley of Virginia, the Union cavalry commander, Philip Sheridan, won a smashing victory against Jubal Early's troops in late September. These victories were reflected in the polls. In September the voters of Maine and Vermont, which then held early elections, gave Lincoln solid majorities. On November 8 the Lincoln-Johnson ticket swept the electoral college by 212 to 21 and won a popular majority over McClellan of 400,000 votes. An important part of the Republican total was the soldier vote. Eighteen states made provision for men in the field to cast absentee ballots. They went overwhelmingly for the party of the Union.

Last Battles, the Last Casualty. The months following the election saw the rapid collapse of southern hopes. On November 15 Sherman and his veteran army left Atlanta heading east for Savannah on the Atlantic coast. Before departing the city, the general ordered everything of military worth burned. The flames got out of control, and a third of Atlanta went up in smoke.

Sherman's "march to the sea" was considered foolhardy by many military experts. He was cutting himself off from his supply bases and moving through the heart of enemy country. It could spell disaster. Sherman believed he could survive, living off the country while cutting a swath of destruction through the heart of Dixie. The general had a theory of warfare that, alas, would see much application in our own day. Winning wars, he believed, was not merely a matter of winning battles and killing enemy soldiers. It was also instilling fear into the enemy people and destroying their

SHERMAN'S MARCH TO THE SEA, 1864

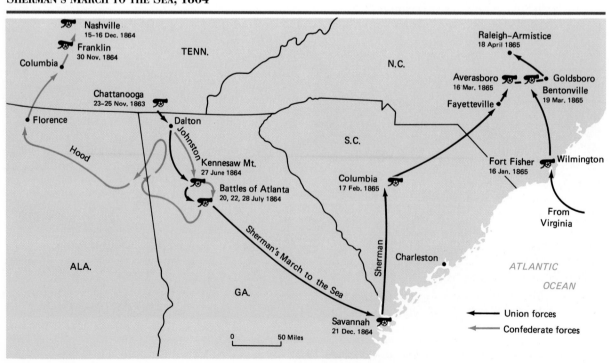

morale. Fortunately, in 1864–1865, this did not mean brutal extermination of civilians. But it did mean massive destruction of property. Sherman's men demolished everything in a fifty-mile belt on either side of their march. One of their favorite targets was southern railroads. Yankee foragers ("bummers") would rip up the iron rails and, over a bonfire of wooden ties, heat them until red hot. Then, while they were soft, they would twist the rails around trees. The men in blue also destroyed fences, crops, and farm houses. Another Yankee target was slavery. Union troops marching to Savannah liberated every black in sight. Before long Sherman's troops were being trailed by a column of thousands of liberated slaves, the able-bodied and lame, the young and old, men and women.

On December 22 Sherman reached Savannah and turned north, heading for a rendezvous with Grant and the Army of the Potomac. Through South Carolina he continued to apply his "total war" tactics. One result was the destruction by fire of Columbia, the capital of the state. In the West, meanwhile, General George Thomas had smashed Hood's army at Nashville. Grant, too, was finally able to achieve the breakthrough he had long sought. During the early weeks of 1865 Grant pressed hard against Lee in Virginia. In early April, with the help of Sheridan's cavalry, he took the important center of Petersburg, which had eluded him for many months. Lee and his army slipped away, but by now southern morale had virtually collapsed. President Davis tried to end talk of surrender by adopting a strict conspiracy law. He also proposed to recruit black troops to shore up the faltering Confederate cause. These men and their families would be promised their freedom in exchange for risking their lives. The Confederate Congress passed a bill to recruit black soldiers but failed to stipulate that they would become free. It is doubtful if black men would have fought for the Confederacy under these terms, but the issue was moot. On April 2 Confederate officials began to flee Richmond to avoid capture by Grant's army. The following day, with the city burning, the Yankees arrived in the Confederate capital. The first blue-clad troops to enter were the men of the all-black Fifth Massachusetts Cavalry.

On April 7 Lee—his army hungry, demoralized, and encircled—asked Grant for terms. On Sunday, two days later, the two commanders met at the crossroads hamlet of Appomattox Court House and agreed on surrender terms. Grant was generous. The Confederate officers and men were to be released on their promise not to take up arms again. The Confederates would surrender all weapons and war material, but the men might keep their personal equipment, including their horses and mules. These, Grant said, they would need to help them "work their little farms." The brief ceremony over, 26,000 Confederates laid down their arms.

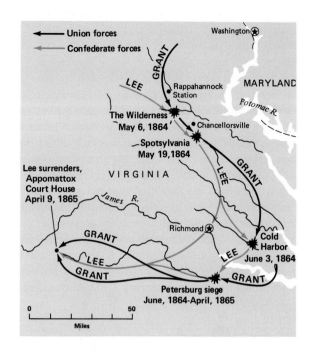

APPOMATTOX, 1865

Lincoln came to the Confederate capital in early April to view the prize for four years's outlay of Union blood and treasure. In the next few days his mind ran much to the problems of political reconstruction, and after his return to Washington he made a major address on the subject. On April 14, 1865, the happy though tired chief executive went with his wife, Mary, and some friends to the theater to see the British comedy *Our American Cousin*. During the third act a dark-haired man entered the presidential box, fired a single shot at Lincoln, and leaped to the stage. Amid the confusion and the shrieks, he shouted something that sounded like "*Sic Semper Tyrannis*" ("Thus always to tyrants"), the Virginia state motto, and escaped. Early the next morning Abraham Lincoln died.

The assassin was John Wilkes Booth, an actor and Confederate sympathizer who, with a few other disgruntled southerners, had concocted a plot to destroy the man they held responsible for Confederate defeat. The plotters also intended to assassinate Seward, Vice President Johnson, and other high Union officials. Booth was cornered in Virginia on April 26 and either shot himself or was shot by a zealous Union soldier. He died before disclosing the full conspiracy; false rumors of complicity by Secretary Stanton or the Confederate leaders soon gained wide circulation.

★ CONCLUSIONS ★

The war was over; but was an era also over? How much difference would the war make in American life? Obviously it ended for all time the threat of national dismemberment through internal forces. Never again, not even during the most severe national crises, would any part of the United States threaten to secede. The war did not transform the United States from an agricultural to an industrial society. That process was already under way before 1860 and would not be completed until well after 1865. Meanwhile, the events of 1861–1865 did fuse the country into a more coherent social and economic whole. It made possible a transcontinental railroad and created a national banking system and a new national currency. It trained thousands of men to manage large-scale operations and mass movements of people and goods—talents that when applied to private enterprise would help to create modern "big business" and further integrate the country. Though it took years beyond 1865 for the full effects to work themselves out, the war also helped to universalize the commercial values of the Northeast. The South would be slow to embrace the new ethos, but for good or ill the rest of the country would find Yankee enterprise and "get-ahead" more acceptable after 1865 than before. Even the intellectuals who had been emphatically critical before 1860 found liberal capitalist society more palatable after the experience of 1861–1865.

Finally, the war destroyed slavery. It did not end problems between blacks and whites; they are still with us today. But it did sweep away an institution that rigidly prescribed the relations of the races and replaced it with alternatives that, however, imperfect, permitted eventual reform and improvement.

★★★★★★★★ FOR FURTHER READING ★★★★★★★★

David H. Donald (ed.). *Why the North Won the Civil War* (1960)
Five historians discuss the social and institutional structure of the Confederacy, the war-making potentials of North and South, northern political parties, military affairs, and Civil War diplomacy.

Benjamin P. Thomas. *Abraham Lincoln* (1952)
Still the best one-volume life of Lincoln. Catches the man as well as the political leader. Although critical where necessary, Thomas admires Lincoln deeply, and successfully conveys to the reader the reasons for his admiration.

Richard N. Current. *The Lincoln Nobody Knows* (1958)
Lincoln has meant many things to many people: Both the abolitionist William Lloyd Garrison and the conservative Mississippi Senator James K. Vardaman claimed him as their own. What was he really like? Current discusses Lincoln's domestic life, religious view, and political goals.

Clement Eaton. *Jefferson Davis* (1977)
This is the best recent biography of the Confederate president. Written by a southern scholar, it is objective and fair. Eaton sees Davis's failure as a Confederate leader as the result of inflexibility.

Bruce Catton. *Mr. Lincoln's Army* (1951); *Glory Road* (1952); and *A Stillness at Appomattox* (1956)
This trilogy is military history at its popular best. Catton captures the sights, sounds, and smells of battle, besides telling us what went on in the minds of the military commanders. The view is from the Yankee side of the line.

T. Harry Williams. *Lincoln and His Generals* (1952)
Lincoln was more than the civilian head of government. He was also commander in chief of all the Union's military forces. Williams's book deals with Lincoln "as a director of war and his place in the high command and his influence in developing a modern command system for this nation."

Adrian Cook. *The Armies of the Streets* (1974)
Spiraling inflation, racial and class resentments, and opposition to the new Union draft brought four days of looting, burning, and lynching of blacks to New York in July 1863. Cook's account of the New York draft riots makes good reading.

George M. Frederickson. *The Inner Civil War* (1965)
The war effected a transformation of northern intellectual life, according to Frederickson. Reformers rejected their anti-institutional, individualistic attitudes as "feeble sentimentalities" and came to favor an uncritical nationalism. After the war they were indifferent to social reform.

Frank L. Klement. *The Copperheads in the Middle West* (1960)
This study treats the Copperheads as the forerunners of Gilded Age agrarian dissenters. Their quarrel with Lincoln and the Republicans, Klement says, was as much over Republican policies favoring business and industry as over slavery and vigorous prosecution of the war.

Margaret K. Leech. *Reveille in Washington, 1860–1865* (1941)
A panorama of life, society, and politics in wartime Washington. Leech writes of high society, southern women prisoners, saloons, hospitals, the Lincoln family, Clara Barton, the famous detective Allan Pinkerton, the look of the capital's streets in wartime—and much else.

Bell I. Wiley. *The Life of Johnny Reb: The Common Soldier of the Confederacy* (1943); and *The Life of Billy Yank: The Common Soldier of the Union* (1952)

Until Wiley wrote these two composite biographies of Confederate and Union soldiers, most published accounts of the Civil War concerned high military officers and grand strategy. Drawn from ordinary enlisted men's letters, diaries, and other records, these are vivid, down-to-earth accounts of the amusements and inconveniences of camp life and the brutal experience of battle as it appeared to the ordinary soldier.

Benjamin Quarles. *The Negro and the Civil War* (1953)

According to Quarles, the real and lasting significance of the black Civil War experience was "the momentum it gave to the ideals of freedom and the dignity of man." The book deals with black Americans in both North and South, and with black soldiers as well as black civilians. Shows black Americans as active on behalf of their own freedom.

Emory M. Thomas. *The Confederate Nation, 1861–1865* (1979)

This study of the Confederacy claims that if the South had won its independence, it would have been as thoroughly transformed by the wartime experience as the North.

Martin Duberman. *Charles Francis Adams, 1807–1886* (1960)

An exemplary biography of a moderate antislavery leader, son of the sixth president, who became United States minister to England during the Civil War and Lincoln's most important diplomatic representative abroad during the years of Union crisis.

MacKinlay Kantor. *Andersonville* (1955)

This historical novel is about the infamous Confederate prison near Americus, Georgia, where almost 13,000 Union soldiers died in the last months of the war. Kantor is at his best in his compassionate portrayal of the perverse commandant, Henry Wirz, the only Confederate official executed at the war's end.

James McPherson. *Battle Cry of Freedom* (1988)

Each generation feels the need to retell the epic of the Civil War. This is the best of the recent crop.

Ralph Andreano (ed.). *The Economic Impact of the American Civil War* (1959)

A collection of articles on the subject of the Civil War as an accelerator of economic growth.

16 ★

RECONSTRUCTION

What Went Wrong?

1863	Lincoln announces his "ten-percent plan" for reconstruction
1863–65	Arkansas and Louisiana accept Lincoln's conditions but Congress does not readmit them to the Union
1864	Lincoln vetoes Congress's Wade-Davis Reconstruction Bill
1865	Johnson succeeds Lincoln • The Freedmen's Bureau is overrides Johnson's veto of the Civil Rights Act • Johnson announces his Reconstruction plan • All-white southern legislatures begin to pass "Black Codes" • The Thirteenth Amendment
1866	Congress adopts the Fourteenth Amendment, but it is not ratified until 1868 • The Ku Klux Klan is formed • Tennessee is readmitted to the Union
1867	Congress passes the first of four Reconstruction Acts • Tenure of Office Act • Johnson suspends Secretary of War Edwin Stanton
1868	Johnson is impeached by the House and acquitted in the Senate • Arkansas, North Carolina, South Carolina, Alabama, Florida, and Louisiana are readmitted to the Union • Ulysses S. Grant elected president
1869	Woman suffrage associations are organized in response to women's disappointment with the Fourteenth Amendment
1870	Virginia, Mississippi, Texas, and Georgia are readmitted to the Union
1870, 1871	Congress passes Force Bills
1875	Blacks are guaranteed access to public places by Congress • Mississippi "redeemers" successfully oust black and white Republican officeholders
1876	Presidential election between Rutherford B. Hayes and Samuel J. Tilden
1877	Compromise of 1877: Hayes is chosen as president, and all remaining federal troops are withdrawn from the South
By 1880	The share-crop system of agriculture is well established in the South

Almost no one has had anything good to say about Reconstruction, the process by which the South was restored to the Union. Contemporaries judged it a colossal failure. To most southern whites Reconstruction was a time when Dixie was subjected to a cruel northern occupation and civilization itself was submerged under an avalanche of black barbarism. For the ex-slaves—or freedmen, as they were called—the period of 1865–1877 started with the bright promise of true freedom and prosperity, but ended in bitter disappointment with most blacks still on the bottom rung of southern society. Contemporary northerners, too, generally deplored these years. They had thought that Reconstruction would change the South. But it had not, and most of them were relieved when the last federal troops withdrew in 1877 and the white South once more governed itself.

Later Americans have not generally thought well of Reconstruction either. From the 1890s to the 1940s most historians assumed that the Republicans who controlled Washington and the southern state capitals after the Civil War were moved primarily by the desire for revenge. Liberal scholars of the following generation rejected this view, but they believed the chance to modernize and liberalize southern society had been missed because the North had neither will nor conviction sufficient to take the bold steps needed. Recently some younger historians have declared that by failing to provide land and power to the freedmen, the Reconstruction process nullified much of the advantage of emancipation. In this view, the North sold out the black people, leaving them little better off than before the Civil War.

Obviously, then, from almost every point of view, Reconstruction has seemed a failure. What went wrong? And was it as bad as most critics have believed?

★ THE LEGACY OF WAR ★

A month or so after Appomattox, Whitelaw Reid, a correspondent for the Republican *Cincinnati Gazette*, went south to see what the war had done to Dixie. Strongly antisouthern, Reid was inclined to belittle claims of southern distress, but even he was struck by the devastation he encountered. Hanover Junction, near Richmond, Reid reported, "presented little but standing chimneys and the debris of destroyed buildings. Along the [rail]road a pile of smoky brick and mortar seemed a regularly recognized sign of what had once been a depot." Not a train platform or water tank had been left, he wrote, and efforts to get the

road in running order were often the only improvements visible for miles. Young pines covered the old fields of wheat and corn, and the crumbling remains of defense works could be seen everywhere.

Others gave similar descriptions. Wherever northern and southern armies had fought, every manmade object bore the scars. Interior South Carolina, hard hit by General Sherman's army, "looked for many miles like a broad black streak of ruin and desolation." In the Shenandoah Valley of Virginia between Winchester and Harrisonburg, scarcely a horse, pig, chicken, or cow remained alive. Southern cities, too, were devastated. Columbia, capital of South Carolina, was a blackened wasteland with not a store standing in the business district. Atlanta, Richmond, Selma, and other southern towns were also devastated. All told, over $1 billion of the South's physical capital was reduced to ashes or twisted wreckage.

Human losses were appalling. Of the South's white male population of 2.5 million in 1860, a quarter of a million (10 percent) had died of battle wounds or disease. Most of these were young men who represented the region's most vigorous and creative human resource. Of those who survived, some were maimed; many were worn out emotionally. "A more completely crushed country I have seldom witnessed," a Yankee officer in the federal occupation force wrote the United States attorney general.

The South's economic institutions were also wrecked. Its banking structure, based on now-worthless Confederate bonds, had collapsed. Personal savings had been wiped out when Confederate currency lost its value. Even more crushing, the region's labor system was in ruins. Slavery as an economic institution—and as a social one—was dead, but no one knew what to replace it with. Many blacks remained on the farms and plantations and continued to plant, cultivate, and harvest. But many others—whether to test their new-found freedom, hunt for long-lost relatives, or just to take their first holiday—wandered the roads or flocked to the cities, abandoning the land on which the South's economy was based.

The physical and institutional destruction of the war was matched by its emotional damage. People in both sections harbored deep resentments. After struggling for independence against the "tyrannical government in Washington" and "northern dominance" for four years, white southerners could not help feeling apprehensive, angry, and deeply disappointed. Now, even more than in 1860, a weak South would be tyrannized by the North, whose arrogance and power were now reinforced by victory and unchecked by any need to compromise. Northerners, for their part, would not easily forget the sac-

Richmond, Virginia, the Confederate capital, being abandoned by the Jefferson Davis government in the last days of the war.

rifices and losses they had suffered in putting down what they considered the illegal and unwarranted rebellion; nor would they easily forgive the "atrocities" committed by the Confederacy. At Andersonville, Georgia, for example, during July 1864, 31,000 Union prisoners had been confined in a sixteen-acre stockade, sheltered only by tents and fed on scanty rations. As many as 3,000 prisoners had died in a month—100 a day. It did not matter that the prisoners' guards received the same rations, that southern prisoners in northern camps were not treated much better, or that bad conditions were made worse by Yankee captives who preyed on their own comrades. To the northern public the Confederate prison officials, and especially the camp commandant, Captain Henry Wirz, were beasts who must be punished. Regarding the South as a whole, John Sherman, an Ohio Republican, spoke for many northerners: "We should not only brand the leading rebels with infamy, but the whole rebellion should wear a badge of the penitentiary, so that for this generation at least, no man who has taken part in it would dare to justify or palliate it."

The American people, then, faced a gigantic task of physical, political, and emotional restoration. By the usual measure, the period of restoration, or Reconstruction, lasted for some twelve years, until 1877. It was a time of upheaval and controversy, as well as new beginnings. In its own day the problems associated with Reconstruction dominated the political and intellectual life of the country, and they have fascinated and repelled Americans ever since.

★ ISSUES AND ATTITUDES ★

It is difficult even today to draw a balanced picture of Reconstruction. Many issues—racial inequality, southern poverty, sectional antipathies and suspicions—are still with us. During Reconstruction people were even more deeply concerned with the role of blacks in the restored nation and the proper relation of the South to the rest of the United States. All agreed that racial and political readjustments were necessary. But how to make them deeply divided the American people, North and South, white and black, Republican and Democrat.

The positions that people took fell roughly into five categories: Radical Republican, northern conservative, southern conservative, southern Unionist, and southern freedmen. Let us allow each of these groups to speak for itself. The monologues that follow are fabricated, but they show what these groups of Americans felt about Reconstruction and wanted to see come out of it. Because they controlled so much of the process, let us start with the Radical Republicans.

Radical Republicans. *"The South must be made to recognize its errors, and southerners must acknowledge that now that they have been defeated, they can no longer decide their own fate. It is now in the hands of the victorious North. Southerners can avoid our anger and show they are prepared to be readmitted as citizens of the United States in a number of ways. At the very least, they must reject their former leaders and choose new ones who have not been connected with the Confederacy. They can take oaths of loyalty to the United States. They can reject all attempts to repay the Confederate debt incurred in an unjust cause. Most important of all, they can accept the fact that the former slaves are now free and must be treated as the political equals of whites.*

"Many former slaves worked and fought for the Union, and we must now help them through the difficult transition to full freedom. As to how this end can best be accomplished, not all of us agree. A few hold that it will be necessary for the freedmen to get land so they can support themselves independently. But we all believe that at the very minimum the freedmen must have the vote and, during the early stages of the change, must be protected against hunger and exploitation. No doubt they will be grateful for the efforts of their Republican friends in defeating the slave power, destroying slavery, and defending them against those who will not accept the new situation. This gratitude will incline them to vote Republican. And that is all to the good. The Republican party is the great hope of the nation. It is the party of freedom and economic progress. It is not afraid to use government to encourage that progress. In a word, it is the party that has, since its founding, proved that it is the best embodiment of both the nation's moral and practical sense."

Northern Conservatives. *"We, the northern conservatives, are generally of the old Democratic persuasion. Most of us opposed secession and supported the war. But we agree that now that the war is over and secession defeated, we must forget the past. Let southerners—white southerners, that is—determine their own fate. It is in the best American tradition to let local communities decide their own future without undue interference from the national government. Let us confirm this great principle of local self-determination, and let us allow the South back into the Union on its own terms.*

"We must not try to force black suffrage or social equality down the throats of the former Confederates. Almost all white Americans believe that Negroes are ill-equipped to exercise the

rights of citizens. The Radicals insist on giving them the vote only because they want to secure continued control of the national government. They want to guarantee the predominance of the values and goals of the Northeast, the nation's commercial-industrial region, against the very different interests and goals of the country's agricultural West and South. It is clearly hypocritical of the supposed champions of the freedmen to be so timid in supporting Negro suffrage in the northern states, where such a stand is politically unpopular and where there are too few Negroes to add to their voting strength. We must reject such hypocrisy and restore peace and tranquillity to the nation as quickly and completely as possible."

Southern Conservatives. *"The war we fought and lost was for a noble cause, and it brought out the best in our southern people. We must never forget the sacrifice and heroism of the gallant men in gray. Perhaps secession was a mistake, but that fact will never diminish the grandeur of our struggle.*

"But let us now get back to the business of daily living. We of the South must be allowed to resume our traditional political relations with the rest of the states. We must be free to determine our own fate with a minimum of conditions. Above all, we must be permitted to steer our own course on race relations. The 'carpetbaggers' who come down from the North looking for easy money, and the southern renegade 'scalawags' willing to betray their own people for the sake of power, are self-serving and contemptible. They do not understand or accept southern traditions.

"True, we must recognize that Negroes are no longer slaves and we must make certain concessions to their private rights, but in the public realm these must be limited by their capacities. Above all, Negroes must not be allowed to exercise political power. They are not the equal of whites. They are ignorant, lazy, improvident, and intellectually inferior. They can be duped and deceived by their professed 'friends' into supporting the Republican party, but actually their interests will be best served by those who have always been the leaders of southern society and who remain the Negroes' natural protectors. Nature dictates that the freedmen of the South remain in subordination, that they accept their humble economic stations and political inferiority, for that is the only way they can function at all."

Southern Unionists. *"At long last we are free to speak our minds! For four long years we have been persecuted and intimidated by the secessionists. Now that they have been defeated, we deserve recognition and favor. Unfortunately the rebels are still in the majority. They say they have accepted the new circumstances of the South, but many of them have not, and we are in a vulnerable position. At the very least we must be protected by our northern friends against hostile unreconciled rebels. Moreover, we should be rewarded for our loyalty to the Union with an important place in the new order.*

"We do not all agree about the role of the Negroes in the South's future, but many of us recognize that they are entitled to

equal political rights now that they are free. Given the vote, they will inevitably—and rightly—look to us for leadership. Ex-rebels may call us scalawags and worse; that is to be expected. But we can help transform the South from a sleepy backward region dominated by the former planter class into a bustling, thriving region of farms, factories, and cities."

Southern Freedmen. *"We are now free men and women and must be accorded all the privileges of free people as expressed in the Declaration of Independence. We contributed to Union victory in war and have earned the right to be treated as equals. We are also the largest group in the South truly loyal to the Union. Southern whites, with some exceptions, cannot be trusted. They are unreconciled to defeat, and if the North fails to protect us and guarantee our rights as free men and women, these ex-Confederates will once more seize power and nullify the Union victory. The federal government, then, must continue for an indefinite period to employ a strong hand in the process of southern Reconstruction.*

"We do not expect white southerners to accept us as social equals; but we must have equality before the law and full civil rights, including, of course, the right to vote. We must also have economic independence, which means not only the right to sell our labor in the open market but also the right to our own land. Thousands of the South's best acres, abandoned by disloyal owners during the war, are controlled either by the Freedmen's Bureau or by the army. Giving us this land would enable us to secure our independence and prevent our being kept in permanently subordinate positions. We also deserve access to education. Literacy is an important tool for achieving economic independence. If the cost of a public school system means that southern state taxes must rise, so be it."

Several of these positions overlapped. Radical Republicans and black freedmen, for example, often agreed on measures to guarantee a successful transition. The position of northern conservatives overlapped that of southern conservatives. But it would clearly be difficult to reconcile those people who wanted to return to prewar conditions as quickly as possible and those who hoped to make social transformation a requirement for readmitting the South to the Union. The diversity of opinion boded ill for the effort to bring together the nation's separated halves. In the next dozen years there would be fierce battles between the contending parties, some almost as passionate as the war itself.

★ PRESIDENTIAL RECONSTRUCTION ★

Even before Lee's surrender in 1865 the Union government had been forced to consider the question of reconstruction. As Union troops advanced into the South, the Lincoln ad-ministration confronted the problem of how to govern the conquered territory and subdued people. In 1862 the president appointed military governors for those parts of four Confederate states under federal control. But while military administrators might suffice for a while, they ran counter to the American tradition of civilian rule and could only be considered a temporary resolution of the problem.

Lincoln's Ten-Percent Plan. Lincoln sought to keep in his own hands the process of restoring southern self-rule and normalizing the South's relations with the rest of the country. Congress had the constitutional right to determine the qualifications of its members and so could accept or reject any new southern Representatives or Senators, but beyond that, he insisted, "reconstruction" should be the president's responsibility. Lincoln no doubt believed this would be more efficient, but he also inevitably preferred wielding the power to guide and control the final stage of reuniting the Union. The president also favored a lenient process, one that would not create too many hurdles to the South's readmission to the Union, impose severe punishment on white southerners, or require unrealistic changes of heart. He agreed, however, that any scheme had to guarantee the South's acceptance of slavery's demise.

Lincoln waited almost a year from the time of the Emancipation Proclamation to announce his plan for reconstruction. Issued on December 8, 1863, his Proclamation of Amnesty and Reconstruction, usually called the Ten-Percent Plan, offered full pardon and full restoration of all rights to white southerners who pledged *future* loyalty to the Union and accepted the abolition of slavery. Excluded from the pardon and restoration were high-ranking Confederate political and military leaders. When such loyal southerners in any rebel state equalled in number ten percent of the voters in the 1860 elections, this group could convene and establish a new state government to supersede the old. The new constitution adopted must abolish slavery but it could also temporarily accept laws for the freed slaves "consistent . . . with their present condition as a laboring, landless, and homeless class." The state governments which met these conditions would be entitled, as far as the president was concerned, to admission to the Union and to representation in Congress.

Lincoln's goals at this point were clearly limited. He had little interest in encouraging a major social revolution in the South. His plan, apparently, was aimed at white southern moderates, former Whigs like himself, who would welcome a return to the Union but might be alienated by any scheme to change the relations of the races too drastically. The Ten-Percent Plan did not please several important groups. Blacks and their allies condemned it for ignoring black suffrage and saying nothing about civil rights for the freedmen. Wendell Phillips, the ardent humanitarian and pre-war abolitionist, noted that it "frees the slave and ignores the negro." Radical Republicans deplored the easy requirements for amnesty. In place of the pledge of *future* loyalty they preferred the "ironclad oath," by which the oath-taker declared that he had never willingly helped the Confederacy. Under the president's scheme, they felt, far too many collaborators with the detested rebellion would be forgiven and escape punishment. As Jacob Howard told his Senate colleagues: "The people of the North are not such fools as to fight through such a war as this . . . and then turn around and say to the traitors, 'all you have to do is to come back into the councils of the nation and take an oath that henceforth you will be true to the Government'."

The Radicals also had constitutional concerns. Lincoln's easy blueprint for southern restoration was based on his feeling that since the rebellion was illegal, the southern states had never been out of the Union and the victors therefore could not constitutionally impose novel conditions on the vanquished for resuming normal federal-state relations. The Radicals saw the legal facts differently. Radical Pennsylvania Congressman Thaddeus Stevens was certain that the southern states had indeed left the Union and were now "conquered provinces." The victorious Union, like any conqueror, could impose any conditions on them it wished. Charles Sumner, equally committed to the Radical cause, had an alternate theory but one which also justified the North in dictating readmission terms: The southern states had committed "suicide" and had reverted to the status of territories.

The differences between the president and Congress came to a head in early 1864 when Louisiana applied for readmission under terms close to Lincoln's blueprint. The situation in the state was confused. In April 1862 the Union army under Benjamin F. Butler had seized New Orleans and a part of southern Louisiana and held it for the Union. The Crescent City, the largest in the South, formerly had enjoyed close commercial ties to the North and many of its merchants were Unionists. It also had a large population of foreign-born whites whose attachment to the Confederacy was never strong. Another Union contingent were the 11,000 free blacks. Other southern cities had free black populations, but none were as prosperous and well educated as in the Louisiana port. These men and women included sugar planters, real estate magnates, and many skilled craft workers. Together this pool of potential loyalists seemed ripe for inclusion in a new state government under the Lincoln plan.

But Louisiana Unionists were divided between conservatives who favored the old order—though with slavery excised—and radicals who hoped that Louisiana could be transformed into a modern, progressive, free-labor community on the pattern of the Yankee North. The state's March 1864 constitutional convention, under the Ten-Percent Plan, produced a blend of both radical and conservative positions. The new frame of state government made New Orleans the state capital, established a minimum wage and nine hour day on all public works, adopted a progressive income tax, and created a system of free public education. But it also rejected black suffrage despite the president's suggestion to Governor Michael Hahn that the vote be given to "some of the colored people . . . as for instance, the very intelligent, and especially those who have fought gallantly in our ranks."

The failure of the Louisiana Ten-Percent government to allow any black voters aroused the Radicals in Congress. In July 1864 they adopted the Wade-Davis Manifesto, replacing the president's leniency and seizing the initiative on reconstruction for the legislative branch.

The Wade-Davis scheme proposed postponing the reconstruction process until a majority of a given state's white males had pledged to support the United States Constitution. Then, elections would be held for a state constitutional convention with only those who had taken the Ironclad oath permitted to vote. In addition, though it avoided requiring black suffrage, the Wade-Davis plan provided guarantees of equality before the law to the freed slaves. Lincoln feared that the measure would force him to repudiate the Louisiana Ten-Percent government and so pocket-vetoed it. But, he said in mock innocence, he had no objection if other southern states chose Wade-Davis rather than his own plan. Senator Ben Wade and Representative Henry Winter Davis promptly responded with a blistering attack. The president, they said, was guilty of "dictatorial usurpation" for defying the judgment of Congress.

Despite the disagreement with Congress, by the time of Appomattox Unionist governments recognized by Lincoln were operating in Louisiana, Arkansas, and Tennessee.

Johnson Takes Charge. Lincoln's assassination profoundly altered the course of political reconstruction. Had he lived, his popularity, prestige, and flexibility might have induced Congress to accept major portions of his plan. Still, it is clear that even he probably would have encountered difficulties in guiding the process. The war had swollen executive power far beyond its former limits, and at the end of hostilities Congress would certainly have fought hard to control so vital a policy as Reconstruction. It seems unlikely that either side would have gotten its own way entirely.

Lincoln's successor had to confront this struggle with Congress, and much else besides, without the martyred president's skills and popularity. Johnson superficially resembled Lincoln. Born within two months of one another, both men came from southern poor-white stock. Neither had much formal education (Johnson's wife taught him to read), and yet they both were strivers driven by fierce ambition. An acquaintance described Andy Johnson's life as "one intense, unceasing, desperate, upward struggle." And both men had succeeded—against great odds. Beginning as local alderman in East Tennessee in 1829, Johnson had moved steadily up the political ladder to the state legislature, to Congress, to the Tennessee state house and then, in 1857, to the United States Senate.

Johnson was not a Republican and had been put on the Union national ticket in 1864 to attract War Democrats. He did not share the strong federal supremacy principles of the Republicans. He was, rather, a defender of local power, even states rights, though he detested secession and the secessionists. Much of his political philosophy derived from his region. East Tennessee was a mountainous part of the state, an area of small farms with few slaves. It's dominant inhabitants were white yeomen who despised the state's privileged planter class and considered secession a plot to perpetuate their power. At the same time, these folk had little respect for blacks. Fierce democrats when it came to the rich and powerful, they drew the egalitarian line at the white race. Blacks need not apply!

Johnson, for all his political success, lacked Lincoln's winning personal qualities. Lincoln was confident in his own abilities and principles. Johnson suffered from severe self-doubts and these made him susceptible to flattery even by avowed enemies. He also lacked Lincoln's gregarious personality. He was a loner with few friends or close advisers. His political ally, Navy Secretary Gideon Welles, said the president's most serious weakness was detachment. He had "no confidants and seeks none." His major decisions apparently were made without consulting "anyone whatever." He was a rigid man. He could be cajoled out of a position, but when defied directly, he refused to budge. This stubbornness, in turn, often pushed his opponents into positions more extreme than they had originally taken and drove them into the waiting arms of Radicals like Wade, Stevens,

An idealized portrait of Andrew Johnson. His photographs show a coarser-featured man, an image more in keeping with his actual origins and early life.

and Sumner. He also lacked well-tuned political instincts. Though he had served in both houses of Congress, he seemed incapable of understanding how jealously congressional leaders guarded their perogatives and how fiercely they would fight him primarily because his office was at the other end of Pennsylvania Avenue.

The president's characteristics became apparent only gradually, however. At first the Radical Republicans, tired of dealing with the wily Lincoln, had rejoiced at Johnson's succession. As military governor of Tennessee during the war he had clamped down hard on secessionists. Recalling his remark that "treason . . . must be made infamous and and traitors . . . punished," they concluded that he would be harder on the South than his predecessor. Just days after Lincoln died a group of Radical leaders met with the new president to express their confidence. "Johnson, we have faith in you," exclaimed Wade of Ohio. "By the Gods, there will be no trouble now in running the government." "I believe," another declared, "that the Almighty continued Mr. Lincoln in office as long as he was useful, and then substituted a better man to finish the work."

During his first eight months in office Johnson had a relatively free hand in formulating Reconstruction policy. Congress was not in session and, although the politicians at home and in Washington did not cease to give advice and make statements, they did not have the proper forum for taking action. A wiser man, especially one who had served in both House and Senate, might have called Congress into special session and consulted its members on the burning issues of the day. But Johnson chose to jealously guard his own power over the momentous question of Reconstruction.

Two proclamations on May 29, 1856, formally announced Johnson's Reconstruction plan. The first offered pardon and amnesty to participants in the rebellion who pledged loyalty to the Union and support for the end of slavery. All who took the oath would have all property confiscated by the Union government during the war, except for slaves, returned to them. Exempted from this blanket pardoning process were fourteen classes of Southerners who were required to apply individually for pardons from the president. These included most high Confederate officials and owners of taxable property worth more than $20,000. This last proviso reflected Johnson's southern yeoman prejudice against the old planter class as the source of disunion and secession.

The second proclamation designated William Holden as provisional governor of North Carolina. Holden was to call a convention to amend the state's existing constitution so as to create a "republican form of government." Voters would be restricted to those who had taken the oath of allegiance; they would not include ex-slaves or any blacks.

Johnson soon extended the same process to six other southern states while also recognizing the new governments of Louisiana, Arkansas, and Tennessee, three states Lincoln had already accepted back into the Union. Johnson made it clear that he expected the conventions to accept the abolition of slavery and pledge not to repay any public debts incurred in the Confederate cause. He also asked them to consider giving voting rights to a few educated and property-holding blacks in order to "disarm" those clamoring for civil rights for ex-slaves. Otherwise they could decide for themselves what sort of government and laws they would adopt.

In the next few months Johnson chose provisional governors from among each unreconstructed state's "loyalists" to manage the process he had prescribed. He often turned to members of the old Whig elite. These men typically had been skeptical of secession but had gone with their states when the decision to leave the Union was irrevocably made. Few favored any changes in the undemocratic and unprogressive systems of the prewar era. None supported civil equality for blacks. The governors wielded broad patronage power and, during their months in office, used it to win the support of the Old South's planter and merchant class regardless of their Unionism or willingness to accept a new social and political order. Meanwhile, each of the unreconstructed states held elections for a convention and adopted a new state constitution. Each acknowledged the end of slavery and all, except stubborn South Carolina, pledged to repudiate its Confederate debts. No state conceded blacks the vote, however, though several revised their formulas for representation to favor the white small farmer counties over the plantation regions. Soon afterward, they held statewide elections for permanent governor and other officials and chose state legislators and congressional delegates. Satisfied that the states had met his conditions, Johnson ordered that the powers exercised by his provisional governors be transferred to the newly-elected state officials.

During the summer and fall conservative white southerners had reason to feel reassured that, despite Johnson's tough talk about disunionists and his disdain for the planter class, the president did not intend to disturb their region's social and political systems. In August he overruled Freedmen's Bureau Commissioner Oliver Howard's Circular 13 setting aside forty-acre tracts of land for the freedmen to farm and ordered the return of land confiscated during the war from disloyal southerners. He also yielded to southern demands for removing black troops, whose presence whites considered a "painful humiliation" and a force for undermining plantation labor discipline. The president scattered pardons wholesale. A large proportion of those excluded from the regular pardon under the $20,000 clause soon applied for special presidential pardon. By 1866 the

Black Reconstruction

Black southerners were not passive participants in the Reconstruction process. In the South they joined the militia companies and the Union Leagues, as well as the Republican party. They also spoke out against their enemies and appealed to their white northern friends for support. The following is an early instance of such an appeal. It is a statement adopted by a black convention held in Virginia in August 1865, soon after the end of the war. Note how many of the things the delegates asked their white allies for were actually granted.

"We, the undersigned members of a Convention of colored citizens of the State of Virginia, would respectfully represent that, although we have been held as slaves, and denied all recognition as a constituent of your nationality for almost the entire period of the duration of your Government, and that by *your permission* we have been denied either home or country, and deprived of the dearest rights of human nature: yet when you and our immediate oppressors met in deadly conflict on the field of battle—the one to destroy and the other to save your Government and nationality, we, with scarce an exception, in our inmost souls espoused your cause, and watched, and prayed, and waited, and labored for your success. . . .

"When the contest waxed long, and the result hung doubtfully, you appealed to us for help, and how well we answered is written in the rosters of the two hundred thousand colored troops now enrolled in your service; and as to our undying devotion to your cause, let the uniform acclamation of escaped prisoners, 'whenever we saw a black face we felt sure of a friend,' answer.

"Well, the war is over, the rebellion is 'put down,' and we are *declared* free! Four fifths of our enemies are paroled or amnestied, and the other fifth are being pardoned, and the President has . . . left us entirely at the mercy of these subjugated but unconverted rebels, in *everything* save the privilege of bringing us, our wives, and little ones, to the auction block. . . . We *know* these men—know them *well*—and we assure you that, with the majority of them, loyalty is only 'lip deep,' and that their professions of loyalty are used as a cover to the cherished design of getting restored to their former relations with the Federal Government, and then, by all sorts of 'unfriendly legislation,' to render the freedom you have given us more intolerable than the slavery they intended for us.

"We warn you in time that our only safety is in keeping them under Governors of the *military persuasion* until you have so amended the Federal Constitution that it will prohibit the States from making any distinction between citizens on account of race or color. In one word, the only salvation for us besides the power of the Government is in the *possession of the ballot*. Give us this and we will protect ourselves. . . .

"We are 'sheep in the midst of wolves,' and nothing but the military arm of the Government prevents us and all the *truly* loyal white men from being driven from the land of our birth. Do not then, we beseech you, give to one of these 'wayward sisters' the rights they abandoned and forfeited when they rebelled until you have secured *our* rights by the aforementioned amendment to the Constitution. . . .

"Trusting that you will not be deaf to the appeal herein made, nor unmindful of the warnings which the malignity of the rebels are constantly giving you, and that you will rise to the height of being just for the sake of justice, we remain yours for our flag, our country, and humanity."

---

president had given out almost 7,000 of these. Scholars have puzzled over Johnson's change of heart. Some have tied it to his susceptibility to flattery from the very people he formally despised. Others suggest that he saw this white leadership class as essential to maintaining order in the South and also as potential allies in his bid for election in his own right as president in 1868. Whatever the reason, by fall's end the president had become the protector of the South's old order, or at least as much of it as could be preserved.

The Johnson Governments. For several months the "Johnson governments" operated without restraint from Washington.

Their deeds dismayed many northerners, strengthened the Radicals, and destroyed any possibility that Congress would accept the president's Reconstruction policy.

Several things especially offended northern Unionists. In the elections for new state and federal officials southern voters turned primarily to qualified opponents of secession, but few real Unionists. Chosen for the upcoming Congress were four Confederate generals, five Confederate colonels, six Confederate Cabinet officers, fifty-eight Confederate Congressmen, and Alexander H. Stephens, vice president of the Confederate States of America. Many of the newly-elected state officials were also tainted with secession. In North Carolina, for example, the former Confederate state treasurer defeated William Holden for governor. It was natural for white southerners to turn to former secessionists for their leaders. To have done otherwise would have acknowledged a completely new order of things, a response that few communities ever accept willingly and none in so short a time. But this blatant display of Confederate sympathies offended many northerners. It even gave the president pause. "There seems, in many of the elections," he wrote in late fall, "something like defiance, which is all out of place at this time."

The new legislatures in turn also provoked northern opinion. Despite the president's recommendations, several refused to ratify the Thirteenth Amendment, passed by Congress in January 1865, that constitutionally abolished slavery in every part of the United States. Mississippi and South Carolina also refused to repudiate their wartime state debts. None of the Johnson governments allowed even a handful of blacks to vote. But worst of all, each of them enacted a set of laws to govern race relations called the Black Codes.

These codes did extend to the freedmen several rights of normal citizens. Marriages between blacks, including earlier slave relationships, were legalized; ex-slaves were allowed to buy, own, sell, and otherwise transfer property; and they were given the right to appear, plead, and testify in court in cases involving fellow blacks. But the codes also placed the freedmen in a position of distinct legal inferiority to whites and sought to give them permanent second-class status in their economic and political relations to whites.

Under the Black Codes, black southerners could not offer their labor freely on the market. Mississippi required workers to produce each January a written document showing they had a contract to work for the coming year. Laborers who left their jobs before a contract expired forfeited any wages already earned and could be arrested. Anyone who offered a job to a laborer who already had a contract could be imprisoned or fined. "Vagrants"—defined as the idle, disorderly, and those who "misspend what they earn"—could face fines or forced plantation labor. Other states' codes were equally oppressive. The South Carolina code forbade blacks from working at occupations other than farming or as servants unless they paid a stiff annual tax. In Florida, blacks who broke labor contracts could be whipped, sold into indenture for up to one year, or placed in the pillory. Louisiana mandated that any dispute between an employer and his employees should be settled exclusively "by the former." In several states blacks were forbidden to bear arms, were subject to more severe punishment for given offenses than whites, and could not live or buy property in specified locations. Most states prohibited interracial marriage. Most rankling of all were apprenticeship laws which allowed the courts to "bind out" black minors to employers for a period of time without their own consent or that of their parents.

One feature of all the legislation passed by the presidential reconstruction state governments was the failure to distinguish between the newly freed and the always free among the black population. Eric Foner, the distinguished historian of the Reconstruction period, has noted that in the British island of Jamaica, where slavery had been abolished in the 1830s, the white minority had been able to ally themselves with the small, educated mulatto class. In the process they had confirmed their power and wealth. The Black Codes, for good or ill, drove the small class of free blacks, many educated and a few prosperous, into the arms

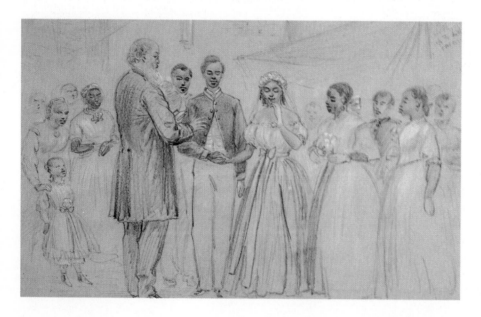

One of the real advances afforded by the emancipation was the legal recognition of black marriages. After 1865 black men and women seized the opportunity to solemnize relationships begun under slavery or to contract new ones. Officiating at this wedding is a chaplain from the Freedmen's Bureau.

of the Radicals and turned them into leaders of their race during the years after 1865.

Blacks eloquently protested the codes. One black man wrote the Freedmen's Bureau: "Surely the law does not Call for Children to be bond out when their peopel is Abel to Keep them." Wrote another: "I think very hard of the former owners for Trying to keep my Blood when I kno that Slavery is dead." One black Union veteran exclaimed: "If you call this Freedom, what do you call Slavery!" But even more consequential was the response of the white North.

At first most white northerners had gone along with Johnson. Except for confirmed Radicals, even Republicans, especially those of Democratic antecedents who opposed enlarged federal power, endorsed his early policies. Democrats were almost uniformly favorable. Also positively inclined were many of the North's business leaders, especially bankers, merchants, and manufacturers who before the war had strong economic ties to the cotton South and now hoped to resume valuable business connections. These men often saw the drive for social change and black suffrage as potential disrupters of southern economic recovery and a threat to profits. As Jay Cooke, the banker who had helped finance the Union cause during the war, noted, the country needed a "plain, simple, common-sense plan" for reconstruction so that it could get back to the business of business.

But for many Northerners, especially those closely identified with the wartime Union cause, and for Radicals generally, the president's plan was deplorable. Some condemned it for its racial injustice. Wendell Phillips prophetically noted that without the right to vote blacks in the South would be consigned to "a century of serfdom." Others appealed to the anti-Confederate feeling of the war period. Henry Winter Davis declared that only black suffrage could destroy "the power of those who rebelled." Nothing so offended this sector of northern opinion as the Black Codes. The *Chicago Tribune* declared that the people of the North would turn one of the worst offending states, Mississippi, into a "frog pond" before they would allow its Black Code "to disgrace one foot of soil in which the bones of our soldiers sleep and over which the flag of freedom waves." Another critic called the codes "an outrage against civilization." Even some white southerners feared that the new legislation had gone too far and would provoke the North into a repressive response. Meanwhile, northern congressmen were receiving almost daily reports from white southern Unionists that the former secessionists were crowing about how they once again had the upper hand and would make life difficult for their opponents. And there were other provocations. During the summer and fall of 1865 the northern press reported frequent attacks on freedmen by whites. Simultaneously northern travelers in Dixie recounted unpleasant experiences with unreconstructed "rebels." Hotels and restaurants often refused them service and individual southerners sometimes insulted them. One Rochester, New York, resident wrote to Secretary of State Seward in November. "The great majority [of southern whites] ae exceedingly sore toward the North and northern people, however much they may sometimes attempt to cover it up."

The outrage of many northerners over the Johnson Governments' policies and the Black Codes should not deceive us about the extent of racial liberalism at this time in the nation at large. Northern Democrats were often blatant racists who had no scruples against appealing to the voters' bigotry and resisted every attempt to confer the franchise on blacks. Republicans, generally, were less prejudiced and, in any case, believed that the freedmen's votes were needed to keep former rebels from regaining power in the South. As Chicago newspaper publisher Charles Dana wrote in September, "as for Negro suffrage, the mass of the Union men in the Northwest do not care a great deal. What scares them is the idea that the rebels are all to be let back . . . and made a power in the government again, just as though there had been no rebellion."

But even many Republicans were reluctant to accord black Americans the full rights of citizenship, at least where they themselves lived. In the fall of 1865 three northern states–Connecticut, Wisconsin, and Minnesota–placed constitutional amendments on their ballots allowing the handful of black males within their borders to vote. The Republican leaders in each state bravely campaigned for the revised franchise laws but they were defeated in all three. A majority of Republican voters supported the changes, but many did not, and together with the Democrats, the Republican bigots had voted the black franchise laws down. In effect then, a majority of *all* white voters opposed letting blacks vote and this reality inevitably tempered the Radical ardor of Republican politicians in districts where elections were closely contested.

★ CONGRESS TAKES OVER ★

By the time the Thirty-Ninth Congress assembled on December 4, 1865, the Republican majority was determined to take over the process of southern reconstruction to assure that rebels would not get their way. Its first act was to reject the Congressional delegations sent by the Johnson governments to Washington. Prompted by the Radicals, the Clerk of the House, Edward McPherson, skipped the names of the newly elected southern congressmen as he called the roll. Immediately after, the two houses established a Joint Committee on Reconstruction to look into conditions in the South and consider whether any former Confederate states were entitled to representation. Consisting of fifteen Senators and Representatives, three of them Democrats, their views spread across the political spectrum, although the "too ultra" Sumner was deliberately excluded.

Despite his policies, Johnson had still not completely alienated the Republican moderates and they listened to his conciliatory annual message with respect. Efforts at this point by a few Radicals to completely replace the president's regimes failed and for a time the Republican congressional centrists took charge. This changed abruptly when moderate Lyman Trumbull of Illinois introduced a bill to extend the life of the Freedmen's Bureau and widen its authority.

Established in March 1865, just before the war ended, the bureau aided refugees, both white and black, found employment for freedmen, and supplied transportation home for those displaced by the war. It had established hospitals and schools and drawn up guidelines for bringing ex-slaves into the free labor market. In enlarging the bureau's scope, Congress gave it the additional power to protect freedmen against discrimination, including the right to punish state officials denying blacks their civil rights, and authorized it to build and run schools for the ex-slaves. Noting that the bill assigned a limit to the bureau's life, it was generally considered a moderate measure.

Not so the second law Trumbull proposed. The Civil Rights bill of 1865 was far-reaching in scope. Representative Henry J. Raymond of New York called it "one of the most important bills ever presented to the House for its action." It declared all persons born in the United States, including blacks (but not Indians), citizens, and specified their rights regardless of race. These included the right to make contracts, bring lawsuits, and enjoy the "full and equal benefit of all laws and proceedings for the security of person and property." To ensure that no state denied citizens these rights, it authorized federal district attorneys and marshalls, as well as the Freedmen's Bureau, to sue in the federal courts. In many ways the law foreshadowed the civil rights measures of the mid-twentieth century.

Johnson refused to sign either bill. The Freedmen's Bureau was, he said in his veto message, a vast patronage boondoggle that would create a horde of bureaucrats to oppress ordinary citizens. It was also too expensive. Moreover, it violated the Constitution; never before had the federal government been called on to provide economic relief to individuals. The president soon after attacked the Civil Rights bill as another unwarranted extension of federal power. The bill was a "stride toward centralization and the concentration of all legislative powers in the national Government."

The fight over the Freedmen's Bureau destroyed the hope of moderates that Johnson could be trusted with Reconstruction. It was the opening round of a struggle that lasted until the end of Johnson's term, with each new battle driving more and more moderates into the Radical camp. Soon after the veto the president further offended Republican leaders by calling Radicals Stevens and Sumner "traitors" and "opponents of the fundamental principles of government." In the end Congress was unable to muster the two-thirds needed to pass the Freedmen's Bureau bill though it managed to override the Civil Rights veto.

The Fourteenth Amendment. While Congress and the President fought for supremacy, the Joint Committee on Reconstruction set to work on its own comprehensive plan to restore Dixie to the Union. Even with the Thirteenth Amendment finally approved by the states and the Civil Rights bill enacted into law, Radicals worried that the rights of black Americans were vulnerable. Certainly, if it proved necessary to rely on the federal courts, there could be little security. Although it was not until April 1866 that the Supreme Court, in the case of *Ex Parte Milligan*, voided the Lincoln administration's wartime imposition of martial law on civilians in Indiana, the justices already seemed hostile to the Republican philosophy of federal supremacy. What would prevent them from striking down the Civil Rights Act or any other measure that Congress passed to protect the freedmen? With this in mind, the first initiative of the Joint Committee was another amendment to the Constitution to put the principles of the Civil Rights bill beyond the reach of the president, the states, and unfriendly federal judges.

As finally hammered out and submitted to the states for adoption, the Fourteenth Amendment contained four clauses, the first two of which were of major significance.

Clause two, concerning suffrage, was not all that the most radical of the Republican leaders wanted. Congress might have declared unconstitutional all political discrimination on racial grounds. Instead it deferred to conservative opinion and continuing northern racial prejudice by a series of evasions. Rather than giving the vote to all adult male citizens, white as well as black, it merely declared that whenever a state denied any twenty-one-year-old male citizen the right to vote, that state's representation in Congress would be reduced proportionately. The South, with its large black population, would now have a strong incentive to grant full voting rights to black males. (Otherwise it would send far fewer representatives to Congress than its total population warranted.) Northern states, however, with few blacks residents, could continue to deny them suffrage without serious penalty. Not until after the adoption of the Fifteenth Amendment (1870) were "race, color, or previous condition of servitude" completely eliminated as legal grounds for denying adult men the vote.

Clause one of the Fourteenth Amendment was actually the more important section, vastly expanding federal power over the states and serving in the end many purposes besides ensuring racial justice in the South. The original Bill of Rights had only limited the power of the federal government over citizens. Now the Constitution would place restraints on the states as well.

The clause defined citizenship to include all those born or naturalized in the United States. This ended a long term dispute between the states and the federal government over who was a citizen entitled to a citizen's rights. It then went on to establish that no state could make or enforce any law that abridged the rights of American citizens, or deprived any person of "life, liberty, or property without due process of law." This meant that individuals could not be executed, imprisoned, or fined by the states except through the normal processes of law with all their constitutionally-protected procedures and safeguards. Nor could any state "deny to any person within its jurisdiction the equal protection of the laws." This meant that no individual or class of individuals could not be treated under the law as inferior to others; no group could have special privileges.

The amendment also contained two minor sections. Clause three denied public office, state and federal, to those who had taken oaths as state or federal officials and then served in the rebellion; the last repudiated any debt incurred in aid of the Confederate cause while at the same time upholding all those incurred in repressing the rebels.

In specifically restricting the franchise to men, the Fourteenth Amendment was a serious disappointment to women's rights reformers. Many had hoped that Union victory would result in enhanced voting rights for women as well as blacks. But many black leaders and friends of the freedmen, fearing prejudice against political feminism would weaken their own cause, insisted that it was now the "Negro's hour." Theirs were the voices that in the end were heeded. Ratification of the Fourteenth Amendment, with its use of the term "male," now implicitly denied women the vote in federal elections.

The suffrage issue split the women's rights movement. Some women's groups and their male supporters accepted the

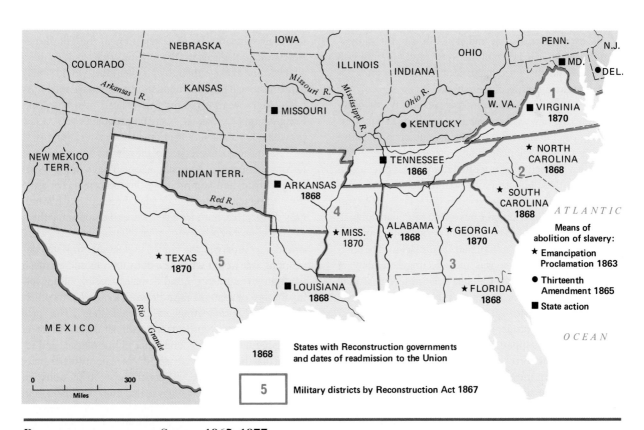

RECONSTRUCTION OF THE SOUTH, 1865–1877

"blacks first" argument. Black Americans had been the most oppressed class of Americans and now deserved first chance. But others rejected the notion that they should allow the struggle for racial justice delay women's progress to full citizenship. Wendell Phillips called the amendment a "fatal and total surrender." Women suffrage activists Susan B. Anthony and Elizabeth Cady Stanton also denounced it. By 1870 two women's rights groups, the more militant New York-based National Woman Suffrage Association, led by Anthony and Stanton, and the more conservative Boston-based American Woman Suffrage Association, led by Lucy Stone and Thomas Wentworth Higginson, had been organized.

★ THE FIRST RECONSTRUCTION ACT ★

To assure adoption of the new constitutional amendment, Congress made its passage by the southern state legislatures a condition of readmission to the Union. But this prod did not work. By the end of 1866 Texas, South Carolina, Georgia, Florida, North Carolina, Arkansas, and Alabama had all rejected it. As the governor of Florida remarked: "We will be taxed without representation, we will quietly endure the government of the bayonet, . . . but we will not bring as a peace offering the conclusive evidence of our own self-created degradation." In fact, the ratification process dragged even in the North, and not until well into 1867 did the amendment receive the necessary approval by three-fourths of the states.

By now the president's abrasive personality and backward-looking views had alienated almost all the Republicans in Congress. But there still remained a nub of conservative Republicans, including men like Secretary of State Seward in his own cabinet, who supported him and his policies. In April 1866 these leaders joined with moderate Democrats to form the National Union Executive Committee. In August they held a National Union Convention in Philadelphia to form a third party based on sectional reconciliation and immediate return of the southern states to the Union. The highlight of the convention was the affecting ceremony of Massachusetts and South Carolina delegates, representing the two sectional poles, marching into the convention hall in pairs, arm and arm.

Though the president gave the National Union movement his hearty support, it came to little. For one thing, the conservative forces could not overcome the impression of southern intransigence created by news from the South. In May an angry white mob invaded the black section of Memphis killing forty-six people. In late July another white mob assaulted delegates to a black suffrage convention in New Orleans. Before federal troops could

arrive, the attackers had murdered thirty-seven blacks and three of their white supporters. Here was proof, if any were needed, that the Radicals were right: The South would never accept the consequences of defeat without northern coercion.

Despite poor prospects, the president campaigned aggressively for the National Union movement in the 1866 off-year elections. Against the advice of friends, he set out on a "swing around the circle," giving speeches in Washington, Chicago, and St. Louis. In these addresses he attacked the Radicals as the country's real traitors, defended the South as loyal, justified his generous pardoning policy, and offered his life to save the Union and the Constitution. Wherever he went, his critics heckled him unmercifully and goaded him into rash, undignified replies. He probably did his cause more harm than good. Radical Republicans won a decisive victory almost everywhere. The new Congress would retain its three-to-one Republican majority.

But even before the Fortieth Congress convened, the second session of the Thirty-ninth, its Republican leaders encouraged by the 1866 election mandate, passed the First Reconstruction Act (also called the Reconstruction Act of 1867).

By December 1866 Johnson had lost all Republican support. As one moderate Senator noted, the "President has no power to control or influence anybody and legislation will be carried on entirely regardless of his opinions or wishes." By now, too, the Johnson governments had forfeited all sympathy by their rejection of the Fourteenth Amendment. Radicals felt the time was ripe to sweep them all away and replace them by a system that would finally express the will of the Union's most progressive forces. As a first step toward imposing the Radical's own blueprint, Congress quickly passed, over the president's veto, a law providing for black suffrage in the District of Columbia.

But the major expression of the new mood was the First Reconstruction Act. As finally adopted after much wrangling, debate, and compromise, the measure swept aside the existing state regimes. It divided the South into five military districts, each under a general, and empowered them to use troops if necessary to protect life and property. They would also supervise the choice of delegates to state conventions that would write new constitutions and establish new state governments. All adult males were eligible for voting for the conventions regardless of race, except those excluded for participating in the rebellion. The new constitutions had to provide for a similar broad electorate for legislature, governor, and other public officials and required that their work be accepted by a majority of the same, color-blind, pool of voters. When the new constitutions had been so ratified, when Congress had approved them, and when the new state legislatures had ratified the Fourteenth Amendment, the states would then be admitted to the Union and their delegations to Congress be seated.

Johnson Impeached.   Radicals suspected that Johnson would do what he could to frustrate the First Reconstruction Act. Through his appointment authority and general executive powers he could, they feared, tilt the balance against them in the South. And before long he did, removing several of the military commanders as too Radical, and issuing orders to others designed to frustrate the will of Congress.

To hedge him in, Congress passed a series of additional measures n 1867. To prevent a gap that the president could take advantage of, in January it approved a bill that called the new Congress into special session immediately after the old one had expired. In March it passed, over Johnson's veto, the Tenure of Office Act requiring Senate consent for the dismissal of all federal officeholders appointed with Senate approval. A third measure, affixed to a military appropriation bill, required that all presidential orders to the army be issued through the general of the army. This happened to be Grant, a man who had come to support the Radical position on Reconstruction. At the same time, to goad dilatory southern voters to take steps under the First Reconstruction Act, Congress passed the Second Reconstruction Act. A Third Reconstruction Act in July tightened control by the five military commanders in the South to initiate the registration of voters and start the machinery for the constitutional conventions mandated by the First Reconstruction Act. A Third Rconstruction Act in July tightened control by the five military commanders over the provisional governments in the South and sought to broaden the rules excluding ex-Confederates from the Reconstruction process.

Yet Radicals in congress still did not believe that they could afford to leave Andrew Johnson at the head of the U.S. government in such a critical period, and in January 1868 they attempted to remove him from office through impeachment. This constitutional procedure, requiring indictment in the House for "Treason, Bribery, or other High Crimes and Misdemeanors" and conviction by the Senate, had seldom been used before even for lesser federal officers and never for a president. When, in January, House Radicals sought an indictment of the president, it was squelched in committee. As yet most moderates did not believe there were grounds for such a drastic process.

But then Johnson handed his opponents their opportunity. In August, during a congressional recess, Johnson had suspended from office Secretary of War Edwin Stanton and appointed Grant as interim Secrecary. In January 1868 the Senate refused to accept Stanton's dissmissal, and Grant, against the wishes of Johnson, stepped down. Defiant, the president once more removed Stanton and replaced him with Lorenzo Thomas. Bjut Stanton, with the urging of congressional Radicals, barricaded himself into his office and refused to leave or to allow Thomas to enter. However ludicrous, the Stanton affair seemed to provide grounds for impeachment that had not existed before. The president, exclaimed one moderate, had "thrown down the gauntlet and says to us plainly as words can speak it: 'Try this issue now betwixt me and you: either you go to the wall or I do." On February 24, 1868, the House formally voted to impeach the president by a strict party vote of 126 to 47.

The impeachment trial, conducted before the Senate

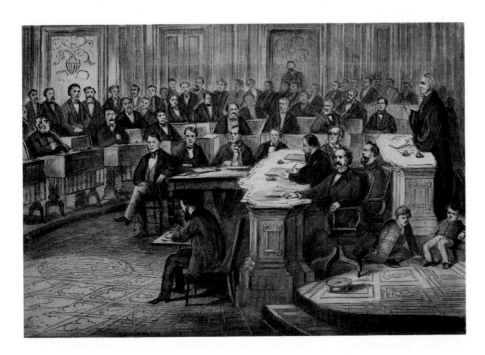

In August 1866 President Johnson announced that "peace, order, tranquility, and civil authority now exist . . . in the United States." Dissatisfied with Johnson's idea of peace and order, the House voted his impeachment less than two years later. Here a packed gallery follows the trial of the century.

sitting as a court, was the show trial of the century. The major charge against the president was his "unlawful" removal of Stanton. Attorne y General Henry Stanbbery, the president's counsel, based his defense on the fact that Stanton had been appointed by Lincoln, not Johnson. Consequently, Stanbery argued, he was not covered by the Tenure of Ofice Act. In any case, the law was probably unconstitutional, and it was the right of the president to test it by violating it and bringing it before the courts. Furthermore, having refused to leave, Stanton was still in office, so no law had actually been broken.

During the six weeks of the trial intense excitement reigned in Washington and the country. Radicals insisted that acquittal would be a victory for rebels and traitors. The president had frustrated the clearly expressed will of the nations duly elected legislators by pardoning rebels wholesale and by appointing officials to administer the Reconstruction Act who would not carry it out as they were required to. He must be stopped. Democrats and Johnson's few remaining moderate supporters within Republican ranks claimed that conviction would mean that Congress had successfully usurped the power of the executive branch. The president's defenders also noted that his removal would have political consequences. The man next in line for the presidency was the president pro tempore of t he Senate, the truculent Radical Benjamin Wade.

On May 16, 1868, Johnson was acquitted by one vote. Most historians believe that he should not have been impeached in the first place. There can be no question that he was stubborn and at times boorish, and that he used his executive power to impede Congress. Nor is there much dispute among scholars today that his racial policies were misguided. In a parliamentary system like Britain's he would have been removed by a legislative vote of "no confidence." But the Founders had deliberately created an independently elected executive with the right to disagree with Congress. It seems unlikely that they intended impeachment to serve as a way to remove an official from office except for breaking the law or for gross incapacity. The Radicals in effect, then, were seeking implicitly to change the Constitution in a vital aspect.

★ RECONSTRUCTION IN THE SOUTH ★

The Election of 1868. Johnson still had almost a year to go before his term ended but achieved little in the months remaining. During this period he spent much of his time maneuvering for the Democratic presidential nomination. The Democrats did not want him. In the West many preferred George Pendleton of Ohio, a Democratic Senator who fa-

vored the "Ohio Idea," a scheme to pay the immense federal debt in paper money ("greenbacks"). This policy, its advocates claimed, would lift a large burden from taxpayers' backs and, at the same time, stimulate the economy and relieve debtors by providing an abundance of money circulation. Eastern Democrats considered the Ohio Idea appalling. Unlike Republicans, they did not regard the federal debt as a "sacred obligation," incurred in the noble cause of preserving the Union. But they deplored what they viewed as the financial skullduggery of paying off public debts by turning on the treasury printing presses. Such a policy would call into question all debts, public and private, shake the financial markets, and set loose the forces of social anarchy. At the Democratic convention in New York the two party wings fought a bitter battle. It took twenty-two ballots before Governor Horatio Seymour of New York, a "hard money" man, nosed out Pendleton. The "soft money" men were able to get the Ohio Idea incorporated into the party platform but as soon as nominated Seymour repudiated it. Seymour, however, did not reject the platform's denunciation of Radical Reconstruction.

The Republicans turned not to their most militant wing but to the center. The acquittal of Johnson had weakened the Radicals and they could not stop the nomination of Ulysses Grant, the great war hero, who before the war had voted as a Democrat. General Grant had not opposed the Radicals' policies after 1865 but he was a pragmatist, rather than a zealot, and reassured the moderates. The Republican platform denounced the Ohio Idea as "repudiation" and a "national crime," and defended the civil rights of the freedmen in the South.

The Democrats campaigned as opponents of Reconstruction. Democratic Vice Presidential candidate Frank Blair denied that Republican Reconstruction was an accomplished fact and claimed that by electing the Democratic ticket "white people" in the South would be restored to power and the new governments organized by Congress would be declared "null and void." Expressing a growing public fatigue with political and social turmoil, Grant assumed a moderate tone with his slogan "Let Us Have Peace."

The election was remarkably close. In the South, armed and violent whites succeeded in intimidating many blacks from going to the polls. In eleven Georgia counties with black majorities no votes at all were recorded for Grant. But the Republicans did manage to carry all but two states in Dixie thanks to black voters and won most of the North. With 53 percent of the popular vote, the ticket of Ulysses S. Grant and Schuyler Colfax won the election.

By the time the new president was inaugurated in early 1869, the governments organized under the congressional reconstruction acts—composed of white and black

Thaddeus Stevens

His enemies in the South accused him of murder, adultery, misanthropy, and treason. His friends in the North considered him a sterling defender of democracy and freedom. His admirers called him "the old Commoner" after the eloquent and witty William Pitt, leader of the British House of Commons. Detractors called him "old Clubfoot" because of his congenital deformity. This man who attracted scandal and controversy all his life was Thaddeus Stevens, leader during Reconstruction of the Radical Republicans in the House of Representatives.

Born in April 1792, Stevens was the second son of a sometime farmer, surveyor, wrestler, and shoemaker who disappeared permanently after the birth of his fourth son. His mother, Sarah, was a religious, strong-willed, and energetic woman who ran the farm and taught her sons to read from the Bible. It was she who showed Thaddeus how to fight failure and finally overcome it. She was a firm believer in the value of education, moving her four fatherless children to Peacham, Vermont, when an academy was founded there.

Thaddeus was a bright boy who justified his mother's faith in him. He was also rebellious, a trait that lasted his entire life. As a senior at the academy, he took part in a theatrical performance "by candlelight," an activity expressly forbidden by the stern puritan headmaster. After signing "articles of submission" stating that he regretted his misdeed, he was allowed to finish school. He graduated from Datmouth in 1814, and in his commencement speech he defended luxury and wealth, claiming they were necessary for progress. Paradoxically, Stevens later attacked the South as a bastion of entrenched privilege and inequality.

In 1815 he went to York, Pennsylvania, where he taught for a year at the local academy and continued his study of law, begun in Vermont. Although the county insisted on a two years' residency requirement for admission to the bar, Stevens thought he was ready after a year because of his previous training. The lawyers of York did not like him and were unwilling to grant him a dispensation, so he crossed the border to Maryland. Here he answered a few questions on Blackstone's *Commentaries*, and a few on evidence and pleading, gave the judge two bottles of Madeira, and received his certification.

Stevens liked Pennsylvania, but did not want to return to York, where he had been snubbed. Instead, he opened his law office in Gettysburg. After a hard first year with few clients, he defended a mentally defective farmhand who had murdered a constable, using insanity as his plea. This was not a recognized defense at the time, and Stevens lost his case. He won himself a reputation for genius and boldness, however, and business poured into his office. He quickly bought himself a horse, a house and property in town, and a farm for his mother in Vermont. By 1830 he had become the largest property owner in the county, had invested in an iron business, and had been elected president of the Borough Council.

During his Gettysburg years Stevens survived an attack of typhoid fever that left him completely bald and added to his feelings of physical inferiority. Although he had many chances to marry, he rejected them all, feeling that his baldness and lameness made him unattractive and that any woman who wanted him must have reasons other than love.

Stevens also became an enthusiastic Anti-Mason, in part because of his rejection at Dartmouth and in York by secret societies. In 1831, in a speech at Hagerstown, Maryland, he attacked the Masons as corrupt, accused them of encouraging crime, and charged them with attempting to stop "the regular action of government." Jacob Lefever, a leading Mason and the owner of a Gettysburg newspaper, who had long been printing anonymous letters blaming Stevens for his supposed part in two recent murders, printed the Hagerstown speech in its entirety with a comment suggesting that Stevens had "blood" on his "skirts." Stevens sued him for criminal libel and damages. Lefever was sentenced to three months in jail and ordered to pay $1,500 in damages.

Despite the Masons' attacks, the Gettysburg townspeople elected Stevens to the state legislature, where he initiated much anti-Masonic legislation. He also made fiery speeches in behalf of an act to extend the free school system of Philadelphia to the entire state. His defense of education for all continued as long as he lived. Just a month before his death he introduced a bill in the House of Representatives "to establish a system of schools for the District of Columbia which shall serve as a model for similar institutions throughout the Union."

While still serving in the Pennsylvania legislature, Stevens became active in the antislavery cause, founding a colonization society and presenting a report in favor of abolishing slavery and the slave trade in the District of Columbia. At the state's constitutional convention in 1837 he refused to sign the final version of the constitution because it restricted suffrage to white males. He also acted as lawyer for fugitive slaves from other states hiding in the Pennsylvania hills. He was, by now, widely recognized as one of the state's foremost abolitionists.

In 1842 Stevens found himself at a personal low point. He had lost his seat in the state legislature and was deeply in debt because of business reverses, losses on massive election bets, and the failure of clients and friends to repay loans. To add to his troubles he was faced with a paternity suit brought by the father of an unmarried woman, a man whom he considered a friend. He was eventually cleared of this charge, but was embittered by this betrayal and his experiences in Gettysburg generally. He moved his residence and law offices to Lancaster, where he regained his fortunes and his reputation as the state's most accomplished lawyer. Here he also acquired a mulatto housekeeper, Lydia Hamilton Smith, who worked for him until he died. People speculated about their relationship; his enemies snidely referred to her as "Mrs. Stevens."

In 1848 Stevens was elected to Congress as a Whig. In Washington he immediately gained a reputation as a firebrand. He denounced slavery as accursed, criminal, and shameful, and condemned northerners who permitted its continuance as fiercely as the southerners who practiced it. His House colleagues, from both sections, were often shocked by his abusive and offensive language, believing it better "suited to a fishmarket" than to the halls of Congress. He fought vigorously against both the Compromise of 1850 and the Fugitive Slave Act. After the shattering defeat of Winfield Scott, the Whig candidate for president in 1852, Stevens left Congress and returned to Lancaster to attend to his legal practice and iron business. Having no legiti-

mate children of his own, he also devoted himself to his nephews, Thaddeus and Alanson.

Though out of Congress, Stevens remained involved in politics, taking an active part in the birth of the Republican party in Pennsylvania. In 1858 he was returned to Congress as a Republican, winning 75 percent of the votes in Lancaster County. In 1860 Stevens was a delegate to the Republican National Convention. He was mentioned for a cabinet post after Lincoln's victory at the polls, but instead stayed in the House, where he became chairman of the powerful Ways and Means Committee. A month after Lincoln's inauguration Confederate troops fired on Fort Sumter, precipitating the War Between the States. Stevens's committee gave the administration staunch support on financial matters. He was largely responsible for the Internal Revenue Act of 1862, which taxed almost every article produced by the Union. He favored the greenback paper currency, issued directly by the United States and backed by the credit of the country rather than by gold.

During the war Stevens was remorseless toward the South. He favored confiscation of captured enemy property and called for war without mercy. Some thought this was in retaliation for the destruction of his iron works during Lee's invasion of Pennsylvania in 1863. He introduced a bill calling for general emancipation, with compensation for loyal slaveholders and the freeing of slaves who wanted to leave their masters or who aided in "quelling the rebellion."

Stevens favored generals who opposed slavery, believing that such men fought better. He hated George McClellan for his indecisiveness and was pleased when Lincoln fired him.

It was on Reconstruction that Stevens left his greatest mark. He and Charles Sumner were the two most prominent Radical Republicans—a group that favored strict terms for southern readmission to the Union, strong measures to guarantee the rights of the freedmen, and vigorous federal intervention to further economic progress. The Radicals had not been satisfied with Lincoln's lenient "ten-percent plan" for readmitting the seceded states to the Union. The harsher Wade-Davis Bill pleased Stevens no better; it was still too lenient.

When Andrew Johnson became president after Lincoln's assassination, Stevens hoped he would join the Radicals. On the surface, Johnson looked like an ally. A former senator from Tennessee, he had remained loyal to the Union and had fought against secessionists as military governor of the state. Both Stevens and Johnson had strong sympathies for the underdog, but where Stevens championed blacks, Johnson limited his compassion to poor whites. Less than two months after Johnson took office Stevens was permanently disillusioned with the president, considering his plans dangerous and his actions "insane." When Johnson proceeded to reconstruct the Union according to his own lenient design, Stevens and his fellow Radical Republicans determined to take over Reconstruction themselves.

On December 1, 1865, Stevens

Republicans and decidedly Radical in temper—had been admitted to the Union, and the Fourteenth Amendment had been incorporated into the Constitution. In a narrow legal sense, Reconstruction was now complete. But in fact, the situation in the newly restored states remained uncertain and tense.

Economic Recovery.   Several important changes had

taken place in the South since April 1865. Physical reconstruction had proceeded at a rapid pace. Damaged southern railroads were quickly rebuilt after Appomattox and the system extended to additional regions. Between 1865 and 1879, 7,000 miles of track were added to the southern rail network. Much of the needed capital was supplied by investors in the North and in Britain, who anticipated a fa-

called together twenty-five supporters to propose a joint committee of both houses of Congress on Reconstruction. The committee would study the condition of the "so-called Confederate States of America," and no member elected to Congress would be admitted until the committee had made its report. When the full Republican caucus met the next night, it unanimously adopted this proposal. When Congress convened later that month, no southerner was seated and the Joint Committee of Fifteen on Reconstruction was established. As chairman of the House faction, Stevens was the dominant member of the committee. He intended to reduce the South to a "territorial condition" and treat it as a "conquered province" over which Congress would have complete control. He also was determined to guarantee the political and, if possible, the social rights of the freedmen. In 1865 and 1866 Stevens urged confiscation of land owned by rich ex-confederates and the transfer of forty acres of this property to each adult ex-slave. Not only would this provide the freedmen with a secure economic position in the South, it would also humble the proud southern elite that Stevens believed had brought the horrors of a brothers' war on the nation.

Stevens saw Johnson as the chief obstacle to the Radicals' policies and determined to get him. In early 1867 he secured passage of the Tenure of Office Act stripping the president of the authority to remove high officeholders who favored congressional Reconstruction. The Radicals also passed a measure requiring the president to issue orders to the army through the general of the army, Ulysses S. Grant, who could not be dismissed without the Senate's consent. The law was intended to filter all orders concerning Reconstruction through Grant, now a supporter of the Radical position.

This legislation set the stage for the impeachment of Andrew Johnson when the president refused to keep Edwin Stanton, a Radical, in his cabinet and ordered him to resign in February 1868. Stevens was in his middle seventies and in poor health by now, but he actively took part in the impeachment proceedings. He bypassed the Judiciary Committee and reported a resolution out of his own Committee on Reconstruction to impeach the president for violating the Tenure of Office Act. "Old Thaddeus Stevens," wrote a contemporary political commentator, "is still keeping himself alive only by the hope of sometime scalping Andrew Johnson ... and watches with a feverish and bilious eye from behind the rampart of his Reconstruction laws the least movement of the enemy." The House voted for impeachment 126 to 47, but when the Senate tried Johnson for high crimes and misdemeanors, the necessary two-thirds majority for conviction fell short by one vote.

Stevens lived only ten weeks after the trial. Many said that his disappointment speeded his decline. This was not true, however. In the short period before his death he continued to work for Reconstruction, a free public school system for the District of Columbia, various railroad bills, and the purchase of Alaska. He died in August 1868 and rested in state in front of Lincoln's statue on the Capitol Rotunda, attended by an honor guard of black soldiers from Massachusetts. After his burial in Lancaster, the Republican party, in a grandiose gesture of respect, formally nominated him for Congress. So loyal were his constituents that he won in November!

Stevens made many fierce enemies during his lifetime. For many years after his death their views of him were widely accepted and he was remembered as an ill-tempered, vindictive, and punitive man who set back the course of sectional reconciliation. Now, following the "second Reconstruction" of the 1950s and 1960s, "the old Commoner" appears as a statesman ahead of his times and an often admirable defender of racial justice. He, of course, preferred to be seen as a great egalitarian. The inscription he chose for his tombstone testifies to his deep concern for all humanity, regardless of race:

I repose in this quiet and secluded spot,
Not from any natural preference for solitude
But, finding other Cemeteries limited as to Race by Charter Rules,
I have chosen this that I might illustrate in my death
The Principles which I advocated Through a long life:

EQUALITY OF MAN BEFORE HIS CREATOR.

vorable business climate in the South. The southern state governments, both the Johnson regimes and the ones established under Congress's formula, also contributed, going heavily into debt to lend money to railroad enterprises. Industry recovered. In 1860 southern cotton mills boasted 300,000 spindles. By 1880 these had increased to over 530,000. Between the same two dates southern manufactures as a whole increased in value almost 55 percent.

Many southerners had expected even more spectacular advances. Now that slavery was dead and the plantation class that had discouraged manufacturing was out of favor, the South, some felt, would flourish industrially. Until the 1880s such hopes were largely unrealized. Still, the rebound of industry and transportation from immediate postwar lows was remarkable.

During the period between 1865 and 1877, agriculture continued to be the chief element in the southern economy, and the war did little to shift southern agriculture from its traditional emphasis on corn and cotton. If anything, cotton became even more important after 1865 than before the war. For a year or two after Appomattox cotton prices remained high. Though cotton was taxed heavily by the federal government—vengefully, southerners believed—high cotton prices helped put money into the pockets of a needy people. It took years to restore cotton production to prewar levels, but by 1878 the South's cotton output had almost reached its prewar peak. Thereafter, it grew steadily, and by the 1890s the region was producing twice as many bales as in 1859.

Tenantry and Sharecropping. By the end of the century the social basis of southern agriculture had been thoroughly transformed. Before the war, defenders of slavery had denied that blacks could function in a free labor market. During the war the Treasury Department, under Secretary Chase's prompting, put this theory to the test in an interesting experiment in the South Carolina Sea Islands near Port Royal. The experiment demonstrated that when exslaves were given land, they made successful farmers. A similar experiment undertaken by Grant at Davis Bend, Mississippi, also proved successful. Unfortunately, neither test benefited the freedmen. The Port Royal venture collapsed when the Treasury Department failed to transfer land title to the freedmen as it had promised, selling the abandoned Sea Island property to the highest bidder instead. The Davis Bend property was returned to planters armed with pardons from President Johnson.

Efforts to create a class of black farm owners in the South did not cease with these two instances. General Rufus Saxton, head of the Freedmen's Bureau in South Carolina, in June 1865 declared he would carve up thousands of acres of land confiscated from rebels into forty-acre homesteads where exslaves, "by faithful industry," could "readily achieve an independence." Thaddeus Stevens and other Radicals in Congress introduced actual legislation to transfer confiscated rebel estates to newly enfranchised blacks. Only landowning, they believed, could protect blacks against exploitation and keep them from being virtually reenslaved. The former slaves themselves yearned to become landowners. "We all know that the colored people want land," a South Carolina carpetbagger declared. "Night and day they think and dream of it. It is their all and all." Whitelaw Reid quoted an elderly black man he had met on his trip to the South: "What's de use of bein' free if you don't own land enough to be buried? Might juss as well stay slave all yo days."

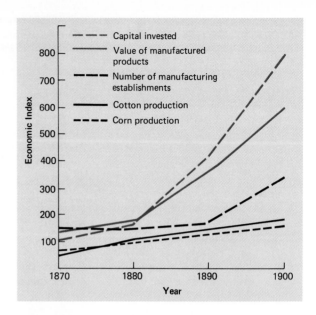

The economic recovery of former confederate states, 1870–1900
Note: Indexed at 1860 = 100. Source: Twelfth Census of the United States, 1990: Agriculture.

Yearnings were often transformed into vivid expectations. Many blacks, hearing about Sexton, Stevens, and the others, came to believe that the government intended to give them "forty acres and a mule," and they were bitterly disappointed when it proved untrue. Some acreage *was* turned over to freedmen. Radical-controlled South Carolina set up a program to sell land on easy terms to ex-slaves. By 1890 the state Land Commission had given some 2,000 black families title to their own farms. In 1866, Congress passed the Southern Homestead Act, providing free land for blacks and whites alike on the federal domain in the former slave states.

In the end, however, a large black yeomen class failed to appear. The lands available in the South for homesteading were isolated and infertile, and few if any black families were able to make a success of farming them. Congress might have followed Stevens's advice and turned over all seized Confederate land to the freedmen. It might even have "nationalized" all southern land and redistributed it as various revolutionary governments have done in our time. But ultimately the Radicals were not so very radical, and their respect for private property rights—even those of ex-rebels—took precedence over their concern for the freedmen. Most were certain that the ballot offered sufficient protection to the freedmen; a social revolution was not needed.

There was another way that freedmen could have become landowners: Black southerners might have accumulated some money and bought land. Southern land prices were low in the 1870s, and a few hundred dollars could

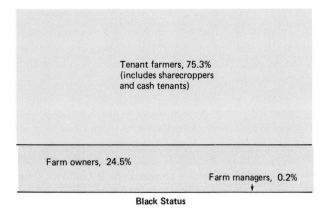

Tenant farmers, 75.3%
(includes sharecroppers
and cash tenants)

Farm owners, 24.5%

Farm managers, 0.2%

Black Status

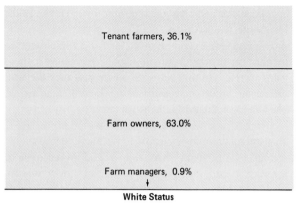

Tenant farmers, 36.1%

Farm owners, 63.0%

Farm managers, 0.9%

White Status

The status of farm operators in former slave states, 1900

have bought a black family a small farm. In 1865, Congress chartered the Freedmen's Bank to support such black self-help efforts. But the bank was poorly managed and could not withstand the financial panic of 1873. When it closed its doors the following year, it took with it over $3 million of hard-won savings from thousands of black depositors. There was still another impediment to freedmen buying land: White southerners believed that if blacks owned land they would not work for white landlords and employers. It is easy to see why they made it difficult for black farmers to buy land even when they could pay cash. Yet despite all the difficulties, by 1880 about a fifth of all black farmers owned their land.

Though only a minority of southern blacks ever became yeomen, they did remain as workers on the land. For a short while after Appomattox most worked for wages under contracts supervised by the Freedmen's Bureau. But this system pleased neither blacks nor their employers. Cash was difficult for landowners to find in the months following the war, so money wages were hard to pay. The bureau tried to guarantee payment, but employers often fell behind in their obligations anyway. The freedmen, of course, resented such treatment and also disliked the harshness with which some bureau agents enforced labor contracts against them. Still more unsatisfactory from the freedmen's point of view was the return to gang work and the planters' close supervision of every aspect of their labor and their lives. The system reminded them too much of slavery and seemed a mockery of freedom.

Out of this mutual dissatisfaction with wage-paid agricultural labor emerged a tenant farmer system that by 1880 had become characteristic of much of the cotton-growing South. Tenantry took many forms and included whites as well as blacks. Thousands of Confederate privates returned home to become, not successful planters, but tenants on lands owned by former slaveholders. Tenants might pay rent either in cash or in part of the crop, typically cotton. Though the system was not as desirable as ownership, a cash tenant was at least free from constant supervision and sometimes could save enough to buy land.

The greater number of tenant farmers, however, especially among the freedmen, were either sharecroppers or share renters. The former had nothing to offer but their labor, and in return for use of the land and a house, usually divided the crop equally with the landlord. A share renter could provide his own seed, mule, and plow as well, and usually got three fourths of what he produced. Linked to tenantry was the crop-lien system, a credit arrangement by which a storekeeper (who sometimes was the landlord as well) would extend credit to the tenant for supplies during the crop-growing season. When the harvest came and the cotton was sold, the tenant would then repay the debt. Buying on credit was expensive since it included an interest charge. It also gave dishonest storekeepers a chance to cheat. Because they kept the books, they had the upper hand and often juggled the debits and credits to suit themselves. Tenants who could not meet their debts could not change the merchant they dealt with; they remained tied to him almost like serfs.

The freedmen's lot represented a missed opportunity for the nation. This is not to say that freedom was not better than slavery. Some blacks managed to become landowners despite all the difficulties. Most were released from the degradation of close personal supervision by whites. Economically they were better off as sharecroppers than as slaves. Roger Ransom and Richard Sutch conclude that whereas slaves received in food, clothing, housing, and medical attention about 23 percent of what whites received, the freedmen after 1865 obtained a full half of total white income. In addition to these economic advances, blacks were now able to make decisions about their economic lives that they never were allowed to make before. Almost all decided that black women would no longer work in the fields; like white women, they would stay home and become proper housewives and mothers. Many black children too left the labor market to attend school. Unfortunately, these gains were a one-time advance, made just after the war. Thereafter, while the country as a whole became richer, black living standards remained stagnant.

Indeed, the sharecrop–crop-lien system proved to be an economic trap for the entire lower South. Because they did not own the land, sharecroppers had no incentive to improve it. Landlords, too, had little incentive, for they could only hope to recover a limited portion of the greater output that might come from additional capital investment. Tenantry also tied the South to a one-crop system and prevented diversification. As one sharecropper complained in the 1880s: "We ought to plant less [cotton and tobacco] and more grain and grasses, but how are we to do it; the man who furnishes us with rations at 50 percent interest won't let us; he wants money crops planted." Failure to diversify also produced serious soil exhaustion that could only be offset by expensive additions of fertilizers. Worse still, cotton prices steadily declined for a generation after 1865, pulling down the entire cotton-tied southern rural economy.

There was still another factor at work that reduced southern income after 1865. The pre–Civil War system of gang labor had been exceptionally efficient. However harsh, it had made southern agriculture the most productive in the nation. Its replacement by tenantry diminished the per-worker output of southern labor. Blacks, even though tenants, might be better off economically after emancipation, but that was because they got a much larger piece of a reduced pie. Whites clearly suffered a decline from their pre–Civil War conditions.

For whatever reasons, the South as a section also experienced a relative decline. As farms in the North and West came to look more prosperous after 1865, travelers in the South reported weed-choked farmyards, sagging, unpainted shacks, and ragged, discouraged-looking people, black and white. With each year Dixie fell further behind the rest of the nation in almost every measure of material abundance and social well-being: literacy, infant mortality, longevity, health, and per-capita income. By 1890, the section that had once led the nation had become America's problem area.

Cultural Change. Whatever the economic effects, the end of slavery brought immense social and cultural gains for black Americans. Black men and women enjoyed a new freedom of movement, which some exercised by going to the cities or decamping for more prosperous parts of the country. At the end of Reconstruction several thousand blacks left the lower South and moved north or west. A particularly large movement of "exodusters" to Kansas after 1878 alarmed southern white leaders, who feared that the South might lose its labor force.

The end of slavery freed blacks to express themselves in ways never before possible. Slavery had not destroyed

They were free, but the economic condition of most black sharecroppers and tenant farmers was not dramatically better than that of slaves. Redistribution of confiscated plantation lands might have improved their lot, but the government, which gave millions of acres to railroads, was not so generous to its newest citizens.

black culture, but it had made it difficult for blacks to demonstrate the full range of their talents and to exercise their organizational abilities. The end of formal bondage released energies previously held in check. Blacks withdrew from white churches in large numbers and formed their own. Particularly successful were the Baptists and Methodists. By 1870 there were 500,000 black Baptists; in 1876 the African Methodist Episcopal church had 200,000 members. These churches gave talented former slaves an opportunity to demonstrate leadership beyond anything previously possible. Unlike politics, which was largely closed to talented black men after 1877, the Protestant ministry continued to provide leadership opportunities.

The end of slavery also expanded educational opportunities for blacks. Before the war slaves had been legally denied education. After 1865 northern educators and philanthropists seized on Dixie as missionary territory to be converted to "civilization." As one Yankee benefactor remarked, South Carolina needed only "freedom and education" to become "another Massachusetts." In the months after Appomattox hundreds of Yankee teachers, hoping to uplift a benighted region, went South to establish schools and bring the blessings of literacy. The Freedmen's Bureau also labored to end illiteracy and sought to train blacks in trades. The most permanent impact was achieved by southern self-help. Before long every southern state, under Radical guidance, had made some provision for educating black children. The southern educational system long remained segregated (except for a time in the cosmopolitan city of New Orleans) and poor; yet the schools managed to make a dent in ignorance. By 1880 a quarter of all blacks could read and write; twenty years later the figure had risen to half. College training for blacks, nonexistent in the South before 1860, became available as well. No blacks were admitted to the established southern state universities, but southern state governments founded separate black colleges and universities. Meanwhile, the Freedmen's Bureau and white philanthropists helped charter such black private colleges as Atlanta University, Fisk University in Tennessee, and Howard University in Washington, D.C. Black education—indeed, all southern education—had a long way to go before it caught up with the North; but compared with the accomplishments before 1860, the gains of the generation following the war were truly impressive.

Yet segregation remained a central fact of life in the South. In 1875 Congress passed a strongly worded Civil Rights Act guaranteeing to all persons, regardless of color, "the full and equal enjoyment of all the accommodations . . . of inns, public conveyances . . . , theaters, and other places of public amusement"; but separation and social inequality persisted; in fact, the separation of the races became more complete than before the war. In most communities, trains, buses, and theaters had white and black sections. In private life the racial spheres were still more exclusive, and blacks almost never entered the homes of white people except as servants. Even southern Radicals seldom treated blacks as social equals.

The Southern Radical Governments.   The greatest disappointment of Reconstruction for black Americans was its political failure. Accepting blacks as political equals was completely unacceptable to a majority of white southerners, and in the end they were able to defeat the goal of the Radical Republicans to make the freedmen equal citizens.

Blacks fully participated in the creation and running of the state governments established by the five military commanders under the terms of the Reconstruction Acts. As prescribed, they voted in the elections for state constitutional conventions, served in those conventions, voted in the state elections for state and federal office that followed, and served in these offices. Blacks, however, did not dominate the Radical Republican regimes that came to power. Even in South Carolina and Mississippi, where the black population outnumbered the white, they held only a minority of political offices. The rest were filled by native-born southern white Republicans and northern-born white immigrants to Dixie.

Blanche K. Bruce, a black man, was Jefferson Davis's able successor as United States Senator from Mississippi.

One of the persistent myths of Reconstruction is that black political officials during the years of Republican rule in the South were unusually corrupt and incompetent. But in fact that was not the case. Among the fifteen black southerners elected to Congress were a number of exceptionally able and well-educated men. Senator Blanche K. Bruce of Mississippi was an effective legislator who, had he been white, would have been a major power in Congress. James G. Blaine, who served with many of the black legislators, said of them: "The colored men who took their seats in both Senate and House. . .were as a rule studious, earnest, ambitious men, whose public conduct. . .should be honorable to any race." On the level of state government, black officeholders ranged from excellent to poor. All in all, as legislators and officials, their successes did not fall noticeably behind those of their white colleagues.

White Republican leaders too have been greatly disparaged. Southern white Republicans—called "scalawags" by their enemies—were denounced by their opponents as "the vilest renegades of the South," as men "who have dishonored the dignity of white blood, and are traitors alike to principle and race."

In fact, many were former Unionists and members of the South's prewar Whig business class who were attracted to the Republican party because they supported Republican pro-business, pro-growth policies. And they were not the tiny minority of the white population that we would expect if they were merely renegades. In 1872, for example, 20 percent of the South's white voters cast their ballots for Republican candidates.

Nor were the northern whites who participated in the Republican state governments the "itinerant adventurers" and "vagrant interlopers" that southern conservatives charged. Called "carpetbaggers," after the cheap carpet-cloth suitcases carried by travelers, many were former Union soldiers who had served in the South and come to like it as a place to live. Others were sincere idealists who were committed to establishing a new social order. Obviously many white southern Republicans—scalawags and carpetbaggers alike—were people who hoped to take personal advantage of new circumstances, but there is no reason to consider them any more venal, corrupt, or self-serving than voters and politicians in general.

On the whole the Radical-dominated southern state gov-

The first colored senator and representatives in the 41st and 42nd Congress of the United States. As a group they acquitted themselves competently.

ernments were remarkably effective and reasonably honest. Of course, measured by the standards of the tightfisted prewar South, they were big spenders and ran up huge debts. But the job of physically rebuilding and adjusting to the new circumstances required a great deal of money. The new governments contributed freely to railroads and other businesses. They established the South's first state-supported school systems and sharply increased public spending for poor relief, prisons, and state hospitals. Though still far behind the North in providing social services, under Radical rule the South began to catch up with the rest of the nineteenth century.

The new Radical governments were also more democratic and egalitarian than were the prewar regimes. The state constitutions adopted under congressional Reconstruction made many previously appointive offices elective and gave small farmers better representation in the legislatures than they had had before the war. They also extended the vote to white males who did not meet the old property qualifications. The new state governments reduced the number of crimes punishable by death and granted married women more secure control over their property, reforms most northern states had adopted before 1860. They swept away the unequal treatment of black workers that had been incorporated into the Black Codes. Some of the Radical regimes even pursued policies that foreshadowed the modern social welfare state. South Carolina financed medical care for its poor citizens. Alabama paid legal fees for poor defendants. Not for another century would the South—or the nation—see anything like this again.

Redemption. Regardless of their accomplishments, many white southerners despised the Radical regimes and accused them of corruption. Some were in fact corrupt, but generally no more than was normal in state affairs during those years. Southern conservatives also disliked the reforms they initiated, because they were new, because they seemed to be Yankee-inspired, and because they were expensive. Landlords, in particular, denounced the new programs for raising taxes on real estate, which before the war had been lightly taxed, if taxed at all. But above all, conservatives found it difficult to accept the Republican-dominated state governments because they were part of the new racial regime. After 250 years of regarding blacks as inherently inferior, the white South could not easily agree to changes that declared a black person the political equal of a white one.

When the Freedmen's Bureau set up schools for blacks, former slaves of all ages flocked to them. Wrote Booker T. Washington, "It was a whole race trying to go to school." The Snow Hill School, here, abandoned classical education in favor of industrial training, which was deemed more appropriate to black needs.

A fierce struggle for political control soon developed in the South between the forces of the new era and those of the old. Radical Union Leagues helped to rally black and scalawag voters in support of Republican candidates for state and local offices. The Radicals also had influential friends in Washington, and after 1869, when Ulysses Grant became president, they had the support of the federal executive branch. That year, moreover, the Republicans forced through the Fifteenth Amendment forbidding any state to deny citizens the right to vote because of "race, color, or previous condition of servitude." Now black suffrage was securely embedded in the Constitution without qualification. For a while the Radical governments succeeded in holding onto political office, especially in states where they were most firmly entrenched—Alabama, Mississippi, Texas, Florida, Louisiana, and South Carolina. But in the end they could not match the experience, self-confidence, and ruthlessness of the defenders of bygone times, who hoped to "redeem" the South from "Black Republicanism."

A major weapon of the "redeemers" was the Ku Klux Klan. Formed in 1866 in Tennessee by young Confederate veterans primarily as a social club, the Klan quickly grew into an antiblack, anti-Radical organization. At the outset it used fear and superstition to intimidate blacks. Hooded, mounted Klansmen would swoop down at night on isolated cabins where blacks lived, making fearsome noises and firing guns. Later they resorted to more violent methods. Klansmen torched black homes, attacked and beat black militiamen, ambushed both white and black Radical leaders, and lynched blacks accused of crimes. During the 1868 presidential campaign Klansmen assassinated an Arkansas congressman, three members of the South Carolina legislature, and several Republican members of state constitutional conventions. Some conservative apologists dismissed the Klan as an organization composed of white riffraff but in fact, as one Radical newspaper noted, it included "men of property . . . respectable citizens."

At its height in the late 1860s, the Klan tide went vir-

The Ku Klux Klan, here depicted on one of its raids, was a brutal enforcer of conservative white views in the reconstruction south.

tually unchecked. Law enforcement officials either looked the other way out of sympathy or felt impotent to deal with the violence. Witnesses of Klan misdeeds were often scared off from testifying against it. In Arkansas and Tennessee, where white Republicans were numerous, hostile governors struck back and damaged the Klan severely. But in other states the Klan created a reign of terror and lawlessness that threatened to undo the entire Reconstruction process. Then in 1870 and 1871 Congress passed three Force Bills, which declared "armed combinations" and Klan terrorist tactics illegal. The bills gave the president the right to prosecute in federal courts all those who sought to prevent qualified persons from voting. For the first time the federal government had defined certain crimes against individuals as violation of federal law. President Grant invoked the measures in nine South Carolina counties, and soon hundreds of Klansmen were indicted for illegal activities.

The Klan quickly declined, but by the 1870s racism was thoroughly institutionalized in Democratic politics. The determination of southern conservatives to render blacks submissive and to take control of the South away from Radicals and their supporters persisted. The redeemers abandoned hooded robes and night rides, but not other forms of intimidation. Typical of their approach was the successful effort in 1875 to return Mississippi to conservative control. There the redeemers ostracized the scalawags and drove many white Republicans to abandon politics or change their party. One who succumbed to their tactics, Colonel James Lusk, told a black fellow Republican: "No white man can live in the South in the future and act with any other than the Democratic party unless he is willing and prepared to live a life of social isolation and remain in political oblivion."

Black voters could not be so easily forced to abandon the party that had served them so well, but here harsher tactics were often effective. Blacks who continued to vote Republican were denied jobs or fired from those they had. More stubborn black Republicans were threatened with violence. During the 1875 Mississippi election thousands of white Democrats armed themselves with rifles and shotguns, and then, to make the message clear, entered the names of black Republicans in "dead books." In Vicksburg, Yazoo City, and other Mississippi towns blacks were shot and killed in preelection fights.

The campaign worked. The Democrats captured the Mississippi legislature and elected the only state official running for statewide office. The Republican governor, Adelburt Ames, faced with impeachment by the new legislature, agreed to resign. Mississippi had been "redeemed." Similar processes took place in several of the other states,

so that by 1876 only Louisiana, Florida, and South Carolina remained under Republican administrations—and these regimes stayed in power only because they were protected by federal troops.

The End of Reconstruction.   Clearly the redeemers were effective tacticians and organizers. But if the commitment of northerners to Radical rule in the South had not been weakening, the redeemers would not have succeeded. The decline of northerners' determination had several sources. To an increasingly large number of Republicans, it began to seem that the defense of the black man was merely an excuse for continued domination by the corrupt wing of their party. Whenever a new scandal was uncovered in the Grant administration—and there were many—it would be covered up by an appeal to Republican unity against the ex-rebels, a process usually referred to as "waving the bloody shirt." The problem of how to deal with blacks and their oppressors always seemed to justify continued Republican ascendancy. By the middle of the 1870s many

Secret societies like the Knights of the White Camelia, the Pale Faces, and the Knights of the Ku Klux Klan organized to frustrate Reconstruction. Describing itself as an "institution of Chivalry, Humanity, Mercy, and Patriotism," the Klan violently intimidated blacks.

Republicans had concluded that abandoning blacks and their friends in the South was better than continuing to uphold the corrupt element in their own party.

Fatigue and racism also played their parts. How long, many northerners asked, could the country invest energy and money to sustain a system that the "best elements" of southern society opposed? Clearly, they said, blacks would never make good citizens, and there was no point in continuing the hopeless battle. Such arguments were reinforced by a growing conviction among northern commercial and industrial groups that peace in the South would be better for business than the political agitation that constantly disturbed the nation.

The end came in 1876. In the presidential election of that year the Democrats nominated Samuel J. Tilden of New York, a stuffy but honest corporation lawyer. The Republican candidate was Rutherford B. Hayes, the equally upright and aloof governor of Ohio. The Democratic platform promised to withdraw federal troops from the South and endorsed traditional Democratic low-tariff, small-government positions. The Republicans declared that they would never abandon the black man and would continue to support positive government, a protective tariff, and "sound money."

The election was so close that the results were challenged. The Democrats claimed they had carried New York, New Jersey, Connecticut, Indiana, and the entire South. The Republicans insisted that the votes of Florida, Louisiana, and South Carolina—the "unredeemed" states—rightfully belonged to them. They also challenged one Democratic vote in Oregon, where electors had split between the two candidates. As in 1824, the election was thrown into the House of Representatives. For the next four months the country's political life was in an uproar as the politicians tried to settle the issue before Inauguration Day in March 1877.

Both sides brought every weapon to bear on the dispute—propaganda, legal maneuvering, congressional com-

Southern black voters after 1865 were alternately courted and coerced by white politicians. The Democrats found force more necessary than did the Republicans to win black votes. In this Radical Republican cartoon two Democrats (the one at right looking remarkably like Jefferson Davis) make no pretense of winning "hearts and minds."

missions, and threats of violence. Some historians believe that one hidden but vitally important issue during the disputed election period was railroads. The Republicans had favored government land grants to encourage completion of the national rail network. The Democrats disliked federal aid, and on many occasions leading northern Democrats had attacked the land-grant policy. At the time of the disputed election, a major grant of special importance to southern commercial and business interests was being considered in Congress. The beneficiary of this gift was the Texas and Pacific Railroad, designed to connect New Orleans and other important southern cities with the Pacific Coast. The rail link, it was believed, would bring wealth to many communities in the South. A Democratic administration, of course, would remove the troops from the remaining unredeemed states and end Reconstruction, but it would also certainly oppose the Texas and Pacific rail project. This reasoning, it is said, led influential southern leaders, many of whom were former Whigs with little love for the Democrats, to seek a bargain with the Republicans.

In return for a promise to remove the troops, to give some high federal office to southerners, and to support a Texas and Pacific land grant, southerners in the House of Representatives agreed to support Republican Hayes. Many scholars believe that this bargain, known as the Compromise of 1877, gave Hayes the election. Others deny that such a wide-ranging agreement occurred. Instead, they argue, the southerners merely traded electoral votes for removing federal troops from the South. There was no economic deal. In any event, soon after Hayes's inauguration as nineteenth president of the United States, the last federal troops were withdrawn from the South. The redeemers quickly moved in. Reconstruction was over.

★ CONCLUSIONS ★

Reconstruction was not an unrelieved disaster. During these momentous years southerners repaired the physical devas-

PRESIDENTIAL ELECTION OF 1876

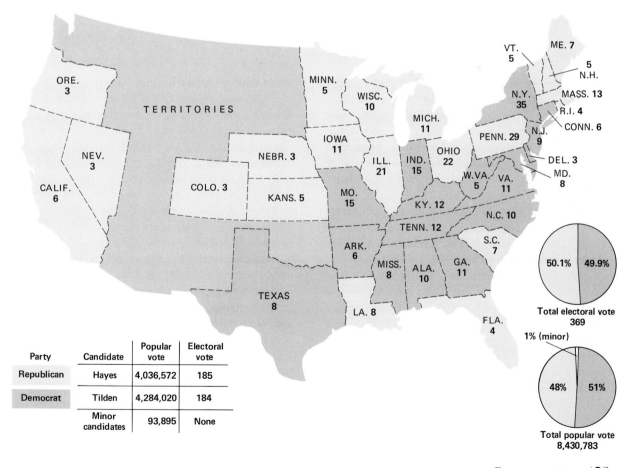

Party	Candidate	Popular vote	Electoral vote
Republican	Hayes	4,036,572	185
Democrat	Tilden	4,284,020	184
	Minor candidates	93,895	None

Total electoral vote
369

Total popular vote
8,430,783

The Compromise of 1877 was a political deal; Hayes was only elected when he, in effect, made promises to end Reconstruction. Neither southern Democrats nor northern Republicans wanted their dealing made public, so they met in secret sessions like this. (Collection of the New York Historical Society)

tation of the war and reestablished their states' constitutional relations with the Union. Meanwhile, black southerners were able to create for themselves important new islands of freedom—freedom to move, freedom to create social and cultural institutions of their own, freedom for black women to leave the fields. They also improved their material well-being. As sharecroppers, blacks kept a larger share of the wealth they produced than as slaves. Also on the credit side were the Radical-sponsored Fourteenth and Fifteenth amendments. Once implanted in the Constitution, they would become the bases for a "second Reconstruction" in our own day.

Yet there is much that is dismaying about Reconstruction. In general, Americans of the era failed to meet the great challenges that faced them. Instead of a prosperous black yeomanry, the South would be left with a mass of impoverished semipeons who for generations would be a reproach to America's proud claims of prosperity and equality. Instead of political democracy, Reconstruction would bequeath a legacy of sectional fraud, intimidation, and shameless racial exclusion. Rather than accelerating southern economic growth, Reconstruction would chain the South to a declining staple crop agriculture and leave

it ever further behind the rest of the nation.

Who was to blame for this failure? One answer is that Americans were trapped by the past. Deep-seated prejudices and memories of slavery blinded most white southerners—and many northerners—to the need for racial justice. Traditional individualism and the commitment to self-help obscured the fact that the special circumstances of black dependence resulting from slavery called for imaginative government aid. And there were the accidents of events and personalities. Would Lincoln have seen realities more clearly? Certainly the succession of Andrew Johnson, a stubborn man of limited vision and conventional racial views, did nothing to solve the unique problems of the day. Refusing to recognize the North's need to exact some penance from the defeated South, he needlessly antagonized even moderates and drove them into the Radical camp. The result was a legacy of sectional hatred that poisoned American political life for generations.

Meanwhile, the nation was turning away from the intractable "southern problem" to what many citizens believed were more important matters. The South and Reconstruction became increasingly remote as the country at large experienced a surge of economic expansion that dwarfed anything of the past.

Eric L. McKitrick. *Andrew Johnson and Reconstruction* (1960)

Andrew Johnson's personality is emphasized in this study of Reconstruction. McKitrick says that Johnson was easily flattered and irrationally stubborn when defied. Most serious of his deficiencies, however, was that he failed to see that the North needed evidence of southern contrition before it could forgive and allow a return to normal relations between the two regions.

Clement Eaton. *The Waning of the Old South Civilization, 1860–1880* (1968)

An excellent short summary of life among the common people and the planter elite in 1860, the effect of the war on southern culture, the postwar white adjustment to freed blacks, economic recovery, and the "cultural lag" especially evident in small towns and rural areas. Eaton concludes that the New South retained much of the old, especially its devotion to states' rights, white supremacy, and the cult of southern womanhood. In the brief generation since this book was written, much has changed, however.

Albion W. Tourgée. *A Fool's Errand: A Novel of the South During Reconstruction* (1879). Edited by George M. Frederickson (1966)

An autobiographical novel by a "carpetbagger" lawyer from Ohio who settled in North Carolina after the Civil War. As a Radical superior court judge, Tourgée was hated by white conservatives for his attempts to bring Ku Klux Klan leaders to justice. His estimate of the role of idealistic carpetbaggers is summed up in his title.

Allen W. Trelease. *White Terror: The Ku Klux Klan Conspiracy and Southern Reconstruction* (1971)

The big, definitive study of the first Klan after the Civil War. This is a potent indictment of the KKK and all its doings.

Joel Williamson. *After Slavery: The Negro in South Carolina During Reconstruction, 1861–1877* (1965)

In this detailed, interesting study of race relations in one key Reconstruction state, Williamson concludes that racial segregation was not wholly a product of "redemption." He also deals with efforts by South Carolina Radicals to provide "land for the landless."

Willie Lee Rose. *Rehearsal for Reconstruction: The Port Royal Experiment* (1964)

The efforts of the northerners who attempted to give the former Sea Island slaves their masters' land are tragicomic in Rose's account. Ultimately the ex-slaves lost the rich cotton lands to their former owners. Yet the temporary success of the Port Royal experiment tells us what might have been if the northern commitment to black freedom and racial justice had been stronger.

Roger Ransom and Richard Sutch. *One Kind of Freedom: The Economic Consequences of Emancipation* (1977)

An important book by two "cliometricians" about how emancipation affected the economic well-being of the freedmen and the South as a whole. Has an interesting discussion of the sharecrop–crop-lien system.

LaWanda Cox and John Cox. *Politics, Principles, and Prejudice, 1865–1866: Dilemma of Reconstruction America* (1963)

A study of presidential Reconstruction that gives the Radicals much credit for idealism and suggests how much politics actually entered into Andrew Johnson's decisions. Reverses the older pattern of blaming the Radicals and praising Johnson.

Leon Litwack. *Been in the Storm So Long: The Aftermath of Slavery* (1980)

Professor Litwack tells us—at somewhat excessive length—what black men and women felt about the new world of freedom after 1863. He shows that their reactions were amazingly diverse and often contradictory.

Herbert Gutman. *The Black Family in Slavery and Freedom, 1750–1925* (1976)

Excellent social history, not only of the slavery period but also of the postslavery experience of black families.

Kenneth Stampp. *The Era of Reconstruction, 1865–1877* (1965)

An excellent overall view of the "new" Reconstruction history. Stampp attacks the myth that Reconstruction meant federal tyranny and "Negro rule." He considers the failure to redistribute property to the freedmen a mistake, but believes the Radicals were governed by idealism rather than greed or pure politics.

C. Vann Woodward. *Reunion and Reaction: The Compromise of 1877 and the End of Reconstruction* (1951)

The dean of southern historians concludes that the agreement to end the presidential election dispute of 1876/1877 was not a bargain made purely in the interest of political peace and orderly government. Rather, it was a behind-the-scenes agreement to exchange continued Republican supremacy for major economic favors to southern business groups. Not all scholars buy his thesis.

Jonathan Wiener. *Social Origins of the New South, 1860–1885* (1978)

A Marxist-oriented study of post-bellum southern society that emphasizes the continued domination of the planter class and the near-slavery of the freedmen.

Eric Foner. *Reconstruction, America's Unfinished Revolution, 1863–1877* (1988)

A wonderfully executed history of Reconstruction that reflects the revisionist research of the past generation as well as the political and cultural perceptions of today. It is a long book, however, (over 600 pages), and the reader could substitute Foner's briefer version, *A Short History of Reconstruction* (1990).

17 ★

THE TRIUMPH OF INDUSTRIALISM

What Were the Causes, What Were the Costs?

1862, 1864	Pacific Railroad Acts
1866	The National Labor Union is established
1869	The Knights of Labor is organized
1873	The Slaughterhouse cases • Financial panic; unemployment climbs to 12 percent
1877	The Compromise of 1877: Rutherford B. Hayes elected president • U.S. Supreme Court decides the Granger cases • Socialist Labor party is established
1880	James A. Garfield elected president
1881	Garfield assassinated; Chester A. Arthur becomes president
1882	John D. Rockefeller forms the first "trust," but it is dissolved by Ohio courts • Edison's first electric generating station opens in New York • The *San Mateo* case
1884	Grover Cleveland elected president
1886	Haymarket Riot in Chicago • Samuel Gompers founds the American Federation of Labor (AFL) • *Santa Clara Co.* v. *Southern Pacific Railroad*
1888	Benjamin Harrison elected president
1890	Sherman Antitrust Act
1892	Grover Cleveland elected president for the second time • Populist party is established
1893	Sherman Silver Purchase Act is repealed • The American Railway Union is organized by Eugene V. Debs
1894	Pullman strike is ended by federal troops
1895	*E. C. Knight* case weakens Sherman Antitrust Act
1896	William McKinley elected president
1897	*Maximum Freight Rates* case
1901	McKinley is assassinated; Theodore Roosevelt becomes president • Eugene V. Debs's Socialist party is founded
1904–12	Socialist party membership increases to 130,000
1913	Federal Reserve System established

Almost every part of the American economy grew at top speed during the post–Civil War period. Mining, construction, commerce, agriculture—all experienced remarkable expansion. Yet the most spectacular advance was in industry. As late as 1880 agriculture still created a larger share of income for Americans than any other source. Ten years later, despite impressive growth, its contribution was surpassed by industry, and by 1900 the total value of goods produced by factories and shops in the United States was twice that of goods produced on farms. In the mid-1890s America became the leading industrial power in the world. In 1913 one-third of all the world's manufactured goods came from American factories.

The explosive surge in industry was the major force behind the country's impressive gains in GNP (Gross National Product), the simplest overall measure of economic growth. Between 1865 and 1908 total GNP grew at an average annual rate of more than 4 percent a year, considerably higher than it has been for most of the period since. By 1908 the total American GNP was eight times that of the year Robert E. Lee surrendered at Appomattox. Population was also increasing in this period. Still, at its end, Americans were producing twice the output of goods and services *per person* each year as at the beginning. Unfortunately, this did not mean that every American was

twice as rich on the eve of World War I as he or she—or, more likely, their forebears—had been in 1865. As we will see, the gains were unequally distributed. But the extraordinary performance at least provided the foundation for broad affluence.

What caused the industrial leap and the economic surge after 1865? Was there some single, predominant factor, or were there a number of separate ones? And did the American people pay a price for the impressive advance? Or was growth essentially cost-free? Let us start with the causes. We shall then consider the price.

★ CAPTAINS OF INDUSTRY ★

If the average educated American were asked to explain the country's late-nineteenth-century economic advance, he or she would probably point to men like Andrew Carnegie, John D. Rockefeller, and "Commodore" Vanderbilt as the principal agents. Even against the gaudy and boisterous background of the era we call the Gilded Age, the image of these big-business tycoons stands out vividly. The image is, in many ways, a negative one: The business leaders of this period were "robber barons" who held the nation for ran-

Entrepreneur Gustavus Swift created a new industry and expanded a national market by bringing western meat to eastern cities. Swift's "dissembly lines" for dressing beef and pork and his improvements of the refrigerator car made more meat available at lower prices to more people.

som to amass their great fortunes; they were crude and vulgar men who flaunted their wealth and their bad taste. Yet to this day many Americans will readily concede that these men almost single-handedly made the United States an industrial giant. Are they right?

A close look at the extraordinary economic achievement of the Gilded Age shows that the great entrepreneurs—those who organized, managed, and assumed the risks of business—were indeed important elements in the nation's spectacular economic success. Entrepreneurship is a major element in virtually all economic growth. To increase an economy's output, it is not enough to add more materials, labor, and machines to the economic mix. Growth also requires applying the initiating, coordinating, and managerial functions to the start of new businesses and the improvement of old ones. The ability to detect an important economic need, slash costs of production, tap new sources of savings, recruit and manage labor, recognize and inspire new talent—these entrepreneurial skills are not common or easy to marshal. When a given society is able to bring these talents to bear, the economy will almost certainly advance more quickly than before.

Gustavus Swift and the Organizing Function. To understand the role of entrepreneurship in the economic growth and change of the post–Civil War period, let us consider several examples. A good place to start is the meat-packing industry.

Before the Civil War a few western cities like Cincinnati were important meat-packing centers. Hogs and cattle were slaughtered on a large scale and pickled in brine to supply merchant seamen and slaves with salt pork and beef. Most fresh meat consumed, however, came from local butchers as it spoiled too quickly to be sent from distant suppliers. Live animals could be shipped by rail or driven on the hoof to city consumers, but they often lost much weight or were injured or killed in transit. Then, in the generation following the Civil War, three developments helped transform the business of supplying the public with meat. First, an increasing proportion of Americans came to live in cities, re-

INDUSTRY, 1860–1890

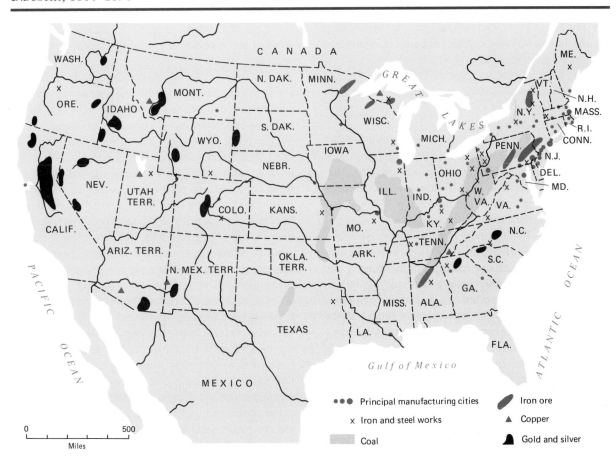

Principal manufacturing cities •••
x Iron and steel works
Coal
Iron ore
▲ Copper
Gold and silver

mote from the farms and from the major grazing areas of the country. Second, an expanding railroad network made the products of the prairies and plains of the West more accessible to urban consumers. Third, in the 1870s refrigerated railroad cars appeared, allowing chilled fresh beef and pork to be shipped long distances without spoilage.

One of the first men to recognize the new possibilities that these changes opened up for the meat industry was Gustavus Swift, a New Englander who came to Chicago as a cattle buyer in the 1870s. Swift saw the advantages of slaughtering cattle close to the grass and corn of the West and shipping the trimmed product to eastern consumers. Such a system would eliminate the losses in shipping live cattle; more important, centralized processing would be more economical. Much of the slaughtering could be mechanized, thereby reducing labor costs, and the animal parts that were normally discarded could be sold to make medicines, sausage casings, fertilizers, leather, and other byproducts. (It would be said of the great hog butchers of the late nineteenth century that they used every part of the pig but the squeal.)

Swift sent his first trimmed chilled beef east by refrigerator car in the mid-1870s. At first he encountered stiff resistance to the unfamiliar product from consumers and from local retailers alike. But in a few years, joined by other packers like Philip D. Armour, Michael Cudahy, and Nelson Morris, he was shipping millions of pounds of meat annually from his Chicago plants and marketing it through a network of branch houses and agents. In 1875 the Chicago packers slaughtered 250,000 cattle; in 1880, 500,000; in 1890, a million.

Thomas Edison and Technological Innovation. Swift's contribution to the economic advance of the period consisted primarily of improving the organization of an existing industry. Thomas Edison developed new technology, adapted it to public needs, and created several whole new branches of manufacturers.

We think of Edison today as an inventor of gadgets—and indeed he was. He improved the telephone and the telegraph, and invented the motion picture camera, the phonograph, and the incandescent light bulb. Yet he was far more than an inspired tinkerer; he was also a first-rate entrepreneur whose skills immeasurably improved the quality of American life and launched a giant new business.

At the beginning of the nineteenth century Americans worked and played almost entirely during daylight hours, and the rhythms of life closely corresponded to the seasonal length of the day. At night city streets were dark. Private homes were also unlighted after daylight, or at most dimly lighted, except on special occasions or if the owners were well off and could afford expensive candles or whale oil

The young Thomas Edison, one of the most inspired of America's inspired tinkerers.

lamps. During the 1850s gas light arrived, but it too was expensive, and its use was confined to city streets and to the upper and middle classes of the larger urban centers, where it was economically feasible to install costly pipes and meters.

The new petroleum industry changed this picture. In the 1840s and 1850s, "rock oil" was a substance extracted from streams and used as a medicine. Its value as an illuminant was understood, but no one was certain that it could be collected in large enough quantities to be useful for lighting. Then, in 1859, a group of businessmen hired E. L. Drake, a former railroad conductor familiar with well drilling, to try to extract oil from the ground in western Pennsylvania. After several weeks of effort Drake struck a major oil pool, proving that it was possible to guarantee a steady supply of the substance. Thereafter, what had been a quack medical remedy became a household necessity. Refined into kerosene, petroleum quickly replaced whale oil and candles as the nation's major source of home lighting.

Kerosene was especially valuable as an illuminant in rural areas, and indeed it is still used on isolated farms and backwoods camps today. But from the outset, the risk of fire in congested city homes, and in stores, hotels, and restaurants, made it unwelcome in the major urban centers. By the 1870s it was widely recognized that electricity would not have this drawback. In fact, it was used already, in the form of arc lights, for illuminating stage productions and city streets. Unfortunately, arc lights were too brilliant and too wasteful of power to be used in private homes. This is where Edison saw his opportunity. If electric light could be reduced to small units, electricity would replace kerosene and gas for home use. Many scientists at the time believed that the feat could not be accomplished. Edison ignored their warnings and at his laboratory in Menlo Park, New Jersey, pushed ahead to develop a practical home electric lighting system.

Edison was interested in more than an efficient long-lasting lamp. He hoped to develop an entire system similar to the profitable gas-lighting systems of the day. Such an arrangement would require a centrally located source of electric power that could serve many lamps, a means to transmit the power efficiently to each lamp, lamps that could be turned on and off without affecting other lamps on the circuit, and finally, a metering arrangement to measure each customer's use of current. Edison's goal was not merely technical; it was also commercial. He had to lure customers from an established workable system—gas—to his own, and at the same time make a profit for private investors.

This difficult enterprise aroused Edison's impressive talents as both businessman and inventor. After securing dependable financial backing, he worked out the technical specifications for an efficient and economically feasible lighting system—with the aid of a trained mathematician. Once he had developed a usable carbon filament for his glass lamp, he built a central generating station on Pearl Street near New York City's financial district, where his success would be sure to attract the attention of the nation's money men. He also developed a simple metering system that enabled the Edison Company to assess charges against users.

The Pearl Street power station began operation on September 4, 1882, and was a brilliant success. During the next few years the Edison Company opened other stations in Boston, Philadelphia, and Chicago. Before long the incandescent lamp had almost totally replaced gas light in towns and cities. In a few years the nation's cities were alive with light, and urban Americans stayed up later to read, talk, dine, and generally enjoy themselves. Eventually electricity came to the farms and rural areas. A whole way of life had been revolutionized by one man's skill, insight, and enterprise.

Andrew Carnegie and Cost Consciousness. Careful cost analysis and ruthless cost cutting were the hallmarks of Andrew Carnegie's entrepreneurship.

Carnegie was the classic self-made man. Arriving in the United States with his family in 1848, the thirteen-year-old Scottish lad first worked in a Pittsburgh textile factory replacing broken threads on the spinning spools for $1.20 a week. In the 1850s, after a stint as a telegraph operator,

Andrew Carnegie at the height of his power and fame.

Carnegie became an assistant to Thomas A. Scott, vice president of the Pennsylvania Railroad. Scott was one of the most creative railway executives of his day. The railroads—with their thousands of employees, millions of dollars of capital, and complex financing and rate-setting problems, as well as their enormous territorial extent—were the first truly modern business organizations. From Scott, Carnegie learned how to deal with a large-scale enterprise and how to save thousands by squeezing pennies.

Carnegie was not an inventor like Edison. He worked with existing technology and processes, but made them show a profit. When he moved from railroading to bridge building and then to iron and steel making during the 1860s, men like Abram Hewitt and Eber Ward had already begun to make steel with the new Bessemer and open-hearth processes. Carnegie was more than willing to spend money on promising investments, and he seized on the new steel-making methods for his Pittsburgh-based Edgar Thomson Works. He was never content with the status quo, however. When new improvements came along, he adapted them, disregarding the costs of scrapping his older but still usable equipment. Carnegie ran his furnaces, hearths, and converters full-blast regardless of replacement costs, and did not let up even when orders tumbled during hard times. He also cut expenses ruthlessly and kept down labor costs by mechanizing as many processes as he could. When faced with the prospect of paying dearly for high-quality coke produced by another firm, Carnegie bought a major coke company and acquired along the way its president, the shrewd Henry Clay Frick, as a partner. Later he bought his own ore fields in the newly opened Mesabi Range of Minnesota. Carnegie recruited a corps of driving young executives and then held them strictly accountable for every penny spent producing steel. One of these men later said: "You [were] expected always to get it ten cents cheaper the next year or the next month." Within a few years Carnegie and his associates had lowered the price of steel so much that it could be used to replace iron, wood, and stone in construction, thus paving the way for marvels of engineering never before possible.

Of all the so-called robber barons, Carnegie was probably the most civic-minded. Like the others, he fought to keep his employees' wages low, but he also believed that rich men were custodians of wealth for society at large. Before he died, the "Star-spangled Scotsman" gave away much of his immense fortune for libraries and to charitable institutions, research foundations, and endowments for peace and international understanding. And his charity was genuine: In Carnegie's day, before the income tax, philanthropy was not tax-deductible.

Capital Creation and J. P. Morgan.   Swift, Edison, and Carnegie faced the problem of raising money to invest in blast furnaces, meat-packing plants, and power stations. Where did these funds come from? Ultimately the source of any money for capital investment must be savings. Swift and Carnegie relied largely on their own savings, derived from the profits of previous and existing enterprises. Many businesspeople, however, were happy to tap the pools of savings set aside by other people.

Fortunately, the savings rate was exceptionally high in the era, far higher than in our own day. Before the Civil War savings ran about 15 percent of national product. By the 1880s this had leaped to about 25 percent. People saved because it was enjoined by religion; they also saved because there was no other way to provide for old age, disease, or accident. Substantial inequalities of wealth and income also help explain the high savings rate. Rich men and women were particularly able to save because their incomes far exceeded their day-to-day needs. These savings usually represented the profits they earned by employing labor. They had money to invest because other people received lower wages and incomes than might otherwise have been possible. Thus millions of ordinary wage earners surrendered potential income to speed economic expansion, though they were seldom consulted directly about the process. In effect, in a society where inequalities of wealth and income existed, a large proportion of the public involuntarily contributed to economic growth.

Piling up savings is not enough, however. These savings must be channeled into the hands of entrepreneurs who have the will and the skill to use them effectively. When the saver and the investor are the same person—as in the case of Carnegie and Swift—there is little problem. But what if the two are different individuals? It is here that various investment institutions come into play.

One of those institutions was the stock market located on New York's Wall Street, where stocks and other securities issued by corporations and governments had been bought and sold since the late eighteenth century. Selling stock was potentially a very useful device for tapping the savings of people with capital. Those who bought "shares" in a business corporation were part owners of the firm and received a portion of its profits without risking losses beyond the extent of their share purchase (limited liability). This system should have been an effective way for entrepreneurs to raise capital, but its value was seriously reduced by the fact that by the end of the nineteenth century the stock exchange had become a sort of gambling casino where speculators—"bulls" and "bears"—bought and sold shares, not to gain profits from corporate earnings, but to make quick killings in "corners," "raids," and other get-rich-quick-maneuvers. Prudent people with capital looked aghast at these risky and shady doings and stayed away from the stock market.

A more successful way to channel savings to investors during these years was through the banks. By using other people's savings deposits or simply by establishing a line of credit for borrowers, bankers were able to provide funds to investors who met their standards of creditworthiness. But the nation's banking structure had serious weaknesses. The National Banking Acts of 1863 and 1864 had created a single, uniform bank note issue and had made this secure by backing it with government bonds. The national banking system was a major advance over the old state bank system, but it had substantial drawbacks. Banks with national charters were not allowed to take land as security for loans, a restriction that limited their value for farmers who only had their land to offer as collateral. Nor could they easily increase the country's money supply to take care of seasonal needs or the steady, long-term growth of the economy, since the amount of their paper money issues depended on their holdings of a limited volume of government bonds. Lacking a central bank of last resort that might provide extra funds when needed, the national banking system was also unable to deal effectively with financial panics or other sudden crises. Not until the Federal Reserve System was established in 1913 were many of these problems solved.

Despite these flaws the regular commercial banks that formed the national banking system served to bring savers and investors together satisfactorily, especially where small amounts of capital were needed. For large-scale capital investment, however, the most effective agent was the investment banker. The need for investment bankers was especially urgent during the Gilded Age, when explosive urban growth and rapidly expanding railroads and industry created an extraordinary need for capital.

Investment banks were generally not part of the national banking system and did not normally engage in the day-to-day business of commercial banking. Instead, they dealt with large borrowers, either government agencies or industrial and transportation promoters interested in raising enormous amounts of capital.

Investment banking did not appear abruptly in the Gilded Age. Before the Civil War a few banking firms had begun to serve as middlemen between the government and savers. They bought government bonds, thus guaranteeing the treasury the money it needed, and then peddled the bonds to the public at a profit. During the Civil War Jay Cooke and Company had assumed many of the risks of selling the giant issues of "five-twenty" bonds that had financed the Union army and navy. Cooke's success in this enterprise helped make him the leading investment banker of the day and encouraged him to move into private investment banking after the war. In the 1870s he became the financial agent of the Northern Pacific Railroad, but became too deeply involved. When the public lost confidence in Northern Pacific securities, Cooke and Company went bankrupt, bringing on the panic of 1873 and six years of hard times.

The public's experience in 1873 did little to create investor confidence in stocks. But by the 1880s things began to change largely because of J. P. Morgan. Morgan often said that his chief asset was trust. The public believed that any promotion orchestrated by J. P. Morgan and Company was apt to succeed. Building on this trust Morgan was able to put together a flock of corporation mergers that combined competing, inefficient, small firms into giants that promised greater efficiency and above all managed, tolerable competition. In the process thousands of investors of the constituent firms often had to be induced to accept stock in the new, larger firm. It was here that Morgan's reputation was indispensable: Only because they trusted the New York banker were they willing to approve the merger. To further reassure stockholders, invariably a Morgan partner remained as a prominent member of the new corporation's board of directors.

Morgan, and the other investment bankers who imitated him, accustomed many prosperous Americans to think of the stock market as a safe place to invest their savings, not merely an arena for wild speculation. The speculative side continued, of course. Periodically thousands of Americans were seized with the notion that "playing the market" was a good way to get rich quick. But by the end

J. P. Morgan. He had a bulbous red nose—carefully obscured in this portrait. Yet his forceful personality comes through.

of the century the stock exchange had also become a vital money market where those with funds came together with those who needed those funds to invest in industry. By 1910 billions of dollars of stock were being bought and sold annually on Wall Street. Much of this trading remained speculative. But a good deal of it represented the constructive meeting of savers who wanted secure returns and promoters who could put these savings to productive use.

★ THE SPOILERS ★

Clearly the entrepreneurship of Swift, Edison, Carnegie, Morgan, and others like them benefited the American people by providing new or cheaper products or by encouraging investment. Though most nineteenth-century businessmen had limited social sympathies and were not above sharp dealing, their efforts helped to increase the income of Americans generally. Not all business leaders, however, were constructive innovators. Some were primarily spoilers who got rich by manipulating finance while cheating investors, bribing politicians, ruining competitors, or rigging prices. Among these spoilers were Jay Gould and John D. Rockefeller.

The Railroads and Jay Gould. The Civil War had delayed railroad construction, but after 1865 the country turned with a will to conquering time and distance with rails and locomotives. In 1865 there were about 35,000 miles of track in the United States. By 1873, after an enormous spurt of construction, this mileage had doubled. During the depression years of 1873 to 1879, railroad growth slowed. Then came the prosperous 1880s, and by 1890 the country had 167,000 miles of track. By 1910, when the rail network was largely complete, America was tied together by 240,000 miles of steel road.

Much of the new construction occurred in the older regions of the country. After 1865, promoters consolidated smaller companies into trunk lines such as the New York Central and the Baltimore and Ohio that allowed freight and passengers to move from the Atlantic to the Midwest without changing from one road to another. Chicago, St. Louis, Kansas City, and Omaha became major rail centers, and from these points other promoters began to push west and south over the rapidly developing prairies. The most spectacular growth, however, was shown by the transcontinentals. In 1869 construction teams from the Central Pacific, driving eastward from Sacramento, and from the Union Pacific, driving west from Omaha, met at Promontory Point in northern Utah, completing the first Atlantic-Pacific railroad connection. By 1890 five major railroads crossed the Great Plains, connecting the Atlantic to the Pacific Coast.

Railroad efficiency was also vastly increased. Relatively cheap steel rails produced by Carnegie and his competitors soon replaced the older iron tracks, allowing the railroads to run larger, more efficient locomotives and cars. Heavier trains created serious braking problems, but these were solved with the adoption of George Westinghouse's air brake in the 1880s. Track gauges—the distances between rails—were standardized in these years so that passengers and freight need not be shifted from one set of cars to another. Meanwhile, George Pullman had invented a new passenger car that was an ordinary coach by day but could be converted into a comfortable sleeping car by night.

Scholars have warned against exaggerating the impact of the railroads on the late-nineteenth-century American economy, but most interpreters believe it was immense. Cheap, all-weather transportation accelerated the decline in shipping costs that had begun during the pre–Civil War period, opening vast new regions to economic exploitation. Lower transport costs allowed commodities to be produced in the most efficient locations and then shipped to consumers all over the country. They enabled each region to specialize in what it did best and exchange its products for those of other regions, further lowering consumer costs. The creation of an integrated national market raised the country's total output per capita substantially.

Some of the people who helped bring this process about were farseeing, creative individuals who risked their own fortunes in opening new areas to settlement. James J. Hill, for example, the promoter of the Great Northern connecting St. Paul with Puget Sound, built his road without the great federal subsidies behind the other transcontinentals. Hill, rightfully called the "Empire Builder," was an uncommon man. Many of the railroad promoters of the age were neither as civic-minded nor as creative as Hill. Most notorious of all was Jay Gould.

Gould was a railroad man, but he built no railroads. Instead he made a fortune by manipulating their financial structure and leaving them debt-ridden and gutted. In 1867 Gould and his friend James Fisk became directors of the Erie Railroad, supposedly as allies of the New York railroad promoter, Cornelius ("Commodore") Vanderbilt, who was seeking to add the Erie to his New York Central to achieve a dominant position in New York City's western traffic. Vanderbilt began secretly to buy up Erie stock to gain a controlling interest.

The new directors, joined by the notorious speculator Daniel Drew, betrayed Vanderbilt. Drew, especially, was a master of "stock watering." As a cattle drover before the Civil War, he had often driven his herds long distances without allowing them to drink, and then, just before arriving at market, let them have as much water as they wanted. When sold to the butchers by weight, the bloated animals brought Drew a handsome profit. Now he and his confederates "watered" the Erie Railroad stock by issuing vast amounts of new securities unjustified by any increase in the railroad's earning capacity. They dumped these shares on the market. The unsuspecting Commodore bought and bought, but could not manage to buy enough to gain control of the railroad. Eventually Vanderbilt discovered the deception and sought help from the courts; the Erie ringleaders did the same. For months the two groups fought bitter legal battles, culminating in Gould's wholesale bribery of the New York State legislature to legalize his acts. Soon Gould lost interest in the Erie and moved onto greener pastures. But the railroad, stuck with millions of shares of watered stock, was never the same. As he turned to new endeavors, Gould jeered: "There ain't nothing more in Erie."

John D. Rockefeller and Monopoly. The career of John D. Rockefeller illustrates another form of business abuse common during these years: monopoly. His manipulations also highlight a general characteristic of the era: Business operated in a permissive legal atmosphere in which the rules were either unclear or unformulated. Some of Rockefeller's actions were not strictly illegal at the time, however unfair or ethically suspect.

Rockefeller's business arena was the oil-refining industry. After Drake's discovery in western Pennsylvania, the

John D. Rockefeller's first oil refinery in Cleveland, Ohio, about 1869.

oil industry had boomed. Prospectors swarmed all over the East and soon discovered oil in western New York, West Virginia, Ohio, and Indiana. By the mid-1870s California, too, had begun to produce petroleum in commercial amounts. The new sources of supply soon generated spectacular growth in the refining industry, which converted crude oil into kerosene, wax, and lubricants. By the early 1870s the refining companies had begun to concentrate near Cleveland, Ohio, a region close to the eastern oil fields with unusually good transportation connections to the country's major population centers.

The refining industry was risky. For a few thousand dollars anyone could set up a simple plant to produce kerosene. As more and more firms entered the business, profits fell to the vanishing point, and many refineries went bankrupt. The intense competition undoubtedly kept prices low and benefited the consumer, but from the refiners' point of view, the results were disastrous.

The petroleum refiners were not the only business people injured by cutthroat competition. In the 1870s the railroads, too, found themselves slashing rates on competitive lines to stay in business. In that decade passenger fares between New York and Chicago dropped dramatically; first-class freight rates over the same route dropped by two-thirds or more. Businesspeople, not surprisingly, found this risky regime unsettling and sought to do something about it. Consolidation of several firms under one controlling firm

was a common response among railroad entrepreneurs. In the 1870s they also tried the "pool," an agreement among several roads with competing routes to divide the traffic according to a formula and avoid rate cutting. Invariably these agreements broke down when one firm or another found it advantageous to break the pool. Because their legality was at best dubious, the pools could not be enforced by law. Industrial firms also tried the pool and several variants, but with similar dubious results.

Rockefeller's campaign to reduce competition in his own industry was more successful than most. In 1870 he and his partners established the Standard Oil Company of Ohio. With a million dollars invested in stills, pipelines, storage tanks, and other equipment, Standard soon became one of the largest refining companies in the country. The technical and managerial skills of the Standard people were important factors in their firm's prosperity. Equally significant, however, was Rockefeller's ability to squeeze cheap rates from the railroads for shipping crude and refined oil. So competitive was the refining business that even a small saving on transportation costs could give one producer an edge over the others. Taking advantage of the railroads' own fierce competition, Rockefeller arranged to provide large-scale shipments of Standard products by a given railroad in return for rebates that would reduce Standard's shipping charges far below the published rates. As a result, Standard Oil grew at the expense of its competitors—many of whom were forced to sell out to their aggressive opponent—and with each spurt of growth further increased its ability to squeeze favorable terms out of the railroad companies.

By 1872 Rockefeller controlled about one-fourth of the country's entire petroleum-refining capacity. Thereafter, Standard Oil went on to establish a virtual monopoly of American refining. By 1880 it controlled between 90 and 95 percent of the country's refining capacity and 92 percent of the crude oil supply of the Appalachian area, the major oil region at the time. In 1882 Rockefeller and his associates formed the first "trust," a company that owned the securities of subsidiary firms and controlled their operations.

Rockefeller's trust was dissolved by the Ohio courts on the grounds that it violated the rights of owners of the individual firms and was "a virtual monopoly of the business of producing petroleum . . . to control the price." But the Standard people reorganized under a New Jersey law that legalized a rather similar device, the holding company, enabling a super company to own stock in several subordinate firms and so control their operations. Thereafter, Standard's share of the industry declined somewhat, but as late as 1911, when the United States Supreme Court ordered the parent holding company dissolved into thirty separate firms, it was still by far the largest producer of refined oil and crude petroleum in the world.

The post–Civil War business leaders were, then, both wreckers and builders. It would be difficult to consider business leadership a major factor in late-nineteenth-century economic growth if all business leaders had resembled Jay Gould or John D. Rockefeller. But others such as Carnegie, Edison, Swift, and Morgan assuredly helped accelerate economic growth.

★ THE INTELLECTUAL FOUNDATION ★

Entrepreneurship was only one component of the economic advances of the Gilded Age. Another was a system of values congenial to material growth.

Not all the mine, railroad, construction, and factory workers of America enthusiastically supported the era's economic developments. Indeed, a substantial minority were reluctant participants. Yet, to an amazing degree, they and the rest of the American public endorsed private profit, hard work, and economic progress.

In part this support can be explained by the realities of Gilded Age American society. As we shall see, the growing economy, however imperfect, did permit a fair degree of improvement in the economic status and income of average wage earners, and a certain amount of movement up the social ladder for their children. These improvements re-inforced the faith of ordinary people in the process. But actual experience was not the whole of it. Faith in the system was buttressed by a mass of ideology, myth, and propaganda that sang the praises—and the inevitability—of the social and economic changes underway.

The Work Ethic. An important cultural accelerator of economic change was the work ethic. In part a residue of Puritan teaching that the elect would reveal themselves by hard work and worldly success, it was reinforced in the nineteenth century by popular writers, preachers, the schools, and opinion makers generally. The work ethic was a value system appropriate to a society that needed a disciplined, hard-working labor force. It proclaimed the virtues of reliability, thrift, sobriety, respectability, honesty, and conscientious performance of duties and obligations. These val-

Horatio Alger, writer of "pulp" novels, was the apostle of the work ethic and its myth of success in late-nineteenth-century America. The title page of his Fame and Fortune *suggests that newsboys and shoeshine boys have their feet on the first rungs of the ladder of success.*

ues were of course rewards in themselves, as were all virtues. But they also produced other rewards. Those who reaped would inevitably sow. According to the famous McGuffey *Readers*, used by generations of American schoolchildren, "he who would thrive must rise at five; he who has thriven, may lie to seven." Popular biographies and novels made heroes of successful strivers. In the potboilers of William M. Thayer and Horatio Alger, the heroes are usually ambitious poor boys who overcome adversity to achieve social respectability and economic security. Alger's 119 formula novels for young people were particularly successful in the Gilded Age. Though obsessed by achievement, in truth Alger's heroes often prosper more by sheer luck than by persistent labor. In one Alger story, for example, "ragged Dick" rescues a child from drowning and is rewarded with a job by the child's father—a banker, it turns out. In another story the young hero finds an enormous gold nugget. Obviously, even the young of the Gilded Age preferred the quick fix. Yet the ultimate lesson Alger conveyed was that toil was both good in itself and profitable. His heroes, however blessed by good luck, are also youths who glory in work. Tom Thatcher is "a sturdy boy of sixteen with bright eyes and smiling, sun-burned face. His shirt sleeves were rolled up, displaying a pair of muscular arms. His hands were brown, and soiled with labor. It was clear that here was no whitehanded young aristocrat." Raised on a steady diet of such edifying tales and myths, millions of Americans were prepared to accept the virtues of the contemporary economic system.

The Defense of Inequality. The work ethic no doubt helped to inculcate values and habits that were useful to employers. Indirectly it also justified unequal rewards, for if hard work was the way to achieve riches, then what divided rich from poor was the quality and intensity of their effort, not birth or good fortune. But there were more direct defenses of the inequalities of wealth as well.

Until close to the end of the century the Protestant ministry often defended the disparities between rich and poor. Henry Ward Beecher told an audience during the 1870s depression: "I do not say that a dollar a day is enough to support . . . a man and five children if a man would insist on smoking and drinking beer. . . . But the man who cannot live on bread and water is not fit to live." In his lecture *Acres of Diamonds*, Baptist minister Russell Conwell delivered the message that material riches were a sign of God's approval, if honestly earned. For the Christian to reject riches was a mistake, for riches allowed the Christian to aid others. Conwell was an enormously popular speaker. During the Gilded Age he traveled to every part of the country and gave his standard talk 6,000 times to many thousands of listeners.

The ministers were not alone in defending the economic inequalities of the time. In the colleges and universities, on the editorial boards of newspapers and magazines, writers, academics, and journalists saw virtues in the competitive spirit of the age and the unavoidable success of some and failure of others. To defend inequality, these men drew on either the ideas of Adam Smith and other economists of eighteenth- and early-nineteenth-century Britain or the newer ideas of Charles Darwin.

Adam Smith and his disciples, writing at the dawn of the Industrial Revolution, sought to demonstrate how the unrestricted pursuit of private gain by individuals must maximize the profit of all. Through a process Smith called the "invisible hand," free play for acquisitive drives would ultimately generate abundance for all. One consequence of free competition was no doubt inequality; some people would gain more than others. But the alternative of government intervention to determine economic outcomes, as under the mercantilist system of the past, was worse. It would merely check growth by discouraging enterprise and by distorting the most efficient ways to produce and to distribute. Laissez faire (hands off) was by far the best policy for government to follow if its goal was economic progress.

Defenders of inequality had used such arguments to support their position long before the Civil War. After 1865 they could also turn to social Darwinism to make their case.

Social Darwinism was an attempt to apply the ideas of the English naturalist Charles Darwin to the social realm. In his monumental work *Origin of Species*, first published in 1859, Darwin proposed a mechanism to explain the great diversity of living plant and animal species hitherto explained by Christians and Jews as God's creation as described in the Bible. According to Darwin, the fierce competition among the multitude of living things for the limited sustenance provided by the environment was the cause of diversity. In this battle, he wrote, individual living things that were stronger, tougher, fiercer, quicker, more intelligent, or more aggressive—in a word, "fitter"—survived to reproduce. The others died, and their lines, with their distinctive qualities, ceased to exist. In this way small differences, when they provided an advantage in the struggle to survive, were encouraged, and gradually living things diverged, at first in minor ways, later in major ways that created whole new species. The process was "progressive" in some sense. Lower gave way to higher, and at the top of the evolutionary ladder was humankind, descended undoubtedly from some common ancestor with the higher animal primates, the apes and gorillas.

To social Darwinists it seemed clear that what applied to the biological world also applied to society: Competition and the "survival of the fittest" constituted the only way to achieve progress. For humankind to advance, economic competition must be allowed a free hand, even if this response meant accepting gross social inequalities and human suffering. Every attempt of soft-hearted philanthropists to interfere with the social evolutionary process by curbing the strong and bolstering the weak was shortsighted and regressive. "Let it be understood," wrote Yale professor William Graham Sumner, "that we cannot go outside this alternative: liberty, inequality, survival of the fittest; not liberty, equality, survival of the unfittest." Sometimes this insistence on laissez faire was carried to preposterous extremes. Herbert Spencer, the English philosopher who traveled extensively through the United States and helped popularize social Darwinist ideas, believed that laws to aid the poor, to provide publicly supported education, to regulate housing, to provide cheap mail service, even to protect citizens against medical quackery were all misguided and certain to lead to social disaster.

It is not clear how seriously the business community took social Darwinism; after all, many of these same men were busily organizing pools and trusts to reduce competition and demanding government aid. Yet at times businessmen echoed the slogans of the professors and philosophers. Rockefeller's son reportedly told a Sunday school audience that "the growth of a large business is merely the survival of the fittest. . . . The American Beauty rose can be produced in the splendor and fragrance which brings cheer to its beholder only by sacrificing the early buds which grow up around it." Even Andrew Carnegie, an atypical business tycoon in so many ways, accepted the necessity for inequality on Darwinian grounds. In his famous work *The Gospel of Wealth*, he startled the reading public by declaring that rich men were only "stewards of wealth" who must give it all back to society. But Carnegie also wrote: "We accept and welcome . . . great inequality of environment; the concentration of business, industrial and commercial, in the hands of a few; and the law of competition between these as being not only beneficial, but essential to the future of the race."

Students of society cannot be certain how ideas such as social Darwinism actually influence human actions and social change. Some believe that ideas possess only limited capacity to influence those who perceive them as contrary to their own advantage. Certainly business people were capable of ignoring their own laissez-faire precepts when it suited their purposes. Other scholars credit ideas with the power to create myths that obscure people's view of their true interests. It is difficult to choose between these positions. Yet it is probably true that in many cases, where they did not fly in the face of clear, firsthand experience, the defense of hard work and inequality, and the propaganda for the self-made man were accepted by workers. These ideas in turn undoubtedly discouraged the expression of dis-

content and helped create a disciplined labor force that contributed to economic growth after 1865.

★ THE ROLE OF GOVERNMENT ★

Anyone who believes that the entrepreneurs of this era were solely responsible for economic progress must account for the active economic role played by government. The federal government stimulated the economy by direct investment, by grants, by tariffs, and by giving business the freedom to do virtually all that it wished. Without this help, growth would undoubtedly have been slower.

Government Aid. At times Washington invested directly in the physical improvements the nation needed. The federal government appropriated funds for post offices, docks, and canal locks, and dredged river channels. In 1874 James B. Eads, already famous for his steel bridge across the Mississippi at East St. Louis, designed federally financed jetties that deepened the lower Mississippi and helped preserve New Orleans's role as a major ocean port. Each year Congress supported such enterprises by a flock of "rivers and harbors" bills. In 1867 these took $1.2 million from the taxpayers' pockets; by 1895 they cost almost $20 million. Local governments, too—by paving streets, constructing sewers, and building hospitals, schools, reservoirs, and aqueducts—contributed to the country's capital growth.

An especially important federal contribution to Gilded Age economic growth was friendly tax policy. After the 1870s the tariff—in effect a tax on consumers—rose in steps virtually without pause until the twentieth century, providing a wall behind which investors could initiate new industries without fear of more efficient foreign competition. Internal taxes also favored investors. For most of this period, import duties and excises on tobacco, whiskey, beer, wine, and other items were the main sources of federal funds. The tax system was quite *regressive*; that is, it took a larger portion of the income of the poor than of the rich. Between 1861 and 1872 the federal government imposed an income tax, a *progressive* tax that rose proportionately with higher income. Had it remained in force, it would have placed more of the tax burden on those with higher incomes. But it was dropped as part of the postwar retreat from heavy taxation; when it was revived again in 1894, it was declared unconstitutional by the Supreme Court. Local governments raised most of their revenues by taxing property, an equally regressive practice. All told, the tax burden fell disproportionately on farmers and on people on the lower rungs of the income ladder, constituting a kind of

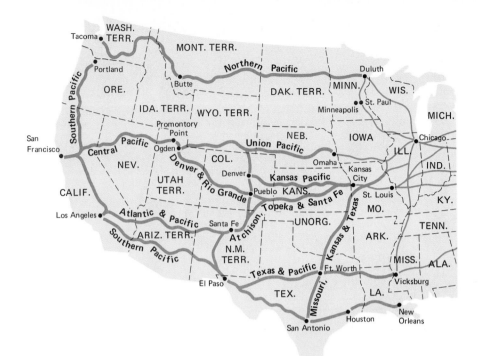

RAILROADS, 1850–1900

subsidy to business and the rich. The system clearly was not egalitarian, but it probably stimulated economic growth: The rich were left with substantial surpluses to invest in land, securities, or business enterprises.

During the post–Civil War decades such wartime Republican initiatives as the Homestead Act (1862), which gave western land to those willing to settle it, and the Morrill Land Grant College Act (1862), which endowed agricultural colleges, stimulated greater agricultural productivity. Federal railroad legislation had even weightier consequences. By 1871, under the terms of the Pacific Railroad Acts (1862 and 1864) and several later railroad land grant measures, the federal government had given private railroad companies over 130 million acres of land in the trans–Mississippi West, about one-tenth of the entire public domain. This vast empire included timber, minerals, and some of the most fertile soil on earth. Individual states contributed 49 million additional acres from their public lands. This huge block of real estate—larger than the state of Texas—was a vital source of funds for the railroads. People with savings, especially rural folk, who would not buy the stocks and bonds of the railroads, did buy their land. Thousands were attracted west to take up farms on railroad lands. Their contribution to the roads' coffers was immense. The average price at which the railroads sold their land was

about $3.30 an acre, bringing the promoters about $435 million in much-needed funds.

The wisdom of the railroad land-grant policy has been debated for many years. Some historians call it a giant giveaway that deprived the American people of a large part of their heritage in order to benefit a few. Railroad promoters certainly made money from the land grants, but the government and the public also benefited: The grants accelerated growth of the West, reduced charges for transporting government goods—a requirement written into each of the grants—and enhanced prices of the land retained by the government adjacent to the railroads. Most important, the policy speeded the process of linking the country together by rail. If the railroads had not had land to sell, few private capitalists would have put their money in ventures so risky as railroads thrown across hundreds of miles of empty space, much of it arid and—until the railroads arrived—virtually worthless. Without the land grants, economic development would have been slower.

Hands Off.   Each of these examples—tariff, tax policy, railroad land grants—is an instance of government's contributing directly to economic development. Eventually, through the federal courts, it also contributed immensely in indirect ways as well.

Steam-driven trip-hammers stamped out metal parts for reapers and other farm machinery at the McCormick factory in Chicago. Machines like these increased workers' productivity, but they also added immeasurably to the hazards of wage earners' lives.

The courts' development of a strong probusiness attitude unfolded slowly. Between 1865 and 1880 the federal courts took the position that the states could restrict the exercise of private property rights in order to protect the health, welfare, or morals of citizens. In the Slaughterhouse cases of 1873, for example, the Supreme Court rejected the contention that the Fourteenth Amendment, which had been passed to safeguard the political rights of black freedmen against state encroachment, also protected the profits and property of individuals and corporations against state regulation. In the Granger cases (notably *Munn v. Illinois*) of 1877, it upheld the right of Illinois to establish maximum rates for storing grain on the grounds that a state, under its legitimate police powers, could regulate any business that embraced "a public interest."

In the 1880s, however, the federal courts began to limit the power of state legislatures to intervene in the operations of business. In the *San Mateo* case (1882) and the *Santa Clara* case (1886)—both involving efforts by California to regulate railroad practices—the Supreme Court reversed its earlier position. The Fourteenth Amendment, it now asserted, did apply to those injured by state economic regulation. Moreover, the amendment's protections applied not just to individuals; they also applied to corporations, which were, the justices said, "persons" under the Constitution. In effect, corporations too could claim that they had been deprived by states of "property" without "due process of law" and appeal for federal protection against regulatory laws. Thereafter, it became more difficult for state legislatures to intrude into the transactions between business and individuals to protect what was perceived as the public interest against the misdeeds of business.

Having diminished the states' right to regulate private business, the federal courts soon clamped down on the federal government too. In the *Maximum Freight Rate* case (1897), for example, the Supreme Court allowed the Interstate Commerce Commission only to determine whether an *existing* freight rate was reasonable, not to set *future* rates, and in the *E. C. Knight* case (1895) it emasculated the monopoly-regulating Sherman Antitrust Act by making it inapplicable to businesses that were involved primarily in manufacture rather than commerce.

By 1900, then, the federal courts had imposed on the nation a hands-off policy toward business enterprise that subordinated state regulatory power to federal law and then crippled Congress's right to regulate as well. The federal government could help business in various ways, but it could not limit business for the sake of perceived public need. The policy disregarded issues of social justice and private power versus public power; later generations would often condemn it harshly. But it also created an environment in which those with capital felt confident of high returns with limited risk. All told, by its generosity toward entrepreneurs, the hands-off policy undoubtedly accelerated the pace of economic expansion.

★ THE WAGE EARNER ★

In discussing the triumph of industry after 1865, we have considered causes. What about consequences? How did laboring men and women, those who tended machines, who went down into the mines, who sawed the wood and dug the foundations, who stoked the furnaces and engines—how did these people fare as the nation accelerated its output, and how did they respond to what they experienced?

If we look only at the cold statistics, the lot of Gilded Age wage earners appears moderately good. Their incomes were growing. Average real wages and annual earnings rose substantially in the half century following the Civil War. One economist has estimated that hourly wages and earnings for American industrial workers, allowing for changes in the purchasing power of the dollar, increased by 50 percent between 1860 and 1890. Another concludes that during the next twenty-five years the increase was another 37 percent. Even omitting individual improvements in skill and increasing experience, then, industrial workers between 1865 and 1914 almost doubled their real income.

But these statistics tell only part of the story. They are only averages, and so mask a great deal of variation. They also disregard many other aspects of the working person's life in this era of pell-mell economic change.

Social Mobility and Financial Rewards. White males made up the majority of the labor force in this era, and we will consider them first. There was a definite cycle in the working lives of most male wage earners. During their late teens, when they took their first jobs, they received the wages typical of unskilled "laborers." But this was usually not their permanent lot. A majority raised their skill levels over the years, and by their forties or fifties they were earning considerably more than thirty years before regardless of the general trend of wage levels. Much of this improvement took place without changing the general occupations they began with. But many workers could count on another mechanism to improve their lot: movement out of the occupation where they started the "race of life." The data on occupational mobility among white American working men suggest overall that movement from unskilled to semi-

Much of the unskilled labor force of early twentieth-century America was foreign-born—like these Russian steel workers in Homestead, Pennsylvania, in 1907.

skilled and even skilled jobs was not uncommon. A study of Boston in the period 1880–1930 shows that of those who began as laborers between 35 and 40 percent ended up higher on the occupational scale, largely in the better-paid, more prestigious, white-collar group. If we look at these Bostonians over *two* generations the results are still more impressive. For the sons of unskilled or semiskilled men who reached adulthood in 1900, some 40 percent ended up in middle-class positions.

We must not exaggerate, however. Horatio Alger and the other myth-makers were defending a system that did not invariably pay off. Mobility and success depended on more than individual effort and merit. We know that the extent of mobility varied, for example, by decade, by ethnic group, and by religious identification. And it was certainly difficult for a poor boy to leap to the very top of the pile. The great tycoons of the Gilded Age were almost all native-born Protestants of colonial stock who received far better educations than did the average American of the day.

Their fathers, moreover, were themselves middle class or rich. On the other hand, the popularity of the rags-to-riches myths depended on a substantial number of Americans seeing mobility as a fact of daily life. As the social historian Herbert Gutman has said in a study of late-nineteenth-century mobility in Paterson, New Jersey: "So many successful manufacturers who had begun as workers walked the streets of the city . . . that it [was] not hard to believe that 'hard work' resulted in spectacular material and social improvement."

We must keep in mind, in assessing the fate of Gilded Age working people, that we are dealing with a "segmented" class. Although the average wage in 1900 was $483 a year, carpenters, masons, and other skilled construction workers often earned as much as $1,250 annually. In 1880, when "laborers" were getting an average of $1.32 a day, blacksmiths received $2.31, locomotive engineers $2.15, and machinists $2.45. The wages of federal employees, clerical workers, and western miners were also above the national

Women were the most harshly exploited adult workers during the Gilded Age and the early twentieth century. In light industries like the garment trade—much of it located in New York City—"sweatshops," such as this, where immigrant women labored, were common.

average. Agricultural workers, even when we take into account that they were commonly fed and housed by their employers, were always poorly paid. In the aptly named "sweated trades" of the big-city garment industry, working people were squeezed hard by their employers—struggling small businessmen who showed little consideration for those whose wages represented their major cost of production.

One reason for low wages in the garment industry was the presence of many female workers. Very few women in these years received wages comparable to those of adult men. A typical woman's wage was the dollar or two a week earned by female domestics who washed, cooked, sewed, and ironed in middle-class homes; women piece-workers in New York and Chicago garment loft factories received under a dollar a day. Fortunately, the picture was not as bleak as these figures suggest. Most women eventually married and ceased to be part of the labor market. Yet for the "spinster" who had to support herself, or the widow with young children, such wages were scandalous.

Black Americans were also paid well below the average. Most were sharecroppers in the South, but the few who had left the farms for the mills or factories were almost all relegated to low-paying, dead-end jobs regardless of their education, skills, or talents. Immigrants, too, at least until they acquired skills and an adequate command of English, received lower wages than skilled and native-born white workers.

Living and Working Conditions. For families at the bottom of the wage pyramid, life was hard. Few Americans went hungry, but many wage earners fought a constant battle to maintain a decent living standard and achieve a little comfort. In 1883 the large family of a railroad brakeman in Joliet, Illinois, reportedly ate chiefly bread, molasses, and potatoes. The family's clothes, a contemporary investigator noted, were "ragged" and the children "half-dressed and dirty." A witness before a Senate committee in 1883 described the home of the typical Pennsylvania coal miner as consisting of two rooms, one upstairs and one down. "The houses are built in long rows without paint on the outside," he reported. "The kitchen furniture consists of a stove and some dishes, a few chairs and a table. They have no carpets on the floor. . . ."

Matters improved over the next generation, as we have seen, and life expectancies as well as income increased. In the industrial state of Massachusetts the average life expectancy of a newborn infant increased from about forty-two years in 1880 to about forty-five in 1920. Much of this improvement reflected lower infant mortality rates, but adults, too, benefited from the advancing living standards. In 1850, twenty-year-old males could count on living a trifle over forty more years; in 1920 they could look forward to about forty-five more years. In the same period the improvement in life expectancies for twenty-year-old women was slightly greater.

Despite these advances the *quality* of the wage earner's life, regardless of income, remained unsatisfactory from a modern viewpoint. Factory hours dropped from about sixty-six a week in 1850 to sixty in 1890. Yet the length of the workday remained a trial for most workers. "I get so exhausted that I can scarcely drag myself home when night

Many American working-class families lived on the edge of subsistence, slipping into poverty if the economy declined or their families grew too large. Heads of families like this one worked sixty to seventy hours a week and often lived in bare, squalid homes.

comes," exclaimed a woman worker in a Massachusetts mill. A working man knew "nothing but work, eat, and sleep," and was "little better than a horse," declared one Pennsylvania factory employee.

Even when hours became shorter, there was the dreary monotony to contend with. Much industrial work consisted merely of repetitive, simple manipulations. At one Chicago packing house at the end of the century, five men were needed to handle just the tail of a steer—two to skin it, another two to cut it off, and one to throw it into a box. How could such mindless work provide any satisfaction? One middle-class reformer who tried factory work in the 1890s summed up the feelings of most industrial wage earners: "There is for us in our work none of the joy of responsibility, only the dull monotony of grinding toil, with the longing for the signal to quit work, and for our wages at the end of the week."

In some ways "progress" made the worker's life worse, not better. Rapid technological change made many skills obsolete. Although the job market as a whole expanded enormously in this period, skilled hands often found themselves replaced by machines. In the iron industry, for example, Andrew Carnegie and Henry Clay Frick pushed relentlessly for new ways to reduce the number of skilled workers in the mills. They succeeded in bringing down production costs, but only at a high price to their workers. Some were discharged; many who remained were forced to accept semiskilled or unskilled work, which reduced their income and made their jobs more monotonous. Some employers adopted Taylorism—that is, the ideas of Frederick W. Taylor, an industrial engineer who had developed his theories while trying to increase the efficiency of the work force at the Midvale Steel Company. Taylor was certain that machine tenders, like machines, could be made to work more effectively if the physical operations they performed were carefully examined and timed. By doing so, wasted motion could be eliminated and output raised. Workers often charged that implementation of Taylorism resulted in speed-ups that made their lives on the job more hectic and difficult.

Industrial work was also unsafe and unhealthy. Even at the end of the era few people understood the effects on health of chemicals, pollutants, dust, and other contaminants. Thousands suffered from chronic illness brought on by industrial conditions. Thousands more died young from silicosis (a lung disease caused by inhalation of rock dust), tuberculosis, cancer, heart conditions, and other work-induced diseases. Industrial accidents were epidemic. Unsafe machinery, mine gases, and explosive, dust-laden air maimed and killed many. Between 1870 and 1910 there were almost 4,000 injuries or deaths at Carnegie's South Works alone. In 1917 the nation's industrial casualty list was 11,000 killed and 1.4 million wounded.

Mechanization made factory labor both more routine and more dangerous. If a man became disabled, his family had to struggle desperately to survive. As government did not provide assistance, injury and unemployment were disastrous.

Society did little or nothing to offset the fearful toll. Before 1900, common law held that if a "fellow servant" was responsible for a job injury, the employer was not liable for damages. And even if injury resulted from direct employer neglect or carelessness, injured workers or their families had to sue to receive compensation. Few could take such an expensive course. Some prosperous working people were able to buy private insurance; but when the chief wage earner was killed or lost the ability to hold a job, most families faced a grim future indeed.

In addition to accidents and sickness, workers had to contend with unemployment produced by periodic hard times. Between 1870 and 1900 there were two serious slumps and several lesser ones. In the first and last of these (1873–1879 and 1893–1897) the proportion of the labor force unemployed ran to over 12 percent, a figure not equaled until the 1930s. During these lean years many working-class families had difficulty keeping a roof over their heads and decent clothes on their backs. Beggars swarmed the streets, and hoboes and tramps rode the rails from town to town looking for work.

Averaged out throughout the Gilded Age, unemployment reduced workers' total income only about 7 percent below a full-employment level. But this burden, too, was not equally shared. For older workers, for blacks, for many unskilled immigrants, depressions were especially disastrous. Considered marginal by employers, they were the first to be fired and the last to be rehired. For the least employable members of the labor force, hard times sometimes meant permanent idleness.

Old age also presented economic hazards for working people. There were no pension systems. Men and women who became too old to work usually had little to fall back on if they lacked personal savings. Private charity was often degrading and stingy. Many aging parents were forced to move in with their children. If retired workers presented a less serious problem for society as a whole during this period than today, it was because men and women had more children to support them, and fewer lived to their later, nonworking years.

To understand the circumstances of the American wage earner during the Gilded Age, it is essential to make distinctions. White, male, native-born skilled workers were the nation's "labor-aristocrats"; many lived in decent comfort, owned their own homes, ate well, and enjoyed some comforts, even a few luxuries. Like all other workers, they were subject to job insecurity and danger and worked long hours; but generally they had reason to praise their society and the economic system that made their moderately comfortable lives possible. It is difficult to calculate the size of this labor elite, but it probably represented between a third and a half of the total nonfarm labor force.

For the other members of the armies of labor—women, blacks, and unskilled, recent immigrants—life was not only precarious but often meager and harsh. The families of the unskilled made up for the primary breadwinner's low wages to some extent by sending everyone to work—young and old, male and female. The prevalence of child labor was one reflection of this need. But this arrangement was a high price to pay for survival. In sum, even though unskilled American workers were probably better off than their equivalents abroad, their lives were not only insecure but also pinched. Life was getting better, but there was still a long way to go before people at the base of the income pyramid could say that America had fulfilled its age-old promise of abundance.

★ WORKING-CLASS PROTEST ★

Given these failings of the economic system, it is not surprising that wage earners expressed discontent. Much of their protest took the form of vague mutterings, angry talk, and absenteeism. But there were organized expressions of discontent as well. These took three forms: trade unionism, political reform, and utopianism.

Trade unionists accepted both the capitalist and the industrial systems—though sometimes with reservations—and sought higher wages, shorter hours, and better working conditions through collective bargaining. If negotiation did not work they were willing to resort to picketing, slowdowns, strikes, and boycotts of employers' goods. The political reformers came in two varieties. The moderate reformers favored separate labor parties to fight for the eight-hour day, workers' compensation laws, safety legislation, and child-labor laws. The militants favored radical parties—socialist or anarchist—that would replace capitalism and private property with some version of the "cooperative commonwealth," either by electoral processes or by violent overthrow. Neither group, however, sought to dismantle the system of large-scale industry and return to a simpler form of production. Those who took the third approach to transforming the existing labor system, utopianism, hoped to convert the industrial worker into a small producer. This utopian position expressed a widespread nostalgic yearning for a relatively recent past in which most Americans had been farmers or self-employed craftspersons.

Before 1860 most trade unions had been local organizations, enrolling workers within a given city. During the prosperous years immediately following the Civil War the national trade union appeared in response to the new coast-to-coast labor market that exposed local wage earners to competition from workers in distant cities. By 1873 there were forty-one national unions with between 300,000 and 400,000 members. These bodies typically sought to organize all the skilled workers in a given "craft"—carpenters, bricklayers, printers, plumbers, iron puddlers, and the like—rather than all the workers in a given industry at differing skill levels. Because times were good and labor tight, these unions managed to squeeze some concessions on wages and hours out of employees.

Paralleling the trade union surge of these early post–Civil War years was the rise of the National Labor Union (NLU), a body expressing both the political activist and utopian sides of the labor movement. Formed by Boston machinist Ira Steward in 1866 as the first nationwide labor *federation*, the NLU at first focused on securing the eight-hour day through state action. Steward believed that the success of the eight-hour principle would not only make the worker's job more tolerable but also help free wage earners from enslavement to the wage system. Under William Sylvis, Steward's successor, the NLU turned to Greenbackism, a scheme for large government issues of paper money to be lent to groups of workers to start their own businesses. The resulting "producers' cooperatives" would enable workers to escape wage earner status and become self-employed small producers in their own right. In 1872 the NLU transformed itself into the National Labor

Reform party and nominated Supreme Court Justice David Davis as its presidential candidate.

Depression of the Seventies.   The panic of 1873 and the depression that followed made jobs hard to get and hurt the trade union movement. Employers, finding that they could hire desperate unemployed men and women willing to accept any terms, became less tolerant of "troublemakers." Union membership nationwide declined from about 300,000 in 1873 to some 50,000 in 1878.

The mid-1870s was a time of bitter labor strife. In January 1874 New York City police charged into a crowd of unemployed workers assembled in Tompkins Square to protest hard times, injuring many. The following year was marked by the sensational trial of the so-called Molly Maguires for the murders of coal mine managers in eastern Pennsylvania and for acts of violence against the mine owners' property. To this day it is not clear whether the violence resulted from class hatreds or ethnic tensions between the Irish Catholic miners and their Welsh and Scottish Protestant bosses. Some scholars believe that the sensational evidence against the Mollies, collected by an agent of the Pinkertons, a private detective agency employed by the owners, was largely concocted so that the principal mine owners could break a miners' union. In any case, when ten Mollies were hanged and another fourteen sent to jail, many middle-class Americans saw their suspicions of labor organizations confirmed.

The middle-class public suffered a still worse shock in 1877 when labor turned to violence. After four years of hard times the eastern and midwestern railroads, to protect their profits, cut their workers' wages and increased their hours. In Baltimore in mid-July the angry workers began to picket; the police dispersed them. Soon after, Baltimore and Ohio workers seized the railroad's terminal and yards at Martinsburg, West Virginia. This spontaneous uprising quickly spread to Pittsburgh, Chicago, Buffalo, and points west, involving several major railroads and thousands of workers. For two weeks it looked as if the country was in the throes of a revolution. In Baltimore militia fired on a mob of workers and youths, killing ten. In Buffalo strikers seized the facilities of the Lake Shore and Erie railroads. In Pittsburgh rioters burned hundreds of freight cars, the Union Depot, and machine shops; looted stores; and engaged in a pitched gun battle with militia. Frightened by these signs of "red revolution," governors and local officials called out state troops and deputized volunteers. The governor of Maryland, panicked by the Martinsburg seizure, called for and got federal troops to protect life and property, one of the earliest examples of such use. By early August the violence had ended, but many conservative Americans were convinced that they had narrowly escaped a major social revolution.

The Knights of Labor.   With the return of prosperity in 1878–1879, labor discontent once more took the form of orderly organizing. The chief beneficiary of the new mood was the Noble Order of the Knights of Labor, a body created in 1869 by a group of Philadelphia tailors led by Uriah S. Stephens. During the mid-1870s the Knights had done little more than survive, but with the return of good times they began to prosper.

At first the Knights operated more like a secret lodge or fraternal order than an ordinary trade union. They provided an environment for social activity and offered life insurance, burial plots, and other benefits to compensate for the uncertainties of the wage earners' life. If they had any general labor policy, it was to encourage producers' cooperatives.

In the early 1880s, under the leadership of Terence V. Powderly, the Knights responded to improved times and the enhanced leverage on employers that resulted. Abandoning their longer-range reform goals, they confronted employers with wage demands backed by strikes or threats of strikes. In March 1885, the Knights forced Jay Gould's Southwest Railroad to cancel a 10 percent wage cut. In the strength of this victory over a hated Gould, the union attracted throngs of new members. In the next two years

The Knights of Labor had problems dealing with race prejudice among its members. Terence Powderly (here introduced by black Knight Frank M. Farrell) was not bigoted, but he had to placate southern members. In the end the Knights endorsed the "civil and political equality" of all citizens, but pledged to avoid interfering in southern "social relations."

membership leaped from a little over 100,000 to almost 730,000.

Here was an opportunity to create a powerful labor movement, but the chance was missed. Powderly and the Knights' other leaders never could decide whether they were organizing a trade union, a lodge, a reform association, or a political pressure group. Nor could they decide whether to recruit black members. Powderly endorsed organizing among black workers, but he denied that he endorsed racial equality and insisted that black members be confined to segregated locals. The Knights could not sustain the momentum of the mid-1880s and soon lost many of its new members.

The final blow to the Gilded Age trade union movement came with the 1886 Haymarket Riot in Chicago. Chicago was a turbulent city of factories, railroad yards, meat-packing plants, and large commercial enterprises. During the spring, at the vast McCormick Harvester Company, one of the city's largest employers, company of-

The labor troubles in Chicago in 1886 were heightened by the activities of a small group of anarchists. The group's fervor is captured in this handbill—in both English and German—for the meeting that would become the Haymarket Riot.

ficials had locked out 1,400 members of the Knights of Labor for demanding an eight-hour day and a $2 daily wage. On May 3, when the company tried to bring in "scabs" to replace the union men, the workers attacked the strike-breakers; the police fired on the workers.

The McCormick dispute marked the climax of a five-year citywide struggle for the eight-hour day, led by the Knights and by an assortment of socialists and labor leaders, that had deeply disturbed Chicago's labor relations. One element in the inflammable mixture was the anarchists, a group of radicals dedicated to destroying all government, along with private property and the wage system. Though few in number, the anarchists had supporters among the city's large German population. Following the police attack at the McCormick company, August Spies, a leading anarchist, issued a circular in German calling on the city's wage earners to "rise in your might . . . and destroy the hideous monster [of capitalism] that seeks to destroy you." The response of the conservative daily press was equally alarmist and overwrought. "A Wild Mob's Work; Wrought Up to a Frenzy by Anarchist Harangues, They Attack Employees" was the headline in the *Chicago Tribune.*

On the evening of May 4, at the anarchists' call, 3,000 men and women gathered at Haymarket Square on the city's West Side. The crowd was disappointing. Many who might have come had been frightened away by Spies's inflammatory words. Yet the meeting was relatively orderly, and the crowd had begun to thin out when the police tried to disperse the small remnant. At this point someone threw a bomb, which exploded among the advancing police. When the smoke cleared, seventy policemen lay wounded. Eventually seven died from the blast.

The forces of law and order reacted blindly and violently. No one ever discovered who threw the bomb, but the public and the authorities blamed the anarchists and, by extension, all "labor agitators," whether radical or not. Hundreds of men were hustled off to jail, and ten anarchists were indicted for conspiracy to commit murder. Seven were sentenced to death after a trial that failed to establish their direct connection with the massacre. In late 1887, four were hanged.

The public outrage at the Chicago bombing shook the entire labor movement. Middle-class people, already convinced by the Molly Maguire trial and the 1877 riots that labor unions were violence-prone, now condemned all unions, even the most moderate and peaceful. To the already weakened Knights, the Haymarket affair was disastrous. Recruiting dried up; timid members quit. The Knights survived for another decade and a half, but after 1886 it became a shadow of what it had been at its peak.

American Federation of Labor.   As the Knights sank, the American Federation of Labor (AFL) rose. Established

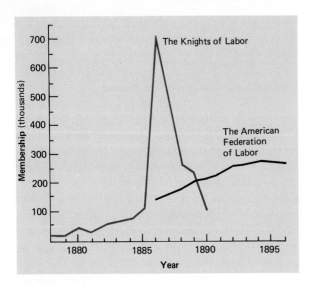

The passing of the Knights of Labor. *Source: Leo Wolman, The Growth of American Trade Unions (1924).*

in 1886 by ex-socialists, including Adolph Strasser, Peter J. Maguire, and Samuel Gompers, the AFL concentrated its efforts on native-born workers in the skilled crafts. As its name suggests, the AFL was a federation of unions. Each of the represented craft workers belonged to the AFL only through their own trade union.

The AFL succeeded for several reasons. First, it confined its organizing efforts to skilled workers. These were the most easily organized because they were not easily fired. A factory owner could replace floor sweepers, machine tenders, and other untrained hands if they demanded too much, but a construction company could not hire carpenters or bricklayers off the street, nor could a printer easily replace its press operators and typesetters. When skilled laborers demanded higher wages, threatened to strike, or insisted that a union be recognized as their bargaining agent, employers had to listen.

The AFL was also successful because it abandoned utopian goals and avoided politics. Samuel Gompers and his lieutenants, though they had once been socialists, believed that political radicalism was dangerous to the labor movement. Skilled workers, they noted, were profoundly wary of radical politics, and any hint of extremism frightened the middle class. The blow that the Haymarket riot had dealt the Knights of Labor convinced the AFL leaders that direct action, radical or not, was unsafe. Moreover, if the government were encouraged to become involved in labor-management relations, as socialists demanded, it might pass measures harmful to labor or seek to impose its decisions on labor disputes. Through the courts the government could easily suppress strikes, boycotts, or other labor actions by injunctions and by citing union leaders for contempt.

Gompers, who served as AFL president almost continuously until his death in 1924, favored "volunteerism" and "pure and simple" trade unionism as the best policies for the AFL. Unions would improve labor conditions by collective bargaining, resorting to strikes if necessary. Workers themselves would be encouraged to vote for labor's political friends, but beyond that, political involvement would be avoided. Seeking to abolish the capitalist system was simply not realistic. It was foolish, Gompers declared, to suppose that people could

go to bed one night under the present system and tomorrow morning wake up with a revolution in full blast, and the next day organize a heaven on earth. That is not the way that progress is made; that is not the way . . . social evolution is brought about. We are solving the problem day after day. As we get an hour's more leisure every day it means millions of golden hours of opportunities to the human family. As we get 25 cents a day wage increase, it means another solution, another problem solved, and brings us nearer the time when a greater degree of social justice and fair dealing will obtain among men.

Joined with this moderate philosophy was a pragmatic program. The AFL fought to extract an eight-hour day from employers along with higher wages and better job conditions. It demanded that employers recognize the union as the "collective bargaining" agent for their employees. Eventually it tried to get a union shop—that is, a promise by management that union membership be a precondition for hiring workers.

Armed with this philosophy and program, the AFL forged ahead, particularly when prosperity returned after the depression of the mid-1890s. Battling against strong opposition by employers, who branded every effort to achieve collective bargaining an interference with the rights of private property, the federation made substantial gains. In 1904 it claimed 1.6 million members out of a total of some 2 million union members in the country. By 1914 it had over 2 million workers in its affiliated unions out of 2.7 million union members altogether. A large majority of blue-collar industrial workers, particularly the unskilled, remained outside the protection that unions conferred; so did most black workers and women. But by the eve of World War I, Gompers and the AFL were powers to be reckoned with in national life.

The Socialist Alternative. Forced to fight conservative employers on the right, the AFL also had to fend off socialists on the left. Before the Civil War, "socialism" and "communism" had sometimes been used as synonyms for the philosophies of utopian communitarians like Charles

The son of a London cigar maker, Samuel Gompers established the American Federation of Labor in 1886. Although he was once a socialist, he came to believe labor's problems should be solved through negotiation with employers, using, if needed, the weapons of strikes and boycotts.

Fourier and Robert Owen. The socialism of the late nineteenth century, however, was largely Marxist.

Marxism was a body of political beliefs and a theory of society that would exert enormous influence over the years. In *Das Kapital* (1867) and other works, Karl Marx had written that material, or economic, relations had always determined human interests and actions. All institutions and values derived ultimately from the way goods were produced and distributed. Religion, family structure, government, literature, arts, and philosophy reflected each era's fundamental economic institutions. Marx also believed that each economic era was marked by a dominant class. Those were the people who controlled the means of production—whether land, as in feudal times, or capital thereafter—and consequently exercised the power and enjoyed the wealth produced by society.

According to the Marxist interpretation of history, capitalism in its early stages had been a progressive force that

had dramatically increased the world's riches. During this period of vitality, capitalists (the bourgeoisie), like other ruling classes, were able to control and dominate all the social, cultural, and political institutions of their society. These were used to bolster the capitalist system, and even those people who were not beneficiaries of capitalism found it difficult to deny its legitimacy.

But this situation, Marx said, could not last. By the mid-nineteenth century capitalism had generated within itself certain "contradictions." Capitalists need consumers. But by limiting the working class (the proletariat) to bare subsistence wages, capitalists had limited their own markets. As the working class became progressively poorer, capitalist societies increasingly were finding themselves with goods that no one would buy. In the near future, Marx predicted, capitalist economies would experience ever more frequent and serious depressions, and these crises would further undermine the workers' conditions. Eventually the proletariat would become "class conscious." They would see their common interests; abandon the ethnic, cultural, religious, and national differences that had kept them apart; and become militant revolutionaries. The "class struggle" would worsen. Finally, the masses would seize the railroads, factories, farms, and banks and nationalize the means of production and distribution. Government, now an agent of the proletariat, would own and manage all.

Following the revolution, profits formerly skimmed off by the capitalists would be used to benefit the masses. Under the new socialist system there would no longer be exploiter and exploited, powerful and powerless. Instead, there would be only one class, the working class, and within it all would be equal. With the class struggle ended and capitalist contradictions eliminated, humanity would prosper as never before under a regime of economic and social justice for all.

To thousands of men and women the Marxist vision was an inspiration. It appealed to the oppressed by holding out hope of a world in which they would enjoy the abundance and freedom seemingly reserved for the rich under capitalism. Its promise of a harmonious society after capitalism appealed to intellectuals by offering a substitute for their lost religious faith. It spoke to artists, writers, and romantic rebels by promising an antidote to what they saw as the crude and vulgar world of bourgeois values.

In the Gilded Age the Marxists competed with several other socialist groups for the allegiance of wage earners and middle-class dissenters. For a while many Americans were attracted to the Nationalist clubs organized by the journalist Edward Bellamy. In *Looking Backward* (1888), Bellamy told of a young man who awakened in the Boston of the year 2000 and found society transformed into a cooperative commonwealth where abundance, cooperation, and leisure had superseded scarcity, competition, and drudgery. An enormous best-seller for a while, *Looking Backward* made socialism of an undogmatic sort temporarily respectable for thousands of middle-class people.

Also prominent for a while were the anarchists, whose activities in the Haymarket riot have been mentioned. Members of the so-called Black International (in contrast with the Marxist Red International), anarchists believed that every effort to regiment or coerce human beings was a denial of freedom. Capitalism was evil, but so was any state or government, no matter which class controlled it. In place of the all-powerful workers' state envisioned by the Marxists, anarchists would substitute voluntary associations of people organized around their jobs. These associations would own the factories, mines, and tools and would cooperate to produce a benevolent and just society.

Although noncoercive in their philosophy, the anarchists were anything but gentle in their tactics. They believed in direct action to destroy the capitalist state. In Europe and America they were notorious for assassinating public officials and throwing bombs to make their antiauthoritarian point.

The Homestead Strike.   Prior to the Haymarket bombing the anarchists and socialists had won small working-class followings in the major industrial centers. At first there were several competing socialist groups; but after its founding in 1877, the Socialist Labor party, under the brilliant but abrasive Daniel De Leon, became the chief socialist organization. As we have seen, the public reaction to the Haymarket riot injured trade unionism; it also damaged the various anticapitalist parties, and for several years they languished as little more than debating societies.

A further blow fell on labor in July 1893 in the form of a searing, violent clash at the Carnegie steel plant at Homestead, Pennsylvania. The issue at Homestead was new technology. Carnegie and Frick had introduced the most modern labor-saving machinery. Claiming that the new equipment would enhance productivity and hence wages for those who worked by the piece, Frick announced that piece rates would be reduced. The Amalgamated Association of Iron and Steel Workers, representing a small group of the most skilled men, refused to accept the new arrangement. At the end of June 1892, joined by the unskilled workers, they went on strike and sealed off the plant.

Frick had no intention of allowing the strikers to close down the Homestead works and advertised for strike-breakers. But how was he to get the new employees to the idle machines? The locked-out workers were sure to block the way. To solve this problem Frick hired 300 armed Pinkerton agents and sent them in two barges up the Monongahela River, which ran along the edge of the Homestead works. Early on the morning of July 6 the Pinkertons tried to slip by the guards posted by the strikers, but they were detected. The strikers let go with rifles and pistols; the Pinkertons returned the fire until the strikers poured oil on the water and lit it. At this point, rather than be burned alive, the Pinkertons surrendered in return for safe conduct. As they departed for the railway station, however, they were badly beaten. All told, five strikers and three Pinkertons died in the savage melee.

Five days later the governor of Pennsylvania sent 8,000 militiamen to the plant and returned it to the company. The Amalgamated then offered to surrender its economic demands in return for recognition of its right to serve as the bargaining agent for the workers. Frick refused. "Under no circumstances will we have any further dealings with the Amalgamated Association," he declared. "This is final." This arrogant attitude, combined with the use of Pinkertons, brought public opinion to the side of the strikers. Though he supported Frick, Carnegie was dismayed by the mayhem and might have forced concessions. But a young anarchist, Alexander Berkman, outraged at Frick, went to his office and shot and stabbed him repeatedly. Frick survived, but public opinion quickly turned against the strikers, ending all possibility of compromise. As one union man noted: "The bullet from Berkman's pistol went straight through the heart of the Homestead strike."

Depression, Pullman, and Socialist Revival.   The depression following the panic of 1893 encouraged further labor violence and gave socialism a renewed impetus. As in the 1870s, unemployment soared and thousands of idle workers tramped the streets or "rode the rails" looking for work. Employers sought to maintain profits and avoid losses by cutting wages. Like all depressions in capitalist societies, that of the 1890s undermined confidence in the system and aroused dissent.

By creating a new charismatic leader, Eugene V. Debs, the Pullman strike of 1894 became an important turning point in the history of American socialism. George Pullman, the inventor of the sleeping car, had established his giant factory outside Chicago and surrounded it with a model community for his employees. With its tree-lined streets, cream-colored brick houses, its gardens and parks, the town of Pullman was a physically attractive place. It was also a repressive place. Pullman insisted on making his town moral, obedient, and profitable. He forbade liquor, spied on his employees, fired workers for running against the candidates he favored for local office, and charged high rents and utility rates. Pullman considered himself a benevolent man, but he acted like a feudal lord of the manor.

In the summer of 1893, when orders for new Pullman "palace cars" began to fall off, Pullman began to fire work-

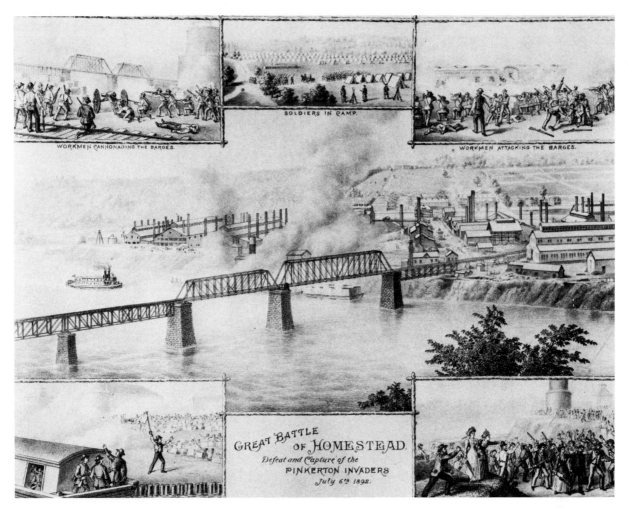

This contemporary scene shows the Carnegie Homestead works in Pennsylvania as they appeared at the time of the great strike of 1892. In each corner of this prostrike engraving are scenes showing the "defeat and capture of the Pinkerton invaders."

ers and cut wages while refusing to reduce rents and utility rates. To defend themselves, Pullman workers began to join the newly organized American Railway Union (ARU) led by a tall, lanky Indianian, Eugene V. Debs. On May 11, 1894, after several unsuccessful attempts to negotiate with Pullman officials, over 3,000 employees walked off the job and asked for ARU support. Debs tried to persuade the Pullman management to talk. When his efforts failed, he reluctantly ordered the ARU switchmen to refuse to attach Pullman cars to trains. The railroad officials responded by dismissing the defiant switchmen. The ARU struck back. By July 1 all twenty-four railroads operating out of Chicago, the nation's rail hub, had shut down.

Despite their anger, the strikers were restrained and orderly. Yet the shutdown of the country's major transportation system frightened the middle-class public. The

Chicago Herald charged: "If the strike should be successful the owners of the railroad property . . . would have to surrender . . . future control to the class of labor agitators and strike conspirators who have formed the Debs Railway Union."

Hoping to break the strike and smash the union, the General Managers Association, representing the major railroads entering and leaving Chicago, hired strikebreakers and asked the federal government for aid, claiming that it was Washington's responsibility to guarantee delivery of the mail, which had slowed in many places when the trains ceased to run. In Attorney General Richard Olney the railroad had a friend in government. A hot-tempered former railroad lawyer who despised labor leaders, Olney quickly ordered federal marshals to Chicago. He also convinced a federal judge to issue an injunction that ordered the union

Pullman Workers' Grievances

The workers in George Pullman's Palace Car Company went on strike in June 1894 after years of accumulated grievances. These included not only the typical labor issues of wages and hours, but also those involving the community of Pullman, the company town where most of the workers lived. The selection below is from a statement issued by the forty-six-member Pullman employee grievance committee to the American Railway Union, the union many Pullman workers had recently joined. It was designed to explain the Pullman workers' decision to strike and to appeal to the ARU for support.

"In stating . . . our grievances it is hard to tell where to begin. You all must know that the proximate cause of our strike was the discharge of two members of our grievance committee the day after George M. Pullman, himself, and Thomas H. Wickes, his second vice-president, had guaranteed them absolute immunity. The more remote causes are still imminent. Five reductions in wages, in work, and in conditions of employment swept through the shops at Pullman between May and December, 1893. The last was the most severe, amounting to nearly 30 percent, and our rents had not fallen. We owed Pullman $70,000 . . . [on] May 11. We owe him twice as much as today. He does not evict us for two reasons: One, the force of popular senti-

ment and public opinion; the other because he hopes to starve us out, to break . . . the back of the American Railway Union, and to deduct from our miserable wages when we are forced to return to him the last dollar we owe him for the occupancy of his houses.

"Rents all over the city [of Chicago] . . . have fallen, in some cases to one-half. Residences, compared with which ours are hovels, can be had a few miles away at the prices we have been contributing to make a millionaire a billionaire. What we pay $15 for in Pullman is leased for $8 in Roseland; and remember that just as no man or woman of our 4,000 toilers has ever felt the friendly pressure of George M. Pullman's hand, so no man or woman of us all has ever owned or can ever hope to own one inch of George M. Pullman's land. Why, even the very streets are his. His ground has never been platted of record, and today he may debar any man . . . from walking in his highways. . . .

"Pullman, both the man and the town, is an ulcer on the body politic. He owns the houses, the schoolhouses, and churches of God in the town he gave his once humble name. The revenue he derives from these, the wages that he pays out with one hand . . . he takes back with the other. . . . He is able by this to bid under any contract car shop in this country. His competi-

tors in business, to meet this, must reduce the wages of their men. This gives him the excuse to reduce ours to conform to the market. . . . And thus the merry war . . . goes on, and it will go on, brothers, forever, unless you, the American Railway Union, stop it; crush it out.

"Our town is beautiful. In all these thirteen years no word of scandal has arisen against one of our women, young or old. What city of 20,000 persons can show the like . . . ? We are peaceable; we are orderly. . . . But George M. Pullman . . . is patiently . . . waiting . . . to see us starve. . . .

"George M. Pullman . . . has cut our wages from 30 to 70 percent. . . . [He] has caused to be paid in the last year the regular quarterly dividend of 2 percent on his stock. . . . [He] . . . took three contracts on which he lost . . . $5,000. Because he loved us? No. Because it was cheaper to lose a little money in his freight car and his coach shop than to let his workingmen go, but that petty loss . . . was his excuse for effecting a gigantic reduction of wages in every department of his great works, of cutting men and boys and girls with equal zeal. . . .

"We will make you proud of us, brothers, if you will give us the hand we need. . . . Teach arrogant grinders of the faces of the poor that there is still a God in Israel, and if need be a Jehovah—a God of battles. . . ."

to cease the strike or be "in contempt of court." The following day, July 3, over the protests of Illinois governor John P. Altgeld, who denied that there was sufficient disorder to require federal intervention, President Grover Cleveland ordered the entire garrison of Fort Sheridan to the city to prevent violence.

The presence of troops and federal marshals infuriated the strikers, and the railway yards were swept by a wave of

shootings and arson. The federal authorities cracked down, arresting Debs and other ARU officials on July 17 for violating the court injunction. Deprived of their leaders, the men gave up and gradually went back to work.

Debs went to prison for six months and thereafter turned against capitalism. In 1901 he became a founder of the Socialist Party of America, an organization that would win a far larger following than Daniel De Leon's Socialist

Eugene V. Debs

For a generation, Eugene V. Debs was the soul of the socialist movement in America. There were other socialist leaders, but no one else so fired the imaginations and raised the hopes of those who accepted the socialist vision at the beginning of the twentieth century.

Debs's American birth was important for the party and movement he headed. Far too many socialist leaders and followers were foreign-born. With his midwestern twang and rangy build, Debs seemed typically American. Actually, his family roots did not go very deep in American soil. His father and mother were both immigrants from Alsace, the German-speaking province of France, who had arrived at Terre Haute in western Indiana in 1851.

Born in 1855, Eugene enjoyed a moderately prosperous middle-class childhood, attending the local private academy and clerking in his father's grocery store. Though his parents were not needy and opposed his decision, Eugene quit school at fourteen to become an unskilled worker for the Vandalia Railroad.

Over the next four years Debs rose to the rank of fireman, but then lost his job during the depression of the mid-1870s. Fortunately, his father succeeded in getting him placed as a clerk in the prosperous wholesale grocery business of a friend. Debs retained a foot in the blue-collar camp by joining the Vigo Lodge of the recently formed Brotherhood of Locomotive Fireman. Yet the lodge was more a fraternal organization like the Masons or Elks than a modern trade union. It was certainly not a militant, class-conscious organization. In 1878, the year after the violent railroad strikes, Debs would tell an approving Brotherhood convention that the firemen's interests were "closely aligned with those of their employers."

The young man of twenty still believed in social harmony as an ideal. One of his friends was William McKeen, president of the Terre Haute and Indianapolis Railroad. Debs praised McKeen as a benevolent employer. McKeen in turn supported Debs when he ran for Terre Haute city clerk on the Democratic ticket in 1879, and again when he ran for the Indiana State Assembly in 1884. During these years the Republican *Express* called the rising young politician "the blue-eyed boy of destiny." In 1885 Debs capped his worldly success by marrying Kate Bauer, daughter of a prosperous Terre Haute druggist.

Despite his upward mobility, Debs refused to abandon his union work. In 1880 he became national secretary-treasurer of the Locomotive Firemen's Brotherhood. He also served as editor of its journal. His ambitious, status-conscious wife kept urging him to accept various business offers, but Debs continued to travel around the country on Brotherhood business. The marriage was not a happy one. The couple could not have children, and this affliction left a gap. Kate Debs took solace in buying a luxurious house in Terre Haute with the proceeds from an inheritance and furnishing it elaborately. She never liked her husband's union and political associates; they were not respectable. Her obsession with material things would prove embarrassing to the country's leading socialist in later years.

During the later 1880s the increasing impersonality of labor-management relations and the erosion of skilled workers' status by new labor-simplifying technology affected Debs's social views. The event that finally liberated him from his earlier ideal of social harmony was the Firemen's strike in 1888–1889 against the Chicago,

Burlington, and Quincy Railroad. The workers were unable to cooperate against an alliance between the railroad and the courts, and they were defeated. The experience convinced Debs that unless working people pulled together, they would never improve their position relative to capital.

In 1893 Debs helped organize the American Railway Union and became its first president. The ARU was soon embroiled in a major strike against James J. Hill's Great Northern Railroad. The following year Debs brought his union into the Pullman strike on the side of the Pullman Palace Car workers. Accused of defying a federal court injunction to stop impeding the mails, Debs and other ARU officials were sentenced to prison terms. The union suffered a blow from which it never fully recovered.

Despite a later myth that Debs himself encouraged, he did not at this time become a socialist. He did emerge from six months in Woodstock prison with a more radical evaluation of American society, yet in 1896 he campaigned for William Jennings Bryan, the Democratic–free-silver candidate for President. Bryan's defeat pushed Debs over the line, however, and in January 1897 he told his associates at the ARU that "the issue is Socialism versus Capitalism. I am for Socialism because I am for humanity." Debs soon maneuvered the remnants of the ARU into forming the Social Democracy of America.

Between 1897 and 1900 Debs came to accept the orthodox socialist class-conflict version of history and politics and became a founding father of the socialist movement. In 1900 the newly formed Social Democratic party nominated him for president, and in 1901 he helped forge the Socialist Party of America out of a collection of socialist splinter groups and factions.

For the next two decades Debs remained the leading figure in the American socialist movement. He was the Socialist party candidate for president in 1904, 1908, 1912, and again in 1920, the last year running his campaign from prison. In the 1912 campaign he received almost a million votes, over 6 percent of the total cast. Debs was a powerful speaker who could hold an audience in his grasp for hours while alternately excoriating capitalism and evoking glowing images of the future Cooperative Commonwealth. Millions, including many who would not "throw away" their votes on a third-party candidate, adored him. To many Americans of the day, he personified the heroic and humane socialist ideal.

Yet within the socialist movement Debs had his critics and opponents. To his right within the party there was Victor Berger of Milwaukee and Morris Hillquit of New York. Both were foreign-born, yet both represented moderate positions. They believed it essential for socialists to work within the existing conservative labor unions, seeking to gain control by influencing members' views. They also believed that socialists must support reform programs in order to appeal to discontented members of the middle class as well as to blue-collar workers.

Debs led the left wing, which endorsed separate radical unions in competition with the American Federation of Labor, was more skeptical of reform, and more "proletarian" in its sympathies than the right wing. Yet Debs had his critics to the left, too. These were people like "Big Bill" Haywood of the Industrial Workers of the World (IWW), who advocated industrial sabotage, the general strike, and overtly confrontationist tactics to bring capitalism to its knees. Debs tried to mediate between these extremes. He did not always succeed, but his charisma and popularity with the rank-and-file members managed to preserve the formal unity of the party.

World War I was a catastrophe for the socialists and for Debs. Some prominent socialists left the party to support the Allied cause even before American entrance into the war, and more resigned when, in April 1917, shortly after America's declaration of war against Germany, the party announced its opposition to the war. During the war the mood of intolerance and superpatriotism led to official repression of socialist publications, government raids on party offices, vigilante actions against socialists, and the arrest and imprisonment of socialist leaders on charges of subversion and attempts to discourage men from registering for the draft. In June 1918, following a speech critical of the United States, Debs was indicted by the federal government for violating the 1917 Espionage Act. He used his trial as an effective forum for his ideas, but he was sentenced to ten years in prison and sent to Atlanta Penitentiary to serve his term.

During the two years Debs actually spent in prison, the party he had helped to found underwent drastic changes. In the decade preceding 1917 more and more of the party membership came to consist of recent immigrants from Finland, Russia, and other parts of eastern Europe. When the Bolsheviks took power in Russia in late 1917, many of these immigrants hailed the event and insisted that the party endorse the Russian Revolution. Before long the "foreign-language federations," with their far-left allegiances, formed a caucus within the party and sought to seize power. In March 1919 the Bolshevik leaders in Moscow ordered the formation of the Third International, with the slogan "Back to Marx" and the name "Communist." One of the first directives issued by the International's leaders was that each of the organized Socialist parties divest itself of any bourgeois, right-wing elements. This encouraged the foreign-language federations to split off from Debs's Socialist party and organize what came to be the American Communist party, leaving behind a depleted and demoralized rump.

At first Debs supported the radicals, but then, while still in prison, he changed his mind. After his release from Atlanta in December 1921, he returned to Terre Haute to be greeted by 25,000 cheering supporters. By this time the early hope that the Socialist party might become a major agent of fundamental change had evaporated. In 1924, recognizing the depleted energies of the party, Debs supported Robert LaFollette's presidential bid on the Farmer-Labor ticket. For this he was bitterly attacked by his former left-wing comrades, now mostly Communists.

Debs had never been a healthy man. Over the years he had suffered numerous breakdowns from mysterious ailments and had taken a series of "cures" at sanitariums. On October 20, 1926, following a massive heart attack, he died in Chicago and his body was brought to Terre Haute. Thousands came to pay their respects, trailing through the parlor of the Debs's house to view the coffin. Eugene's brother Theodore, Theodore's wife and daughter, and other family members greeted the mourners. Debs's widow, Kate, remained upstairs in her room, however. To the very end she could not help expressing her disapproval of her husband's disreputable associates.

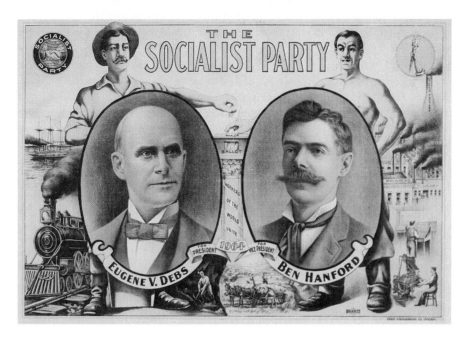

A poster for one of Eugene Debs's earlier presidential campaigns.

Labor party. During the remainder of his life, Debs would embody both the best and the worst in American socialism. Generous, humane, and fiery in defense of justice, he was also a stubborn visionary who lacked the ability to manage a party racked by bitter internal disagreements. Despite his failings, under Debs's leadership the Socialist Party of America grew rapidly before World War I, winning the support of many German and Jewish wage earners and even some rural and small-town people in the Midwest. It also attracted a following of authors, ministers, and professional people. Between 1904 and 1912 the party increased its dues-paying membership from 20,000 to 130,000; in 1912 Debs received 900,000 votes, 6 percent of the total, when he ran for president. The party did even better on the local level, electing several congressmen and a half-dozen mayors in cities like Scranton, Milwaukee, and Syracuse.

Still, the Socialist Party of America never captured the support of a majority of American wage earners. Unlike the French, Italian, German, and British Socialist parties, it never truly challenged the leading moderate parties for control. Some scholars have blamed this comparative failure on the Socialists' tendency to fight among themselves over minor points of Marxist theory. Others contend that American capitalism was too self-confident, too competent, and too powerful to be successfully challenged. Another view emphasizes the power of cultural indoctrination, such as the Horatio Alger myth or the work ethic, to dissuade American workers from accepting radical ideas.

The most convincing answer, however, points in a different direction. No doubt factionalism and strong capitalist resistance weakened the Socialist party in the United States; but European socialists, who faced the same difficulties, prospered. In contrast to European workers, however, American wage earners, especially the native-born, were not class-conscious. Well paid by comparison with industrial workers in other lands and just a generation or two off the farm, they expected to prosper and move up the social ladder. Many owned some property and could not accept a philosophy that predicted inevitable class conflict and the increasing misery of wage earners under capitalism. Immigrant workers were not much better as potential recruits for socialism. Most had difficulty enough adjusting to American cities and American industry without making further trouble for themselves, and they avoided "labor agitators." Despite their initially low status, they too expected to rise socially and economically. All told, the relative prosperity of the United States and people's expectations for improvement were strong antidotes to radical politics. As the German sociologist Werner Sombart noted at the turn of the century, socialist "utopias" in America inevitably foundered "on the reefs of roast beef and apple pie."

★ CONCLUSIONS ★

As we consider the reasons for the nation's economic surge a century ago, several distinct factors come into view. Creative industrial tycoons gave a strong push to America's forward leap. Their skill, intelligence, drive, and even ruthlessness furthered the growth that propelled the Republic past its rivals. But besides the builders who added to the nation's efficiency, innovation, and technology, there were the spoilers who milked the achievements of others solely for their own advantage. And the tycoons—builders or spoilers—could not have created an industrial nation alone. Working people, accepting the conventional wisdom of the age, labored hard, believing that success and security would reward their efforts. It is also clear that without government's substantial contributions, despite the theories of laissez faire and social Darwinism, progress would have been far slower.

Clearly many of the men and women who lived through these tumultuous years were ground down by the great economic machine they were helping to build. The pain they experienced was expressed in the violence of the Pullman, Homestead, and railway strikes, and in the organized political efforts meant to effect change. Yet we must not exaggerate the extent or depth of discontent among wage earners. Many found their lives satisfactory and, with reason, looked forward to better times. Despite the agitation and the occasional violence, it remains true that most Americans retained their faith in the "system" and refused to accept radical solutions to the problems they faced. This ultimate faith was expressed in the continued vitality of the economy and the mainstream political parties and in the growth of cities and the nation as a whole.

★★★★★★★★ FOR FURTHER READING ★★★★★★★★

Edward C. Kirkland. *Dream and Thought in the Business Community, 1860–1900* (1956)
This intellectual history of Gilded Age businessmen is based on their private correspondence, congressional testimony, and published writings. Seeking to avoid stereotypes, Kirkland presents their thoughts on the economy, government, the civil service, public schools, philanthropy, and the universities.

Matthew Josephson. *Edison* (1959)
According to Josephson, Edison's Menlo Park laboratory was his greatest invention: It was the first industrial research laboratory, applying scientific theory and technical knowledge to practical problems.

Harold C. Livesay. *Andrew Carnegie and the Rise of Big Business* (1975)
This small jewel of a book makes Carnegie's role in the post–Civil War economic surge clear. It is not a full biography, but it makes the economic man and his accomplishments come alive.

Frederick Lewis Allen. *The Great Pierpont Morgan* (1949)
A breezy, entertaining biography of Morgan that succeeds in defining his place in American economic life. Allen makes complex financial deals easy to understand.

Irvin G. Wyllie. *The Self-Made Man in America: The Myth of Rags to Riches* (1954)
Wyllie follows the myth of the self-made individual from colonial times to 1929. He describes the continuing power of the myth in the face of some hard statistics suggesting that to go from rags to riches was a rare achievement.

Theodore Dreiser. *The Financier* (1912)
The hero of this novel is modeled after the Gilded Age streetcar magnate Charles Yerkes. A superb historical document: Dreiser understands the sort of driven and aggressive man Yerkes was and perceives the relationship between business and politics in this era. Dreiser actually admires Yerkes for his powerful will.

Herbert Gutman. *Work, Culture, and Society in Industrializing America* (1976)
A collection of essays, written at different times, by a leading social historian. It emphasizes the experience of working-class life in the half century following 1865. An important, though uneven, book.

Stephen Thernstrom. *Progress and Poverty: Social Mobility in a Nineteenth-Century City* (1964); and *The Other Bostonians: Poverty and Progress in the American Metropolis* (1973)
The first of these two books deals with Newburyport, Massachusetts; the second with Boston. Both seek to determine the extent of social mobility for working people and the middle class in nineteenth-century America. In Newburyport, a small city, Thernstrom finds that movement up the social and occupational ladder for wage earners was modest and difficult, though it took place. In Boston, on the other hand, it was remarkably easy, especially for native-born Americans, Northern Europeans, Protestant immigrants, and Jews, though slower for blacks and Irish Catholics. Both studies are important.

Stanley Buder. *Pullman: An Experiment in Industrial Order and Community Planning, 1880–1930* (1967)
This is as much an urban as a labor history. It tells the story of the town of Pullman and views it as an example of unsuccessful paternalism.

David Montgomery. *Beyond Equality: Labor and the Radical Republicans, 1862–1872* (1967)
An interesting attempt to connect the Gilded Age labor movement to the egalitarian ideas of the 1860s Radical Republicans.

Daniel Walkowitz. *Worker City, Company Town: Iron and Cotton Worker Protest in Troy and Cahoes, New York, 1855–1884* (1978)
A study of two New York industrial towns with different ethnic mixes and with different property distribution patterns. Walkowitz links the differing response to labor conditions of each wage earner community to its distinctive

social milieu. Though seemingly narrow in scope, the study makes for interesting reading.

David Brody. *Steelworkers in America: The Nonunion Era* (1960)

Brody shows not only what produced discontent among American steelworkers before 1919, but also what encouraged labor's stability and acquiescence. A model study.

Harold C. Livesay. *Samuel Gompers and Organized Labor in America* (1978)

Another good biography by Livesay, this time of a leading labor statesman. The book goes beyond biography, however, and tells us much of the evolving labor movement, particularly the AFL, during the years 1890 to 1920.

Daniel T. Rogers. *The Work Ethic in Industrial America, 1850–1920* (1975)

Examines the intellectual defense of hard work and steady application that accompanied industrialization in the United States.

Daniel Bell. *Marxian Socialism in the United States* (1962)

Bell, although at one time a Marxist himself, was critical of socialism by the time he wrote this brief book. Though one must keep his biases in mind, this short history of American socialism is valuable.

Nick Salvatore. *Eugene V. Debs: Citizen and Socialist* (1982)

This is the best biography of Debs. Written by a scholar sympathetic to, but not uncritical of, the Socialist leader.

Charles Francis Adams, Jr., and Henry Adams. *Chapters of Erie* (1866)

The classic account of the chicanery of Jay Gould and his confederates. The work of patrician descendants of Presidents John Adams and John Quincy Adams, it was written by two men who knew the Gilded Age business community despite their origins.

Maury Klein, *The Life and Legend of Jay Gould* (1986)

Professor Klein attempts the difficult here: rehabilitating the reputation of Jay Gould. He almost pulls it off.

18*

THE GILDED
AGE CITY

*What Did It Offer,
and to Whom?*

1860–1910	American cities, as defined by the Census, increase in number from 392 to 2,220
1871	The Great Chicago Fire
1872	New York's Boss Tweed is indicted and jailed
1878	Asphalt paving introduced in Washington, D.C.
1880	Salvation Army introduced from England • James A. Garfield elected president
1881	Garfield assassinated; Chester A. Arthur becomes president
1882	Chinese Exclusion Act passed in response to organized labor's fear of cheap labor
1884	Grover Cleveland elected president
1888	Benjamin Harrison elected president
1892	Cleveland elected president for the second time
1894	Immigration Restriction League • Coxey's Army marches on Washington to protest unemployment
1896	William McKinley elected president
1897	First subway line is built, in Boston
1899–1904	Mayor Samuel "Golden Rule" Jones institutes municipal ownership of utilities in Toledo
1900–10	Eight million immigrants arrive
1901	McKinley assassinated; Theodore Roosevelt becomes president
1907	Congress appoints Dillingham Commission to investigate immigration
1914	Birth control advocate Margaret Sanger is forced to leave the country

The city has been a central element in civilization for perhaps 5,000 years. In fact, cities seem to "equal" civilization, for it has been in urban settings that humanity has produced most of the ideas, artifacts, art, and science that we identify as essential marks of civilized life.

Throughout much of history, however, city populations have constituted only a small part of any given society as a whole; until the years following the Civil War, the United States was no exception to this rule. As late as 1860 only 20 percent of the nation's population was urban. The most heavily urbanized sections of the nation were the New England and Middle Atlantic areas, where industrialization had already taken hold and thousands of farm people, both native- and foreign-born, had been drawn to the factories, docks, shops, and countinghouses of both old towns and new ones. Elsewhere, particularly in the West and the South, most Americans continued to live on villages and farms.

The Civil War slowed city growth somewhat, but thereafter it resumed at a breakneck speed. Between 1860 and 1910 the number of "urban places" increased from 392 to over 2,200. In 1860 New York and Philadelphia were the only American cities with more than half a million inhabitants. By 1910 these communities, along with the "prairie colossus," Chicago, had over a million residents each, and five other cities had grown to 500,000 people. During that fifty-year stretch the urban share of the country's population went from 20 to 46 percent. The Northeast remained the most urban part of the nation: Massachusetts and Rhode Island were about 90 percent urban; Connecticut, New York, New Jersey, and Pennsylvania were over 60 percent urban. But urbanization had spread far beyond the areas that had first felt the pull of industry and commerce. In the Midwest, Illinois, Ohio, Michigan, Wisconsin, Indiana, Missouri, and Minnesota were almost 46 percent urban—the 1910 national average. The Far West and Pacific Coast were not far behind, and by 1910 Colorado, Washington, and California were all either ahead or just behind the national average.

What forces explain this rapid urban growth? What brought millions of people from the farms of America and from distant regions of the world to the cities of the United States in these years? And how did the millions of new urban dwellers prosper in their new homes?

★ IMMIGRATION ★

One major factor that set urban populations soaring in the half century following the Civil War was the influx of foreign-born newcomers. In the 1880s more than 5 million people entered the United States. The severe depression of the 1890s reduced the number of immigrants substantially, but between 1900 and 1910 over 8 million more foreigners arrived. Many of these people eventually returned home, either disappointed with America or so successful that they could live well in the "old country" on what they had made here. Yet most immigrants, by far, remained in America, and by the end of the century most of them made the cities their home.

America's Attractions. Like previous immigrants, Gilded Age arrivals came because of both "pushes" and "pulls." The chief "pull" of America, for late-nineteenth-century immigrants as for their predecessors, was economic. Immigrants from every land were attracted by the possibility of improving themselves in some material way. Only a minority were drawn by America's reputation for religious and political freedom. Through letters from previous arrivals and from the newspapers and magazines in their native lands, immigrants were remarkably well informed about American economic conditions. During hard times in the United States, such as the mid-1890s, foreigners stayed home. During good times, such as the 1880s and the first decade of the twentieth century, the flow of immigrants became a flood.

The United States actively encouraged immigration. During the 1850s western mining companies had brought in Chinese workers to dig for gold in California and Nevada. In the 1860s the Central Pacific Railroad imported 10,000 Chinese to help construct the first transcontinental line. After its completion many of these laborers remained to build other western railroads and to swell the populations of San Francisco, Sacramento, Denver, and other towns. In Texas, Arizona, New Mexico, California, and Colorado, railroad employers recruited many Mexicans from across the border to work on repair and construction crews; many other Mexicans came to work picking fruit, cotton, lettuce, and tomatoes in the Southwest and on the Pacific Coast.

The railroads encouraged immigration in other ways, too. Endowed with enormous land grants, they looked abroad for settlers to convert their acreage into cash. The Illinois Central, the Northern Pacific, and other railroads scattered colorful brochures advertising their lands across Europe and established offices in major European cities where railroad representatives offered advice to would-be immigrants and described the favorable terms available to those willing to come. Thousands took the bait.

Other businessmen sought to use the 1864 Contract Labor law to attract workers from abroad. Designed to remedy an anticipated labor shortage, this measure had authorized employers to hire foreign workers under an agreement that guaranteed passage money, a specified wage, and defined working conditions. The law was not effective. Though only a few hundred skilled workers were brought to the United States under its provisions, trade union pressure induced Congress to repeal it in 1885 (the Foran Act).

A more fruitful source of foreign labor was the *padrone* system used to recruit Italian labor for eastern mines, factories, and construction projects. *Padroni* were Italian-American middlemen, frequently connected with small immigrant banking firms, who signed up gangs of Italian laborers in southern Italy at fixed wages and paid for the workers' passage. In the United States the *padrone* arranged with an American employer to supply workers at a sum that gave him a profit. In the early years, when the United States was still an unfamiliar destination for Italians, the system was useful in providing immigrants with food, board, and advice. The *padroni*, however, often took advantage of the trusting men they recruited, charging them high prices for what they provided while keeping them in virtual slavery. Fortunately, when the Italian-American community had put down firm roots and would-be immigrants could turn to relatives and friends for advice and help, the system declined.

Though immigration was to some extent "guided," then, the great majority of European arrivals needed little encouragement to join the burgeoning industrial market of America. Letters from relatives and friends, talks with townspeople back in the "old country" for a visit, or information supplied by government agencies and shipping companies was enough to draw people by the thousands to Genoa, Trieste, Bremen, Le Havre, Odessa, Salonika, Oslo, or Liverpool to take ship for the United States.

Despite the obvious attractions of America, fewer immigrants would have crossed the Atlantic or the Pacific if not for the plummeting prices of ocean fares and the growing speed of ocean travel. Here the steamship made the difference. During the 1860s the introduction of large and fast steam vessels with auxiliary sail reduced transatlantic crossing times from as long as three months to as little as ten days. A dozen shipping companies—British, German, Italian, Dutch, and French, as well as American—soon entered the transatlantic trade, and their fierce competition quickly brought passenger rates down.

The Push: The New Immigrants.   Like the "pull" to America, the "push" was predominantly economic. Until the 1890s most European immigrants came from northern Europe—Britain, Germany, and Scandinavia. In each of these countries agriculture had been hurt by competition from the newer grain-growing regions of Canada, the United States, Argentina, and Australia. Unable to compete with the lower production costs in these new lands, European landlords squeezed out the peasants and introduced machinery. To make matters worse, the 1870s and 1880s were times of severe drought in parts of western and central Europe. Overseas competition, combined with nature's ill favor, drove thousands of Swedes, Germans, and Britons to seek havens in the United States.

The push from northern Europe soon slackened. By the 1890s northern European agriculture had adjusted to the overseas competition. At the same time, rapid industrialization in Sweden and Germany, plus falling birthrates throughout northern Europe, provided new opportunities for displaced farm people in their own nations' factories and mines. Meanwhile, growing militarism in Germany led to official efforts to discourage the emigration of young men. British emigration continued; but more and more, the Irish, Scottish, English, and Welsh found the British "dominions"—Canada, Australia, New Zealand, and South Africa—more attractive than the United States.

After 1890 a wave of immigrants from southern and eastern Europe more than offset this northern European decline. These so-called New Immigrants were a diverse lot. Many were Slavic peoples—Czechs and Bohemians, Poles, Ukrainians, Slovaks, Serbs, Croatians, Ruthenians, and Russians—from the Hapsburg Empire (Austria-Hungary) or from Russia, the empire of the Romanov czars. Many were southern Europeans, with the largest number from Italy, though there were many Greeks as well. Other eastern Europeans included Hungarians and Rumanians. From the Turkish dominions came Armenians and Syrians. A large group of New Immigrants consisted of Jews from either Austria-Hungary or imperial Russia. Many of the Slavs and virtually all the Italians were Roman Catholic, and for the first time there were substantial numbers of Orthodox Catholics among the new arrivals.

Until late in the century America had meant little to these people. It was too far away and too expensive to reach. Besides, the Hapsburgs, the Romanovs, and the Ottoman Turks had refused to allow their subject peoples to leave for fear of reducing their military forces or their tax rolls. Toward the end of the century Austria, Russia, and Turkey abandoned their opposition to emigration. At the same time, as we have seen, ocean passage rates and travel time declined sharply. In addition, the blight of overseas agricultural competition, which had attacked the countries farther west a decade or so earlier, finally spread to eastern Europe.

Though the push was largely economic, political and religious factors also played a part in propelling people from the czarist and Ottoman lands across the Atlantic. No country in Europe was as backward, as illiberal, and as authoritarian as Russia. The czars often treated non-Russian

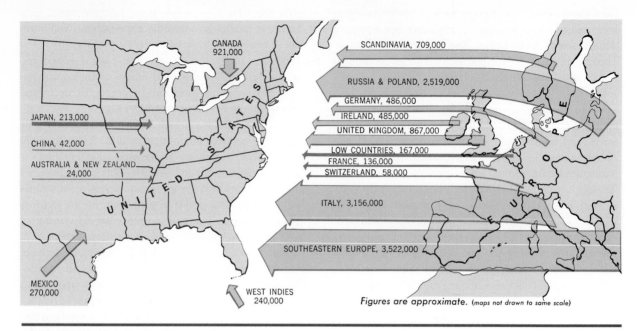

CANADA
921,000

JAPAN, 213,000

CHINA, 42,000

AUSTRALIA & NEW ZEALAND
24,000

MEXICO
270,000

SCANDINAVIA, 709,000

RUSSIA & POLAND, 2,519,000

GERMANY, 486,000

IRELAND, 485,000

UNITED KINGDOM, 867,000

LOW COUNTRIES, 167,000

FRANCE, 136,000

SWITZERLAND, 58,000

ITALY, 3,156,000

SOUTHEASTERN EUROPE, 3,522,000

WEST INDIES
240,000

Figures are approximate. (maps not drawn to same scale)

SOURCES OF IMMIGRANTS, 1900–1920

subjects harshly. After 1870 thousands of German Pietists, who had settled in southern Russia during the eighteenth century, fled when the czars withdrew their privileges. A much larger group of refugees from the czars' domain were Jews who had resided in Russian lands since the Middle Ages. Never treated as full equals, they had managed to survive as craftworkers, innkeepers, small merchants, and manufacturers. After 1880, however, a wave of laws excluded them from public office, universities, agricultural pursuits, the professions, and other activities. The government also incited anti-Jewish riots (pogroms) that resulted in hundreds of deaths and the devastation of whole communities. Meanwhile, in the Ottoman Empire, the Turkish government began to persecute brutally its Christian Syrian and Armenian minorities.

These changes, taken together, produced a drastic shift in the source of the immigrant streams: Most now came from southern and eastern Europe. In 1880 a mere 17,000 immigrants to the United States came from Austria-Hungary; by 1907 there were almost 340,000. Only 5,000 Russian subjects immigrated to America in 1880; in 1907 over 225,000 arrived. In 1880 some 12,000 Italians came to the United States; in 1907, over 285,000. Northern European immigration showed the opposite trend: In 1880 the number from Britain, Germany, and Scandinavia totaled 295,000; by 1907, when total immigration was almost three times as great, it was down to 199,000.

From Farms to Cities.   The ocean crossing remained unpleasant for poorer immigrants until well into the twentieth century. Unable to pay for private cabins, they traveled below decks in "steerage," jammed in with hundreds of others. Rough seas brought seasickness. At times cholera epidemics swept the ships, killing scores and so frightening American officials that the federal government imposed quarantines, shutting down all transatlantic immigration for substantial periods.

Most European immigrants came through New York, Boston, New Orleans, Baltimore, or Philadelphia, with New York far in the lead. Before 1892 most New York–bound immigrants passed through Castle Garden, a facility established at the tip of Manhattan Island by New York State officials. In 1892 the federal government took over the responsibility for receiving immigrants and replaced Castle Garden with a new facility at Ellis Island in New York harbor. Here new immigrants were asked their names, ages, occupations, places of origin, literacy, and financial status. They were also examined by doctors to see that they were not carriers of infectious diseases. At Ellis Island, too, immigrants first made contact with the many societies established by their compatriots to offer advice and services and to keep them out of the hands of swindlers eager to cheat "greenhorns" of their money and possessions.

Once in America, the immigrants had to consider their ultimate destinations. During the 1870s and 1880s thousands of Germans, Scandinavians, Poles, and Bohemians went to the wheat regions of Minnesota, the Dakotas, Nebraska, and Kansas, where they bought land from the railroads. Then, as the nation shifted from an agricultural to an industrial economy, the immigrants were increasingly drawn to the cities and their factories.

Specific immigrant groups tended to concentrate in certain industries and occupations. There were several reasons for this: because their compatriots who had come to America earlier worked in the particular industry, because it was related to a business they were familiar with, or because they had settled in a region dominated by a specific industry. French Canadians crossed the border from Quebec to the nearby New England textile towns, where they displaced many of the Irish, who had earlier replaced the New England mill girls. Jews from Russia and Poland who had been skilled tailors in Europe entered the garment industry of New York, Rochester, and Chicago. Italians, coming from a land notable for stonemasons and workers in marble, concentrated in the construction industry; Slavs, from nations with mines, entered mining and heavy industry; the Portuguese from maritime Portugal and the Azores moved into the New England fishing industry.

Nativism.   The new pattern of immigration that emerged toward the end of the century disturbed many Americans. Some deplored the immigrants' urban concentration, seeing it as a deterrent to their assimilation into the mainstream of American life. Concentrated in tight-knit ghettos, they would be slow to lose their alien ways and become "good Americans." Immigrant organizations were also concerned, and Jewish and Catholic societies sought to deflect recent arrivals among their co-religionists from the cities to rural areas. Many native Americans resented the unfamiliar appearance and ways of the newcomers. The novelist Henry James, visiting Boston after spending many years in Europe, felt out of place as he walked the city's streets. While strolling on fashionable Beacon Hill one Sunday, James observed groups of men and women in their best clothes walking and "enjoying their leisure." "No sound of English . . . escaped their lips; the great number spoke some rude form of Italian, the others some outlandish dialect unknown to me. . . . The types and faces bore them out; the people before me were gross aliens to a man, and they were in serene and triumphant possession."

The resentment was not confined to elite, old-stock Americans like James. The New Immigrants frequently

Were poor immigrants a resource? Steel king Andrew Carnegie, himself an immigrant, believed they were. In fact, he estimated that each one was worth $1,500. Immigrants labored in mines and mills, built railroads and bridges, farmed the land, and bought products of the nation's factories.

clashed with the Old Immigrants of the pre–Civil War generation or with their half-assimilated children. In 1877, during the hard times that followed the panic of 1873, Irish-American workers in San Francisco attacked Chinese businesses and the docks of the Pacific Mail Steamship Company, the firm they held responsible for importing the "coolie" immigrants from Asia to undercut their wages. Local businessmen organized a Committee of Public Safety and with the aid of federal authorities quashed the rioting, but not before four men had died. Soon afterward Denis Kearney, a native of Ireland's County Cork, helped organize the Workingmen's Party of California, an organization dedicated to improving the lot of the city's working people, but also committed to eliminating the Chinese from the community. Kearney denounced the rich railroad and mining magnates of California, but his speeches usually ended with the cry: "And whatever happens, the Chinese must go!"

The anti-Chinese movement in California was not unique. Spokesmen for organized labor feared "coolie labor," and indeed any cheap labor, whether from Europe or Asia. Passage of the Foran Act in 1885, repealing the Contract Labor Law of 1864, was, as we saw, largely the result of trade-union pressure. In 1882 similar pressure induced Congress to pass the Chinese Exclusion Act prohibiting the immigration of Chinese laborers for ten years. This measure was renewed several times, and Chinese exclusion was made permanent in 1902. Not until 1943 were foreign-born Chinese allowed to take up legal permanent residence in the United States.

Anti-immigrant sentiment in these years, however, was not primarily economic in origin. Most native-born Americans had little to fear from the New Immigrants, for they generally took the low-paid, unskilled, dirty jobs that no one else wanted. Nativist feelings, rather, had roots that were largely cultural. No American denied that the United States was composed of past immigrants and their descendants. But many native-born people were certain that the New Immigrants were inferior to the immigrants of the past. They seemed more alien and illiterate. They came, it was said, from more backward lands where democratic institutions were unknown. A larger proportion of them were Catholic or Jewish, and hence further removed than earlier arrivals from the American Protestant tradition. They were responsible for the increased disorder, violence, and vice of the cities. The New Immigrants, moreover, did not intend to stay, the critics said. Many were birds of passage, men without wives or families, who would make their fortunes in America and return to their native lands. They refused to go to the farms, the indictment continued, congregating instead in the big cities, where they retained their foreign ways, turned to crime, and succumbed to insanity, epilepsy, or other nervous or emotional disorders that severely taxed local health facilities.

The hostile response to immigrants was reinforced at the turn of the century by the racist theories of men like Josiah Strong and Madison Grant, who proclaimed the natural superiority of "Nordics" over "Mediterraneans," "Alpines," and other darker-haired, darker-eyed white people of southern and eastern Europe. Racist ideology and traditional prejudice against foreigners led in 1907 to the appointment by Congress of the Dillingham Commission to investigate immigration. Its voluminous report confirmed all the common negative stereotypes. The commission described the Old Immigrants as "ideal farmers" and people "imbued with sympathy for our ideals and . . . democratic institutions." By contrast, the more recently arrived southern and eastern Europeans were "different in temperament and civilization from ourselves." Serbo-Croatians had "savage manners," Poles were "high-strung," southern Italians had "not attained distinguished success as farmers." Generally, the report endorsed the common view of the inferiority of the New Immigrants and branded them undesirable.

The Dillingham Commission's report was full of errors. It disregarded the differences among nationalities except when these could be held to their discredit. But the new arrivals were not all alike. The illiteracy rate was high among Italians, low among Bohemians. Greeks returned to their homeland in some numbers, but few Jews of the czar's empire did, for Russia was violently anti-Semitic. Many New Immigrants were unskilled; but the Armenians were more skilled than the Germans arriving at the same time.

Whatever the reality, many old-stock Americans continued to believe in the inferiority of the most recent immigrants and supported nativist organizations dedicated to reducing the flow of immigrants or limiting their role and that of their children in American public life. In the 1880s and 1890s, the American Protective Association (APA) demanded that noncitizens be excluded from political power and attacked "the diabolical works of the Roman Catholic church." In 1894 a group of New England blue bloods organized the Immigration Restriction League with a program to impose literacy tests on the new arrivals, many of whom, the League believed, could not pass such a test. The League was blunt in expressing its goals. According to one prominent member, Americans must decide whether the country was "to be peopled by British, German, and Scandinavian stock, historically free, energetic, progressive, or by Slav, Latin, and Asiatic races, historically downtrodden, atavistic and stagnant."

The League failed in its main goals before the 1920s. In 1896, and again in 1913 and 1915, Congress passed measures requiring that all immigrants be able to read and write either English or their own language. Each time, however, the president vetoed the measure. Though many Americans feared the foreign deluge, others opposed restriction. Businesspeople resisted an end to the seemingly inex-

A large unidentified office, about 1900. An increasingly complex society needed more literate white-collar workers, and so proved willing to finance high school education out of public funds.

haustible supply of cheap labor, and the National Association of Manufacturers constantly lobbied against restrictions on immigration. Old-fashioned liberals, who prized America's tradition as a haven for the world's poor and oppressed, also fought efforts to end free immigration. In the end the doors remained open. Though Congress whittled away at free movement from Europe by passing laws excluding immigrants with chronic diseases, those with records as criminals or prostitutes, and those with known anarchist views, drastic limitations on transatlantic immigrants would wait until a later day.

Buckwheats and Hayseeds.   City streets were crowded not only with the foreign-born; they were also jammed with men and women straight off the nation's farms. Just as there were "pushes" and "pulls" in the movement of immigrants to America, there were similar factors in the exodus from the nation's farms and villages to Gilded Age cities.

The lure of the city for rural people is a persistent theme in the history of the Western world. Cities were no doubt wicked; they were dangerous. But they were also vivid places where life was full of excitement and color. Compared with the sleepy village or farm, the city—with its well-stocked stores, its bustle, its amusements, its street life, and its brilliant lights—was a joy. The novelist Hamlin Garland recalled that everything about Chicago was interesting when he arrived there as a young farm boy: "Nothing was commonplace, nothing ugly." In *The City*, a 1909 play by popular playwright Clyde Fitch, one character exclaims: "Who wants to smell new-mown hay, if he can breathe gasoline on Fifth Avenue instead!"

And besides the urban glamor, there were irresistible economic pulls. Jobs, of course, were primary. Thousands of young rural people came to the cities to work as clerks, secretaries, bookkeepers, and salespeople. Farm boys also were drawn to the mills and factories to tend machines, stoke furnaces, and supervise other hands. At his plants in Pennsylvania Andrew Carnegie liked to hire "buckwheats," lads from the nearby countryside. These young men, he believed, made the best workers in the mills. For young Americans with special career interests, the cities were indispensable. To talented musicians, artists, writers, actors, or performers of any kind, only the largest cities of the land could provide the training, the experience, and the appreciative audience they needed and craved.

The push also applied to rural youths—"hayseeds" in the vocabulary of the day. If the cities were fascinating, the farms and villages often were not. Hamlin Garland wrote about the "sordidness, dullness, triviality, and . . . endless drudgeries" of rural life. In his short story "Up the Coulee" one of his characters complains: "Anything under God's heavens is better'n farmin'." But even if a farm youth wanted to stay and till the soil, it was often difficult. Because farm families were large, rural fathers could not provide land for all their sons. There was the option of going west, but as we shall see, through much of the late nineteenth century, agriculture was a troubled industry even on the newer western lands.

In the Northeast the farmers' problems were compounded. With the completion of the transportation network, it became ever more difficult for the old, rocky fields of New England and the Middle Atlantic states to compete with the rich soils of the Great Plains and the prairies. In certain places northeastern farmers were able to adjust to the new competition. In many areas, however, they and their children simply abandoned the land that their ancestors had occupied for generations and went off to the nearest big city. As the census of 1890 showed, the counties in two-fifths of Pennsylvania, one-fourth of New Jersey, about five-sixths of New York, and a very large part of New England had declined in population during the 1880s. A French visitor who traveled through Pennsylvania and New England in the early 1890s noted: "Sloven farms alternate with vast acreages of territory, half forest, half pasturage." Farm buildings "partly in ruins testify at once to the former prosperity of agriculture and to its present collapse."

★ THE URBAN SETTING ★

The Physical Environment. Whether from Italy or Iowa, Austria or Alabama, all newcomers found urban life in the Gilded Age replete with problems. American cities in the years immediately following the Civil War were generally harsh, dirty, congested places. The streets were unpleasant. Many cities had miles of dirt roads, dusty in summer, muddy in winter, and filthy at all times owing to the large numbers of horses. Nor was the sky above any better. The soft coal widely used for heating and industrial fuel darkened city air with soot. In the 1890s the ash from its steel and glass factories often brought twilight at midday to Pittsburgh.

Until the end of the century few American cities had adequate public water supplies or decent sewer or street-cleaning services. In 1880 Baltimore, with 330,000 people, had "no sewers to speak of . . . , all chamber slops [being] deposited in cesspools or privy vaults." A newspaper report on Chicago in the same year declared with unusual directness that "the air stinks." Just after the Civil War, Memphis was described as an open sewer.

Housing presented the most serious urban problem. Newcomers to the city struggled to find decent dwellings at affordable prices. Many were forced to take the dilapidated houses formerly occupied by the middle class, who had fled the squalor and congestion of the inner city. The originally spacious rooms of these older structures were cut up into small, cramped apartments for people who could pay only $8 or $10 a month for rent. Others found room in shoddily constructed new buildings. In New York at the end of the century over a million people lived in tenements of five to six stories with shallow air shafts on either side to provide a little light to interior rooms. These structures, called "dumb-

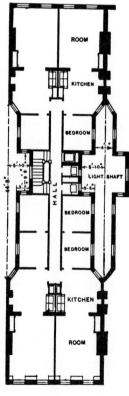

This floor plan of a "dumbbell" tenement explains the name but leaves much unsaid. Each unheated apartment housed at least one family, allowing the landlord to charge rent for as many as 700 people in a single block of dumbbells. The "hall" was less than three feet wide, and the light shafts—often used to dispose of garbage—were a fire hazard. Like most tenements, the dumbbell had a way of looking dilapidated as soon as it was built.

bell tenements" because their floor plans revealed a long, narrow waist where the air shafts were placed, had only one bathroom for every twenty inhabitants, a situation that endangered the health and undermined the comfort of the inhabitants. Chicago, too, was full of substandard housing. Although the Great Fire of 1871 created the opportunity to construct comfortable apartments for working people, the city permitted builders to throw up block after block of shanties and ugly two-decker flats on the burned-over land.

As cities grew, it became increasingly difficult for people to get to stores, workplaces, and recreation areas. Congested downtowns, full of wagons, carriages, and pedestrians, made the movement of goods a nightmare. Long before the era of the automobile, downtown city streets experienced colossal traffic jams.

Well before the Civil War the country's largest urban centers had ceased to be "walking cities," in which everything was accessible for people moving on foot, and had adopted the horse-drawn "omnibus" and, a little later, the horse-drawn streetcar on rails. After the war many more communities expanded beyond comfortable walking-city size and adopted animal power for transportation. Using a horse-drawn vehicle was faster than walking, but it had many drawbacks. The cars were often crowded and stuffy. Riders were packed in like "smoked hams in a corner grocery." In 1864 a newspaper described a streetcar trip as an experience in "martyrdom." Public transportation also compounded the sanitation problem. The thousands of horses trotting the city streets created enormous piles of droppings, and the resulting smells and clouds of flies made the summer, especially, an ordeal for city dwellers.

The Immigrant Adjustment.   Newcomers to the city also faced a harsh and disruptive social environment. For foreign immigrants the challenge was particularly severe because they had to make a double adjustment, acquiring the ways of both America and the city simultaneously. Most eastern and southern European immigrants were rural peasants who found the cities alien places. Here were no one-story cottages, but multifloor apartment dwellings. Here you did not light your candle or oil lamp or cut wood for your cooking stove; you turned on a switch or stopcock and paid utility bills to the gas or electric company. In Chicago, Cleveland, or New York, you did not throw your garbage to the pigs; you placed it in refuse cans for the sanitation department. And how different it was to earn a living and get from place to place! Immigrants, in a word, had to abandon the familiar customs and practices of Europe's rural villages and learn how to survive in the vast impersonal metropolis.

For some groups social and institutional adjustment was especially difficult. Southern Italians, for example, had no tradition of group cooperation. At home loyalty had been given to the family and the village, not to the larger society. Even the Italian nation, a recent political creation, did not evoke a strong shared response. In America, however, being Italian set one apart and forced one to acknowledge a group identity. Unused to self-help and communal associations, Italian immigrants from diverse regions had to learn for the first time to cooperate. It has been said that people from Naples, Calabria, and Sicily became Italians only in America.

Some groups were spared the double adjustment. The Jews, in particular, had already become acclimated to urban life before they arrived. In both Russia and Austria-Hungary, many had been town dwellers with occupations readily transferable to the cities of America. In addition, they had a strong group cohesion forged through centuries of persecution. Unlike the Italians, they brought to America community associations and fraternal groups to help ease their adjustment.

The economic problems were the most urgent ones the immigrants encountered in the American "urban wilderness." Most groups of newcomers included a professional and business class. The Jews in the garment industry not only worked as cutters and sewing machine operators but also owned many of the shops. Italians became building contractors employing Italian workers. Because all groups retained a strong loyalty to the customs, cuisine, and language of their native land, a few enterprising people with a little capital established restaurants, groceries, theaters, bookstores, and assorted businesses catering to their compatriots. The newcomers also preferred to turn to their own kind for professional help, and immigrant doctors, lawyers, priests, and rabbis found ample demand for their services. By 1914 the typical American city was crowded with street signs in Polish, Italian, Yiddish, Chinese, Spanish, and other languages that advertised the wares of ethnic shopkeepers and the services of ethnic professionals.

Many of the cities' foreign-born remained unskilled or semiskilled workers for most of their lives. Yet social mobility studies of the Gilded Age city paint a complex picture. In Boston the British and other northern Europeans, as well as the Jews, moved up rather rapidly from unskilled to skilled jobs; some even graduated into the ranks of the business class or the professions. The Irish and Italians, in contrast, lagged behind both native American newcomers to Boston and more mobile immigrant groups. In New York, on the other hand, according to one study, both Jews and Italians moved ahead almost equally fast and both achieved large gains in income and status in a rather short time. In Atlanta immigrants raised their status with remarkable speed, says one scholar, far faster than the city's large black population.

The Boston Poor

Not every city dweller in the Gilded Age, not even every working-class person, was miserably housed, of course. But in this era, when rural Americans and immigrants poured into the country's cities, decent living accommodations were denied many people. For decades following the Civil War few middle-class Americans worried much about the "slums." But then, toward the end of the century, a new urban reform movement appeared, led by men and women who believed that much of the cities' misery could be blamed on the wretched hovels inflicted on the urban poor. One such reformer was Benjamin O. Flower, a Boston journalist and publisher. The following is a description of Boston's North End from a book-length report called *Civilization's Inferno* that Flower wrote in 1893.

"The first building we entered faced a narrow street. The hallway was as dark as the air was foul or the walls filthy. Not a ray or shimmer of light fell through transom or sky-light. The stairs were narrow and worn. By the aid of matches we were able to grope our way along, and also observe more that was pleasant to behold. It was apparent that the hallways or stairs were seldom surprised by water, while pure, fresh air was evidently as much a stranger as fresh paint. After ascending several flights, we entered a room of undreamed of wretchedness. On the floor lay a sick man. He was rather fine looking, with an intelligent face, bright eyes, and a countenance indicative of force of character. No sign of dissipa-

tion, but an expression of sadness, or rather a look of dumb resignation peered from his expressive eyes. . . . There, for two years, he had lain on a wretched pallet of rags seeing his faithful wife tirelessly sewing, hour by hour and day by day, and knowing full well that health, life and hope were hourly slipping from her. This poor woman supports the invalid husband, her two children and herself, by making pants for leading Boston clothiers. No rest, no surcease, a perpetual grind from early dawn often far into the night. . . . Eviction, sickness, starvation—such are ever-present spectres, while every year marks the steady encroachment of disease, and the lowering of the register of vitality. . . .

"The next place visited was the attic of a tenement building even more wretched than the one just described. The general aspects of these houses, however, are all much the same, the chief difference being in the degrees of filth and squalor present. Here in an attic lives a poor widow with three children, a little boy and two little girls. They live by making pants at starvation wages. Since the youngest child was two and a half years old she has been daily engaged in overcasting the long seams of garments made by her mother. . . . There, on a little stool, she sat, her fingers moving as rapidly and in as unerring a manner as an old experienced needle-woman.

"Among the places we visited were a number of cellars or burrows. We descended several steps into dark, narrow passageways, leading to cold,

damp rooms, in many of which no direct ray of sunshine ever creeps. We entered one room containing a bed, cooking stove, rack of dirty clothes and some broken chairs. On the bed lay a man who had been ill for three months with rheumatism. This family consists of father, mother and a daughter in her teens, all of whom are compelled to occupy one bed. They eat, cook, live, and sleep in this wretched cellar and pay over fifty dollars a year in rent. This is a typical illustration of life in this underground world.

"In another similar cellar or burrow, we found a mother and seven boys and girls, some of them quite large, *all sleeping in two medium-sized beds in one room*; this apartment is also their kitchen. . . . Their rent is two dollars a week. The cellar is damp and cold; the air is stifling. Nothing can be imagined more favorable to contagion both physical and moral than such dens as these. Ethical exaltation or spiritual growth is impossible with such an environment. It is not strange that the slums breed criminals, which require vast sums yearly to punish after evil has been perpetrated; but to me it is an ever-increasing source of wonder that society should be so short-sighted and neglectful of the condition of its exiles, when the outlay of a much smaller sum would ensure a prevention of a large proportion of the crime that emanates from the slums; while, at the same time, it would mean a new world of life, happiness, and measureless possibilities for the thousands who now exist in hopeless gloom. . . ."

The crucial factor affecting the immigrants' economic progress apparently was education. Those who were illiterate or who could not speak English were easily exploited. People who had nothing to sell but physical brawn stayed on the bottom rungs of the economic ladder. Immigrants

understood the importance of education very well and flocked to night schools where, after a hard day's work, they attempted to learn English and reading and writing. The more enterprising or energetic succeeded. Others failed, defeated by age, bad luck, or personal inadequacy. Those who

One of Ash Can School's pictures of city streets. George Luks's Hester Street, a portrait of New York's Lower East Side in 1905.

did not, or could not, acquire a basic education generally remained part of the large mass of urban poor.

Pressures on the Family.   The traditional father-dominated, home-centered rural family changed substantially in the new city environment. On the farms and in the rural villages, whether of America or Europe, fathers worked close to their families. Even in the smaller cities this proximity was elusive, and as the urban centers grew, the physical distance between home and work became ever greater. The advent of the horse-drawn streetcar enabled many of the more prosperous working-class men to commute to their jobs. Although the "streetcar suburbs" provided space for recreation and some of the pleasantness of the countryside, the long commuting time meant that a man spent longer periods than ever away from his wife and children. With fathers so often absent, young men, in particular, lost close contact with a model of how to deal with the adult world, and many found the process of adjusting to work and adulthood more difficult than in earlier days.

The gap between generations encouraged by city life was even greater among immigrants than among the native-born. The children of European peasants and laborers encountered very different customs and habits from those their parents had known in the "old country." Growing up in the city streets and attending American schools, the second generation often developed different values. Girls picked up attitudes that were at odds with strict European views of the proper role for unmarried women. Children who knew

English and felt familiar with American life fared better in the new environment and could use the language more effectively than their parents. Boys often found work when their fathers could not. Adolescence is at best a turbulent time of revolt against parental control; in the cultural clash between foreign-born parents and native-born children, families were frequently shaken to their foundations.

The city not only weakened the structure of the family but also reduced its size. It took a lot of money to raise children in the city. Farmhouses could sprawl almost indefinitely without affecting the family's expenses for shelter. But in the cities working-class families could not afford large apartments and painful congestion was common. Benjamin Flower, a philanthropist-editor, described a woman and her seven children who lived in one room in Boston's North End. In 1899 housing expert Lawrence Veiller noted a New York tenement block of four- and six-story dwellings in which almost 3,000 people lived in thirty-nine buildings.

Nor were children the economic asset in the city that they were in the country, where they were an important part of the work force. Working-class urban families were forced to put their children to work at odd jobs. Some children worked alongside their parents at garment making or some other "sweated" trade conducted in the home. But compulsory education laws and the difficulties of finding wage-paying work for boys and girls meant that they were not as self-supporting as rural children.

The cost of raising a family in the city encouraged fam-

For poor immigrant families, privacy was unknown. Whole families shared a single bed, and they often squeezed boarders into their homes for extra income. Children frequently worked long hours at some "home industry" with their parents to bring in enough income to support the family.

ily limitation. Fertility rates in the United States had been declining for generations in both towns and countryside. Toward the end of the nineteenth century the constraints of the urban environment provided new incentives to family limitation.

The growing trend toward smaller families offended social conservatives. Moralists and religious leaders frequently denounced efforts to disseminate birth-control information as sinful. In 1873, at the urging of "purity" crusader Anthony Comstock, Congress classified birth-control information as obscene and excluded it from the mails. Toward the end of the century, however, Margaret Sanger, a visiting nurse on New York's East Side, launched a campaign to provide poor women with scientific birth-control information. Defenders of old-fashioned morality attacked Sanger, and denounced the whole family-limitation movement as "race suicide." Sanger persisted but was forced to flee the country in 1914 for distributing the pamphlet *Family Limitation*. She later returned and organized the American Birth Control League, which became the leading agency of the birth-control movement in the United States.

Margaret Sanger's effort, initially directed at the slum family, achieved its greatest success among middle-class women and those working-class women most anxious to move into the middle class. Its effect on their lives was profound. With fewer children in the family, they were relieved from long years of childbearing and child nurture. Together with new labor-saving devices for the home such as the gas range and hot piped-in water, the decline in family size freed many women from lifelong household drudgery. Some directed their released energies to civic work or self-improvement. Women's clubs, literary societies, and discussion groups proliferated and became potent forces for political and social reform in the early twentieth century.

Changes in family responsibility also enabled middle-class women to join the labor force in growing numbers. Until late in the nineteenth century few middle-class women worked outside the home, since, schoolteaching aside, the jobs available to them were largely in domestic service or low-paid factory work. By the 1890s, however, urban service jobs were expanding rapidly, and thousands of middle-class women could become retail salesclerks, bookkeepers, typists, bank tellers, and secretaries. By 1914 city streets were thronged with working women going to and from their jobs in downtown offices and stores.

Family limitation had mixed social consequences. In smaller families children were less often neglected. And with fewer mouths to feed, the family was more prosperous. Children could be allowed to stay in school until they were better prepared for the "race of life." Married women often found their lives more rewarding and the bonds of marriage less confining.

But the change in family size also had a dark side. The family as an institution lost some of its cohesion. In 1867, when divorce laws were strict and divorced people ostracized, only 10,000 divorces were granted in the entire country. By 1907, as a result of divorce-law reforms and the more

Most immigrant children learned to read and write and to understand the ways of their new country in public and parochial schools. But parents like this Italian immigrant father also helped their children acquire the skills needed to get ahead in the new land.

permissive moral climate, there were 72,000 divorces, a rate over three times as great per capita. Whether viewed as a social calamity or liberation, divorce had become a more widely accepted feature of American life.

Crime, Vice, and Loneliness.   All newcomers to the American Gilded Age city encountered social pathologies. Cities were schools of crime and disorder, with gangs of cardsharps, pickpockets, purse snatchers, and thieves. Then as now, poor people were the major victims of city crime. They were also its chief perpetrators, especially of violent crimes. A city disease, crime was also a way of "making it" in America. Street boys stole from stores, passers-by, and drunks. In Chicago, an observer noted, the newsboys who gathered in the courtyard of the Hearst Building to pick up the evening papers were also petty thieves.

Those young men, it seems, usually gambled away what they stole, but other slum dwellers used their illegal gains to get ahead. Crime, in sociologist Daniel Bell's phrase, was a "queer ladder of social mobility" for some of the urban poor. It was also typically American: It fit the American ideal of self-employment and called forth the "manly" virtues of courage and physical skill.

Prostitution also plagued the cities of this period. The Gilded Age was a particularly prudish era in sexual matters. Except in the medical profession, the physical relations between men and women were seldom discussed by decent people. "Good" women were expected to be indifferent to sex. By itself this distaste for sex might have encouraged prostitution; but in addition the cities attracted multitudes of young women looking for jobs and respectable marriages. Although many achieved their goals, others failed and fell prey to madams, shady saloonkeepers, and others who took them in and led—or forced—

them into prostitution. Periodically, reformers and crusaders would rise up against the "white slave" trade and close the brothels, but they would generally spring up again.

A pioneer in the birth-control movement of the early twentieth century, Margaret Sanger offended traditionalists and inspired reformers. In 1914 she was indicted for violating the laws against obscenity by mailing birth-control information. Here she poses for photographers after her arraignment at court.

Respectable people deplored the city saloon as a haunt of vice and drunkenness, but it met an urgent urban social need. American cities were lonely places for the thousands of men and women who arrived without family or friends. To offset the isolation of their lives, newcomers to the city joined lodges, church organizations, ethnic societies, and veterans' groups. In the 1890s settlement houses, where the poor could find educational and recreational facilities, helped create community feeling in the city neighborhoods. The local tavern often served the same purpose. Church leaders and moralists might rail, but to many isolated men the saloon was a place where they could find companionship for the price of a glass of beer.

The saloon, the settlement house, the fraternal order, and the ethnic society proved inadequate in providing moral and emotional support for city dwellers, especially those without families. Even the churches often failed. Catholics and Jews were quick to provide for their own religious needs, and every immigrant quarter was dotted with small churches and synagogues, many of which were unpretentious storefront establishments. But Protestants often neglected their less-fortunate members. With their base in older rural America and the prosperous middle class, the Protestant denominations frequently found it difficult to understand or cope with the problems of poor city dwellers.

Disturbed by the demoralization in the city centers, in the 1880s Protestant reformers launched the Charity Organization movement. Hundreds of middle-class women became volunteer "friendly visitors" to slum families to advise them how to save, how to use their money, how to dress, and how to keep clean. They accomplished little. The Salvation Army was more successful in aiding the cities' outcasts. It set up hundreds of soup kitchens, shelters, lodging houses, and "rescue missions" in the run-down areas of many cities to provide meals and a place to stay for the homeless. The YMCA and YWCA also sought to help. But none of these efforts solved the problems created in the cities by the breakdown of traditional ties to family, neighbors, and other social groups. By the end of the century every city had its "skid row," where lonely men and women in cheap rooming houses lived out narrow hopeless lives amid squalid surroundings.

Suburbanization. In part the failure to deal successfully with the problems of the city was the consequence of suburbanization. Many middle-class, old-stock Americans chose to escape the problems of congestion, decrepit housing, noise—and newcomers—by leaving them behind and fleeing to new, middle-class neighborhoods. The earliest suburbs appeared in the 1850s when the railroads first provided fast connections between country home and city office for a small group of prosperous merchants. The coming of the streetcars in the post–Civil War period made it possible for less affluent folk to buy suburban private homes. Richer people could afford large, detached private houses with sizable backyards and front lawns. The lower-middle-class and skilled blue-collar workers made do with two- or three-family dwellings such as those constructed in Boston's "streetcar suburbs" of Roxbury and Dorchester. With another family or two to pay rent, a clerk, foreman, or skilled machinist could afford to live along the tree-shaded avenue of a suburb rather than on the grimy streets of downtown.

The suburbanization of these years was not a mass movement; that would come with the advent of the motor car in the 1920s. But it did make a dent in city congestion. In Milwaukee, for example, 34 percent of the population lived within a mile of the city's business core in 1880; by 1900 this figure had fallen to 17 percent. During much of the nineteenth century the cities kept these people as taxpayers by annexing the suburbs and so maintained their solvency. After 1920, when the suburbs resisted political union with the central cities, the exodus of the middle class would have serious social and economic consequences for those who remained behind.

★ CITY GOVERNMENT ★

Contemporaries might argue over the social and physical virtues of cities, but few cared to defend their politics. Lord James Bryce, an English observer of Gilded Age America, in fact considered American cities "the worst governed in Christendom."

The critics' chief target was the city machines—political organizations designed to perpetuate a faction or party in office. Each machine was led by a "boss," who might or might not serve as mayor but who, regardless of his official title, dominated the city government. Beneath the boss was a collection of faithful aides—the ward or precinct captains ("ward heelers") and various rank-and-file hangers-on—who performed the machine's essential function of mobilizing the vote for its mayoral and city council candidates. The machines kept the loyalty of their retainers by providing them with jobs, often sinecures that paid well but did not require serious effort or any demonstrated competence.

The purpose of the machine was to win and retain office. But for what? Reformers, champions of "good government," insisted that the machine's only goal was to milk the city treasury or to confer under-the-counter favors on business people and purveyors of vice for the personal gain of its members. The boss and his henchmen, they said, were at heart little more than racketeers. And their methods were no more savory than their goals. Machines, the reformers noted, won the support of voters by wholesale bribery and corruption. They paid the poor $5 or $10 each for their votes; they stuffed ballot boxes with false returns; they brought in "floaters" from other communities to vote in city elections; they illegally naturalized aliens to cast ballots for the machine and against its opponents. In short, as "good-government" people saw it, the machines were essentially diseased organs that had to be cut out of the body politic if city life was to be improved.

The Machine in Action.   The reformers were not entirely fair. The machines performed important functions that could not be handled by the more formal institutions of the day. New York in the 1870s illustrates how they operated and why they became so deeply entrenched.

In the years immediately following the Civil War, the country's largest city was governed by a confused jumble of overlapping agencies. It had a board of aldermen, a board of councilmen, twelve supervisors, and a separate board of education—all with power to make decisions in various spheres without the mayor's approval. The police commissioners were appointed not by the mayor or by any city agency but by the governor of the state, as were the commissioners of Central Park and of the fire department. The system was a "hodgepodge," declared James Parton, a contemporary critic, that made New York virtually ungovernable.

Into this confusion stepped William M. Tweed. Tweed was not the gross, predatory figure depicted in the savage cartoons of reformer Thomas Nast. Neither was he the model of an upright public servant. Tweed and his hench-men bilked the city treasury of millions of dollars collected largely in the form of kickbacks from private contractors, who provided the city with supplies and services at rigged prices and then secretly returned some of their take to the machine and its leaders. In building the fabulously expensive New York County Courthouse, for example, three-fourths of the total cost of $12 million represented profit to the ring composed of Tweed and the other officials of Tammany Hall, the New York Democratic machine. One estimate puts Tammany's total thefts at between $45 million and $200 million.

But Tweed and his Tammany henchmen did not take without giving. Tweed made the chaotic, aimless political system of New York respond to the pressing needs of its citizens. Did shippers need improved docks? Tweed would get new powers for the city to build them. Did working people need a rapid transit system? Tweed would see that transit promoters could acquire private property for the right-of-way. Did households need new sewers or a better water supply? Tweed would use his influence in the state capital so that the city could borrow to provide them.

Other cities had versions of Tweed. In St. Louis Ed Butler was the conduit through which most of the urban capital improvements flowed. In Philadelphia the ring under boss David Martin organized the granting of contracts for city services in an efficient and orderly manner. Chicago's Republican boss, William Lorimer, helped the city obtain streetcar lines and expanded gas services. In Cincinnati boss George B. Cox stemmed the social disorganization that set in after 1880 and provided the city with remarkably efficient administration.

Reformer Thomas Nast was to plague Tammany Hall's Boss Tweed long after Tweed's imprisonment. Years later, after Tweed had escaped abroad, Spanish authorities arrested him on kidnapping charges. Apparently they had seen an old Nast cartoon showing Tweed beating a child.

The machines were not only useful devices for getting new sewers, improved lighting, and transit lines; they were also informal welfare organizations, providing services today supplied by local, state, and national government agencies. Although cities of that time had official almshouses, orphanages, hospitals for the insane, and even refuges for drunkards, these were dreary and oppressive places avoided by the poor. Churches and private philanthropic organizations also sought to help the poor, yet their aid remained grossly inadequate for such large numbers of needy.

The machines helped offset the failings of the contemporary welfare system. Because they controlled massive amounts of patronage, they could find jobs for the unemployed in the police department, the fire department, the schools, or the sanitation service. Civil service rules seldom applied to these jobs, and the local ward captains reserved them for their favorites. The machines also supplemented

the incomes of the poor—providing coal during the winter, turkeys at Thanksgiving and Christmas, and free medical services—and fed money into private charities. During his term as state senator, Tweed, a Protestant, pressured the New York legislature into appropriating funds for the Catholic charities and parochial schools that many of his poor city constituents relied on.

The city machines were also buffers between the poor citizen and the law. Much of what was accounted illegal in the contemporary American cities was victimless crime: gambling, drinking on Sunday, "blood" sports such as cockfighting or bare-knuckled boxing, and sex for money. Not all Americans believed that these activities should be considered illegal, and many continued to engage in them. When, during a sudden surge of civic virtue, the authorities clamped down on saloons, gambling, or vice, people were arrested for practices that they considered at worst venial sins. Where could they turn for help? The obvious an-

The ward captain, or "heeler," was the neighborhood leader of the Gilded Age city machine. His job was to disperse the benefits that the machine used to win and keep voters' loyalty. Shown here is the annual outing of Tammany Hall's Timothy D. Sullivan Association on a summer day in New York.

swer was the precinct captain, who could "speak to" the judge. Even better, the machine could quash the spasm of virtue before it developed. City machines were understanding of human weaknesses, as reformers seldom were, and overlooked transgressions that did not unduly disturb public order.

The machines, then, often functioned both as social service organizations and as shields between city people and the barbs of city life. As Tammany leader George Washington Plunkitt explained, a ward captain was always obliging: "He will go to the police courts to put in a good word for the drunks and disorderlies or pay their fines, if a good word is not effective. He will feed the hungry and help bury the dead." Martin Lomasney, a Boston machine leader, explained it more philosophically: "I think that there's got to be in every ward somebody that any bloke can come to—no matter what he's done—and get help. *Help, you understand; none of your law and justice, but help*."

Goo-Goos. Of course the machines were not purely altruistic. In return for these services they expected gratitude that could be turned into votes at election time, as well as a certain acceptance of graft and corruption. The public's acquiescence was finite. Eventually Tweed, for example, ran up bills that the voters would not tolerate. When a disgruntled former Tammany leader decided to tell all, the commercial and financial leaders of the city, joined by good-government reformers ("goo-goos" to their enemies) and an outraged citizenry, mounted a campaign to cut Tweed down. In the election of 1871, although Tweed himself was reelected to the state senate, most of his cronies lost their races for state and local office. In 1872 the reformers elected to the mayor's office William F. Havemeyer, a wealthy sugar refiner and one of their own. Tweed himself was indicted on criminal charges and sent to jail. On his release he was rearrested to stand trial in a civil action to recover the sums he had stolen. He fled to Spain, was returned to New York, and sent to jail again, where he died in disgrace in 1878.

Under Havemeyer the reformers attempted to run the city on economical and honest principles. They cut back on hundreds of patronage positions in the city service departments and eliminated many construction projects. Thousands of workers lost their jobs. With Tweed no longer in Albany to manage the necessary legislation, the state ceased to appropriate money for private and religious charities. Ticket-fixing, "speaking to" judges, and gifts of coal and turkeys also stopped, as did the tolerance for the petty law-bending of working-class life. This moralism and the cuts in patronage and services cost the reformers the support of the poor, and bossism soon returned in the form of "Honest" John Kelley. As leader of Tammany Hall, Kelley was a more scrupulous man than Tweed; but he, too, an-

chored the machine squarely on the support of the city poor and dispensed favors and services with a ready hand.

The pattern of spendthrift machine followed by tight-fisted reformers and spendthrift machine once again was repeated over and over in American cities during the Gilded Age. The poor often preferred open-handedness to economy, ethical tolerance to the moralism of the reformers. If municipal reform movements before the 1890s were generally short-lived, it was due as much to the reformers' limitations as to any perversity on the part of city voters.

★ A BETTER PLACE TO LIVE ★

Many of the difficulties faced by city dwellers after the Civil War were the result of extraordinary growth that outran the capacity of cities to solve their problems. Urban citizens had to turn to makeshifts, including the city machines, to meet their needs. They often had to accept inferior facilities and services as well. By the 1880s, when the cities finally began to catch up with their problems, city life began to improve.

Physical Improvement. A part of the advance was the upgrading of the physical environment. The introduction of asphalt in the 1870s made city streets cleaner and safer. Asphalt was cheaper than cobblestone or brick and more durable than wood blocks; it soon became the standard paving material for cities.

Waste-disposal problems were not as easily solved; yet as the years passed, matters improved. In 1887 Los Angeles, a city without a major river to use for dumping waste, built a sewage treatment plant. Chicago stopped the pollution of Lake Michigan, the source of its drinking water, by reversing the direction of the Chicago River so that it flowed into the Mississippi. In the landlocked Midwest several cities turned to incinerators to dispose of waste. Most of these schemes only postponed the difficulties or imposed them on some other community downstream. But they were better than those that had preceded them.

One of the great urban triumphs of the age was the provision of pure water. By the time of the Civil War many cities had systems for piping water into homes. After the war, following the discoveries of Koch and Pasteur that bacteria are powerful disease-causing agents, cities began to filter and chlorinate their water. By the time of World War I, every American city had pure drinking water, and death rates from cholera, typhoid, and other water-borne diseases plummeted. Combined with milk pasteurization and other new health measures, these advances drastically reduced urban mortality rates, especially among the young.

Abraham Ruef

In 1883, Abraham Ruef graduated from the University of California at Berkeley with a senior thesis called *Purity in Politics*. At Hastings Law School he and some friends founded the Municipal Reform League to study city problems and find ways of solving them. Twenty years later, as boss of the San Francisco Republican machine, Ruef pleaded guilty to charges of extortion and spent four years at San Quentin prison.

This reformer-turned-boss was born in San Francisco in 1864, two years after his parents emigrated from France. Though the son of immigrants, Ruef's childhood was affluent. His father became a successful storekeeper on Market Street and a real estate dealer who listed himself in the city directory as "capitalist." Abraham himself was a precocious student who spoke seven languages and graduated from Berkeley with high honors and a major in Greek and Latin.

Ruef stumbled into politics. In 1886 he was admitted to the California bar and opened a law office in the Bay city. Soon after, he found himself at a Republican club meeting in his home district attended by only two others— a boardinghouse owner and a saloon-keeper, the two district leaders. The two men, Ruef later claimed, told him that the large, intelligent crowd that had attended had just left, and they induced him to write a newspaper article describing the successful party gathering. Whether out of appreciation of the young lawyer's literary imagination or his gullibility, they soon made Ruef captain of two Republican precincts and got him elected as delegate to the municipal convention of 1886. Ruef's political career was launched.

San Francisco's leading Republicans soon noticed this bright, cocky lawyer. They may have bridled at his pretensions, but his seniors in the machine found his cultivation and refinement a welcome contrast to the vulgarity and ignorance of the typical machine hack. For his part, Ruef realized the value of the machine in bringing him into contact with public officials, judges, and successful fellow lawyers. Before long he began to dream of becoming United States senator.

Though initially Ruef preferred the good-government faction of the party, he soon judged the reformers "apathetic" and "drifted" to the side of the machine. "Whatever ideals I once had," he later confessed, "were relegated to the background." Ruef quickly became the local Republican boss of San Francisco's Latin Quarter, the raffish, bohemian district of the Bay city.

Boss Ruef displayed all the skills and talents of his breed. He systematically cultivated the different ways to collect votes. He joined every social club he could find. He understood the endless demands of the district's people for charity and bought tickets to every benefit. He made friends with the judges at the police court so he could help his constituents in trouble with the law. He also paid court to the city's tax assessors to help local business people and property owners when tax time came around. He even established useful contacts at the coroner's office so he could get a death report changed to suit a political ally. Ruef understood that every function of government provided an opportunity to do a favor for a constituent. But he also had other political assets. His sense of humor endeared him to the voters. On one occasion at a political rally, he noticed that the audience had a supply of eggs to throw at him when he got up to speak. "Throw all the . . . eggs at one time," Ruef told the crowd, "so that we can get down to business."

In 1901 Ruef founded the Republican Primary League to help influence the course of an important three-way mayoral contest. The city had just weathered a huge dockworkers', sailors', and teamsters' strike that had idled 40,000 workers and tied up 200 ships in the harbor. When Mayor James D. Phelen finally decided to call in the police to protect strikebreakers, a riot had broken out that ended in bloodshed. The strikers, outraged at the use of police, formed a new party of their own—the Union Labor party—to take control of the city government, and received the support of William Randolph Hearst's powerful paper, *The Examiner*.

Ruef allied his League with the new party and then hand-picked his friend and client Eugene Schmitz as its candidate. A violinist, composer, and director of the Columbia Theater orchestra, Schmitz, as president of the local musicians' union, qualified as a friend of organized labor. Meanwhile, the Republicans, dominated by the Southern Pacific Railroad, had picked city auditor Asa Wells as their candidate; the Democrats chose a member of Phelen's entourage, Joseph S. Tobin.

Schmitz's campaign, managed by Ruef, emphasized fair play for labor, public ownership of utilities, and economy in government. Energized by deep working-class resentments against the recent police brutality, the Union Labor party won. Schmitz's fellow musicians expressed their elation at the results by parading around the city playing their instruments with gusto. But no one was more pleased than Ruef. The new party, he wrote, would be "a spark . . . which would kindle the entire nation. . . . [It would be] a throne for Schmitz as Mayor, as Governor—as president of the United States. Behind that throne, I saw myself its power, local, state—nation. . . ." Schmitz, in office, did not actually seek city ownership of public utilities, yet labor did benefit from his friendly attitude. During the streetcar strike in 1902 working people considered his role "fair and fearless." His tight rein on the police allowed labor to win this dispute and many later ones. Under Mayor Schmitz San Francisco would earn the reputation as the "tightest closed-shop town" in the United States. In 1903 the violinist-mayor won a resounding reelection.

As Schmitz prospered, so did Ruef. During the day the "Curly Boss" could be found in his law offices, putting in long hours dealing with clients and constituents. At night he held court at the Pup, a French restaurant downtown. Ruef did not drink or smoke, but he was vain and drove a sporty automobile he called the "Green Lizard." He never married, and his nocturnal headquarters were said by his enemies to be an "institutionalized house of assignation."

Much was also said about his political morals. Both at his office and at the restaurant, Ruef allegedly collected bribes camouflaged as payments for legal services, from the United Railroad, the Pacific State Telephone and Telegraph Company, and the Home Telegraph Company, in exchange for political favors. He and his friends also collected tribute from dairies, real estate brokers, insurance adjusters, auctioneers, produce dealers, and proprietors of restaurants, theaters, gambling houses, saloons, and brothels.

By 1903 the good-government forces, led by Fremont Older, the reformist editor of the *San Francisco Bulletin* and friend of former Mayor Phelen, had resolved to oust Schmitz and break Ruef's grip on the city government. The two men, Older insisted, were false friends of the working people and were utterly corrupt. Soon editorials were appearing in the *Bulletin*

almost daily, attacking the "boodlers" and "grafters" who were running the Bay city. Older's denunciations of Ruef spared nothing. Even his legal work for the city's prominent French restaurants was immoral. These establishments, he noted, had family eating rooms with good food on the first floor, but no respectable woman would be seen on the second, with their private dining rooms, or on the third, with their accommodations for prostitutes and their clients.

The campaign of Older, Phelen, progressive reformers, and antilabor city businessmen to dump Schmitz in 1906 failed; the Mayor won a smashing reelection victory. But Older persisted. Later that year he visited President Theodore Roosevelt in Washington and procured the services of Francis J. Heney, special assistant to the United States attorney general. With the support of Rudolph Spreckels, one of the city's most prominent business leaders, Older and his friends raised $100,000 to investigate Ruef's deal to build an electric trolley streetcar line. Aside from their suspicion that it was a corrupt deal, they also objected to the overhead wires that they claimed would mar the city's natural beauty. At the same time they proposed on alternate scheme of their own: streetcars powered by an underground moving cable.

The earthquake and fire that ravaged the Bay Area in April 1906 drove the corruption and transit system issues from people's minds. Schmitz proved to be an able leader in the crisis, and Ruef served on the Committeee on Reconstruction. For the moment it seemed that all hostilities would be suspended. But while the city remained preoccupied with physical reconstruction, Ruef's associates got an ordinance passed authorizing their overhead trolley streetcar. When the public discovered the coup there was a huge outcry amplified by new allegations of money distributed to secure

a favorable telephone company franchise. Ruef's plans for building a "greater" San Francisco, charged a city newspaper, were essentially "plans for a greater Ruef."

By this time Older and his associates felt they had enough evidence to proceed to trial. Some of this material had been obtained by a "sting" operation wherein an agent for the reformers had enticed some of the city's supervisors into taking bribes and then promised them immunity in return for testimony against the boss. Ruef tried to forestall the trial, but in November 1906, he, Schmitz, and a flock of their colleagues were indicted for graft.

In exchange for partial immunity, Ruef confessed and implicated several prominent California business leaders in his deals. This did not help him. Chief Prosecutor Heney decided that the confession was entirely self-serving and untrue, and withdrew the immunity offer. The trial was one of the most sensational on record. Prosecution documents were rifled, witnesses suborned, jurors bribed, and incriminating evidence hidden away. A supervisor's house was blown up, and the chief prosecutor was shot in the courtroom by a juror he had revealed to be a former convict. Someone even kidnapped Older and spirited him away to Santa Barbara, but the kidnapper lost his nerve and refused to carry out his commission to kill him. Heney was eventually replaced by a young California lawyer, Hiram Johnson, who later went on to become Governor of the state and a leading progressive in the United States Senate.

In the end the prosecutors obtained only four convictions. Three of these were reversed, and only Ruef ended up going to jail. On March 7, 1911 he entered San Quentin to begin his sentence of fourteen years.

Agitation for his release began almost immediately. Many people felt that with corruption so pervasive in San Francisco, it was unfair to single out Ruef. Foremost among the doubters was Fremont Older, who had been so instrumental in getting Ruef convicted. Older apparently had come to believe that Ruef had been victimized by a corrupt political environment for which all the citizens of San Francisco were to blame. He also felt that by reneging on the promise to grant Ruef partial immunity, the prosecution had used tactics as despicable as those of the defense. A few months after Ruef entered San Quentin, Older visited him, asked his forgiveness, and promised to work for his parole.

As part of his release strategy, Ruef agreed to write his memoirs, which Older would publish in the *Bulletin*. In May 1912, the paper ran the first installment of Ruef's "The Road I Traveled: An Autobiographic Account of My Career from University to Prison, with an Intimate Recital of the Corrupt Alliance between Big Business and Politics in San Francisco." In September, when the account reached the period of the trial, the memoirs stopped. Older had decided that if Ruef's side were published it would raise too many hackles and weaken the public sympathy that had been aroused by the early parts. Instead, Ruef began a new series entitled "Civic Conditions and Suggested Remedies," in which the corrupt boss proposed a series of civic reforms.

Ruef spent three more years in prison. While there Older served as custodian of his estate, and appeared at San Quentin to take him home the day he was released. Ruef left San Quentin in the fall of 1915 and spent the rest of his life in San Francisco, devoting all his time to the real estate business. Although he never reentered politics, his name would appear in the press from time to time in connection with various business schemes, like his project to remove the alcohol from wine without destroying its taste, or his more successful venture, a restaurant at Fisherman's Wharf. At one point he was charged with renting one of his hotel properties to a prostitution ring, but he proved that he had evicted these tenants as soon as he discovered their business.

By the 1920s Ruef had restored most of his fortune. In the Depression, however, he suffered severe business reverses. When he died of a heart attack on February 29, 1936, he was bankrupt.

New Ideas in Housing and Architecture. The most intractable urban problem—the lack of adequate housing for the working class—became the concern of philanthropists during the 1870s. Alfred T. White, a successful Brooklyn businessman and engineer, became convinced that landlords' profits and decent housing for the poor were compatible. Pursuing "philanthropy and 5 percent," he completed his Home Buildings near the Brooklyn waterfront in 1877. These attractive structures accommodated forty families in apartments two rooms deep, ensuring good light and ventilation; they included a bathroom for each family. Although his projects attracted the attention of civic-minded men and women all over the country, White's experiment did not revolutionize building practices. Developers continued to throw up jerry-built structures that crammed human beings into dank, dark apartments with few amenities.

Clearly better design was not enough; but until the 1890s philanthropists had no other approach. Then, as part of the emerging "progressive" mood, reformers began to mobilize the power of government to protect the urban citizen against the unrestrained profit motive. In New York, the community with the worst housing problem, reformers secured a series of state tenement laws culminating in the measure of 1901, which outlawed the dumbbell structure and established more stringent minimum housing guidelines. Chicago, too, revised its housing code in 1898 and 1902 to impose higher standards on builders. Still, housing for the poor continued to be overcrowded and squalid.

Architects, philanthropists, and reformers soon began to focus their attention on improving other city facilities. Before the 1890s American cities had few open spaces. Office buildings, city halls, and courthouses were often ugly structures scattered about the downtown areas without plan or order. Above the city streets unsightly tangles of telegraph and telephone wires crisscrossed the sky. Many city streets were blighted by elevated trains that clattered overhead and plunged the surface below into gloom.

A few cities had escaped the blight. Following the Civil War, Washington was transformed from a village of shanties into a spacious, tree-lined city appropriate for a national capital. New York had reserved land for the great Central Park in the heart of Manhattan, designed by the landscape architects Frederick Law Olmsted and Calvert Vaux. Kansas City constructed a $10 million system of parks and boulevards. Most cities, however, had not shown such foresight and had sold their open land to developers, who covered it with solid blocks of apartment houses or office buildings.

Toward the end of the century new attitudes began to gain public acceptance. The change was ushered in by the White City, erected in Chicago to house the great Columbian Exposition of 1893. Inspired by its gleaming neoclassical structures, architects and urban planners launched the City

In general, the "White City" at the 1893 Chicago World's Fair mimicked ancient Rome. This view of the "Grand Court" makes it look like Venice.

Beautiful Movement to bring aesthetic order and distinction to American cities. During the next generation scores of American cities built elaborate civic centers composed of neoclassical buildings to house city agencies. These structures, usually grouped around a large landscaped plaza, provided spacious open areas for urban dwellers in Cleveland, San Francisco, St. Louis, San Diego, and other cities.

This period also saw the birth of the skyscraper as a characteristic American architectural expression. The offspring of engineering and economics, the skyscraper conserved downtown land by combining the new technology of steel, which permitted tall structures without space-wasting thick walls, and the electric elevator. Although it started as an engineering innovation, it soon became a distinctive architectural style, worthy of aesthetic consideration.

City Transit.   Transportation also improved as the century approached its end. In the 1870s New York had built its first "el" (short for elevated railway), a steam railroad raised on columns above the city streets. Chicago and other cities had quickly followed suit. The el was fast, but it was also dirty and unsightly. Pedestrians on the street below were subjected to a steady rain of soot and ash, while the el structure created a ribbon of blight along every avenue it traversed.

Help came during the 1870s. The cable car, first adopted in San Francisco in 1872 to meet the special needs of that hilly city, was an early attempt to provide a clean transport system for city-dwellers. Traction for the cable car was supplied by great revolving reels that pulled long cables running beneath the street. Each car was attached to the moving cable by a grip that reached down through a slot between the rails. Then, in the late 1880s, Frank

Sprague, a naval engineer and former colleague of Edison's, built the first electric streetcar system in Richmond, Virginia. The Sprague streetcar drew its power from an overhead "trolley" held against a power wire by a spring arrangement. Fast, smooth, and nonpolluting, the electric trolley car was an immediate success. By 1895, some 850 lines were operating, carrying passengers from home to office, stores, factory, and amusement parks. Many longer interurban lines connected towns and cities in a dense network that blanketed the populous East and parts of the metropolitan West. Especially admired was the system of "red cars" that stretched like spokes from the central hub of Los Angeles to the surrounding satellite communities of southern California.

The final improvement was the subway, which combined electric traction with an underground right-of-way unobstructed by pedestrians or other traffic. Boston became the first city to acquire an underground transit system when it dug a mile-and-a-half tunnel for its trolleys under its downtown streets in 1897. New York opened the first true underground railroad in 1904 when it completed the first fifteen-mile stretch of what would eventually become the most extensive subway system in the world. Philadelphia and Chicago, too, acquired subways before World War I.

Schools for Newcomers.   As the country approached the new century, cities also began to cope better with the mass of newcomers who poured in from every part of the world. The major agency for Americanizing the new arrivals was the city school system.

When we look back at urban schools of the Gilded Age, we are struck by their strict discipline, narrow view of subject matter, and limited physical facilities. Nonetheless,

*As time passed, conditions in the cities began to improve. Streetcars, for instance, in-
creased job possibilities for poorer citizens by making transportation to areas far from
their homes faster and easier. These vehicles needed tracks in the street so horses could
pull them more easily.*

they were successful in teaching the basic skills that society needed. Unlike today, the schools in large cities often
performed better than those in rural or suburban areas.

Americanizing the immigrants and their children was
a difficult and impressive accomplishment of the schools.
A cultural gap often existed between the children in city
classrooms and their teachers. At times the teachers literally did not speak the pupils' language, and textbooks made
no concessions to the pupils' backgrounds. Yet many immigrant children overcame this gap. Mary Antin, a young
Russian-Jewish immigrant, writing in 1912, told how the
Boston schools had made her into a "good American." Mary
sat "rigid with attention" as her teacher read the story of the
Revolutionary War. As she learned "how the patriots
planned the Revolution, and the women gave their sons to
die in battle, and the battle led to victory, and the rejoicing
people set up the Republic," it dawned on her "what was

meant by *my country*." She, too, was an American citizen,
and the insight changed her life. Mary went on to become
a successful writer.

Not every immigrant child was so successfully
Americanized. Many, finding the schools alien and uncongenial, resisted their influence. Some dissenters believed the
schools were taking away the children's sense of their own
heritage and leaving them stranded between two cultures.
Horace Kallen, a prominent teacher and social philosopher,
conceived an alternative approach to the problem of
American social and cultural diversity. His "cultural pluralism" celebrated a "democracy of nationalities, co-operating
voluntarily and autonomously in the enterprise of [American]
self-realization through the perfection of men according to
their kind." He hoped men and women of diverse backgrounds could retain their heritages while sharing important
common values and attitudes. Few schools in these years

New York at about the turn of the century. Note the three simultaneous means of transportation: horse-drawn carriage, cable car, and el.

heeded Kallen's advice, yet they managed on the whole to ease the transition from immigrant to American.

Reform with a Heart. The schools' contribution toward easing the cities' social problems was supplemented by other agencies. The most comprehensive effort took the form of a new kind of humane political reform. During the 1870s and 1880s, as we have seen, urban reformers had emphasized economy and efficiency over social justice and had often offended the urban poor. If any group of city politicians was concerned with the well-being of the city masses, it was the bosses who ran the machines. This division—shady politicians with a heart and honest reformers with a balance sheet—did not entirely cease with the advent of the new century. During the Progressive Era that began in the mid-1890s, one group of reformers continued to be more concerned with economy and efficiency than with social justice, as we shall see in Chapter 23.

But there was another thread to the urban reform movement that developed in the 1890s. As public-spirited citizens became aware of the failings of the Gilded Age city and of previous reform philosophies, they began to acquire a more sophisticated understanding of what had to be done. The result was compassionate urban reform and movements for social justice in cities like Detroit, Cleveland, Toledo, and Milwaukee.

In Detroit, Mayor Hazen Pingree was the agent of the new reform. Pingree was a rich but self-made manufacturer of shoes. Although of Protestant Yankee background himself, he rode into office as the reform mayor of multilingual and predominantly Catholic Detroit in 1890 following the indictment of several Democratic aldermen for taking bribes.

At first Pingree differed from the traditional reformers more in style than in substance. Although he emphasized reducing "the extravagant rate of taxation," he was not a rigid puritan. He avoided the usual goo-goo attacks on the voters' cultural preferences. In the style of the old ward leaders, he launched his first campaign by a round of drinks with the boys at Baltimore Red's Saloon.

Pingree learned, however, that his constituents required more than social tolerance. They also demanded that he acknowledge their economic needs. Pingree soon became their champion against "the interests." He attacked the street railway monopoly for its high fares and die-hard labor policies. During an 1891 street-railway strike, the mayor sided with the strikers against the company. Following the panic of 1893, he initiated a much-publicized "potato-patch" plan by which the city turned over vacant lots to needy families so that they could raise vegetables to help support themselves. The mayor also shifted some of the city's tax burden from Detroit's citizens to the corporations that did business with the city.

Toledo's equivalent of Pingree was the colorful Samuel ("Golden Rule") Jones. Jones began a program of city ownership of water, gas, and electric utilities; put to a popular vote such questions as extending city franchises to private companies; and inaugurated a major expansion of the system of parks, playgrounds, and municipal baths. Like Pingree, Jones refused to go along with the conventional reformers' prejudice against working-class customs, amusements, and presumed vices. He rejected demands that he close the saloons and put drunks in jail. When local ministers asked him to drive prostitutes out of the city, he asked them pointedly: "To where?"

For reform groups in Milwaukee, too, efficiency was less important than the general welfare. Until the mid-1890s the city's reformers had been of the traditional goo-goo type. But during the hard times following 1893, when the utility companies tried to raise their rates while refusing to pay local taxes, reformers' attitudes changed. Outraged by the arrogance of the state's utility tycoons, they sought allies among the working class in a concerted attack on privilege. A decade and a half later the Socialists took control of the city from the middle-class reformers when Emil Seidel became mayor and instituted a regime that combined good government and social justice. During the years of Socialist control the city enacted a minimum wage for all city employees and established a permanent committee on unemployment. In addition, Seidel expanded the public concert program, established commissions on tuberculosis and child welfare, and encouraged the use of the public schools for after-hours social, civic, and neighborhood clubs.

★ CONCLUSIONS ★

During the half century following the Civil War, American cities exerted a powerful pull on the peoples of the world. Glamour, culture, excitement, and, above all, jobs drew millions of rural men and women, foreigners and natives, to the cities of the country. For a while the deluge overwhelmed many urban centers. City services and facilities were poor, making life for the newcomers uncomfortable and unhealthy. City government, designed for a simpler era, was inadequate, opening the way for political machines. Newcomers found city life unsettling and damaging to individual personality and to family structure. Poverty and crime were the consequences of this unsettled life, and there were few social services to help.

American cities never became paradises. But by the early years of the twentieth century, they were better places to live than they had been a half-century before. Billions of dollars were spent for sewers, streets, aqueducts, and other municipal services, improving the health and comfort of citizens. Electric streetcars and subways brought fast, clean, and relatively comfortable transportation. Best of all, new leadership by people with a strong sense of responsibility toward the voters made government more efficient without sacrificing the values and interests of the great mass of working-class citizens. Many problems remained; in later years much that was gained would be lost. But for a while, around the year 1910, the American city had become an interesting, a relatively livable, place. In 1905 the reformer Frederic C. Howe could call the American city "the hope of democracy."

★★★★★★★★ FOR FURTHER READING ★★★★★★★★

Maury Klein and Harvey A. Kantor. *Prisoners of Progress* (1976)
The authors briskly describe American industrialization and the growth of cities between 1850 and 1920. They depict the clash of cultures in the city and describe the lives of the rich, the poor, and the in-between. They also deal with city planning and urban reform movements of the day. Well illustrated.

Sam B. Warner. *Streetcar Suburbs: The Process of Growth in Boston, 1870–1900* (1962)
Originally separate towns, Roxbury, West Roxbury, and Dorchester were bound to Boston by the streetcar after the Civil War. Public transportation thereafter molded their physical and social structure. Warner describes the developing economic and social segregation of city and suburbs as the middle and upper classes left Boston, spurred on by the "rural ideal."

Thomas Kessner. *The Golden Door: Italian and Jewish Immigrant Mobility in New York City, 1880–1915* (1977)
A case study of urban social mobility for two important New Immigrant groups. In lucid prose that makes this careful statistical study easy reading, Kessner demonstrates extraordinary material progress for Gilded Age immigrants in the nation's largest metropolis.

Philip Taylor. *The Distant Magnet: European Immigration to the U.S.A.* (1971)
This volume by an English scholar deals with European immigration to the United States for the whole period from 1830 to 1930. It is especially good on the European "pushes" of immigration.

Stanford Lyman. *Chinese Americans* (1974)
A brief treatment of the Chinese-American experience by a sociologist. Tells of the constant tension in Chinese-

Americans between desires for community and ethnic integrity on the one hand and for acceptance in the wider world of Caucasian America on the other.

Matt S. Meier and Feliciano Rivera. *The Chicanos: A History of Mexican Americans* (1972)

A brief survey of the whole sweep of Mexican-American history. Described by one reviewer as "coherent and readable."

John Higham. *Strangers in the Land: Patterns of American Nativism, 1860–1925* (1955)

An interesting account of anti-immigrant attitudes and movements from the Civil War to the end of unrestricted European immigration in the mid-1920s. Higham demonstrates how the European immigrant often became a scapegoat when Americans suffered a loss of confidence as a result of depression, war, or some other crisis.

Abraham Cahan. *The Rise of David Levinsky* (1917)

One of the best of the immigrant novels. Written by a Jewish immigrant journalist and editor who came to New York's Lower East Side, it vividly describes sweatshops, problems between the established German Jews and the newer arrivals from eastern Europe, and conflicts between generations in immigrant families. For David Levinsky the materialism of American life and its moral and ethical confusion are mixed with opportunity, intellectual stimulation, and financial success.

Seymour Mandelbaum. *Boss Tweed's New York* (1965)

Tweed was not a good man, but he *was* a useful one—as Professor Mandelbaum shows in this study of Thomas Nast's favorite villain. Using his "communications" model of urban bossism in the late nineteenth century, the author shows how Tweed brought together various important groups in New York to get things done.

Zane Miller. *Boss Cox's Cincinnati* (1968)

Cox, too, was useful, but more enlightened and honest than Tweed. In this description of Cox's achievements Miller makes Cincinnati's boss into a rather admirable character.

Humbert Nelli. *The Italians in Chicago, 1880–1930* (1970)

A model study of an urban ethnic group of the New Immigration following 1880. Nelli disposes of many stereotypes, especially the one of ethnic solidarity. His south Italians find that they are Italian only after they have lived for several years in Chicago.

Melvin Holli. *Reform in Detroit: Hazen Pingree and Urban Politics* (1969)

Pingree was the "potato-patch mayor" of Detroit who fought the transit magnates and brought reform with a heart to his city. A well-written and interesting study of late Gilded Age urban reform.

Theodore Dreiser. *Sister Carrie* (1900)

Sister Carrie recounts the experiences of a young rural woman who comes to Chicago to make her fortune. She succeeds—by choosing, and using, the right lovers. An early exponent of naturalism in fiction, Dreiser was concerned mostly with the battle between primitive drives and moral principles within each of us. Along the way he tells us much about the urban jungle of the Gilded Age. The novel was banned for indecency when it first appeared.

Gunther Barth. *City People: The Rise of Modern City Culture in Nineteenth-Century America* (1980).

A fine treatment of the culture of Gilded Age American cities.

19 ★

THE TRANS-MISSOURI WEST

Another Colony?

1849	Bureau of Indian Affairs formed
1851	Federal government begins negotiating treaties for small Indian reservations in place of "the Indian Frontier"
1862	The Homestead Act • The Morrill Land Grant College Act
1864	The Chivington Massacre at Sand Creek • Lincoln reelected
1865	Sioux War on the Plains • Lincoln assassinated; Andrew Johnson becomes president
1866	"Long drive" of cattle, from Texas to railroad sites to expand market to East begins
1867	Federal peace Commission creates reform policies to assimilate Indians to white civilization • Patrons of Husbandry founded
1868	Ulysses S. Grant elected president
1873	The Timber Culture Act
1876	Custer's Last Stand at Little Big Horn
1877	Rutherford B. Hayes becomes president • The Desert Land Act
1880	James A. Garfield elected president
1881	Garfield assassinated; Chester A. Arthur becomes president
1884	Grover Cleveland elected president
1887	The Dawes Severalty Act designed to make Indians individual landowners • Severe winter destroys cattle boom on the Great Plains
1888	Benjamin Harrison elected president
1890	Massacre at Wounded Knee Creek
1892	Cleveland elected president for the second time
1893	Financial panic begins depression
1896	Presidential election between "goldbugs" and "silverites"; McKinley elected president over Bryan
1901	McKinley assassinated; Theodore Roosevelt becomes president
1902	The National Reclamation (Newlands) Act is passed to develop irrigation
1904	Roosevelt elected president
1905	The California Fruit Growers' Exchange introduces Sunkist products

America has had many "Wests." During most of the colonial period, the West was the forested region beyond the settled Atlantic coastal plain. On the eve of the American Revolution, the West was the great valley across the Appalachian Mountains. For the generation preceding the Civil War, it was the land between the Mississippi and the Missouri. The "last West" of 1865 to 1910 was the vast expanse of territory stretching from the Missouri River to the Pacific Ocean.

In the last West, as on America's previous frontiers, people with a basically European culture came into contact with an unfamiliar human and natural environment. As they adapted to western realities, the settlers often came to resent the power the East held over the country and their lives. Easterners, they felt, did not understand the country's newest region or its problems; they were only interested in milking the frontier and its people. Between the Civil War and the turn of the century, many western Americans came to view themselves as inhabitants of a colony, exploited by people who lived thousands of miles away.

To a certain extent, the last West *was* treated as a colony of the East. Western mining companies held their board meetings in New York or Chicago, not in Denver, Butte, or Boise. The great cattle ranches of the Great Plains and Great Basin were often owned by Bostonians, New Yorkers, or even French and English investors. Indian policies and land policies were not made in "the territories"; they were made in Washington by people who did not seem to understand either Indians or western needs or wishes. When a cartoonist in the 1890s pictured America straddled by a huge cow grazing on the Great Plains and being milked in New York, westerners knew what he meant.

The men and women who settled the trans-Missouri West would eventually feel almost as alienated from Washington, D.C., Boston, and Chicago as had the white colonists of Massachusetts and Virginia from the England of George III. Howard Lamar, historian of the West, notes that by 1889 "every territory in the West was calling its federal officials colonial tyrants and comparing its plight to that of the thirteen colonies." Eventually, in alliance with the South, they would rise up in a major political revolt against the urban East. Unlike the American Revolution 120 years before, however, the uprising would fail and discontent would subside. Yet for a while the nation would be startled by the sectional resentment and tension it revealed.

How did this antagonistic East-West relationship develop? What was the basis for western discontent following the Civil War?

★ SETTLEMENT OF THE LAST WEST ★

The Land.   The last West was a vast and diverse area of some 1.2 million square miles, approximately two-fifths of the entire nation. Its eastern third, the Great Plains, is a level plateau gradually rising toward the west like a table tilted up at one end. In its eastern portion—through the central Dakotas, Kansas, Nebraska, Oklahoma, and Texas—rainfall in normal years is twenty inches or more, sufficient for grain crops. West of this band a few elevated spots such as the Black Hills of South Dakota catch the moisture-laden winds coming from the west. Elsewhere the rainfall is usually too scanty for ordinary farming. Before the land was settled, except for stream borders and a few favored spots where trees grew, the ground was covered with grass—long grass in the more humid eastern parts, short "buffalo" grass in the drier western half. Without trees or hills, the area lacked shelter from constant winds that often brought fierce blizzards in winter and turn grass and grain to dry straw in a few days during the blazing hot summers.

As settlers moved west across the Great Plains, 600 miles beyond the Missouri River, they suddenly encountered a great escarpment rising like a wall—the lofty, forested Rocky Mountains. The Rockies form the eastern rim of several shallow but extensive basins. The largest is the Great Basin, which consists of most of present-day Nevada, western Utah, northern Arizona, and the extreme southeast of California. This region is almost a true desert. Besides the Colorado, there are few rivers with outlets to the oceans. Before dams and irrigation, water flowed only briefly, after occasional cloudbursts. Rivers generally petered out into "sinks" or ended in shallow lakes that evaporated during the dry season, leaving behind white alkaline "flats."

The narrow band of the Cascade and Sierra Nevada mountains form the western rim of the harsh basin region. Their eastern slopes are arid, but the western slopes catch the moisture-laden Pacific winds and are heavily forested. Between the Cascade-Sierra range and the coastal hills of Oregon, Washington, and California are several broad valleys: to the north, the valleys of Puget Sound and the Willamette River; to the south, in California, the great Central Valley.

Beyond the coast ranges, a narrow coastal plain, scarcely more than a thin ribbon of beach in many places, borders the Pacific. From San Francisco Bay northward, the climate of the Pacific Coast region resembles that of northwestern Europe, with rainy, relatively warm winters and cool, drier summers. South of San Francisco, the climate is Mediterranean: warm all year with little cloud cover and only sparse winter rains.

The Exploitation Ethic.   In the years immediately following Appomattox most Americans saw the West as a treasure-trove waiting for human exploitation. A handful of clear-sighted bureaucrats sought to preserve scenic portions of the West from "improvement" and in 1872 they succeeded in getting Congress to set aside 2 million acres of northwestern Wyoming as Yellowstone National Park, the first of the nation's national parks. But such men were a distinct minority. And even they were far from perceiving the virtue of wilderness as such. During the discussion of the Yellowstone bill, Ferdinand Hayden, sometimes called father of the national park system, emphasized the value of the region primarily as the site of natural curiosities—"decorations"—such as geysers, rather than as a specimen of raw nature. One major supporter of the proposed park was the banking firm of Jay Cooke, financiers of the Northern Pacific Railroad, which ran to the region. Cooke and his colleagues saw the park as a magnet for passengers on their railroad. And even after passage of the bill many Americans considered its value dubious. In 1883 Senator John J. Ingalls

of Kansas declared "the best thing the Government could do with the Yellowstone National Park" was "to survey it and sell it as other public lands are sold."

Still, by the 1880s a wilderness sensibility had begun to infiltrate the minds of well-educated men and women. In 1886 promoters of the Cinnabar and Clark's Fork Railroad Company, in aid of mining interests, sought to get Congress to allow tracks to be built across Yellowstone Park land. During the debate Congressman Lewis Payson declaimed that he could "not understand the sentiment which favors the retention of a few buffaloes to the development of mining interests amounting to millions of dollars." But a majority of his colleagues felt otherwise. Representative William McAdoo of New Jersey noted that the park had been created so that people might find "in the great West the inspiring sights and mysteries of nature that elevate mankind and bring it closer communion with omniscience." The railroad's request for a right-of-way was rejected by a vote in the House of 107 to 65.

Yet until early in the twentieth century such views continued to be rare; the wilderness preservation perspective remained that of a small group of unusually sensitive men and women. For most, the West was a great cornucopia of timber, gold, grass, oil, and copper to be skimmed off its surface or extracted from its bowels.

Railroads were not only transportation companies; they were also land-selling companies, as these brochures advertising cheap land in the Plains attest.

Settlement Patterns. The settlers of the last West and their patterns of settlement were as varied as the land they had to adapt to. The earliest part of the last West to be settled was the Pacific Coast. The fertile soils of the Willamette Valley of Oregon attracted midwestern farmers in the 1840s, and in the 1850s gold brought thousands to California by ship around Cape Horn or overland by wagon train. By 1860 two Pacific Coast states had entered the Union: Oregon with 52,000 people and California with 380,000.

The Great Basin and Rocky Mountain regions were settled as much from the West as from the East. During the 1850s the easy pickings in the Sierra gold streams of California had ended. Gold remained, but it was either buried under many layers of silt or embedded in quartz rock. Ordinary prospectors did not have the capital or expert knowledge to extract the metal from these deposits and were forced to leave gold mining to corporations. During the later 1850s and through the next decades, displaced California miners and prospectors spread through the Great Basin and Rocky Mountain regions from Mexico to Canada, their bedrolls, shovels, pans, supplies, and rifles piled on a burro or mule. News, or even rumors, of a strike brought prospectors rushing from all directions to stake claims along reported gold streams. There they would join crowds of men, and a few women, from the East who were new to the game. Many of the gold-seekers were black; many more, especially among the Californians, were Mexican or of mixed Indian-white parentage; and there were many Celestials, as the Chinese were called. No one racial group had a monopoly of either the sweat or the luck of the mining frontier. As in California, only a few struck it rich. Most of the others drifted off in quest of new bonanzas.

The settlement pattern in the Great Plains was more conventional. Most settlers on the Plains came from the agricultural Mississippi Valley immediately to the east. These people were farmers and farmers' children seeking lands cheaper than those available in the Midwest. During the 1880s Iowa, Missouri, and the five states of the Old Northwest lost a million of their sons and daughters to the Great Plains region.

Joining these ex-midwesterners were immigrants from Ireland, Canada, Germany, and Scandinavia, as well as former black slaves fleeing southern sharecropping. Travelers in the eastern part of Dakota Territory reported that Norwegian was spoken more often than English. And despite the initial hostility of white Kansans, black farmers eventually acquired some 20,000 acres of rich Kansas farmland.

Plains settlers usually came as individuals or members of family units, but part of the migration was sponsored or even subsidized by outside agencies. In the Great Basin, for example, Mormon missionaries were responsible for drawing thousands from the East and from Europe to Utah and the so-called Mormon Corridor, stretching from Idaho to Arizona. The transcontinental railroads attracted easterners and Europeans to their lands on the Plains by colorful brochures advertising $4-an-acre land, free seed, and free agricultural advice. In later years farmers would denounce the railroads for their greed and their exploitive practices. But the railroad companies were initially a big help to those who came west to farm the lands that Congress had granted them, and were an important factor in the settlement of the last West.

★ INDIANS OF THE LAST WEST ★

To the Indian tribes of the trans-Missouri West, the whites were unwelcome intruders. The Great Plains alone were inhabited by over 125,000 Indians in mid-century. About 75,000 of these were former woodland people—including the Blackfoot, Assiniboine, Sioux, Cheyenne, Arapaho, Crow, Shoshone, Pawnee, Kiowa, and Comanche—who had moved into the Great Plains from the East several hundred years before and adopted nomadic ways. These tribes shared the region with an almost equal number of Indians of the so-called Five Civilized Tribes (Cherokee, Choctaw, Chickasaw, Creek, and Seminole), who had been transplanted by government order before the Civil War from their traditional lands in the Southeast. In the Oregon region there were some 25,000 Nez Percé, Spokane, Yakima, Cayuse, Chinook, Nisqually, and other peoples. Texas contained 25,000 Lipan, Apache, and Comanche Indians; while in California and New Mexico Territory there were 150,000 Native Americans, distributed among the Ute, Pueblo, Navajo, Apache, Paiute, Yuma, Mojave, Modoc, and a flock of smaller coastal tribes, collectively called "Mission Indians," who had been gathered by the Spanish friars into settlements centering around mission churches during the preceding century.

The Western Cultures. These Indians, like those farther east, were diverse in their cultures, economies, religion, and political arrangements. The Navajo and Apache of the Far Southwest were mostly nomadic hunters, though they practiced some agriculture as well. They acquired much of their food by stealing the sheep, goats, and horses of their neighbors, Indian and white. Along the Rio Grande and its tributaries were the Hopi, Zuñi, and other "Pueblo" peoples, who practiced irrigation agriculture and lived in villages of adobe and stone structures that resembled modern apartment houses. The Hopi and Zuñi had warded off the Spaniards and the Mexicans during the eighteenth and early

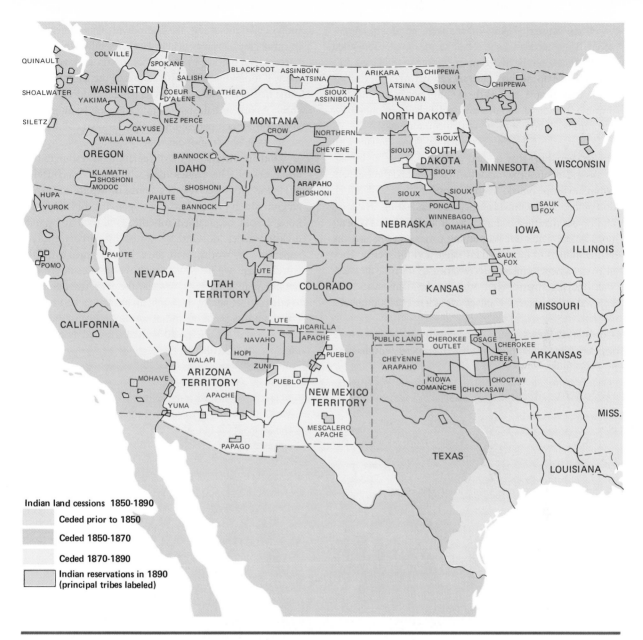

INDIAN RELATIONS BEYOND THE MISSISSIPPI, 1850–1890

nineteenth centuries and, by adopting evasive policies of passive resistance, would manage to fend off American influences, too. As a consequence, unlike many other tribes, they were able to avoid the social and cultural breakdown that whites generally brought.

The Indians of the Northwest—the Oregon-Washington region—included the coastal fishing peoples, who consumed salmon, traveled the sea in hollowed-out canoes, lived in timber lodges, wore clothing made of bark, and engaged in elaborate social ceremonies (potlatches) that involved competitive destruction of physical wealth to estab-

lish social status. To their east were tribes like the Nez Percé, whose material culture was transitional between that of the Plains and that of the coastal peoples. The Nez Percé lived in brush lodges, wore skin garments, and both fished for salmon and hunted elk, deer, and mountain sheep for food.

The Plains Indians were the classic "Indians" of American frontier legend: tall, bronzed, with straight black hair, high cheekbones, and prominent curved noses. At the eastern fringes of the Plains some tribes practiced agriculture. Farther west, where the rainfall diminishes, they were nomadic hunters.

These western Plains Indians were formidable opponents. They traveled light. Their homes were skin-sided teepees that could be folded up in minutes and loaded on a pony to be set up quickly again miles away. Unlike the Indians of the East, people such as these could not be subdued by burning their crops and destroying their villages; they grew no crops, and did not live in settled communities.

The vast buffalo herds provided the Plains Indians with almost everything they needed to survive. They ate buffalo steaks and tongues; they made their clothing and their teepees of buffalo hides; buffalo "chips" (droppings) were their fuel; and buffalo sinews provided their cord and string. The guns and horses that they had acquired from Europeans generations before made buffalo hunting easier and enabled the Plains Indians to increase their range and prosperity. They also made them formidable adversaries. By the time the westward-moving Americans encountered the Plains tribes, they enjoyed little military advantage over them except numbers.

Conflicting Views. Indian and non-Indian societies were separated by a wide cultural gulf. White society emphasized individual rights and goals. The individual took precedence over the group. By contrast, Indians generally subordinated personal ambitions to the tribe's needs and goals, and merged individual identity into that of the tribe. The tribe came first even when it involved parent–children relationships. As one Indian shaman told a French Jesuit missionary: "You French people love only your own children; but we love the children of our tribe."

Indian attitudes toward the land and resources were also different. The white settlers who came west conceived of land as an object. It was a source of wealth, a means to an end. Much like a plow or a wagon, it could be owned, bought, sold, bequeathed, inherited, and used up by an individual owner. Most Indians saw land as part of the sacred, superhuman, world. Men must live in peace with that world, must live in balance with nature. Resources must not be squandered. Land was also the collective possession of either tribe, family, or clan. If an individual had any special claim to a piece of land, it was only because he or she used it. Land left idle could be redistributed among other members of the tribe.

This is what an Indian war party actually looked like. The Indians shown here are Atsinas, members of a branch of the Arapaho tribe of Plains Indians, photographed at the beginning of this century by Edward Curtis.

The nomadic ways of the western Plains tribes compounded Indian-white differences over land ownership. Nomads must wander far and wide in search of food and cannot respect artificial boundaries established by deeds and laws. Because they exploit the land *extensively* for hunting and food gathering, rather than *intensively* for farming, they need vast amounts of space. What seemed to whites an enormous surplus of land was barely enough to provide a Cheyenne or a Sioux tribe with sufficient food.

Washington, the Indians, and the Settlers. In dealing with the Indians, the federal government often showed no more understanding of Indian realities than the whites who went west. Until 1871 the Washington authorities accepted the fiction that the tribes were independent Indian "nations" that, like other sovereign states, could be dealt with through diplomatic negotiations and treaties. This view was useful to white Americans because the disparity in power between the United States and the individual tribes made it possible to impose conditions that favored whites. In exchange for some blankets, food, tools, a few rifles, or a little cash, the Indians were pressured into surrendering vast stretches of valuable land. If the government could not extract a favorable agreement from the current Indian leaders, it would find some dissident group to deal with that could be bribed or coerced. Federal authorities would then announce that the agreement reached with the malcontents represented the collective will of the tribe. Nor did the federal government respect the treaties it signed with the Indians as it did those concluded with foreign nations. When local western interests—miners, ranchers, farmers—found a treaty inconvenient, they could often induce the government to abrogate it. At times the whole treaty system seemed nothing more than a façade for exploitation. As a governor of Georgia at one point expressed it: "Treaties were expedients by which ignorant, intractable, and savage people were induced without bloodshed to yield up what civilized people had the right to possess by virtue of that command of the Creator delivered to man upon his foundation—be fruitful, multiply, and replenish the earth, and subdue it."

Until the 1850s the federal government had tried to maintain a permanent Indian frontier beyond the Mississippi where no whites could trespass. But the opening of California and Oregon to settlers soon made a shambles of the plan, and the government replaced it with the "reservation" policy. In place of a solid wall of Indian communities blocking off white settlement and passage westward, the tribes would be concentrated in compact tracts. Here, supposedly, they would be protected from white exploiters and taught the ways of agriculture and other "civilized" arts and practices.

The new policy was embodied in a collection of treaties negotiated with the tribes by the Indian Bureau, a division of the Interior Department. Under these treaties, the tribes agreed to surrender much of the land they claimed in exchange for clear title to smaller tracts and payments of cash and other gifts. The reservation policy was accompanied by serious troubles. White settlers on the scene often begrudged the Indians even the reduced plots of ground the treaties gave them, while many of the Indians fiercely resisted the government's efforts to deprive them of their traditional range.

The most important of these treaties were those concluded with the Plains tribes at Forts Laramie and Atkinson in 1851 and 1853, respectively. Under their terms, the Indians promised to dwell in peace with the whites and with one another forever and to allow the whites to build roads through their territory. The treaties also defined precisely the boundaries of each tribe's lands. These boundaries would later become the bases of the Plains reservations.

The Indians and the Civil War. The Civil War converted the last West into a battleground between Indians and whites and between Confederate and Union sympathizers. At first the war stripped the West of troops as federal garrisons were withdrawn to cope with the rebellion. Then, as volunteers filled the gap, more blue-clad soldiers than ever appeared in the Plains and Great Basin. This boded ill for the Indians. The Union volunteers were more determined fighters than the lackluster regulars they replaced. Many were from the West itself and were fierce Indian-haters. Meanwhile, despite the war, whites continued to enter the region, drawn by a series of gold strikes in the Pacific Northwest, the eastern flank of the Sierra Nevada range, and the foothills of the Rockies.

No group suffered as much from disturbed wartime conditions as the Civilized Tribes of Indian Territory (Oklahoma). Many owned slaves and sympathized with the South. A minority, however, favored the Union. Both groups sought to avoid being drawn into the white man's quarrels but failed. At one point Cherokees wearing Union blue slaughtered Cherokees wearing Confederate gray. Several regiments of Creek, Seminole, and Cherokee fought with the Confederate forces at the Battle of Pea Ridge in 1862.

Nor did the remainder of the West escape the bitter turmoil of the war period. In Minnesota seething Sioux discontent with the reservation policy boiled over into a major Indian war that cut a bloody swath through the new state. Meanwhile, in the far Southwest, General James Carleton and Kit Carson, colonel of the New Mexico territorial volunteers, clashed with the restless Navajo and forced them to settle down at Bosque Redondo reservation, a barren region where many died of exposure, disease, and malnutrition. The worst disaster of the wartime Indian "troubles" was the notorious Chivington Massacre in Colorado Territory.

This dreadful event was a by-product of territorial politics. The Colorado Cheyenne were one of many Indian tribes that resisted surrendering title to their land and withdrawing to territory designated by the whites. Their stubborn resistance to displacement enraged territorial governor John Evans and Colonel John Chivington of the Colorado volunteers. Both men nursed political ambitions and saw the Indians as impediments to the territory's progress toward statehood and national political roles for themselves.

Warfare broke out in Colorado in the spring of 1864 when Cheyenne chief Black Kettle defied a government order to remove his tribe to a small reservation in the eastern part of the territory. Instead, Black Kettle began to raid mining camps and attack mail coaches. By the fall the Indians decided that they had done enough damage and sued for peace. The whites, especially local territorial residents, were unreceptive, feeling that the Indians had not paid the full price for their raids and attacks and must be further punished. When for a time the Third Colorado, under Colonel Chivington, hesitated to resume the attack, the firebrands ridiculed it as the "Bloodless Third." Fearful of public contempt, Chivington changed course. On November 29, at dawn, the Third Volunteers swooped down on 500 sleeping Cheyenne at Sand Creek. Black Kettle tried to surrender, but the volunteers ignored the Indians' white flag. The militia shot and killed 450 Cheyenne, two-thirds of them women and children, and scalped and mutilated many. The brave victors of Sand Creek soon after paraded through the streets of Denver to the cheers of the citizens. "Colorado soldiers have again covered themselves with glory," trumpeted the *Rocky Mountain News*.

On the northern plains, too, the government tried to apply a military solution to the "Indian problem" during the war years. Here General John Pope, the man responsible for the Union debacle at the Second Battle of Bull Run, treated all the tribes as enemies, and after Sand Creek, many of them were. In the spring of 1865, just as the Confederacy began its death throes, the Sioux, Cheyenne, and Arapaho went on the offensive, burning ranches and stagecoach stations, plundering wagon trains, tearing up telegraph wire, and stealing cattle. Pope sent massive forces with ponderous supply columns to subdue the Indians. The Indians easily eluded the soldiers, while the troops in turn suffered much from the bitter Plains weather. In the end the campaign petered out with little accomplished. Fortunately, the Indians by this time were weary of the struggle and ready to make peace.

Developing an Indian Policy. The end of the Civil War marked a watershed in the government's Indian policy. The Republicans who dominated policy-making after 1865 were, as we have seen, more strongly committed than their predecessors to racial justice. They were also strong nationalists who believed in the integration of all racial elements into the community. The Chivington Massacre, moreover, had shocked many sensitive men and women and convinced them that major reforms were needed.

These new attitudes opened a major gap between the regions on how to deal with the Native Americans. Easterners might now be convinced that a "peace policy" was the best approach to the Indian problem, but recent events only confirmed western convictions that the government in Washington was too feeble to put down the Indian menace. When Senator James R. Doolittle of Wisconsin arrived in Denver in the summer of 1865 to represent the Senate Indian Committee, he quickly learned how wide the East-West disagreement was. At a public meeting in Denver's opera house Doolittle attempted to explain the peace position that was now taking hold in the East. Should the Indians, he asked, be firmly placed on reservations and taught to support themselves or should they be exterminated? Doolittle assumed that the question answered itself. But, as he later reported, his rhetorical question was followed by "such a shout as is never heared unless upon some battle field—'Exterminate them! Exterminate them!'"

The new approach also created a rift between civilians and the military. Having seen what force could do against an implacable white enemy, the victorious Union generals saw no reason why it should not be used against a lesser foe, the Indians. The divisions in opinion widened when Red Cloud's Cheyenne, Arapaho, and Sioux warriors ambushed a detachment of U.S. troops under Captain William Fetterman in late 1866 near Fort Philip Kearny in Wyoming. Fetterman and his whole force of eighty-two men were killed.

In the end the peace advocates and the reformers prevailed. In 1867 Congress established a commission to end violence on the Plains. The commissioner's attitudes were those that would mark reformers' views for the next half-century. They wanted peace with the Indians and hoped to see them prosperous and content. But this meant that the Indians must conform to white ways. The reformers saw the reservation policy as a progressive system that would compel the Indians to surrender their nomadic life, settle down as farmers, and shift from "barbarism" to "civilization." To help the Indians assimilate white culture, the government would provide schools to teach them English, agriculture, and mechanical skills, and would bring them the blessings of the Christian faith. Until they became self-supporting, they would be supplied with food, blankets, tools, and clothing. There was another side to this apparent generosity: A thoroughgoing reservation policy would open large tracts of Indian lands to white settlers.

The commissioners met with the Kiowa, Comanche, Cheyenne, and Arapaho in 1867 and, after bribes, threats, and cajolery, induced them to accept reservations in western Oklahoma on lands confiscated by the Civilized Tribes as punishment for their support of the Confederacy. The next year the Sioux signed the Treaty of 1868 at Laramie, Wyoming. In exchange for the government's abandonment of a mining road through their lands and the usual promise of blankets, rations, and other handouts, they agreed to lay down their arms and accept a reservation in western South Dakota. Federal officials extracted similar agreements from the Shoshone, the Bannock of Wyoming and Idaho, and the Navajo and Apache of Arizona and New Mexico.

The peace policy did not work any better than previous strategies. Whites continued to covet Indian lands and encroached on the reservations. The government itself violated the agreements, often failing to come through with the promised food and blankets. The efforts to Christianize the Indians offended their religious sensibilities. To make matters worse, the Bureau of Indian Affairs soon became a hotbed of corruption. The commissioner of Indian affairs was invariably a political appointee, almost always a party hack. He and his agents often used money allotted for Indian supplies to line their own pockets. Effective administration was further undermined by the division of responsibility between civilian officials and the army. In 1871 when Congress abandoned the policy of dealing with the Indians by treaty as separate nations, it made little difference. Violent confrontation between the army and the Indians continued to be a chronic element in Indian-white relations in the last West.

The Final Indian Wars. One of the gravest blows to the Indians' survival and autonomy was the destruction of the great buffalo herds they depended on. The slaughter of the buffalo was not a deliberate effort to subdue the Indians. Many were killed to supply meat for the crews working on the transcontinental railroads that began to cross the Plains

Most of the treaties between the United States government and the Indian nations were coerced. In this stiffly posed 1867 photograph, Louis Bogy, commissioner of Indian Affairs, apparently interprets the terms of the treaty in his left hand to chiefs of the Sauk and Fox tribes, who lived in the upper Mississippi Valley. The Indians finally surrendered 157,000 acres of their fertile lands in exchange for $26,574 and about three times as much less desirable land in Oklahoma.

soon after the war ended. Others fell to "sportsmen" who came to the Plains to stalk the great beasts for the thrill of it. Eventually, random slaughter gave way to more purposeful and profitable hunting to satisfy the demand for leather and buffalo robes. During the 1870s buffalo hunting became a major Plains industry and it was soon clear to everyone that the buffalo were on their way to extinction. "From the way the carcasses are strewn over the vast plains," wrote a traveler in these years, "the American bison will soon be numbered among things of the past." He was almost right. By 1883, 13 million animals had been destroyed. When an eastern museum expedition arrived on the Plains that year to obtain specimens for its collection, it found only 200 animals still alive.

The destruction of the buffalo virtually ended the Plains Indians' nomadic ways. Without the herds the Indians became ever more dependent on the government for handouts, or else were forced to take up an alien agricultural way of life to support themselves. For a generation more the Indians resisted giving up their traditional life. Resentment against the reservation policy festered.

Meanwhile, the last years of the nineteenth century were marked by a chain of white provocations. In the mid-1870s, gold prospectors invaded the Sioux reservation in the Black Hills of South Dakota. At first the federal authorities tried to exclude the whites. When the prospectors persisted, the government attempted to buy back or lease Sioux lands containing the gold diggings. The Indians defied the authorities and were declared renegades.

The Sioux turned for leadership to Sitting Bull, a chieftain of imposing appearance and fierce determination who had long spurned the white man's gifts and promises. Sitting Bull had only contempt for the Sioux who had accepted life on the reservations. "You are fools to make yourselves slaves to a piece of fat bacon, some hardtack, and a little sugar and coffee," he taunted his weak-willed brothers. Allied with Chief Crazy Horse, he encouraged the rebels and was soon being pursued by soldiers under the command of General Alfred Terry. On June 25, 1876, a detachment of Terry's troops led by the reckless George Custer attacked the Sioux camp at the Little Bighorn River. Sitting Bull's warriors were waiting and pounced on Custer's men. By the time Terry's forces came to the rescue, Colonel Custer and all 264 of his men were dead.

Though an immense moral victory for the Indians, Custer's defeat ultimately hurt their cause. More soldiers flooded into the Plains, and the government forced the Sioux to surrender much of the Black Hills region to the whites. During the next fourteen years almost all the tribes as yet untamed were compelled to accept confinement on the reservations. But discontent continued to seethe. The final pitched battle—though not the last violence—of the 400-year Indian-white war in North America took place in December 1890 at Wounded Knee Creek on the Sioux reservation in South Dakota.

The Indians at Wounded Knee had gathered for religious purposes. The chronic resentments among the Sioux and other Plains tribes had encouraged an Indian revival movement spread by a Paiute Indian prophet named Wavoka. Wavoka preached a new religion that promised the Indians a paradise where they would be free of the whites and where they would live forever in peace and prosperity

An army inspector and his family pose with a group of Indians. The exploitation of the Plains Indians did not stop with their removal to reservations. Many died awaiting money the government promised for their support. Sitting Bull was reduced to traveling with Buffalo Bill Cody's Wild West Show.

amidst their ancestors, without sickness or suffering. This Indian Garden of Eden could be attained by practicing love, hard work, and peace with the whites, and by participating in the Ghost Dance, a ceremony of spiritual renewal emphasizing singing and dancing to the point of trance.

The Ghost-Dance religion appealed tremendously to the despairing Plains Indians, for it promised liberation from white oppression and a bright new age. The movement worried the white authorities, who, despite its professions of peace, saw it as a possible incitement to violence. Their nervousness converted a possibility into a reality. When the commander of the U.S. Seventh Cavalry tried to disarm a group of Sioux at Wounded Knee, someone fired several shots. A bitter hand-to-hand fight ensued. When the Indians broke through the army's line, the troops fired at them with hotchkiss cannons, killing at least 150, including many women and children.

The New Reformers. After 1870 Washington became increasingly convinced that the solution to the Indian problem was assimilation. During these years influential congressmen and their constituents, particularly in the East, became aroused to the plight of the Indians by the writings of Helen Hunt Jackson. Her 1881 book, *A Century of Dishonor*, recounted the doleful record of American Indian policy since independence and created a large public in favor of reform.

The active Indian reformers of the 1870–1900 period—people like former antislavery leaders Wendell Phillips and Harriet Beecher Stowe, and explorer-anthropologist John Wesley Powell—were well-meaning men and women who found the western Indians worthy objects of their compassion and social consciences. But like the peace commissioners of 1867, they had little regard for traditional Indian ways. Even Powell, who described the reservations as "pen[s] where a horde of savages are to be fed with flour and beef, to be supplied with government blankets from the Government bounty, and to be furnished with paint and gew-gaws by the greed of traders," saw no substitute for "civilizing" the Indians.

The Indian reformers were influential people who succeeded in getting their views incorporated into major new legislation. To train Indians in white ways, Congress established special Indian schools both on the reservations and off. There Indian children were separated from their language and their culture and taught to read and write English and learn trades that presumably would help them prosper on the reservations.

The reformers also succeeded in changing the land laws to suit their theories of Indian assimilation. The Dawes Severalty Act of 1887 gave the president the power to order Indian lands surveyed and divided into 160-acre plots.

In this vivid portrait of Sitting Bull we can see the determination and strength that led to the United States cavalry's greatest defeat—Custer's disaster at Little Big Horn in 1876.

These would be allotted to each head of family, with additional amounts for minor children. If the land was suitable only for grazing, the plot size could be doubled.

The law broke with Indian tradition. Each adult male Indian was to become an individual landowner; the tribe would no longer own the land collectively. Indians would, it was hoped, become independent farmers on the white American model. To help ensure that the Indians would not quickly lose their land to sharpers, it was to be held in trust tax-free for twenty-five years. Individuals who took the allotments would in time become citizens of the United States and no longer be considered members of autonomous Indian "nations." The Dawes Act did not cover the Five Civilized Tribes, but under the Curtis Act of 1898 similar policies were applied to them.

Easterners and westerners generally welcomed the Dawes and Curtis acts, but for different reasons. The humanitarian reformers, with their assimilationist views, called the Dawes Act the "Emancipation Proclamation for the Indian." Westerners rejoiced because the laws reduced tribal holdings and allowed them to acquire additional Indian lands. For the Indians, the results were almost en-

Sitting Bull

Sitting Bull was the son of Returns-Again, a chief of the Hunkpapa, a tribe of the Teton, the western division of the proud Sioux Nation. Born in 1831 in what is now South Dakota, the young boy was first called Slow. The name described his deliberate way of doing things. Even as an infant, for example, he would examine carefully a piece of food placed in his hand before putting it in his mouth.

Slow got his adult name when he was fourteen. The Sioux were a warlike people. Their clashes with their Indian neighbors were often motivated by their quest for horses. They were also a vital part of Sioux culture with much of the tribe's life taken up with war dances, preparations for war, lamenting for the dead and wounded, and distributing spoils of raids on other tribes.

To the Sioux fighting was a glorious sport. Sioux braves achieved status by striking the first blow, or *coup*, against an enemy in battle, whether the blow was a mere touch with a stick or an actual thrust with a weapon. Yet it was a bloody sport. Once the *coup* had been achieved, the Sioux fought to kill and spared neither men, women, nor children. They often mutilated their victims by removing ears, scalps, fingers, or genitals as souvenirs of their successes.

It was on a raiding expedition against the Crow in 1845 that Slow made his first *coup*, and in recognition he was given the new adult name *Ta-tan'-ka I-yo-ta'-ke*, Sitting Bull. At fourteen the Indian lad was a man.

Thereafter Sitting Bull rose in the esteem and affection of his people as a brave, vigorous, and generous man. His first contact with whites came in 1864 at Kildeer Mountains in present-day North Dakota when the western Sioux clashed with army troops on a punitive expedition following Indian attacks on settlers in Minnesota. Thirty Indians died in a series of skirmishes with the soldiers, but most escaped. Sitting Bull, present in the thick of the fight, was not impressed with the quality of the white fighting men. They did "not know how to fight," he said. "They are not lively enough. They stand still and run straight; it is easy to shoot them."

After the Sand Creek Massacre of 1864, the Sioux joined the Cheyenne for a campaign along the Platte River to avenge Chivington's savagery. During the fighting Sitting Bull proved his prowess against the whites and soon was recognized as a chief not only of his own Hunkpapa, but also of other western Sioux tribes.

For a time in the mid-1860s Sitting Bull directed the aggressive energies of the Sioux against his Indian foes, the Crows, Mandans, Flatheads, Hohe, and Rees. But he did not forget the white danger. Sitting Bull had become a leader of the "hostiles," the Indians who resisted the whites' reservation policy. The Indians, he believed, must be allowed to continue their nomadic, hunting ways, and must never agree to settle down to farm or take the white man's food, blankets, and other handouts. In these immediate postwar years, like other leaders of the northern Plains tribes, he demanded that the whites close their road across the northern Plains, burn and evacuate the forts in the region, stop the steamboats from ascending the Missouri and its tributaries, and expel all white intruders except traders.

The Sioux got much of what they wanted in the Treaty of 1868, a document that reflected the conciliatory mood of the post–Civil War peace policy. Under this agreement the government abandoned its road through the new Great Sioux Reservation, promised to destroy its forts within the Sioux lands and exclude all whites, except those who obtained tribal permission to settle or pass through. But in return the Indians agreed to abandon their nomadic life and settle down on the reservation near the Indian agencies where they were under protection and supervision of the white Indian agent.

Despite the government's concessions Sitting Bull refused to surrender the old ways. In 1869 he led his warriors on raiding expeditions against the Crows and the Flatheads in which many warriors fell. He refused to settle near the Indian agency. In 1872 and 1873 the Sioux skirmished with soldiers escorting Northern Pacific Railroad surveying parties through Sioux lands. After these incidents Sitting Bull and his friend Crazy Horse, of the Oglala Sioux, resolved to adopt a new policy toward whites: "If they come shooting, shoot back."

One of the white officers in these battles was General George Armstrong Custer, a brave, but flamboyant and foolhardy, veteran of the Civil War. In 1874 General Philip Sheridan, of Civil War cavalry fame, sent Custer with a thousand soldiers, along with miners and journalists, to explore the Black Hills region of the Sioux reservation, where, rumors had it, there were rich gold deposits. The Indians protested that this expedition violated the Treaty of 1868, but the authorities refused to yield.

The reconnaissance had tragic consequences. Custer's miners confirmed that there was gold in the Black Hills streams, though not in lavish amounts. The expedition also found fertile, well-watered land, and abundant timber in the region's valleys and mountain slopes. Custer's report, though cautious, was like a lightning bolt in a dry forest. The country was in the midst of a severe business recession with thousands of men seeking jobs and some way of earning a living. News of the Black Hills' resources set off a rush of miners and would-be settlers to the Dakota region.

The influx of whites clearly violated the Treaty of 1868, and the Indians loudly protested. The army made a half-hearted attempt to drive out the miners, but in the end allowed them to stay. In 1875, the government decided to negotiate a new treaty that would remove the Black Hills from Sioux control. The government's incentive was an extension of the period of federal aid and handouts. Under the 1868 agreement this was supposed to last for a limited time while the Indians transformed themselves into settled farmers. The process had failed; the Sioux and other buffalo hunters despised farming as unworthy of true men. Unfortunately, the buffalo on which their nomadic existence had depended were fast disappearing. They found cattle herding more congenial, but it did not provide sufficient food and money for them to become self-supporting. Taking advantage of the Indians' continued need for government largess, federal officials, at a meeting with the Sioux at the Red Cloud agency, offered to give the Indians $400,000 a year for mining rights in the Black Hills or $6 million for their outright sale. Sitting Bull, one of the chiefs present, had already rejected any surrender of Indian lands and the meeting failed to accomplish anything.

The government now decided to use force. In December 1875 the Secretary of the Interior ordered all Indians to report to the reservation agencies or face the government's displeasure. In 1876, after the hostile Sioux had failed to comply, General George Crook sent several expeditions to break their will. Prime target during

the spring foray was the camp where Sitting Bull and Crazy Horse had gathered under their command Sioux from almost every tribe as well as hundreds of other Plains Indians who hated both the white man and the reservation policy. In mid-June, Crook's men fought an inconclusive battle at the Rosebud River with Sioux and Cheyenne led by Crazy Horse.

The second punitive expedition produced the greatest military disaster in the long history of the western Indian wars. This foray was led by General Alfred Terry, with Custer second in command. When Terry reached the Tongue River he divided the Seventh Cavalry into two columns, one under Custer, and ordered it to advance on the Indian camp.

Custer did not know that he was about to poke his nose into a hornet's nest. More than 10,000 Indians, including 4,000 fighting men, were encamped near the Little Bighorn River. Custer's force numbered a scant 500 men, and he further weakened his command by placing almost two-thirds of it under other officers, Major Marcus Reno and Captain Thomas Weir.

Early on the afternoon of June 25, 1876, the 140 dismounted cavalrymen of Reno's force approached the Indian encampment. The Sioux and Cheyenne attacked, forcing Reno back. Meanwhile, Custer and his men advanced on the camp from the north. The Indians were desperate to protect their women and children and fell on the soldiers with ferocity. Much of the fighting was hand-to-hand, a whirling confusion of shouts and shots enveloped in a dust cloud stirred up by frantic men and lunging horses. This time the Indians ignored *coups* and fought to kill from the start. Reno heard the sounds and saw the smoke of battle, but he did not come to his superior's rescue. In a brief, savage hour Custer and all 264 of his men lay dead. It was the greatest victory that the

Plains Indians had ever won over the white men.

The victory at the Little Bighorn could not alter the fate of the Plains tribes. Though there was some talk of forming an Indian confederacy that would stop the encroachment of the whites, this never came about. Nor would it have made any difference. There were a thousand whites ready to replace every one of Custer's fallen men.

In the wake of "Custer's last stand" another Indian commission forced the Sioux to surrender the Black Hills and accept other onerous revisions of the 1868 Treaty. The original treaty had solemnly promised that there would be no changes unless three-fourths of the adult Indian males had agreed. This provision was simply ignored and the government pronounced the new treaty in effect when the principal chiefs had signed it.

Sitting Bull and his hostiles remained at large and were not a party to this pact. During the winter following the Little Bighorn battle the army continued its campaign to force Sitting Bull and his followers to settle down. At one point General Nelson Miles and Sitting Bull conferred face-to-face and the chief told the general that no white man had ever loved an Indian and that no true Indian had ever failed to hate the white man. Despite Sitting Bull's belligerent response, Miles succeeded in detaching several thousand Indians from the hostile group. Even Crazy Horse defected, but Sitting Bull refused and fled across the border into Canada where the Americans could not touch him.

During the next few years Sitting Bull and his followers remained encamped just north of the international boundary, making occasional raids across the border to hunt buffalo and attack white settlers. Finally, in 1881, their resolve undermined by hunger and exhaustion with incessant fighting, the chief and his remaining followers surrendered to the American authorities.

For a time they were placed under guard at Fort Randall, in South Dakota, and then moved to the Standing Rock agency on the Sioux reservation. During his last years Sitting Bull remained a thorn in the government's side. He demanded extra rations and cattle, even horses and buggies, for himself and his followers. In 1889, when the government once more revised the treaty with the Sioux, further reducing their lands, he again resisted, though this time with words rather than arrows or bullets. Soon after, he took up and encouraged among his people the new Ghost-Dance religion.

As preached by the Paiute Indian prophet Wovoka, the Ghost Dance was a peaceful faith. In Sitting Bull's version, however, the new Indian messiah, when he returned to earth in 1891, would exterminate the white man. It is not clear whether Sitting Bull believed the Ghost-Dance prophecy, or whether he was only seeking to use it to restore his authority among the Sioux, but it frightened the already nervous white authorities.

On December 15, 1890, the reservation police, a force made up of "tame" Indians, came to arrest Sitting Bull for continuing to encourage the Ghost-Dance ceremonies. As he was preparing to accompany them, the old

chief shouted "I'm not going. Come on! Take action!" At this signal, Catch-the-Bear, one of his followers, fired a shot that hit Lieutenant Bull Head in the right side. The lieutenant fired back, hitting Sitting Bull. A confused melee followed, and at the end Sitting Bull lay dead.

Scholars often date the end of the nineteenth-century Indian Wars from the Wounded Knee massacre of December 29, 1890. In fact, the wars had really ended two weeks before when the great Hunkpapa chief, Sitting Bull, the fierce defender of his people's heritage, fell before the bullets of the tame Indians wearing the white man's uniform.

---

tirely negative. Government agents often prevented them from claiming the best lands. The long-term exemption of Indian lands from local taxation led several states to refuse to provide schools and other services to Indians, and despite its promises, Congress did not come through with adequate funds to offset this loss.

As agencies of "civilization," too, the acts were failures. The tribes lost their cohesion without many Indians becoming strong, self-sustaining individuals. Caught between two cultures, Indians often turned to drink, petty crime, and idleness. Though the twenty-five-year trust period written into the original laws supposedly protected the Indians from sharpers, the laws were amended so often that many Indians lost their property to speculators for a song. Between 1887 and 1934, Indian-owned lands were reduced from 139 million to 47 million acres. Without means or livelihoods, many Indians became charges of the public authorities.

By the 1920s it had become clear that the reformist Indian policies adopted after 1870 were bankrupt. A number of white Americans, most notably the progressive social reformer John Collier, began to perceive that forced assimilation degraded the Indians' heritage and deprived them of their culture without providing a satisfactory alternative. Working through the American Indian Defense Association, Collier and his supporters demanded that the Dawes policy be replaced. The government should guarantee basic civil rights to Indians, confer limited self-government on the reservations, end paternalism, and encourage the preservation of Indian traditions and culture. When Collier became com-

missioner of Indian affairs in 1933, he promptly set about changing Indian policy. The chief legislative embodiment of his work was the Wheeler-Howard Act of 1934, which repealed the allotment policy, recognized the right of Indians to organize for "the purposes of local self-government and economic enterprise," and stated that the future goal of Indian education should be to "promote the study of Indian civilization, arts, crafts, skills, and traditions."

Passage of this Indian Reorganization Act did not solve all the Indians' problems. Indians continued to be poor; infant mortality rates on the reservations remained appalling; Indians were still treated, especially in the West, as second-class citizens; there was little that intervened to reduce the erosive effect of white culture on Indian values. But by 1934 it could be said that mainstream America was finally beginning to reverse the damaging trends of the past.

★ THE MINING FRONTIER ★

The gold seekers whose invasion of Indian lands in the mid-1870s had tripped off the Sioux uprising were representatives of the new far western mining frontier. There had been mining and mineral booms before in America—in California during the 1850s, and in the Pennsylvania oil regions a few years later. But none had been so extensive or would leave so deep an imprint on regional social development and on the collective American imagination.

Dawes Act

From the perspective of white reformers, the Dawes Severalty Act of 1887 was an ideal, long-overdue measure that would assimilate the tribal Indians into the mainstream of American life. It would, Amherst College's benevolent president Merrill E. Gates declared, make the Indian "intelligently selfish." It would get him "out of the blanket and into trousers—and trousers with a pocket in them, and with a pocket *that aches to be filled with dollars!*" The actual effects were different, but the measure stands as a monument to the failed good intentions of white reformers toward the country's native American peoples.

"An act to provide for the allotment of lands in severalty to Indians on the various reservations, and to extend the protection of the laws of the United States and the Territories over the Indians, and for various other purposes.

"Be it enacted, That in all cases where any tribe or band of Indians has been, or hereafter shall be, located upon any reservation created for their use, either by treaty stipulation or by virtue of an act of Congress or executive order setting apart the same for their use, the President of the United States be, and he hereby is, authorized, whenever in his opinion any reservation, or any part thereof of such Indians is advantageous for agriculture and grazing purposes to cause said reservation, or any part thereof, to be surveyed, or resurveyed if necessary, and to allot the lands in said reservation in severalty to any Indian located thereon in quantities as follows:

"To each head of a family, one-quarter of a section;

"To each single person over eighteen years of age, one-eighth of a section; and,

"To each orphan child under eighteen years of age, one-eighth of a section; and,

"To each other single person under eighteen years now living, or who may be born prior to the date of the order of the President directing an allotment of the lands embraced in any reservation, one-sixteenth of a section; . . .

"SEC. 5. That upon the approval of the allotments provided for in this act by the Secretary of the Interior, he shall . . . declare that the United States does and will hold the land thus allotted, for the period of twenty-five years, in trust for the sole use and benefit of the Indian to whom such allotment shall have been made, . . . and that at the expiration of said period the United States will convey the same by patent to said Indian, or his heirs, . . . discharged of such trust and free of all charge or encumbrance whatsoever. . . .

"SEC. 6. That upon the completion of said allotments and the patenting of the lands to said allottees, each and every member of the respective bands or tribes of Indians to whom allotments have been made shall have the benefit of and be subject to the laws, both civil and criminal, of the State or Territory in which they may reside; . . . And every Indian born within the territorial limits of the United States who has voluntarily taken up, within said limits, his residence separate and apart from any tribe of Indians therein, and had adopted the habits of civilized life, is hereby declared to be a citizen of the United States, and is entitled to all the rights, privileges, and immunities of such citizens, whether said Indian has been or not, by birth or otherwise, a member of any tribe of Indians within the territorial limits of the United States without in any manner impairing or otherwise affecting the right of any such Indian to tribal or other property. . . ."

Mining Communities. The spillover of prospectors from the California gold streams first reached north into British Columbia. In 1859 the search was deflected to the region around Pike's Peak in western Colorado. In a few months a new town, Denver, appeared under the shadow of the Rocky Mountains. Soon afterward two prospectors in the mountains surrounding the Carson River valley in northwestern Nevada Territory hit "pay dirt." Called the Comstock Lode after a gabby drifter who claimed to be its discoverer, the gold strike was one of the richest on record. The district immediately became the magnet for thousands of California miners, and Virginia City—a settlement of tents, lean-tos, and prefabricated frame structures—rose mushroomlike from the desert in a few weeks.

The Comstock Lode discovery was followed by strikes on the Snake River in northwestern Idaho. In 1863 gold was found at Last Chance Gulch in west-central Montana. The next major precious metal strike was that in the Black Hills of South Dakota during the 1870s. Coeur d'Alene in northern Idaho followed in the early 1880s. This was the last of the major rushes in the contiguous forty-eight states. But at the very end of the century fabulous finds would be made in the Canadian Yukon and in Alaska, marking the last episode of the mining frontier.

This picture dates from the late 1800s. Obviously, not much has changed from the 1849 gold rush in extracting the precious metal from the ground.

The mining communities that grew up around the strikes have become a vivid part of the American legend. They were places of great variety where every nation, race, and class could be found. The California diggings, reported Louisa Clappe, were "a perambulating picture gallery" where one could hear English, French, Spanish, German, Italian, and many Indian tongues spoken on the streets. They were also violent. The gamblers and hangers-on who followed the gold frontier were often unruly dissolute men and women. But violence and crime also flowed from the refusal of the federal government to provide either laws or law enforcement. The western answer was the vigilance committee, a group of local worthies who, without benefit of legal trial, hanged the worst of the trouble-makers as an example to the rest.

Slow in providing law enforcement officers for the territories, the federal government was also remiss in responding to demands for statehood in the mining regions. When Congress failed to act on Colorado's petition, settlers in 1859 organized the Territory of Jefferson with an elected

governor and legislature. Congress rejected this initiative, and not until 1876, when the community was well beyond the frontier stage, did it admit Colorado to statehood.

Big Business and Mining. The tent camps and the vigilance committees were only passing phases of the western mining boomtowns. In some cases the next stage was abandonment. In scores of communities, when the richer ores gave out, the miners, storekeepers, and camp followers departed, leaving ghost towns of rusting machinery, decaying buildings, and empty mine shafts.

Many mining communities, however, became permanent towns and cities. Denver, Lewiston, Coeur d'Alene, and Butte developed into substantial places with schools, churches, opera houses, and police forces. The mining industry also stimulated the growth of regional supply, shipping, and outfitting centers such as Seattle, Spokane, and Tucson.

The change from raw mining camp to sedate city seldom took place without a major shift in the mining busi-

Alaska gold rush, camp scene, about 1900. Note the horse mired in the deep mud.

ness that sustained the local economy. As in California in an earlier period, after the loose nuggets and flakes had been skimmed off by men panning the streams and washing earth through cradles, gold mining became a heavily capitalized industry that required deep shafts and expensive machinery. Silver extraction required complex refineries. Still more expensive to produce were the copper and lead found throughout the Great Basin and Rocky Mountains regions. These ores required deep mines, crushers, and complex chemical processes—operations that depended on heavy infusions of capital, trained mining engineers, technicians and chemists, and a permanent force of wage-earning miners and smelter workers.

The capital needed by the postpioneer mining industry was seldom available from local sources. Much of the costs of sinking shafts and erecting mills and refineries in the fabulous Comstock Lode district, for example, came from San Francisco capitalists. These men extracted millions in profit from the Comstock, and with the proceeds built great mansions on Nob Hill overlooking the beautiful city on San Francisco Bay. One Californian who made a fortune in Nevada silver was George Hearst, whose son, William Randolph, would become a powerful New York press lord at the end of the century. In the 1880s Meyer Guggenheim, a lace manufacturer of Philadelphia, began to

invest in the Leadville silver district of Colorado and soon became a major economic force in the state. In Montana the copper kings—William A. Clark, Marcus Daly, and Frederick Heinze—built Butte into a major copper-smelting center. Clark represented local capital, but Daly was allied with the Anaconda Copper Company, an eastern corporation with many English investors. Phelps Dodge, a New York firm, owned large copper mines and refineries in Arizona.

During the last years of the century, eastern capitalists battled bitterly over control of the western mining industry. Chief antagonists were Daniel Guggenheim, son of Meyer, and Henry H. Rogers, an early associate of John D. Rockefeller, whose American Smelting and Refining Company (ASARCO) sought to establish a monopoly of copper smelting by absorbing the Guggenheim interests. The Guggenheims fought back. After the dust had cleared, Daniel Guggenheim and his brothers controlled ASARCO, which they ruled from its headquarters in New York City.

Although outside control over local resources would later fan westerners' discontent, the opening of the western mines added enormously to the country's resources. By 1900 the United States was one of the world's largest producers of gold, silver, copper, lead, and zinc. Politically and financially, the production of gold and silver would be of

Creede, Colorado, a silver boom town in the Rockies, sprang up in a canyon so narrow there was only room for one main street. During the flush times of the early 1890s, Creede grew by several hundred people a day; by 1900 it was a virtual ghost town.

immense significance. The flood of gold would facilitate the adoption of the international gold standard in the last half of the century. But at the same time, the even greater proportional increase in silver production would depress its price relative to gold and profoundly disturb the nation's monetary affairs.

★ THE CATTLE KINGDOM ★

Just east of the mining regions another economic frontier was taking shape. During the two decades that followed the Civil War, cattle raising became the major activity of the Great Plains, attracting eastern and even European investors. Even more than the mining frontier, the cattle kingdom would become an American epic.

Longhorns and Long Drives. The Plains cattle industry began in the Texas grasslands, where, before the Civil War, Mexican ranchers had pastured immense herds of wild, rangy animals. When Americans entered the south Texas area, they brought new breeds of cattle with them. These

mingled with the Spanish-Mexican variety to produce the famed Texas longhorn, a wiry, resourceful creature that could survive winter on the open grasslands by digging through the snow with its hooves to the nutritious dried grass beneath.

The Civil War severed the Texas cattle industry from its major markets—eastern leather manufactures and New Orleans beef buyers. During these fallow years the cattle ran wild on the Texas grasslands, and by 1866 there were an estimated 5 million head on the state's southern prairies. Meanwhile, the rest of the country, having reduced its cattle stock to meet the Union army's needs, was starved for beef. In Texas, cattle were selling for $4 a head, while in the eastern cities they were worth as much as $40 and $50.

Returning Confederate veterans saw this imbalance and soon after Appomattox began to consider ways of getting Texas cattle to eastern consumers. By this time the Missouri Pacific Railroad had reached Sedalia, Missouri, 700 miles north of San Antonio, the heart of the Texas cattle country. If cattle could be driven on the hoof to the railroad, they could then be shipped east. In March 1866 a group of Texas ranchers and Iowa and Kansas businessmen launched the first of the classic "long drives" of range cat-

Many of the hard working "hands" in the cattle raising areas of the "Last West" were black. Only now is Hollywood and the media generally beginning to acknowledge the existence of black "cowboys."

tle north to railhead to satisfy the eastern market for beef and hides.

The Texas cattle drives became annual affairs. In a standard drive, a half-dozen mounted "cowboys" under a "trail boss" guided each band of a thousand or so unruly longhorns across open country accompanied by "chuckwagons" to carry food and equipment and a "horse wrangler" to care for the mounts. The way was often beset with difficulties. Besides mud, swollen streams, and rough terrain, there were hostile humans to contend with. The Sedalia Trail passed through Indian territory where resentful tribesmen often stampeded the herds. Even more troublesome were Missouri farmers, who feared that the invading longhorns carried the dread Texas fever and would infect their own cattle. Turning out in force, they engaged in shootouts with the Texans. Despite these obstacles, cattle that got through sold for $35 a head in Sedalia, providing a clear profit for the ranchers.

It did not take long for an enterprising businessman to see how the system could be improved. In 1867 a cattle dealer from Illinois, Joseph G. McCoy, established a depot at Abilene in central Kansas along the Kansas-Pacific Railroad, where "the country was entirely unsettled, well watered, [and with] excellent grass." There ranchers could pen their animals and arrange for their sale to buyers, who would then ship them east by rail. The route north to Abilene by way of the Chisholm Trail passed through country farther west than the Sedalia Trail and avoided irate farmers. Between 1867 and 1871 some 1.5 million head of Texas cattle were driven to Abilene for shipment east.

The day of the Chisholm Trail was brief. The railroads brought to the West farmers and settlers who opposed the Texas cattle drive. When the area around Abilene became too densely populated, the drive was deflected farther west to Ellsworth on the Kansas-Pacific line. Later the "cow towns" of Newton and Dodge City were developed along the Santa Fe Railroad.

The Kansas cow towns, like the mining camps, were rowdy places. It was hard to maintain law and order among the transient "cow poke" population. Cowboys were a diverse lot of ex-Confederate and ex-Union soldiers, former slaves, Mexicans, and Indians who rode the range twelve hours a day looking for strays. At spring roundup they worked hard roping and branding the unmarked calves. On the long drives cowboys spent as many as four months in the saddle, keeping the cattle moving and preventing stampedes. The work was dirty, hard, lonely, and unhealthy. No wonder that when he was paid several months' wages in Dodge City or Abilene at the end of the long drive, the cowboy went on a roaring spree—drinking, gambling, debauching, and sometimes shooting up the town.

Boom and Bust. Stimulated by expanding markets, the Texas cattle industry soon spread over a large part of the Lone Star State. Then, as the railroad penetrated further into the central and northern Plains, thousands of Texas cattle were driven north to stock the newly accessible region. By the early 1870s the central and northern Plains were covered with ranches.

As fully developed during the late 1870s and early 1880s, the range cattle industry of Colorado, Wyoming, Montana, Idaho, and the western Dakotas relied on free use of the public land and on weather mild enough for the cattle to graze outdoors on the open range all year. The cattle used the public domain at no cost to the ranchers, who, in effect, were subsidized by the government with free land, grass, and water. All the ranchers had to do was wait as their cattle multiplied and put on weight. In the spring they rounded up their herds and shipped the mature animals east at a good profit.

For a decade the cattle kingdom flourished, sustained by high prices and low costs. "Cotton was once crowned king," exulted a contemporary editor, "but grass is now." The free, adventurous, and individualistic life of the Plains rancher proved a powerful magnet for outsiders. Easterners, like the impetuous young New Yorker, Theodore Roosevelt,

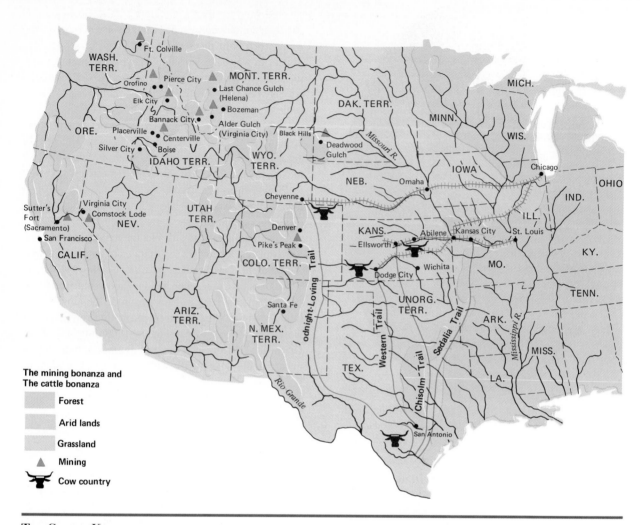

The mining bonanza and
The cattle bonanza

Forest

Arid lands

Grassland

▲ Mining

🐂 Cow country

THE CATTLE KINGDOM

bought land on the Plains and became ranchers. So did
Europeans, especially Englishmen and Scots. And many outsiders who did not come themselves sent their capital. When
a committee of the British Parliament reported 33 percent
profits in American ranching, money from Britain poured in
by the millions. In 1883 twenty cattle-raising corporations
capitalized at $12 million were formed in Wyoming alone.

By 1885 farsighted people began to suspect trouble
ahead. Each year the range grass became thinner as more
and more cattle grazed the Plains. To prevent personal disaster, ranchers began to fence off areas of range with barbed
wire—invented in 1874—though this was illegal on publicly owned land. They also formed livestock associations
to regulate the number of cattle grazed, exclude intruders,
and protect the herds against rustlers and wolves. Despite
these efforts, by the mid-1880s the Plains were overstocked.
So numerous were cattle shipments that prices began to
tumble. Some ranchers, seeing the handwriting on the wall,

sold off their herds and got out, further depressing prices.

Then nature struck. From 1875 to 1885 the weather
had been unusually mild and rainy on the northern Plains.
In 1886 it changed. That summer was hot and dry; by fall
the cattle, lacking decent forage, were weak. In November
the blizzards came. January 1887 was the worst winter
month that anyone could remember, with record snows and
temperatures dipping at times to seventy degrees below
zero. Thousands of cattle were buried alive by the drifts.
Others froze to death standing upright. Unable to get to the
grass beneath the snow, crazed animals poured into the
streets of several towns and tried to eat everything in sight.
When the terrible winter ended, hundreds of carcasses were
carried down the streams by the spring freshets, bearing
with them the fortunes of their owners.

The cattle industry survived on the Plains, but it was
never the same. Many of the cattle corporations went bankrupt, a process that drove out many distant eastern and

Union Stockyards in Chicago in 1878, as the city was becoming "hog butcher to the world."

European investors who could not supervise their investments closely. Under the control of local people the industry was transformed. Even more land than before was fenced in. Ranchers began to raise hay for winter feed and replace the wiry longhorns with Herefords and other breeds that would produce more meat per animal. Some ranchers, recognizing that sheep were hardier than cattle, turned to wool production, though others fought the sheep invasion as a threat. The life of the cowboy changed, too. Now he spent less time in the saddle and more digging post holes and stringing barbed wire. The cowboy became a "ranch hand." Meanwhile, wheat farmers began to intrude from the east, driving the cattlemen into the more isolated portions of the Plains. The ranching industry survived, but as a smaller, more localized, and more rational industry than during the heyday of the open range.

★ WESTERN LAND POLICIES ★

Cattle ranchers were not the only people to capitalize on liberal land policies. The federal government—always vital in determining who got land and how it was used—played a particularly important role in the apportionment of land in the last West, for almost all of it was public domain, acquired by war, purchase, or treaty. From 1862 to the end of the century, Congress gave away or sold vast amounts of these western lands under inconsistent policies designed to satisfy a variety of interests. In the end the small western farmers who were supposed to benefit from these policies felt betrayed, and they were convinced that outside speculators and the government's distance from western realities were responsible.

Land Acts of the 1860s. From the earliest years of the republic, Jeffersonian agrarians and other champions of the small farmer class had struggled to distribute the public domain in small parcels at low prices to actual settlers. The passage of the 1862 Homestead Act fulfilled their dream by providing that any adult head of family or person over 21 could acquire, free of cost, 160 acres of surveyed federal land if they resided on the land for five years and cultivated it.

In reality, only a fraction of the immense public domain ever got into the hands of small farmers free of charge. At the same time it was giving land to bona fide settlers, the

"Doing a land office business" has become a cliché for holding a fabulously successful sale. In this 1885 photograph of the United States Land Office in Garden City, Kansas, we can see where the phrase originated.

government was distributing large parcels for other public purposes. The 1862 Morrill Land Grant College Act conferred on each state a portion of the public domain in proportion to its congressional representation to be used for state-run agricultural colleges. Most of the land went to populous eastern and midwestern states where agriculture was subordinate to industry. The railroad land grants of the 1860s and 1870s were another instance of land excluded from homestead entry. In addition the federal government handed out land to encourage the construction of wagon roads and gave away millions of acres to states that entered the Union after 1862. Nor did it cease outright land sales. In 1862 some 84 million acres of federal lands were on the market for cash.

Spokesmen for small farmer groups complained that free homesteads were largely an illusion; much of the best land was available only by cash purchase, whether from the land grant colleges, the railroads, the states, or the federal government. And they were right. Between 1862 and 1904 only some 147 million acres of land passed to farmers under the Homestead Act; in that same period more than 610 million acres were sold for cash.

Nor was the Homestead Act itself free of abuses. By law, every homesteader was supposed to cultivate and dwell on the land before taking legal title. Actually, many who filed claims never met the requirements honestly but got legal possession through fraud. One dishonest practice was for employers to file claims for their hired hands and then, when these were "proved up," purchase the parcels for a purely nominal amount. In this way many farmers, ranchers, and timber-cutters acquired far more under the Homestead Act than the 160 acres envisioned.

Acts Tailored to Western Land Problems. The Homestead Act also took no account of the special land problems of the arid Great Plains and Great Basin. In the humid East and parts of the Midwest 160 acres were sufficient to support a farm family, for yields per acre were high where rainfall was abundant. West of the ninety-eighth meridian, however, rain was sparse and crop yields were low. The 160-acre allotment was too small for the "dry farming" cultivator on the eastern edge of the Plains; for the rancher who grazed hungry cattle in the drier portions of the region, it was impossible; each animal required 40 acres of grazing land to survive.

Following the Civil War Congress passed a series of measures to deal with the special land problems of the West. One, the Timber Culture Act of 1873, allowed farmers with 160-acre homesteads to take out papers on another 160 acres of adjacent land on the condition that they agree to plant trees on some portion of it. In theory, trees would encourage rain and so make the plains less arid. In reality, the tree-planting provision was largely ignored; the effect was to give Plains farmers about 10 million additional acres of dry land.

The Desert Land Act of 1877 was also designed to accommodate the land laws to the arid West. Most scholars, however, consider it a giveaway to the cattle companies. Under its provisions lands could be bought for a down payment of 25 cents per acre if the purchaser agreed to irrigate a full section (640 acres) within three years. After meeting the requirement the purchaser could pay an additional dollar per acre and own the whole parcel. Unfortunately the law allowed purchasers to assign the acreage to others even before they had met the irrigation requirement. Thousands of acres thus passed to the cattle companies with few public benefits.

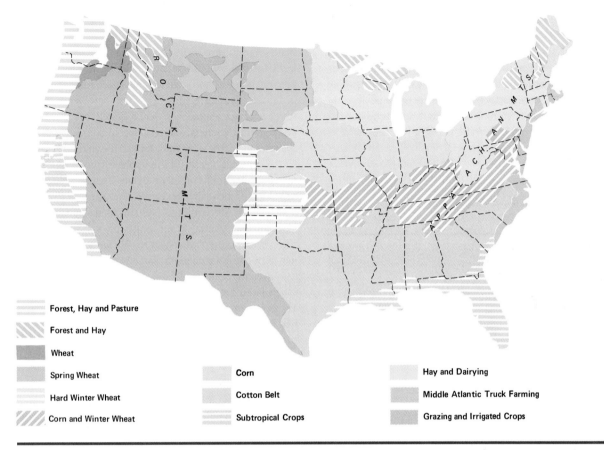

Agricultural Regions of the United States

Forest, Hay and Pasture

Forest and Hay

Wheat

Spring Wheat

Hard Winter Wheat

Corn and Winter Wheat

Corn

Cotton Belt

Subtropical Crops

Hay and Dairying

Middle Atlantic Truck Farming

Grazing and Irrigated Crops

Still another measure, the Timber and Stone Act of 1878, violated the spirit of the Homestead Act. The law applied to lands "unfit for cultivation" and "valuable chiefly for timber or stone." After declaring that the land in question contained no useful minerals, any citizen could buy up to 160 acres at $2.50 an acre. Few small farmers benefited from the law. Instead, through various forms of fraud, large tracts ended up in the hands of timber companies.

In dealing with the climatic realities of the arid West, federal policy inevitably reflected the knowledge and values of the day. Today we are skeptical of large dams and irrigation systems. They may for a time "make the deserts bloom," but their long-term effects on desert ecology are often disastrous and, in many cases, they produce only temporary benefits. After years of being soaked with alkaline river water, the irrigated soil becomes chemically poisoned and unproductive. Around the world thousands of acres of irrigated land have been abandoned as useless.

Still, we should not blame our forebears for what they could not know. In the National Reclamation, or Newlands, Act of 1902 the federal government believed it was adding to the West's, and the nation's, wealth. And, in the short run, it was.

The law provided that a reclamation fund be established from the proceeds of federal land sales in the arid states and territories, the fund to be used for building dams, water channels, and other irrigation facilities in these states. The public lands so irrigated would be reserved for small farmers in tracts of 160 acres under the same provisions as the 1862 Homestead Act. Water users were to pay water-use fees and reimburse the government for its capital outlays over a ten-year period. The reclamation fund, thus renewed, would become available for other projects in succeeding years.

Under the Newlands Act a score of dams were constructed, including Roosevelt Dam in Arizona and Idaho's Arrowrock Dam, and thousands of acres were irrigated and reclaimed from the desert. Less successful than the engineering feats were the social results. Many settlers found that they could not pay the government's charges. Much of the land passed to large holders, though periodically the government sought to provide relief for the hard-pressed small farmers.

To many western citizens, the land laws seemed generally to benefit land speculators and midwestern cities, while the western family farmer got the leftovers. Indeed, there were some large corporate farms in the wheat lands of the Northwest, and certainly much of the country's mineral and timber lands fell into the hands of corporations. But the greatest speculators were actually the small farmers themselves, who often took more land than they needed and reaped large profits on the excess when they sold it. Nevertheless, the legend of the evil outside land speculator helped shape much of the political reaction of the later nineteenth century. Here was still another reason to denounce the East and demand relief from "oppression."

★ FARMING IN THE LAST WEST ★

Indians, miners, cattlemen—all these groups could show how imposed eastern policies were inappropriate to western needs. For the Indians, certainly, the inadequacies were devastating. But ultimately it was the farmers' grievances that became the most unsettling.

Plains Agriculture. The Great Plains presented special difficulties for the would-be farmer. Along its eastern fringes precipitation was adequate for cultivation methods familiar in the older farming regions. Elsewhere, however, rainfall was scarce and new approaches were required. In many regions underground aquifers offered hope of supplementing the sparse rainfall. These could be tapped by windmills powered by the constant breezes of the unobstructed Plains. During the 1880s windmills raised on pylons became a characteristic feature of the plains landscape. Another way to conquer aridity was by "dry farming," a system based on planting seeds far apart and covering plant roots with a dust mulch after each rainfall to preserve moisture. Dry farmers also adopted new drought-resistant grain, some brought from Russia.

Even in regions of adequate rainfall, transplanted easterners faced difficulties they had not encountered at home. The most serious perhaps was the absence of stone and timber. Except for a few cottonwoods, willows, and hackber-

Women are often left out of the story of western homesteading. This picture by Harvey Dunn helps reestablish their critical role.

Mechanized agriculture in the West was encouraged by the absence of trees. In eastern Washington State in 1900 wheat was harvested efficiently by enormous combines drawn by huge teams of horses.

ries along stream banks, the Great Plains were treeless. Furthermore, the soils were deep and stone-free. What could settlers use for fencing their fields and building their barns and dwellings?

During the 1860s agricultural experts touted hedges as fencing for cultivated fields. But before hedging could come into wide use, barbed wire appeared. A barbed-wire fence required only a few timber uprights; the rest was iron wire, a few rolls of which could enclose hundreds of acres. One contemporary listed the advantages of barbed wire: It "takes no room, exhausts no soil, shades no vegetation, is proof against high winds, makes no snowdrifts, and is both durable and cheap."

To solve the shortages in housing material, early Plains settlers used squares of sod cut from the thick Plains grass. These were piled up to make walls along the edges of deep holes dug into the ground. The roof of such a house was also sod, placed on brush and cottonwood rafters. Warm in winter and cool in summer, these half-buried structures were also dirty, and during heavy rains they leaked badly. Yet they served some families for many years and were even used for schoolhouses and other public buildings. Eventually, when the railroads came, timber from the East and Far West made frame structures possible. In time the houses of the Plains began to resemble those in the Midwest.

The Plains environment presented still other problems. In 1874 swarms of grasshoppers descended on the region

from the Dakotas to Texas, consuming grain, vegetables, bark, clothes, and even the handles of plows and pitchforks. During the 1870s and early 1880s, however, rainfall was generally sufficient in the region, and with the confinement of the Indians to reservations and the arrival of the railroads, people swarmed into western Kansas, Nebraska, and the Dakotas to grow grain for the East and Europe. Then the late 1880s ushered in a decade of extremely dry conditions. Crops drooped and died, and whatever survived the parching winds was consumed by insects. Farmers and their families fled the searing sun during the early 1890s and returned east with the sides of their wagons sardonically inscribed: "In God We Trusted; In Kansas We Busted!"

Yet many farmers persisted and ultimately prospered. Once labor shortages—another chronic problem on the Plains—had been solved by the invention of special harvesting and threshing machines, Plains farming became enormously productive. It was *extensive* agriculture that cultivated vast acreages using little labor. It focused on wheat, the crop best suited to grasslands and, owing to its durability, to production far from consumers. By 1899 the United States was producing over 600 million bushels of wheat a year, much of it from the Great Plains. In 1870 the wheat belt had been centered in the older Midwest. By 1899 Minnesota, North Dakota, South Dakota, and Kansas were among the top five wheat producers.

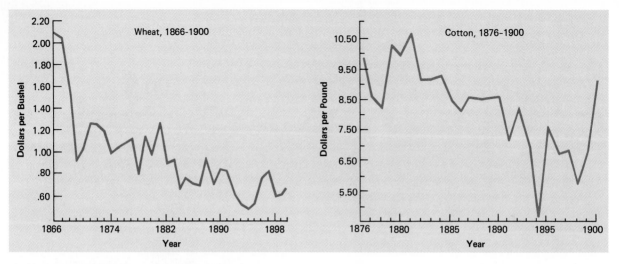

Wheat and cotton prices in the Gilded Age. *Source: Historical Statistics of the United States, Colonial Times to 1970.*

Pacific Coast Agriculture. As the Plains became the nation's wheat belt, the Pacific Coast emerged as the country's fruit and vegetable belt. California land was initially used for cattle ranching and wheat production, often on "bonanza" farms of more than a thousand acres. The Pacific Northwest states, too, at first concentrated on grain and cattle, though never on such a large scale as California.

Gradually, as transportation to the East improved and it became possible to preserve perishables by refrigeration, agriculture on the Pacific Coast became more diversified, taking advantage of the region's mild climate. Oregon began to supply the San Francisco market with apples, pears, peaches, plums, and grapes. In Washington the arrival of the Northern Pacific Railroad in the 1880s stimulated the production of apples and pears in the state's eastern valleys.

Meanwhile, California was developing into a significant specialty agricultural region. Grapes had been grown there long before the Americans arrived, but in the 1860s and later, after the arrival of German and then Italian immigrants, the wine industry grew rapidly. During the 1870s and 1880s the vineyards were almost wiped out by an insect pest, but were saved when resistant grapevine species were developed. By 1900 California produced 19 million gallons of wine, over 80 percent of American output.

Citrus fruit, too, had been grown in California during the Spanish period. The fruit, however, was inferior and consumed only locally. Then in the 1870s Brazilian navel oranges were introduced on irrigated fields in southern California. When refrigeration came in the 1880s, navels picked during the early winter could be shipped all the way to the East Coast. Summer-ripening Valencia oranges, introduced somewhat later, enabled the growers to produce year-round.

The citrus industry at first was plagued by haphazard marketing. Shipments spoiled or got lost; at times the market was glutted, at other times it was undersupplied. To deal with these problems, the growers tried to form cooperatives during the 1880s. The middlemen who marketed the crop blocked this effort, but then in 1893 the growers organized the Southern California Fruit Exchange, which later became the California Fruit Growers' Exchange and marketed its product under the brand name Sunkist. The Exchange brought stability to the industry.

★ FARM DISCONTENT AND WESTERN REVOLT ★

Viewed from a broad economic perspective, the development of American agriculture during the generation following the Civil War was a success story. In quantity, acreage, output per person and per acre, the advances were spectacular. Largely because of the mechanized farms of the Great Plains, wheat production tripled between 1860 and 1899. In the older Midwest, states like Illinois and Iowa shifted from wheat to hogs and cattle, feeding them on the country's huge corn harvests—840 million bushels of corn in 1860, 2.7 billion bushels in 1900. In cotton and livestock the increases were equally dramatic. The nation's farm labor force continued to rise in absolute numbers until 1910, but the increase in farmers was far smaller than the expansion in their output, for new technology, new plant science, the land-grant colleges, and the Department of Agriculture all helped to increase productivity at a rapid pace. The result was that the United States became an agricultural cornucopia, capable of producing cheap grain, meat, and fiber, not only for its own exploding urban population, but also for much of the industrializing Atlantic world. So efficient was American farm production and marketing that it undermined British, French, and German cultivators and led to loud European demands for protection against the "American menace."

And yet there was another tale that competed with this agricultural success story: The post–Civil War American farmers were discontented and were in full-scale revolt against the perceived oppression of rural America by the rich and the powerful residing in the cities.

Farm Problems. The grievances behind the insurgency were broad-ranging in their scope. According to farm spokespersons, farmers were victimized by bankers and mortgage companies that kept interest rates high and squeezed farmers and other borrowers and debtors through "hard money" policies that restricted the country's money supply. The typical American farm, they claimed, was mortgaged to the hilt, and the moneylenders and bankers showed no mercy in foreclosing when the farmer could not pay. Farm advocates also insisted that the prices of the goods that cultivators bought were kept artificially high by tariffs and monopoly practices, whereas prices they received for their unprotected crops fell steadily. They charged that middlemen's costs—for transporting farmers' products to market, for storing their grain, for milling their flour, and ginning their cotton—all rose during this period. The parasitic railroads, farm processors, grain and cotton brokers, and all the others grew fat while they grew poor. Beyond these economic grievances, spokespersons for "agrarianism" expressed fears that those who "fed them all," the nation's cultivators, were losing influence and the new "money power" was in the driver's seat.

Today, economic historians are puzzled by the charges leveled by farm advocates during these last years of the nineteenth century. For one thing, they note, farmers did not all fare alike economically. Pacific Coast farmers prospered by adopting fruit and vegetable crops. Prairie farmers of Iowa and Illinois switched from wheat to corn and hogs and made decent profits. East Coast and Great Lakes truck and dairy farmers found profitable markets in the cities.

As for claims of financial oppression, this too is puzzling. It is true that interest rates were higher in the West and South—the country's premier farm areas—than in the Northeast. But this difference can be explained by the shortage of savings in the two staple-crop regions and the higher risks of farming than manufacturing or commerce. Nor were American farm borrowers poor peasants turning to moneylenders to stave off starvation. Most of the money that farmers borrowed was for barns, fences, plows, harvesters, and other improvements, all items that were needed to increase productivity and income. The loans they contracted were, in effect, no different from the loans of any other small businessperson. Nor were the oppressive farm mortgages as universal as the critics claimed. Even in the wheat belt, no more than 39 percent of the farms were burdened with mortgages

in 1890, though the figure was higher in Kansas and Nebraska. As for the legendary wicked urge to foreclose, this was not common. The banks and the mortgage companies that lent farmers money were not interested in acquiring farm acreage; they often extended the repayment terms of loans more than once to avoid having to foreclose.

The claims that falling prices were contrived deliberately by a cabal of bankers and money power monopolists to squeeze the nation's "producers" are equally dubious. All prices fell during the generation following the Civil War. This meant the prices the farmers paid as well as those they received. Not only did wheat, cotton, pork, beef, and tobacco decline, but so too did iron, coal, clothing, railroad and interest rates, farm machinery, barbed wire, and lumber. There is no good evidence that the "terms of trade" between the producers of food and fiber and the providers of the services and manufactured goods that they used shifted significantly against the nation's rural tillers in these years. Moreover, the price declines were not only an American phenomenon; they were common to the entire world. If there was a conspiracy to force down prices, the conspiracy was evidently worldwide in its scope.

Nor is it clear that monetary forces were responsible for the great deflation of the late nineteenth century. This was an era when *real* costs were going down. Each year the furnaces that created steel, the locomotives and boxcars that hauled freight, and the plows and combines that produced grain became more efficient and their products less expensive in terms of labor and matériel. Even the middlemen's real costs declined owing to greater efficiency. When, in the 1890s, the Russians sought to make their grain more competitive in the world market, they sent a delegation to the United States to learn how American brokers and grain handlers managed to get the American wheat crop to market at such low cost. Some scholars do believe that late-nineteenth-century price declines can be traced to a slow increase in the money supply. But few believe that this was deliberately engineered by a collection of conspirators. And in any event, the case for excessively slow money growth is not proven.

Agrarianism. And yet we are left with the reality of turbulent farm discontent in the generation following the Civil War. How can we explain it?

First, let us note that the agrarian insurgency of the period was confined primarily to the wheat- and cotton-growing areas. Dairy farmers, corn-hog farmers, and truck farmers were generally proof against the insurgent appeal. In large part this was because they sold their products to domestic consumers in the fast-growing cities. Though their prices declined like all others, they were more stable than many.

Stability—or rather its absence—is one possible answer to the riddle of insurgency in the wheat and cotton belts. Grain and cotton farmers were subject to a degree of uncertainty that other producers did not experience. These cultivators sold their crops in a world market where they competed fiercely with other nations. Europeans bought not only the grain of the American prairies and plains, but also the wheat of Canada, Australia, Argentina, and Russia. They bought cotton from the American South; they also could buy it from Egypt, India, and Brazil. By the end of the nineteenth century the entire world was knit together in a single market for nonperishable agricultural goods, and prices were established by countless impersonal transactions between buyers and sellers.

The system was a tremendous boon to consumers. Everywhere they benefited from the declining cost of food and fabric. But, of course, however successful in lowering their own costs of production to offset world price declines, farmers would have been better off if prices had risen. Of greater significance, however, was the painful experience of price instability. The American farmer's own output was only one factor affecting world crop prices. A bumper wheat crop in the American Plains could be expected to lower world grain prices. But it might be more than offset by a dearth in, say, Argentina, that would push prices up. And, of course, the reverse might also occur: An American farmer, expecting good prices after a short crop, might be bitterly disappointed if Australia or the Russian Ukraine had a bounteous harvest. The net effect was that farmers found themselves on a rollercoaster over which they could exercise no control. The villains were actually impersonal market forces, but these were not as satisfactory as flesh-and-blood villains of the sort that farmers saw or heard about every day—the bankers, railroad officials, politicians, and farm machinery manufacturers.

Clearly, like the wage earners discussed in Chapters 17 and 18, American farmers as a group faced difficult problems adjusting to the demands and circumstances of a new industrialized, urbanized era. Some of their problems were exaggerated, but some were also real. No one could deny the distress of sharecroppers in the South, penalized often by a vicious social and racial system that placed them at the mercy of powerful and privileged planters and landowners. Land in America, moreover, bore a disproportionate share of the national tax burden; personal property and personal income was lightly taxed or entirely tax-exempt. Though railroad rates generally went down, in noncompetitive areas, often in the West and South, the railroad managers tried to make up for the "cutthroat" competition on major trunk lines by charging all that the local traffic would bear. Finally, agriculture as a way of life had lost standing. More and more the cities had seized on the imaginations of Americans. This explained, in part, the exodus of the young from the rural areas. It also accounted for the increasing references to "rubes," "hayseeds," and "appleknockers" in the metropolitan press. As the nation urbanized, American farmers felt more and more left behind.

Moved by such forces and feelings, in the generation following the Civil War farm advocates launched a campaign to arouse the sympathy of the nation for a war against the oppressors and exploiters. Claiming to speak for the entire rural community, and playing on resonant Jeffersonian chords, they created a social philosophy based on agrarian distress and rural rights that can best be labeled *agrarianism*.

Agrarianism exalted the farmer as the only true citizen, the backbone of the nation, the heart of the "producing masses." Agrarians gradually expanded the concept to include the ever-growing number of wage earners and sought to construct a farmer-labor alliance of producers, whose plight was said to be shared by the nation as a whole. On the other side, agrarians personalized the enemy as the "money power" or the "bloated middlemen." These "plutocrats," they said, had seized control of the economy and through various hidden financial arrangements had imposed their will on the nation. The United States was fast becoming the land of a rich few and an impoverished, exploited, and powerless many.

Though agrarian advocates sought to universalize their protest, much of their indictment had a sectional edge. Both the Great Plains and the South regarded themselves as colonies in bondage to the "East." It was the East that was the source of credit, and it was eastern moneylenders and bankers who charged the high interest rates the "producing sections" paid. The railroads had their headquarters in Boston, New York, Philadelphia, or Chicago, and it was in these eastern and large midwestern cities that the freight rates that squeezed cotton and wheat farmers were set. Easterners—or Europeans—also owned the land and marketed the crops, the agrarians said. The farm-machinery manufacturers, the barbed-wire producers, and the other industrialists who made the equipment western and southern farmers needed to survive were easterners with headquarters in Chicago, Indianapolis, or Richmond. Furthermore, the East dominated the major political parties and through them the government. Policies regarding the Indians, finance, money, tariffs, and land were not made by the people of the West and South, who were most directly concerned. They were made by the representatives of the eastern "money interests," who sought only their own gain.

Whether true or false, whether exaggerated or exact, the agrarian indictment of plutocracy and the East had become a powerful political force by the end of the century. The discontents that built up over the years in the West and South emerged in a series of political movements from the 1870s until the end of the 1890s. Like socialism among wage earners, these were all reactions against the perceived

This poster shows farmers as living a potentially idyllic existence. Their actual position was less fortunate, and they created Granges to push for political solutions to their problems. Although "Granger Laws" eventually regulated railroad and grain elevator rates, farm problems remained severe through the end of the century.

abuses that accompanied the great economic and social changes that marked the era.

Agrarian reformism differed from socialism in many ways, however. First, though like Marxism it considered labor the source of all value, it was distinctly American in origin, borrowing heavily from the Jefferson-Jackson emphasis on the small landholder and the "producer." Second, though the agrarian reformers sought to win support among eastern wage earners, their appeal fed largely on southern and western discontents, especially those of cultivators. Finally, the agrarian reformers were never enemies of private property and a profit system. Their complaint was with the way capitalism had supposedly been rigged in favor of the few and against the many. Their desire was not to end profit and property but to make sure that the benefits of both were more widely distributed among the masses of the people.

The Grangers. To solve their problems, some farmers during the Gilded Age, like some wage earners, turned to collective action. In the early 1870s they flocked to local "Granges" of the Patrons of Husbandry, a social-fraternal order founded in 1876. At first the Granges were primarily social and educational organizations. Farm life was isolated and lonely, and farmers and their wives welcomed the chance to socialize and listen to lectures at the local Grange hall.

As midwestern farmers became increasingly dependent on middlemen and railroads, the Grangers became politically active. Joining with many eastern merchants and business people who also disliked the railroads' high and often arbitrary freight charges, they supported state laws to regulate railroad companies and grain elevator firms. In states like Illinois, Iowa, Wisconsin, and Minnesota, where political power was balanced between the major parties, the pro-Granger men in the state legislatures were able to enact the regulatory laws the Patrons of Husbandry supported.

The patrons were also active in various cooperative ventures to improve the economic standing of farmers. In several midwestern states Grange agents negotiated purchases of large quantities of supplies from merchants or manufacturers at special low prices and passed these savings along to Grange members. In 1872 a group of merchants formed Montgomery Ward and Company for the specific purpose of dealing with the Grangers. Grange agents also secured price reductions from some farm machinery manufacturers. Efforts to produce farm machinery cooperatively failed, however; the managers of Grange manufacturing enterprises lacked experience and were unable to meet the aggressive competition of established private firms.

The Alliances. By the late 1870s the Grange had ceased to be anything more than a social-educational organization, but farmers did not abandon political or economic organization. New agrarian Alliances soon appeared that were more militant than the Patrons of Husbandry.

The Alliance movement began in the mid-1870s when small rancher-farmers in central Texas organized a secret club to catch horse thieves, collect stray cattle, and fight the large ranchers who ignored the rights of their smaller neighbors. The scheme soon spread to the rest of the state and grew in strength and ambition. In 1886 the Texas Alliance, borrowing ideas from the Greenback party of 1884, revealed a program calling for opposition to landholding by foreigners, for stiff taxes on railroads, and for paper money. These political demands threatened to split the Alliance until Charles W. Macune brought the opposing sides together.

Macune went on to become a major leader in a regional Southern Alliance that incorporated the Arkansas Wheel and a large Colored Alliance composed of black tenant farmers and sharecroppers. By 1890 the Southern Alliance had a million members.

Farm discontent in the prairies and Great Plains led to similar efforts. By 1890 the Northwest Alliance, organized a decade earlier, had expanded to fifteen states, with particularly heavy concentration of membership in Kansas, Nebraska, the Dakotas, and Minnesota.

Toward the end of the 1880s the Alliances began to emphasize politics rather than cooperatives. Alliance-affiliated candidates running on platforms favoring the "producers" over the bankers, merchants, and manufacturers won election as either Democrats or Republicans to state legislatures in the South and West. In several states they captured one of the major parties and compelled it to endorse farmers' programs. But the Alliance-controlled state legislatures achieved relatively little. They enacted some legislation regulating railroads and businesses, but these measures were largely ineffective. Alliance-dominated state governments were frequently led by political novices who were easily outmaneuvered by the seasoned politicians of the regular parties. When the Alliance leaders were not simply duped, they were sometimes handicapped by a limited vision of what government could or should do. Too often, in the words of the Tennessee Alliance, they considered the "Jeffersonian noninterference theory of government" to be the "wisest" and refused to employ state power in positive ways.

Frustrated by their initial experiences with politics, Alliance leaders concluded that the fault lay in relying on the Democrats and Republicans. Instead, the farmers should organize their own party, one that would be free of the old-line politicos, who seemed indifferent at heart to the needs of rural people.

★ CONCLUSIONS ★

The development of the last American frontier made an enormous difference in the nation's history. The exploitation of the trans-Missouri West added immense resources to the country's economic base. The cattle and mining frontiers also added to the raw material for American literature and legend. For the American Indian, development of this area was the final defeat in almost three centuries of bitter conflict with people of Old World origins.

The last West was also the focus for the last truly serious threat of sectional disunity. Along with the cotton South, it was indeed in some ways a colony of the Northeast. Eastern money controlled its resources; eastern attitudes affected its Indian policy; eastern politicians decided its political fate. By the end of the century, moreover, western and southern grievances had created a sense of apartness, of distinctiveness, that contributed to a mighty political revolt. This sense was reinforced and given focus by a group of agrarian thinkers who drew their ideas from the Jefferson-Jackson tradition of the early Republic. Scholars may argue over the validity of western grievances or whether western leaders properly identified the causes of their section's difficulties. But there can be no question that by 1890 in the West and the South a powerful wave of discontent was gathering. Before the new century began, it would sweep over the nation, threatening to push aside long-standing political alignments and shift the country's balance of power.

✦✦✦✦✦✦✦ FOR FURTHER READING ✦✦✦✦✦✦✦

Walter P. Webb. *The Great Plains* (1931)

The classic study of the Great Plains. Describes the physical environment of the Plains region, its native inhabitants, and the efforts of people of European ancestry to conquer it. Webb shows the important ways in which geography and climate modified transplanted institutions.

Fred A. Shannon. *The Farmer's Last Frontier: Agriculture, 1860–1897* (1945)

This older work is still the indispensable study of agriculture in the generation following the Civil War. Shannon is more than a scholar in this book; he is also an advocate of southern and western farmers in their struggles with the railroads, the manufacturers, and middlemen. In some ways *The Farmer's Last Frontier* is the baseline from which all later works on the post–Civil War "farm problem" are derived.

Allan G. Bogue. *Money at Interest: The Farm Mortgage on the Middle Border (1955)*; and *From Prairie to Corn Belt* (1963)

Two revisionist treatments of the post–Civil War farmer's difficulties. Bogue denies that eastern moneylenders were greedy or made excessive profits from western farmers. He also claims that corn belt farmers did very well for themselves in the late nineteenth century. Neither of these books should be read for recreation.

Everett Dick. *The Sod-House Frontier, 1854–1890* (1954)

The subtitle of this book is: "A Social History of the Northern Plains from the Creation of Kansas & Nebraska to the Admission of the Dakotas." It summarizes quite well the contents of the work. This is old-fashioned social history—and it is lively.

Rodman W. Paul. *Mining Frontiers of the Far West, 1948–1880* (1963)

This brief book combines excellent scholarship with a sense of the romantic aspect of the great western mining bonanzas. Has first-rate illustrations.

R. K. Andrist. *The Long Death: The Last Days of the Plains Indians* (1964)

A skillful overview of the tragic destruction of the Plains tribes by the encroachment of "civilization." The work of a talented journalist.

Robert W. Mardock. *Reformers and the American Indian* (1970)

Surveys the Indian reformers through to the Dawes Act of 1887. Mardock ties their efforts to the antislavery movement that most of them had participated in. They were sincere, he says, but their vision was limited and culture-bound.

Ernest Staples Osgood. *The Day of the Cattlemen* (1929)

Old, but good. A brief study of the range cattle industry of the northern Plains, this is 250 pages of instruction and entertainment.

Robert Utley. *The Lance and the Shield: The Life and Times of Sitting Bull* (1993)

An impressive new scholarly treatment of Sitting Bull and his tribe and also, along the way, a reexamination of Indian–white relations after the Civil War.

Robert Dykstra. *The Cattle Towns* (1968)

This book is an up-to-date, unromantic, but interesting study of the cattle towns—Dodge City, Abilene, Ellsworth, Caldwell, and Wichita—between 1876 and 1885. Written by an urban historian, it emphasizes the nature of town life in the cattle communities and talks as much of dry-goods merchants as of cowboys and dance-hall girls.

Gene M. Gressley. *Bankers and Cattlemen* (1966)

The subtitle of this book is "The Stocks-and-Bonds, Havana-Cigar, Mahogany-and-Leather Side of the Cowboy Era." That is as good a description as one could find of this study of the western cattle industry from 1870 to 1900.

John D. Hicks. *The Populist Revolt: A History of the Farmers' Alliance and the People's Party* (1931)

This is the standard older treatment of late-nineteenth-century agrarian insurgency. Hicks sees the Populists as the forerunners of twentieth-century American liberalism.

Hamlin Garland. *Main-Travelled Roads* (1891)

The characters in this collection of short stories are pitiful victims of a harsh environment and unjust laws. Garland, who settled with his parents on the Iowa prairie, learned early that "farming is not entirely made up of berrying, tossing the new-mown hay, and singing 'The Old Oaken Bucket' on the porch by moonlight."

Frank Norris. *The Octopus* (1901)

The fortunes of western farmers were tied to the railroads, the grain elevator operators, the Chicago Board of Trade, and the weather. In this description of California wheat growers in the Central Valley, the Southern Pacific Railroad is depicted as "a giant parasite fattening upon the lifeblood of an entire commonwealth."

Robert Utley. *The Last Days of the Sioux Nation* (1963)

The best, most complete treatment we have of the Ghost-Dance uprising and the Wounded Knee massacre.

Gene Clanton. *Populism: The Humane Preference in America, 1890–1990* (1991)

This is a powerful defense of Populism as a humane alternative to mainstream politics of the 1890s. By a scholar who has spent much of his career investigating Kansas Populism.

20★

REPUBLICANS AND DEMOCRATS

What Made Gilded Age Politics Work?

1861	The United States goes off gold standard
1873	With the Coinage Act, or the "Crime of '73," Congress drops silver from the coinage system
1875	The "Whiskey Ring" scandal
1877	Rutherford B. Hayes is elected president in Compromise of 1877
1878	The Bland-Allison Act
1879	The United States returns to gold standard
1880s	More than 80 percent of the electorate turns out to vote in presidential elections
1880	James A. Garfield elected president
1881–82	The "Star Route" scandals
1881	Garfield is assassinated; Chester A. Arthur becomes president
1883	The Pendleton Act establishes the Civil Service Commission
1884	Grover Cleveland elected president
1886	*Wabash, St. Louis and Pacific Railway Co. v. Illinois*
1887	The Interstate Commerce Act creates the Interstate Commerce Commission (ICC)
1888	Benjamin Harrison elected president
1890	The Sherman Silver Purchase Act • The Sherman Antitrust Act • The McKinley Tariff Act
1892	People's party (Populist) is formed • Grover Cleveland elected president for the second time
1893	Financial panic leads to depression
1894	The Wilson-Gorman Tariff Act
1896	William McKinley elected president, defeating William Jennings Bryan
1897	Almost half of federal employees are under Civil Service rules

The Gilded Age, so the story goes, was the era of triumphant Republicanism. The party that won the Civil War retained its tight hold on the nation's decision-making processes and succeeded time and again in electing its candidates to office against a divided and demoralized Democratic opposition. The reasons for Republican success were both ideological and practical, this view holds. The "Grand Old Party" (GOP) was the party of big business and relied on the support of the great postwar tycoons for the financial means to achieve electoral victory. In return it handed out favors lavishly to its backers in the form of tariffs, land grants, and other probusiness measures. In this version of the period, the Democrats, hampered by their record of opposition during the Civil War, remained a minority party whose appeal lay with those voters, both rural and urban, who opposed the strong-running currents of industrialism that seemed to be conquering the nation.

This interpretation emphasizes the economic basis for party politics. Men voted for one party or the other because it expressed their economic interests and they expected their party's program to benefit them in material ways. By implication the Republicans were consistent winners because more Americans found their program of encouraging industrial growth to their liking, whereas the Democrats, identified with traditional rural values, seemed backward-looking and unprogressive. This view also implies a class separation of the parties. The Republicans, it says, were the party of the prosperous, the strivers, the respectable; the Democrats, the party of the poor, the unsuccessful, and the dispossessed.

These generalizations collide head-on with the real facts of Gilded Age politics. One of the most striking characteristics of the political system between the end of Reconstruction and the 1890s was the failure of either party to dominate national politics. True, every president during these years except Grover Cleveland was a Republican, but almost all federal elections were close. In 1880 Republican James Garfield defeated his Democratic opponent, Winfield Scott Hancock, by only 7,000 popular votes. Four years later Cleveland, a Democrat, defeated James G. Blaine by under 25,000 votes out of 10 million cast. Only for three short periods during this era did the same party control the presidency and both houses of Congress. In only one congressional election between 1878 and 1888 inclusively did more than 2 percentage points separate the total Democratic and Republican votes.

On the local level the picture was more complex. In parts of northern New England and regions elsewhere settled by New Englanders, the Republicans were consistently in firm control. The South, except for a few Republican pockets mostly in the old Unionist regions, was solidly Democratic. In these areas one party almost totally dominated the local political scene.

On the whole, however, the close political contests of the Gilded Age not only refute the notion that there was a minority party and a majority party; they also call into question the view that the parties represented distinct and antagonistic economic interests. If one party—the Republicans—represented big business, and the other—the Democrats—the mass of the people who did not benefit from the legislation demanded by big business, how could the Republicans ever have won? How many businessmen—big or little—were there in the country? Surely not enough to guarantee Republican success even 50 percent of the time. As most voters were either small farmers or wage earners, something is also clearly wrong with the idea that the country was divided into rich Republicans and poor Democrats. But is this commonsense deduction confirmed by the facts? And if it is—if Gilded Age politics was not a contest between the rich and the poor—what did the parties stand for?

★ THE ECONOMIC ISSUES ★

As we saw in Chapters 17 and 18, the Gilded Age was a time of headlong industrialization and urbanization. People were moving from country to city, from East to West, and from agriculture to industry and commerce. The lives of millions of men and women were being transformed both for good and for ill. Social inequality, slums, depressions, the difficulties of adjusting to urban life, and many other new issues arising out of the pell-mell economic transformation were being thrust to the surface of national life. Reflecting these crosscurrents, three important economic issues entered political discourse: the tariff, the money supply, and government regulation of private enterprise. None of these divided the nation along clear party lines.

The Tariff. Traditionally, the Democrats were the party of free trade; the Republicans the party that endorsed protection of domestic industry. In the years immediately following the Civil War, however, the two parties seldom confronted one another directly on the tariff issue. Both were too divided internally. Western Republicans, more closely tied to agriculture than industry, were less enthusiastic about a high tariff than were eastern Republicans. Pennsylvania Democrats, who represented the state with the largest commitment to heavy industry, were almost in-

CONSISTENCY OF THE VOTE, 1876–1892

variably protectionists, unlike Democrats from, say, commercial New York or agricultural Mississippi.

During Reconstruction and for some years thereafter, tariff rates gradually rose to levels never reached before. But not until 1888 did the tariff become a contested issue in a presidential campaign. The 1888 election seems to confirm the traditional view of a big-business-oriented GOP and a mass-oriented Democratic party. Democratic President Grover Cleveland made "tariff reform"—that is, downward revision—the key plank in his reelection platform. The Republicans took a strong stand for the tariff and fought the campaign on the issue.

The Republican candidate, Benjamin Harrison of Indiana, was a former United States senator and the grandson of Old Tippecanoe, William Henry Harrison. A dignified figure with a gift for words, he was nonetheless colorless and lacking in warmth before crowds. One newspaper reporter called him "the man who never laughs." Provided by manufacturers with what then seemed unlimited funds, he waged a successful "front porch" campaign despite his austere personality. Delegations came to visit Harrison at his home in Indianapolis and listened to his prepared statements—usually homilies that played on religion, patrio-

tism, and freedom—which were then disseminated to the country by the Republican party press. The strategy was hard on Harrison's front lawn, but the results demonstrated its political effectiveness. Harrison toppled the incumbent by winning an electoral college majority, although he fell behind Cleveland by 100,000 popular votes. Apparently Republican protectionism had met Democratic free trade head-on and beaten it.

But if we look closely at the election of 1888, it becomes clear that it was neither a serious test of party commitment nor of public attitudes toward tariffs. Cleveland's running mate, Allen Thurman of Ohio, was a protectionist, and during the campaign Cleveland himself retreated from his antiprotectionist stand. "We have entered upon no crusade for free trade," he declared. The Democrats, if victorious, would arrange tariff schedules with the "utmost care for established interests and enterprise." The Republicans, too, wavered. In the industrial East they emphasized the high-tariff plank of their platform, but in the West they told the farmers that the GOP was the soul of moderation on the tariff.

Besides this waffling on issues, many other considerations affected the 1888 election. The age and feebleness of

The tariff was not the central issue in the flagrantly corrupt election of 1888. Instead, such problems as the return of captured Confederate flags and Cleveland's veto of veterans' pension bills dominated debate. The Republican victory was narrow, especially in Indiana, where votes that had once cost only $5 sold for as much as $20.

the Democratic vice presidential nominee, Allen Thurman, dismayed many voters. As usual, moreover, the Democrats of New York proved to be more interested in fighting one another than their common Republican foe. Finally, president Cleveland lost some usually Democratic Irish votes when the British minister to Washington, representing the traditional enemy of Irish patriots, foolishly allowed it to come out that he preferred Cleveland to Harrison. These factors make it hard to demonstrate that Republican victory was a mandate for a high tariff—or for any other policy.

Never again during the Gilded Age did the tariff come as close as in 1888 to becoming a clear-cut election issue. The tariff reform bill initiated by Cleveland in 1888 ended as the McKinley Tariff of 1890, which set rates higher than ever before. In 1894, after Cleveland had returned to office, his administration attempted once more to lower rates. The Wilson-Gorman Tariff that resulted was the product of considerable lobbying in the Senate, where eastern Democrats imposed 634 amendments that effectively raised the duties. This bill was so timid in its attack on protection that the disappointed president allowed it to become law without his signature.

Finance. National finance was another matter that might have separated the parties. But between 1865 and 1896 it seldom did. The issue was a complicated one. The advocates of "soft money" believed that the country's supply of

money and credit was too restricted. A minority of the soft-money people favored reforming the banking system to make it more flexible and capable of expanding its issues and its credit. More of the soft-money group were Greenbackers, who believed the nation's economic problems were caused by a shortage of government-issued paper currency. There were still $400 million of the Civil War federal greenbacks in circulation, but this amount was fixed by law and was not enough for an expanding economy. With a static money supply and a growing volume of business transactions, the country, Greenbackers said, was experiencing a severe money shortage that deflated prices and raised interest rates. This deflation was harmful to farmers, industrial wage earners, and all debtors and borrowers.

On the other side were the advocates of "sound money" or "hard money," who deplored any attempt to inflate the currency. Their opponents, they said, were demagogues whose policies would shake the public's trust in the economic system and dislocate all commercial relations. The soft-money people were inflationists whose policies would push up the prices of all commodities and injure every citizen whose income was fixed. The hard-money people insisted that a fixed money and credit supply had to be maintained for the sake of stability and order, and the best way to achieve this goal was to ensure that paper money—if needed at all—be made and kept redeemable for gold on demand at the banks and at the treasury. To the sound-money group the gold standard was the very foundation of the international economy, if not of modern civilization itself.

From the end of the Civil War to the end of the century, the hard-money and soft-money forces fought a series of battles. The first was over reducing the wartime issue of greenbacks and making them redeemable in gold. The soft-money forces prevented the former, but in 1879, under the prodding of hard-money groups, the country returned to the gold standard it had abandoned in 1861, thereby making all the federal greenbacks redeemable in gold on demand.

The second round of the long struggle, the battle over silver, also ultimately went to the hard-money forces. Silver had been part of the nation's currency ever since Alexander Hamilton's day, when it was established along with gold as part of the coinage system. At that time it was legally exchangeable with gold at a ratio of fifteen ounces of silver to one of gold. In the 1830s the ratio was altered to sixteen to one. But this change was insufficient to match the actual relative value of the metals on the open market, where gold and silver were bought and sold like wheat, coal, or corn. Because the government's stated value of silver was lower than its price on the open market, it became profitable to melt down silver coins and sell them as metal. As a result, by 1860 the country was on an actual gold standard—that is, only gold circulated as coin, and only gold was in fact used to back the country's paper money.

The discovery of huge silver deposits in the West after the Civil War lowered the price of silver relative to gold in world markets. By 1876 the official sixteen-to-one exchange rate now *overvalued* silver and made it the cheaper metal with which to pay debts. The soft-money men noted this development and also saw that silver's growing abundance offered the chance for the country to increase its money supply, stimulate the economy, lower interest rates, and raise all prices. Silver must, they declared, supersede gold as the world monetary standard.

Unfortunately, from the soft-money point of view, the potential benefits of abundant silver had supposedly been thrown away in 1873 when Congress had "demonetized" silver—dropped it from the coinage system. The soft-money advocates charged that this "Crime of '73" had been carried out by corrupt manipulators to frustrate debtors and "producers" while benefiting creditors and all those whose profits were advanced by high interest rates and price deflation. Especially implicated in the "crime," they held, were British bankers, who preferred this "expensive money" because it suited their creditor needs and advanced the interests of their own nation. These men, they said, had sent agents to Washington to bribe congressmen when the 1873 Coinage Act was being considered.

The money question, in its various forms, would disturb political life for a generation following the Civil War. But until 1896, when William Jennings Bryan made it the key Democratic plank in his first presidential race, it would not become a party issue. Greenbackers were to be found in both parties; so were "free silverites," who wanted silver "remonetized" at the old sixteen-to-one ratio. The same was true of gold-standard advocates: Some were Democrats, others Republicans. There was a slight bias toward the gold standard among Republicans and a similar bias toward the greenback–free-silver position among Democrats. But both parties had hard-money and soft-money wings.

Section rather than party or class was generally the distinguishing characteristic of the two groups of advocates. Western congressmen, either from the silver-mining area or from the debtor agricultural regions, tended to be soft-money men, as did representatives of the agricultural South, regardless of party. Democratic and Republican politicans from the commercial states and, by and large, the industrial regions of the northeast and the Midwest, concerned that greenbacks and free silver would push up the cost of living for wage earners and disturb business relations, favored the gold standard. The money question, then, *was* tied to economic interests, but it did not divide the nation along lines of rich and poor, Democrat and Republican.

The battle between the silverites and "goldbugs" was politically joined at a number of points. In 1878 the silverites won a partial victory with the passage of the Bland-Allison Act, requiring the treasury to buy not less than $2 million nor more than $4 million of silver monthly and coin it into silver dollars at the old ratio of sixteen ounces of silver to one of gold. The Bland-Allison Act was not a party issue: In the Senate 62 percent of the Republicans and 73 percent of the Democrats supported the bill. The silver coin authorized by the Bland-Allison Act did expand the money supply by a small amount, but the inflationary effect was undetectable and the agitation for silver continued. In 1890, after the value of silver metal had fallen still further relative to gold, the silverites—now reinforced by a bipartisan group of senators from several newly admitted, far western mining states—succeeded in pushing another silver measure through Congress, the Sherman Silver Purchase Act. This law required that the treasury buy virtually the entire yearly domestic output of silver and turn it into silver certificates. But even this massive addition of silver to the currency did not topple the gold standard. With a gold reserve of $100 million, the treasury, under both Democratic and Republican secretaries, was able to redeem all currency—greenbacks, small coins, silver dollars, and the new silver certificates—in gold, thereby frustrating silverites' hopes. Not until after the panic of 1893 did the accumulation of silver coin and silver certificates threaten to undermine the gold standard. At this point, as we will see, it was shored up and saved, with bipartisan support.

Government Regulation. The third major economic issue of the Gilded Age was government regulation of private enterprise. This problem, too, did not divide the parties. Nor did it divide the American people. After the Supreme Court declared in the 1886 *Wabash* case that the state legislatures were incompetent to regulate interstate railroads, federal regulation seemed unavoidable and received wide support among farmers as well as among business interests who required cheap transportation to ensure profits. Even the railroads were not totally opposed to regulation. Far better to have some guidelines on rates and practices, the railroad leaders said, than the anarchy and cutthroat competition for freight and passengers that often prevailed in the transportation business.

Pushed by these allied forces and led by Senator Shelby Cullom of Illinois and Congressman John Reagan of Texas, Congress passed the Interstate Commerce Act in 1887. This measure established the first federal regulatory body, the Interstate Commerce Commission (ICC). The ICC was given apparently ample powers. It could compel the railroads to desist from agreements to divide traffic to avoid competition, from discriminating among customers in setting rates, from charging more for short than for long hauls, and from granting the sorts of rebates and kickbacks that had helped make Rockefeller rich. The act also gave the ICC power to examine the books of railroad corporations and required the roads to file annual financial reports and adopt a uniform accounting system.

The law had some grave weaknesses, however. Time would show that all regulatory commissions tended toward co-option—taking on the principles and goals of the industries they were created to regulate. But the Interstate Commerce Act was particularly flawed. The ICC could not *set* rates, and its orders did not have the force of a court's. To compel a railroad to desist from some outlawed practice, the ICC had to institute proceedings before a federal judge. The federal courts turned out to be generally unfriendly to effective regulation. In the 1897 *Maximum Freight Rate* case the Supreme Court virtually annulled the Interstate Commerce Act.

What does the formation of the ICC tell us about Gilded Age politics? Although traditionally the Democrats favored a laissez-faire policy and the Republicans advocated strong government, the Interstate Commerce Act was a bipartisan law. Of the two original sponsors, Cullom was a Republican and Reagan a Democrat. The bill passed both houses of Congress by large margins, and yeas and nays cut across party lines.

The same bipartisanship applied to the other major federal law designed to place public reins on private business, the Sherman Antitrust Act of 1890. The Sherman Act was Congress's reaction to a wave of public anxiety over the dangers of monopoly. This fear went back to the earliest years of the republic, when Jeffersonians and Jacksonians had warned of concentrated economic power. After 1865 it inspired the western Greenbackers and farmers' groups to push for "Granger" legislation regulating railroad, grain elevator, and warehouse corporations.

In the Sherman Act of 1890 Congress responded to the public anxiety about trusts and monopolies by declaring illegal "every contract, combination in the form of trust or otherwise, or conspiracy, in restraint of trade or commerce among the several states, or with foreign nations." Anyone who made such an agreement was to be punished by a fine of up to $1,000 and a year in jail; anyone injured by such an agreement might sue for triple damages in the federal courts. The measure, like the Interstate Commerce Act, was scarcely one that separated the parties; the vote by which it was adopted in Congress fell one short of complete unanimity!

The conclusion is clear: The major economic issues of the Gilded Age were not party issues. This does not mean that economic matters played no role in Gilded Age party politics. That would be almost inconceivable. Both parties contained a variety of economic pressure groups—farmers, workers, bankers, merchants, industrialists—that fought for control. It was *within* the parties rather that *between* them that economic conflict took place, and until 1896 it proved impossible for any pressure group to dominate completely either the Democrats or the Republicans.

★ THE AMERICAN LOVE OF POLITICS ★

Despite the absence of major differences between Democrats and Republicans on economic matters, American voters during the Gilded Age were passionate political participants. Voter turnouts during these years were enormous. Everywhere but the South, where thousands of black voters were effectively deprived of the right to vote after 1877 and where the Democratic nominee was the guaranteed victor, a far larger proportion of the eligible voters cast ballots than today. During the 1880s, for example, more than 80 percent of the voters went to the polls during presidential election years. In 1896 this figure soared to more than 95 percent in the five states of the Old Northwest—Ohio, Indiana, Illinois, Wisconsin, and Michigan. In local elections, too, the proportion of the eligible voters who voted was greater than today.

These citizens were not only enthusiastic participants; they were also dedicated partisans. "Independents" in those years were treated with contempt as people without spirit or commitment, and few voters were willing to accept the label. Obviously Americans considered it important whether one party or the other won. But given the party overlap on economic matters, the question is: Why?

Politics as Recreation. Entertainment was one force that helped drive the political machinery. Americans of this era enjoyed relatively little leisure time. Most worked on Saturdays, and even Sunday was not a day of rest for everyone. Besides the Fourth of July and Washington's Birthday, there were few legal holidays. Thanksgiving was not celebrated outside New England, while in New England, Christmas, considered a "papist" feast, was just another day in the calendar. A political rally gave working people one of the few occasions to take time off. Employers might not like it, but few dared say no when an American male citizen asserted his God-given right to hear a political speech.

One reason for enthusiastic political participation during the 1880s was the spectacle that politics provided. Here we see a gaslit parade staged for the St. Louis Democratic convention of 1888.

Elections aroused extraordinary interest during the Gilded Age. This picture is of New York's Printing House Square on November 4, 1884. The thousands of spectators are awaiting the announcement of returns on the Cleveland-Blaine contest—despite the rain that may have helped Cleveland win.

Besides providing an excuse to avoid work, political campaigns were diverting. Gilded Age politics was a sport for both spectators and participants. In the absence of television, motion pictures, and professional athletics (except baseball, which had already become the national game), politics was a lively amusement. Contemporaries frequently acknowledged this fact. One reporter described a Republican political rally in Cambridge City, Indiana, in 1876 as "a spectacle no foreign fiesta could equal." Even though most people could not hear the distant speaker, General Harrison, they were perfectly content, for it was "the holiday diversion, the crowds, the bravery of the procession, the music and the fun of the occasion they came chiefly to enjoy." As one late-nineteenth-century observer noted: "What theater is to the French, or the bull fight . . . to the Spanish, the hustings [election campaigns] and the ballot-box are to *our* people."

In part the excitement derived from the closeness of the contests, which, like a tight baseball pennant race, brought out the partisans of both sides in record numbers. When, after 1896, the Republicans forged far ahead of their Democratic rivals and the excitement declined, voter turnouts dropped off sharply.

Like all exciting and well-patronized spectator sports, Gilded Age politics had to have its stars, its heroes, its villains. Many of them were colorful characters. There was James G. Blaine, Republican senator from Maine, the "plumed knight," magnetic, charming, combative, brilliant, and corrupt. His sworn enemy, Roscoe Conkling, Republican senator from New York, was a strutting "turkey-gobbler," whose gorgeous plumage of yellow shoes, scarlet coat, waistcoat with gold lace, and green trousers entranced the voting public and amused his Senate colleagues. There was Thomas B. Reed, the 300-pound-speaker of the House. Ponderous in body but quick in mind, Reed was one of the wittiest men in America and tossed off aphorisms as funny as Mark Twain's: "A statesman is a dead politician"; "One with God is always a majority, but many a martyr has been burned at the stake while the votes were being counted." Men like these alternately delighted and dismayed the voting public and helped sustain the enthusiasm for the Gilded Age politics.

Politics as Morality Play. The metaphor of Gilded Age politics as a sport is useful up to a point. To some Americans—the "best men"—politics during these years seemed rather to be a profound moral drama. It was, these latter-day Puritans believed, a contest between good and evil. The evil was personified by the political rogues who had risen to the top after the Civil War and had perverted the once-virtuous republic. The good was personified by men like themselves—disinterested, dedicated, scrupulous, and expert, who wished only the public good and who, if allowed to govern, would restore America to a state of grace.

Almost all the "best men" were young, though they included some survivors of antebellum reform battles. Many came from the country's most distinguished families: Charles Francis Adams, Jr., and his younger brother, Henry, were the grandsons of one president and great-grandsons of another. Several, however—such as the righteous Carl Schurz and the self-righteous E. L. Godkin—were self-made or foreign-born. Almost all were university educated; most were men of cultivation and refinement.

The "best men" disapproved of contemporary American political life. They believed that both parties were corrupt, and although they were generally nominal Republicans, they avoided partisan allegiance. Almost alone among the politically active people of the era, they voted for candidates and platforms rather than parties and gloried in being "independent." Their tone was one of almost constant outrage—an attitude that often amused the general public. One subscriber to the independent *New York Evening Post* noted that she always felt safe with the paper on her doorstep: "It just lay there and growled all night."

However exaggerated or humorless the response of the "best men" to contemporary politics, their indignation had much to feed on. Scandal after scandal marred state and national politics in the Gilded Age. In many states rings of dishonest businessmen united with corrupt politicians to control the legislatures. In New York the Erie Ring of Jay Gould and his allies bought and sold legislators like cattle. In Pennsylvania it was said that when Thomas A. Scott, president of the Pennsylvania Railroad, finished his business with the state government, the legislature at Harrisburg adjourned. At the federal level the Whiskey Ring, an unholy alliance of federal officials and distillers, bilked the treasury of millions of dollars in revenue taxes. In 1881–1882, the federal authorities uncovered a gang of Post Office personnel that awarded generous contracts to private parties to deliver mail to remote areas (the "Star Routes") in return for kickbacks.

Much of the corruption originated in the desire of businessmen to secure valuable favors that only government could confer. To this extent it is valid to interpret Gilded Age politics as an instrument that served the needs of an aggressive capitalist system. Sometimes, however, the politicians themselves initiated corrupt deals. An example of this were the "strike bills," making illegal some common business practice, that were constantly introduced in the state legislatures. The politicians never intended the bills to pass, but anxious businessmen were willing to pay good money to make certain they did not. After the sponsoring politicos had been properly paid off, the strike bills died quietly in committee.

Corruption spread even to elections. Every year, following some local or national political contest, the newspapers carried long accounts of bribery, stuffing of ballot boxes, illegal voting by aliens, and the use of "floaters," who, to tip a close election, crossed state or county lines to vote illegally. Most of the electoral chicanery took place in the cities and involved local offices. But there were also numerous instances of corruption in national elections, and not all occurred in large urban centers where the foreign-born could be blamed. In fact, one of the most flagrant instances of chronic electoral dishonesty in this era took place in Adams County, Ohio, a rural community composed mostly of old-stock Americans. There, beginning in the 1870s, virtually the entire voting population sold their votes to the highest bidder. Given the near equal strength of parties, it is likely that more than one presidential election was won by voting fraud.

The greatest failing of all, however, as seen by the independents, was the spoils system, which had first emerged during the Jackson era but had come to full flower during the Gilded Age. It grew out of a problem that Americans have never fully solved: how to pay for party government.

Should the party system be supported by ordinary citizens through small contributions and through voluntary labor? Must it be financed by the rich or by special-interest groups seeking to influence legislation? Or, as many Americans have recently come to believe, should it be supported by public funds?

Under the spoils system of the Gilded Age, parties were in effect financed by the government, though scarcely in the form advocated by reformers today. Government support in these years took the form of job patronage, and vast amounts of patronage were available. Government was a major growth industry. Between 1865 and 1891 the federal payroll expanded from 53,000 to 166,000. Even the lowest-paid federal employees earned from two to three times the annual income of privately employed unskilled workers, and they normally spent only eight hours a day at their jobs, in contrast with the ten- to twelve-hour workdays common in private industry.

Men and women, not surprisingly, eagerly sought federal employment. Would-be officeholders worked hard for political candidates and expected patronage appointments in return. Once on the job, appointees were willing to contribute further effort and a portion of their salaries ("assessments") to keep their party in office lest a victorious opposition deprive them of their positions.

The system was wasteful and often inefficient. Although government was becoming ever more complex and technical, the spoils system made flattery, party loyalty, and political knowhow the sole measures of merit. Moreover, when competent people did gain office, they seldom kept their jobs long enough to learn their duties and perfect their skills. At the beginning of each administration the civil service, and consequently the whole federal government, was immobilized while the president sorted out the patronage claims of party supporters all over the country. The spoils system also encouraged outright corruption. Men and women frequently paid cash for their jobs, and advertisements like the following were not uncommon in Washington newspapers during the 1880s:

WANTED—A GOVERNMENT CLERKSHIP at a salary of not less than $1,000 per annum. Will give $100 to anyone securing such a position.

WANTED—BY TWO YOUNG LADIES situations in Government office; will give first month's pay and $10 monthly as long as retained.

The independents condemned the spoils system and demanded civil service reform that would substitute merit (determined by examination) for party loyalty, and tenure in office for constant rotation. But the spoils system was so deeply rooted in American politics that it was difficult to eradicate, although federal officials sometimes adopted merit schemes for their own departments or divisions. In

Both parties long resisted civil service reform, but after Garfield's assassination they could not ignore the clamor for change. The Pendleton Act, by establishing the merit system, made it difficult for politicians to favor members of their families, a practice lampooned in this 1890s cartoon.

James G. Blaine

James G. Blaine traveled two paths, wrote one of his biographers, "one in the daylight that was straight, one in the dark that was twisted as a ram's horn." An idol to millions in his day, Blaine epitomized to many others all that was venal and corrupt in American political life in the Gilded Age.

Blaine was born in Pennsylvania in 1830 of Irish stock. On his father's side he was descended from a line of Scotch-Irish Presbyterians who came to America from Ulster in the 1740s. His mother's family was Irish Catholic from County Donegal. James himself was raised as a Protestant, though his mother never forsook her Catholic faith. His mixed religious background would affect his career in an age when religion was an important determinant of political preference.

Almost from the outset the young Pennsylvanian exhibited the democratic politician's essential qualities: geniality, eloquence, humor, and an excellent memory for names and faces. At Washington College, which he entered at the startling age of thirteen, both his fellow students and his instructors thought him charming. People were drawn to him in a way that gave meaning to the popular adjective of the day: "magnetic."

After graduation, Blaine became an instructor of mathematics and classical languages at a military academy at Georgetown, Kentucky, where many of his students were as old as he was. It was there that he met Harriet Stanwood, a teacher at the local "female seminary," and married her in 1850. Harriet was a New Englander with family roots in Maine. The connection would prove as important as the marriage was happy.

In 1854, after a short stay in Philadelphia, Blaine was offered an opportunity by Harriet's brothers to edit the *Kennebec Journal*, and he left his native state to spend the rest of his career in Maine. Most ambitious young men went west to seek opportunity; Blaine reversed the direction.

Because all newspapers were then party organs, Blaine's editorship of the *Journal* inevitably thrust him into politics. He had arrived in Maine at the time when the Whigs, his original party, were breaking up. Blaine and the *Journal* soon became ardent Republicans, defending the new party's positions on slavery, the tariff, and the territorial issue. In 1859 he became chairman of the Maine Republican State Committee, a post he retained for over twenty years.

Maine was a small state at a far corner of the continent. But it had advantages for Republican politicians with national ambitions. It was a "rock-ribbed" Republican state and could be counted on to reelect its Republican officeholders over and over again. In Congress this practice guaranteed seniority and national prominence.

In 1862, after three terms in the Maine legislature, Blaine was elected to the United States House of Representatives. He arrived in Washington the following year to take part in the exciting events of the Civil War and Reconstruction eras. Blaine was a Radical Republican who distrusted the "rebels" even after they had laid down their arms. He was not an extremist, however, and frequently clashed with Thaddeus Stevens, leader of the most militantly antisouthern Radical faction. Though Blaine was willing to take strong positions, he kept the respect of his colleagues and in 1869 they elected him Speaker of the House, one of the most powerful positions in the federal government.

Blaine presided over the House with a degree of good nature and fairness that won the respect of even the Democrats. But he did make one enemy: the arrogant, supercilious, opinionated Republican congressman from Utica, New York, Roscoe Conkling. In 1866 Blaine and Conkling got into an argument over a bill to create a permanent provost marshal's office in the army. Conkling was sarcastic about Blaine's views on the issue under discussion. Blaine responded in kind, describing Conkling's "haughty disdain, his grandiloquent swell, his majestic, supereminent, turkey-gobbler strut," and concluding that the New Yorker, compared to the truly eloquent Henry Winter Davis to whom he had been likened, was as "mud to marble, dunghill to diamond, a singed cat to a Bengal tiger, a whining puppy to a roaring lion." Conkling never forgave Blaine, and the two men's enmity would affect the course of Gilded Age politics.

During Grant's administration (1869–1877) Blaine became leader of the Republican "Half-Breeds," along with James Garfield and John Sherman of Ohio, and George F. Hoar of Massachusetts. Slightly younger than the "Stalwarts," led by Conkling, John A. Logan of Illinois, Zachariah Chandler of Michigan, and Simon Cameron of Pennsylvania, the Half-Breeds were also less committed to defending traditional Republican obligations to the freedmen and to invoking the Civil War as the basis of party politics in the post-1865 period. But Half-Breed–Stalwart differences over policy were less important than their battles over patronage and appropriations.

It was during the 1876 presidential campaign that Blaine's reputation for financial honesty suffered its first serious blow. Grant's second term was over and he did not as yet harbor third-term ambitions. The field was wide open for another Republican and many believed Blaine the logical choice. But fate intervened when, in April 1876, a director of the Union Pacific Railroad reported that Blaine had received a permanent loan of $64,000 from the UP against the worthless collateral of some Little Rock and Fort Smith Railroad bonds. In effect, the Union Pacific had given Blaine a large gift of money.

The House committee appointed to investigate the charges soon received information that one James Mulligan had letters by Blaine that implied that the Maine congressman had accepted securities in return for favors to the railroad. When Mulligan came to Washington to testify, Blaine intercepted him at his hotel and walked off with the letters Mulligan had intended to give the committee. The following day Blaine himself wove the letters selectively into a brilliant speech on the House floor that obscured the most incriminating portions. The performance dazzled the public, and convinced his partisans that their hero had thoroughly vindicated himself.

But Blaine never fully cleared his name, and at the Republican convention in Cincinnati he saw the presidential nomination go to the governor of Ohio, the colorless but honest Rutherford B. Hayes. It was at Cincinnati that Robert Ingersoll, in the course of his nominating speech, used the phrase "the plumed knight" to describe Blaine. It became his nickname, often used with irony by his detractors.

In 1877 the Maine legislature sent Blaine to the United States Senate. Here he spent most of his time locked in battle with Conkling and positioning himself for 1880. As the struggle for the nomination began, it seemed like a contest between Grant, with his Stalwart supporters, and the Half-Breeds led by Blaine. In the end the Grant and Blaine forces deadlocked and the nomination—and the election—went to Garfield, a friend of Blaine's.

Blaine had not found the Senate as congenial as the House and he welcomed his appointment by Garfield as secretary of state. In the State Department Blaine was a diplomatic activist who believed that American influence in the Western Hemisphere and elsewhere must be expanded. His aggressive support of American interests abroad earned him the label "Jingo Jim." He also acted as Garfield's chief domestic adviser and used his influence to remove his Stalwart enemies from influential office. In New York this led to wholesale dismissals of Conkling's supporters. Whatever satisfaction Blaine felt at Conkling's discomfiture was short-lived. On July 2, 1881, an embittered Stalwart shot the president, who died two months later, leaving Chester A. Arthur, a New York Stalwart, as his successor. Blaine remained in office for a few months more but then resigned to return to private life and write his political memoirs.

As 1884 approached, the "Blaine legion" of loyal supporters once again prepared to make their idol president. This time they got further than ever before. Blaine won the party nomination at Chicago on the first ballot and, for the sake of party peace, chose Stalwart John Logan as his running mate. His opponent in the contest was Governor Grover Cleveland of New York.

To an unusual extent the race turned on Blaine's honesty. By now a substantial portion of the country's educated class, voters often nominally Republican, were "Mugwumps," who felt that the Republican party had lost its moral bearings and existed only for the sake of patronage and plunder. Cleveland was considered a reformer because as governor he had opposed the New York Democratic machine and conducted an honest state administration. The Mugwumps—led by Carl Schurz, former secretary of the interior; George William Curtis of *Harper's Weekly*; E. L. Godkin of the *Nation*; and others—attacked Blaine as corrupt and

a spoilsman. No party, declared Schurz, had any right to expect victory at the polls "without respecting that vital condition of our greatness and glory, which is honest government."

At one point it looked as if the anti-Blaine forces would lose their moral advantage. In July a Buffalo newspaper published an article telling of Cleveland's illegitimate child. This revelation created utter dismay in the reformers' ranks until they rationalized it away as an isolated transgression and one that, in any event, lay in the private rather than the public sphere.

In September the Mugwumps found further ammunition to use against Blaine—a complete, uncensored transcript of the Mulligan Letters, including items not available in 1876. One was a letter from Warren Fisher, Jr., a promoter of the Little Rock and Fort Smith, dictated to Fisher by Blaine, absolving the then Speaker of all blame in the Union Pacific loan incident. Blaine's own letter requesting Fisher to help him had ended with the incriminating phrase "burn this letter." When the Fisher letter and the others were published in the anti-Blaine papers, they confirmed the worst suspicions about Blaine's corrupt relations with the railroads.

In the end Blaine lost the election to Cleveland because the hotly contested state of New York went to the Democrats. Many observers had expected Blaine to carry New York's Irish voters and with them the state. His Catholic lineage, his anti-British attitudes, and his personal warmth and charm were all supposed to be particularly appealing to Irish-Americans. Unfortunately, he failed to reprove the disparaging "Rum, Romanism, and rebellion" charge made against the Democrats by the Reverend Samuel Burchard and consequently lost Irish votes. He had also offended many working men by appearing at "Balshazzar's Feast" in New York, a banquet given in his honor by some of the nation's best-hated "money kings." The two mistakes clearly lost him more than the 1,200 votes that gave the Empire State and the election to the Democrats.

Blaine was not finished with public life. Though his health was poor, he accepted the post of secretary of state once again when it was offered him by Benjamin Harrison in 1889. His second stint as secretary represents America's resumption of a vigorous foreign policy, now more in tune with the public mood. Blaine was especially interested in displacing Great Britain from economic leadership in Latin America, and to this end sought to create an informal "Pan-American" union with the United States as "elder sister."

Though his three years in the State Department under Harrison stand out from the low plain of nineteenth-century American diplomacy, the period was not personally fulfilling. The Blaines resided during the winters in a house close to the State Department, formerly owned by William Seward. They escaped the Washington summer heat at their home in Bar Harbor on the Maine coast. The Blaine's marriage remained happy, but tragedy struck when their eldest son, Walker, died of pneumonia at only thirty-five. Soon after, their eldest daughter, Alice, also died, and in a little over a year their second son, Emmons, was dead as well. Nor did Blaine find much satisfaction in his relations with his chief. Harrison was a distant and aloof man whose personality clashed with that of the outgoing, genial Blaine. In June 1892 Blaine re-

signed his post in a brief, cool letter. Harrison's acceptance was equally brief and formal. Neither man expressed any personal esteem for the other.

Blaine's health had been fast declining and he did not have many months left. The Blaines went to Bar Harbor for the summer of 1892 and then, in the fall, returned to the Seward House in Washington. Suffering from gout and Bright's disease, Blaine took to his bed. Bulletins about his health appeared in the newspapers and the faithful Blaine legion, who had worshiped the man for thirty years, gathered before his house to express their loyalty. He died on January 27, 1893, three days short of his sixty-third birthday. His life had indeed followed two paths, "one in the daylight" and "one in the dark."

1871 President Grant established a commission to study a merit system and recommend a practical program of civil service reform. These moves accomplished nothing. Then, in 1883, after the assassination of President James Garfield by Charles Guiteau, a disappointed office seeker, Congress passed the first federal civil service law, the Pendleton Act. It forbade the assessment of federal employees, made appointments contingent on competitive examinations, and regularized promotions and linked them to demonstrated competence. Presidents Arthur and Cleveland placed some 20,000 federal jobs on the "classified list" of those covered by the new rules. By 1897, when William McKinley became president, 86,000 employees—almost half the federal civil service—were recruited by examination, promoted by merit, and protected by tenure.

The number of men and women who saw national politics as a battle between the forces of light and the forces of darkness never amounted to more than a small minority. But they were a very influential group. Through the pages of Edwin L. Godkin's *Nation* and other journals of criticism and opinion, their views entered the homes of the educated middle class. The independents became a sort of conscience for the nation, and few well-read Americans could entirely resist the feeling that what they supported was virtuous and what they opposed evil.

★ THE BASES FOR PARTY AFFILIATION ★

Viewing Gilded Age politics as an exciting game or as a moral drama tells us something about how and why the political system worked: Americans of this era may not have had much faith in the party system as a way to achieve their economic or material ends, but they did enjoy it as a spectacle. This interpretation does not tell us, however, what distinguished the average Democrat from the average Republican.

The Civil War Legacy.   The Civil War, its antecedents, its Reconstruction aftermath, and the long memories of these emotion-stirring events, helped forge links of shared affection and antagonisms that contributed to party identification.

Republicans regularly "waved the bloody shirt" to appeal to Union veterans and northerners generally. In a typical demagogic bloody-shirt tirade, Republican Oliver Morton of Indiana roared:

Every bounty jumper, every deserter, every sneak who ran away from the draft calls himself a Democrat. . . . Every man who labored for the rebellion in the field, who murdered Union prisoners by cruelty and starvation, . . . calls himself a Democrat. Every New York rioter in 1863 who burned up little children in colored [orphan] asylums, who robbed, ravished, and murdered indiscriminately . . . calls himself a Democrat. In short, the Democratic party may be described as a common sewer, and loathsome receptacle, into which is emptied every element of treason North and South, every element of inhumanity and barbarism which has dishonored the age.

Even when they abandoned the black population of the South to the conservative white "redeemers," Republicans felt guilty about it and were quick to react when southern mistreatment of blacks became too blatant. As late as 1890 a Republican House of Representatives passed a "force bill" designed to reimpose federal supervision of national elections so that blacks were not totally disfranchised by the southern states. Republicans also furiously denounced Grover Cleveland, the first Democratic president since Buchanan, when he returned captured Confederate battle flags to the southern states as a gesture of sectional reconciliation. Black voters, though not numerous in either section owing to disfranchisement in the South and sparse

numbers generally in the North, remembered their champions, Abraham Lincoln and Thaddeus Stevens, and were among the most loyal Republicans in the entire nation.

The Democrats also capitalized on Civil War and Reconstruction memories. In the white South hatred of "Black Republican" emancipation and later Radical Reconstruction policies created a powerful and long-lasting Democratic solidarity. Any white man who voted Republican was branded a traitor by Democratic politicians. By the 1880s, except for a few small dissenting pockets in the former anti-secession mountain regions, it was hard to find a Republican voter in the South. Winning the Democratic nomination for office became tantamount to election. Thousands of transplanted white southerners in the Midwest, sharing the South's racial attitudes, also voted Democratic.

One key component of the Republican coalition was Union veterans. Not only were they energized by bloody-shirt appeals; they were also shamelessly bribed by Republican administrations. Prodded by the Union veterans' organization, the Grand Army of the Republic (GAR), successive Republican Congresses appropriated millions of dollars in pensions for former Union soldiers and their wid-

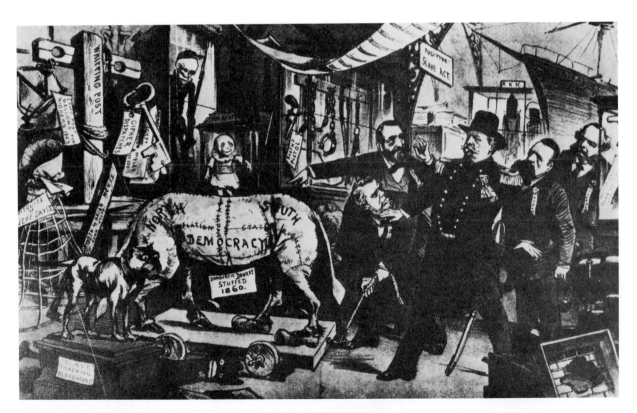

This Republican cartoon, depicting Cleveland surrounded by Democratic leaders, enthusiastically waves the bloody shirt, reminding northerners of the supposed traitorous past of the Democratic party.

ows and dependents. By 1899 the total paid annually by the U.S. Treasury amounted to almost $157 million. One scholar has called the Union veteran pension policy the beginning of the social welfare state in America.

Religion, Race, and Nationality. With each passing year the political hold of the Civil War became a little fainter, especially among northern voters. Yet party loyalty remained intense, and only the most extraordinary scandal or the most lackluster candidate could drive the average voter away from his traditional party allegiance. What tied the voters to their parties so firmly?

Many historians now believe that ethnic and religious factors forged the tightest bonds of Gilded Age party loyalty. During these years the United States was an exceptionally diverse nation. By the 1880s the German, Irish, and Scandinavian immigrants of the 1830–1870 period had put down roots and had emerged as an important political force. In addition, there were now many second-generation, American-born children who combined an understanding of the American political system with a continuing loyalty to their ethnic and religious traditions. It is no surprise, then, that in the generation following the Civil War, cultural loyalties and tensions played a special role in political life.

Religion apparently shaped party loyalties more than nationality or ethnic background. Whatever their national origins, members of the "liturgical" churches, which emphasized "right belief" over personal regeneration, were generally Democrats. The most numerous of the liturgical church groups were the Catholics who since the days of

Jefferson had found a political refuge in the more "popular" of the two parties. Led by religiously tolerant and pragmatic men, the Jeffersonians and then the Democrats had welcomed the Catholic French, Germans, and Irish who crossed the Atlantic before the Civil War, and had catered to their needs. These needs, in part, had been material and practical, and, as we have seen, the predominantly Democratic machines in the cities helped the immigrants with jobs, handouts, and legal aid.

Both parties played this game, but concessions to cultural differences were more difficult for the Republicans, and their Whig predecessors, to make. Catholics wanted more of America than material advantages. They also wanted freedom to pursue their religion, which meant not only formal freedom to worship but also a share of local taxes for Catholic parochial schools and the right of Catholic chaplains to serve in state hospitals and penal institutions. And they wanted the freedom to pursue their customs, which meant being able to consume wine, beer, and whiskey without excessive restriction and to enjoy a "Continental" Sunday without being harassed by the "blue laws" that shut down businesses, forbade work, and banned recreation in many American cities and towns on the Sabbath. Members of other churches that emphasized ritual and well-defined dogma shared these preferences with Catholics; thus Lutherans, Jews, Episcopalians, and Catholics were frequently allied. But Catholics were the largest single bloc of liturgical voters in the country.

Republicans, like their Whig forebears, generally resisted the cultural and religious pressures of the liturgical faiths. The difficulty was not exclusively bigotry but a lat-

State aid to private Catholic schools won support from Tammany Hall, and Republicans charged the "Romish Church" was using the Democratic party to overthrow the American school system. Here Thomas Nast portrays crocodiles with Catholic bishops' miters attacking wholesome innocents, presumably Protestants, while Tammany bosses look on approvingly.

ter-day puritanism that was an essential ingredient in the makeup of rank-and-file Republican voters. Both Whigs and Republicans, each party in its own day, represented evangelical America. Whig-Republican voters were drawn heavily from members of churches that emphasized inner regeneration, personal reformation, and "right behavior." They were mostly native-born Baptists, Methodists, Presbyterians, and Congregationalists; but some were foreign-born Pietists who, like their native-born counterparts, tended to consider politics a vehicle for imposing their moral vision.

In the 1850s evangelicals had helped found the Republican party dedicated to the containment and ultimate extinction of sinful slavery. Through the remainder of the century Republican zeal for public and private virtue was expressed in demands for blue laws and restrictions on the manufacture and sale of liquor and the suppression of "blood" sports such as cockfighting and boxing. Republicans also insisted on strict separation of church and state, since the alternative, they felt, was to allow Catholic influence on public institutions.

Catholics, as well as many Lutherans, resented these efforts to restrict their personal freedoms and limit their influence. Unlike evangelicals, they believed that what citizens did in their personal lives was no business of the state. They also believed that far too many state-supported institutions, though supposedly nonsectarian, were actually dominated by pietistic Protestants. The Democrats naturally took advantage of these resentments. In 1881 the Ohio state Democratic platform declared that the Democrats favored "the largest individual liberty consistent with public order, and . . . opposed legislation merely sumptuary." John ("Bathouse") Coughlin, a Chicago Democrat, warned the voters: "A Republican is a man who wants you t' go 't church every Sunday. A Democrat says if a man wants t' have a glass of beer on Sunday he can have it. Be Democrats unless you want t' be tied t' a church, a schoolhouse, or a Sunday school."

If political puritanism had stopped at the blue laws and equally mild expressions, it might not have polarized the voters. But it did not. In the 1880s the antiforeign, anti-Catholic American Protective Association (APA) demanded the exclusion of noncitizens from American political life, attacked "the diabolical works of the Roman Catholic Church," and pledged to fight for the "cause of Protestantism." During the 1890s the APA bulled its way into several local campaigns as an unacknowledged, but not unrecognized, ally of the Republicans and a champion of "true Americanism" against "aliens" and "papists." However impatient liturgical voters might become at times with their traditional party allegiances, or however tempted to vote for a particularly attractive Republican candidate,

such virulent anti-Catholic and antiforeign sentiment confirmed their view "that personal liberty . . . [was] surely only safe with the Democratic party in power."

Church affiliation and nationality determined not only the voters' party preferences but also those of officeholders. In the 1893 lower house of the Wisconsin legislature, for example, all eight German Catholics were Democrats, as were twelve of the fifteen Irish Catholics and ten of the thirteen German Lutherans. On the other hand, the Republicans were predominantly Scandinavian, British (English, Scottish, and Scotch-Irish), and Yankee Protestants. These ethnic differences between the two parties produced divergent voting patterns in the legislature. Wisconsin Democrats and Republicans agreed on most economic issues, but they fought over social questions. These disagreements were at times so sharp that the atypical Democratic legislator—say, a British Protestant—or the atypical Republican legislator—say, an Irish Catholic—might desert his party on a roll call concerning regulation of liquor or some similar issue to vote with British Protestant or Irish Catholic colleagues of the opposite party.

Although religion was a major determinant of political affiliation, its role in politics was not invariably overt. Politicians recognized that religious conflict violated American ideals of tolerance and that bigotry was politically explosive. Yet local campaigns for legislators, governors, and municipal officials were often thinly disguised confrontations of the opposing liturgical and evangelical points of view. The 1875 gubernatorial campaign in Ohio, for example, was fought ostensibly over the question of greenbacks and inflation. Actually, an important hidden issue was whether Catholic chaplains would be allowed to minister to Catholic convicts in the state prisons.

At other times the religious issue was undisguised. In Wisconsin in the 1890s German Lutherans sharply criticized the Bennett Law, which required all children to attend schools where instruction was in English, seeing it as an attack on their German-language parochial schools. Catholics, with parochial schools of their own, joined the German Protestants in protesting the Republican-sponsored measure. For a while the Bennett Law controversy threatened to disrupt Wisconsin political life. Not until the Democrats repealed the bill was the issue laid to rest.

Religious differences were expressed more often in local political affairs than in national politics, largely because the federal government at the time had little to do with grass-roots social issues such as liquor regulation, education, blue laws, and the other matters that impinged directly on the daily lives of citizens. Yet the national parties were as much defined by cultural-religious issues as the local parties. This effect can be explained by the structure of the party system during the Gilded Age. Far more than today, the major parties were built from the bottom up. Only in presidential election years did the national party machinery become more important than the state, city, and county organizations—and then, generally, only for the brief span of the presidential campaign. Between national elections *Democrat* and *Republican* were little more than labels for collections of state and local organizations. Almost always, the person who voted for a Republican for mayor, state legislator, or governor would also vote for a Republican for Congress and for president. The result was that the national parties were polarized along the same ethnic-religious axis as the local ones, regardless of presidential campaign issues.

The Election of 1884.   Yet even national party politics were not entirely free from direct ethnic or religious confrontation, and at times religion became a significant issue in a national campaign. The most important of these occasions was the 1884 presidential contest between Grover Cleveland and James G. Blaine.

If any visible issue separated Cleveland and Blaine, it was honesty. In 1876 Blaine, the Republican nominee, had damaged his reputation badly by apparently using his power and influence as Speaker of the House of Representatives to procure a land grant for the Little Rock and Fort Smith Railroad. In a dramatic appearance before the House, Blaine had denied the charges against him and had seemed to show that certain incriminating letters from him to the railroad directors in fact proved his innocence. Reading selections from these so-called Mulligan Letters, Blaine created the impression that he had done nothing wrong, and he avoided disgrace. But the charges would not die. Blaine entered the 1884 presidential race with the smell of corruption clinging to him. Then Democratic headquarters in New York received a packet of new letters showing that Blaine's defense in 1876 had been a clever dodge. In mid-September, at the height of the campaign, these letters were published, setting off a major furor.

By contrast, Cleveland seemed above moral reproach, at least in his public life. As mayor of Buffalo and governor of New York, he had endeared himself to the advocates of clean government by taking a stand against the machine politicians and for honest, economical government. In 1884 this record won him the support of the "best men," who deserted the Republicans and worked for Cleveland's election. The Republicans called the turncoats Mugwumps—a derisive term supposedly of Indian origin.

Late in the campaign the Republicans discovered that as a young man Cleveland had fathered an illegitimate child. They were quick to publicize this personal transgression. During the last days of the campaign marching Republicans in New York chanted enthusiastically: "Ma! Ma! Where's my

Pa? Gone to the White House, Ha! Ha! Ha!" The damaging effect of the revelation was blunted, however, by Cleveland's candid admission of his moral slip and by the fact that he had willingly provided financial support for the child.

Despite his clean political record and the support of the Mugwumps, Cleveland fell behind Blaine as the campaign neared its end. New York was the crucial state, and it seemed to be leaning to Blaine. In this situation the Irish vote could determine the winner. Blaine was a Republican, and the Irish did not normally vote Republican. But he was a Republican with a difference: Although a Protestant himself, his mother was a Catholic and his cousin the head of a convent. Moreover, as secretary of state during James Garfield's brief administration, Blaine had badgered and baited the British, had "twisted the lion's tail," a time-honored practice among politicans interested in cultivating the Irish vote. Combined with his personal charm, his kindness, and his verbal brilliance, these acts made him an attractive candidate even to those who seldom voted Republican.

Then, in the last days of the campaign, one of Blaine's supporters undermined his advantage with a foolish remark that deeply offended Catholic voters. The occasion was a meeting between the candidate and Protestant ministers in a hotel lobby in New York. The Reverend Samuel Burchard, in a short address greeting the candidate, remarked: "We are Republicans and don't propose to leave our party and

The 1884 presidential campaign was particularly scandal-ridden. The Republicans thought they had a winning issue when they discovered that Democrat Grover Cleveland had fathered an illegitimate child. In the end Cleveland had less cause for dismay than this Republican cartoon suggests.

identify with the party whose antecedents have been rum, Romanism, and rebellion." The statement, if we discount its obvious hostility, was an accurate description of the Democratic party, most of whose members were opposed to strict liquor regulation, were Catholic, or were southerners. But it violated one of the basic commandments of American political life: Do not insult a man's religion. Blaine, tired and inattentive at this late stage in the campaign, failed to rebuke Burchard, and the remark went out to the country over the wire services.

In a matter of hours gleeful Democrats were distributing Burchard's statement in handbills and posters, and it was plastered over all the newspapers. On Sunday, November 4, Catholic clergymen denounced the slur from their pulpits. On election day, the following Tuesday, Blaine lost New York state by 1,200 votes, and with it the election. The chagrined Republican later told some friends: "I should have carried New York by 10,000 if the weather had been clear on election day, and Dr. Burchard had been doing missionary work in Asia Minor or Cochin China."

Actually, it is not clear precisely what caused Blaine's defeat. Many things could have accounted for Cleveland's hairbreadth victory in New York. But whatever its practical significance, the Burchard slur suggests the power of religious and cultural biases, even at the national level, in Gilded Age politics.

Women were particularly active in Populist politics. Mary Elizabeth Lease, a Kansas lawyer, was among the most effective Populist speakers. She caught the nation's attention when she told Midwest farm audiences to "raise less corn and more hell."

★ PARTY REALIGNMENTS ★

For fifty years cultural values and memories of the Civil War had forged bonds between the voters and the two major parties that were extraordinarily strong. But not every American believed that the Democrats and the Republicans exhausted the range of political possibility. By the 1890s, in fact, there were those who would be singing the words of a new political song: "Good-Bye, My Party, Good-Bye." The discontented westerners and southern farmers discussed in Chapter 19 would break away from the major parties, and in the process inadvertently create a new political era, one dominated by the Republicans.

The Populist Party. In 1892 leaders of the Farmers' Alliances and assorted political dissidents launched the People's Party of the U.S.A., or Populists, at a convention held at Omaha, Nebraska. The Populist leaders were agrarians representing a coalition of sections; the preamble to the new party's platform delivered an agrarian message. The nation was on the verge of ruin as a result of wealth concentration and the power of bondholders, usurers, and millionaires, it said. "A vast conspiracy against mankind" had been "organized on two continents" and was "rapidly taking possession of the world." As a result of this conspiracy, the nation's money supply was totally inadequate for its business, and the consequences were "falling prices, the formation of combines and rings, and the impoverishment of the producing class." The two traditional parties had let the people down. Now, in the impending political campaign, they proposed "to drown out the outcries of a plundered people with the uproar of a sham battle over the tariff, so that capitalists, corporations, national banks, rings, trusts, watered stock, the demonetization of silver, and the oppression of the usurers may be lost sight of."

The Populist platform itself called for "free and unlimited coinage of silver" at a sixteen-to-one ratio with gold, a money supply of at least $50 per capita, a graduated income tax, and a postal savings bank for small savers afraid of private banks. To limit the power of the transportation and communications corporations, the Populists demanded government ownership of the railroads and of the telephone and telegraph systems. The party's land plank demanded that aliens and the railroads be compelled to give up excess land. A section tacked on as an afterthought called for the secret ballot, restrictions on immigration, and an eight-hour work-

What's Wrong with the Major Parties

By the 1880s discontent with the major political parties was growing among several groups in the nation. In the West and South the dissent was led by the Farmers' Alliances. Eventually the mood of dissatisfaction with the Democrats and Republicans exploded as the Populist Revolt of 1892–1896. The document below is by a leader of the Northern Farmers' Alliance and expresses the disenchantment of many agrarians with the two major parties. It is clear that the chief complaint of the writer is with the parties' financial principles. Note also the speaker's moralism.

"The Republican party was born of the spirit of opposition to chattel slavery. It was this principle that gave it life, vitality and power. While this contest was waging it was grand in its conception of right and justice. It taught the inconsistency of slavery growing on the tree of liberty, that the two could not be blended in one harmonious setting; that the cries of the mother who was compelled to part

with her child did not harmonize with the songs of heaven; that the groans of the woman compelled to become a mother without being a wife were not consistent with the teachings of Christianity; that this was intended by the fathers of American liberty to become, and indeed in truth, a free land; that it was a Union of States having a common interest, that it was a land of free churches, free schools and free men. When the contest for these principles was over, and chattel slavery went down amid the boom of artillery, the rattle of musketry and groans of the dying, the Republican party emerged from the conflict with a prestige and glory that commanded the admiration of the world. Flushed with victory, they said in the pride of their heart—like the king of Babylon—see, we have done all this.

"Then the work of despoiling began. . . . The glory of the Republican party has departed. Their bright sun has set in the hopeless misery which their financial policy has entailed upon an enterprising people. Their record on

contraction of the currency, national banks, back salary steals, credit strengthening act, funding schemes and demonetization tendencies should have consigned them to political oblivion long ago, and would, but there was no power that promised any better, and the people were in the hands of corporations and combinations. . . .

". . .Since the war [the Democratic party has] aped the policy of the Republican party on every issue of vital interest to the great masses of the people. They have voted for contraction; they have favored national banks; they have aided the Republicans in their funding schemes; they have voted and worked to strike down silver; they have bowed to Baal; they have worshipped Mammon; they have built unto themselves false Gods, and set them on the hill-tops of freedom; they have courted aristocratic establishments; they have partaken of the spoils; they have received bribes; they have forsaken their principles, and their glory is departed from them forever. . . ."

day for government workers. Populists wanted the tools of direct democracy placed in the people's hands. Citizens should have the power to instigate laws directly by the initiative petition and the right to pass proposed legislation by actual referendum, without the need for Congress and the legislatures to act. And the voters should elect the president and United States senators directly; their choice should not be made by the electoral college or the state legislatures.

The Populist platform of 1892 was in many ways a forward-looking document. Several provisions foreshadowed the programs of the early-twentieth-century progressives and even the New Deal and the modern welfare state. Its overall thrust was the desire to make government more responsive to the popular will, limit the power of large corporations, and reduce some of the worst disparities of wealth. At the same time, it did not directly challenge the existing regime of private property. It is not surprising that several leading social-

ists of the day dismissed the Populists as a "bourgeois party" composed of petty agrarian capitalists.

As the delegates at Omaha adjourned, they faced the difficult task of convincing the voters to drop their traditional allegiances and join their new political organization. The problem promised to be especially difficult in the South, where a third party could crack the white solidarity established by Democrats in the 1870s and maintained by their equally conservative successors, known as the Bourbons. Conservative whites feared that if the Populists successfully challenged the "lily white" Democratic party, blacks might regain a foothold in southern political life.

Some southern Populists were indeed eager to gain black votes. In Georgia Tom Watson promised black voters that if they stood "shoulder to shoulder" with the Populists, they would have "fair play and fair treatment as men and citizens, irrespective of color." In Texas two black men were elected to the Populist executive committee. In North Carolina blacks were given a visible role in the 1892 presidential campaign. But the Populist commitment to racial equality was limited. Populists in southern state legislatures did not differ noticeably from the Bourbons in their desire to keep blacks "in their place," nor were they particularly sensitive to the special social problems that blacks faced beyond those they shared with poor whites. In Tennessee the Alliance members of the legislature endorsed measures to eliminate remaining black voters from election rolls. Tom Watson's *People's Party Paper* supported proposals to segregate blacks from whites on the state's railroads.

In the 1892 presidential election the Populist candidate, James B. Weaver, a former Union general, conducted an energetic campaign. Unfortunately for the Populists' chances, sectional biases left from the Civil War were still strong. Weaver's Union record made him unwelcome in the South. The surviving southern Republicans were willing to vote Populist, but most southern Democrats, whatever their economic or social sympathies, feared breaking the solid white front against restored black rule. On the western Plains the new party did better: In several states the Democrats, the weaker of the two parties, fused with the Populists and ran local candidates on joint "Popocrat" tickets while continuing to support Grover Cleveland for president. In several western states the Democrats merely stole the Populists' thunder by adopting platforms endorsing Populist principles. In the end the Populist ticket won over 15 percent of the vote in the Deep South and higher percentages in the silver-producing mountain states and parts of the Great Plains. Weaver received over 1 million out of 12 million votes cast, or about 8.5 percent. Cleveland won, but the Populist vote promised—or threatened—much for the future.

Unrest Under Cleveland.   Cleveland's second term (1893–1897) was marked by social unrest more stormy than anything the country had seen since the Civil War. In the spring of 1893 the stock market crashed, ushering in a devastating depression. Labor disturbances broke out in many parts of the country as workers struggled desperately to keep their jobs or prevent cuts in pay. It was this climate of fear and anger that set off the Pullman strike of 1894 (described in Chapter 17).

Another manifestation of the times was Coxey's Army, a march of the unemployed on Washington in 1894. Organized by Jacob S. Coxey, an ex-Greenbacker, the march sought to dramatize the plight of the jobless and advertise Coxey's scheme for a federal works program financed by a paper-money issue of $500 million. The experts ridiculed the idea, and when Coxey's 400 bedraggled men arrived in Washington, federal officials arrested their leaders for trampling the Capitol grass.

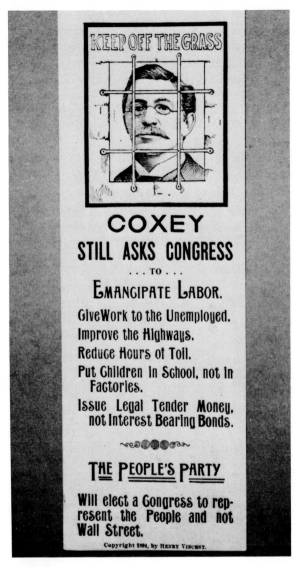

The Washington police arrested Jacob Coxey and several of his followers when they trespassed on the Capitol lawn. But he and his "army" had a serious program to end unemployment and promote economic recovery after the panic of 1893.

The reaction of the Cleveland administration to the distress of the laboring population was at best unimaginative. The president believed that Populist agitation and the government's piling up of silver—required by the Sherman Silver Purchase Act—had set off the panic of 1893 and the resulting economic depression by frightening business and shaking public confidence in the ability of the government to pay its obligations in gold. Whether valid or not, in fact this fear was fast becoming a financial danger in itself. Hoarders were withdrawing more and more gold from the banks and the treasury, and before long the nation would be forced off the gold standard. To stop the gold drain and reassure public creditors, Cleveland pressured Congress to repeal the Sherman Silver Act. Simultaneously he sought to shore up the treasury's gold reserve by selling bonds to the public for gold coin. The public bought the bonds, but then brought more paper money to the treasury to be redeemed for gold. Gold went in one treasury door and out the other. Ultimately, by getting the international investment bankers to guarantee delivery of foreign gold, Cleveland saved the gold standard, but his tactics only confirmed the belief of millions of southerners and westerners that J. P. Morgan, "Wall Street," and the European banking family of the Rothschilds owned the country.

It is against this background of depression, unemployment, and suspicious dealings with the international financiers that we must view the momentous election of 1896. By 1895 the country was restless and uneasy. Many Americans, especially in the West and South, believed that the United States was fast falling under the sway of the "money power." These sections could not be ignored. In the generation since the Civil War the South had regained some of its self-confidence and the West had become an important force in the nation's economic and political life. In 1889–1890, North Dakota, South Dakota, Montana, Washington, Idaho, and Wyoming had been admitted to the Union, adding to

Congress twelve senators who endorsed the West's view of politics and increasing the political power of the silver-mine owners, the chief financial backers of free-silver candidates. For thirty years or more the country's social and economic institutions had been undergoing fundamental change as the United States moved from farming and rural life to industry and cities. Yet despite socialists, anarchists, Greenbackers, and now Populists, the country's political life had changed little. Would the forces of political change now succeed or be beaten back? In the end the American people rejected major alterations in the status quo, but only after a political battle that aroused, among many conservative citizens, fears of anarchy and revolution.

"Bryan! Bryan! Bryan!" Despite the Populists, the arena in which the contending forces fought out their differences was the Democratic party. On one side were the Democratic goldbugs, mostly from the Northeast and the Midwest, who believed that civilization itself rode on the gold standard. On the other side were the many western and southern Democrats, who were equally convinced that humanity could survive and prosper only if silver were restored to the currency system. The Republicans also had silver and gold wings, representing western and eastern attitudes, respec-

Though they criticized Bryan's religious rhetoric, the Republicans had their own pious slogan: "In God we trust, in Bryan we bust." The election's religious flavor is ironic because the issues of 1896 were, ultimately, economic.

tively. But the proponents of silver were stronger among the Democrats.

In addition to their clashing financial views, silverites and goldbugs, particularly within the Democratic party, differed over more fundamental matters. Free-silver Democrats were often indistinguishable from Populists in their agrarian values, their support of direct democracy, of taxes to equalize wealth, and of government regulation of large corporations. Goldbug Democrats resembled the most conservative Republicans in their political and social views.

In June 1896, the Republicans nominated William McKinley of Ohio on a platform pledged to a high tariff, a gold standard (although promising to consider silver if acceptable by international agreement), and an aggressive foreign policy. The gold-standard plank was a bitter disappointment to the Republican silverites, and Senator Henry M. Teller of Colorado and his western friends walked out of the convention.

Bryan ran for president three times. This is a poster from his 1900 second campaign, but you can still see echoes of the first in the slogans.

At the Democratic convention in Chicago the silverites were in the majority. Senator Richard ("Silver Dick") Bland of Missouri was the front-runner as the delegates arrived. But a young ex-congressman from Nebraska, William Jennings Bryan, was also a serious contender. The young Nebraskan had spent many months rounding up support for himself and silver, writing letters, speaking before silverite audiences and Democratic groups, and cultivating the Farmers' Alliances. Rising as the last speaker before the convention voted on whether to endorse a gold-standard or a free-silver platform, he launched into what is probably the most influential address in American party history.

Bryan preferred to avoid polarizing the nation and the party. In answer to the previous speaker, a defender of gold, he pointed out that the man who worked for wages, the "merchant at the crossroads store," the farmer, and the miner were also "businessmen." All were the same and must be treated the same. But then he made clear that the money question did indeed drive a sharp wedge between Americans. "We say not one word against those who live upon the Atlantic Coast, but the hardy pioneers who had braved all the dangers of the wilderness . . . are as deserving of the consideration of their party as any people in this country. . . . It is for these that we speak." He continued:

> You came to tell us that the great cities are in favor of the gold standard; we reply that the great cities rest upon our broad and fertile prairies. Burn down the cities and leave our farms, and the cities will spring up again as if by magic; but destroy our farms and the grass will grow in the streets of every city in the country.

Now followed the moving conclusion that gave the name "Cross of Gold" to the address. If the gold men insisted on the gold standard, the silverites, supported by the "producing masses" and the "toilers everywhere," would fight them to the end. Raising his hands to the sides of his head, with fingers extended, Bryan thundered: "You shall not press down upon the brow of labor this crown of thorns, you shall not crucify mankind upon a cross of gold."

As Bryan finished, he stretched his arms out horizontally, as if crucified himself. For several seconds the crowd was silent, then it burst into frenzied shouts and cheers: "Bryan! Bryan! Bryan!" Amid flying hats and waving handkerchiefs, the delegates lifted the speaker onto their shoulders and carried him off the platform. On July 10, 1896, the Democrats chose Bryan as their candidate and Arthur Sewall, a silverite Maine businessman, as his running mate.

The Election of 1896. What would the Populists do now? At their convention in St. Louis soon after the Democrats had adjourned, they faced a dilemma. Bryan claimed to speak for social justice, but his emphasis was heavily on silver. Many Populists saw free silver as an exaggerated issue. What about popular election of senators, a progressive income tax, government ownership of railroads? According to the Populist journalist Henry Demarest Lloyd, silver was the "cowbird" of the insurgent movement. It would deposit its eggs in another bird's nest and when its young were born they would evict the offspring of the original parents. In effect, silver would crowd out the other issues.

Moreover, Bryan was a Democrat. To southern Populists, especially, the Democrats were the enemy. After fighting the Bourbons for so long, how could they now fuse with them on the candidate at the top of the ticket?

On the other hand, Bryan could win, whereas no Populist could. And, though not a Populist himself, he was a champion of the people and could be expected to fight for social reform. And besides, if he won with the Populists' support, he would be in their debt and they would undoubtedly occupy influential places in the new administration.

Despite misgivings, delegates to the St. Louis convention gave Bryan their nomination as president. Unable to support banker Arthur Sewall, however, they selected Georgia's fiery Tom Watson, one of their own, as their vice presidential nominee.

The campaign that followed was one of the bitterest on record. Both major parties split. A large group of conservative Democrats refused to endorse Bryan and organized a separate "gold" Democratic ticket with John M. Palmer of Illinois at its head. "Silver" Republicans endorsed the Democratic candidates, Bryan and Sewall.

Obviously the underdog, Bryan campaigned hard. Consciously or not, he sought to change the foundation of Gilded Age party alignments. Playing on the hard times, he labored to overcome evangelical allegiance to the Republicans by appealing to class and economic interests. With silver, he declared, times would get better, prosperity would return, and wealth inequalities would be reduced.

Bryan appealed to traditional Republicans by speaking the language that Americans of pious Protestant background understood. Bryan himself was a devout Protestant, raised on the Bible and old-time religion. His earliest ambition had been, he said, to be a Baptist minister; when he became a lawyer and a politician, he never ceased being a preacher. As the Cross of Gold speech implied, free silver to him was more than an economic position; it represented justice and virtue. Gold, on the other hand, was not just the metal of the creditors; it was the source of injustice and oppression. "Every great economic question," Bryan declared as he crisscrossed the country, was "in reality a great moral question." Through the Midwest he called on goldbug sinners to "repent." Wherever the Nebraskan went he was received as an evangelist. In the South and on his beloved prairies, the people treated his rallies like great religious

"Sound Money" was the Republican cry in 1896. But so was a higher tariff.

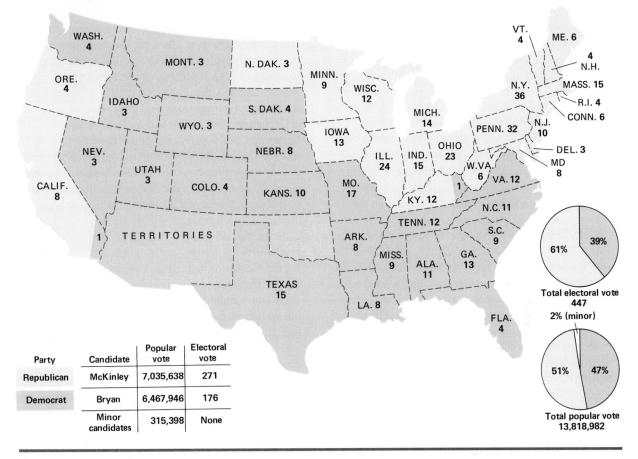

Party	Candidate	Popular vote	Electoral vote
Republican	McKinley	7,035,638	271
Democrat	Bryan	6,467,946	176
	Minor candidates	315,398	None

Total electoral vote 447
2% (minor)

Total popular vote 13,818,982

THE ELECTION OF 1896

camp meetings. The Democratic campaign of 1896 was a crusade.

The Republican campaign was a countercrusade. To conservative Americans, Bryan and his forces were dangerous radicals. Postmaster General William L. Wilson declared that the silver leaders were "socialists, anarchists and demagogues of a dangerous type. . . ." A writer to the *New York Times* asserted that "within six months of Bryan's election mobs would be rushing up and down our streets howling for bread." If Bryan tried to make the free-silver cause a moral issue, so did his opponents. Clergymen denounced free silver as immoral. The *Chicago Tribune* declared that the gold position was a matter of simple honesty. "It is in no respect a question of politics, but of moral principle. It is taking the commandment, 'Thou Shalt not Steal'. . . , and applying it to the Nation."

The goldbugs had the tremendous advantage of money. The Republican national chairman was Cleveland industrialist Mark Hanna, a close friend of McKinley. Hanna was spectacularly effective in convincing the business community to write checks for McKinley and other antisilver candidates. The one important business group that might have contributed to Bryan, the silver-mine owners of the moun-

tain states, proved surprisingly stingy (the price of silver having dropped). To make up for the lack of money, Bryan had only his fierce energy and enormous eloquence.

In the end these were not enough. The public perceived the election as the most critical since 1860 and turned out in record numbers. But the consequence was a resounding defeat for Bryan. The Democratic candidate won 6.5 million popular and 176 electoral votes to McKinley's 7.1 million and 271.

The nature of the vote reveals much about the social and sectional tensions of the 1890s. In New England, the Middle Atlantic region, and the states of the Old Northwest where the Democrat Cleveland had done well in 1892, Bryan carried not a single state. On the Pacific Coast he carried only Washington. In the Great Plains he did much better, taking Kansas, Nebraska, South Dakota, and Missouri. Bryan's real support, however, came from the South and the mountain states. In the South traditional Democratic voters joined with Populists to give Bryan the large majorities that Democratic candidates could invariably count on from the former Confederacy. In the mountain states, however, the Bryan sweep represented a major shift, best explained by the Democratic focus on silver.

If we look more closely at the details of the returns, it becomes even clearer that section rather than class determined how Americans voted in 1896. Despite Bryan's appeal to all "producers," city people voted strongly Republican, except in urbanized mining centers like Butte, Boise, and Denver, where those concerned over monetary issues made up an influential portion of the population. One possible explanation for his failure to win city votes is that Bryan's evangelical fervor repelled many of the urban Catholics and Lutherans who usually voted Democratic. On the other side, Republicans who normally offended Catholic and other liturgical voters were careful to avoid stepping on ethnic toes. Instead, unity and tolerance were major Republican themes. "We have always practiced the Golden Rule," declared McKinley: "the best policy is to 'live and let live.'" There were also economic factors. Rather than splitting the rich from the poor, the self-employed and professional classes from the wage earners, the threat of free silver forged a bond across class lines. Eastern working men saw no advantage for themselves in cheap money. The Republican promise that a new tariff would bring prosperity and "the full dinner pail" seemed more likely than the millennium promised by Bryan.

Nor did Bryan appeal to all rural Americans. Wisconsin dairy farmers, California citrus growers, Iowa and Illinois corn-hog farmers, and New Jersey truck gardeners, for example, saw little reason to take a chance on free silver. Prices for pork, milk, cheese, oranges, and vegetables were good; these farmers had no desire to fiddle with the country's monetary and financial system.

Scholarly partisans of Bryan had charged that the Republicans used coercion to win wage-earner votes for McKinley. Republican employers, they say, threatened to fire Bryan supporters or close their own businesses if the Democrats won. There is indeed evidence of such business pressure. Bankers threatened to call in farm mortgages. The railroads declared they would be forced to shut down if foreign investors were scared away by free silver. Many businessmen were panicked by the free-silver issue and made extravagant statements expressing their fears. But this pressure was probably not decisive. In the end, Bryan and free silver lost because their appeal proved primarily southern and western.

★ CONCLUSIONS ★

The facts are clear: The Republican party did not dominate the political life of the nation during the Gilded Age; nor did the successes it scored imply the triumph of big business over agriculture, labor, and the other interests that made up the country's socioeconomic system. Americans were not indifferent to the economic questions raised by rapid industrialization: the tariff, currency backing, and government regulation of industry. But opposing groups worked within each party to achieve their ends.

In defining themselves politically, moreover, most American voters apparently paid more attention to cultural and religious matters than to class or economic ones. The Democrats, as the party of cultural laissez faire, appealed more to Catholic and other liturgical voters who preferred to keep politics out of private life. The GOP, as the party of "God and morality," to use a Democratic critic's phrase, appealed to those evangelical Protestant groups who saw politics as a vehicle for creating a more virtuous society. Section and race also defined the two Gilded Age parties. White southerners did not easily forget that the "Black Republicans" had crushed the Confederacy, abolished slavery, and tried to impose black suffrage. Northern Union veterans and southern blacks remembered the same things, but with greater affection and to the opposite political effect.

Cultural values and memories maintained the alignment of the parties in the Gilded Age, but the discontent of southerners and westerners disturbed that balance. When Bryan gave voice to many of their complaints as the Democratic candidate in 1896, he weakened the traditional party ties, alienating many Catholic and Lutheran voters as well as eastern workers. After 1896 the Republicans would grow in strength.

That year also marked a change in farmers' fortunes. When prices for cotton and wheat began to rise after the 1896 election, western and southern cultivators lost interest in political insurgency. Farmers continued to be concerned about the abuses of middlemen and the high cost of credit; they still worried about the declining quality of rural life. But they ceased to talk of political revolt. By 1900 the Populist party was dead, and political insurgency as a sectional phenomenon was over.

Although the Populists had often been naive in their analyses and solutions, the problems of industrialization and urbanization they had complained about were real and did not go away. Serious social and economic abuses by the powerful, and inequalities of wealth and power, continued. As the new century began, more and more eastern and urban Americans who had rejected Bryan would come to see that he and his supporters had grasped some important part of American reality. Populism foreshadowed the growth of twentieth-century liberalism. But before resuming the political struggles, Americans would turn their attention to overseas affairs in a way that they had not since the earliest days of the nation.

H. Wayne Morgan, (ed). *The Gilded Age: A Reappraisal* (1970)

Twelve contributors write on civil service reform, labor, the robber barons, science, the currency question, the party system, Populism, foreign policy, popular culture, and the arts. Morgan pulls together the threads with an introduction that emphasizes growing national unity.

Richard Jensen. *The Winning of the Midwest: Social and Political Conflict, 1888–1896* (1971)

Using statistical data, Jensen demonstrates how political affiliations during the Gilded Age were often determined by social and religious values rather than by pocketbook issues. You will find this a challenging example of the "new" political history as practiced by historians armed with computers. For another good example of this genre, see Paul Kleppner, *The Cross of Culture: A Social Analysis of Midwestern Politics, 1850–1900 (1970)*

John G. Sprout. *"The Best Men": Liberal Reformers in the Gilded Age* (1968)

A fine study of Gilded Age reform focusing on the Liberal Republican movement of 1872 and the later Mugwumps. Sprout sees these people as out of touch with the harsh realities of their time and he calls their brand of reform the "politics of nostalgia."

Irwin Unger. *The Greenback Era: A Social and Political History of American Finance, 1865–1879* (1964)

Deals with post–Civil War finance as an example of who controlled political power in the Gilded Age. The author of *These United States* tends to be partial to this work.

David Rothman. *Politics and Power: The United States Senate, 1869–1901* (1966)

Rothman shows how the United States Senate changed from a leaderless group of politicians during Reconstruction to a tightly organized and immensely powerful "millionaires' club" by the beginning of the twentieth century. He analyzes recruitment patterns for Senate seats, state party structures, and lobbying practices.

Morton Keller. *Affairs of State: Public Life in Late-Nineteenth-Century America* (1977)

A meaty book, one that attempts to show how the social and economic transformation of the nation between 1865 and 1900 was reflected in its political life. Deals with changes in state as well as national government and with law as well as politics. Keller sees the Civil War as expanding the scope of government for some years following 1865.

Matthew Josephson. *The Politicos, 1865–1896* (1938)

The classic older treatment of Gilded Age politics. According to Josephson, the political leadership of the period was thoroughly unprincipled. Politicians either blackmailed businessmen for their own gain or, after the civil service reform of the 1880s, were the corrupt tools of big business.

Thomas Beer. *The Mauve Decade: American Life at the End of the Nineteenth Century* (1926)

Another classic treatment of the Gilded Age. "Americans have no political ideas," writes Beer. "They follow leaders who attract them or know how to manage them. The kind of political leaders they like are human circuses." In other words, Beer endorses the concept that Gilded Age politics was a kind of spectator sport.

Allan Nevins. *Grover Cleveland: A Study in Courage* (1932)

The Gilded Age has not inspired political biographers, despite the color of its politicians. The best political biography for the era remains this older work by a master of narrative history, Allan Nevins.

Mark Twain and Charles Dudley Warner. *The Gilded Age* (1873)

Fictional Senator Dilworthy (modeled on a real senator, the corrupt Samuel C. Pomeroy of Kansas) exclaims: "I think I can say, and say with pride, that we have some legislatures that bring higher prices than any in the world." This satire of the "all-pervading speculativeness" in business life and corruption in politics gave the Gilded Age its name.

Mary R. Dearing. *Veterans in Politics: The Story of the G. A. R.* (1952)

A study of the Civil War Union veterans' organization, the Grand Army of the Republic, as a political pressure group and a bulwark of the Republican party after 1865.

Richard Hofstadter. *The Age of Reform: From Bryan to FDR* (1955)

The first third of this important and influential interpretation of American reform deals with Populism. Hofstadter sees Populism as a backward-looking movement of men and women who were trying to restore a vanished rural age. He says they were also much given to conspiracy theories to explain why the times were out of joint.

John D. Hicks. *The Populist Revolt: A History of the Farmers' Alliance and the People's Party* (1931)

This is the standard older treatment of late-nineteenth-century agrarian insurgency. Hicks sees the Populists as the forerunners of later liberalism.

Lawrence Goodwyn. *Democratic Promise: The Populist Movement in America* (1976)

An impassioned defense of the Populists against their detractors (such as Hofstadter). Despite the breadth of coverage implied by the title, this is really a study of southern Populism.

Louis W. Koenig. *Bryan: A Political Biography of William Jennings Bryan* (1971)

The best one-volume biography of Bryan. Fair without being enthusiastic. By a political scientist, but good nonetheless.

Paul Kleppner. *The Cross of Culture: A Social Analysis of Midwestern Politics 1850–1900* (1970)

Kleppner's book is the pioneer study of Gilded Age cultural politics. Interesting but not a conventional "good read."

21★

THE AMERICAN EMPIRE

Why Did the United States Look Abroad?

1853–54	Commodore Perry opens American-Japanese trade
1867	Secretary of State Seward negotiates the purchase of Alaska and American control of the Midway Islands
1868	Ulysses S. Grant elected president
1869–70	Grant attempts to annex Santo Domingo
1877	Rutherford B. Hayes becomes president
1878	Coaling station at Pago Pago established
1880	James A. Garfield elected president
1881	Garfield is assassinated; Chester A. Arthur becomes president
1883	Congress appropriates funds to build modern naval vessels
1884	Grover Cleveland elected president
1887	The U.S. secures a naval base at Pearl Harbor
1888	Benjamin Harrison elected president
1890	The McKinley Tariff Act • Alfred Thayer Mahan's *The Influence of Sea Power upon History* published
1892	Grover Cleveland elected president
1893	American planters organize coup d'état in Hawaii • Frederick Jackson Turner's *The Significance of the Frontier in American History* published
1895	U.S. disputes British claims in Venezuela
1896	William McKinley elected president
1898	The *Maine* is sunk in Havana harbor • Congress declares war on Spain • Congress votes to annex Hawaii • Treaty of Paris: Spain surrenders the Philippines, Puerto Rico, and Guam, and frees Cuba
1899–1900	Secretary of State Hay writes the Open Door Notes • The Boxer Rebellion
1899–1902	Emilio Aguinaldo leads a guerrilla war against the American occupation of the Philippines
1901	McKinley assassinated; Theodore Roosevelt becomes president • The Platt Amendment affirms American right to intervene in Cuba • The Hay-Pauncefote Treaty allows the United States to build a Central American interocean waterway
1903	Hay-Bunau-Varilla Treaty gives the United States the Canal Zone
1904	Roosevelt states Monroe Doctrine Corollary

*I*n April 1898 Albert Beveridge, a young, ambitious Indiana Republican, spoke to Boston's Middlesex Club on the occasion of former President Grant's birthday. The Spanish-American War had just been declared, and although the fighting had scarcely begun, Beveridge looked ahead to what would follow the expected American victory.

American factories are making more than the American people can use; American soil is producing more than they can consume. Fate has written our policy for us; the trade of the world must and shall be ours. . . . We shall establish trading posts throughout the world as distributing points for American products. We will cover the ocean with our merchant marine. We will build a navy to the measure of our greatness. Great colonies governing themselves, flying our flag and trading with us, will grow about our posts of trade. Our institutions will follow our flag on the wings of our commerce. And American law, American civilization, and the American flag will plant themselves on shores hitherto bloody and benighted, but by those agencies of God henceforth to be made beautiful and bright.

In this brief burst of oratory Beveridge summarized virtually every motive that contemporaries—and later scholars—would advance for America's overseas thrust during the generation following the Civil War. The American people needed markets for their surplus manufactures and farm products; they envisioned the glorious Stars and Stripes waving around the globe; they foresaw American civilization conferring immense benefits on the "benighted" peoples fortunate enough to fall under United States dominion. And all this was to be accomplished by the "agencies of God." Glory, Gold, and God all justified an American empire in 1898—as they had a Spanish empire in 1498 and a British empire in 1598.

The resemblance between historical phenomena spread over 400 years is striking, and it is tempting to assume that not much had changed in the interval. But nineteenth-century Americans were not fifteenth-century Spaniards or sixteenth-century Englishmen. Even if they had the same general motives for expansion as their predecessors, these motives were expressed in different ways and were present in different proportions. How can we explain America's expansionist impulse during the years immediately preceding our own century?

★ THE BACKGROUND ★

Viewed one way, post–Civil War expansionism seems an extension of the American past. For 250 years following the first permanent European settlements along the Atlantic Coast, the American people had pushed steadily westward toward the Pacific. Americans often think of this movement as the filling in of an empty continent and the conquest of nature. But the vast interior of North America was not devoid of people: It was occupied by several million Indians, who resisted the settlers' thrust and were pushed aside. Parts of what later became the United States, moreover, were under the sovereignty of European nations, and Americans used aggressive diplomacy and military force to incorporate these areas into the United States. In one sense, then, the overseas thrust following 1865 was merely a continuation of what had preceded. Having run out of "Wests," expansionist Americans sought new frontiers on other continents and on the islands off their shores.

Besides noting this continuity with the past, any theory of post–Civil War expansionism must consider the immediate international context. Expansionism is an expression of unequal power. As the Western world's advantage over the non-Western world increased during the nineteenth century, the temptation to use that advantage grew irresistible. The closing decades of the century witnessed the last burst of European colonialism. In Africa, the Pacific Islands, and East Asia the European powers were on the move, seizing territory, until the remotest regions were firmly under European control. All the great Western nations, as well as newly westernized Japan, vied for influence and trade in China, a vast but weak and disintegrating empire and a potentially rich market for industrial goods. America in these decades surpassed its competitors on every index of wealth; inevitably, this view holds, it felt the same urge as the other industrial nations to impose its will on others.

Post–Civil War expansionism clearly had an economic dimension. Marxist analysis asserts that modern imperialism can be explained as a way that strong, advanced capitalist nations avoid serious internal problems by preying on weak, precapitalist ones. In the Marxist view such advanced societies reach an economic saturation point through years of development. They have difficulties finding markets for their goods and outlets for their capital at home, and so turn to weaker societies to exploit. In this way—through imperialism—they are able to stave off social upheavals and achieve internal stability.

This description may fit European imperialism, but it clearly does not explain the American equivalent. Until well into the twentieth century the United States was itself more of an economic colony than an economic imperialist. Few Americans had investments abroad; rather, millions of European pounds, francs, and marks were invested in American railroads, government bonds, and land. Nor did the United States depend on foreign markets for its economic survival. The enormous home market was far from saturated with goods. American agriculture, it is true, relied on foreign consumers; but the consumers were in countries such as Britain, France, and Germany. These nations were in no danger whatever of becoming America's colonies.

And yet we cannot dismiss economic motives entirely. Even though the American economy did not depend on foreign trade, much less colonies, during hard times like the late 1870s and the early 1890s, many business people, farmers, and politicians became fearful that unless the country could find overseas outlets for its surplus goods, it would be forced to keep its machines, factories, and labor force idle. It is the rhetoric of these periods that lends itself to the theories of Marxist economic determinists. In reality, business people and farmers seldom believed that actual colonies, politically controlled by Washington, were essential to the country's economic health; but they did demand that the American government do what it could to open markets for American goods abroad. Groups of intellectuals and some politicians then carried the prescription for prosperity one step further: Why not guarantee captive markets and outlets for surplus capital by actual political control? These men, few in number but often in positions of power and influence, would form a vanguard for imperialism after 1865.

★ THE BEGINNINGS OF AMERICAN OVERSEAS EXPANSION ★

The story of American overseas expansion does not begin abruptly in 1865. Before the Civil War southerners had strongly favored the absorption of Spanish-controlled Cuba into the United States, and in 1854 President Pierce had offered Spain $130 million for the island. In the same decade American adventurers and soldiers of fortune had fomented revolutions in Central America with the purpose of annexing territory to the United States. In the Far East the United States had pursued an aggressive policy of encouraging American trade, which culminated in the two visits of Commodore Matthew Perry and an American naval squadron to Japan in 1853–1854. Perry forced the Japanese government, virtually at gunpoint, to open its doors to foreign trade and traditional diplomatic relations.

The Civil War brought these expansionist activities to a sudden halt. Both South and North were too caught up in the battle for survival to concern themselves with overseas adventures. But after Appomattox, despite the continued distractions of Reconstruction, Americans once again looked with interest toward the surrounding oceans and the lands that dotted and bordered them.

Foreign Policy Under Seward. The man who gave concrete shape to this revived interest in the outside world between 1865 and 1869 was Secretary of State William Henry Seward, chief formulator of American foreign policy during the presidency of Andrew Johnson. Seward's interest in American expansion had its practical, strategic side. The nation's difficulties in dealing with the Confederate ships raiding northern commerce during the Civil War had convinced him that the United States must have naval bases and coaling stations scattered around its perimeter to fend off any future naval aggressor. But Seward's interest was also based on a romantic vision of a benevolent American empire that resembled the Manifest Destiny of the 1840s. In 1867, in a burst of poetry surprising in a man so practical and businesslike, Seward announced:

> Our nation with united interests blest,
> Not content to pose, shall sway the rest;
> Abroad our empire shall no limits know,
> But like the sea in boundless limits flow.

Before he could consider expansion, however, Seward had to attend to the nagging problem of European intrusion into the Western Hemisphere. In 1863, while the United States was preoccupied by the Civil War, the French had established a puppet regime in Mexico under Archduke Maximilian of Austria and had sent troops to support him against Mexican patriots led by Benito Juárez. The French occupation of Mexico was a clear challenge to the Monroe Doctrine of 1823, which stated that any attempt by the major European powers "to extend their system to any portion of this hemisphere," would be considered "dangerous to . . . [the] peace and safety" of the United States. When the war ended, Seward told Napoleon III, the French emperor, that the United States would no longer tolerate Maximilian's rule in Mexico. Growing opposition at home, the cost of maintaining troops in America, and the threat of the seasoned Union army just across the border induced the French to withdraw their support of the puppet regime in 1867. Shortly thereafter, Maximilian was captured by Juárez's forces and executed.

Seward's success in expelling the French was applauded by the Mexican people. For once, the Monroe Doctrine had served Latin America as an effective shield against European aggression. Seward's fellow citizens were also delighted at having forced Napoleon III to abandon his ambitions in the Western Hemisphere.

But neither Latin Americans nor citizens of the United States greeted Seward's expansionist moves as warmly. Most Americans had other things on their minds than overseas possessions and were either indifferent or stubbornly opposed to empire building. When Seward tried to buy land for a coaling station in Santo Domingo (the Dominican

Republic), Congress refused to support him. He also could not get Congress to approve a treaty to purchase the Danish West Indies (now the U.S. Virgin Islands). Critics of the secretary had a field day with these island-shopping trips. A mock advertisement in a New York newspaper ran: "A Few West India Islands Wanted.—Any distressed persons having a few islands to dispose of in the Spanish Main can find a purchaser by applying to Washington D.C. . . ." The only islands that Seward ever managed to acquire were specks of land a thousand miles west of Hawaii: the Midway group. Seward's only major success was Alaska.

"Seward's Folly." Alaska, in Russian hands for many years, had been exploited by the Russian-American Company for its furs. By the mid-nineteenth century the fur trade had begun to decline, and the Russian government faced the prospect of having to rescue the company from bankruptcy. It was also feared that in a war with Great Britain, Russia would not be able to protect her distant colony. Uncertain of Alaska's defenses and unwilling to support it financially, the czar decided to sell it to the United States.

The American secretary of state was more than willing to talk terms. Seward saw Alaska not only as a base for American naval defense in any Pacific war but also as a way station to the Far East and the potential markets of China. But many outspoken Americans, including many in Congress, were opposed to acquiring a distant, unknown,

This 1867 cartoon showing President Johnson and Secretary of State Seward welcoming "our new senators" pokes fun at "Seward's Folly," the purchase of Alaska from Russia. Many Americans had little faith in Alaska's ability to become a modern community. (Note: The penguin on the left was not found in Alaska; it was an Antarctic bird!)

and apparently worthless chunk of land. Those who had ridiculed Seward's Caribbean interests promptly labeled his new scheme "Seward's Folly" and the territory itself "Seward's Icebox." A weekly newspaper reported that the benefits of buying Russian America included a bracing climate, a promising ice crop, and cows that gave ice cream instead of milk. At the very least, many Americans felt, the $7.2 million that the Russians wanted was a high price for half a million square miles of desolate mountains, ice, tundra, and scrub forest.

Seward responded with a major sales campaign. He secured testimonials from experts describing the region's vast resources. He collected statements from the newspapers of 1803 attacking the Louisiana Purchase to show his opponents as foolish, timid men without vision or foresight. With the help of Charles Sumner, the influential chairman of the Senate Foreign Relations Committee, he induced the Senate to pass the treaty annexing Alaska. When the House of Representatives balked at appropriating the necessary money, the Russian minister plied the reluctant House members with cash. In the end it all worked out. On October 18, 1867, the American flag was raised over the Russian fort at Sitka. Alaska was now American territory.

A Stronger Navy. Then for almost two decades following Seward's retirement, the American people turned inward. In 1869–1870 the Senate rejected President Grant's attempt to annex all of Santo Domingo, and thereafter the expansionist impulse subsided. During the 1870s and 1880s much of the nation's energy was consumed in filling in the rest of the continent with farms, railroads, mines, factories, and new cities and towns. With so much of the interior still undeveloped, there seemed little reason to seek out new lands across the seas. So remote and unimportant did America's foreign relations appear that as late as 1889 the *New York Sun* could half seriously suggest doing away with the diplomatic service as "a costly humbug and sham" that did "no good to anybody."

Yet even during this low point of diplomacy, there were rumblings of a revived interest in foreign concerns and a new aggressiveness toward the outside world. At first the new mood manifested itself as anxiety about American naval impotence. Of the 1,900 vessels in the fleet in 1880, only 48 could fire a gun. Citizens began to wonder how the country could protect itself against foreign attack.

In 1878 the new concern led to a treaty with the ruler of the island of Samoa establishing an American naval coaling station at Pago Pago. In 1883 Congress authorized four new steel ships capable of defending the country's coasts, adding the high-seas battleships *Texas* and *Maine* to the fleet in the next few years. These additions made Americans breathe a little easier, but the American navy remained primarily a defensive force.

The battleship Maine was a product of the "new navalism" just beginning in the 1880s. This 1880 photograph shows it under construction at the Brooklyn Navy Yard. Its building was an example not only of the change in America's international outlook, but also of the new technology of steel construction. But note the wood scaffolding.

Then, in the 1890s, the United States began to construct a high-seas fleet that could support an ambitious foreign policy. The inspiration for the "new navalism" was the writings of Captain Alfred Thayer Mahan, a career naval officer who in 1886 went to teach at the Naval War College at Newport, Rhode Island. Mahan believed that nations must either expand or die, and that naval power was the key to expansion. In *The Influence of Sea Power upon History*, published in 1890, he described how Britain had become the greatest nation in the world by seizing command of the seas. America must now strive to equal Great Britain or accept eventual decline.

Mahan's book enjoyed a great vogue. It confirmed the views of those who were ready to look outward; it convinced many who remained dubious of colonialism that the country must have a navy second to none. Spurred on by Mahan's ideas, during the 1890s the United States built numerous fast vessels with long cruising ranges, capable of meeting an enemy anywhere in the world. By the end of the decade the naval building program had created a high-seas fleet consisting of seventeen steel-sided battleships, along with six armored cruisers and numerous modern smaller craft.

"Jingo Jim" Blaine.   Navalism, though a sign of change, did not end the country's isolationism, and Americans as a whole remained uninterested in foreign concerns. James G. Blaine, secretary of state under James Garfield (1881) and again under Benjamin Harrison (1889–1892) felt differently. Blaine was not a man to sit in his office and shuffle papers. Jingo Jim* was particularly interested in Latin America. Like many Americans since Monroe's day, he believed that the United States had a special big-brother role to play in the Western Hemisphere, and he advocated stronger ties among the nations of the New World, a policy he referred to as "Pan-Americanism."

---

*A *jingo* was an aggressive patriot willing to fight at the drop of a hat to protect the nation's interests. The term comes from a British song of the late 1870s expressing a combative attitude toward Russia during an international crisis.

Blaine's interest in Latin America combined altruism and economic gain in roughly equal parts. The United States imported from Latin American countries almost $100 million worth of goods more a year than it exported to them. Although it bought large quantities of foodstuffs and raw materials from its southern neighbors, they continued to buy most of their manufactured goods from Europe. Blaine hoped to divert the flow of Latin American trade from Europe to the United States, but he feared that improved economic relations would be impossible if the Latin American nations continued to squabble constantly among themselves. If the United States could act as a peacemaker and a stabilizing influence in the Western Hemisphere, everyone would benefit. Good deeds would bring good profits.

In 1881, Blaine called an inter-American conference to meet in Washington to further these goals. Before it could assemble, President Garfield was assassinated. Blaine soon resigned as secretary of state, and his successor in the State Department canceled the conference. Blaine got another chance during the second round of his "spirited diplomacy" under President Benjamin Harrison. In October 1889 representatives of seventeen Latin American states convened in Washington at Blaine's invitation. The results, from Blaine's point of view, were mixed. The delegates rejected the secretary's pet project, a Western Hemisphere customs union designed to increase United States–Latin American trade and curtail trade with Europe. They also turned down his proposal for establishing procedures to handle inter-American disagreements. The conference was not a total failure, however. It set up the Pan American Union as a clearinghouse for distributing information and furthering cooperation between Latin America and the United States, and it provided a model for further hemispheric solidarity.

A New Frontier.   Blaine's career suggests that even during this low point in diplomacy, Americans never completely lost their interest in international affairs. But a vague interest is a long way from expansionism. Then, in the last two decades of the century, thoughtful men and women began to reconsider fundamentally their country's place in the world.

The process was inspired by a paradoxical mixture of arrogance and fear. During the 1880s and 1890s a sense of crisis seized many middle-class Americans. The country seemed to be in turmoil. Populism, labor unrest, and growing radicalism were threatening the nation's stability. What was responsible for these dangers and what could be done about them? As they struggled for understanding, many people turned to political seers and social prophets for help. In these years they encountered a persistent theme: The United States had run out of physical space.

James G. Blaine was much beloved and much despised, about par for a Gilded Age politician.

This new idea found several expressions. Its most influential spokesman was the historian Frederick Jackson Turner who, in 1893, in a paper delivered to the American Historical Association, announced that the frontier experience was over. According to Turner the frontier had ended in 1890 when the Census Bureau had ceased to mark the line on its official maps where population dropped to less than two persons per square mile. For almost three centuries, he noted, the "West" had provided a constructive outlet for social discontents and had encouraged social and political democracy. Now it was gone and a vital chapter in American history had closed. Turner did not propose moving the American frontier overseas, but he raised in the minds of the educated the frightening prospect of growing inequality and social chaos if America could not find some alternative to continental expansion.

The Reverend Josiah Strong made the solution explicit. In his popular book *Our Country* (1885) he asserted that since the free land was gone, the United States would soon "approximate European conditions of life," marked by class conflict and gross inequality. To avoid these afflictions, America must leap the oceans and find new frontiers abroad where its civilization would have room to expand. "I believe it is fully in the hands of the Christians of the United States, during the next ten or fifteen years," wrote Strong, "to hasten or retard the coming of Christ's kingdom in the world by hundreds, and perhaps thousands, of years. We of this generation and nation occupy the Gibraltar of the ages which commands the world's future." Though Strong's vision combined Protestant missionary zeal and American expansionism, his advocacy of expanded foreign missions was lost in the defense of American destiny.

Strong and Turner derived their insights from history and sociology; another group of expansionist thinkers extracted theirs from science, or pseudo-science. Social Darwinists, as we saw in Chapter 17, viewed the competition among nations and peoples as a necessary continuation of the struggle for survival that fueled biological evolution. In this struggle the strong would win and gain dominion and the weak would fail and be enslaved. The result might appear immoral and heartless, but it would further human progress.

At its most extreme, social Darwinism tipped over into the "scientific" racism of Madison Grant, John Fiske, John W. Burgess, and others. These men believed in the "natural superiority" of the Nordic and Anglo-Saxon peoples. Grant, who was associated with the Museum of Natural History in New York, used notions of the superiority of northern Europeans primarily to justify immigration restrictions. Other racists insisted that this superiority gave Americans the right to rule "inferior peoples." Fiske, a philosopher and historian, noted that the Anglo-Saxons had always been conquerors. Now, in the nineteenth century, they could not give up their "sovereignty of the seas" and "their commercial supremacy." Burgess, a professor of political science at Columbia University, taught his students that people of English origin were particularly well suited to the establishment of national states and were destined to impose their political institutions on the rest of the world.

In future years, when Americans considered the morality of colonialism, they would ease their consciences by recalling the inherent "inferiority" of the world's brown-skinned and black-skinned races. Ironically, racism could also be used to argue against maintaining colonies. When it came time to decide whether to keep the Philippines, the spoils of the Spanish-American War, some of the most unashamed racists in the country advised against trying to incorporate the millions of "little brown brothers" into the nation's body politic.

The Foreign Policy Elite. The Americans who read the works of Turner, Strong, Grant, and the other expansionist scholars belonged to the literate middle class. Their interest in foreign policy was probably marginal to their lives, and although their views were important, they did not directly affect foreign policy decision making. Closer to that process was what one scholar has called "the foreign policy elite." These were people scattered across the nation who were seriously concerned with what went on in the world. Strategically located in government, journalism, the universities, the professions, and business, they influenced public opinion, Congress, and the State Department out of proportion to their numbers. Their concerns were not primarily economic but grew out of their cosmopolitanism and their interest in world affairs.

Many members of this elite were admirers of imperialist France or England, and French or English policies shaped their attitudes toward American foreign policy. To many it seemed a shame that the United States, as strong as any of the great European colonial powers, had so far held back. America's restraint, they said, had encouraged Europe to consider it unimportant in international affairs outside the Western Hemisphere. Few European countries, they noted, assigned ambassadors to Washington, being content with ministers or lesser diplomatic representatives. A colonial empire promised to end this inferiority and propel the United States into the ranks of the world powers, where they believed it belonged.

★ HAWAII AND VENEZUELA ★

Toward the end of the 1880s, then, expansionist sentiment and national assertiveness began to reemerge among the decision-makers and the public at large. Early in the 1890s the phrase "Manifest Destiny" began to appear once more in political platforms; in 1893 Congress created the rank of ambassador to replace that of minister. Yet for some years Americans' interest in overseas matters would continue to vacillate as the experience with Hawaii illustrates.

Ambivalence About Expansion. The strategic value of the Hawaiian Islands had been recognized ever since their discovery by Captain James Cook in 1778, and Americans had been active there for many years. In the early nineteenth century American merchant ships en route to China often stopped at the beautiful islands for fresh water and supplies. In 1820 the first American missionaries arrived and devoted themselves to bringing their Christian faith to the native Polynesian peoples. Whalers soon came to the island kingdom, and the whaling crews, long without women, helped to undo the missionaries' efforts to improve Hawaiian morals.

The sons of the missionaries, along with other American settlers attracted to the islands, made sugar growing rather than soul saving their chief concern and eventu-

Alfred T. Mahan

No single person, of course, was responsible for American expansionism at the end of the nineteenth century. The events that culminated in the war with Spain in 1898 and the acquisition of an American empire are bound up in an intricate criss-cross of forces, institutions, values, personalities, and accidental circumstances. Yet no explanation of the nation's post–Civil War outward thrust can ignore the role of a tall, balding, intellectual naval captain, Alfred Thayer Mahan.

Mahan's father was an army officer and engineering professor at the military academy at West Point when Alfred was born in 1840. If Alfred's story had been typical, he would have become an army officer himself. But Professor Mahan and his wife did not believe that a military life was desirable for their son and sent him to Columbia College in New York for a conventional education. Alfred, for his own part, had developed a fascination for the sea from his boyhood reading and defied his parents' wishes. In 1856 he convinced his local congressman to appoint him to the United States Naval Academy at Annapolis.

Acting Midshipman Mahan, with two years of college, was ahead of most of his classmates and was therefore given advanced standing at the academy. This advantage alone would have made him unpopular with his classmates, but in addition, Mahan was a reserved young man more interested in reading than in the rough games of the typical Annapolis cadet. He also had a priggish streak. Upperclassmen were expected to report lowerclassmen for infractions of the rules. However, they exempted themselves from the practice. Mahan insisted on treating his fellow seniors like everyone else, and was soon on speaking terms with few of them.

In June 1859 Mahan graduated from the academy and was assigned to the frigate *Congress* for his first long tour of sea duty. His experience on the *Congress* taught him much about ships and navies in the age of sail, knowledge that would be invaluable to him when he undertook his histories of sea power. While on station off the coast of Brazil, the crew of the *Congress* learned of the secession of the southern states and the ship quickly returned home.

Lieutenant Mahan spent most of the next four years on blockade duty off the Confederate coast. Though vital for Union victory, the duty was routine and monotonous. One event of the war stood out for Mahan, however. In December 1864, while serving with Admiral Dahlgren's squadron off Georgia, he was able to present his father's greeting to William Tecumseh Sherman, Professor Mahan's former student at "the Point," when his army reached Savannah after their march to the sea.

The end of the war was followed by the precipitous decline of the U.S. Navy. Appropriations were drastically cut and thousands of officers and men left the service. Ships were neither repaired nor replaced. By 1874, a military publication noted, the navy was "a heterogeneous collection of . . . trash."

During these years of retreat Mahan served aboard a succession of creaky vessels in Europe, the Far East, South America, and other places. In June 1872 he married Ellen Evans of New York. Like all navy wives, Mrs. Mahan was forced to accept her husband's long absences at sea, punctu-ated by leaves and occasional longer periods of shore duty. She was not happy with the arrangement, but she kept busy raising the Mahan children and serving as hostess when the captain was at home.

In these early postwar years Mahan was opposed to expansion and an aggressive foreign policy. During the 1884 Blaine–Cleveland presidential campaign, he thanked God that the jingoistic Blaine was not president. "If that magnetic statesman were in office," he wrote a friend, "I fancy that American diplomats would be running around in the [ships'] with lighted candles."

But American attitudes toward expansion, including Mahan's, would soon change. In 1885 Admiral Stephen Luce induced the navy to establish the United States Naval War College to help revitalize the service. This would be a sort of graduate school for commissioned naval officers where they would study naval history and tactics. Many "old sea dog" types opposed the scheme, and for its first decade the War College, located in Newport, Rhode Island, was under constant attack. But Luce prevailed and appointed Mahan to his faculty to teach naval tactics.

Mahan took most of a year off to prepare for his new task. During these months he read widely in naval and general history and took extensive notes for his forthcoming lectures. These notes his wife typed up until he had a large volume of 400 pages. The course proved a success. Mahan's own lectures at the War College were supplemented by talks of visiting scholars. One of these was the young civil service commissioner, Theodore Roosevelt, who had written a scholarly history of the naval War of 1812. The

Mahan-Roosevelt encounter brought together two men who would become leaders in the new expansionism.

Despite the War College's success, its enemies managed to cut its budget and merge it with the adjacent Torpedo Station. Fortunately the emerging "new navalism" soon rescued both the War College and Mahan. In 1889 Harrison's secretary of the navy, Benjamin Tracy, induced Congress to make the War College a permanent navy installation with a new building for its own use at Newport. The supervisor of construction would be Captain Mahan.

Over the next few years, while Mahan was overseeing this project and giving lectures, he published the book that brought him fame. It was a study of how sea power had governed history during the years when Britain was establishing its overseas empire through its domination of the seas. *The Influence of Sea Power upon History, 1660–1783* made an implicit plea not only for a powerful American navy but also for colonies. The road to glory for the United States, Mahan suggested, was the route that Britain had pioneered.

By this time Mahan had become an unabashed expansionist. He had formerly believed, he later noted, that colonies required large standing armies and that these in turn made free government difficult. But his study of Britain's experience had convinced him that great empires were created by navies, not armies, and this was not incompatible with democratic rule. He had also come to believe that the British Empire had benefited the peoples it had governed and ultimately the world. Surely a similar venture by the United States would have similar benevolent results. During the early 1890s, in a succession of articles and letters to newspapers, Mahan endorsed

the construction of the new "dreadnought" type battleships, American annexation of Hawaii, the conversion of the Caribbean into an American lake, the construction of an isthmian canal across Panama, and other policies that became vital parts of the expansionist platform.

In 1892 Mahan completed a sequel to his first sea power book, *The Influence of Sea Power upon the French Revolution and Empire*, which recounted the effect of navies on the momentous events in Europe between 1793 and 1812. This work was even more influential than the first. Widely praised in the United States by the advocates of a bigger navy, it also evoked a strong response elsewhere. The young, headstrong German emperor Wilhelm II considered it a masterpiece and had copies in translation placed in German naval libraries. Mahan's ideas helped to inspire the German naval expansion that so frightened and antagonized the British in the closing years of the century.

In 1893, despite the efforts of his many political friends and admirers to keep him ashore where he could pursue his scholarly studies, Captain Mahan was ordered to sea as commander of the cruiser *Chicago* under Admiral Henry Erban, head of the European station. The three-year tour of duty turned into a personal triumph. Wherever the ship docked, Mahan was feted. In England banquets, attended by members of the royal family, were given in his honor. Erban felt slighted and responded by submitting a negative report on his chief subordinate. The captain, he declared, was not interested in "ship life or matters," and he was "therefore not a good officer." Mahan protested against this evaluation, but in truth it was accurate.

The European tour was Mahan's last sea duty. He returned to the United

States in 1895, and the following year retired from the navy to devote the remainder of his life to scholarship. In 1898 he returned to active duty for a short while to head the strategy board supervising naval operations in the war against Spain. The board actually had little influence on the course of events that led to the great American naval victories in the Philippines and off Cuba, but Mahan could take satisfaction in his part in the naval revival that had provided the country with the modern vessels that made the victories of Dewey and Sampson possible. In the debate over the peace Mahan was also an influential voice on the side of those who wanted to keep what America had seized from Spain.

Mahan spent his last years in New York City. He continued to lecture at the Newport War College and to write. In 1902 he was elected president of the American Historical Association, the historical guild's highest honor. Four years later, though on the retired list, he was promoted to the rank of rear admiral. In 1914 Mahan was induced by J. Franklin Jameson, a noted historian, to come to the Carnegie Institution of Washington as scholar-in-residence. This last chapter in his life did not last long. Mahan had been ill with a weak heart for some time, and on December 1, at the Washington naval hospital, he died.

The tributes and assessments quickly poured in. His friend, former president Theodore Roosevelt, called him "one of the greatest and most useful influences on American life." A foreign newspaper labeled him "the greatest naval historian of the nineteenth century." But the most pithy, and in some ways the most accurate, evaluation was one by a small-town paper: "The super-dreadnoughts are his children, and the roar of the 16″ guns are but the echoes of his voice."

Queen Liliuokalani was actually less benevolent than this picture suggests.

Suddenly the rosy Hawaiian economic situation changed. The McKinley Tariff of 1890 removed the duty on all sugar entering the United States, thus ending Hawaii's advantage over its competitors in the American market. The islands' economic boom collapsed. Almost simultaneously Queen Liliuokalani succeeded her brother to the Hawaiian throne, determined to restore much of the royal power he had surrendered to American advisers. The new queen was violently anti-American. Adopting the battle cry "Hawaii for the Hawaiians," she launched a campaign to end all foreign influence in her kingdom. In 1893 she proclaimed a new constitution that disfranchised all white men, except those married to native Hawaiian women, and gave the queen dictatorial powers.

The Americans in Hawaii now had both political and economic reasons for seeking annexation to their mother country. They promptly organized a "Committee of Safety," staged a coup d'état, and established a provisional government with themselves in control. To intimidate Queen Liliuokalani, the American minister to Hawaii, John L. Stevens, on the pretext of protecting American property, deployed marines from the cruiser U.S.S. *Boston* outside the queen's palace.

Unable to counter this show of force, the queen abdicated. Stevens then proclaimed the islands an American protectorate and triumphantly wrote the State Department: "The Hawaiian pear is now fully ripe and this is the golden hour for the United States to pluck it." The American-dominated provisional government soon applied for annexation to the United States, as Texas had sixty years before under similar circumstances.

Less than a month after the queen's overthrow, President Harrison signed an annexation treaty with representatives of the rebel government. Unfortunately for the annexationists, Grover Cleveland succeeded to the presidency before the Senate could act on the treaty. The new president—upright, principled, conscientious—was a figure from the nonexpansionist past. Reluctant to involve the country in a new policy of acquisition, he was also skeptical of the morality of the takeover by the American residents. Accordingly, he withdrew the treaty from the Senate and sent James H. Blount as his personal representative to the islands to investigate the circumstances of the queen's downfall.

Annexationists attacked Cleveland's scrupulous actions. A New York newspaper accused him of turning back "the hands of the dial of civilization." But when the Blount report arrived in Washington, it confirmed Cleveland's worst suspicions. Blount scolded Stevens for interfering in Hawaii's internal affairs and declared that a large majority of the native Hawaiian voters opposed annexation. Cleveland now determined to restore the queen to her

ally came to own much of the land. The strong American presence and the strategic location of the island chain inevitably aroused the interest of the United States government. Seward soon added the annexation of Hawaii to his other ambitious schemes. But few Americans were interested and nothing was done. Then, in 1875, the United States agreed to allow Hawaiian sugar, unlike that from other foreign lands, to enter the United States duty free. As a result, the islands' sugar plantations expanded and their economy soon became dependent on the profitable American market. The Hawaiian government, meanwhile, came under the influence of the American planters and businessmen who had brought prosperity to the kingdom. In 1887 the United States renewed the sugar agreement and received the right to use Pearl Harbor as a naval base.

throne. But when she declared her intention to decapitate the revolutionaries as soon as she could, he withdrew his support, allowed the Americans to remain in power, and recognized the provisional government as the legitimate authority of the Republic of Hawaii. Until its annexation to the United States in 1898, Hawaii remained an independent republic controlled by its American residents.

The Monroe Doctrine Reasserted.   The Hawaiian affair points up the unassertive side of American public opinion and the cautious side of American foreign policy. But the jingoist, aggressive side soon took hold under the impact of depression, fears about the closing of the frontier, and the influence of Mahan, Strong, and the social Darwinists.

This more combative attitude was displayed in the Venezuela incident of 1895. Independent Venezuela and the English colony of British Guiana, both on the Caribbean northern shore of South America, had long disputed their common boundary. From the beginning of this controversy, the Venezuelans had sought American support and had taken pains to depict the British as callous aggressors against a weaker nation.

Matters came to a head in 1894 when the British government refused President Cleveland's offer to arbitrate the dispute. The American State Department had become suspicious that British machinations in Central America and French intrigue in Brazil showed renewed European interest in Latin American colonies. The Royal Navy had recently landed troops in Nicaragua and extracted $360,000 from its government on the pretext that the British consul had been insulted. The incident, made doubly offensive to Americans by the British admiral's remark that the Monroe Doctrine was a myth, had set off a strong anti-British response in the American press. The American government's anxiety was further increased by the realization that if the British won the boundary dispute with Venezuela, they would control the mouth of the Orinoco and gain commercial priority in the large area of the continent drained by that river. Britain's refusal to accept American offers to settle the dispute only confirmed anti-British prejudices.

Not surprisingly, the United States sided with Venezuela. Early in 1895 Congress passed a resolution denouncing British claims in Venezuela. Secretary of State Richard Olney backed the resolution in a strong letter to

Though Cleveland moved cautiously on the Hawaiian matter, he and Olney did not consult Venezuela before intervening in its border dispute with England. The cartoon is obviously an American view; a heroic Uncle Sam is defending the "poor" Latin Americans against attack by aggressive European powers.

the American minister in London. Brusque and aggressive in Olney's usual manner, the note insisted that America's interest in the dispute was legitimate under the Monroe Doctrine. After defending the right of the United States to guarantee the independence of Latin American republics, the secretary launched into a blunt declaration of American power that startled the British. "Its infinite resources," he boasted, "combined with its isolated position render [the United States] the master of the situation and practically invulnerable against any or all other powers." Olney concluded by demanding that the issue be submitted to arbitration and that Britain respond before Congress met later in the year.

The British prime minister, Lord Salisbury, denied the applicability of the Monroe Doctrine and, offended by Olney's tone, rejected the call for arbitration with a brusqueness almost equal to Olney's. President Cleveland replied that if Britain refused arbitration, the United States would impose a boundary line and defend it militarily if necessary. Amid a wave of anti-British enthusiasm throughout the United States and Latin America, Congress approved Cleveland's plan and quickly appropriated $100,000 for a boundary commission. Anglophobes and jingoes eagerly anticipated war with Great Britain.

Fortunately for world peace, sober second thoughts soon took hold on both sides of the Atlantic. By now Britain had begun to fear an aggressive German empire that was challenging British naval supremacy and had recently sided against the British in their dispute with the Boer settlers in South Africa. Rather than take on both the United States and Germany, Lord Salisbury chose to conciliate Washington. In the United States, once the initial excitement had passed, a peace faction composed of clergy, business leaders, financiers, and journalists prevailed. Britain and Venezuela eventually agreed to accept arbitration; but by the time a decision was handed down in 1899, the whole dispute had been virtually forgotten.

★ CUBA LIBRE ★

The second Cleveland administration (1893–1897) was a time of transition between an isolationist and a more expansionist attitude toward the rest of the world. The issue that triggered the shift in outlook was Cuba.

That rich island, as well as Puerto Rico, had remained under Spanish rule long after the rest of Spain's once-great empire in the New World had disintegrated. The Cubans, however, were not satisfied to accept subordination to a declining European power. In 1868 they began a ten-year uprising to gain independence. Cuban rebels, some of them naturalized American citizens, appealed to the United States for help. But despite a number of minor diplomatic brushes with Spain, the United States refused to be drawn in, and the revolt eventually subsided.

Revolution in Cuba. For seventeen years the Cuban revolutionary spirit remained dormant. Then, in the early 1890s, harsh Spanish rule, its effects amplified by a severe crisis in the Cuban sugar industry, goaded the Cubans to revolt once again. This time the insurrectionists not only attacked Spanish soldiers and officials but also set fire to sugar plantations and cattle ranches, hoping that Spain would capitulate if nothing of value was left on the island. Cuban patriots living in the United States organized groups called "juntas" to aid the rebels and provoke trouble between Spain and the United States.

Spanish authorities under General Valeriano Weyler ("The Butcher") rounded up thousands of suspected rebels and sympathizers, including women and children, and confined them in concentration camps. Despite his reputation, Weyler did not intend mass murder, but unsanitary conditions and rebel interference with the food-supply systems made the concentration areas death camps. According to the American consul-general in Havana:

> Four hundred thousand self-supporting people, principally women and children [have been] transformed . . . into a multitude to be sustained by the contributions of others, or die of starvation, or of fevers resulting from low physical condition. . .without change of clothing and without food. Their homes were burned, their fields and plant beds destroyed and their livestock driven away or killed.

American Sympathies. As in all revolutions and civil wars, both sides were brutal and destructive, yet almost without exception the American people condemned Spain and supported the Cuban rebels. It used to be said that our sympathies were determined by our economic interests in the island. But there is little evidence to support this assertion.

Actually, most American business interests were opposed to political involvement in Cuba. With the depression of 1893–1897 just coming to an end, war was the last thing the business community wanted. Today we tend to see war as an economic stimulus, but in the late 1890s it seemed more likely to produce a financial panic and another depression. As relations with Spain worsened, the business press attacked any drastic action that would "impede the march of prosperity and put the country back many years."

Some farm spokespersons and part of the agricultural press did take a strong prointerventionist stand, but that they did so for economic reasons is doubtful. Even if farm-

An apostle of national prosperity, President McKinley was more interested in the country's recovery from the 1893 depression than in challenging Spain in Cuba. Here he is trying to keep the jingoes from killing the golden goose.

ers yearned for expanded overseas markets and generally favored an aggressive foreign policy, it is difficult to see what advantages they would have derived from war. Working people usually shared the views of their employers: A war with Spain would hurt business and therefore labor.

And yet by April 1898 most Americans—farmers, business people, wage earners, and others—favored intervening in Cuba despite the risk of war with Spain. Why? Clearly Americans were outraged at Spanish cruelty and sympathized with the Cuban underdogs. These feelings were reinforced by America's own anticolonialist past: The Cuban people seemed to be fighting the same battle for freedom that Americans had fought 120 years before.

But natural sympathies were not enough. During the nineteenth century Americans sympathized with virtually every foreign group they perceived as persecuted and with every anticolonial movement. Yet the United States had managed to avoid going to war against the oppressors. Fortunately for the Cuban rebels, American sympathies were strongly amplified by the activities of the "yellow press," especially William Randolph Hearst's *New York Journal* and Joseph Pulitzer's *New York World*. During the late 1890s the two press lords fought a bitter war in which truth took a back seat to circulation. Each sought to provide a daily diet of atrocity stories detailing Spanish brutality, for that sold papers. Both were unscrupulous, though Hearst was probably even less principled than his rival. According to one story, when an American artist sent to Cuba to illustrate the insurrection reported that things were quiet, Hearst shot back: "You furnish the pictures and I'll furnish the war."

Shown is William Randolph Hearst, the young newspaper publisher who helped propel the United States into war in 1898.

War Becomes Unavoidable.   Yet war seemed only a remote possibility when William McKinley was inaugurated in March 1897. The new president shared the business community's reluctance to jeopardize returning prosperity and declared in his inaugural address that war must be avoided

A contemporary artist's horrific vision of what the destruction of the battleship Maine *looked like.*

"until every agency of peace has failed; peace is preferable to war in almost every contingency." But McKinley could not control events. Ordinary public opinion was running against him, and the foreign policy elite considered his course cowardly and unworthy. The young New Yorker Theodore Roosevelt, for one, believed McKinley was as spineless "as a chocolate éclair." Early in 1898 a key group of congressional Republicans agreed to push the president for a war resolution, promising to join with the Democrats and sponsor one themselves if he did not yield. The religious press, viewing the issue in Cuba as a fight between Cuban virtue and Spanish beastliness, also demanded that the American government intervene to end the atrocious situation.

The Spaniards seemed to be their own worst enemies. In January 1898 the Spanish minister to the United States, Enrique Dupuy de Lôme, a well-meaning but indiscreet grandee, wrote an imprudent letter to a friend in Cuba expressing his contempt for McKinley and admitting that Spain was negotiating in bad faith over a proposed trade treaty with America. A Cuban patriot stole the letter from the desk of the recipient in Havana and sent it to Hearst, who promptly published it in his newspapers. The outraged public demanded that de Lôme be sent home. The minister instantly resigned in hope of mending the situation, but the damage was done. The American people now had even more reason than before to picture the Spaniards as arrogant and deceitful.

De Lôme's blunder was soon followed by an even bigger blow to Spanish-American relations. In January 1898 the American government sent the battleship *Maine* to Havana. The visit was officially "friendly"; the ship was only there to protect American lives and property following a serious local riot. The captain and the crew of the vessel were treated courteously by Spanish officials in Havana, though the visit naturally aroused some suspicion. Then, on February 15, a tremendous explosion rocked the ship, sending it to the bottom of the harbor with the loss of over 260 lives.

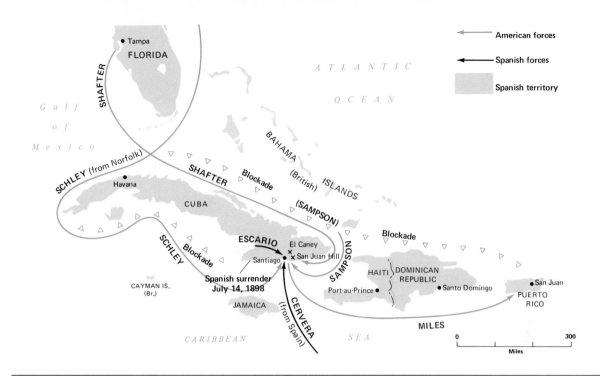

THE SPANISH-AMERICAN WAR IN THE CARIBBEAN

No one has ever solved the mystery of the *Maine*'s destruction. Spanish authorities disclaimed responsibility for the sinking. When American divers examined the hull of the ship, they concluded that the explosion had come from outside and could not be the result of a burst boiler, as the authorities in Havana implied. But neither they, nor anyone else, could determine who had done it.

Regardless of who or what sank the ship, most Americans considered it an act of war. Agreeing with Theodore Roosevelt's theory that the *Maine* had been "sunk by an act of dirty treachery on the part of the Spaniards," they demanded immediate retaliation. Jingoes had a field day. Mass rallies were held all over the country at news of the atrocity. People marched through the streets, chanting, "Remember the *Maine*. To Hell with Spain!" The yellow press, of course, insisted that Spain be punished with all the force of America's might.

McKinley could not resist the growing pressure to intervene. He promptly instructed the American minister in Madrid to demand that the Spanish government grant an armistice to the rebels and end the cruel concentration camp policy. Spain would have until October to accept these terms. If it did not, the United States would impose a settlement. The Spanish government was caught in a dilemma. To bow to the American ultimatum would antagonize many of its own citizens; if it refused to give in, it would certainly find itself at war with the United States. For a while it wavered, but finally, on the advice of the pope, it agreed to grant an armistice and abolish the concentration camps.

Spain had given the United States virtually everything it had asked for, but it was not enough to avoid war. American opinion now would not be satisfied with anything less than an independent Cuba—"Cuba Libre." The president was still reluctant to intervene, but he, too, was caught in a dilemma. In Congress the pressure to declare war was becoming irresistible; even if he did not request a declaration of war, there were signs that Congress would go ahead without him. Moreover, if he held back, the Democrats would charge him with weakness and jeopardize his chances of winning reelection in 1900.

On April 11 McKinley sent a war message to Congress. The United States, he said, must protect the lives and property of American citizens and put an end to the "barbarities, bloodshed, starvation, and horrible miseries. . .right at [its] door." Intervention was justified, the president claimed, by the "very serious injury to commerce, trade, and business of our people, and by the wanton destruction of property and devastation of the island." In addition, it was of "utmost importance" to end a disturbance which was a "constant menace to our peace and entails upon this Government an enormous expense."

Considering the intensity of the war fever, Congress acted surprisingly slowly. On April 19 it passed four resolutions defining the nation's war policy. They were: (1) that

Dismounted black cavalry supporting the Rough Riders at the Battle of Qarimas near Santiago, Cuba.

Cuba must be free; (2) that Spain must withdraw from the island; (3) that the president could use the armed forces to obtain these ends; and (4) that the United States would not annex Cuba. The commitment to nonannexation—the Teller Amendment—was approved without a dissenting vote. On April 25, 1898, Congress formally declared war on Spain.

★ THE SPANISH-AMERICAN WAR ★

The war with Spain was short and cheap. Few American lives were lost; more soldiers died at Custer's Last Stand than from battle wounds in the entire Spanish-American conflict. Moreover, the war was over in a few months and peace concluded by December 1898. As wars go, this one was also a financial bargain: It cost the United States only

$250 million. John Hay, soon to be secretary of state, called it a "splendid little war," and from the point of view of most Americans, the successes of their country's armed forces, particularly the navy, were splendid indeed.

Quick Victory. As assistant secretary of the navy, Theodore Roosevelt had anticipated war with Spain and prepared to attack Spain in the most exposed parts of its scattered empire. Acting in the absence of his superior, he had dispatched Commodore George Dewey and the Asiatic squadron to China even before McKinley delivered his war message. When Congress declared war, Dewey immediately sailed for the Philippines, a Spanish possession in the China Sea. Commanding six modern vessels of the new fleet, Dewey attacked and sank the whole Spanish Asiatic squadron in Manila Bay without losing a ship and hardly a man. The navy soon repeated Dewey's Pacific triumph in the Caribbean. In July the main United States naval detachment in Cuban waters smashed the Spanish squadron in a brief battle off Santiago. Again, American losses were minimal: one killed, one wounded.

The army's performance was considerably less impressive. For years its main job had been to contain and control the Indians in the West, and it was a comparatively small force. When war came, the War Department had to recruit and train a large number of volunteers, including Roosevelt's band of western cowboys and eastern gentlemen who enlisted as the "Rough Riders." Secretary of War Russell A. Alger botched the job of organizing and supplying the new recruits. Amid incredible confusion, 17,000 ill-equipped soldiers were embarked from Tampa, Florida, and landed near Santiago in southeastern Cuba. After several sharp skirmishes, including the Rough Riders' famous charge up San Juan Hill, the Americans captured the heights overlooking the city. On July 17, following the Spanish naval defeat, the Spanish military commander surrendered his troops. Soon afterward the American army occupied Puerto Rico without opposition.

The Spoils of War. By the end of July the Spanish government was ready to sue for peace. Delegates from the United States and Spain met in Paris in October to work out final details. Spain had already agreed to give Cuba its independence and to cede Puerto Rico and the Pacific island of Guam to the United States. The issue that blocked quick agreement was the fate of the Philippines. Although Dewey had sunk the Spanish Asiatic fleet and demolished Spanish power in the islands, he lacked troops and waited offshore for reinforcements before occupying Manila, the capital city. Meanwhile, Britain and Germany assembled naval squadrons nearby, ostensibly to protect the interests of their citizens in the Philippines but actually to claim the islands if the United States proved uninterested.

Before the war Americans had paid little attention to the Philippines; few even knew where they were. Now, suddenly, they found themselves up to their ears in international complications over these exotic islands. What should they do with them? Particularly disturbing were the designs of Germany. Since its unification twenty years before, Germany had become an aggressive colonial power, rummaging around for new territories all over the world. This lust for empire had seldom disturbed Americans before, but the Philippines were a different matter. The United States had fought for the islands; the Germans had expended nothing for them. Why allow them to fall into undeserving hands?

Moral and practical considerations also encouraged the United States to hold on to the islands. Whatever the business community felt at the war's start, it was now convinced that the Philippines would be a useful base for es-

tablishing closer trade relations with China. In July 1898, moved by a new, war-generated expansionist fever, Congress had finally annexed Hawaii. Add the Philippines and the United States would have a convenient set of stepping-stones across the Pacific to the Asian mainland. As Senator Henry Cabot Lodge noted, controlling the port of Manila would be "the thing which will give us the eastern trade." Many Americans also believed it would be inconsistent and irresponsible to have fought to free Cuba from Spanish tyranny and ignore the similar plight of the Filipinos. Besides, what a field for missionary effort the islands promised to be! Ignoring the fact that most Filipinos were already Catholics, McKinley found this opportunity to advance Christian civilization a compelling reason to hold on to the islands. He had been troubled by the fate of the Philippines and its people, he later told a church group,

This 1899 German cartoon makes fun of a hypocritical Uncle Sam. Protesting against imperialism, he erects a diplomatic skyscraper that dwarfs the works of other western nations. The title means "either Caesar or Nothing!"

Anti-Imperialism

America's outward thrust during the last years of the nineteenth century did not go unchallenged at home. A sizable portion of the American people saw it as a violation of the country's most precious traditions and a dangerous precedent. In June 1898, people of this persuasion met in Chicago and formed the Anti-Imperialist League to fight what they considered the jingoism and aggressiveness of the expansionists. The following is the core of the Anti-Imperialist League platform adopted at the League's October 1899 Chicago convention.

"We hold that the policy known as imperialism is hostile to liberty and tends toward militarism, an evil from which it has been our glory to be free. We regret that it has become necessary in the land of Washington and Lincoln to reaffirm that all men, of whatever race or color, are entitled to life, liberty, and the pursuit of happiness. We maintain that governments derive their just powers from the consent of the governed. We insist that the subjugation of any people is 'criminal aggression' and open disloyalty to the distinctive principles of our Government. . . .

"The United States have always protested against the doctrine of international law which permits the subjugation of the weak by the strong. A self-governing state cannot accept sovereignty over an unwilling people. The United States cannot act on the ancient heresy that might makes right.

"Imperialists assume that with the destruction of self-government in the Philippines by American hands, all opposition there will cease. This is a grievous error. Much as we abhor the war of 'criminal aggression' in the Philippines, greatly as we regret that the blood of Filipinos is on American hands, we more deeply resent the betrayal of American institutions at home. The real firing line is not the suburbs of Manila. The foe is of our own household. The attempt of 1861 was to divide the country. That of 1899 is to destroy its fundamental principles and noblest ideals. . . .

"We propose to contribute to the defeat of any person or party that stands for the forcible subjugation of any people. We shall oppose for re-election all who in the White House or in Congress betray American liberty in pursuit of un-American gains. . . .

"We hold, with Abraham Lincoln, that 'no man is good enough to govern another man without that man's consent. When the white man governs himself, that is self-government, but when he governs himself and also governs another man, that is more than self-government—that is despotism. . . . Those who deny freedom to others deserve it not for themselves, and under a just God cannot long retain it.'

"We cordially invite the consideration of all men and women who remain loyal to the Declaration of Independence and the Constitution of the United States."

---

until in answer to his prayers for divine guidance he had suddenly seen what must be done:

> We could not give them back to Spain—that would be cowardly and dishonorable. . . . There was nothing left for us to do but take them all and to educate the Filipinos, and uplift and civilize them and Christianize them, and by God's grace do the very best by them, as our fellow-men for whom Christ also died.

After reaching this inspired and practical conclusion, McKinley told the American negotiators in Paris to insist that the whole island chain be given to the United States. Spain resisted at first, but in exchange for $20 million it surrendered the Philippines, along with Puerto Rico and Guam, and at the same time confirmed Cuban independence.

The Anti-Imperialists.   The Treaty of Paris, especially the provision ceding the Philippines, set off a storm of protest in the United States. Although the war had shifted American public opinion as a whole in the direction of imperialism, there were still many opponents of expansion. Mugwump reformers, who had fought for civil service reform and sound money during the 1880s, along with many intellectuals and clergymen, believed that colonies were immoral and expensive. America, these anti-imperialists were certain, would be denying its finest ideals and traditions if it continued the quest for colonies. "America had something better to offer mankind," lamented Professor Charles Eliot Norton of Harvard. "These aims she is now pursuing . . . [are a] desertion of ideals which were not selfish or limited in their application but which are of universal worth and validity." By searching for colonies, America had "lost her unique position as a potential leader in the progress of civilization" and had "taken her place simply as one of the grasping and selfish nations of the present day." Other anti-imperialists were more angry than sad about the nation's desertion of its ideals. "God damn the United States for its vile conduct in the Philippine Isles," wrote the philosopher William James. If the United States made the islands a colony, it would leave the Filipinos with nothing: we could "destroy their own ideals," he declared, "but we can't give them ours."

Not all anti-imperialists were idealistic, however. Carl Schurz, for instance, feared that racial problems would overwhelm the United States if it incorporated the Philippines and parts of the Caribbean into its domain. Could the nation, he asked, absorb "immense territories inhabited by white people of Spanish descent, by Indians, by negroes, mixed Spanish and Indians, mixed Spanish and negroes, Hawaiians, Hawaiian mixed blood, Spanish Philippinos, Malays, Tagals?" These people were "savages and half-savages": they were all "animated with the instinct, impulses and passions bred by the tropical sun." "What will become of American labor and the standards of American citizenship?"

The most active opponents of colonialism banded together to form the Anti-Imperialist League, which tried to prevent American negotiators from signing the Treaty of Paris. When this effort failed, the league turned its atten-

tion to the Senate, where the fight for ratification promised to be long and bitter. In the course of a few months it mailed thousands of propaganda pieces denouncing colonialism and badgered senators and other politicians to stop the treaty.

Ratification of the Treaty of Paris. In the end the anti-imperialists failed. Despite misgivings, most Americans favored the treaty and the new American policy it implied. The decision to ratify in the Senate, however, was certain to be very close. Under a barrage of cajolery, persuasion, and pressure from McKinley and other administration leaders, almost all Senate Republicans pledged to support the treaty. But Democratic votes, too, were needed for passage.

William Jennings Bryan seemed to hold the key to success. Though defeated in 1896 and now a private citizen, he continued to exert great influence among fellow Democrats. Bryan was not an imperialist, but he threw his support behind the treaty, believing that ending the war was more important than the details of the settlement. He naively assumed the United States would give the Philippines its

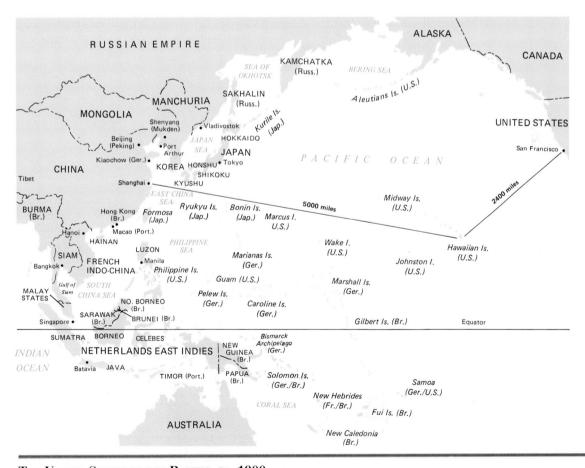

The United States in the Pacific, ca. 1900

freedom almost immediately. Enough Democrats went along with Bryan to carry the treaty 57 to 27, just one vote more than needed for ratification.

★ IMPERIAL AMERICA ★

The Treaty of Paris did not end the controversy over expansionism. Bryan still opposed overseas colonies and hoped to make the election of 1900 a referendum favoring return to the country's old, nonimperial ways. But American presidential elections seldom revolve about a single issue. In the end, the election of 1900 turned on silver, reform, prosperity, and the achievements of the first McKinley administration. Bryan's resounding defeat revealed little of what the American public felt about overseas expansion: Even the anti-imperialists split their votes between the two candidates.

Meanwhile, events in the Philippines were demonstrating the dangers and costs of America's new imperial course. Two days before ratification of the Spanish treaty, full-scale fighting broke out between the Filipinos, led by Emilio Aguinaldo, and the American forces attempting to establish American sovereignty in the islands. Eventually the United States was forced to fight a full-scale colonial war to put down the Filipino patriots. Not until mid-1902 were the 70,000 army regulars able to capture Aguinaldo and pacify the islands. The Philippines Insurrection was America's first land war in Asia, and like Vietnam in the 1960s, it was marked by savage atrocities on both sides.

In the years following 1902 the United States sought to make amends in the Philippines by introducing land reform, establishing local self-government, and improving educational facilities. In 1902 Congress created a Philippine legislative assembly, though the governor of the islands remained an American. But the ugly war experience was a disturbing one and made Americans all the more uneasy in the role of colonial power.

During the next twenty years the nation vacillated between its liberal and its imperial tendencies. In 1900, under the Foraker Act, Congress authorized limited self-government for Puerto Rico. By the Platt Amendment to the Army Appropriation Bill of 1901, it directed the president to withdraw American forces from Cuba. Yet Cuba was not to be truly free. According to the Platt Amendment, it could not enter into any treaty that would impair its sovereignty, nor could it contract debts beyond its capacity to pay. Also, the United States might intervene in the island's internal affairs to maintain law and order. Until the outbreak of World War

The American Navy, built during the 1880s and 1890s, destroying the Spanish fleet at Manila Bay during the Spanish-American War.

I the United States continued to waver, sometimes aggressively seeking overseas advantages, sometimes appearing indifferent to them, and at other times supporting weak nations against greedy European powers.

Relations with Latin America. America's attitude toward its closest neighbors in Latin America during these years was that of a strict older brother: It would protect them against outsiders, but they must behave or face American wrath. This policy worried and offended Latin Americans; Yankees considered it necessary for their peace of mind. The United States was the only great power in the Western Hemisphere, and Americans found this situation comfortable. Any hint that a European country was trying to extend its influence into the Western Hemisphere set off immediate alarm bells in Washington.

Sometimes this proprietary attitude operated to the advantage of America's smaller neighbors. Without American protection, a number of the weaker Latin American states would almost certainly have fallen again into the hands of one or another of the great European powers. Yet Latin America undoubtedly paid a high price for this protection. The United States insisted that its strategic, political, and economic interests came first, and often demonstrated this attitude in ways that left a legacy of resentment.

A characteristic instance of American highhandedness occurred in 1903. During the recent conflict with Spain the U.S.S. *Oregon* had taken many weeks to sail from Puget Sound around Cape Horn to come to the defense of the exposed and anxious East Coast. The ship's slow progress had underscored the advantages of a canal across the isthmus that joined North and South America. With the war over and America the uneasy owner of a new Pacific empire, a canal seemed even more vital.

Two obstacles blocked the way. The Clayton-Bulwer Treaty, signed with Great Britain in 1850, had denied the United States exclusive control over an isthmian canal. This hurdle was overcome by the 1901 Hay-Pauncefote Treaty with Britain, which gave sole right to the United States to build, control, and fortify a Central American waterway. Location was the second problem. Two routes were possible: one through Nicaragua and one at Panama. A factor favoring Panama was the enormous labor already expended by the French, who, under the leadership of Ferdinand de Lesseps, builder of the Suez Canal, had been hacking and digging their way unsuccessfully through the fever-ridden jungles and mountains of the isthmus since the 1880s. When the French offered to sell their rights and equipment for $40 million, Congress accepted.

But another difficulty now loomed. Panama was part of Colombia. Before construction could begin, Colombia would have to agree to the arrangement. In January 1903 the United States concluded a treaty with Tomás Herrán, the Colombian minister in Washington, giving the South American republic a one-time $10 million payment and $250,000 annually for the rights to build the canal and to lease a canal zone six miles wide along the right-of-way for ninety-nine years. When the treaty reached the Colombian Senate, however, it was defeated. The Colombians had two major objections: The treaty gave the Americans too much

The biggest engineering problems faced by the Panama Canal builders were the "cuts," the deep gorges that had to be sliced through the ridges across the isthmus. This is a view of the difficult Culebra Cut.

power over a portion of their territory, and they saw no reason why they should not receive the $40 million that was promised to the French canal firm.

President Theodore Roosevelt considered the Colombians' action abominable. These people, he shouted, were "jack rabbits" and "contemptible little creatures." They were "imperiling their own future," and the United States might have to teach them a lesson for their own good. Equally upset were the agents of the French canal company, who saw the promised $40 million escaping their grasp, and those residents of Panama who looked forward to the prosperity that the canal would bring and feared that it would now be built in Nicaragua.

In the end, the French agents, the Panamanians, and Theodore Roosevelt combined to assure a Panama route. Although they had revolted against Colombia in the past, the Panamanians had never succeeded in gaining their independence. Now, encouraged and financed by the French canal company, they rose once again. Fortunately for the insurgents, the U.S.S. *Nashville*, an American warship, had conveniently arrived just a day before the revolt broke out and was docked at Colón on Panama's Caribbean coast. Inspired by this scarcely disguised support, the rebels quickly overcame the feeble Colombian military forces and

in a matter of hours proclaimed an independent Panamanian republic. To no one's surprise, Roosevelt immediately concluded an accord with the new government. For the same financial terms offered Colombia, the United States was granted the right to build a canal through a ten-mile-wide zone where it would exercise "all the rights, power, and authority" it would possess "if it were the sovereign of the territory."

With the political details out of the way, work on the gigantic engineering project began. Using mammoth steam shovels and thousands of black laborers drawn from the Caribbean islands, as well as better-paid whites from the United States, American engineers dug, blasted, and chopped their way across the isthmus. Hundreds of lives were lost to yellow fever until Colonel William C. Gorgas wiped out the mosquito-breeding places at Colón and Panama City and eliminated the disease from the isthmus. On August 15, 1914, the interocean canal connecting the Atlantic and Pacific, the dream of three centuries, was formally opened to world shipping.

Roosevelt also acted aggressively elsewhere in Latin America. Many of the smaller Latin American countries, he felt, had acted irresponsibly and thereby had endangered the safety of the hemisphere. Debt default and political

Americans had long been fascinated with China, both as a land of mystery and as a vast potential market for American products. This elaborate display of Chinese splendor drew huge crowds at the St. Louis Exposition in 1904.

chaos in the weaker countries were inviting European nations to intervene to protect their citizens and their investments. By American reasoning, if the Caribbean and Central American republics expected the United States to defend them against the European powers—as indeed they did—they could not expect their protector to ignore their misdeeds. In 1904, when several European nations threatened to blockade the Dominican Republic until it paid its debts, Roosevelt decided to lay down the law. In his "corollary" to the Monroe Doctrine, he announced that "chronic wrongdoing" by Latin American countries or political "impotence" that resulted in serious disorder might force the United States to "exercise. . .police power, and compel it to intervene in the offending nation's internal affairs." While the Roosevelt Corollary prevented takeovers by European nations, it also gave the United States an excuse to intrude at will into Latin American affairs.

The Open Door in China.   The United States often took advantage of its power to overawe its weaker hemispheric neighbors, but its role in the Far East was, on the whole, more benign. After acquiring Hawaii and the Philippines, the nation eagerly awaited the opening of the supposedly vast China market. It never materialized: The Chinese people had neither the wealth nor the tastes for America's major exports. Nevertheless, Americans remained hopeful and were anxious to prevent China from being carved up by Japan and the major European powers into exclusive "spheres of influence" where others could not trade.

But American interest in China went beyond trade. Americans were fascinated by China's ancient civilization, art, and customs. They also considered the Celestial Empire a promising field for missionary effort. The first American missionaries had arrived in China before the Civil War, bringing Western science and learning along with Protestant Christianity. However contemptuous they were of Chinese "heathenism," the missionaries deeply sympathized with the long-suffering Chinese people and conveyed their compassionate feelings to pious churchgoers at home. By the end of the nineteenth century millions of Americans—notwithstanding considerable hostility to those Chinese living in the United States—considered China an arena for benevolence, not one for crass economic and political exploitation.

For many years American policy toward China was marked by this combination of self-interest and compassion. After China's defeat by Japan during the First Sino-Japanese War (1894–1895), the great powers renewed their demands for political and economic concessions. The United States, which had no designs on Chinese territory, feared that the Western nations would completely carve up the decaying empire, destroying Chinese sovereignty while excluding the United States commercially. Encouraged by the British, Secretary of State John Hay in 1899 sent notes to the major colonial powers asking for assurances that they would not demand special trading privileges in China. Most gave Hay evasive answers, but he chose to interpret these as acceptance of his "open door" principle, which rejected exclusive "spheres of influence" and held that all nations must be free to trade throughout China. In 1900, following suppression of the antiforeign Chinese Boxers by an international army, the United States converted the principle of economic parity to one of defending the Chinese nation against European annexation. In a circular letter of July 1900 Hay declared that it was "the policy of the United States government" to "bring about. . .peace to China" and to "preserve Chinese territorial and administrative entity. . . ."

The Open Door policy was a perfect mirror of American ambivalence. Unprepared by its history and traditions to take up the burdens and responsibilities of blatant colonialism, the United States sought to protect its share of the Chinese market in some less costly way than political control. At the same time, Americans sincerely sympathized with the Chinese people and sought to preserve Chinese sovereignty. But whatever the motives, the concern of the United States for an independent China would serve on more than one occasion to keep it from being dismembered by the European colonial powers and an expansionist Japan.

★ CONCLUSIONS ★

Many elements contributed to the outward thrust of the post–Civil War generation. The impulse that had carried the American people 3,000 miles across the North American continent continued to operate even after the Pacific was reached. Much as the earlier expansion had been fortified by the quest for gain, so the later one was reinforced by the desire for trade and expanded investment opportunities. Altruism, however misguided and arrogant, also influenced America's interest in foreign lands. Americans continued to believe that they had unique gifts—political freedom and material abundance—to offer other peoples. The American role in China, Hawaii, and the Philippines, in particular, expressed this mixture of the crass and the idealistic.

But post–Civil War expansionism also contained new ingredients. The desire to achieve big-power status by collecting colonies, as had the western European countries, augmented the older Manifest Destiny. So did the fear that now that continental expansion had ended, the United States must seek out new territory or cease to prosper and grow. The aggressiveness of the American government, particularly toward Latin America, reflected the new mood of big-power assertiveness: Great powers cut a wide swath in their own neighborhoods; they did not allow themselves to be defied by troublesome pygmies.

And yet Americans never wore the mantle of imperialism very comfortably. A rich nation of continental proportions, the United States needed to throw its weight around, but less so than nations that had fewer natural resources and smaller home markets. Less strongly impelled by necessity, the United States was also more restricted by its traditional liberal anticolonial values and by its fears that overseas acquisitions could not be incorporated into the Union as equal partners with the older states. In the new century just opening, the world would see many further instances of American forbearance and even generosity toward weaker nations combined with manifestations of self-serving interest, and would be puzzled by the course of the Great Republic.

✦✦✦✦✦✦✦✦ FOR FURTHER READING ✦✦✦✦✦✦✦✦

Walter LaFeber. *The New Empire: An Interpretation of American Expansion, 1860–1898* (1963)
A study of late-nineteenth-century American expansionism by a scholar who believes that "economic forces [were] the most important causes" of the expansionist impulse.

Ernest R. May. *American Imperialism* (1968)
May ascribes the major cause of American expansionism near the end of the nineteenth century to the appearance of a foreign policy elite inspired by the example of Britain, France, and Germany.

Walter Millis. *The Martial Spirit: A Study of Our War with Spain* (1931)
A fine older narrative history of the origins, course, and results of the Spanish-American War. Millis sees the war's origins in the gradual development of a warlike spirit that derived from a mixture of boredom, greed, politics, and the yearning for glory.

Julius W. Pratt. *Expansionists of 1898: The Acquisition of Hawaii and the Spanish Islands* (1936)
Pratt criticizes the view, common in his day, that the Spanish-American war was the work of business groups anxious to acquire markets. He gives far more credit to new currents of thought that he calls the "new Manifest Destiny."

Graham A. Cosmas. *An Army for Empire: The United States Army in the Spanish-American War* (1971)
This study of the army and the War Department during the war with Spain seeks to refute the usual picture of bungling and general incompetence. Cosmas believes that, given the realities of time and the difficulties of tropical warfare, the army did rather well.

Kenton J. Clymer. *John Hay: The Gentleman as Diplomat* (1975)
A study of Secretary of State John Hay's thought about such matters as race, expansion, England, and China. Clymer sees Hay as a patrician with a strong leaning to Britain. He denies that Hay's Open Door policy was primarily intended to protect China from rapacious foreign powers.

Margaret Leech. *In the Days of McKinley* (1959)
A superb "life and times" of McKinley that emphasizes his presidential years. Leech spends much time on the relations between McKinley and his invalid wife, but she also deals colorfully with the events surrounding Cuba and the Spanish-American War.

Howard K. Beale. *Theodore Roosevelt and the Rise of America to World Power* (1956)
An effective, if not always fair, attack on TR for his jingoism and imperialistic arrogance. In truth, TR is often condemned out of his own mouth.

Joseph Wisan. *The Cuban Crisis as Reflected in the New York Press* (1934)
Wisan probably exaggerates the significance of the Hearst-Pulitzer circulation battle in New York as a cause of the Spanish-American War. But his study of public opinion formation does tell us much about American values and prejudices, and how prowar groups played on them.

Frank A. Freidel. *Splendid Little War* (1958)
The words and pictures of news correspondents, artists, and photographers tell the story of the war in Cuba. Freidel's 300 illustrations include some by Frederic Remington. Others are charming photographic efforts by cadets fresh out of Annapolis.

Robert Beisner. *Twelve Against Empire: The Anti-Imperialists, 1898–1900* (1968)
Beisner studies twelve prominent Americans who opposed the Spanish-American War, including William James, "Czar" Thomas Reed, and Andrew Carnegie. All upper-class Republicans or former Mugwumps, they believed that acquiring unwilling colonies ran counter to American principles and would threaten democracy at home.

Leon Wolff. *Little Brown Brother* (1961)
War in the Philippines lasted from 1898 to 1902, but after 1898 the United States fought not Spain but Filipino guerrillas. Wolff describes the methods army officers with Indian-fighting experience used to persuade "our little brown brothers" to accept American control. He also treats the growing controversy at home over army atrocities and the costs of the prolonged conflict.

Thomas J. McCormick. *China Market: America's Quest for Informal Empire, 1893–1901* (1967)

In this New Left interpretation of American expansion in the Pacific, McCormick proposes that the government refused to solve the problems of overproduction by dealing with underconsumption at home. Instead, he says, the American economic and political leadership sought a tariff to promote exports and an Open Door agreement designed to assure American domination of the China market.

David C. McCulloch. *The Path Between the Seas: The Creation of the Panama Canal, 1870–1914* (1977)

A lively account of the building of the great isthmian canal, from the early French effort to the final success under the auspices of the United States. Fine narrative history. McCulloch is an honest scholar who describes the greed, incompetence, and chicanery that accompanied the construction as well as the intelligence, hard work, and heroism.

22★

CULTURE IN THE AGE OF THE DYNAMO

Were Materialism and High Culture Compatible?

1851	The YMCA is established in the United States
1858	The National Association of Baseball Players is founded
1859	Darwin's *The Origin of Species* published in England
1870–82	Printing processes improve, enabling newspapers to print more news daily • The Associated Press and the United Press are founded • Pulitizer begins "yellow journalism" in the *New York World*
1870–90	American school of art, led by Winslow Homer
1876	American Library Association is founded and lobbies for local communities to support free public libraries
1880	William Le Baron Jenney designs the first skyscraper
1883	Brooklyn Bridge is completed • Metropolitan Opera House opens
1884	Mark Twain's *Huckleberry Finn* published
1893	The Chicago World's Fair
1895	Stephen Crane's *The Red Badge of Courage* published
1896	First showing of a commercial motion picture in a legitimate theater
1900	Theodore Dreiser's *Sister Carrie* published • "Tin Pan Alley" marks the beginning of the popular music trend • 240 Ph.D.s are awarded, beginning the expansion of graduate schools and professional education • Frank Lloyd Wright begins functional modernism in architecture
1903	First World Series
1904	Pragmatist philosopher John Dewey institutionalizes major changes in the education system • The Henri "Ashcan" school marks the trend toward modernism in painting
1913	The Armory exhibition exposes Americans to the works of Cézanne, Van Gogh, Picasso, Matisse, and Duchamp, as well as the Henri group
1915	Over 80 percent of all children attend school as a result of compulsory attendance laws

In the half century following the Civil War the United States, as we have seen, became a nation of cities and factories. Millions bent their energies to making money, developing skills, surviving, or getting ahead. It was an era when young men went to work at fourteen, spent ten or twelve hours a day on the job, and received no yearly vacation; when young women commonly devoted even longer hours to cooking, cleaning, and washing for large families, their own or someone else's.

In such a time few men and women could think of much more than the daily round. Ordinary Americans had little time and energy left for "the finer things"—for "serious" literature, music, art, and other so-called embellishments of life. Nor did people of wealth seem to be in any better shape to appreciate or pursue the arts. The American rich were not leisured gentlemen and ladies whose family wealth had been earned by some aggressive ancestor and who had themselves mellowed into "cultivation" and appreciation of beauty for its own sake. There were such people—survivors of colonial merchant families in the North and of the planter aristocracy in the South—but they had been superseded in numbers and wealth by the upstarts, the "new men"—the Rockefellers, Goulds, Carnegies, Swifts, Hearsts, and Guggenheims—who had clawed their way to the top of the economic pile and thrown the old elite into deep shadow.

Among the small intellectual class, especially in the opening years of the period, there was despair at the possibility of high cultural achievement in a nation so obsessed with practicality and swamped with materialism. In 1874 Edwin L. Godkin, a transplanted Anglo-Irishman who edited the prestigious *Nation*, declared that his adopted country suffered from a "chromo civilization"; like the popular colored prints of the day (chromolithographs), its colors were gaudy and false.

To some, America's democracy seemed almost as hostile to cultivation and good taste as its materialism. In a famous passage the novelist Henry James made it clear why he had fled his homeland to live in England. The United States, he noted, "had no sovereign, no court, no personal loyalty, no church, . . . no diplomatic service, no country gentlemen, nor old country houses, . . . nor ivied ruins, no great universities. . . ." In short, it had few, if any, old, privileged institutions and few of the men and women that such institutions produced. These were the only interesting subjects to the writer, in James's view, and lacking them, America could never create a great literature.

James's critique was meant as a general indictment of America's cultural and intellectual potential. How could a society so immersed in wealth-getting, and so dedicated to

equality at all costs, make room for the arts? How could it be expected to think creatively? How could Americans even find the leisure to amuse themselves? To critics such as James there was an irreconcilable conflict between materialism and culture, whether the "high" culture of sophisticated trained artists and thinkers or the popular culture of ordinary people.

And yet in the half century following Appomattox the United States experienced a cultural flowering that compares favorably with any that preceded or followed. The country produced a flood of authors, painters, architects, thinkers, and educators who made it one of the cultural centers of the Western world. There was also an exuberant and vigorous growth of "low" culture—the song, dance, theater, and amusements of average men and women—that became a powerful attraction to people of other lands.

How did the nation manage to avoid the dire predictions of such critics as Henry James? How did it manage to combine wealth-getting, industrialization, and urbanization with literature, painting, music, sports, educational progress, and the creation of new ideas? How did it manage to avoid a "chromo civilization"?

★ LITERATURE ★

The Genteel Tradition. Post–Civil War Americans had an impressive literary heritage to build on. In the years between 1800 and 1860, in New England especially, the United States had experienced a literary birth that had astonished the world. But many of the outstanding figures of the prewar days did not survive the Civil War. Hawthorne, Cooper, Irving, Thoreau, and Poe were all dead by 1865. The aura of their reputations, however, persisted, so that New England, especially the Boston-Cambridge area, for some time continued to be the literary capital of the nation. Here were published two of the country's chief journals of culture—the *Atlantic Monthly* and the *North American Review*. Along with the *Nation* and *Harper's Weekly*, published in New York, these were the arbiters of literary taste among the educated elite. The Boston-Cambridge area also was home to Longfellow, James Russell Lowell, and Charles Eliot Norton, all of whom taught at the country's most prestigious university, Harvard.

These men and these publications defended what the philosopher George Santayana would call the "genteel tradition" in literature. They believed that art, and especially fiction and poetry, must represent the spiritual, the pure, and the noble, for literature was a moral medium, not merely an aesthetic one. Literature should not report life as it actually was; that would include much that was sordid and mean. Rather, it must try to transform life into something higher and more refined. In poetry the genteel tradition called for pseudo-classical epics or romantic lyricism that imitated either the Roman poet Horace or the English romantics Keats and Shelley. The genteel novelist believed that nothing could be recounted that might offend the ears of a middle-class maiden. Lowell in fact declared that no man should write what he was unwilling for his young daughter to read. Evil existed in the fiction of the genteel authors, of course, but it was without detectable social cause, personified by evil men and women, and always, in the end, defeated. Sex was so buried under flowery romanticism that a traveler from another solar system who read a genteel novel might not have known that men and women were biologically different.

The exemplars of the genteel tradition included a few survivors from the great years of prewar New England, like Lowell, and also a new group of writers. With the exception of Thomas Bailey Aldrich, whose sentimental *Story of a Bad Boy* (1870) is still read, these critics, poets, and novelists are deservedly forgotten. Yet for a while during the last thirty years of the nineteenth century, they sought to impose a set of values on American literary taste that denied all the great changes of the nation's recent history. One of them, George Boker, in 1882 expressed in verse his disapproval of Gilded Age America and his view that poets must defend traditional values:

> We poets hang upon the wheel
> Of Time's advancement; do our most
> To hide its inroads, and reveal
> The Splendors which the world has lost.
>
> Science and Avarice, arm and arm,
> Stride proudly through our abject time;
> And in their footsteps, wrangling, swarm
> Their own begotten broods of crime.

Another defender of the waning past, Hamilton Wright Mabie, protested that the emerging new "realistic" literature seemed bent on "crowding the world of fiction with commonplace people whom one could positively avoid coming into contact with in real life; people without native sweetness or strength, without acquired culture or accomplishments, without the touch of the ideal which makes the commonplace significant and worthy of study."

Regionalism. But even as Boker and Mabie were composing these lines, writers were supplanting their pallid, genteel assumptions. The first fiction writers to defy post–Civil War gentility were those who insisted on de-

picting American regional reality with all its coarse vigor and liveliness.

One of the new voices came from the mining camps of California and depicted a way of life that had just recently passed. In 1867 Bret Harte, a transplanted easterner who had come to California in 1854, published "The Luck of Roaring Camp," a short story, in the San Francisco–based *Overland Monthly*, a new magazine that he edited himself. The story concerned the hard-bitten miners and dance-hall girls of a Sierra mining camp who are bequeathed a baby. The plot was less important, however, than the cast of characters; each has a rough exterior and speaks the way people in the mining camps did indeed speak. Few are "good" people in the usual sense. It was this quality of apparent authenticity that made the story an instant sensation and Harte a celebrity. In the next few years his other stories about the mining camps, including "The Outcasts of Poker Flat," "The Idyl of Red Gulch," and "Tennessee's Partner," were widely applauded as examples of honesty in literature. In fact, much sentimentality remains in Harte's characters; even the most villainous and degraded have hearts of gold. Yet Harte's work was a milestone on the way to a more realistic literature.

Over the next few decades the vein of regionalism that Harte had first mined attracted other authors. The Midwest had Edward Eggleston, whose series of books—*The Hoosier Schoolmaster* (1871), *The Circuit Rider* (1874), *Roxy* (1878), and others—depicted rural Indiana with a sharp eye for local color and a true ear for regional speech. In the South, George Washington Cable wrote brilliantly about Creole New Orleans in *Old Creole Days* (1879) and *The Grandissimes* (1880). The southern mountain people of the Great Smokies and the Cumberland plateau found their literary portraitist in Mary Noailles Murfree, who published under the pseudonym of Charles Egbert Craddock. Joel Chandler Harris wrote about poor Georgia whites and even poorer Georgia blacks. His "Uncle Remus" stories depicted black farmers honestly and accurately, though Harris emphasized humor rather than the very real oppression that blacks labored under in the Gilded Age South. The East, too, had its local colorists. Sarah Orne Jewett began to write stories of the village and farm people of southern Maine during the 1860s. Her novel *The Country of the Pointed Firs* (1896) has been described as "the best piece of regional fiction to have come out of nineteenth-century America." Another local colorist of the East was Mary Wilkins Freeman, whose stories dealt with the people of rural Massachusetts.

Mark Twain. The most talented of all the regional authors, one who far exceeded them in depth and universality, was Samuel Langhorne Clemens, alias Mark Twain.

By the time this photograph of Mark Twain was taken (1906), he had become an adored national monument. Nevertheless, he was a tortured man who never could reconcile his contempt for wealth with his need for luxury and worldly success.

Mark Twain shared with the local colorists their love of dialect, their focus on rural and small-town "types," their humorous emphasis. A native of Missouri, he fought briefly in the Confederate army, and then, in 1862, departed for the gold diggings at Virginia City, Nevada, where he became a reporter and feature writer for the *Territorial Enterprise*.

In 1864 Mark Twain went to California, where he achieved fame for a story using the same mining-camp material as Harte, "The Celebrated Jumping Frog of Calaveras County" (1865). But Twain was far more talented than Harte. Combining the traditions of the frontier tall tale with an uncanny ear for speech, and at times a sense of the tragic, Mark Twain ultimately became an author of international stature. At the beginning of his career, however, he capitalized on his capacity to make people laugh. In books such as *Innocents Abroad* (1869) and on the lecture circuit, which occupied much of his time and earned him large fees, he told jokes and funny stories, and in general seemed to be interested solely in amusing people.

Mark Twain's more serious side became evident in his later books. In three of these he turned to his own youth and to the upper South before the Civil War, describing the joys and the agonies of youth. The first of these, the novel *Tom Sawyer* (1876), is about a boy growing up in a town very much like Sam Clemens's Hannibal, Missouri. Tom is no paragon, but a realistic boy given to laziness and romantic dreaming, yet capable as well of loyalty and courage. *Life on the Mississippi* (1883) is a superb nonfiction account of the great days before the Civil War when the steamboat dominated commerce on the South's rivers and the steamboat captain was almost a Renaissance prince. Mark Twain's greatest novel, *Huckleberry Finn* (1885), was a sequel to *Tom Sawyer*. But Huck is a more interesting boy than Tom—less conventional, more genuine, less spoiled by romantic illusion, more spontaneous. The novel also is more sensitive to fundamental human issues. Huck helps Jim, a black slave, escape from bondage and refuses to betray him, though Huck is troubled by a sense that he is defying his own community. Clemens, though a southerner himself, portrayed Jim as an even braver, more manly personality than Huck.

Despite his genius and his willingness at times to choose truth over romantic convention, Mark Twain never fully escaped from the literary conventions of the Gilded Age. Even his best works contain much sentimentality and cheap farce. He eventually turned to vapid historical romance and developed a tendency to flaunt an adolescent melancholy. Only in *The Gilded Age* (1873), written in collaboration with Charles Dudley Warner, did he use contemporary industrial America as his theme. The novel recounts the adventures of a cast of sharpers, confidence men and women, and corrupt Washington politicians in the crass years immediately following the Civil War, when businessmen wanted favors and government had them to confer. The book caught the moral and aesthetic shoddiness of the day so well that it gave its name to the whole postwar era. Yet Mark Twain never repeated the performance, and while the nation marched rapidly into the industrial age, he continued to write about antebellum Missouri or England and France in the Middle Ages.

In his later years Mark Twain became a national institution much beloved by Americans. When he died in 1910, the nation sincerely mourned. Yet despite his fame and popularity, in many ways he was a tragic figure whose enormous talents never found a truly worthy theme.

Realism. As the century progressed, other men and women would come closer to fitting their talents to vital modern materials. Leader of the move toward realism was William Dean Howells, an Ohio-born author and editor who came to Boston in 1867 to become editor of the *Atlantic Monthly*. Howells was the first westerner to edit this pillar of New England gentility, and he brought a breath of fresh air to the publication. Though he never fully liberated himself from the prudishness of the day, Howells insisted on new principles for judging literature. A novel, he declared, must be "true to the motives, the impulses, the principles that shape the life of actual men and women." As editor and critic, he praised the work of such early American realists as John William De Forest, whose *Miss Ravenel's Conversion from Secession to Loyalty* (1866) has been described as the best Civil War novel ever written. He welcomed newer talents such as Hamlin Garland, whose bitter stories of western farm life, *Main-Travelled Roads*, appeared in 1891. He was also receptive to the realism of Émile Zola in France and Henrik Ibsen in Scandinavia, and introduced these authors to American readers.

A talented novelist in his own right, Howells practiced what he preached. In *The Rise of Silas Lapham* (1885) he described a self-made millionaire manufacturer who finds that his simple western ways cause social difficulties for himself and his family in Boston. The novel is one of the earliest portrayals of a businessman by an American author.

The violent Haymarket affair in Chicago produced a personal crisis for Howells. The sentencing to death of the five anarchists in 1887 seemed to him "civic murder" and awakened his social conscience. In his next business novel, *A Hazard of New Fortunes* (1890), Howells's business characters are less amiable and sympathetic, and his canvas expands to include poor working people, a German-American socialist, and a violent streetcar strike. Howells never became a Marxist, but he did come to believe that unrestrained capitalism was not the most desirable economic system. In *A Traveler from Altruria* (1894) and *Through the Eye of the Needle* (1907), he built on Edward Bellamy's utopian novel *Looking Backward*, positing socialist alternatives to a dog-eat-dog economic system.

A major American literary figure not easy to classify is Henry James. James had an extraordinarily acute sense of the nuances in human relationships, and his characters are men and women in comfortable circumstances whose lives revolve about the subtleties of taste, class, and nationality and crises of personal integrity. His settings are generally European, but his characters are often American, and the tensions in many of his best works—*The American* (1877), *The Portrait of a Lady* (1881), *The Wings of the Dove* (1902), and *The Golden Bowl* (1904)—arise between simple but honest and intelligent Americans, often young women, and sophisticated but corrupt and devious Europeans. It is difficult at first glance to see in James's work much of Howells's realism. James seemed little interested in the vast social changes sweeping the Western world. Yet there is in his fiction none of the "picturesqueness" that his criticism of the American literary scene, as previously quoted, seems to prize, nor does he suffer from the false sentimentality of the genteel authors. His people, though well-bred and worldly, are recognizably real human beings with the complex personalities found in daily life.

Women Writers and the New Woman. By the 1890s a new breed of women authors had made gender an issue and an inspiration in literature. American women had been successful and admired authors as far back as the colonial era. During the early nineteenth century women had dominated the field of the popular novel, and several women writers, Louisa May Alcott, Harriet Beecher Stowe, and Margaret Fuller, for example, had made permanent contributions to the nation's literary canon. After the Civil War women entered the front ranks of literature.

The female local colorists—Jewett, Murfree, Freeman—though focused on polite and picturesque surfaces, at times expressed the emotions of the "New Woman" beginning to emerge as the century wound down. In Jewett's *A Country Doctor* (1884), one character notes that many women are unsuited for motherhood; another protests against society's effort to "bury the talent that God has given me." Other women authors went beyond the limited local colorist genre in expressing the full range of women's yearnings. Among the novelists, Ellen Glasgow, a Virginian, wrote about her native section with special attention to the false gentility of southern womanhood. Edith Wharton, a descendant of New York's old Knickerbocker families, wrote with exquisite sensibility of heroines caught between the vulgar new rich and the decaying upper class. But the novelist who best exemplified the New Woman was Kate O'Flaherty Chopin, a widow and mother of six, who despite her own experience—or because of it—raised explicit questions about women's roles as wives, mothers, and lovers. Chopin's novel, *The Awakening* (1899), offended the more prudish critics as "sex fiction" for its focus on women's sexual feelings. The hostile response, including refusal of librarians in her native St. Louis to circulate it, crushed Chopin's spirit.

One writer of this period, the poet Emily Dickinson, attained after her death in 1886 an almost mythic place in our literary history. A spinster who lived quietly and obscurely in the small town of Amherst, Massachusetts, Dickinson was able to create a fresh poetic voice by deliberately cutting herself off from her immediate male-dominated social milieu and carving out a separate corner for herself. Her verse is full of inverted syntax, metrical experiments, and startling switches of sensory experience that foreshadowed much of poetic modernism. Little of her work appeared in print in her own lifetime. It remained to our century to discover her originality.

Naturalism. As the end of the century approached, Howells's rather mild realism gave way to something more vigorous and more brutal—naturalism. Though the realists sought to describe the day-to-day world of work, class, and ordinary people doing ordinary, everyday things, they retained an essentially sunny view of life. Not so the naturalists. These authors perceived life as sordid and vicious. Modern science and social science, they held, showed that all things were determined including the lives and deeds of ordinary people. In their novels men and women are mere atoms in the grip of forces beyond their control or even understanding. Their endings are generally tragic. Naturalist novels were not invariably set in cities, but almost always the naturalist authors focused on the emerging industrial-urban order, and even their rural characters are people whose lives are entangled in the vast social changes that characterized the closing years of the nineteenth century.

One young writer who explored the relationship between large social currents and the lives of rural Americans was Hamlin Garland, a "son of the middle border," the prairie region undergoing momentous and jarring change during the 1870s and 1880s. In *Main-Travelled Roads* (1891) and *Prairie Folks* (1893), Garland told of the bitter failures and intense hardships of rural life, and of farm people crushed both by cruel nature and by even crueler human oppressors. Stephen Crane's *Maggie* (1893), subtitled *A Girl of the Streets*, is about a young woman in the slums of New York. Maggie is destroyed by the poverty, drunkenness, and crime of her environment. The picture is one of brutality and sordidness so frankly rendered that no publisher would risk it; Crane had to finance its publication himself under a pseudonym. Crane, who died young, would write one masterpiece, *The Red Badge of Courage* (1895), the story of a young soldier in the Civil War experiencing his first taste of battle. Born in 1871, Crane had no firsthand knowledge of the war; but the tale is a magnificent evocation of courage, cowardice, death, and violence under fire.

Another naturalist novelist was Theodore Dreiser. An Indianian who came from a background of poverty and scandal himself, Dreiser was a crude stylist but a writer of great cumulative power. His characters, unlike Crane's Maggie, are often strong people; but they, too, are at the mercy of their circumstances, their appetites, their drives, their yearnings. Carrie, of *Sister Carrie* (1900), is an ambitious young woman who uses men, is corrupted by them, and then destroys them in turn as she climbs her way up the social ladder. The hero of *The Financier* (1912) and *The Titan* (1914), modeled after Charles Yerkes, is Frank Cowperwood, an unprincipled big businessman driven by a lust for power that allows nothing and no one to stand in his way; although he triumphs over all his enemies, he is no more master of his destiny than the tragic Maggie.

Other authors of these years who played on the theme of powerful forces molding people include two Californians, Frank Norris and Jack London. In *McTeague*

(1899) Norris depicted a simple-minded San Francisco dentist who is gradually overwhelmed by material failure and tragically driven to murder. *Vandover and the Brute* (1914) is the tale of a man afflicted by illness who turns into a beastlike creature. *The Octopus* (1901) concerns the wheat farmers of California's Central Valley and their struggles with the railroad. Norris sympathized with the farmers, but as a naturalist, he tried to avoid praise or blame. All the characters, heroes and villains alike, are in the grip of forces they cannot control. London, though an avowed socialist, worshiped the power of the individual, and in adventure books set in Alaska—*The Call of the Wild* (1903), *White Fang* (1905)—as well as in works dealing with driven men—*The Sea Wolf* (1904)—he glorified the superman. Modeled on philosopher Friedrich Nietzsche's "blond beast," these brutal, arrogant, commanding characters, acting like elemental forces, sweep lesser beings aside.

★ PAINTING AND ARCHITECTURE ★

In two other areas of the arts, painting and architecture, we encounter the same movement from romantic gentility to an attempt to come to terms with the emerging modern world. In both, as in literature, some of the results are lasting and impressive achievements.

Romanticism to Modernism. American painting during the 1860s and 1870s was dominated by borrowed European romanticism, and Europe of the "Old Masters" remained for many years the measure of good taste in painting. When the first American museums were established in the decades surrounding the Civil War, their collections were almost exclusively paintings by European artists of the Renaissance and the seventeenth century. By the 1870s rich Americans had begun to buy paintings, sculpture, and other art objects as a mark of "culture" and sophistication, but almost invariably these were the works of established figures. The enormous collections accumulated by J. P. Morgan, Henry Clay Frick, and others brought much-needed cash to impoverished European gentry with family pictures to sell, but they benefited living American artists scarcely at all.

At the beginning of the post–Civil War era most American painters received their training in France or Germany, where they learned to paint in the romantic manner. Men like James McNeill Whistler and John Singer Sargent in fact preferred Europe as their permanent homes. During the years from 1875 to 1890 a more distinctively American school appeared, led by Winslow Homer, John La Farge, and Thomas Eakins. At their best these men painted vigorously honest portraits of professional men,

These paintings by Winslow Homer (left) and John Sloan (below) reveal how the sensibilities of visual artists changed in the half century following the Civil War. In Homer's 1866 painting, the upper-middle-class subjects, the balanced composition, and the croquet game itself all reflect the genteel tradition that dominated American art. The "Ashcan" painter Sloan depicted urban working-class life without sentimentality or disapproval. The woman in this 1911 painting does not seem distressed by the large family wash.

sportsmen, Americans at play. Their work was realistic in the sense that it was direct and vivid, but it was not contemporary. Its subject matter lacked relevance to the world in which most Americans lived.

At the beginning of the twentieth century a new school of painters began to come to terms with the emerging urban-industrial America. The core of this group consisted of Everett Shinn, George Luks, John Sloan, and William Glackens, all of whom had been newspaper illustrators in Philadelphia in the 1880s. Trained to capture events in quick, vivid images, as news photographers do today, they developed a keen eye for city scenes and city types. In the early 1890s the Philadelphia group came under the tutelage of Robert Henri, a teacher at the Pennsylvania Academy of Fine Arts. Henri had received his training in Europe but had been influenced by the French impressionists rather than the earlier romantics. Impressionists avoided sharp lines and photographic realism. Instead, they relied on the sort of visual shorthand that the eye in real life detects and the mind converts into reality. Toward the end of the decade Henri and his four disciples, one by one, moved to New York, where they were joined by Maurice Prendergast, Arthur B. Davies, and Ernest Lawson.

The Henri circle considered the conventional American painting of the day anemic and feeble, suitable for interior decoration, "merely an adjunct of plush and cut glass." Their own work was vigorous and real. Their subjects were certainly contemporary. They depicted prize fights, ordinary people waiting for taxis and streetcars, pigeons wheeling over tenement roofs, children at play in city streets, urban backyards, and the New York el at rush hour. Their technique often bordered on caricature. People were fat, frumpy, often coarse-looking. The critics attacked their work as harsh and vulgar. When, in 1904, six of the group exhibited at the National Arts Club, a conservative critic described them as portraying "an outlook where nature is seen under her most lugubrious mood, where joyousness never enters . . . and where unhealthiness prevails to an alarming extent." Before long the Henri group was being derided as the "Ashcan school." Offended by the tight rein imposed on artists by the conservative National Academy of Design, which excluded them from its prestigious exhibitions, eight Ashcan painters held their own show at the Mac-Beth Gallery in New York in 1908. The show immortalized "the eight" and marked a new era in American painting.

In 1913 the Henri group, and the still more radical Postimpressionists, sponsored a major showing of the best new European and American work at the Sixty-Ninth Regiment Armory in New York. Here for the first time a large number of Americans saw the works of Cézanne, Van Gogh, Picasso, Matisse, and the cubists, who seemed to have abandoned representation entirely. The sensation of the show was Marcel Duchamp's *Nude Descending a Staircase*, a cubist painting that by a succession of closely overlapping flat plane figures suggested the motion of a woman walking from the top to the bottom of a flight of stairs. One critic called the Duchamp painting "an explosion in a shingle factory." Another labeled the whole exhibit an exercise in "incomprehensibility combined with symptoms of paresis."

Despite the attacks, the Armory exhibit was an immensely influential event in American art. In New York and in the other cities where the paintings were shown, they attracted immense crowds. Most people came to smirk, but many stayed to marvel and appreciate. In all, 235 of the

The Armory Show sponsors, recognizing how controversial their exhibition would be, tried to win friends by offering the press a free beefsteak dinner. The menu, signed by prominent sponsors, features the scandalous Duchamp painting, Nude Descending a Staircase.

paintings were eventually sold. The market for modern art boomed, and American taste was given a tremendous push toward modernism.

Architecture. The years immediately following the Civil War found American architecture particularly out of tune with contemporary life. Designers of public buildings were still creating Greek temples or combining elements of so many traditional European styles that no clear label could be given them. A similar eclecticism marked domestic architecture for the rich. French chateaux, Elizabethan half-timbered cottages, small Roman temples—or frequently mixtures of all three—were what rich businessmen commissioned. Meanwhile, the ordinary middle-class family bought a balloon-frame house constructed of wood uprights and siding stuck together with nails, and decorated, if at all, with wooden "gingerbread" trim.

By the 1880s and 1890s many critics had become disenchanted with American architecture. Charles Eliot Norton, professor of fine arts at Harvard, told his students that "we have, as a nation, painfully displayed our disregard of the ennobling influence of fine architecture upon national character." Norton and his colleagues were the

Though they originated in Chicago, skyscrapers were quickly adopted in crowded Manhattan. In this view of the Flatiron Building we can see the steel frame as yet incompletely encased by its masonry sheath.

equivalents of the genteel literary critics, who saw art as a means for improving public virtue. Yet what they endorsed was a higher level of performance than was common in their day.

To some extent the plea for a finer aesthetic in building was answered by a group of young men—including Stanford White, Charles McKim, Daniel Burnham, and William Robert Ware—who studied in Paris and returned with finely honed skills that enabled them to reproduce accurately the traditional styles of the past. They could design Renaissance and Elizabethan homes for the rich, as well as Gothic buildings for colleges. But, the critics asked, in what sense were these *American* buildings?

A few utilitarian objects had somehow escaped the almost universal blight of inappropriate overdecoration. At

the 1876 centennial celebration in Philadelphia, the Corliss engine, a monster machine, had been admired not only for its power but also for its clean lines. The Brooklyn Bridge, completed in 1883, delighted almost everyone by its airy simplicity. But on the whole there was little relationship, in either building or household and industrial design, between the use of structures or objects and their appearance. Nor, as the 1870s ended, had architects yet taken new technology—cheap steel, electricity, and the telephone—into account.

The first signs of change came in the 1880s when a group of Chicago architects began to develop a new way of looking at building. During this decade the Windy City was caught up in a frenzy of construction, both to restore structures destroyed in the fire of 1871 and to build new ones to meet the space needs of the nation's fastest-growing metropolis. In the midst of this building boom William Le Baron Jenney designed the first true skyscraper.

There had been tall buildings in the past, of course— churches, lighthouses, public buildings—but these had been both expensive and impractical. Walls of high buildings had to be very thick at the base to bear the enormous weight of the masonry above. Windows on the lower stories had to be small, making it difficult to light interiors. The thick lower walls also reduced sharply the structure's usable space. Finally, the inconvenient stairs of high buildings made space at the top virtually unrentable.

The new buildings of Jenney, Louis Sullivan, Ernest Flagg, Cass Gilbert, and others used steel, electric light, and the electric elevator to get around these problems. Steel, especially, revolutionized construction. Instead of heavy, weight-bearing walls, architects needed only a frame of light, interlocked steel beams. To these they attached thin walls of brick or stone veneer. With electricity and fast elevators, such a building could provide convenient, usable space at much lower cost than an equivalent masonry structure. Because the skyscraper could be erected to virtually any height, designers could go up rather than out and so reduce the outlay on expensive downtown land.

At first skyscrapers, like other American structures, ignored the design implications of technology. They were decorated with classical pillars; many were made to look like overblown Gothic cathedrals. Gradually, however, a new attitude appeared that held that a structure's design and appearance should honestly reflect its function. In the words of Louis Sullivan, "Over all the coursing sun, *form ever follows function*, and that is the law." A building should not disguise its use, but proclaim it boldly and honestly. In line with this new perception, Henry Hobson Richardson, though known for his adaptations of the Romanesque style, designed structures like Marshall Field's wholesale store (1885–1887)—square, simple, and solid, without fussy lines or details borrowed from traditional European styles. Sullivan's best works were the Schiller Building (1891–1892) in Chicago and St. Louis's Wainwright Building (1890–1891).

Frank Lloyd Wright, Sullivan's pupil, translated his mentor's theories into domestic architecture. Wright had learned not only from Sullivan but also from the Japanese, whose simple, light domestic buildings with adjustable spaces he had observed at the 1893 Chicago World's Fair. After establishing his new Chicago office in 1894, Wright developed his ideas concerning the close relation of form, use, materials, and site. These became the basis for his famous prairie houses—long, low structures to match the terrain of the flat Midwest. Wright broke with the past by avoiding traditional elements of exterior design, and he built the homes of local stone and timber that suited their locations. Critics hailed Wright's work as strikingly innovative, yet at first few patrons came to him. Not until the 1920s did Wright's form of architectural modernism begin to attract widespread public acclaim.

★ POPULAR CULTURE ★

It is possible, then, to trace the gradual response of artists to the realities of the American social and economic scene in the half century following the Civil War. A similar pattern of adaptation to an emerging urban-industrial environment can be observed in popular culture, entertainment, sports, and recreation.

Spectator Sports.   As more and more Americans moved to the cities, they found that the world of play as well as the world of work had changed. Country people engaged in sports, of course. They swam, fished, played versions of baseball. Yet rural labor offered so many opportunities to exercise in the open air that country residents had less reason to crave organized games than town people.

Smaller American urban centers were in some ways ideal places for sports. They had both many open spaces for games and enough people of like mind to make up teams. The largest cities, however, presented serious problems. True, there were both the people and the need for outdoor recreation, but space was often unavailable and so, too, was leisure. As we have seen, few American cities had preserved open space in their congested centers. Not until the very end of the nineteenth century did cities open playgrounds for children and add sports and exercise programs to school curricula. Insufficient leisure remained a deterrent to sports for a longer time. As late as 1890 the average workweek for American factory workers was sixty hours; until the mid-

1920s it was still fifty. Few wage earners had paid vacations. Most worked every day except Sunday, and in many cities evangelical Protestant groups had succeeded in imposing blue laws that kept theaters and ball parks closed on the Sabbath. Only gradually as the old century gave way to the new did pressure from Catholics, nonbelievers, working people, and various secular groups force city officials to permit Sunday sports and amusements. Increasingly, sports became incorporated into city life. But most urbanites were caught up in the movement as spectators rather than personal participants.

An exception to this generalization was the bicycle of the 1890s. Early bicycles had been bizarre contraptions with giant front wheels and tiny rear ones. They tipped easily and only daredevils would ride them. The safety bicycle with two equal-size wheels changed the bicycle's clientele to ordinary people, and by the 1890s thousands of "wheelmen" (and women) were taking Sunday trips to the country carrying picnic lunches with them. Before long the new bicycle-riding public was demanding better roads of local and state governments. But the bicycle fad was the exception; most Americans in the new urban age were content for professionals to play while they watched.

The first of the nineteenth-century sports to be commercialized was baseball, a game that had evolved out of several centuries-old children's games. By the 1850s amateur baseball clubs had become common in the cities and towns. Their matches soon attracted spectators, and reports of their encounters began to appear in the newspapers. Before long the teams were erecting high fences around their playing fields and charging spectators for admission to underwrite the cost of equipment, uniforms, and travel to rival communities.

The next steps in commercializing baseball came quickly. In 1858 the National Association of Baseball Players was organized, and in 1869 the Cincinnati Red Stockings began to pay salaries to players. In 1876 the National League of Professional Baseball Clubs—with teams in New York, Philadelphia, Hartford, Boston, Chicago, Louisville, Cincinnati, and St. Louis—superseded the amateur organization. In the next few years more teams joined the National League, and in 1899 a group of promoters organized the American League. The two leagues struggled for supremacy for a few years and then amicably agreed to coexist. In 1903 the champions of each met in the first World Series; the American League's Boston Red Sox beat the National League's Pittsburgh Pirates. Baseball attendance grew rapidly in the early part of the new century, and in the 1913 World Series gate receipts for the five games reached $326,000. In 1908 the popular song "Take Me Out to the Ball Game" marked the triumph of baseball as the country's most popular sport.

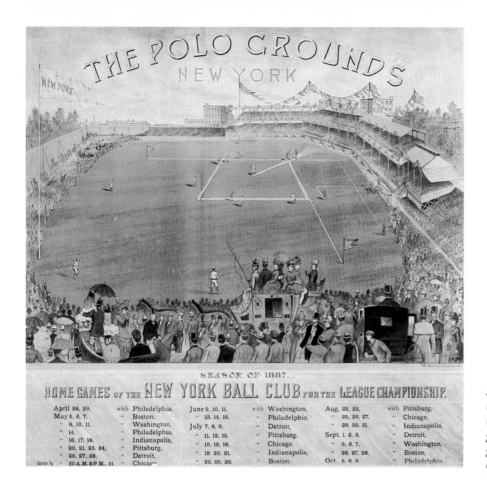

Football and boxing, though popular, failed to match baseball's popularity during these years. Until the 1920s football remained a game played in colleges by amateurs and patronized by upper-middle-class people, often graduates of one of the schools. Yet toward the end of the century college rivalries encouraged active recruiting of players, often poor sons of immigrants. By 1917 critics were charging that the supposedly amateur game had become commercialized with hidden subsidies to players, vulgar hoopla, and expensive stadiums—in addition to excessive violence.

Because of its brutality, boxing carried a stigma as a "blood" sport in these years. Few women and few respectable men attended matches, and in some cities boxing was forbidden. Yet the sport was popular among working men, especially recent immigrants and second-generation Americans in the big cities. When John L. Sullivan returned to his native Boston after knocking out Jake Kilrain in a harrowing seventy-five round, bare-knuckle fight in 1889, the city's Irish turned out in force to honor him as an ethnic hero.

The new spectator sports not only diverted city people but also filled them with pride. Professional sports were rel-atively democratic. The lists of outstanding players or champions in a particular sport record the growing assimilation and acceptance of newer-stock Americans. At the beginning the names are Anglo-Saxon; by the 1890s they are German and Irish; by 1910 or 1920 they are increasingly Italian, Spanish, and Jewish. Clearly, professional sports provided an escalator upward for each new European group in America.

Most professional sports retained the "color bar," however. Black players were excluded from major league baseball and forced to play in black leagues, where salaries were low, equipment poor, and ballparks mere fenced fields. College football was somewhat more open in the North, though when northern teams played rivals in the South, they benched their black players in deference to southern prejudices. The least segregated major spectator sport was prize fighting; in 1908 Jack Johnson, a black man, defeated Tommy Burns, a white Canadian, to become heavyweight champion of the world. But even boxing was not free of prejudice. The white public resented Johnson's reign as champion and yearned for a "white hope" to defeat him. Johnson's marriage to a white woman made him even more unpopular, and when he was defeated by Jess Willard, a white American, the white public cheered.

Culture in the Age of the Dynamo   609

The bicycle craze of the 1890s, like its equivalents today, spawned hobbyist magazines. (Collection of the New York Historical Society)

Women were even more restricted in their sports role than blacks. Prevailing American attitudes of the Gilded Age and the early twentieth century held sport to be a masculine occupation. Middle-class women shared in the bicycle craze of the 1890s and played genteel games like croquet and lawn tennis. Working women and working-class housewives had little time for these, though some joined their husbands, brothers, and fathers in attending sports events. Women participated in professional sports exclusively as spectators. Nowhere in these years was there a professional women's team that attracted paying customers.

Mass Entertainment. Music, the theater, the circus, and the amusement park were other ways in which city people in the half century following the Civil War filled their limited leisure time and softened the rough edges of their daily lives.

The amusement park was in part an outgrowth of the streetcar lines. In an effort to encourage weekend business, the "traction" companies established resorts on the outskirts of the towns they served. Chicago had Cheltenham Beach and later White City. Boston had Paragon Park; San Francisco, The Chutes; St. Louis, Forest Park Highlands;

Philadelphia, Willow Grove; and New York, Coney Island. On Sundays city people flocked to these parks to hear concerts, watch balloon ascensions and bicycle races, and patronize the "rides," including the Ferris wheel, the roller coaster, and others. Here Americans ate hamburgers and hot dogs for the first time.

Before World War I "classical" music had not been fully absorbed into American life. The elite could hear chamber music, symphonies, and opera in some cities, but it was music composed by foreigners and often performed by foreigners. Popular music was home grown. During the post–Civil War years, writing popular songs to be sold as sheet music and played and sung at the parlor piano became a successful profession for a score of composers. By 1900 most of the songwriters and their agents were located along New York's Twenty-eighth Street, "Tin Pan Alley." The label soon became the nickname for the lucrative popular music business.

Some of the most successful composers, Gussie Davis for one, were black. Others, including Edward Marks, Monroe Rosenberg, and Irving Berlin, were Jewish. During the 1890s Scott Joplin and other black composers introduced ragtime into popular music. "Rags" were instrumental pieces written for either piano or band, rather than pieces for singing. They combined elements of traditional white music, the syncopation of urban black music, and the street music of the white underclass. In the hands of Joplin, a Texas-born black man with formal musical training, they were often complex, sophisticated works. Joplin wrote thirty-nine rags and was widely imitated by other composers, black and white alike.

Jazz, like ragtime, had roots in the black city ghettos. Its original home was New Orleans, where blacks had long been a vital part of the cultural scene. Black wind musicians played at funerals and other important occasions, both solemn and joyous, and freely improvised on melodies from traditional French and American marches and popular songs, combining them with ragtime-style syncopation drawn from the black musical experience. Black singers, pianists, and instrumentalists also played in the raffish saloons and brothels of Storyville, the New Orleans red-light district. Here one heard both ragtime and "the blues," a mournful vocal form related to rural black spirituals, but usually concerned with less uplifting themes: crime, betrayal, sexual passion. It was in Storyville that such inspired performers as Ferdinand ("Jelly Roll") Morton, Louis Armstrong, Joseph ("King") Oliver, and "Ma" Rainey got their start.

When military authorities closed the Storyville brothels in 1917, supposedly to protect servicemen from venereal disease, New Orleans musicians dispersed in all directions. Some became performers on the passenger river-

New Yorkers in the 1890s amused themselves at Steeplechase Park in Coney Island. Almost every city in America had its equivalent in this era.

boats that still plied the Mississippi. Eventually they settled in the emerging black ghettos of Chicago, St. Louis, Kansas City, Memphis, and New York where they played in the nightclubs and speakeasies that Prohibition had spawned. They also began to make phonograph records. Young white musicians found "Jass" exciting and some began to imitate the black players. At their best they created the lively new Chicago Style, which, like the original, relied on improvisation and spontaneity. At their worst they watered it down and prettied it up. The music of Paul Whiteman, the "King of Jazz," was a slick, contrived sort of popular music that suited the palates of a middle-class white audience. The Whiteman style was generally what the white public knew as jazz during the 1920s.

Popular music in this period often shared billing with other entertainment on stage. In the minstrel shows, a form of "review" dating from before the Civil War, songs, dances, and comedy routines exploited black stereotypes and black musical themes. There were a few all-black minstrel shows, but troupes such as Christy's Minstrels featured white people with faces darkened with burnt cork. Such groups were seldom concerned about authenticity. Black people were depicted as happy, amiable "darkies." During the 1860s a

hundred such companies toured the country performing minstrel shows to large audiences.

By the 1880s the minstrel show, rooted in an earlier, simpler era, had been replaced by vaudeville, which offered much greater variety. A typical vaudeville performance consisted of as many as thirty brief acts—dances, comic skits, songs, acrobatics, animal stunts, juggling, magic. Like the minstrel show, it was a showcase for popular songs. It also offered talented young men and women from newer immigrant stock—Jewish, Spanish, Italian, Irish—opportunities to win fame and fortune as performers. The vaudeville show was especially popular among the new urban audiences. They did not need to know English to enjoy a juggler or a magician, and the costumes and music created a glamorous image, briefly transforming the narrow, impoverished world of slum dwellers.

The motion picture was even better suited to the growing urban audience. Its basis was a set of technical advances that combined a flexible medium for photographic emulsions, a camera that could take a fast series of still frames, and a projector that could send these through a magnifying lens onto a screen to create the impression of live motion. Edison did much of the work in joining these elements,

By 1910 Americans had developed the movie habit. For urban newcomers, especially the hordes of immigrants, silent films offered cheap, accessible entertainment. Even children—as this view outside a New York city nickelodeon suggests—found movies irresistible.

though at first he saw little but an amusing toy in his invention and was happy to license exhibitors to show thirty-second films in penny arcades. The first films were merely scenic views or bits of action—dancers, acrobats, boxers. Soon the exhibitors discovered more profit in such racy material as *Taking a Bath, What the Bootblack Saw,* and *Dolorita's Passion Dance.* Motion pictures began to tap a more general audience in 1896 when the first film was shown in a respectable theater, Koster and Bial's Music Hall in New York. Soon vaudeville managers began to add a filmed "act" to the live performances they presented.

The audience for the new medium proved enormous. Live theater was expensive, and relied on conventions that sometimes baffled untutored audiences. There was also the language barrier. Some immigrant communities established theater in their own tongue, but for others the only alternative was the inaccessible English-language stage. The early movies were silent and told their simple stories with broad gestures and giant images. No one, no matter how ignorant of English or deficient in education, felt excluded from the action. Once the medium's success was assured, Edison attempted to impose a monopoly by insisting his patent rights be respected and charging movie makers high fees to use his cameras and projectors. He did not succeed. Before long dozens of small picture makers, using equipment of their own make or imported from Europe, were

shooting films in backyards and makeshift studios. Many were Jewish businessmen who were quick to recognize the potential of the new medium.

There soon was a similar proliferation of exhibitors. By 1900 hundreds of exhibitors were showing films in empty stores, town halls, school auditoriums—almost anyplace they could assemble some chairs in a darkened room. These early movie houses were often called "nickelodeons." They charged five cents for an eight-minute showing of a humorous, exciting, or exotic incident. Most of these primitive sketches were created on the spur of the moment by directors, camera operators, or other employees of the many small firms formed to provide material for the nickelodeons.

This impromptu approach to filmmaking soon gave way to more deliberate efforts. In 1903 Edwin Porter of the Edison company produced *The Great Train Robbery*, telling a story of some complexity, in almost a full reel of film. Soon two other firms, Vitagraph and Biograph, were imitating Porter. Equipment became better, theaters more permanent and comfortable, and films more impressive artistically. By 1905 many of the classic film genres—western, comedy-romance, crime, travelogue, science fiction—had become established.

At first many of the film companies were located in the East, close to the established pool of actors and technicians. But the East had many drawbacks. Land for studios in the big eastern cities was expensive. When producers began to shoot outdoors, they were hindered by the cold and rainy eastern weather. The East was also close to the Edison "film trust," which pursued a policy of suing every company that did not pay a substantial fee for the privilege of making films. To escape the trust and to take advantage of cheap space and sunny weather, William Selig, a Chicago producer, moved his company to southern California in 1907. Soon Selig was joined by others. By 1912 the Los Angeles suburb of Hollywood had become the nation's filmmaking capital.

By this time, too, the audience for motion pictures had grown to between 10 million and 20 million annually. Also fully developed was the star system, which relied on popular performers to pull customers in each week. Among the earliest stars were Tom Mix, Mary Pickford, Charles Chaplin, "Bronco Billy" Anderson, William S. Hart, Mabel Normand, Buster Keaton, Pearl White, and Theda Bara. These actors commanded fabulous salaries, a fact which added to their glamour and enhanced their public adulation.

Eventually the motion picture audience grew more sophisticated and began to demand more than superficial dazzle and excitement. Talented people soon met the more exacting demands. In the years after 1910, D. W. Griffith worked for the Biograph studio and helped to make its films a superior product. Griffith was the first producer-director who truly understood the new medium and successfully exploited its unique potential. In 1915 he produced, for the then-immense figure of $100,000, *The Birth of a Nation*. Concerned with the tribulations of Reconstruction, the movie was blatantly racist and pro–Ku Klux Klan. It aroused fierce opposition among blacks and white liberals wherever it was shown, but it was an immense popular success—and from a purely artistic perspective, deservedly so. Twelve reels long, it made effective use of the fadeout, the dissolve, crosscutting, the close-up, and the long-shot. In the special theaters where it was shown, orchestras accompanied the action. However deplorable ideologically, *The Birth of a Nation* set a new standard of artistic and technical excellence for the entire film industry.

★ EDUCATION ★

In their various ways, then, the arts, both "high" and "low," responded to the transformation of America from a rural and agricultural society to one marked by cities and industry. The educational life of the nation between the Civil War and World War I revealed a similar shift. In the process it managed simultaneously to become more democratic, create more stringent cultural and intellectual standards, and serve the nation's infatuation with material progress.

The Public Schools. The greatest change in education in the half century following 1865 was its sheer expansion. In 1870 about 7 million pupils were enrolled in public day schools; by 1915 there were over 18 million, with another 1.5 million in private schools, mostly Catholic parochial institutions. Not only had the number increased; so had the proportion of the school-aged population attending school. By 1915 well over 80 percent of all young people were attending classes of some sort. School outlays rose even faster than enrollments, growing to $605 million, or $31 annually per pupil, in 1915.

Many factors helped produce the increasing expenditures and numbers. In 1860 few states in the South had systems of public education. By the end of Reconstruction, however, southern states had joined the rest of the country in accepting responsibility for supporting elementary schools. Meanwhile, in the large cities a parallel system of parochial schools sprang up, largely to serve the nation's growing Catholic population. More and more states also made school attendance compulsory. In 1881 nineteen states and territories in the North and West had compulsory attendance laws; by 1898 there were thirty-one. At the same time legislatures raised school-leaving ages and made the school year longer.

All these changes added substantially to the taxpayers' bills. But education seemed well worth the cost to this generation of Americans. As the nation's economy grew larger and more complex, not only was education easier to pay for, it was also more essential. With each passing year business needed more and more young men and women who could calculate receipts, add figures, write letters, and follow written instructions. With well-paying jobs requiring a high degree of literacy becoming more common, staying in school became attractive to the young.

The growing need for managerial and clerical personnel increased the demand for public high schools. Before the Civil War, Massachusetts was the only state that had authorized a system of high schools supported by public funds. Secondary education elsewhere was the domain of the private "academy," which charged tuition to young women preparing for the teaching profession and young men preparing for college. After 1865 several states followed Massachusetts's lead. At first local taxpayers resisted the new burden on the grounds that no community owed its citizens an education beyond the elementary level. In 1874, however, the Michigan Supreme Court upheld a state law allowing citizens of local school districts to tax themselves for the purpose of establishing public high schools. Thereafter, with the legal roadblocks eliminated, other states followed suit; by 1915 there were more than 11,000 public high schools in the United States with over 1.3 million pupils.

Initially the curricula of the public high schools emphasized the same liberal arts and classic languages that were dominant in the private academies. Before long, however, school administrators introduced commercial programs, including typing, bookkeeping, and accounting. Latin and Greek gave way to modern foreign languages. Even more "practically" oriented were the vocational classes that began to invade the high schools under the prodding of the National Society for the Promotion of Industrial Education. In 1917 Congress—recognizing the value of teaching "manual training," including carpentry, printing, home economics, mechanical drawing, and agriculture—passed the Smith-Hughes Act providing subsidies to the states to underwrite vocational and industrial skills courses for high school students.

Higher Education.   During these same years the United States became a world leader in college and university education. Before the Civil War the typical American college was a small church-related institution that prepared young men for the ministry or for the learned professions. Most had a few hundred students, a single classroom building, a museum containing stuffed and preserved animals, and a library of a few hundred books, mostly on religion, tucked into some corner. Faculties were small, and many of the professors were ministers who doubled in science and modern languages—if these subjects were taught at all.

After the Civil War change came swiftly. The Morrill Land Grant College Act (1862) provided funds for a new class of agricultural and technical colleges, many of which developed into major universities. At the same time vast sums flowed from the swollen fortunes of post–Civil War business tycoons to establish new colleges and universities and revive old, sleepy ones. Under the guidance of a new breed of college president, curricula altered rapidly to provide students with training in the sciences, modern languages, and the new social sciences, as well as vocational courses such as accounting and engineering. In the 1880s president Charles W. Eliot of Harvard introduced the elective system, ending the requirement of tightly prescribed

The burgeoning high school system of the late nineteenth century was designed to produce office workers as well as better-educated citizens. Here we see the typing class in an 1899 Washington, D.C., high school.

Women scientists were rare before our own day, but not unknown. Here is chemist Ellen Swallow Richards (first row right), sitting as part of a group portrait of the faculty of the Massachusetts Institute of Technology (MIT) around 1900. The first woman to graduate from the institute, she was also the first to serve on its faculty.

courses and allowing students to choose their own program within broad limits.

Another important change was the expansion of higher education for women. Before 1860 only a handful of institutions allowed women to take college degrees. After the Civil War these limits were quickly swept away as women's colleges proliferated and state universities opened their doors to men and women on an equal basis. In the older elite schools—the so-called Ivy League—women were admitted to sister institutions with separate faculties, courses, and buildings. In the state schools they sat in the same classrooms with men, though they used separate dormitories and were subject to stricter rules of decorum.

The most important advance in higher education during this period was the appearance of the research university and the graduate school. Before the Civil War, though some professors occasionally performed experiments or engaged in scholarly pursuits, research was not considered a part of faculty duties. During the 1840s and 1850s, however, a number of Americans studied in Germany, where they encountered a different system. German universities were not just glorified academies. They were institutions where young men were trained in the techniques of discovering new knowledge and where faculty members were themselves engaged in pushing forward the frontiers of science and scholarship.

Americans trained in the German universities carried the new idea to their native land, and after the Civil War these seeds bore fruit in the modern American university. The first institution founded on the German model was Johns Hopkins, which opened in Baltimore in 1876. Hopkins was primarily a graduate school where the sciences, social sciences, and humanities were treated as scholarly disciplines. The new university taught by the seminar system, wherein a prominent scholar and a small group of advanced students worked on a common set of problems. The result for the student was published research and the new degree of Ph.D. (Doctor of Philosophy).

Hopkins was soon widely imitated. Clark University, founded in 1887 at Worcester, Massachusetts, also patterned itself on the German model. At the same time, existing institutions—Harvard, Yale, Columbia, Chicago, Cornell, Michigan, Wisconsin, and Minnesota among them—set up graduate schools for training scholars and scientists. In 1900 some 240 doctoral degrees were conferred on American students, and the degree was well on its way to becoming the "union card" of the college teaching profession. Meanwhile, however imperfectly, the best American universities were being transformed into communities of creative men, and some women, dedicated to the quest for new fundamental understanding and practical knowledge.

Professional Education and Professionalism. The process by which college teaching was transformed from a field for amateurs to one dominated by trained and "credentialed" experts was paralleled in other professional areas. In part the trend was inspired by the sheer accumulation of knowledge, which forced each field to divide into ever-narrower specializations. This trend was most apparent in the social sciences, where by the end of the century the old "moral philosophy" had been broken down into economics, sociology, psychology, and political science. Professionalization was also a consequence of efforts by occupational groups to raise their status and income by restricting entry into the field, usually by credentialing procedures in the name of higher professional standards.

In law and medicine training through apprenticeship gave way in these years to formal education in law and medical schools. In medicine, at first, this led to an enormous proliferation of inferior schools, some mere diploma mills where students acquired M.D. degrees for a fee and perfunctory work. Doctors trained at these schools were seldom competent in the medical advances of the period, though no doubt some of them made adequate general practitioners. In 1910 a report by Abraham Flexner, supported by the Carnegie Foundation, exposed widespread abuses in medical education and led the American Medical Association to push for the closing of inferior schools and the upgrading of others. The effects were drastic. The number of medical graduates dropped from over 5,000 yearly between 1900 and 1906 to about half that number in 1922. Critics charged that the true purpose of the upgrading was to restrict the number of physicians in order to prevent over-competition. Yet the changes did indeed improve the level of skills among doctors.

Legal training also improved, though the overall effect was less restrictive. During these years more and more universities established law schools with three-year courses of study. At first, students could begin legal training after high school. Gradually, however, the better law schools insisted on college preparation, and in the 1870s Harvard introduced the case method, a system of learning legal principles by studying actual cases decided by the courts. Lawyers also began to specialize. Increasingly, especially in the larger cities, university-trained lawyers joined corporate law firms where they spent most of their time preparing contracts and mergers and almost never appeared in court.

The process of professionalization soon spread to many other areas. The usual pattern was for some occupational group, feeling dissatisfied with their incomes, social status, and prevailing intellectual levels, to band together in a professional association. The association would then set new standards for education and training and often, in connection with the universities, establish a degree program to be required of all future entrants into the profession. Another step in many cases was to induce state governments to accept the new standards and require them of new entrants to the field. Finally, an examination administered by the state would be imposed on those seeking to practice the profession under state license. In this way such diverse groups as teachers, nurses, engineers, accountants, social workers, dentists, pharmacists, optometrists, and others raised themselves to professional status. As in the case of doctors, their professionalization improved the level of service for the public, but also increased the cost of those services. A final beneficiary of professionalization was the universities, which acquired crowds of students eager to gain professional degrees and the training needed to pass professional licensing exams.

Informal Education for the Masses.   Not all the educational progress and expansion of these years took place in formal schools. Adult Americans by the millions found self-education enjoyable and sought opportunities to acquire books and instruction outside the schools.

One of the most successful forms of adult education was the Chautauqua Assembly, an institution devoted to bringing learning and instruction to large numbers of people without formal requirements and degrees. Chautauqua began in 1874 when a Methodist clergyman, John H. Vincent, established a summer camp and school for Sunday school teachers in western New York. By the 1880s Chautauqua had left its religious focus behind and had become a sort of informal college where for ten summer weeks thousands of men and women gathered to hear learned and lively speakers such as economist Richard T. Ely; psychologist G. Stanley Hall, president of Clark University; philosopher William James; and historian Herbert Baxter Adams. Chautauqua also offered courses more useful in daily life. Indiana author Edward Eggleston described the enormous range of Chautauqua's offerings:

> You can learn Greek, Latin, Hebrew, and for aught I know Choctaw here. You can learn . . . Penmanship and Pedagogy and Exegetics and Homiletics and History and Rowing and Piano Music and fancy bicycling and singing and athletics and how to read a hymn in public and the art of writing family and Business letters and everything else except dancing and whist.

Chautauqua had no formal ideology or philosophy; but as the century advanced, it tended to feature speakers who represented new ideas that challenged the intellectual pieties of the age. Many of the clergymen represented the new social gospel, which called on Christians to aid the weak and oppressed. Chautauqua economists like Ely rejected extreme laissez-faire doctrines and were friendlier to organized labor than their predecessors had been. Chautauqua speakers also favored women's suffrage, the peace movement, and even socialism. In fact, the Chautauqua Assembly of the 1890s and the first decade of the new century was a major center for disseminating the ideas that would be called "progressive." This effect was enhanced in 1904 when Chautauqua established summer seminars in small towns all over the country. These were held in communities for a week at a time and usually conducted in tents. In addition, the Chautauqua Assembly established more permanent summer camps, modeled after the New York original, in such places as Boulder, Colorado.

An even less formal dispenser of knowledge was the public library. Before the Civil War the few tax-supported free libraries had been concentrated in a handful of eastern cities. Elsewhere avid readers had either bought books or borrowed them from those who could afford private libraries. The few large libraries that existed had primitive systems of classification that reduced their value to users. After the war, under the leadership of Melvil Dewey and W. F. Poole, the American Library Association (founded 1876) developed classification systems that were immense aids as libraries grew in size. The association also lobbied for tax support, and by 1898 eighteen states had authorized local communities to impose taxes to support public libraries. In 1881 Andrew Carnegie began his program of contributions to public libraries, which eventually dotted the nation with "Carnegie libraries" from the Atlantic to the Pacific. By 1900 there were over 9,000 free public libraries in the country, with nearly 50 million volumes.

Paralleling this development was the rise of the research library. By the end of the century, owing to generous gifts or legislative appropriations, institutions such as the Library of Congress, the New York Public Library, the Newberry Library in Chicago, and the Cleveland Public Library had become centers of scholarship in the humanities. College and university libraries, too, burgeoned as American institutions of higher learning moved into the forefront of scholarship and research. By the eve of World War I the largest American university libraries had surpassed in size those of European institutions founded many centuries earlier.

★ THE NEW JOURNALISM ★

Newspapers on the eve of the Civil War were very different from their counterparts today. For one thing they were smaller, usually only sixteen to twenty pages long. In part this was because they contained a fraction of the advertising they do today, but it also reflected skimpier coverage of national and international events. News-gathering facilities were primitive. Foreign news, in the absence of the transat-

lantic cable (which was not successfully laid until 1866), took weeks to arrive. Domestic news was transmitted more quickly, but only a few of the very largest urban papers had reporters outside their home cities, and usually only in Washington and the state capitals. For coverage of any American community but their home towns, newspaper editors were forced to copy stories from other newspapers received by exchange in the mail.

The newspaper of 1860 was different from its modern version in other ways, too. It had no pictures; it was not yet possible to print photographs on newsprint. There were a few illustrated weeklies, but they relied on woodcuts or copper engravings, which could not be prepared quickly enough for the daily press. There were no comic strips, syndicated news columnists, food columns, horoscopes, or advice to the lovelorn. Anyone reading an 1860 newspaper today would also be impressed by the relative sedateness of the coverage. Editors reported crimes and disasters, but usually in a sober, matter-of-fact way. Most of their space was filled with political news from Washington, the state capital, and the local board of aldermen. Reported in enormous detail, these stories are valuable for a political historian today, but may well have induced instant sleep in contemporary readers.

New Trends in Newspapers.   By the early years of the twentieth century, newspaper publishing had undergone a revolution. Part of the impetus for change came from the growth of city population, which created a new, concentrated market for news, information, and entertainment. Part was the result of new technology that helped with gathering, packaging, and distributing news.

The new technology came from widely scattered developments. At the end of the 1870s the modern typewriter, capable of printing both upper- and lower-case letters, appeared. A decade later Ottmar Mergenthaler invented the linotype machine, eliminating the need to set type painfully by hand. Cheap pulp paper came into wide use about the same time, as did processes for fast reproduction of illustrations and photographs. The telephone, invented in the 1870s by Alexander Bell, a Scottish-born teacher of the deaf, was in wide use by the 1890s and proved an invaluable tool for information gathering.

New sorts of news-collecting and news-packaging agencies also facilitated change. In the 1840s a group of New York editors conceived the idea of pooling information and selling it to subscribers. Out of this grew the Associated Press, with information-gathering facilities in major foreign capitals and in many American news centers. The United Press followed in 1882. In 1884, S.S. McClure, an inventive publisher, established "Newspaper Features," providing ready-made syndicated columns, short stories, and a "woman's page," for subscribing papers.

The new yellow journalism of Hearst and Pulitzer was brash and readable. The city room of Pulitzer's New York World, *with its shirt-sleeved editors and reporters, captures some of the informality and hectic pace of the late-nineteenth-century urban newspaper.*

Taking advantage of these changes was a group of aggressive editors. One of them, Joseph Pulitzer, was a man of broad social sympathies who retained his respect for journalism even while he appealed to popular taste. An Hungarian refugee who arrived in the United States in 1864 with hardly a penny, Pulitzer became active in St. Louis publishing and in 1878 acquired the St. Louis *Post-Dispatch*. He soon made the ailing paper a success and with the money he accumulated bought the *New York World*.

As editor of the *World*, Pulitzer helped create what critics would call "yellow journalism." His paper emphasized "human interest" stories—crime, corruption, disasters, strange reversals of the usual order of things, sudden luck, and the like. The *World* printed illustrations showing "X— where the Body Was Found." Its headlines ran to: "Baptized in Blood," and "Death Rides the Blast." Pulitzer also attracted readers by promotional schemes, such as dispatching the "girl reporter" Nellie Bly in a world-circling race to beat Jules Verne's fictional hero of *Around the World in Eighty Days*. He was also the first editor to print a comic strip, R.F. Outcault's "The Yellow Kid," printed in yellow ink, which provided the name for Pulitzer's approach to the newspaper business.

Pulitzer's yellow journalism was enormously successful. When he acquired the *World*, its circulation was 15,000. By 1898 he was selling a million papers a day. He soon acquired a flock of imitators, including the Scripps brothers, with papers in Detroit, Cleveland, St. Louis, and Cincinnati, and William Randolph Hearst in San Francisco. In 1895 Hearst came to New York, determined to outdo Pulitzer. He

introduced his own comic strips, "The Katzenjammer Kids" and "Happy Hooligan," and then stole "The Yellow Kid" from Pulitzer. Before many months his *New York Journal* was engaged in a full-scale circulation war with the *World*, with each editor attempting to outsensationalize the other. In later years Hearst acquired or established newspapers all over the nation and even set up his own press service. By the early years of the twentieth century he had become the nation's most powerful "press lord," using a formula of sensationalism plus human interest that usually lacked Pulitzer's saving grace of concern for the underdog.

Magazines. Magazines also responded to the new technology and new urban mass market for reading material. Most of the successful magazines before the Civil War had been highly literate small-circulation publications intended for the educated middle and upper class. In the 1880s a number of magazine publishers tried, like Pulitzer and Hearst, to take advantage of new printing technology and city audiences. Dutch-born Edward W. Bok turned the recently established *Ladies' Home Journal* into a success by offering light fiction, pieces on interesting personalities, "Talks With Girls," and house plans, as well as articles on food, fashions, and house care—and all for 10 cents a copy. Samuel S. McClure took advantage of drastically reduced printing costs and growing advertising revenues to launch a mass-circulation magazine of general interest, *McClure's*. In 1893 the first copy, selling for 15 cents, appeared. Soon after Frank Munsey launched *Munsey's*, followed quickly by

Hearst's *Cosmopolitan*, both priced at 10 cents. Until McClure hit on the muckraking formula in 1903 (described in Chapter 23), all three mass-circulation magazines relied on good illustrations and popular, skillful authors to attract enough readers to make a profit despite their low price. And they succeeded. By the end of the century magazine readership had expanded to over five times that of the 1870s.

★ NEW MODES OF THOUGHT ★

In the half century following the Civil War the way Americans thought about their world and about society underwent an enormous shift. Not all Americans were equally affected by the changes, of course. Inevitably, many continued to accept the received wisdom of their predecessors; some actively fought the new trends. But a substantial group of urban, educated men and women adjusted their thinking to a flood of new ideas, many of them derived ultimately from the theories of the English naturalist Charles Darwin.

We have already seen in Chapter 17 how the ideas of Darwin served as a prop for laissez-faire thinking. In this role Darwinian ideas played the conservative function of reinforcing accepted belief, including social inequality. Yet Darwinism had a profoundly disturbing tendency as well, unsettling old attitudes and ways of thinking about society.

American social thought at the end of the Civil War had been "formalistic." Attitudes toward society and social values tended to be rooted in some kind of received wisdom transmitted from the past. This wisdom, it was assumed by thinkers of the day, was based on universal characteristics or principles that changed little over time. To understand the world, to prescribe policies for society, one merely had to reason logically from these first principles. To a very large extent formalistic thinkers assumed a static, rather than dynamic, reality, and held tight to precedent and tradition when considering the lot of humankind.

Reform Darwinism.   The advent of Darwin, stressing change and flux, seriously undermined this way of thinking. As we have seen in Chapter 17, in the form of social Darwinism it was a conservative concept buttressing laissez-faire social policies and economic inequality. But evolutionary thought could also be used to reinforce opposite social views. Many social thinkers perceived Darwinism as a force for progress and democracy. Darwinian ideas, they said, demonstrated the power and beneficence of change. Institutions, like species, were not static; they evolved. Indeed, society was far more like a living organism that experienced growth and mutation than like a machine that conformed to fixed motions prescribed by the nature of its

original design. Institutions, then, must be allowed to change. In fact, said these "reform Darwinists," they must be encouraged to change so as to maximize human welfare.

One man who found a progressive lesson in Darwinism was the sociologist Lester Ward. Ward believed that evolution implied cooperation as well as competition. Advance to higher forms and higher institutions did not necessarily emerge from a hands-off policy. A man who had spent many years as a federal civil servant, Ward did not fear government. Society's ultimate goal, he believed, should be "the scientific control of the social forces by the collective mind of society." Similarly, Richard T. Ely used Darwinism to support the idea that government should play a positive role in the economy. One of the founders of the American Economic Association (1885), Ely, unlike most contemporary academic economists, endorsed trade unions and believed the state was "an educational and ethical agency whose positive aid is an indispensable condition of human progress."

A still more radical break with the economic formalism of the past emerged from the fertile mind of the Norwegian-American Thorstein Veblen. Veblen rejected the economic "first principles" associated with the laissez-faire economists of England. These assumed that people made decisions based on rational self-interest and that people's efforts to maximize their material advantages explained how the economy operated. Nonsense! Veblen said. People behaved as illogically in the economic sphere as in others. They were more often impelled by inherited drives and historically transmitted cultural values than by the desire to maximize wealth or profit. In *The Theory of the Leisure Class* (1899) Veblen demonstrated to his own satisfaction that the great business magnates of the day were impelled as much by the primitive drives for status and emulation as by rational calculation. In later books he spoke about the "instinct of workmanship" as the wellspring of true economic progress. Veblen's major intellectual contribution, however, was to create a new school of "institutional" economics that substituted the study of economic practices evolving over time for model-making based on supposed first principles.

Legal thinking, too, felt the impact of the evolutionary revolt against formalism. Here the outstanding figure was Oliver Wendell Holmes, Jr., associate justice of the Supreme Court (1902–1932) and one of the great legal minds of his generation. Holmes attacked the idea that the law was unchanging, a static set of rules struck off by some great intellect in the past or the incontestable collective wisdom of the ages. Such a view, he stated in *The Common Law* (1881), was merely a convenient defense of the past. All law, even that embodied in revered documents like the federal Constitution, incorporated views that had evolved gradually in response to the needs of particular periods and

Social Darwinism

Conservatives justified the inequalities of the social order in late-nineteenth-century America in several ways. One of the more popular was recourse to "social Darwinism," a theory that held that in human society, as in the natural world, the struggle for survival was the only way that progress was achieved. The theory was drawn from the "evolutionary" ideas of Charles Darwin, the eminent English naturalist, as spread through the writings of the English philosopher Herbert Spencer. Among Spencer's disciples in the United States, none was more forceful than William Graham Sumner, an Episcopal priest-turned-college professor, whose 1883 book, *What Social Classes Owe to Each Other*, is excerpted below.

"The humanitarians, philanthropists, and reformers, looking at the facts of life as they present themselves, find enough which is sad and unpromising in the condition of many members of society. They see wealth and poverty side by side. They note great inequality of social position and social chances. They eagerly set about the attempt to account for what they see, and to devise schemes for remedying what they do not like. In their eagerness to recommend the less fortunate classes to pity and consideration they forget all about the rights of other classes; they gloss over all the faults of the classes in question, and they exaggerate their misfortunes and their virtues. They invent new theories of property, distorting rights and perpetuating injustice. . . . When I have read certain of these discussions I have thought that it must be quite dishonest to own property, quite unjust to go one's own way and earn one's own living, and the only really admirable person was the good-for-nothing. The man who by his own effort raises himself above poverty appears, in these discussions, to be of no account. . . .

"We owe it to the other [person] to guarantee rights. Rights do not pertain to *results*, but only to *chances*. They pertain to the *conditions* of the struggle for existence, not to any of the results of it; to the *pursuit* of happiness, not to the possession of happiness. It cannot be said that each one has a right to have some property, because if one man had such a right some other man or men would be under a corresponding obligation to provide him with some property. . . .

"The only help which is generally expedient . . . is that which consists in helping a man to help himself. . . . Now, the aid which helps a man to help himself is not in the least akin to the aid which is given in charity. If alms are given, or if we 'make work' for a man, or 'give him employment,' or 'protect' him, we simply take a product from one and give it to another. If we help a man to help himself, by opening the chances around him, we put him in a position to add to the wealth of the community by putting new powers in operation to produce. . . .

". . . The class distinctions [in society] simply result from the different degrees of success with which men have availed themselves of the chances which were presented to them. Instead of endeavoring to redistribute the acquisitions which have been made between the existing classes, our aim should be to *increase, multiply, and extend the chances*. Such is the work of civilization. . . ."

groups: "the felt necessities of the time, the prevalent moral and political theories, institutions of public policy, avowed or unconscious, even the prejudices which judges share with their fellow men, have a good deal more to do than the syllogism in determining the rules by which men should be governed." When the law corresponded to existing circumstances and filled current needs, there was no reason to quarrel with it. But it must change, must evolve, with the times, said Holmes. When it lagged behind, when it was out of touch with modern conditions and needs, it merely served as a brake on progress. Holmes was seconded by Roscoe Pound, dean of Harvard Law School, whose "sociological jurisprudence" called for "putting the human factor in the central place and relegating logic to its true position as an instrument."

In the discipline of history we find the same critical spirit during the years following 1890. The scholars of the New History found Darwinism useful as a weapon against the prevailing tradition of their discipline. American historical studies as promoted by Herbert Baxter Adams had emphasized the extent to which characteristic American institutions were planted as "germs" by northern European settlers. Thus the New England town meeting and ultimately the nation's democratic legislatures were survivals of ancient German assemblies. There was no sense in the work of Adams's students that the American environment had substantially altered those germs. Then in 1893 Frederick Jackson Turner delivered his famous address before the Chicago meeting of the American Historical Association and turned the study of American history on its head. "American democracy," Turner declared, "was born of no theorist's dream; it was not carried in the *Susan Constant* to Virginia, nor in the *Mayflower* to Plymouth. It came out of the American forest, and it gained new strength each time it touched a new frontier." Here, then, was an evolutionary view of American institutions, one that took seriously the three centuries of experience on American soil.

Turner eventually developed a theory of change that emphasized the molding effect of the physical environment. Charles Beard believed that class was more important. In his pioneering *An Economic Interpretation of the Constitution* (1913) Beard sought to demonstrate that the framers of the federal Constitution were not demigods free of class prejudices and interests and concerned only with dispassionate justice. Rather, he said, the Constitution was a document constructed by a coalition of merchants, speculators, and assorted businessmen to defend private property; it was based on the principles and interests of their class. By relating the Constitution to its time, Beard confirmed Holmes's view of the historical relativity of the law.

Pragmatism. The new spirit of dissent from static and excessively abstract ways of viewing social institutions also affected the most abstract of all areas of thought, philosophy. The new approach was pragmatism, and its major practitioners were John Dewey and William James.

Like many literate Americans of this era, the pragmatists were profoundly impressed by the success and prestige of the natural sciences and sought to make philosophy as useful a tool as physics, chemistry, or engineering. The old view, they noted, held that truth was an abstract, fixed reality. It assumed that there was some ultimate measuring rod to which statements or beliefs corresponded. But this was not so. Truth, in reality, was a quality that changed, evolved, as relationships were viewed from different perspectives or as an idea was employed for different purposes. To the pragmatists, most of the ideas about ultimate realities that had concerned philosophers and other thinkers over the centuries simply had no real answers, except formal and inconsequential ones. What men and women needed to know was *what difference did it make* whether this was true or that was false. The value of an idea, then, was not in its truth or falsity in the traditional sense, but in what consequences flowed from believing it or applying it. Thus in *The Varieties of Religious Experience* (1902) William James tackled the age-old problem of the existence of God and the truth of traditional religion by asserting that belief or doubt could only be validated by showing whether they brought comfort and hope. Truth was related to consequences and could not be understood in any other way. In an unfortunate and misunderstood, but vivid, phrase, James declared that it was "the cash value" of an idea that counted.

Because true ideas were those that had desirable effects in the world around us, the purpose of thought was not to contemplate eternity but to solve problems and serve as a guide to some practical course of action. In John Dewey's version of pragmatism the model of all truth-seeking was the experimental method of the natural sciences. Social and political ideas could not be tested by rigorous experiments, perhaps, but social and political thinkers, like natural scientists, could ask about the consequences of choosing course *A* as opposed to course *B* and act accordingly.

The pragmatic approach was experimental, practical, relativistic, and evolutionary. To the pragmatists the world was not rigidly laid out and determined. It was, rather, incomplete, ongoing, open, diverse, and turbulent—very much like the urban-industrial America of the day—and the task of philosophers and other thinkers was to find solutions to the problems of real people in the real world.

As a whole, pragmatism was a method or approach rather than a fully rounded system with precise prescriptions. Yet in one area, education, Dewey sought to apply his ideas directly. He believed that the education of the day was excessively static, mechanical, and irrelevant to the new society he saw emerging around him. Rather than memorizing by rote, he wanted students to be actively involved in learning. Dewey's disciples, the "progressive" educators, called this kind of teaching "learning by doing." He also believed that teachers should spend less time on books and more on showing students how to get along with one another so that they could ultimately make society less competitive and exploitive.

Besides a new pedagogical approach, pragmatic education demanded new subject matter suited to a new age. The traditional curriculum emphasized Latin and Greek, polite literature, ancient history, and formal mathematics as training for the mind. In the modern age, the pragmatists said, men and women must be trained for jobs, for solving personal problems, and for performing the civic duties of an industrial society. The history taught should be the past of the students' own society; geography, that of their own city and neighborhood. Dewey was also sympathetic to vocational education. Students should learn how to operate machines, cook and sew, and set type. Out of the new school would come new citizens who would know how their world worked, be prepared to perform the tasks it required, and be able to lead it along more humane paths.

Dewey first introduced these new attitudes and approaches into the experimental school at the University of Chicago during the 1890s. In 1904 he came to New York to join the faculty of Columbia University. At Teacher's College, a division of Columbia, Dewey profoundly influenced an entire generation of professors of education and through them thousands of student teachers. Eventually

William James

Few men epitomize the American spirit at its best so well as William James, the philosopher and experimental psychologist. Optimistic, tolerant, generous, liberal, practical, and forward-looking, he transformed these attitudes into a major philosophical approach that we call *pragmatism*. Though at times expressed in the technical jargon of academic philosophy, pragmatism was a distillation of the American experience of subduing a continent, creating a people, and conferring wide abundance.

William James was the grandson of a Scotch-Irish immigrant, also named William, who arrived in America in 1789 and made a fortune in business in Albany, New York. His son, Henry, was afforded the leisure of a gentleman by his father's wealth, but he rejected his father's dour Presbyterian Calvinism. Henry James the elder devoted his life to literature, conversation, social reform, and the pursuit of spiritual fulfillment. The young William, his first child after his marriage to Mary Robertson Walsh, grew up in a household where Emerson, Thoreau, Bryant, Greeley, Tennyson, Carlyle, and Mill were frequent guests, and the great theories and ideas of the age were discussed more often than the price of eggs or the best way to remove a clothing stain.

William's father was physically as well as intellectually and spiritually restless. The family never seemed to settle down anyplace. The Jameses traveled often, and William and his younger siblings, including Henry Jr., the future novelist, lived for long periods in Albany, New York, Boston, London, Paris, Berlin, Geneva, Florence, and other places. The children attended schools of many different kinds, for their father had advanced ideas about the proper nurture of

young people and was constantly trying out new schemes. It was an unusually cosmopolitan experience for a young American, but it never undermined William's quintessentially American values.

When William reached adulthood he was forced to consider a profession. His father favored science; William preferred painting. For a time William studied under the artists William M. Hunt and John La Farge in Newport, but after a year concluded that he was not greatly gifted as a painter and in 1861 entered the Lawrence Scientific School at Harvard. Here he studied chemistry and physiology and in 1864 entered the Harvard Medical School. He did not earn his M.D. degree until 1869.

The delay was caused by indecisiveness and poor health. In 1865 William took nine months off to join an expedition to the Amazon region to collect plant and animal specimens. Back at Harvard, he met the young war veteran Oliver Wendell Holmes, Jr., then resuming his law studies after three years fighting the Confederates. James thought "Wendell" a "first rate article," but disagreed with his friend's overemphasis on thought. "Feeling counts," he retorted, thus announcing a principle that would remain fundamental to his philosophy throughout his life.

Another major delay in his formal education occurred soon after. James was attracted to the scientific side of medicine, but did not like bedside visits with patients and daily hospital rounds. He found the work dull and tiring, and began to suffer severe back pains. He became deeply depressed and thought at times of suicide. In April 1867 he took another leave of absence from Harvard and sailed for Europe to "take the baths" at the

German and Austrian spas and immerse himself in German science to rest his troubled spirit.

The year and a half abroad neither improved his health nor resolved his career uncertainties. He returned to Cambridge and obtained his medical degree, but found it impossible to settle down as a doctor. For almost three years James drifted, still depressed and beset by physical maladies. He also began to experience fierce attacks of dread and panic. He finally achieved a psychological breakthrough when he read an essay by the French philosopher Charles Renouvier, on the freedom of the will, that cut through his despair and made him feel it was possible to mold one's life as one wished; the human being was not simply a woodchip tossed about aimlessly by the currents of the world.

James's emotional recovery coincided with a renaissance at Harvard under its new president, Charles W. Eliot, one of James's old teachers. In 1872 Eliot appointed James to an instructorship in physiology at the college, and for the next ten years James taught comparative anatomy, hygiene, and physiology to Harvard undergraduates. But he did not teach his subjects in a conventional way. By this time he had become convinced that there was no easy way to separate body from mind. His own experience had taught him that thoughts and feelings had a profound influence on bodily functions. Out of this came a growing interest in psychology, then a new subject in the college curriculum. In 1875 he offered a course on the "Relations Between Physiology and Psychology." The course was soon transferred to the department of philosophy, and in 1880 James himself joined that department.

The 1870s and 1880s were decades of growing satisfaction for

James personally and professionally. In 1878 he married Alice Howe Gibbens, an intelligent, competent, and interesting Boston schoolteacher, the daughter of a country doctor. The marriage was a rare success. They had five children, four of whom lived to maturity. Alice proved a supportive, though not infinitely tolerant, wife. She had saved him from hopeless neurasthnia, he later declared. William also took great pleasure in the literary success of his brother, Henry, who during this decade achieved fame as a novelist.

During the 1880s James's major intellectual preoccupation was a psychology text he had contracted for in 1878. He did not intend to supply a mere rehash of the accepted principles, though the publisher would have been content with that. Instead, he hoped to break new ground. Writing such a work, however, proved to be a gigantic task, and *The Principles of Psychology* did not appear until 1890, when it attracted wide acclaim as a new view of the way the mind worked.

James saw the mind as essentially a tool with which the individual dealt with his or her environment. It was not some mystical entity; it had a biological basis and, like all biological appurtenances, had evolved over time. In divorcing the idea of mind from older concepts, James went so far as to declare that what we perceive as emotions are really only the biological responses—rapid pulse, thumping heart, churning stomach, sweaty palms, and so forth—that are *associated* with emotions. Some of James's readers felt that he had reduced human beings to unfeeling robots, but that was never his intention. To the end of his life he refused to accept this sort of crude materialism because it seemed deterministic, suggesting a closed universe and the impossibility of human beings changing things or mastering their own fate.

During the decade following the publication of the *Principles* James

made philosophy his field, with the issue of "how we know" his special interest. Here he encountered two competing philosophical schools. The first, *rationalism*, held that we know first principles instinctively because they are emanations from God. We then ultimately deduce from these all the other aspects of reality. The second, *empiricism*, rejected deduction from first principles and held instead that all knowledge comes from observation of discrete events and phenomena. James liked the empiricists' skepticism of grandiose systems that purported to explain everything, but he was impatient with their refusal ever to generalize. Empiricism's rejection of principles left the world a buzzing confusion and seemed both cold and arid. It was from a desire to preserve the best of both theories that James evolved his pragmatism. In the process he borrowed much from his Harvard colleague, the philosopher Charles Pierce, who had made "everything is to be tested by its practical results" his philosophical guide.

James's first big philosophic project was a book on religion. He could not accept traditional religious views as the exact truth. But he also found atheism and agnosticism unacceptable because they deprived the individual of the comfort of religion. In the essays collected in *The Will to Believe* in 1897, he asserted that individuals had the right to accept any view of the universe, whether "provable" or not, that provided the emotional support they needed. James himself followed this principle. However much the scientist, for example, he was also a spiritualist who believed it possible to communicate through "mediums" with the dead.

At the end of the nineteenth century James found himself drawn into political controversy. He was a democrat who had enormous respect for the free and egalitarian institutions of his native land. He deplored the seizure of the Philippines after the Spanish-

American War as a repudiation of American traditions of self-rule for all people. These views drew him into the anti-imperialist movement, which was dedicated to keeping the United States from joining the Western nations' race for empire.

James's major contribution to philosophy came in the last decade of his life, though it was foreshadowed many years earlier. In a series of lectures given in 1907 he elaborated the theory of pragmatism associated with his name. James expressed impatience at many of the age-old controversies about the "truth" of particular ideas or propositions. These would never be settled. But that was irrelevant, for what was important was not whether some concept was true in some supposedly final, ultimate way, but whether believing it *made a difference* and whether it was useful in human terms. As a Darwinian, James linked this view to the idea of an evolving universe, one that never reached a final, static form, but was perpetually open to change. Truths, then, were working hypotheses that we could use for our purposes. Critics charged that this reduced truth to personal opinion and made any view, any belief, as good as any other. James responded that it merely required that each person's view meet the test of workability, that it have "cash value." In the hands of a younger group of philosophers associated with John Dewey at the University of Chicago, pragmatism became a system called "instrumentalism," of subjecting social ideas to the scientific method.

James's last years were marked by both sunlight and shadow. His books and lectures were enormously popular and successful and he received international recognition. Frequent trips to Europe and to California, visiting professorships and lectureships, generous praise by much of the world's intellectual community, brought variety and satisfaction. Distinguished men and women from all over the Western world came to visit the Jameses in Cambridge or at their summer places in the Adirondacks and New Hampshire. His family life was happy. Alice, as always, was warm and supportive, and his children brought him pleasure. But for the last decade of his life James was afflicted with a severe heart condition; in 1909 he began to suffer serious chest pains. As a doctor, he knew how serious his condition was, but he could not relax or slow his pace. In early 1910 the Jameses sailed for Europe to visit Henry, now living permanently in England. William was sick during much of the time and the Jameses returned home in August, with William failing, and made their way to their New Hampshire summer house. On the evening of August 26 Alice recorded in her diary: "William died just before 2:30 in my arms. I was coming in with milk and saw the change. No pain at the last and no consicousness. . . . Poor Henry, poor children."

these young men and women fanned out across the nation, carrying the message of progressive education and spreading it to virtually every school system in the country.

Religion and Modernism.   Darwinian ideas were profoundly disturbing to many people. Not all scientists accepted them. Louis Agassiz, a distinguished Harvard zoologist, and James Dwight Dana, the nation's leading geologist, for example, both rejected Darwin's theory. Still more hostile were traditional Christians, both laypeople and ministers.

In 1865 religion played an immensely important role in the way Americans regarded the world. Of the nation's 36 million people, about 4 million were Catholic and perhaps a tenth that many were Jewish. The rest were nominally Protestant, although probably less than half were active church members. Christian, predominantly Protestant, ideas powerfully affected the way Americans thought about the world and their place in it.

Most Christians, but especially Protestants, placed the Bible at the center of their faith as God's revealed word. To the more orthodox the biblical account in *Genesis* of how God created the world and all its creatures in six days and how all humans were descendants of the first human pair, Adam and Eve, was literally true. Darwinian ideas challenged the Bible's authority by proposing slow, natural processes for events that Scripture describes as under the immediate guidance of God and as happening in a brief period of time. Evolution also connected humankind to lower creatures in the biological realm. If Darwin was right, the Bible could not be literally true. In itself this conclusion was unthinkable, but its human consequences were also disturbing. If humans were derived from animals they were part of the "brute creation" reather than creatures made in God's own image and set above other living things. Evolution not only contradicted the Bible, it also seemed to strip humans of their special unique dignity.

Traditional Protestant belief was also under attack from

The now-familiar uniform of the Salvation Army was a welcome sight in the city slums of the late nineteenth and early twentieth centuries. As part of their evangelizing work, Army volunteers provided food, shelter, and other necessities to the homeless and destitute.

a different quarter, as scholars in England, France, and Germany began to examine the Bible as a historical document. Exponents of the so-called Higher Criticism depicted the Scriptures as a work of men living in distinctive historical settings and compiled over generations. It did not represent God's exact words, they said, so much as the thoughts of inspired poets, chroniclers, philosophers, and prophets. As such it was not infallible, nor was it to be taken literally. Though the Higher Criticism originated abroad, it quickly won disciples among the American Protestant clergy and laity.

Some clergymen—including popular Brooklyn preacher Henry Ward Beecher, Lyman Abbott, President James McCosh of Princeton University, and others—found it possible to accept simultaneously both the essential truth of Christianity and the views of the Darwinians. Yet many Protestants, especially among the more evangelical denominations with rural roots, saw Darwin's ideas and the Higher Criticism as unproved theories that endangered true religion. To counter these forms of modernism the traditionalists insisted on certain basic principles as essential to Christian belief, and in 1910 they published a pamphlet, the *Fundamentals*, that enumerated five points as the foundation of true Christian faith: the infallibility of the Bible, Jesus' virgin birth, His resurrection, His atonement for humankind, and the inevitability of His second coming. In the following decades those who belonged to fundamentalist denominations that accepted the "Five Points" would wage an intense battle to halt the erosion of traditional Protestantism and the growth of the modernism they perceived as false, dangerous to society, and threatening to human salvation.

Religion and Social Justice. Another challenge to traditional Protestantism that arose during the 1870s and 1880s came from clergymen and laypeople who believed that Protestantism had retreated too far from the old Puritan zeal to make the world a better place and had lost contact with the urban poor. As a result, they felt, the United States was becoming a society of pagans who associated the church only with privilege.

One response to this perceived failure was the "social gospel" movement. To ministers such as Washington Gladden, William Bliss, and Walter Rauschenbusch, it appeared that Christianity had failed the poor by emphasizing the problem of personal salvation excessively. Religion to traditional Christians, Gladden explained, was "too much a matter between themselves and God." Yet true Christianity was social as much as individual. It required righteous dealings with other people, not merely concern for personal salvation. To the social gospel preachers it seemed essential that the churches take stands on social issues and defend the weak and oppressed from those who exploited them. As early as the 1880s Gladden endorsed trade unions and the right to strike. Bliss, an Episcopal minister influenced by the Christian socialists of England, organized an American society of Christian socialists in 1889. Rauschenbusch denounced the competitive economic system and supported one based on the cooperative ideal.

Social gospel ideas were especially powerful among the Unitarians, Episcopalians, Methodists, and Congregationalists—the denominations that were also most open to the Higher Criticism and new scientific ideas generally. In 1905 thirty-three social gospel–oriented denominations, representing millions of communicants, banded together in the Federal Council of Churches of Christ in America. The council endorsed the abolition of child labor, and the adoption of the six-day workweek, workers' compensation for injury, old-age insurance, a living wage for workers, and other social reforms.

Other Protestants responded to the poverty and demoralization of urban centers in more conservative ways. The Salvation Army, an evangelical body founded in England by William Booth and brought to America in 1880, sought to rescue drunkards, petty criminals, prostitutes, and other outcast men and women in the slums. At first the Army focused on the traditional evangelical methods of calling sinners to repentance and personal reform. To attract people to meetings, the Army deployed its forces on slum street corners and in city downtowns, armed with trombones and drums. After the sermon at the Army's "shelter," those who stayed could count on a free meal. By the 1890s the Salvation Army had begun to establish slum employment bureaus, provide cheap lodging for vagrants, and perform other social services.

The Young Men's Christian Association (YMCA) was a more middle-class organization. Founded in England, the "Y" was brought to the United States in 1851 and devoted its labors to preserving the Christian faith of young men newly arrived in the city. It provided reading rooms, religious classes, and clubs. It also offered gymnasiums and eventually established inexpensive hotels where young male newcomers to the city could stay until they found more permanent homes. In 1858 the Young Women's Christian Association (YWCA) was formed to provide the same mixture of nondenominational Protestantism and urban social services to women.

★ Conclusions ★

The cultural life of the United States underwent a colossal transformation in the half century following the Civil War. On every level, from the heights of academic philosophy to the everyday amusements of ordinary men and women, culture adapted to the new urbanism and to the changes in technology and in political and economic institutions that swept the nation.

The cultural effects of the new forces were both direct and roundabout. The movie industry was clearly a product of post–Civil War urbanization. It also depended on inventions possible only after years of technological advance. Other changes, however, were affected by the new forces in more oblique ways. Many of the ideas adapted to the emerging world of industry and cities derived from Darwinian evolution. Yet evolutionary theory itself was a product of scientific change and growing concern for the problems of a postagricultural society. It is significant that Darwin got his central idea of the struggle for survival from a book by the English economist-demographer Thomas Malthus, who was concerned about the population explosion that accompanied the English Industrial Revolution.

Were the cultural adaptations to the new forces cheap and vulgar? Did Gilded Age America become a "chromo civilization"? So many changes are involved that it would be difficult under any circumstances to answer these questions. The problem is made worse by the fact that we are seeking to evaluate ideas as well as artistic expression.

In the case of the arts, surely the changes of the period 1865–1915 were "progressive." In literature, for example, it is difficult not to applaud the eclipse of insipid gentility by a robust realism; in architecture it is difficult to defend the imitative old guard against the innovative Louis Sullivan and Frank Lloyd Wright. In these cases, as in many others,

adaptations unleashed new creative energies. In the area of popular culture, too, the changes of the period were surely advances. Admittedly, the early movies, yellow journalism, and Tin Pan Alley music, to name a few examples, were generally naive, sensational, or lurid. Yet whatever their initial failings, in time the popular new media and forms of entertainment improved.

Changes in the realm of ideas, however, cannot be seen as a simple matter of progress. The struggle between the progressive thinkers and the formalists, for example, represents merely one round in a battle between competing views of the world, humanity, and God that has been fought in the Western world for hundreds of years. No irrefutable factual basis exists for deciding that one was right and the other wrong. If the formalists were rigid, their opponents could be such flexible relativists as to deny or undermine all moral and intellectual guideposts. Perhaps, for example, the law had to change to suit new circumstances, as Holmes and Roscoe Pound declared. But law that changed at every passing social whim or fad clearly had no claim to moral or intellectual respect. The uncertainty and ultimate subjectivity of conclusions about these approaches can be gauged by the continued existence today of arguments over these same issues.

Meanwhile, as the new century began, the reform impulse reflected in the social gospel, pragmatism, and reform Darwinism began to quicken. Before long the nation would embark on a new political crusade informed and inspired by the ideas of James and Dewey, Holmes and Pound, Ward and Ely.

******** **FOR FURTHER READING** ********

Morton White. *Social Thought in America: The Revolt Against Formalism* (1957)
This is not an easy book. Written by a Harvard philosopher who has made American thought his province, it is by far the best study of the changes in social thought as molded by Darwinism in these years.

Richard Hofstadter. *Social Darwinism in American Thought* (1944)
This work deals not only with the conservatives who used Darwin to defend the social and economic status quo, but also with those, like Lester Ward, who used evolutionary ideas to defend reform. Recently Hofstadter's linkage of Darwinism with Gilded Age businessmen has been challenged.

Lawrence Vesey. *The Emergence of the American University* (1965)
This is the best one-volume study of the new currents in graduate and professional training that arose during this period. There are also many good histories of individual universities—such as Johns Hopkins, Cornell, Columbia, University of Chicago, Harvard, and Yale—that were in the forefront of the new trends.

Lawrence A. Cremin. *The Transformation of the School: Progressivism in American Education, 1876–1957* (1961)
Written by the outstanding historian of American education, this book examines the roots, the course, and the eventual transformation of the "progressive movement" in education that John Dewey helped to launch. Cremin ties changes in educational practice to changes in society and new ways of thinking.

Alfred Kazin. *On Native Grounds* (1942)
A brilliant interpretation of American literature from the 1890s onward. The first third of the volume deals with the "Search for Reality" during the years from 1890 to 1917.

Henry Steele Commager. *The American Mind: An Interpretation of American Thought and Character Since the 1880s* (1950)

An interpretive survey of American thought and the arts from about 1880 to about 1920. Covers an enormous range of topics, with a bias in favor of the new trends in each area discussed.

Arthur M. Schlesinger. *The Rise of the City, 1878–1898* (1933)

This older book is still one of the few good treatments of popular culture as a whole during the Gilded Age. It should be supplemented by the appropriate sections of Russel Nye's *The Unembarrassed Muse: The Popular Arts in America* (1970), which covers a much larger period.

Oliver W. Larkin. *Art and Life in America* (1949)

This work covers far more than the period of this chapter, and so can be consulted selectively by the student of the Gilded Age. Larkin seeks to tie the trends in the visual arts with social change in general. Well illustrated.

John Burchard and Albert Bush-Brown. *The Architecture of America: A Social and Cultural History* (1966)

What applies to Larkin's book also applies to this work.

Lewis Mumford. *The Brown Decades: A Study of the Arts in America, 1865–1895* (1931)

This still readable and useful book was a ground-breaking attack on Victorian architecture and a defense of the "modern" trend. Written by one of the deans of architectural history.

W. A. Swanberg. *Citizen Hearst* (1961)

A colorful, critical biography of William Randolph Hearst, one of the creators of yellow journalism, by an outstanding popular biographer.

Sidney Hook. *John Dewey* (1939)

An intellectual biography of Dewey by one of his most articulate disciples.

Burton Bledstein. *The Culture of Professionalism: The Middle Class and the Development of Higher Education in America* (1976)

Bledstein makes a linkage between the ambition of the mid-nineteenth-century American middle class, the development of the professions, and the rise of the university. The author rides his thesis too hard, but we do learn much about these interrelated events.

Justin Kaplan. *Mr. Clemens and Mark Twain* (1966)

An outstanding literary biography. As the title suggests, Kaplan sees Mark Twain as a deeply divided personality, a man who both wanted wealth and success and despised all that they represented.

Gunther Schuller. *Early Jazz* (1968)

The best discussion of jazz from its origins to the early 1930s. By a fine modern composer.

23★

PROGRESSIVISM

What Were Its Roots and What Were Its Accomplishments?

1874	Women's Christian Temperance Union established
1890	Jane Addam's Hull House opens in Chicago • National American Woman Suffrage Association is formed in a merger of two older groups
1892	Grover Cleveland elected president
1895	Booker T. Washington's Atlanta Compromise Address
1896	*Plessy* v. *Ferguson* legalizes segregation • William McKinley elected president
1899	The National Consumers' League is formed
1900–06	Governor La Follette of Wisconsin establishes state primaries and taxes railroads
1901	McKinley assassinated; Theodore Roosevelt becomes president
1902	Roosevelt's antitrust campaign begins
1903	Congress establishes the Department of Commerce and Labor and the Bureau of Corporations
1904	Roosevelt elected president
1905	W. E. B. Du Bois launches the Niagara Movement
1905–07	Most states limit or outlaw child labor
1906	Congress passes Hepburn Act, Meat Inspection Act, and Pure Food and Drug Act
1908	William H. Taft elected president • Aldrich-Vreeland Emergency Currency Act
1909	Ballinger-Pinchot controversy • The Payne-Aldrich Tariff • National Association for the Advancement of Colored People (NAACP) founded
1910	The Mann-Elkins Act • The Mann Act
1911	*Standard Oil Co.* v. *United States*
1912	Woodrow Wilson elected president
1913	The Sixteenth and Seventeenth amendments follow a federal income tax and direct election of senators • The Federal Reserve Act • Underwood Tariff
1914	The Federal Trade Commission Act • The Clayton Antitrust Act • World War I begins in Europe
1916	Wilson sponsors the Federal Farm Loan Act, the Kern-McGillicuddy Act for federal employees, and the Keating-Owen Act limiting child labor

lowly, as the new century began its first decade," wrote editor William Allen White from the vantage of 1946, "I saw the Great Light. Around me in that day scores of young leaders in American politics and public affairs were seeing what I saw, feeling what I felt. . . . All over the land in a score of states and more, young men in both parties were taking leadership by attacking things as they were in that day."

White's "Great Light" was the desire to change American society that historians have called the Progressive movement. In the years between the beginning of the new century and America's entrance into World War I, men and women of all national backgrounds and classes felt the urge to improve life for themselves and for their fellow citizens. They did not join any one organization; they had no single leader, no neat, well-defined set of goals. Their support of change was not always unselfish. Most groups—whether intellectuals, professionals, wage earners, or farmers—understandably placed their own concerns first or believed their own concerns were everybody's. Nevertheless, the social sympathies of many progressives would be broad, encompassing many groups besides themselves.

The new views first appeared in the cities during the 1890s. A little later they came to the statehouses. Finally, about 1904 or 1905, they arrived in Washington. When they did, they were given the name "progressivism," and they helped transform the nation. How can we explain this sudden passion for reform? What made so many people conclude that things had to change? What did the reformers want, and what did they accomplish?

★ UNCERTAINTIES ★

Fear of Bigness. If any single concern united the forces of reform during the opening years of the twentieth century, it was the fear of inflated, uncontrolled private economic power. The sense of being at the mercy of great aggregations of private wealth and privilege was not new; it was as old as the republic and had never ceased to affect political perceptions. In the early years of independence it had taken the form of Jeffersonian concern over the new "paper aristocracy" created by Hamilton's funding program. In the Jackson era it evolved into fear of the "monster bank," the Second Bank of the United States. After the Civil War agrarian concern over the "money power" and the railroads sounded the same theme. All these views attest to a powerful and pervasive "populistic," antimonopoly streak in the American political consciousness.

In each of these early instances the opposition to "monopolists" had come predominantly from small producers—farmers, independent artisans, small manufacturers. That was inevitable; until late in the nineteenth century most Americans had belonged to one of these occupational groups. By the 1880s and 1890s the nation had spawned a large class of urban wage earners, salaried professionals, and white-collar workers, but by and large they had refused to join the populistic movements of the period; it had been the small farmers of the South and West who had formed the backbone of the People's Party and the free-silver movement. The failure of the Populists and Bryan in 1896, as we saw, can be explained by their inability to rally the urban voters to their cause.

Progressivism, the new, early-twentieth-century attack on concentrated power and wealth, originated in, and found its chief support among, the very groups that Populism and Bryanism had failed to ignite. Many small-town and rural men and women would call themselves progressives in these years, but the movement would be led by middle-class urbanites widely supported by the city working class. What had happened in one short decade to change the perception of millions of city dwellers, blue collar and middle class?

One answer is that the shift of attitude was sparked by the acceleration of business consolidation during the closing years of the nineteenth century. But that was not enough. Business mergers and concentration had taken place earlier as well and had not concerned the mass of middle-class Americans. Why did the process this time arouse the fears of the urbanites who had not been moved by Bryan and Populism?

The Growth of Trusts. In the generation following the Civil War the economic integration of the nation was brought to swift completion by the final burst of railroad building. As the cost of shipping goods to distant customers declined, local markets evolved into regional markets and then into national markets. Firms grew larger as they sought to serve the growing number of customers, many now living in the burgeoning cities. For a time business competition intensified. And for a time prices dropped. However beneficial to consumers, this regime did not please producers and, as we saw, they tried to stabilize market shares and prices through pools, trusts, mergers and other arrangements to avoid "cutthroat" competition.

Late-nineteenth-century business consolidation came in two bursts. The first began in the 1870s and culminated in the formation of the Standard Oil Company. It was this round that had spurred the anxiety of the Grangers and the Alliances. It ended abruptly with the panic of 1893 and the

Businessmen celebrate the merger of feuding steel companies into United States Steel in 1901. At its birth the company produced 65 percent of America's steel; by the eve of World War I, the company's gross income exceeded that of the U.S. Treasury.

depression that followed. Then, beginning in 1896, the merger movement revived, primarily among industries that catered to the exploding urban market.

The second merger wave, as midwifed by J. P. Morgan and other investment bankers, came to a grand climax between 1898 and 1902. In those five years 2,500 large firms combined into huge ones. Every day, it seemed, formerly competing businesses were being consolidated into new, ever larger "trusts." In 1901 the process culminated with the formation of United States Steel, the world's first billion-dollar corporation.

Americans watched the consolidation process with apprehension. Trusts seemed to be everywhere. Not only were there monopolies in banking, railroads, and farm machinery—combinations that Grangers, Greenbackers, and Populists had been attacking for a generation—but in iron and steel, sugar refining, petroleum, meat-packing, can manufacturing, tobacco, public utilities, copper, and many other industries that directly affected city consumers. In 1904 financial analyst John Moody listed 318 trusts, with total capital of over $7.2 billion, "covering every line of productive industry in the United States."

The New Urban Consumers. Almost all Americans deplored the trend toward ever greater concentrations of private economic power. But to urbanites the trusts appeared particularly threatening. Many city people, of course, were

producers who turned out manufactured goods in small or large shops. But many others were now white-collar workers—professionals, clerks, accountants, office workers—whose connections with a product were indirect at best. To an increasing extent urban Americans, especially those of the middle class, viewed themselves more as consumers than producers.

The perception was a new one for Americans in 1900. Earlier most had been farmers. Even though American farmers had never been fully self-sufficient, they had been able to supply many of their own needs. They had slaughtered their own hogs and cattle, raised their own fruits and vegetables, and produced their own eggs and milk. Even urban folk had been less at the mercy of others in the simpler days before 1900. They had been closer to the country suppliers of their needs, and these needs had been less complicated. Through most of the nineteenth century average Americans had burned wood from their own woodlots in their stoves, read by candlelight or firelight, communicated with their friends face to face, gone to work on foot, and doctored themselves with nostrums from their own gardens or from a local medical practitioner. In all these matters they had relied on themselves or on someone they knew well.

For city dwellers in 1900 this self-reliance was a thing of the past. The economy had become more complex. The food they consumed, for instance, was now supplied by remote corporations—meat-packers, canners, millers, and other food processors. Formerly, they could avoid an un-sanitary butcher and boycott a short-weighing grocer—if, indeed, they had to buy from them at all—for these were local people whose practices were known. But now producers were giant corporations located hundreds of miles away that could not be held to account for their products. No doubt, the huge firms were efficient distributors and producers, but could they be trusted? Dishonest meat packers could and did doctor spoiled beef to make it appear fresh. Firms processed lard and suet as butter and packed turnips in syrup to be sold as canned peaches or pears.

Nor was this all. City dwellers now relied on public utilities to light their houses, fuel their stoves, and transport them from their homes to their offices and shops. But the gas and lighting companies had legal monopolies through franchises and could squeeze customers as they pleased. The traction companies that ran the streetcars and elevated railroads corrupted city officials to secure exclusive charters, and then provided poor and expensive service.

The dependence on others extended to personal health. When ill, city dwellers now counted on "patent medicines," bottled or packaged concoctions they saw advertised in the newspapers and magazines. Drug companies marketed useless and sometimes harmful potions, fortified with alcohol or even opium for every disease known—and for several invented by the patent medicine purveyors themselves. In short, urban consumers were at the mercy of others and were exceptionally vulnerable to deception and exploitation. The economist Richard Ely in 1905 expressed his chagrin at the new era: "Under our present manner of living, how many of my vital interests must I entrust to others! Nowadays the water main is my well, the trolley car is my carriage, the banker's safe is my stocking, and the policeman's billy is my fist."

Dependence and deception were bad enough, but consumers of this period also faced remorselessly rising prices. For a whole generation after 1897 the nation escaped major depressions such as those of the 1870s and 1890s. But the income gains that Americans made in these years were partly offset by the steady inflation that reversed the trend of the previous decades. Beginning about 1902, consumer prices started a steady rise that did not end until the 1930s. Deflation following the Civil War had hurt farmers and other producers; now inflation hurt consumers. Everyone who went to the corner grocery store or butcher or who paid a utility bill or bought a load of coal soon became painfully aware of the new trend. "All the host of men who are not engaged in the actual production or delivery of material things," lamented one observer of rising prices in 1903, "how will they fare?" In the opening years of the new century everyone wanted to know who was responsible for the "high cost of living." The answer seemed inescapable to many; the monopolies.

The new consumerism was a particularly effective political glue. As one journalist pointed out in 1913: "In America to-day the unifying . . . force is the common interest of the citizen as a consumer of wealth. . . ." The producers were "highly differentiated," but "all men, women, and children who buy shoes (except only the shoe manufacturer) are interested in cheap, good shoes." Because consumers were "overwhelmingly superior in numbers than [sic] producers," consumer consciousness, this writer was certain, formed the basis for a political revolt of vast proportions that the politicians would not fail to note.

Besides their exposed position as consumers, urban people still confronted the special problems and hazards of the city environment. Large cities provided men and women with more opportunities to learn, grow, and amuse themselves. But for wage earners they were also places where crime, vice, loneliness, and poverty flourished. In the 1870s and 1880s, as we have seen, the city poor had often turned to the political machines to protect them against the hard edges of urban life; by the 1890s many had come to believe that urban reform might be in their interests. The urban middle class, meanwhile, saw city government as inefficient and wasteful. Why could it not be run like a business, though obviously one dedicated to the public interest, rather than profit? Dissatisfaction with city government further fueled the desire for progressive reform.

Farmers, Blacks, and Women.   The addition of urbanites to the ranks of the nation's uneasy and restless citizens may well have been the crucial trigger to progressivism. But city people would not be alone in their search for reform during the next few years. Although farmers would profit from the higher prices after 1900, they still faced many difficult problems. Railroad officials and farm machinery manufacturers remained arrogant and arbitrary; credit for farmers was still in short supply; country life continued to fall behind city life in its amenities. These persistent problems left rural Americans dissatisfied, and at times their voice would imbue progressivism with a strong agrarian tinge reminiscent of Populism.

We cannot categorize all the reform elements as rural and urban, producer and consumer. Groups defined in other ways were also part of the progressive coalition. In these years many women, especially of the middle class, found their lives limited in ways that no longer seemed acceptable. By now thousands of women were high school and college graduates, but there were few outlets for their talents and energies. Law, medicine, and teaching no longer formally barred women. But women lawyers and doctors labored under severe handicaps imposed by the men who dominated these professions. There were thousands of female schoolteachers, but the higher-status positions in ed-

This 1889 cartoon, showing the bloated money-bags looking over the shoulders of U.S. senators, caught the public's skeptical mood toward the United States Senate. Long before the Muckraking era, Americans were obviously concerned with the dangers of money in politics.

ucation as college instructors and school administrators were virtually closed to women. Except in a few states women still could not vote or hold office. Many educated women with unused talents and energies joined women's clubs and spent their time discussing art, high culture, and great ideas. Women were active in church affairs. A few middle-class or wealthy women also did "charity work" among the poor. Yet as the new century opened, many talented women felt that society was not properly using their skills and brains, and it made them receptive to social and political change.

Black Americans, too, found much to complain of as the new century dawned. In the South blacks were deprived of voting rights either by intimidation or by ingenious legal dodges. All through Dixie the system of legal segregation prevailed. There were separate public facilities for "white" and "colored," and invariably the "colored" bathrooms, schools, drinking fountains, waiting rooms, and hospital facilities were far inferior to the white ones. Worst of all was the brutal regime of lynchings. Each year scores of blacks accused of criminal offenses were taken from local jails and hanged, burned, or maimed by white mobs unwilling to wait for the slow processes of law.

Blacks were better treated in the North. Few communities north of the Mason-Dixon line imposed legal segregation. But unofficial segregation, especially in housing, was common. Northern blacks also suffered from discrimination in jobs, college admissions, and professional education, and were often treated shabbily by whites in ordinary social relations. As the twentieth century began, a new generation of college-educated black urban leaders appeared, determined to make white Americans grant black citizens their constitutional and God-given rights.

Some historians have seen progressivism as a predominantly middle-class movement. Yet is is clear that it embraced recent immigrants, factory workers, and slum dwellers as well. In fact, for a time almost all Americans came to consider themselves progressives in some sense. Progressivism by about 1910 was definitely "in the air," a fact that helps to explain its complexity and its seeming inconsistencies. No coalition so large could have been all of a piece or definable in a single sentence.

★ THE OPINION MAKERS ★

The Progressive movement owed much to the intellectual and cultural currents that had appeared in the last decades of the nineteenth century. The revolt against formalistic thinking and against conservative social Darwinism in the 1880s and 1890s prepared the way for jurists, academics, politicians, and, ultimately, ordinary literate citizens to demand social legislation designed to protect the weak and to control private economic power. Many of the new thinkers—including Oliver Wendell Holmes, Jr., John Dewey, and Charles Beard—were also reformers. But their contribution to reform was primarily through their ideas rather than their personal activities. Writers and painters also contributed to the new political mood. Though the literary and artistic modernists often claimed to be mere observers, in fact they generally aligned themselves with political dissent and lent their prestige to reform. Moreover, their depictions of railroad abuses, big-business chicanery, and the poverty and sordidness of life in the slums and on

Ida Tarbell

Ida Tarbell could never decide whether she was a muckraker or a historian. Today her contributions to history are largely forgotten; we remember her only as a muckraker. She may have been, in fact, the first of the muckrakers.

Tarbell belonged to that special breed of journalists and writers who shaped the way early twentieth-century Americans perceived their society. Their exposés of corrupt municipal governments, patent medicine deception, the revolting conditions in meatpacking plants, the unscrupulous business practices of trusts, the exploitation of child workers, and the venality of the American Senate, among other issues, produced the agenda for the reform movement we call progressivism.

Ida Tarbell was born during the financial crisis of 1857 in a log cabin in northwestern Pennsylvania. Her mother, Esther, a descendant of Sir Walter Raleigh, was a schoolteacher whose own mother insisted she give up her career when she got married. Her father, Franklin, was a farmer who, at the time of his first daughter's birth, was in Iowa looking for promising land on which to settle down with his family. The panic closed the bank where the Tarbell savings were deposited and compelled Franklin to return home on foot without buying the farm, teaching to earn money as he traveled across Illinois, Indiana, and Ohio. By the time he arrived home, Ida was already eighteen months old and greeted the father she had never seen by telling him, "Go away, bad man."

Franklin Tarbell still intended to move the family to Iowa, and for the next three years he saved his money. Then came the oil strikes in Erie County and all thought of moving ceased.

With "rock oil" gushing from the ground in vast amounts, storage space was in short supply. A skilled carpenter, Franklin constructed a new kind of wooden tank that could hold over a hundred barrels of oil without seepage. By the summer of 1860 he had established a profitable shop for building such tanks near the well that gave him his first order. He also built a house adjoining the shop, and it was there that Ida and her baby brother, Will, spent the next ten years. The log cabin where she had been born was near trees, streams, and flowers; the new house was encircled by oil pits and derricks and smelled of gas. Ida was often scolded and spanked for exploring her surroundings and climbing on the derricks in the front yard. After a few months she tried to run away, but could not find the road to her grandmother's farm. Her new home made her a rebel. "This revolt," she confessed in her autobiography, "was a natural and righteous protest against having the life and home I had known, and . . . loved, taken away without explanation and a new scene, a new set of rules which I did not like, suddenly imposed." This spirit of defiance remained with her throughout her life.

Her questing and independent personality was reinforced by her family environment. Her parents were ardent antislavery Republicans who followed the Civil War closely in *Harper's Weekly, Harper's Monthly,* and the *New York Tribune.* Her earliest memory of concern for things outside her own world, as well as her first "realization of tragedy," occurred when President Lincoln died. Her father and mother sobbed on hearing the news, shut up their house, and put black crepe on all the doors. Her parents also welcomed to their home reformers and crusaders, whether prohibitionists, women's suffragists, or independent oilmen fighting Rockefeller. Her mother, who had never reconciled herself to the loss of her own teaching career, was also deeply concerned with improving the lot of the poor and hungry, and for a while felt drawn to socialism. A further boost to Ida's doubting nature came in high school when she developed a strong scientific curiosity. She was then faced with the problem of trying to reconcile her religious beliefs with the contradictions she found in studying science. In an age when only a handful of women went to college, her father and mother encouraged her to get the higher education she needed to become a biology teacher.

In 1876 Ida went to Allegheny College in nearby Meadville, Pennsylvania. Although the institution was nominally coeducational, Ida was the only girl in the freshman class. The head of the natural science department was impressed with her dedication and allowed her to use the college microscope. He also permitted her to experiment with the electrical apparatus in the laboratory. When she graduated four years later, she found that there were few opportunities for women in science and took a teaching post at the Poland Union Seminary in Ohio. There she taught foreign languages as well as geology, botany, geometry, and trigonometry—on both high school and college levels. After two tiring years that left her no time to use her beloved microscope, she left teaching and went back to her parents' house.

Though she wanted to go on to further study, her father was now in financial trouble. Standard Oil, the biggest refiner, had made an arrangement with the railroads. In exchange for all of Standard's enormous business, they would give the company a secret rebate on freight rates. This reduced Standard's overhead and allowed it to sell its oil at cut-rate prices. Standard's competitors, particularly the independents like Franklin Tarbell, could not market their oil because they could not obtain the cheap freight rates. Many oilmen simply gave in to the inevitable and sold out to the larger company. Ida's father resisted, but in 1882 he was forced out of business. "It was not the economic feature of the struggle in the Oil Region which deeply disturbed . . . me," Ida wrote many years later. "It was what it was doing to people themselves, . . . to my father and mother and their friends. It was the divided town, the suspicion and greed and bitterness and defeats and surrenders." At twenty-four, Ida was discouraged, feeling that she was faced with only two choices: marriage or becoming resident spinster in the family home. Neither appealed to her.

At this point her luck changed. Reverent T. L. Flood, publisher of a monthly magazine, offered her a job on his staff. *The Chatauquan* had a circulation of 40,000 and the right views on government, temperance, labor, monopoly, and feminism. Ida immediately accepted and moved back to Meadville, where the monthly was put out. Although she was hired on a temporary basis, she soon became a permanent staff member, doing everything from copy editing to advertising. Before long she was writing unsigned columns on current events as well. Her first byline appeared in 1886 under the title "The Arts and Industries of Cincinnati." Unfortunately Flood wanted her to stick to editing, and Ida, by now tired of the circumscribed world of western Pennsylvania, decided to resign and move to Paris. When she told the publisher she was going to France to write, he told her rudely: "You're not a writer; you'll starve."

Undaunted, in 1891 Ida and two friends left for Paris, where they took inexpensive rooms in the Latin Quarter. She went to lectures at the Sorbonne, did research at the Bibliothèque Nationale on women's role in the French Revolution, began a biography of the female revolutionary Madame Roland, and wrote columns for Pittsburgh, Chicago, and Cincinnati newspapers. She was thrilled when *Scribner's Magazine* bought one of her stories for $100. In the summer of 1892, S. S. McClure visited Paris and interviewed Tarbell. He immediately hired her to translate French newspaper articles into English and write her own stories when needed by his publishing syndicate and his new magazine. McClure was particularly interested in scientific discoveries, and Ida had a field day interviewing Pierre Janssen, the builder of the Mont Blanc observatory; Alphonse Bertillon, the inventor of a criminal identification system; and Louis Pasteur, the famous French bacteriologist. In 1893 McClure asked her to return to the United States and commissioned her to write a lengthy biography of Napoleon, to be serialized in his magazine. After her first installment appeared (the full-length biography was eventually issued in book form), McClure assigned her to do a biography of Abraham Lincoln. By 1896 the popularity of Tarbell's series on Napoleon and Lincoln had raised the magazine's circulation and helped assure its success.

By the beginning of the century the magazine had acquired a permanent staff of young and talented reporters and writers. Reform was already in the air and McClure was prepared to unleash them on the abuses that seemed to flourish everywhere. But he insisted that his staff be factual, accurate, and fluent. With the advantage of weekly, rather than daily, publication, there was no reason why journalists could not be held to high standards. McClure's reporters included Tarbell, Ray Stannard Baker, Lincoln Steffens, and William Allen White. This was the core of the influential group whom Theodore Roosevelt would soon dub the "muckrakers."

McClure knew that business monopoly was one of the problems that already troubled the American public. The huge business conglomerations frightened and confused people. The reporters thought it would be timely to pick out one industry to analyze—its origins, its growth, its strong-arm tactics, its combinations, "and so on, until it is finally absorbed into a great Trust." After a great deal of discussion the staff finally decided that they would choose the "greatest [trust] of them all—the Standard Oil Company." Tarbell was picked for the assignment, partly because of her family's experiences with Standard Oil, partly because she was such an assiduous collector of facts, and partly because Ray Baker declined the job.

In 1901 Tarbell started her research. The work was designed to be impartial, with material both favorable and critical, and Tarbell insisted that she had an open mind. "We were neither apologists nor critics," she wrote in her autobiography, "only journalists intent on discovering what had gone into the making of this most perfect of all monopolies." But as she got deeper into the project, important documents in the company's archives vanished, her father's former colleagues refused to speak to her, and she was physically threatened. One pamphlet that she tried to locate was *The Rise and Fall of the South Improvement Company*, published in 1873, that detailed how the company, under an earlier name, had conspired with railroads to get payments for each barrel of oil shipped by its competitors, and illicit information about shipments by its rivals. All the copies in circulation had abruptly disappeared. Finally Ida found one in the New York Public Library and learned how Rockefeller had actually bought the charter of the South Improvement Company to secure the enormous range of business powers granted it by the state of Pennsylvania. The only right he was not given was that of banking, and he soon rectified this by buying the National City Bank of New York.

Tarbell's additional research included interviews with the Industrial Commission, the Interstate Commerce Commission, and Henry Rogers, a Standard Oil partner. She went to services at the Euclid Avenue Baptist Church in Cleveland to get a look at Rockefeller in person, and was amused to see that he wore a skullcap to cover his baldness. The project, which took five years to complete, was published in nineteen articles in *McClure's* and then as a two-volume book in 1904. Much of what Tarbell wrote has been confirmed by more recent scholarship.

By the time the Standard Oil series concluded, Ida Tarbell was famous and sought after. She was insulted, however, at being excluded from the Periodical Publishers' Dinner, an all-male affair that McClure, Baker, and Steffens, as well as other colleagues, attended. "It is the first time . . . ," she wrote, "that the fact of petticoats has stood in my way and I am half inclined to resent it." Although she researched and wrote about the status of women and chose a career over marriage, she never became a women's rights or suffrage activist. In fact, in two separate series on women she publicly opposed giving the vote to women on the grounds that suffrage would not cure all of society's ills, as the activists claimed, and that women did not pay enough attention to the values of home and family. When pressed by feminist critics, she finally confessed her position as "a kind of instinct. It is no logic or argument. . . ."

In 1906 Tarbell helped lead a staff revolt at *McClure's* over the founder's management policies, business practices, and personal philandering. The upshot was that she, Baker, Steffens, White, and Finley Peter Dunne left *McClure's* and bought a competitor, *The American Magazine*. It was for this latter publication that she wrote her series on tariff abuses. She also shifted from a negative to a positive attitude toward business after she visited Henry Ford's factories and was impressed by his mass-production techniques, his fair wages, and his benevolent treatment of his workers. In 1914 and 1915 she wrote a series in *The American Magazine* in favor of Frederick Taylor's scientific management methods in industry. In the same year she published a series on women in *Women's Home Companion*, and this ended her full-time affiliation with *American Magazine*.

In 1916 Tarbell, dividing her time between her New York apartment and her Connecticut farm, became a freelance writer, and continued this career until the end of her life. She served on the Women's Committee of the Council of National Defense in World War I, and as a member of President Wilson's Industrial Conference. In 1919 she covered the Paris Peace Conference and published her only novel. Throughout the 1920s she wrote on Lincoln and his family, and on Elbert H. Gary, the founder of United States Steel. She also visited Italy to observe Mussolini's regime. In 1930 she was elected the first woman member of the Authors' Club. She was a supporter of the New Deal, endorsing the National Recovery Administration and social security. She contributed a volume, *The Nationalizing of Business*, to the distinguished *History of American Life* series. In 1939 she published *All in the Day's Work: An Autobiography*. Five years later, at the age of eighty-seven, still in full possession of her mental faculties and working on *Life After Eighty*, she died of pneumonia. Ida Tarbell was buried in the Pennsylvania oil country in a cemetery in Titusville near her forebears.

---

the farms, helped reinforce the public perception that the nation was in crisis and must be restored.

The Muckrakers. The antiformalists, the pragmatist philosophers, the liberal Darwinians, and the new literary and artistic realists set the mood for the reform movement. But it was a group of talented editors, journalists, and essayists known as the muckrakers who give a sharp focus to the public's fears and discontent.

The muckrakers aimed dazzling spotlights into every dark cranny of American political and social life to reveal the gross abuses that existed. They owed their name to Theodore Roosevelt, who often sympathized with their aims but considered their passion for uncovering dirt and wrongdoing excessive. TR likened them to a morose character in John Bunyan's *Pilgrim's Progress* who "continued to rake to himself the filth of the floor" even when offered a "celestial crown."

Exposé journalism was not an invention of the Progressive Era. Toward the end of the nineteenth century, newspapers, in their effort to help newcomers interpret the city environment, had increasingly resorted to exposing local political and business abuses. In 1894 Henry Demarest Lloyd had described in lurid detail the abuses of Standard Oil in his book *Wealth Against Commonwealth*. Yet it was not until after 1900—when lower printing costs, the new mass audience educated by the public high schools, and the capacity to produce magazines in vast numbers all came together—that true exposé journalism appeared. Thereafter periodical publishers became more willing than ever to pay good prices for well-written and well-researched articles on controversial, dis-

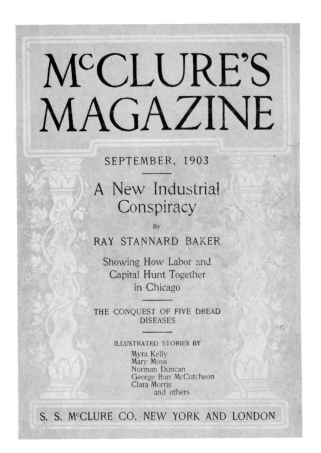

MᶜCLURE'S
MAGAZINE

SEPTEMBER, 1903

A New Industrial
Conspiracy

By
RAY STANNARD BAKER

Showing How Labor and
Capital Hunt Together
in Chicago

THE CONQUEST OF FIVE DREAD
DISEASES

ILLUSTRATED STORIES BY
Myra Kelly
Mary Moss
Norman Duncan
George Barr McCutcheon
Clara Morris
and others

S. S. MᶜCLURE CO. NEW YORK AND LONDON

McClure's, Cosmopolitan, *and many other turn-of-the-century magazines were the voices of muckraking reporters. Their sensational attacks on powerful institutions sold millions of copies, guaranteeing McClure and other publishers enormous profits.*

turbing, or sensational subjects that would grip readers and keep them coming back for more.

Samuel S. McClure, a shrewd and ebullient Irishman, was the first publisher to take advantage of the new opportunity. His instinct for profitable journalism was sound, if at times disconcerting. He would have paid well, one wit observed, for a "snappy life of Christ." McClure did not intend to create a new kind of journalism; he wanted to sell magazines. But his practice of hiring talented writers and reporters to investigate various aspects of American life produced a journalistic revolution. In October 1902 *McClure's* carried an article by a young Californian, Lincoln Steffens, entitled "Tweed Days in St. Louis." It described the efforts of a young district attorney to prosecute the corrupt St. Louis Democratic machine. The November issue carried the first installment of a series by journalist Ida Tarbell exposing the monopolistic practices of the Standard Oil Company. Early in 1903 Ray Stannard Baker's article on unfair labor practices appeared. The public took notice of these

articles, and McClure found himself selling more magazines than he had ever believed possible. Before long other publishers, observing their rival's success, rushed to hire men and women with a talent for uncovering wrongdoing and writing about it in a colorful and exciting way.

What followed was the greatest outpouring of exposé journalism in American history. Eventually the muckrakers probed into every national abuse: uncontrolled sale of patent medicines; the shady doings of stock market manipulators; the extent of businessmen's efforts to corrupt legislatures, city councils, and Congress; the harsh treatment of labor; the disgusting and unsanitary conditions in the meat-packing industry; the profiteering of the "beef trust"; the exploitation of child workers; the savage treatment of defenseless young women by purveyors of vice; the behind-the-scenes effort of the "money trust" to manipulate the entire American economy. Some of the muckrakers' output does not stand up to careful rechecking. But it touched the public's exposed nerves, confirmed its uneasiness, and gave direction to its unfocused fears.

The New Republic Group. The muckrakers seldom saw far beneath the surface, nor did they generally offer profound solutions to the problems they uncovered. But there were also in these years more sophisticated thinkers who perceptively analyzed the nature of unrestrained private power and the vulnerability of the ordinary citizen, and suggested thoughtful remedies.

Three of these—Walter Lippmann, Herbert Croly, and Walter Weyl—expressed their views through a crusading new magazine, *The New Republic.* The older liberalism, the three precocious philosophers pointed out, assumed a social system of small producers, no one of whom could overawe and oppress the others. Although the Jeffersonians and their successors feared excessive private power, they had seldom actually faced it. In their day any group that attempted to gain excessive power was certain to find itself checked by others of equal strength and influence. If government had any role to play in maintaining a balance of forces in such a simple society, it was only as a disinterested policeman that would keep the various groups from hurting one another.

Now Americans lived in an age of giant corporations. Few people were small farmers or self-employed artisans. Although most still yearned for a past when people had done more or less as they pleased, that was no longer possible. Any effort to restore the past of small producers by breaking up the great corporations would fail and only make the economy less efficient. Instead, *The New Republic* writers said, liberals must accept bigness and insist that government be given a positive role in guiding the great corporations and regulating the economy for the general good.

If all else failed, government must be allowed to take over, manage, and run the giant trusts. Herbert Croly called this approach the "New Nationalism." In effect, he declared, Hamiltonian, big-government means must be used to achieve Jeffersonian, egalitarian ends.

★ PROGRESSIVISM ENTERS POLITICS ★

Muckraking journalists helped direct the attention of literate urban Americans to the ills of society and reinforced the uneasiness they felt at their exposed positions. What could they do to reduce their vulnerability? Answers began to appear as early as the 1890s.

The Cult of Efficiency in City Government. The first expressions of progressivism appeared at the local level. In the cities the "reform with a heart" that emerged in the 1890s (discussed in Chapter 18) was one aspect of the new reformist mood. A little later a group of city reformers emerged with somewhat different goals and a different clientele. Most of these people were professionals—engineers, lawyers, doctors, teachers, journalists—who believed that cities were much like large business firms and could be run effectively if subject to scientific management principles. Their motto, and their god, was efficiency.

In part, this "cult of efficiency" reflected the growing prestige of science and technology in these years. In industry, as we saw in Chapter 17, this same spirit was reflected in Taylorism—the meticulous examination and timing of industrial workers' motions in order to increase productivity. In part, too, the efficiency-oriented urban reform impulse was a throwback to the old economy-minded reform of the 1870s and 1880s. Like this earlier version, it seemed to ignore the urban wage earner class.

In the efficiency reformers' view there was no Democratic or Republican way to clean the streets or provide police protection or pure water. City government, accordingly, should be nonpartisan. Rather than elected mayors, cities should be headed by "managers" or "commissioners" who would run them on business principles designed to provide good value for the taxpayers' money. This may well have been desirable; all city people obviously benefited from inexpensive and efficient city services. But there is evidence that at times the new city government schemes, whatever their intentions, by making government nonpolitical, deprived the urban ethnic blocs and blue-collar workers of much of their former political influence.

In the 1890s the new city reformers organized the National Municipal Reform League and formulated a model city charter, which they hoped cities and state legislatures would adopt. Their first actual success came in 1901 when Galveston, Texas—following a catastrophic hurricane—adopted the commission plan. Under this scheme city government was turned over to a board of five commissioners chosen on a nonpartisan basis and at-large, rather than by wards, to eliminate old-fashioned politics from the selection process. The board combined the role of mayor and city council in one body. By merging functions and by eliminating party politics from consideration, the commissioners hoped to run city government like an efficient business. Still another idea was the city-manager scheme first adopted in Staunton, Virginia, in 1908. City managers were hired professionals who presumably knew how to run an urban community. They were hired by an elected city council and paid to manage the city much as a corporation might hire an executive to run the firm. By the 1920s several dozen cities, usually small or middle-sized, had adopted one or the other of the new municipal government schemes.

The Social Progressives. The Progressive movement reached beyond city hall, down into the neighborhoods and slums. There men and women dedicated to changing the urban environment established a network of neighborhood voluntary associations designed to improve the lives of the poor. These "social" progressives formed the most militant wing of the Progressive movement. Many were inspired by the social gospel of Walter Rauschenbusch or the Christian socialism of Washington Gladden. They were for the most part recruited from among the idealistic young people who poured from the secondary schools and colleges in the last years of the nineteenth century. Particularly prominent among them were the new college women who sought to use their skills, education, and energies for something more fulfilling than the self-improvement of women's clubs. Many of these young people became voluntary charity workers or took up the new profession of social work. An especially dedicated contingent threw in their lot with the urban poor and went to live in settlement houses in the noisome slums that dominated the cities' centers.

Settlement houses were places where slum children could go for recreation and entertainment; where mothers could learn about nutrition, scientific child care, and household management; and where fathers could learn vocational skills, improve their English, prepare for citizenship, and meet other men to discuss city or community problems. Beginning with the Neighborhood Guild on New York's Lower East Side and Hull House in Chicago, settlements began to spring up during the 1890s in all the major cities. Hull House, under the leadership of Jane Addams, and New York's Henry Street Settlement, run by Lillian Wald, were the most prominent, but there were scores of others in every large city.

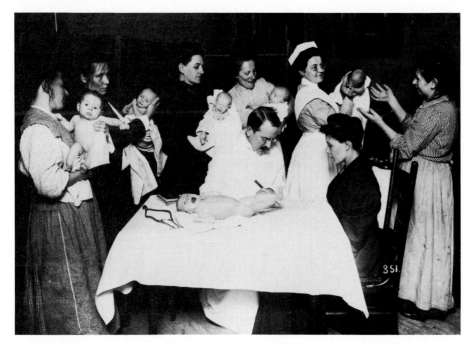

Settlement houses provided many services for the city poor. This settlement house in Chicago dispensed medical services for local infants. Such work may have contributed to the declining infant mortality rate of the early twentieth century.

Most of the people who used the settlements were European immigrants and their children, but the settlement workers were also concerned with the problems of black city dwellers. Frances Kellor of New York's College Settlement helped organize the National League for the Protection of Negro Women after she discovered how young black farm women were lured to the cities by promises of good jobs and then harshly exploited by employers or forced into prostitution. Another white social worker, Mary White Ovington, established a settlement in a New York black slum. Mexican-Americans, too, benefited from the movement. The College Settlement in Los Angeles, located in a Mexican district, sought to provide the local poor with facilities for recreation and education and legal aid.

The settlements soon became springboards of social reform. Middle-class reformers living among the poor quickly learned that many of their problems could be solved only by legislation. In Chicago Jane Addams regularly supported city reformers who dared to challenge the city machine. Addams worked for tenement legislation as well as improved educational and recreational opportunities for the urban working class. She and her counterparts in other communities regularly joined in citywide efforts to eliminate vice and reduce crime. Much of the support that the reform mayors of the 1890s and early twentieth century received came from the settlement workers.

As women's clubs caught the new reform spirit, they too became sources of reform in neighborhoods and cities. The clubs were especially active in the fight for honest city government, but middle-class women also battled for consumers and worked to help the urban poor. In 1899 a group of upper-middle-class women established the National Consumer's League, which threatened to boycott employers who did not adhere to fair employment practices. The league also labored to improve community health through licensing of food vendors and supported measures to protect urban consumers against retail fraud. Many local laws that now protect consumers are traceable to the efforts of these first consumer advocates almost a century ago.

Progressivism in the States.   Only so much could be accomplished on the neighborhood or city level, however, and in the end the reformers had to turn to the state legislatures to achieve their goals. Until the 1890s state governments all too often had been little more than junior partners of large business corporations. Despite the flurry of Granger laws in the 1870s, legislators and governors remained subservient to the great railroads, utility companies, and other corporations that exploited their constituents. Many were notoriously corrupt men who accepted money and other gifts from business people and did their bidding without concern for the public interest.

For years reformers had denounced the "unholy alliance" of state government and big business characteristic of the Gilded Age. Their voices went unheeded. Then the panic of 1893 exposed many of the flaws in the country's economy and pointed up the dangers of unregulated economic power as never before. Public opinion soon began to change.

The revelation came with particular force to the people of Wisconsin, a state dominated by a Republican machine that had always worked hand-in-glove with the major corporations. The depression of 1893–1897 severely jolted Wisconsin's economy. By the winter of 1893–1894 more than a third of the state's wage earners were unemployed. Meanwhile, the hard-pressed utility firms refused to pay their taxes and raised their rates to city consumers to offset declining revenue. To make matters worse, the distress of the unemployed and consumers were accompanied by revelations that a clique of bankers had been embezzling funds from depositors and stockholders. As the citizens of Wisconsin looked around them, they were shocked by the contrast between the continued affluence of a small group of men and women based on influence and corruption and the worsening plight of the average citizen.

The Wisconsinite who best understood the growing public outrage and disquiet was the ambitious young Republican lawyer Robert M. La Follette. The combative and eloquent La Follette had already run against the state machine for governor and failed. In 1897 he was seeking new issues and quickly saw that he could win wide public support by championing the citizenry against arrogant, irresponsible economic power. Defeated once more in 1898, he was finally swept into office two years later.

La Follette's victory was followed by a wave of legislation that made Wisconsin the pioneer in statewide reform and the "laboratory" for progressive lawmaking. First on the new governor's list of changes was a state primary system that permitted the voters to bypass the party bosses and nominate their own candidates for state office. His second measure was a railroad tax that shifted some of the burden of supporting government from farmers and wage earners to the previously untaxed railroad corporations and their stockholders. He later supported a state railroad commission to regulate the rates that the railroads could charge.

In 1902 La Follette ran for reelection. In his first successful campaign he had stressed his Republicanism, albeit a reform variety. This time he appealed for nonpartisan support and got it. Virtually all Wisconsin citizens, not just Republicans, by now feared the power of the "interests." Vulnerability cut across ethnic lines, and many Catholic voters abandoned their earlier allegiance to the Democratic party to vote for the reformer. La Follette's resounding reelection victory helped eclipse the old party politics of the Gilded Age.

In 1905 the young governor was elected to the United States Senate by the state legislature—still the normal procedure for election of senators. But Wisconsin continued to be a center of progressive reform. Under "Battle Bob's" successors, the state adopted two new instruments of "direct democracy" to reduce the power of the political boss–big-business alliance. The first of these, the *initiative*, was a procedure enabling voters to introduce legislation without waiting for legislators to do so. The *referendum* allowed voters to accept or reject, by a direct ballot, certain laws passed by the legislature. Progressives hoped that the two political innovations would allow the voters to bypass or overrule legislatures controlled by powerful economic interests and gain a greater say in the political process. The state also established a public utility commission to protect consumers against gouging by gas companies and power and light companies. Working closely with social scientists from the University of Wisconsin, successive state administrations enacted a workers' compensation act for injured or disabled wage earners and a state income tax to make wealthier citizens bear a larger part of the community's tax load. They established a board of public affairs to protect vital natural resources from corporate exploiters. The thrust of the whole reform wave was to ensure that ordinary citizens would be protected against the hazards of a vast, impersonal economy subject to the whim of private capital.

The "Wisconsin idea" captured the attention of millions of Americans. The muckrakers took notice of Battle Bob and transformed him into a figure of national importance. Other states soon adopted Wisconsin's program. In Oregon William S. U'Ren, who had in some ways anticipated La Follette, added other direct-democracy measures to the Wisconsin idea. U'Ren sponsored the *recall*, which enabled voters to remove corrupt or incompetent officials from office, and supported the secret ballot, to replace the prepared party-printed ballot that the voter selected in full view of everyone, including the local party precinct captain.

Much of the new legislation was designed to protect citizens in general. A good deal of it was aimed specifically at weaker groups in society. Beginning with Illinois in 1899, for example, many states established special courts for juvenile offenders. Between 1905 and 1907 two-thirds of the states enacted laws limiting the hours of child labor or outlawing paid labor for young children. Both juvenile offenders reform and child labor restrictions were part of a larger "child saving" movement that included providing germ-free milk and play facilities as other elements. Working women, too, were increasingly surrounded by state regulations intended to prevent employer exploitation and abuse. The states also limited the working hours of men employed in exhausting or hazardous occupations like baking and mining. More and more states joined Wisconsin in adopting workers' compensation insurance schemes, though in truth, in part, this was at the behest of business firms increasingly beset by lawsuits instigated by injured workers. As an expression of the most advanced social vision there was even talk of publicly funded health and unemployment insurance. But these extreme proposals did not get very far.

Southern Progressivism. In 1912 Robert La Follette remarked that he "did not know of any progressive sentiment of any progressive legislation in the South." The Wisconsin

Robert La Follette (second from right) took his progressive views to the people of Wisconsin in this special campaign train. It was successful, and La Follette went to the statehouse in Madison. His performance as governor promised him a successful national career.

leader was only revealing a common Yankee ignorance of Dixie. From many southern statehouses, beginning early in the century, progressive governors launched effective attacks against railroads, utility companies, insurance firms, and other business groups that seemed to be exploiting the region and its citizens. In Alabama there was Braxton Bragg Comer, a wealthy Birmingham manufacturer, banker, and landowner, who joined the progressive fold when he discovered that the state's railroads, controlled by directors in Chicago and New York, were personally hurting him economically. What began as a private grievance soon grew into a public-spirited crusade. As governor, Comer expanded the authority of the state railroad commission and reduced passenger and freight rates. In Arkansas, Attorney General Jeff Davis initiated scores of suits against insurance companies, tobacco firms, and oil companies, charging them with unfair, monopolistic practices and price-fixing.

Southern progressives were often openly anti-Yankee, aiming their sharpest barbs at "Wall Street" and "foreign"—that is, northeastern—corporations, which sucked profits out of the South and gave nothing in return. At times skeptical southern progressives twitted their colleagues for reluctance to attack such home-grown abuses as child labor, when doing so might discourage the growth of local industry. But the South had its advanced social reformers, too. The Southern Sociological Congress—composed of ministers, urban humanitarians, and middle-class clubwomen—worked to improve the lot of the region's children, the handicapped, consumers, and prisoners. The congress could claim credit for only a small amount of advanced social legislation, but it brought together men and women of

like mind and helped to create the "southern liberal" type, whose efforts would help transform the region in later years.

Black Americans. The Sociological Congress worked to improve race relations, but by and large southern progressivism was "for whites only." A number of prominent southern politicians—James K. Vardaman and Theodore G. Bilbo of Mississippi, for example—managed to combine a desire to protect white yeomen farmers from the corporations with a violent antiblack rhetoric that poisoned the racial atmosphere. Even southern primary laws, widely adopted early in the century, did blacks little good. Southern progressives, arguing that the conservative southern Bourbons used the black vote to reinforce privilege, excluded blacks from the primaries. Thereafter black political influence in Dixie, much reduced already from Reconstruction times, declined almost to zero.

Meanwhile, as progressive laws poured from southern state legislatures, the "Jim Crow" system, which kept the races strictly segregated, expanded into every corner of the region's daily life. Blacks and a few white liberals tried to check the process through legal action. But the Supreme Court ruling in the landmark *Plessy* v. *Ferguson* (1896) decision that segregation was legal as long as the facilities provided each race were equal in quality, frustrated their efforts. Far worse, lynching continued and even grew as a savage weapon of terror to keep blacks in "their place."

Militant egalitarians at times blamed the South's continued oppression of its black citizens on southern black acquiescence. Their target was Booker T. Washington, who, well into the new century, wore the mantle of black leadership in Dixie.

Washington had risen to prominence in the 1890s as a protégé of southern whites. Born into slavery, he had been sent by white philanthropists to Hampton Institute in Virginia, a glorified trade school, but one of the few existing all-black institutions of higher education. In 1881 whites chose him to head a school for black youths at Tuskegee, Alabama. Washington made Tuskegee into a flourishing institution emphasizing industrial education, modeled on the work-ethic, self-help principles of Hampton. In 1895 he achieved national prominence with an electrifying address at the Atlanta Cotton States Exposition. Speaking to a white audience, he proposed that blacks accept disfranchisement and racial segregation in exchange for the right to advance economically and be unmolested in their persons and property. This so-called Atlanta Compromise immediately impressed white southerners as a useful rationalization of existing practices. Thereafter the white establishment made Washington the "spokesman" for his race and the quasi-official dispenser of white philanthropy and political patronage to blacks.

Washington's Atlanta Compromise surely acquiesced in segregation and appeared to encourage black passivity in the face of mistreatment. It undoubtedly reinforced the southern caste system. But Washington was by no means a complete "Uncle Tom." Although projecting a public image of meekness, behind the scenes he quietly fought segregation, lynching, and debt peonage. In 1900 he raised money to test southern laws disfranchising blacks in the federal courts. When President Theodore Roosevelt gave dishonorable discharges in 1906 to three companies of black soldiers for refusing to identify the leaders of a riot in Brownsville, Texas, Washington went to the White House to intercede for the wronged men, though without success.

Despite such efforts, to a new group of urban black intellectuals Washington seemed all too willing to surrender fundamental black rights and to consent to permanent second-class citizenship. Among this group were the Boston editor William Monroe Trotter, T. Thomas Fortune of the New York *Age*, the Jacksonville minister J. Milton Waldron, and, the most prominent member, W. E. B. Du Bois. The Massachusetts-born Du Bois was one of the first black men to receive a Ph.D. from an American university. An early advocate of black liberation from white economic and cultural domination, he insisted that black Americans must run their own businesses, provide their own professional services, write their own books, and create their own art. In 1903, in *The Souls of Black Folk*, he attacked Washington as a man who had "practically accepted the alleged inferiority of the Negro," and urged prominent black Americans to cease flattering the white South and to speak out on the race issue. Du Bois at this stage of his life was scarcely a democrat. A proud and sensitive man, he believed that black salvation

Throughout his long life (1868–1963), W. E. B. Du Bois's thinking anticipated developments in black positions on race. The first black to receive a Ph.D. from Harvard, he helped start the Niagara Movement and then the NAACP, advocated Pan-Africanism, lost faith in integration, became a Communist, supported Black Power, and finally moved to Africa.

rested with the "Talented Tenth" of liberally educated black men and women.

In 1905 Du Bois and Trotter convened a meeting at Fort Erie, Ontario, near Niagara Falls, to raise a militant voice against black oppression. The convention issued a manifesto demanding true manhood suffrage, the end of racial discrimination, the freedom of blacks to criticize American society, and free access for blacks to liberal education as well as to vocational training. Incorporated as the Niagara Movement, the group continued to meet annually for several years to defend black rights and demand that white America practice its professed principles of equality.

By 1908 Washington's counterattack and the growing divisions among the militants themselves had reduced the Niagara Movement's momentum. By this time, however, a group of white progressives had concluded that something must be done to end the brutality and injustice committed against black Americans. Among this group were Oswald Garrison Villard, grandson of the abolitionist William Lloyd Garrison; the social workers Jane Addams, Lillian Wald, and Mary White Ovington; Chicago lawyer Clarence Darrow; novelist William Dean Howells; and John Dewey, the Columbia philosopher. In 1909 these white progressives joined with the Niagara Movement militants to establish the National Association for the Advancement of Colored People (NAACP), which immediately sought to defend the legal and constitutional rights of blacks wherever they were threatened or denied. The modern movement for racial equality was now under way.

Female Progressives.   Women were among the most active workers for social reform before and during the Progressive Era. They fought for improved labor laws, for consumer protection, for better race relations. One major cause that attracted many reform-minded women in these years was temperance. The battle to contain and perhaps end for all time the social and moral evil of drunkenness had engaged the attention of American women for many years. In 1874 female reformers had organized the Women's Christian Temperance Union (WCTU). After the turn of the century, in alliance with the predominantly male Anti-Saloon League, it propagandized in the schools and churches against alcohol and lobbied for state laws outlawing the production, sale, and consumption of beer, wine, and whiskey. In later years temperance advocates and prohibitionists

would often uphold the social status quo; but in the early years of the twentieth century such temperance reformers as Frances Willard and Anna Shaw were strong advocates of child-labor laws and other progressive legislation.

No cause, however, engaged the energies of women reformers so completely as the issue of suffrage for women themselves. For decades women suffragists had been struggling for the right to vote. Successes had been few. Most men and many women saw enfranchising women as a violation of nature and a threat to the family. Little was achieved before the Civil War. Then, during Reconstruction, when the suffrage issue surfaced once again, women suffragists chose to defer their struggle until the fight for black civil rights was won.

The battle proved long and hard. In 1869 Susan B. Anthony and Elizabeth Cady Stanton, both pre–Civil War women's suffrage leaders, organized the National Woman Suffrage Association. This group scored some successes in the West. By 1896 Wyoming, Utah, Colorado, and Idaho had granted women the vote. Meanwhile, a more conservative group of women, including Lucy Stone and Julia Ward Howe, had formed the American Woman Suffrage Association. In 1890 the two organizations merged under the presidency of Stanton as the National American Woman Suffrage Association (NAWSA).

By the opening years of the twentieth century, new and more militant suffragist leaders had appeared, such as Carrie Chapman Catt and Anna Howard Shaw. These

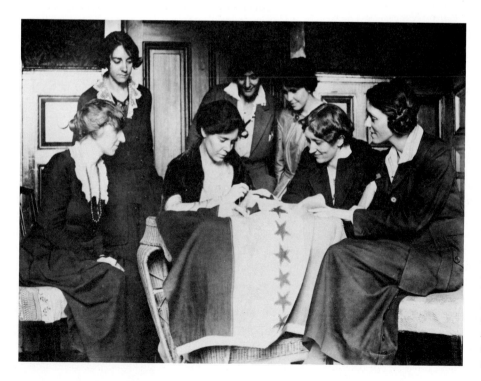

Women's rights leader Alice Paul sews the ratification star on the flag of the National Women's Party, celebrating the 1920 ratification of the Nineteenth Amendment, which gave women the vote. Paul also authored the unsuccessful Equal Rights Amendment, a source of great controversy more than a half century later.

Progressivism   643

women introduced a greater degree of professionalism into the suffragists' work and streamlined NAWSA's operations.

To NAWSA's left was a cluster of social feminists who demanded more than the vote. There must also be fundamental changes, they said, in women's relations with men, the economy, and the family. Charlotte Perkins Gilman argued in *Women and Economics* (1898) that women's subordinate economic role had stunted their personalities and damaged their effectiveness as wives and mothers. Gilman demanded economic equality and proposed communal child-care centers to liberate women from economic dependence on men. Crystal Eastman, an active suffragist, also advocated sexual emancipation of women and free dissemination of birth-control information and devices. In 1914, Eastman and Alice Paul, a young Quaker activist, organized the Congressional Union to agitate for a suffrage amendment to the Constitution in place of a state-by-state approach. The new militants were not bound by the decorum of their elders, and they adopted the flamboyant tactics of English suffragists, which included mass marches, chaining themselves to lampposts, and prison fasts. In the elections of 1914 and 1916, Paul's group (organized as the National Women's Party in 1916) campaigned to punish the Democrats, the party in power, for failure to support a suffrage amendment. Resistance continued, however, and victory for women's suffrage would be delayed for four more years.

★ PROGRESSIVISM CONQUERS THE NATION ★

Progressivism was largely a local phenomenon at first. By the opening years of the new century, community halls, city council chambers, and state capitols were alive with people imbued with the new awareness of social problems and impatient with stand-pat institutions and leaders. But all was quiet along the Potomac. Then events moved quickly.

In 1898, four months after his much-publicized charge up San Juan Hill in the war with Spain, Theodore Roosevelt was elected governor of New York. Although he had been the candidate of Thomas C. Platt, the state's Republican boss, his administration brought little joy to the state machine. As governor, Roosevelt appointed honest people to office and supported bills to tax public utilities. Unhappy with his choice, and anxious to get him out of New York, Platt maneuvered Roosevelt into accepting second place on the 1900 Republican ticket with William McKinley. McKinley and Roosevelt won a landslide victory in 1900 over Bryan and Stevenson.

On September 6, 1901, while on a visit to the Pan-American Exposition in Buffalo, McKinley was shot by Leon Czolgosz, a demented anarchist. The president died a week later. Suddenly, at forty-two, Roosevelt found himself the youngest man yet to occupy the presidential office.

The new president was a remarkable man. A graduate of elite Groton and Harvard, TR was a literate man whose histories, *The Naval War of 1812* and *Winning of the West*, can still be read with profit today. He was also a man of frenetic action who forced even the most distinguished guests at his country home, and at the White House itself, to join him on jogs about the countryside while he shouted his views of politics, art, and economics. Though capable of dashing off reviews, speeches, books, and articles, and holding his own with distinguished scholars, he also enjoyed living with the cowboys of western Dakota and spent long, happy months in the wilds of three continents hunting, exploring, and collecting zoological specimens. TR had a juvenile streak that often led him to snap judgments. One distinguished foreign observer remarked to an American friend: "You know your president is really six." An intense nationalist, Roosevelt identified the United States with virtue and tended to see other nations and other races besides the "Anglo-Saxon" as inherently inferior. Despite his failings—and perhaps partly because of them—Roosevelt charmed and delighted the American public, and his personal appeal would rub off on the programs he supported.

Roosevelt's First Term.   The conservative Republican "Old Guard" did not trust Roosevelt. When Roosevelt's name was first proposed for vice president on the 1900 Republican ticket, Senator Marcus (Mark) Hanna warned that if TR received the nomination, only one life would stand between the country and a "madman." Yet TR at first adopted a prudent and moderate course. His first annual message to Congress proved so conventional that the *New York Evening Post* declared that it might have been composed by "a man of sixty, trained in conservative habits." Yet there were some elements of the future progressive agenda in his recommendations for a cabinet-level department of commerce and labor to protect labor's rights and to publicize inflated corporate earnings, and for stronger measures to protect the country's forests and conserve its natural resources. Even closer to the emerging progressive program was his request for increased power for the feeble Interstate Commerce Commission to help guarantee fair treatment to shippers.

Congress eventually gave TR much of what he asked for. In 1902 it passed the Newlands Act, which set aside money from federal land sales in the arid West for dams and canals to irrigate the land (see Chapter 19). In 1903 it established the Department of Commerce and Labor, incorporating a Bureau of Corporations empowered to subpoena information from industry that could then be used for antitrust suits under the Sherman Antitrust Act. That same year Congress passed the Elkins Act outlawing rebates to favored shippers and giving the federal courts the power to issue injunctions ordering railroads to desist from practices that benefited some shippers at the expense of others.

Despite these successes, reform-minded observers considered Roosevelt's initial legislative performance disappointing and timid. In his executive capacity, however, he proved bolder and startled the nation in 1902 by ordering Attorney General Philander Knox to file suit against the Northern Securities Holding Company for violating the Sherman Antitrust Act.

Here was a new spirit indeed. The Northern Securities Company was a combination put together by J. P. Morgan, James J. Hill, E. H. Harriman, and the Rockefellers that merged into one giant firm most of the railroads in the northwestern corner of the nation. If ever a business trust promised to "restrain trade" and impose an economic stranglehold on millions, this was it. Now, after twelve years, the Sherman Antitrust Act was finally to be used for its intended purpose. Soon after, Knox also indicted Swift and Company, the Chicago meatpackers, for conspiring with its competitors to fix prices.

The liberal press and the growing contingent of reform-minded citizens hailed the antitrust suits with delight. Morgan, however, was dismayed by the Northern Securities indictment. How could the president act in such an arbitrary way? The uncrowned king of Wall Street did not see himself as a mere private citizen subject to ordinary law, and he told the president: "If we have done anything wrong send your man to my man to fix it up." Roosevelt was not swayed and the suit proceeded to a successful conclusion in 1904, when the Supreme Court ordered the dissolution of the Northern Securities Company.

The *Northern Securities* case, the Swift suit, and later suits against Standard Oil and the American Tobacco Company gave TR the reputation of being a trustbuster and an uncompromising foe of big business. Actually, Roosevelt distinguished between "good trusts" and "bad trusts." The first obeyed the law and did not use their power to squeeze

One reason for TR's success as a politician was that he enjoyed the political game. Clearly it would be hard to dislike anybody with such an infectious grin.

the consuming public; the latter knew no such restraint. "Bad trusts" should be punished, but "good trusts" should be left alone because large firms were more efficient than small ones. Besides, TR felt, the country could as soon reverse the Mississippi spring flood as stop the processes of corporate growth. On the other hand, the nation need not allow the floods to surge unchecked. Instead, it could "regulate and control them by levees," preventing misuse of corporation power. In fact, though he rejected Morgan's overtures, TR was not adamantly opposed to negotiations with big business. In 1905, for example, he struck a bargain with Elbert Gary, board chairman of U.S. Steel. If Gary cooperated with an investigation of his company, then any wrongdoing detected would be reported to him to correct before the government commenced a suit.

Clearly TR was at most a qualified opponent of big business. He was an equally qualified friend of organized labor. Like many middle-class Americans of the day, the president feared socialism and at times confused it with trade union activity. As New York governor, he had sent state militia to put down disorders that had followed a labor dispute. Yet far more than most of his predecessors, TR believed that unions had a legitimate place as agencies to protect wage earners. By this time even conservative men such as Mark Hanna, the Cleveland industrialist and senator who had been a close adviser to McKinley, were willing to join such organizations as the National Civic Federation, a body that brought together business people, civic leaders, college presidents, and labor leaders for joint action to make the economy more efficient and promote good labor-capital relations.

Roosevelt demonstrated his sympathetic attitude toward organized labor early in his first term. In May 1902, after months of arguing with the coal-mine owners in eastern Pennsylvania over higher wages, union recognition, and an eight-hour day, the United Mine Workers, led by John Mitchell, walked off their jobs. The anthracite coal they produced was the major source of heating fuel along much of the Atlantic Coast. If the strike dragged on through the summer and fall, there would be no coal for winter and millions of householders would suffer. Yet for months the mine owners arrogantly refused to negotiate. In reply to critics, George F. Baer, spokesman for the mine owners, haughtily declared that the "rights and interests of the laboring man will be protected and cared for not by labor agitators but by the Christian men to whom God has given control of the property rights of the country." When someone proposed that Archbishop John Ireland of St. Paul be brought in as mediator, Baer retorted that "anthracite mining is a business, and not a religious, sentimental, or academic proposition."

Roosevelt and a majority of the voters were offended by the owners' willingness to risk the public's welfare for their own gain. In early October, as winter approached,

Roosevelt invited the union leaders and the mine operators to Washington to discuss a settlement. At an all-day conference Mitchell declared his willingness to negotiate with the owners directly or to abide by the decision of a presidential arbitration commission—if the owners also agreed to accept its decision. The owners refused to budge. Their spokesman assault Mitchell personally and demanded that the president use federal troops to end the strike.

Outraged by the stubbornness of the operators and their discourtesy toward Mitchell, Roosevelt threatened to seize the mines and run them as federal property. Faced with the president's determination, the mine owners finally yielded. At another White House conference representatives of the miners and the operators agreed to a settlement. The men would go back to work; and a five-man commission consisting of an army engineer, a mining engineer, a businessman, a federal judge, and an "eminent sociologist" would be appointed by the president to arbitrate differences. The eminent sociologist Roosevelt selected was a union leader: E. E. Clark of the Brotherhood of Railroad Conductors, a novel choice for the day. The commission granted the miners their wage increase and some reduction in hours, but not union recognition. It was at best a mixed result, but to many Americans it was, as TR described it, a "square deal." The settlement established an important new precedent: From now on, the national government would be a factor to reckon with in disputes between capital and labor that vitally affected consumer interests.

The New Nationalism. With a "Square Deal" for all Americans as his rallying cry, Roosevelt ran for reelection in 1904. Tired of two defeats in succession under Bryan's banner, the Democrats nominated the conservative New York judge Alton B. Parker. The change did not help. TR won an impressive victory with 56 percent of the popular vote.

Roosevelt soon moved significantly to the left, responding to the changing mood of the American people, as well as to his growing political confidence now that he had been elected president in his own right. By this time a contingent of Republican progressives, including La Follette, Senators Albert Cummins of Iowa, Albert Beveridge of Indiana, Moses Clapp of Minnesota, Joseph Bristow of Kansas, and William E. Borah of Idaho, had arrived in Washington from the states where they had long been active in local reform movements. In later years they would be joined by other Republican progressives such as Hiram Johnson of California and George Norris of Nebraska. In addition, an increasing number of Democrats, caught up like their rivals in the surge of reform zeal, were prepared to support legislation to protect the public against "the interests." The opposition promised to be formidable, how-

TR viewed as a conquering hero in 1904 after his resounding election victory. Actually, his great achievements still lay ahead. (Collection of the New York Historical Society)

ever. The Republican stand-pat Old Guard—led by Senators Nelson W. Aldrich, Orville Platt, and John C. Spooner—were still powerful and would resist fiercely every attempt to alter the status quo.

Despite the stand-patters, during his second term Roosevelt was able to get some notable progressive legislation on the books. In 1906 he induced Congress to pass the Hepburn Act, for the first time giving a government agency—the Interstate Commerce Commission, in this case—the power to set rates for a private business. The bill allowed the commission to inspect the books of interstate railroads before setting rates. It also outlawed the practice of issuing free passes with which the railroads had bribed politicians. The bill was not a complete victory for the reformers. The railroads, through Aldrich, succeeded in inserting a provision giving the courts power to overturn commission-set rates. Nevertheless, the law was an important addition to the federal arsenal against business abuses.

Two other important regulatory measures passed in 1906 provided direct federal protection to consumers. For years reformers had attacked irresponsible meat-packers and food processors. In the government itself Dr. Harvey Wiley, chief of the Department of Agriculture's Bureau of Chemistry, had long warred against the patent medicine quacks and demanded that drug preparations be labeled to show their contents. Wiley supplied most of the data for "The Great American Fraud," a sensational muckraking article on the drug companies by Samuel Hopkins Adams, published in *Collier's* in 1905. An even more effective blow for consumer protection came in 1906, when the young socialist author Upton Sinclair published his lurid novel *The Jungle*. Sinclair's description of the filth of the Chicago meatpacking plants, of men falling into the lard vats and being rendered into cooking fat, and of packers injecting spoiled meat with chemicals and selling it to city saloons for their free lunch counters revolted the public and turned the stomach of the president himself.

After checking Sinclair's charges, TR threw his support behind a meat inspection bill then in Congress. Although the bad reputation of American beef had hurt their sales abroad, the meat-packers resisted the bill's passage strenuously. Only when the president warned them that he would publish the results of an official investigation of Sinclair's charges did they yield, though not without extracting concessions. The bill that Roosevelt signed into law as the Meat Inspection Act on June 30, 1906, provided for government supervision of sanitary practices in meat-packing plants, but the cost of the inspection would be borne by the treasury. On the same day, the years of agitation for drug regulation also bore fruit when TR approved the Pure Food and Drug Act requiring that the contents of food and drug preparations be described on their labels. Now at least the public could tell what it was getting when it bought "Brown's Iron Bitters" or "Horsford's Acid Phosphate."

Conservation. Among the progressives' many contributions to the quality of American life none was so impressive as their efforts to conserve the nation's natural resources. Conservation appealed to a wide range of citizens. One group was composed of lovers of nature who gloried in the forests, mountains, and lakes and considered the unspoiled wilderness a delight in itself, one capable of renewing the soul and the spirit. Led by Scottish-born naturalist John Muir and groups such as the Sierra Club of California, these "preservationists" insisted that the country's natural heritage be protected against any sort of defilement and preserved intact. Another group—the "conservationists"—was more pragmatic in its goals. Led by Chief Forester Gifford Pinchot, an upper-class Pennsylvanian trained in foresty and land management, these "conservationists" worshiped efficiency and sought the "best use" of resources. They had little patience with those who considered nature inviolable. Best-use conser-

vationists of the Pinchot variety believed the natural endowment must be exploited, but exploited rationally, scientifically, so that it would remain available to future generations. They noted the destruction of the buffalo, the disappearance of the enormous Great Lakes forests, the erosion of the soil everywhere, and the neglect of usable resources, and called for scientific resource management. At times the preservationists and the conservationists fought one another, but they also cooperated to battle the great lumber and mining companies, which they accused of putting profit ahead of the nation's long-term interests. At times, too, they found themselves at odds with ranchers and other western groups that resented eastern attempts to interfere with the traditional free-wheeling way they exploited the land.

Both preservationists and conservationists embodied the growing realization, as the nineteenth century closed, that the country's last frontier was rapidly filling in. As we saw, the emerging new sense of finite unspoiled space inspired creation of Yellowstone National Park in 1872. Yellowstone would be the precedent for setting aside other tracts of exceptionally scenic land as permanent recreation areas. In 1890, after strenuous efforts by Muir and other

The panic of 1907, though short, was frightening; it led Americans to rethink the country's banking and currency structure. This crowd—some looking worried, some unconcerned—is gathered outside New York's Trust Company of America in the early hours of the panic.

preservationists, Congress created Yosemite National Park in California, embracing one of the most beautiful natural spots in North America. Eventually the United States would create a national park system unequaled in the world. And the conservationist-preservationist impulse to exclude resources from exploitation went beyond scenic sites. In 1891, the Forest Reserve Act withdrew federally owned forests from the public domain and exempted them from private purchase. Under the act's provisions, President Benjamin Harrison would create 13 million acres of "forest reserves." These would later be called "national forests."

As an authority on wildlife and a lover of the outdoors, Roosevelt became a champion of the conservation movement. Closer to Gifford Pinchot than to John Muir—though he respected the Scottish mystic and considered him his friend—Roosevelt approved such "best use" projects as the 1902 Newlands Act. In 1905 he transferred the government's forest reserves from the Department of the Interior to the Department of Agriculture, where Chief Forester Pinchot could supervise their management. Two years later he and Pinchot saved millions of additional acres of public-domain forest and several important power sites from western timber companies by placing them in the forest reserves or designating them as ranger stations. In 1908 the president called a National Conservation Conference of forty-four state governors and hundreds of experts to consider resource-management problems.

The Panic of 1907. Although the economy generally was healthy during the Progressive Era, in 1907 the country only narrowly averted a serious depression. During the years immediately preceding, the economy had expanded rapidly. Combined with the trust movement, this growth had absorbed enormous pools of savings. By the middle of 1907 credit was so tight that New York City found it difficult to borrow money from the public to meet its needs. Then, at the end of October, a major New York bank closed its doors, setting off a wave of panicky deposit withdrawals from other banks. If matters had taken their usual course, the panic would have spread to the stock market and then to the nation's other credit agencies. In the absence of a central bank, this in turn would have tripped off a major depression. Fortunately, the combined action of the treasury, which deposited $35 million of the government's surplus in various private banks, and large loans by J. P. Morgan and other private bankers to troubled financial institutions stopped the panic in its tracks. A business downturn did follow, but it was both brief and shallow.

Morgan and the treasury had saved the day; but in the wake of the scare, many Americans began to ask what could be done to avoid future panics. In 1908 Congress passed the Aldrich-Vreeland Emergency Currency Act, making

$500 million in new currency available to certain national banks that deposited bonds with the treasury and establishing a congressional commission to investigate the deficiencies in the country's banking system and to recommend changes.

Taft's Misfortunes. Theodore Roosevelt left the White House in March 1909 convinced that William Howard Taft, his hand-picked successor, would carry on in his progressive steps. He had reason to be confident. The ponderous, 350-pound Taft—a former federal jurist, Commissioner of the Philippines, and secretary of war—had campaigned in 1908 on his predecessor's record. With the popular Teddy behind him, Taft defeated William Jennings Bryan, once again the Democratic candidate, though he fell short of Roosevelt's vote in the West.

Affable, well-liked, but indolent, Taft did not really want to be president. His was a judicial rather than an executive temperament. At one point he said that if he could be made a common pleas judge in Hamilton County, Ohio, he would be content to remain there all his life. His obesity hampered him. He ate gargantuan meals and then fell asleep at the table even with guests present. It made him a figure of derision.

Taft was pledged to continue TR's progressive policies, but at heart he was a conservative. He and his attorney gen-

TR chooses his successor. Carrying the mountainous William Howard Taft on his shoulder this way would have been quite a feat!

eral, George W. Wickersham, would be reasonably energetic in enforcing the Sherman Antitrust Act, for it was the law of the land. Indeed, Taft brought more suits against trusts than either Roosevelt or Wilson, Taft's progressive successor. But he was at best a timid reformer who refused to dramatize his policies or rally public opinion in their favor. When opposed by the party's Old Guard, Taft usually retreated.

Roosevelt had scarcely left office to go big-game hunting in Africa when the new president managed to alienate the progressives in his own party, turning them into fierce opponents. Taft's problems with the Republican "insurgents" began when, in fulfillment of a campaign pledge, he asked Congress to consider lowering tariffs. By 1909 tariff revision seemed long overdue. With brief and minor exceptions, taxes on foreign imports had risen steadily since the Civil War. Perhaps, as protectionists claimed, the ever-rising tariff had kept out foreign competition, enabling American industry to prosper. But, reformers charged, it had also been costly to the American consumer. The Dingley Tariff of 1897 had pushed import duties to their highest level in history and had inflated the price of everything the public wore, ate, and used. Indeed, some critics insisted that the Dingley Tariff explained the rising prices that Americans had been experiencing since the turn of the century. To make matters worse, they said, the high tariff was the "mother of trusts," encouraging the great industrial combinations that further gouged the public.

Prompted by the party's recent campaign pledge and the president's request, in 1909 the Republican House passed a tariff revision bill sponsored by Sereno E. Payne, cutting rates sharply. This bill ran afoul of Rhode Island's Nelson Aldrich when it came to the Senate. Aldrich, a businessman himself as well as a stand-patter, transformed the House bill drastically by throwing out most of the lowered schedules. Taft was appalled by the Payne-Aldrich Bill, but he left the fight against it to the Senate Republican insurgents.

Day after day, during the hot Washington summer, La Follette, Albert Beveridge, Jonathan Dolliver, Moses Clapp, and other midwestern Republican progressives attacked the Payne-Aldrich Bill. Taking up each of the schedules in turn, they showed how the Senate version would raise costs to the consumer and benefit only the trusts. The Aldrich measure, La Follette declared, would assuredly continue the thrust of the previous tariff. That law had encouraged monopoly, and with competition gone there was now "shoddy in everything we wear and adulteration in everything we eat." The country, Beveridge admitted, had to protect wage earners and manufacturers, but it was "a high concern . . . to the prosperity of our people as a whole that a just and equal consideration . . . be shown the consuming public."

The progressives' fight was gallant but futile; the Aldrich rates prevailed. The results might have been different if the president had intervened, but Taft refused to use his influence to defeat the measure. When it came to his desk with the Aldrich changes intact, he signed it into law. Soon afterward he called it "the best tariff measure the Republican party has ever passed."

The president's response shocked progressives. The midwestern Republican insurgents considered Taft's performance a repudiation of TR's policies and the party's promises to the public. In short order the reformers found new cause for dismay in the president's handling of the Ballinger-Pinchot controversy.

Taft's secretary of the interior was Richard A. Ballinger, a Seattle attorney with close ties to western mining and lumbering interests. As secretary, Ballinger restored lands to commercial exploitation that Roosevelt had removed from entry, interfered with the Reclamation Service, and canceled an agreement giving the Forest Service control over forest preserves on Indian lands. In each of these actions he clashed with Pinchot, who was still Chief Forester and who, somewhat self-righteously, considered himself the special guardian of the public against selfish business interests.

The argument between Ballinger and Pinchot came to a head when government-owned coal lands in Alaska were transferred to a Morgan-Guggenheim syndicate. Pinchot believed that this was a blatant giveaway of public resources, and he accused Ballinger of being in cahoots with the despoilers of the public domain. Rather than confining his criticism to memos to the president, Pinchot made public speeches all over the country attacking his department chief. He also leaked information to the newspapers pillorying Ballinger, and by inference condemning Taft himself. Eventually Pinchot clashed head-on with the president, who fired him while retaining Ballinger. Pinchot was now a progressive martyr, and his treatment another reason to distrust Taft.

The insurgent Republicans also clashed with Taft over congressional reorganization. They had long feuded with the Republican Speaker of the House, the profane, hard-drinking "Uncle Joe" Cannon, a man fiercely opposed to progressive legislation. Soon after Pinchot's dismissal, Cannon began to deprive the party rebels of committee chairmanships they had earned by seniority. The insurgent Republicans resolved to break his power and turned to the president for support. Taft disliked Cannon but declined to help the insurgents, claiming that the Speaker was too deeply entrenched to be ousted. The rebels refused to give up. At the opening of the March 1910 congressional session, led by George Norris, a young progressive Republican from Nebraska, they joined with anti-Cannon Democrats to strip the Speaker of his power to appoint members to the all-important House Rules Committee and deprived him of his own place on it. Some of the insurgents would have been happy if Cannon had also been deposed as Speaker, but they had to be content with limiting his ability to undercut progressive legislation.

By mid-1910, then, Taft had thoroughly alienated the progressive, largely midwestern wing of his party. In truth, the president's record on progressive measures was not all bad. He supported the Mann-Elkins Act (1910), which gave the Interstate Commerce Commission the power to suspend railroad-initiated rate changes if they seemed excessive and also authorized government supervision of telephone, wireless, and telegraph companies. That same year he endorsed a "postal savings" scheme to allow small savers, often victimized by private bank failures, to place their money in the safekeeping of the federal post office. He also threw his considerable weight behind the Sixteenth Amendment to the constitution, which authorized a federal income tax, and signed the Mann Act (1910), which prohibited the interstate transportation of women for purposes of prostitution. Yet on most of these issues Taft so equivocated that he received little credit from the insurgents. Perhaps worst of all, in their eyes, the lethargic, ponderous, dull chief executive was not the dynamic, joyous, charismatic TR. One progressive publication put its dismay in verse:

> Teddy, come home and blow your horn,
> The sheep's in the meadow, the cow's in the corn.
> The boy you left to tend the sheep, is under the
> haystack fast asleep.

Republican Split. The progressive Republicans rapidly deserted Taft. In May 1910 Pinchot met with Roosevelt, who was touring Europe on his way back from Africa, and filled his ears with news of Taft's transgressions. By the time TR returned to the United States, his cordial feelings for his protégé had decidedly cooled. The last straw was the administration's revelation, in the course of an antitrust suit, that during the 1907 panic Roosevelt had allowed U.S. Steel to buy the Tennessee Coal and Iron Company without protest, though the purchase enhanced the firm's monopoly position in steel. Roosevelt believed that the move had been justified to restore business confidence when it was badly shaken, but the leak made him appear a tool of Morgan.

Besides his growing doubts about Taft's political wisdom and loyalty, TR simply could not abandon politics. In 1910 he was only fifty-two and still overflowing with energy. Permanent retirement seemed unthinkable. He had served only one elected term, even though he had been president for almost eight years, so tradition did not bar his reelection. Under the barrage of the anti-Taft insurgents,

Declaring himself "strong as a bull moose," Roosevelt made the 1912 election a three-way race. Ironically, all three candidates were progressive to one degree or another. Notice the moose biting the Republican elephant's rear end.

Roosevelt quickly warmed to the idea of opposing the president for the 1912 Republican nomination.

By this time TR had read Herbert Croly's *The Promise of American Life* (1909), which crystallized the activist view of the government's role that he had played with for some years. In a speech at Osawatomie, Kansas, in August 1910, TR used Croly's phrase, "the New Nationalism," to describe a federal government that, rather than forbidding combinations or attempting to break them up, would seek to "control them in the interest of the public." This New Nationalism would also place the well-being of the public ahead of property rights. "Every man," TR told his Kansas audience, "holds his property subject to the general right of the community to regulate its use to whatever degree the public welfare may require." Here was an endorsement of government paternalism and control beyond anything previously espoused by a major-party candidate. It distanced Roosevelt still further from the president.

Not all Republican progressives favored Roosevelt. Many, especially in the Midwest, preferred Wisconsin's La Follette. In January 1911 the midwesterners had organized the National Republican Progressive League to advance progressive ideas and promote La Follette's candidacy. Roosevelt refused to join. For a while the two men jockeyed for leadership of the party's progressive wing, but then, unable to compete with TR's broad national appeal, La Follette dropped out of the race.

Throughout the spring of 1912 Roosevelt and Taft battled for Republican convention delegates. TR won in the states, mainly western, that used the new presidential primaries to choose convention delegates. Taft swept the states in the South and East where tightly controlled conventions, dominated by party regulars, made the delegate choice. At the convention in Chicago the Republican National Committee, controlled by the Taft men, refused the Roosevelt forces' claim to a large block of disputed convention setas, giving almost all of them to Taft. The Roosevelt delegates walked out, leaving the convention firmly in the president's hands.

Roosevelt and his friends were not through. Early in August, 2,000 men and women, many of them distinguished social workers, settlement house leaders, and state and local reformers, assembled in Chicago to organize the Progressive party and nominate Roosevelt for president. The delegates selected Hiram W. Johnson of California as their vice presidential candidate. The platform of the Progressive party—or Bull Moose party, as it was called after TR's remark that he felt as energetic as a bull moose—was the most radical ever proposed by a major party, foreshadowing almost all of the modern American welfare state. Taking many of the emerging progressive ideas and carrying them several steps further, it endorsed direct popular election of United States senators; presidential primaries; the initiative, referendum, and recall in federal matters; women's suffrage; the recall (by citizens' petitions) of state court decisions; tariff reduction; a commission to regulate interstate industry, not just interstate commerce; a more stringent pure food and drug law; old age pensions; minimum wage and maximum hours laws; and the prohibition of child labor. The closing words of TR's acceptance speech conveyed the crusading mood of the new party. "Our cause," the candidate thundered, "is based on the eternal principles of righteousness, and even though we who now lead for the first time fail, in the end the cause itself will triumph. . . . We stand at Armageddon and we battle for the Lord."

THE ELECTION OF 1912

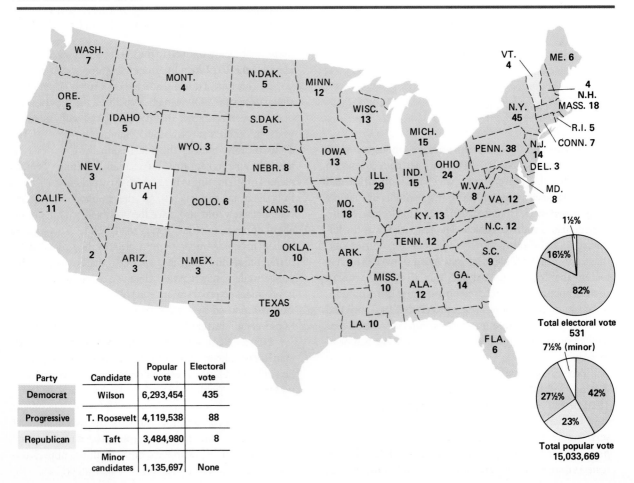

Party	Candidate	Popular vote	Electoral vote
Democrat	Wilson	6,293,454	435
Progressive	T. Roosevelt	4,119,538	88
Republican	Taft	3,484,980	8
Minor candidates		1,135,697	None

The Election of 1912. Meanwhile, the Democrats had nominated Woodrow Wilson, former president of Princeton University and, most recently, progressive governor of New Jersey. The son of a Presbyterian minister from Virginia, Wilson was a slender, scholarly man who joined stubborn self-righteousness with an eloquence unequaled since Lincoln and a vision of human potential unmatched since Jefferson. In 1910 the New Jersey Democratic bosses had selected him as a figurehead candidate for governor, but he had gone on to repudiate his sponsors and make an impressive record as a strong, liberal leader who brought staunchly conservative New Jersey into the progressive era. At the 1912 Democratic convention in Baltimore, Wilson faced the formidable opposition of the progressive Speaker of the House, Missouri's Champ Clark. Wilson had Bryan's support, and his friends were able to win over the leaders of the big-city machines. The contest was close, however; it took forty-six ballots to reach a decision.

During the next few months the country experienced the liveliest presidential battle since 1896. The contest was really between Roosevelt and Wilson, with Taft lagging badly from the very beginning. During the weeks of campaigning the conflicting ideologies of the two front-runners were thrown into sharp relief. TR trumpeted the message of the new Nationalism: Bigness as such was not bad; it only became bad when it injured the public and the national interest. Government could, and should, regulate private economic interests. Government also had a responsibility to protect citizens in many other aspects of daily life and reduce life's uncertainties and hazards. Wilson, a man from the Jeffersonian tradition of limited government, fought back with his New Freedom, much of it inspired by the liberal Boston lawyer Louis D. Brandeis. The New Nationalism was "big-brother government," Wilson charged. "You will find," he told a Buffalo audience of working men, "that the programme of the new party legalizes monopolies and systematically subordinates workingmen to them and to plans made by the Government. . . ." Like the Bull Moosers, Wilson believed that concentrated private economic power was a danger to the American public; he differed from them in holding that the way to salvation lay in breaking up these monopolies by vigorous antitrust action. TR's response to the New Freedom was blunt: It was "rural toryism," he declared, more suitable for a simpler age than for the twentieth-century world.

Wilson won the election by a plurality. The public loved Teddy, but many progressives were suspicious of his newfound radicalism, especially since he had allowed a Morgan partner, George Perkins, to play an important role in the campaign as fund-raiser and organizer. In the end TR received the votes largely of the Republican progressives; Taft, of the Republican stand-pat core. Wilson, on the other hand, won the votes of both Democratic progressives and traditional conservative Democrats. Eugene V. Debs took 900,000 votes for the Socialists. For the first time since 1897 a Democrat would occupy the White House, but only because a third party had split the opposition.

The New Freedom in Action. As president, Woodrow Wilson proved to be a strong leader. Disregarding the precedent established by Jefferson in 1801, he appeared before Congress in person to read his annual message. His proposals were less bold than his presentation. Wilson's first major concern was the tariff, which, he reminded Congress, had long fostered monopolies and exposed the consuming public to oppressive prices. The structure of "privilege" and "artificial advantage" must be destroyed and American businesses compelled to compete with their rivals in the rest of the world. Wilson was determined to do what Taft had failed at in 1909.

The fruit of the president's efforts was the 1913 Underwood Tariff. This measure substantially lowered the nation's tariff walls for the first time since the Civil War. To make up for the expected loss of federal revenue, Congress took advantage of the recently adopted Sixteenth Amendment and included a graduated income tax in the measure. Lobbyists for manufacturing and other special-interest groups resisted passage of the tariff bill, but Wilson fought back. Lashing out at the "industrious and insidious" lobbyists, he accused them of seeking to "create an artificial opinion and to overcome the interests of the public" for their own selfish ends. His counterattack jarred the Senate, and the bill passed.

Wilson's next important achievement was the Federal Reserve Act. The failings of the country's banking system had engaged the attention of the business community and farmers for fifty years. The national Banking Acts of the Civil War Era had failed to create a central bank to regulate the supply of money and credit and extend help to hard-pressed local commercial banks in time of crisis. Nor had the national banking system provided the flexible currency that could expand to meet the needs of the economy during peak periods like harvest time or the Christmas season, and then contract during quiet months. Farmers condemned the system for forbidding federally chartered banks to lend on mortgages, the only security for loans that they generally possessed. Yet agrarians feared a system that would be centralized in New York and tightly controlled by Wall Street.

As finally passed in 1913, the Federal Reserve Act was a compromise between the centralizers and agrarians, the supporters of government rule and those who favored private control. It created twelve district banks, whose directors were chosen by both private bankers and the

Progressive Party Platform, 1912

In 1912 the progressive agenda at its most liberal was incorporated into the platform of the Bull Moose, or Progressive, party. The new party was made up of ambition and personal grievances as well as idealism; without the anger of Theodore Roosevelt at his protégé President Taft, there might not have been such an organization. Yet however derived, the party attracted all the most advanced progressives. Its 1912 platform is a summary of what these liberal men and women envisioned for the good society of the future. It is a remarkable foreshadowing of mid-twentieth-century liberalism.

"The conscience of the people, in a time of grave national problems, has called into being a new party, born of the nation's sense of justice. We of the Progressive party here dedicate ourselves to the fulfillment of duty laid upon us by our fathers to maintain the government of the people, by the people, for the people. . . .

The Rule of the People

" . . . In particular, the party declares for direct primaries for the nomination of State and National officers, for nation-wide preferential primaries for candidates for the presidency; for the direct election of United States Senators by the people . . . ; with responsibility to the people secured by the initiative, referendum and recall. . . .

Equal Suffrage

"The Progressive party, believing that no people can justly claim to be a true democracy which denies political rights on account of sex, pledges itself to the task of securing equal suffrage to men and women alike.

Corrupt Practices

"We pledge our party to legislation that will compel strict limitation of all campaign contributions, and expenditures, and detailed publicity of both before as well as after primaries and elections. . . .

The Courts

"The Progressive party demands such restriction of the power of the courts as shall leave to the people the ultimate authority to determine fundamental questions of social welfare and public policy. . . .

Administration of Justice

" . . . We believe that the issuance of injunctions in cases arising out of labor disputes should be prohibited when such injunctions would not apply when no labor disputes existed. . . .

Social and Industrial Justice

"The supreme duty of the Nation is the conservation of human resources through an enlightened measure of social and industrial justice. We pledge ourselves to work unceasingly in State and Nation for:

"Effective legislation looking to the prevention of industrial accidents, occupational diseases, overwork, involuntary unemployment, and other injurious effects incident to modern industry;

"The fixing of minimum safety and health standards for the various occupations. . . ;

"The prohibition of child labor;

"Minimum wage standards for working women, to provide a 'living wage' in all industrial occupations;

"The general prohibition of night work for women and the establishment of an eight-hour day for women and young persons;

"One day's rest in seven for all wage workers. . . ;

"The abolition of the convict contract labor system. . . . ;

"Standards of compensation for death by industrial accident and injury and trade disease, which will transfer the burden of lost earnings from the families of working people of the industry, and thus to the community;

"The protection of home life against the hazards of sickness, irregular employment and old age through the adoption of a system of social insurance adapted to American use. . . ;

"The establishment of industrial research laboratories to put the methods and discoveries of science to the service of American producers;

"We favor the organization of the workers, men and women, as a means of protecting their interests and of promoting their progress. . . .

Conservation

" . . . We believe that the remaining forests, coal and oil lands, water power and other natural resources still in State or National control . . . are more likely to be wisely conserved and utilized for the general welfare if held in public hands.

"In order that consumers and producers, managers and workmen, now and hereafter, need not pay toll to private monopolies of power and raw material, we demand that such resources shall be retained by the State or Nation, and opened to immediate use under laws which will encourage development and make to the people a moderate return for benefits conferred. . . ."

government. The entire system was placed under the weak overall supervision of a central Federal Reserve Board in Washington. The district banks would hold the reserves of member banks—the local commercial banks that did the day-to-day business of the nation. By lending money to member banks at low interest rates, or alternately by limiting such loans by charging high interest ("rediscount") rates, the district banks could regulate credit and the money supply to suit the economy's seasonal needs and head off financial crises. The new system also allowed member banks to lend on farm mortgages. Despite the serious failings that time would reveal, the new system seemed a great improvement over the old.

The third major item on Wilson's first-term agenda was antitrust legislation to fulfill his campaign promise to break up the monopolies. Over the years the government's antitrust drive had been blunted by the federal courts. Most recently, in its 1911 "rule of reason" decision (*Standard Oil v. United States*), the Supreme Court had declared that only "unreasonable" restraints on interstate commerce were illegal; from now on a case of monopoly must be blatant to be subject to antitrust prosecution. But that was not all. For over a decade the federal courts had been treating labor unions as "combinations in restraint of trade," subject to antitrust prosecution. They had even issued injunctions (as in the 1894 Pullman strike) compelling unions to cease strikes and boycotts or face federal contempt-of-court charges. In the hands of the courts the Sherman Antitrust Act had become a union-busting weapon.

To protect organized labor's rights, help consumers, and get around the courts' limitations on antitrust actions, Wilson proposed two new measures. The first established the Federal Trade Commission (1914) to replace Roosevelt's Bureau of Corporations. The FTC was given powers to procure data from corporations and issue cease-and-desist orders against abuses like mislabeling, adulteration of products, trade boycotts, and combinations to fix wholesale prices. The new commission would be the public's watchdog against the trusts. The second measure, the Clayton Antitrust Act (1914), strengthened the Sherman Antitrust Act in several ways. It prohibited firms from charging one price to one customer and a different price to another when such discrimination tended to foster monopoly. It forbade contracts that required buyers not to do business with sellers' competitors. It also declared illegal most "interlocking directorates," a device by which one group of corporate directors headed several firms simultaneously. Similarly, a corporation was prohibited from acquiring stock in other corporations when the transaction threatened to reduce competition. A final provision—called by AFL president Samuel Gompers "labor's Magna Carta"—declared both labor unions and farmers' cooperatives ex-

empt from the antitrust laws and limited the right of federal courts to issue injunctions in labor disputes.

Another important change during Wilson's first months in office—one that was a general progressive initiative rather than Wilson's alone—was the adoption of the Seventeenth Amendment to the Constitution (1913): Henceforth all United States senators would be elected by direct vote of the people in each state rather than by the state legislators. No longer, the reformers felt, would the Senate be a bastion of conservatism that could ignore public opinion and protect the big corporations.

Wilson's Failings. Despite the president's successes, his first few years disappointed some of the most advanced progressives. He declined to support women's suffrage and at first refused to fight for a child-labor law. Nor was he as fierce an opponent of trusts as he had promised to be during the campaign. Like TR before him, he bargained with big corporations, agreeing not to prosecute them for combining to restrain trade if they would modify their behavior in some acceptable way.

But the most conspicuous defect of Wilson's first administration was its attitudes toward black Americans. The new president was a Virginian by birth and had lived much of his early life in the South. His party, moreover, was strongly southern in its makeup, and many of his closest advisers were white southerners. The new administration had few ties to the black community. Once in office, it abruptly cut off much of the political patronage that the Republicans had conferred on black supporters. In addition, one by one, federal departments and agencies in Washington began to segregate their remaining black workers, imposing on the federal government the Jim Crow system that permeated the South. Eventually, following loud protests from black leaders and their white progressive allies, the president tried to undo some of the damage. But it was too late. By the end of his administration the nation's capital had become a full-blown southern city in its racial practices.

Wilson Shifts Left. Wilson's first three years in office produced mixed results from the progressive perspective. And after passage of the Clayton Act of 1914, the president appeared to lose interest in pushing further progressive legislation. Then, as the 1916 election approached, his reformist enthusiasm revived.

The reason for the change was primarily political. Wilson had won in 1912 because the Republicans, who usually had been the majority party during these years, had been split between Taft and Roosevelt. By 1916 TR had returned to the GOP of his youth, virtually killing the Bull Moose party. To win, Wilson concluded, he would have to

A portrait of President Woodrow Wilson in 1921, just before he left office, a sick and beaten man.

attract former Bull Moosers, and this meant moving to the left. Hitherto his brand of reform—the New Freedom—had emphasized the restoration of free competition as a way to protect the ordinary citizen against private power. He had avoided the social legislation that required expansion of federal authority. Now Wilson shifted ground.

To aid farmers, who despite the Federal Reserve Act still had unmet credit needs, he supported the Federal Farm Loan Act of 1916. This measure established twelve Federal Farm Loan banks to lend money at low rates to farmers who joined certain farm loan associations. A bolder innovation was the Keating-Owen Act (1916), which discouraged child labor by prohibiting interstate traffic in goods manufactured by the labor of children under sixteen years of age. This prohibition, progressives believed, would virtually end child labor, for few manufacturers could afford to sell their products solely within their own state. Still other advanced progressive measures the president pushed were the Kern-

McGillicuddy Compensation Act (1916) providing workers' compensation for injured federal employees, and the Adamson Act (1916) establishing an eight-hour day and time-and-a-half overtime pay for railroad workers. Though these new laws applied to only limited groups of employees, they represented a long step toward federal regulation of the labor market.

One additional move rounded out Wilson's shift to the left in 1916: the nomination of his friend Louis D. Brandeis as Supreme Court justice.

For years Brandeis had been one of the best-known labor lawyers in the country. His work in establishing arbitration procedures in the New York garment industry had been hailed as a model approach to labor-capital relations. In 1908, in the case *Muller v. Oregon*, his brief for the state against an employer challenging an Oregon law that limited the working hours of women had been called a progressive landmark. In the *Muller* case, Brandeis had not merely cited legal precedents to bolster his reasoning, but had also mustered arguments drawn from sociology to demonstrate that long work hours were detrimental to the health of women and seriously injured society as a whole. The "Brandeis brief" had saved the Oregon law and established an important precedent for defending future social legislation.

The Brandeis nomination raised a storm. The Supreme Court in 1916 had only one progressive member, Oliver Wendell Holmes, Jr., and the nation's liberals cheered the prospect of Brandeis joining him. But conservatives, including ex-president Taft and the American Bar Association, fought the nomination with every ounce of their strength. Running through much of the opposition was a barely disguised streak of anti-Semitism. Despite the powerful opposition, Wilson fought hard for his friend and adviser, pulling all the strings he could. His success earned him additional gratitude from progressives of both parties.

By late summer of 1916 the Progressive movement had largely run its course. By now the public's attention had shifted from domestic issues to the question of war or peace. In a few months the country would embark on a crusade to make the whole world safe for the kind of liberal society that the progressives had been trying for a decade or more to construct at home. In the process the domestic reform impulse would lose its spark.

★ CONCLUSIONS ★

Between 1890 and 1917 more and more Americans became fearful of unrestrained private power. As the nation became ever more tightly knit together, giant corporations had become essential for providing the products people needed for a comfortable life. As growing numbers came to live in the cities, they became increasingly dependent on large firms for virtually everything they consumed. Seeking to protect themselves, urban Americans of all classes adopted a new political outlook, one that resembled views earlier held by rural reformers such as the Populists and the free-silver Democrats.

The progressives took much from Populism. Their primary enemy was similar—the trusts, the monopolies—and they borrowed the familiar rhetoric of an earlier rural age when they attacked "the interests." Especially in Wilson's New Freedom, we find echoes of Jefferson and Jackson in attitudes and ideas. Progressives also revived the Populist concern for direct democracy to bypass corrupt legislatures. Yet the addition of urban and middle-class people to the reform cause altered its quality. Progressivism was more so-phisticated than Populism. Borrowing from the liberal social Darwinists and the new efficiency-oriented professionals, progressives abandoned monetary cure-alls and developed new ideas of direct government action to solve social ills. Inevitably they focused on city problems and on wage earners, though rural grievances were not ignored. Especially in its New Nationalism guise, progressivism pointed the way to future reform in a complex urban society.

Progressivism was not a complete success even in its own terms. It did not end the dangers inherent in a society with large inequalities of wealth and power; it did not end the insecurity that afflicted many Americans. It would remain to a later generation to tackle these problems again, with somewhat greater success. The failure cannot be blamed solely on the progressives themselves. They were innovators and their support, while wide, was often thin. Americans were not yet accustomed to the idea of a strong, positive state that could override entrenched private rights if need be, a situation underlined by the frequency with which the federal courts overturned, and would continue to overturn, progressive regulatory legislation. In their battles to change society, progressives were often forced to accept half a loaf rather than none at all. Much progressive legislation proved inadequate, not because of a failure of the progressive vision, but because of insufficient progressive power.

Yet progressivism also had inherent limitations. The prophets of efficiency clearly had a limited vision of a better society. Placing economic savings before human needs, they believed that reform consisted primarily in making political as well as economic machinery work better. Nor were progressives as a whole free of the prejudice that marked their predecessors. A few demanded that black Americans be included in the progressive agenda. But most, including the two progressive presidents, believed in the superiority of the white race, and within it the superiority of its North European branch. Clearly, not all those who called themselves progressive were in the forefront of their times. Many who were essentially conservative in nature climbed aboard the progressive bandwagon once it started to roll. It seems that at times this charge can be applied to both Roosevelt and Wilson. Wilson's racial attitudes and failure to support women's suffrage, and TR's desertion of the Bull Moosers in 1916, surely point in this direction. And even at their most advanced their answers now seem naive. It is not, after all, as easy to end serious social and economic inequalities as they believed. Nevertheless, the progressives of 1900–1917 were the first generation to grapple with the new problems of an increasingly urbanized nation. For all their failings, they laid the foundation for much that would follow.

Richard Hofstadter. *Age of Reform: From Bryan to F.D.R.* (1955)
The middle portion of this interpretation of American reform movements deals with progressivism. Urban and middle-class in origin, according to Hofstadter, the movement failed to achieve real reform because its members distrusted organized labor and immigrants and were obsessed with threats to their own status from both the left and the right.

Lincoln Steffens. *Autobiography* (1931)
The famous muckraker eventually became disillusioned with the liberal values that motivated progressivism, concluding that capitalism itself was responsible for political corruption and social oppression. Includes many anecdotes about business executives and political leaders of the Progressive Era.

James Harvey Young. *The Toadstool Millionaires: A Social History of Patent Medicines in America Before Federal Regulation* (1962)
Before the Pure Food and Drug Act of 1906, quacks and crooks sold pills, powders, and liquids in bottles shaped like pigs, Indian maidens, and Founding Fathers. This funny and tragic tale of the gullible public and the patent-medicine manufacturers will tell you something about modern advertising.

Allen F. Davis. *Spearheads for Reform: The Social Settlements and the Progressive Movement, 1890–1914* (1967)
Concentrating on three cities—New York, Chicago, and Boston—Davis shows the frustration of settlement workers' efforts for social justice in the wards. He evaluates their success in citywide and national politics, especially their influence on education, housing, unions, and female and child labor.

David Thelen. *The New Citizenship: Origins of Progressivism in Wisconsin, 1885–1900* (1972)
This well-written monograph on progressivism in Wisconsin emphasizes the role consumer anger and frustration played in launching the new reform movement. The depression of the 1890s, says Thelen, made the state's corporations squeeze consumers and awakened deep resentment of their power.

August Meier. *Negro Thought in America, 1880–1915* (1963)
An analysis of the thought of Booker T. Washington, W. E. B. Du Bois, and other black leaders on politics, economics, migration, colonization, racial solidarity, and industrial and elitist education.

James Weldon Johnson. *Autobiography of an Ex-Coloured Man* (1912)
This is a fictional composite autobiography of blacks before World War I by a black composer and lyricist, lawyer, a founder of the NAACP, and chronicler of Harlem. Best known for its depiction of life on Manhattan's West Side and its appreciation of ragtime, this book was prophetic of the Harlem Renaissance in which Johnson took part.

Henry F. Pringle. *Theodore Roosevelt* (1931)
Pringle's long and graceful biography follows the many TRs: sickly boy, university dude, reformer in New York City, Dakota rancher, Washington office seeker, Rough Rider in Cuba, president, Bull Mooser, and anti-Wilsonite.

Upton Sinclair. *The Jungle* (1906)
Sinclair, a socialist, lived among the Chicago meatpackers during their strike in 1904. He intended this novel to arouse the nation's indignation about the packers' working conditions. Instead, his nauseatingly detailed descriptions of the meat prepared for public consumption turned the nation's stomach. The Meat Inspection Act of 1906 was the result.

Roy Lubove. *The Progressives and the Slums* (1962)
Focusing on New York City, Lubove has written a fine study of how the progressives dealt with one of the key social problems of the day—the slums. An important and interesting book.

William Harbaugh. *The Life and Times of Theodore Roosevelt* (1975)
Pringle's biography reads better than Harbaugh's, but the latter's is more up to date and more in tune with recent scholarship.

Samuel P. Hays. *Conservation and the Gospel of Efficiency: The Progressive Conservation Movement, 1890–1920* (1959)
This was a ground-breaking book when it appeared and is still important for the serious student of progressivism. Hays is one of those scholars who emphasize the progressive obsession with efficiency. His focus here is on the conservationist group within the larger environmental movement.

John D. Buenker. *Urban Liberalism and Progressive Reform* (1973)
Buenker believes that we must not ignore the interest in, and support of, progressivism by urban working people and their political spokespersons in Congress and the state legislatures. He shows that these leaders were as strongly in favor of the graduated income tax and direct election of senators, for example, as they were of legislation limiting working hours and regulating tenements.

George Mowry. *The California Progressives* (1951)
This study of progressivism in a banner progressive state helped introduce the thesis that the progressives were middle-class citizens suffering from acute social anxiety as a result of threats to their status. Hofstadter borrowed heavily from Mowry in his *Age of Reform*.

Arthur Link. *Woodrow Wilson and the Progressive Era* (1954)
Still the best study of the Wilsonian phase of progressivism. Link admires his subject, but he can also see his flaws.

Aileen Kraditor. *The Ideas of the Woman Suffrage Movement, 1890–1920* (1965)
A study of the thought of the women's suffrage movement leaders during the final drive that brought success. Contains an enlightening analysis of the way racism affected the goals of the white, middle-class women who led the women's suffrage movement.

William O'Neill. *Everyone Was Brave: A History of Feminism in America* (1971)
A lively, intelligent discussion of feminism with an especially good section on feminist politics in the Progressive Era.

24★

WORLD WAR I

Idealism, National Interest, or Neutral Rights?

1914	American marines occupy Veracruz, Mexico • World War I begins in Europe; Wilson calls for American neutrality
1915	Marines occupy Haiti • Germany declares a war zone around the British Isles • U-boats sink the *Falaba*, the *Lusitania*, and the *Arabic*, all with loss of American lives • Wilson initiates the preparedness program to enlarge the army and the navy
1916	Wilson orders General John Pershing and 6,000 troops to Mexico to capture Pancho Villa • Colonel Edward House promises American intervention if deadlock on Western Front continues • U-boat sinks the *Sussex* with resulting American injuries; Germany suspends submarine warfare • Wilson reelected on "He kept us out of war" platform • Marines occupy the Dominican Republic
1917	Germany resumes submarine warfare and the United States severs diplomatic relations • British intelligence intercepts the "Zimmermann telegram" • Wilson orders the arming of American merchant ships • The Russian Revolution • Congress declares war on Germany; the War Industries Board, the War Labor Board, and the Committee of Public Information manage the war effort at home • Congress passes the Espionage Act
1918	The Sedition Act • Postmaster General Albert Burleson excludes publications critical of the war from the mails • The Justice Department indicts socialist leaders Eugene Debs and Victor Berger on charges of advocating draft evasion • Wilson announces his Fourteen Points • Germany collapses and armistice ends the war
1919	Peace conference at Versailles; League of Nations incorporated into treaty
1919–20	Congress rejects the Versailles Treaty
1920	The states ratify the Nineteenth Amendment providing for women's suffrage • Warren G. Harding elected president • Harding signs separate peace treaty with Germany in lieu of Versailles Treaty

As Americans read their newspapers over morning coffee on June 29, 1914, many wondered: "Where is Sarajevo?" The day before, in that remote Balkan town in present-day Bosnia a fanatical Serbian nationalist had shot and killed Archduke Francis Ferdinand, heir to the Austro-Hungarian throne. Few people could have anticipated how their lives and those of millions of others would be affected by the archduke's murder in that backward and unruly corner of eastern Europe.

Within six weeks the major European powers were at war. First, Austria demanded that Serbia suppress the nationalist movement it had allowed to flourish on its soil. The Serbs appealed for support to their Slavic big brother, Russia; the Austrians in turn asked Germany to come to their aid. Tied by a bewildering tangle of alliances and agreements, both public and secret, all the large nations of Europe were quickly drawn into the dispute, with France, Russia, and Great Britain (the Allies) on one side, and Germany and Austria-Hungary (the Central Powers) on the other. Before many months Japan and Italy had joined the Allies; and the Ottoman Empire (Turkey) and Bulgaria, the Central Powers. By the end of 1914 great armies were smashing at one another in Europe with the most lethal weapons that twentieth-century technology could devise, while on the high seas and in the air hostile navies and air fleets grappled in fierce and deadly combat.

President Wilson officially responded to the tragic events in Europe in mid-August. Americans, declared the president, must be "neutral in fact as well as in name during these days that are to try men's souls." We must, he pleaded, "be impartial in thought as well as in action, must put a curb on our sentiments as well as upon every transaction that might be construed as a preference of one party to the struggle before another." Thirty-one months later the same man would appear before a joint session of Congress to ask for a declaration of war against the Central Powers.

What had happened in those months to bring the peaceful and self-satisfied Republic into this "most terrible of wars"? Why did the United States and its people not heed the president's early advice and remain neutral both "in thought" and "in action"?

★ WILSON AND THE WORLD ORDER ★

To understand American involvement in World War I, we must consider Wilson's view of the world and America's place in it. Progressive foreign policy came in two main varieties. Some progressives, like Theodore Roosevelt and Albert J. Beveridge, were aggressive internationalists who believed the United States must play a vigorous role in world affairs and serve as a force for international balance and morality. Others, like Senators Robert La Follette of Wisconsin and Hiram W. Johnson of California, were isolationists who feared that excessive United States involvement in concerns beyond its borders would interfere with reform at home. Both the progressive internationalists and the progressive isolationists agreed that enlightened, liberal capitalism was the most benevolent social system in the world; all others fell short of the happy balance of individual freedom and equality.

Wilson's foreign policy views fluctuated between these poles. At times he seemed to believe progressive democracy was for domestic consumption only. On other occasions he acted as if it was for export as well. In addition, his attitudes were infused with an intense moralism derived from his Calvinist forebears and his father, a devout Presbyterian minister. To complicate matters further, like every national leader, he had to remember always his country's vital interests and defend them against any threatening power. To satisfy all these imperatives Wilson walked a tightrope, and his resulting unsteadiness and hesitation opened him to charges of inconsistency and even hypocrisy.

When he became president in 1913, Wilson's interest in domestic reform far outweighed his concern for international affairs. Yet he had misgivings. The world was at peace when he took office, but Europe, steeped in its age-old rivalries and tangled in its web of alliances, seemed poised on the edge of violence. Shortly before his inauguration the president-elect told a friend that it would be ironic if he had to spend most of his time as president attending to foreign affairs. His premonition proved sound.

Moral Diplomacy. Wilson chose William Jennings Bryan as his first secretary of state. The long-time titular leader of the Democratic party was not a professional diplomat, but Wilson distrusted such men. Bryan was, rather, a fervent pacifist, a man who had worked long in the cause of peace and who shared Wilson's view that America must serve as the world's "moral inspiration." Bryan's first official exertions for world peace came in 1913 and 1914, when he negotiated conciliation treaties with twenty-one nations. The parties to these treaties agreed to submit all international disputes to permanent investigating commissions and to forgo armed force until the commission had completed its report.

A similar idealism infused other aspects of Wilson's early diplomacy. Both Bryan and his chief opposed using the American government to serve the interests of American businesses abroad. Under Taft, Wilson's predecessor, the government had supported the participation of American bankers in a multinational consortium to build railroads in China. Feeling that the arrangement might undermine China's fragile sovereignty, Bryan withdrew the government's support. The two foreign-policy makers also induced Congress to repeal a 1912 law that had exempted American coastal vessels from paying tolls on the Panama Canal, a law that violated the Hay-Pauncefote Treaty and its promise of equal treatment for all nations.

But Wilson never forgot the country's "vital interests"; where they seemed to be involved, and where the risks appeared small, he was sometimes insensitive to moral considerations. In the Caribbean, which the United States considered an American lake, Wilson and his chief lieutenant proved as overbearing as Roosevelt. In 1913 Bryan negotiated a treaty with Nicaragua giving that small nation $3 million for exclusive American rights to construct a second Atlantic-Pacific canal. The Bryan-Chamorro agreement, not ratified until 1916, made the strategically located Central American republic a virtual satellite of the United States, with little control over its own foreign affairs or its international economic relations. In 1915 and 1916 the United States intervened militarily in Haiti and the Dominican Republic—in the first to put down disorder, in the second to prevent the European powers, especially Germany, from landing troops to protect their citizens and collect unpaid debts. In each of these cases Wilson believed that he was merely holding America's less scrupulous neighbors to universal standards of order and honesty. To outsiders it appeared that the United States was imposing its will on countries too weak to resist the American giant.

Mexico.   In Mexico the United States managed to combine blatant self-interest and idealism in a particularly confusing way. For a generation following 1880 Mexico was ruled by dictator Porfirio Díaz. Díaz had encouraged foreign investment in Mexican mines, oil wells, and railroads; by 1913 American businesses had poured over a billion dollars into his country. Though this infusion of capital helped the middle class, ordinary Mexicans remained as poor, illiterate, and oppressed as in Montezuma's day.

In 1911 Díaz's enemies among the country's liberal intellectuals toppled him from power and made Francisco Madero president. Madero tried to effect sweeping democratic reforms and restore constitutional liberties denied by Díaz. His policies aroused the hostility of the Mexican landed aristocracy, the army, and the Catholic Church. Two years later Victoriano Huerta, Madero's chief military adviser, seized the government and had Madero murdered.

Great Britain, Germany, and France had already officially recognized Huerta when Wilson took office. Many

A minister's son and a historian, Wilson had been president of Princeton University. As president of the United States, he continued to lecture and preach. Here, symbolically, he instructs a rather skeptical Mexico in the principles of true democracy.

Americans, including business people with investments in Mexico, advised Wilson to follow suit. He refused. The United States, like other nations, traditionally recognized established governments no matter how they gained power or what their internal policies were. In Wilson's eyes, however, Huerta was a "butcher" who did not represent the "eighty-five percent" of the Mexican people who were "struggling toward liberty." Instead of according diplomatic recognition to the Huerta government, Wilson proclaimed a new policy toward revolutionary regimes in Latin America: The United States would not recognize any new government unless it was "supported at every turn by . . . orderly processes . . . based upon law, not upon arbitrary or irregular force."

Wilson disclaimed any intention of intervening in Mexico, but he quietly sought to isolate the new Mexican tyrant by pressuring the British into withdrawing their recognition. He also stationed American naval vessels off Mexico's major ports to stop arms shipments to Huerta while allowing arms to get through to his enemies. Eventually, he hoped, Huerta might be pushed out by some champion of liberal rule like Venustiano Carranza, an associate of Madero who had raised the banner of revolt in the northern part of the country.

Wilson's policies led to trouble. In April 1914 crewmen of an American naval vessel were arrested by an Huertista officer when they went ashore at Tampico. Although they were soon released, the American naval commander, Admiral Henry Mayo, demanded that the Mexican officer be punished and that the commander of the port give the American flag a twenty-one-gun salute as a sign of respect. The Mexican commandant apologized and promised disciplinary action against his subordinate, but refused the salute.

The incident now seems trivial, but Wilson made it an issue of principle. Appearing before Congress, he asked for authority to compel the Mexicans to show respect for American rights. At this point, a German vessel began to land arms for Huerta at Veracruz. To prevent this, Admiral Mayo shelled the city and ordered it occupied by marines. In the fighting that followed, over a hundred Mexicans lost their lives.

In explaining the Veracruz disaster, the president maintained that he meant only the best for the Mexican people and hoped to see them establish a new order based on "human liberty and human rights." Wilson then lectured the Mexicans on how they should arrange their affairs. Mexico would have to redistribute land to equalize the condition of rich and poor. The country would continue to need foreign capital, too, but foreign corporations should not be allowed to exert excessive power and influence in Mexican affairs. This prescription for Mexico's future, though worthy of the best sort of American progressive, revealed the progressives' limitations. Ignoring Mexico's legacy of deep class antagonism and bitter ideological conflict, Wilson had assumed that the fundamental social change required of an "underdeveloped" nation might be effected as peaceably and amicably as progressive legislative reform in the United States. Still more imperceptive was the president's conclusion that the United States had the right to prescribe for Mexico at all. The Veracruz incident was an excellent demonstration of how American intrusion, even in a good cause, could produce disastrous consequences for its intended beneficiaries.

Meanwhile, the Veracruz attack had outraged all patriotic Mexicans, raised Huerta's stock among his own people, and cast the United States in the role of a brutal aggressor. It looked as if the Wilson administration would now be forced into the folly of war with Mexico. The president was rescued from this fate when Argentina, Brazil, and Chile (the so-called ABC powers) offered to mediate. In May 1914 the United States, Mexico, and the ABC powers met at Niagara Falls, Canada, and thrashed out a compromise that averted war.

But war with Mexico soon threatened again. Unable to resist the growing pressure at home and abroad, Huerta fi-

nally resigned, and power in Mexico City passed to Carranza. Once in office, however, Carranza was faced by a revolt among his own followers led by Francisco ("Pancho") Villa. Hoping to goad the United States into some overt action against Mexico that would unite the Mexican people against the "gringos" and help his chances to seize the government, Villa ordered his men to attack American citizens both in Mexico and across the border.

American indignation quickly reached a new peak. Whatever they felt following the Tampico and Veracruz incidents, virtually all Americans now agreed that the United States must take strong action. In March 1916, after 35 Americans had been massacred by Villista soldiers on both sides of the border, Wilson ordered General John J. Pershing to enter Mexico with 6,000 troops. The wily Villa eluded the American army, however, while drawing it deeper and deeper into Mexican territory.

Carranza, whose regime the Wilson administration had informally recognized in October 1915, had reluctantly given the Americans permission to enter Mexico to capture Villa. But the Mexican president was appalled by the size of the expedition and the depth of the American penetration. Pershing, it appeared, was not pursuing a bandit; he was invading a friendly nation and violating its sovereignty. War was averted at the last minute only when Wilson, realizing that the United States had far more pressing concerns in Europe, ordered Pershing to return to Texas. The president then sent Ambassador Henry Fletcher to Mexico and formally recognized the Carranza administration.

With this move Wilson ended the threat of war with Mexico. Warned off by Pershing's military failure, he had resisted the temptation to make a popular war, although it probably would have guaranteed his reelection in 1916. Though his bungling caused anti-American feeling to run high in Mexico for years, his support for Carranza and his newfound determination to avoid war despite sharp provocations allowed the revolutionaries to establish control. The Mexican situation revealed the principal elements of the Wilson foreign policy: moralism, self-interest, missionary interventionism, and a deep reluctance to make war. These contradictory urges would also be apparent in the American approach to the war in Europe.

★ NEUTRALITY AND PUBLIC OPINION ★

Wilson's call for neutrality in August 1914 had evoked a loud "amen" from the American public. Almost no one wanted to become directly involved in Europe's quarrel. Americans had a traditional distaste for the complicated alliances formed among the European nation-states. Moreover, America was now a nation of immigrants, and war would inflame conflicting sympathies with Old World countries, causing social tension and unrest. Finally, there were many pacifists who deplored all war regardless of the causes.

Americans Take Sides. Though most Americans wished to avoid war, they were not as emotionally removed from European concerns as they thought. And how could they be? Millions of citizens had been born in one or another of the belligerent nations and found they could not escape the ideological and emotional commitments of their heritage. Recent arrivals from England, Scotland, and Wales retained their affection for Britain and hoped to see it remain mistress of the seas. On the other side, the large German-American population still had strong attachments to the "fatherland" and cheered for the Central Powers. The picture was greatly complicated by the immigrants from Austria-Hungary and Russia. These sprawling empires contained millions of Poles, Czechs, South Slavs, Finns, Jews, and many other groups who suffered under repressive governments. Immigrants from the Hapsburg and czarist lands, despising the Austrian and Russian regimes, prayed for their defeat. The Irish further complicated this tangle of responses; many hated Britain as their mother country's centuries-long oppressor and hoped that England's troubles could be turned to Ireland's advantage.

Old-stock Americans looked askance at the continued attachment of newer arrivals to their native lands and ac-cused them of putting European concerns ahead of American ones. The "hyphenates," they said, were not acting as loyal Americans. Yet they, too, took sides. Aside from a small but prestigious group of intellectuals who respected German culture and scholarship or disliked the pervasive English influence on American life, most old-stock Americans were pro-Ally. Such people read the classics of English literature and admired English law and parliamentary institutions. Many of them tended to feel affection for France as well, remembering with gratitude French aid during the Revolution. The sophisticated set, which included many of the country's opinion makers, was fascinated with French fashions, food, and thought.

Partisanship for the Allies went beyond sentiment and aesthetic preference, however. England and France were democracies tied to the United States by a common bond of liberalism and egalitarianism. In an era of revitalized enthusiasm for liberal principles at home, Britain's and France's democratic institutions seemed especially worthy of support. This natural sympathy of progressive Americans was to some extent offset by the revulsion they felt toward tyrannical and backward czarist Russia, but Russia was very remote and seemed, at most, a junior partner of the western Allies.

Germany's conservatism, militarism, and arrogance confirmed American preferences. A nation dominated by Prussian discipline and obsession with social order since its unification in 1871, Germany had allowed its imperial ambitions to swell to gigantic proportions under Kaiser Wilhelm II. Since 1898 American military and naval lead-

Pershing leads his troops across the Rio Grande into Mexico on a search for revolutionary Pancho Villa. Although Pershing's expedition failed. Wilson eventually promoted him to general and gave him command of the American Expeditionary Force in Europe.

ers had become increasingly worried about a German threat to the Western Hemisphere. As recently as 1910 the Navy General Board had estimated that Germany was probably America's most dangerous potential enemy. Opinion makers and the foreign policy elite shared the fear of German aggressiveness and power, and many other citizens could not help feeling that Germany's defeat would benefit America and democratic principles everywhere.

All told, a majority of Americans were pro-Ally from the outset. At no time would intervention to help Germany be a conceivable option. The best that the Central Powers could expect was American neutrality. From the beginning, however, the British and French had reason to hope that the United States could be turned into an active ally, willing to supply arms and even men to help them defeat their opponents.

The Propaganda War. Both sides sought to sway American opinion, the Allies for intervention, the Central Powers for neutrality. Before long they were waging a fierce propaganda battle in which truth often took a backseat to expediency. The *New York Times* would call the European conflict the "first press agents' war."

In the lively struggle for American minds the Germans labored under serious handicaps. The British and French controlled the transatlantic cables, which transmitted European news to the American press, leaving the Germans with only the still-primitive wireless for getting their message to the American public. The Central Powers were also inept. German war propaganda emphasized hate and destruction—an approach that often aroused more revulsion than sympathy. Some of the most effective Allied efforts to win American approval consisted of reprinting German hate propaganda against Britain and France.

More important in repelling American opinion than German words were German deeds. Germany opened its military campaign on the Western Front by invading little Belgium, thereby violating an international agreement of long standing. The German chancellor then contemptuously referred to the treaty as a "scrap of paper." When patriotic Belgians challenged the occupiers, the German authorities retaliated by executing Belgian civilians—some 5,000 in the course of the war—and by burning the old university town of Louvain.

If the Germans seemed clumsy and brutal, the Allies seemed adroit and forebearing. The British in particular spoke the language of Americans, literally and figuratively. Instinctively, they knew how to arouse American sympathies. They were quick to blow up German atrocities to enormous proportions. In 1915 the British government issued an official report signed by James Bryce, a distinguished historian and respected former British ambassador to Washington, describing in gruesome detail the torture, mutilation, and murder of Belgian civilians, especially women and children. The report concluded that under the German occupation "murder, lust, and pillage prevailed . . . on a scale unparalleled in any war between civilized nations in the last three centuries." Many of the atrocity stories were unfounded; others were grossly exaggerated. Nevertheless, the Bryce Report convinced many Americans that the Germans were savage "Huns" who deserved the condemnation of the entire civilized world.

The Administration's Partisanship. In some ways the Allies' strongest supporter in America was the president himself, despite his appeal for neutrality. Ever since his early manhood, when his admiration for British political institutions had led him to write *Congressional Government*, praising the English parliamentary system, Wilson had been an Anglophile. As president he felt close to the leaders of the Liberal party in England, whose program of social welfare in the years immediately preceding the war had closely paralleled his own.

The president tried to be neutral, but his true feelings often showed through his reserve. He once told the British ambassador that everything he loved most in the world depended on Allied victory. He remarked at another point to his private secretary that "England is fighting our fight. . . . I will not take any action to embarrass England when she is fighting for her life and the life of the world." In addition, Wilson and his closest advisers, Colonel Edward M. House and later Robert Lansing, took seriously the threat of German expansionism and looked to Britain and France to check the German emperor's ambitions. Ever since the Spanish-American War, when Britain alone among the European powers had supported the United States, makers of American foreign policy had regarded England as a bulwark against the ambitions of expansionist Germany. This feeling remained a major, though unspoken, cornerstone of American foreign policy from the late 1890s onward. This informal alliance would influence American policymakers after August 1914.

★ NEUTRAL RIGHTS ★

Despite the pro-Ally bias of the American people and their government, American entrance into the war could have been avoided if it had not been for the issue of neutral rights. Although propaganda, admiration of the democracies, and fear of imperial Germany all worked to erode American determination to stay clear of the war, it was the issue of neutral rights that ultimately brought the United States in.

Today, when warfare seems to have no rules, it is difficult to believe that Americans once took seriously the concept of neutral rights. But in 1914 they did.

In the early twentieth century, as during the Napoleonic Wars a hundred years before, the United States found itself the major neutral power in a world divided into two warring camps, each determined to defeat the other no matter what the cost to bystanders. The United States, however, expected European belligerents to observe the rights traditionally due neutral nations in wartime. Under these rules vessels owned by neutrals had the right to carry unmolested all goods except contraband. Contraband normally meant arms and munitions, with commodities such as food, textiles, and naval stores explicitly exempt. Neutrals also had the right to trade freely with all belligerents, although they might be legitimately intercepted and turned back by an effective surface blockade maintained outside a belligerent port. If a neutral merchant or passenger ship was stopped by such a naval blockade, however, the blockading power was responsible for the safety of the passengers and crew of the detained vessel.

Wilson, in his characteristic way, gave the long-standing American policy of defending neutral rights a new moral emphasis. The right of neutral citizens to go wherever they pleased, sell whatever they pleased, to whomever they pleased, subject only to the recognized rules of war, he said, was more than a legal abstraction or a matter of profit. What was at stake was the fundamental structure of the international order. This structure must be based on well-defined inviolable rules, which in turn must be derived from the basic principles of respect for human life and fair treatment of all peoples and nations.

Still, no matter how pro-British or how determined he was to guarantee American rights, for many months following the outbreak of the war, Wilson saw no reason to intrude into European affairs. By remaining neutral, America might exert a strong moral force to end the fighting quickly and then help establish new relations among nations based on disarmament, arbitration, and international justice. A neutral America, Wilson declared, would be "fit and free to do what is honest and disinterested and truly serviceable for the peace of the world."

Allied Violations of American Rights. From the beginning of the war, both the British and the Germans disregarded what Americans considered their rights on the high seas and in international trade. The British severely limited American commerce with the Central Powers by extending the definition of contraband to include almost everything that might be useful to German survival. They stopped American vessels and forced them to go to British ports for thorough and time-consuming searches instead of allowing them to be examined at sea. They planted mines in the North Sea, endangering all neutral ships routed through the area. They set up blacklists of American firms suspected of trading with Germany through other neutral nations, and threatened these firms with the loss of English business.

As a major supplier of goods and credit, the United States had the power to retaliate against the British and force them to relent. Soon after the war broke out, the British and the French had placed immense orders with American firms for arms, grain, cotton, and other supplies. In the beginning the Allies paid cash; but when cash ran low, they requested loans from American bankers. Secretary of State Bryan at first considered credits to the Allies a breach of neutrality and refused to sanction them. Gradually he retreated, and in October 1914 Wilson informed the National City Bank and the Morgan Company that he would not oppose bankers' credits to finance Allied war orders. By early 1917 Americans had lent Great Britain over $1 billion and France $300 million more. Had Wilson wished, he might have threatened to restrict loans or asked Congress to embargo munitions to belligerents unless the Allies complied with American demands. He justified his failure to use this powerful weapon of coercion—one employed by Thomas Jefferson in 1807—on the grounds that neutralizing the Allied advantage of control of the shipping lanes to Europe would be equivalent to helping the Central Powers. But it is difficult to avoid the conclusion that the president was less willing to enforce neutral rights against the Allies than against their enemies.

There were reasons beyond pro-Ally feelings for discriminating between British and German violations of American rights, however. Whatever it did, England avoided injuring too many American interests simultaneously lest an outcry from too many groups at once force retaliation. The English were also careful to blunt the edge of their actions. When placing cotton on the contraband list produced a loud protest from southern cotton growers, for example, the British agreed to buy enough cotton to make up for the lost German-Austrian market. On numerous occasions, moreover, they promised to compensate American businesses for losses after the war. But the most compelling reason for distinguishing between the Allies and the Central Powers was that Allied policies hurt only American pocketbooks; German policies took American lives.

Submarine Warfare. The chief German naval weapon was the U-boat (*Unterseeboot*), a tiny submarine armed with torpedoes and one small deck gun. U-boats could creep up on their targets unseen and sink them without warning. But because they were small and thin-skinned, they could not risk surfacing to warn of their intentions, to search for contraband, or to care for civilians aboard the vessels they sank.

U.S.A.
1917

NORWAY

FINLAND
Indep. July, 1917

Lake Ladoga

Oslo

Helsinki

Petrograd

Stockholm

SWEDEN

ESTONIA
Indep.
Feb. 1918

NORTH SEA

Battle of Jutland
May-June, 1916

DENMARK

LATVIA
Indep.
Nov, 1918

Riga

RUSSIA
1914

Edinburgh

BALTIC SEA

Riga offensive
Sept, 1917

Smolensk

GREAT BRITAIN
1914

Copenhagen

LITHUANIA
Indep. Feb, 1918

Memel

Kiel

Konigsberg

Vilna

London

Hamburg

Danzig

Minsk

NETH.

Amsterdam

Berlin

Masurian Lakes
Sept, 1914

Tannenberg
Aug, 1914

Brussels

Cologne

GERMANY
1914

POLAND
Indep. Nov, 1918

Pinsk

BELG.
1914

Leipzig

Warsaw

Brest-Litovsk

Kiev

GERMAN INVASION
AUG-SEPT, 1914

Dresden

Lublin

Paris

Mainz

Prague

Lemberg

Metz

Rhine R.

Cracow

GALICIA

LUX.

Strasbourg

BAVARIA

Munich

Danube R.

Vienna

UKRAINE

FRANCE
1914

Berne

SWITZ.

Piave June, 1918

Pressburg

Graz

Budapest

Odessa

Vittorio-Veneto
Oct-Nov, 1918

AUSTRIA-HUNGARY
1914

Milan

Trieste

Genoa

Venice

RUMANIA
1916

BLACK SEA

SPAIN

BOSNIA

Belgrade

Bucharest

Danube R.

ITALY
1915

Sarajevo

CORSICA

Withdrew from
Triple Alliance 1914

MONTENEGRO
1915

SERBIA
1914

BULGARIA
1915

Rome

Sofia

Constantinople

SARDINIA

Naples

ALBANIA

OTTOMAN EMPIRE
1914

Salonika

Gallipoli

PORTUGAL
1916

GREECE
1916

Dardanelles campaign
1915-1916

Smyrna

SICILY

Athens

CRETE

1916   Date of entry into the war

———   Maximum advance of the Central Powers

– – –   Maximum Russian advance

••••••   Line of the Brest-Litovsk Treaty Mar, 1918

———   Armistice lines, eastern front Dec., 1917

0   500

Miles

Central Powers   Allied Powers   Neutral Powers

WORLD WAR I

German U-boats were fragile vessels that could not be used effectively if forced to obey traditional rules of naval warfare. This reality placed Germany on a collision course with the neutral United States.

German U-boats could indeed strangle England—but only by attacking all shipping, naval or merchant, enemy or neutral, found in the waters off the British Isles, thereby endangering civilians and deeply offending international opinion.

Chancellor Theobald von Bethmann-Hollweg and a few other German leaders foresaw that a "shoot-on-sight" U-boat policy would lead to serious problems with the United States. Nevertheless, in February 1915 the German government announced that it would authorize its submarines to sink without warning all ships found within a large war zone surrounding the British Isles.

The American State Department immediately denounced these "unprecedented" tactics and declared that the German government would be held to "a strict accountability" for any action that injured Americans or their property. The Berlin authorities remained unmoved. A month later a German submarine sank the British passenger liner *Falaba*, killing an American citizen. Bryan urged the president to forbid Americans to travel in the war zones, at least on belligerent ships; but Wilson refused on the grounds that to do so would surrender a valid American right. A far worse tragedy took place in May when the British luxury liner *Lusitania* was sunk off the Irish coast by a German submarine, with a loss of 1,198 lives, 128 of them American. Before the vessel left New York, the German authorities had advised Americans to avoid belligerent ships, but the actual attack had come totally without warning.

The sinking of an unarmed passenger liner, with such wholesale destruction of life, profoundly shocked Americans. "From the Department of State," the *New York Times* trumpeted, "there must go to the imperial Government in Berlin a demand that the Germans shall no longer make war like savages drunk with blood." For days afterward editorials denounced the attack as "criminal,"

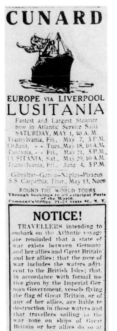

Americans thinking of embarking on the Lusitania *were warned of the dangers, but the decision to brave them or stay out in safety was their own. Secretary of State Bryan argued that Wilson's insistence on the right of neutral citizens to travel anywhere would result in the loss of lives and, ultimately, in war.*

"bestial," "uncivilized," and "barbarous." "Condemnation of the act," the *Literary Digest* summarized, "seems to be limited only by the restrictions of the English language."

In the days immediately following, there was some loose talk of war with Germany. But the public was not ready to plunge into the European bloodbath, and before long most Americans concluded that strong words would be sufficient to check German atrocities. On May 13 Wilson dispatched a note to the German government demanding an apology for the brutal act. Germany must also renounce future attacks on merchant and passenger vessels and would be held responsible for any infringement of American rights on the high seas. The Germans expressed regret for the American dead, but defended the sinking as an act of "self-defense" because the *Lusitania* had carried arms that would have been used against German soldiers. In a second, stiffer note, Wilson insisted that the Germans give up submarine warfare entirely. A third note threatened to sever diplomatic relations if another passenger ship was attacked.

Bryan considered the second *Lusitania* note an ultimatum to Germany that if she did not abandon U-boat warfare, the United States would go to war. A pacifist, he resigned in protest. Wilson replaced him with Robert Lansing, a man of a very different stripe, who believed that German success "would mean the overthrow of democracy . . . , the suppression of individual liberty, the setting up of evil ambitions . . . , and the turning back of the hands of human progress two centuries." Lansing's leadership of the State Department strengthened the pro-Ally groups and undoubtedly helped steer the country into war.

The conflict between the Central Powers and the United States remained unresolved when the Germans struck again in mid-August 1915, sinking the *Arabic*, another unarmed British passenger liner, and killing two Americans. The sinking brought to a climax the battle between the cautious Chancellor Bethmann-Hollweg and the German admirals, who wanted to continue unrestricted submarine warfare. This time the German emperor sided with the moderates and assured the State Department that his navy would stop attacking *passenger* ships without warning and in the future would provide for the safety of passengers and crews. The German government suspended submarine warfare against passenger vessels.

The War Spirit Rises. The *Arabic* pledge prevented a break in diplomatic relations with Germany, but it did not fully comply with Wilson's demands. The German government had not agreed to exempt cargo vessels from attack and had not apologized for the *Lusitania* sinking. It also had not offered reparations for lost American lives.

While these grievances festered, Americans were treated to new demonstrations of what seemed outrageous German behavior. Shortly after the *Arabic* sinking, an American Secret Service agent picked up a briefcase carelessly left by a man on the Sixth Avenue elevated railroad in New York. The contents revealed its owner, Dr. Heinrich F. Albert, as head of a widespread German operation in the United States to influence American opinion and sabotage munitions factories and shipyards producing war matériel for the Allies. At almost the same time, the British released captured documents that disclosed German-Austrian plans to foment labor stoppages at American armament plants. Soon afterward the United States accused two German diplomatic attachés of spying and sent them home; another German agent was indicted for blowing up a bridge; and still others were held responsible for various unexplained explosions and accidents in American factories and war plants.

The sensational revelations of German undercover activities deeply antagonized the American public. Brutalities in Belgium and sinkings on the Atlantic were distant events that affected few citizens directly. Bombings and spying brought the terrible war to America's shores. By mid-1915 many citizens had begun to fear that the nation could not avoid entering the fight.

The changing public mood manifested itself in a "preparedness" movement to rearm the United States for any eventuality. Not all the preparedness advocates favored "intervention"; some professed to believe that if the country was strong militarily, it would not have to fight. But many were militant anti-Germans who thought war unavoidable, or even desirable, and wanted to ensure that when it came, the country could fight effectively. The most militant leader of the preparedness-interventionist group was former president Theodore Roosevelt, who went around the country calling Wilson "yellow" for holding back on rearmament and for not taking a stronger line against the Germans. At one point, in his typically intemperate way, TR recommended that if war came, peace advocate Robert La Follette should be hanged forthwith.

A strong peace contingent confronted the preparedness movement. Besides the Quakers and members of other traditional "peace churches," the opponents of war included a fair proportion of the progressive community, who believed that domestic reform would be forgotten if the country became embroiled in a war. Women progressives were particularly prominent in the peace movement. War, asserted Harriot Stanton Blatch, represented the male principle of physical force and would be ended only when the "mother viewpoint" prevailed in international diplomacy. Socialists were even more strongly opposed to the preparedness campaign and intervention than progressives.

The war in Europe, they held, was a battle between rival capitalist imperialists in the outcome of which the world's working class had no vital interest.

At first Wilson himself was skeptical of the preparedness movement, but his growing anger at Germany and belief that preparedness was politically popular soon changed his mind. In mid-summer 1915 the president finally asked his naval and military advisers to draw up plans for an enlarged army and navy. On the basis of these proposals, in November he recommended that Congress approve a $500 million naval building program and expand the army to 400,000 men.

Even as he readied the nation for the possibility of war, Wilson struggled to avoid it. In early 1915 he had sent Colonel House to Europe to try to bring the belligerents together around the peace table. House was ignored. In January 1916 Wilson sent the colonel back to Europe for the same purpose, determined this time that if either side refused to parley, the United States would use its "utmost moral force" to compel the reluctant party to accept compromise terms that would include disarmament and a world peacekeeping organization.

Once again, House accomplished little. The warring nations wanted no part of peace except on their own terms. Despite the stubbornness of both Allied and German leaders, House made some startling promises to Britain and France that exceeded the president's instructions. If the 1916 Allied effort to break the military deadlock on the Western Front failed, and if Germany appeared to be winning, the United States, House told the British and French leaders, would intervene to prevent Allied defeat.

The Sussex Pledge. German-American relations took a turn for the better early in February 1916 when the German government finally expressed regret for the sinking of the *Lusitania* and offered to pay an indemnity for lost lives. But the pendulum soon shifted once more when a U-boat torpedoed the unarmed French steamer *Sussex*, injuring a number of Americans.

Pushed by his advisers and by public indignation, Wilson shot off a note to the German government declaring that unless it ceased all attacks on cargo and passenger ships, the United States would immediately break off diplomatic relations. With Bethmann-Hollweg and the moderates still in control, the German government gave the so-called *Sussex* pledge: It would abandon its practice of shooting on sight in all cases except those involving the enemy navy. The pledge was qualified, however. The Germans would honor it only if the United States compelled the Allies to abide by the rules of international law. Wilson accepted the *Sussex* pledge, knowing that it would be im-

possible to force the Allies to comply with Germany's conditions. But peace was preserved temporarily, and the president, still unprepared for American intervention, was grateful for the respite.

For some time following the *Sussex* pledge, the Germans acted in exemplary fashion. Meanwhile the British seemed determined to arouse the president's and the public's wrath. They seized American packages and parcels to look for contraband, opened and read letters to and from America, and refused to allow American shipowners to use British coaling facilities unless they submitted to British inspection. They also brutally suppressed the Easter Rebellion in Ireland. The execution of the Irish rebels against British rule appalled Americans and seriously damaged Britain's image as a defender of democracy. War talk ebbed as Americans had second thoughts about the Allied cause.

The Election of 1916. For the next few months public interest in foreign affairs was eclipsed by the excitement of a presidential election. In 1916 Wilson faced a Republican nominee, U.S. Supreme Court Justice Charles Evans Hughes, who did not have to split his vote with the Progressive party candidate as had Taft in 1912. Hughes was an attractive candidate. As counsel for the Armstrong Committee, he had established a solid reputation as a progressive crusader by helping to prosecute New York insurance companies for fraudulent practices. He had enhanced his reputation as a progressive during two terms as governor of New York. Then, in 1910, he had become an associate justice of the United States Supreme Court where he had upheld state power to regulate business.

Despite Hughes's appeal, Wilson was reelected. The president's success in part derived from his late turn to the left, as discussed in Chapter 23. But even more, the campaign outcome turned on the issue of war and peace.

Hughes had the difficult task of holding together a party deeply divided between a pro-Ally interventionist wing and a large number of German-American supporters. A poor speaker, he seemed to waver on the issues to please every segment of the voting public. The Democrats were more forthright. "He kept us out of war" was their campaign slogan. A Democratic ad in the *New York Times* reminded voters:

> You are working;
> —*Not Fighting!*
> Alive and Happy;
> —*Not Cannon Fodder!*
> Wilson and Peace with Honor?
> or
> *Hughes with Roosevelt and War?*

This Wilson campaign truck carries most of the 1916 Democratic platform on its sides. Although his success in keeping the nation out of war was important to voters, Wilson was also running on his progressive domestic record.

The election was close. Hughes carried the Northeast and much of the Midwest. Wilson took the South, the mountain states, and most of the Pacific Coast. Because of slow returns from California, not until Friday following the Tuesday balloting was President Wilson assured of four more years in the White House.

The Road to War. Wilson's reelection was a vote for peace. No doubt Americans as a whole were pro-Ally, despite Britain's recent blunders. Yet they still wanted very much to keep out of the war. In the wake of his victory Wilson

decided to make one last effort to force both sides to hammer out a compromise settlement. Late in December 1916 he sent notes to the belligerents asking them to state their war aims and offering again to mediate. He warned both sides that only a "peace without victory" would last. Any other "would leave a sting, a resentment, a bitter memory upon which terms of peace would rest . . . only as upon quicksand." The president's words were prophetic, but neither side was willing to stop fighting and talk terms.

German-American relations now moved swiftly toward a final crisis. By the end of 1916 the military stalemate in

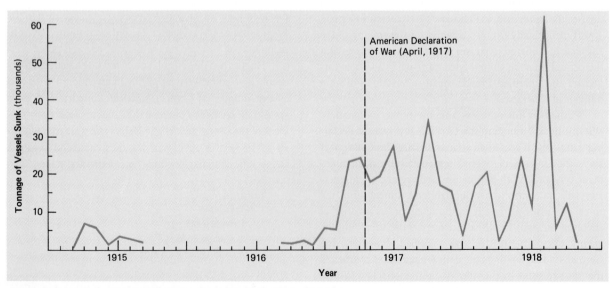

American losses to the German submarine campaign, 1915–1918. (*U.S. Navy Department, American Ship Casualties of the World War, 1923*).

Europe was becoming intolerable to the German leaders. Continued frustration weakened the moderates and strengthened the military. At a momentous conference in January 1917 the aggressive generals told Kaiser Wilhelm that the United States could never send enough men to Europe to break the impasse. Because it was already providing the Allies with as much war matériel and financial aid as it could, America would make little difference if it formally joined the enemy. Moreover, Germany was now so well supplied with U-boats that if the submarine captains were not required to observe the rules imposed by concern for neutral opinion, they could deliver a knockout blow to the Allies in short order. The generals' analysis was convincing: Germany chose unlimited submarine warfare. This choice virtually guaranteed that American ships would be involved in incidents on the high seas and the American people would be drawn into the war.

On January 31, 1917, the German ambassador in Washington informed Secretary of State Lansing that

Germany would direct its U-boats to sink without warning all ships, both neutral and enemy, found in the eastern Mediterranean and in the waters surrounding Great Britain, France, and Italy. The new German order totally repudiated the *Sussex* pledge. True to his promise, Wilson severed diplomatic relations with Germany. Most Americans, even many of Wilson's former critics, supported his decision. Volunteers began to show up at army enlistment centers.

Wilson still hoped to avoid hostilities and refused Lansing and House's advice to prepare for war. While he deliberated, rallies all over the country demanded American forbearance and further negotiations before taking the final step. Much of the president's and the public's remaining doubt was dispelled by the revelation of a secret note from the German foreign secretary, Arthur Zimmermann, to the German minister in Mexico proposing that if the United States and Germany came to blows, Mexico should ally itself with Germany and help persuade Japan to switch its

WORLD WAR I: THE WESTERN FRONT

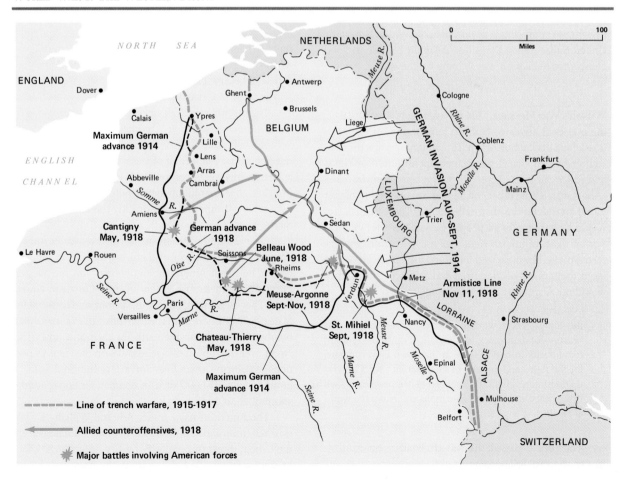

allegiance to the Central Powers. In the event of victory, Mexico would be rewarded with its lost territory in Texas, New Mexico, and Arizona. Intercepted by British intelligence, the "Zimmermann telegram" pushed Wilson over the line. The day following the receipt of the incriminating document he asked Congress for authority to arm American merchant ships and employ "any other instrumentalities or methods" to protect American interests on the high seas. When the isolationists in the Senate, led by La Follette and George W. Norris of Nebraska, threatened to talk the measure to death, Wilson released the telegram to a shocked and furious public. Carried along by a wave of public indignation, the House gave Wilson the power he wanted. But the Senate isolationists blocked action despite Wilson's condemnation of them as a "little group of willful men, representing no opinion but their own."

Wilson refused to be stopped, and on March 9 he announced that he was arming American merchant vessels under his authority as commander-in-chief. Soon after, three American merchant vessels were sunk by submarines, with heavy loss of life. Public outrage now reached a new pitch, and even some prominent socialists demanded war. In the minds of many Americans, final doubts about the Allied cause evaporated when a liberal uprising in Russia overthrew the autocratic government of the czar. Now if the United States joined the Allies, it would be able in good conscience to claim it was fighting on the side of democracy.

Wilson's War Message. On the evening of April 2, 1917, the president appeared before a joint session of Congress to ask for a declaration of war. He could not escape the conviction, he said, that German contempt for American rights and American lives, displayed by the bestial, unrestricted U-boat war, left no other course. But he appealed to higher moral considerations than self-defense. The United States would be fighting for all people, he said, for the "vindication of right, of human right" against "autocratic governments backed by organized force." As the American people faced the months of "fiery trial and sacrifice" ahead, they would not forget that they were struggling for

> the things which we have always carried nearest our hearts—for democracy, for the right of those who submit to authority to have a voice in their own Governments, for the rights and liberties of small nations, for a universal dominion of rights by a concert of free peoples as shall bring peace and safety to all nations and make the world at last free.

The Senate passed the war declaration on April 4. House approval followed on April 6.

★ THE WAR ★

America was finally in! In London, Rome, and Paris crowds cheered the news and drank toasts to the United States and its great president. Sagging Allied spirits soared. At home most socialists and a number of midwestern isolationists still opposed the war. Senator Norris charged that the war's sole cause was economic and that Americans would be "sacrificing millions of . . . [their] countrymen's lives in order that other countrymen may coin their lifeblood into money." Many German-Americans, Irish-Americans, and a small minority of intellectuals remained skeptical of the Allied cause. But on the whole the American people embraced the war wholeheartedly and accepted the sacrifices it required.

Mobilization. Now, the nation's resources had to be mobilized. Americans had not expected at first to send large numbers of men to the fighting fronts, but it soon became clear that the Allies could not fight on without American troops. The liberal Russian Revolution of March 1917 had been followed by the Bolshevik Revolution of October 1917. The Bolsheviks soon opened peace negotiations with the Germans, freeing the German troops and equipment that had been fighting Russia to move to the Western Front. As this huge army was transferred to face the French and British, it became clear that only American forces could offset the surge in German strength.

The first military draft since the Civil War provided the needed manpower. It worked surprisingly well. Scrupulously administered by local civilian draft boards, it did not arouse the feeling of class discrimination that had appeared fifty years before. With its help the army grew from 200,000 to 4 million men. Draftees were sent to thirty-two training camps and were quickly transformed into soldiers.

Over 2 million American troops eventually went to France, and 1.4 million of them saw action on the front lines. The lot of American "doughboys" on the Western Front was as miserable as that of their European equivalents. They faced mud, rain, cold, vermin, and constant fear of death. They huddled in the trenches while fierce artillery bombardments shook the earth for days at a time. They "went over the top" in savage assaults on the enemy's positions, sacrificing their lives for a few hundred yards of ground. About 50,000 died in combat; an equal number succumbed to disease.

The American navy, under Admiral William S. Sims, escorted troop and supply vessels to France and helped end the U-boat threat to Britain. For every American soldier it brought safely to the fighting front, the navy had to guar-

The Great War

Many months before President Woodrow Wilson, Robert Lansing, Bryan's successor as secretary of state, had come to the conclusion that imperial Germany was a menace to America and to democracy. Lansing was not shy about presenting his views. In the selection below he tells the president how he perceives Germany under the Kaiser and how the United States should respond. The date of the memo is July 11, 1915, almost twenty months before the American declaration of war.

"I have come to the conclusion that the German Government is utterly hostile to all nations with democratic institutions because those who compose it see in democracy a menace to absolutism and the defeat of German ambition for world domination. Everywhere German agents are plotting and intriguing to accomplish the supreme purpose of their government.

"Only recently has the conviction come to me that democracy throughout the world is threatened. Suspicions of the vaguest sort only a few months ago have been more and more confirmed. From many sources evidence has been coming until it would be folly to close one's eyes to it.

"German agents have undoubtedly been at work in Mexico arousing anti-American feeling and holding out false hopes of support. The proof is not conclusive but is sufficient to compel belief. Germans also appear to be operating in Haiti and San Domingo and are probably doing so in other Latin American Republics.

"I think that this is being done so that this nation will have troubles in America and be unable to take part in the European War if a repetition of such outrages as the *Lusitania* sinking should require us to act. It may even go further and have in mind the possibility of a future war with this Republic in case the Allies should be defeated.

"In these circumstances the policies we adopt are vital to the future of the United States and, I firmly believe, to the welfare of mankind, for I see in the perpetuation of democracy the only hope of universal peace and progress for the world. Today German absolutism is the great menace to democracy. . . .

"The remedy seems to me to be plain. It is that Germany must not be permitted to win this war or to break even, though to prevent it this country is forced to take an active part. This ultimate necessity must be constantly in our minds in all our controversies with the belligerents. American public opinion must be prepared for the time, which may come, when we will have to cast aside our neutrality and become one of the champions of democracy.

"We must in fact risk everything rather than leave the way open for a new combination of powers, stronger and more dangerous to liberty than the Central Allies are today."

---

antee the arrival of fifty pounds of supplies and equipment daily. Ultimately millions of tons of food, munitions, vehicles, medicines, clothing, guns, horses, and fuel were ferried from American ports to Le Havre, Bordeaux, Calais, Brest, and Boulogne, with minimal loss from U-boats.

The War Effort at Home.   This enormous military and logistical effort was made possible by the effective mobilization of economic and emotional resources at home. The war cost the United States $33 billion, including $9 billion of loans to the Allies. About a quarter of this huge sum was raised by taxes. The war taxes were highly progressive, taking up to 75 percent of the largest incomes. Inheritance taxes of 25 percent, an excess-profits tax of 65 percent, and a variety of excise taxes also helped spread the burden throughout the population. The rest of the money came

from banks and from campaigns to sell Liberty Bonds, which not only paid for the war but also helped whip up enthusiasm for the war effort.

The billions, however, had to be effectively deployed. For this purpose the Wilson administration borrowed a page from the New Nationalism progressives by setting up a collection of new federal war agencies. By the end of the war these administrative bodies were exerting many new powers and had achieved extraordinary control over the economy. They also anticipated a number of governmental structures and measures of the New Deal and provided precedents for the mobilization effort of World War II.

Food production burgeoned under the direction of Food Administrator Herbert Hoover, who had supervised food relief to ravaged Belgium earlier in the war. Americans voluntarily observed "wheatless" and "meatless" days in a

Montgomery Flagg, a popular illustrator of the day, produced this saccharine poster urging boys and girls in 1917 to help the American war effort by saving money.

remarkably effective campaign to conserve food. The Food Administration guaranteed an attractive price for the entire 1917 wheat crop, causing a dramatic jump in the number of acres planted with wheat. Vegetable gardens appeared everywhere, and exotic meats such as horse and rabbit were introduced into the wartime diet. The Food Administration was a great success, and it played no small part in Hoover's popularity after the war.

The War Industries Board, headed by Wall Street broker Bernard Baruch, performed well after a slow start. American arms and clothing factories equipped the American doughboy better than any other soldier in the world. American shipyards struggled, not always successfully, with the crucial task of replacing Allied vessels sunk by U-boats. The board built new production facilities and converted existing ones for war purposes, developed new sources of raw materials, served as purchasing agent for the Allies, standardized thousands of items, and established strict economic priorities.

Meanwhile, the United States Railroad Administration took tight control of the country's rail transportation, now called on to carry millions more passengers and tons of freight than in peacetime. The administration combined railways into regional units, limited unnecessary passenger travel, standardized rates and schedules, and gave priority to munitions and war matériel over nonessential goods.

Fuel Administrator Harry A. Garfield became a virtual dictator over the nation's fuel supply. When a coal shortage immobilized thirty-seven munitions ships in New York harbor during the bitterly cold winter of 1917–1918, he closed down all civilian manufacturing plants to release their coal for the ships' use. The Fuel Administration also asked automobile owners to conserve gasoline for trucks carrying vital goods.

The war overstimulated the economy. Unemployment melted away, and men and women were soon working long

Drafting 4 million men into the armed forces opened up an employment gap on the home front. These women making cartridges at Bethlehem Steel were typical of thousands who joined the work force in 1917–1918.

hours at good pay. But despite high taxes and the Liberty and Victory Loans that drained off much excess purchasing power, prices rose sharply and offset many of the workers' gains. It soon became apparent that labor would have to be regulated, along with other sectors of the economy, to ensure uninterrupted work, prevent strikes for higher wages, and provide the highest priority for war industry. To attain these goals, Wilson created the War Labor Policies Board. By granting recognition to labor unions and establishing generally favorable working conditions for wage earners, the board imposed labor peace during the war. It prohibited strikes, but it also forced management to negotiate with the unions. Under these policies the AFL and other unions expanded their membership to over 4 million, a 50 percent increase over 1914.

One firm principle of the War Labor Policies Board was that women should have equal pay for equal work in war industries. High wages, encouraged by wartime labor shortages and labor board policies, soon drew thousands of women into the labor force. Thousands of women also went "over there" to France with the doughboys, working as ambulance drivers and nurses and representing organizations such as the Salvation Army and Red Cross. The war accustomed American women to working outside the home and accelerated their economic independence.

Blacks also made economic gains. With millions of men in the armed forces and European immigration at an all-time low, the American labor force fell drastically just at the time when the economy needed labor most. To meet the shortage, employers were forced to lower their barriers to black workers. Thousands of black men and women were soon leaving southern farms for the high wages of the northern war plants.

Even children were recruited to help in the war effort. This sentimental poster, put out by U.S. Food Administrator Herbert Hoover, was designed to encourage "victory gardens." With more Americans growing their own fruits and vegetables, more farm produce was available for shipment to troops and the Allies in Europe.

The all-black 369th Regiment was the first American unit in France and came under longer continuous fire than any other American army unit in World War I. The regiment was called the "Hell Fighters" by the Germans, who were awed by its fighting qualities.

George Creel

World War II came abruptly with death from the sky over Pearl Harbor; the Civil War arrived with a bombardment of the United States fort in Charleston Harbor. Both attacks shocked the American people and united them at least temporarily behind the effort to defeat the enemy.

In 1917 war came only after two and a half years of debate that left a nation unsure of itself and its goals. Millions of Americans had little reason to love Britain or Russia, two of our chief allies; many others had strong reason to love Germany, their *Vaterland*, our chief enemy. Thousands of Americans opposed all wars; thousands more opposed all "capitalist wars." Given these facts, many influential prowar Americans feared that the nation would be unable to mobilize itself for the hard struggle ahead. It was for this reason that on April 13, 1917, just a week after the war declaration, President Woodrow Wilson issued an executive order creating the Committee on Public Information (CPI) and appointed George Creel of Denver to head it.

Creel was a good choice, a man with the experience and the values that the task seemed to require. His father was a former Confederate officer who never got over the South's defeat and, while his wife supported the family by running a boardinghouse, slowly drank himself to death. George Creel became a journalist as a teenager and for a while published a small crusading newspaper in Kansas City. In 1909

he moved to Denver to edit first the flamboyant *Denver Post*, and then the *Rocky Mountain News*.

Creel was a full-fledged progressive who used his journalism to advance the "people's cause" against the "interests." At one point he got into trouble by recommending that eleven Colorado state senators with close ties to exploitive business groups be lynched. Creel also had liberal social views. Elected police commissioner in 1912, he applied the legal theories of the famous Denver judge, Benjamin Lindsey, to the evil of urban prostitution. Rather than arrest the women or merely drive them from the city, he organized a rehabilitation center for them, headed by a sympathetic woman.

In 1916 Creel wrote a book, *Wilson and the Issues*, that became a major item in the president's reelection effort. The work depicted Wilson as nobly struggling to avoid war, yet always determined to protect the interests of the United States. It "mightily pleased" the president and he rewarded Creel with the appointment to head the CPI.

As director of the new agency, Creel tried to avoid encouraging hysteria or abandonment of America's liberal and humane values. In March 1918 he wrote to a progressive Democrat: "I shall support every necessary measure directed to the supreme end of defeating . . . the unholy combination of autocracy, militarism, and predatory capitalism that rules Germany and threatens liberty

and self-government everywhere. . . . [But] I ask and expect support only of those who believe that for the sake of political liberty and social progress, America must win this war while it consolidates at home every position won from the forces of reaction and political bigotry." Creel's hopes would be disappointed.

Even before the CPI began to beat the drums of patriotism, Americans had been gripped by a spasm of intolerance and irrational fear. Between 1914–1916, when the United States had become a major supplier of munitions to the Allies, German agents had been active on this side of the Atlantic. Once the United States entered the war, among the unthinking, it was easy to equate the antiwar opposition of German-Americans, pacifists, and socialists with espionage. Some conservatives seized on the socialist issue to stigmatize all political views left of center, including progressivism, as anti-American. Congress encouraged the fearful mood by passing a series of repressive measures including the Espionage Act and the Trading-with-the-Enemy Act. These made aiding the enemy, obstructing military recruitment, or preaching disloyalty crimes punishable by stiff sentences. They established a Censorship Board to screen messages between United States citizens and citizens of foreign countries, and imposed severe penalties on anyone who uttered, wrote, or published "disloyal, profane, scurrilous, or abusive language about the form of gov-

One of the most important wartime agencies was the Committee on Public Information (CPI), established to "mobilize the mind of the world." To Wilson the fight for people's minds, the "conquest of their convictions," was just as urgent as the military effort.

To lead the propaganda war he chose George Creel, a progressive journalist with a gift for storytelling and platform oratory. Creel mobilized thousands of people in the arts, advertising, and motion pictures to "advertise America." Under Creel's urging, some of the most talented

ernment of the United States, or the Constitution of the United States, or the military or naval forces of the United States, . . . or any language intended to bring the form of government of the United States . . . into contempt, scorn, contumely, or disrepute." One of Wilson's appointees to the Censorship Board was George Creel.

A chief function of the CPI was to distribute government releases. Officials saw this as a way of keeping the public well informed, but inevitably the CPI held back as much information about the war as it disseminated. Besides this indirect censorship, the CPI laid down prohibitive guidelines for news that should not be published under any circumstances and news of dubious propriety. Though the CPI had no power to punish, its rebuke to papers that violated its guidelines was inevitably coercive and a damper on the free flow of information to the American public. Creel's interference with the free operation of the press made him the target of countless attacks. Some of these he deserved, but often he was merely the scapegoat for administration opponents who feared to attack the president himself.

Far more important than censorship was the CPI's work as a propaganda agency. Creel hoped to clarify the nation's war goals and mobilize the public to achieve them. He solicited free space from newspaper and magazine publishers and filled it with patriotic articles, advertisements for Liberty Bonds, and attacks on the "Prussianism" that would sweep the world if the Kaiser was not stopped.

The CPI created a Division of Pictorial Publicity with the illustrator Charles Dana Gibson in charge. Gibson and his recruits from the art world created hundreds of posters, cartoons, and magazine illustrations depicting heroic American soldiers and sailors, patriotic American housewives, and bestial-looking German "Huns."

One of Creel's most inspired schemes was the Four-Minute Men. These were 75,000 volunteers who delivered short rousing speeches urging such patriotic acts as bond purchases, food conservation, and donation of binoculars to the navy. They laid out American war aims, explained the workings of the draft, and told their audiences how to sustain morale. They often described German atrocities against civilians in Belgium. The volunteers spoke in school auditoriums, movie theaters, and opera houses, in every language current among the polyglot American population.

Two of the CPI's most powerful allies in molding public opinion were the movie industry and academe. Anxious to demonstrate their patriotism, the movie moguls quickly offered their services to the CPI. Creel was happy to take up the offer, and during the war the CPI and Hollywood collaborated on a series of documentaries and feature films. One of these was *Our Colored Fighters*, designed to appeal to black audiences. Another was *The Kaiser, the Beast of Berlin*, a no-holds-barred anti-German attack that attracted long lines to the theaters where it played. In addition, the CPI employed stars like Mary Pickford, Douglas Fairbanks, and Theda Bara to sell Liberty Bonds.

The nation's scholars and academics lent themselves to Creel's goals. The CPI's Division of Civic and Educational Cooperation, headed by Dean Guy Stanton Ford of the University of Minnesota Graduate School, employed some of the nation's most prominent historians and social scientists to churn out hundreds of pages of war propaganda in the guise of scholarship. Like almost all the wartime propaganda, this material glorified the American cause and disparaged imperial Germany, its values, and its institutions. The division's most widely circulated pamphlet was the German-language version of *American Loyalty by Citizens of German Descent*, a work that testified to the patriotism of the German-American population. Yet much of the CPI's effort to avert ethnic bigotry within the country failed. In the end the anti-German propaganda encouraged the intolerance that was sweeping the United States.

After the war Creel defended Wilsonian internationalism and the League of Nations. He moved to San Francisco in 1926 and became a member of the city's cultural elite. During the New Deal period he held posts with the WPA and other government agencies, but he broke with Roosevelt during World War II. The president and his colleagues, he believed, were too lenient toward the enemy. In his old age Creel became an intense anticommunist. For most of his life he had tried (though not always successfully) to avoid simplistic ways of thinking. But now he lost his sense of balance and came to exemplify the intolerance his enemies had, on the whole unfairly, ascribed to him many years before when he headed the Committee on Public Information.

artists in the country designed Liberty Loan and recruiting posters. An army of lecturers, called "Four-Minute Men," delivered pithy lectures all across the country on subjects like "Maintaining Morals and Morale," "Why We Are Fighting," and "The Meaning of America." "There was no part of the great war machinery that we did not touch," Creel wrote after the war, "no medium of appeal that we did not employ . . . to make our own people and all other peoples of the world understand the causes that compelled America to take up arms."

Progressive impulses survived on the home front through 1917, as when these women's suffragists marched in Washington, D.C. In fact, the women's rights movement found new unity during the war.

Civil Liberties During the War. Creel's campaign was immensely effective in whipping up enthusiasm for the war and Wilson's announced goal of making the world "safe for democracy." War fervor also unleashed a wave of intolerance against those who did not show the proper patriotic spirit or who harbored pacifist or socialist attitudes.

Quick to sense the new superpatriotic mood, Congress passed the Espionage Act and the Trading-with-the-Enemy Act in 1917. The Espionage Act imposed severe penalties on persons found guilty of obstructing recruitment, aiding the enemy, or encouraging anyone to be disloyal or insubordinate or to refuse duty in the armed forces. Under it the postmaster general could exclude from the mails any material he deemed treasonable or seditious. The Trading-with-the-Enemy Act authorized the government to confiscate and run German-owned businesses and to censor international communications and the foreign-language press. In 1918 Congress passed the Sedition Act, declaring "disloyal" or "seditious" all talk against the war and making "profane, scurrilous, or abusive language" about the Constitution, the flag, or the armed forces a crime.

In the months before war was declared, Wilson had warned of the intolerance it might bring. After April 1917 his administration clamped down hard on dissenters. Postmaster General Albert S. Burleson excluded from the mails publications opposed to the war. In *Schenck v. U.S.* the Supreme Court upheld the conviction of a man for mailing circulars that urged draftees to refuse military induc-

tion. In war, said Justice Oliver Wendell Holmes, Jr., speaking for the majority of the Court, such material posed a "clear and present danger" to the nation and could by law be suppressed. In 1918 the Justice Department indicted and secured the convictions of Eugene V. Debs and Victor L. Berger, the Socialist party leaders, on the charge of encouraging draft evasion.

Local officials joined the repressive chorus and fined and imprisoned those who spoke out against the war. Meanwhile, vigilante groups and self-appointed guardians of the country intimidated "slackers" and supposed subversives. In the Pacific Northwest their target was often the Industrial Workers of the World (IWW), a radical labor group with a strong following among western miners and loggers.

One of the war's casualties was ethnic tolerance. With Creel's CPI portraying the German enemy as "Wolves of Kulture," "Prussian Curs," and "Beasts of Berlin," superpatriots were encouraged to attack their German-American neighbors. Many schools and colleges suspended the teaching of German. To superpatriots sauerkraut became "liberty cabbage" and German measles "liberty measles."

The prevailing mood of intolerance found another easy target in the nation's black citizens. The influx of southern blacks into war plants created severe tensions in overcrowded northern cities. Despite their important contribution to the war effort, black Americans suffered acts of abuse and violence and economic exploitation. In East St. Louis in mid-1917 hatred exploded into a bloody race riot in which forty blacks were clubbed, beaten, stabbed, and hanged.

As if to counterbalance the decline in tolerance, the war gave a massive push to the women's suffrage movement. In 1916 Alice Paul converted her Congressional Union into the National Woman's Party (NWP), and during the presidential election she and NWP attacked Wilson and the Democrats for failure to act on the suffrage issue. Meanwhile, using gentler means, Carrie Catt of the National American Woman Suffrage Association managed to convert the president himself to the cause.

Still, Congress and much of the male public resisted. The suffragists appealed to the nation's conscience with slogans like "Democracy Begins at Home," and advertised the giant contributions women were making to the war effort. Alice Paul and her group used more aggressive tactics, including throwing picket lines around the White House. District of Columbia officials carted the picketers off to jail, but this only succeeded in making a flock of suffrage martyrs and arousing sympathy for their cause.

At last, in January 1918, the House of Representatives, anxious to further national unity during wartime, passed the women's suffrage amendment to the Constitution by precisely the two-thirds majority needed. The Senate took another year and a half to approve the amendment, and not until August 1920 was it ratified by three-fourths of the states. But without the impetus of war, women would have been forced to wait far longer for the right to vote.

★ MAKING THE PEACE ★

The American Expeditionary Force (AEF) under the command of General John J. Pershing began to arrive in France in July 1917, though it saw little fighting before early spring

On his way to Versailles, Wilson is showered with flowers. This warm reception suggested that Europeans would accept the League of Nations, the international manifestation of his ideas on constitutional government.

1918. In March 1918 the Germans, strengthened by the armies brought west from Russia, attacked on a broad front, engaging the Americans in May and June around the town of Château-Thierry and at Belleau Wood, fifty miles from Paris. In September the American First Army, some 500,000 strong, pushed back a German salient at Saint-Mihiel. Between late September and the armistice on November 11, 1.2 million Americans were committed in the Meuse-Argonne campaign around Verdun, a thrust coordinated with major British and French attacks along the front. On November 1 the Americans broke the German line. Beaten on the battlefield and on the verge of collapse at home, the Germans began talking of peace.

Wilson's Hopes for the Future. The Central Powers' defeat was in part a military failure. But it also was the result of deteriorating morale. By late 1918 the German will to re-

---

WILSON'S PLAN FOR A LASTING PEACE

THE FOURTEEN POINTS	SUPPLEMENTARY POINTS
From the Fourteen Points Address to Congress, January 8, 1918	*From Speeches Delivered between February and September 1918*

THE FOURTEEN POINTS

1. "Open covenants of peace, openly arrived at" and an end to secret diplomacy.
2. Absolute freedom of navigation upon the seas . . . alike in peace and in war."
3. "The removal, so far as possible, of all economic barriers" to free trade.
4. Reduction of armaments "to the lowest point consistent with domestic safety."
5. An "absolutely impartial adjustment of all colonial claims" giving equal weight to the interests of the colonial populations and "the equitable claims" of the imperial governments.
6. "The evacuation of all Russian territory" and cooperation to allow Rusia "the independent determination of her own political development and national policy and assure her of a sincere welcome into the society of free nations under institutions of her own choosing."
7. German evacuation of Belgium and restoration of full sovereignty.
8. "All French territory should be freed" and Alsace-Lorraine, taken by Prussia in 1871, should be returned to France.
9. "A readjustment of the frontiers of Italy . . . along clearly recognizable lines of nationality."
10. Autonomy for the peoples of Austria-Hungary.
11. Evacuation of Rumania, Montenegro, and Serbia: international guarantee of the political and economic independence of the Balkan states; and Serbian access to the sea.
12. Autonomy for the subject nationalities within the Turkish Empire and free passage through the Dardanellas for ships of all nations.
13. An independent Poland with "free and secure access to the sea."
14. A "general association of nations."

SUPPLEMENTARY POINTS

15. Base "each part of the final settlement . . . upon the essential justice of the particular case and upon such adjustments as are most likely to bring" a permanent peace.
16. An end to bartering "peoples and provinces . . . as if they were mere chattels and pawns."
17. Determine "every territorial settlement . . . in the interest and for the benefit of the populations concerned," and not as a compromise "amongst rival states."
18. Attempt to satisfy "all well-defined national aspirations."
19. "The destruction of every arbitrary power anywhere that can . . . disturb the peace of the world."
20. Conduct of nations "to be governed . . . by the same principles of honor and of respect for the common law of civilized society that govern the individual citizens."
21. Special interests "not consistent with the common interest of all" nationals cannot become the basis for any settlement.
22. No alliances or special understandings will be allowed within "the League of Nations."
23. "There can be no speical, selfish economic combinations" or economic boycotts except as used by the League of Nations for discipline.

sist had been seriously undermined by expectations of a generous peace as laid out in Wilson's Fourteen Points.

Announced in a January 1918 speech while the fighting was still at an indecisive stage, the Fourteen Points was a blueprint for the postwar world. Wilson sought to deal with several immediate, war-connected issues. Germany would have to abandon all occupied territories in France, Russia, and Belgium; Austria would surrender territorial gains in the Balkans. All nations would agree to respect neutral rights on the high seas. The American president also sought to address and correct the fundamental causes of the war still raging. Armaments would be sharply reduced to prevent future destabilizing arms races; Serbia would be given access to the sea; the repressed aspirations for nationhood among the peoples of the Turkish, Austrian, and German empires would be satisfied; Italy's frontiers would be altered to incorporate Italian-speaking people living outside its existing borders; the conflicting colonial claims of the great powers would be adjusted with due regard to the rights of the colonial populations themselves.

On a still more abstract level, Wilson proposed to remake the international order so that future disputes among nations could be kept from deteriorating into war. The president was here expressing American liberal idealism and, critics would say, American naiveté. He attacked "private international understandings" and demanded in their place "open covenants of peace, openly arrived at." He called for "the removal, as far as possible," of all international economic barriers and the establishment of "equality of trade conditions among all the nations consenting to the peace." His most visionary "point" was "a general association of nations . . . for the purpose of affording mutual guarantees of political independence and territorial integrity to great and small states alike." Wilson concluded with an assurance to the Germans that the United States did not desire their destruction or humiliation. America would welcome them into the family of "peace-loving nations" if they demonstrated their clear desire for peace by overruling the "military party and the men whose creed is imperial domination."

Central Powers' spokesmen derided the Fourteen Points as propaganda and almost a year more of fighting and dying would follow. Then, following the 1918 German military failure on the Western Front, Wilson's hopeful and generous terms broke the Central Powers' will to fight. That fall events moved swiftly. On October 27 the Austrians notified Wilson that they would be willing to conclude a separate peace. The next day the sailors of the German Imperial Navy mutinied at their base in Kiel when ordered to sail for a desperate showdown battle against the British fleet. The revolt soon spread to other German garrisons and towns. On November 9 the German kaiser abdicated and went into exile; Germany was proclaimed a republic. By this time German officials had already agreed to surrender terms at Compiègne in northern France. These incorporated much of the Fourteen Points but also imposed punitive German reparations for war damages. On November 11 at 11 A.M. the guns fell silent; World War I, the Great War, was over.

Versailles. On January 18, 1919, the Allied leaders met at Versailles, near Paris, to determine the shape of the peace. Wilson was there in person. Although he was widely criticized for his precedent-shattering decision to leave the United States while in office, the president insisted that only his physical presence could ensure that the victors would accept a just and secure peace.

Wilson was received like a savior in Europe. Wherever he went, enormous crowds turned out to cheer him. In Paris 2 million people lining the Champs-Elysées rained flowers and bouquets as he drove down the boulevard in his open automobile. The people of Europe were honoring not only the man. Wilson represented American idealism and the possibility of a more decent and democratic world system. Even the defeated Germans seemed willing to entrust their future to his hands.

But while the common people of Europe applauded the president, his chief Allied colleagues—Georges Clemenceau of France, David Lloyd George of Britain, and Vittorio Orlando of Italy—remained skeptical. To these unsentimental men Wilsonian idealism was all very well to shore up faltering Allied morale and weaken the German will to fight, but it seemed impractical as the basis for an international settlement. The major Allied powers wanted Germany condemned as a war criminal, totally disarmed, and forced to pay stiff indemnities that could be used to rebuild the devastated Allied economies. France, in particular, feared the might of a restored Germany and demanded guarantees that the attack of 1914 would not be repeated. The European Allies were also determined not to surrender any of their gains, including the German colonies that they had seized during the war. Finally, they were suspicious of the principle of self-determination. Could the confused patchwork of nationalities in eastern Europe really be sorted out into functioning nations? Reinforcing all anxieties and doubts was the specter of Russian Bolshevism hovering over a continent devastated by war and shaken by the breakup of old empires. In early 1919 a succession of far left Marxist groups had seized power in Hungary and parts of Germany. Would these revolts spread? As the victorious Allied leaders conferred amid the splendors of Louis XIV's palace at Versailles, it seemed vital to move quickly or face Bolshevik-inspired revolutions throughout eastern and central Europe.

Wilson soon discovered that he could not force the

European powers to accept his Fourteen Points without drastic modification. The French refused to consider any matter that threatened their quest for secure borders. The British would not hear of the "freedom of the seas." Several of the European Allies wanted a slice of the overseas German empire and they all wanted the German aggressor punished and forced to pay financial compensation for their losses. The president was not happy with the changes his colleagues demanded, but he went along with most of them, convinced that the League of Nations, his "general association of nations," would eventually right many of the injustices of the peace settlement.

The terms of the resulting treaty were a severe disappointment to idealists all over the world. The agreement allowed German-speaking peoples to be absorbed into the newly created nations of Poland and Czechoslovakia. Much of the Tyrol went to Italy, placing people who considered themselves Austrians under a foreign government. The German possessions in Africa and Asia were parceled out among the European Allies. And, disastrously, Germany was forced to accept complete responsibility for the war—"war guilt," it was called—and to pay crushing reparations (ultimately set at $33 billion) to the victors. Unmentioned in the treaty were Wilson's idealistic calls for disarmament, tariff reductions, and freedom of the seas.

Throughout the Versailles deliberations Wilson worked tirelessly for the point he considered the cornerstone of his peace proposals, the League of Nations. As finally hammered out, the League Covenant established two bodies: a general assembly composed of all member nations, and an executive council to consist of the United States, the British Empire, France, Italy, Japan, and four other countries to be elected by the assembly. These bodies would listen to disputes among member nations and dispense international justice. The League's decisions would be enforced first by world opinion; then by economic sanctions against the international wrongdoers; and finally, if necessary, by the use of military forces contributed by member nations. In addition, the League would help adjust minor disputes between citizens of different countries through a permanent International Court and seek to improve world social standards through an International Bureau of Labor.

As Wilson labored at Versailles during the winter of 1919, his support at home eroded. Before leaving for Europe he had put his prestige on the line by asking the American public to endorse the Democratic party in the 1918 congressional elections as a mandate. When the voters gave the Republicans control of the Senate, his enemies claimed that they had repudiated the president's leadership. Wilson had further antagonized his political opponents by appointing

Wilson found the Senate—whose three foremost League of Nations opponents are pictured here refusing to give "Peace" their seat—less willing to consider the League than the war-weary Europeans. The surge of sentiment against the League was in part a result of Wilson's inattention to political details, but it marked a more significant event: the reemergence of American isolationism.

only one Republican to the peace commission that accompanied him to Paris, although treaty ratification in the Senate would require the support of both parties.

Now, as news of the emerging treaty's provisions filtered back to the United States, his opponents took sharp aim at its specific proposals. Irish-Americans were soon attacking the failure of the treaty to further the cause of Irish freedom from Britain. Italian-Americans complained because Italy had not been awarded the Adriatic city of Fiume (now Rijeka). German-Americans denounced the war-guilt clause that made their ancestral land a self-confessed criminal nation. Jingoes and superpatriots claimed that the treaty would compromise American sovereignty. Isolationists insisted that the League would commit the United States to an overly active role in world affairs.

After two months of hard negotiating at Versailles, Wilson returned briefly to the United States to discover that the still uncompleted treaty had come under withering fire. Thirty-seven senators, led by Henry Cabot Lodge of Massachusetts, had signed a "round robin" declaring that they would not vote for the treaty without amendment. Lodge and his fellow dissenters feared the loss of American autonomy under the League. Lodge himself also personally despised Wilson. The treaty had enough no votes to defeat it; clearly a bitter battle was in prospect.

Despite his disappointing reception at home, the president returned to Europe for further negotiations in an optimistic mood, certain that the American people—if not the Senate—shared his vision of a new world order. To accommodate his critics, however, he had the League Covenant modified to allow any member nation to withdraw from the organization and to refuse colonial trusteeships if it so wished. The League would also keep hands off member nations' domestic tariff and immigration policies and avoid intruding into regional arrangements like the Monroe Doctrine. The treaty, incorporating the revised League Covenant, was ratified by the delegates in the Hall of Mirrors at Versailles on June 28, 1919. Soon afterward Wilson departed for home to fight for its ratification.

The Battle for the League. The president found the opposition to the treaty and the League stronger and more determined than ever. Yet public opinion was by no means all negative. There were still some who shared Wilson's vision of a new liberal world order in which aggressive nations could be restrained by collective action. Scores of newspapers, labor leaders, and representatives of farm and women's organizations—much of the old progressive coalition—supported Wilson's League, fearing that the peace would otherwise prove fragile. Wilson counted on people like these to get the treaty through the balky Senate.

But by this time Senator Lodge had developed a clever strategy to defeat the League. He would not oppose it directly but would demand a series of "reservations." (Reservations, unlike amendments, would not have to be approved by other League members.) Most of these would be moderate enough to attract support from a number of fence-sitting senators. But Lodge foresaw that Wilson and his supporters would reject them. If he maneuvered the treaty-adoption process in the right way, Lodge believed, he might get its own supporters to defeat it.

First, Lodge called hearings that consumed many weeks. By the time the interested parties had finished their wordy testimony, the protreaty public had begun to lose interest. Wilson fought back. Although thoroughly exhausted by the arduous negotiations in France, he decided to take his case directly to the American people. For three weeks the aging president toured the country, speaking before large audiences in support of his work at Versailles. Soon after a speech at Pueblo, Colorado, Wilson collapsed and had to cancel the remainder of his trip. Following his return to Washington, he suffered a severe stroke that partially paralyzed him. For months he was unable to work, and during this period his wife and the cabinet took over most of the duties of the presidential office. Though Wilson's strength gradually returned, he never fully recovered, and he remained irritable and quick to take offense. The illness exaggerated Wilson's stubbornness and heightened his belief in his cause.

Wilson's illness proved fatal for the treaty. By the time he returned to Washington, Senator Lodge had appended fourteen "reservations" to the Versailles agreement. These actually altered the document only in detail. But the obstinate president saw them as serious modifications that "emasculated" his work, and he insisted that his supporters vote against the modified treaty. They did. At the same time the isolationists refused to accept the original treaty. It looked as if the agreement hammered out at Versailles was finished.

The treaty and the League were not yet dead, however. Under public pressure the Senate was forced to reconsider its decision. In March 1920 the modified treaty was once more put to a vote. Wilson again proved rigid and unyielding. He insisted that the treaty with reservations be defeated. "Either," he declared, "we should enter the league fearlessly, accepting the responsibility and not fearing the role of leadership which we now enjoy, contributing our efforts towards establishing a just and permanent peace, or we should retire as gracefully as possibly from the great concert of powers by which the world was saved." Wilson's supporters were loyal to him again, but they did his cause a fatal disservice by defeating the treaty for the last time.

In the election of 1920 the Democrats endorsed the Versailles agreement; their presidential and vice presidential candidates, Governor James M. Cox of Ohio and the young Franklin Delano Roosevelt of New York, respectively, were League supporters. The Republican platform hedged on the League, and the G.O.P. candidate, Senator Warren G. Harding of Ohio, evaded the issue.

The ailing Wilson sought to make the election a referendum on the League. It was a wasted effort, for the public was tired of war and progressivism and great crusades. Campaigning for "normalcy," Harding won by a landslide of 16 million votes, enabling the isolationists to claim that the American people had repudiated internationalism. The new Harding administration eventually signed a separate peace treaty with Germany officially ending the hostilities, but the United States never entered the League of Nations.

★ CONCLUSIONS ★

The outcome of World War I was profoundly disillusioning to those Americans who shared Wilson's view of their country as a missionary nation ordained to carry the blessings of liberal democracy to every part of the world. Most citizens, however, were not deeply committed internationalists, and after 1918 were happy to return to the business of their daily lives. They might agree with Wilson that the world deserved a better international order, but far more than the idealist in the White House, they had supported the war as the only way to teach a lesson to the nation that had ridden roughshod over American "rights." Both the ordinary citizen's modest goal of fending off a brutal attacker who used barbarous U-boat warfare to gain his ends and the president's more exalted vision of a "new world" were needed to bring the United States into the great conflict. But the simple defeat of Germany was enough to satisfy the average American, and Wilson's hopes remained unfulfilled. America, having entered the war from a position of self-proclaimed moral authority, was forced to recognize that there were limits to what could be accomplished with great wealth and missionary zeal. The unworkable settlement reached at Versailles, the failure of the League of Nations, and the resurgent American isolationism that followed World War I—all these contributed to the causes of World War II, an even more colossal tragedy.

By 1919 progressivism, which had dominated the first two decades of the twentieth century, was in deep eclipse. The battle to defeat Germany had consumed the emotions that had helped fuel the crusade against trusts and unregulated private power. At home wartime intolerance had broken up the broad progressive coalition by pitting American against American. In the prewar decades the issues of trust control, more responsive government, and consumer protection had united Americans. Now the nation was about to enter an era when cultural issues and prejudices would deeply divide them from one another.

★★★★★★★★ FOR FURTHER READING ★★★★★★★★

N. Gordon Levin. *Woodrow Wilson and World Politics: America's Response to War and Revolution* (1968)
Levin maintains that the "effort to construct a stable world order of liberal-capitalist internationalism"—safe from "imperialism of the Right" and "revolution of the Left"—was basic to Wilson's foreign policy and all subsequent American policy-making.

Robert E. Quirk. *An Affair of Honor: Woodrow Wilson and the Occupation of Veracruz* (1962)
Quirk's treatment of the Tampico incident and the shelling and occupation of Veracruz by American marines is brief and well written.

Walter Millis. *Road to War: America, 1914–1917* (1935)
Writing when most citizens believed that America's entry into World War I was a mistake, Millis blames Allied propaganda, American businessmen, and anti-German prejudice for dragging the nation into an unnecessary conflict. *Road to War* was a Book-of-the-Month Club selection in 1935 and helped create the isolationism that characterized the thirties.

Arthur S. Link. *Woodrow Wilson and the Progressive Era, 1910–1917* (1954)
Half of this book is devoted to Wilson's foreign policy and the advent of war with the Central Powers. Link is far more sympathetic to Wilson than is Millis; he sees the president as motivated by idealism and a sincere desire to stop brutal aggression.

Frederick Luebke. *Bonds of Loyalty: German-Americans and World War I* (1974)
Luebke describes the unfair treatment of German-Americans during 1917–1918.

Ralph Stone. *The Irreconcilables: The Fight Against the League of Nations* (1970)
This is the best study of Lodge and his anti-League colleagues.

Randolph S. Bourne. *War and the Intellectuals: Collected Essays, 1915–1919.* Edited and introduced by Carl Resek (1964)
A collection of essays by a man who opposed America's entry into World War I. Bourne, a brilliant political commentator, ridicules the tendency of many of his fellow intellectuals to justify American intervention in progressive and moral terms. Why did the United States fight? Because, Bourne says, "War is the health of the State."

John Dos Passos. *Three Soldiers* (1921)
Three young men of very different temperaments and backgrounds meet in an army training camp and go to war. Dos Passos traces their spiritual destruction in this novel.

Erich Maria Remarque. *All Quiet on the Western Front* (1929)

The narrator and author of this novel was a German private serving in the trenches of the Western Front. Like Dos Passos, Remarque recounts the death of spirit and passion in living men under the extreme conditions of trench warfare.

Florette Henri. *Black Migration: Movement North, 1900–1920* (1975)

This is a sympathetic survey of the migration of 1.25 million blacks from the South, the "hard-luck place," to northern cities, where wages were higher and jobs more plentiful. The author discusses blacks' economic status, their leaders and goals, the development of ghettos, and the national progressives' neglect of black needs.

Ernest May. *The World War and American Isolation, 1914–1917* (1959)

A balanced study of American entrance into World War I. May has looked not only at American documents, but also at Allied and German ones. It is particularly fascinating to see what the German leaders were saying as Wilson was acting to stem unrestricted U-boat warfare.

Robert Ferrell. *Woodrow Wilson and World War I, 1917–1921* (1985)

The best one-volume study of Wilson and the war. Ferrell celebrates Wilson's soaring idealism but also criticizes his stubbornness and racial bigotry.

25★

THE TWENTIES

*Happy Adolescence
or Decade of Stress?*

1913	Henry Ford introduces the moving assembly line in his automobile plant
1916	Wilson is reelected president • The Federal Highways Act
1917	The Eighteenth Amendment provides for national Prohibition
1919	The Volstead Act enforces Prohibition • Steelworkers strike unsuccessfully for union recognition • Attorney General Palmer breaks miners' strike • Race riot in Chicago
1920	Palmer orders Department of Justice agents to jail 4,000 aliens suspected of radical activities • Warren Harding elected president • Pittsburgh station begins commercial radio broadcasting
1920–21	Postwar recession
1920–29	Unemployment and low profits beset the New England textile industry, coal mining, railroads, and agriculture; 1.2 million leave farms for cities
1921	The Sacco and Vanzetti trial • The American Plan is designed by the National Association of Manufacturers to resist unions • The Immigration Act establishes national quotas for first time
1921–23	Congress exempts farmers' cooperatives from antitrust laws and regulates middlemen's rates
1921–31	Treasury Secretary Andrew Mellon shifts the tax burden from the rich to the middle class
1922	The Fordney-McCumber Act raises tariff rates
1923	Harding dies; Calvin Coolidge becomes president • The Teapot Dome scandal
1924	Coolidge elected president • The Johnson-Reed Immigration Act establishes stricter immigration quotas
1925	Scopes trial • Ku Klux Klan membership reaches 3 million
1927	Sacco and Vanzetti executed • Charles Lindbergh makes first transatlantic solo flight • Marcus Garvey, black leader of "Back to Africa" movement, is deported
1928	Herbert Hoover elected president
1929	Southern mill owners defeat United Textile Workers' union drive • Automobile production reaches five times that of 1915 • National Origins Act further limits immigration
1930	Union membership falls to 3.6 million, down from a high of 5 million in 1920

To many of the men and women who reached adulthood after Versailles, the 1920s would seem a time of exuberance, vitality, zany creativity, and bounding prosperity. Novelist F. Scott Fitzgerald called the twenties "an age of miracles, . . . an age of art," when world leadership "passed to America." It was "the greatest gaudiest spree in history." Joseph Wood Krutch, one of the decade's bright young men, later recalled that he and his fellow journalists and critics "were . . . fundamentally optimistic, . . . gay crusaders. . . . The future was bright and the present was good fun at least." Many of the serious scholars of the day also liked the new era. "We are approaching equality of prosperity more rapidly than most people realize," declared Harvard economist Thomas N. Carver in 1925.

Contemporary judgment was not all on one side, however. The novelist Sinclair Lewis considered the nation's heart hollow and sick in the 1920s. H. L. Mencken, a persistent critic of American life, thought only a tiny minority escaped the sham and stupidity of daily life in twenties America. After months spent in Muncie, Indiana, during 1924 interviewing citizens and investigating social conditions, sociologists Robert and Helen Lynd concluded that "Middletown's" people had failed to adjust to rapidly changing technology. Change had produced serious "friction spots" that people tried to relieve with boosterism and police repression.

What were the 1920s really like? Was it an era of happy adolescence when Americans, released from puritanical restraints and blessed with newfound abundance, responded creatively and joyously to a new world? Or was it a period of friction, repression, and painful adjustment covered over with a glittering but thin veneer?

★ THE SWING TO THE RIGHT ★

One way to view the twenties is to see it as a time when diversity replaced unity. During the Progressive Era Americans were in general harmony on the big issues. They shared a fear of big business and joined the crusade to check irresponsible power and protect the "common man." World War I projected this crusading mood out to the rest of the world and reinforced the voluntary unity of the preceding decade and a half with overheated patriotism. But the war also exhausted the national zeal to right wrongs and opened ideological and cultural fissures. With the armistice the consensus came apart. Americans lost their sense of a common foe and abandoned their concern for social justice. In its place they substituted pursuit of the good life as each individual defined that term.

The Retreat to Privatism. The new mood of privatism and retreat affected politics first. By 1919 many progressive reformers were tired and disillusioned. Much of the great progressive crusade, it seemed, had ended in triviality. Walter Weyl of the *New Republic* despaired that the person "who aspired to overturn society, ends by fighting . . . for the inclusion of certain books" in a village library. Walter Lippmann, Weyl's colleague, summed up the new attitudes, and expressed his own waning political faith: "The people are tired," he wrote, "tired of noise, tired of politics, tired of inconvenience, tired of greatness, and longing for a place where the world is quiet and where all trouble seems dead leaves, and spent waves riot in doubtful dreams of dreams." At times disillusionment with the liberal past was carried to extremes. During the 1920s, the crusading muckraker Lincoln Steffens became for a time a defender of the Italian fascist dictator Benito Mussolini.

Progressivism did not entirely disappear, however. Its legacy of concern for efficiency survived in Herbert Hoover's Commerce Department, which worked to eliminate wasteful practices in private industry and government. In New York Governor Alfred E. Smith successfully continued many progressive welfare programs. And the conservation ideal, well represented by Horace Albright, superintendent of Yellowstone National Park, remained before the public's mind. In Congress during the decade some fifty representatives and senators from the Midwest and South fought big-business domination of political life. Senators George Norris and Robert La Follette continued to demand that government protect the weak from the rich and powerful. But most of this dissent lacked a universal vision, and in the case of the farm bloc, all too often degenerated into a defense of narrow agricultural interests against urban ones. These survivals were at best a pitiful remnant of the once all-pervasive progressive impulse.

Isolationism, which had been in eclipse since the 1890s, once again became the dominant public sentiment in foreign policy. Not that the country cut all ties with the rest of the world. On the contrary, during the 1920s, under Harding, Coolidge, and Hoover, the government aggressively fostered outlets for American goods and capital abroad. But few Americans believed it necessary to become involved politically in the affairs of distant countries. The United States never joined the League of Nations, and after long dickering it failed to become a member of the League's Court of International Justice. The one foray into European concerns was the Kellogg-Briand Pact of 1928 to "outlaw war," jointly initiated by Aristide Briand of France and Secretary of State Frank Kellogg and eventually signed by sixty-two nations. The pact provided no penalties for violators and was little more than a pious expression of hope.

During the 1920s American foreign-policy makers virtually ignored Europe while devoting their attention to the Western Hemisphere and the Far East. The major goal of the State Department was to promote international stability in the regions. At the beginning of the decade the United States still pursued the policies of Roosevelt and Wilson in the Caribbean, landing marines in several small Latin American countries to put down disorders and protect American lives and property. But gradually, under the leadership of two different secretaries of state, Charles Evans Hughes and Frank Kellogg, the nation backed away from intervention in Latin America. The United States would continue to defend its Latin neighbors against Old World aggression, but it would no longer assert so aggressively the right to intervene in their internal affairs.

Harding's Presidency. The swing in political mood was best expressed by Senator Warren G. Harding of Ohio. Speaking to a Boston audience early in 1920, the senator declared that the nation needed "not heroism, but healing, not nostrums but normalcy, not revolution, but restoration, not agitation but adjustment, not surgery but serenity, not the dramatic but the dispassionate, not experiment but equipoise, not submergence in international duty but sustainment in triumphant nationality." It is difficult to say precisely what Harding meant by these alliterative pairings, but the general drift was clear: The country was tired of all the excitement, commitment, and dedication of the previous decade and Americans wished to retreat to a quieter, less demanding, more private world.

And Harding was right about the public mood. Americans indeed wanted "normalcy." They particularly

This portrait catches Warren G. Harding in a dignified mood. He was a handsome man, but more likely to be disheveled than suggested here.

wanted to forget the Wilson administration, with its constant calls to virtue and international responsibility. By the end of his second term Wilson, his health broken, had lost control of his administration, and the public was treated to the gloomy sight of an embittered old man allowing affairs to drift.

Harding reflected the best and the worst of postwar America. He was amiable, kind, and neighborly, as befitted a small-town newspaper editor. But he was also provincial, seldom seeing beyond the American Midwest, and morally shoddy, bringing illegal liquor and a mistress into the White House while president. The contrast between him and the cerebral, sternly upright, and inaccessible Woodrow Wilson suited the public mood. In 1920, when the Republican National Convention deadlocked between General Leonard Wood and Governor Frank O. Lowden of Illinois, Harding carried off the nomination as the most "available" man. Against Democrats James Cox of Ohio and Franklin Roosevelt of New York, Harding and his running mate, Calvin Coolidge of Massachusetts, scored the most sweeping victory in a presidential election to that time.

Harding was an indifferent president. As he told a newspaper reporter, he could not hope to be the best president, but he would be happy if he were remembered as the best-liked. He did select for his cabinet talented men such as Charles Evans Hughes, the 1916 Republican presidential candidate, and Herbert Hoover, wartime food czar and administrator of Belgian war relief. Also to his credit was his generous release of Eugene V. Debs from prison where the Wilson administration had put him during the war. Harding successfully carried out the public mandate to reconcile government and business interests. During his administration, Washington became the friend and ally of business. The president himself supported the Fordney-McCumber Tariff (1922), which raised import duties far above those of the Underwood Tariff of 1913. He also pushed for a bill to subsidize the American merchant marine, which, now that the war was over, could not compete with the merchant fleets of other nations.

The Harding legislative record had a prominent debit side as well. Though government-business reconciliation was probably unavoidable after 1918, the administration proved far too willing to give capital its way. The president allowed Secretary of the Treasury Andrew Mellon, a Pittsburgh industrialist and one of the world's richest men, to pursue "soak-the-poor" policies. Like most businessmen and many politicians of this era, Mellon believed that the nation's well-being depended on the proper climate for business investment and incentive. Convinced that the high corporate and personal income taxes imposed in 1917 and 1918 to finance the war were hampering enterprise, he persuaded Congress to eliminate the wartime excess-profits tax and to reduce income tax rates at the upper levels while leaving those at the bottom untouched. Between 1920 and 1929 Mellon won further victories for his drive to shift more of the tax burden from high-income earners onto the backs of the middle and wage-earning classes.

Except for Hoover and Hughes, and Agriculture Secretary Henry C. Wallace, most of Harding's appointments were deplorable. The president's criteria for selecting his advisers were those of a good-natured glad-hander: The appointee had to be a good fellow, cheerful, a regular guy. The results of this loose policy were predictable. As attorney general, his old friend Harry M. Daugherty distributed government favors with a free hand. The "Ohio gang" presided over by Daugherty's close friend Jesse Smith dispensed Justice Department pardons and paroles, granted businessmen immunity from antitrust prosecution, and bestowed government appointments on any who would pay a price. To head the Veterans' Bureau, the president selected Charles R. Forbes, a man he had met on vacation and liked. Forbes sold supposedly surplus blankets, sheets, and medical supplies of veterans' hospitals for a song—and a kickback. Worst of all was Albert B. Fall, secretary of the interior. Soon after taking office, Fall got the secretary of the navy to turn over the government's naval oil reserves to the Interior Department. Then, disregarding the country's long-term interests, Fall promptly leased the Elk Hills (California) oil reserve to Edward L. Doheny of the Pan-American Petroleum Company and the Teapot Dome (Wyoming) reserves to Harry F. Sinclair. In exchange Doheny "lent" Fall $100,000 in cash, and Sinclair gave Fall's son-in-law $200,000 in government bonds.

Harding was probably unaware of the Teapot Dome frauds and the other unsavory doings of his subordinates. In subsequent months, Fall would be convicted of accepting bribes, and Forbes would be sent to prison. However, the president would never learn about these events. In June 1923 he had set out on a speaking tour of the West Coast and Alaska. In San Francisco, on the way home, he suffered a stroke and died in his hotel bed.

Coolidge Does Little. As inward and dour as Harding had been outgoing and friendly, Vice President Calvin Coolidge, who now became president, was also an exceptionally indolent man. As governor of Massachusetts he had done little to attract attention outside the state and seemed merely another local politician. Then, in September 1919, when the Boston police went on strike, leaving the city exposed to unchecked crime and chaos, Governor Coolidge captured national notice by declaring that there was "no right to strike against the public safety by anybody, anywhere, anytime." These blunt words expressed the public's own growing impatience with labor unrest and won

Calvin Coolidge was admired for his stubborn Yankee character, a relief from the shabby glad-handing of his predecessor. But he was also known for his tightfistedness: The title of this cartoon from the end of his presidency is "Mr. Coolidge refuses point-blank to leave the White House until his other rubber is found." He was also probably the laziest man ever to occupy the White House, sometimes sleeping as many as fourteen hours a day.

Coolidge the Republican vice presidential nomination the following year.

As president, Coolidge restored the public's faith in the honesty of the executive branch. He appointed two outstanding attorneys as prosecutors of the government's case against the Teapot Dome culprits, thus bypassing Daugherty, the corrupt attorney general. He soon replaced Daugherty with the distinguished former dean of the Columbia University Law School, Harlan Fiske Stone. The White House itself, hitherto the scene of hard-drinking, poker-playing cronyism, became a more dignified place with Coolidge and his charming and cultivated wife, Grace, as its occupants.

Otherwise Coolidge slept away most of his five years in office. During his term the watchword of government was "do nothing." The administration avoided new programs, balanced its budgets, and reduced the national debt. This inaction pleased business, but it ignored pressing social and physical needs of the country. The nation acquired a major new road system and hundreds of new schools, courthouses, and other public facilities; but the burden of constructing them was thrown largely on the states. Farmers

found the new president a disappointment. Hoping for substantial assistance from the government to help them out of economic difficulties brought about by the contraction of war-inflated agricultural prices, they were dismayed when Coolidge twice vetoed congressional farm assistance plans.

But to be fair, Coolidge did suit the public mood. On balance, most Americans liked what they saw: dignity in the White House and a president who knew when to let well enough alone. When Coolidge ran for president in his own right in 1924, he won by a large majority over the combined votes for La Follette on the Progressive Farmer-Labor ticket and Democrat John W. Davis, a conservative corporation attorney from New York.

★ "New Era" Prosperity ★

Republican electoral success in the twenties was assured by the country's growing prosperity. By 1925 the economy was generating a flood of commodities beyond anyone's dreams, and most Americans could see little reason to challenge the party that stood watch over the affluent New Era.

In fact, the decade opened with a brief depression. Government spending during the war had produced a boom that poured money into the pockets of millions of Americans. For a year following the armistice, good times continued and eased the return of 4 million men to the civilian economy. The bubble burst in 1920. As Europe recovered and restored its devastated fields and factories, its reliance on American exports declined. At the same time American consumers, appalled by sky-high prices, held off buying. Down came prices with a resounding crash, a collapse that particularly hurt farmers.

The hard times soon passed. By 1923 unemployment—which during our own day has hovered between 6 and 7 percent—was only about 3 percent of the labor force. Thereafter the economy surged. Growth of total GNP reached an average of 7 percent a year between 1922 and 1927. Even allowing for price changes, the income of the average American would be a third higher in 1929 than in the last prewar years. The gross national product reached heights never before attained. Total output in 1929 would be 75 percent higher than in 1909.

The Consumer Durables Revolution. The great economic expansion of the middle and late 1920s was in part stimulated by readily available credit. Interest rates remained low through the decade. Thousands of citizens could and did borrow money to invest in factories and productive machinery, buy houses, and acquire expensive

The Twenties   693

Cities had known traffic jams in the age of the horse and wagon. But they got much worse—and spread to the suburbs as well—after the automobile became supreme in the 1920s.

goods "on the installment plan." Foreigners borrowed extensively from American bankers, and the borrowed dollars soon came back to pay for imported American automobiles, electrical equipment, petroleum, wheat, and corn.

More fundamental than cheap credit in explaining the boom was a major structural change in the economy. Between 1910 and 1920 average family income reached the point where many Americans had substantial amounts of discretionary income, that is, money left over after buying necessities, such as food and shelter. For the first time, a relatively large number of consumers could afford services and goods that had always been beyond their reach. Many middle- and working-class women could now buy silk, or at least rayon, stockings and pay for the services of beauty parlors and hairdressers. Middle-class families could "eat out" more often, go to the movies, and hire household help. Most important, American consumers could now buy expensive "durables" like radios, vacuum cleaners, washing

machines, electric irons, refrigerators, and, above all, automobiles. In 1929 automobile production was five times greater than it had been fourteen years earlier, and there were over 23 million registered passenger cars. Theoretically, every American could be out taking a drive at the same moment, and on some summer Sundays it often seemed as if they all were. So extensive and important was this development in consumption pattern that many scholars consider it a "consumer durables revolution."

The total impact of these new markets was immense. Demand for consumer durables called forth billions of dollars of investment in new plants and factories, creating jobs and income for building contractors, architects, electricians, bricklayers, and a host of people directly involved in construction. The indirect effects, especially of the automobile, were also immense. Cars needed roads. Until the 1920s, despite some improvement to please the bicyclists of the 1890s, the typical American highway was a dirt track leading from the farm to the local railroad depot. Now the states, aided by matching federal outlays under the Federal Highway Act of 1916, poured billions into new, hard-surfaced, all-weather roads. At the end of the 1920s the nation had an unequaled network of 275,000 miles of asphalt and concrete intercity highways.

Investment in roads was only the beginning. To meet the demands of automobile manufacturers and users, investors directly financed steel, rubber, glass, and petroleum-producing facilities. The automobile also gave birth to a new generation of suburban communities now made accessible to city wage earners by the family car and the paved highway. Within ten years new "automobile suburbs" grew up in a ring beyond the streetcar suburbs of an earlier period.

Growing industrial efficiency also fueled the economic boom. In 1913 Henry Ford had introduced the moving assembly line in his Detroit automobile plant. During the war the need for speed to supply the fighting fronts and offset a chronic labor shortage led to increasing acceptance of mass-production techniques using standardized, interchangeable parts. Meanwhile, the principles of Frederick W. Taylor, which reduced management to a precise "science," spread to more and more industrial concerns. All these elements combined increased labor productivity dramatically. By one estimate, the amount of labor time needed for a given unit of industrial output shrank 21 percent between 1920 and 1929.

Business and Labor. Still another cause—as well as effect—of prosperity was the new public attitude toward private enterprise. Americans had far greater respect for business and business people during the 1920s than during the Progressive Era. At times their good opinion approached reverence. "The man who builds a factory builds a temple," intoned President Coolidge, and "the man who works there worships there." Henry Ford, the creator of the Model T and the person who perhaps did more than any other to bring about the consumer durables revolution, was listened to respectfully when he held forth on such matters as diet, world peace, and reincarnation. In a 1925–1926 best seller *The Man Nobody Knows*, an advertising executive could find no better way to convey the glory of Jesus than by describing him as a first-rate entrepreneur who "picked up twelve men from the bottom ranks of business and forged them into an organization that conquered the world." The clergy itself was saturated with business values. Typical sermon titles of the 1920s included "Christ: From Manger to Throne," "Public Worship Increases Your Efficiency," and "Business Success and Religion Go Together." Preachers were admonished by parishioners and church superiors to "preach the gospel and advertise."

The uncritical public support of business hurt organized labor. During the progressive years and the war, mid-

One of the fathers of modern advertising, Bruce Barton was also a glorifier of the 1920s business ethic. His best seller The Man Nobody Knows *made Jesus into a successful executive and so gave religious sanction to contemporary business practices.*

dle-class Americans had learned to accept organized labor and at times even supported it against business. Now the pendulum swung back. Without public support, the unions suffered a succession of defeats when they attempted to organize various sectors of industrial labor. In 1919, the steelworkers lost a major strike to gain union recognition from the large steel firms. In 1929, mill owners defeated the efforts of the United Textile Workers to unionize southern cotton workers.

American business mounted a vigorous campaign to roll back trade unionism. Under the 1921 American Plan businessmen were encouraged to use labor spies to ferret out and report on union activities. They were also advised to hire strikebreakers if unions tried to shut them down and to spread propaganda among their employees to discourage union organizing. Behind the plan was the National Association of Manufacturers (NAM). Formed in 1895 primarily to lobby for tariffs and other favorable industrial legislation, during the 1920s the NAM spent most of its energies to defeat trade unions.

An unfriendly federal government and biased federal courts also contributed to labor's declining fortunes. The steel strikers lost in 1919 in part because Attorney General A. Mitchell Palmer dispatched federal troops to the United States Steel plant at Gary, Indiana, to protect strikebreakers. Shortly thereafter Palmer broke a mine workers' strike.

In 1922 Attorney General Daugherty had a federal judge issue an injunction against idle railroad shopworkers, forcing them back to work. Under Chief Justice William Howard Taft, the former president, the Supreme Court gutted the provision of the Clayton Act exempting unions from antitrust prosecution and made it possible once again for employers to attack union activities as illegal restraints of trade. In these years Justice Louis D. Brandeis and Oliver Wendell Holmes, Jr., frequently upheld the unions, but their dissenting voices were seldom heeded.

In this atmosphere it is not surprising that labor unions languished. In 1920, as a result of wartime expansion, the number of organized workers had reached over 5 million; almost 20 percent of all nonagricultural workers belonged to labor unions. Soon, under the combined pressure of employers' attacks, public fear of radicalism, and an unfriendly government, union membership dropped to 3.6 million. For the remainder of the decade, it hovered around this figure, while the labor force grew rapidly. By 1930 scarcely 10 percent of nonfarm workers belonged to unions.

The Depressed Industries. The boom of 1923–1929—"Coolidge prosperity," the Republicans called it—was wide and deep enough to make Americans willing to accept the conservative, probusiness values of the day. But prosperity was by no means universal. Unemployment remained high and wages low in several chronically sick industries. Miners of soft coal experienced hard times throughout the decade. The railroad industry was depressed, and the railroad companies laid off workers. Cotton manufacturing also failed to benefit from prosperity. To survive in the face of stiff competition, many textile companies moved from New England to the southern Piedmont region, where labor and land was cheap and where they could put up new mills with the latest and most efficient equipment. New England communities whose livelihood depended on the cotton mills were devastated. And the new opportunities for southern workers hardly offset New England's loss. The southern mill communities were often squalid places. Upton Sinclair reported that at Marion, South Carolina, most mill workers' homes lacked running water or toilets. Old newspapers served as wallpaper.

The most seriously depressed of all economic sectors was the most competitive one: agriculture. In 1925 there were still 6.5 million American farms, and growers of wheat and cotton faced millions of foreign competitors as well. During the war farmers had borrowed heavily to buy more land and upgrade their equipment to take advantage of high wartime prices. When farm prices dropped 40 percent at the end of 1920, farmers were still saddled with large interest payments but now had less income. Yet intense competition for the consumer's dollar forced them to continue buying machines like tractors, which reduced their production costs but put them still further in debt.

Farmers responded to the agricultural depression in several ways. During the 1920s over 1.2 million people abandoned agriculture, most of them to go to the cities and their growing suburbs. The black migration out of the rural South became a flood, though many blacks were responding as much to new opportunities in northern manufacturing as to depressed conditions in the cotton fields. Farmers also turned to politics, as they had in the past. Except for La Follette's unsuccessful 1924 effort to create a farmer-labor alliance, however, they turned to pressure-group rather than third-party politics. The congressional farm bloc obtained legislation to ease agricultural credit, exempt farmers' cooperatives from antitrust prosecution, and regulate the rates various middlemen charged. The main difficulty, however, was low farm income. To remedy it the bloc proposed the McNary-Haugen plan. This scheme required the federal government to buy farm surpluses at prices that would guarantee growers a good income. The surpluses would then be sold abroad at the lower world price, with the loss made up from a small fee paid by each farmer. Twice the McNary-Haugen Farm Relief Bill was passed by Congress, and twice Coolidge vetoed the measure on the grounds that it favored a special group of citizens and constituted undue interference with free markets. Though the scheme never became law, it familiarized Americans with the principle of farm price supports, which a more innovative decade would enact into law.

★ OLD AND NEW AMERICA ★

During the 1920s, then, the United States was not exempt from economic difficulties and class antagonisms. Yet relatively few Americans saw anything seriously wrong with the class or economic arrangements of their society. Support for the Socialist party, a useful barometer of American economic dissatisfaction in the early twentieth century, dwindled as working- and middle-class citizens lost interest in radical action. In 1928 Norman Thomas, the Socialist party's presidential candidate, received only 267,000 votes; William Z. Foster, of the new Communist party, only 49,000.

Still, the 1920s were scarcely harmonious. Americans fought bitterly over many issues, but they were primarily social and cultural ones. As in other periods of prosperity, the questions that set citizens apart involved religion, ethnicity, race, cultural attitudes, and styles of life, rather than class or economic ideology.

Despite the confusion of voices debating the decade's values, we can identify two general divisions of opinion, separated by a deep cultural chasm. On one side were the forces of New America. New America was urban and professed to be urbane. It was also in part modernist and free-thinking in religion and was apt to be liberal or, occasionally, radical in politics. It was also culturally liberal. At the level of ordinary people, this often translated into "fun-loving" hedonism. Farther up the ladder cultural liberalism was associated with avant-garde or modernist taste in the arts. New America accepted freer sexual standards and was "wet"—that is, it considered drinking alcohol a matter better left to private conscience. On the question of drinking, though not necessarily on the other issues, New America found itself allied with urban Catholics. Old America, on the opposite side of the chasm, was small town–rural and proud of its simplicity and homeyness. In religion it was Protestant, and at its most conservative, fundamentalist. In political matters Old America tended to be conservative, and in matters of taste and morals, old-fashioned. It rejected the "looser" sexual practices of New America. As for drinking, Old America considered it either a social evil or a sin that must be restricted or actually prohibited by the authorities.

Not every person was clearly on one side of the line or the other, of course. Old America and New America were both loose clusters that at no point had any formal embodiment in a single organization. And yet, to a surprising degree, these two sets of attitudes can be found consistently ranged against each other in the passionate cultural war that raged throughout the 1920s.

Wets versus Drys. A major cultural battlefield of the twenties was Prohibition. The liquor questions had roiled American politics since before the Civil War. In the 1870s Frances Willard and a number of like-minded women had founded the Women's Christian Temperance Union (WCTU). Two decades later reformers interested in strengthening the family, business people anxious to upgrade the quality of the work force, and citizens concerned about alcoholism as a health problem organized the Anti-Saloon League. By 1915 the league and the WCTU had induced fifteen states in the South, Midwest, and Far West to prohibit the production and sale of "demon rum."

Although the state-by-state campaigns had been modestly successful, much of the country, especially the Northeast, was unlikely ever to accept Prohibition; the big cities in the industrialized states were home to too many New Americans—Catholics, worldly sophisticates, and social liberals—who considered it tyrannical for the state to dictate what a person could or could not drink. Also opposed were the brewers and distillers, loudly seconded by the saloonkeepers and proprietors of hotels and restaurants, who stood to lose business, if not their very livelihoods, if

Americans were not permitted their beer, wine, and whiskey. Not all rural Americans were drys. In the South, especially, there was a venerable tradition of illegal distilling—and consumption—of moonshine. Still the South, along with the Midwest, was the center of prohibitionist sentiment.

World War I helped the prohibitionists override their opponents and outlaw liquor nationally. Temperance organizations proclaimed that brewing and distilling consumed badly needed grain. They played on the public's concern for the morals of the young men drafted into the army and took advantage of the fact that many brewers were of German origin and hence in bad repute. In 1917 Congress passed the Eighteenth Amendment, outlawing the manufacture, sale, and transportation of intoxicating liquors one year after its adoption. In January 1920, after state confirmation, national Prohibition went into effect.

The Volstead Act of 1919 supplemented the Eighteenth Amendment by declaring any beverage containing more than 0.5 percent alcohol illegal and establishing a Prohibition Bureau for enforcing the law. But at no time during the Prohibition Era did Congress ever give the bureau enough money to do its job. Nor were city and state authorities particularly willing to spend money to enforce the federal law. Some states passed their own "baby Volstead acts," but their enforcement, too, was generally poorly funded and weak. Americans continued to drink.

Poor enforcement was as much a symptom as a cause of Americans' continuing homage to John Barleycorn. Many of those who supported Prohibition did so only for the sake of appearances or to guarantee someone else's good behavior. In a famous quip humorist Will Rogers remarked that the people of one thoroughly dry state would "hold faithful and steadfast to Prohibition as long as the voters [could] stagger to the polls." In fact, by adding an element of the forbidden to the usual attractions of drinking, Prohibition made alcohol consumption appealing to new sorts of people. In former days the "better" people seldom consumed intoxicating beverages, except a little wine at dinner. Now hard (distilled) liquor became a significant part of urban–middle class life. Alcohol consumption overall apparently declined during the 1920s and with it such diseases as cirrhosis and alcoholic psychosis as well as arrests for public drunkenness. But the "noble experiment" also replaced the tea party with the cocktail party as a social diversion and made it a mark of distinction between the urban sophisticate and the puritanical, small-town "rube."

It has been argued that whenever a community forbids a practice that many people favor, it opens the door to other forms of lawbreaking. This formula held true in the Gilded Age, when laws against prostitution, gambling, and Sunday sports led to urban police corruption; it did so again in the

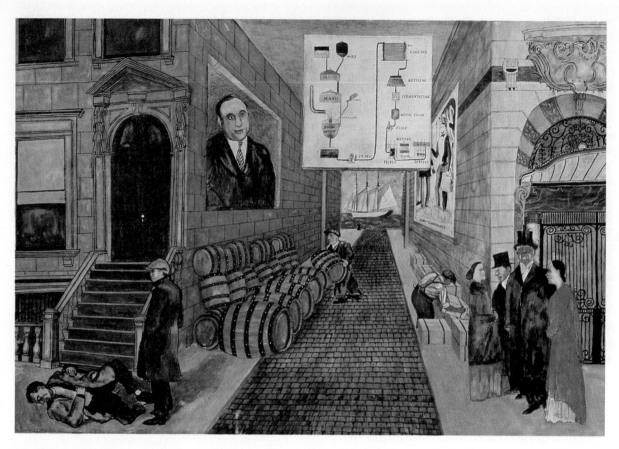

Ben Shahn, a "message" artist in the 1930s, here tells of the evils of Prohibition, including drunkenness and Al Capone. He also gets in a swipe at the rich.

1920s. The United States might forbid the manufacture and sale of intoxicants, but Canadians, Mexicans, and Europeans did not. Alcohol transported by truck across the borders or landed clandestinely by boat produced huge profits for rumrunners. Once in the country, its distribution and sale were taken over by bootleggers, who were also happy to furnish customers with "moonshine," "white lightning," "bathtub gin," and other potent—and often dangerous—native American concoctions.

Prohibition not only encouraged lawbreaking; together with the fast automobile and the Thompson submachine gun, it helped create organized crime. To accommodate the thousands of citizens who wanted alcohol and were willing to pay for it, enterprising and ruthless men organized liquor distribution networks that rivaled major legitimate business enterprises in their complexity and efficiency. Just as successful businessmen often diversified, successful bootleggers, organized into "families" under strong and brutal leaders, extended their operations into prostitution, gambling, and the "protection" racket.

The mobs brought new violence to the cities. When one tried to invade another's territory, the result was often gang warfare that left scores dead. In the 1929 St. Valentine's Day massacre, for example, six members of Bugs Moran's North Side gang were gunned down by unknown rivals in a Chicago garage while waiting for a shipment of bootleg liquor. Periodically, crusading district attorneys, goaded by the newspapers or citizens' groups, cracked down on the gangsters. But indictments and convictions were hard to get. Members of rival gangs refused to testify against their opponents; honest citizens were intimidated; officials, judges, and juries were bought off. Al Capone, the Chicago gang lord, foiled every attempt to bring him to justice and was only convicted when Eliot Ness of the U.S. Justice Department's special squad of "untouchables" found evidence against him of income tax evasion.

Eventually the connection between Prohibition and organized crime induced many Americans to change their minds about the Eighteenth Amendment. But throughout the 1920s millions of citizens continued to consider

Citizens and resident aliens suspected of having Communist sympathies board the Ellis Island Ferry. The "red scare" was closely linked with restrictions on immigration, and in California was justification for suppressing unions among Mexican and Asian workers.

Prohibition a "noble experiment" that would advance national well-being and purify the country's morals. The "drys" agitated constantly to increase appropriations for Volstead Act enforcement; the Anti-Saloon League maintained lobbyists in Washington and the state capitals to ensure that lawmakers did not relax their vigilance. No group endorsed the noble experiment as vigorously as the Protestant clergy, especially those of the conservative evangelical denominations. In many communities the weekly Sunday sermon became the occasion for denouncing the wicked wets and defending the values of Old America against its enemies. Nevertheless, by the end of the decade the dry forces were losing ground, and each day more and more people came to believe that the noble experiment had failed.

Immigration. During the war superpatriotism and suspicion of foreigners had run rampant in the United States. Tensions reached a new pitch after the armistice as Europeans sought to escape the devastation of their homelands by fleeing to the United States. European immigration soared, quadrupling between 1919 and 1920 and almost doubling again in 1921.

To Old America the new wave of foreigners seemed a serious threat. The immigrants were largely Catholic and Jewish and hence religiously alien. They were also certain

to be "wet." Neither Catholics nor Jews considered drinking sinful, and judging by those who were already here, they would oppose Prohibition.

Some of the new arrivals were also radicals—or so many Old Americans believed. Ever since the war and the Bolshevik Revolution, many traditional Americans had become deeply concerned with radicals. Soon after the armistice a wave of bombings, set by anarchists and "reds," and an epidemic of strikes had made the Bolshevik call for world revolution seem a real threat. Public fear was encouraged by Attorney General A. Mitchell Palmer, who blamed violence and the labor troubles on alien extremists. Palmer's views, his opponents believed, were influenced by his ambition for higher political office. In January 1920 Department of Justice agents rounded up 6,000 men and women, mostly eastern European aliens on suspicion of radical activities, and threw them into unsanitary, overcrowded cells. There, in violation of their civil rights, they were kept for weeks without explicit charges being placed against them. Despite Palmer's assertion that a radical uprising was imminent, the police discovered no explosives and only three handguns among the hapless radicals. Eventually the courts released most of the prisoners.

By the end of Palmer's term of office in early 1921, the "red scare" had abated as the forces of common sense took

The "Red Scare"

More than once in our history Americans have been seized by a wave of hysteria over the danger of internal subversion. One such occasion was shortly after World War I, when the success of the Bolsheviks in Russia raised the specter of radical revolution in many Western countries.

The "red scare" of 1919–1920 was fed by the chief legal officer of the United States government, Attorney General A. Mitchell Palmer. Under Palmer, the Justice Department imprisoned thousands of suspected radicals and began deportation proceedings against those who were not citizens. In the selection below Palmer justifies his actions in terms that appealed to the intolerant mood of the day.

"Like a prairie-fire, the blaze of revolution was sweeping over every American institution of law and order a year ago. It was eating its way into the homes of the American workman, its sharp tongues of revolutionary heat were licking the altars of the churches, leaping into the belfry of the school bell, crawling into the sacred corners of American homes, seeking to replace marriage vows with libertine laws, burning up the foundations of society.

"Robbery, not war, is the ideal of communism. This has been demonstrated in Russia, Germany, and America. As a foe, the anarchist is fearless of his own life, for his creed is a fanaticism that admits no respect of any other creed. . . .

"Upon these two basic certainties, first that the 'Reds' were criminal aliens, and secondly that the American

Government must prevent crime, it was decided that there could be no nice distinctions drawn between the theoretical ideals of the radicals and their actual violations of our national laws. . . .

"My information showed that communism in this country was an organization of thousands of aliens, who were direct allies of [Leon] Trotsky [a leader of the Bolshevik Revolution]. Aliens of the same misshapen caste of mind and indecencies of character . . . were making the same glittering promises of lawlessness, of criminal autocracy to Americans that they had made to the Russian peasants. . . . How the Department of Justice discovered upwards of 60,000 of these organized agitators of the Trotsky doctrine in the United States, is the confidential information upon which the Government is now sweeping the nation clean of such alien filth. . . . In my testimony before the sub-committee of the Judiciary Committee of the Senate . . . I had fully outlined the conditions threatening internal revolution in the nation that confronted us. . . .

"One of the chief incentives for the present activity of the Department of Justice against the 'Reds' has been the hope that American citizens will, themselves, become voluntary agents for us, in a vast organization for mutual defense against the sinister agitation of men and women aliens, who appear to be either in the pay or under the criminal spell of Trotsky and Lenin. . . .

". . . [W]hat will become of the United States Government if these alien radicals are permitted to carry out

the principles of the Communist Party as embodied in the so-called laws, aims and regulations? . . . There wouldn't be any such thing left. In place of the United States Government we should have the horror and terrorism of bolshevik tyranny such as is destroying Russia now. Every scrap of radical literature demands the overthrow of our existing government. All of it demands obedience to the instincts of criminal minds, that is, to the lower appetites, material and moral. The whole purpose of communism appears to be a mass formation of the criminals of the world to overthrow the decencies of private life, to usurp property that they have not earned, to disrupt the present order of life regardless of health, sex or religious rights. By a literature that promises the wildest dreams of such low aspirations, that can occur in only the criminal minds, communism distorts our social law. . . .

"These are the revolutionary tenets of Trotsky and the Communist Internationale. Their manifesto further embraces the various organizations in this country of men and women obsessed with discontent, having disorganized relations to American society. These include the I.W.W.s [Industrial Workers of the World, a radical trade union], the most radical socialists, the misguided anarchists, the agitators who oppose the limitations of unionism, the moral perverts and the hysterical neurasthenic women who abound in communism. The phraseology of their manifesto is practically the same wording as was used by the Bolsheviks for their International Communist Congress."

hold. But through the entire decade fear of Bolshevism remained a central component of antiforeign feeling among traditional Americans.

No event threw this connection into more vivid relief than the agony of Nicola Sacco and Bartolomeo Vanzetti, two Italian-born anarchists who were convicted in 1921 of having robbed and murdered a shoe factory paymaster and his guard in South Braintree, Massachusetts. To this day there is still disagreement over whether the two men were guilty of the crime. It is clear, however, that the judge who officiated at their trial and presided over a number of the review hearings was strongly prejudiced against foreigners

Ben Shahn, who supported Sacco and Vanzetti's battle for vindication, here in The Passion of Sacco and Vanzetti depicts their ultimate defeat. The man in the cap and gown is Harvard president A. Lawrence Lowell, who chaired a committee of investigation that supported the guilty decision of Judge Thayer's court.

and radicals; during their trial, Judge Webster Thayer privately called them "those anarchist bastards." And he was not alone. To many Old Americans the men were aliens, both in their "race" and their views.

The liberal community, however, rallied around the two Italian radicals. Led by Walter Lippmann and Felix Frankfurter, liberals and intellectuals turned the defense of Sacco and Vanzetti into a crusade for free speech and common justice. Meetings, petitions, lobbying, civil disobedience—all the accoutrements of modern political agitation—were deployed to drum up support for retrial or pardon of the two prisoners. The issue so deeply divided public opinion that one Sacco-Vanzetti supporter, the novelist John Dos Passos, described the opposing sides as "two nations." The liberals succeeded in getting the case reconsidered several times. But on August 22, 1927, after final appeals for clemency were rejected, both men were electrocuted. Most Americans probably applauded the result, but to the political left, in both America and around the world, their execution seemed judicial murder.

It would be unfair to dismiss the arguments for restrictions on immigration as entirely unworthy. The United States could not have continued an open door policy on immigration indefinitely. Yet clearly it was in large part ethnic bigotry and political hysteria that slammed shut the immigration door, and the restriction legislation reflected these attitudes. In 1921 Congress limited for a one-year period the number of new arrivals of each nationality to 3 percent of that group present in the country in 1910. In 1924 it passed the Johnson-Reed Immigration Act. This law limited immigration to 154,000 persons annually, assigning national quotas that strongly favored northern and western over southern and eastern Europe. Great Britain and Ireland were to have almost 45 percent of the total immigration allotment, and Germany and Scandinavia much of the rest. Italy, Poland, and Russia—the major sources of recent immigrants—were left with ludicrously small quotas. The 1921 law and the Johnson-Reed Act ended the three centuries of free European immigration that had marked American history. It also enshrined into law the prejudices of native-born Old America against persons who, by their mere presence, seemed to be altering the customs, habits, and beliefs of the United States.

Black Pride. From the perspective of Old America, one of the most disturbing changes in postwar American society was the growing assertiveness of blacks. During the war thousands of black soldiers had served their country in France, where they had encountered a racially more liberal society than their own. When they returned home, their experience only heightened long-standing resentments of segregation and bigotry. At times black veterans became targets of violence. In 1919 alone, ten were lynched in southern states, several while still in uniform. Thousands of southern blacks expressed their desire for a better life by leaving for the North. By 1930 Chicago would have over 230,000 black residents; New York, over 327,000; Philadelphia, over 219,000; and Detroit, over 120,000.

Most blacks who came north found jobs, though seldom the best-paying or most attractive ones. The typical black worker in the North during the 1920s was an unskilled factory worker or day laborer. In increasing numbers black women replaced Irish and German women as domestics in middle-class urban homes.

The transplanting of thousands of southern rural families to northern slums caused painful social problems. Black families were placed under many of the same pressures as the immigrant families of the recent past. Children, once physically close to parents, now lost touch as fathers and mothers went to work away from the home. Low income created further strains. Poverty in the northern city seemed worse at times than in the rural South.

The black migration to northern cities brought racial tensions in its wake. Many whites resented and feared the new arrivals and fought to exclude them from their neighborhoods. In Chicago racial antagonisms built during the summer of 1919 and exploded into a furious race riot in late July when a black teenager, swimming off a Lake Michigan beach that whites considered their preserve, was stoned and drowned. Within hours gangs of white and black youths were battling one another and beating innocent bystanders. For thirteen days the city was torn by riot, arson, and vandalism, with the authorities unable to stop the destruction. When the casualties were finally counted, the death toll stood at almost 40, with over 500 injured and thousands of dollars of property destroyed.

Despite the troubles and difficulties, a few blacks discovered opportunities for achievement and fame in northern cities. Sociologist and historian W. E. B. Du Bois, poet and critic James Weldon Johnson, and painter Henry Ossawa Tanner had already established themselves in American life. But the black achievements of the 1920s outshone anything that had come before. Harlem, in upper Manhattan, became a black Athens where poets, writers, painters, musicians, and intellectuals gathered from all over the country and from other parts of the world. Among the Harlem Renaissance writers were Claude McKay, a Jamaican, who wrote eloquently and bitterly about the repression of blacks; Jean Toomer, an author of realistic stories about black life; and Countee Cullen, a master of delicate lyric poetry. Most impressive of all was Langston Hughes, a poet, novelist, and short-story writer of rare power who could employ humor as well as satire and argument to defend his race and express its hopes.

The 1920s was also an era when black musicians began to attract the attention of white Americans. Although they seldom gave it a second thought, whenever a white "flapper" and her "lounge lizard" boyfriend danced the Charleston or Black Bottom, they were celebrating the vitality of black musical creativity in the 1920s. This was the decade when jazz broke out of the black community and began to find an appreciative audience around the world. Within the black community itself, great performing artists like the trumpeter Louis Armstrong, trombonist Kid Ory, and the powerful blues singer Bessie Smith were immensely popular. Their records sold millions of copies among the "cliff-dwellers" of Harlem, Chicago's South Side, and the other urban black neighborhoods.

Among blacks the combination of renewed racial pride and the problems of adjusting to the new urban environment gave rise to a Back-to-Africa movement that resembled Jewish Zionism. The leader of the movement was Marcus Garvey, a native of Jamaica in the Caribbean who came to New York in 1916 to establish an American branch of his Universal Negro Improvement Association. Garvey's appeal was particularly strong among working-class urban blacks, who did not feel at home in the NAACP, the middle-class black defense organization. Like more recent black leaders, Garvey told blacks to be proud of their race. Everything black was admirable and beautiful; and the blacker a man or woman, the better. Because America was unalterably white and racist, Garvey declared, blacks should return to Africa and there erect a new empire befitting their potential. The black middle class considered these ideas incredible; but among the urban black masses straight from the rural South, Garvey's message was electrifying. They flocked to become knights of the Nile, dukes of the Niger and Uganda, and members of the Black Eagle Flying Corps or the Universal Black Cross Nurses, under the association's auspices.

Garvey was stopped by federal officials, who accused him of mail fraud in his effort to raise funds for a black shipping line. Tried by a liberal white judge who was a member of the rival NAACP, he was sentenced to five years in jail. After being released from prison by President Coolidge, he was deported as an undesirable alien in 1927 and died in obscurity in 1940. Despite his failure, he had blazed a black separatist trail that other black leaders would follow over a generation later.

The Sexual Revolution. Sexual behavior was yet another issue that divided the two Americas. No matter how fiercely traditionalists might protest, the nation's sexual values were changing quickly, especially among the young.

Women were at the forefront of this change, yet while they were leading the revolt against traditional sexual

An outstanding figure of the Harlem Renaissance, Langston Hughes was deeply concerned about the ill treatment of black Americans by their white fellow citizens. Yet in his writing he avoided the angry voice of a later generation of black writers. "America never was America to me," he wrote in a poem whose title sums up his plea: "Let America Be America Again."

individuals, not as overgrown children or fragile dolls. In the 1920s respectable wives, mothers, and daughters began to smoke, a habit that till then had been confined to men or to women of ill repute. They also began to drink as never before. The new cocktail party introduced a feminine element to social drinking, previously an all-male preserve.

Far more shocking was the new female sexual assertiveness. For women who reached their late teens or twenties between 1919 and 1929, sex was not so obviously linked to marriage and children as it had been for their mothers. Influenced by a popularized version of Sigmund Freud's theories concerning the primacy of the sexual instinct and the emotional dangers of sexual repression, many young women began to insist that they were as entitled as men to the pleasures of physical love and the free choice of sexual partners. The incidence of premarital sex increased sharply, especially among well-educated women. Adultery also became more common. Even when young women did not "go all the way," they were far more relaxed in their social relations with men than before. Young women of respectable families "petted"; they refused to be chaperoned; they danced cheek to cheek.

The "flapper," as the liberated young woman of the 1920s was called, also insisted on greater freedom in her dress and appearance. In contrast to the "womanly" long skirt, sweeping picture hat, rounded bosom, tight natural waist, and petticoats of the past, her skirt was cut off at the knee to reveal a long stretch of silk- or rayon-stockinged leg. Her waistline was high, her bosom flattened, her underclothes minimal, her cloche hat brimless. In 1913 a typical woman's outfit consumed nineteen and a half yards of cloth. In 1925 it required a scant seven. Hair, previously grown long and worn down the back or pinned up, was cut short and "bobbed" or "shingled." To offset the tomboy effect of her dress and reassert her femininity, the flapper painted herself as respectable women never had before. "Beautician" soon became a new professional class catering to the new twenties woman.

Older people, particularly those of traditional America, predictably deplored the new trends in dress and behavior among the female young. Smoking by women was the "beginning of the end," according to one male social critic. Dr. Francis Clark of the Christian Endeavor Society denounced modern dances as "impure, polluting, corrupting, debasing." One clergyman proclaimed: "We get our [dress] styles from New York, New York from Paris, and Paris from Hell." Legislators joined the disapproving chorus. In 1921 the Utah legislature considered a bill to fine or imprison any woman whose skirts were higher than three inches above the ankle.

Notwithstanding the new, more liberated 1920s woman, families continued to be strong social units. In fact,

taboos, they were losing their political punch. Once the battle for female suffrage was won, the women's rights movement began to retreat. The League of Women Voters succeeded the National American Woman Suffrage Association; but after arousing some initial enthusiasm for its program of enlarged economic rights for women, it lost support. Alice Paul's more aggressive National Woman's party, with an equal rights amendment to the Constitution as its major goal, survived into the 1920s; but with only 8,000 members, it had little influence. Observing the dismal turnouts of women at the polls, female political activists wryly asked themselves whether the struggle to get the vote had been worth the trouble.

The feminists should not have been so hard on their sisters. They had not abandoned their challenge to the status quo. Having won the right to vote, women activists and rebels turned their attention elsewhere and became the agents of fundamental change in the social realm. Young women, especially urban, middle-class women, began to demand in ever-larger numbers that they be treated as adult

John Held, Jr., a famous 1920s illustrator, drew this book jacket for a collection of F. Scott Fitzgerald stories. Held touches on a set of famous twenties cultural icons: jazz music, flappers, social drinking by the young, and women smokers.

marriage became more popular than ever, a trend marked by the decline in the average age of marriage. These marriages, however, were often different from their predecessors. They were more apt to be "companionate," relationships in which the partners were relatively equal and felt mutual respect and regard. They also provided a better opportunity for free sexual expression by both partners than their Victorian equivalents.

The Media Assault on the Small Town.   In explaining the erosion of the traditional sexual code, moralists often pointed to the debasing effects of the media. Novels like *Flaming Youth* (1923) by Walter Fabian, *This Side of Paradise* (1920) by F. Scott Fitzgerald, and *Moon-Calf* (1920) by Floyd Dell glorified the wild pursuit of pleasure by the young. In the early part of the decade Hollywood studios put out a flood of films with such suggestive titles as *Up in Mable's Room, A Shocking Night, Sinners in Silk,* and *Her Purchase Price.* One producer described his films as replete

with "neckers, petters, white kisses, red kisses, pleasure-mad daughters, sensation-seeking mothers . . . the truth—bold, naked, sensational." Actually, compared with the explicit sexual display of recent "X-rated" films, these productions were almost prudish, but they brought down the wrath of the moralists and censors. To avoid local legal re-

One of the screen idols of the 1920s was the glamorous Gloria Swanson. This poster for one of her movies epitomizes Hollywood's exploitation of sophisticated naughtiness to sell its product.

Rural Oregonians listening to the radio in July 1925. The new wonder exposed small town Americans to a big-city media invasion the likes of which it had never encountered before.

pression, the movie industry in 1922 chose a "czar"—Warren Harding's postmaster general, Will H. Hays—to lay down guidelines of taste and decorum. The Hays Office rules ended the rash of cheap exploitation movies. Critics charged that they also lowered the intellectual and artistic level of Hollywood films to that suitable for a sheltered child of twelve. In 1930 the movie industry adopted a "production code" to guarantee that motion pictures would not offend the most prudish tastes.

The moralists undoubtedly exaggerated the social impact of the movies. But they were not entirely wrong. Popular media helped undermine the values and culture of Old America even when they did not directly attack them. Good roads and the automobile had reduced the isolation of America's rural areas and small towns. Now the movies brought to the smallest communities an image of sophisticated urban life that appealed intensely to American youth. Young people learned what passed for romantic technique among worldly men and women. "It was directly through the movies that I learned to kiss a girl on her ears, neck, and cheeks, as well as her mouth," wrote one young man. After long exposure to the fantasies of Hollywood, one small-town girl told a social researcher that her "daydreams . . . consist of clothes, ideas on furnishings, and manners." Such young people were not easily induced to accept the sexual taboos, dress customs, and social values of their communities.

Radio, too, put small-town values under serious pressure. The basic technology of radio was invented before World War I, but the medium was delayed by the war and did not come into its own until 1920, when Station KDKA in Pittsburgh began to broadcast commercially. By 1929 over 10 million American families owned receiving sets.

Radio broadcasting might have been placed under government control, as in most of Europe. Instead, it became a private industry dependent on advertising for revenue. In 1927 the federal government did step in to assign station wavelengths to avoid chaos, but it did little to compel broadcasters to serve the public. Advertisers who paid the bills and naturally wished to attract the largest audiences were far more inclined to pay for "Roxy and His Gang" or "Amos 'n Andy" than for serious discussion or the Metropolitan Opera. Commercial broadcasting surrendered an opportunity to elevate public taste, yet it exposed listeners to a high level of professionalism that did much to undermine the confidence and morale of village America. How could a community amateur hour outdo the "Ipana Troubadours"? How could the local high school dance band compete with Paul Whiteman, coming "live from New York"?

Rebel Artists.   Nor was the decade free from more direct assaults on traditional cultural values. The big cities, especially New York, were the havens of sophisticates who projected a barely disguised contempt for rural, small-town America. The bohemians of the shabby-chic apartments and refurbished town houses of Greenwich Village in lower Manhattan felt themselves escapees from small-town culture. They expressed their new freedom through hard-drinking, free sex lives, socialism, and devotion to the avant-garde in the arts and thought.

The bohemians of the twenties considered American culture hopelessly provincial. Europe, with its greater intellectual and artistic depth, seemed far more interesting. Many, including Ernest Hemingway, F. Scott Fitzgerald, Edna St. Vincent Millay, and Gertrude Stein, felt so alienated that they left the country, most to go to Paris.

Edna St. Vincent Millay

My candle burns at both ends;
It will not last the night;
But ah, my foes, and oh, my
    friends—
It gives a lovely light!

This quatrain became a rallying cry for the "flaming youth" of the 1920s, young men and women who experimented with new patterns of living, drinking, dressing, and sexual expression. Its author was Edna St. Vincent Millay, and her poem caught the essence of her own tempestuous life.

Edna St. Vincent Millay was born in Rockland on the Maine coast, on February 22, 1892. The poet's mother, Cora Buzzelle Millay, was an unconventional woman in her own right and set the stage for the drama of her daughter's life. A New Englander with literary and musical inclinations, she was determined that her three daughters, Edna, Norma, and Kathleen, be given the opportunity to fulfill themselves in a way that she was unable to. "My frustration," she declared, "was their chance." In 1900 she scorned custom by divorcing her husband, Henry, a school principal, and moved to Camden, Maine, a resort town on Penobscot Bay, where she supported her children by working as a district nurse.

When her daughters were little, Cora worked only at night so that she could be with them during the day. By the time Edna was twelve, her mother began to take on "live-in" cases, which meant she was away for days or weeks at a time. Edna was made responsible for all the household chores and her sisters' upbringing. She tried to prepare nutritious meals, but sometimes when there was no money, supper would consist of milk and the wild blueberries they had just picked. The three girls washed the dishes singing Edna's composition, "I'm the Queen of the Dishpans." At night Edna would play the piano or tell her sisters stories she made up. The three girls depended on one another and were particularly affectionate and close-knit throughout their lives.

Though often absent, when she returned, Cora worked feverishly to get her house and children in order. She baked, cooked, preserved, gardened, made new clothes or mended old ones, and caught up on the girls' progress in school and music lessons. Edna remembered her childhood as extraordinarily happy. "Meseems it never rained in those days," she wrote later. The absence of a father, however, probably contributed to Edna's later distrust of men and her doubt of love's permanence, a motif that often appeared in her poetry.

At thirteen, having skipped eighth grade, Edna entered Camden High School and immediately joined the literary magazine, which published her autobiographical essay "The Newest Freshman," as well as her poems. In her senior year she became editor. When she graduated from high school she had no intention of going to college. There was little money to pay for an education, and her mother disapproved of college for creative "genius." Instead, using her typing and shorthand skills, Edna worked part-time as a secretary for tourists and spent the rest of her time keeping house for her sisters.

In 1912 Edna entered a poem about nature and survival in a poetry contest. She came in fourth. The poem was published with the others and many readers and critics wrote in claiming that Millay's work was the best in the collection. During the following summer she read it at a party at the Whitehall Inn, a large resort hotel in Camden. One of the listeners was Caroline Dow, head of the National Training School of the Young Women's Christian Association, who was so impressed that she convinced Edna to consider college and promised to obtain the necessary financial aid.

Edna spent the winter of 1913 in New York City, preparing for her entrance into Vassar College the following fall. Although she lived in the protected environment of the National Training School, she plunged into New York's cultural life. She attended the controversial Armory Show of avantgarde art, watched Sarah Bernhardt in *Camille*, and was invited to meetings, teas, and luncheons at the Poetry Society of America. She rode the double-decker New York buses with poet Sara Teasdale and explored the city with Salomon de la Selva, a young Nicaraguan poet teaching poetry at Columbia. "Recuerdo," written many years later, commemorates her trips on the Staten Island ferry and picnics with de la Selva.

Millay entered Vassar in September 1913, four years older than most of the incoming students. Already acclaimed for her literary talents, and unusually independent and self-reliant as a result of her unsupervised childhood, she chafed at Vassar's strict rules of conduct for its young ladies. The college limited absences and cuts, required attendance at chapel, and prohibited smoking. It permitted young men on campus only on Sundays, and closely chaperoned them until they departed. "I hate this pink-and-gray college." Edna wrote to an older male friend. "They trust us with everything but men. . . . [A] man is forbidden as if he were an apple." A few months later, however, she wrote home that she was "crazy about the college." Although Edna made good use of her four years at Vassar, she broke every college rule she could. She cut classes regularly, came late to those she attended, missed chapel frequently, and smoked in a nearby cemetery. Just before her graduation she went for a car ride with some friends, and did not get back the same night. The faculty voted to suspend Millay indefinitely, forcing her to postpone her degree. This meant that she would have to miss graduation, though she had already composed the music and words for the Baccalaureate Hymn. Fortunately, the senior class circulated a petition on her behalf and the liberal president, Henry MacCracken, lifted the suspension, enabling her to graduate and attend the ceremonies.

With her B.A. in hand, Millay moved to New York in 1917, where she rented a tiny apartment in Greenwich Village. The Village had already become America's bohemia. Here lived the sculptors, the painters, the poets, the playwrights, the actors and actresses, the political radicals, and those who just wanted to escape conventional society. These people drew up their own codes of sexual and social mores. "We held the same views of literature and art," reminisced Floyd Dell, the popular Village novelist and playwright, "we agreed in hating capitalism and war. And, incidentally, of course, we agreed in disbelieving in marriage. We considered it a stupid relic of the barbaric past. . . ."

Edna was determined to find work as an actress to support her writing. She auditioned for Dell's play, *The Angel Intrudes*, then being rehearsed by the Provincetown Players, a theater group established to perform radical, controversial, and noncommercial plays. Dell was so charmed by the "slender little girl with red-gold hair" that he not only gave her that part, but others in subsequent plays. He also became the first of her many lovers and, in spite of his declarations against marriage, wanted to make his relationship with her legal and permanent.

Claiming she was "nobody's own," Millay refused on the grounds that marriage would tie her to one person. Women, she insisted, should have the right to love as freely and casually as men. She was also afraid that if she married and got involved with babies and domestic responsibilities, she would not have time for her poetry. The love affairs that came after Dell were similar in pattern. They started quickly and intensely and were followed by a period of idyllic companionship. The promising beginning ended, however, in bickering and fighting, possibly fueled by Edna's fear of being hemmed in. In this stage she cast around for a new flame, before the old had been entirely extinguished.

By 1920 every Villager knew Edna St. Vincent Millay, as the "beautiful young actress at the Provincetown" or "America's leading woman poet." She brought her popular and pretty sisters and her mother down to the Village to live with her. Not only did she continue acting, but the Provincetown Players produced her own poetic drama, *Aria da Capo*, with her sister, Norma, playing the lead. Most of her income, however, came from stories and poems that she published under the pseudonym Nancy Boyd. In 1920 she met Edmund Wilson, a rising young literary critic, who fell in love with her and got her work printed in the prestigious *Vanity Fair*. In the same year Millay published her first book of sonnets, twenty poems that expressed love from a woman's viewpoint, but without the sentimentality or romanticism that usually characterized female love poetry. *A Few Figs from Thistles*, with the "burning candle" quatrain, also appeared that year and established her as the spokesperson of the convention-flaunting postwar generation. During this period Millay was burning her own candle at both ends. She was working hard, eating irregularly, getting little sleep, drinking too much, and under emotional strain from pursuing and being pursued.

That same momentous year Edna and her family moved to Cape Cod for a summer of plain living, good eating, sea breezes, and sun. Edmund Wilson came to Truro to ask her to marry him. Edna, confessing that she was worried about money and the future, for a while considered it. In the end, however, she accepted an offer from *Vanity Fair* that took her to Europe. Millay sailed for Paris on the *Rochambeau* on January 21, 1921, forsaking, at least temporarily, her family, her theatrical career, and her importuning suitors. She joined the flood of young American literary expatriates—including Hemingway, Fitzgerald, Ezra Pound, and Gertrude Stein—who believed that Europe offered a kind of creative excitement and cultural freedom missing even from Greenwich Village.

Millay spent two years in Europe traveling and writing, but she could not escape the men who found her irresistible. Not only did she have to fend off a new flock of European lovers, but Wilson appeared in Paris to resume his marriage campaign. News reached her of both her sisters' weddings, and despite her many suitors, she felt unbearably lonely. In 1922 she received an advance for a novel and used it to bring her mother to Paris to keep her company. At this point, after years of eating poorly, Edna's stomach began to trouble her. Her mother took her to England to nurse her. There she worked on her novel, ate well, and exercised both on horseback and on foot. She still felt ill, and in the winter of 1923 she and her mother returned to the United States.

Millay was living in a small apartment in the Village when she won the Pulitzer Prize for poetry, based on *Figs*, eight new sonnets, and a long poem, "The Ballad of the Harp Weaver," on the impermanence of love. The prize made her America's foremost woman poet and she was soon a celebrity whose activities were followed at every step like a movie star's. Thousands of young Americans who read about her in the gossip columns quoted her and tried to imitate her. All this notoriety exhausted her and she continued to feel sick. With gratitude, Edna accepted the invitation of a friend to visit at her country house in Croton-on-the-Hudson.

Croton was then a sort of "suburb of Washington Square" where a group of political liberals and radicals had homes, including John Reed, Max Eastman, Stuart Chase, and Doris Stevens, a militant suffragist author. It was at a party at Stevens's that Edna was reintroduced to Eugen Boissevain, a Dutch coffee and sugar importer, whose former wife had been the beautiful Inez Milholland, a lawyer and suffragist. Boissevain, now a widower, loved the company of creative people and was himself a feminist.

He and Millay fell instantly in love, and Boissevain resolved to spend the rest of his life taking care of the poet and nurturing her creativity. "Anyone can buy and sell coffee," he declared, "but anyone cannot write poetry." At last Edna had met the right man. The newspapers had a field day with the decision of a confirmed "free spirit of romance" to wed. "Has Happiness Come to Repay/Fair Edna St. Vincent Millay?" asked the title of a five-column article in the *Chicago Times*. It was subtitled "She Married As She Lived—On a Moment's Impulse." The moment's

impulse lasted twenty-six years, until Boissevain's death in 1949.

Eugen's first concern was Edna's health. He took her to doctors to diagnose her fatigue and illness. When they decided an operation was necessary, he insisted she marry him before going to the hospital. They were married by a justice of the peace in Croton and then drove to New York for Edna's operation. Before she went into surgery she declared: "If I die now, I shall be immortal." After she recuperated, Eugen and Edna moved into a narrow brick house at 75½ Bedford Street, in the heart of the Village.

In November 1923 Millay appeared at a rally commemorating the seventy-fifth anniversary of the Senaca Falls Equal Rights Meeting. At the unveiling of a statue in honor of Mott, Anthony, and Stanton, she read "The Pioneer," a poem written for the occasion and dedicated to Inez Millholland. During the winter of 1924 Millay toured the United States, reading her poems to audiences who came to see what the "bohemian poetess" looked like and how many of her more scandalous poems she would read. When the tour was over, she and Eugen visited the Orient and Hawaii, returning to Bedford Street early in 1925.

On Bedford Street they were constantly sought after by admirers and friends. On May 1, 1925, the Ashcan Cats, a group of students from Barnard,

including future anthropologist Margaret Mead and poet Leonie Adams, brought Millay a May basket made up of moss, wild flowers, and twigs from Bronx Park. After they placed the basket on the doorstep, they shouted: "We want Edna!" and were delighted when she opened the door, dressed in a long bathrobe. She shook hands with each of them and asked their names, which she then diligently repeated. Much as she enjoyed this sort of attention and admiration, however, she began to feel that life in New York was too hectic for her to work.

In 1925 the Boissevains bought a farm in the Berkshire foothills at Austerlitz, New York, which they named "Steepletop." Here they planned to spend the rest of their lives, Millay writing and Eugen farming and landscaping as well as cooking, cleaning, and doing the laundry. The only problem was that Steepletop was not near the sea, which they both loved. To remedy this lack, in 1933 they bought Ragged Island in Casco Bay in Maine, and spent part of every year on their island. It is obvious that this woman who epitomized the frenetic Jazz Age also had a deep yearning for tranquility.

At Steepletop Edna worked on the libretto for an opera commissioned by the Metropolitan Opera Company, with music by Deems Taylor. *The King's Henchman* premiered on February 17, 1927, before an audience glittering with

---

Some who stayed, as well as a few who left, wrote novels that ridiculed and condemned the life of the American small town. Sinclair Lewis's *Main Street* (1920) recounts the story of a young woman who moves to "Gopher Prairie," a typical small town. There she resolves to reform her neighbors' tastes, values, and politics, but is instead defeated by their ignorance and materialism. Sherwood Anderson's *Winesburg, Ohio* (1919) depicts the small-mindedness, hypocrisy, and secret vice that Anderson believed afflicted provincial Americans.

American writers and intellectuals ridiculed not only the small towns but also the entire culture of Old America.

H. L. Mencken, the acid-tongued social critic of the *Baltimore Evening Sun*, took aim at almost everything in his native land and shocked traditional Americans by his irreverence, elitism, and attacks on established beliefs. Mencken reserved his sharpest barbs for the "booboisie," the absurdly crass and puritanical middle class he was convinced inhabited the country's heartland. Sinclair Lewis followed *Main Street* with *Babbitt* (1922), a novel about a businessman in a middle-sized midwestern city whose material success and irrepressible boosterism masked deep doubt about his own worth. *Babbitt* is a memorable portrait of a troubled person in a shallowly optimistic society ob-

celebrities from every field. Enthusiastic applause followed each act, and when the opera finally ended, the ovation lasted twenty minutes. "I thank you," responded Edna, "I love you all." Afterward critics called it "the best American opera we have ever heard," and one reviewer said she was the "young sovereign of the written word."

Later that year Edna went to Massachusetts to protest the impending execution of Sacco and Vanzetti, two Italian anarchists accused of robbery and murder. Like many other American intellectuals of the day, she believed that they were the victims of prejudice against both Italians and radicals. The execution was set for August 23, 1927, and Massachusetts Governor Alvan Fuller had earlier denied an appeal for clemency. On August 22 thousands of protesters began to gather on Boston Common. Millay and John Dos Passos led a demonstration of writers and poets. Millay was picked up by the police, thrown into a patrol wagon, and taken to a police station, where she was formally charged with "sauntering and loitering." Her husband arrived in time to bail her out. Later that day she made a personal appeal for clemency in an audience with Governor Fuller. At night she read a poem called "Justice Is Denied in Massachusetts" to a crowd in the shadow of Old North Church. Just before the execution at midnight, Millay wrote a letter to Fuller, which was hur-

riedly delivered to the statehouse. "There is need in Massachusetts of a great man tonight," she pleaded. "It is not yet too late for you to be that man." The electrocution took place as scheduled, and the next day Edna was fined $10 for her part in the demonstration.

Over the next ten years Edna and Eugen spent most of their time at Steepletop or Ragged Island. Edna was in poor health and probably drinking too much, but she continued to write and publish her poetry. In 1929 she was elected to the prestigious National Institute of Arts and Letters; in 1931 she received a national prize for a collection of poems. Throughout the thirties she was active at her craft and also worked on a translation from the French of Baudelaire's decadent *Flowers of Evil*. By the middle of the decade her feverish life had truly begun to catch up with her and she felt ill much of the time. In addition, although her poetry continued to sell and receive critical acclaim, reviewers began to criticize her work and her popularity diminished. In 1936 a manuscript of a play she had written was destroyed in a hotel fire on Sanibel Island. During the summer she injured the nerves of her back in an automobile accident. Her last years were full of unwelcome drama and worries. Both Edna and Eugen drank too heavily and their friends became very concerned for them.

During World War II Edna wrote nothing but propaganda poetry. She was no mere apologist for America, however, and warned that when the soldiers returned, they must beware of "the very monster which they sallied forth to conquer and quell." During the summer of 1944, weakened by years of frail health and worried about money because of her husband's financial setbacks, she had a nervous breakdown. She was confined to Doctors Hospital for a long time and could not write for two years. In August 1949 her husband died after a stroke following an operation for lung cancer. Millay started drinking relentlessly after the funeral and once again suffered a nervous collapse, spending many more months in the hospital. On her release, she resumed her writing, but she had little time left. In October 1950 she collapsed of a heart attack at Steepletop. A friend found her there the next afternoon, halfway up the stairs, a glass of wine and a page of poetry nearby. Her epitaph might have been her own beautiful lines:

Down, down, down into the
    darkness of the grave
Gently they go, the beautiful, the
    tender, the kind;
Quietly they go, the intelligent, the
    witty, the brave.
I know. But I do not approve. And I
    am not resigned.

---

sessed by gadgets and profits. Its hero's name gave a new word for conformity to the English language. Another powerful indictment of the nation's materialism was *An American Tragedy* (1925) by Theodore Dreiser, a tale of the corrupting effect of ambition for wealth and position on a weak young man.

F. Scott Fitzgerald was a more subtle denigrator of America's false values. A chisel-featured midwestern Irish-Catholic who had attended elite Princeton, Fitzgerald was alternately attracted and repelled by the life of the American upper bourgeoisie in the 1920s. He never lost his fascination for the rich and their doings, but in *The Great Gatsby*

(1925) he brilliantly depicted the dry rot at the heart of America's business civilization in the person of Jay Gatsby, a man who destroys himself in pursuit of wealth and glamor.

Another critic of American civilization was Ernest Hemingway, a representative young man of the "Lost Generation," who had fought in World War I and had returned to find "all Gods dead, all wars fought, all faiths shaken." In *The Sun Also Rises* (1926) he portrays a group of young Americans wandering through Europe seeking a substitute for the ideals of the past that now seemed hollow and insincere. In this first book and such later works as *A Farewell to Arms* (1929), in muscular, unadorned prose,

Sinclair Lewis's knowledge of small-town midwestern life came from his own childhood in Sauk Centre, Minnesota, and was deepened by a long car trip he and his wife took through the heartland on the way to San Francisco in 1916.

Hemingway depicts characters struggling against the hypocrisies of the world and forced to find heroism and authenticity in their private lives.

Drama also became a vehicle of protest against the conventionality of the decade. In Eugene O'Neill, the most important figure of the "little theater" movement, the United States produced its first playwright of international distinction. O'Neill and the stage designers, producers, and other writers connected with the Provincetown Players (at that time performing in Greenwich Village) sought to convert the American theater from mere commercial entertainment into a vehicle for expressing serious ideas. With such productions as Elmer Rice's *The Adding Machine* (1923), satirizing the emptiness of modern commercial life, and O'Neill's *Desire Under the Elms* (1924), debunking American puritanism, the little theater groups looked critically at American life.

Not all men and women of talent and genius in this decade were so negative about their world. There were those who dealt with timeless human themes, wrote hymns of praise to nature, or celebrated regional virtues. In Robert Frost, America found a poet who expressed profound love for the beauties of rural New Hampshire. Willa Cather wrote moving novels and stories about the lives of passionate, vibrant, and decent men and women living in preindustrial America. Edith Wharton continued to compose novels about upper-class New York that were both sensitive and satiric.

Among the best-selling authors of the twenties the mood, as in the past, was upbeat and unruffled. To the purveyors of popular romances, historical melodramas, and comic entertainments, the world seemed bright and wholesome—or else

thrillingly, if shallowly, wicked. Nevertheless, the more characteristic literary voice of the decade disapproved of the prevailing folkways of America, and the most original thinkers and artists were generally sharp critics of their nation.

★ CONFRONTATION ★

Old America watched with pain, frustration, and anger the influx of immigrants, the new assertiveness of blacks, the frivolous and "immoral" behavior of the young, the rise of organized crime, and the ridicule and naysaying of the novelists. America, it seemed to them, was being taken over by people with nothing but contempt for the values and beliefs that had made the nation great. The "intellectuals and liberals," declared one defender of the old ways, had "betrayed Americanism" and created "confusion in thought and opinion, a groping and hesitancy about national affairs and private life alike." Old America seized on every sign that all was not lost. The successful solo flight of Charles Lindbergh to Paris in 1927 touched off a wave of hero worship unequaled since Washington's day. "Lindy," the clean-cut, blond young American from the Midwest, demonstrated that something survived of the noble past. His achievement, noted one social critic, showed "that we are *not* rotten at the core, but morally sound and sweet and good!" Old America fought back against modernity, setting off a series of confrontations that alternately disturbed and fascinated the nation.

The Klan Reborn. At its most disruptive and aggressive, Old America's counterattack took the form of a revived Ku Klux Klan. The Klan of Reconstruction days had not long survived the federal government's attack during the 1870s. But it lived on in the South's collective memory as the heroic savior of white culture and the enemy of "ignorant" blacks and their "rascally" carpetbagger allies. This view of the Klan was reinforced and widely disseminated when, in 1905, it was incorporated into a popular historical novel, *The Clansman*, by Thomas Dixon. In 1915 the novel became the basis for D. W. Griffith's spectacular film *Birth of a Nation*.

The movie stirred the imagination of William Simmons, an Atlanta Methodist preacher, sometime salesman, and professional organizer of fraternal orders. Soon after seeing it in Atlanta, he set about establishing a new "high class order for men of intelligence and character," which he named after its Reconstruction predecessor. The war's superpatriotism and intolerance helped swell the Klan's ranks to several thousand, all dedicated to defending white Protestant America against blacks, "aliens," and dissenters. After 1918, with the help of Edward Young Clarke and Elizabeth Tyler, two skilled publicists, Simmons

Nightriders, in Virginia, out for a daytime drive with their ladies, 1921. This second incarnation of the Klan had a larger political base than the first.

capitalized on the pervasive postwar anxiety over social change to recruit members for his new organization.

The Klan represented the most extreme ideological fringe of traditional, white, native-born America. Utterly devoted to white supremacy, it held Catholics and Jews to be aliens, under obligation in one case to the pope and in the other to an international anti-Christian conspiracy. The Klan also considered itself a defender of traditional public morals. It endorsed Prohibition and denounced the illegal liquor traffic; it attacked prostitution and sexual laxity; it warned wife beaters and criminals to cease their nefarious doings; it stood for "100 percent Americanism" and opposed all forms of radical ideology.

During the 1920s the Klan became a political force in the rural parts of the nation, especially in the South, Midwest, and Far West. It even penetrated the big cities, where it appealed to white Protestants recently arrived from rural areas, who felt lost amid the social and ethnic diversity that surrounded them. The Invisible Empire entered politics in many states and cities. At one time it virtually controlled the governments of Indiana and Oregon. Denver and Dallas fell under its sway; in Denver it succeeded in defeating the reelection bid of the famous liberal judge, Ben Lindsey.

For a time it looked as if the Klan could not be stopped. By 1925 there were 3 million Klansmen, and their presence was felt almost everywhere. Daytime Klan parades of sheeted, robed men, and nighttime rallies under immense fiery crosses became common in many American communities. Some Klansmen, no doubt, were well-meaning if misguided men who sincerely believed they were upholding decency and traditional values. Others joined the Klan because it was economically or politically expedient. Yet many lawless and viciously racist people hid behind Klan regalia to commit crimes against blacks, supposed radicals or social deviants, and Jews and Catholics. Intimidation, boycotts, tar and feathering, and even murder, were all part of the Klan arsenal.

Outraged by Klan atrocities, various Catholic, Jewish, black, and liberal groups fought back. Many big-city newspapers, led by the *New York World*, denounced it. Even many conservative Protestants, frightened by its divisive influence on the nation, resisted the Klan.

This counterassault was aided by the hypocrisy of Klan leaders. Thousands of dollars poured into Klan coffers, but much of the money stuck to the fingers of Klan officials. Even more damaging were instances of sexual laxity by several prominent Klan leaders. For an organization that denounced the ethical slackness of the times and appointed itself the guardian of community morals, the financial and carnal weaknesses of its leaders were damaging blows.

By 1925 or 1926 the Klan was in retreat; by 1930 it was practically dead. But it had established a precedent, and in later years, when social tensions once more intensified, it would again become a vehicle for hate, intolerance, and mindless superpatriotism.

The Klan fight was only one of many battles pitting Old and New Americans against each other. Two others were the Scopes trial in Dayton, Tennessee, in 1925 and the presidential election of 1928.

The Scopes Trial.   The Scopes trial brought to a boil the simmering dispute between the liberal Protestantism and secularism of the big cities and the fundamentalism of Old America. Fundamentalism was not a new force in American life. Ever since the Gilded Age, conservative Protestants, as we saw in Chapter 22, had attacked Darwin's teachings and defended orthodox Christian views to check what they saw as the erosion of old-fashioned Bible religion and the growth of atheism.

Bryan (left) was an attorney
for the prosecution at the
Scopes trial, but Darrow had
him called as a defense witness to try to poke holes in his
literal interpretation of the
Bible. The Scopes trial was the
last political battle of Bryan's
long and frustrated career; he
died shortly afterward.

Education became a major battleground between the conservative fundamentalists and the liberal modernists. Conservatives held that the schools had to be kept from purveying skepticism and irreligion; modernists held that teachers had to be free to teach the latest theories of science, wherever they led. Inevitably, Darwinism and evolution became the focus of a furious battle over the schools between the Old and the New America.

The confrontation came to a head in 1925 when the Tennessee legislature passed the Butler Law, which made the teaching of Darwin's theory of evolution illegal in state-supported public schools and colleges. Many Tennesseans had had misgivings about the measure but had been afraid to oppose its passage. In the small town of Dayton, however, a young high school biology teacher named John Scopes proved more courageous. When a group of local rebels suggested casually over lemon phosphates at Robinson's Drug Store that he challenge the law, Scopes reluctantly agreed. Several days later he lectured to his class on evolution and was arrested.

The response of outsiders to Scope's arrest was startling. The venerable William Jennings Bryan volunteered to help the prosecutor protect traditional America from the theory that humanity had evolved from lower forms of life. The American Civil Liberties Union (ACLU), an organization dedicated to free speech that had been itching to challenge the Butler Law, joined the prominent liberal lawyer Clarence Darrow in helping the defense. All the major wire services set up shop in sleepy Dayton. Reporters representing the major newspapers poured into the town. So did many curiosity seekers and hundreds of local farmers. The square in front of Dayton's courthouse became a bustling county fair with hawkers of soft drinks, souvenirs, fans, books, and religious tracts everywhere.

Scope's guilt was never in question; he had violated the letter of the law. But Darrow and the ACLU were far more interested in striking a blow against what they believed to be the irrationality and ignorance of traditional America than in establishing their client's innocence. At one point Darrow declared that his purpose was to "show up Fundamentalism . . . to prevent bigots and ignoramuses from controlling the educational system of the United States." Enraged, Bryan responded that his purpose was to "protect the word of God against the greatest atheist and agnostic in the United States."

Neither side came off well in the encounter. Bryan was revealed as grossly misinformed about modern science; Darrow showed himself to be a cocky smart aleck. The trial ended in a draw. The jury found Scopes guilty and fined him $100, but the state supreme court later threw out the verdict on a technicality. The law remained on the books, and its violator went free. Still, though the results were anticlimactic, the Scopes trial provided a window into the forces contending for America's cultural soul.

The Election of 1928. Equally dramatic and more momentous for the country was the 1928 presidential election. The contestants were Secretary of Commerce Herbert Hoover and Alfred E. Smith, the progressive Democratic governor of New York.

The two men seemed complete opposites. Smith was an extrovert who loved clubhouse politics and enjoyed the company of men and women from all walks of life. Hoover

Al Smith waves to his supporters during a 1928 rally. Although he lost the election, his party would win the next five with the support of the coalition Smith assembled. Voter turnout was 30 percent higher in 1928 than in 1924.

was a painfully shy man who seldom evoked warm personal affection. Smith was a natty dresser who made his trademark the striped suit and the brown derby that had been high fashion in his youth. Hoover's clothes were almost always conservative, well cut, and black. Smith's formal education was slight, Hoover was a mining engineer, a graduate of Stanford University, and a world traveler. Most important of all, Smith's origins were urban, Irish-Catholic, and wet. Hoover was a Quaker from the tiny hamlet of West Branch, Iowa, of mixed English-German stock, who believed Prohibition was "a great social and economic experiment, noble in motive and far-reaching in purpose."

Many Americans distrusted Al Smith and what he stood for. Good government voters had reservations about his Tammany Hall affiliations. Drys deplored his stand on liquor and the Volstead Act. Snobs winced at his imperfect education. Rural voters questioned his knowledge of farm problems. Westerners doubted he cared about their section. But among traditional voters it was his Catholicism that awakened the most misgivings. Sophisticated critics charged that Catholics did not accept venerable American traditions such as the separation of church and state and did not support secular public education. At the lowest level there was the Klan's unthinking prejudice against Catholicism as a perversion of Gospel Christianity and an evil international conspiracy. One Vermonter expressed the anti-Smith position succinctly when he prayed that "the good Lord and the Southland [might] keep us safe from the rule of the Wet, Tammany, Roman Catholic Booze Gang."

In fact no Democrat could have won in 1928. However they might differ over short skirts, the pope, liquor, and immigrants, most Americans agreed that the country had never been so prosperous. During the campaign, while some Republicans attacked Smith's religion and his personal attributes, others, including the Republican nominee himself, played up the blessings of good times. "Given a chance to go forward with the policies of the last eight years," Hoover intoned in his acceptance speech, "we shall with the help of God be in sight of the day when poverty will be banished from this nation." Elect the Great Engineer, Republican campaign slogans declared, and there would be a "chicken in every pot and two cars in every garage." Good times, added to the fear of Catholicism, made the Republican ticket unbeatable in November 1928.

Nevertheless, the Democratic candidate did exceptionally well in the cities. If thousands in the South and the rural West and North voted against him because of his Catholicism, thousands of others in the northern cities voted for him for the same reason. Catholic women, especially, many of whom had not voted in the two previous presidential elections, came to the polls in record numbers in 1928 and voted Democratic. In some Irish and Italian election districts in New York City, Smith received 97 or 98 percent of the total vote! Viewing the campaign in the context of American party history from the Civil War to the present, Smith's candidacy marks a point where the urban immigrant vote, which had been loosened from its nineteenth-century Democratic moorings by World War I and Republican New Era prosperity, became more strongly fastened to the Democrats than ever before. Hoover carried 40 of the 48 states, with 444 electoral votes and over 21 million popular votes, to Smith's 87 electoral votes and 15 million popular ones. For the first time since Reconstruction, Texas, Florida, North Carolina, Tennessee, and Virginia went Republican. On the face of it, it was a Democratic disaster. In reality, it was the beginning of a great resurgence that would soon make the Democrats the party of the normal American majority.

★ CONCLUSIONS ★

Herbert Hoover took the oath of office in March 1929. In his inaugural address he told the American people that he had "no fears for the future of the country." The years ahead were "bright with hope." However wrong he proved to be, Hoover was expressing the optimism that many Americans felt, and he and they apparently had good reason for their sunny expectations.

The decade was a period of unusual achievement. For the middle class and upper levels of American wage earners, it was a breakthrough into a new affluence. It was also a time of expanding freedom for women, young people, and intellectuals, and it was a creative age in the arts.

But the decade had a darker side. It was a time of contraction for farmers and of severe material limits for the semiskilled and unskilled. But above all it was also a decade of bitter cultural and social strife. Between 1919 and 1929 an older, rural, traditional, native, fundamentalist America collided with a newer, urban, modernist, foreign-born, non-Protestant America. The Klan, immigration restriction, Prohibition, political intolerance, and organized crime were all ugly manifestations of that cultural clash.

And now a new force was about to intrude into the cultural battleground. Eight months into Hoover's term the stock market collapsed, altering the lives of millions of Americans and the course of the nation's history.

★★★★★★★ FOR FURTHER READING ★★★★★★★

Frederick Lewis Allen. *Only Yesterday: An Informal History of the 1920s* (1931)
This 1932 best-seller vividly sketches the politics, morals, fashions, heroes, business, and arts of the "bally-hoo" twenties. Allen popularized the theory that the collapse of Wilsonian idealism left Americans disillusioned and discontented, prey to Mah-Jongg, Freudianism, marathon dances, and real estate speculation in Florida.

Irving Bernstein. *The Lean Years* (1960)
A history of the American worker from 1920 to 1933. Bernstein describes the very different responses of organized and unorganized workers to change, the role played by employer associations, and the courts' use of injunctions to break strikes.

Ray Ginger. *Six Days or Forever?* Tennessee *v.* John Thomas Scopes (1958)
Ginger analyzes the cultural and political background of the Tennessee law and the subsequent "monkey trial." His sharp, witty portraits of Darrow and Bryan are entertaining, and quotations from the court proceedings make this book valuable for research as well as good general reading.

William E. Leuchtenburg. *The Perils of Prosperity, 1914–1932* (1958)
Brief and beautifully written. Leuchtenburg treats the cultural conflicts of the 1920s, industrial development, labor, morals, and the nature and limits of the decade's prosperity. He emphasizes the confrontation of the city and the small town, believing it to be the key to understanding America in these years.

Robert S. Lynd and Helen M. Lynd. *Middletown: A Study in Modern American Culture* (1929)
In this classic sociological study of Muncie, Indiana, during the 1920s, the Lynds examine the effects of mass production, the car, electricity, and advertising on attitudes toward work, leisure, education, the family, and the community.

Robert K. Murray. *Red Scare: A Study in National Hysteria, 1919–1920* (1955)
A fine study of the post–World War I Palmer raids. Murray is highly critical of the attorney general's brutal disregard of civil liberties.

William Manchester. *Disturber of the Peace: The Life of H. L. Mencken* (1951)
A state legislature once prayed for his soul. College presidents blamed him for undergraduate suicides. Mencken retorted that America needed a wave of suicides among college presidents. Superpatriots, public officials, intellectuals, reformers, and "homo boobiens"—none were safe from Mencken's gibes.

Roderick Nash. *The Nervous Generation: American Thought, 1917–1930* (1970)
Nash writes of the uncertainty and contradiction in American thinking about war, democracy, the nation, aesthetics, nature, humanity, and ethics during the 1920s. He also examines the heroes, popular literature, moral and social crusades, and religious life of the period.

Andrew Sinclair. *Prohibition: Era of Excess* (1962)
Sinclair explores the social and psychological forces behind the enactment and repeal of Prohibition. Considering the

events of those thirteen dry years, he judges Americans to be born extremists with strong compulsions to make and break laws.

Edmund Moore. *A Catholic Runs for President, 1928* (1956)
A good treatment of the Smith–Hoover contest.

Joan Hoff Wilson. *Herbert Hoover, Forgotten Progressive* (1975)
Portrays Hoover as a progressive, rather than the reactionary New Dealers believed him to be. It is not clear whether the thesis rehabilitates Hoover or diminishes progressivism.

Norman Furniss. *The Fundamentalist Controversy, 1918–1931* (1954)
Discusses the Scopes trial and much else regarding the conservative Protestant surge of the twenties.

Paula Fass. *The Damned and the Beautiful: American Youth in the 1920s* (1977)
The title is misleading; this is really a book about college youth in the twenties. But on that subject it is the last word. If you think some of your own peers are not serious enough about their education, be assured that they are dedicated scholars compared with "Betty Coed" and "Joe College" of the 1920s.

Geoffrey Perrett. *America in the Twenties: A History* (1982)
A brilliant account of a period that has often inspired brilliant writing. One of Perrett's major themes is the contrast between the Old and New America that characterized the era.

26 ★

THE NEW DEAL

Too Far or Not Far Enough?

1929	Depression begins with financial panic on Wall Street • President Hoover increases federal spending on current projects but avoids deficit spending
1930	4 million Americans are unemployed • Hawley-Smoot Tariff
1932–35	Drought makes Great Plains a "dust bowl"
1932	Congress establishes the Reconstruction Finance Corporation (RFC) • Dispersal of the Bonus Army • Franklin D. Roosevelt elected president
1933–35	First New Deal
1933	Roosevelt orders a four-day "bank holiday" • New Deal legislation and agencies: Emergency Banking Act, Agricultural Adjustment Act (AAA), National Industrial Recovery Act (NIRA), Public Works Administration (PWA), National Recovery Administration (NRA), Home Owners Loan Corporation (HOLC), Federal Emergency Relief Act, Civilian Conservation Corps (CCC), Federal Deposit Insurance Corporation (FDIC), Tennessee Valley Authority (TVA), Civil Works Administration (CWA)
1934	Securities and Exchange Commission established • Conservative Democrats and wealthy Republicans form the anti-Roosevelt Liberty League
1935–38	Second New Deal
1935	Legislation: Emergency Relief Act, National Labor Relations (Wagner) Act, Social Security Act, Public Utility Holding Company Act, Revenue (Wealth Tax) Act, Banking Act, Frazier-Lemke Farm Mortgage Moratorium Act, Resettlement Administration Act, Rural Electrification Act • The Supreme Court strikes down the NIRA • Committee on Industrial Organizations (CIO) formed • The Supreme Court invalidates the AAA • Huey Long is assassinated • Benny Goodman organizes his own orchestra
1936	Roosevelt reelected president • Soil Conservation and Domestic Allotment Act
1937	Roosevelt's attempt to "pack" the Supreme Court • General Motors Corporation and United States Steel recognize unions as the bargaining agents for their employees • Chicago police kill ten while breaking up a strike against Republic Steel • The Farm Security Administration established • Wagner-Steagall Housing Act
1938	Agricultural Adjustment Act • Food, Drug, and Cosmetic Act • Fair Labor Standards Act

The New Deal, that wide-ranging political response to the massive social and economic crisis of the 1930s, has always been controversial. Contemporary conservatives called it "socialistic" and denounced it for destroying fundamental American liberties. Contemporary radicals condemned it for preserving America's capitalist institutions and the inequalities of wealth and power that went with them. Critics from both ends of the political spectrum continue to attack it today. According to several conservative scholars, the New Deal delayed recovery from the Great Depression by frightening the business class that might have invested and restored economic momentum. At the other end of the political scale, historian Barton J. Bernstein notes that the "liberal reformers of the New Deal did not transform the American system; they conserved the protected American corporate capitalism. . . . There was no significant redistribution of power in American society, only limited recognition of other organized groups, seldom of unorganized people."

But the New Deal wins the great middle. A majority of scholars and well-informed laypeople today probably agree that Franklin Roosevelt and his policies saved capitalism by pruning its excesses and made possible its later record of beneficial economic growth without extreme fluctuations. The New Deal in its day, they would say, also prevented much human suffering and over the years helped moderate the enormous disparities of wealth and power.

Was the New Deal's role in American life positive or negative? Did the New Deal fall short of the goals it set for itself? Were its goals too limited? Did it really create as many problems for our society as it solved? To answer these questions we must look at the difficulties the nation faced during the Great Depression, and for this purpose we must turn back to the closing months of the New Era.

★ BOOM AND BUST ★

The year 1929 was a dazzling one for American capitalism. By almost every measure the economy had never performed so well. Automobile production reached almost 4.5 million units, 800,000 more than in 1928; steel production climbed to 5 million tons above the year before. Manufacturing output as a whole reached an all-time peak. Late in the summer the stock market soared to a historic high, with shares in American corporations selling for prices never before attained. When economists got around to figuring out the gross national product for 1929, they would put it at over $104 billion, or $857 for every man, woman, and child—25 percent higher than a decade before.

Life for millions of Americans seemed good as the 1920s drew to a close. Over 20 million of the nation's 30 million families had automobiles. Radios were prized possessions in over 10 million households; many people were beginning to acquire electric washing machines and refrigerators. Almost half of all American families owned their own homes, and over two-thirds had electric power—twice the proportion of a decade previously. Never before had so many enjoyed so much. Despite some persistent dark spots, few Americans doubted that 1929 was a charmed year.

Abruptly, the spell broke. In the weeks following Labor Day the stock market, which had been rising at an unprecedented rate for three years, plunged and plunged again. On Thursday, October 24, a record-breaking 13 million shares changed hands at prices so sharply deflated that $9 billion in investments were wiped out in that single day. Thousands of investors and speculators scrambled to sell rapidly falling stocks for whatever they could get. The New York banking houses, led by J. P. Morgan, Jr., tried to stem the tide as Morgan's father had done in the panic of 1907, but this time the effort failed. On October 29, 16 million shares were sold, with prices down an average of 40 points.

For the next two and a half years the 1920s "bull market" deflated. At times there were rallies, but they were short-lived. By July 1932 stock prices had reached bottom at a fraction of their former value and would recover only very slowly. During the long slide over $70 billion of investments and paper wealth were wiped out, $616 for every person in the country!

Causes of the Depression.   Americans often blamed the stock market crash for their plight. The blame was not entirely misplaced. The Crash impaired for years the ability of American business and industry to raise money by borrowing from banks or selling stock. If the blind optimism of stock market investors during the New Era had helped cause the Crash, the equally blind pessimism following the Crash helped prolong the Great Depression.

The stock market crash, however, was only the most visible cause of economic collapse. The 1920s had been a time of economic growth, but that growth had depended on an unstable balance of factors. New markets for automobiles, radios, refrigerators, and other durables had induced businesses to invest vast sums to expand production. In addition, governments had poured more billions into roads, bridges, and other capital improvements, while private citizens, now able to rely on the family automobile for quick transportation to city jobs, bought homes in the burgeoning suburbs. Pushed by the consumer durables revolution, construction, steel, cement, petroleum, rubber, and

October 29, 1929, the Day of Judgment—or so it seemed. The financial structure that had supported the New Era's prosperity collapsed, generating a tidal wave of misfortune that affected every American.

scores of other industries boomed, creating jobs and income for millions of urban Americans. Most people came to see the new affluence as normal and to assume that it would never end. President Hoover shared the prevailing confidence that somehow America had discovered the formula for permanent growth and prosperity.

Both the president and the people were wrong. Few contemporaries discerned that the boom was sustained by the special circumstances of the consumer durables revolution and could not outlast it. And the end of the revolution was inevitable. With 50 percent of the nation's income going to only 20 percent of its families, the market for expensive consumer durables, though wider than in the past, was strictly limited. When all those who could afford the new car or the new radio had satisfied their needs, demand had to decline. By 1927 or 1928 these effects were already being felt and manufacturers were beginning to cut production and lay off workers. A spiral was now set in motion: Fewer new orders for goods led to fewer jobs; the unemployed in turn could not buy what the factories produced and so orders further declined.

This pattern was soon evident in many enterprises. Building starts, the most sensitive barometer of economic conditions, leveled off in 1926 and dropped sharply in 1929. Expansion in the public sector also reached its limits: The new road network was largely complete, and the need for new highways became less urgent. State highway departments were soon investing less and hiring fewer people. Over all, the massive push to invest, which had fed the economy since World War I, had lost its momentum.

The international economy also contributed to the decline. The burdens of war debts and tariff barriers were becoming harder and harder to bear as the decade neared its end. England and France had emerged from World War I owing enormous debts to America. Their foreign investments drastically reduced, they no longer received the interest and dividends that had formerly enabled them to buy American goods. Lower American tariff barriers might have permitted them to sell more in the United States, in turn allowing them to buy American commodities and pay their American debts. But, as we have seen, the United States raised tariffs during the 1920s, a policy that made it increasingly difficult for the British, French, and other Europeans to sell their goods in America, buy American exports, and pay their American creditors.

Britain and France saw German reparations as the way out of their dilemma. If the Germans could be compelled to pay the $33 billion indemnity set by the postwar Allied Reparations Commission, all would be well: German reparations could then be used to buy American coal, wheat, steel, and automobiles. The sum was unrealistic. The Germans could not pay it, and in two successive stages (the Dawes Plan, 1924, and the Young Plan, 1929) the payments were pared down and stretched out. For a while large-scale lending by American banks took up the remaining slack, enabling the former Allies to buy American goods on credit. By 1928, however, the bankers were beginning to have second thoughts about foreign loans. The whole shaky structure of foreign trade was now in jeopardy.

Finally, the Wall Street bull market was itself a cause of serious instability in the 1920s economy. During the early 1920s many corporation stocks sold at low prices relative to the dividends they yielded; that is, whatever the price of the stock, each dollar invested repaid healthy dividends. A few years of good returns brought a flood of investors into the market, and the huge sums of money they invested helped finance spectacular industrial growth. After 1926, however, many investments were on paper only; that is, many of the investors were speculators gambling heavily with borrowed money. Under the rules of the day, stock could be bought with as little as 10 percent down, a practice known as buying "on margin." The rest of the money

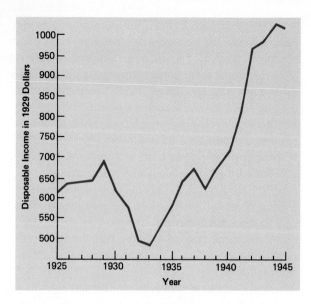

Per capita disposable income, 1925–1945. *Source: Historical Statistics of the United States, Colonial Times to 1970.*

needed to make up the purchase price could be borrowed from a broker, who in turn would borrow it from a banker. This system put billions of borrowed money into the market and drove up stock prices, producing a glut of paper wealth. Speculators paid outrageous prices and borrowed beyond their ability to repay on the blithe assumption that prices would keep going up and rescue them. If stock prices were to fall, however, all the players in the system—speculators, brokers, and bankers—would be locked together

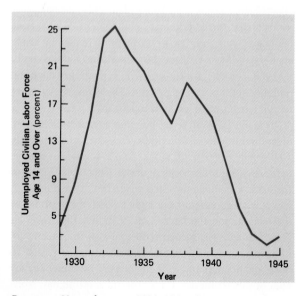

Percentage Unemployment, 1929–1945. *Source: Historical Statistics of the United States, Colonial Times to 1970.*

and fall together. The speculators, unable to pay back the loans from the brokers, would default. When enough speculators defaulted, brokers would be unable to pay off the bank loans, and would also default. When enough speculators defaulted, the banks would be in trouble. The chain of failures would depress stock prices even more, further reducing the value of holdings and the ability to avoid default all along the chain.

The Great Depression. The collapse of the stock market when business was already weakened by declining consumer demand and a shaky international economy brought the entire economy down with a resounding crash. Credit became tight, and interest rates soared. The Federal Reserve Board, which could have eased the situation by lowering the interest rate charged to member banks, took no action to shore up the banking system. To save themselves, banks cut off credit to businesses and foreign borrowers. All trade slowed, but foreign commerce, which had been sustained largely by constant infusions of American credit, was hit especially hard.

The collapse of the world's principal source of credit upset the entire international system. The trading nations had used a currency exchange system pegged to the price of gold, which now collapsed. As the gold standard fell apart, values of goods and currencies fluctuated wildly, making people millionaires one minute and paupers the next. To protect their economies from the chaos in exchange rates, nations resorted to strict trade barriers and tariffs. Under the double blow of trade restrictions and collapse of the currency exchange system, international trade declined to a trickle. By mid-1930 the Great Depression had been exported from America and was virtually worldwide.

Now came the turn of the commercial banks. Frightened depositors rushed to withdraw their savings. Bank after bank failed as the "runs" forced even solvent institutions into bankruptcy. In November 1930, a total of 256 banks with deposits of $180 million closed their doors. Most severely affected were the financial institutions of the farm areas where bank failures had been numerous even in the 1920s.

The shock to general investor confidence overshadowed all other effects. The Crash badly frightened the people who made the economy's major decisions to invest. Why take a chance when things looked so grim? By 1932 gross private domestic investment had sunk to one-ninth the 1929 amount.

Consumers, too, turned timid after the Crash and ceased to make their indispensable contribution to the economy. By wiping out billions of dollars in assets, the Crash instantly reduced the expenditures of the thousands of upper-income families headed by men and women who

The Great Crash and ensuing Great Depression spared neither working-class nor middle-class people, though clearly the former suffered more absolute deprivation. The Depression's near universality made it an exceptionally potent political force.

had bought stock. Though not numerous enough to make a difference to farmers or to manufacturers of soap, shoes, and hairpins, their belt tightening cut sharply into the sale of luxury automobiles, golf clubs, and expensive restaurant dinners. The Crash also had a disastrous effect on ordinary consumers. Few were directly hit by the market collapse, but their confidence in the economy rapidly waned. Here the nation's very affluence hurt it. In former times consumers had had little choice about whether to spend or not because almost all of their income went for necessities. But in this rich era of mass markets for expensive durables and other former luxuries, they could cut expenditures—and did. People put off vacation trips and decided not to buy new radios, cars, or refrigerators; all consumer durables sales plummeted. The most durable of all durable goods—houses—could be deferred the longest, and new housing sales dropped off disastrously.

The economic retreat quickly became a rout. Deferring purchases and investment at first was largely voluntary, but it soon became inescapable. As unsold inventories built up in stores and showrooms, retailers reduced their orders to manufacturers and suppliers. They in turn lowered their in-vestment goals, cut back on production, slashed wages, and fired employees. Unemployment shot up. By the end of 1930 over 4 million men and women were out of work. Many more were working part-time or for sharply reduced wages. Families whose breadwinners lost their jobs cut their budgets to the bone. Total demand now declined still further, establishing a vicious downward spiral of economic deflation.

If commodity prices had fallen as far and as fast as consumer income, goods might have continued to move, and workers might have kept their jobs. Prices did fall in certain areas of the economy. Where there were many competitive producers, most notably in agriculture, prices plummeted. Between 1929 and 1933 agricultural prices dropped 56 percent, but the output of farm products and the number of farmers and farm laborers remained almost the same. The plunge in the price of produce was unfortunate for farmers, but it kept farm production and farm employment high and prevented widespread hunger. In segments of the economy where there were relatively few producers and competition was limited, however, prices stayed high. Automobiles remained expensive—about $600 for the average vehicle both in 1929 and in 1932. Because most people could not buy cars, production—and employment—fell. By 1932 automobile output had dropped to 25 percent of the 1929 figure, and the number of automobile workers had declined to under 40 percent of the 1929 total.

The Human Toll. The Great Depression was a human disaster of colossal proportions. Despair spread through every part of the country and penetrated every walk of life. By the winter of 1932–1933 a quarter of those Americans who wanted work were without jobs. The situation of blue-collar wage earners, who had few resources to cushion them against adversity, was the worst. Millions of factory hands and construction workers tramped the streets looking for work or waited in lines for handouts from charity organizations. But hard times did not respect class lines. Small business owners went bankrupt as their customers dwindled. Lawyers had fewer clients, and the clients they retained could not afford to pay high fees. Doctors and dentists discovered that many of their patients put eating before health care. The sharp decline in building and construction left architects without clients.

Private agencies were not equipped to handle the thousands of destitute families who applied for help. Nor could state and local governments provide relief. During the Depression three states and hundreds of municipalities went bankrupt trying to cope with widespread want at a time when tax revenues were declining. Few, if any, Americans died of starvation. But many went hungry, and doctors saw thousands of cases of malnutrition.

Many artists of the 1930s found the Depression a fascinating subject. Here, in Shoeshine, *George Grosz sums up the era's economic misery in the person of a huddled shoeshine boy.*

What did the unemployed and their families do to survive? Most blue-collar Americans had little to fall back on. When a family's savings had been exhausted, day-to-day survival became precarious. Men and women borrowed money from pawnbrokers, from friends, or against insurance policies, until all sources dried up. In past times Americans had often dealt with their problems by abandoning them. And so it was again. Many young men and women took to the road, traveling from hobo jungle to hobo jungle by freight train, dodging railroad police, begging, or working at ill-paying odd jobs. So many were riding the rails by 1933 that railroad officials decided to accept the inevitable and told their guards to look the other way. Some of the unemployed tried setting up small undercapitalized stores. Others sold apples on the streets. These pathetic efforts became symbols of pluck and determination, but they seldom succeeded.

One of the most urgent problems of the unemployed and their families was housing. Without income, a family could not pay the rent or the mortgage. A common sight on city streets was the dispossessed family sitting disconsolately on their streetside furniture, not knowing where to go. (A joke that made the rounds in 1933 was a version of an old classic. Bill asks Mike: "Who was that lady I saw you with last night at the sidewalk café?" Mike replies: "That was no lady; that was my wife. And that was no sidewalk café; that was my apartment furniture.") Thousands of Americans moved in with friends or relatives. On the outskirts of every large city the unemployed and their families moved into squatters' settlements thrown together from loose boards, packing crates, sheet tin, and cardboard. In Oakland, California, jobless men set up housekeeping in surplus sewer pipes. In western Pennsylvania unemployed steelworkers kept warm by sleeping in the big coke ovens of the idle steel plants. For the first time migration from country to city was reversed as young men and women returned in droves to the rural homestead.

Among the most unfortunate victims of the Great Depression were many of the nation's 12.5 million blacks. In the North, where black Americans had only recently

Private charities tried to relieve the effects of poverty and unemployment during the 1930s, but were overwhelmed by conditions. Here black children in Harlem line up to receive food from a Catholic agency.

found a toehold in industry, they were often the first to lose their jobs when employers cut back their work force. Besides, construction, bituminous coal mining, and domestic service, which provided employment for large numbers of blacks, were among the occupations that were particularly depressed. In April 1931, some 35 percent of the black workers in Philadelphia were unemployed, compared with 24 percent of white wage earners.

In the South the lot of the black population was even bleaker. The economic crisis provided a new basis for white bigotry. In Houston black and Mexican-American relief applicants were regularly turned down by officials. In Atlanta, in 1930, a group of Klanlike "Black Shirts" paraded downtown carrying banners inscribed "Niggers, back to the cotton fields—city jobs are for white folks." Things were no better in the cotton fields. In 1931 the price of cotton slumped to 4.6 cents a pound, the lowest since 1894. Producers of cotton, farmers and sharecroppers, black and white alike, suffered severely. Early that year a Red Cross worker in a rural cotton-growing area of Arkansas found that more than half the homes he visited did not have enough food to last forty-eight hours.

Life Goes On. Yet a majority of Americans continued to work and to provide their families with the necessities of life. They even managed to enjoy themselves. During the winter of 1929–1930 a craze for miniature golf took hold, and by the summer of 1930 thousands of Americans were tapping golf balls through drainpipe tunnels and over little bridges. By 1930 radio had produced its first superstars: Freeman F. Gosden and Charles J. Correll, both whites, who amused listeners with their comic stereotypes of the ignorant but cunning black characters Amos 'n Andy. The theater flourished as well. In the fall of 1931 the big Broadway hit was *Of Thee I Sing*, a musical spoof of American politics. Equally popular that season was George White's *Scandals*, featuring Rudy Vallee singing "Life Is Just a Bowl of Cherries."

Through the worst years of the Depression, Hollywood continued to prosper. During the 1930s, 85 million Americans went to the nation's 17,000 movie houses each week. While the country lived on short rations, movie moguls like Louis B. Mayer and Sam Goldwyn and stars like Carole Lombard, Greta Garbo, Clark Gable, Joan Crawford, and James Cagney earned thousands of dollars a week. The public did not seem to mind Hollywood's affluence. The movies provided an escape from the drabness and worries of their lives, and they were grateful.

Reading was another form of escape during the Great Depression. Publishers were equal to the challenge of hard times. Using the high-speed presses employed by magazines, along with glued bindings and paper covers, they reduced the price of reprints to as little as a quarter. Before long the public was buying millions of "pocketbooks" and other paperbound volumes by such entertaining writers as Hervey Allen (*Anthony Adverse*, 1933), Pearl S. Buck (*The Good Earth*, 1931), Edna Ferber (*Show Boat*, 1936), James Hilton (*Lost Horizon*, 1933, and *Goodbye, Mr. Chips*, 1934), and the biggest best-seller of all, Margaret Mitchell, whose "moonlight and magnolias" epic of the Old South, *Gone with the Wind* (1936), sold 8 million copies by the time of her death. Paralleling the paperback revolution was the picture magazine revolution ushered in by *Life* magazine in 1936. Mixing brilliant photography with the breezy verbal style developed by Henry Luce and his *Time* editors, *Life* and its imitators provided the American public with light-hearted glimpses of culture, customs, and costume, as well as grimmer "photo-essays" of the world in distress.

Popular music, too, helped people, especially the young, get through the bleak days. New Orleans–type jazz had gone into eclipse with the end of good times, though here and there black, and a few white, musicians continued to play Dixieland or Chicago-style jazz in small ensembles. By the early 1930s black arrangers, including Edward ("Duke") Ellington, Fletcher Henderson, and Sy Oliver, had adapted jazz to the big-band format. Then, in 1935, clarinetist Benny Goodman created a sensation with a new sort of big-band dance music, "swing." Thousands were soon dancing the Lindy Hop, the Suzie-Q, and the Big Apple to the arrangements of Tommy Dorsey, Glenn Miller, and Count Basie, as well as the King of Swing himself. In 1938, swing became a part of "culture" when the Goodman band gave a sensational concert at New York's Carnegie Hall.

★ HOOVER AND THE DEPRESSION ★

Though a few Americans prospered and others managed to squeeze some pleasure from life, millions found their lives contracting with each passing day.

As we view the era from the present, the reaction of the federal government seems limited and slow. But we must recognize that it took months before anyone could assess how serious the damage had been, and, in any case, there was a very strong presumption that self-righting forces would soon assert themselves. Besides, orthodox economic doctrine held that government could, or should, play only a limited role in financial crises.

Federal Inaction. President Herbert Hoover was one of the more ardent believers in the necessity for business to regulate itself. His rigid adherence to the ideas of rugged individualism was perhaps appropriate to the prosperous twenties, but it now proved disastrous. Republican orthodoxy held that periodic depressions were natural and inevitable and represented a sort of cathartic for the economy. Secretary of the Treasury Andrew Mellon proposed doing nothing whatever and allowing the downturn to bottom out by itself. "Liquidate labor," Mellon advised, "liquidate the farmers, liquidate real estate. It will purge the rottenness out of the system. . . . Values will be adjusted and enterprising people will pick up the wreck from less competent people."

Hoover was never as committed to inaction as his treasury secretary. In November 1929 he called a series of conferences of business and labor leaders and local government officials to consider the economic crisis. At his urging they pledged to maintain wages, desist from strikes, and continue the existing level of investment and local public works spending. Simultaneously, because he was convinced that the collapse of confidence was an important component of the slump, Hoover went to great pains to project optimism. The "fundamental business of the country," he told the public several days after the Crash, "is on a sound and prosperous basis." What the country needed, he later declared, was a "big laugh" or a "great poem" to make people "forget their troubles and the Depression." The collapse was certain to be short-lived if everyone retained faith in the system and resolved to buy and invest as in the past.

As the dreary months passed, each worse than the preceding, voluntary efforts to maintain spending, employment, and investment levels became inadequate. The obvious solution was a public works program to get the unemployed back on the job and put money into the hands of consumers and investors. Hoover did increase the federal government's planned outlays for public projects, and because federal tax revenues had plummeted, he could not avoid a deficit in doing so. But he steadfastly refused to allow the government to adopt a deliberate policy of borrowing money to finance massive public works. In his view, such a procedure would force it into competition with weakened private industry for limited investment funds and injure the economy further. Actually, by 1930 or 1931 business confidence was so thoroughly riddled that virtually no business person wanted to borrow; there was no need for the president to worry about the government outbidding private industry for limited capital.

Hoover was not alone in his failure to perceive the appropriate policies for a time of mass unemployment and underused capital equipment. Few people during the Depression understood that the only cure for the collapse of private business expectations was for the federal government to stimulate the economy by deficit spending—

spending beyond what it took in in taxes. The rigid belief in a balanced budget, shared by Republicans and Democrats alike, had to die a bitter death before the government would use deficit spending to aid economic recovery.

Hoover was even more reluctant to use federal funds to relieve human misery than to stimulate recovery. The president argued that it was dangerous to make people dependent on federal handouts. For a man whose early public reputation was earned as relief administrator for Europe during and immediately following World War I, Hoover seemed strangely insensitive to his fellow citizens' misfortunes. Aid to the unemployed, he believed, must come from voluntary organizations and local governments, not from Washington. Hoover's view disregarded realities. Private religious and charitable organizations could not come close to meeting the needs of the vast army of the unemployed; cities, counties, and states found themselves overwhelmed by demands on their resources. Only the federal government could deal with a disaster that deprived millions of the nation's families of their fundamental means of support.

Hoover's Programs. The president never endorsed direct federal outlays for relief, but gradually he came to see that something more than private talks with business and labor leaders, sprinkled with public smiles, was necessary to check the economic slide. As he considered the causes of the nation's plight, Hoover concluded that they originated abroad. To help restore the international economy, in 1931 he proposed a one-year moratorium on German reparations and the intergovernmental debts of the former Allies.

This effort to restore international trade was a wise, if limited, move. But Hoover was inconsistent. The previous year, against the advice of the country's best economists, he had accepted a traditional Republican solution to economic difficulties and signed the Hawley-Smoot Tariff Act, which raised the already high American protective wall and further weakened international trade.

By late 1931 Hoover finally recognized that the federal government must intervene directly in the domestic economy to get the country moving again. In his State of the Union message to Congress, he proposed establishing a Reconstruction Finance Corporation (RFC) to lend federal funds to business on the theory that the loans would check the economic slide, restore confidence, and increase employment. Congress created the RFC in 1932 and gave it a $500 million appropriation with authority to raise $1.5 billion more by borrowing. These funds it could lend to faltering banks, railroads, savings and loan associations, and industrial firms. In addition, the president signed into law measures providing new capital to federal land banks, liberalizing the credit-granting powers of the Federal Reserve

System, and establishing home loan banks to refinance home mortgages.

Hoover's liberal opponents labeled his program, particularly the RFC, a "breadline for big business" that only indirectly touched the plight of ordinary men and women. To be fair to Hoover, his moves—though tardy and insufficient—were steps in the right direction. But Hoover got little credit from the public for his vigorous actions in the last two years of his administration. The president lacked the popular touch. Characteristically, through the worst years of his term, he continued to wear formal clothes when dining at the White House, even when he and his wife were alone. As the economic clouds became ever darker, the president's popularity plummeted. Soon people were referring to empty pockets turned inside out as "Hoover flags," shantytowns on the outskirts of cities as "Hoovervilles," and newspapers wrapped around the body for warmth as "Hoover blankets."

The Bonus Expeditionary Force. Most difficult to forgive, in the public's estimate, was the president's treatment of the Bonus Army. World War I veterans were among the "forgotten men" of the Depression. In 1924 Congress had authorized a "delayed bonus" for veterans, to be paid in 1945. In 1931, over Hoover's veto, Congress liberalized the law to allow veterans to borrow immediately up to 50 percent of the amount ultimately due them. This money was gratefully accepted but quickly spent, and veterans, like most Americans, continued to suffer from the winding down of the economy. "Why wait until 1945 for the rest of the bonus?" veterans wondered. In June 1932 several thousand former doughboys, calling themselves the Bonus Expeditionary Force (BEF), arrived in Washington, D.C., to demand the remainder of the bonus immediately.

Most of the veterans camped out in tents and shacks at Anacostia Flats, a vacant area on the edge of the city. They asked to see the president, but he refused to have anything to do with them. When Congress rejected a new bonus bill, 15,000 veterans resolved to "stay till 1945." The men, many of whom had brought their wives and children, were orderly and sober. There were a few radicals and troublemakers among them, but most were prepared to wait patiently for Congress to act. As the congressional session drew to a close, however, tensions mounted. Hoover was reluctant to involve the federal government in what he considered a local police problem; but when the District commissioners asked for federal help, the president called in the army.

The troops evicted the veterans from some abandoned buildings in the city and then, despite Hoover's orders not to cross the river to the main BEF encampment, General Douglas MacArthur ordered his men onto Anacostia Flats. Firing tear gas in every direction, the soldiers put the tents and the shanties to the torch and drove the BEF out of the camp with bayonets and sabers. Over a hundred people were injured in the melee, and two infants died of tear gas inhalation.

The scene at Anacostia shocked many Americans. Men who had served their nation well in 1917–1918 had been treated like dangerous revolutionaries. Hoover's standing, already low, dropped still further. The president was not responsible for ordering the attack; but he had refused to see the BEF leaders and he shared the blame for the outcome.

Hoover Defeated.　The Bonus Army was not the only episode of social confrontation during the first years of the Depression. Desperate midwestern farmers organized a "farm holiday" movement during mid-1932 that stopped shipments of food to cities, halted the forced sale of farms whose impoverished owners had fallen behind in tax payments, and dumped underpriced milk into gutters. In parts of the country hungry men looted stores and food delivery trucks. Early 1932 saw 3,000 unemployed men march on Henry Ford's River Rouge plant to demand jobs. Police used tear gas to stop them, and then opened fire with revolvers and a machine gun, killing four.

Still more ominous to conservatives was rising public interest in socialism as a solution to the crisis. Big business, which had claimed so much credit for good times, now bore the brunt of the public's wrath when times turned bad, and angry voices began to denounce capitalism as a cruel fraud against humanity. In September 1932 the Marxist journal *New Masses* published a symposium in which prominent intellectuals Edmund Wilson, Clifton Fadiman, Sherwood Anderson, Upton Sinclair, and others declared that social-

Before New Deal programs began to operate, private charities were almost the sole sources of relief for the jobless. Louis Ribak in Home Relief Station *shows how often they were sources of humiliation to the poor.*

ism alone could save the country. Two months later the Socialist party candidate for the presidency, Norman Thomas, received 880,000 votes, the largest Socialist vote since 1920.

There is no way of telling how far the disenchantment with capitalism might have carried the American people if the nation had been forced to endure four more years of Hoover. Despair might have pushed Americans into communism or into a right-wing dictatorship such as emerged in central Europe in response to similar pressures. But, through the two-party system, Americans had an orderly and constitutional way to express their anguish, and they used it.

During the last two years of Hoover's administration the Democrats made steady political gains. In the congressional elections of 1930 they came close to winning control of both the House and Senate. The Democratic candidates did not offer drastic alternatives to the Republicans. In fact, many of them held political and economic views as conservative as Hoover's. Yet they could not be considered responsible for the economic debacle, and that in itself was enough to lure voters into the Democratic camp.

In the end the public got more than it expected. By early 1931 the Democratic presidential front-runner was Franklin D. Roosevelt, the governor of New York. FDR had achieved a commendable record in Albany by continuing the progressive policies of Al Smith. An only child born to comfort at Hyde Park, New York, Roosevelt had developed the confidence and poise that came with an assured position in society and the love of a doting mother. Though from an upper-class, old "Knickerbocker" family, he was a Democrat. In 1912 he supported Wilson for president and in 1913 went to Washington as assistant secretary of the navy. As a Wilson supporter, Roosevelt received the vice presidential nomination of his party in 1920. During the 1920s he contracted polio and for the rest of his life was unable to walk without assistance. The experience confirmed FDR's sense that any obstacle could be overcome with enough determination. Encouraged by his strong-willed wife, Eleanor, he refused to give up politics. In 1928 he ran for governor of New York and was elected, although Smith, the party's chief, went down to defeat in the presidential race. In 1930 Roosevelt was reelected governor in a landslide. Surrounded by astute political managers, a proven vote-getter in the nation's most populous state, FDR won the 1932 Democratic presidential nomination handily.

Hoover had little difficulty securing renomination. Though many Republicans had misgivings about the president, they could not deny their leader the chance for a second term. In a lackluster convention the president and vice president were renominated without opposition.

The campaign that followed was not an inspiring one. Neither party platform was especially bold or innovative. Nevertheless, Roosevelt promised increased aid to the unemployed and endorsed government involvement in electric power generation, national resource planning, and federal regulation of utilities and the stock market. The Democrats also favored the repeal of Prohibition. Hoover warned that Roosevelt's election would worsen the country's economic plight; but everywhere he went, he was greeted with hoots, catcalls, and hostile demonstrators accusing him of killing veterans or of personally causing the country's economic catastrophe. He soon became his party's worst liability, a man exuding gloom from every pore. On election day, as expected, Roosevelt and the Democrats were swept in with 23 million votes to Hoover's 16 million. FDR captured 282 counties that had never gone Democratic before. Both House and Senate also went overwhelmingly for the Democrats.

★ FDR's New Deal ★

In the four months between the election and Roosevelt's inauguration, the economy plunged to a new low. During the early weeks of 1933 virtually every bank in the country stopped paying its depositors or tottered on the verge of doing so. To stave off legal bankruptcy, by March 4 the governors of thirty-eight states had been forced to declare bank holidays, allowing the banks to close their doors rather than acknowledge insolvency. By the eve of the inauguration* it seemed that the whole financial structure on which American capitalism rested was about to crumble.

During these dismal lame duck weeks President Hoover tried to enlist Roosevelt's cooperation on emergency measures. But even at this early point FDR favored more vigorous action to revive the economy and more humane measures than Hoover believed necessary and proper. The president-elect listened to Hoover's suggestions, but, unwilling to tie his hands, he refused to commit himself and his administration to anything.

The First Hundred Days. Roosevelt's inaugural speech of March 4 set the tone for the early months of what would be called the New Deal. He proposed federal public works measures, legislation to redistribute population from the cities to the country, to force up the prices of agricultural

---

*Until the Twentieth Amendment to the Constitution was adopted in 1933, the president was inaugurated in early March. The amendment was intended to shorten the "lame duck" period between presidential elections and the beginning of a new presidential term.

produce, to end home and farm foreclosure, to cut costs at all levels of government, to improve and make more efficient relief measures, and finally, to tighten federal regulation of banking and stock speculation. His specific proposals were less important than his tone and manner, however. In a confident, resonant voice the president told the American people that "fear itself" was the chief danger and that they must regain their confidence and self-esteem. If they worked hard, pulled together, and submitted to sacrifice and discipline, all would be well. He hoped that the normal balance of authority between Congress and the executive could be maintained in the days to come, but the crisis might call for expanded presidential authority. If necessary, he declared, he was prepared to ask for broad emergency powers similar to those he would need if the nation were facing a foreign invasion.

The response to the inaugural address was remarkable. In the succeeding days the White House received a half-million letters and telegrams from people who were deeply moved and cheered by the president's words. "It was the finest thing this side of heaven," wrote one citizen. "It seemed to give the people, as well as myself, a new hold on life," exclaimed another. Actually, Roosevelt had not moved much beyond what he had proposed during the campaign, but he had conveyed to the public some of his own jaunty optimism and had given people the feeling that there was now a strong hand at the helm.

Despite his generalities and brave words, Roosevelt had few specific remedies in mind. He was not a brilliant econ-

omist or a man with a clear-cut set of principles to guide him. At times these deficiencies would create confusion and lead to serious mistakes. But FDR had some impressive assets, notably his openmindedness and willingness to experiment. "Take a method and try it," he advised. "If it fails, admit it frankly and try another." And he had gathered around him a talented array of advisers, a so-called Brain Trust—drawn from the universities, from law, and from the social work profession—who could supply him with the ideas he himself lacked.

The new president's first move, on March 5, was to order the nation's banks closed. The four-day bank holiday was accompanied by an order that, in effect, took the country off the gold standard. Four days later, acting with the enthusiasm it had never shown Hoover, Congress passed the Emergency Banking Act, confirming the bank closings and providing for an orderly reopening of those that proved sound. The administration's bold action reassured the American people, who expressed their confidence in the president when the banks reopened by redepositing the cash they had earlier withdrawn in panic.

The bank holiday was the first shot of a whirlwind hundred-day war on defeatism, despair, and decline such as Americans had never witnessed before. The assault was marked by confusion and contradiction and did not end the Depression. But it did check the decline and restore a sense of forward motion to the American people.

The president's major goal during the First Hundred Days was to turn the economy around. To do so he pro-

A naive depiction by Mexican artist Miguel Covarrubias of the pomp surrounding FDR's inauguration in 1933. Notice the angels of hope with their trumpets over his head.

posed two key measures, the Agricultural Adjustment Act (AAA) and the National Industrial Recovery Act (NIRA). The AAA (1933) was the New Deal's major effort to deal with the acute farm crisis. Based on the ideas of Secretary of Agriculture Henry A. Wallace and others, it sought to raise farm prices by creating scarcity. The measure provided that farmers who agreed to reduce their output or acreage of seven basic commodities would be compensated for their sacrifice from the proceeds of a special tax levied on food processors (millers, meat-packers, canners, and so on). Because prices normally rise when the supply of a product shrinks, the administration expected the reduction in farm output to check the price slide and ultimately raise farm income.

The NIRA (1933) was intended to restore industrial prosperity by ending the deflation of prices and wages and reestablishing the balance among competing sectors of the economy. Like the AAA, it was a retreat from the idea of free competition and accepted limitations on output as a key to

renewed prosperity. The bill established the National Recovery Administration (NRA) with power to negotiate codes of "fair competition" for the nation's major industries with representatives of industry. These codes would set prices and assign production quotas to individual firms. Though the authors of the law added language expressing concern over creating monopolies that could squeeze consumers, in reality the measure represented a suspension of antitrust principles. Labor, too, was handed a gift. Section 7(a) of the NIRA required that every code provide for collective bargaining for labor and comply with presidential guidelines for minimum pay rates and maximum working hours. Tacked on to the NIRA as Title II was a provision establishing a Public Works Administration (PWA) with a $3.3 billion budget to undertake large-scale public construction projects.

The two major recovery measures fell far short of their goals. By the time the AAA went into effect in the spring of 1933, southern farmers and sharecroppers had already

The "dust bowl," an ecological disaster created by years of bad land management plus bad weather, was a major problem of the Depression era. It displaced thousands of Plains farmers, but it also helped raise depressed farm prices.

planted many acres of cotton, and in the corn belt millions of sows had produced their annual litters. To keep this supply of fiber and food from coming to market and further weakening prices, the Department of Agriculture had to persuade cotton growers to uproot a quarter of their crop. In September 1933 it induced farmers to destroy 6 million pigs. Some of the pork was given to people on relief. Nevertheless, the wholesale destruction of commodities at a time when people were hungry and ill-clothed seemed irrational to many Americans.

More serious were the long-term social effects of the AAA. Reducing cotton production squeezed sharecroppers off the land. Those who remained, both black and white, were often deprived by landlords of the federal cash due them.

Despite the AAA's failings during the two years following its passage, farm income more than doubled. Some of the gains consisted of direct payments to farmers for cutting production; some came from the higher prices that reduced output produced. But the AAA was responsible for only a part of the advance. Higher wheat prices, for example, owed as much to the great drought that parched the Great Plains between 1932 and 1935 as to government programs. The drought turned a vast area stretching from Texas to the Dakotas into a "dust bowl," where the skies were obscured by blowing topsoil and crops withered. Thousands of tenant farmers in Oklahoma and Arkansas were up-

rooted. Imprecisely called Okies, many became "gasoline gypsies" and set off in jalopies for the warmth, jobs, and presumed easy living of southern California. The sharp drop in wheat production added substantially to the impact of the AAA wheat program. When the federal judiciary declared the tax on food processors unconstitutional, the AAA's major crop-reduction features were reincorporated into a new law, the Soil Conservation and Domestic Allotment Act (1936).

Unlike the AAA, the NIRA was almost a complete failure. The flamboyant NRA administrator, General Hugh S. Johnson, had hoped to use the Public Works Administration (PWA) established by the NIRA to beef up demand by putting people to work. But Roosevelt handed over the agency to Secretary of the Interior Harold Ickes, depriving Johnson of one of his tools for success. Working with what he had, Johnson succeeded in bullying the nation's largest industries into writing codes of fair practices. These agreements contained some progressive labor features, including mandatory collective bargaining for employees and limitations on child labor. In return for these, however, the NRA authorized price-fixing and output limitations and allowed big business to adopt policies that discriminated against small firms.

But the greatest disappointment of the NRA was that it failed to stimulate industry. The government gave its pro-

Rural poverty, especially in the South and southern Plains, drove many people to seek a better life in California. "Okies," as they were called by contemptuous observers, loaded their meager belongings onto rattletrap vehicles and headed west, many ultimately to become prosperous citizens of their adopted state.

gram a symbol—a blue eagle—and a slogan—We Do Our Part. Blue eagle parades wound through the downtowns of a score of cities; blue eagle stickers were plastered over store and factory windows. For a time the ballyhoo boosted investor confidence and consumer morale and kept the Depression from worsening. But the agency established no effective machinery by which to restart silent mills and factories, and industrial production remained stalled. When in May 1935 the Supreme Court struck down the code-making sections of the NIRA as unconstitutional, few people, even in the administration, mourned its passing.

Fiscal Stimulus. It is easy to see today why the two major recovery measures failed. In addition to their unfortunate side effects, they did little to increase investment rates or consumer spending. Under the circumstances, only the government, by disbursing large receipts, could have given the economy the stimulus it needed.

The treasury under Roosevelt did spend more money than it took in. The RFC funneled money into banks to help them expand their loans. The Home Owners Loan Corporation (HOLC) dispensed billions of dollars to savings and loan associations to refinance mortgages. The PWA, which survived the Supreme Court's invalidation of the NIRA, poured millions into major federal works pro-

jects. Between 1933 and 1939 the agency built 70 percent of the new schools and 65 percent of the new city halls, sewage plants, and courthouses constructed. It was responsible for more than a third of all the nation's new hospitals. It funded university libraries, the Lincoln Tunnel connecting New York and New Jersey, the causeway linking the Florida Keys to the mainland, and many other outstanding construction projects.

Whatever his critics charged, however, Roosevelt was never a deliberate "spender." He believed that a little "pump priming" by government could be useful, but he worried about running the treasury consistently in the red. "I doubt if any of his reform legislation," a Roosevelt adviser wrote in 1936, "would give him as much satisfaction as the actual balancing of the budget." Federal spending exceeded federal income in every year of the New Deal, but the deficits were always incidental to relief; they were never part of a deliberate program. Nor were they ever large enough to spark a complete recovery. At their maximum, in 1936, treasury deficits totaled a scant $4.4 billion, scarcely enough to make up for weak investment by the private sector or even to offset the simultaneous spending cutbacks of impoverished city and state governments. Few in the Roosevelt administration had read the apostle of deliberate deficit spending—John Maynard Keynes—though Marriner

The WPA under Harry Hopkins sought to rescue people in the arts, as well as other Americans, from idleness during the Depression. Moses Soyer here, in Artists on WPA, depicts a room full of WPA painters using their skills and earning some money in the process.

Eccles, a Utah banker who headed the Federal Reserve Board, was an instinctive Keynesian.

Relief.　By far the largest outpouring of federal funds throughout the New Deal Era went to jobs and relief for the unemployed. Although conservative in fiscal matters, FDR—unlike Hoover—put the welfare of ordinary men and women before a balanced budget.

As part of the First Hundred Days, Congress established the Civilian Conservation Corps (CCC). The corps took 2.5 million idle young men on relief rolls and put them to work on public lands at $30 a month planting trees, building forest ranger stations, clearing branches, and restoring historic battlefields. Congress also passed the Federal Emergency Relief Act, creating the Federal Emergency Relief Administration (FERA) and appropriating $500 million for local and state relief agencies to distribute to the unemployed. Administering the program was a fast-talking, poker-playing young social worker, Harry L. Hopkins, who believed that jobs, rather than outright charity, were needed to restore individual morale and self-respect. In late 1933 Hopkins persuaded Roosevelt to establish the Civil Works Administration (CWA) with funds drawn from FERA and the PWA to put the unemployed directly on the federal payroll. By mid-January 1934 the CWA was providing 4 million men and women with a steady paycheck averaging $15 a week.

Needless to say, CWA was popular with the unemployed. It was also popular with local storekeepers and other small business people, who quickly felt the stimulating effect of new paying customers. But the president worried that it was too expensive and would create a permanent class of government dependents. By summer Roosevelt had shut down the program and returned relief to the local governments.

It did not remain there. In January 1935 Roosevelt asked Congress for $5 billion to support other work relief programs. The men would be employed on various government projects at wages higher than the straight dole under FERA, but lower than the amount paid by CWA. Congress responded to the president's request and made the largest single appropriation in the nation's history. The questions now were who would spend this great sum, and how? Secretary Ickes wanted it devoted to long-term projects under his PWA. Hopkins wanted it for short-term projects like those of his CWA. The two men fought like spoiled children. In the end Roosevelt recognized that quick relief was the need of the hour and allotted most of the funds to

The New Deal was a builder as well as a make-work employer. It helped improve the country's infrastructure in the midst of a severe depression. Shown here is William Gropper's mural "Construction of the Dam."

a new agency, the Works Progress Administration (WPA), under Hopkins's direction.

For the remainder of the Depression, the WPA was the major distributor of government funds to the unemployed and an important stimulant to the economy. Government spending, however incidental, pushed up the GNP and cut into unemployment. By 1935 the number of jobless had declined from almost 13 million, or 24.9 percent of the labor force, to 10.6 million, a little over 20 percent of those seeking work.

The relief programs cannot be measured solely by their statistical consequences. True, much of the WPA outlay went to make-work projects. But Hopkins was an imaginative man with broad cultural and human sympathies who saw that artists, writers, intellectuals and performers were also victims of the economic collapse. Under his direction the WPA sponsored programs to put these people to work enriching community life, while preserving their own skills. Hundreds of musicians were paid to perform in school auditoriums and community halls. Artists were hired to paint murals for the new federal courthouses and post offices built with PWA funds. Writers were set to work compiling state guidebooks. Many talented men and women—including Saul Bellow, Ralph Ellison, Richard Wright, and Arthur Miller—owed their starts to the Federal Writers Project or the Federal Theater Project under the WPA. The WPA also established a National Youth Administration to give part-time work to college and high school students to enable them to complete their studies.

Reform and Innovation. Much of the first two years of the New Deal was devoted to emergency legislation to revive the economy and relieve public distress. But the president had promised reform and innovation, too, and he came through on his promises. A series of New Deal measures sought to end stock market abuses by placing the management of Wall Street under the new Securities and Exchange Commission (SEC). The banking system was made more secure and stable by creation of the Federal Deposit Insurance Corporation (FDIC) to ensure depositors' accounts and prevent the sort of panic withdrawals that had almost destroyed the banking system following the Crash.

THE TENNESSEE VALLEY AUTHORITY

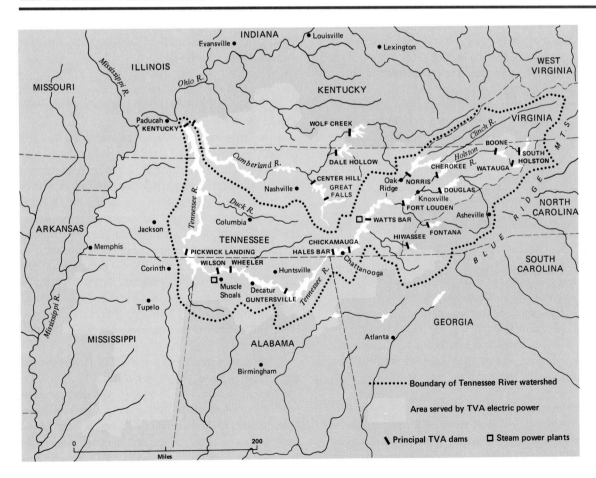

The most important innovation of the First Hundred Days was the Tennessee Valley Authority (TVA). In the tradition of the old progressives, Roosevelt was a conservationist who placed an almost Jeffersonian value on nature and rural life. In his inaugural address he had proposed the more effective use of the nation's land and natural resources. In May 1933 he secured congressional approval of the TVA, a resource-management project long advocated by Senator George Norris of Nebraska and other conservationists who were dismayed at the physical and social deterioration of the potentially rich Tennessee River valley and the waste of its precious water resources.

The TVA was given the authority to build dams, manufacture fertilizer, undertake soil conservation and reforestation measures, and join with local authorities within the seven-state valley in various social improvement projects. Between 1933 and 1944 the TVA built nine major dams, which not only brought low-cost light and power to valley homes and farms but also provided new recreational facilities. Cheap power attracted large industries to the region, especially during World War II. Together with reforestation and soil conservation, inexpensive electricity helped reverse the valley's long decline, turning it into one of the most prosperous parts of the South.

For all its benefits the TVA clearly represented an old-fashioned sort of conservation. From a modern ecological point of view its virtues seem limited. Its disruption of the natural environment and its focus on maximizing energy use would not get high marks today. In fact, it is doubtful if the project could have passed the environmental impact tests imposed on new developments today. But for decades the TVA would be cited as a triumph of the New Deal at its best.

★ FRIENDS AND ENEMIES ★

The early months of the New Deal were a hectic time. The public wavered between fear and hope, still stunned by the economic catastrophe but encouraged by the new surge of energy in Washington. Congress gave Roosevelt almost everything he wanted without looking too closely at the cost or questioning the wisdom of his proposals. As the months passed, however, opposition mounted at both ends of the political spectrum, and by 1935 Roosevelt and the New Deal were beset by critics and enemies.

Thunder on the Right. Despite the new legislation to regulate the banks and Wall Street, FDR was not a foe of business. Many of his advisers, particularly Professor Raymond Moley of Columbia, were conservative men who

endorsed business-government cooperation. Their views had been incorporated into the NIRA. Unfortunately for FDR, once the worst of the economic crisis had passed and business people lost their fear of total collapse, many began to accuse the New Dealers of unwarranted interference with the economy, fiscal irresponsibility, and socialist leanings. In August 1934 a group of conservative Democrats and executives of Du Pont, General Motors, and other large corporations organized the Liberty League to fight the New Deal and prevent the "further aggrandizement of an ever spreading governmental bureaucracy."

At the same time a more formidable conservative challenge came from the Supreme Court. Composed of men whose average age was over seventy, the Court was dominated by some of the most tradition-bound conservatives in the American bar. On May 27, 1935, in the *Schechter* case, it struck down the NIRA on the grounds that it unconstitutionally conferred legislative power on the executive branch. Shortly thereafter, in *United States* v. *Butler*, the Court invalidated the AAA on the grounds that the processing tax that provided the fund to pay farmers was not a true tax but a means to regulate production. The AAA, the Court's conservative majority declared, granted the government powers far beyond any that the Constitution intended. If the principle of the AAA were allowed to stand, federal taxing power could be used to regulate industry throughout the United States.

The Attack of the Left. The conservative assault on the New Deal was only half the story. Roosevelt also came under attack from the political left.

The Depression gave American Marxism a new lease on life. Most Americans retained their faith in private property and a market economy, but some intellectuals, artists, journalists, academics, and trade union leaders came to believe that capitalism was doomed and that the only hope for America lay in a public takeover of the means of production. To many skeptics the apparent success of the Soviet "experiment" clinched the argument. While capitalism was reeling in the United States, the Soviet economy was forging ahead under Joseph Stalin's Five-Year Plans. Capitalism generally, it seemed, was in its final death throes while Soviet socialism had solved the problems of growth, unemployment, and economic equality. Surely Russia was the model to follow.

American Marxists attacked the New Deal as too little too late. The Socialist party leader, Norman Thomas, at first was friendly to Roosevelt. By 1935, however, the socialists were denouncing the New Deal as "the greatest fraud among all the utopias." Whether right or wrong, the American socialists were at least their own masters. Not so the Communists. Earl Browder, head of the Communist party of the United States, echoed whatever Moscow's current attitude toward the Western capitalist democracies happened to be. In 1934, during the so-called Third Period of International Communism, Browder called the New Deal "a program of hunger, fascization, and imperialist war." Then, after 1935, the Soviet leaders, frightened by the rise of Hitler and Nazism in Germany, shifted the Moscow "line" to a "United Front" policy of cooperation with the Western democracies to stem the dictators. In short order, Browder and his colleagues ceased their attacks; the New Deal became acceptable.

The Neopopulists. The Socialists and Communists were at most an annoyance to Roosevelt. The real political challenge from the left came from a collection of neopopulists in the dissenting tradition of the West and South. Closest to the Populist heritage was Senator Huey Long, the Louisiana Kingfish. An earthy man who wore pink suits, called fellow officeholders "dime-a-dozen punks," and conducted public business in pajamas and a silk bathrobe, Long was also a shrewd politician who knew that the times cried out for a savior. As governor of Louisiana he had forced the state's corporations to pay a larger share of taxes than they had before and had used the money to build bridges, hospitals, mental institutions, and schools. To carry out his program, Long had employed any weapon at hand, including physical intimidation, political blackmail, and kidnapping.

Father Coughlin, the "radio priest," gathered an enormous following with his weekly "Golden House of the Little Flower" broadcasts. Every week he received more mail than Roosevelt.

In 1932 Long came to Washington as a Democratic senator. At first he supported the president, but he soon concluded that the New Deal was too friendly to big business. In part the argument between Long and Roosevelt was a clash between two strong and ambitious men. But they also disagreed ideologically. The Kingfish professed to be a radical egalitarian. He wanted to "share the wealth" by taxing away all large incomes and fortunes and giving every citizen a lump sum of $5,000 and a guaranteed income of $2,000 a year. Many Americans dismissed the Share Our Wealth program as an unworkable scheme that was more likely to produce chaos than solve the nation's problems. But Long's proposal to make "every man a king" appealed to millions of ordinary people. Roosevelt considered Long a demagogue and one of the most dangerous men in America, and by the beginning of 1933 he and the administration were at war.

Another outspoken critic of the New Deal was Father Charles E. Coughlin, a Catholic priest from Royal Oak, Michigan. Coughlin's radio broadcasts of sermons and commentary had begun in the late 1920s, and by 1933 the golden-voiced "radio priest" had an audience of millions. Like Long, he first supported the New Deal but turned against FDR when the president refused to endorse inflationary measures to end the Depression. In late 1934 Coughlin formed the National Union for Social Justice, a pressure group advocating silver inflation and the nationalization of power, oil, light, and natural gas companies, and ultimately the seizure of the banks as well. At various times he was denounced by Catholic prelates for his rhetorical excesses, especially his anti-Semitism; but secure in the support of his own bishop, he continued to attack Roosevelt and those he called the "money-lenders."

A third Populist challenge came from an aging California physician, Francis E. Townsend. Townsend was a generous man with a tender heart. Outraged by the lack of public concern for the elderly victims of the Depression, he proposed that all persons over sixty be given pensions of $200 a month on condition that they retire and "spend the money as they get it." The scheme, he declared, would simultaneously remove thousands of older workers from the overcrowded job market and inject millions of dollars of fresh purchasing power into the economy.

The Townsend Plan quickly won a following among older people and was incorporated into a bill introduced in Congress in early 1935. Critics attacked the measure as unworkable and unfair to the great majority of Americans under sixty. Many of its opponents were conservatives who saw the plan as socialistic, but Frances Perkins, the secretary of labor, also derided the scheme as crackpot. The *Townsend Weekly*, the doctor's editorial voice, soon responded with an angry attack on the administration.

The Roosevelt Coalition. Fortunately for FDR, he had also won hordes of friends. By 1935 millions of Americans had reason to thank the New Deal and the Democratic party for their help. Creative men and women were grateful for the opportunity under the WPA to do productive work and maintain their skills and talents. Young people were grateful for the dole from the National Youth Administration that allowed them to stay in school and prepare for careers; they were glad to be taken off the city streets by the CCC and given the chance to earn some money working in the forests and national parks. Thousands of middle-class homeowners sang Roosevelt's praises for sparing them the humiliation of eviction from their homes through a timely HOLC loan. Unemployed factory workers could thank the president for the relief payments that kept them from hunger. For many millions of citizens, the federal government for the first time seriously touched their lives and the touch seemed protective and benign.

Black Americans were especially grateful to Roosevelt and his party. Not that the administration's policies were ideal. The AAA programs, as administered, had hurt black sharecroppers. Moreover, Roosevelt, who needed southern votes in Congress, was unwilling to attack the racial caste system of the South. He endorsed a federal antilynching bill, but then refused to fight for it and allowed it to be filibustered to death in the Senate. Nevertheless, not since Reconstruction had black Americans received as good a shake from their government as now. Blacks shared in WPA programs; the National Youth Administration helped many hundreds of young black men and women. When the New Deal adopted a slum-clearance program, blacks would become prominent beneficiaries of the new public housing. New Dealers, moreover, were often solicitous of black pride. Eleanor Roosevelt and Secretary Harold Ickes, particularly, accorded recognition to talented black men and women, supported black aspirations, and sought to further the cause of civil rights. When the Daughters of the American Revolution refused to allow the distinguished black contralto Marian Anderson to sing at Washington's Constitution Hall, Secretary Ickes invited her to use the steps of the Lincoln Memorial for an open-air concert. Black Americans appreciated the benefits of the New Deal and ignored its deficiencies. By 1935 many had broken their traditional Republican ties and shifted their votes to the Democratic column.

By late 1935 organized labor had also joined the Roosevelt camp. During the 1920s the unions had declined in power and numbers. After 1924 leadership of the labor movement rested in the conservative hands of William Green, Samuel Gompers's successor as head of the AFL.

Eleanor Roosevelt was an ardent champion of the nation's poor, causing wealthy conservatives to label her, like her husband, a traitor to her class. Here she encourages a group of farmers about to begin new lives under a program of the Resettlement Administration, one of the boldest experiments of the New Deal.

Hoover Hits Back

Roosevelt and the New Dealers succeeded in creating a political coalition that included broad segments of the American people. They did not convince all Americans that they had found the correct formulas for national health, however. One of the outspoken dissenters was former president Herbert Hoover. Here, speaking on the eve of the Roosevelt landslide of 1936, Hoover attacks the New Deal and his opponent of four years before, and expounds the Republican philosophy of "freedom" against what he portrays as the New Deal doctrines of centralized power and "personal government."

"Through four years of experience this New Deal attack upon free institutions has emerged as the transcendent issue in America. All the men who are seeking for mastery in the world today are using the same weapons. They sing the same songs. They all promise the joys of Elysium without effort.

"But their philosophy is founded on the coercion and compulsory organization of men. True liberal government is founded on the emancipation of men. This is the same issue upon which men are imprisoned and dying in Europe right now. . . .

"I gave the warning against this philosophy of government four years ago from a heart heavy with anxiety for the future of our country. It was born from many years' experience of the forces moving in the world which would weaken the vitality of American freedom. It grew in the four years of battle as President to uphold the banner of free men.

"And that warning was based on sure ground from my knowledge of the ideas that Mr. Roosevelt and his bosom colleagues had covertly embraced despite the Democratic platform.

"Those ideas were not new. Most of them had been urged on me. . . .

"I rejected the notion of great trade monopolies and price-fixing through codes. That could only stifle the little business man by regimenting him under the big brother. That idea was born of certain American Big Businesses and grew up to be the NRA.

"I rejected the scheme of 'economic planning' to regiment and coerce the farmer. That was born of a Roman despot 1,400 years ago and grew up into the AAA.

"I refused national plans to put the government into business in competition with its citizens. That was born of Karl Marx.

"I vetoed the idea of recovery through stupendous spending to prime the pump. That was born of a British professor.

"I threw out attempts to centralize relief in Washington for politics and social experimentation. I defeated other plans to invade States' rights, to centralize power in Washington. Those ideas were born of American radicals. . . .

"I rejected all these things not only because they would not only delay recovery but because I knew that in the end they would shackle free men. . . .

"It was not until after the [1932] election that the people began to awake. Then the realization of intended tinkering with the currency

drove bank depositors into the panic that greeted Mr. Roosevelt's inauguration.

"Recovery was set back for two years, and hysteria was used as the bridge to reach the goal of personal government. . . .

"The people knew now the aims of the New Deal philosophy of government.

"We propose instead leadership and authority in government within the moral and economic framework of the American system.

"We propose to hold to the Constitutional safeguards of free men.

"We propose to relieve men from fear, coercion, and spite that are inevitable in personal government.

"We propose to demobilize and decentralize all this spending upon which vast personal power is being built. We propose to amend the tax laws so as not to defeat free man and free enterprise.

"We propose to turn the whole direction of the country toward liberty, not away from it. . . .

". . . [D]o not mistake. Free government is the most difficult of all government. But it is everlastingly true that the plain people will make fewer mistakes than any group of men no matter how powerful. But free government implies vigilant thinking and courageous living and self-reliance in a people.

"Let me say to you that any measure which breaks our dikes of freedom will flood the land with misery."

Green did little to counteract the decline in union membership and influence that had begun in the 1920s; nor did he do anything to bring the millions of new industrial wage earners into organized labor's house. There were a few industrial unions in the nation. Among them were the feeble United Mine Workers under the unpredictable John L. Lewis and two unions of garment workers, predominantly Jewish and Italian, under Sidney Hillman and David Dubinsky. But these leaders and their unions were exceptional. Most factory workers and miners were unorganized.

The Depression further weakened organized labor. Membership dropped as union workers lost their jobs. Desperate men and women turned to unauthorized, or "wildcat," strikes in hope of preserving their wages and their jobs. But with millions unemployed and the economy steadily worsening, the position of labor was pitifully weak, and these efforts invariably failed.

Then came the NIRA and its Section 7a, authorizing collective bargaining in industries that adopted NIRA fair-practice codes. Roosevelt was at first indifferent to organized labor. But many prominent New Dealers, particularly Senator Robert F. Wagner of New York and Secretary of Labor Frances Perkins (the first female cabinet member), were strongly prounion. The administration established to enforce the NIRA labor provision pursued a vigorous policy of encouraging labor unions and collective bargaining. Before long thousands of workers, inspired by labor organizers' claim that "the president wants you to unionize," were flocking into both old and new labor organizations, glad to oblige the president and certain that he wished them well.

★ THE WELFARE STATE ★

Roosevelt did not respond to attacks from both ends of the political spectrum by moving toward the middle. The assault from the right annoyed him, but he expected it. The criticism of the left was more wounding. FDR considered himself left of center, and when challenged by the neopopulists, he worried about his liberal credentials and feared he might lose his popular support.

The first New Deal had been devoted largely to recovery and relief. Of the two goals, only the second had met with any large measure of success. In 1935 growing opposition and the sense that the New Deal had stalled caused Roosevelt and his advisers to veer left with a new program to weaken the power of big business, equalize opportunity, and increase economic security. In a burst of energy known as the Second Hundred Days, or the Second New Deal, they transformed the nation by creating the modern welfare state.

The stimulus for the new tack may have been immediate problems, but the inspiration was derived from the reform impulse of the early twentieth century. Many of its authors were old progressives or their later disciples. Justice Brandeis, one of the key figures of the Second New Deal, had been Woodrow Wilson's mentor, and Brandeis's protégé, Felix Frankfurter, was a prominent figure in the new drive. Other people in the Roosevelt administration were also old progressives. The feisty "old curmudgeon" with the sharp tongue, Harold Ickes, was a former Bull Mooser. Frances Perkins had been a settlement house social worker and social justice reformer before World War I. In local government, where the New Deal relied on friendly administrators to carry out its wishes and create grassroots support for its programs, there were many former progressives in high office. The mayor of New York City between 1933 and 1945 was the bouncy, exuberant Fiorello La Guardia, a former progressive Republican congressman who helped deliver New York City's votes for Roosevelt each time he ran for president. Congress was full of surviving progressives, many of them midwestern Republicans, who supported New Deal reform measures despite their Democratic inspiration. Some of these progressives personally disliked Roosevelt, but they could not stop the New Deal from appropriating many of their ideas.

The Second New Deal elevated the progressive social welfare programs that had been largely confined to the states before 1917 to the national level. Now the federal government would not only complete the job of taming the "vested interests" but also make Washington the guardian of the weak and unfortunate and the source of security for all Americans.

In June 1935 the president sent Congress a list of "must" legislation consisting of four crucial items: a social security bill, a measure to replace the collective bargaining provision of the defunct NIRA, a banking regulation proposal, and a new progressive income tax with rates that rose sharply as income increased. In addition, he demanded that Congress pass several important secondary measures to expand social and economic benefits for various segments of the nation.

Labor's New Charter.   Over the next few months FDR got almost all that he asked for. In July Congress passed the first of the major measures, the National Labor Relations Act, also called the Wagner Act, after its chief congressional sponsor, Senator Robert Wagner of New York. It became the charter of the modern American labor movement.

The new law established a permanent National Labor Relations Board with the authority to supervise elections to determine whether workers in an industry wanted union representation. Their union, if approved, would become the

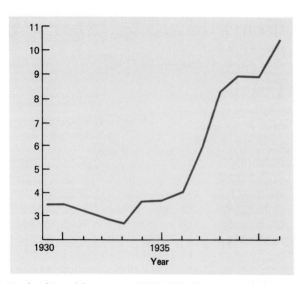

Membership in labor unions, 1929–1941. *Source: Historical Statistics of the United States, Colonial Times to 1970.*

legal collective bargaining agent for its members, whether employers liked it or not.

The Wagner Act would prove a powerful weapon in the struggle to organize the nation's miners and factory workers. But obstacles remained. For years American industrialists had bitterly and successfully opposed unions. Using labor spies, strikebreakers, strong-arm methods, and legal injunctions, they had checked efforts of their employees to win collective bargaining rights. They were now certain to fight back.

Nor could the industrial unionists expect much help from the AFL. William Green and the heads of the powerful craft unions that made up the AFL considered the growth of industrial unionism a threat to their own power. They were also contemptuous of the semiskilled workers of predominantly southern and eastern European stock who labored in the mills and mines. At the 1935 annual AFL convention Green and his friends refused to support the principle of industrial unionism. In response, dissenters Sidney Hillman, David Dubinsky, and John L. Lewis set up the Committee for Industrial Organization. Until 1938, when it became the Congress of Industrial Organizations, the CIO remained within the AFL. It received little support from Green and his lieutenants.

The steel industry was the first target of CIO organizers. The smaller companies resisted, and on Memorial Day, 1937, outside Republic Steel, strikers and the police clashed violently, leaving several strikers dead and many injured. The giant of the industry, United States Steel, however,

quickly capitulated, signing an agreement with the steelworkers recognizing the union as their bargaining agent in March 1937. The automobile industry was tougher, but it, too, yielded. In February 1937, after a series of dramatic sit-down strikes in which workers refused to leave the plants until their demands were met, General Motors surrendered and recognized the United Automobile Workers. Ford Motor Company, under the fiercely individualistic Henry Ford, held out for many more months, using toughs and spies to break the union drive. In 1940 Ford too capitulated. By the eve of World War II the entire auto industry had been unionized.

By 1941, as a result of the Wagner Act and the doggedness of Lewis, Hillman, and other leaders of industrial labor, the number of men and women belonging to unions had swelled to a record 8.4 million—23 percent of the nonfarm labor force. It would not be easy for the politicians to ignore labor representatives again. The successful organizing of industrial labor was a power shift as dramatic as any that had taken place since the Civil War.

Social Security. The next piece of "must" legislation passed during the Second Hundred Days, the Social Security Act (1935), had consequences for American life that were even more far-reaching than those of the Wagner Act. From the beginning of the century, advanced progressives had advocated a system of social security for the unemployed, the handicapped, and the aged. Other nations had adopted such schemes, but in the United States health, the problems of employment, and old-age uncertainties, were left to the individual or to private charities to solve. Besides creating personal insecurity, the lack of social insurance guaranteed that even a small economic setback would produce a sharp drop in consumer demand. Workers who lost their jobs had little to fall back on and quickly ceased buying. The economy then weakened still further.

The Social Security Act established a system of unemployment insurance under the joint administration of the states and the federal government, financed by a payroll tax levied on employers. It also set up a pension scheme for retired people over sixty-five and their survivors to be paid for by a tax levied equally on both employers and employees. Finally, it provided federal funds to the states to aid them in caring for the destitute blind and for delinquent, crippled, dependent and homeless children; and in setting up public health programs, maternity care, and vocational rehabilitation services.

The United States had finally joined the ranks of the other advanced industrial nations in providing economic security for its citizens. But at best it was a qualified commitment. Roosevelt toyed with the idea of recommending a comprehensive health insurance scheme for his Social

Fiorello H. La Guardia

The New Deal was a political upheaval that resounded through the whole of America, affecting the politics of cities and states as well as the nation's. In New York, the country's largest metropolis, it was personified not by the patrician Democrat in the White House, but by a Republican of Italian-American ancestry, Fiorello H. La Guardia.

The Little Flower (his first name in Italian) was, as one of his biographers says, Brotherhood Week all by himself. His father, Achille, was a lapsed Catholic from Foggia in southern Italy; his mother, Irene Luzatto Coen, was a moderately observant Jew from Trieste on the Adriatic. Fiorello was born in New York's Greenwich Village in 1882, two years after his parents arrived in the United States. He grew up in western military posts, where his father served as army bandmaster. He always considered Arizona his native state, and throughout his career as a New York political leader wore western string ties and a high-crowned Stetson hat.

The young La Guardia imbibed his democratic political principles from an improbable source: the pages of Joseph Pulitzer's *World*. Though the paper arrived in Prescott, Arizona, almost a week late, young Fiorello avidly read its socially conscious columns and editorials and absorbed Pulitzer's sincere concern for the underdog. His years in the West were formative for La Guardia, but they ended in 1898 when Sergeant Achille La Guardia set off to fight the Spaniards, only to be struck down by the "embalmed beef" that the Quartermaster Corps served the troops. Discharged from the army as unfit for service, Achille took his family to Trieste, where they moved in with Irene's widowed mother. There, in the Italian-speaking part of Austria-Hungary, and later in Budapest, Fiorello got a job as a U.S. consular representative and learned seven languages.

La Guardia returned to the United States in 1906 and for a while worked as an interpreter for the immigration service at Ellis Island. He went to night law school and opened a law office in New York. The experience did not enhance his views of lawyers or judges. The ones he met were invariably associated with Tammany Hall, the New York Democratic machine, and were invariably dishonest, ignorant, or stupid. La Guardia himself stayed free of the machine and its corrupting patronage by establishing ties with the Italian-Jewish garment worker unions. In 1909–1910 he helped to settle a major garment industry strike and received much favorable attention.

In 1914 Fiorello, a Republican out of hatred for Tammany, received his party's nomination for Congress. The choice meant little; no Republican had ever won in the 14th District, and the weak Republican organization gave him no help. He lost, but his impressive showing won him appointment as deputy state attorney general by the Republican governor. Two years later he won the same congressional seat, largely through the votes of Italian-Americans who resented the Irish-dominated Democratic machine and wanted to see one of their own in office.

The first Italian-American ever to sit in Congress, La Guardia arrived in Washington in time to vote for war against Germany and Austria-Hungary. During the war the young congressman took a leave and joined the air corps. He was sent to Italy to learn to fly and to establish liaison with America's Italian ally. La Guardia never became a very good pilot, but he utterly charmed the Italians with his American bumptiousness and exuberance. He returned home a decorated hero in 1918, in time to win reelection for a second term, but then resigned to run successfully for president of the New York Board of Alderman. In 1921 he sought the Republican nomination for mayor but was defeated. The following year, however, he was returned to Congress from a new Manhattan district, and then reelected to three more terms.

La Guardia was a political maverick in every way. At a time when the country as a whole had become conservative, he retained his skepticism of big business and joined with Senator George Norris of Nebraska to prevent sale of the Muscle Shoals waterpower site to private utility companies. When the country turned isolationist, he fought for the League of Nations. When most Americans were still convinced that Prohibition was a "noble experiment," he sought to have the Volstead Act repealed. La Guardia was considered a troublemaker by his colleagues. The practice of the day allowed congressmen to introduce bills on Wednesdays to benefit constituents under "unanimous consent." It was understood that these would not be challenged. La Guardia had no patience with such boondoggles at the taxpayers' expense and regularly raised objections, thereby forcing a vote. He did not endear himself to his fellow representatives.

During the boom years of the 1920s men like Norris, Robert La Follette, and La Guardia were ignored. Though he served seven terms in Congress, La Guardia never received coveted committee chairmanships, and never was entirely happy with his job in Washington. In 1929 he ran for mayor of New York against the Democratic incumbent, Jimmy Walker. Walker spent more time in nightclubs than in his City Hall office. He was a heavy drinker and a womanizer who had left his wife for a showgirl mistress. He was also politically corrupt. But he suited the devil-may-care spirit of the Jazz Age, and he swamped the gadfly little congressman by almost half a million votes.

The Crash and the Depression abruptly changed the fortunes of the country's political insurgents. In the liberal Congress elected in 1930 La Guardia joined with western progressives to push through important legislation. He jointly sponsored the Norris–La Guardia Anti-Injunction Act outlawing "yellow-dog" contracts (agreements by employees, signed as conditions of employment, not to join unions) and forbidding federal court injunctions in labor disputes except when they threatened to become violent. The new law eliminated a major weapon that management had for years wielded against organized labor.

The Depression irreparably tarnished the luster of "Beau James," the playboy mayor of New York. In 1931 a commission under the patrician judge Samuel Seabury revealed Mayor Walker as an unvarnished crook who had taken thousands from people doing business with the city. The mayor had stored $1 million of his illegal gains in a safety deposit box. When the Seabury investigation finished its work, Walker abruptly resigned and sailed off to Europe.

Walker was gone, but Tammany remained. To challenge the machine, the good-government forces, composed primarily of upper-middle-class professionals and business leaders, organized a Fusion party. Their natural candidate was Seabury himself, but the judge, anxious to preserve the objectivity of his continuing investigation, refused to run. Seabury instead endorsed La Guardia, who also received the support of the New York City Republicans and of the president, Franklin Roosevelt. Though a Demo-

crat, Roosevelt liked La Guardia and despised Tammany.

La Guardia won with a 250,000-vote majority. On January 1, 1934, in the oak-paneled study of Judge Seabury's luxurious Upper East Side townhouse, the Little Flower took the oath as ninety-ninth mayor of New York.

His first task was to save the city from bankruptcy. New York, like almost all American cities in this the fifth year of the Great Depression, confronted intolerable burdens with drastically reduced means. A million unemployed people depended on the city Department of Public Welfare for food and shelter, but the city was broke. Five hundred million dollars of short-term city obligations were past due, and the bankers would not lend New York another dime. As the new mayor began his term, over 140,000 city teachers, firefighters, police, and sanitation workers faced the prospect of payless paydays.

La Guardia got the state legislature to grant the city fiscal autonomy and allow it to consolidate departments to cut expenses. The arrangement reassured the bankers, and New York was able to borrow again at reasonable rates. The mayor's friendship with FDR also paid off. Federal money soon began to flow into the city's coffers.

With the financial crisis past, La Guardia could devote his energies to reform. The Little Flower was the best mayor the city ever had. He was compassionate, dynamic, honest, candid, amusing, and effective. He made it clear right off who was boss. "In this administration," he told the Tammany-dominated Board of Aldermen, "I am the majority." He rejected all patronage appointments, even of Fusionists who had worked for his election. Merit alone counted. There was not, he said, "a Republican or a Democratic way to collect garbage." His appointees to high city office were almost invariably the top people in their field, and he

never let them relax their vigilance. On one occasion he telephoned his sanitation commissioner at 3 A.M. to find out if he had a snow-alarm plan in place. "Sure," the startled official replied. "I'm called as soon as the first flake falls." "Wonderful," the mayor responded. "Stick your head out of the window." The commissioner did; there was a raging blizzard under way. Like other officials who committed boners, the commissioner got a polished sheep shank as a trophy.

La Guardia was a ruthless antivice and anti–crime crusader. He cracked down on illegal gambling and, to the dismay of some, drove burlesque from the city. He imprisoned hoodlums who preyed on legitimate business people, and he supported the efforts of New York's crusading district attorney, Thomas Dewey, to break the power of racketeers. He told the city police at one point: "I want you to put so much fear into the heart of every crook in New York that when he sees a cop he'll tip his hat."

The mayor carried into his office the same sensitive social conscience he had shown as a congressman.

La Guardia procured millions of dollars of federal money for public housing to replace the most squalid of New York's slums. During the bitterly cold winter of 1934 he opened the city's armories to the homeless and heatless. He established a large covered market in the city for the hundreds of pushcart peddlers who had to face inclement weather and police harassment. He was also a master builder. He and his parks commissioner, Robert Moses, often with federal aid, built dozens of bridges, scores of schools, hundreds of playgrounds and parks, and the city's two major airports.

The mayor was a newspaper reporter's delight. He was funny. When, in 1945, New York newspaper deliverers went on strike, the mayor turned up at the city's municipal radio station to read the comics over the air to the city's children. It was a memorable performance. "Ahh! what do we have here? The gardener! Stabbed! . . . But Dick Tracy is on the trail!" When the city was legally forced to allow the pro-Nazi German-American Bund to stage a rally in Madison Square Garden, the mayor assigned only Jewish policemen to maintain order. When Commissioner Moses had tried the tactic of resigning to force concessions from him once too often, the mayor had a pad of forms printed reading: "I, Robert Moses, do hereby resign as _____, effective _____." The next time Moses swept into his office with a resignation threat, La Guardia handed him the pad and said: "Here, just fill in the blanks." La Guardia was theatrical. He was always at the scene of the crime, the fire, or the disaster—often wearing the hat of the city service in charge.

La Guardia's three terms as mayor (1934–1946) coincided almost exactly with FDR's reign. The two political leaders worked closely together. La Guardia seldom came back from Washington without some spoils for the city in his pocket. Roosevelt could always count on Fiorello to use his popularity to win votes for New Deal measures in Congress and for himself every four years at the polls. FDR was also grateful for the mayor's effective neutralizing of Tammany, always an embarrassment to him. In many ways, what La Guardia accomplished in New York was a little New Deal that helped to bind the city's voters to the new Democratic coalition.

By the time his third term ended, La Guardia had lost interest in the mayor's office. After FDR died in 1945,

his successor, Harry Truman, appointed La Guardia head of the United Nations Relief and Rehabilitation Administration, the agency for rescuing and resettling the millions of Europeans made homeless by the war. The work was not congenial, and he soon resigned. Though only sixty-three, his health was now poor. In the spring of 1947 his severe back pain was diagnosed as cancer of the pancreas, a virtually incurable disease.

On September 20 Fiorello La Guardia died. When they opened his safety deposit box, they found $8,000 in war bonds. The only other asset he could pass along to his wife, Marie, and their two adopted children was a heavily mortgaged modest house in the Bronx. The Little Flower had lived the exemplary life he preached after all!

Security package but backed off when the American Medical Association, representing the nation's doctors, attacked it as "socialized medicine." And even in the areas where it intruded, the Social Security legislation's applicability was limited. The old-age pension plan originally excluded farm workers and the self-employed, for example. A later generation would plug some of the gaps and beef up the amounts, but it would also allow the vast expansion of the aid-to-dependent-children provision into a sort of dole that critics insisted created a permanent class of healthy adult "welfare" clients incapable of taking care of themselves.

Additional "Must" Legislation. Other legislation of the Second Hundred Days also fulfilled or reinforced old progressive promises. The Public Utility Holding Company Act gave the federal government control over interstate transmission of electricity and gas. It also conferred on the new Security and Exchange Commission power over monopolistic corporate holding companies. To help equalize income, the Wealth Tax Act increased estate and gift tax rates and imposed stiffer levies on high-income recipients. The final "must" law was the Banking Act of 1935, which

strengthened the federal government's control over the Federal Reserve System and gave the hitherto weak Federal Reserve Board a more effective voice in the management of the country's monetary affairs.

Several measures of the Second New Deal were designed specifically to improve the quality of rural life. In May 1935 Congress established a Rural Electrification Administration (REA). In a few years this agency brought electricity to millions of the nation's farms, created large new markets for electrical appliances, and dramatically changed the lives of farm families. The Soil Conservation and Domestic Allotment Act of 1936 rescued the crop-limitation features of the AAA by paying farmers not to grow "soil-depleting" crops. The Frazier-Lemke Farm Mortgage Moratorium Act extended farm mortgages for three years to save farmers from foreclosures.

Conservatives often criticized New Dealers as "planners," a term equivalent among some critics to socialism. In reality, besides the Tennessee Valley Authority, the Resettlement Administration (RA) was one of the few deliberate New Deal attempts at social planning, in this case to eliminate the chronic problem of rural poverty.

Though America never came close to revolution during the Depression, it did not escape disorder. Here we see a riot on Union Square in New York in 1930 growing out of a labor protest organized by radicals.

Established by Roosevelt as part of Federal Emergency Relief Administration, the RA sought to move farmers from unfertile, "submarginal" land where they lived at bare subsistence level to farms where they could support themselves in modest comfort. At government expense, subsistence farmers would receive better acreage, low cost loans, and expert advice. Under Rexford Tugwell, one of Roosevelt's liberal brain trusters, the underfunded agency succeeded only in relocating some 4,000 poor farmers and share-croppers. Tugwell, in fact, was more interested in establishing "greenbelt" towns around the major cities where urbanites could escape from the poverty and pathologies of the metropolises to a merged rural-urban environment that had the best qualities of both. But here too the achievement was modest. Owing once again to insufficient money, he succeeded in establishing only three such planned towns. The RA's successor, the Farm Security Administration (established by the 1937 Bankhead-Jones Farm Tenancy Act), took on the special task of converting tenant farmers into farm owners. It too was starved for money and made little dent in the problem of rural poverty. Despite their modest results, both the RA and the Farm Security Administration experiments demonstrated a potential for direct social planning by government rarely encountered previously, and seldom again, in American history.

★ END OF THE NEW DEAL ★

By the end of the Second Hundred Days the 1936 presidential race was well under way. Roosevelt easily won his party's renomination. The Republicans turned to Governor Alfred M. Landon of Kansas, a modest, likable man with progressive leanings. To the left of the Democrats—or to the right, some insisted—was the Union party, whose nominee, William Lemke of North Dakota, was a farmer-laborite in the Populist tradition. In all likelihood Huey Long would have headed the third-party ticket had he not been assassinated by one of his many Louisiana enemies in September 1935.

The campaign outcome was never really in doubt. By now a new political coalition had formed around Roosevelt, composed not only of the Democratic party's traditional southern, Catholic, and ethnic voters but also of blacks, Mexican-Americans, intellectuals, and organized labor. Many of these people were the beneficiaries of New Deal programs. They also admired FDR as a man and a leader. Millions listened to his "fireside chats" on the radio and felt that their government cared.

Conservatives charged that Roosevelt was a dictator who had gathered into his hands unheard-of powers over every aspect of American life. They denounced the "bloated" federal bureaucracy and warned that "big government" would soon overawe every other institution. They were not entirely wrong. No American administration had ever achieved such dominion over the economy and over so many people's lives. The combination of big government and a vigorous leader who had a rare rapport with the people focused more attention on Washington than ever before.

Whatever drawbacks time would disclose in this arrangement, in 1936 relatively few Americans took the conservatives' warnings seriously. In November they turned out in record numbers and expressed their enthusiastic support of the Democrats. Roosevelt carried every state in the union except rock-ribbed Republican Maine and Vermont and won the most impressive popular mandate in American political history: almost 28 million votes to Landon's 17 million. In the congressional contest the results were equally lopsided. When the new Congress convened, the Democratic side of the House was so crowded that many of the new Democrats were forced to sit with the opposition.

In his second inaugural address Roosevelt promised to extend New Deal social and economic programs to meet the needs of the "one-third of a nation" that was "ill-housed, ill-clad, ill-nourished." It was a call for a new burst of reform. He secured a part of what he wanted. In September 1937 the National Housing Act (Wagner-Steagall Act) launched a generation of federal slum clearance and public housing projects for the urban poor. The Agricultural Adjustment Act of 1938, without the unconstitutional processing tax, restored the crop-limitation provisions of the first AAA and made farm price supports a permanent feature of the American economy. The Food, Drug, and Cosmetic Act of June 1938 strengthened the consumer-protection features of the progressives' Pure Food and Drug Act of 1906. The Fair Labor Standards Act established for the first time a federally determined minimum hourly wage and a maximum workweek for millions of workers in occupations involved in interstate commerce. But the Fair Labor Standards Act was the last important piece of New Deal legislation. Thereafter New Deal legislative initiatives ceased. The effort to overhaul America and promote recovery had run out of steam.

Given Roosevelt's overwhelming mandate in 1936 and the top-heavy Democratic majority in Congress in 1937 and 1938, this outcome is startling. Yet we can understand its sources by considering where the nation was at this point. Despite every New Deal effort, the economy had failed to make a complete recovery. During 1937 the nation's output

Many Americans were disturbed by Roosevelt's plan to "pack" the Supreme Court, and some enemies of the New Deal believed he was planning to impose one-man rule on the nation. His attempt might have succeeded had not the Court reversed its stands on several issues. Said one wit: "A switch in time saved nine."

forged ahead, but unemployment remained at 7.7 million, some 14.3 percent of the labor force. The gains made, moreover, had been accompanied by sharp price rises. Fearing inflation, in June Roosevelt cut back sharply on federal spending and threw the economy into an unexpected tailspin. By the following year unemployment was back to 10.4 million, 19 percent of the work force. Roosevelt quickly increased relief and other outlays, and checked the descent, but by this time it had become clear to everyone that the country had not solved its chronic unemployment problem.

The persistence of a depressed economy undoubtedly damaged New Deal zest and morale. Nothing seemed to work—or work well—and the administration seemed to have no new ideas. FDR's inability to get the economy going again injured his prestige within his own party. Divisions between northern liberals and southern conservatives, which had been papered over by the mutual concern for recovery, now broke through. Within months of the November electoral victory, the Democrats were in disarray, squabbling with one another and uncertain which way to turn.

At this point Roosevelt launched an ill-advised attack on the Supreme Court. FDR saw the Court as a bastion of judicial conservatism. It had struck down the AAA and the NIRA, and no matter how imperfect these measures had been, he resented the Court's actions. It had also declared unconstitutional the Frazier-Lemke Act, a measure designed to protect farmers against bank foreclosures, and several other New Deal measures. What it would do with the major social legislation of 1935–1936 no one knew, but the president feared the worst.

The justices were almost all elderly men, and Roosevelt could have allowed resignations and deaths to change the Court's complexion. Instead, in February 1937 he asked Congress for the power to name up to six new judges, one for each incumbent who refused to resign after reaching seventy years of age. This scheme to "pack the Court" with more liberal judges stirred up a storm. Predictably, conservatives saw it as an attempt to subvert the Constitution. Even many liberals, including Justice Brandeis, balked at the proposal. When the Court, perhaps intimidated by the president's stand, unexpectedly sustained several crucial pieces of New Deal legislation and several liberal state laws, the Court-packing bill's congressional support melted away. In late July the Senate sent the bill back to the Judiciary Committee, where it quietly died. The president had suffered a major legislative defeat, almost his first, and the blow to his prestige was damaging. Thereafter, as confidence in Roosevelt's leadership waned, southern Democrats would increasingly side with conservative Republicans against their own party's leader.

The loss of support was also expressed by the public at the polls. In the 1938 congressional elections, hoping to regain his liberal majority in Congress, Roosevelt urged the voters to defeat conservative Democrats in the congressional primaries. Many voters resented the interference in local politics and ignored the president's wishes. In the elections themselves the Democrats lost eighty-one seats in the House and eight in the Senate. Such losses by the party in power in midterm national elections are not unusual, and in any case the Democratic majority of 1936 was too lopsided to last. Nevertheless, the election suggested that many citizens had lost confidence in the man and the party they had turned to to save them and the country. In the turbulent years that followed, Roosevelt continued to be admired as the country's savior; but for all intents and purposes the New Deal was incapable of further innovation.

★ CONCLUSIONS ★

The New Deal did not create a revolution. The United States remained a capitalist nation after 1938. But it would be capitalist with a difference. In the words of John Maynard Keynes, Roosevelt had made himself "the trustee" for all those who sought "to mend the evil of our condition by reasoned experiment within the framework of the existing social system." Never again would Americans be completely exposed to the uncertainties of a freewheeling economy modified only in favor of powerful business groups. The government's ability to restore full employment by massive deficit spending was still unproved. But after 1939 it would be difficult for any president to insist that the business cycle had to work itself out no matter what the human cost.

Even more important, the New Deal created permanent safeguards against another collapse and against private insecurity with unemployment insurance, old-age pensions, a strengthened Federal Reserve System, price supports for farmers, and the minimum wage. Perhaps Roosevelt could have done more to reduce the inequalities of wealth and power. A more rigorous system of progressive taxation—without loopholes—and a better-funded and more sustained welfare program might have created a more egalitarian society. But that he could have achieved a socialist society, as later critics have implied—even assuming that this goal was desirable—is doubtful. Public fear in 1933 did give FDR a broad mandate for change and experiment. Yet few Americans would have supported anything so much against the national grain as federal ownership of industry and the banks. And if, in panic, they had endorsed such measures, they certainly would have regretted and reversed their action once they had regained their confidence.

In reality, only a small minority of Roosevelt's aides were radicals, and in the end his New Deal preserved capitalism. It did so by reviving hope, providing the nation with a sense of forward motion, and preventing mass misery. In retrospect, it is easy to see that the New Deal was precisely what the majority of Americans wanted.

In the process of creating the modern welfare state, there were losses as well as gains. Federal power and executive authority were both greatly expanded. Few, except the hidebound conservatives who opposed virtually every New Deal measure, could see the dangers in this change as the 1930s came to an end. Only time would reveal to what extent FDR had encouraged an "imperial presidency." But there can be no doubt that by his programs and his awesome charisma he had helped expand federal and presidential power to the detriment of local and congressional autonomy. Meanwhile, as the 1940s loomed, the country began to turn away from domestic concerns and direct its attention to the threatening events taking place beyond its shores.

✸✸✸✸✸✸✸ FOR FURTHER READING ✸✸✸✸✸✸✸

John Kenneth Galbraith. *The Great Crash, 1929* (1955)
This account of the great Wall Street panic of 1929 explains its causes and effects without resorting to technical jargon. Galbraith discusses the weaknesses of the banking structure, the spirit of speculation, and the dishonesty of highly placed men.

Peter Temin. *Did Monetary Forces Cause the Great Depression?* (1976)
Temin tackles the question raised by the economic school that emphasizes the importance of the money supply in major economic cycles: Was it money mismanagement that produced the Depression? He concludes that the answer is essentially no, and he accepts the Keynesian view that weak investment was the culprit.

William E. Leuchtenburg. *Franklin D. Roosevelt and the New Deal, 1932–1940* (1963)
In this excellent short history of Roosevelt and the New Deal, Leuchtenburg maintains that Roosevelt assumed "that a just society could be secured by imposing a welfare state on a capitalist foundation."

Richard H. Pells. *Radical Visions and American Dreams: Culture and Social Thought in the Depression Years* (1973)
Confronted by the devastation of the early Depression, intellectuals and artists sought radical alternatives to the beliefs and values of the 1920s. In an extraordinarily well-written analysis of articles, books, novels, plays, and films of the 1930s, Pells seeks to demonstrate an underlying conservatism in the thought of the intellectual elite.

Studs Terkel. *Hard Times: An Oral History of the Great Depression* (1970)
Here Terkel records his interviews with miners, farmers, migrant farm workers, corporation presidents, a "Share Our Wealth" organizer, hobos, and teachers. The unavoidable poverty of the Depression created feelings of confusion, shame, and guilt in many of these people.

Robert S. Lynd and Helen M. Lynd. *Middletown in Transition: A Study in Cultural Conflict* (1937)
The Lynds returned to Muncie, Indiana, to study its experience of the Depression. (See Chapter 25's reading suggestions.) They found that its citizens believed the Depression to be a temporary problem that did not require radical changes in the economic system.

James Agee and Walker Evans. *Let Us Now Praise Famous Men* (1941)
Evans's photography complements Agee's sensitive, compassionate record of the daily lives of three white tenant cotton farmers in Alabama during the hard years of the 1930s.

Theodore Rosengarten. *All God's Dangers: The Life of Nate Shaw* (1974)
An aged black Alabama cotton farmer tells of his years as a sharecropper in a world dominated by white landlords, bankers, fertilizer agents, gin operators, sheriffs, and judges. Central to his story is his participation in the Alabama Sharecroppers Union during the Depression, for which he was shot by white lawmen and jailed for twelve years.

Tom Kromer. *Waiting for Nothing* (1935)
An estimated 2 million Americans were homeless wanderers during the Depression, and Kromer was one of them. This autobiographical novel describes the constant degradation of down-and-outers: Panhandling, soup lines, job hunting, imprisonment for vagrancy, and the sermons and lice-ridden bunks of the "missions" were their lot.

Robert E. Sherwood. *Roosevelt and Hopkins: An Intimate History* (1948)
Only about a third of this dual biography concerns the New Deal years. But that third is one of the best brief histories of political leadership during the Depression. Written by a well-known playwright who was also a speechwriter for FDR.

James M. Burns. *Roosevelt: The Lion and the Fox* (1956)

The best discussion of Roosevelt as a domestic leader. Also works as a biography. Burns describes FDR's early life and his preparation for ultimate greatness.

Paul Conkin. *The New Deal* (1967)

A strong attack on the New Deal from the vantage of the political left. Conkin sees it as an instance of missed opportunities to equalize wealth and power in the United States.

John Steinbeck. *The Grapes of Wrath* (1939)

The best novel of the Great Depression. Recounts the story of midwestern farmers fleeing the Depression by heading west to California, and their reception there. Strongly pro–New Deal.

Michael Bernstein. *The Great Depression: Delayed Recovery and Economic Change in America, 1929–1939* (1989)

The most recent discussion of the causes of the Great Depression. Rather technical at times, but agrees with the author of *These United States* at many points. Recommended.

Frank Freidel. *Franklin D. Roosevelt: A Rendezvous with Destiny* (1990)

A one-volume distillation of decades-long research and writing on Roosevelt by the dean of Roosevelt scholars. This volume will probably have to serve as Freidel's final word on the subject.

Lizabeth Cohen. *Making a New Deal: Industrial Workers in Chicago, 1919–1939* (1990)

A first-rate study of ethnic life and ethnic politics in Chicago during the New Deal era and the decade immediately preceding. Says New Deal substituted class for race as the key factor in how Chicago's wage earners voted.

27 ★

WORLD WAR II

Blunder, or Decision in the National Interest?

BUY THAT INVASION BOND!

1904	Japan defeats Russia, takes control of Korea and Manchuria
1908	Root-Takahira Agreement
1921–22	Washington Conference • Benito Mussolini rises to power in Italy, imposing Fascist regime
1928	Kellogg-Briand Pact
1931–32	Japan reoccupies Manchuria
1932	Franklin D. Roosevelt elected president
1933	Adolf Hitler ends Weimar Republic and becomes German chancellor, imposing Nazi rule
1936	Hitler occupies the Rhineland • FDR reelected
1937–38	Japan invades China
1938	Hitler annexes Austria • Munich Pact cedes Czechoslovakia's Sudetenland to Germany
1939	Germany occupies the remainder of Czechoslovakia • The Soviet Union and Germany sign a nonaggression pact • Germany invades Poland; Great Britain and France declare war on Germany
1940	Germany conquers Norway, Denmark, Belgium, Luxembourg, Holland, and France • Japan, Italy, and Germany sign a military and economic agreement forming the Axis alliance • FDR reelected
1941	Lend-Lease Act • Germany invades the Soviet Union • Roosevelt and Churchill issue Atlantic Charter • Japan bombs Pearl Harbor; U.S. declares war on Japan; Germany and Italy declare war on U.S. • Manhattan Project begins • Fair Employment Practices Act • Hitler begins extermination of Jews
1942	Roosevelt orders the War Department to confine Japanese-Americans on West Coast • Battle of Midway checks Japanese Pacific advance • Women's Army and Navy corps (WACS, WAVES) established
1943	Allies defeat the German Afrika Korps, invade Sicily; Soviets stop Germans at Stalingrad • "Big Three" in Teheran • MacArthur and Nimitz close in on Pacific islands • California and Detroit race riots
1944	Normandy invasion • Japanese launch first kamikaze attacks • FDR reelected
1945	Yalta Conference • MacArthur recaptures Philippines • Germany defeated • FDR dies; Harry S. Truman becomes president • Atomic bombing of Hiroshima and Nagasaki • Soviets declare war on Japan • Japan surrenders

December 7, 1941, dawned partly cloudy over the Hawaiian island of Oahu, 2,200 miles southwest of San Francisco. At Pearl Harbor, base of the United States Pacific Fleet, eight battleships, nine cruisers, twenty destroyers, and forty-nine other American naval vessels lay in their berths or were at dry dock. It was Sunday, and many of the crew members were on weekend liberty. Elsewhere on the island Army Air Corps planes sat idle. Not one was in the air. Crews were away or asleep in the barracks. Some were attending religious services. The planes were disarmed and parked in clusters to prevent possible sabotage.

Suddenly at 7:55 A.M. Pearl Harbor burst into flames as Japanese torpedo planes and bombers unleashed tons of explosives onto the American ships tied up in Battleship Row. At the military airfields American planes were sitting ducks for the attackers. Only forty American pursuit planes took to the air to challenge the enemy. Meanwhile, several Japanese midget submarines, having sneaked through the harbor net, were launching torpedoes at every target in sight. Two hours later, when the attack ended, much of America's Pacific naval and air power had been destroyed.

In that brief, hellish interval 2,400 American sailors, marines, soldiers, airmen, and civilians died; 8 battleships were sunk or badly damaged; and 183 planes were lost. If the aircraft carrier force had been berthed rather than at sea, the destruction of American naval power would have been almost total. Still, it was the worst naval disaster in American history.

A few minutes after news of the raid reached Washington, Japanese Ambassador Kichisaburo Nomura and special envoy Saburo Kurusu met with Secretary of State Cordell Hull. They had been instructed to inform Hull just prior to the attack that their government had broken off negotiation of the serious differences then existing between the United States and Japan. Tokyo did not want to alert American forces, but hoped to avoid the charge of having struck without warning. Unfortunately, the diplomats' instructions arrived late.

On December 8, at a little after noon Eastern Standard Time, President Roosevelt appeared before a tense joint session of Congress to ask for a declaration of war against Japan. The country, he declared, would never forget that the Japanese had attacked while their emissaries were talking peace. December 7 was a date that would "live in infamy." With only one dissenting vote, Congress declared war against Japan. On December 11 Germany, Japan's ally, declared war against the United States; Italy, the third Axis power, immediately followed. The crowded and tragic events of four days had finally brought the United States into the greatest war in history.

How did the country arrive at this tragic point? In early December 1941 few Americans doubted that the United States had been treacherously attacked and had no choice but to defend itself. The war stilled the discordant voices that for three years or more had debated war or peace. After 1945 Americans resumed the argument. A majority continued to believe that the nation had been placed in mortal danger by the Axis powers; the attack on December 7, 1941, they insisted, was merely the culmination of Axis plans to enslave all free peoples. A minority denied the danger from Germany, Italy, and Japan and concluded that the United States had blundered into the war or had even been pushed into it by scheming men. Who was right? Was American entrance into war a mistake that might have, and should have, been avoided? Or was it the only way the United States could have protected itself and its vital interests against a pack of dangerous aggressors intent on destroying democracy and freedom?

The disaster of Pearl Harbor had roots that reached back to the beginning of Japanese-American relations and were entangled with historical developments on at least three continents—Asia, America, and Europe. The Japanese attack and the great war that followed were the culmination of events that began as much as a century earlier and involved the relations of one half of the industrialized world with the other.

Friction with Japan. American interests in the Far East dated from early in the nineteenth century. At first these had focused on China, a United States trading partner and an object of American philanthropic and missionary concern. American-Japanese relations began in the 1850s when Captain Matthew Perry of the United States Navy forced the Japanese to abandon their traditional isolation and open trade relations with the West. Perry's visit thrust Japan into the modern world. To avoid Western domination the Japanese were soon imitating not only the West's parliamentary institutions, universal education, and industrialization but also its aggressive nationalism and imperialism. In 1895 Japan wrenched Korea from China. In 1904 it went to war against czarist Russia over China's loosely attached northern provinces and defeated the Russian colossus in a brief and bloody confrontation.

American-Japanese relations in the early twentieth century deteriorated. The United States supported the Japanese against the Russians in 1904–1905. But when, at Portsmouth, New Hampshire, President Theodore Roosevelt helped bring the Russo-Japanese War to an end by compromise, the Japanese blamed the United States for depriving them of the gains they considered their due. Matters worsened two years later when the San Francisco Board of Education placed Japanese students in segregated schools. A blow to their pride, this action outraged the Japanese. Theodore Roosevelt patched things up with the so-called Gentlemen's Agreement: The school board would cancel its order, and the Japanese government would not issue any more passports to would-be immigrants to the United States. The issue was superficially settled, but by this time feelings between the two nations had been rubbed raw. In succeeding years there would be talk, particularly in the Hearst press, of the "yellow peril" in the Far East.

In the next few years Japanese and American interests would frequently clash in Asia. In the 1908 Root-Takahira Agreement, the Japanese agreed to accept the American view that China must remain independent and retain its territorial integrity. But to the Japanese it seemed that the United States and the other Western powers—"have" nations with abundant resources either at home or within their own empires—were trying to keep them—a "have-not" nation, without oil, coal, iron, and copper—from becoming a great power. Densely populated and confined to a small, resource-poor island chain, Japan felt it must have the resources of China and Southeast Asia or remain weak. For this vigorous nation to be confined to a small group of islands while other powers seized control of the rest of the non-Western world would be not only demeaning but also detrimental to Japan's vital interests.

During World War I the Japanese took advantage of Europe's preoccupation and presented China with the so-called Twenty-one Demands (1915), which would have reduced China to a Japanese protectorate. American protest forced the Japanese to back off. The Washington Armament Conference of 1921–1922 further reined in Japan. Called by Secretary Hughes to help stabilize international relations in the Far East, the conference resulted in the Four Power Treaty by which France, the United States, England, and Japan pledged to respect one another's possessions in the Pacific. A Nine Power Treaty concluded among the same four, along with four smaller European nations plus China, promised to respect Chinese territorial integrity and the Open Door principle.

America's Pacific Fleet was decimated in the Pearl Harbor attack. The jumbled mass of wreckage in the foreground is the remains of two destroyers. Behind it rests the Pennsylvania, one of the few capital ships in the harbor to escape heavy damage.

For a while Japanese ambitions diminished, and relations with the United States improved. At the end of the 1920s, however, Japanese militarists and extreme nationalists gained control over their country's affairs and launched a more aggressive policy toward China. In 1931–1932 the militarists provoked an "incident" with China and seized its rich northern province of Manchuria, converting it into a puppet state, renamed Manchukuo. The United States viewed Japan's aggression against its weaker neighbor as a violation of Japan's agreements. But distracted by the Depression and unwilling to take action stronger than the American public would then support, Washington limited itself to diplomatic protests. In January 1932 Secretary of State Henry L. Stimson, reasserting John Hay's Open Door policy of a generation before, announced that the United States would not recognize any act that impaired the "territorial and administrative integrity of the Republic of China."

The Stimson Doctrine put Japan on notice that the United States would oppose its China policy, but it did not deter the Japanese military leaders. Early in 1932 Japanese army units clashed with Chinese troops in Shanghai, and during the fighting thousands of Chinese civilians were killed. In 1937, following a shooting incident at the Marco Polo Bridge near Peking, the Japanese began a piecemeal occupation of the Chinese Republic. Before long their armies had seized major Chinese cities and torn large chunks of the republic from the control of Chiang Kai-shek, leader of the Kuomintang, China's ruling party. In 1938 the Japanese announced a "new order" in the Far East based on thinly disguised Japanese domination of the whole region.

The Rise of Fascism in Europe. Meanwhile, an even more dangerous group of aggressors had appeared in Europe. In Italy, where bitter conflict between Communists and conservatives had undermined the parliamentary system, Benito Mussolini seized power in 1922 in the name of law and order. "Il Duce" and his Fascists before long brutally eliminated their opponents, established a centralized totalitarian regime, and revealed their aggressive foreign

FASCIST EXPANSION IN EUROPE, 1935–1939

policy. In 1935 Fascist Italy attacked Ethiopia, one of the few still independent African nations, and conquered it. The moving plea of Ethiopia's emperor, the eloquent Haile Selassie, to the League of Nations brought economic sanctions against Italy. However, these were weakly supported by member nations and the United States and did not deter Mussolini.

Authoritarian governments resembling Fascist Italy's spread through eastern and southern Europe following the collapse of the international economy in the early 1930s. Clearly, Versailles and the various secondary treaties that had ended World War I had not stabilized the Continent. The boundaries drawn by Wilson and his colleagues had created several small nations out of the ruins of Austria-Hungary and the czarist empire; few of these had democratic traditions or the social institutions to support parliamentary government. By the early 1930s Hungary, Poland, Yugoslavia, and the Baltic states, along with Bulgaria, Rumania, Albania, and Greece, all had authoritarian regimes. Many of the new states were not viable economically or politically, and their weaknesses would be a permanent temptation to their greedy, more powerful neighbors.

Most dangerous of all, the postwar settlement failed to create a stable German democracy. By blaming Germany for the war, imposing vast indemnities on the German economy, and forcing the German nation to disarm, the Versailles treaty left a legacy of intense bitterness. German nationalists held the Weimar Republic, successor to Kaiser Wilhelm II's regime, responsible for the degrading treaty and never became reconciled to it. The Weimar leaders in turn never developed much confidence in the republic's parliamentary institutions or in their ability to govern a people without a democratic tradition.

Despite these problems, for a few years in the late 1920s the German people experienced a period of prosperity and cultural creativity under their new government. When the bottom fell out of the world economy in 1929, however, the inability of the Weimar regime to stop Germany's downward economic spiral destroyed the public's fragile confidence. Right-wing and Communist groups quickly took advantage of the situation to attack democracy. By 1930 Weimar's enemies, on both the extreme left and the extreme right, were engaged in a life-or-death struggle to see who could destroy the democratic republic first and impose its own ideology, Communist or Fascist, on the German nation.

The victor in the competition was Adolf Hitler, a fanatical right-wing German nationalist whose National Socialist (Nazi) party proclaimed its intention to repudiate Versailles and the galling military restraints and financial burdens it had imposed on Germany. The new Third Reich would restore German pride and German might. Like Italy's Fascists, the Nazis glorified the state and expressed contempt for democracy and parliamentary institutions.

Indeed, Hitler's contempt for parliamentary institutions and hatred of liberal values went beyond even Mussolini's. The Nazis were rabid racists who carried ideas of Nordic supremacy to a chilling conclusion: All other peoples were inferior beings who must ultimately bow to the *Herrenvolk*, the superrace of northern Europe. In Hitler's view the Jews, especially, were inferior beings who were responsible for most of Germany's calamities. Blaming the Jews for Germany's defeat in 1918, Hitler promised the German people that he would punish the Jews, destroy the Communists, and make Germany a powerful nation once more.

Few Americans had paid much attention to events in Germany before 1933, but Hitler and the Nazis could not be ignored. Once head of the German state, the new chancellor renounced the armaments limitations of the Versailles treaty and began to rearm Germany. He swept away parliamentary government and either assassinated his democratic and leftist opponents or threw them into concentration camps. Finally, he instituted a reign of terror against Germany's Jewish population that sent thousands of the nation's most talented scientists, writers, musicians, doctors, and scholars fleeing to western Europe and the United States.

From the start Hitler's lust for territory and dominance was scarcely concealed. In 1936 he reoccupied the Rhineland, which had been demilitarized by the Versailles treaty. That same year he and Mussolini concluded an alliance of mutual support (the Rome-Berlin Axis). In 1937 the two dictators intervened in the civil war in Spain, siding with the Fascist strongman Francisco Franco against the coalition of liberals, socialists, Communists, and anarchists (the Loyalists) who supported the Spanish Republic. In 1938 Hitler began his campaign to reincorporate all German-speaking territories in Europe into "Greater Germany" by annexing Austria. Hitler's next target was Czechoslovakia, a democratic republic formed in 1918 from parts of the Austro-Hungarian Empire that contained several million Germans in its Sudetenland region.

Americans watched Hitler's course with dismay. Not all saw fascism-nazism as a serious danger. Some Catholic Americans and conservatives preferred Hitler's client, Franco, to the Spanish Loyalists. A small number of Italian-Americans and German-Americans endorsed the dictators of their respective mother countries. There was even a very small contingent of old-stock Americans who believed that nazism represented the "wave of the future." Yet undoubtedly the great majority of Americans deplored and feared what they saw taking place in central and southern Europe.

Hitler's progress disturbed his European neighbors even more than Americans. Under the Nazis Germany once

Adolf Hitler in 1938 at a major Nazi party conference at Nuremberg. He was about to provoke the greatest war in history.

more was becoming an expansionist nation that threatened the balance of power in Europe. But England and France, traumatized by their enormous human and financial losses in World War I and deeply troubled by the domestic repercussions of the worldwide Depression, were reluctant to take a strong stand against the German threat. When, in early 1938, Hitler demanded that Czechoslovakia turn over the Sudetenland to Germany, the Czechs asked the Western democracies for aid. British Prime Minister Neville Chamberlain and French Premier Édouard Daladier refused. Believing they could successfully appease the Germans, they agreed, at a conference with the German dictator at Munich in September 1938, to support Hitler's demands on the Czechs. Unable to confront Germany alone, the Czechs were forced to surrender the Sudetenland.

Chamberlain returned home from Munich convinced that appeasement would work and that the Munich Pact would bring "peace in our time." It did not. In March 1939 German forces occupied the rest of now defenseless Czechoslovakia and set up a puppet regime. Hitler soon made territorial demands on his eastern neighbor, Poland. By this time only the near-blind could believe that Hitler

and Mussolini did not pose a serious threat to the peace and stability of Europe. In April 1939 Britain and France signed a mutual assistance pact with Poland promising to come to its aid if attacked.

Roosevelt and the Interventionists.   Though most Americans deplored the rise of the dictators and the European retreat from democracy, they did not agree on their implications for the United States. Liberals and leftists saw a rising tide of authoritarianism about to submerge free government everywhere. Even many conservative Americans feared that German, Italian, and Japanese expansionism would upset the delicate international balance of power long maintained by Britain and France, throwing the world into turmoil. The Nazis seemed particularly dangerous. When Hitler violated the Munich Pact, Americans were forced to confront the possibility that he could be stopped only by force.

Yet few Americans wished, in the mid- to late-1930s, to see the United States become directly involved. By this time American isolationism had hardened into an ideology that deplored all foreign wars and all foreign entanglements. The American people had no vital interests in these transoceanic conflicts, isolationists believed, and in the past they had been duped into joining them by munitions manufacturers, bankers, and other cunning, self-serving manipulators.

Between 1934 and 1936 isolationist views were reinforced by the Senate Munitions Investigating Committee hearings probing the origins of World War I. The committee, chaired by Senator Gerald P. Nye, concluded that those who profited from munitions manufacture had encouraged United States involvement in the war. In the wake of the Nye Committee hearings, Congress passed a series of Neutrality Acts requiring the president in the event of war to embargo arms shipments to belligerents, forbid American citizens to sail on belligerent ships, and deny bankers the right to extend credit to warring powers. By avoiding the policies of 1914–1917, the United States could stay out of any future war. By 1937, according to an opinion poll, 94 percent of the American people favored nonintervention abroad regardless of who the combatants were or how just their cause.

President Roosevelt from the outset was more interventionist than most Americans. A disciple of Admiral Alfred Thayer Mahan and Woodrow Wilson, FDR believed in America's responsibility as a great power to cooperate with other nations to achieve a stable world order. During the 1920s he moved with the drift of American public opinion to isolationism, but the rise of the dictators quickly revived his internationalist convictions. At what moment Roosevelt and his advisers concluded that the dictators must be stopped is unclear. As early as 1933 he tried to induce Congress to prohibit the sale of arms to aggressor nations. In 1935, in the interest of world security, he tried to get the United States admitted to the World Court. Congress, dominated by isolationists, rejected both schemes.

Frustrated in Europe, Roosevelt worked to strengthen the United States against "the aggressors" by establishing closer ties with Latin America. His Good Neighbor policy, built on the efforts of his Republican predecessors, was designed to create "hemispheric solidarity." During his first term of office FDR renounced the Platt Amendment, which had allowed the United States to intervene in Cuban affairs. At two Latin American conferences in 1933 and 1936, the United States reinforced the pledge (given in the 1928 Clark Memorandum) to cease intervening in the affairs of Central and South America. Before long the United States had ended its remaining occupations of Caribbean nations. The Good Neighbor policy would pay dividends: When war came, almost all the Latin American countries would support the United States against its enemies.

During his second term, as the international situation darkened, the president turned to face the aggressors di-

rectly. In 1937, following Japan's attack on China, he denounced "international lawlessness" and suggested that nations contributing to "international anarchy" be "quarantined"—isolated and walled off by the rest of the world. By this time the president clearly considered Germany, Italy, and Japan potentially dangerous adversaries; in private conversations he referred to them as the "three bandit nations."

Ideology influenced Roosevelt's views. The totalitarian and militaristic regimes of Germany, Italy, and Japan represented everything a liberal democrat despised: repression, racism, and brutality. The president, moreover, was surrounded by advisers who saw Hitler as antichrist, embodying every primitive, irrational, reactionary current in Western society. But there were also more self-interested motives at play. Ever since the late nineteenth century the United States had relied on the Western European nations, especially Britain, to impose stability in the world outside the Americas. With England and France threatened by Germany, and the Japanese on the rampage in the western Pacific, the president feared for the safety of the United States. What would happen if Britain and France could not check Hitler? A triumphant Germany to the east, allied with a triumphant Japan to the west, would leave the United States a besieged outpost in the middle of a hostile and dangerous world.

By this time most Americans shared FDR's opinion of the dictators. A Gallup poll in mid-1939, following Germany's occupation of Czechoslovakia, showed that 65 percent of Americans endorsed a boycott of Germany and Italy, and 55 percent wanted the Neutrality Acts revised to aid the democracies. Few citizens favored their nation's direct involvement, however. There seemed little need. If war were to erupt, Britain and France would surely win. But even if they did not, the American fortress could hold out indefinitely against the victorious dictators, safe behind its ocean moats, patrolled by its powerful navy.

★ THE EROSION OF AMERICAN NEUTRALITY ★

In the fall of 1939 American complacency would be put to the test. On September 1, after signing a nonaggression pact with the Soviet Union's Joseph Stalin, his former archenemy, Hitler attacked Poland. Two days later Britain and France, having pledged their support to Poland, declared war on Germany.

On September 3, Roosevelt delivered a fireside chat to the American people. Like Wilson in 1914, he promised to expend "every effort" to avoid war. Consciously diverging from his predecessor, however, he refused to ask Americans to "remain neutral in thought as well." As required by the neutrality legislation, he forbade the export of arms to the belligerents. But on September 21 he called a special session of Congress to ask for repeal of the arms embargo.

Roosevelt's tactics when Congress met typified his cautious behavior in dealing with his isolationist opponents. The president knew they would use anti–New Deal feelings to win support for their position and he kept out of sight while others carried the burden of getting repeal through Congress. Meanwhile, behind the scenes he used his patronage to bring fellow Democrats into line. The strategy worked. On October 27, by a vote of 63 to 30, the Senate replaced the arms embargo of the Neutrality Acts with a "cash-and-carry" policy that permitted the British and French to buy war matériel as long as they paid cash and transported their purchases in their own ships. A week later the House accepted the revision, 243 to 181.

Hitler Conquers Europe. Had the war against Hitler gone well for the Allies, the United States could have preserved its neutrality. It went badly. Poland fell to the German invaders in five weeks. For several months thereafter an ominous quiet hung over Europe. During the "phony war," as the isolationists contemptuously called it, nothing happened to indicate that the major European powers were locked in a life-or-death struggle. Then on April 9, 1940, the German army struck at Norway and Denmark. Denmark fell virtually without a shot. Norway, with the aid of British and French troops and naval units, fought bravely against the invader but was quickly subdued. On May 10 German armored units smashed across the borders into Belgium, Luxembourg, and Holland. In a week German armored columns were sweeping across northern France toward Paris.

The British and French fought back, of course, but their armies were overwhelmed by the fast-moving German tank columns supported by terrifying Stuka dive bombers. The German *Blitzkrieg* destroyed French military resistance in a few weeks. By the end of May the British forces in France were pinned against the English Channel near Dunkirk by a tightening ring of German tanks and artillery. The British and French were able to hold the German tanks at bay long enough for an armada of small ships to rescue their entrapped troops from the flaming beaches, but most of their equipment had to be left behind. On June 10 Paris surrendered, and Italy entered the war as Germany's ally. On June 22, with more than half their country in German hands, the French, now led by Marshal Henri Philippe Pétain, an arch conservative, signed an armistice with the Germans that allowed the invaders to occupy the whole northern half of the country and the Atlantic coast. Some Frenchmen refused to surrender, however, and rallied around the free French leader, Charles de Gaulle, who established a London-based government-in-exile. Before long the Free French and the Pétain government located at Vichy were battling for control over the French overseas empire.

In a little over three months Hitler had conquered Norway, Denmark, Luxembourg, France, Belgium, and Holland, and had almost destroyed the power of mighty Britain. He had done in a few weeks what his imperial predecessor, Wilhelm II, had been unable to accomplish in four years of war. Americans were stunned by the rush of catastrophic events. *Time* magazine in its issue of May 20, 1940, reported American opinions as appalled but determined. Among the crowds that gathered on Boston's Washington Street to read the fast-breaking news bulletins, the talk was: "We'll be in it if it keeps up six months." In California "many . . . talked of U.S. naval participation in the war; and a feeling of inevitability was widespread." Even in Omaha, in the heart of the strongly isolationist Midwest, the magazine reported people saying: "It looks like we can't keep out."

Roosevelt's reaction to the Nazi triumph was swift: He asked Congress for vast sums for rearmament, including funds for 50,000 planes a year and a "two-ocean navy." By October Congress had appropriated $17 billion to strengthen the nation's weak defenses. In September it had authorized peacetime compulsory military service for the first time in American history. On October 16, 1940, some 6.5 million young men registered for the draft and prepared to go to training camps to become soldiers.

Meanwhile, the Germans had launched the Battle of Britain, an all-out air attack designed to soften England up for invasion. During the summer of 1940 German aircraft bombarded the British Isles by day until the losses exacted by the gallant but badly stretched Royal Air Force made these raids too costly. In early September the Luftwaffe began night raids that set London and other English cities ablaze. The British people suffered grievously but held on. Sustaining them were the words of their eloquent prime minister, Winston Churchill, who had succeeded Chamberlain after the Allied defeat in Norway. A master of English prose, Churchill declared that if the British Empire lasted a thousand years, men would say: "'This was their finest hour.'" He promised victory though the cost would be "blood, toil, tears, and sweat."

Britain's brave struggle aroused the admiration of virtually all Americans. News from Europe for the first time was relayed instantaneously to the United States by short-wave radio, creating a sense of participation impossible in an earlier day. From London Americans heard Edward R. Murrow and other American correspondents describe the Nazi air attacks while sounds of air-raid sirens, anti-aircraft guns, and bombs filled the background. They also heard the defiant and moving words of Churchill. As they listened to the broadcasts, most Americans found it impossible not to feel that they themselves were cowering with the British under the rain of German bombs.

Roosevelt's Third Term. By mid-1940 few Americans doubted that Britain's plight was desperate, and many believed that their country was next on Hitler's list after he had gobbled up and digested his enemies in Europe. In the spring, supporters of England, New Deal liberals, and what would later be called the eastern intellectual establishment, organized the Committee to Defend America by Aiding the Allies. Its chairman was the old Kansas progressive William Allen White. That fall a Gallup poll showed that half the voters were willing to help England "even at the risk of getting into war." Yet the isolationist voice remained powerful and insistent. In early September of 1940 a group of isolationists organized the America First Committee, composed of philosophical isolationists and conservatives with a fringe of Anglophobes, Roosevelt haters, and pro-Nazi anti-Semites. For the next year the two groups waged a bitter war for the minds of the American people.

Meanwhile, the country found itself in the middle of another presidential campaign. After keeping everyone guessing for months, FDR concluded that the survival of liberal policies and the nation's safety during the international crisis required his strong hand at the helm. Having effectively eliminated all potential party rivals, Roosevelt left the Democrats with no choice but to break with the two-term tradition and nominate him for a third time.

The 1940 Republican nominee was Wendell Willkie, a utility magnate from Indiana whose sincerity and boyish charm appealed to younger, less conservative Republicans. Fortunately for the country's unity, Willkie proved to be as much of an internationalist as Roosevelt. He denounced the president's gift of fifty overage destroyers to England in exchange for bases in British North American possessions (September 3) as "the most dictatorial and arbitrary act of any President in the history of the United States." But on the whole, the two candidates were careful to avoid arguing over foreign policy.

Toward the end of the campaign, however, Roosevelt uttered some words that would later make his friends cringe. In a speech in Boston in late October he promised his audience that American men would not go overseas to fight. "I have said this before," he declared, "but I shall say it again and again and again: Your boys are not going to be sent into any foreign wars." FDR would have been elected in any case; in the midst of the grave world crisis Americans were not inclined to exchange the veteran leader for a novice. But the promise helped. On election day Roosevelt carried 38 states to Willkie's 10 and won a popular majority of 27.2 million votes to his opponent's 22.3 million.

Lend-Lease. During the next full year of peace Roosevelt deliberately maneuvered the country ever closer to war, certain that the United States could not avoid confronting the

After France's fall, American admiration and support for Britain were reinforced by the fortitude the British showed in the face of the German blitz. Pictures like this one, showing Londoners bedding down in the city's subway to escape the Nazis' bombs, created an outpouring of sympathy in the United States.

dictators. A month following the election Churchill wrote to FDR, laying out Britain's plight in stark outline. The desperate prime minister warned that the well-being of the American people was "bound up with the survival and independence of the British Commonwealth of Nations." British sea power protected the United States against its enemies. But it was spread very thin and might collapse entirely if the Pétain government at Vichy turned over the French navy to the Nazis. Furthermore, if the Nazis gained control of the French fleet, they could then threaten Latin America. Nor was this all. In the Far East Japan was taking advantage of French, Dutch, and British weakness and inability to protect their Asian possessions by expanding its power and influence. Britain did not need American manpower, said Churchill, but it did need to guarantee that American supplies could get through the tightening German submarine blockade. Churchill pleaded for American naval assistance and for an end to the cash-and-carry system. Britain was running short of money. Cash-and-carry was a great improvement over the embargo, but more direct help was needed if Britain was to continue to serve as a bulwark against the Nazi scourge.

Churchill's letter was a masterly plea that played effectively on Roosevelt's deepest fears. The president quickly responded. On December 17 he called a press conference and, after puckishly informing the assembled reporters that there was no particular news that day, he proceeded to tell them a parable. Suppose, he said, my neighbor's home catches on fire and he needs my garden hose to put it out. Do I bargain with him over the cost of the hose? Obviously not. I give it to him and then say: "I want my garden hose back after the fire is over." If it is damaged, you replace it "in kind."

Soon afterward in a fireside chat, Roosevelt prepared the ground for his new aid scheme by warning the public of the critical danger to civilization posed by the Axis powers and explaining the need for the United States to become the "arsenal of democracy." In January 1941 he submitted the "lend-lease" bill to Congress. The measure broke sharply with the country's isolationist past. It authorized the president to "lend" military equipment to any country "whose defense the President deems vital to the defense of the United States" and provided $7 billion for the purpose, the largest single appropriation in the nation's history. Most Americans apparently favored the measure, but the great power it seemed to confer on the chief executive made them uneasy. The bill immediately came under withering attack. Senator Burton K. Wheeler of Montana called lend-lease the "New Deal's Triple A foreign policy" that would "plow under every fourth American boy." The isolationist *Chicago Tribune* called it "a bill for the destruction of the American Republic . . . [and] a brief for an unlimited dictatorship . . . with

power to make war and alliances forever." Administration officials retorted that Britain faced invasion within three months and without such aid would be defeated. If the British navy were destroyed or seized, the United States would be in serious danger.

Both sides had a point. Wheeler was being grossly unfair, and the *Tribune's* attack was as much anti-Roosevelt, anti–New Deal as a legitimate defense of the Constitution. But in later years many Americans would come to regret the erosion of congressional control over foreign policy that began under FDR. Yet the president was not consciously attempting to usurp power; he and his advisers were expressing their honest fears. And most informed citizens supported them. After a furious battle the congressional isolationists were defeated. On March 11 Roosevelt signed the lend-lease bill into law. In a few weeks the $7 billion of war matériel that Congress had authorized began to flow to Britain.

United States Aid Increases. The additional aid provided by lend-lease had little immediate effect. During the spring of 1941 Americans held their breath as Germany and Italy smashed the Yugoslavs and the Greeks and forced the British to retreat almost to the Nile in North Africa. Meanwhile, Britain was losing the Battle of the Atlantic, as German submarines sent vast quantities of American munitions and supplies to the bottom of the ocean. Could nothing be done to stop the Axis?

In Washington, Roosevelt was uncertain what course to take and moved cautiously. On April 9 he concluded an agreement putting Greenland, a Danish colony, under United States protection, thereby extending American naval patrols partway to Britain. His advisers urged him to use the United States Navy to convoy arms all the way to Britain, but the president held back. On May 13 he agreed to shift part of the Pacific Fleet to the Atlantic. In mid-May he told Secretary of the Treasury Henry Morgenthau, Jr.: "I am waiting to be pushed into the situation."

On May 27 Roosevelt proclaimed an unlimited national emergency giving him expanded powers over the economy. He followed this move in June by an executive order freezing Axis assets in the United States and placing German and Italian ships in American ports under federal control. Each action brought the nation a little closer to outright belligerency, but still the president was reluctant to throw the country's full weight behind Britain. He believed war must come; but fearing the wrath of the isolationists, he felt unable to start it himself. Instead, he waited impatiently for the Germans to move offensively against the United States.

Hitler carefully avoided a showdown with America. However outraged at United States aid to Britain, he looked the other way, for he had other things in mind. Four thousand miles from Washington, on the plains of eastern Europe, German and Soviet troops faced one another along a common border that ran through what had once been the independent republic of Poland. For almost two years the two countries had maintained an uneasy marriage of convenience. Then, on June 22, 1941, in fulfillment of his long-cherished ambition to destroy communism and expand German power eastward, the Nazi dictator sent his tanks, aircraft, and troops hurtling across the border toward the heart of the Soviet Union.

In London and Washington the Nazi attack provoked a quick response. The British and Americans could have ignored Russia's plight. The Soviet Union, after all, was the seat of international communism, and many people in both countries considered it little better than Nazi Germany. These anti-Soviet feelings had been reinforced by the 1939 Nazi–Soviet pact and by the brutal Soviet invasion of small, democratic Finland in the winter of 1939–1940. Yet neither the British nor the American governments hesitated very long to offer help to the Russians. Two days after the German attack Roosevelt promised aid to the Soviet Union. In the fall a British-American mission traveled to Moscow

English ordinance personnel unpack American revolvers delivered under the terms of lend-lease, the program for supplying the Allies with desperately needed weapons. If American equipment made its way to the fighting fronts, could American soldiers be far behind?

to determine Soviet war needs. Soon afterward the United States pledged $1 billion in lend-lease matériel to the embattled Russians; by the end of the war American aid had grown to $11 billion in value.

Although he welcomed Russia as a new ally against Hitler, Roosevelt could not lose sight of Britain and the Atlantic. In July he sent troops to occupy Iceland and announced that the American navy would escort British-bound supplies as far east as that strategic island. The following month the president met Churchill on a ship off Newfoundland. Out of that meeting came the Atlantic Charter. This document affirmed and expanded upon the Wilsonian ideals of self-determination for all people, freer international trade, cooperative efforts for world prosperity, freedom of the seas, disarmament, and "freedom from fear and want." The charter was a moving declaration of liberal principles, but its real significance was its linkage of America and Great Britain in a common set of world goals.

Bit by bit, Roosevelt was pushing the United States toward a direct confrontation with Germany. He did not confide his goals to the American people, and that lack of candor has troubled even his firmest admirers. Yet the president was not seeking power or glory. FDR was certain that the fate of civilization depended on Hitler's defeat, and he felt he must do whatever was necessary to guarantee that defeat. Yet he feared taking a divided people into war and was still convinced that the enemy must act first.

Events seemed to be moving the way FDR hoped in the fall of 1941. Soon after his return from Newfoundland, a German U-boat commander off the coast of Iceland, believing his vessel to be under British attack, launched two torpedoes at the United States destroyer *Greer*, which had been tracking the submarine and radioing its location to the British. The *Greer* returned the fire. Roosevelt (neglecting to mention that the *Greer* had been engaged in unneutral activities) called the incident an act of "piracy legally and morally," adding that from now on American naval vessels would "shoot on sight" at any German submarine found between Iceland and North America. On October 9, 1941, he asked Congress to modify the Neutrality Acts further to permit the arming of American merchant vessels. Early in November, after the Germans had torpedoed the destroyer *Kearney* and sunk the U.S.S. *Reuben James* with heavy loss of life, Congress authorized the arming of American merchant vessels and removed restrictions on their carrying cargoes to belligerent ports.

By mid-November the United States was in a virtual naval war with the Germans. Yet a substantial minority of the American people still hoped to avoid full-scale military intervention. As recently as August the House had voted to extend the draft period an additional eighteen months by a margin of a single vote. Isolationist sentiment in Congress was powerful enough to prevent easy passage of the modifications of the Neutrality Acts. In the Senate the president's majority was only 50 to 37; in the House, 212 to 194.

The continuing isolationism troubled Roosevelt. What if the Germans avoided further serious incidents? How could Americans be brought, united, to the point of war? The problem stumped the president. As his friend and biographer Robert Sherwood later wrote: "He had no tricks left. . . . The bag from which he had pulled so many rabbits was empty." Fate—and the Japanese—would soon solve the problem for the president and the undecided nation.

Miscalculations in the East. Roosevelt and his advisers misunderstood and underestimated the Japanese. Japan had a deep emotional involvement in its East Asian expansionist policies. It also feared that without the resources of Manchuria, China, and the East Indies, it could not survive as a great power. It would not be easy to get the Japanese to back down in China, or the Far East generally, without the use of military force. In addition to underestimating Japan's commitment to expansionism, the American government did not take Japan seriously as a military opponent. Americans knew that Japanese industry was capable of producing the shoddy trinkets and gewgaws that flooded the five-and-dime stores of the day. But could it produce modern weapons?

Although it underestimated the Japanese, the American government, believing Hitler the more dangerous threat, at first sought to appease Japan. Having neither the steel nor the petroleum to maintain a modern war machine, the Japanese had to rely on imports. Until the fall of France, the United States, over the protest of China's many American friends, supplied much of them. When the Japanese began to pressure the Vichy French for bases in Indochina and threatened the Dutch in the oil-rich East Indies, however, the American government imposed licensing requirements on the export of American oil and scrap metal and forbade the export of aviation gasoline.

These moves goaded the Japanese into seeking allies elsewhere. In September 1940 Japan signed an agreement with Italy and Germany, converting the Rome-Berlin Axis into the Rome-Berlin-Tokyo Axis. The agreement pledged the three nations to support one another's plans to establish a "new order" in Europe and a "Greater East Asia" in the Far East. If any one of them was attacked by a fourth power—with which it was not then already at war—the others would go to its aid. The Soviet Union, which the Japanese feared, was specifically exempted from this provision, making it clear that it was aimed at the United States. In effect, if the United States attacked either Japan or one of the European Axis nations, it would find itself with a two-ocean war. The American government responded to this threat by prohibiting the export of scrap iron and steel outside the Western Hemisphere.

As yet, neither the Americans nor the Japanese were prepared for a showdown. In March 1941 the moderate government of Prince Fumimaro Konoye opened conversations with Secretary of State Hull in Washington to prevent an irreparable break between the two countries. The Japanese were willing to make minor concessions but not, as Hull demanded, to evacuate China. As the talks dragged on, the Japanese, who already controlled northern Indochina, moved to seize the rest of the French colony. In July 1941 Japan forced the Vichy government to grant it bases in southern Indochina, close to the East Indies and British Malaya. Shortly thereafter, Roosevelt ordered all Japanese assets in the United States frozen, virtually ending trade between the two nations. This move was quickly followed by the order of the governor of the Dutch East Indies embargoing Dutch oil to Japan.

By showing Japan how dependent it was on foreign sources of raw material, the Americans and Dutch hoped to give the Japanese government pause. Their moves had the opposite effect. During the remaining months of peace two groups of Japanese leaders—the military chiefs on one hand and the royal family on the other—battled over what policy to pursue toward the United States. Among the military leaders, the army generals were most confident and militant. The admirals, though convinced that Japan had little chance to win a war with America, favored a massive surprise blow that would so damage American military power that the United States would be forced to give Japan a free hand in East Asia. The American refusal to supply Japan with oil would soon cripple the Japanese war machine, the admirals said. Why not seize the oil wells in the Dutch East Indies and the vital rubber and tin of Malaya? Because such a move would certainly bring an American declaration of war, it would be advisable to open with a surprise knockout punch against the American navy. Prince Konoye and Emperor Hirohito opposed this aggressive course except as a last resort.

In August, Konoye proposed a meeting with President Roosevelt to iron out Japanese-American differences. Secretary Hull distrusted the Japanese, however, and the meeting was never held. But the American government was not anxious for a showdown, and for a while strung Prince Konoye along. In October, his credibility with his own people damaged by American delays, Konoye resigned in favor of the more militant war minister, Hideki Tojo.

Tojo was determined to break the deadlock between the two nations or attack. On November 5 the Japanese government resolved to adopt the admirals' policy unless the United States and Great Britain halted their aid to the Chinese and allowed Japan access to oil and other vital raw

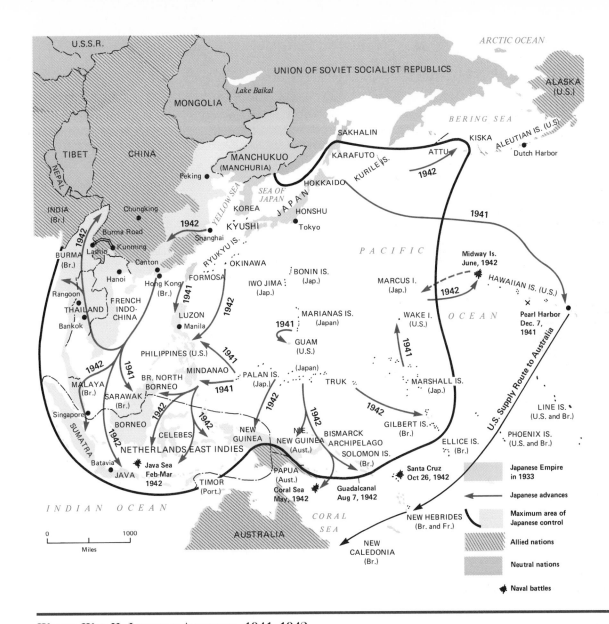

WORLD WAR II: JAPANESE ADVANCES, 1941–1942

materials from America and Southeast Asia. In return, Japan would agree to withdraw its troops from the French possessions when the war with China was over and would eventually leave China itself. On November 25 Admiral Isoroku Yamamoto ordered the navy strike force to put to sea, subject to last-minute recall.

The United States refused to accept the final Japanese terms. America could not, Hull believed, end its aid to Chiang Kai-shek; we were too firmly committed to a stable Chinese republic to desert him. Moreover, the Japanese could not be trusted to evacuate China.

The American government had broken the top-secret Japanese "purple cipher" code by this time and knew from intercepted messages that unless a settlement with the United States was soon reached, Japan would launch an attack against American or British-Dutch forces somewhere in the Pacific. The American government assumed that the blow would land in Southeast Asia and alerted the United States military commanders in Hawaii and the Philippines. On the morning of December 7, Washington time, Army Chief of Staff General George C. Marshall sent radiograms to San Francisco, the Canal Zone, Hawaii, and the Philippines, warning of an imminent attack. Electrical interference delayed the radio message to Hawaii, and it had to be sent by cable. By the time it arrived at the Western Union office in Honolulu, the bombs were falling over Pearl Harbor. On

Americans were horrified—and suddenly unified—by Japan's surprise attack on Pearl Harbor. But the Japanese were unified too, and certain they were in the right. An English-speaking Japanese pilot aboard Admiral Yamamoto's carrier strike force drew this prophetic cartoon before he and his fellow pilots set out to attack Pearl Harbor.

December 8 the United States declared war on Japan. Three days later the Germans and Italians ended American uncertainty regarding the European conflict by declaring war on the United States. The titanic struggle over intervention was finally over: A united American people were now heart and soul in the crusade to stop Hitler and the other aggressors.

★ MOBILIZATION AND SOCIAL CHANGE ★

World War II was the most costly war in American history. Between December 1941 and the Japanese surrender in the late summer of 1945, almost $300 billion was poured into the war effort. Sixteen million men and women served in the armed forces. Of these, almost 300,000 died in combat; another 700,000 were wounded.

The government, as we saw, had begun raising a military force before Pearl Harbor. Late in 1940 the first peacetime draftees were inducted into service. Most found the process of becoming a soldier exciting but painful. After induction the new GI—so called because of his "government issue" uniform and gear—was shipped off to a training camp for eight weeks or more of "basic training," followed by ei-

ther advanced infantry training or, if he was qualified, for instruction in some specialty. The voluntary branches of the service—Navy, Marine Corps, Coast Guard, and Army Air Corps—conducted similar training operations.

Most young Americans found it difficult to adjust to the armed forces. They were fed well, and the transformation of many once-skinny adolescents into well-muscled young men amazed their families and friends when they returned home on their first leave. But they did not like military discipline and despised the hard, dirty jobs of obstacle-course running, calisthenics, bivouacking, and marching—not to speak of KP (kitchen police) and guard duty. The War and Navy departments tried to make the hardships acceptable by providing libraries, movies, and religious services. Church and volunteer organizations sponsored camp dances to which young women were invited. Yet complaints about the military's stupidities and foul-ups became the mark of the wartime citizen-soldier; SNAFU, an acronym usually politely interpreted as situation normal, all fouled up, was added to the American vocabulary. Nevertheless, as time would show, American youths would make fine soldiers when well led. They would go through the hell of war griping all the way, and yet fight bravely when they had to.

Racism on the Home Front. Pearl Harbor was a tremendous shock to American confidence. For days after the frightening news from Hawaii, Americans peered anxiously at the skies, expecting to see bombers overhead with Japan's rising-sun emblem on their wings. In the early weeks following December 7 there were air-raid scares in several cities.

The fears were aggravated by an unbroken string of Japanese victories that followed the initial Pearl Harbor attack. On the West Coast something close to panic seized Americans in these early months. Jittery citizens, certain that the resident Japanese-American population was a potential "fifth column," demanded their removal from the exposed Pacific Coast. Fear was reinforced by racism and greed. Long the targets of bigotry, the Japanese were envied for their economic success. Many whites coveted their property, much of it rich farmland.

For a time Washington officials resisted the pressure for relocation by West Coast congressmen and state officials, including the zealous California attorney general, Earl Warren. But they soon yielded. On February 19, 1942, Roosevelt signed an executive order allowing the War Department to "prescribe military areas . . . from which any or all persons may be excluded." Within weeks thousands of Issei (immigrant Japanese) and Nisei (American-born Japanese) were forced to sell their homes, businesses, and farms, often at a fraction of their true value, and move to detention centers in isolated areas of inland states such as Utah, Arizona, and Arkansas.

Though these centers were a far cry from the concentration camps of Nazi Europe, they were a disgrace to American democratic principles. Despite harsh living conditions, most of the imprisoned people survived the war; remarkably, many of them retained their loyalty toward the United States.

By comparison, the government treated other enemy nationals generously. Italians and Germans, even those not citizens, were left alone. Leaders of the pro-Nazi German-American Bund, along with a handful of native-born Fascists, were indicted under the antisubversive Smith Act of 1940, which imposed tighter controls over aliens and made it a crime for any person or group to teach the overthrow of the government by violent means. But the extreme anti-Germanism that characterized World War I did not surface. Nor was there very much of the superpatriotism that abounded during the earlier war. Antiradical sentiment declined sharply. The Communist party, which had denounced Roosevelt as a warmonger during 1940 and early 1941, hailed him as a hero after the Soviet Union was attacked by Hitler. Thereafter, the American Communists threw themselves into the war effort with great fervor. Impressed by the patriotic enthusiasm of the Communists and deeply moved by the heroic struggle of the Russian people against Hitler, Americans avoided most of their antiradical excesses of 1917–1918.

Of course, the war did not turn the country into a democratic paradise. Besides the hostility toward the Japanese, antagonism surfaced toward Mexican-Americans. In June 1943 some young Mexican-Americans attacked

Some 110,000 people of Japanese descent—many of them American-born and citizens—were rounded up in California, Washington, Oregon, and Arizona, and sent to "relocation camps" following the Pearl Harbor attack. The move, spurred by panic and bigotry, was almost without precedent in American history, and was a blot on an otherwise good record on civil liberties during the war.

U.S. sailors on liberty in Los Angeles. The Chicano youths had been wearing "zoot suits"—flashy outfits with broad-shouldered jackets, tightly pegged trousers, and wide-brimmed flat hats. The sailors retaliated by beating up every zoot-suiter they could find. It was, *Time* magazine said, "the ugliest brand of mob action" in California "since the coolie riots of the 1870s." Hundreds were injured before the violence ended.

Blacks, too, fell victim to wartime social stresses. War brought a mixture of good and bad to black Americans, much as it had in 1917–1918. During peacetime rearmament defense contractors had resisted hiring black workers. When A. Philip Randolph, president of the all-black Brotherhood of Sleeping Car Porters, threatened in May 1941 to organize a mass march on Washington to protest this exclusion, Roosevelt established the Fair Employment Practices Committee (FEPC). Thereafter, the FEPC and the pressure of urgent war orders forced open the employment doors to black Americans. Black men and women by the thousands soon found jobs in the tank factories of Detroit, the steel mills of Pittsburgh, the shipyards of Puget Sound, and the aircraft factories of southern California, Texas, and Kansas.

Economic progress for blacks during the war was not matched by major advances in other areas of American life, however. More black soldiers than ever before became commissioned officers, and for the first time blacks were admitted to the Marine Corps and to the navy at ranks higher than mess boy. But through most of the war they were kept in segregated military units. Their obvious second-class status injured black military morale. In the South and at army camps in the North, serious tensions developed between black servicemen and neighboring white civilians. In Detroit, where thousands of blacks and newly arrived southern whites lived and worked side by side, racial friction set off a bloody race riot in mid-1943 that left 30 people dead, 800 injured, and over $2 million in property destroyed.

Despite their mistreatment, black Americans were loyal and patriotic. Hitler's virulent racism, of course, was particularly repulsive to black Americans; but many of them might have been attracted to the Japanese if only because they were nonwhites fighting the white Western nations. A tiny minority did find the Japanese cause appealing; the overwhelming majority, however, supported the war effort. Like other Americans, black citizens bought bonds, worked in war plants, and collected scrap metal and rubber. Thousands of black troops fought in Europe and the Pacific, albeit in segregated units. In Italy the all-black Ninety-ninth Fighter Squadron achieved a distinguished record in air combat against the German Luftwaffe.

Yet many black Americans remained skeptical of the great war to make the world safe for freedom, and black leaders put the nation on notice that it could not continue to treat black people as badly as it had in the past. Rather than opposing the war effort, however, they called for the "Double V"—"victory over our enemies at home and victory over our enemies on the battlefields abroad." Ultimately, black people would have to fight for their own civil rights, black leaders declared. As Walter White, head of the NAACP, noted, the majority of black soldiers would "return home convinced that whatever betterment of their lot is achieved must come largely from their own efforts.

Black Americans fought in segregated units in World War II, just as they had in World War I. Here the Army Air Force's all-black 99th Fighter Group assembles at the beachhead of Anzio, Italy.

Woman war workers made up for the manpower shortage during World War II.

They will return determined to use these efforts to the utmost."

Pressures on the Family. The war was hard on American families. Married men had been exempted from the peacetime draft; but in 1943, when the need for manpower reached its peak, even fathers were inducted. The wartime industrial boom also strained family relations. Much war industry was located in the South, the Southwest, and the Pacific Coast states. Whole families from the Northeast and Midwest moved to remote parts of the nation to work in war plants, but sometimes male workers left their wives and children behind to move in with parents or other relations. Between 1940 and 1945 the number of families headed by a married woman with her husband absent rose from 770,000 to almost 3 million.

Young wives and mothers made the best of a bad situation, but the best was often not very good. Women were lonely and sought out one another's company. Some inevitably found other male companionship, and marriages broke up. More than a few GIs received "Dear John" letters telling them that other men had taken their place.

Many young women found the war an opportunity. In 1942 Congress authorized the Women's Auxiliary Army Corps (the WACS, after *auxiliary* was dropped from the title), and later established the WAVES, the navy equivalent. In all, a quarter of a million young women donned military uniforms and served as clerk-typists, technicians, jeep drivers, or nurses at home and behind the front lines.

Many women went to work to keep busy, to supplement their incomes, or to help the war effort. "Rosie the Riveter" in overalls and cap became a familiar figure in every American industrial community. The nation admired her type, but working mothers compounded the problems caused by absent fathers. Children often did not get proper care. Agnes Meyer, wife of the *Washington Post* publisher, observed their plight in California:

> In the San Fernando Valley . . . where several war plants are located, a social worker counted 45 infants locked in cars of a single parking [lot]. In Vallejo the children sit in movies, seeing the same film over and over again until mother comes off the swing shift and picks them up. Some children of working parents are locked in their homes, others are locked out.

During the war juvenile delinquency soared. Crime as a whole dropped, but juvenile arrests increased 20 percent in 1943. In San Diego, a major aircraft-manufacturing center and naval base, 55 percent more boys were charged with crimes in 1945 than in the previous year; the arrest rate for girls climbed 355 percent.

The pressures on families were particularly severe where there was an especially heavy concentration of war

On the home front speedy production was essential to victory. This ship was completed in ten days, a remarkable feat that brought FDR (in the foreground, left) to the Portland, Oregon, shipyard where it was accomplished.

industry. In such areas housing was in short supply, and families had to live in trailers or Quonset huts. Classroom space was often limited, and schools were forced to hold double sessions. The government provided money for "war-impacted" areas, but it was not enough to improve conditions created by the influx of new people.

To a degree, all civilians paid a price for the war. After Pearl Harbor the government clamped down on automobile production and housing construction. It soon began to ration rubber tires and later restricted gasoline consumption. Racetracks, motels, and vacation resorts lost business; but passenger railroad service boomed. Metals, deflected into war production, disappeared from many familiar items, and consumers had to accept familiar commodities made of wood or plastic. Rationing of meat, sugar, coffee, butter, and cooking fats—all needed by the armed forces or requiring essential shipping to import—began in 1942. Rationing of clothing began at about the same time. The housing, gasoline, and rubber shortages produced hardships, but the food and clothing rationing were relatively easy to accept. Meat was often hard to get, but once people stopped hoarding things they thought would become scarce, they generally discovered that they had ration

"points" for more items than they either needed or could afford. Compared with the experiences of besieged Britain or embattled Russia, life in wartime America remained easy.

Economic Prosperity.   The war's most important effect on the home front was the boost it gave the economy. By 1941 lend-lease and defense spending had reduced unemployment to less than 10 percent of the civilian labor force, the lowest figure since 1930. By 1943 it was down to a nominal 1.9 percent. The gross national product leaped, and by 1943 the country enjoyed a per capita GNP some 70 percent higher than in the "miracle" year 1929. Even when purely military items are subtracted, Americans were better off economically by the middle of the war than in the most prosperous peacetime era. In essence, by forcing the government to forsake a balanced budget, the war made up for lagging private consumption and investment.

Everyone welcomed the return of prosperity, but a new danger, inflation, soon appeared. The public had billions of extra dollars to spend; but because much industrial capacity was diverted to military needs, there was relatively little to spend it on. The absence of expensive consumer durables such as automobiles, household appliances, and new homes put great added pressure on the prices of those goods that were available.

To deal with this imbalance of commodities and cash, the government raised taxes drastically. Beginning with the first "defense" budgets in 1940, Congress lowered the personal income tax exemption, raised tax rates sharply, and established the excess-profits tax for business firms. In June 1943 the treasury began withholding income taxes from paychecks. Forty-four percent of the cost of the war was paid with tax money; for the first time most working Americans paid income taxes.

To further reduce the danger of inflation, the government once again issued war bonds. As in World War I, bond sales campaigns also helped whip up support for the war effort and nurtured civilian morale. In September 1942 the treasury launched its first war-bond drive with a massive advertising campaign in print and on radio. Prominent athletes, politicians, and literary figures contributed their names and services to the enterprise. The most effective support for these drives came from Hollywood stars, who were credited with selling bonds worth $834 million in the first drive alone.

Neither taxes nor bond sales were sufficient to skim off all the excess purchasing power, and prices soon began to rise. The largest increases, over 30 percent, occurred between 1940 and 1942. Then in 1942 Congress established the Office of Price Administration (OPA) and the War Production Board, with the power to ration scarce raw materials, set wage rates, and fix wholesale and retail com-

Price Controls

The first economic effect of the outbreak of war in December 1941 was to put everyone back to work. Before long, however, the flood of federal war spending began to produce enormous pressures on prices. By mid-1942 prices and wages were being closely regulated by the government through the Office of Price Administration to prevent runaway inflation.

Not every American accepted the regimentation that this system entailed. One of the objectors was John L. Lewis, president of the powerful United Mine Workers' Union. Lewis believed that his men's wages had been fixed *after* prices had already risen, thus depriving them of considerable income. On the other hand, he charged, nothing was being done to limit business profits. Roosevelt responded to Lewis's attempt to scuttle price-and-wage controls by the Executive Order below, issued in early April 1943. (His proposal, at the end of the order, to increase taxes, was never adopted by Congress.)

"The Executive order I have signed today is a hold-the-line order.

"To hold the line we cannot tolerate further increases in prices affecting the cost of living or further increases in general wage or salary rates except where clearly necessary to correct substandard living conditions. The only way to hold the line is to stop trying to find justifications for not holding it here or not holding it there. . . .

"All items affecting the cost of living are to be brought under control. No further price increases are to be sanctioned unless imperatively required by law, . . . any further inducements to maintain or increase production must not be allowed to disturb the present price levels; such further inducements, whether they take the form of support prices or subsidies, must not be allowed to increase prices to consumers. . . .

"On the wage front the directions in the order are equally clear and specific.

"There are to be no further increases in wage rates or salary scales beyond the Little Steel formula [a 15 percent increase authorized in 1942], except where clearly necessary to cor-

rect substandards of living. Reclassifications and promotions must not be permitted to affect the general level of production costs or to justify price increases or to forestall price reductions. . . .

"Some groups have been urging increased prices for farmers on the ground that wage earners have unduly profited. Other groups have been urging increased wages on the ground that farmers have unduly profited. A continuance of this conflict will not only cause inflation but will breed disunity at a time when unity is essential. . . .

"We cannot stop inflation solely by wage and price ceilings. We cannot stop it solely by rationing. To complete the job Congress must act to hold in check the excess purchasing power. We must be prepared to tax ourselves more—to spend less and save more. The details of new fiscal legislation must be worked out by the appropriate committees of the House and of the Senate. The executive department stands ready to submit suggestions whenever the committees desire."

---

modity prices, rents, and other charges. From April 1943 to August 1945 retail prices rose only 4.2 percent, a figure that seems remarkable today.

Admittedly, the public paid a hidden cost for price stability. The amount of regimentation and paperwork was enormous. Labor was forced to accept wage regulations that deprived it of the advantages that a tight labor market would otherwise have conferred. Profits, too, were closely controlled, but—many liberals complained—not tightly enough. The government essentially paid war contractors what they asked without looking too closely at costs— "Cost-Plus," it was called.

Yet the scheme got the job done. Under a succession of "dollar-a-year" men called in from private industry to run various superagencies, war production burgeoned despite

bottlenecks, labor and raw material shortages, strikes, and union disputes. Between 1940 and 1945 United States factories turned out 300,000 aircraft, 5,425 merchant ships, 72,000 naval vessels, 87,000 tanks, 2.5 million trucks, 372,000 artillery pieces, and 44 billion rounds of small-arms ammunition. The country truly became, as Roosevelt had promised, the arsenal of democracy.

★ THE FIGHTING FRONTS ★

The months immediately following Pearl Harbor were a time of disastrous American and Allied retreat. In quick succession, the Japanese invaded and captured Singapore,

Wherever the Nazis conquered, they murdered and destroyed. Here soldiers of the German occupation army in Warsaw round up Jewish civilians for deportation to the concentration camps and eventual execution.

Hong Kong, the Dutch East Indies, and Burma. In May 1942, after a long siege of the Bataan Peninsula and Corregidor Island, near Manila, they compelled the surrender of a combined force of Americans and Filipinos. Before the final collapse, however, the American commander, General Douglas MacArthur, was rescued and brought to Australia to lead the defense and reconquest of the South Pacific. Despite these critical losses, Roosevelt and his advisers, believing Hitler the more dangerous enemy, accepted the British commitment to Europe first. The war against Japan would be a holding operation until American factories and training camps had provided enough arms and men to deal with Hitler and the Japanese simultaneously.

Unlike the British, who favored an indirect attack on Germany, either through Africa or against Europe's "soft underbelly" along the Mediterranean, Roosevelt and Chief of Staff Marshall wanted a major buildup of Anglo-American strength in Britain, followed by a direct thrust into the heart of German-occupied Europe across the English Channel. In the end British and American strategies were combined, but the decision probably spread Allied strength too thinly and lengthened the war.

Early in 1942 the first American GIs arrived in Northern Ireland. They were the vanguard of millions of American soldiers and airmen who poured into the United Kingdom to prepare for the cross-Channel attack. At the end of the year the United States and Britain undertook Operation Torch, an invasion of North Africa that pitted Allied troops against combined German and Italian forces commanded by General Erwin Rommel.

Meanwhile, the Allies were winning a vital battle in the Atlantic. By the use of destroyers, aircraft, and new sub-marine-detection equipment, and by the sheer productivity of American shipyards, losses to the U-boats were either cut drastically or made up, though not before millions of tons of Allied shipping went to the bottom.

The year 1942 was the darkest of the war, but it also marked the turning of the tide. At the Battle of the Coral Sea (May 7–8) American carrier planes stopped the Japanese advance southward toward Australia. A month later (June 3–6) they inflicted an even greater defeat on the Imperial Navy at the Battle of Midway, sinking 4 Japanese carriers and shooting down 275 enemy aircraft. Midway shifted the balance of naval strength in the Pacific permanently to the United States. Soon afterward, American marines, soldiers, and naval forces invaded the Japanese base on Guadalcanal island, opening a three-year "island-hopping" counteroffensive against the Pacific enemy.

In Europe, however, Hitler held on tenaciously. He had subjugated millions of Europeans, from France in the west to European Russia in the east. His treatment of these people, especially the Slavs of eastern Europe and the millions of Jews who had fallen into Nazi hands in Poland, occupied western and central Europe, and the Soviet Union, was savage. Hitler considered the Slavs and Jews subhuman, and he treated them like vermin. Many were shipped to slave-labor camps where they were worked to death. Far worse, in late 1941 the Nazi SS (*Schutzstaffel*, an elite military corps) began the "final solution to the Jewish problem": the mass extermination of Jews—men, women, and children. By the time the war ended, almost 6 million Jews—along with hundreds of thousands of Russians, Poles, Gypsies, and other "inferior beings"—had been shot, starved, or gassed to death in such concentration camps as Auschwitz, Treblinka, and Majdanek. This event—the Holocaust—is one of the most horrifying pages in recent human history.

Wartime Diplomacy. The war effort required complex interactions among nations allied as much by necessity as by affection and shared values. Relations among the Western Allies were relatively good. Roosevelt did not get along with the touchy Free French leader de Gaulle, but Britain and the Commonwealth countries (Canada, South Africa, Australia, and New Zealand) cooperated closely with the United States. Roosevelt and the half-American Churchill, both extroverts, got along famously. With its vast manpower and industrial output, America was clearly the senior partner. If the British resented that seniority, they recognized its inevitability.

Generally speaking, relations with China were good, too. Roosevelt believed that under Chiang Kai-shek China had the makings of a great power, once freed of the Japanese yoke. In 1942 he and Churchill agreed to abandon the remaining special privileges their nations held in China. In

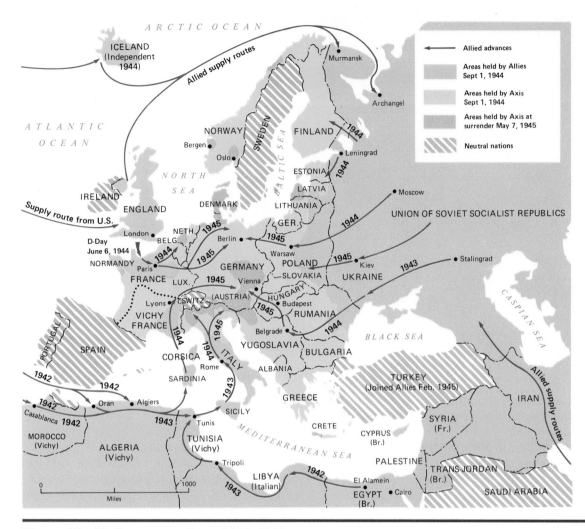

WORLD WAR II: CLOSING THE RING, 1942–1945

November 1943, at Cairo, the two Western allies and China agreed to exact "unconditional surrender" peace terms from Japan if the Allies won the war, and resolved to return to the Chinese territories like Manchuria, Formosa (Taiwan), and the Pescadores, which Japan had wrenched from her in past years.

Relations between the Western partners and the Soviet Union were not so cordial. In 1943 the Russians dissolved the Comintern, the central body of the international Communist movement, as a gesture of cooperation with the West. Nevertheless, Stalin remained suspicious of Britain and the United States, and they of him. The mutual Soviet-Western distrust dated from the years of the Russian Revolution (1917–1919), when Britain, France, and the United States, along with Japan, had sent troops to support the enemies of the Bolsheviks in order to keep Russia in the

war against imperial Germany. Thereafter, suspicion had been kept alive by continued competition between capitalists and Communists in the world arena.

Though Hitler's invasion of Russia temporarily eclipsed East-West differences, the war itself created grounds for mutual distrust. Stalin suspected that Roosevelt and Churchill would be content to see the Soviet Union and Nazi Germany destroy each other on the Eastern Front. Starting in late 1941, he repeatedly demanded that Britain and America open a second front in Western Europe, to relieve the pressure on Soviet troops. That the Allies delayed the opening of that second front until the invasion of Normandy in June 1944 was a chronic sore point with the Soviet Union.

Still, suspicion did not prevent cooperation. In October 1943 Secretary of State Hull, British Foreign Secretary Sir Anthony Eden, and Vyacheslav M. Molotov,

It is not difficult to guess who is winning this game of World War II dominoes. Note the benign figure of "Uncle Joe" Stalin to the right. His image would soon become much more sinister in the perception of Americans. (It is a mark of the times, perhaps, that the "good guys" are depicted smoking!)

the Soviet foreign minister, met in Moscow to discuss wartime problems and consider postwar reconstruction. The ministers agreed to establish a European Advisory Commission to formulate policy for Germany after victory and to set up a world organization to maintain international peace. One knotty problem that they could not solve was the postwar fate of Poland. Britain and the United States were committed to returning the Polish government-in-exile, then in London, to power when the war ended. The Soviet Union preferred a government friendlier to itself. The issue was not settled at Moscow and continued to rankle; but as a token of good faith, Stalin promised to join the war against Japan as soon as Germany was defeated. At Teheran, Iran, a month later, Churchill, Roosevelt, and Stalin met personally to confirm the results at Moscow and plan joint military operations against the common foe.

The Defeat of Germany. By the time of the Teheran meeting, Soviet fortunes had begun to improve. The initial German offensive against Russia had carried Hitler's armies to the gates of Moscow by September 1941. In the course of their eastward drive they had killed, captured, or wounded some 2.5 million Soviet troops, virtually wiped out the Soviet air force and tank corps, destroyed enormous quantities of war matériel, murdered thousands of civilians, and laid waste to hundreds of Russian cities.

But during the winter of 1941–1942 the Soviets counterattacked, forcing the Germans to retreat at some points.

In the spring the German offensive resumed, and by fall Hitler's armies had penetrated to Stalingrad, on the Volga River, and Maikop, in the Caucasus. During this critical period vast Allied air fleets based in England dropped tons of bombs on Germany and German-occupied territories. These raids devastated the civilian population of Germany but did little to relieve pressure on the Russians or impair the German war effort.

The war on the Eastern Front turned in February 1943 when the Russians forced the German forces at Stalingrad to surrender. In August the annual German summer offensive was stopped dead by the Soviet armies and then reversed. In the spring of 1943, in North Africa, the combined British and American forces led by generals George S. Patton and Bernard Montgomery, under the overall command of General Dwight D. Eisenhower, dealt the final blow to Rommel's Afrika Korps. Rommel was rescued to fight again, but on May 13 some 250,000 Axis troops surrendered to the British and Americans. In early July the Allies invaded Sicily. The king of Italy soon announced the resignation of Mussolini and negotiated the surrender of Italy. Mussolini was rescued by German troops and placed at the head of a puppet Italian regime. Meanwhile, British and American troops had invaded the Italian boot, only to encounter fierce and effective opposition from the entrenched Germans, who retreated slowly while inflicting heavy casualties on the Allies.

The following year, 1944, was the beginning of Nazi Germany's end. In January, in the east, the Russians freed

Not until June 1944 were Germany's western enemies able to engage it on land. Here we see American troops wading ashore on the Channel coast of France. The place was Omaha Beach, the landing area where the Americans met the fiercest resistance. American casualties were heavy.

Leningrad from a devastating two-and-a-half-year siege and began their major westward drive. By February they had crossed the 1939 Polish-Russian frontier. In Italy the stalled Allied advance resumed, and on June 4 the American Fifth Army liberated Rome; then in August the British marched into Florence.

By this time Eisenhower had launched Operation Overlord, the long-awaited second front in France. The cross-Channel attack began before dawn on the morning of June 6, when a colossal armada of Allied warships, transports, landing craft, and concrete caissons that could be converted into artificial ports approached the French coast in Normandy. After several days of ferocious fighting, the beachheads were secured. For six weeks the Germans were able to contain the Allies. Then, at the end of July, the American Third Army under George Patton broke out and began the drive east toward Germany. On August 15 the United States Seventh Army landed on the French Mediterranean coast and advanced north to attack the Germans from behind. On August 25 the Free French Second Armored Division liberated Paris.

The end of Hitler's empire was in sight. In October American troops crossed onto German soil. The Germans rallied briefly at the Battle of the Bulge, but in March American armies leaped the Rhine in force and dashed eastward. Meanwhile, the Russians, too, had crossed into Germany. On April 22, 1945, they reached Berlin. Rather than face defeat, Hitler committed suicide in his underground Berlin bunker. On April 25 American and Russian troops met at Torgau on the Elbe. On May 7 the German military commander accepted unconditional surrender at Allied headquarters. The war in Europe was over.

Yalta. In February 1945, as Germany's collapse neared, Stalin, Churchill, and Roosevelt met once again, this time at Yalta in the Soviet Crimea. Out of their deliberations emerged a set of important arrangements that helped mold the postwar world. The Yalta conference results fall into two parts: a series of arrangements announced soon after the meetings, and a number of secret provisions not even revealed to Congress.

In their public pronouncements the three leaders agreed to cooperate militarily until Germany's unconditional surrender and then to establish four occupation zones in the defeated nation, one for each of the major powers plus France. These would remain under military control until a final peace settlement with Germany down the road. They agreed to root out nazism from Germany so that its people could eventually join the community of peaceful nations. They announced that they would meet in San Francisco in April 1945 to draw up the charter for a "United Nations" world organization that would replace the League of Nations. In the countries liberated from the Nazi yoke, provisional governments would be established composed

George S. Patton

General George S. Patton once wrote: "War is very simple, direct and ruthless. It takes a simple, direct and ruthless man to wage war." Everyone who knew Patton recognized that he was describing himself.

Patton was destined to be a soldier. One of his ancestors had been a Revolutionary War general; his grandfather, the first George Patton, had commanded a regiment of Virginia infantry during the Civil War and had died of battle wounds in 1864. His father attended the Virginia Military Institute (VMI), though he became a California lawyer and politician rather than a regular army officer. As a child, George was fascinated by military history and military heroes and read about them voraciously while growing up on his father's ranch near Pasadena. He eventually developed the strange sense that he had been a soldier in many previous incarnations—with Caesar in Gaul, with the English at Crécy, and with Napoleon at Jena and Austerlitz.

The young Patton spent his childhood riding horses and learning the classics by heart. In 1904 he entered West Point. Though bright—even intellectual—he was poor in mathematics and took five years to graduate, and then only in the middle of the class. Fortunately, he had money, both through his own family and through his wife, Beatrice Ayer, a New England heiress, and this would help the young second lieutenant's army career despite his undistinguished record at "the Point." While other young officers in the peacetime army were forced to get ahead on their merits, Lieutenant Patton entertained lavishly and often provided his superiors with mounts from his stable of thoroughbreds.

But Patton had more than generous hospitality to offer. He was well-read, literate, and charming. He was also colorful and impetuous. In 1916 he served as aide to John ("Black Jack") Pershing, commander of the army expedition sent into northern Mexico to capture Pancho Villa, and attracted wide attention by killing three of Villa's bodyguards in a Wild West–type shootout.

Patton liked to dress the part of military hero. Tall and erect, he wore high, shiny cavalry boots, starched cavalry breeches, a well-tailored khaki wool shirt, and a tie neatly tucked into his shirt between the second and third buttons. Strapped to his hips in open holsters, he carried two pearl-handled revolvers.

In 1917 Patton fought with the American Expeditionary Force in France in a new military branch, the tank corps. He won several medals, and was promoted to the rank of colonel, but was severely wounded before the final drive against the Germans. He returned to the boredom of peacetime army service in 1919, and during the next twenty years occupied himself largely with polo, riding, writing articles on the art of war for military journals, and attending every army school available. During the late 1930s he attracted the attention of George C. Marshall, the army deputy chief of staff.

Marshall regarded Patton as hot-tempered and insubordinate, but also as brave and aggressive. When America began to rearm to meet the growing German and Japanese threats, he saved Patton from oblivion by assigning him a prominent role in the revival of the army's tank force.

When war broke out Marshall gave Patton command of the First Armored Corps, and in October 1942 he and his men landed in North Africa to wrest the region from the Vichy French and their German masters. Patton's own men, though green and half-trained, fought well. But other American troops, pitted against the veterans of Erwin Rommel's Afrika Korps, were whipped badly at Kasserine Pass in Tunisia. Hoping to restore morale, General Dwight Eisenhower, in overall command of the British-American forces, sent Patton to the Tunisian front. He performed as expected. Taking command from his beaten predecessor, he clamped down on the lax practices previously allowed. Because too many officers were reporting late to duty each morning, he closed the officers' mess at 7:30 A.M. He also insisted that all personnel under his command, including the nurses, wear their steel helmets at all times. Patton did not leave compliance to chance. He personally gathered up violators and, after chewing them out en masse, told them they could either pay a $25 fine or be court-martialed. It was even rumored that he peeked into unit latrines to see if men answering the call of nature did so with their helmets firmly on their heads. Patton's tactics were not always appreciated, but they were effective in restoring morale and infusing fighting spirit into the Tunisian front troops.

In July 1943 Patton led the American forces in the invasion of Sicily from North Africa. His superior in the campaign was British Field Marshal Bernard Montgomery, a cautious man whose indecisiveness angered and frustrated the American. Patton's pent-up rage boiled over in August when, on a series of visits to Sicilian military hospitals, he slapped and kicked several American soldiers awaiting evacuation for what he considered malingering and cowardice. Eisenhower forced Patton to apologize when he got wind of these incidents, but he tried to keep them from the American people. In November, however, the story was leaked by the radio commentator Drew Pearson and produced a storm of public outrage. Americans who felt that citizen-soldiers of a democracy should not be abused by their officers demanded that Patton be relieved of command. Eisenhower thought Patton too good a soldier and refused, but he also denied Patton the coveted command of the great cross-Channel invasion of France being prepared for 1944.

In March 1944 Patton was assigned to command the U.S. Third Army in England as a subordinate of Omar Bradley, the American general in charge of the invasion. He and his men did not land on the beaches of Normandy on D-Day, June 6, 1944, but arrived weeks later, when the Anglo-American forces were penned up in the Cotentin Peninsula, unable to break out of the pocket and sweep south and east to destroy the Nazis and liberate Europe. On August 1 Patton's tanks punched through the German line at Avranches and burst out into open country. The Third Army rolled up the enemy into Brittany to the west and simultaneously sliced through the German lines to the south and east. The triple-pronged tactic was probably a mistake. Though made worse by the caution and tardiness of the British and Canadians on the eastern end of the Normandy front, the thrust into Brittany slowed the American advance eastward and prevented the encirclement at Falaise of most of the German army in France.

By mid-September Patton's army had dashed to the east as far as the Franco-German border, but then ground to a halt for lack of supplies and gasoline, much of which had been commandeered by Montgomery for *his* drive eastward. Patton was forced to mark time while the Germans themselves prepared a counterblow. At this point—if the supplies had been available and if Bradley and Eisenhower had given him the go-ahead signal—the war could probably have been quickly won. Instead, just before Christmas, having squeezed every available man, gun, tank, and plane, from their depleted resources, the Germans attacked the Americans in the Ardennes Forest.

The Battle of the Bulge was Germany's last gasp on the Western Front, but it produced a near disaster for the American army. The blow fell on General Courtney Hodges's First Army, which reeled back fifty miles and threatened to crack. At Bastogne 18,000 Americans were surrounded by the German forces. They refused to surrender, though greatly outnumbered. Eisenhower called on Patton for help, scarcely believing he could turn his Third Army, oriented eastward toward Germany, northward in time to aid Hodges and save the besieged Americans troops. But Patton shifted direction in a few days and launched a powerful counterattack against the Germans from the south that lifted the Bastogne siege and broke the Wehrmacht's offensive.

This was the last major military effort the Germans were capable of. They were now too exhausted by five years of war against half the world to continue more than a token fight. By March 1945 Patton and his colleagues had driven to the Rhine. Soon after, the Anglo-American troops were slicing through Germany virtually without opposition, while the Russians, coming from the opposite direction, were steamrolling over the few ill-equipped troops the Germans could still muster. Patton was one of those American officers who hoped that American troops could drive on to Czechoslovakia and exclude the Russians. But on April 16 he was ordered to turn south to prevent the Nazis from retreating to a supposed "redoubt" in the mountains, where, it was feared, they would hold out to the bitter end. In the end the Soviets liberated the Czechs from Nazi control and ultimately made the country into a Soviet satellite.

The Third Army's last day of fighting was May 6, 1945. It was also George Patton's. Following the German surrender Patton was placed in charge of the program in Bavaria to uncover and punish ex-Nazi leaders, but he was now convinced that the Russians were a greater danger to America and urged a German-American alliance to drive the Russians back across the Soviet border. It is not surprising that the Bavarian denazification program was a conspicuous failure. Patton was soon at the eye of a storm over his seemingly pro-Nazi position, and shortly after was removed from his command and placed in charge of a largely paper army as punishment.

In December, scarcely six months after the war's end, Patton suffered a broken neck in an automobile accident. Twelve days later, at the army hospital at Heidelberg, he died of a blood clot on the lungs. He was buried at the big American military cemetery at Hamm in Luxembourg, alongside 6,000 other men of the Third Army that had done so much to destroy the power of Hitler's savage empire.

"The Big Three" met for the last time at Yalta in February 1945. There they discussed the United Nations and the partition of Germany, boundaries and political arrangements in eastern Europe. Two months later, Roosevelt, already looking frail, died.

of all "democratic elements" to be chosen by free elections. The future Polish government, they declared, would be made up largely of the pro-Soviet provisional government established at Lublin, rather than the London-based, pro-Western government-in-exile. Poland's postwar boundaries would be shifted westward at the expense of Germany, and in Yugoslavia, the pro-Soviet guerrilla leader, Josef Tito, would lead the future provisional government.

The secret clauses, not revealed until much later to the world public, contained an agreement on mutual repatriation of Soviet and American prisoners of war swept up by the respective UN armies. It included a voting formula for the Big Four nations in the UN Security Council to come after the San Francisco meeting. Most important of all, it agreed that the Soviet Union would declare war on Japan "in two or three months after Germany . . . surrendered." In return for helping Britain and the United States to defeat Japan, the Soviet Union would receive from Japan the Kurile Islands and the southern half of Sakhalin on the Pacific. In

addition, it could establish an occupation zone in the northern half of Korea, establish a Soviet protectorate over Outer Mongolia, and be allowed special privileges in Manchuria and other parts of northern China, notwithstanding America's long-standing policy of protecting China's "territorial integrity."

Roosevelt's concessions to the Soviet Union at Yalta have since been sharply criticized. Eventually the Soviet Union would establish puppet regimes in Poland and eastern Europe generally, and strengthen its position in the Far East. But the Yalta Conference was not to blame for this outcome. By the time of Yalta, Soviet troops had swept across Poland and were already entering Germany in great force. Nothing could have kept the Soviet Union from imposing its will on Poland or the Balkan and Danube regions. As for the concessions in the Far East, the American atomic bomb had not been successfully tested and no one could foresee that by the time Germany surrendered, Japan would be on its knees and Soviet aid not needed. In February 1945

Roosevelt faced the prospect of having to launch a huge amphibious invasion of the Japanese islands, and he believed that Soviet help would be vital to that campaign. Roosevelt knew that the Russians had driven a hard bargain at Yalta, but he did not see how it could have been avoided. As he told a close adviser shortly after the conference: "I didn't say it was good. . . . I said it was the best I could do."

The Last Days of the Pacific War. Meanwhile, there was still a war to win in the Pacific. From 1943 to 1945 the United States mounted a score of bloody and expensive amphibious operations. Moving from the east under the command of Admiral Chester Nimitz, American naval task forces thrust deep into Japanese-controlled areas. Under cover of carrier bombers and fighters and the big guns and rockets of the battleships and cruisers, waves of marines and army troops landed on the island beaches and smashed Japanese resistance. After Midway the Japanese navy no longer controlled the open seas, but it continued to be effective against the landings, especially as American forces neared Japan itself. On October 25, 1944, the Japanese launched their first kamikaze attacks—suicide missions of untrained pilots willing to fly their bomb-loaded planes directly into American invasion ships. Meanwhile, MacArthur's forces, coming from their bases in Australia to the south, made a series of brilliant end runs around Japanese-controlled islands, leaving large pockets of imperial troops behind to be mopped up at leisure.

The Japanese fought desperately for every scrap of coral reef. Even when overwhelmingly outnumbered and at the end of their strength, they refused to surrender. Whole Japanese garrisons went to their deaths in suicide charges against the Americans. Where the terrain permitted, Japanese troops retreated to interior caves and mountains and fought to the last man. The Pacific fighting was always on a smaller scale than in Europe or North Africa, but it was more vicious and proportionately more costly. At Iwo Jima, 775 miles from the main Japanese island of Honshu, over 4,500 Americans lost their lives early in 1945. Japanese casualties were even greater: Over 21,000 of the emperor's finest troops died defending the small dot of land.

In late February 1945 MacArthur's forces marched into the wrecked Philippine capital, Manila. Soon marines and army units invaded Okinawa, 360 miles from the Japanese main islands. This attack was the largest amphibious operation of the Pacific war and also one of the costliest. Kamikaze planes sank or badly damaged 30 American vessels, and Japanese ground troops inflicted almost 40,000 casualties, including over 11,000 deaths, on the invaders before the Americans could take the island.

Once in American hands, Okinawa was converted into a powerful air base in preparation for the invasion of the Japanese home islands. By now Japan was in desperate straits. Many Japanese cities were in ruins, the Imperial Navy rested on the bottom of the Pacific, and the surviving parts of the empire that had supplied Japan with vital raw materials were either in American hands or inaccessible because of devastating American submarine attack on vital shipping lanes. Yet the Japanese still had the will and the means to fight. On the main islands 2 million troops and 8,000 kamikaze planes awaited the final American attack. If the experience of Okinawa, Iwo Jima, Guadalcanal, and the other islands was an accurate foretaste of Japanese determination to resist, the Americans could expect hundreds of thousands of casualties in any invasion attempt. MacArthur worried that his men would face a fanatical enemy prepared to sacrifice every Japanese subject rather than surrender.

The First Nuclear Attack. After the capture of Saipan in July 1944, American B-29 superfortresses began the systematic bombing of Japanese cities that culminated in the nuclear destruction of Hiroshima and Nagasaki on the Japanese main islands of Honshu and Kyushu. The long course that led to these atomic attacks began quietly in 1939, when a group of scientist-exiles from Hitler's Germany informed Roosevelt that the Nazis were preparing to construct a new bomb of unimaginable destructiveness, based on the newly discovered process of uranium fission. The United States, they declared, must undertake a program to develop an atomic bomb before Germany could succeed. In mid-1940 Roosevelt turned the proposal over to a newly formed National Defense Research Committee.

After Pearl Harbor the government launched the so-called Manhattan District Project. At three major centers hundreds of scientists and technicians, headed by J. Robert Oppenheimer, searched for ways to build an atom bomb. The cost ran to almost $2 billion, but the engineering problems were gradually solved.

As the war approached its end in 1945, Niels Bohr, Albert Einstein, and several other scientists concluded that the bomb would not be needed and, fearing a postwar international atomic weapons rivalry, they sought unsuccessfully to stop the Manhattan Project. By the time the first atomic bomb was exploded experimentally at Alamogordo, New Mexico (July 16, 1945), the decision to use the bomb against Japan had been the subject of much heated debate in high government circles and among atomic scientists. Opponents of the bomb argued that the Japanese were on their last legs and would sue for peace shortly with or without the atomic bomb, especially if the Allies allowed the emperor to remain on the throne. In any case, why not demonstrate the bomb's power on some dummy target and

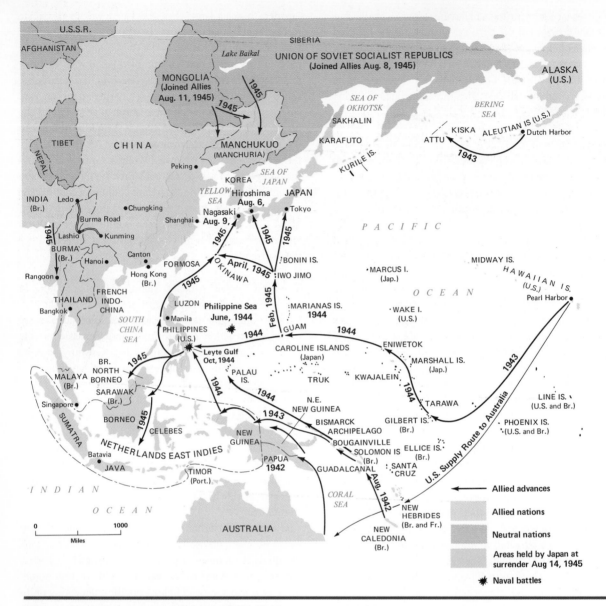

WORLD WAR II: ASSAULT ON JAPAN, 1942–1945

so spare many lives? Proponents of dropping the bomb noted that the United States had warned the Japanese in late July that unless they accepted Allied "unconditional surrender" peace terms, they would suffer "prompt and utter destruction." The warning had been spurned as "unworthy of public notice." As for providing a demonstration of the bomb's potential, only two bombs were available, and no one knew for sure that they could be used under combat conditions. If a demonstration were arranged and the bomb failed to go off, the Japanese would become more firmly committed than ever to fighting to the end. And if the casualties had been so high

in the outlying islands, what would they be like when American troops landed on the sacred home islands?

The decision to use the bomb would not be made by FDR. In 1944 Roosevelt had been elected to a fourth term. His running mate was Senator Harry S. Truman of Missouri, who had achieved prominence as Senate investigator of abuses in war production. Roosevelt barely survived two months of his new term. In early April 1945 he died of a cerebral hemorrhage in Warm Springs, Georgia, worn out by twelve years of office during some of the nation's most trying and momentous times.

One month after its destruction by an atomic bomb, the heart of Nagasaki was nothing but a mass of debris. Sixty-five thousand people were killed or wounded in the surprise attack.

Truman scarcely knew the atomic bomb existed when he took the oath of office. Once he learned of the bomb's power, he was determined to use it, convinced that invading the Japanese home islands could be a colossal bloodbath. The new president had no doubt that the atomic bomb represented the fastest way to end the war with the fewest American casualties.

Early on the morning of August 6, 1945, the B-29 Superfortress *Enola Gay* left Tinian Island for Japan. The plane and its two escorts arrived over southern Honshu at dawn. At 8:15 the bomb was released over Hiroshima. Sixty seconds later the *Enola Gay* crew watched in disbelief as an immense fireball rose over the city and slowly turned into a mushroom cloud.

For the bustling city of Hiroshima it was a moment of unspeakable horror. Hundreds of people simply vanished from the face of the earth, incinerated by the intense heat. Others were torn to pieces. Thousands, unshielded from the flash, were severely burned. All told, over 60,000 people died in the first few minutes of the attack. Others, exposed to high radiation, sickened and died later. The entire center of the city was flattened except for a few reinforced concrete structures.

Now the war moved swiftly toward a conclusion. Two days after the Hiroshima attack, the Soviet Union declared war on Japan and sent troops across the Manchurian frontier. On August 9 another atomic bomb was exploded over Nagasaki, killing another 35,000 Japanese. By this time the Japanese leaders were meeting to consider surrender. The military advised fighting to the bitter end, but the emperor vetoed the idea. Assured at the last minute that Hirohito would not be forced to abdicate, the Japanese accepted Allied surrender terms. On September 2, aboard the battleship *Missouri* anchored in Tokyo Bay, the Japanese signed the capitulation that ended the most devastating war in history.

★ CONCLUSIONS ★

During the two days of official jubilation that marked VJ (Victory-Japan) Day, few people asked themselves why the nation had gone to war. Thereafter, speculation ballooned as many of those who had at first opposed the war sought to justify their positions or to take intellectual revenge on their opponents.

Those critics asserted that the United States had no vital reason to join the anti-Axis coalition. Only Roosevelt's need to escape the political and economic impasse confronting the New Deal or, alternately, his unwarranted and grossly exaggerated fear of Hitler's designs, led him to favor American involvement. Nor was the president honest in his actions, they said. While denying that he wanted war, he was actively turning the United States into the anti-Axis arsenal and maneuvering the Japanese into a position where they had to attack the United States or surrender their vital interests. Some suggested that Pearl Harbor was the result of a conspiracy by the administration to turn public opinion in favor of war: By ignoring the intercepted Japanese messages, these critics said, the government made the American navy a sitting duck for Japanese bombs.

As we have seen, these charges are, at best, half-truths. By 1941 the president undoubtedly believed that war was unavoidable. But he wanted to fight Hitler, not Tojo; the Japanese could be attended to eventually after Germany's defeat. The Pacific war *was* a blunder, but only in the sense that Roosevelt preferred to contain the Japanese while taking care of the Nazis first, and Pearl Harbor forced the United States to fight both simultaneously.

Nor was the president seeking primarily to evade a political impasse. Roosevelt's fear of the dictators predated the New Deal's political and economic difficulties. FDR was a Wilsonian who believed in collective security and detested authoritarian regimes long before the problems of his second term stopped the New Deal in its tracks. It was Hitler's astonishing and alarming successes that awakened his concern after 1937, not political frustration. The president was indeed less than candid in his tactics. While denying that he favored war, he was goading the Nazis into attacking American ships. But however mistaken he was in not taking the voters into his confidence, his purpose was governed by his concern for free American institutions.

And still another qualification is in order. Roosevelt's view of the Axis danger was not his alone; it was shared by a majority of Americans. The president was more eager than many of his fellow citizens to intervene, but the public was treading closely on his heels. Every move FDR made to aid Britain—cash-and-carry, the destroyer deal, lend-lease—was strongly endorsed by the American public. By the late summer of 1941 Hitler had either frightened or antagonized an overwhelming majority of the American people. They were not yet ready to take the final plunge, but they did not have very far to go. In the end it was Germany's brutality, contempt for humanity, and apparent threat to every nation's independence, not Roosevelt's duplicity, that was responsible for America's intervention in World War II.

******** **FOR FURTHER READING** ********

William Langer and S. Everett Gleason. *Challenge to Isolation, 1937–40* (1952); and *Undeclared War, 1940–41* (1953)
These weighty studies support the view that war between Germany and the United States was inevitable. They are defenses of the Roosevelt foreign policy, and critics have claimed that they are in effect "official histories," that is, treatments that express the official United States government view.

James M. Burns. *Roosevelt: The Soldier of Freedom* (1970)
Sees foreign policy before and during the war through Roosevelt's eyes. Burns believes that FDR foresaw the danger Hitler posed to America and validly sought to stop him.

Robert Dallek. *Franklin D. Roosevelt and American Foreign Policy, 1932–1945* (1979)
A monumental study (540 pages) covering all of Roosevelt's foreign policy. Complete and exhaustive. Fine for the serious student.

Charles A. Beard. *President Roosevelt and the Coming of the War, 1941* (1948)
Written by the dean of American progressive historians just before his death, this book indicts Roosevelt for bringing on an unnecessary war in 1941 to revive the flagging fortunes of his party and the New Deal. A book both fiercely criticized and fiercely defended.

Samuel Eliot Morison. *The Two-Ocean War: A Short History of the United States Navy in the Second World War* (1963)
A condensation of the multivolume history Morison wrote for the navy. Morison had the good fortune to witness much actual sea action in both the Atlantic and Pacific, so this well-written account is often based on firsthand knowledge.

Barbara Tuchman. *Stilwell and the American Experience in China, 1911–1945* (1971)
General "Vinegar Joe" Stilwell brilliantly commanded American forces in China until 1944, when Chiang Kai-

shek had him recalled for advocating increased aid to Chinese Communist forces. This book illuminates the little-known war in the Far East and helps to explain why the Chiang government eventually collapsed.

Dwight D. Eisenhower. *Crusade in Europe* (1948)

An account in Eisenhower's own words of the American war effort in Europe that led to the final defeat of the Germans.

John Morton Blum. *V Was for Victory: Politics and American Culture During World War II* (1976)

Shows the greed, bigotry, dishonesty, and stupidity as well as the selflessness, goodwill, patriotism, and intelligence of Americans "back home" during the war.

Richard Lingeman. *Don't You Know There's a War On? The American Home Front, 1941–45* (1970)

Lingeman's book is lighter fare than Blum's and better at catching the flavor of American civilian life during the war.

Audrie Gardner and Anne Loftis. *The Great Betrayal: The Evacuation of the Japanese-Americans During World War II* (1969)

A critical account of an event that weakened the moral position of the United States in a war against the enemies of freedom.

James P. Baxter. *Scientists Against Time* (1946)

In few wars did scientific research play so decisive a role as in World War II. This popular history of the Office of Scientific Research and Development tells how industrial and university scientists worked with the military to develop improved radar, antisubmarine devices, rockets, blood substitutes, and medicines.

John Hersey. *Hiroshima* (1946)

Hiroshima has become a classic. It is a factual account of how the first atomic bombing affected six survivors: a clerk, two doctors, a poor widow with three children, a German missionary priest, and the pastor of a Japanese Methodist church.

John Toland. *The Rising Sun: The Decline and Fall of the Japanese Empire, 1936–1945* (1970)

An American journalist-scholar tells the story of Japan's tragic try for world greatness. A gripping account by one with intimate knowledge of what was happening in Tokyo. Sympathetic to Japan.

Robert Leckie. *Delivered from Evil: The Saga of World War II* (1987)

A well-written journalistic history of the war—all fighting fronts. Makes the war, in all its horrors, a vivid story.

28★

POSTWAR AMERICA

Why So Security Conscious?

1944	Bretton Woods Conference • Congress passes the GI Bill of Rights
1945	United Nations charter approved • Potsdam Conference • Roosevelt dies; Truman becomes president
1946	Winston Churchill's "Iron Curtain" speech • The Chinese civil war resumes • U.S. gives $3.75 billion in aid to Britain and $11 billion to the United Nations Relief and Rehabilitation Administration
1947	Truman orders the FBI to locate "bad security risks" in government • Congress endorses the Truman Doctrine, voting $400 million in military and economic aid to Greece and Turkey • Taft-Hartley Act • Congress creates the Central Intelligence Agency (CIA) • Cold War begins
1948	Congress approves the Marshall Plan • Berlin Airlift supports West Berlin against Soviet takeover • Executive order desegregates the armed forces • Truman elected president
1949	North Atlantic Treaty Organization (NATO) organized • The Soviet Union explodes its first atomic bomb • People's Republic of China established under Mao Tse-tung; Nationalists retreat to Taiwan
1950	GNP rises above its wartime peak • Alger Hiss convicted of perjury • Senator Joe McCarthy begins campaign against alleged American Communists • McCarran Internal Security Act passed over Truman's veto
1950–53	The Korean War
1952, 1953	The United States and the Soviet Union explode hydrogen bombs
1952	Dwight D. Eisenhower elected president
1954	*Brown v. Board of Education* • Army-McCarthy hearings; Senate condemns McCarthy
1954–1959	Housing legislation makes credit available for home buying, accelerating the middle-class move to the suburbs
1955	Montgomery bus boycott; Martin Luther King, Jr., rises to national prominence
1956	Interstate Highway System construction begins • Eisenhower reelected
1957	Federal troops enforce desegregation of Little Rock, Arkansas, Central High School
1960	John F. Kennedy elected president

Sometimes a book expresses the essence of a time so well that it captures the imagination of a wide public. One such work was *The Lonely Crowd: A Study of the Changing American Character*, by David Riesman, Reuel Denney, and Nathan Glazer, published in 1950.

According to Riesman and his associates, Americans had once been "inner-directed" people, guided through life by values learned in their youth. But most Americans were now "other-directed." They were no longer sure of themselves. What they did and said depended on what their peers were doing and saying; they were anxious to fit in, to conform to a group average. Using the technical imagery of the new postwar era, Riesman described the change as the shift from people with internal gyroscopes to those with internal radar sets.

Riesman was not contrasting individuality with a new conformity, but that is how *The Lonely Crowd* was understood, for conformity was what the public saw on every side. The spirit of adventure seemed to have gone out of American life in the 1950s, and safety appeared the only sensible course. Even young people, social observers said, were now sedate, at least in matters that counted. They were committed to security. Theirs was the "silent generation," aspiring to little more than a secure job, a new car in the garage, and a house with two smiling and obedient children in the backyard. Moralists of the generation that had experienced the Depression and the war, finding almost none of the usual irresponsibility and callowness of youth to complain about, lamented that young people seemed crushed and dispirited. As the literary critic Leslie Fiedler observed: "The young, who should be fatuously but profitably attacking us, instead discreetly explain, analyze and dissect us. How dull they are!"

Fiedler's barb implies the survival of an older group of intellectual naysayers. And there were such people. Fiedler obviously was one. Yet most of the thinkers of the "fifties," as we may conveniently refer to the decade and a half following VJ Day, were celebrators. American writers and intellectuals of the 1920s and 1930s had been critics of their society. Some had been Marxists as well. But during the postwar decade and a half this skeptical mood changed drastically. In religious thought beliefs emphasizing humanity's limitations and the inevitability of imperfection and injustice in this world became more common. In political thought the ideological battles of the 1930s waned, and pragmatism—once a liberating approach—became narrowly practical and a force for rejecting change and reform. In history, sociology, and political science American scholars ceased to be adversaries and began to praise their society, sometimes uncritically. When Daniel Bell published *The End of Ideology* (1960), he coined an epitaph for the intellectual life of the period.

Why had Americans become so timid? Why had they lost their taste for political change and social reform? Why did they reject achievement and fear self-expression? What made this the decade of the safe thought, the safe course, the safe life?

★ THE POLITICS OF DEAD CENTER ★

Timidity and fear of change clearly permeated political life from 1945 to 1960. Regardless of who was president, governing seemed little more than a holding operation. Reformers would find the fifties disappointing. The public was cautious and divided. Every step toward reducing inequalities of income and status and expanding the safeguards against life's mischances would be hard-fought. And in some areas the nation would actually retreat from the gains of the 1930s.

Liberalism did not die, however. The major trade unions, with more members than ever before, remained an important liberal force. The CIO's Political Action Committee continued to fight for higher minimum wages, expanded Social Security, federal health insurance, and racial justice. A liberal press, although a minority voice, survived from the previous decade. And the universities continued to be bastions of liberalism, though some of the more stylish campus intellectuals became conservatives.

Liberalism did not lack capable leaders after 1945. Philip Murray of the CIO and Walter Reuther of the United Automobile Workers continued to battle for greater social and economic equality and more effective security. So did Eleanor Roosevelt; after her husband's death she became the figure around whom many surviving New Dealers rallied. In 1947 she joined with economist John Kenneth Galbraith, historian Arthur Schlesinger, Jr., Minneapolis mayor Hubert H. Humphrey, labor leaders Reuther and David Dubinsky, and others to organize Americans for Democratic Action (ADA), a group dedicated to greater social justice and an expanded welfare state.

The Man from Missouri. Harry S. Truman, who inherited Roosevelt's job, was himself a throwback to an earlier, more liberal era. The temper of the times, however, frustrated his New Dealism and severely diminished what he could accomplish.

Truman was an interesting though limited man. Though a protégé of Thomas J. Pendergast, boss of the

Kansas City, Missouri, Democratic machine, his record as a country judge was a good one, and in 1934 he was elected to the United States Senate. As a freshman senator, Truman identified himself with the New Deal wing of his party. During his second term he achieved national stature by uncovering several sensational cases of waste and corruption in defense procurement, and in 1944 he replaced the erratic and visionary Henry Wallace as FDR's running mate.

Truman was unprepared for his abrupt elevation to the presidency in April 1945. He had not been admitted to the inner war councils of the administration, and FDR's death, he later declared, hit him so hard it felt as if "the moon, the stars, and the planets" had landed on his head. Despite his dismay, the new president moved quickly to take up the reins of domestic policy. Days after the Japanese surrender he submitted to Congress a legislative program that contained the essential features of what he would later call the Fair Deal, in imitation of Roosevelt's New Deal. Among his proposals were an extension of unemployment benefits to ward off a depression; continued support of the U.S. Employment Service to help returning veterans get jobs; a permanent Fair Employment Practices law to ensure equal job rights to minorities; retention of price and wage controls to prevent runaway inflation; an increase in the minimum wage from 40 cents to 65 cents an hour to maintain consumers' purchasing power; a large public works program to build roads, hospitals, and airports in order to provide jobs; "broad and comprehensive housing legislation" to give returning GIs places to live; government aid for small business; continued agricultural price supports for farmers; an expanded Social Security system; a bill to guarantee full employment; and, eventually, a national health insurance program.

Liberals applauded Truman's agenda. It seemed to contain something for everyone in the liberal coalition: minorities, wage earners, old people, farmers, consumers, and small business people. But they soon discovered that Truman was quick to propose but bewildered by the task of pushing his program through Congress. At the same time he seemed suspicious of Roosevelt's New Deal advisers, people with good liberal credentials, and turned instead to old cronies from his Kansas City days, men who seemed to one liberal editor "a lot of second-rate guys trying to function in an atom bomb world."

A crucial test of the president's liberalism came with the battle over what eventually became the Employment Act of 1946. Fighting for the bill was a flock of liberal journalists, lawyers, and economists who believed that wartime experience had confirmed John Maynard Keynes's theories that the level of employment could be managed by government spending policies. Conservatives, opposed to unbalanced budgets and big government, succeeded in getting

Here Ben Shahn depicts Truman and Dewey in 1948: They did not *make beautiful music together.*

the administration's proposal to guarantee full employment bottled up in the House. Liberals, by now virtually all committed Keynesians, called on Truman to appeal to the public over the heads of congressional conservatives and use his influence to garner votes in Congress. The president complied, but without apparent conviction, and the measure that finally passed as the Employment Act of 1946 was a weak one. It established a Council of Economic Advisors to inform the president about the state of the economy and recommend economic policies, and set up a Joint Economic Committee of Congress to perform similar functions. Absent from the bill was the commitment to *full* employment, and the explicit authorization of deficit spending when needed to achieve that end, that liberals desired. Instead, it declared that it was "the continuing policy and responsibility" of the federal government "to use all practicable means" to promote "*maximum*" employment, production, and purchasing power, and this requirement was so qualified as to seem meaningless. As the liberal magazine *The New Republic* wrote: "Alas for Truman, there is no bugle in his voice."

Liberals were disappointed again during the president's fight for price controls. They had hoped that wartime price regulations would be retained to protect middle- and lower-income consumers against serious postwar inflation. Conservatives opposed price controls, claiming that they merely fostered government bureaucracy and meddling and encouraged producers and retailers to keep goods off the market, thus guaranteeing shortages. When Congress passed a weak price-control bill, the president vetoed it, leaving the country without any price regulation at all. Prices of still-scarce civilian commodities, especially beef, quickly soared, rising faster in a few weeks than they had during the four years of war. The frightened Congress now became more receptive to a stronger bill, but Truman failed to fight effectively for one and signed a measure not much better than the first one. To make matters worse, the president used the powers granted him by the bill inconsistently. When his control board ordered a roll-back of beef prices, ranchers refused to ship cattle, creating a beef famine that had the public up in arms. Truman held out for a few weeks, then ordered the end of price controls on beef. Meat reappeared in stores, but at prices that shocked consumers. Once more the president seemed exposed as an ineffectual, confused, and inexperienced man.

The steady and rapid rise in prices in the postwar months injured all consumers, but few could make their discontent felt as effectively as trade unionists. In January 1946 the steelworkers, under Philip Murray, demanded a wage increase and threatened to strike if they did not get it. On January 19, some 800,000 workers walked off the job, not to return for eighty crippling days. The following April John L. Lewis of the United Mine Workers led 400,000 coal miners out of the mines to force the coal operators to meet his demands for a miners' welfare fund. Truman ordered the government to take over the mines but then met the union's demands. Soon afterward the president tried to avert a strike of railroad workers by threatening to seize the rail lines and have the army run them. The threat did not work and, faced with the prospect of the country shutting down, the president went before Congress to announce that he intended to draft the striking railroad workers into the army if they did not return to their jobs. The original speech threatened to "hang a few traitors" if the railroad brotherhoods did not relent. Fortunately, calmer heads prevailed and, as delivered, the address was somewhat more temperate. But Truman's toughness worked. As he was reading his speech he was handed a note by his adviser Clark Clifford. It read: "Mr. President, agreement signed, strike over." Truman glanced down at the scrap of paper and then told the joint session of Congress: "Gentlemen, the strike has been settled."

The labor troubles left a bad taste in everyone's mouth. The labor leaders felt Truman had been too tough; the middle class felt he had not been tough enough.

The voting public was probably less concerned than ardent liberals by Truman's failure to round out the New Deal. But many Americans were dismayed by his feeble leadership, inconsistency, and apparent lack of direction. They also resented his public profanity and his tendency to shoot verbally from the hip. In the 1946 congressional elections the Republicans made "Had Enough?" the party's slogan. The voters responded with a resounding "yes," electing a Republican Congress for the first time since 1930.

Election: 1948.   They quickly discovered that they had gotten more than they bargained for. The public mood was more conservative than during the Great Depression, but it was not reactionary. Yet the Eightieth Congress seemed intent on dismantling the New Deal and in short order made fierce enemies among important blocs of voters.

In June 1947, fired up over recent strikes and strike threats, Congress struck back at organized labor by passing the Taft-Hartley Act. This measure made illegal the "closed shop" and secondary boycotts: Labor unions could no longer force employers to hire only union members, nor could they boycott employers to prevent them from doing business with other employers on a union hit list. It allowed states to pass "right to work" laws permitting them to outlaw "union shops," that is, agreements where workers, *after* being hired, had to join the union. Further, the law allowed the government to impose a sixty-day cooling-off period on would-be strikers, legalized injunctions against strikes that threatened national health and safety, ended the practice whereby employers collected dues for the unions, required unions to disclose their financial practices, and imposed an anti-Communist loyalty oath on union officials. The law represented a major check to the power conferred on unions by the New Deal, and organized labor would make its repeal their chief legislative target for the next generation.

The same Congress frustrated the president in other ways, too. It refused to abolish racial segregation in the armed forces by statute and rejected his recommendations for a fair employment practices act to eliminate discrimination in firms with federal contracts.

Truman helped reestablish his liberal credentials by vetoing the Taft-Hartley measure, though Congress easily overrode him. He also accomplished by executive order the armed forces desegregation and the fair employment hiring practices that Congress refused to enact.

Truman capitalized brilliantly on the conservative record of the Eightieth Congress in his campaign for a full presidential term in 1948. His major opponent was the governor of New York, Thomas E. Dewey, a member of the

Truman

Democratic gains from election of 1944

Dewey

Republican gains from election of 1944

Thurmond

THE ELECTION OF 1948

northeastern liberal Republican establishment. But he also faced challenges from both extremes of the political spectrum. To his right was Senator J. Strom Thurmond of South Carolina, candidate of the States' Rights Democratic party ("Dixiecrats"), a new organization of rebellious southern Democrats strongly opposed to Truman's racial liberalism. To his left was the former vice president, Henry Wallace, running on the Progressive party ticket supported by left-liberals, Soviet sympathizers, and those who feared that Truman's foreign policies would lead to war. In the end neither Thurmond nor Wallace proved formidable, but from the outset Dewey appeared impossible to beat. Fortunately for Truman, Dewey was a stiff, overcontrolled man who reminded one observer of the little spun-sugar groom on top of a wedding cake. The Republican candidate's chief difficulty, however, was the negative record of the Republican Eightieth Congress.

Through the late summer and into the fall, Truman traveled 22,000 miles by train and spoke 271 times, often to small audiences in villages and whistle stops from the back of his observation car. The president attacked the "do-nothing Congress" and warned that those who had benefited from the New Deal—farmers, wage earners, ethnic Americans, and blacks—would lose all their gains if Dewey and his party won. The public took heed of his words and came to admire his pluck. Across the country the crowds began to shout "Give 'em hell, Harry!" at the game little man with the awkward gestures and rough syntax. The result was one of the greatest upsets in American presidential history. All the polls had predicted that Truman would lose; he beat Dewey by a popular plurality of 2 million votes and carried most of the South and West.

The Fair Deal. The American people had announced that they did not want to return to the "bad old days" of Herbert Hoover. It soon became clear that they did not want to go forward very far or very fast, either. The next four years disappointed those who looked for further liberal change. In his State of the Union message soon after the election, the president unveiled his program for domestic reform. His Fair Deal, foreshadowed by his 1945 proposals to Congress, aimed merely at rounding out the limited welfare state inaugurated by Roosevelt. But Congress, dominated by a coalition of conservative northern Republicans and Dixiecrat Democrats, refused to give him what he wanted. Little of the Fair Deal passed. Congress defeated Truman's farm program (the Brannan Plan), which replaced farm price supports by a system of farm income subsidies, rejected the administration's effort to add health insurance to the Social Security system, and ignored its scheme to provide federal aid for education. The only concessions that Truman could extract were a higher minimum wage, an extension of Social Security coverage to an additional 9 million citizens, and a Housing Act (1949) for slum clearance and low-cost federal housing. All chance of significant domestic change evaporated when high administration officials, including the president's aide, Harry Vaughan, St. Louis Collector of Internal Revenue James Finnegan, and Assistant Attorney General T. Lamar Caudle, were accused of selling their influence to people who wanted government favors. Truman himself was innocent of these misdeeds, but in the midterm elections of 1950 the Republicans picked up many additional seats in Congress.

The Republican Decade Begins. In March 1952 Truman announced that he would not be a candidate for reelection. This decision threw the Democratic nomination wide open for the first time since 1932, and it went to the one-term governor of Illinois, articulate, witty, and patrician Adlai E. Stevenson, the man favored by the party's liberal northern wing.

At the Republican convention the party regulars and conservatives supported Senator Robert A. Taft of Ohio, son of the twenty-seventh president and a man of rare intelligence but little personal warmth. The moderate wing and those who prized victory over ideological purity wanted Dwight D. Eisenhower, the hero of the great crusade in Europe. Ike was an attractive figure. Benevolent in mien, bland but reassuring in speech, he seemed to be everyone's kindly if slightly bumbling father. The general had no known politics; but he was clearly a patriot and a moderate, and he seemed certain to prove an irresistible candidate. After adopting a conservative platform, the Republican convention turned to Eisenhower. As its vice presidential candidate it chose an eager young senator from California, Richard M. Nixon, whose reputation as an aggressive campaigner and hard-line anti-Communist had recently brought him to national prominence.

The race that followed had more than its share of surprises. When it was disclosed that Nixon was the beneficiary of a businessmen's fund to help pay his political expenses, it looked as if the Democrats had a winning issue. But Nixon maneuvered out of the tight spot. Appearing on nationwide television, he explained that he had not received any personal benefit from the fund. He was not a rich man, he told his viewers. His wife, Pat, unlike the mink-coated wives of men in the Truman administration, wore a "Republican cloth coat." He had accepted one gift while in office: a black-and-white cocker spaniel, which one of his two young daughters had named Checkers. No matter what anyone said about that transaction, he was not going to give Checkers back!

The response to the "Checkers Speech" was overwhelming and positive. Most voters liked the homey, sentimental quality of the talk, and the public clamor guaranteed that Nixon would not be dropped from the ticket. In fact, the entire Republican campaign sounded a note of wholesome domesticity and traditionalism that the public found congenial. By contrast, Stevenson seemed too smart, too irreverent. He was amusing, no doubt, but could a witty man—and a divorced one at that—be trusted? By the end of the campaign the Republicans were making the Democratic candidate and the men around him seem vaguely un-American. They were "longhairs," "highbrows," and—a new term tailored to fit the baldpated Stevenson— "eggheads." The clincher came in October, when Eisenhower promised that if elected he would go to the Far East to help end the Korean War. Stevenson, in his characteristic way, quipped that if elected, *he* would go to the White House. In the end the Eisenhower-Nixon ticket won with a 7-million-vote margin.

"I Like Ike." In domestic matters Eisenhower was an indifferent, even lazy leader. Ike allowed his staff, headed by Sherman Adams, former governor of New Hampshire, to conduct most day-to-day business while he spent many happy hours on the golf links, especially after his heart attack in 1955. In later years the president declared that he had intended to "create an atmosphere of greater serenity and mutual confidence," and he accomplished his end. His opponents attacked him for his indolence, but most voters found it soothing.

Ideologically, Ike was a moderate conservative. He opposed deficit spending as "fiscal irresponsibility" and considered New Deal–Fair Deal social programs "creeping socialism." His cabinet was heavily weighted with businessmen, one of whom, Defense Secretary Charles E. Wilson of General Motors, offended many liberals by his remark that "what is good for the country is good for General Motors, and what's good for General Motors is good for the country." *The New Republic*, taking account of Labor Secretary Martin Durkin, an official of the Plumbers and Steamfitters Union, dubbed Ike's cabinet "eight millionaires and a plumber."

Eisenhower's policies tended to favor business and the growing suburban middle class over blue-collar wage earn-

Here "Ike" is making a campaign speech to the Republican National Convention in 1952. The slogan was platform enough for victory in November.

complex." This close alliance of defense industry and government was in some ways unavoidable, he noted; it was also a potential danger to the country's liberties. It was a strange conclusion for a military man, but his warning would be remembered and often praised by dissenting citizens in later years.

The Guard Changes. Prevented by the new Twenty-second Amendment (1951) from renominating Ike, the Republicans turned to Richard Nixon as their candidate in 1960. The Democratic front-runner as the campaign for the nomination began was Senator Hubert H. Humphrey of Minnesota. Opposing Humphrey was the young Democratic senator from Massachusetts, John F. Kennedy. Like Al Smith, Kennedy was a Catholic. But as a Harvard graduate, naval hero, and son of a rich and conservative businessman, he was poles apart from the poor boy from New York's Lower East Side. Kennedy's effective young staff was generously supplied with Kennedy family money and conducted a brilliant campaign. After overcoming party fears that voters would reject a Catholic candidate as they had in 1928, Kennedy won the Democratic nomination.

The presidential race itself was close. Nixon was the more experienced man. Liberals considered him too conservative, and even many middle-of-the-road voters judged him unprincipled. They remembered his devious smear tactics against past opponents and called him "Tricky Dick." But his long years in office, his close association with the beloved Ike, and his proven anticommunism gave him an early edge. By contrast, for all his glamour, Kennedy seemed too young and unproven. Moreover, although anti-Catholicism had declined, it still remained a potent force in the South and Midwest.

In the end the race became a popularity contest. Some of Nixon's initial advantage faded after a series of television debates established that the younger, handsomer man was also more adept at parrying difficult questions. Kennedy, moreover, was able to defuse the issue of his Catholicism by discussing his religion frankly and making it clear that he supported the separation of church and state. "No Catholic prelate," he stated, "should tell the president (should he be Catholic) how to act." Strongly backed by blacks, Catholics, Jews, and the big-city machines, and aided by a recession that had begun in 1960, Kennedy squeaked into office by a wafer-thin 118,000-vote margin over Nixon.

Even in politics, then, the fifties were a time when the public avoided activism and change. The period was bracketed by two moderately liberal presidents. But the first, Truman, had won election in his own right by the narrowest of margins, although he had the tremendous advantage of incumbency; the second, Kennedy, almost certainly

ers and city dwellers. Between 1954 and 1959 a series of housing acts made credit for home buying more readily available, accelerating the middle-class flight to the suburbs. In 1956 Congress passed the Highway Act, which authorized $32 billion for an immense interstate highway system financed by a federal gasoline tax. The measure, though much needed, further drained the central cities. Moreover, by destroying the passenger traffic of the railroads, it made suburbanites still more dependent on the wasteful, polluting private automobile. In later years many Americans would come to regret these changes, but at the time they clearly suited the fast-growing suburban middle class.

In 1956 the general ran for reelection with Stevenson his opponent once more. The team of Eisenhower and Nixon won an even greater victory than in 1952, despite the misgivings many Americans had about Ike's shaky health. During his second term the president spent more time than ever on the golf course. Yet at times Ike could rise above his indolence and natural conservatism. In his parting words to his fellow citizens, he warned against the "military-industrial

would have lost without overwhelming Catholic support. The voters did not want to turn back the clock, but neither did they want unsettling change. Except on the racial front, where the New Dealer–dominated Supreme Court acted without direct public sanction, political activism declined and unresolved problems piled up.

★ THE GOOD LIFE ★

Prosperity was a major prop of 1950s conservatism. And its impact was all the greater for being unexpected and hard-won.

Between 1941 and 1945, for many long, often grim months, 12 million GIs had yearned for the day when they could return to normal lives. Their dreams and goals were understandably domestic. After the pain and danger, they craved the tranquillity and happy pursuits of family, home, and successful careers. Many women, after months working the swing shift and living with parents and in-laws in temporary accommodations, looked forward to starting families and enjoying domestic routines in their own homes.

This vision of private satisfaction, so appealing and powerful to ex-soldiers and their wives or girlfriends, left a deep impression on the values of the postwar generation. After 1945 the average age for marriage dropped sharply, birthrates soared, and family sizes swelled. In 1945 the country had 37.5 million households; by 1960 there were almost 53 million. In 1954 *McCall's* magazine would coin the word *togetherness* to describe the new commitment to a close family life revolving about children, one-family suburban houses, and home entertainment.

The year of victory itself was a time of difficult new personal beginnings, of course. Children long fatherless and wives long without husbands had to adjust to an important new figure in the house; men had to get used to the company of women and children once more. Former GIs had to wind down and come to grips with—or forget—their war experiences. Yet most were able to make the difficult emotional adjustment to peace.

Avoiding a New Depression. They were also able to make a successful economic adjustment. During the final stages of the war Americans had begun to worry about what the defeat of Germany and Japan would mean for the economy. Knowledgeable observers forecast cataclysm once the stimulus of gigantic government spending ceased. Economist Leo Cherne envisioned hungry veterans roaming the streets in packs, fomenting strikes and rioting. Ordinary Americans, remembering the days of Depression breadlines, shuddered.

To prevent disaster, in 1944 Congress passed a measure popularly known as the GI Bill of Rights. This law extended to all honorably discharged veterans several benefits, including generous monthly allowances for education; loans to purchase farms, businesses, or homes; and unemployment compensation of $20 a week for a maximum of fifty-two weeks. Millions of veterans became members of the "fifty-two, twenty club" until they were able to find jobs. Thousands of others started small businesses financed by government loans. Every ex-GI who entered college or a recognized trade school was entitled to $500 a year for tuition and $75 a month for personal support while attending school. Millions of veterans poured into the nation's colleges and universities. The GI Bill of Rights ultimately cost the government $14.5 billion; but it eased the problem of postwar readjustment and, more significantly, created a giant pool of educated, trained people that would serve the economy well in the years to come.

The Rage to Consume. Luck also played a part in preventing economic catastrophe. During the war high wages and acute shortages of new homes and consumer durables had forced the public to save money. By the end of 1945 the American people had piled up $134 billion in cash, bank accounts, and government bonds. The public might have held on to this money, but the postwar mood was anything but frugal. Having gone without the good things of life for so long through the Depression and the war, Americans now seemed unwilling to deny themselves anything. In the closing months of the war advertisers reminded their customers that civilian products would shortly become available. "There's a Ford in your future," announced the car manufacturer. A month before Japan's surrender General Electric advertised its "all electric kitchen-of-the-future." The breathless advertising copy noted that the dishwasher "washes *automatically* in less than 10 minutes. And the Disposall disposes of food *electrically*—completely eliminates garbage."

The immense pent-up demand ensured that there would be no repetition of 1929–1933. After an initial period of scarce consumer goods and devastating price increases, industry completed its conversion to peacetime production and caught up with demand. During the first full year of peace only a little more than 2 million cars were produced—fewer than in 1934. In two years that output almost doubled. Americans soon came to consider many new items essential for the good life. General Electric's prophecy came true: By the end of the decade the public was buying 225,000 automatic dishwashers and 750,000 electric disposals a year. In 1946 the first electric clothes dryers appeared, and housewives began to order them enthusiastically.

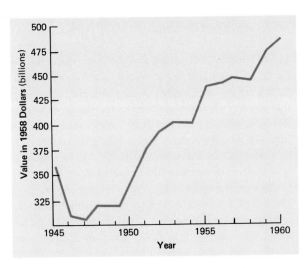

Gross national product, 1945–1960. *Source: Historical Statistics of the United States, Colonial Times to 1970.*

One electronic gadget not foreseen by GE would be even more momentous. In 1939 the Radio Corporation of America had tentatively offered for sale the first home television sets. The war stopped further growth in the industry, but after Japan's surrender the market took off. In 1948 RCA and other domestic manufacturers turned out a million sets; in 1956, almost 7.5 million. By 1960 almost half of all American homes had one or more television sets.

The new industry not only created jobs but also delivered a powerful social and cultural impact. Hollywood shuddered as families gave up their Saturday nights at the movies to watch "sitcoms" or variety shows. Television proved to be more than an entertainment medium. It was capable of providing instruction, though parents complained that its reliance on dramas steeped in violence was dangerous to young children, and educators and professors were certain that young TV viewers were losing their capacity to read. Local as well as major national and international events came "live" into the living rooms of millions of viewers. Television affected how the public perceived politicians. It made a difference in the 1960 election and also helped bring down Senator Joseph McCarthy, as we shall see.

The drastic increase in the number of families made new housing the nation's most pressing postwar need. At first private industry responded to this demand ineptly. For months following VJ Day thousands of returned veterans and their families lived in army surplus Quonset huts or moved in with their parents. Then came William J. Levitt and his imitators. Levitt used standardized components and automatic equipment to create housing "tracts" or "developments" on a gigantic scale. His houses were virtually all the same, but they had the indispensable modern conveniences and a price of $10,000, payable in thirty years on an FHA or GI home mortgage. They sold briskly. Levitt's two largest developments were on Long Island and in eastern Pennsylvania, but his methods quickly caught on. Before long there were "Levittowns" in every part of the country, each boasting the same rows of houses with picture windows, small front lawns, and tree-bordered streets full of playing children.

And so the postwar depression did not materialize. Despite brief recessions—in 1949, 1953–1954, and 1959–1960—the GNP grew at an average annual rate of 3.2 percent during the fifties, higher than for many past periods. Prices rose, but after 1950 at less than 2 percent a year for the remainder of the decade. The good health of the economy owed little to direct government policy. Far more important, at least at the outset, was the enormous pent-up domestic demand, cheap international raw materials—including petroleum—and America's unique position after 1945 as the only great industrial power capable of meeting the needs of war-ravaged Europe and Asia. Over the entire post-1945 period, moreover, the sheer size of the government sector of the economy and the existence of unemployment insurance, old-age pensions, and federal deposit insurance, introduced elements of stability that had been absent before 1930. Whatever the reasons, prosperity helped convince Americans, as in the 1920s, that there was little need to tamper with existing political arrangements.

Suburbia Triumphant. The postwar economy slowed slightly during the late 1950s, but it did not stop. Economic expansion dramatically altered the quality of American life. As the economy grew, its structure changed. By 1960, occupations like farming, mining, and even manufacturing had sharply declined in relative importance; more and more Americans worked at service jobs like advertising, technical and clerical services, publishing, accounting, and teaching. Particularly dramatic was the drop in farm workers: from 9 million to 5.2 million between 1940 and 1960. Increasing numbers of Americans ceased to wear overalls and uniforms on the job; more and more went to work in skirts, white shirts, and gray flannel suits. By 1960, for the first time in history, there were more white-collar than blue-collar Americans.

The new white-collar class developed a characteristic lifestyle centered around suburban living. The pattern was home- and child-oriented. Wives became experts in house decoration, gardening, and meal planning. Husbands took up handicraft hobbies like carpentry and boat building. A "do-it-yourself" craze swept the suburbs as much to accommodate the new domestic interests of men as to help keep down the high cost of home repairs. The doings and

"Levittown," wherever located, was geared to the family. This picture was certainly staged, but it does capture the daytime demographics of the new suburbs of the 1950s—women and babies. The only men around are the "diaper service" truck drivers.

problems of children became major new concerns of suburban parents. They worried about their offspring more than in the recent past when simple economic survival overshadowed difficulties about schools, dating patterns, orthodontics, and "cultural advantages." With so many children in the house and some money to spare, parents discovered the babysitter problem for the first time.

The suburban pattern of life was not confined to white-collar people; it was shared by better-paid skilled blue-collar workers. For both groups it was often a heavy financial burden. Many married women went to work to help out, especially after 1950. Between 1950 and 1970 the percentage of married women who worked went from 23.8 to 40.8 percent. During the 1950s, at least, few of these working wives were looking for personal fulfillment; caring for home and children remained their ideal. But a job to supplement the family income until husbands completed school on the GI Bill or received a promotion seemed unavoidable if the precious new lifestyle was to be maintained.

★ THE OTHER HALF ★

The shift of population from central city to suburb was one of the dramatic social developments of the 1950s. Yet millions of people remained in the central cities; many rural or semirural folk moved into the urban neighborhoods emptied by the lure of the suburbs.

Urban Poverty. Some of the newcomers were, as in the past, Europeans—refugees from postwar poverty and disorder. During the decade Congress passed a number of measures that admitted GI "war brides" and several hundred thousand displaced persons, refugees from Europe's wasteland. (Not until 1965 did the country fully eliminate the national quotas that discriminated in favor of northern Europeans.)

Most of the arrivals in the central cities, however, were blacks from the South and people of Hispanic background. Their experiences in some ways repeated those of earlier newcomers to American cities. Largely unskilled, they, too, took the lowest-paying jobs; they, too, moved into housing rejected by the middle class; they, too, were victims of prejudice and discrimination. Like their predecessors, they found themselves caught in a web of poverty, crime, and family disruption and were blamed for their afflictions.

Most Americans assumed that the latest arrivals—like the Irish, Germans, Jews, Italians, Poles, and other European groups of the past—would move up in society as they acquired skills. It took longer than expected. First they needed unskilled or semiskilled jobs, and mid-twentieth-century America did not offer as many of these as in the past. A construction worker now had to know how to operate a bulldozer; he could no longer merely wield a pick and shovel. The few unskilled jobs that did exist paid so little that they were unsuited to people with families to support. Thousands of Puerto Rican, Mexican, and black women found jobs as domestics, waitresses, and hospital attendants; but their husbands, brothers, and sons often looked vainly for decent-paying work. And even when newcomers had some skill, they often found that their way up was blocked by unions whose members were hostile to them or wanted to save the declining number of skilled blue-collar jobs for their relatives.

Civil Rights. Despite the continuing poverty of many minorities, the 1950s did see major advances in civil rights. The war had made a considerable difference for America's racial and religious minorities. By pointing up in ghastly relief the fruits of Nazi racism, it shamed many Americans into reconsidering their own behavior and attitudes. Hostility toward Japanese-Americans, whose spectacular fighting record in Italy during the war was widely acclaimed, rapidly dissipated. Jews, the Nazis' chief victims, also experienced a new kind of acceptance. And the wartime mingling of Americans of all kinds in a common struggle reduced traditional anti-Catholic prejudice.

Black Americans benefited least by the wartime changes. In the South segregation imposed by state and local

Braceros *were Mexican farm hands brought into Texas and the Southwest to help solve the acute shortage of labor in agriculture. Though supposedly only temporary residents of the United States, many stayed permanently. They were followed by thousands of other Mexican immigrants to the Southwest, both legal and illegal.*

laws continued. Hospitals, theaters, buses, trains, playgrounds, parks, and other public accommodations maintained separate facilities for blacks and whites, mandated by local and state ordinances. Prodded by a new generation of liberal federal judges, southern states by the 1950s were making an effort to upgrade black schools so that they could meet the "separate-but-equal" test of *Plessy* v. *Ferguson*. But almost everywhere they remained both separate and inferior. Worst of all, lynching and other kinds of racial violence survived in the South.

The situation for blacks in the North was better. The movement of thousands of black Americans out of the South, where they had been effectively disfranchised, to northern cities, where they could vote, enormously in-

creased their political influence. In most northern communities there was no legal bar to the schools that black citizens could attend or theaters, hotels, restaurants, or sports events they could patronize. On the other hand, many white northerners continued to believe that blacks were inherently inferior. Their prejudice informally accomplished many of the same ends that statutes did in the South. Whites excluded blacks from private social clubs; restaurant and hotel managers refused to accept black patrons. Landlords' prejudice forced blacks to accept inferior housing even when they could afford better. Few blacks, no matter how well qualified, could find skilled professional work. The AFL craft unions, making up the building trades, excluded black workers. Only a few industrial unions, like

A vivid instance of "Jim Crow" segregation in the south. The scene in this 1939 picture still applied in the 1950s. Separate was not equal.

Walter Reuther's United Automobile Workers, did not discriminate against black members. Although black talent was often recognized in the arts and in sports, even there bigotry persisted. In baseball, presumably the "national sport," there were no black players in the major leagues until 1947. In that year Branch Rickey, the courageous owner of the Brooklyn Dodgers, signed Jackie Robinson to play second base, finally breaking the major leagues' longtime color bar.

The struggle for black civil rights engaged many white liberals, but most of the burden was carried by blacks themselves. During the 1940s Walter F. White, secretary of the NAACP, and A. Phillip Randolph, president of the Brotherhood of Sleeping Car Porters, fought for legislation that would benefit blacks. Among their goals were a federal antilynching bill, an end to poll taxes in federal elections, and the outlawing of discrimination in work under government contract. The NAACP initiated a succession of suits aimed at breaking down segregation sanctioned by southern state and local laws.

By 1950 black citizens were growing ever more discontented as they watched the snaillike pace of change in race matters. The political system, however well it responded to the wishes of the white middle class, seemed incapable of meeting blacks' needs. Congress was paralyzed by the resistance of the well-organized southern Democratic bloc to any change in the racial order. The Republicans owed little to black voters and seemed indifferent to their problems.

The Warren Court.   Into this void stepped the branch of government traditionally the least democratic and the least responsive to public pressures: the federal courts. Beginning in 1953, the Supreme Court was led by Chief Justice Earl Warren, an Eisenhower appointee. Most of the other justices were holdovers from the New Deal and stood for an earlier liberalism. Composed of judicial activists who were willing to extend the Court's power into areas hitherto considered legislative concerns or beyond the reach of law, the Warren Court broke through the legal barriers to racial change.

Even before Warren's appointment, the Court, under NAACP goading, had begun to restrict segregation in housing and in graduate and professional education. Then, in 1954, came its momentous decision in the case of *Brown v. Board of Education of Topeka*, ably argued for the NAACP by black attorney Thurgood Marshall. Resting its decision on the findings of sociologists and psychologists that separate schooling inevitably stigmatized black children, the Warren Court declared that segregation in the public schools was a denial of the Fourteenth Amendment's requirement that the states accord to every person "equal protection of the laws." "We conclude," the chief justice wrote, "that in the field of public education the doctrine of 'separate but equal' has no

The Supreme Court's decision in Brown v. Board of Education *in 1954 was a triumph for civil rights and for the NAACP, which fought the legal battle for desegregation. Lawyers for the NAACP (chief attorney and future United States Supreme Court Justice Thurgood Marshall is in the center) express their feelings at the news of the Court's decision.*

place. Separate educational facilities are inherently unequal." The Court had spoken, and in the next decade it would speak many times again until the system of legal segregation had been totally dismantled in every part of national life.

The road to equality would be long and difficult, however. In the border states of the upper South compliance with the *Brown* decision was generally good. School segregation in practice remained, but it was based on deeply embedded patterns of residential segregation and no longer had the sanction of law. In the lower South the decision produced a storm. The more respectable conservatives organized white citizens' councils—"uptown Ku Klux Klans," their critics called them—to defeat the Court's order by boycotts and other economic weapons against both black and white supporters of desegregation. The Klan itself revived and used violence and threats of violence to prevent compliance with the *Brown* decision. At Little Rock, Arkansas, in 1957 the Klan supported Arkansas governor Orval Faubus when he defied a court order that black students be admitted to Central High School. Eisenhower could not allow such blatant disregard of the law of the land and used federal troops to guarantee admission of the black children.

Yet the president was not a civil rights enthusiast. He was willing to march with the times, but he did not care to lead the parade. He would later call his appointment of Earl Warren as chief justice "the biggest damnfool mistake" he had ever made.

Grass-Roots Protest. Legal action was the preferred tactic of the NAACP against legal segregation. Other civil rights leaders recognized that it required more than a court order to achieve desegregation and turned to grass-roots civil disobedience instead.

The civil disobedience approach represents the rise of a new black leadership. The black community in the South had changed in the previous fifty years. Despite the crippling caste system, black southerners were better educated in 1950 than in 1900; there was now a substantial black middle class of clergymen, teachers, students, small-business owners, and professionals, men and women better prepared to defend their race than their predecessors. Inevitably such leaders perceived that their experience resembled the struggles of oppressed colonial peoples around the world and that the tactics used to evict the European imperialists might be applied to the American South. It is no accident that well-read black college students would be particularly effective agents of social protest.

The new approach first attracted national attention in December 1955, when Rosa Parks, a black seamstress and activist, weary from her day's work, refused to give up her seat on a crowded Montgomery, Alabama, bus to a white man as the Jim Crow law required. Mrs. Parks was arrested and fined $10. Black community leaders, waiting for a case to test Montgomery's segregation ordinances, quickly organized a boycott of the city bus company. The city authorities struck back by arresting the boycott leaders, including the twenty-seven-year-old Reverend Martin Luther King, Jr., a Georgia-born, northern-educated Baptist minister. Blatant white racists went further. The Ku Klux Klan bombed King's house and burned several black churches. Despite the reprisals, day after day, Montgomery's black community refused to patronize the buses, the determined people getting to work on foot or by car-pooling. Some blacks were tempted to meet violence with violence, but King, an adherent of Mohandas Gandhi, India's pacifist liberator, headed them off. "We must love our white brothers," he advised, "no matter what they do to us."

The bus company was soon in serious financial difficulties but resisted yielding to the boycotters. While Montgomery's black citizens protested with their feet, the Rosa Parks case worked its way through the courts. A year later, on December 20, 1956, the U.S. Supreme Court ordered the end of segregation on the Montgomery bus system. The black protesters had won.

The Montgomery bus boycott raised King to the front rank of civil rights leadership. His eloquence and courage had sustained the protesters through difficult times. It also made nonviolent civil disobedience the central strategy of the civil rights movement. In 1957 King and his followers established the Southern Christian Leadership Conference in Atlanta as agent of a concerted nonviolent, biracial campaign to challenge the remaining bastions of Jim Crow and restore the voting rights the white South had denied its black citizens for almost a hundred years.

The grass-roots efforts were intended to keep southern race discrimination clearly before the court of public opinion. King and his colleagues on the Southern Christian Leadership Conference never doubted that white support was needed if racism was to be defeated and America ever to become a colorblind society. As the civil rights hymn proclaimed: "White and black together" would "overcome some day." Fortunately the civil rights leaders could count on broad white support. By the 1950s many middle-class whites had come to accept the conclusions of social scientists and anthropologists that race differences were culturally derived and that discrimination was costly, irrational, and unjust. With his dazzling eloquence, cultivated mind, and disarming message of Christian love, King was particularly well equipped to capitalize on liberal white attitudes.

Meanwhile, civil rights leaders continued to seek redress on the level of federal law and policy. In September 1957, after beating back a filibuster by Senator J. Strom Thurmond, Congress passed the first of several measures designed to restore voting rights to black southerners. The Civil Rights Act of 1957, the first such legislation since Reconstruction, set up a six-member Civil Rights Commission and a Civil Rights Division of the Department of Justice. The commission was to investigate complaints that voting rights had been denied. The Civil Rights Division could then prosecute authorities who were found responsible. A weak measure that had been rendered toothless by southern opposition, it was strengthened somewhat by the 1960 Civil Rights Act, which required voting registrars to retain their records for some months following an election so that they could be examined by federal officials. Both laws provided the government with modest weapons to end black disfranchisement. But as the 1960s began, the slow and painful process of restoring rights guaranteed by the Fourteenth and Fifteenth Amendments almost a century before had just begun.

The fifties retreat of white Americans to private satisfactions can be explained in part by the payoff of an affluent society that fulfilled people's hopes beyond their expectations. Yet there was something else that contributed to conformity. As millions of Americans surrendered to the pleasures of a consumer society, a great anxiety remained: the threat of nuclear holocaust. This fear would reinforce the inward turning of the American people and encourage a political and social philosophy that avoided all criticism of the nation and its dominant capitalist, middle-class values. Cold War fears, when superimposed on the more positive values of togetherness and career building, made Americans yea-sayers and self-celebrators to a degree almost unique in their history.

The United Nations. Few Americans after 1945 expected their nation to withdraw from world affairs as it had following Versailles. To avoid this possibility, leading internationalists had labored during the war years to commit the country to various forms of world cooperation. In 1944, at Bretton Woods, New Hampshire, American and other anti-Axis diplomats signed agreements for an international bank and a world monetary fund to stabilize international currencies and rebuild war-torn economies. In November 1945

the Senate endorsed "an international authority to preserve peace," an act, the *New York Times* noted, that undid "a twenty-four-year-old mistake."

The work of the internationalists was realized in the conference at San Francisco, April–June 1945, called for at Yalta. There, 282 delegates representing the 50 nations arrayed against the Axis powers organized the United Nations, modeled after the League of Nations. The UN charter established a General Assembly composed of all member nations, which would be the ultimate UN policy-making body. It also set up an eleven-nation Security Council, consisting of five permanent members—the United States, Great Britain, the Soviet Union, France, and China—and six others elected by the General Assembly for two-year terms. Each permanent member was given the power to veto Security Council decisions. The Security Council would meet in continuous session and would be the chief agency for settling disputes among member nations.

The creation of the UN was a triumph for the old Wilsonian ideal of international cooperation to preserve world peace. But it could not disguise the discord that had long been growing between the Soviet Union and the West or settle all the conflicts brewing in the troubled postwar world.

An Unsettled World. Clearly the international balance following VJ Day was very different from the past. Western Europe, long the world's power center, emerged after 1945

Forlorn residents of Nuremberg, in 1945, wait for something to happen. The United States responded with the Marshall Plan, which helped rebuild the shattered heart of Western culture. On the twentieth anniversary of the plan, the German government initiated the German Marshall Fund to support cultural exchange between the United States and Europe.

profoundly enfeebled and shaken. France, defeated by the Nazis in 1940, was demoralized and faced with the serious problem of reestablishing national unity and a political consensus. Germany and Italy were shattered societies where children begged on the streets and women sold themselves to American GIs or Soviet soldiers for packs of cigarettes and chocolate bars. Most disturbing of all, victorious Britain was impoverished and incapable of holding its vast empire together. All over the Continent misery prevailed. Millions of displaced persons wandered across Europe looking for a place to live and ways to reconstruct their lives. The physical scars of war marked every city and town. Hunger and disease afflicted populations weakened by wartime privations and continuing shortages. Winston Churchill scarcely exaggerated when he described Europe in 1945 as "a rubble heap, a charnel house, a breeding ground of pestilence and hate."

In Eastern Europe, too, the prewar balance had been upset. The Nazi invasion of Poland and the Soviet Union had been devastating. Millions of Russians, Jews, Poles, and others had died in combat or been shot, gassed, or starved to death by the Nazi conquerors. Cities had been totally de-

The benevolent-looking Chiang Kai-shek, leader of Nationalist China both during and after the war. His critics called him a devious, tyrranical man who condoned corruption and brooked no opposition.

stroyed by the warring armies. The political equilibrium had also been profoundly altered. Before 1939 a group of independent nations, including the Baltic states (Lithuania, Latvia, and Estonia), Finland, Poland, and Rumania, had walled the Soviet Union off from the rest of Europe. The regimes in these countries, as well as the next tier to the west, were generally unfriendly to the USSR. After 1945 the picture was transformed. During the last year of the war Soviet forces had swept as far west as central Germany. They had defeated the Finns and occupied Poland, the Baltic states, Rumania, Czechoslovakia, most of the Balkans, as well as part of Austria. When the war ended, the Soviets shared occupation zones in Germany and Austria with the Western Allies; had established pro-Soviet "satellite" regimes in Poland, Hungary, Rumania, Bulgaria, Albania, and Yugoslavia; had incorporated the Baltic states into the Soviet Union; and had extended the USSR's official borders westward by annexing eastern Poland and compensating the Poles with territory in eastern Germany. Finland and Czechoslovakia remained independent, but the former did so only at the price of avoiding policies that offended the Soviet Union, while the latter's autonomy would be short-lived.

Meanwhile, the decline of Western Europe had created a power vacuum in Asia and Africa. In the Far East the Japanese military successes of 1941–1943 had stripped away the myth of white superiority and had wakened dormant nationalist feelings in Indonesia, Ceylon (Sri Lanka), Indochina, Burma, India, and Malaysia. In the Middle East and North Africa, Arab nationalism, long held in check by France and Britain, began to seethe. In sub-Saharan black Africa, too, by 1945 Western-educated intellectuals were demanding an end to European colonial rule.

The most troubled nation of all in the Orient was China. During the war the United States, Great Britain, and even the Soviet Union had supported the Kuomintang, the Nationalist government under Chiang Kai-shek. Though Chiang's regime still had the support of many liberal, Western-educated Chinese in 1945, increasingly it had come under the domination of corrupt bureaucrats, privileged landlords, and rich merchants. It had failed to win the support of the Chinese peasantry and seemed unable to deal with China's industrial backwardness and social inequalities.

For many years Chiang's chief opponents had been the Chinese Communists led by Mao Tse-tung. In the portion of north China they controlled, the Chinese Communists had given land to the peasants and established an honest, though authoritarian, administration. They had also been more effective than the Kuomintang in fighting the Japanese. Hoping to combine the best of both regimes, President Truman sent General George C. Marshall to China in December 1945 to end the Nationalist-Communist rift. Although Marshall succeeded briefly in bringing Chiang and Mao together, by mid-1946 their arrangement broke down, and China was soon in the midst of a devastating civil war.

And even in the Americas the postwar era was troubled. In the Latin countries south of the United States, authoritarian regimes, often run by generals, along with gross poverty and inequality, encouraged social resentments and political restlessness.

Sources of the Cold War. The postwar instability in Europe, Asia, Africa, and the Americas set the stage for competition between the only two nations still powerful—the United States and the Soviet Union. Eventually all four continents became arenas for the chronic rivalry between the two and their respective allies. Their conflict soon became a worldwide struggle waged by diplomacy, propaganda, economic warfare, and military threat and intimidation. Occasionally the Cold War would erupt in actual combat, though fortunately for humanity, only through surrogates, never between the two superpowers directly.

The causes of the Cold War were complex, and undoubtedly both the Soviet Union and the United States contributed to them. The people and leaders of both nations were certain that they, and they alone, represented international justice and a better life for humanity. Both believed that their system alone must ultimately prevail. Viewed objectively, the Cold War was the attempt of two superpowers to ensure their own safety and protect what they perceived as their vital interests in the dramatically transformed international environment after 1945. Yet the two sides were not symmetrical. The Soviet Union was an outsider nation, aggrieved by a sense of exclusion from a central role in world affairs. It resembled, after 1945, a self-made millionaire blackballed from the best private clubs by the established elite and determined to achieve its rightful place. The Soviet leaders always nourished a thinly disguised sense of inferiority toward America and this fueled their belligerence. The United States, on the other hand, was the successor to the Western European nations as the world's power center. This role at times encouraged arrogance. The relation of outsider to insider was inevitably confrontational. The Soviet Union, to achieve its goals, had to alter the existing world order; the United States need only preserve it.

The asymmetry went beyond strategic relationships. The two systems were not morally equal. The United States and the USSR were poles apart in their political cultures. America, for all its imperfections, was a democratic society with a functioning multiparty political system and a large private sphere protected by traditions of individual liberty and personal rights incorporated into fundamental law. The Soviet Union was an oppressive, totalitarian society where boundaries between the public and private spheres were weak and political and economic control were centralized at the top in a single all-powerful Communist party and an unresponsive, rigid bureaucracy.

To make matters worse, during the immediate postwar years the ruler of this sprawling, untidy, monolithic country, Joseph Stalin, was a ruthless and paranoid dictator who had swept aside all his domestic enemies and imposed a regime on the Soviet people that made the czars' autocratic reign seem liberal and benevolent by comparison. Before, during, and after the war, Stalin's secret police arrested thousands of men and women who were accused, usually on the flimsiest evidence, of being enemies of the state and sent to brutal prison camps or summarily executed. During his last years he became a half-mad recluse who locked himself in the Kremlin and imagined plots against his rule. Even after Stalin's death in 1953, his successors, though never as bad, continued to repress their own people and support the tyrants in the Soviet satellite nations who imitated their masters in Moscow. The USSR continued to be a prison for scores of national groups swept up originally by the czars and compelled to accept the domination of the Slavic Great Russians who ruled from Moscow or St. Petersburg.

The conflict between the superpowers began well before the end of World War II, though during the war itself the Soviets and the Western powers had cooperated militarily and maintained a show of friendship that papered over serious disagreements. And for some Americans the friendship went beyond mere show. Many Americans sincerely admired the brave Soviet people in their brutal struggle with the Nazi invaders, a struggle in which they lost over 20 million lives. Then, as Soviet troops broke the back of the German army and pushed westward into Poland, the Baltic states, and the Balkans, questions of postwar boundaries, spheres of influence, and relations between the Soviet Union and its immediate neighbors became sources of contention.

By the time of the Big Three's Potsdam Conference in July 1945, the postwar world was already taking shape. Churchill, defeated for reelection by the British voters before Japan surrendered, was replaced at the conference by British Labour party head, Clement Atlee. President Harry Truman came in place of the fallen Roosevelt. During the conference, Truman received word that the scientists of the Manhattan Project had successfully tested an atomic bomb. Roosevelt had believed he could charm Stalin. Truman, influenced perhaps by the sense of America's awesome new strength, took a more skeptical approach to the Soviet dictator. The conferees agreed to little of consequence, and most pending issues between the democracies and the Soviet Union remained unresolved.

Determined to eliminate all unfriendly regimes from the Soviet Union's western borders, Stalin moved rapidly toward establishing political dominion over Eastern Europe and permanent division of conquered Germany. With the Red Army holding all the territory Stalin coveted, his allies had no choice except to concede Soviet gains. The American people, led by Roosevelt to believe that he could handle Stalin, were bitterly disappointed when Eastern Europe was "lost" to the Communists under Truman. Britain, which had entered the war in response to Hitler's attack on Poland, was particularly anguished over Stalin's refusal to restore free institutions in Russia's western Slavic neighbor.

Most Western Europeans and Americans, except those who openly sympathized with Communist ideology, were alarmed by this westward shift of Soviet power, seeing it as a direct threat to their own nations. The Soviets, and their supporters in the West, argued that they could not allow the "Socialist Motherland" to be surrounded by hostile states as in the past. And, in any event, they said, the new Communist regimes within the Soviet orbit expressed the will of the local people far better than the aristocratic and semifascist ones that had existed in 1939. The United States generally avoided direct challenges to Soviet actions in Eastern Europe. But Communist advances in the Third World would trip off a more aggressive response.

The Third World presented both opportunities and dangers to both superpowers. With France, Britain, Hol-land, and Japan too weakened to maintain empires, who would benefit from the political changes bound to come in their former colonies? The United States had never been a major colonial power like France or Britain, and during the post-1945 occupation of Japan it had demonstrated an attractive zeal for encouraging free, liberal institutions abroad. Could it now capitalize on the goodwill it possessed to win the emerging Third World nations over to Western-style liberal capitalism? But the Soviet Union also had advantages. It, too, had taken little part in the earlier race for overseas colonies, and so could claim to be free of imperialist taint. The people in almost all these emerging societies were desperately poor, and would be attracted by drastic schemes to redistribute land and end the privileged status of local elites. The Soviet Union sought to identify itself with these changes. Communism would be the vehicle for creating more just societies after political freedom was achieved. Many Third World intellectuals, moreover, were strongly influenced by Marxist ideas, which promised quick modernization without the complexities and inconveniences of democratic institutions. Moreover, the middle class—the traditional backbone of liberal democracy that might have offset these groups—was tiny and weak.

In any struggle over the "nonaligned" world, then, it was not clear who would win. Some Americans, and perhaps some Soviet leaders, did not see the world as a simple polar division of "East" versus "West." But clearly during

THE COLD WAR, 1955

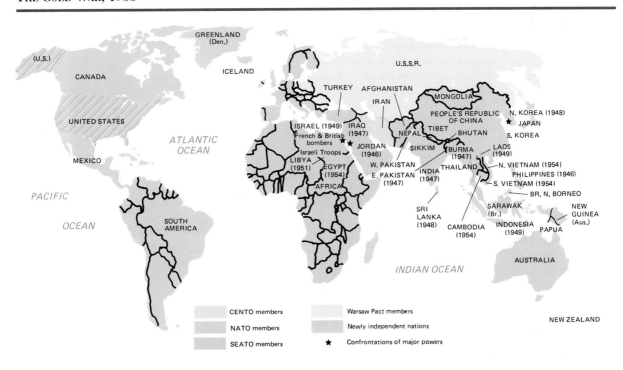

CENTO members

NATO members

SEATO members

Warsaw Pact members

Newly independent nations

★ Confrontations of major powers

the immediate postwar period most Americans and Soviets found it difficult to imagine that nations could be permanently nonaligned or that there might be "blocs" of nations both non-Soviet and non-Western. Either "they were for us, or against us," opinion leaders on both sides seemed to believe. It was a certain formula for confrontation.

Inexperience, too, helped bring on the Cold War. Both antagonists found themselves the only great powers left in a world otherwise composed of has-beens and would-bes, and neither was equipped by history or tradition to handle this situation well. Soviet foreign policy in the fifties bore a marked resemblance to the czars' traditional quest for warm-water ports on the Mediterranean and Pacific and for secure western borders. American policymakers continued to believe that all people craved democracy and private property as much as Americans did.

Containment. The end of World War II brought rapid international change. The Soviet Union moved not only in Eastern Europe, to secure its western borders, but also in southern Europe, to gain access to warm-water ports. In 1945 it demanded that neighboring Turkey cede to it several frontier districts and allow Soviet control over the Dardanelles, the all-important strait connecting Soviet Black Sea ports with the Mediterranean. In the following year Greece was torn apart by a Communist-led revolt sustained by supplies sent by Stalin and Marshal Josip Broz Tito, the leader of the Yugoslav Communists. Meanwhile, after 1945 the French confronted a strong independence movement in Indochina under Ho Chi Minh, the founder of the Indochina Communist party. In 1947, nationalists, inspired by Mohandas Gandhi, ousted the British from the Indian subcontinent and established the new republics of India and Pakistan. In 1949, the Dutch were forced to recognize the independence of the United States of Indonesia formed out of their East Indies colony.

The Soviets seemed likely to make major inroads into war-damaged, impoverished, and demoralized Western Europe too. Yet at first the United States was slow to recognize Europe's plight. In 1946 Congress authorized a

POSTWAR ALLIANCES IN EUROPE AND THE MIDDLE EAST

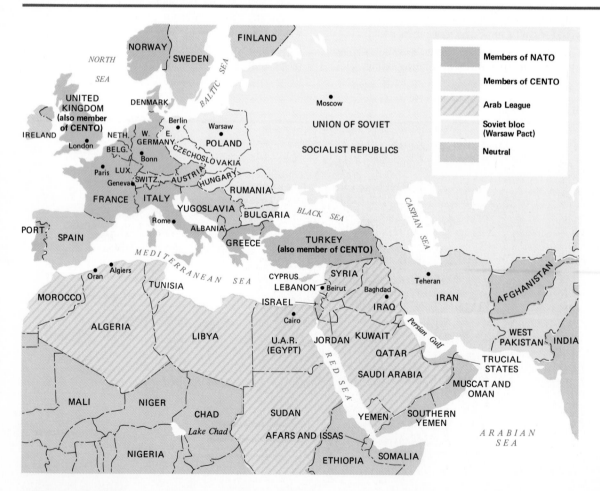

$3.75 billion loan to Great Britain and contributed to the United Nations Relief and Rehabilitation Administration (UNRRA), which funneled money and supplies to starving Europeans. This generous effort was not enough, however, and by 1947 Europe seemed on the verge of chaos.

Americans were sincerely concerned with the suffering of Europe's people. They were also worried that poverty and social disruption were playing into the hands of the Communists. Americans deplored the Soviet domination of Poland, the Balkans, and Eastern Europe. They perceived the creation in 1947 of the Cominform, the Moscow-based association of world Communist parties, as a revival of Communist agitation and subversion outside Soviet borders. Soviet policy probably did not anticipate direct control of France, Italy, or Great Britain. Nevertheless, Moscow was certain to take advantage of Western Europe's weakness to win support for pro-Soviet parties and to reduce the influence of America's friends. Even a neutral Europe would be an enormous defeat for the United States and a corresponding gain for the Soviet Union.

During the first two years of peace a growing chorus of Western leaders warned that something must be done to stop Soviet expansion. In March 1946 Winston Churchill told an audience at Fulton, Missouri, that an "iron curtain" had "descended across the continent of Europe" behind which Communist tyranny reigned supreme. Elsewhere "Communist fifth columns" were threatening Christian civilization. A little over a year later George F. Kennan, a senior American diplomat, asserted that the Soviet Union was committed to an "aggressive intransigence with respect to the outside world." American policy, he advised, must be one of "long-term, patient, but firm and vigilant containment of Russian expansive tendencies."

The first significant move to implement containment and wall in the spreading "red tide" came during the cruel winter of 1946–1947 when Europe seemed about to sink into the abyss. In February 1947 the British government told George Marshall, now Truman's secretary of state, that the situation was becoming desperate in Greece and Turkey. Britain itself was laboring under austerity measures as severe as those of wartime and could no longer continue its traditionally active role in the eastern Mediterranean. On March 12 Truman asked Congress for $400 million in aid for the two beleaguered nations. Under the leadership of Republican Senator Arthur H. Vandenberg of Michigan, Congress endorsed the Truman Doctrine and made the appropriation. Massive aid to Greece and Turkey, combined with the break in 1948 between Tito and the Soviet Union, which blocked Russian aid to the Greek guerrillas, soon ended the Communist threat in both countries. The Truman Doctrine established a precedent that would inspire American foreign policy for the next forty years.

The Marshall Plan. The next installment of containment was the Marshall Plan. With the Soviet Union checked in Greece and Turkey, there still remained the threat of sub-

American Marshall Plan money helped rebuild a badly damaged Europe brick by brick and, in doing so, cemented an alliance that dominates the international policy of the West to this day.

version in Western Europe. Americans met this danger with an economic recovery program first broached by Secretary of State Marshall in June 1947. To restore "the confidence of the European people in the economic future of their own country and of Europe as a whole," Marshall proposed a gigantic joint economic recovery effort by Europe and the United States. The Western European response was enthusiastic. In July an all-European conference convened in Paris, formed the Committee for European Economic Cooperation, and agreed on a recovery program financed jointly by the United States and the European nations. The American call for a cooperative effort did not exclude the Soviet Union, although the prospect of Soviet participation made American officials uneasy. The Soviets, suspicious and wanting no part in any program that would strengthen Western capitalism, came to the conference; but when Molotov discovered he could not disrupt the meeting, the Soviet delegates walked out.

Americans did not support containment unanimously. Walter Lippmann, the dean of American journalism, called it a "strategic monstrosity" and feared that it was a blank check for American entanglement in every conflict around the world. Senator Taft believed the Truman Doctrine would only exacerbate East-West tensions, and other conservative critics called the Marshall Plan (officially the European Recovery Program) "Operation Rathole" and a "share-the-American-wealth plan." Critics on the left often agreed with these attacks and had other objections as well. Some were appalled by the inclusion in ERP of Spain, where the Fascist Franco regime still ruled. Friends of the Soviet Union considered it a danger to world peace. Former Vice President Henry Wallace dubbed it the "Martial Plan." But anti-Communist public opinion, reinforced by farmers' and manufacturers' zeal for enlarged export markets, endorsed the administration proposal. In March 1948 Congress voted to fund the European Recovery Program, and in a few weeks vessels laden with grain and vital manufacturers were steaming for Europe.

In all, the United States contributed $12.5 billion to European recovery. It was not pure generosity. Shorting up Western Europe served America's strategic interests and helped bolster the American economy. However motivated, the Marshall Plan's results were spectacular. By 1950 Western Europe's economic output had outstripped that of 1939, the last prewar year, by 25 percent. Non-Communist Europe was beginning a dramatic economic surge that would carry living standards far beyond anything dreamed of before the war. The political effects were invaluable, too. As poverty receded, so did communism. By 1950 the fast-recovering nations were confident once again, and the growth of the Western European Communist parties had been effectively checked.

The Marshall Plan was accompanied by other moves to stiffen European resistance to Soviet and internal Communist pressures. Britain, France, and the United States were determined to restore an independent German state. In 1948 they stabilized the German currency and soon after created out of their occupation zones a West German Federal Republic with its capital at Bonn. Checked in their hopes of further westward expansion and fearful of a revived and militant Germany, the Russians reacted strongly. In June 1948 they imposed a blockade on all traffic into the western sector of Berlin, a city deep inside Soviet-occupied eastern Germany. To save Berlin and prevent its complete takeover by the Soviet East German satellite, the United States sent vital supplies into the city by plane. The Berlin Airlift lasted for more than ten months, until the Russians withdrew their barricades and allowed the city to be supplied once more by railroads and highways. In October 1949 the Soviets transformed their German occupation zone into the German Democratic Republic (East Germany) under firm Communist control.

Moves and Countermoves. During these critical postwar years the two superpowers played a deadly game across the board of Europe. In February 1948 a Communist coup d'état in Prague, Czechoslovakia, turned the only Eastern European country with a democratic regime into another Soviet satellite. In September 1949 the USSR exploded its first atomic bomb. Knowledge that the Soviets were capable of waging atomic war sent shock waves through the Western nations.

The Prague coup and the Berlin blockade goaded the Western powers into a defensive response. In April 1949 Belgium, Canada, Denmark, France, Great Britain, Iceland, Italy, Luxembourg, the Netherlands, Norway, Portugal, and the United States formed the North Atlantic Treaty Organization (NATO). Each NATO member pledged to go to war if any other member were attacked. Conservative Republican senators fought the NATO treaty, but with the support of Senator Vandenburg, the leading Republican internationalist, it passed. For the first time the United States had committed itself to an international alliance in time of peace.

The Soviets did not take what they considered Western provocation lying down. Especially fearful of NATO moves to include West Germany in the Western alliance, in 1955 they organized the Warsaw Pact, a military alliance of Albania, Bulgaria, Czechoslovakia, East Germany, Hungary, Poland, and Rumania with the USSR.

Despite these moves and countermoves, the West and East moved slowly toward a mutual accommodation in Europe. Crises continued, however. Until 1971 Berlin would remain a Western hostage in Soviet–East German hands, periodically triggering dangerous confrontations. Americans were slow to accept Soviet domination in Eastern Europe. In January 1953 Secretary of State John Foster Dulles declared in a television broadcast that people in the Soviet satellite nations could "count on" the United States. Soon afterward he had his supporters in Congress introduce the "captive peoples" resolution; it implied that America would aid anti-Soviet forces in Eastern Europe. When anti-Soviet Hungarians rose up in revolt in 1956, however, and demanded the departure of Soviet troops and an end to Soviet control, the United States refused military aid and allowed the Hungarian "freedom fighters" to be crushed brutally by Soviet might. The tragic failure of the Hungarian uprising clarified the limits of American commitment: The United States would fight for NATO and West Germany; it would not go to war to liberate the "captive peoples" of the East.

The Arms Race. Adding to the uncertainties of balance-of-power politics, and coloring almost every international event, was the threat of a direct armed clash between the two superpowers and the possibility of nuclear cataclysm. Although Stalin had professed indifference to the American atomic bomb when he officially learned of it, the Soviets were actually frightened by their adversary's new weapon. They quickly put their best technical brains to work and imported German scientists to help overtake the West. When the United States proposed international control of atomic weapons in 1946, the USSR rejected it on the grounds that it would freeze the weapons regime while the

Americans were still ahead. The Soviet atom bomb project was helped by extensive Soviet wartime espionage in Britain, Canada, and the United States that had revealed the techniques needed to produce uranium-235 and the mechanisms to set it off. The Russians would have acquired a working bomb under any circumstances. Still, in September 1949, when President Truman announced that the Soviet Union had exploded its first atomic weapon, many Americans were certain that spying had greatly speeded the Soviet drive for nuclear parity.

The Soviet race for the bomb was only the first phase of the great superpower struggle to achieve arms supremacy by every means possible. At first each side sought bigger and better bombs. In 1950, over the protests of Robert Oppenheimer and other prominent scientists, the American government ordered the Atomic Energy Commission to develop the far more destructive hydrogen bomb. On November 1, 1952, the first H-bomb was exploded at Eniwetok, an atoll in the Marshall Islands. Within ten months the Soviet Union exploded its own hydrogen bomb, thus ending America's brief nuclear advantage.

Over the next few years both sides set off dozens of H-bombs to test their effectiveness and improve their capacity. It soon became obvious that the H-bomb was indeed a "hell" bomb that made it theoretically possible to destroy the entire world. Each test explosion, moreover, released large amounts of radioactive strontium-90 into the atmosphere, threatening to cause thousands of deaths from cancer in future generations.

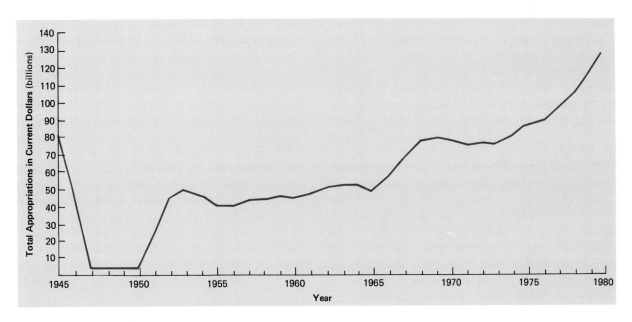

National defense outlays, 1945–1980. *Source: Historical Statistics of the United States, Colonial Times to 1970 and Statistical Abstract of the United States 1980.*

Once both superpowers had acquired weapons of unimagined power, the arms race shifted to delivery and detection systems. During the early 1950s the United States maintained a 270,000-person Strategic Air Command, which kept a constant patrol of B-29 bombers in the air, each one carrying H-bombs. The Russians did not try to compete with SAC but sought to outflank the United States by developing guided missiles. Soviet engineers succeeded in producing unmanned, radar-guided rockets that could travel great distances and hit their targets within an error of a few miles. To counteract the Russian intercontinental ballistic missiles (ICBMs), the United States established a chain of radar stations, the DEW (distant early warning) line across northern Canada. At the same time American scientists worked furiously to close the "missile gap." They succeeded in late 1958, when an American Atlas rocket traveled from Florida to hit its target on Ascension Island 6,325 miles away.

Missiles and H-bombs did not preclude heavy investment in conventional weapons. American budget outlays for planes, tanks, artillery, atomic submarines, and other "defense" items went from $13 billion in 1950, when it was about one-third of the total federal budget, to $46 billion in 1960, when it was half.

Added to the outlays on military hardware were vast disbursements for other Cold War safeguards. In July 1947 Congress passed the National Security Act unifying the army, navy, and air force under a single secretary of defense, establishing the National Security Council (NSC) to advise the president on issues necessary to American safety, and setting up a Central Intelligence Agency (CIA) to gather information deemed essential to American security abroad. Over the next three decades the CIA became the major American spy agency, and its epic battle of wits with its East Bloc counterparts became legendary, reviving the whole genre of spy novels and movies. Unfortunately, in the name of American security, the CIA engaged in activities that seemed to exceed its mandate. Over the years the public learned that it had plotted to assassinate hostile foreign rulers and "destabilize" unfriendly foreign governments; had covertly subsidized academics, students, and journalists to fight the intellectual battles against communism; had sowed "disinformation" among Americans to confuse the enemy. The CIA's defenders claimed that the United States, facing a totally unscrupulous enemy, had no choice but to fight fire with fire. But many Americans felt uncomfortable with its sometimes amoral activities. Along with other Cold War agencies, such as Radio Free Europe and the Voice of America, the CIA, moreover, cost billions of dollars, though its budgets were hidden in other federal expenditures to conceal the extent of its activities from the Soviet enemy. The NSC also contributed to increased Cold War outlays.

In early 1950, the National Security Council, in a top secret report (NSC 68), warned the president of the Soviet threat in dramatic terms. The Cold War, NSC 68 declared, was "in fact a real war in which the survival of the world [was] at stake." The United States must be prepared to rearm on a massive scale, a recommendation that would soon be carried out.

A vocal minority of Americans deplored the economic costs of the Cold War. On the political right, it seemed that economies might be possible without weakening American defense. During the Eisenhower administration, Secretary of State John Foster Dulles advanced the doctrine of "massive retaliation" with atomic weapons against any Soviet challenge as a way of keeping down costs. Rather than trying to match the Soviet Union man for man, gun for gun, and tank for tank, we should deploy an arsenal of H-bombs and threaten to use it when they defied us. Critics of the secretary's views noted that it would turn every confrontation with the USSR into a possible atomic war. Given another Dulles policy, "brinkmanship"—bringing each crisis with the Soviet Union to the edge of war—the emphasis on atomic weapons seemed a certain prescription for world disaster.

But the most determined critics of the full-court-press arms race were on the left, not the right. Pacifists, women's civic groups, liberal scientists and academics, and political radicals of most sorts denounced the massive armaments outlays. In 1957 a group of liberal academics, journalists, intellectuals, and assorted peace activists organized SANE (the National Committee for a Sane Nuclear Policy) to press for strong international controls of nuclear weapons. The next year a group of pacifists founded the Committee for Nonviolent Action. Some of the "stop-the-arms-race" groups emphasized the dangers of war from the race itself. International arms competitions inevitably were self-fulfilling prophecies; they would *cause* war. Others emphasized the draining effect of armaments expenditures on civic life. The money that poured with such abandon into weapons could be far better used to restore the nation's crumbling cities, provide social services to the poor, improve its schools, and make the United States a better place to live. Some advocated arms controls; others believed the only way to save the world was for the West to risk unilateral disarmament.

The protests did make an impression. Although the peace groups did not get the United States to renounce the arms competition, by playing on the widespread health concerns of people around the world, they did induce the superpowers to sign a treaty in 1963 forbidding atmospheric testing of nuclear weapons. Their continued pressure, moreover, created a widespread international demand for arms limitations that would eventually bear fruit.

And yet the arms race continued. Most Americans were reluctant to allow the Soviet Union and its allies a major arms advantage over the Western countries and endorsed the costly outlays. Before long, as Eisenhower had anticipated, many people—workers, scientists, engineers—and whole communities acquired a vital stake in continued massive defense spending. Some Americans came to consider an end to the Cold War a greater threat than its continuation.

Containment in Asia.   In Asia, meanwhile, the United States found itself facing a new danger. Since the end of the war it had sent $2 billion in aid to Chiang Kai-shek in China with little result. Much of the war materiel meant for Chiang was sold off by corrupt Kuomintang officials and ended up in the hands of either profiteers or the Chinese Communists. The Kuomintang soon lost the confidence of the Chinese people. Although the United States had done its diplomatic best, and even though the Soviet Union, fearing a rival in Mao Tse-tung, had supported Chiang, by 1948 Mao's Communist forces were sweeping all before them. In December 1949 Chiang, his entourage, and his remaining troops fled the mainland to reestablish the Republic of China on Taiwan (Formosa), off the south coast of China. Now unchallenged on the mainland, Mao and his supporters set up the People's Republic of China (PRC) with its capital at Beijing. Many Americans were certain that the "free world" had suffered a grievous and avoidable defeat. Hundreds of millions of Chinese, it appeared, had now been added to the Communist side of the scales.

During the Chinese civil war Americans associated with the "China lobby" and an Asia-first policy had supported direct military intervention to prevent the Communist takeover. The Truman administration had rejected the idea, convinced that a land war in Asia would be a bottomless quagmire that would drain the nation's strength and could not be won. Even after the Communist victory the American government sought to avoid a direct military role in East Asia as a strategically insupportable position. We could defend Europe but, it seemed, not Asia, too, where we had no strong allies and where the appeal of communism to the impoverished masses was exceptionally powerful. In January 1950 Secretary of State Dean Acheson declared that the United States did not consider Taiwan, mainland Southeast Asia, or South Korea essential to American security. If any of these places were invaded, the "initial resistance" would have to come from those attacked.

Acheson did not intend to give the Communists the green light for further expansion, but that was a possible effect of his pronouncement. Since shortly after World War II, Korea, for years a brutalized Japanese possession, had been divided into Soviet and American zones at the thirty-

eighth parallel, pending its eventual reunification. By 1948 there were two governments in Korea: a Republic of Korea (ROK) in the South led by Syngman Rhee, elected president under UN supervision, and a People's Republic in the North, closely allied with the Soviet Union. In 1949 the United States withdrew its last remaining troops from the South, leaving the ROK unprotected.

Soon after Acheson's statement the North Koreans—apparently with Stalin's approval—concluded that it was time to reunite Korea under their own auspices. On June 25, 1950, some 95,000 Soviet-armed North Korean troops crossed the thirty-eighth parallel in a massive invasion of the Republic of Korea, which was still formally under United Nations control. Reversing his administration's previous position, Truman acted decisively to stop what he considered a blatant act of aggression. The United States immediately called an emergency session of the UN Security Council, from which the USSR had temporarily withdrawn its representative. On June 27, unimpeded by a Soviet veto, the Security Council asked all members of the United Nations to contribute "such assistance to the Republic of Korea as may be necessary to repel the armed attack and restore international peace and security in the area." By this time President Truman had already instructed General Douglas MacArthur, Supreme Allied Commander in Japan, to send military assistance to the ROK defenders. Yet the UN resolution was invaluable. Because of it, the United States would be fighting a "police action" in Korea as agent of the UN. Not only would it receive valuable material aid from other UN members, but outside the Communist Bloc no nation would accuse it of imperialist motives.

The initial North Korean attack quickly overran most of the South, pushing ROK and American forces into a tight pocket around the port of Pusan. There they held on desperately until reinforcements began to arrive from Japan and the continental United States. On September 15, 1950, MacArthur made an end run by sea around the North Koreans and began to sweep the enemy northward. By October he had reached the thirty-eighth parallel. Here he might have paused; but certain that the Chinese would not intervene, he drove past the old border all the way to the Chinese-Korean boundary at the Yalu River.

Mao Tse-tung had threatened to support the North Koreans if they appeared certain to lose, and by October MacArthur's troops began to encounter Chinese military units. Despite these signs of Chinese intentions, in November 1950 MacArthur launched a final offensive to crush all remaining North Korean resistance. He drove his men into a gigantic Chinese trap. Masses of Chinese troops overwhelmed the ROK and American forces and for a while threatened to capture thousands. MacArthur succeeded in extricating the bulk of his army but was forced to retreat to

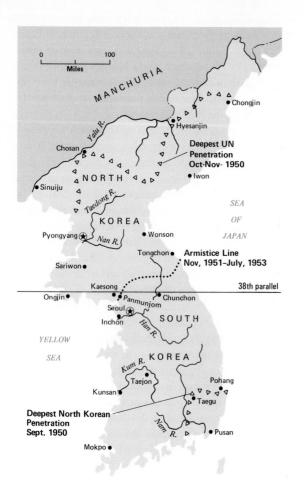

The Korean War Arena

a line close to the thirty-eighth parallel. There the two armies settled down to a cruel and costly static trench warfare that resembled the Western Front during World War I.

From the moment the Chinese intervened, MacArthur advocated expanding the war to destroy the enemy's staging areas and sources of materiel. This might mean "unleashing" Chiang Kai-shek and letting him attack the Chinese mainland, or bombing Chinese bases in Manchuria. If these acts brought the Soviet Union into the war, so be it. Truman and his advisers, as well as many liberal opinion makers, found this prospect dismaying, and the president warned the general to desist from his bellicose pronouncements. In March 1951, Truman sought to open peace negotiations with the Communists. In response, MacArthur publicly threatened to escalate the war against the Chinese, a move that scuttled all possibility of talks. Several weeks later he wrote a public letter to House Republican leader Joseph Martin declaring "there is no substitute for victory," and urged the United States to shift its

strategic priority to Asia. Truman now concluded that the general had allowed his years as benevolent dictator in Japan to go to his head and removed him from command. He replaced him with General Matthew Ridgeway, a man who obeyed orders.

MacArthur's dismissal shocked many conservatives, who judged it a sign of weakness in the cosmic struggle against the great international Communist threat. Many ordinary Americans agreed with them. When the general returned home he was welcomed as a hero. Thousands lined the streets of major cities as he passed through on his way to Washington, and Congress invited him to speak to a joint session. Conservative Republicans were soon talking about nominating him for president in 1952.

MacArthur's firing cleared the way for peace talks. In July 1951, at Kaesong, the United Nations and Communists opened armistice negotiations. These were broken off in August and then resumed at Panmunjom. The cease-fire discussions dragged on fruitlessly for two years while hundreds of Americans died in vicious patrol actions along the static front line. At home, frustrations grew. Not until after Stalin's death in March 1953 was the stalemate ended and agreements reached. On July 26 the truce documents were signed at Panmunjom and fighting ceased.

Nothing much had been accomplished. A generation later Korea remained divided along a line just a few miles from the June 1950 border between South and North. Meanwhile, the American people had paid dearly for the Korean War. At home the country had returned to a war footing. Congress had revived the draft and expanded the armed forces to more than 3 million men. The decision to restore a conventional military force proved expensive and pushed the military budget to over $50 billion by 1952. The economy, which had been in the doldrums in 1949, quickly revived and then began to overheat. By 1951 prices had risen about 12 percent despite the government's efforts to hold them down by price controls like those in World War II. The total cost in lives and wealth was immense for a struggle that had achieved so little. The United States had suffered 135,000 casualties (including 33,000 killed) and spent an estimated $54 billion.

★ A SECOND RED SCARE ★

The Cold War and the Korean conflict profoundly affected the national mood. It had been the proudest boast of patriots before 1945 that America had never lost a war. With the advent of nuclear weapons, however, final victories seemed impossible. Nuclear war promised mass slaughter, if not the total destruction of all life on the planet. There

Even as North Koreans and Americans were negotiating an armistice at Panmunjom, the fighting continued. Here American troops are moving toward the front while Korean refugees flee in the other direction.

were a few "tough-minded" people who, under the banner "Better dead than red," advocated a nuclear "first strike" against the Soviet Union. At the other extreme were those who reversed the slogan to "Better red than dead" and favored "unilateral"—that is, one-sided—disarmament. Few Americans cared to accept either devastating nuclear war or certain surrender to the Soviet Union, and the unresolvable world crisis tried the patience of millions of citizens.

Heightening this frustration was the feeling that the new enemy was maddeningly elusive. Hitler, Mussolini, and Tojo had been straightforward military aggressors, and the danger they posed had been clear for all to see. These and other past enemies had challenged the United States frontally, and Americans had marshaled their energies and finished them off. But the Cold War was fought through surrogates and by subversion, espionage, and propaganda. Few Americans knew much about the emerging Third World of former colonial states, and did not recognize that their lack of democratic traditions, absence of a substantial middle class, and deep resentment against the West made them unlikely candidates for U.S.-style governments. They tended to see the Soviet Union behind every social upheaval

in Asia, Africa, or Latin America. And indeed, the Soviet Union did use Third World wars of "national liberation" to expand its power and influence.

During much of the 1950s, moreover, the Communists appeared to be winning the struggle for world control. Disinclined to make distinctions among Chinese Communists, Yugoslav Communists, and Soviet Communists, many Americans thought the whole world was turning uniformly "red." Because communism was obviously an evil, atheistic, brutal force that all right-thinking people must abhor, how could its success be explained? Besides the visible enemy there must be a disguised and hidden one that operated internally in the West to undermine anti-Communist resistance. Confusing the democratic socialism espoused by Britain's Labour party and the various social democratic groups of Western Europe with communism, it could seem to many conservative Americans that dangerous ideologies were expanding and the West was being undermined and subverted. The enemy was an invisible presence, it appeared, hiding behind familiar institutions and secretly supported by respectable people in high places in the United States and Europe. However simplistic this analysis of the Cold War, during the 1950s it gained wide currency among unsophisticated Americans.

The Enemy Within. Frustration, suspicion, and fear set off a repressive reaction. The public mood during the 1950s was clearly overwrought, but it was also true that the Soviet Union supported extensive espionage operations in the United States. In 1950 the British uncovered the doings of Klaus Fuchs, a German refugee atomic physicist who had been employed at Los Alamos on the Manhattan Project during the war and had transmitted atomic secrets to the Soviet Union. The trail of Fuchs's betrayal soon led to David Greenglass, an enlisted man at the Los Alamos Atomic energy center. Greenglass accused his brother-in-law and sister, Julius and Ethel Rosenberg, of passing secrets to the Russians. Although many people believed them innocent, the Rosenbergs were eventually convicted of espionage and executed in what became an international *cause célèbre*. In March 1950 Judith Coplon and her Soviet agent-lover, Valentin Gubitchev, were convicted of spying. Gubitchev was deported and Coplon sentenced to jail.

Most disturbing of all was the apparent betrayal of the country by a prominent public servant, Alger Hiss, president of the Carnegie Endowment for International Peace. During the 1930s Hiss had been a New Dealer who had served in the State Department. He had then been a delegate to the UN, and had accompanied Roosevelt to Yalta. In 1948 Whittaker Chambers, an admitted former Communist, told the House Committee on Un-American Activities (HUAC) that during the 1930s he and Hiss had been members of a Soviet spy ring in Washington and that Hiss had given secret government documents to the Russians. Summoned before HUAC, Hiss was subjected to close questioning by Congressman Richard Nixon and others, but he denied that he had ever known Chambers or stolen official secrets. Because of the statute of limitations, Hiss could no longer be indicted for espionage. He sued Chambers for libel, however, and in the libel suit Chambers produced new evidence that Hiss had been a spy. The federal government now tried Hiss for perjury, and in the second of two trials he was found guilty and sentenced to five years in prison.

The Hiss-Chambers case was one of the pivotal political events of the early postwar period. Many Americans were deeply disturbed that a man so generously honored by his nation should, apparently, have betrayed it. Conservatives would use the Hiss case to attack their foes to the left. Hiss's actions, they said, were symptomatic of the whole New Deal. Alien to the American way, it had represented "twenty years of treason." Nor had the betrayal ceased. The Democrats were still protecting traitors. The Truman administration, charged Congressman Nixon, "was

extremely anxious that nothing happen to Mr. Hiss." On the pro-Hiss side feelings were equally impassioned. The far left considered Hiss an innocent martyr to Cold War hysteria, and at times even moderate liberals reacted to the charges of Chambers and others as if Soviet espionage against the United States was inconceivable or that such spying could ever pose a threat to the nation.

McCarthyism. But besides the valid fear of spying, there was a parallel, less legitimate, fear of subversion. Often the public confused the two, with many people failing to distinguish between stealing military secrets and merely advocating ideas that were, or seemed to be, pro-Communist or pro-Soviet or simply "un-American." Before long the country was in the grip of a full-scale panic that endangered the civil liberties of many Americans.

The Truman administration was in part responsible for the hysteria. Fearful of attacks by conservative opponents as "soft on communism," Truman issued Executive Order 9835 in March 1947 establishing a program to eliminate "disloyal" federal employees who, because of their politics or their personal or sexual traits, might pose security risks. As part of the same executive order, he authorized the attorney general to indict eleven top officials of the American Communist party on charges of violating the Smith Act of 1940 by advocating overthrow of the government by force. After a tumultuous trial in New York, all the defendants were convicted and sentenced to prison. Their defenders, whether civil libertarians or political sympathizers, claimed that no one could take seriously the threat to the nation's political stability of the few thousand Communists.

The president did not want the antisubversive drive to go too far, however. In 1950 he vetoed the McCarran Internal Security Act requiring registration of Communist and Communist-front organizations, excluding from the country would-be immigrants who belonged to a totalitarian party, forbidding the employment of Communists in defense work, and providing for the internment of radicals during national emergencies. "In a free country," Truman declared in his veto message, "we punish men for the crimes they commit, but never for the opinions they have." These were stirring words, but Congress overrode his veto. Whether he acted out of conviction or from fear, Truman cannot escape blame for having stimulated, through his earlier "anti-Communist" moves, the excessive reaction to internal subversion that marked the decade. Nor was the president the only liberal who, through timidity or miscalculation, piled fuel on the anti-Communist blaze. At one point Senator Hubert Humphrey, for example, proposed a bill to outlaw the Communist party. Other liberals, while refusing explicitly to support the intolerant mood, declined to attack it publicly, thereby lending it their tacit support.

Joe McCarthy

The career of Senator Joseph R. McCarthy of Wisconsin was a Cold War artifact. McCarthy was an undistinguished member of the upper house faced with a stiff fight for reelection when he happened on the anti-Communist issue in 1950. Thereafter, he became a power in the land, winning reelection handily in 1952, and striking fear into the hearts of his political enemies by his grip on the imaginations and loyalties of millions of Americans. The following is the heart of McCarthy's famous Wheeling, West Virginia, Lincoln Day speech of February 1950 wherein he first broached the issue of "treason" in high places.

"Six years ago, at the time of the first conference to map out the peace—Dumbarton Oaks—there was within the Soviet orbit 180,000,000 people. Lined up on the antitotalitarian side there were in the world at that time roughly 1,625,000,000 people. Today, only 6 years later, there are 800,000,000 people under the absolute domination of Soviet Russia—an increase of over 400 percent. On our side, the figure has shrunk to around 500,000,000. In other words, in less than 6 years the odds have changed from 9 to 1 in our favor to 8 to 5 against us. This indicates the swiftness of the tempo of Communist victories and American defeats in the cold war. As one of our outstanding figures once said, 'When a great democracy is destroyed, it will not be because of enemies from without, but rather because of enemies from within.'

"The truth of the statement is becoming terrifyingly clear as we see the country losing each day on every front. . . .

"The reason why we find ourselves in a position of impotency is not because our only powerful potential enemy has sent men to invade our shores, but rather because of the traitorous actions of those who have been so well treated by this Nation. It has not been the less fortunate or members of minority groups who have been selling this Nation out, but rather those who have had all the benefits that the wealthiest nation on earth has had to offer—the finest homes, the finest college education, and the finest jobs in Government we can give.

"This is glaringly true in the State Department. There the bright young men who are born with silver spoons in their mouths are the ones who have been worst. . . .

"When Chiang Kai-shek was fighting our war, the State Department had in China a young man named John S. Service. His task, obviously, was not to work for the communization of China. Strangely, however, he sent official reports back to the State Department urging that we torpedo our ally Chiang Kai-shek and stating, in effect, that communism was the best hope of China.

"Later, this man—John Service— was picked up by the Federal Bureau of Investigation for turning over to the Communists secret State Department information. Strangely, however, he was never prosecuted. However, Joseph Grew, the Under Secretary of State, who insisted on his prosecution, was forced to resign. Two days after Grew's successor, Dean Acheson, took over as Under Secretary of State, this man—John Service . . . was not only reinstated . . . but promoted. . . .

"Then there was a Mrs. Mary Jane Kenny, from the Board of Economic Warfare . . . , who was named in an FBI report and in a House committee report as a courier for the Communist Party while working for the Government. And where do you think Mrs. Kenny is—she is now an editor in the United Nations Document Bureau.

"This, ladies and gentlemen, gives you somewhat of a picture of the type of individuals who have been helping to shape our foreign policy. In my opinion the State Department . . . is thoroughly infested with Communists.

"I have in my hand 57 cases of individuals who would appear to be either card-carrying members or certainly loyal to the Communist Party, but who nevertheless are still helping to shape our foreign policy. . . .

"As you know, very recently the Secretary of State proclaimed his loyalty to a man [Alger Hiss] guilty of what has always been considered the most abominable of all crimes—of being a traitor to the people who gave him a position of great trust. The Secretary of State in attempting to justify his continued devotion to the man who sold out the Christian world to the atheistic world, referred to Christ's Sermon on the Mount as a justification and reason therefore, and the reaction of the American people to this would have made the heart of Abraham Lincoln happy.

"When this pompous diplomat in striped pants, with a phony British accent, proclaimed to the American people that Christ on the Mount endorsed communism, high treason, and betrayal of a sacred trust, the blasphemy was so great that it awakened the indignation of the American people.

"He has lighted the spark which is resulting in a moral uprising and will end only when the whole sorry mess of twisted, warped thinkers are swept from the national scene so that we may have a new birth of national honesty and decency in Government."

Senator Joseph McCarthy uses "visuals" to show supposed power of communism in the United States as Joseph Welch expresses his skepticism.

It was perhaps inevitable that a demagogue would appear to exploit Americans' fears and suspicions for his own purposes. The man was Joseph R. McCarthy, the Republican junior senator from the once proudly progressive state of Wisconsin. Like many demagogues, McCarthy had his attractive side. He genuinely liked people and could never understand why they despised him. Though he was a scrappy man, willing to take on anyone, he did not make his political foes into personal enemies. But he was also a liar, a petty tyrant, a crude opportunist, and an insensitive boor who could not comprehend that a democratic society required a modicum of civility and political decency to function.

In early 1950 McCarthy was in political trouble. Elected to the Senate over a weak opponent in the extraordinary 1946 Republican sweep, he had not made an impressive record. In fact, he had acquired a reputation as a crude opportunist who exchanged votes and influence for favors from business groups. In two years he was up for reelection and he would not be able to count on the special circumstances that had enabled him to win Wisconsin's liberal voters the last time. Clearly, the junior senator had to find an issue that would give him broad exposure and a

good press if he wanted to stay in Washington. He quickly found his issue in the rising anti-Communist concerns.

In Wheeling, West Virginia, on February 9, while on a speaking tour for Republican candidates in the 1950 campaign, he opened his own reelection drive with a speech devoted to the dangers of communism at home and abroad. The United States, he told the local Republican women's club, found itself "in a position of impotency" in international affairs because of "the traitorous actions" of men in high government posts. The State Department, especially, was "thoroughly infested with Communists," bright young men from the privileged class who had betrayed their country. He could, he said, name 205 members of the State Department whom the secretary of state knew to be members of the Communist party.

McCarthy could do nothing of the sort. His list was largely concocted and based on sources long out of date. But the press began to take notice of his sensational charges, and the country was soon in an excited mood. President Truman and Secretary of State Dean Acheson angrily denied the senator's claims. On Capitol Hill McCarthy's Senate colleagues asked him for proof. In response he carried out the feeble charade of reading some unconvincing documents that at many points completely exonerated the supposed culprits. The presentation was so shoddy that even the Republican leaders, who had at first welcomed his charges as likely to discomfit the Democrats, were embarrassed. Soon afterward, while testifying before a Senate subcommittee, McCarthy announced dramatically that the "top Soviet espionage agent" in the United States was Owen Lattimore, a professor of Far Eastern affairs at Johns Hopkins University, who had been a State Department adviser on China policy. The testimony of witnesses failed to support McCarthy's claims, but many Americans, deeply chagrined at the recent "loss" of China, were willing to believe that Lattimore and men like him had betrayed the nation. For days the senator made the headlines. In a few short months the word *McCarthyism* had been added to the language as a term for irresponsible mudslinging and defamation.

Civil libertarians notwithstanding, McCarthy and his cause were genuinely popular. Opinion polls in 1950 showed that the senator had the approval of 50 percent of the American people. Thereafter his popularity grew. McCarthy's views appealed strongly to many Catholics, whose hatred for Communist atheism and materialism went very deep. He also drew considerable working-class support by playing on class resentments, choosing as his favorite targets people of elite background like Hiss, Acheson, and Lattimore. McCarthy's strong political base was confirmed when, in the 1950 congressional election, he came to Maryland and helped defeat Democratic Senator Millard Tydings, one of his severest critics. His strength with the voters made McCarthyism an effective weapon for conservative Republicans to use against liberals and Democrats. As such it was sanctioned by many GOP leaders, including Mr. Republican himself, Robert Taft. So pervasive was McCarthy's popularity that even liberal Democrats had to reckon with it. In the early 1950s the young Massachusetts congressman John F. Kennedy noted that "Joe . . . may have something."

McCarthyism became a mood and an attitude that penetrated many layers of American life, with malign consequences. Besides McCarthy's own probes, the House Committee on Un-American Activities and the Senate Internal Security Subcommittee regularly investigated Communist infiltration of the universities, the churches, private industry, and the media. HUAC's well-publicized hearings usually focused on very visible fields such as the movies, the universities, and the unions. It forced men and women under subpoena to answer charges, often anonymous, that they had been members of "subversive" organizations. These groups were not necessarily formally Communist; they might be "Communist fronts" included on the attorney general's "list" of several hundred suspect organizations. HUAC did not punish offenders directly, but

many of those called before the committee lost their jobs and their reputations.

Private organizations and local officials quickly joined the antisubversive chorus. The broadcasting industry refused to hire anyone for radio or television work who was listed in *Red Channels*, a volume compiled by three former FBI agents that purported to identify all entertainers and media writers with past or existing radical affiliations. In Hollywood there were unofficial blacklists of performers, screenwriters, and directors whom no studio would touch. The theater, too, was rife with accusers and lists of "disloyal" people. Universities imposed loyalty oaths on faculty; states and local governments, on clerks, typists, laborers, and officials.

The prevailing hysteria over Communist and subversion cast a dark shadow over American life. Among performers, artists, and intellectuals, some of whom had been attracted to radical politics during the 1930s, the fear of attack and the possible consequences for their careers and personal lives squelched creativity. Many former leftists convinced themselves that they had been wrong about socialism—or even liberalism—and retreated to conservatism or became profoundly apolitical. With the whole left end of political and social ideology either silenced or converted, the tenor of the country shifted to the right. The witch-hunts destroyed many artistic and intellectual careers, but even ordinary citizens were deeply affected. When vigilantes were attacking every dissenting view and every dissenter as Communist, it seemed wise to keep silent and repress any opinion that could be considered irreverent. Fear of attack as a dangerous subversive, then, reinforced the 1950s tendency to focus on domestic joys and confirmed the American retreat into privatism.

After Eisenhower's victory and McCarthy's reelection in 1952, observers expected the senator to quiet down. The Republicans were now in office, and attacks on government officials would hurt his own party. But he refused to stop. In February 1953 he accused officials of the United States Information Agency, the information arm of the State Department, of attempting to undermine the American propaganda war against the Soviet Union. Panicked, Secretary of State John Foster Dulles ordered hundreds of books by authors of "doubtful loyalty" removed from the agency's shelves.

McCarthy's Downfall. With his popularity at its peak, the Wisconsin senator launched an attack on the army. His initial target was Secretary of the Army Robert T. Stevens, whom he accused of condoning the promotion of Irving Peress, an army dentist who had once been a member of the radical American Labor party. The promotion was actually a routine reranking of all drafted medical personnel,

Jack Kerouac

Jean-Louis ("Jack") Kerouac would be a hero to young rebels trying to escape the stifling conformity of the 1950s. He was also a "mamma's boy" who invariably returned from his misadventures to the safety and comfort of Gabrielle Lévesque Kerouac ("Mémêre").

Jack Kerouac always believed that his ancestors were noble Celts from Cornwall who later settled in France. The truth is more prosaic. Jack's parents, Leo and Gabrielle, were both born in Quebec of peasant stock and emigrated with their families to New England as small children. They were part of the flood of French Canadians who crossed the U.S. border seeking better livelihoods than afforded by the thin soils of the St. Lawrence Valley. When Jack was born in 1922 his parents were living in the old mill town of Lowell, Massachusetts, where Leo ran a print shop.

The three formative influences of Jack's childhood and youth were the death of his older brother, Gerard, when Jack was four, his discovery of the novels of Thomas Wolfe when he was fifteen, and football at Lowell High School. Gerard's tender, long-suffering character left his little brother with an image of saintly purity that would always attract one pole of his personality. Wolfe's sprawling, disorderly style would be Jack's literary inspiration. Varsity football at Lowell High in his teens would be his ticket of escape from the narrow world of immigrant Massachusetts.

In 1939 Columbia University offered Kerouac a football scholarship, and he arrived in New York in the fall to attend Horace Mann, a Columbia-affiliated prep school, to make up deficient academic credits and put on some weight. Kerouac's college football career was short-lived. In 1940 he played for the Columbia freshman squad but broke his leg and spent the rest of the year on campus in a cast. When he returned to school the following September he played briefly for the varsity, but quit the team when Coach Lou Little relegated him to a line position. Meanwhile, the United States had entered World War II, and Kerouac joined the merchant marine as a cook's galley helper and went on one trip to Greenland. He returned for a brief stint at Columbia and then quit for good. In early 1943 he was inducted into the navy but was discharged for psychiatric reasons: He could not obey orders.

Kerouac learned little from Columbia, but New York would become a major focus of his life. In 1943 the elder Kerouacs moved to New York, where Leo and Mémêre both got jobs. Jack divided his time between their apartment in Queens and that of Edie Parker, an attractive art student from Michigan, who lived in the Columbia neighborhood. At Edie's he met a crowd of young bohemians, including Lucian Carr, a Columbia freshman from St. Louis, and his friend, Allen Ginsberg, another Columbia student from Paterson, New Jersey. Through Carr, Kerouac also met an older man, William Burroughs, who, like Ginsberg, was physically attracted to Carr.

His new friends were different from anyone Kerouac had encountered before. They were cultural rebels with a streak of surrealism in their nature. On a visit to Burroughs's Greenwich Village apartment, Carr, imitating André Gide's *acte gratuit*, chewed up a beer glass. To continue the game, host Burroughs served his guests a plateful of razor blades. Burroughs also introduced Kerouac to Oswald Spengler's celebration of Western civilization's decay, *The Decline of the West*. Nineteen forty-five was also the year that Jack married Edie (the marriage was brief and unhappy); started to take Benzedrine, a powerful stimulant; and discovered Bop, the new, "cool" form of jazz that black musicians such as Dizzy Gillespie, Charlie Parker, Miles Davis, and Thelonious Monk were beginning to play in New York. It was from the "hipster" fans of Bop—young people who despised the "square world" of postwar America—that Kerouac and his friends borrowed the term "beat" to describe their cultural stance.

Toward the end of that momentous year Leo Kerouac was diagnosed as having stomach cancer. Jack came back to Queens to help his mother nurse him. His father's death in May 1946 plunged Jack into gloom, but shortly after he began to write *The Town and the City*, his first novel. An even more important event of the first full postwar year was Jack's meeting with Neal Cassady, a young man who came to represent heroic freedom and inspired the book that made Kerouac famous.

Cassady was essentially a juvenile delinquent. He had been raised by a wino father in a Denver flophouse. He began to steal cars at fourteen, and by the time he reached twenty had stolen over 500. After reform school in New Mexico he decided that he wanted to write and came to New York in the fall of 1946, determined to enter Columbia.

To Kerouac, Cassady represented the vital life force and liberation from conventional morality. Jack admired his friend's sexual freedom, his western openness, his physical fearlessness. He seemed a "mad genius of jails and raw power." The two planned a car trip west together, but then, in March, Cassady suddenly returned to Denver with his sixteen-year-old wife and a stolen typewriter. That summer both Kerouac and Ginsberg turned up in Denver. The visit with Cassady was not a success, and Kerouac went on to San Francisco after a few weeks for his first stay of many in that lively, creative city. In July he returned to Mémère in Queens, finished his 1,100-page novel, and met John Clellon Holmes, another aspiring writer. The two young men got along well, and it was in a discussion of their generation that Kerouac would remark, "I guess you can call us a beat generation," one weary "with all the forms, all the conventions." Holmes later wrote a novel about Kerouac and "the Beats" called *Go*.

While *The Town and the City* made the rounds of the publishers, Kerouac took courses in literature at the New School and began a novel about a long-distance car trip. In October Cassady turned up in New York with a brand-new silver-colored Hudson Hornet, and he and Kerouac set off on a marathon drive that took them south to visit Burroughs in Louisiana, across Texas to Tucson, and on to San Francisco. The two young men hurtled across the landscape of fifties America, exhilarated by the sheer joy of moving fast. The impressions collected on this trip, when merged with the earlier car manuscript, became the building blocks of Kerouac's most famous novel, *On the Road*.

By the mid-1950s, in isolated pockets across America, young men and women were declaring their independence of their society's conventionality and timidity. Few of them were "creative." Most were merely consumers of culture, but this culture was intensely antagonistic to middle-class fifties values. "Beatniks" sought a particular personal style. They assumed a "natural" look. They dressed in working-class style: jeans, open-necked plaid shirts, workshoes. They led freer sex lives; they often smoked mari-juana; they listened to Bop; they struck poses of personal "coolness"—uninvolvement—including indifference to politics.

There were also more creative Beats. In New York, Los Angeles, and especially San Francisco, small clusters of young, cool poets and novelists gathered together to provide mutual support for their writing. In San Francisco, a refuge for mavericks and bohemians ever since Gold Rush days, the Beat poets reached a critical mass under the aegis of a former Chicagoan, Kenneth Rexroth, and Lawrence Ferlinghetti, a San Francisco poet who ran a combined bookstore–publishing house called City Lights that became a haven for the city's Beats. Both Kerouac and Ginsberg were in the Bay Area in October 1955, just in time to be included in a Rexroth-sponsored poetry reading at the Six Gallery in an old San Francisco garage. Jack himself was only a spectator, but it was here that Ginsberg first read his long poem "Howl," a work that became the anthem of the cultural left for a generation and made Ginsberg famous.

Jack was soon to make his own very large literary splash. In September 1957 Viking Press published *On the Road* to rave reviews in *The New York Times* and other leading newspapers and magazines. Written on a continuous roll of typewriter paper in a twenty-day burst of creative energy fueled by oceans of coffee, the novel recounted the adventures of "Dean Moriarty" and "Sal Paradise" as they rolled frenetically across the continent in Moriarty's tail-finned behemoth, drinking in the essence of American vitality. Soon after, following articles on them in *Harper's Bazaar, The New York Times, Evergreen Review*, the *Nation*, and other publications, the Beats became culture heroes to the rebellious young and curiosities to their conventional elders of fifties America.

Kerouac spent much of the remaining 1950s as a restless wanderer shuttling among New York, San Francisco, North Carolina, Mexico, Florida, Long Island, and Tangier in Morocco. He was often in the company of Cassady, Ginsberg, Burroughs, or one of the new Beat poets. At least half the time he stayed with Mémère in several different places. Kerouac became a devotee of Zen Buddhism and wrote about his Zen friend Gary Snyder in *The Dharma Bums*, a book finished in ten mammoth typing sessions. He wrote a flock of other works in the 1950s and early 1960s, but few were taken seriously by the critics.

As Kerouac's stock fell, Allen Ginsberg's rose. Ginsberg became a prophet who, as the sixties unfolded, adapted to the new political rebelliousness of the young. Unlike Kerouac, who grew more conservative and misanthropic as he got older, Ginsberg moved politically left and became a gentle, nonviolent guru-radical. He also became an apostle of the new "psychedelic" drug culture, while Kerouac's mind-bender of choice remained alcohol—and ever larger quantities of it. In 1967 Kerouac moved with his mother and third wife back to Lowell, and then to St. Petersburg, Florida. In 1968 Neal Cassady collapsed and died in Mexico after overindulging in liquor and drugs. By now Kerouac's own health had deteriorated. The former varsity football player had become, at forty-six, a bloated, seedy alcoholic. On October 20, 1969, as he sat in front of his TV set with a can of tuna fish and a small bottle of whiskey, Jack suffered a massive intestinal hemorrhage. Eighteen hours later he died in surgery.

When they heard the news, reporters rushed to interview Allen Ginsberg at his upstate New York farm. Ginsberg started to quote William Blake's lines, "The days of my youth rise fresh in my mind," but he was too choked to finish. When the journalists left, he inscribed on a tree with a hunting knife: "Jack Kerouac, 1922–1969."

but in the next few weeks McCarthy made the cry "Who promoted Peress?" as famous for a while as "Remember the *Maine*." The army responded by accusing McCarthy of using his influence to gain preferential treatment at Forth Monmouth for G. David Schine, a draftee who had been a member of the senator's staff and a protégé of Roy Cohn, his committee counsel.

Eventually Congress voted to hold an investigation before McCarthy's own committee with Republican Senator Karl Mundt of South Dakota presiding. On April 22, 1954, the hearings commenced, and when they were over eight weeks later, McCarthy had to all intents and purposes run his course. Before the glaring lights of the television cameras, the senator seemed like a scowling Hollywood villain. He badgered witnesses and insulted them; he constantly interrupted the proceedings with points of order and irrelevancies.

The army's special counsel—a puckish, deceptively mild-mannered Boston lawyer named Joseph N. Welch—proved to be the senator's undoing. To weaken Welch's credibility, McCarthy chose to attack one of Welch's young Boston associates for his membership, years before, in the National Lawyer's Guild, a Communist-front organization. The young man had been dropped from Welch's hearing staff because of this association, but Welch had forgiven him his youthful indiscretion and retained him in his law firm. He saw no reason to bring the attorney's past to the attention of the public. When McCarthy broached the subject, Welch turned on him furiously: "Let us not assassinate this lad further, Senator. You have done enough. Have you no sense of decency, sir, at long last? Have you no sense of decency?" When he had finished his impassioned denunciation, the audience in the hearing room cheered. Even more important, television viewers in the living rooms and the neighborhood bars also cheered.

McCarthy's stock quickly plummeted. On December 2, 1954, the Senate passed a resolution condemning him for bringing the Senate into disrepute. The censure motion entailed no legal penalties, but from that day on, his colleagues shunned him, and when he rose to speak, they left the Senate chamber. Worst of all, the media began to ignore him. No matter what he said, he could no longer make the headlines. On May 2, 1957, he died of a liver ailment, unlamented by most Americans.

McCarthy's Legacy. McCarthy himself was dead, but in various guises the feelings he fed on and the movement he helped launch survived. In 1958 a Massachusetts candy manufacturer named Robert Welch founded the John Birch Society, a far-right anti-Communist organization. Welch and his followers insisted that the entire nation was riddled with secret Communists. From 60 to 80 percent of the world had already fallen to the Communists, they said, and the United States, having rejected Christian orthodoxy, rugged individualism, and free enterprise, was virtually lost as well. According to Birch Society members, everything since Herbert Hoover represented a conspiratorial effort to undermine Christian American civilization, and even the Eisenhower administration was actively aiding the forces of communism.

Despite attacks by public officials, journalists, scholars, and aroused citizens, the Birch Society flourished. Well supplied with money from southwestern oil, cattle, and electronics magnates, it attracted intolerant fundamentalists, people obsessed with the Communist danger, and, seemingly, every opponent of change or novelty. Local chapters of the society fought against the fluoridation of drinking water, instigated recall elections against liberal school board members, attacked "subversive" college professors, demanded the impeachment of Chief Justice Earl Warren, and resisted efforts to impose gun controls. Allied with the society were the Christian Anti-Communism Crusade, led by Australian preacher Fred Schwarz, and the Christian Crusade, led by another Protestant minister, Billy James Hargis. Neither Welch nor his associates were Nazis, but some active anti-Communists also belonged to George Lincoln Rockwell's American Nazi party or some similar neo-Nazi hate group. Others joined semisecret paramilitary organizations like the Minute Men, which collected arms and held drills in expectation of an imminent Soviet invasion or an internal Communist takeover.

McCarthyism also affected American foreign policy. Fear of attack by professional anti-Communists at times forced policymakers to pursue a hard line against communism even when it did not best serve American interests. America's refusal to accord diplomatic recognition to Communist China, for example, was in part a response to pressure from the McCarthyite witch hunters. Even more serious, perhaps, fear of being attacked for "losing Indochina", as Truman had "lost China," would, as we shall see, help lure Lyndon Johnson into one of the most unfortunate military escapades in American history.

The Election of 1960. McCarthyism was still alive when the political pendulum swung to the Democrats. With the ever popular Ike about to retire, 1960 was a good chance for the Democrats to win the White House once again. They had a decent array of candidates as the nomination season began. The loquacious liberal senator from Minnesota, Hubert Humphrey, had the support of organized labor and the party's old-line New Dealers. Adlai Stevenson, though a two-time loser, still had the hearts of many younger Democrats. Lyndon Johnson of Texas, the powerful Senate Majority Leader, parading as a westerner rather than a son of Dixie, hoped to win a deadlocked convention. Most interesting of all, in many ways, was the young, handsome senator from Massachusetts, John F. Kennedy.

Kennedy's qualifications for president were not overwhelming. The oldest surviving son of Joseph Kennedy, a multimillionaire business tycoon and Wall Street operator, he seemed to be more interested in wine, women, and song than in public service. He had returned from the war a young navy hero and had been pushed by his power-hungry father to run for Congress. As a member of the House and then the Senate, Kennedy had been a mediocre legislator, not well respected by his colleagues. Many strong liberals within the party considered him too conservative. He had even tepidly endorsed McCarthy. But his most serious disqualification was his religion. The Kennedys were Catholics and the last time a Catholic had run for president—Al Smith in 1928—he had been badly beaten. Anti-Catholicism, though abated since 1928, still ran strong in the rural Midwest and the South, and it did not seem likely that a Catholic, even in 1960, could overcome the ingrained prejudice of the heartland.

But Kennedy had many things going for him as well. He was handsome, well-spoken, well-educated, and rich. The rich part was important, for money talked eloquently in politics even in 1960. The Kennedys could pay for chartered jets, TV time, and newspaper advertisements to swamp their opponents. The key Democratic primary was in West Virginia where Kennedy went head-to-head with his chief rival, Humphrey, in a state overwhelmingly Protestant. When Kennedy won it was assumed that the contest was all but over. The Kennedy forces went on to the Los Angeles convention and won on the first ballot. In a stunning show of *Realpolitik* they turned to the wheeler-dealer Texan, Lyndon Johnson, to balance the ticket.

The Republicans chose Vice President Richard Nixon as their candidate. Nixon was not a beloved man. Liberals considered him a junior McCarthy for his anti-Communist work on the House Committee on Un-American Activities and the prosecution of Alger Hiss. He also seemed unprincipled and had earned the nickname "Tricky Dick." But as vice president he had acquired some stature as a foreign-policy expert. The public best remembered the "kitchen debate" with Soviet leader Khrushchev when, at a gleaming model American kitchen on exhibition at a Moscow trade fair, Nixon had scored points for American capitalism. Nixon defeated his chief rival for the nomination, New York Governor Nelson Rockefeller, but not before compromising his independence by going to the governor's apartment and accepting conditions on foreign and domestic policy to win Rockefeller's support. Henry Cabot Lodge, Jr., the UN ambassador, got the Republican vice presidential slot.

The contest was the most exciting in a decade. Nixon campaigned as the beloved Eisenhower's successor and heir apparent though the president, who never liked Nixon, gave him only lukewarm support. Nixon plugged his own experience, especially in foreign affairs, and called his opponent a lightweight. The vice president never mentioned Kennedy's Catholicism, but clearly it was on the minds of many devout traditional Protestants. Kennedy partially neutralized the issue by appearing before the Greater Houston Ministerial Association in September and eloquently endorsing the separation of church and state.

Many observers believe the contest was decided by a series of TV debates between the two candidates during September and October. In the first one, especially, Kennedy, though the younger man, seemed poised and articulate whereas Nixon appeared nervous and tired. Kennedy's telegenic quotient, moreover, far exceeded his opponent's. The election marked the true onset of the "tube" as the key media instrument in American politics.

In the end the election was one of the closest on record. The Massachusetts senator received only some 100,000 more popular votes than Nixon out of almost 69 million cast, and he carried fewer, though larger, states than did his adversary. Kennedy may have been weaker than even these figures suggest. Some evidence suggests that in both Texas and Illinois the Democratic machines altered the popular votes in favor of the party's candidate. Nixon might have challenged the results but chose to accept them rather than force a major constitutional crisis.

⋆ CONCLUSIONS ⋆

Well into the 1960s Americans remained a timid, insecure people. Having suffered through the nation's worst depression and its most agonizing war, they could not help regarding the postwar era as an improvement. With all its flaws, prosperity was real, and they turned from politics to revel in the pleasures of growing abundance and domesticity. The pursuit of private goals and satisfactions and the avoidance of controversy after 1945 was to some extent, then, a predictable consequence of the surprising success of the postwar economy.

It was also the result of fear. The Soviet Union seemed like a colossus astride half the planet. Moreover, for the first time since the Ottoman threat to Christendom in the seventeenth century, the West had to reckon with the competition of non-Europeans with values and cultures different from its own. And there was no way Americans could deal with these challenges militarily. America's only effective weapon was the atom bomb, but its use was ruled out by the instincts both of humanity and self-preservation.

The only valid response to this impasse probably was patient diplomatic and intellectual struggle. But Americans are not a patient people, and the resulting frustration and anxiety brought out their worst side. McCarthyism was the major expression of that frustration. McCarthyism in turn engendered further fear. Why, most would-be dissenters asked, stick one's neck out? People who spoke up would be labeled Communists, and once so labeled, their lives and careers would be blighted. Intimidated by public events that seemed to threaten their safety, and exposed to the pleasures of consumerism as never before, Americans turned inward and sought private, safe satisfactions.

Despite the appeal of privatism and prudence, by the mid-1950s acute observers could detect signs of change. In 1956 a popular sociologist, John Keats, wrote *The Crack in the Picture Window*, attacking suburbia as deadening to the mind and spirit. By the end of the decade a new cultural bohemia composed of "Beat" poets and novelists had begun to appear in San Francisco and New York. For bohemians, the Beats were unusually apolitical and "cool," but they took drugs, wore sandals, and were sexually promiscuous. Clearly, times were beginning to change.

✶✶✶✶✶✶✶ FOR FURTHER READING ✶✶✶✶✶✶✶

Dean Acheson. *Present at the Creation* (1969)
This is Secretary of State Acheson's own account of his State Department experiences from 1941 to 1953. It is, not surprisingly, a strong defense of the Truman Doctrine, the Marshall Plan, NATO, and the Korean intervention.

Athan Theoharis. *Seeds of Repression: Harry Truman and the Origins of McCarthyism* (1971)
Theoharis blames the liberals for McCarthyism rather than the political right.

Thomas C. Reeves. *The Life and Times of Joe McCarthy: A Biography* (1982)
A masterly and unfailingly interesting biography by a careful scholar.

Alan Weinstein. *Perjury: The Hiss-Chambers Case* (1978)
A definitive study that concludes that Hiss was guilty as charged.

Walter LaFeber, *America, Russia, and the Cold War* (1975); and David Horowitz, editor, *Containment and Revolution* (1967)
These two books are "revisionist" studies of the Cold War that strongly endorse the view that American policy was the predominant, and avoidable, cause of the confrontation with the Soviet Union. The Horowitz work is an anthology of New Left—and some Old Left—writings on aspects of American foreign policy from 1917 to the mid-1960s. It treats the United States as a counterrevolutionary force in the world during that period.

Daniel Yergin. *Shattered Peace: The Origins of the Cold War and the National Security State* (1977)
American policy toward the Soviet Union since the 1940s was governed by two distinct views, says Yergin. One, identified with FDR, saw the possibility of U.S.-Soviet accommodation. The other, the view of certain groups within the State Department, saw no possibility of compromising with an aggressive, expansionist power. The United States after 1945 vacillated between these two positions.

Alonzo Hamby. *Beyond the New Deal: Harry S. Truman and American Liberalism* (1973)
This solid volume is a defense of Truman and Truman liberalism. Hamby sees the latter as a valid adaptation of the New Deal.

Charles C. Alexander. *Holding the Line: The Eisenhower Era, 1952–1959* (1975)
A good summary of domestic and foreign policy in the Eisenhower years. The title suggests the author's view of the Eisenhower administration.

Douglas T. Miller and Marion Nowak. *The Fifties: The Way We Really Were* (1977)
The authors have little patience with those who would romanticize the 1950s. They see it as a time of real but neglected problems. In their eagerness to restore the critical balance they probably are too harsh on Americans during that decade.

David Riesman, Reuel Denney, and Nathan Glazer. *The Lonely Crowd: A Study of the Changing American Character* (1950)
The influential study that made Americans worry about the loss of "inner direction." An important cultural document.

Scott Donaldson. *The Suburban Myth* (1969)
Most intellectuals and social observers despised the post–World War II suburbs. Donaldson examines this phenomenon. He also disagrees with his colleagues. Suburbs, he believes, were the most realistic solution of the mid-twentieth-century housing problem.

Richard O. Davies. *The Age of Asphalt: The Automobile, the Freeway, and the Condition of Metropolitan America* (1975)
We Americans are so dependent on cars and highways because we love to move about and because, in 1956, Congress decided to build a gigantic interstate highway system. Davis describes the reason for the Highway Act and discusses the neglected alternatives that might have eased our energy and urban crises.

Richard Rovere. *Senator Joe McCarthy* (1959)

Like most political reporters, Rovere is fascinated by McCarthy's career. This is the standard liberal account of McCarthy by the late political correspondent of *The New Yorker* magazine. For a conservative treatment, far more favorable to the Wisconsin senator, see William F. Buckley, Jr., and L. B. Bozell, *McCarthy and His Enemies* (1954).

Richard Kluger. *Simple Justice: The History of* Brown v. Board of Education *and Black America's Struggle for Equality* (1975)

The best single volume on the civil rights movement in the 1950s. Focuses on the famous 1954 school desegregation decision of the Supreme Court.

Bruce Cook. *The Beat Generation* (1971)

Cook's thesis is that the Beat movement of the 1950s anticipated much of the cultural and political radicalism of the 1960s. In the poems and novels of Jack Kerouac, Allen Ginsberg, Gregory Corso, and others, the author finds the disdain for authority, the antimilitarism, and the taste for mysticism, sensuality, and drugs that also characterized the later "Age of Aquarius."

Jack Kerouac. *On the Road* (1957)

Experience was everything to the Beats, and this attitude explains their constant need to move, to be on the road. A novel of characters frantically moving across the American landscape of the 1950s.

Ralph Ellison. *Invisible Man* (1952)

A beautifully written, convincing, and often amusing novel of the coming of age of a young black man who is caught up in—and then dumped by—the Communist party. He learns that he will have to "stay in the dark" as an invisible man.

Max Hastings. *The Korean War* (1987)

An English military historian seeks to rescue the Korean War from what he considers recent neglect. This lively review of the Korean "police action"—based on interviews as well as documents—depicts the conflict as a dress rehearsal for Vietnam, with many of the same frustrations and confusions. Yet at the same time Hastings does not condemn those who insisted that the United States had to intervene to save the South Koreans from the invaders from the North. With all its faults, he says, the present South Korean regime is better than the one that would have replaced it if the Communists had won.

J. Ronald Oakley. *God's Country: America in the Fifties* (1986)

A very readable survey of America in the flush 1950s when the United States was an economic colossus. Oakley shows that all was not necessarily well in the Garden of Eden, what with racism, the Cold War, and Joe McCarthy.

29★

THE DISSENTING SIXTIES

Why Protest in the "Great Society"?

1954	French defeated at Dien Bien Phu; Geneva Accords
1957	Russians launch Sputnik into orbit • Martin Luther King, Jr., founds the Southern Christian Leadership Conference (SCLC)
1959	Castro overthrows Batista regime in Cuba • U-2 incident
1960	Student Nonviolent Coordinating Committee (SNCC) founded • Birth-control pill introduced • John F. Kennedy elected president
1961	Peace Corps founded; Kennedy announces the Alliance for Progress • CIA and anti-Castro Cubans launch the Bay of Pigs invasion of Cuba • Berlin Wall built • Kennedy sends American troops to Vietnam
1962	Cuban Missile Crisis
1962, 1963	Attorney General Robert Kennedy enforces integration of state universities in Mississippi and Alabama
1963	Civil rights demonstrators numbering 250,000 march on Washington • Kennedy assassinated; Lyndon Johnson becomes president
1964	Johnson launches the "War on Poverty" • China explodes its first atom bomb • Congress passes the Civil Rights Act • Tonkin Gulf Resolution
1964–65	Berkeley Free Speech Movement sets precedent for major campus revolts
1965	Johnson orders the bombing of North Vietnam • Great Society Legislation and agencies: Elementary and Secondary Education Act, Medicare, Department of Housing and Urban Development (HUD), Omnibus Housing Act, Voting Rights Act, National Foundations of the Arts and Humanities, Higher Education Act, Metropolitan Area Redevelopment Act, Truth in Lending Act
1965–67	Black riots in Los Angeles, Detroit, Newark
1966	Highway Safety Act • Betty Friedan organizes the National Organization for Women (NOW)
1968	My Lai Massacre • Martin Luther King and Robert Kennedy assassinated • Street riots at Democratic National Convention in Chicago • Richard Nixon elected president
1969	American Indian activists occupy Alcatraz Island • Woodstock and Altamont rock festivals • Americans land on the moon

In April 1968 a group of young actors appeared in a new musical at the Biltmore Theater in New York. The play, *Hair,* glorified every rebellious, nonconformist theme of the decade. *Hair* announced that the Age of Aquarius was at hand, that "harmony and understanding" and "crystal revelation" would soon prevail. A song called "Sodomy" described the delights of oral sex and masturbation; "Air" detailed the horrors of air pollution; and "Walking in Space" was simultaneously about the space program and "tripping" on drugs. The musical theme of "Hare Krishna" was borrowed from a Hindu sect whose adherents could be seen ringing bells and chanting on the streets of large American cities. The high point of the performance came at the end of the first act, when members of the biracial cast removed all their clothes while singing "Beads, Flowers, Freedom and Happiness."

To a Rip Van Winkle of 1948 awakening twenty years later, *Hair* would have been a profound shock. Radical in politics, "liberated" in social vision, ecstatic and orgiastic in cultural texture, it was almost the antithesis of the values Americans had accepted in the years between 1945 and 1960. Then, only in the darkest corners of American life had there been a hint that such things existed. But in 1968 the members of the *Hair* cast became culture heroes who, according to theater critic Clive Barnes of the *New York Times,* expressed "the authentic voice of today."

How had this startling turnabout come to pass? America in the 1950s was a prosperous, self-satisfied society. Why did it change so drastically, so quickly? Was it primarily the inexorable swing of the cultural pendulum: having moved so far to conformity, could it only move to revolt? Did prosperity, as in the past, breed its special forms of discontent with the status quo? Were outside forces and events responsible?

★ Politics in Camelot ★

The decade began with a breath of fresh political air. The thousand days of the Kennedy presidency have been likened to Camelot, the mythical court of King Arthur where, "for one brief shining moment," an enchanted realm existed. The new president was young, the first chief executive born in the twentieth century. The advisors he brought to Washington in early 1961 were like himself—dashing, bright, charming, full of confidence that there were new answers to old problems. They worked hard and they played hard, and the public enjoyed watching them. We now know that the president was not the personal paragon of the Camelot legend. He was, in fact, a reckless womanizer and a compulsive pill-popper. But for the first time since FDR, the White House became a lively and interesting place, and the public delighted in the change.

Kennedy appealed especially to the idealism of young people. In his inaugural address he noted that a "torch" had "been passed to a new generation of Americans, born in this century," who would not "permit the slow undoing of those human rights to which this nation has always been committed." One of his first moves was to propose a Peace Corps of young men and women who would invest their skills and part of their lives in working abroad among the sick and poor of Third World nations. Soon afterward he announced the Alliance for Progress, a foreign aid proposal to pump $20 billion into Latin America to raise economic output and redistribute it among the hemisphere's poor and oppressed.

Kennedy Foreign Policy. However idealistic in tone, Kennedy's Alliance for Progress did not fundamentally alter "containment" as the dominant American foreign policy. The Alliance, after all, was intended as much to prevent Communist-led revolutions in the Americas as to improve the lot of the Latin American peoples. Yet Kennedy and his advisers also brought new ideas to American foreign policy.

In his 1960 campaign Kennedy had warned that his Republican predecessor had allowed the Soviet Union to build more missiles than the United States. This "missile gap" threatened the nation's security. After taking office he found that the gap did not exist. But the new president had more substantial objections to Eisenhower's weapons policy as well. The Eisenhower administration, he claimed, had relied far too much on nuclear weapons. Rather than spend the money for conventional arms, the Republican president and his chief foreign-policy adviser, John Foster Dulles, had built up stockpiles of hydrogen bombs. This meant that in the event of international crisis, America's only possible response was threat of nuclear retaliation. Such a threat might validly be used to deter the Soviet Union from, say, a major attack on NATO, but what about other, lesser, Soviet advances? Around the world—in Berlin, Cuba, the Middle East, and Asia—were areas where United States and Soviet interests clashed. We clearly could not use "massive deterrence" to discourage Soviet aggression at such pressure points, for the risks of nuclear holocaust were simply too great for the gains that could be expected. In effect, then, the lack of conventional military forces left the United States without any practical way to deal with the sort of small Soviet actions that the future would bring. Such shortsightedness only guaranteed successful Soviet subversion all over the world.

To avoid the unacceptable alternatives of holocaust or surrender, Kennedy and Secretary of Defense Robert McNamara urged a "flexible response." The United States must build up its conventional forces and prepare itself to use counterinsurgency tactics so it could tailor its response to the extent of the threat. To implement the new policy, the Kennedy administration expanded the army from eleven to sixteen combat divisions and began retraining troops for jungle and guerrilla fighting. This was expensive, and during the Kennedy years the defense budget grew by 25 percent.

Early Tests. The first attempt at counterinsurgency was a fiasco. Carrying out an operation planned by the Eisenhower administration, in April 1961 the president authorized a tiny amphibious military group of anti-Castro Cuban refugees to land in Cuba at the Bay of Pigs. The CIA had persuaded Kennedy that a small invading force would trigger a general uprising that would easily topple Fidel Castro, the leader who had overthrown the Cuban dictator Batista in 1959 and installed an anti-American revolutionary regime in Havana. But the uprising did not materialize, and the invaders were quickly pinned down on the beach.

Not wishing to involve the country more deeply in an embarrassing enterprise, the president refused to provide American air and military support to rescue them. In a matter of days they were all killed or captured, and the United States found itself condemned before the world as an ineffectual bully.

Kennedy's first direct contact with the Soviets was not much happier. Soviet Premier Nikita Khrushchev, Stalin's successor, was a blunt outspoken man. He represented a break with the brutal tyranny of his predecessor, but he was equally suspicious of Western motives and did not intend to surrender any of his nation's interests. He had met with Eisenhower at Geneva in 1955, in the first U.S.-Soviet "summit." The meeting had produced nothing concrete, but its cordial and cooperative tone cheered the world, uneasy about the superpower rivalry. This "spirit of Geneva" quickly dissipated, however, when, in November 1958, Khrushchev escalated Cold War tensions over Berlin.

That city, divided between East and West, was a Communist sore point. Between 1949 and 1958 almost 3 million Germans had fled Communist East Germany for West Germany, and to prevent further loss of productive people the Communist authorities had sealed off most of

If any American president ever was charismatic, John Fitzgerald Kennedy was. Intelligent, youthful, handsome, and articulate, he possessed all the equipment for successful leadership except maturity. Those who hoped that this would come in time were to be tragically disappointed.

the two Germanies' common frontier. Berlin, however, remained open, and its Western zone continued to be a magnet for disaffected East Germans. Hundreds escaped daily to West Berlin, and each person who fled the German Democratic Republic advertised the superiority of the capitalist over the Communist way of life. Related to the problem of Berlin was the refusal of the Western powers to sign a peace treaty that accepted the division of Germany, and their insistence that they would deal only with the Soviet Union, not the East German authorities, in matters concerned with Berlin. On November 10, 1960, Khrushchev announced that the Soviet Union intended to transfer authority over the eastern zone of Berlin to the East German authorities, thus forcing the Western powers to deal with them. Implied was the possibility of another Berlin blockade.

Fortunately, the Soviet premier soon after withdrew his threat, and for a time the danger of superpower confrontation over Berlin receded. In May 1960 Eisenhower and Khrushchev met in Paris for another summit. It was ill-starred. Just before the meeting the Soviets announced that they had shot down an American U-2 spy plane over the Soviet Union and captured its CIA employee pilot, Francis Gary Powers. Ike might have denied his personal involvement, but instead admitted his responsibility for the espionage operation. On May 17, Khrushchev denounced the spy flight and canceled the summit. In January he ominously declared his country's "unlimited support" to "peoples fighting for their liberation." The Cold War, in the form of "wars of national liberation," would, it seemed, now be extended around the world.

Kennedy's encounter with Khrushchev at Vienna in June 1961 was a grim experience. From the Bay of Pigs fiasco, the Soviet leader had apparently concluded that the young American president was weak and could be bullied. Khrushchev was abrupt, even insulting. Berlin was a "bone in the throat" of the Soviet Union. If the Western powers failed to sign an agreement that accepted the legitimacy of the German Democratic Republic, he would turn over administration of Berlin to the East German authorities, who might then end free communication between the city and West Germany. If the United States chose to go to war over this, so be it. When Khrushchev returned to Moscow he delivered a number of warlike speeches and raised the Soviet military budget.

Though shaken by Khrushchev's threats, Kennedy refused to be intimidated. Back at home, he asked Congress for an additional $3.5 billion for defense, announced the call-up of army reserves and National Guard units, and urged Americans to build bomb shelters. Public anxiety soared.

Meanwhile, in Berlin the stream of refugees to the West became a flood. To staunch this hemorrhage, East German authorities on August 13, 1961, abruptly blocked all traffic between the city's zones and the next day began to erect a high wall of brick, concrete blocks, and barbed wire. For the next twenty-eight years the Berlin Wall would symbolize the barriers separating the two Cold War antagonists.

For a while longer the tension over Berlin continued. In early September the Soviets resumed nuclear testing on a massive scale, releasing enormous quantities of radioactive matter into the atmosphere. In retaliation Kennedy authorized the resumption of American nuclear testing, though only underground. Then Khrushchev backed down. At the end of the month in Moscow he told a visiting diplomat from Belgium, a NATO nation: "I'm not trying to put you in an impossible situation; I know very well that you can't let yourself be stepped on." In mid-October he informed the Communist Party Congress that the Western powers appeared conciliatory and he, accordingly, would defer a peace treaty with East Germany. The second Berlin crisis was over.

The Cuban Missile Crisis. But Khrushchev recklessly forced one more confrontation in his war of nerves against the United States and its young president. The Soviet leader knew that the United States actually far surpassed the Soviet Union in its ability to deliver nuclear weapons. Hoping to equalize the imbalance and to protect Cuba against American attack, a year and a half after the Bay of Pigs invasion he sent Soviet troops and technicians to Cuba. These Soviet forces brought with them two sorts of missiles: strategic SS-4s of medium range capable of reaching Washington and New York, and short-range tactical missiles that could destroy any American invasion force landing on Cuba's beaches. The strategic missiles remained under Moscow's direct control, but the Soviet commander in Cuba was authorized, without Moscow's approval, to launch the tactical missiles to stop an American invasion if he felt it necessary. As the military experts—Soviet, Cuban, and American—concluded thirty years later, this was a formula for world nuclear disaster. If the Americans, having discovered the medium-range SS-4s, had decided to invade, the American troops would have been wiped out by the tactical nuclear weapons. In that event the United States would undoubtedly have retaliated with its own nuclear weapons and the world would have found itself immersed in its worst horror, a nuclear holocaust.

Even without full knowledge of the risks, Washington recognized that the world stood on the edge of disaster. From the moment American intelligence revealed the presence of the missiles in mid-October, the National Security Council met in continuous session to debate what course to take. Air Force General Curtis LeMay favored an immediate attack on Cuba. Defense Secretary McNamara and the

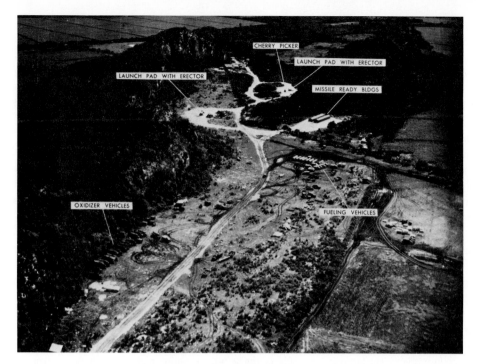

LAUNCH PAD WITH ERECTOR

CHERRY PICKER

LAUNCH PAD WITH ERECTOR

MISSILE READY BLDGS

OXIDIZER VEHICLES

FUELING VEHICLES

This Department of Defense photo shows a missile base in Cuba. President Kennedy used such photos on television to explain the crisis to the nation, and Ambassador Adlai Stevenson displayed them on the floor of the United Nations.

president's brother, Attorney General Robert F. Kennedy, favored a blockade of the island to prevent the missiles still on their way by ship from being landed. The president rejected the aggressive LeMay course. On the evening of October 22, 1962, he appeared on national television to tell the American people about the Soviet missiles and explain that the government had decided to "quarantine" Cuba to prevent delivery of more missiles. If the Soviets tried to run the blockade, the American navy would shoot.

The announcement startled the nation and the world. Never before had the two superpowers found themselves on such a collision course. A wrong move by either might thrust the world into nuclear war. Americans generally supported the president's course, but outside the United States many people blamed Kennedy for gambling with the very existence of humanity.

What would the Soviets do when their missile-carrying ships, fast approaching Cuba, encountered the American blockade? For four days the world waited apprehensively. In Cuba, Soviet technicians worked feverishly to complete the missile launch pads, and began to assemble crated Soviet bombers. Washington kept NATO leaders informed of minute-by-minute developments. The world held its breath. Then the break came. On October 26 Khrushchev sent a long message to the American government acknowledging for the first time that Soviet missiles were being installed in Cuba. The Soviet Union, Khrushchev stated, would send no more missiles if the United States agreed not to attack Cuba. At the same time

he released publicly an offer to remove the missiles from Cuba if the United States would remove its missile bases from Turkey. Overtly ignoring the issue of Turkish bases, Kennedy agreed not to attack Cuba if the Soviet missiles were taken out. Khrushchev did not insist on his terms. The crisis was over.

A wave of relief swept the country; Kennedy's popularity, which had suffered from the Bay of Pigs blunder, rebounded strongly. The Soviets removed the missiles, but their technicians lingered, and Castro rejected on-site inspection of the former bases. The United States soon after quietly dismantled its Turkish bases. Though Kennedy and Khrushchev had averted global destruction, Cuba, as a Soviet ally just ninety miles off the coast of Florida, would remain a sore point for American policymakers. In later years the Cubans would be accused of trying to export revolution to other parts of Latin America and of endangering American interests in the Western Hemisphere and in West Africa.

Vietnam Intervention Begins. Even as world attention focused on Cuba and Berlin, a larger confrontation was developing in Southeast Asia. Vietnam might have remained just another Cold War pressure point but for Kennedy's and McNamara's new "flexible response" policy. This policy tempted the United States into a prolonged military involvement in Southeast Asia that would prove disastrous.

The setting for the American debacle was Vietnam, Cambodia, and Laos, nations carved out of French

Indochina in the years following the Japanese surrender in 1945 and made "associated states" of the French Union—that is, French protectorates. In the northern part of Vietnam, however, Ho Chi Minh, a Communist nationalist, refused to accept French rule. Ho established a "Democratic Republic" ruled from Hanoi and claimed to speak for all Vietnamese, including those in the south. The French fought Ho and his Vietminh forces, but in 1954 they were defeated at Dien Bien Phu. Soon after, they agreed to a division of Vietnam along the seventeenth parallel, pending a 1956 election that would decide the future government for a united country. This decision was ratified by a meeting of the major powers at Geneva, but the election was never held. Fearing that a free ballot might topple his anti-Communist regime, South Vietnamese Premier Ngo Dinh Diem dithered and delayed and, when the Eisenhower administration failed to exert pressure to coerce him, postponed the election indefinitely.

The defeat of the French awakened American fears of further Communist expansion in Southeast Asia. As Eisenhower explained in 1954, the countries of the region were like "dominos"; if "you knock over one . . . the last one . . . will go over very quickly." That September the United States negotiated a treaty with Australia, Great Britain, France, New Zealand, Thailand, the Philippines, and Pakistan pledging joint action of the eight nations against Communist aggression in the region. Though designed to emulate NATO, SEATO (the South East Asia Treaty Organization) lacked a unified military command and proved ineffectual in checking East Asian Communist expansion.

During the last half of the fifties the United States under Eisenhower refused to send troops to the region but supplied war materiel and economic aid on a large scale to pro-Western or neutral regimes in Laos, Cambodia, and South Vietnam to help them resist Communist takeovers. The policy was at best a partial success. In Laos the Pathet Lao, a Communist-led nationalist movement, grew more powerful and threatened to overthrow the neutralist government. In South Vietnam the Diem regime in Saigon failed to pacify the country. Diem and his supporters proved corrupt and unpopular with the country's Buddhists and peasantry and before long the Vietcong (called by its friends the National Liberation Front), a Communist guerrilla movement supplied with arms by Ho Chi Minh in North Vietnam, began to attract a following among the rural people. To alarmists it looked as if the Saigon government would soon fall and be replaced by a Communist regime that would unify Vietnam, North and South, under Communist rule.

Kennedy, like Eisenhower, accepted a containment policy for Asia and, despite misgivings, for a time continued to help Diem against his Communist enemies. Unlike his predecessor, however, JFK was willing to send American personnel as well as money and supplies. In May 1961 he dispatched 400 Special Forces troops, trained in counterinsurgency tactics, to South Vietnam. Yet Kennedy's commitment, too, was ultimately limited. He rejected the recommendation of General Maxwell Taylor and presidential adviser Walter W. Rostow later that year that he send 10,000 American combat troops to help defeat the Vietcong. Still, JFK seemed incapable of resisting the dangerous feeling that just a little more help might do the trick. By October 1962 over 16,000 Americans were in South Vietnam advising and assisting the Diem government, and, though none of these were combat troops, the number of Americans injured or killed had reached almost 600.

The Kennedy administration could not refrain from intervening in South Vietnamese affairs in other ways. In late 1963, convinced that Diem had lost the support of his people, the president gave the green light for a coup to a group of generals who had the South Vietnamese leader assassinated. Unfortunately the roster of military men who replaced him would prove no more competent or honest—and no more capable of rallying the South Vietnamese people to the side of the anti-Communist regime in Saigon against the Vietcong.

JFK and Civil Rights. On civil rights the administration's record was mixed. Kennedy had received his margin of victory in 1960 from blacks in the North. But he also feared driving white southerners out of the Democratic party. Under his brother Robert's aegis, the Justice Department enforced provisions of the 1957 and 1960 Civil Rights Acts and helped get thousands of black southerners on the voting rolls. The administration also compelled conservative governors Ross Barnett of Mississippi and George C. Wallace of Alabama to admit black students to their state universities in 1962 and 1963. Yet it lagged behind the civil rights leaders in its commitment to racial justice and often advised them to go slow.

The administration's caution particularly offended the new breed of young activists who were beginning to come to the fore as the sixties unfolded. The sixties brand of civil rights militancy dated from February 1, 1960, when four black students at North Carolina Agricultural and Technical College at Greensboro took seats at the Jim Crow lunch counter of the local Woolworth. They were denied service; the lunch counter, the manager told them, was for whites only. The next day the students returned with friends and resumed their sit-in. Day after day they continued their protest against segregation despite the catcalls and jeers of unfriendly whites. In a few days the press took notice and the sit-in movement spread all over the South.

The activism of black college students encouraged the formation, under King's sponsorship, of the Student

The 1963 March on Washington was for civil rights, but as several of these signs show, it was also a demonstration for jobs.

Nonviolent Coordinating Committee (SNCC). SNCC at the outset accepted the Southern Christian Leadership Conference (SCLC) commitment to a nonviolent, biracial approach to civil rights, but it was not clear how long the young militants would accept the guidance of their elders.

Nineteen sixty-one was the year of the freedom rides when white and black civil rights activists, under the auspices of the Congress of Racial Equality (CORE), traveled through the South by bus to challenge the segregation policies of the interstate bus companies. White supremicists threatened the freedom riders, and in South Carolina and Alabama white toughs beat them severely. The activists appealed to the Justice Department to protect them from their assailants. The government complied, but too slowly to suit the young activists. The riders had to cut their agenda short.

Yet at times the administration's intervention served the civil rights cause well. In 1961 King and the SCLC launched their Birmingham campaign to open up jobs in the Alabama city to blacks and end downtown segregation of eating places and other public facilities. SCLC's campaign was based on a shrewd estimate. King knew he must touch the liberal conscience of the nation to succeed. In

Birmingham the authorities cooperated. City officials threw King in jail, and police chief Eugene "Bull" Conner used high-pressure water hoses and snarling attack dogs against children marching to protest Birmingham's segregation policies. The public watched the TV images in horror. The president said the events in Birmingham made him "sick," and sent Justice Department officials to negotiate a settlement with the business community and the city authorities that gave the SCLC most of what it wanted.

The culmination of the nonviolent, biracial phase of the civil rights movement came in the summer of 1963 when more than 200,000 civil rights supporters, black and white, came to Washington to demonstrate for "jobs and freedom" and to express their support of a pending new civil rights bill. Kennedy was afraid the march might frighten moderate opinion and do more harm than good. At first he advised against it. His fears were misplaced. At the Lincoln Memorial the enthusiastic and orderly crowd were deeply moved by King's "I Have A Dream" address, a speech that expressed the noblest aspirations of the civil rights movement for a society where skin color would no longer have any significance. The demonstration helped win passage of the pending bill, but only in July 1964 after Kennedy himself was dead. As enacted under his successor, the sweeping Civil Rights Law of 1964 barred discrimination in public accommodations, authorized the Justice Department to commence suits to force desegregation of schools and other public facilities, outlawed job discrimination based on race, color, religion, national origin, or sex, and reduced the power of local voter registration boards to disqualify black registrants on the basis of literacy.

King was now at the very peak of his career. In January 1964 *Time* named him Man of the Year. In October 1964 he would win the Nobel Peace Prize.

The New Frontier.   Kennedy's New Frontier was at best a modest success. He succeeded in pushing through Congress an extension of the number of workers covered by the minimum wage, increases in minimum wage and Social Security payments, and the Housing Act of 1961, which pumped nearly $5 billion over four years into preserving urban open spaces, developing mass transit, and building middle-income housing. He also got Congress to raise unemployment compensation benefits and provide aid to economically depressed areas. In a bold anti-inflationary move Kennedy "jawboned" the steel companies out of a sudden price increase.

Yet much of the New Frontier program failed to pass. Congress defeated his bill to provide funds for school construction and scholarship aid for college students. It also defeated a health insurance plan for the aged and measures to help unemployed youth, migrant workers, and commuters. The most important Kennedy initiative in domestic affairs was a tax cut designed to stimulate the economy by putting more money into the hands of consumers. Many liberals, led by economist John Kenneth Galbraith, felt that an increase in government spending for schools, hospitals, better housing, and social welfare programs was the best way to attack the recession inherited from the Eisenhower period. But the administration chose a cut in government income instead, the line of least resistance. As usual in the case of Kennedy's domestic proposals, the measure moved slowly. A year after its introduction the tax cut was still wending its way through Congress.

It would be hard to give the Kennedy administration the highest grades for its handling of domestic and foreign affairs. Yet despite his mixed record, Kennedy's popularity grew. The public remembered his successes and forgot his failures or blamed them on Congress. Young Americans identified with him and his wife. In 1963 Camelot was still untarnished.

The president was not universally loved and admired, however. The far right, particularly strong in the South and Southwest, despised him. The reemerging left saw him as

a conservative and a cold warrior. When, in November 1963, the president and his wife set off on a political peacemaking trip to Texas, he was warned that he might encounter trouble. Shortly before, Adlai Stevenson, then ambassador to the United Nations, had been verbally abused and spat on in Dallas.

The president ignored the advice and went to Texas. In Dallas, while his motorcade traveled through downtown streets lined with surprisingly friendly crowds, the president was shot by a sniper. He was rushed to the hospital, where he was pronounced dead a half hour later. His apparent killer, Lee Harvey Oswald, was an unstable leftist who had spent some years in the Soviet Union and had been active in the pro-Castro Fair Play for Cuba organization. Oswald had admitted nothing when, two days later, before the eyes of millions of horrified television viewers, he was shot by Jack Ruby, a shady Dallas nightclub owner who apparently saw himself as an avenging angel.

Few events in what would be an extraordinarily catastrophic decade so shocked the American people. The assassination in Dallas had not only killed an American president but it had also struck down a young hero whose career had come to symbolize all that was best and most worthy in American life. To the young, especially, his death

The president and the first lady in Texas on November 22, 1963, just before the tragedy. Vice President Lyndon Johnson is beaming in the background.

seemed a bitter tragedy. In the somber hours between the murder and the burial at Arlington National Cemetery, television's uninterrupted coverage of the events helped draw the nation together as a family united by a shared grief.

In the months that followed, dismay over the assassination gave way to uneasiness and frustration. President Lyndon Johnson, hoping to allay remaining public doubts about the murder, appointed an investigative commission headed by Chief Justice Earl Warren. In September 1964 the commission reported that Oswald was indisputably the culprit and had acted alone. Many Americans accepted the Warren Report, but a large minority suspected that it was incomplete or even a cover-up. Many young people found it difficult to believe that the deed had not involved some right-wing conspiracy. There were too many loose ends, they insisted; too many questions unanswered. In the next few years, as the toll of assassinated leaders grew, more and more Americans would find it hard not to believe that there was an evil plot to kill off the nation's great popular champions.

★ THE AFFLUENT SOCIETY ★

Though a decade of turmoil both at home and abroad, the 1960s were also a time of growing affluence and rising economic expectations. During these years the country enjoyed the longest sustained economic boom in its history, with the Gross National Product increasing at the rate of 4 percent annually, well above that for the preceding fifteen-year period. By 1970 the GNP, measured in 1958 dollars, had risen from $488 billion to $722.5 billion, an increase of 48 percent in average per capita real income. Unemployment did persist, and toward the end of the decade prices began to rise at a fast clip. Yet through most of the 1960s, the public's sense of economic well-being surpassed even that of the previous decade.

The 1960s was the decade when the promise of a mass consumer society finally seeped down to a majority of the American people. In every objective index of comfort the nation forged ahead. Dishwashers, freezers, clothes dryers, garbage disposals, color television—all luxuries in the 1950s—became almost universal possessions among middle-class Americans by 1970.

International Trade. One of the essential components of 1960s prosperity was burgeoning international trade. Under the General Agreement on Tariffs and Trade (GATT) of 1947, international trade barriers progressively declined. At the same time, the United States dollar served, as gold had in the past, as an international monetary standard. Under the influence of GATT and a stable exchange

medium, world commerce grew enormously. During the 1960s German cars, Japanese cameras and electronic equipment, Italian shoes and typewriters, and French wines and perfumes flooded the American market, while American computers, jet passenger aircraft, machinery, wheat, and soybeans flowed back the other way. Simultaneously, petroleum and the other raw materials necessary for industrial production moved at low prices to the developed nations from the Third World, helping to guarantee cheap production of industrial goods.

The Knowledge Industries. The enormously accelerated accumulation and diffusion of knowledge also helped to fuel the decade's economic surge. In some ways this knowledge explosion was the payoff from years of previous scientific advances. It also owed much to the great postwar outlays for research and higher education. In 1950 Congress had established the National Science Foundation to encourage research, especially in areas related to national defense. By 1957 outlays for research and development (R&D) by public and private organizations had reached almost $10 billion annually. Meanwhile, the country's higher education system surged dramatically. In 1940, the last full peacetime year, there were 1.5 million college students; by 1950 there were 2.6 million.

From the mid-1950s on, the country's support of what would later be called the "knowledge industries" was dazzling by any previous standard. Some Americans complained that the public schools were not teaching children to read or to calculate and blamed it on John Dewey's disciples, the "progressive educators." But most citizens were proud of the job the nation was doing. Their complacency was suddenly shattered when, in October 1957, the Russians put a hollow steel ball called Sputnik into orbit around the earth. Having long considered themselves the world's most scientifically and technologically advanced people, Americans were dismayed to discover that they had been abruptly pushed off their pinnacle by their chief international rival.

For the next few years Americans subjected themselves to one of their periodic agonizing reappraisals of education. A dozen books were soon echoing the complaints of earlier critics about American educational failings. Articles appeared in all the popular magazines informing readers that Russian high school students did not waste their time taking courses in marriage and the family, driver education, or social dancing, but spent long hours at chemistry, biology, physics, and mathematics. The dismay produced quick response. By 1970 federal appropriations for research had almost tripled, and federal funding of higher education was four times as high as it had been ten years earlier. Industrial firms, universities, and foundations also invested billions

One of the greatest feats of modern technology was the landing of men on the moon in July 1969. This picture of astronaut Edwin "Buzz" Aldrin was taken by fellow moonwalker Neil Armstrong, whose reflection is visible in the visor of Aldrin's helmet.

in basic scientific research and the development of new products. With research and industry booming, a college education became even more valuable than in the past. With the postwar "baby-boom" generation reaching their late teens, there were also more eligible college-age students. By 1970, some 7 million young men and women were enrolled in colleges and universities, an increase of nearly 500 percent in little more than a generation.

The Impact of Science and Technology. The scientific and technological advances that flowed from the laboratories were often dramatic. Linus Pauling, James Watson, H. Gobind Khorana, and others discovered how the gene, the basic unit of heredity, was constructed. Besides solving one of the great mysteries of life, genetics bore fruit—literally— in a great surge in the output per acre of rice, corn, and wheat, producing in the Third World the Green Revolution. The electronic computer became a powerful tool for solving mathematical and scientific problems and controlling production processes. Soon computers were being used to do everything from building H-bombs to guiding auto-

mated factories, recording checks, and helping libraries keep track of their books and universities of their students. And there was much more. The textile industry adopted new high-speed looms and developed new synthetic fibers. A long list of thermoplastics filled needs hitherto met at higher cost by natural materials. The subsonic passenger jet, first introduced in the early 1950s, replaced the propeller plane in the 1960s and shrank the world to half its former size. Meanwhile, the space program, begun under the auspices of the National Aeronautics and Space Administration (NASA) to challenge the Soviet Union, yielded unexpected scientific dividends. Communications satellites were launched, and new metals and alloys and miniaturized computer elements developed to solve the problems of space travel found surprisingly down-to-earth commercial and technical uses.

Medicine, too, made giant strides in these years. An arsenal of new antibiotic drugs, X-ray techniques, isotope tracers, computerized studies of environmental factors in disease, and other applications of the new science markedly improved the nation's and the world's health. In the 1950s researchers developed vaccines to fight polio. In 1963 they introduced a measles vaccine. Heart disease and cancer remained major killers, and indeed lung-cancer deaths from smoking soared, but the death rate from infectious diseases plummeted.

These medical advances, combined with better nutrition, produced a healthier, longer-lived population than ever before. Life expectancy for a newborn baby rose from 68.2 years in 1950 to 70.9 years in 1970. At the later date it was considerably higher for women (74.8) than for men (67.1) and for whites (71.7) than for blacks (65.3). Still, the improvement was substantial for every segment of the population.

The rapid expansion of the economy and the great surge in technology had costs. American life became increasingly bureaucratized as the federal government expanded its power and size and as private business concentrated itself into giant corporations. Much of the new technology was damaging to land, water supplies, and the air people breathed. By the end of the decade these environmental drawbacks had produced a powerful impulse to protect the public that came to be called the ecology movement.

★ THE RISE OF DISSENT ★

A majority of Americans in the 1960s, then, were living better, longer, and fuller lives than at any time in the past. Through the entire decade, the polls would show, most citizens continued to consider their country the most decent and benevolent in the world. But the great gains of the 1960s clearly left many Americans behind and failed to impress others. Before the decade was out, the country would experience a full-scale insurgent movement by blacks, students, women, American Indians, and many other groups.

The Sources of Dissent. The revolt had complex roots. In the political realm it was fueled by the decline of repressive McCarthyism and the emergence of a new generation less certain than their elders that the Cold War was inevitable. These young people had been raised in the affluence of postwar suburbia, and never doubted that at its best America was capable of providing all its people with the means to lead fulfilling and interesting lives. Yet as they looked around them they perceived racism, inequality, repression, and international belligerence that seemed to belie the nation's professed values. Less aware than their parents of the fragility of postwar prosperity, they rejected the self-congratulation of the 1950s and demanded change. With so many of these idealistic and dissatisfied young people going to college, the nation's campuses became potential political bombs.

Socially and culturally, too, the nation was ripe for dissent by the mid-1960s. A new, more permissive attitude toward sex was foreshadowed by the investigations in the late 1940s and early 1950s of Dr. Alfred C. Kinsey and his associates, which showed Americans as far less traditional in their sexual behavior than the conventional wisdom taught. Even more important, perhaps, was the advent of oral contraceptives in 1960. Besides reducing the birthrate, "the pill" reduced the chances of unwanted pregnancies, and so encouraged sex outside marriage. More permissive sexual values were also encouraged by the declining power of communities to censor books, movies, and magazines. Beginning with a 1952 decision holding that films were covered by the First Amendment's guarantee of free speech, the Supreme Court extended the principle so that a book, play, or motion picture had to be "utterly without redeeming social value" to be regarded as obscene. Soon long-banned erotic classics were available at bookstores, and before long it became clear that even works with social values no one could detect could be legally published and sold. In 1968, in recognition of the new situation, Hollywood dropped its old, self-imposed censorship code and adopted a rating system that placed films in categories ranging from *G* for family movies to *X* for out-and-out pornography.

The ground for the changes of the mid-1960s was also prepared by a new mood among the nation's artists, writers, and thinkers. During the immediate postwar period the nation's intellectual and cultural leaders had been conservative and conformist. By the end of the 1950s this began to change. One sign of the shift was the appearance of "Beat" bohemias in San Francisco, Los Angeles, and New York. To the Beat poets and writers—Allen Ginsberg, Lawrence Ferlinghetti, Jack Kerouac, and William Burroughs—the life of "square" America seemed deadening and oppressive, and they demanded in their works, and exemplified in their actions, freer, less inhibited lives.

Another sign was the advent of radical social thinkers, such as the sociologist C. Wright Mills, the social psychologist Paul Goodman, and the neo-Marxist philosopher Herbert Marcuse. In their various ways, each of these men condemned existing society as oppressive, repressive, and rife with inequalities of wealth and power. In 1960 Mills gave general currency to the term "New Left" to describe a new radical mood among the young intellectuals and students that he detected emerging in the United States and around the world.

Popular culture, too, especially music, both expressed and stimulated the new dissent. In the 1950s singers such as Woody Guthrie and Pete Seeger reinforced the 1930s connection between folk music and the political left. Rock-and-roll, a merger of black rhythm and blues and electronics, burst on the scene in the mid-1950s with Bill Haley's

Four young men who helped create the 1960s cultural revolution. The Beatles here depicted in a satiric mood.

From Civil Rights to Black Power.

During the 1960s dissenters of every race and every political and cultural persuasion would draw inspiration from the black civil rights movement. Many white radicals would first perceive the flaws in American society and institutions as workers on campuses or in the South for SNCC, CORE, SLCC, or some other civil rights organization.

But direct white participation would not last much beyond 1966. From the outset of the postwar civil rights movement there had been an undercurrent of black nationalism, black separatism, which rejected cooperation with whites and acceptance of what were perceived as white values. During the forties and fifties, here and there in the black urban ghettoes, a group called the Black Muslims (the Nation of Islam) had won disciples for a set of beliefs that labeled Christianity a "slave religion," denounced whites as "blue-eyed devils," and proclaimed the superiority and primacy of black people. Led by Elijah Muhammad, the Black Muslims, much like Marcus Garvey before them, sought to instill racial pride and racial separatism into the black population. By the early sixties the Black Muslims' most articulate spokesman was Malcolm X, a former convict converted to the Nation of Islam while in prison. Malcolm denied he was a racist, but his rhetoric seemed angry and it frightened many whites.

The influence of the Black Muslims was reinforced by anticolonial movements in the Third World. Young black activists (and many white ones) found inspiration in these struggles to overthrow the white European overlords. Through the works of Che Guevara, a lieutenant of Fidel Castro, and Franz Fanon, a black doctor who fought against the French in the Algerian war for independence, they learned the uses of violent assault on oppression as well as the value of Marxist analysis to explain the bases for oppression.

Even more important than these cultural influences in transforming the civil rights movement was the growing frustration of blacks over the slow advance toward racial equality. By 1965 virtually all of the legal barriers to black public access in the South had been swept away. Jim Crow was virtually dead. Blacks, moreover, were voting in record numbers in the South. Nationally, there was also a great surge of black college students and black workers in jobs like retail sales, public services, bank clerks, and other white-collar areas where few black faces had ever been seen before. But major inequalities remained. Black Americans were poorer, sicker, less literate, and more badly housed than whites. Thousands of black youths were unemployed and, seemingly, unemployable.

These problems were more difficult to solve than the legalized racial discrimination of the recent South. Federal and state civil rights laws did not end private prejudice or

"Rock Around the Clock." Soon after, Elvis Presley, a white southerner, gave rock a strong sexual cast.

Rock was the music of the rebellious young. The most successful rock group of the sixties, the Beatles, wore the long hair and mod clothes of angry English working-class adolescents. The Rolling Stones, also an English group, and Jefferson Airplane, the Grateful Dead, Country Joe and the Fish, and other whimsically named American groups wore the "love beads," Indian headbands, and gaudy jeans that soon became trademarks of youthful cultural revolt. Eventually some rock groups began to dabble directly in political matters. When the Rolling Stones came out with "Street-Fighting Man" in 1968, the more moderate Beatles responded with "Revolution." Folk singers like Joan Baez and Bob Dylan became increasingly political. Dylan's "The Times They Are A-Changin'" would become an anthem of youth rebellion.

Beginning in 1965 with Watts in Los Angeles, each summer for five years saw violent riots in the black ghettoes of American cities. Young black men, especially, vented their anger against the oppression of the larger society. These angry blacks are confronting a National Guardsman in Newark, New Jersey, in 1967.

successfully guarantee equal access to jobs and housing or full acceptance of equal social relations. They certainly did not overcome all at once the severe cultural handicaps that afflicted the black, inner-city ghetto population. The disparity between promise and fulfillment created intense strains. In the ghettos high expectations coexisted with modest actual achievement. It was an explosive mixture.

In August 1965, as the final major installment of sixties civil rights legislation, President Lyndon Johnson signed the Voting Rights Act, authorizing federal voter registration in districts where local officials had kept the number of registered voters below half the voting-age population. Five days later a riot exploded in the black Los Angeles suburb of Watts, tripped off by charges of police brutality. Twenty-eight blacks died; property damage reached $200 million. The violence of Watts shook Martin Luther King and confirmed his resolve to shift his focus from the South to the northern ghettos and their problems of jobs and housing. In January 1966 he established a SCLC headquarters in Chicago and launched a series of marches through white neighborhoods in support of equal housing laws. The Chicago campaign failed. White Chicagoans perceived it as a threat to their neighborhoods and resisted bitterly. They jeered the marchers and pelted them with stones and other missiles. Meanwhile the ghetto violence seemed to become institutionalized. During the "long, hot summers" of 1966 and 1967 the ghettos of Newark, Cleveland, Detroit, Chicago, and scores of other cities erupted in paroxysms of burning, looting, and attacks on the police sent to quell them. Many of the casualties came from poorly trained, trigger-happy police, national guardsmen, or federal troops.

The ghetto riots helped polarize the civil rights movement. Though King tried to respond to the disappointments of the northern ghettos, increasingly, among the younger activists, he and his message seemed too timid. In 1966 SNCC replaced its moderate head John Lewis with militant Stokely Carmichael; CORE replaced James Farmer with militant Floyd McKissick. Both new leaders endorsed "black power," a position that abandoned nonviolence and black-and-white-together in favor of black separatism. SNCC and CORE quickly told their white members to leave and continue the fight for racial equality through their own all-white organizations. That same year, in the Oakland, California, ghetto, two students at a local community college, Huey Newton and Bobby Seale, formed the "Black Panther Party for Self-Defense," a paramilitary organization avowedly dedicated to forcing the Oakland police to respect the black community's rights. Dressed in black leather jackets and black berets and openly carrying rifles, the Panthers frightened many whites and antagonized the police. Before long they were engaged in murderous shootouts with police in Oakland, Chicago, and other cities.

Student Activists. Not all whites were offended by the new black militancy. To many younger white activists, already radicalized by their experiences during the 1964 Mississippi Freedom Summer campaign, by support of SNCC actions in college towns, and by other civil rights actions, Carmichael and McKissick seemed brave, prophetic figures. Excluded from further direct participation in the militant civil rights movement, many turned their eyes to their home turf, the college campuses.

Another critical element in the rise of student radicalism was the accelerating war in Vietnam. By the middle of the decade American involvement had become massive and manpower needs could only be filled by a draft. At first young men were exempt from the draft merely for attending college. Then it became necessary for them to pass a

Martin Luther King, Jr.

The birthdays of only three Americans have become national legal holidays. One is that of George Washington, father of his country; another that of Abraham Lincoln, preserver of the Union. The last is the birthday of a black American, Martin Luther King, Jr., the most powerful and effective leader of the post–World War II civil rights revolution.

King was born in Atlanta, Georgia, in 1929 at a time and in a place not favorable for a young black male. Racism and its legal reflection, segregation, permeated every corner of southern life. Martin escaped almost all of this. The Kings belonged to the small black elite of Atlanta. Martin's father, Martin Luther King, Sr., was a respected, influential Baptist minister, the pastor of one of Atlanta's richest and most prestigious black churches, Ebenezer Baptist. Martin's family lived in a large house provided with all the most modern amenities. He and his small circle of equally prosperous friends—the children of doctors, lawyers, academics, morticians, and small business people—attended the best black schools in the city, and many, including Martin, went on to Morehouse College, the liberal arts school affiliated with the black community's greatest symbol of achievement, Atlanta University.

Yet even such a sheltered life could not spare King or his parents the cruel snubs, insults, and penalties of being black in racist, segregated Atlanta. When Martin was eleven a white woman walked up to him in a local department store and, without warning, slapped his face. "The little nigger stepped on my foot," she later explained. It was a small incident but it revealed the depth of white contempt for blacks in the 1940s South.

"Daddy" King wanted Martin to enter the ministry and become copas-

tor at the Ebenezer Church and eventually succeed him. But Martin demurred. He wanted to expand his intellectual horizons before settling down comfortably as head of a large and prosperous southern congregation. In 1948 he went to Crozier Theological Seminary in Pennsylvania and earned his Bachelor of Divinity degree, graduating first in his class. In 1955 he earned his Ph.D. at Boston University with a dissertation comparing the concepts of God in the thinking of two contemporary Protestant theologians. In Boston Martin met and married the beautiful Coretta Scott, a young Alabama woman then training as a singer at the New England Conservatory of Music.

Before getting his doctorate, Martin accepted a parish. The Kings moved to Montgomery, Alabama, where Martin became pastor of the Dexter Avenue Baptist Church. He and Coretta had been in the Alabama capital only a year when they found themselves thrust into the middle of a momentous struggle over segregation that would make Dr. King the most famous and powerful civil rights leader in America.

Like all southern cities, Montgomery was thoroughly segregated along racial lines. All public facilities had white and black sections. Almost without exception the facilities available to blacks were inferior to those provided whites. Any black person who refused to obey the city ordinances prescribing the racial divisions was committing a misdemeanor and subject to fine and imprisonment.

Then, on Thursday afternoon, December 1, 1955, Rosa Parks, a dignified black woman, boarded a Montgomery city bus to return home after a day's work as a seamstress in a downtown department store. She took

her seat, as prescribed, in the black section at the rear. But when more whites got on, the blacks in the front row of their section were asked to surrender their seats, as prescribed by law, to the new white passengers. Rosa Parks refused to move. The bus driver called the police and Mrs. Parks was arrested and fingerprinted.

The arrest triggered a strong reaction among Montgomery's black leaders. Ever since the *Brown* school desegregation decision in 1954 they had determined to challenge the city's Jim Crow system. The arrest of Mrs. Parks, a respectable middle-aged lady, promised to make an excellent case. In a matter of hours Montgomery's civil rights activists had decided on a boycott of the bus company until all black bus riders were treated as the equals of whites. Though King was a newcomer to Montgomery and just settling into his new duties and responsibilities, he was elected chairman of the Montgomery Improvement Association, the group formed to run the boycott, with the Reverend Ralph Abernathy of the First Baptist Church as his chief lieutenant.

Planned for a single day, the boycott lasted for almost thirteen months. Black passengers, the chief users of the buses, walked to work or made do with the Improvement Association's car pools. The bus company and the city authorities fought back. They procured injunctions; they harassed King and the other boycott leaders with minor traffic violation charges and threw them into jail; they invoked an ordinance to prevent black taxi drivers from transporting passengers at the same low rates charged by the bus company. At the end of January someone bombed King's home, and Mrs. King and the children barely escaped death. Despite the provocation, the young minister admonished blacks not to resort to violence. "We want to love our enemies," he told a black audience. "We must love our white brothers no matter what they do to us." Though inspired primarily by the Christian concept of charity, these words contained a trace of Mohandas Gandhi's nonviolent civil disobedience philosophy, *Satyagraha*, that King had encountered at Crozier Seminary.

Victory at Montgomery was ultimately won by the courage and sacrifices of the city's black citizens. But it was also helped immeasurably by the Supreme Court decision of November 1955 declaring that Alabama's state and local laws upholding segregation in transportation were unconstitutional. On Friday, December 21, the Montgomery city buses were officially desegregated. The long battle was over.

The Montgomery victory made Martin Luther King a national leader. He was soon in demand wherever black activists needed his eloquence, his leadership, and his ability to attract media attention to their plight. A literate man, he wrote widely for the national press on the goals of the civil rights movement and, despite a killing schedule of speaking engagements and personal appearances, authored several eloquent books. In 1957 he helped to found the Southern Christian Leadership Conference (SCLC), and for the remainder of his life this organization, located in Atlanta, was his chief base of operations. In 1959 King's Gandhian convictions were powerfully reinforced by a trip to the places in India where the saintly Mahatma had actually practiced his nonviolent precepts.

Montgomery proved to be only one of a hundred battles to dismantle the huge edifice of segregation that loomed over the South. During the 1960s the civil rights movement that King helped lead could count on wide liberal support in the North and in Washington. John F. Kennedy owed

black voters a debt for his hairline election victory in 1960. Yet relations between the Kennedy administration and King were, at best, touchy. During 1961–1962 King and the SCLC sponsored a series of "Freedom Rides" in conjunction with the militant Congress of Racial Equality (CORE) and the equally militant Student Nonviolent Coordinating Committee (SNCC) to test the compliance of southern towns with court rulings desegregating bus terminals. Once beyond the border states, the Freedom Riders were met by angry white mobs who burned the buses and beat many of them mercilessly. King and the other civil rights leaders demanded that federal marshals intervene to ensure the Freedom Riders' safety, and were deeply disappointed when the attorney general, the president's brother, Robert, was slow to respond.

King had his share of failures. In Albany, Georgia, the authorities were able to blunt the drive he led to end segregation and improve the job opportunities of black workers by a policy that combined evasion and careful avoidance of police brutality. By the time King left the small city little had changed. King and his colleagues had greater success in Birmingham, the New South's industrial showcase. Here the city's safety commissioner, T. Eugene ("Bull") Connor, was a hothead racist who used brutal tactics against the protest marchers organized by King and his colleagues to dramatize the discrimination practiced against the city's black population. Connor's police attacked marchers and demonstrators with night-sticks, cattle prods, vicious dogs, and high-pressure hoses. The most shocking attack was directed against a thousand black children marching from the Sixteenth Street Baptist Church to downtown. Public outrage forced the active intervention of the Kennedy administration and much of the business community. Powerful men in Washington and in

New York corporate offices contacted friends and associates in Birmingham and demanded that the scandal be stopped. On May 10 the city capitulated and signed an agreement with the civil rights leaders desegregating department stores, promising accelerated hiring of black workers, establishing a biracial committee to plan additional desegregation, and dropping charges against all those arrested in the demonstrations.

The Birmingham victory was capped by the mass march on Washington of August 1963. Organized by CORE, SCLC, SNCC, and the National Urban League, and cosponsored by white liberal organizations, the march was the biggest civil rights demonstration of all time. Over a quarter of a million people, white and black, came to the nation's capital for the purpose of supporting a major civil rights bill pending in Congress. The high point of the enormous rally was King's ringing "I Have a Dream" address at the Lincoln Memorial, which lifted the hearts of everyone present with its vision of a democratic society where "all God's children, black men and white men, Jews and Gentiles, Protestants and Catholics," would "be able to join hands and sing in the words of that old Negro spiritual, 'Free at last! Free at last! Thank God almighty, we are free at last!'"

Though he would achieve international recognition when he was awarded the Nobel Peace Prize in 1964, never again would Martin Luther King come so close to personifying black America's aspirations. By this time rifts had appeared within the civil rights movement. To King's right were the conservative NAACP, which emphasized lawsuits to end discrimination, and the Urban League, which favored education and persuasion. Both believed that street demonstrations and marches were dangerous and unproductive. To King's left was SNCC, which had accepted nonviolence as a tactic, but not as a principle. Blacks, the young SNCC workers believed, could not be expected to turn the other cheek when brutalized by white supremicists. Still further left were the Black Muslims, who demanded complete withdrawal from any association with "white devils," and proclaimed the superiority of blacks over whites. King also had little appeal for the unorganized militants in the northern cities, who saw nothing to recommend in a Christian nonviolent approach to the frustrations of ghetto life. Besides ideological differences, many in the civil rights movement resented King's eminence and believed that he and his associates encouraged the view that Martin Luther King, Jr., *was* the civil rights movement. Some of these people called King "de Lawd" behind his back.

After 1963 King and SCLC began to slip in influence. SCLC played only a secondary role in the voter registration drives and freedom schools organized by SNCC and CORE in the Deep South during the summer of 1964. It recouped somewhat when King helped lead the voter registration drive at Selma, Alabama, in early 1965. King's adversary this time was Sheriff Jim Clark, a man as hot-tempered as Birmingham's Bull Connor. He wore a big badge on his lapel with the word "Never." Clark's men shocked the nation when they used tear gas and clubs

against 500 blacks crossing the Pettus Bridge on their way to the Alabama state capital to present their grievances to Governor George Wallace. Seventeen of the marchers were seriously hurt and forty were hospitalized. The violence at Selma brought a wave of white liberals to the city for a second march in defiance of a court order. This time, faced with state troopers, King stopped the marchers just after they crossed the bridge. For this he was criticized by many militants. But the Selma Campaign had done its work. In its wake President Johnson announced that he was sending a tough, new voting rights bill to Congress.

After Selma SCLC ran into increasing difficulties. In the summer of 1965, beginning with Watts in Los Angeles, the northern black ghettoes began to explode. King deplored the violence but could neither prevent it nor repudiate the rioters. He also found it difficult to deal with the growing separatism of black militants who rejected the integrated society he envisioned and, under the banner of "black power," repudiated the nonviolence he preached. Finally, there was the Vietnam War. King was appalled by the war, but felt that to join SNCC and other leftists civil rights groups in demanding that the United States leave Vietnam would risk destroying his ties with the Johnson administration. Ultimately, he took the principled

course and in 1967 proclaimed the folly and injustice of Vietnam.

When the end came, King was shifting his focus from segregation and voting rights—issues primarily relevant to the South—to poverty, job discrimination, and substandard housing—issues primarily of concern to the northern urban ghettoes. In 1966 and 1967 SCLC launched a campaign to force the city of Chicago to improve the housing of the city's black poor. In early 1968 King and his colleagues drew up plans for a march on Washington to demand a $12 billion "economic bill of rights" from Congress. But before the Poor People's Campaign could be launched, King was induced to come to Memphis to lend support to a sanitation workers' strike against the city.

King visited the city several times during the early spring of 1968 to help the predominantly black garbage collectors. On the evening of April 4, as he prepared to go to dinner, he stepped out on the balcony of his motel. A shot rang out and King fell dead. The killer was a white escaped convict whose motives have never been fully explained.

Martin Luther King was buried under a marble tombstone inscribed: "Free at Last, Free at Last, Thank God Almighty, I'm Free at Last."

---

test and maintain good grades. Besides this intense academic pressure, there was the guilt that exempted students felt for escaping danger while nonstudents, both black and white, were sent off to Southeast Asia to fight and die. The cast of *Hair* proclaimed the injustice of this arrangement when they sang: "War is white people sending black people to make war on yellow people to defend the land they stole from red people." Some students tried to avoid the war by seeking conscientious objector status. Others left for Canada. Many, however, channeled their personal dilemma into an angry political movement to get the United States out of the Vietnam conflict in any way possible.

Also contributing to student militancy was the physical setting in which students found themselves in these years. The baby boom following World War II altered the age structure of the country so that by the mid-1960s a majority of Americans were under thirty. This demographic change, combined with the expansion of opportunities in business and science, guaranteed that campuses would be jammed. Strained by the huge enrollments, they inevitably became more impersonal and bureaucratic. Students soon felt that they were only numbers rather than human beings. Joined with the other radicalizing cultural and political forces, this alienation produced an explosive combination on many college campuses.

The first student blowup occurred at the University of California at Berkeley, where a mixture of bohemia, drugs, pacifism, leftist politics, and overcrowding existed earlier than in most places. There, in the fall of 1964, the university administration withdrew the right of students to use an off-campus area as a free-speech enclave and a staging ground for civil rights forays into the surrounding community. Many white Berkeley students had been active participants in the civil rights movement both in the South and the Bay Area. Confronted with the ban, they exploded. On December 2 a thousand students singing "We Shall Overcome," the civil rights hymn, took over the administration building and refused to leave until the university agreed to cancel its order. The authorities called in the police, who arrested hundreds of protestors. For the next three months the campus remained in an uproar while the leaders of the Free Speech Movement and the administration fought over free expression and an ever-wider range of issues including university government, classroom overcrowding, and restrictions on students' private lives.

Berkeley soon became the precedent for a rash of student upheavals that spread across campuses from coast to coast. Many students saw university administrations as oppressive agencies that were a prototype of all governments—except those few in the Third World that, they believed, truly represented the people. The war in Vietnam and the supposed complicity of universities in the war effort soon became principal campus targets.

Organized opposition to the war began with the "teach-ins" on college campuses in 1965. Teach-ins were followed by "peace marches" in many cities, which brought together thousands of pacifists, antiwar liberals, student radicals, and other concerned citizens. Radical students burned draft cards and mobbed recruiters from the armed forces and companies engaged in war production when they came to interview students on college campuses. They also denounced their universities' role in war planning and weapons research.

After 1966 many of the campus upheavals were led by the Students for a Democratic Society (SDS). Formed in 1959, SDS, at the outset, avoided dogmatic theories. The SDS members proclaimed the need for personal freedom and individual autonomy and condemned both capitalism and Soviet-style communism for depriving people of their liberty. They usually avoided violence. When police came to remove students occupying buildings at Berkeley, Columbia, and elsewhere, the students, following the precepts of the civil rights movement, went limp and allowed themselves to be dragged off to jail.

Beginning in 1966–1967, the SDS, by now the major organizational expression of the New Left, became increasingly militant. It mounted strikes against recruiters

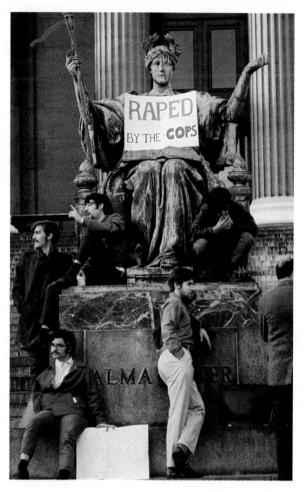

The year 1968 was one of the most intense for student militancy. One of the activists' targets was Columbia University. When the police evicted the SDS activists from the Columbia administration building, students placed this sign on "Alma Mater," the university's personification.

from Dow Chemical, manufacturer of the napalm used in Vietnam, and ROTC (Reserve Officers' Training Corps); demanded student participation in university decisions; and attacked university policies as racist or sexist. (Ironically, feminists would soon attack SDS itself as sexist.) In general, SDS sought to radicalize the student body in the belief that students were the leaders of the future and would eventually move on to radicalize the society at large. In 1968, between January 1 and June 15, SDS and other radical groups organized 221 major student demonstrations on 101 campuses involving 40,000 students.

Port Huron Statement

The major organized expression of the radical student movement during the 1960s was SDS, Students for a Democratic Society. Formed in 1959 as the student auxiliary of the old socialist League for Industrial Democracy, it eventually broke away from the staid parent organization and eventually became a byword for campus radicalism. By the end of the sixties it had evolved into the urban guerrilla group called the Weathermen.

In 1962, long before its final violent stage, SDS issued a manifesto expressing the new mood of dissent among young college students. The document, composed largely by Tom Hayden, then a recent University of Michigan graduate, was adopted at an SDS convention at Port Huron, Michigan. It catches the spirit of SDS when it was still young and more strongly influenced by Jefferson than by Marx. The selection below is the Port Huron Statement's preamble.

"We are people of this generation, bred at least in modest comfort, housed now in universities, looking uncomfortably to the world we inherit.

"When we were kids the United States was the wealthiest and strongest country in the world; the only one with the atom bomb, the least scarred by modern war, an initiator of the United Nations that we thought would distribute Western influence throughout the world. Freedom and equality for each individual, government of, by, and for the people—these American values we found good, principles by which we could live as men. Many of us began maturing in complacency.

"As we grew, however, our comfort was penetrated by events too troubling to dismiss. First, the permeating and victimizing fact of human degradation symbolized by the Southern struggle against racial bigotry, compelled most of us from silence to activism. Second, the enclosing fact of the Cold War, symbolized by the presence of the Bomb, brought awareness that we ourselves . . . might die at any time. We might deliberately ignore, or avoid, or fail to feel all other human problems, but not these two, for these were too immediate and crushing in their impact, too challenging in the demand that we as individuals take the responsibility for encounter and resolution.

"While these and other problems either directly oppressed us or rankled our consciences and became our own subjective concerns, we began to see complicated and disturbing paradoxes in our surrounding America. The declaration 'all men are created equal . . .' rang hollow before the facts of Negro life in the South and the big cities of the North. The proclaimed peaceful intentions of the United States contradicted its economic and military investments in the Cold War status quo.

"We witnessed, and continue to witness, other paradoxes. With nuclear energy whole cities can easily be powered, yet the dominant nation-states seem more likely to unleash destruction greater than that incurred in all wars in human history. Although our own technology is destroying old and creating new forms of social organization, men still tolerate meaningless work and idleness. While two-thirds of mankind suffers under-nourishment, our own upper classes revel amidst superfluous abundance. Although the

The Counterculture. Both SDS and the New Left sought political change primarily, but simultaneously American middle-class youth were in revolt against bourgeois behavior, dress, and expression. Middle-class conventions, they announced, were brutally repressive tools by which a frightened society dominated by the middle-aged controlled people's dangerous instincts and in the process reduced human potential. Unlike the New Left, the counterculture lacked an organizational center, though at different times the Yippies, the Mayday Tribe, and other colorfully named groups would claim to speak for it.

The counterculture's chief practitioners were called "hippies," from hip, a jazz musician's expression meaning knowledgeable or "with it." Hippies displayed their contempt for middle-class values by wearing tattered jeans, sandals, and beads; displaying an abundance of hair; and cultivating a casual way of speaking. Hippies adopted an aesthetic outlook that emphasized natural things. They wore flowers in their hair and around their necks and referred to themselves as "flower children." They considered material possessions fetishes of the "straight culture," and furnished their own "pads" with a few castoffs.

As we have seen, old sexual values, a major target of the counterculture, were already changing when the hippies appeared on the scene. But as the 1960s wore on, and as the counterculture influenced the mainstream, practices that seldom had been talked about and had been relegated to the sexual underground were now celebrated and placed on display. In Tom O'Horgan's play *Futz* one character had sexual intercourse with a pig. "X-rated" movies brought the

world population is expected to double in forty years, the nations still tolerate anarchy as a major principle of international conduct and uncontrolled exploitation governs the sapping of the earth's physical resources. Although mankind desperately needs revolutionary leadership, America rests in national stalemate, its goals ambiguous and tradition-bound instead of informed and clear, its democratic system apathetic and manipulated rather than 'of, by, and for the people.'

"Not only did tarnish appear on our image of American virtue, not only did disillusion occur when the hypocrisy of American ideals was discovered, but we began to sense that what we had originally seen as the American Golden Age was actually the decline of our era. The worldwide outbreak of revolution against colonialism and imperialism, the intrenchment of totalitarian states, the menace of war, overpopulation, international disorder, supertechnology—these trends were testing the tenacity of our own commitment to democracy and freedom and our abilities to visualize their application to a world in upheaval.

"Our work is guided by the sense that we may be the last generation in the experiment with living. But we are a minority—the vast majority of our people regard the temporary equilibriums of our society and world as eternally functional parts. In this is perhaps the outstanding paradox: we ourselves are imbued with urgency, yet the message of our society is that there is no viable alternative to the present. Beneath the reassuring tunes of the politicians, beneath the common opinion that America will 'muddle through,' beneath the stagnation of those who have closed their minds to the future, is the pervading feeling that there simply are no alternatives, that our times have witnessed the exhaustion not only of Utopias, but of any new departures as well. Feeling the press of complexity upon the emptiness of life, people are fearful of the thought that at any moment things might be thrust out of control. They fear change itself, since change might smash whatever visible framework seems to hold back chaos for them now. For most Americans, all crusades are suspect, threatening. The fact that each individual sees apathy in his fellows perpetuates the common reluctance to organize for change. The dominant institutions are complex enough to blunt the minds of their potential critics, and entrenched enough to swiftly dissipate or entirely repel the energies of protest and reform, thus limiting human expectancies. Then, too, we are a materially improved society, and by our own improvements we seem to have weakened the case for further change.

"Some would have us believe that Americans feel contentment amidst prosperity—but might it not better be called a glaze above deeply-felt anxieties about their role in the new world? And if these anxieties produce a developed indifference to human affairs, do they not as well produce a yearning to believe that there is an alternative to the present, that something *can* be done to change circumstances in the schools, the workplaces, the bureaucracies, the government? It is to this latter yearning, at once the spark and engine of change, that we direct our present appeal. The search for truly democratic alternatives to the present, and a commitment to social experimentation with them, is a worthy and fulfilling human enterprise, one which moves us and, we hope, others today. On such a basis do we offer this document of our convictions and analysis: as an effort in understanding and changing the conditions of humanity in the late twentieth century, an effort rooted in the ancient, still unfulfilled conception of man attaining determining influence over his circumstances of life."

depiction of oral sex acts to every large city's downtown theaters. Homosexuality, too, ceased to be a shameful aberration in the eyes of many Americans. Toward the end of the 1960s more and more homosexuals and lesbians began to "come out of the closet" and acknowledge their sexual preferences.

The counterculture seized on these tendencies and magnified them. Hippies believed in freer sex lives and an end to sexual taboos. Gatherings of counterculture people at times included displays of mass nudity and even public sexual intercourse, as at the rock-and-roll festival near Woodstock, New York, in August 1969. Hippies refused to be "uptight" about homosexuality and lesbianism. They also experimented with communes where everything, including sexual partners, was shared, and accepted cohabitation without marriage as normal.

Like sex, drugs offered a new way for young men and women to flaunt their disdain for middle-class life. For the first time in American history large numbers of middle-class white youths began to experiment with substances that had only been used in the ghetto or in bohemia before. Marijuana became a staple among the hippies, replacing alcohol, a substance identified with "square" culture. As marijuana use spread, it became difficult to impose severe criminal penalties on users and eventually in many communities possession or use of "grass" ceased to be treated as more than a misdemeanor. In the early 1960s two Harvard psychology instructors, Timothy Leary and Richard Alpert, had experimented with a new chemical substance, lysergic acid diethylamide (LSD), which they believed capable of "expanding" human consciousness and enabling people to conquer their "inner space." Soon LSD and other consciousness-altering drugs were incorporated into the hippie revolt against bourgeois society.

The hippie phenomenon was short-lived, the hippie enclaves in San Francisco, New York's East Village, and elsewhere, after the 1967 "summer of love," quickly deteriorated into squalid youth slums where mental disturbance induced by "speed" and LSD marked personal relationships. The hippie style—of talk, dress, and behavior—soon became commercialized and hence tainted in the eyes of counterculture purists. Meanwhile, the great rock music festivals degenerated into saturnalias of drugs and violence. The commune movement for a while became the refuge for the more idealistic counterculture people. Young men and women who rejected "square" culture withdrew to remote rural places where they could experiment with ways of living that spurned conventional middle-class material striving, traditional family relations, and hidebound relations of the sexes. But then the commune movement also deflated. The cause was often practical. As one former commune member described his experience: "We were together at the level of peace and freedom and love. We fell apart over who would cook and wash the dishes and pay the bills."

Liberation. The student political left soon followed the counterculture in a downward spiral. Toward the end of the decade SDS was infiltrated with Marxist ideology, some borrowed from Maoist China, some from the guerrilla movements of Latin America and other parts of the Third World. Frustrated by the continuation of the Vietnam War and its failure to expand its base of support, in 1969 SDS surrendered its vision of participatory democracy and adopted the notion of a vanguard party of the political elect

who alone could see and advance the social needs of the people. In June, at its annual convention in Chicago, SDS split in two over abstract issues of who would make the hypothetical revolution. One faction, the Weathermen, led by Mark Rudd, Bernadine Dohrn, and Bill Ayers, fought with the Chicago police during the "Days of Rage" in October 1969. Thereafter its members became underground terrorists determined to attack "imperialist Amerika" from within. Over the next few years the Weathermen would be responsible for dozens of bombings of government facilities and corporate offices. In February 1970 a Weathermen bomb factory in a Greenwich Village townhouse erupted when someone connected a wrong wire, killing three Weathermen leaders. The resort to violence, the declining economy, and a recognition that revolution was still a long way off combined to finish off what remained of the New Left.

Both the New Left and the counterculture were defunct as movements by the early years of the 1970s, but they left behind important traces. Social and political conservatives would later charge that they fostered deplorable tendencies: irresponsible sexual behavior, a permissive attitude toward drugs, and skepticism toward authority and hierarchies in all spheres. To some observers today, the 1960s seem the source of much of the social malaise that characterizes recent American life. Others consider it almost a golden age that broke down the stifling pieties of the 1950s and ushered in a liberated era. In some ways, especially for those who lived through the era, it was a watershed that forever after left its mark on their values and attitudes.

Whatever conclusion one reaches about the insurgency of the 1960s, certain things are clear. The protests of white and black radicals and hippies broke through the perceived

United Farm Workers union leader César Chávez was an important voice in the swelling chorus of Mexican-American protest. The union's strikes against California grape and lettuce growers received the support of many non-Hispanic liberals, who participated in boycotts of the growers' products.

limits of the "system" and created a new sense of the possible among many outsiders. Among ethnic minorities, the example of the black civil rights movement inspired Mexican-Americans, Puerto Rican-Americans, and Indian-Americans (Native Americans) to organize movements for political recognition and an end to discrimination.

Mexican-Americans were the largest of these groups, numbering over 6 million in California, the Southwest, and the Chicago area. A few were descended from the original Spanish-speaking population of the 1840s Mexican Cession. Most, however, were recent immigrants from Mexico. Chicanos occupied the same low social and economic position in the Southwest that blacks did in the South. They worked as domestics and took unskilled factory jobs. As migrant farm laborers, they picked lettuce, tomatoes, fruit, and other crops in California's fertile valleys.

Beginning in the 1960s, a new generation of Chicano leaders began to demand better treatment for their people. In New Mexico, Reies Tijerina's *Alianza* organization insisted that lands in the Southwest that originally had belonged to Mexican-Americans be returned to them. Tijerina accomplished little, but César Chavez was more effective. As leader of the California grape pickers, he forced the grape growers to accept unionization of their largely Chicano work force. Chavez then moved on to organize the lettuce pickers. In both endeavors he was helped by consumer boycotts of nonunion grapes and lettuce by sympathetic liberals and radicals.

The 1960s was a decade of revived self-awareness and assertiveness for American Indians as well. Even after passage of the 1934 Wheeler-Howard Act (see Chapter 19) Indians remained a depressed part of American society. Infant mortality rates on the reservations continued to be appalling; Indians continued to be treated as second-class citizens; white culture continued to erode traditional Indian values. After World War II the federal government sought to improve conditions on the reservations. In 1946 Congress established the Indian Claims Commission to settle outstanding Indian claims against the United States from the very beginning of the federal government. In 1953, by a joint resolution, it authorized "termination" of all federal benefits and controls over the tribes. Over the next six or seven years both aspects of federal-Indian relations were drastically reduced. Though the ostensible purpose of termination was to end federal paternalism and accord the Indians equality with other citizens, the process was often harmful. Before long the National Congress of American Indians was protesting that termination had become primarily a way of lowering federal costs rather than of benefiting the Indians. The process was soon slowed, but not before it had raised up a new class of Indian leaders more militant than any in the recent past.

On the reservations these leaders were primarily concerned with health conditions, poverty, poor education, religious autonomy, and resource development. Many had been working to improve the lot of their tribes since the end of World War II. In the cities, to which many Indians had been drawn from the 1950s onward, the leaders were often young activists inspired by the civil rights movement of blacks and Chicanos. These young activists resorted to propaganda and demonstrations to convince white America that it had treated Indians unjustly in the past and must make restitution. F. David Edmunds and Vine Deloria, Jr., wrote Indian history from an Indian viewpoint, siding with Sitting Bull against Custer and with the Apaches against the cavalry. In 1969 a group of young activists occupied the abandoned federal prison on Alcatraz in San Francisco Bay and demanded that it be converted into an Indian cultural center. In 1970 the American Indian Movement (AIM) emerged as the center of the young urban militants.

The New Feminism.   Potentially the most powerful of the 1960s liberation movements was the new feminism. From a feminist perspective, the immediate post-1945 period had been depressing. As we saw in Chapter 28, following World War II many Americans had turned toward domesticity and togetherness. For middle-class women this meant devoting more attention than ever to the responsibilities of suburban homemaking. The cultural impulse was reinforced by large families that confined women to the home for a longer period than at any time since before the first World War.

Despite these forces, the number of married women with jobs increased during the 1950s, but these jobs were seldom personally rewarding or well-paying. In part the low pay and meager satisfactions resulted from women's limited skills; on the whole women did not have the training or work experience of men. But they also derived from what would later be called sexism: Even when women had equal qualifications they were not given the pay or recognition that men received. Occasionally in the 1950s a feminist voice from the past was raised to protest the narrowing horizons for women, but most women seemed to accept the new mood quietly, without protest.

Sex discrimination, feminists would note later, was often indirect and subtle. Society in the 1950s treated girls and women as second-class human beings. Female children, they said, were "programmed" from the earliest age to assume that they were emotionally and mentally weaker than men. So successful was this process that women themselves believed, consciously or not, that they were inferior and professed to find total satisfaction in nonassertiveness and the traditional roles of wife and mother.

As the 1950s drew to a close, the situation began to change. By 1960 millions of women had gone through college. There they had been exposed to psychological, anthropological, and sociological concepts that identified many supposedly feminine characteristics as primarily the result of upbringing. Educated women were confronted with the contrast between their training and the routine lives they led, either as housewives or as "gal Fridays" to some male executive. By this time, too, the precedent of black liberation had illuminated the path that the nation's largest "minority" could take.

The first signs of the new feminism appeared early in 1963 when the President's Commission on the Status of Women, a Kennedy creation, issued a report urging job equality, day-care centers, and paid maternity leave for women. The intellectual breakthrough for the new feminism came that same year when Betty Friedan, a housewife and mother, published *The Feminine Mystique*. An eloquent attack on the silken bondage imposed on women, the book described dissatisfaction with the stultifying life of the housebound wife and mother as "the problem that has no name." Like most feminist activists of the past, Friedan, a Smith College graduate, spoke mainly for the educated middle class. But among this group her message rang very loud, and the book became a best-seller. In 1964 the emerging new mood was further encouraged by the Civil Rights Act, which forbade job discrimination based not only on race, but also on sex. The law unleashed a flood of complaints by women to the Equal Employment Opportunity Commission established under the act to monitor compliance with its provisions. In June 1966, feminists organized NOW, the National Organization for Women, with Friedan as its first president.

NOW was a moderate voice in the new feminism. Composed largely of college-educated and professional women, it worked through the courts and the legislatures to bring "women into full participation in the mainstream of American society" with the right to exercise "all the privileges and responsibilities thereof in truly equal partnership with men. . . ." It did not target men as the enemy or seek to restructure the family or society as a whole except to achieve equal treatment for women.

To the left of NOW were more militant *liberationist* groups, derived primarily from the student New Left. Operating under various names, women's liberationists developed a profoundly radical critique of Western society as hopelessly male-dominated. "Patriarchy," they held, rather than capitalism, was the source not only of female oppression but of all oppression in the world, and its destruction was a prerequisite for the liberation of all humankind. Radical feminists had little respect for conventional women or for the conventional family. A vocal minority were lesbians with a separate agenda from more traditional women. Women's liberationists employed such attention-getting tactics as "guerrilla theater"—street demonstrations in the form of political drama—and disruption of "sexist" rituals. In September 1968 radical feminists would picket the Miss America Pageant in Atlantic City as a woman-degrading event. Myth notwithstanding, the demonstrators did not burn their bras, but they did toss other supposed symbols of female bondage—corsets, eyelash curlers, high-heeled shoes—into a "freedom ash can."

The radical feminists also introduced "consciousness-raising" as a tool for rallying support for their cause. This activity brought discontented women together in small groups for intense sessions of personal self-revelation designed to uncover grievances against male oppressors and "patriarchy." They served as group therapy and no doubt helped women to face, or escape, painful marriages and other unhealthy relationships with men. But they also provided a steady stream of recruits for the new feminist movements.

Gay Liberation.   Another late manifestation of the new liberation mood was the gay rights movement. Homosexuality had always existed in American society, of course, but gay men and lesbian women had carefully hidden their sexual preferences in the face of "straight" society's stern disapproval and laws that made many homosexual practices criminal offenses. In many large cities homosexuals congregated in their own neighborhoods and developed their own cultural and social institutions where they could be comfortable. Gays often led double lives: one at home, where they felt free; and one at work, where they felt compelled to conform to the straight world's expectations. This enforced concealment, added to the legal hazards, created a deep sense of resentment and the feeling among homosexuals that they, too, constituted an oppressed minority.

By the mid-1960s male and female homosexuals had formed defense organizations of various kinds for mutual support. Then came a crucial event in the response of homosexuals to their circumstances. In June 1969 the police raided the Stonewall Inn, a homosexual bar in New York's Greenwich Village. Gays, who usually accepted such raids as a normal part of existence, this time fought back. A riot broke out that lasted far into the night and continued the next day. This battle marked the end of homosexual acquiescence and the beginning of the Gay Liberation movement. In its wake militant gays began to "come out of the closet" and demand that the laws against free sexual expression and practice and those denying gays equal employment and other rights be removed from the statute books.

An Adversary Culture.   The tensions, pressures, and ideologies of the 1960s helped create an adversary response among the nation's artists and intellectuals. Freed from the political fears of the 1950s and inspired by the militancy of students, blacks, ethnics, and women, American writers, painters, and intellectuals began once again to question, ridicule, and satirize their society and its values.

American movies in these years reached a new level of intellectual maturity as the function of providing escapist entertainment was taken over increasingly by TV. In movies such as *Who's Afraid of Virginia Woolf?* (1965) and *The Graduate* (1967), director Mike Nichols poked fun at widely accepted assumptions—that fulfillment could be found in work, that men and women should behave as their age and status prescribed, that marriage made people happy. Stanley Kubrick turned a similar critical and disillusioned eye on the American political and military establishment in *Dr. Strangelove*. Released in 1964, following the Cuban missile crisis and an upwelling of anxiety over nuclear testing, the movie depicted in broad, gallows-humor strokes the triggering of World War III by a demented right-wing general who believed that "they" (the Communists) were destroying his "precious bodily fluids." The kind of violence depicted in the nightly TV reportage of Vietnam became an integral part of film during these years. *Bonnie and Clyde* (1967), directed by Arthur Penn, made heroes of two 1930s bank robbers and showed in full color the gory effects of a rifle bullet hitting a woman's head. *Easy Rider* (1969) was a counterculture epic about two young men who set out to cross the country by motorcycle to peddle heroin. Along the way they visit a New Mexico commune and have sexual adventures in New Orleans. On the way back to California, while in the Deep South, they are killed by malicious "rednecks," who spot them as intruders into their America. Toward the end of the decade the science-fiction movie came into its own. But unlike the "space operas" of the 1970s, the sixties films were skeptical of the brave new world in store for humanity. Kubrick's *2001: A Space Odyssey* (1968) showed not only the grandeur of the new scientific world that was evolving but also its chilling dehumanization as computers seize control.

And even TV, though reserved for the mass "family" audience, began to develop some bite. In 1961 Newton Minow, Federal Communications Commission chairman, referred to television as a "vast wasteland." Dominated by quiz shows and "sitcoms," the medium did nothing to challenge its audience. The typical sitcom of the 1950s, such as *Father Knows Best*, portrayed the orderly world of a middle-class white family whose problems were confined to solving disputes among siblings and deciding what dress daughter should wear to the prom. By the late sixties there were signs of change. *Rowan and Martin's Laugh-in* hit the top of the ratings with sophisticated sexual humor. The Smothers Brothers' comedy show contained political satire.

Prime-time dramas, too, moved a small distance from the bland, upbeat material of the past.

But TV had its chief impact on the era in its reportorial role. During the decade the TV screen brought shocking real events into people's living rooms: the assassination of President Kennedy; the murder of Lee Harvey Oswald; executions of Vietcong sympathizers; the rioting at the 1968 Democratic convention in Chicago. One could flip from the news to conventional TV drama without changing one's seat in a way that blurred the distinction between truth and fiction. The breakdown of this distinction worried educators. Would the next generation be able to tell the difference between image and reality?

Writing also began to merge fact and fiction in a disconcerting way. During the decade three major authors, Truman Capote, Norman Mailer, and Tom Wolfe, began to practice a literary form that fused the factual and the fictional. Capote's *In Cold Blood* (1965) described the murders of a Kansas family and the pursuit, capture, conviction, and execution of the killers. Capote, like the other practitioners of this genre, seemed to know everything that went on in the heads of his characters, even ones he never met. In *Armies of the Night* (1968) Mailer imposed a novelistic form on an account of the antiwar Pentagon march of October 1967. Tom Wolfe's *Electric Kool-Aid Acid Test* (1968) depicted the evolution of the drug culture on the West Coast through invented dialogue and scenes that Wolfe re-created from second-hand reports. Science fiction, too, at times became a vehicle for interweaving fact and fiction. Kurt Vonnegut's *Slaughterhouse 5* (1969) portrayed a man who "comes unstuck in time" and experiences the mass slaughter in 1945 of German civilians by the RAF in Dresden.

Distinctions among art forms eroded as well. In the visual arts traditionally separate forms like comics and advertising were merged to create Pop Art. The work of the two major Pop artists, Andy Warhol and Roy Lichtenstein, protested against the materialism and shallowness of American culture while at the same time seeming to celebrate it. Claes Oldenburg's huge paintings of hamburgers, when hung in the same museum with Rembrandts and French Impressionists, mocked the pretensions of the museums themselves.

Theater experimented with new forms and new subject matter. The Theater of the Absurd sought to break down the boundaries between audience and players by having actors circulate through the auditorium and by inviting viewers to join the actors on stage. The new experimental companies, such as the San Francisco Mime Troupe, the Living Theater group, and the Open Theater, also used pantomime, ritual, masks, and other nontraditional devices to communicate their message. The message itself was often radical. Barbara Garson's *MacBird* (1966) was an updating of Shakespeare's *MacBeth* with Lyndon Johnson cast in the role of the bloody king of Scotland. Arthur Kopit's *Indians* (1969) bitterly assailed white treatment of Native Americans. *The Connection* (1959), by Jack Gelber, depicted the anguished world of junkies and criminals. Nudity became a staple of some of the new plays. *Hair* had a nude scene. Richard Schechner's Performance Group production of *Dionysius in '69* invited the audience to suggest sexual acts that it would like to see the actors carry out on stage.

The cultural mood, then, was experimental, critical, and hostile to traditional forms and conventions. But the arts were influenced not only by the dissenting political and social mood of the 1960s but also by the decade's affluence. During the 1960s the high arts began for the first time to develop something like a mass audience. Foreign travel, widespread college education, and higher incomes created a new audience for classical music, the dance, museum-going. Government agencies such as the National Endowment for the Arts helped disseminate high culture beyond the normal orbit of a half dozen major cities through subsidies for local orchestras, dance companies, and museums.

★ THE JOHNSON YEARS ★

Many Americans were appalled, even frightened, by the sudden upsurge of political and cultural radicalism during the 1960s though the dissenters were never more than a minority. Yet when Lyndon Johnson took office, in 1963, most citizens were positively inclined toward change in two areas: race and economic inequality. The bombing of black churches in the South, "Bull" Connor's use of police dogs and fire hoses against black demonstrators in Birmingham, the persistence of widespread national poverty as revealed by Michael Harrington in his startling book *The Other America* (1963)—these things made many middle-class citizens ashamed and receptive to a major legislative effort to end them. The Johnson years saw enactment of a flood of legislation that promised to bring American life in line with the new insistence on social justice.

The Great Society. Lyndon B. Johnson was in many ways the antithesis of his predecessor. Middle-aged, homely, coarse, and self-made rather than young, handsome, elegant, and patrician, Johnson's image was unattractive to many Americans and impaired his ability to lead the nation.

Yet he was incomparable as a legislative leader. His long years as Senate minority and then majority leader had honed to a fine edge his talent for getting laws enacted. As president his skills were put to good use. A congressman who resisted the president's legislative demands got the "Johnson treatment." The legislator was marched into Johnson's office, seated next to the towering Texan, and subjected to a powerful verbal assault of jokes, promises, threats, cajolery, and ego stroking, along with thumps, squeezes, and pokes. Few men could hold out against the treatment for very long, and in the course of his five years as president, Johnson initiated more important reform legislation than any chief executive since Franklin D. Roosevelt.

Johnson's program was more than an updating of the New Deal. The president was a long-time admirer of Roosevelt, and he hoped to complete and round out the welfare state that FDR had launched between 1933 and 1938. Invoking the memory of his martyred predecessor, the new president got Congress to enact many of the measures that were pending when Kennedy died. In January 1964, following through on a Kennedy initiative, Congress passed the Economic Opportunity Act. The law established an Office of Economic Opportunity (OEO), and under Sargent Shriver, JFK's brother-in-law, the OEO launched a "War on Poverty" designed to reduce illiteracy, end unemployment among inner-city youths, improve depressed conditions in the Appalachian area, sharpen skills among the poor, and provide capital to minority businesses. One provision of the new measure authorized the OEO to set up community-action groups that would give local-area people a hand in designing and running new antipoverty programs. Such participation, the theory held, would instill in the poor a new sense of confidence and ultimately help them help themselves.

Johnson also convinced Congress to enact the tax reduction that Kennedy had asked for, a measure that gave the economy a much-needed jolt. In the summer of 1964, as we saw, Congress passed a strong civil rights act giving the federal government new authority to protect the voting rights of black citizens.

The president quickly made his mark as an effective domestic leader and was rewarded with his party's 1964 nomination, with Hubert H. Humphrey, Minnesota's liberal senator, as his running mate. The Republicans chose Senator Barry Goldwater of Arizona along with an obscure New York congressman, William Miller. Goldwater was a handsome, likable man, but he represented the extreme right wing of his party. His supporters claimed that they were offering the country "a choice, not an echo." The choice, it seemed to many voters, was to dismantle the Social Security system, sell the New Deal's Tennessee Valley Authority to private interests, and return to Hooverism. Given the Republican candidate's bellicose foreign-policy statements and his affection for uniforms and air force bombers, his election also promised an enlarged Vietnam involvement that few Americans wanted. Goldwater made matters worse by his inept public statements. When many moderate Americans were still worried about the John Birch Society and extremists in general, Goldwater told them, "extremism in the defense of liberty is no vice! And . . . moderation in the pursuit of justice in no virtue!"

The Democrats did not play fair. At the very time Johnson was considering escalating the American commitment in Vietnam, he was denouncing Goldwater as a warmonger and promising to "seek no wider war" in Southeast Asia. Johnson won with 61 percent of the popular vote, better even than FDR's 1936 triumph. A year later a bitter joke would make the rounds: "I was told if I voted for Goldwater we would be at war in six months. I did—and we were!"

With this landslide victory to work with, Johnson embarked on one of the most ambitious legislative programs in history. His Great Society, though it rounded out parts of the New Deal, was very much a product of a confident, prosperous era. Its funding depended on a constant growth of federal revenues as the economic boom kicked personal and corporate income into ever higher ranges. It sought to do more than just improve material security and well-being. As the president described it in May 1964 at the University of Michigan, the Great Society was one where the "order of plenty" Americans now enjoyed could be used "to enrich and elevate our national life and to advance the quality of our American civilization." The Great Society would be

where every child "finds knowledge to enrich his mind and . . . enlarge his talents"; where leisure was a "welcome chance to build and reflect"; where "the city of man serves not only the needs of the body but the desire for beauty and the hunger for community"; where people could "renew contact with nature" and where they were "more concerned with the quality of their goals than the quantity of their goods."

After the election, buoyed by Democratic majorities in the Eighty-ninth Congress unequaled since 1937, Johnson made remarkable progress in fulfilling his promises. In the spring of 1965, overcoming long-standing Catholic-Protestant disagreements over parochial schools, Congress passed the $1.3 billion Elementary and Secondary Education Act appropriating for the first time federal money for the support of local schools. In July, Congress broke the logjam on federal health care created by the organized medical profession, by enacting Medicare for federal pensioners and Medicaid for the poor. A month later the Omnibus Housing Act set up a rent supplement program for low-income families. Recognizing the cities' special needs Congress established the Department of Housing and Urban Development (HUD). The president promptly appointed as its head Robert C. Weaver, who became the nation's first black cabinet member. Later, in September, the

LBJ visits a farm family, 1964. The fourth "accidental" president of the century inherited power at a time when the nation's mood was changing from confident to self-critical and distrustful. Johnson's War on Poverty eventually failed when commitment to its goals evaporated.

The Dissenting Sixties 841

president signed a measure establishing the National Endowments for the Arts and for the Humanities to subsidize artists, writers, composers, painters, and scholars and provide aid to local cultural institutions. Clean air and clean water acts to improve the environment followed soon afterward, as did a Higher Education Act providing the first federal scholarships for college students, the Highway Safety Act, the Model Cities Demonstration and Metropolitan Area Redevelopment Act to revive and reconstruct decaying city centers, and a measure to subsidize noncommercial educational television and radio broadcasting. Still more Great Society legislation included the Truth in Lending Act to protect consumers in credit transactions, and the Voting Rights Act of 1965.

Some of these measures were hastily drawn and ultimately proved unworkable. Some provided opportunities for "rip-offs" of the government. Critics charged that many of the War on Poverty programs pumped more money into the pockets of consultants and administrators than ever got to the poor. Most controversial of all were the programs initiated by community-action groups. Local officials disliked them because they often bypassed city hall and reduced the mayor's power. Other critics charged that they were used by white radicals and black militants to encourage confrontation and radicalize the poor. The whole welfare state expansion during these years would come under conservative attack for perpetuating a "culture of poverty." Rather than providing the means for the poor to pull themselves out of poverty, said critics, it encouraged dependence through successive generations. Liberal and left-wing critics pointed to different failings. Although domestic social programs were the fastest-growing category in the federal budget during these years, the amount allotted to individual projects, they said, was often too little.

But clearly the Great Society had a credit side as well. Among the War on Poverty programs, almost everyone agreed that Head Start, which paid for educational enrichment of poor preschool children, made a difference in the success of those children in later years. The Great Society also revitalized the nation's cultural institutions, helped low- and moderate-income students pay for college, enabled cities to rebuild their centers, made automobiles safer, and enfranchised thousands of black citizens in the South. Medicare and other programs for the aged and retired virtually ended the serious problem of poverty among older Americans.

The Johnson administration can also be given credit for advances in space exploration. In May 1961, Kennedy had set the goal of, within the decade, "landing a man on the moon and returning him safely to earth." Propelled by the urge to beat the Soviets to the punch, the moon-landing program's success was assured under Johnson. The space competition was attacked by the left as a program that starved needed social programs here on earth. Many black Americans considered it a white man's enterprise of no great interest to them. And there were critics among the scientists as well: The scientific community, some said, could have learned as much about the solar system by using far cheaper unmanned rockets. Still, most Americans found the space race fascinating, and the TV audiences for the Apollo launchings ran into the many millions. By the end of Johnson's full term, Frank Borman, James Lovell, Jr., and William Anders had orbited the moon ten times. On Christmas Eve 1968 they transmitted television greetings to earth from seventy miles above the moon's forbidding surface. It was now only a matter of months before the first human beings would place their feet on some other part of the universe besides Mother Earth.

Quagmire in Vietnam. However mixed his record of domestic accomplishments, Johnson would have been treated more gently by contemporaries and historians if not for Vietnam. For all his personal failings and his inability to win the affection of the American people, LBJ was a man of vision and sincere human sympathies. He was capable of crude manipulation and hypocrisy, but he also deserves a place alongside Wilson and the two Roosevelts in the American liberal pantheon.

But Vietnam irretrievably damaged the president and destroyed his post-1964 "consensus." Johnson was a foreign affairs novice. He believed his close advisers, military and civilian, when they told him, as they constantly did, that great progress was being made in defeating the Vietcong and only a few more divisions of soldiers and a little more money would do the trick. He was also a captive of the past. Like many of his generation, he viewed Vietnam in terms of the "lessons" learned from Hitler in the 1930s. If you did not stand up to the enemy, if you appeased him, as Chamberlain had appeased Hitler at Munich, he would consider you weak and take advantage of you. Applied to Vietnam, this analogy meant that if the Communist forces were allowed to conquer South Vietnam, one by one the other nonaligned or pro-Western nations of Southeast Asia would fall to Communist control. This logic was faulty. Ho Chi Minh was not ruler of a powerful militarized nation such as 1938 Germany. Ho's ally, the Soviet Union, might have expansionist tendencies of uncertain dimensions, but there was no evidence that Ho himself had designs on any part of Asia beyond former Indochina. Yet the domino effect was a convincing notion to the president and to many other Americans as well. Truman had been charged with "losing" China; Johnson was determined that similar charges not be leveled at him. "I don't want it said of me that I was the president who lost Vietnam," he remarked.

THE VIETNAM WAR AREA

The president's first step down the slippery path was the Gulf of Tonkin Resolution he induced Congress to pass in August 1964 following a reported attack on American naval vessels off the Vietnam coast. To this day it is uncertain that the assault ever took place, but Congress almost unanimously authorized the president to "take all necessary measures to repel any armed attack against the forces of the United States." Thereafter, Johnson treated the resolution as the virtual equivalent of a declaration of war.

The 1964 presidential campaign, as we saw, muted the Vietnam issue. Then, early in 1965, following a Vietcong attack on a U.S. airbase at Pleiku, the administration

bombed North Vietnam to induce the Ho Chi Minh government to withdraw support from the Vietcong forces in South Vietnam. When operation "Rolling Thunder" proved ineffective, Johnson increased the number of American military advisers to the South Vietnamese army and in April dispatched the first American ground combat troops to Vietnam.

All through 1965 and 1966 Johnson increased the pressure on the Vietcong and North Vietnamese in hopes of forcing a settlement that would preserve South Vietnam as an anti-Communist bastion under the pro-American leaders Nguyen Van Thieu and Nguyen Cao Ky. In April 1966 the United States sent B-52s to bomb Hanoi, the North Vietnamese capital, and Haiphong, the major North Vietnamese port of entry for supplies from the Soviet Union. Meanwhile, on the ground, United States marines and army units fought a guerrilla war in the jungles and rice paddies. The fighting was dirty work in every sense of the term. The American military used body counts to chart their progress. The Vietcong, refusing to meet the Americans head-on, chose to hit and run, slipping away into the jungle when confronted by superior forces. South Vietnamese villagers were often caught in the middle and were attacked by both sides. American guerrilla-warfare experts tried to establish secure areas free of "the Cong," but the villages seldom remained secure for very long. Too many villagers considered the guerrillas less dangerous than the Americans or the corrupt officials of the Thieu government, or simply could not resist Vietcong threats.

There were atrocities on both sides. The Vietcong set off bombs on the streets of Saigon that killed innocent civilians. They tortured and murdered South Vietnamese villagers, policemen, teachers, and Catholics who opposed them. Americans also committed atrocities. In March 1968 an American army unit under Lieutenant William L. Calley, Jr., attacked My Lai, a village of 600 people suspected of harboring Vietcong, and massacred virtually every inhabitant. The Defense Department attempted to cover up this crime, but it became known when a former member of Calley's unit informed several high government officials. Calley was eventually tried, but received a light sentence.

By 1968 the United States had sunk into a dirty, divisive, expensive war. As in the Korean conflict, there seemed to be no way to conclude the fighting. Bland, reassuring government statements were undercut daily by television broadcasts from the battlefields that showed no cause for optimism.

As the war dragged on month after month, it began to blight the economy. Johnson was at first afraid to ask Americans to pay for the war directly, lest any economic sacrifice make it even less popular than it already was. Yet by 1967 it was costing the country $25 billion a year. This

Many Americans realized that the Vietnam War was far from won when the Vietcong were able to mount a major offensive during Tet, the celebration of the Vietnamese Lunar New Year, in 1968. The attackers almost succeeded in penetrating the heavily protected United States Embassy in Saigon, actually managing to blow a hole in the outer wall.

sum, on top of Great Society domestic programs, produced what then seemed gigantic budget deficits: $8.7 billion in 1967 and $25.2 billion in 1968. Finally, the president asked for higher taxes to siphon off excess purchasing power, but by then the damage was done. Until 1966 yearly consumer price increases had remained below 2 percent. In 1966 they rose to 3.4 percent and in 1968 to 4.7 percent. Good times continued, measured by employment and output, but the dollar was becoming one of the war's casualties.

Organized protests against the war, as we have seen, were begun by college students in 1965. In early 1966, J. William Fulbright of Arkansas, chairman of the Senate Foreign Relations Committee, conducted televised hearings on the war during which he grilled Secretary of State Dean Rusk remorselessly and exposed many of the weaknesses of the prowar "hawk" position. Before long, liberal and radical clergy began to demand an end to the Vietnam slaughter. In early 1967 Martin Luther King, Jr., made a "Declaration of Independence" from the war, declaring that it was "time to break silence." Soon after this he led the New York Spring Mobilization parade, and he and black militant Stokely Carmichael denounced the war before an audience of cheering antiwar protesters. In 1967 Father Daniel Berrigan and his brother, Philip, priests who carried the new Catholic liberalism further than most, organized the Catholic Ultra-Resistance.

Most Americans continued to support the war. Many were angered by the protesters and considered them traitors. Bumper stickers reading "America: Love it or leave it" began to appear on the streets and highways. The American Legion, the Veterans of Foreign Wars, and the conservative Young Americans for Freedom organized rallies where the demonstrators carried signs: "Bomb Hanoi," "We Love America," "My Country—Right or Wrong." Even many anti-Communist liberals continued to believe that abandoning South Vietnam would destroy the credibility of American foreign policy and play into Soviet hands.

After 1967, however, support for the president's policies eroded rapidly. Even those Americans who favored the containment policy began to conclude that the war was becoming far too costly economically and morally, and probably could not be won.

The greatest blow to hawk confidence came in early 1968 when, during the Vietnamese Lunar New Year (Tet), the Vietcong and North Vietnamese launched a major offensive against Saigon and other South Vietnamese cities. After fierce and bloody fighting, the attack was checked and the attackers forced to pay a high price, but Tet made a mockery of the administrations' confident propaganda. Until this point many Americans had found it possible to believe that the war, however protracted, was being won. Tet seemed to show that the enemy was, if anything, growing in strength.

Soon after Tet, even Johnson began to have doubts. He now saw that the war was getting out of hand and must, if continued, rip the country apart. The presidential election of 1968 was at hand, and Johnson, his credibility and popular support seriously eroded, faced a formidable challenge within his own party.

The 1968 Election. The president's challengers for the Democratic nomination were Eugene J. McCarthy of Minnesota and Robert F. Kennedy of New York. Both were United States senators, liberals, and Irish Catholics. Both opposed the Vietnam War. In most other ways, however, they were different. McCarthy, a former Catholic seminarian, was a philosopher and poet. A witty and learned man, he was also aloof and cerebral. To the Minnesota senator, the war was a moral evil that must be fought as one fought sin. Kennedy, the former president's younger brother, was a man of action. He, too, detested the war—but as much for what it was doing to the nation's morale and self-respect

THE ELECTION OF 1968

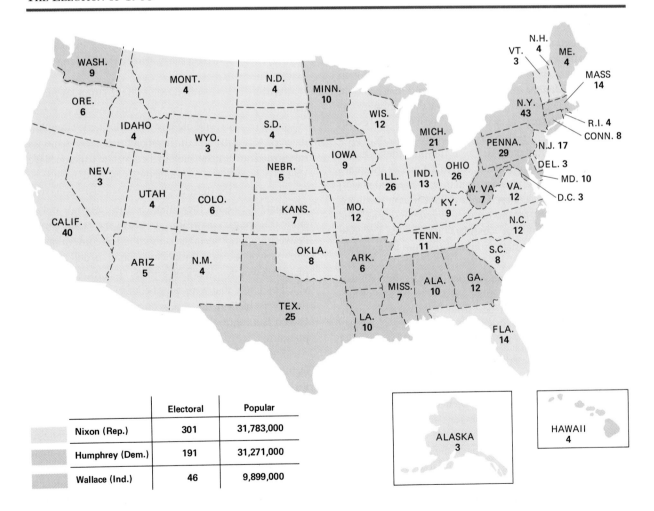

	Electoral	Popular
Nixon (Rep.)	301	31,783,000
Humphrey (Dem.)	191	31,271,000
Wallace (Ind.)	46	9,899,000

as for its conflict with moral law. McCarthy attracted many students and academics who appreciated his ethical stance. Kennedy could communicate more readily with blue-collar workers and blacks. Wearing the still-shining mantle of Camelot, he projected a warmer image as friend of the masses.

McCarthy was first in the field against Johnson. When Kennedy refused to be enticed into running, the Minnesota senator reluctantly announced his candidacy. Few expected that he could make much headway against an incumbent president, but in the New Hampshire Democratic primary in March thousands of students turned out to ring doorbells, make phone calls, and stuff envelopes for him. The results were startling: The challenger received only a few hundred votes less than the president. Having concluded that Johnson was beatable, Kennedy now also entered the race.

By early 1968 Johnson had decided to renounce another full term. In late 1967 he had replaced Secretary of Defense Robert McNamara, a Kennedy holdover, with the debonair Clark Clifford. Clifford, and the informal group of foreign-policy advisers known as the "Wise Men," had told him after the Tet offensive that the war was unwinnable. They advised reducing the American military commitment. Reluctantly accepting their position, Johnson refused to grant the request of General William Westmoreland for an additional 206,000 troops. He also realized that he could encourage a negotiated peace if he ceased the bombing campaign and withdrew himself from public life. In any event, if he continued to seek reelection, he decided, he would only suffer a humiliating defeat in the primaries. On the evening of March 31, in an address to the nation announcing a bombing halt and a peace initiative, he concluded with the words: "I shall not seek, and will not accept, the nomination of my party for another term as your president." The two Democratic antiwar candidates now began the long struggle through the state primaries to secure the nomination.

Before the campaign's end two tragedies intervened. The first took place in Memphis, where Martin Luther King, Jr., had gone to support a local strike of the predominantly black city garbage collectors. King's nonviolence was under attack by black-power militants, but he was about to open a new phase of his career by leading a poor people's campaign. He never did. On April 4, 1968, he was shot and killed by James Earl Ray, an escaped white convict who may have been in the pay of white supremacists. Black ghettoes around the country exploded in rage and despair. Twenty blocks of Chicago's West Madison Street went up in flames. Black neighborhoods in Detroit, Cincinnati, and Minneapolis erupted. From their offices on Capitol Hill congressmen could see the flames and smoke from Washington's burning buildings and stores.

The second tragedy came on June 6. Following a successful battle against McCarthy in the California primary, Kennedy was shot by a confused Arab national named Sirhan Bishara Sirhan during his victory celebration in Los Angeles. The senseless violence of these two events encouraged the view that something had to be done to extricate the nation from the contaminating brutality of Vietnam. The United States seemed to be at the edge of anarchy.

The forces that converged on Chicago for the Democratic convention in late August represented an explosive mixture. Now that Johnson was gone, the hawks had gathered around Vice President Humphrey, who, however much he disliked the war, had become Johnson's heir apparent, tied to his policies by loyalty and dependence. On the other side were the combined antiwar groups representing McCarthy and the delegates who had supported Kennedy. In the city's streets and parks were the Yippies (Youth International Party), politicized counterculture protestors led by Jerry Rubin and Abbie Hoffman, along with New Left radicals, antiwar students, and pacifists. Some young people, as Jerry Rubin would later admit, were intent on rioting to show up the "politics of death" represented by the traditional party system. In response, Chicago's Mayor Richard Daley warned that "as long as I am mayor, there will be law and order."

Within the convention hall itself the Humphrey forces triumphed. Supported by the remaining hawks, union leaders, party regulars, and big-city power brokers, Humphrey defeated McCarthy and the insurgent peace forces and was nominated on the first ballot. In the streets of Chicago Mayor Daley's police and the antiwar activists collided in battle before the eyes of the delegates and the shocked public, who watched the gassing, the clubbings, the trashings, and the stone-throwing on television. To many viewers the contrast between political business as usual in the convention hall and burly policemen propelling young people through plateglass windows was final evidence that America was divided by forces that were out of control. In great numbers the voters blamed the chaos on the Democrats and on Hubert Humphrey; his campaign was in deep trouble from the start.

Meanwhile, in Miami, in a convention as bland as the Democrats' was violent, the Republicans nominated Richard M. Nixon. The nomination was a spectacular comeback. In 1962 Nixon had run for governor of California and had been beaten by the incumbent, Edmund Brown. After his defeat, in an intemperate outburst accusing the press of "kicking him around" during the campaign, he had said he would never run for office again. Soon after, Nixon joined a New York law firm to spend his remaining days making money and enjoying the pleasures of private life. He could

Even Richard Nixon could inspire enthusiasm, at least before Watergate. Here he is seen campaigning for president in 1968. He won, but it was close.

not stay out of politics, however, and soon started the comeback campaign that finally brought him victory at the Miami convention.

The 1968 presidential contest was a close one. Many observers felt that the Democrats had destroyed themselves in Chicago by their bitter, divisive in-fighting and the rioting in the streets. The Republicans, on the other hand, worried about defection on the right to Governor George Wallace of Alabama, running as the American Independent party candidate on a platform of law and order, pushing the war until victory, and clamping down on dissenters and civil rights activists. To avoid losing the South and the conservatives to Wallace, Nixon promised Senator Strom Thurmond of South Carolina that if elected he would keep the nation strong militarily, work for a less activist Supreme Court, and slow the pace of desegregation. It was with Thurmond's urging that Nixon selected Spiro T. Agnew, the little-known governor of Maryland, as his running mate.

At the start of the campaign the Republicans were well in the lead. But as November approached, the traditional Democratic coalition of ethnics, blacks, eastern liberals, and union members began to rally around Humphrey. Had the campaign gone on for just a few days longer, the ticket of Humphrey and Senator Edmund S. Muskie of Maine might have pulled ahead. But the surge came too late. On November 5 Nixon won by 31.7 million votes (301 electoral) to Humphrey's 31.2 million (191 electoral) and Wallace's 9.9 million (46 electoral). Richard Nixon would be the thirty-seventh president of the United States.

★ Conclusions ★

During the 1960s the United States attained a level of material well-being beyond anything dreamed of in the past. Affluence altered the dominant public mood. Among minorities, already mobilized to secure their long-denied basic civil rights, it aroused a sense of fury and hurt at exclusion from the benefits of abundance. Among members of the middle class it encouraged a spirit of generosity. If there was plenty to go around, then why not distribute some of its benefits to those who could not make it by themselves? Generosity, reinforced perhaps by guilt, and underscored by the sweeping 1964 victory of Lyndon Johnson over Barry Goldwater, set off a wave of social reform not equalled since the New Deal.

Yet despite the nation's prosperity, or rather because of it, the decade witnessed a wave of social criticism. Especially among the privileged young, the America of bounding wealth and conspicuous consumption seemed an unlovely place of bureaucratic rigidity, meaningless relationships, manipulation, and aesthetic squalor. Their disgust with their society was in turn reinforced by a distant and apparently pointless war. Thus, some of the chief beneficiaries of prosperity were among the very people who despised it the most. Their excesses in turn would outrage those who still held to traditional values and attitudes and force the dissenters on the defensive. The election of Richard Nixon in 1968 expressed that outrage.

✷✷✷✷✷✷✷✷ FOR FURTHER READING ✷✷✷✷✷✷✷✷

William O'Neill. *Coming Apart: An Informal History of America in the 1960s* (1971)
A witty, highly readable, and opinionated overview of the mores, politics, culture, and thought of the 1960s. Both entertaining and informative.

Irwin Unger and Debi Unger. *1968: Turning Point* (1988)
A panorama of the 1960s from the perspective of its culminating year. Strongly recommended.

Morris Dickstein. *Gates of Eden: American Culture in the Sixties* (1977)
This work demonstrates what a bright scholar can do with the popular culture of the 1960s. Written by a professor of literature who is young enough to have been at the center of things himself during the 1968 student uprising at Columbia University.

Theodore Roszak. *The Making of a Counter Culture: Reflections on the Technocratic Society and Its Youthful Opposition* (1969)
Both a description of the 1960s counterculture phenomenon and an influential part of it. Roszak's attitude is very positive toward the 1960s cultural left.

Arthur M. Schlesinger, Jr. *A Thousand Days: John F. Kennedy* (1965)
A highly sympathetic portrait of the Kennedy presidency by a professorial participant in it. Written with grace and verve.

Doris Kearns. *Lyndon Johnson and the American Dream* (1976)
A fascinating combination of psychological study, biography, and memoir, written by a scholar who enjoyed Johnson's trust and confidence from 1967 to his death in 1973. Kearns quotes the private man at length and demonstrates how his personal behavior affected the course of the Great Society and American policy in Vietnam.

Frances FitzGerald. *Fire in the Lake: The Vietnamese and the Americans in Vietnam* (1972)
American policy in Vietnam was based in part on ignorance of Vietnamese history and society. FitzGerald discusses the Vietnamese people and their history with great sympathy. A complex and rather difficult book.

David Halberstam. *The Best and the Brightest* (1972)
A sharply critical account of the foreign policy "establishment" under Kennedy and Johnson and how its members entangled the United States in the Vietnam War.

Michael Harrington. *The Other America: Poverty in the United States* (1962)
This short book is said to have influenced Kennedy's thinking and led him to propose a federal program anticipating Johnson's War on Poverty. Harrington rediscovered poverty in America after the other experts had said it no longer existed.

Betty Friedan. *The Feminine Mystique* (1963)
This is the feminist "Declaration of Independence" of the 1960s. In this book Friedan, a leader of the women's movement, devastatingly attacked the 1950s cult of female domesticity and left it a shambles among most intellectuals and a large proportion of college-educated women.

Lyndon B. Johnson. *The Vantage Point: Perspectives of the Presidency, 1963–69* (1971)
Johnson defends his administration's policies—not only the Great Society programs, but also the continued intervention in Vietnam.

Norman Podhoretz. *Why We Were in Vietnam* (1982)
The author, a leading neoconservative intellectual, makes the best case possible for American involvement in Vietnam.

George Herring. *America's Longest War: The United States and Vietnam, 1950–1975* (1986)
A scholarly treatment of the Vietnam War. Herring was a dove who believed that America's containment policy, as displayed in Vietnam, was "fundamentally flawed in its assumptions."

Allen Matusow. *The Unraveling of America: A History of Liberalism in the 1960s* (1984)
A critical examination of 1960s political liberalism as seen from the left. Matusow views the Kennedy-Johnson New Frontier–Great Society era as seriously damaged by exaggerated rhetoric and limited commitment to the goals of equality.

Nancy Zaroulis and Gerald Sullivan. *Who Spoke Up? American Protest Against the War In Vietnam, 1963–1975* (1984)
A blow-by-blow account of the anti–Vietnam War movement. Encyclopedic.

Herbert Parmet. *Jack: The Struggles of John F. Kennedy* (1980); and *JFK: The Presidency of John F. Kennedy* (1983)
A more balanced assessment of Kennedy and his administra-

tion than Schlesinger's. The first volume is better than the second.

W. J. Rorabaugh. *Berkeley at War: The 1960s* (1989)
The best treatment of the free speech movement as well as the later struggles in Berkeley between the radicals and the authorities.

Alice Echols. *Daring to Be Bad: Radical Feminism in America, 1967–1975* (1989)
The author considers radical feminism "the most vital and imaginative force within the women's liberation movement." Partisan, obviously, but interesting and valuable.

David Garrow. *Bearing the Cross: Martin Luther King, Jr., and the Southern Christian Leadership Conference* (1986)
Not so eloquent as Stephen Oats's *Let the Trumpet Sound* (1982), but better balanced on King.

Taylor Branch. *Parting the Waters: America in the King Years, 1954–63* (1988)
An effective invocation of the early, more successful years of the civil rights movement. A prize-winning work.

Eric Goldman. *The Tragedy of Lyndon Johnson* (1969)
Written by the White House "intellectual in residence," a Princeton historian, this critical book, though written in 1968, is in many ways still the best narrative account of the Johnson administration.

Matt S. Meier and Feliciano Ribera. *Mexican Americans, American Mexicanos* (1994)
A brief overview of the whole span of Mexican–American experience in the Southwest. Readable.

30 ★

THE UNCERTAIN SEVENTIES

Why Did the Right Fail?

1960	Organization of Petroleum Exporting Countries (OPEC) is formed
1969	Paris peace talks on Vietnam begin • Nixon orders the secret bombing of Cambodia • Strategic Arms Limitation Talks (SALT) begin in Helsinki • Americans land on the moon • Nuclear Nonproliferation Treaty
1970	United States invades Cambodia • Four students killed by National Guard in antiwar demonstration at Kent State University in Ohio • Congress repeals the Gulf of Tonkin Resolution
1971	The *New York Times* publishes the "Pentagon Papers" • Nixon imposes wage-and-price controls • Berlin Accord
1972	Nixon visits China • Congress passes the Federal Election Campaign Act • Nixon visits Moscow; The U.S. and the Soviet Union ratify arms limitation treaties • Watergate break-in • Nixon reelected in landslide
1973	Truce in Vietnam • Senate Select Committee holds public hearing on Watergate; House Judiciary Committee begins hearings on impeachment resolutions • Vice President Agnew resigns in disgrace; Gerald Ford becomes vice president • Israel and Egypt go to war, touching off Arab oil embargo • Abortion legalized by Supreme Court in *Roe* v. *Wade*
1974	Arab oil embargo ends, but OPEC raises oil prices drastically • House Judiciary Committee recommends impeachment of Nixon; Nixon resigns; Ford becomes president; Ford pardons Nixon
1975	North and South Vietnam are reunited
1976	Bicentennial celebrations • Jimmy Carter elected president
1977	SALT II talks collapse • Carter launches "moral equivalent of war" on United States dependency on foreign oil • Camp David Accords
1978	Panama Canal Treaties
1979	SALT II agreement • Three Mile Island nuclear power plant disaster • Shah of Iran exiled • 66 American hostages taken by Khomeini's followers in Iran • Russia invades Afghanistan
1980	Ronald Reagan elected president

In January 1969 a new conservative administration came to power in Washington seemingly dedicated to dismantling the Great Society, slowing the pace of social change, and pushing back the tide of world communism. Between that date and the end of the 1970s American public opinion would, by and large, support such a conservative agenda. Yet very little of it would be achieved. Indeed, by the opening of the 1980s the United States, in the eyes of many committed conservatives, had retrogressed. By then the welfare state seemed more deeply entrenched than ever, the courts were upholding new principles of racial equality, and the United States had recognized Red China and achieved at least a superficial détente with its archenemy, the Soviet Union.

How had such results come about? How had Richard Nixon, the man who epitomized conservative anticommunism, managed to perpetuate the welfare state that he and his followers despised and to replace the hard-line anticommunism of recent American policy with a more flexible approach?

★ THE NIXON PRESIDENCY ★

Richard Nixon was one of the most puzzling and inconsistent men to occupy the White House. Some of Nixon's personal qualities could be explained by his difficult childhood. The second of five sons, he saw two of his brothers die of tuberculosis. His father was a hot-tempered man and a financial failure. His mother, a Quaker and a woman with an especially sweet nature, could not save him from his father's frequent anger. The contrasting personalities of his parents helped mold the extremes of Nixon's own character: one side self-pitying and vindictive, particularly in the face of frustration; the other generous, even idealistic.

Both sides of Nixon's nature could be detected in his approach to public issues. He could support welfare reform, environmental protection laws, and reconciliation with Red China and the Soviet Union, for example. But he could also seek to weaken civil rights protection, encourage the illegal political acts we call Watergate, and attempt to cover them up to protect his administration. His enemies, remembering his aggressive partisan style, seldom found it in their hearts to forgive him for anything. Adlai Stevenson would describe "Nixonland" as a place of "slander and scare, of sly innuendo, of a poison pen, the anonymous phone call, and hustling, pushing, shoving—the land of smash and grab and anything to win."

Nixon's initial appointments deserve mixed reviews. His tough, partisan side was reflected in his choice of John Mitchell, his former New York law associate, as attorney general. His inner White House circle was dominated by people who placed loyalty to their chief above all other considerations. White House chief of staff, H. R. Haldeman, was a rigid right-winger. A powerful force in the Nixon administration, he guarded his chief from all contact with people who disagreed with administration policy. Chief White House adviser on domestic affairs was John Ehrlichman, a former Seattle lawyer. Both men agreed with Nixon that in politics anything goes; that winning was all that counted. They also shared with their boss a deep suspicion of the "eastern establishment," a vaguely defined circle of elite liberal leaders who, they believed, dominated the press, the universities, and the upper reaches of the professions and American business.

Among Nixon's advisers there was also another side, however. Daniel Moynihan, assistant for urban affairs, was one of the more imaginative men in American political life. Henry Kissinger, Nixon's national security adviser and later secretary of state, though he harbored a streak of deviousness, was an unusually adept diplomat with a vision influenced by his deep knowledge of history. Other competent men whom Nixon would appoint to high office included Treasury Secretary John Connally and Secretary of Defense Melvin Laird. Unfortunately, the inner circle of White House aides under Haldeman and Ehrlichman—men without wide experience of elective office and government—often exerted disproportionate influence on administration policy.

Détente Nixon was far more interested in foreign policy than in domestic affairs; it was as an international statesman that he hoped to make his mark in history. Foremost, he and Kissinger sought to stabilize relations with the Soviet Union by a policy called *détente*. Unfortunately, détente had no precise limits, and many Americans, eager to end the anxieties of the Cold War, were quick to believe that superpower rivalry might be ended once and for all.

However commendable their goals, the Nixon–Kissinger diplomatic style disturbed many observers. Kissinger believed in secret "back channel" negotiations with foreign representatives that bypassed the State Department. Although he was at first only the president's national security adviser, Kissinger, rather than Secretary of State William Rogers, was the chief foreign-policy maker. All too often the State Department head, the cabinet officer officially responsible for directing foreign affairs, was treated as little more than a high-level bureaucrat capable only of shuffling diplomatic papers. This awkward situation was rectified in 1973 when the German-born Kissinger became Rogers's successor.

However ill-defined, the Nixon–Kissinger policy made substantial progress toward reducing superpower tensions. During the summer of 1969 American prestige had soared when astronaut Neil A. Armstrong took the first step on the moon while millions around the world watched the momentous event on television. Soon after, Nixon visited the Soviet Balkan satellite, Rumania. As he rode through the streets of Bucharest, the American president was wildly cheered by large crowds. In November 1969 Nixon and Soviet president Nikolai Podgorny signed the Nuclear Nonproliferation Treaty with sixty other nations. Those countries possessing nuclear weapons pledged not to transfer them to other nations. The nonnuclear nations promised to refrain from developing such weapons. In 1971 and 1972 the perennial problems of Berlin and the two Germanies was finally settled by the Berlin Accord: Britain, France, the United States, and the Soviet Union agreed to cease threatening communications between Berlin and West Germany. They also formally recognized the existence of two separate German nations.

Another major step in the détente process came in May 1972, when Nixon visited the Soviet Union, the first American president ever to do so. The visit produced a series of agreements pledging the two nations to improve commercial relations and cooperate in the scientific, medical, and environmental realms. It also led to the signing of the SALT I (Strategic Arms Limitation Treaty) agreements negotiated over several years by the two powers. SALT I enshrined as superpower policy what had already been accepted for some time by default: the check on nuclear war would be deterrence or, as critics preferred to call it, MAD, mutually assured destruction. Implicit in this policy was the conviction that no nation would launch nuclear weapons at another if it meant national suicide. The core agreement of SALT I was the Anti-Ballistic Missile (ABM) Treaty forbidding virtually all defensive weapons capable of shooting down hostile ICBMs. It also included agreements to limit the construction and deployment of new offensive missiles. The world was still a long way from nuclear disarmament; all the superpowers had done was to slow the arms race somewhat. Still, SALT I seemed a lessening of Cold War rivalries and dangers and the world applauded.

The People's Republic of China. Even more remarkable in some ways than détente with the Soviet Union was the breakthrough in relations with the People's Republic of China. Until Nixon became president, the United States had treated Communist China as an outcast. It had refused to recognize the Chinese mainland regime and had vetoed every attempt to admit the People's Republic to the United Nations. As far as the United States was concerned, China was the Republic of China on Taiwan where Chiang Kai-shek's Nationalists had fled after the Communist mainland victory in 1949 and created a prosperous if authoritarian regime. American troops were stationed on Taiwan to provide military support if the Chinese Communists should ever attempt to invade the island of Taiwan.

Nixon, John Erlichman (center), and Arthur Burns, the president's economic advisor, shown in a rather glum moment.

The situation was peculiar. There were good reasons to dislike the regime in Beijing. Communist methods were often brutal. Following the civil war against the Nationalists, the Communists had executed thousands as class enemies and, during the so-called Cultural Revolution of the 1960s, had let loose a brutal reign of anarchy intended to purge the nation of all non-Communist elements. The new regime, on the other hand, had also freed China of the worst of the economic misery of the past and had forged a functioning, if repressive, social order on the mainland. China, with its 800 million people, was clearly a major power, and its existence could not be wished away.

Not only was America's China Policy unrealistic; it was also harmful to this country's interests. Although his enemies accused him of being a crude anti-Communist ideologue, Nixon recognized that world Communist unity was a myth. China and the Soviet Union, though once closely allied, were since Stalin's death adversaries. Each nation was suspicious of the other, and periodically Soviet and Chinese military forces clashed along their extended common border in Asia. It seemed foolish not to take advantage of the Sino-Soviet rift and use one Communist nation to check the goals and ambitions of the other. Indeed, an opening to China seemed an essential ingredient of achieving stable relations with the Soviet Union.

Soon after the 1968 presidential elections, the Red Chinese indicated to Nixon their desire to smooth over Sino-American differences. Before long both countries were holding secret meetings in Warsaw. Early in 1971 the Chinese invited an American Ping-Pong team visiting Japan to tour the People's Republic and play Chinese teams. In July 1971, Nixon startled the world by announcing that he had been invited to visit the People's Republic of China and would go there sometime in the early part of the following year. In October, the United States for the first time abstained from vetoing the admission of Red China to the United Nations. The Beijing government was promptly seated and the Taiwan regime's representatives expelled.

Not all Americans liked what was taking place. To the far right the reconciliation with Red China and abandonment of Taiwan seemed a surrender to communism. Most Americans, however, accepted the move as sensible and long overdue. Many of Nixon's liberal critics noted ruefully that it could only have been carried off by a conservative with a reputation as a militant anti-Communist.

On February 21, 1972, Nixon, his wife, and a large presidential entourage arrived in Beijing by plane. Scores of American reporters and the TV media were present, and millions of viewers in the United States watched the American president shake hands with Premier Chou Enlai. The discussions that followed with Chou and Communist party chairman Mao Tse-tung, China's aging top leader, were largely exploratory; little of a concrete nature was accomplished except for an agreement to withdraw American troops from Taiwan. Much of the Nixon's time was spent in sightseeing and banqueting. But the meeting was momentous symbolically. Television pictures of Nixon toasting Chou, quoting chairman Mao, and strolling

Richard Nixon and Chinese Premier Chou En-lai toast each other during Nixon's famous 1972 trip to Beijing.

along the Great Wall made clear to the American people that the policy of ignoring the world's most populous nation was finally ended.

"Peace with Honor".

The worst of the foreign policy past, however, still held on in Vietnam. Nixon came into office when the war appeared to be winding down. In March 1968 Johnson had vetoed any further American troops for Vietnam. The next month, following his decision to stop the bombing of North Vietnam, peace talks between North Vietnam and the United States opened in Paris. Months of controversy over seating the Vietcong followed, and not until January 1969, just days before Johnson left office, did serious peace talks begin. The war continued, however. The North Vietnamese had no intention of abandoning their goal of destroying the Saigon regime and reuniting Vietnam under their firm control and pursued the policy of "fighting while negotiating."

The new American administration had no interest in continuing the war. Nixon at one point declared: "I'm not going to end up like LBJ, holed up in the White House afraid to show my face on the street. I'm going to stop that war. Fast." But, like his predecessor, the president also wanted

to avoid the charge that he had "lost" South Vietnam to the Communists. America must somehow disengage, but it must preserve an independent South Vietnam to keep its reputation and pride intact. Nixon called this "peace with honor;" his critics called it foolish, among other things.

Nixon resolved to use every means to force the North Vietnamese to accept a compromise position. At one point, to intimidate the Hanoi government, he spread the view that he was a Communist-obsessed nuclear madman capable of blowing up the world if he did not get his way. In March 1969, he secretly ordered the massive bombing of Cambodia—a supposedly neutral nation—to hamper Communist operations in South Vietnam. At the same time, however, he announced that the United States would adopt the policy of "Vietnamization": It would gradually shift military responsibility to the South Vietnamese, and begin to withdraw American combat troops.

The militant antiwar forces at home refused to believe that Nixon intended to disengage. The president talked peace, they said, but the fighting and dying continued. America should leave immediately. "Out Now" was the only valid policy. Then, in late April 1970, the president sent

In May 1970, Ohio National Guardsmen who had been called in to quell disorder on the campus of Kent State University fired on protesting students. Four students died, and the university became a byword among those who opposed the Vietnam War.

American forces on a sweep through Cambodia to attack bases, which, he claimed, were refuges for Vietcong guerrillas. This apparent escalation of the fighting electrified the antiwar movement. In response, protest demonstrations erupted on scores of college campuses. At one of these, Kent State University in Ohio, National Guardsmen fired live ammunition at student antiwar demonstrators killing four and wounding eleven. This attack seemed to confirm every charge of government repression and brutality. Hundreds of American campuses shut down to protest the Kent State killings and to allow students to mobilize against the detested war. In June, Congress itself reacted to the new antiwar surge by repealing the 1964 Gulf of Tonkin resolution that Johnson had used as a legal equivalent of a declaration of war.

By now even many of the government's Cold War experts were convinced that the war was evil. In June 1971, Daniel Ellsberg, a former Pentagon official, made public a collection of stolen classified documents describing the slow steps to American entrapment in the Vietnam morass and the deception of the public that accompanied the escalation. The Justice Department indicted Ellsberg and tried to get publication of the "Pentagon Papers" in the *New York Times* legally stopped. The move failed. A still worse sign of growing discontent was the deteriorating morale of American soldiers in the field. While Vietnamization steadily reduced the number of fighting men, it damaged the spirits of those who remained. What was the point of risking one's life in a war that was winding down? More and more combat troops sought to avoid risks. They disobeyed orders or "fragged" officers by rolling live hand grenades into their tents while they slept. Others turned to drugs to make the time till their tour of duty ended pass more quickly. Even supporters of American Vietnam policy began to fear that the war was destroying the American military.

In 1972, with only a few thousand American combat troops remaining in South Vietnam, the Communists launched a major offensive to destroy the Saigon government led by Nguyen Van Thieu. Unwilling to allow them a military victory, Nixon ordered the resumption of massive bombing of North Vietnam and the mining of Haiphong harbor, the port of entry for most of the arms and supplies from the Soviet Union. It looked as if the escalation pattern of the past would be repeated once more. Fortunately, by this time, both the Chinese and the Russians were more anxious for better relations with the United States than for North Vietnamese good will, and they told Hanoi that it must act more reasonably. Meanwhile, the Saigon government, reassured by a billion dollar gift of American military hardware to help it defend itself against a Communist takeover, also proved more amenable to negotiation.

These events finally broke the Paris peace talks logjam. In January 1973 the United States, South Vietnam, and the Vietcong–North Vietnamese signed an agreement to end the fighting. The document provided for the release of all American prisoners of war, a cease-fire between Hanoi and Saigon, the withdrawal of all remaining U.S. military personnel, massive American economic aid to South Vietnam, and a flock of complicated arrangements intended to reconcile the South Vietnamese government and the Vietcong. Nixon and Kissinger claimed that this agreement would preserve the separate existence of South Vietnam.

Whether they believed this is not clear. Nixon's defenders claim that he and Kissinger actually hoped to give the Saigon regime a fighting chance to survive by providing U.S. economic aid and promising to intervene again if North Vietnam violated the truce. The fault, they say, lay with a dovish Congress that refused to vote the funds or make the guarantees. In fact, determined to prevent a repetition of Vietnam, in late 1973 Congress adopted the War Powers Act, requiring congressional approval for any use of military force except in a national emergency. But in any case the aid was not forthcoming, and by April 1975 Communist forces had overwhelmed the South Vietnamese army and occupied all of the Vietnam, forcibly uniting North and South under their harsh regime. They had finally achieved their goal of thirty years.

The wretched war was finally over but at immense cost to all participants. Vietnam was devastated—physically, economically, socially. Literally millions of Vietnamese—civilians and soldiers—had died; over 46,000 Americans had lost their lives. At home the war had left a bitter taste in everyone's mouth. At first, those who had opposed the war could boast that their efforts had helped end the killing and destruction and replaced a repressive government with a more popular one. It soon became clear, however, that the Hanoi government was as benighted as its enemies had long charged and that the people of South Vietnam would be worse off than before. The North Vietnamese conquerors rounded up thousands of the Saigon regime's friends and sent them to forced labor or "reeducation" camps. Over 1.4 million refugees fled the country, many in small boats. Thousands settled in the United States. In early 1978 the Vietnamese attacked Cambodia, precipitating an inconclusive war with China. Today Vietnam remains one of the poorest, most backward nations in all of East Asia, an embarrassment to all who supported its struggle to win control over the south.

Those people who had cheered the American cause in Vietnam could extract little more satisfaction from the result. The war seemed to demonstrate the nation's impotence: It was the first war that America had lost, and it undermined the nation's confidence in itself.

Finally, the war's ambiguous outcome would also color the debate over future American foreign policy. Some citizens would see Vietnam as a lesson in limits: The United

States could not expect to police events everywhere; it must confine its role to matters that affected its vital interests closer to home. Others would view it as an instance of how defeat would inevitably follow loss of nerve and confidence. For a time the first group would predominate, and during the mid-1970s American foreign policy would enter a phase that observers called neo-isolationist.

Courting the Backlash Vote. In domestic affairs Nixon looked two ways. In part, he acted as the agent for reversing the social and political trends of the 1960s. His 1968 election campaign had been based on the idea that there was a "silent majority," mostly composed of nominal Democrats who were fed up with many of the social trends of the day. If the Republicans emphasized the social issues over the bread-and-butter ones, the silent majority's disgust could be used to forge a new and unbeatable Republican majority.

The theory was politically sound. Since the late sixties a backlash—a powerful negative reaction—to that decade's social and political liberalism had been emerging. Angry backlash voters, generally middle-aged and white, felt that traditional institutions and values were being destroyed. Many were "ethnics," the children and grandchildren of the immigrants of the 1880–1920 period, who believed that the government was showing the sort of favoritism toward blacks that their own forebears had never experienced. Others were old stock white Protestants, particularly well represented in the South and West, who feared the collapse of traditional Christian morality under the assault of the counterculture, drug abusers, and sexual outsiders. Backlash voters were dismayed by rock music, long hair, "pot," and sexual permissiveness. They were usually aggressive patriots who suspected the antiwar forces of disloyalty and considered student activists spoiled brats who deserved to be spanked. They feared the street violence of the cities and were appalled by the "porn shops" and X-rated movies that had sprung up in urban areas. They were skeptical of the new, assertive feminism that seemed to deny gender differences and to blame men for all of women's misfortunes.

Backlash voters blamed much of what seemed wrong with the times on the liberal Supreme Court. In a cascade of decisions, the Court had, in their view, enshrined liberal and anti-Christian values as the law of the land. *Miranda* v. *Arizona*, in the guise of protecting the rights of accused criminals, had weakened the power of the police to deter crime. *Engel* v. *Vitale*, in the guise of defending the separation of church and state, had forbidden prayer in the public schools and encouraged atheism. *Swann* v. *Charlotte-Mecklenburg Board*, in the guise of "racial balance," had condoned busing children to distant schools and undermined local control over public schools. Worst of all, there was *Roe* v. *Wade*.

In the name of expanding the right to privacy, the 1973 decision had struck down state antiabortion laws and permitted abortion on demand during the first trimester of pregnancy. In effect, in *Roe* v. *Wade* the justices had condoned baby murder.

Nixon and his advisers found many backlash views personally congenial. Administration officials wore American flag pins on their lapels and cultivated a reverent demeanor toward traditional American values. The backlash also promised to be political gold, and after 1969 the administration set out to woo—as political analyst Kevin Phillips had advised in *The Emerging Republican Majority*— all "Middle Americans," whether Democrats or Republicans. The president and vice president made themselves spokesmen for backlash and antiliberal views. Campus radicals, declared Nixon, were "bums." As for crime and disorder, ordinary citizens he said, "have had it up to here." Vice President Spiro Agnew toured the nation denouncing "rad-libs," the "nattering nabobs of negativism," and "troglodytic leftists." "The disease of our time," he said, "is an artificial and masochistic sophistication—

Not everyone loved Vice President Spiro Agnew. But "hard hats," blue-collar workers who resented antiwar and civil rights activists and campus militants, made him their hero.

the vague uneasiness that our values are false, and there is something wrong with being patriotic, honest, moral and hard-working."

The campaign to restore presixties values was more than rhetorical. Following the president's lead, federal officials eased up on the enforcement of desegregation processes in the South. In March 1971 Nixon asked Congress to halt "forced busing" of children from neighborhood schools to more distant ones to achieve racial balance. In April he directed veterans' hospitals to cease abortions for ex-servicewomen. The president frequently called for "law and order" and sponsored several bills and measures to strengthen the hand of judges and the police. Nixon and his advisers believed, as had Johnson, that antiwar and New Left dissenters were encouraging the Vietcong and the North Vietnamese to continue their fight. The administration cracked down hard. During a May 1970 antiwar march on Washington, Attorney General Mitchell threw thousands of demonstrators into jail and detention compounds. The Justice Department indicted scores of pacifists and student activists for crimes of conspiracy to commit crimes. The defendants won most of these cases, but the legal defenses depleted the energies and financial resources of the antiwar movement.

Unlike Republicans in the past, Nixon looked for support to the white, formerly solid Democratic South. During the 1968 Republican convention he had promised conservative Dixie leaders to defer to traditional white southern feelings and wishes in regard to appointments, and after the election he tried to keep his word. In early 1969 he nominated Judge Clement F. Haynsworth, Jr., of South Carolina to the U.S. Supreme Court. The Democratically controlled Senate was anxious to preserve recent civil rights gains. When it discovered that Haynsworth had officiated in cases in which he had a personal financial interest, it used this as the basis for rejecting his nomination. Nixon then sent forward the name of Florida federal judge G. Harrold Carswell. Antilabor and racially conservative, the new nominee was a man whose decisions had frequently been reversed by higher courts. The Senate rejected this appointment too. Nixon eventually succeeded in getting confirmed another presumed conservative, Harry Blackmun. Blackmun was a northerner, but the president's efforts on behalf of southerners Haynsworth and Carswell were appreciated by conservative white voters in Dixie.

Nixon helped to slow the movement for social change. The student revolt subsided; the hippies gradually disappeared; antiwar protest did not last much beyond 1973. Still, the results did not satisfy backlash voters. Drug abuse reached into the high schools of suburban America, teenage pregnancies soared, crime and disorder spread, and movies and books continued to deal with sexually explicit themes.

Backlash voters would remain dissatisfied, and would continue to search for ways to restore the nation to old-fashioned virtue.

Domestic Moderation. Yet Nixon did not send the American ship of state into full reverse. Those who had hoped that the Republican president would decrease the size and reach of the federal government were disappointed.

Nixon left intact most Great Society welfare programs. In fact, during his administration, many programs received better funding than before. In 1968 federal social welfare expenditures had totaled $142 billion; in 1974 they reached $229 billion. Nixon even added programs to the Johnson roster. He signed into law the Supplementary Security Income Act that guaranteed a check each month for elderly, blind, and disabled Americans who were not otherwise entitled to a federal pension. He also endorsed a drastic welfare reform proposal by Daniel Moynihan, a Democrat who had served under Kennedy and Johnson, to provide a $1,600-a-year minimum income to each poor family from federal funds. The measure, many hoped, would end forever the inequalities and indignities that beset the existing "welfare system" and cut through the bureaucratic tangle that encumbered it. Though it never made it through both houses of Congress, the Family Assistance Program was a bold departure that probably deserved a better reception.

Nixon's management of the economy was another surprise to those who expected him to pursue traditional Republican approaches. Nixon inherited several difficult economic problems from the Johnson administration. By 1971 inflation was running about 5 percent a year, a figure that then seemed unacceptable. The economy was also in a slump. On the recommendation of Treasury Secretary John Connally, in August the president announced a number of new policies that violated traditional Republican econmomic principles. There would be a ninety-day freeze on all wages and prices, to be enforced by control boards. The man who had remembered with distaste his own World War II experiences with the Office of Price Administration was now, himself, imposing the first peacetime wage and price controls on the nation! The United States would also abandon the gold standard, a conservative sacred cow, by ending the policy, ever since the Bretton Woods agreement, of making the American dollar convertible into gold in international exchanges. Closing the "gold window" ended the era of fixed international exchange rates that had helped to mend and then stimulate the world economy after 1945. Experts would later say that the move accelerated inflation and retarded economic growth.

The New Environmentalism. In some ways the most unexpected of all Nixon's domestic policies was his endorsement of the new environmentalism, however qualified. Franklin Roosevelt had been a conservationist in the Pinchot–Teddy Roosevelt tradition. FDR sought to harness the neglected hydroelectric resources of the rivers, make the forests more productive, and restore the Plains dust bowl to fertility. But among naturalists, biologists, and social philosophers a new ethic was taking hold. Drawing on the ideas of predecessors like Henry David Thoreau and John Muir, and on new scientific insights regarding the interrelatedness of living things, they had come to believe that "development" was often a violation of nature's law and in the end hurt more than helped. Humans, they said, were part of an "ecosystem," a web of life that extended far beyond them, and they must esteem all living things and respect the balances of nature. As Aldo Leopold, an influential Wisconsin environmentalist, wrote in the 1940s: "We abuse land because we regard it as a commodity belonging to us. When we see land as a community to which we belong, we may begin to use it with love and respect." A "land ethic," he said, must supersede the "merely economic attitude toward land."

Few people read Leopold and his colleagues, but the public mind was alerted to some of the new ideas by a 1962 book by Rachel Carson, a naturalist with the U.S. Fish and Wildlife Service. *Silent Spring* blew the whistle on DDT, the potent insecticide that had been lauded as a breakthrough in insect control when it first appeared. Written with grace and a sensitive feel for nature, the book described the long-term and roundabout lethal effects of DDT on wildlife, especially birds, through the food chain and the dangers of carelessly introducing such potent poisons into the natural environment. For every reader of the best-seller who caught the message of nature's interrelatedness there were many more undoubtedly roused by the threat to human health. *Silent Spring* was followed by a flood of books, magazine articles, and TV reports informing the public of how humans interacted with the natural environment and advertising the dangers of pollution from a host of industrial and agricultural processes.

The new environmental sensibility drew on several social trends of the early 1970s. The collapse of the sixties student insurgency had left many idealistic young people stranded without an ideological anchor. Some of the erstwhile student radicals and countercultural activists found a new home in the environmental movement, which for them had the attraction of a strong antibusiness, antiestablishment undercurrent. For a time there was even talk of an anticapitalist "Green" party organized around ecological issues in imitation of the 1970s politicized environmental movement in Western Europe. Feminists too were drawn to environmentalism. Many claimed a connection between a female view of Mother Nature as fecund, nurturing, and benevolent and a male view of the natural world as hostile, begrudging, and challenging. Feminists explained that "conquest" was the metaphor for American continental expansion because men had dominated the process. Carrying the metaphor further, they often depicted the male-dominated westward movement as a "rape" of the environment. Such attitudes, they insisted, must now be abandoned and amends made. Many of the new views went on display on Earth Day, April 22, 1970, when a coalition of environmental groups held a one-day nationwide celebration of unspoiled nature and proclaimed the need to stop the environment-despoiling "development" juggernaut.

It is not likely that Nixon absorbed much of the advanced new sensibility, but he did respond to growing public fears of environmental hazards. Soon after Earth Day he approved the Clean Air Act of 1970 establishing a billion-dollar air pollution control program and imposing tighter emission standards on automobiles. He also signed the Occupational Safety and Health Act establishing a new agency to oversee new standards of health and safety for workers in the job environment. Following a serious oil spill off Santa Barbara, California, Nixon approved the Water Quality Improvement Act of 1970 imposing penalties for pollution of ocean and inland waters. In October of that year Nixon created the Environmental Protection Agency (EPA) to administer the various government antipollution programs.

The 1972 Election. The president's economic policies were driven primarily by short-term considerations. Nothing, including inflation and a weak dollar, must stand in the way of his reelection in 1972. In retrospect it is difficult to see why the administration was so apprehensive. The Democrats were in thrall to the "new politics" of the late 1960s, which expressed the political consciousness of the student insurgency, the antiwar movement, civil rights activism, and the various liberation groups. Their choice for president in 1972 was Senator George McGovern of South Dakota, a figure who represented the party's most liberal wing, now supported by a minority of voters. McGovern won the nomination under new convention rules requiring each state delegation to reflect separate voter blocs—youth, women, minorities, as well as white males—in approximate proportion to their numbers in the general populace. The Democratic delegates at Miami were probably a better cross section of the country's citizens than in past conventions, but many traditional Democrats—white southerners, blue-collar Catholics, older people, trade unionists—felt left out. It soon appeared that many of them either would not vote or would vote Republican.

A more effective campaigner than McGovern might have reunited his party after the convention, but the sena-

John Dean, on the far right, with his wife just behind him, spills the beans to the Ervin Committee. The president, he said, had been party to a cover-up for eight months.

tor proved to be inept. He selected Senator Thomas Eagleton of Missouri as his running mate without a careful background check. When Eagleton admitted that he had been hospitalized for mental illness, McGovern first rallied to Eagleton's side and then dropped him for former Peace Corps director Sargent Shriver. The Democratic candidate also stumbled over his welfare reform plan, revealing his own uncertain grasp of a guaranteed annual income scheme that many found extravagant. By early fall the polls were pointing to a Democratic disaster.

With the Democrats obviously fumbling away the election, Nixon could avoid the political rough-and-tumble and act "presidential." By fall the economy was firmly in hand under phase one of Nixon's wage and price control program. The GNP was up; unemployment and inflation were down. The results were predictable. Nixon won 60.8 percent of the popular vote, a tiny fraction below Lyndon Johnson's 1964 landslide, and all the nation's electoral votes except those of the District of Columbia and Massachusetts.

★ WATERGATE ★

The mandate was one of the most stunning on record, and it appeared that Nixon was set for four more years of impressive achievement. It was not to be. On June 17, 1972, almost six months before the election, five men had been arrested at the Washington, D.C., headquarters of the Democratic National Committee in the Watergate housing complex; two accomplices were caught outside. All seven were obviously attempting to rifle the Democrats' files for information, but why was not clear. Only much later did their motives become known: They were trying to steal incriminating information on an illegal payment by the reclusive millionaire Howard Hughes to a close Nixon friend or to find some dirt on the Democrats that could be used as blackmail to prevent disclosure of the Hughes deal.

Although one of the captured culprits was James W. McCord, Jr., a security consultant to the Committee to Reelect the President (CRP), and two others had White House connections, no information damaging to the administration came to light before the election. When questioned by reporters in mid-June, White House press secretary Ron Ziegler called the Watergate break-in a "third-rate burglary" that had nothing to do with the administration. McGovern struggled to make a campaign issue of Watergate, but could prove little. The public and the press ignored his charges, and Watergate did not affect the outcome. Then, by the time of Nixon's second inauguration, the story behind the break-in began to emerge. As the media revealed the facts, the president's reputation and the fate of his administration sank like a stone.

In January 1973 the seven accused Watergate burglars came before federal District Court Judge John Sirica. Though a lifelong Republican and a Nixon supporter, Sirica aggressively grilled the defendants himself. If they cooperated with Senator Sam Ervin, Jr.'s Senate Select Committee, recently appointed to investigate the Watergate affair, he would consider leniency, Sirica said. Under this pressure McCord soon revealed to the Ervin committee investigators that the president's counsel, John Dean, and Jeb Magruder, of the CRP staff, were both involved in Watergate. Before long the rush to secure immunity by confessing to the United States attorney threatened to become a stampede.

Early in April both Dean and Magruder began to tell the federal prosecutors all they knew, disclosing that Haldeman, Ehrlichman, and Mitchell had tried to hide the administration's role in the break-in. In effect, three of Nixon's closest associates were seeking to obstruct justice, a clearly indictable crime. On April 30, the president learned that Dean intended to accuse him of attempting to hide the administration's responsibility for Watergate. At this point Nixon announced that he had accepted the resignations of Haldeman, Ehrlichman, and Attorney General Richard Kleindienst, and had fired Dean. He also directed the new attorney general, Elliot Richardson, to appoint a special prosecutor to probe Watergate. Richardson named Archibald Cox of the Harvard Law School to the post.

Early Disclosures.   When the Ervin committee opened its televised Watergate hearings in May 1973, viewers watched a steady parade of witnesses who revealed the administration's disreputable efforts, through CRP (called CREEP by the unfriendly media), to crush its political opponents and illegally hide its acts. Other judicial agencies and the press, led by *Washington Post* reporters Bob Woodward and Carl Bernstein, exposed other serious misdeeds.

The list of actions eventually uncovered—actions that violated civil liberties, broke the laws governing political financing, and undermined respect for the law and the political process—was a long one. Watergate began as part of a "plumbers" operation financed by CRP to "plug" information leaks perceived as damaging to the administration. But it soon ballooned far beyond this.

Administration operatives had broken into the office of Daniel Ellsberg's psychiatrist looking for evidence to use against him in his trial for leaking the classified "Pentagon Papers."

Ehrlichman had sought to influence the presiding judge in the Ellsberg case by hinting to him that he might be appointed FBI director. (The White House effort backfired; when the attempt to suborn the judge came out, charges against Ellsberg were dismissed.)

White House representatives had paid large sums of cash to the Watergate burglars after they were arrested to keep them silent on the connection between the break-in and CRP.

Acting director of the FBI, L. Patrick Gray, had destroyed evidence in the Watergate case. The FBI had also shared information from its Watergate investigation with White House counsel Dean, though the White House itself was clearly the target of the investigation.

The Nixon reelection committee had engaged in "dirty tricks" to disrupt the campaigns of several Democratic candidates during the 1972 primaries.

CRP had collected large sums of cash from corporations with promises of favors, or threats of retaliation, in violation of federal law, and had then tried to conceal it.

The White House had drawn up an "enemies list" of administration adversaries in the media, the universities, and the entertainment world. These people were to be harassed by Internal Revenue Service audits and by other means.

One of the Watergate burglars, E. Howard Hunt, had forged State Department messages to implicate the late President John F. Kennedy in the assassination of Vietnamese leader Ngo Dinh Diem. This was designed to besmirch the reputation of President Kennedy's brother, Ted, a potential Nixon presidential rival.

The administration had engaged in illegal wiretapping, even of its own officials, to ferret out national security and political leaks.

The president himself had taken dubious tax breaks for contributing his personal papers to the Library of Congress and had used federal funds to make improvements on his personal homes in Florida and California.

The most telling testimony before the Ervin committee came from John Dean, who claimed that the president had known of the illegal break-in for eight months and had tried to cover it up, even offering executive clemency to the burglars if they would keep quiet. But Dean's testimony could not be corroborated. Then, on July 16, Alexander Butterfield, a former presidential assistant, revealed that since 1971 all conversations in the president's Oval Office and in the Executive Office Building had been taped, and all the president's phones had been linked to recording devices. Now, everything that John Dean and others had disclosed in their testimony could be checked against the actual record.

The president immediately tried to block access to the tapes. For a full year, until the Supreme Court announced its crucial decision against him on July 24, 1974, his lawyers asserted that "executive privilege," needed to preserve the president's freedom of action, permitted him to keep the tapes of vital White House conversations confidential.

When the Ervin committee hearings concluded, the burden of uncovering the remaining facts about the break-in and alleged cover-up shifted to special prosecutor Archibald Cox. In July, Cox subpoenaed nine tapes. Nixon refused to surrender them, and Cox went before Judge Sirica to demand that they be produced. In late August, Sirica ordered Nixon to comply. The president's lawyers promptly appealed to the District of Columbia Circuit Court, which upheld Sirica's order.

Nixon Fights Back. On October 20, 1973, Nixon ordered Attorney General Richardson to fire Cox. Richardson refused, as did his deputy, and both resigned. Solicitor General Robert Bork, now acting attorney general, finally performed the deed.

This "Saturday Night Massacre" produced a storm of criticism. The White House was deluged with telegrams denouncing the president and his actions. *Time* magazine, a conservative journal, in the first formal editorial in its fifty-year history declared "the President should resign." Even prominent Republicans began to wonder out loud whether Nixon would not have to go. On October 30 the House Judiciary Committee began to consider impeachment charges against him.

Taken aback by this ferocious reaction, Nixon retreated. On October 23 he agreed to obey Sirica's order to deliver the tapes. On November 1 he appointed a new special prosecutor, Leon Jaworski, a conservative Texas attorney. But then the president's lawyers revealed that two of the tapes requested did not exist and that another, of a crucial June conversation with Dean, contained an 18-minute gap as the result of an "accidental" erasure. By this time few Americans believed anything the president said, and most doubted that the erasure had been an accident.

Meanwhile, Vice President Agnew was having his own troubles with the law. Accused of income tax evasion and of accepting payoffs for favors to contractors when he was governor of Maryland, he resigned from office on October 10, 1973. Immediately after, under terms of the recently adopted Twenty-fifth Amendment to the Constitution, Nixon nominated House Minority Leader Gerald Ford of Michigan as Agnew's successor. Ford took the oath of office on December 6, 1973, as the new vice president. Now, if Watergate did force Nixon out, the country would at least have an honest man in his place.

Impeachment. Other bombshells soon went off. In late April 1974, in response to a subpoena from the House Judiciary Committee, Nixon released 1,200 pages of edited transcripts of White House tapes. This was the public's first glimpse of what the president and his advisers had actually been saying and doing about Watergate. The view was appalling. The transcripts revealed Nixon as a profane, confused, and bilious man, willing to use any tack against his enemies and prone to mean-spirited and bigoted remarks. Worse than this, several conversations seemed to confirm his role in abetting a cover-up.

On May 1 the House Judiciary Committee denied that the release of the edited transcripts constituted full compliance with its subpoena. Jaworski's office had also subpoenaed tapes, and on May 20 Judge Sirica ordered Nixon once more to comply. The president's counsel appealed his decision to the Supreme Court.

That uneasy summer as Americans watched the unfolding drama, matters came to a head. First, the Supreme Court unanimously ruled that Nixon must release all the tapes asked for by Jaworski. For reasons that would soon become clear, Nixon resisted the Court's order, but then relented. The process of transcribing the tapes began. On July 24 the Judiciary Committee began televised debates on articles of impeachment. A few days later it voted to recommend to the full House of Representatives three articles of impeachment: (1) that Nixon had obstructed justice by his role in the Watergate cover-up; (2) that he had misused federal agencies in violation of the rights of American citizens; and (3) that he had withheld information subpoenaed by the House Judiciary Committee. On August 5, 1974, Nixon released transcripts of three talks between him and Haldeman recorded on June 4, 1972, a scant week after the break-in. The tapes showed that the president clearly had conspired to obstruct justice. Here was the "smoking gun" that could not be explained away, and Nixon's remaining congressional supporters, including stalwart conservative Senator Barry Goldwater, now abandoned him. Facing almost certain impeachment by the full House, Nixon resigned as president on August 8 effective at noon the next day. On August 9, 1974, Gerald Ford took the oath of office as the new president.

Causes and Effects. The Watergate crisis had its roots in a complex set of circumstances. To Nixon's combative and suspicious personality must be added the growth of presidential power since the New Deal. Nixon twisted executive powers granted FDR and his successors to deal with the Great Depression, World War II, and the Cold War, and used them crudely against his political enemies. These powers, visibly manifested in the squads of planes, helicopters, limousines, and other trappings of "an imperial presidency," increased the influence and power of the executive at the expense of the other branches of government. Under Nixon the administration, moreover, confused itself with the American government itself. This position made it possible for the president and his White House inner circle to see their political opponents as national traitors entitled to no consideration. Nixon and his advisers were also victims of the paranoid Cold War mentality that at times excused unacceptable activities if done for the sake of "national security." By the early 1970s, for example, the FBI and CIA had grown into semiautonomous fiefdoms that collected vast files on private citizens considered disloyal, opened private mail, and engaged in dirty tricks operations of its own against suspected subversives. In such an atmosphere it is no wonder that the White House itself should adopt a no-holds-barred attitude toward its opponents.

The postmortems on Watergate would vary widely. Some Americans saw reasons for optimism in the outcome of Watergate. The "system had worked," they said; the villains had been caught and punished, and honest, constitutional government had been restored. Others were not so sure. Nixon had, after all, been reelected in a landslide and might easily have gotten away with it all if a very few lucky events had happened differently. Many Americans could not avoid feeling more cynical than ever about the honesty of politicians and more skeptical about the effectiveness of the nation's political system.

One thing is perfectly clear: Watergate ended whatever hope remained that Nixon would turn back the clock politically. Those voters who had believed that Nixon would lead the country back to traditional values felt bitterly betrayed. Liberals rejoiced that "Tricky Dick" had got his comeuppance.

The Ford Interlude.   America's only nonelected president, Gerald Ford, assumed office at a time when the nation desperately craved an end to distrust and uncertainty. Ford seemed the right man to start the healing process. A stolid legislator who had served in the House of Representatives for many years without special distinction, he was nevertheless an open, decent, and generous man whom most Americans quickly came to like.

The public's respect for Ford the man was not, however, matched by its view of Ford the president. Physically awkward and a wooden speaker, Ford squandered much of the public's trust at the start of his presidency by granting a pardon to Nixon, thereby cutting off any further legal action against the ex-president. Though in his remarks announcing the pardon Ford emphasized personal compassion toward Nixon and his determination to end the controversy and distrust caused by Watergate, many citizens suspected a secret agreement between the two men: Ford would get the vice presidency and promise a pardon if Nixon was forced to resign.

In foreign affairs, the area where his predecessor had achieved the most, Ford continued the initiatives of the recent past, retaining Kissinger as secretary of state and continuing to push détente. Gradually, however, high hopes for mutually advantageous arrangements with the Soviet Union dissipated. Soviet-American cultural exchanges helped dis-

pel Cold War views that Russians were ogres, but Soviet violations of its own citizens' rights and mistreatment of its Jewish population offset such gains. Besides, the Soviet Union seemed determined to pursue its expansionist ends through surrogates. When, for example, the African nation of Angola, newly independent from Portugal, collapsed into civil war, Soviet-armed Cuban troops supported the Angolan Marxists' drive to take control.

In domestic affairs Ford was even less successful. In response to a serious business recession following the spectacular hike in oil prices that accompanied the fourth Arab-Israeli war in 1973, he endorsed a tax cut and sought lower interest rates. By the fall of 1975 national output began once more to rise, but large pockets of unemployment remained.

In his early months as president, Ford had shown little interest in running for a full term. But as he settled into the job, he changed his mind and announced his candidacy for the 1976 election. By the bicentennial year the economy news to help his campaign.

The 1976 Election.   Ford supporters in 1976 believed the president deserved a vote of confidence for having restored Americans' faith in their government. But the bad smell of Watergate lingered on with many Americans convinced that Washington was tightly controlled by wheeler-dealers and politicians on the take. Even the president, though personally liked, seemed tainted by the supposed "deal" with his predecessor.

The public's disgust with the "mess in Washington" helped the nomination campaigns of two outsiders, Ronald Reagan of California and Jimmy Carter of Georgia. Reagan, a former Hollywood actor turned conservative politician, had been an effective governor of California. He had placed his conservatism aside when necessary and compromised with his opponents to get things done. Carter was an Annapolis graduate who, after a stint in the navy, had grown peanuts in Georgia and served a single term as his state's governor. A pious Baptist, his record marked him as a fair-minded man who, unlike many southern politicians of the past, hoped to end the South's racial conflicts and reduce discrimination against blacks. Neither candidate had served in Congress or the executive branch of the federal government nor had they any significant experience in foreign affairs. Both, accordingly, could claim to be untouched by the dirt that besmirched Washington insiders.

Despite the Reagan challenge, Ford got the Republican nomination at Kansas City and selected Senator Robert Dole of Kansas as his running mate. Carter won the Democratic nomination on the first ballot in New York and balanced his ticket by choosing as his partner Senator Walter Mondale of Minnesota, a liberal and a close former associate of Hubert Humphrey. In November, the support of black voters and white southerners, along with traditional Catholic and Jewish voters, helped carry the Carter-Mondale ticket to victory. At the time many observers saw the Carter-Mondale vote as a reassembly of the old New Deal coalition, and a return of the voters to a more liberal outlook. It now seems clear that it was a special case of post-Watergate disgust with the Republicans added to a temporary revival of the "solid South," which was determined to elect the only southerner since before the Civil War to win a major party nomination (if we except Lyndon Johnson, a Texan).

★ SEVENTIES' DISCONTENTS ★

Jimmy Carter had his work cut out for him. The nation he would lead was one buffeted by cross-currents, uncertainties, and uncomfortable challenges to its self-confidence and its leading position in the free world.

The celebration of the two-hundredth anniversary of American independence on July 4, 1976, was symbolic of the public's insecurities and hesitations. There had been talk of a major international exposition at Philadelphia or some other large city to proclaim, as a century before, America's achievements to all the world. It proved impossible to bring

off such a celebration. The America of 1976 was far richer than in 1876, but many people lacked the easy confidence in the political and economic future that prevailed a century earlier. The bitterness of Vietnam lingered, and thousands of antiwar movement veterans doubted that America had much to boast about. Spokespersons for blacks, Indians, and other minorities insisted that they, the perennial outsiders, had scant reason to celebrate 200 years of nationhood. The country, of course, did not let the day go unmarked. In New York City a fleet of sailing ships from all over the world drew throngs of spectators to the harbor and banks of the Hudson River. Millions more watched "the tall ships" on television. In San Antonio a longhorn cattle drive, commemorating the days of the Texas cattle trails, was the celebration centerpiece. In Washington, D.C., half a million people watched a parade down Pennsylvania Avenue. Other communities had their own moving and eye-catching ways of commemorating the great event. But all told, it seemed primarily a party by the white middle-class mainstream, with millions of others standing on the sidelines.

Blacks and Hispanics. As the 1970s began their downward slope, the predominant mood among black Americans was one of disappointment. The previous decade had promised so much and, in truth, some of it had been achieved. Legal segregation was dead. Nowhere could the

New York City, of course, was not the only community to celebrate the bicentennial of independence. But as the nation's biggest city and its media center, its "tall ships" got the most attention.

law be used to bolster exclusion of blacks from public places or services or to enforce separation of the races. Even in the South blacks voted without restraint and were becoming a force to be reckoned with in southern politics. By the early 1980s, in many big cities—Cleveland, Chicago, Washington, D.C., Los Angeles, Philadelphia, and Atlanta—the mayors would be black.

There had also been sweeping economic and social advances for black Americans. The number of black college students had risen from 141,000 in 1960 to 718,000 in 1980, a shift from about 6 percent of enrollments to almost 10 percent. Black median family income had grown from $3230 in 1960 to $12,674 in 1980. Yet the picture was at best mixed. The gains since 1960 had not ended black poverty; nor had they eliminated the differences between black and white family incomes. At the end of the 1970s the average black family was still only 60 percent as rich as its average white counterpart.

A new disturbing feature of the racial picture was the appearance of a two-tier social structure in the black community. By 1980 there was a new black middle class of professionals, government workers, skilled white-collar employees, and business managers. But at the same time there was an expanding "underclass" of unemployed ghetto-dwellers who seemed stuck in the groove of poverty, welfare, drug dependence, and—at times—crime.

Many sociologists believed that faulty family structure was the key factor in producing this result. The black mid-dle class, they said, derived primarily from intact, two-parent families; the underclass was composed primarily of mothers without husbands—many mere teenagers—and their young children. Since the 1960s single-parent, female-headed families had grown disproportionately among all social sectors in the United States as a result of soaring divorce rates and teenage pregnancy. But the phenomenon was more severe among blacks than any other group. In such one-parent families—especially those headed by young, poorly educated women—the processes of child nurture and social conditioning needed to produce competent young people were apparently absent. Family failure in turn fostered successive generations of citizens who were unable to cope with jobs or their personal lives and who became chronically dependent on social welfare services.

Unfortunately, no one knew for certain why the black family had weakened so disturbingly. Some observers blamed it on the welfare system. By encouraging dependency it accelerated the breakup of families, they said. Conservatives often blamed it on the cultural excesses of the 1960s. These allegedly had undermined conventional sexual morality and family values and condoned teenage premarital sex and teenage pregnancies. Others pointed the finger at the black middle class for failing to provide the leadership and the role models needed by the black poor. Another school ascribed it to persistent racism that permeated American society and by undermining morale con-

"Little Havana," the Cuban enclave in Miami, was refuge to thousands of middle-class people fleeing Fidel Castro's Caribbean tyranny.

tinued to hobble the ambitions of black young people. Still another class of analysts believed it derived from structural change in the economy. The jobs that paid, during the seventies, were no longer the unskilled and semiskilled labor that had served as ladders upward for working people in the past. Now, they noted, the economy needed men and women who could program computers, sell securities, draw up plans for sales campaigns, and design sophisticated machines. Those without the necessary education or work habits were inevitably relegated to dead-end jobs that provided neither the income for a reasonable family life nor the psychological and emotional bases it required. Whatever the reasons, by the 1980s it seemed that black ghetto families—with thousands of exceptions—were failing to meet the needs of their offspring and many ghetto-dwellers seemed unable to escape from poverty, illness, and despair.

Hispanic Americans, by and large, improved their lot during the 1970s, though they too remained behind the average in most measures of well-being and progress. During the decade their numbers increased enormously, both absolutely and proportionately. By 1980 over 14.5 million Americans identified themselves as of "Hispanic" origins, an increase of 61 percent for the decade. The states with the largest number were California, Texas, New York, Florida, New Jersey, and New Mexico.

Many Hispanics, including all Puerto Ricans, were American citizens by birth. Others were naturalized. But there was also a very large group of "undocumented" immigrants without visas or immigration clearances who had fled the poverty of Mexico, Central America, the Caribbean, or South America to find jobs and a better life in the United States. Many undocumented Hispanics were employed in low-paying service jobs in hospitals, restaurants, or offices, and in unskilled construction and factory work. In fact, many of these industries could not survive without them.

Though most Hispanic Americans were poor, there were pockets of notable Latin economic success. In the Miami area, for example, Cuban exiles from Castro's Marxist regime—most middle-class people with skills and capital—had reestablished themselves comfortably in their new American homes and were respected if not always liked by their "Anglo" neighbors.

Another racial group, Asians, had increased spectacularly during the 1970s. By 1980 there were 800,000 Chinese, 700,000 Japanese, 774,000 Filipinos, 350,000 Koreans, and 260,000 Vietnamese in the United States. The Asians had generally done well in their new country. Many had opened small businesses—produce stores, restaurants, dry cleaning establishments—others had become successful musicians, scientists, and computer experts. Like some white groups before them, Asians had benefited from supportive families and respect for education. Asian students

studied hard and gained admission in large numbers to the country's best colleges and universities. By the mid-1980s admissions officers at Ivy League institutions and some of the elite state universities would be accused of establishing de facto quotas for Asian-Americans to give everyone else a chance.

As in past eras, however, the newcomers to America in the sixties and seventies were not integrated into American society without friction. On the Texas Gulf Coast, "Anglo" and Vietnamese fishermen clashed in a series of violent incidents. Some middle-class people resented the academic success of Chinese and Japanese students. Hispanics too aroused rancor. In Miami, for example, blacks felt bitter about the success of the Cubans. In the Southwest and California some whites feared that Anglo ways would be submerged under a wave of illegal Hispanic immigration. In many communities in the Northeast and Southwest the use of Spanish as a language of instruction in the public schools became a divisive issue. Whites feared the displacement of English. Hispanic-Americans, on the other hand, worried about their children's loss of the Spanish language and with it their cultural heritage.

The concern over illegal immigration went beyond mere bigotry. Cheap imported labor promised to depress American wage standards; the immigrants, some said, would overburden welfare services. In fact, there was evidence that the undocumented immigrants paid more in taxes to federal and local governments than they received in benefits. And besides, in most cases they performed the unskilled, often dirty jobs, that native-born Americans would not take. Yet it seemed clear that the nation could not tolerate borders that anyone could cross at will, and some controls had to be extended over immigration. In 1986 Congress passed the Simpson-Rodino Act imposing fines on employers who hired undocumented immigrants, but at the same time granting a general amnesty to all illegal immigrants who had arrived in the United States before January 1, 1982. The law required that newcomers apply for amnesty, but compliance was slow, and it was not clear whether the measure would end the frustration many Americans felt about unregulated immigration.

Women. In some ways the most important social issues of the 1970s concerned women. In the early 1960s feminists had argued that women should be free to choose roles other than that of "homemaker." By the late 1970s thousands had by entering the labor market in record numbers. In 1965, some 37 percent of all women over sixteen were employed; by 1978 the figure was 50 percent. Single women had worked in substantial numbers for many years. The new working woman contingent for the first time, however, included thousands of married women with children. Only

During the 1970s women even made it to West Point, the U.S. Military Academy, where the nation trains its future army officers.

19 percent of women with children under age six had worked in 1960; by 1980 the figure had reached 45 percent.

Many of these jobs represented serious careers. Women in record numbers flooded into law, medicine, science, college teaching, journalism, computer programming, and other professional fields. They also flocked to the graduate business schools and joined large firms as executive trainees. By the mid-1980s, the list of women who had attained prominent positions in business, professional life, and government service had grown long indeed: Jeane Kirkpatrick, Ambassador to the United Nations; Governor Ella Grasso of Connecticut; Mayor Jayne Byrne of Chicago; Sandra Day O'Connor, associate justice of the U.S. Supreme Court; Geraldine Ferraro, Democratic vice presidential candidate in 1984; Hannah Gray, president of the University of Chicago; Sherry Lansing, executive of Twentieth-Century-Fox. Even the military service academies at West Point, Annapolis, and Colorado Springs opened their doors to women in the 1970s, as did the armed services in all their branches, except a few involving direct combat.

Yet women had not reached equality with men in the job market. Women's salaries were lower, and relatively few women were found in top-executive positions. Women activists charged that the major cause of this shortfall was "sexism"—sex discrimination. And clearly there was some of this, especially in subtle forms. But others pointed to women's delayed educations, greater job instability, and overall lower expectations as important factors in slowing their advance.

The flood of women into the labor market inevitably imposed strains on society as a whole. Increasingly, the "typical" American family no longer consisted of dependent children, a working father, and a mother at home to do the family cooking and cleaning. By the late 1970s only one in five families followed this pattern, and many conservative observers wondered what the change would do to child-

Congresswoman Geraldine Ferraro was the first woman ever to receive a major party vice presidential nomination. It did not help the ticket; the Democrats were defeated.

rearing practices and the shape of family dynamics. Feminists and liberals demanded better and cheaper child-care facilities so that mothers could work without fear that their children's health, safety, and development would suffer.

Marriage patterns changed too. During the 1970s marriage seemed to be going out of style. In 1960, there were 148 marriages for every 1,000 women between the ages of fifteen and forty-four. By 1980 there were only 108. To some extent this change reflected the replacement of the legal spouse with the "live-in" partner with no necessary net loss of stability. In many cases, however, it represented a decline in real commitment by young people to permanent relationships. And even among the legally married, commitment was down. In 1960 the divorce rate had been 2.2 percent per thousand people. By 1970 it reached 3.5 percent, and by 1980 had climbed to 5.2 percent. In 1980 there was almost one divorce for every two marriages, twice the proportion of twenty years earlier.

Families were not only less stable; they were also smaller. The baby boom of the 1950s and 1960s was over. In 1960 there had been almost 24 births per thousand Americans. In 1970 this figure was down to 18.4. In 1976 it had further fallen to 14.8. Social observers speculated on the reasons for the birthrate decline. Some emphasized the selfishness of many young adults, especially the "Yuppies," young, upwardly mobile professionals. Children cost money and interfered with career goals, especially of female Yuppies. Others saw it as an inevitable product of a rich, advanced urban society. It was part of a long-term trend, they said, only briefly interrupted by the post–World War II baby boom, and it was worse in other advanced industrial nations like West Germany and Japan than in the United States.

Affirmative Action.   Despite the efforts of the "disadvantaged" to achieve equality, then, racial minorities and women continued to occupy positions below white males on the economic ladder. Ending discrimination by itself was not enough, argued some activists and social critics. Minorities and women had suffered so much from past bias, that even if overt discrimination were totally eliminated these groups would not be able to catch up in the foreseeable future. What was needed was not merely *equal opportunity*, but *equal results*. This required, at least as a temporary measure, "affirmative action"—that is, giving preferential treatment to minorities and women in job hiring, promotions, and admissions to training, apprenticeship, and professional programs.

Affirmative action was beset by difficulties. Should all employers or institutions be automatically compelled to prove they gave preferential treatment to minorities, or only those that provably practiced discrimination? And how could such proof be established? Was it sufficient to show that given employers had fewer minority employees than their general proportion of the population, or did intent to discriminate have to be demonstrated? Opponents of affirmative action called it reverse discrimination. Not only did it disregard "merit" as the measure of success; it also hurt those who, by accident of birth, did not belong to officially designated disadvantaged groups. It was, moreover, inherently sexist and racist because it assumed that members of such groups could not make it on their own in America as others had in the past. Opponents also claimed that it stigmatized those accorded special treatment as people who did not fully deserve their success. Most deplorable of all, in the view of affirmative action's enemies, were hard "quotas"—fixed numerical or proportional requirements for hiring, promoting, or admitting specific groups without regard to other considerations. If quotas became the norm, they said, success in life would become primarily a function of biology.

Despite the opposition, under Nixon's labor secretary, George Shultz, the government established affirmative action plans for blacks and selected ethnic groups in all firms submitting bids for government contracts (the Revised Philadelphia Plan). These firms, as well as labor unions, would have to seek out minority workers or members aggressively. During the 1970s the policy was further extended by federal court interpretation to women and then applied to a host of additional private firms, to universities, to foundations, and to other employers. Opponents challenged the principle in court with mixed results. In the *Bakke* decision of 1978 the Supreme Court struck down a University of California Medical School affirmative action rule that denied admission to a white applicant—Allan Bakke—while accepting less qualified nonwhites. Yet the Court did not declare affirmative action invalid, only that the university's method of achieving it—through a rigid quota system—was illegal. The following year, in the *Weber* case, the Court ruled that private employers could adopt voluntary affirmative action plans to eliminate "manifest racial imbalance."

Women's groups in the 1980s sought to establish another principle, "comparable worth," to improve women's relative economic standing. Claiming that many traditional women's jobs—secretarial, teaching, and so forth—paid less than many jobs traditionally held by men—truck driving, plumbing, construction work, for example—though requiring no less training, skill, or general competence, they demanded that employers be required by law to equalize pay scales. Critics said comparable worth was a purely subjective concept fraught with difficulties. It would be expensive, hurt men, and applying it, moreover, would amount to imposing administered wages on the nation. Yet by the mid-1980s several state governments had adopted the scheme for their employees over the protest of many taxpayers.

ERA and Abortion. The hottest social issues of the seventies and eighties were the Equal Rights Amendment and abortion.

First officially proposed by Alice Paul's National Woman's Party in the 1920s, the ERA stated simply that "equality of rights under the law shall not be denied on account of sex." Introduced into every session of Congress from 1923 onward, it had been rejected many times. In 1972, with the new feminism gathering momentum, Congress finally approved it by the constitutionally required two-thirds majority and sent it along for ratification to the legislatures of the states.

At first the ratification process moved swiftly. Thirty-two of the necessary thirty-eight states approved the amendment in a little over a year. Then the opposition began to rally. In early 1973 Phyllis Schlafly, a lawyer and mother of six, organized a "Stop ERA" campaign. Schlafly and her allies attacked the amendment as damaging to women's rights in divorce, claimed that it mandated women's military service in the event of war, and even asserted that it precluded separate male and female public bathrooms. The opponents of ERA touched a deep pool of antifeminist feeling in women themselves. Studies would show that wives and mothers not working outside the home, and even many who did solely for the income, often viewed feminists as hostile to the family values and personal relationships that gave their own lives worth. The state ratifications soon ceased and several states even rescinded their earlier approval. By 1979, the original expiration date, ERA had still not gotten the three-fourths vote it needed. Congress extended the deadline for another three and a half years, but it still failed to get the requisite adoptions. In 1982 ERA was declared dead, though it remained on the feminist agenda for the future.

The abortion issue provoked still stronger reactions. On one side of the question were those who applauded the 1973 Supreme Court decision, *Roe v. Wade*, legalizing abortion during the first three months of pregnancy. The pro-abortion forces—a coalition of feminists and liberals—considered the decision a rational extension of the right of privacy and a validation of an individual woman's right "to control her own body." They called their position "pro-choice." Opponents of legal abortion—traditional Catholics, evangelical Protestants, Orthodox Jews, and political conservatives—called abortion murder. They identified themselves as "pro-life." There were many positions in between these extremes, and most Americans probably be-

Not all women liked the new feminism. Phyllis Schlafly, herself a successful lawyer, was one who objected to most of the feminist agenda.

Roe v. Wade

In 1973 the United States Supreme Court issued a momentous decision striking down a Texas statute making abortion a crime. A pregnant unmarried woman, given the name Jane Roe to protect her identity, who wanted an abortion had sued the Dallas district attorney in 1970, claiming that the Texas antiabortion law was a violation of her right to privacy under the federal Constitution. The case was finally decided in the Supreme Court by an opinion written by Associate Justice Harry Blackmun.

Justice Blackmun not only struck down the Texas law but all others with similar provisions, arguing that they were medically out of date, that they no longer expressed the common view of the community, and that they did indeed violate the constitutional rights of pregnant women to privacy. Though the decision did not make all abortions legal, it did open the door to widespread use of abortion to limit births and thereby created a major social controversy that still roils the nation.

"In view of all this, we do not agree that, by adopting one theory of life, Texas may override the rights of the pregnant woman that are at stake. We repeat, however, that the State does have an important and legitimate interest in preserving and protecting the health of the pregnant woman, whether she be a resident of the State or a nonresident who seeks medical consultation and treatment there, and that it has still *another* important and legitimate interest in protecting the potentiality of human life. These interests are separate and distinct. Each grows in substantiality as the woman approaches term and, at a point during pregnancy, each becomes 'compelling.'

"With respect to the State's important and legitimate interest in the health of the mother, the 'compelling' point, in the light of present medical knowledge, is at approximately the end of the first trimester. This is so because of the now-established medical fact, referred to above . . . , that until the end of the first trimester mortality in abortion may be less than mortality in normal childbirth. It follows that, from and after this point, a State may regulate the abortion procedure to the extent that the regulation reasonably relates to the preservation and protection of maternal health. Examples of permissible state regulation in this area are requirements as to the qualifications of the person who is to perform the abortion; as to the licensure of that person; as to the facility in which the procedure is to be performed, that is, whether it must be a hospital or may be a clinic or some other place of less-than-hospital status; as to the licensing of the facility; and the like.

"This means, on the other hand, that, for the period of pregnancy prior to this 'compelling' point, the attending physician, in consultation with his patient, is free to determine, without regulation by the State, that, in his medical judgment, the patient's pregnancy should be terminated. If that decision is reached, the judgment may be effectuated by an abortion free of interference by the State.

"With respect to the State's important and legitimate interest in potential life, the 'compelling' point is at viability. This is so because the fetus then presumably has the capability of meaningful life outside the mother's womb. State regulation protective of fetal life after viability thus has both logical and biological justifications. If the State is interested in protecting fetal life after viability, it may go so far as to proscribe abortion during that period, except when it is necessary to preserve the life or health of the mother.

"Measured against these standards, Art. 1196 of the Texas Penal Code, in restricting legal abortions to those 'procured or attempted by medical advice for the purpose of saving the life of the mother,' sweeps too broadly. The statute makes no distinction between abortions performed early in pregnancy and those performed later, and it limits to a single reason, 'saving' the mother's life, the legal justification for the procedure. The statute, therefore, cannot survive the constitutional attack made upon it here."

longed somewhere in the middle, accepting abortion as desirable under many circumstances, but deploring its necessity.

From 1973 on, antiabortionists sought to limit women's access to abortion in several ways: by requiring that minors obtain prior parental consent to the procedure; by denying welfare recipients the right to federally subsidized abortions; by trying to limit conditions under which abortions could be legally obtained to cases where the pregnancy resulted from rape or incest, or where the birth threatened the life of the mother. By the end of the 1970s pro-lifers were demanding passage of the Human Life Amendment, a measure to prohibit abortion and place it beyond the jurisdiction of the courts and also to forbid some forms of birth control.

In the 1980 elections the bitter abortion debate would turn several local and state campaigns into single-issue battles. Interest groups devoted solely to the antiabortion po-

Militant "pro-choice" advocates parading in the early 1970s in New York. Note the "laissez-faire" sign at left. Was this an appeal to economic conservatives?

sition would spend large sums to convince voters to support selected candidates on the basis of their abortion stands. Later in the decade there would be a rash of abortion clinic bombings instigated by extreme pro-life militants frustrated by their inability to stop by legal means what they considered a "slaughter of the innocents."

The "Me" Generation. While some Americans continued to do battle over major social and political issues, others turned away from public concerns and issues. Some retreat was probably inevitable given the intense social activism of the 1960s, but it was also encouraged by the unusual difficulty of the problems of the seventies and early eighties. Unable to find easy formulas to inform their responses to pressing public issues, many people simply turned to cultivating their personal gardens. The journalist Tom Wolfe called the mid-1970s the era of the "me generation," a period when people placed personal fulfillment and pleasure before other considerations. Historian Christopher Lasch called the phenomenon the "new narcissism," a mood, he said, that suited the new "age of diminishing expectations." Lasch was obviously mistaken in his diagnosis, for in the form of the Yuppie the selfish mood would afflict young men and women even in the prosperous mid-1980s.

One sign of the new narcissism was the extraordinary new interest in physical culture. Americans had long allowed their health to suffer through lack of exercise and poor eating habits, and no doubt reformation was long overdue. By itself, however, this did not explain the remarkable interest in "natural" diets, "working out," and jogging that appeared in the late 1970s. Another cause of the health-exercise craze was the new obsession with self. Still another manifestation of this "me" mood was the growth of a multitude of new psychological mental health therapies. Affluent young urbanites flocked to teachers of "primal scream," EST, Rolfing, and other therapeutic programs that promised emotional comfort or personal fulfillment. Others sought satisfaction in one of the host of new religious cults such as Sun Myung Moon's Unification Church, L. Ron Hubbard's Scientology, Baghwan Shree Ravneesh's Oregon commune, the Hari Krishnas, or Jim Jones's People's Temple. Cults provided many young men and women with a sense of purpose and community. They also lent themselves to fraud, manipulation, charlatanism, and fanaticism. Americans would be deeply shocked when, in November 1979, over 900 of Jones's American followers committed mass suicide in their settlement in Guyana at the behest of their unbalanced leader.

Sun Belt versus Snow Belt.   One of the most important social trends of the seventies and early eighties was the shift of population, wealth, and leadership from the long-dominant northeastern quarter of the country—the so-called Snow Belt—to the South and West—the Sun Belt.

For a century or more the region stretching from southern New England through the Middle Atlantic states and on through the Old Northwest had been the richest, most populous, and culturally creative part of the United States. It had harbored the nation's most productive industries—clothing, steel, textiles, automobiles, electronics, rubber. Its largest cities had been the centers of the nation's cultural life, sheltering its major museums, universities, publishing houses, symphony orchestras, theater, and dance companies.

The balance began to shift during the 1960s and accelerated thereafter. As more and more Americans retired to live on pensions, they chose to leave behind the cold winters of the Northeast and Midwest. Immense retirement communities sprang up in California, Florida, and Arizona. Industry, too, particularly light industry and industry connected with defense, found the warmer climate, abundant land, cheaper nonunionized labor, and lower taxes of the South and West an advantage. Under four presidents from the region—Lyndon Johnson of Texas, Richard Nixon and Ronald Reagan of California, and Jimmy Carter of Georgia—government seemed to favor the Sun Belt through tax and defense-contract policies. Texas, Louisiana, and California, for a time, would also profit from the energy crisis of the late 1970s. With their large reserves of oil and natural gas,

these states could offer cheap energy to business and individuals alike. Congress magnified this advantage when it decontrolled most natural gas and petroleum prices in 1978. Though the avowed purpose of the decontrol measure was to encourage greater energy exploration and production, one effect promised to be an enormous transfer of income from energy consumers in the Snow Belt to energy producers in the South and West.

All this was anticipated by economists as early as the 1960s, but the message was driven home by the figures provided by the twentieth census. The preliminary results, announced on the last day of 1980, showed small increases, or even declines, in the populations of the northeastern and midwestern states during the previous decade. By contrast, already massive California grew by 17.7 percent; Nevada by almost 64 percent; Texas by 26.4 percent; Arizona by almost 53 percent, and Florida by more than 41 percent. While the population of many older Snow Belt cities stagnated or declined, Phoenix, Albuquerque, Tucson, Houston, Dallas, San Antonio, Miami, Tampa, San Diego, and San Jose leaped ahead. For the first time in history, moreover, the nation's population center had moved west of the Mississippi River, to southeast Missouri.

The statistics both confirmed previous trends and foreshadowed new ones. Political power would clearly shift with population. When Congress was reapportioned, New York, Illinois, Ohio, and Pennsylvania would lose seats in the House of Representatives, and Texas, California, Florida, and Arizona would gain several seats each. Because the newer regions were more conservative politically than

This spectacular city-scape (Houston, Texas) suggests how scarce oil in the 1970s benefited the oil-rich Sun Belt region.

the older Snow Belt, this obviously meant a rightward trend in the nation's political climate. Besides politics, the nation's cultural life was certain to be affected. Already the Snow Belt's near-monopoly of high culture—painting, music, dance, and theater—had been loosened, partly through the National Endowment for the Arts and its counterpart in scholarship and literature, the National Endowment for the Humanities. Since their founding in 1965 as part of Lyndon Johnson's Great Society, these two federally funded bodies had pumped large sums of money into universities, theatrical and dance companies, and orchestras located outside the old Snow Belt cultural centers. Their efforts had been effective. By the early 1980s, universities in the Mountain states, Texas, and the Far West were matching the prestige and creativity of those of the East, while local culture in the Sun Belt was flourishing as never before.

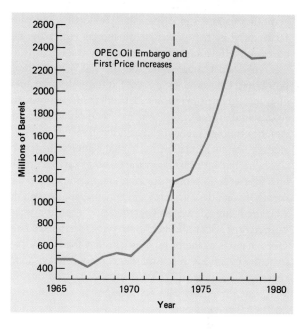

American oil imports, 1966–1979. (*Source: Statistical Abstract of the United States 1980*).

★ THE ENERGY CRISIS AND THE SEVENTIES' ECONOMIC MALAISE ★

The growth of the Sun Belt and decline of the Snow Belt were tied to profound problems facing the United States in the 1970s. The country was perturbed not only by the Vietnam defeat, Watergate, and social strife, but also by an acute energy crisis.

Oil and the American Way of Life. For Americans, the "pursuit of happiness" has traditionally meant the quest for increasing material abundance based on advanced technology and industrial preeminence. In the 1970s, however, the world's industrialized nations confronted the problem of growing resource dearth. Such crucial metals as platinum, silver, tin, copper, and nickel—all needed in modern industrial products and processes—seemed to grow scarcer. Most serious was the oil shortage. To many Americans in the late 1970s the mile-long lines to buy scarce gasoline at prices soaring into the stratosphere seemed to foretell the end of an affluence they had come to accept as part of their national heritage.

The energy problem had evolved over several decades. By the post–World War II era, energy in the rich industrial nations had become synonymous with oil, and by the 1950s much of the world's supply came from the Middle East. The oil wells were located primarily in Saudi Arabia, Kuwait, Iran, and Iraq, but their contents were extracted, refined, and marketed by seven giant Western oil companies, five of them American. These companies had helped finance and develop the oil fields and for many years took the lion's share of the revenues they yielded.

After World War II the collapse of Western hegemony and the growing militancy of Arab nationalism led the Middle Eastern rulers to reconsider their agreements with the Western oil companies. This impulse toward economic self-assertion was influenced by the Arab confrontation with Israel, viewed by Arab nationalists as a Western neocolonial intrusion into Islam. At first the Middle Eastern rulers demanded and got an increase in the royalties they received from the Western oil companies. Then, in 1960, the major oil-producing nations, led by the Middle Eastern countries, organized a cartel, the Organization of Petroleum Exporting Countries (OPEC), for the purpose of setting world petroleum prices and greatly increasing the profit for themselves.

In the early 1970s political and economic events aided OPEC's monopoly pricing effort. The Western nations, including the United States, increased their oil consumption, becoming ever more dependent on imported energy sources. In the years between 1971 and 1973 alone, America quadrupled its oil imports, mostly from the Middle East. The flood of American demand would help create a world seller's market.

Then, in October 1973, two Arab nations, Egypt and Syria, suddenly attacked Israel. The OPEC nations were meeting in Vienna during the October War, and when the United States backed Israel the OPEC countries responded furiously by boosting the price of oil from $3 to $5 a barrel and announcing an oil embargo against the United States and other nations supporting Israel. Suddenly the United States faced its first peacetime oil shortage since the discovery of petroleum more than a century before.

The uncomfortable winter of 1973–1974, with its cold homes and long gas lines, passed. But the embargo made it clear that America had become dependent for energy on the Arab world. The October War itself had other effects on America's energy situation. After heavy casualties on both sides the conflict ended with a United Nations–supervised cease-fire but no decrease in the hostility between Arabs and Israelis and no prospect for a long-term peace settlement. Though the Egyptians and Syrians had not won the war, their limited success had increased Arab unity and buoyed Arab self-confidence. In the years that followed, the OPEC nations would be far more effective than in the past in acting in concert to control the oil market. Their dominance of a resource vital to the West and their hostility toward an American ally—Israel—raised the ominous prospect that they would someday be able to hold American foreign policy hostage. Soon after the October War, President Nixon announced that the United States would begin working toward energy independence.

Energy Alternatives.   For a time the energy crisis forced Americans to consider their future as a people of plenty. Some concluded that we must accept "limits." The United States, they said, had been living beyond its means for many years. Now the age of abundance was over. Some of this school anticipated a "no-growth economy" and predicted that the country would face years of rising social tensions as groups fought over their slices of a diminished economic pie. Environmentalists were a prominent faction within the limits circle. Some seemed almost to welcome the oil crunch. The energy crisis, they said, demonstrated the need to keep population growth low and find ways to conserve energy and resources. By changing our goals from crude expansion of GNP to other, more ecologically sound priorities, we could avoid disappointment and frustration, they promised.

At the other extreme were those who refused to face the facts of change. Some of these people believed that the oil companies had contrived the energy shortage to increase their profits. Others blamed the continuing dearth on the environmentalists who, they said, resisted every attempt to find new energy sources in the name of safety or ecological balance.

Whatever their conclusions, the energy crisis reinforced Americans' sense of malaise brought on by the Vietnam defeat and Watergate. Besides impotence abroad and corruption at home, it seemed we now had to face for the first time the possibility of long-term material limits. America appeared to have passed its prime; it could no longer achieve all the goals it set for itself.

Such signs plagued American motorists in the summer 1979. The 1979 gas famine, caused in part by the overthrow of the shah in revolutionary Iran, pointed up the long-term energy crisis the nation faced.

In its actual energy policies the government pursued a middle course. Congress clamped a fifty-five-mile-per-hour speed limit on drivers and prescribed minimum gas mileage requirements for car manufacturers. It offered tax credits to homeowners who insulated their houses to conserve fuel. It also passed measures to encourage the development of alternative energy sources, such as geothermal, wind, and solar power. In July 1979, President Jimmy Carter would ask Congress to fund a synthetic fuels program to free Americans from dependence on foreign energy sources.

Americans also conducted a major debate over nuclear power. Lauded by some as the complete solution to America's energy problems, nuclear power came under increasing fire on environmental and safety grounds as the seventies advanced. The critics' arguments were given frightening relevance by an accident at Three Mile Island nuclear power plant near Harrisburg, Pennsylvania, in March 1979, which for a time threatened to produce a "meltdown" of the nuclear core. Had that occurred, thousands of lives might have been lost and property in the billions contaminated for decades.

An air view of the Three Mile Island nuclear reactor in Pennsylvania a few days after it malfunctioned and scared the wits out of millions of Americans.

The near disaster intensified the nuclear power debate. Supporters of nuclear energy pointed out that the overall safety record of the industry had been good. Opponents insisted that the accident confirmed the unsuitability of the nuclear solution of the energy problem. Moreover, power from the atom raised difficult issues of nuclear waste disposal. During the next few years environmentalists, organized in various "alliances," conducted a crusade against nuclear power that helped delay construction of new plants and imposed stricter safety standards on old ones. The assault raised the costs of construction so that by the 1980s the building of new nuclear power plants stopped, and several almost completed plants had to be abandoned.

Turmoil in the Economy. The public's disquiet over energy and environmental problems was enormously magnified by the relentless rise in general consumer prices. By mid-1979 the average American family had to earn almost double its 1970 dollar income to achieve the same standard of living. In effect, the value of the dollar had fallen to half its worth from a decade before.

By the end of the decade inflation had become self-perpetuating. People asked: "Why wait to buy when the price will only be higher tomorrow?" This attitude sent millions of Americans rushing off to department stores and discount houses to snap up appliances, clothing, sports equipment, and goods of every kind with their credit cards. The buying spree added fuel to the inflationary surge. It also reduced personal savings. There was little incentive to put money into savings accounts when the gain from interest earned was certain to be more than offset by its loss of value. The drop in personal savings in turn reduced the pool of funds available for building new houses, factories, and equipment and thus slowed the rate of growth in output. It also made the United States increasingly dependent on foreign sources of capital for financing private industry and even to help service the large federal debt.

Experts puzzled over the causes of the inflation. Many pointed to the skyrocketing energy costs that entered into the prices of all goods and services. Others emphasized rising wages. Labor was able to extract higher wages from employers without commensurate increases in labor productivity, and these costs could be simply passed along to consumers because in many areas competition was purely nominal. Still others took their cue from the conservative economist Milton Friedman, who insisted that an excess of cheap money and credit, permitted by the Federal Reserve system and reinforced by large federal deficits, explained the powerful inflation surge.

One difficulty in dealing with inflation was that keeping prices low seemed to depend on keeping unemployment high. Prices would come down only if the economy flattened. Cutbacks in government spending would reduce overall demand for goods and services. Increases in interest rates would discourage investment and consumer buying. Both together should push up the jobless rate, but at the same time reduce inflation. Many liberals opposed such policies for that very reason. Better higher prices than mass unemployment, they argued.

But the argument seemed pointless. Inflation versus unemployment was a formula that no longer seemed to work. At the end of the 1960s the unemployment rate had been less than 4 percent. By 1975 it was up to almost 8 percent. Thereafter it fell, but in 1980 it rose again, averaging over 7 percent of the labor force. In past eras, with so many wage earners out of work, prices would fall or at least remain level. Now, however, unemployment was accompanied by continued inflation.

The combination of high inflation and high unemployment, called *stagflation* by phrase-makers, could not easily be explained. Some experts claimed it was a false problem. Unemployment was actually not as great as it seemed. Many of the unemployed were now women who moved into and out of the job market with great frequency. This flux raised the unemployment figures, but the joblessness of such workers did not affect prices as would un-

The handsome, articulate mayor of San Antonio, Henry Cisneros, a symbol of Hispanic-American progress. He would become President Clinton's secretary of housing and urban development in 1993.

A combination of "Pacific Rim" competition and the tight money policies after 1979 to stop inflation produced long lines at the unemployment insurance offices. Detroit, the nation's auto capital, was especially hard hit.

Yo-yo Ma

Asian-Americans have achieved renown in science, technology, medicine, and music. In the international musical world few, however, have won such universal acclaim as the Paris-born cellist of Chinese ancestry, Yo-yo Ma, who now makes his home in Winchester, Massachusetts.

Yo-yo Ma's paternal grandparents were landowners in Ningbo, a city south of Shanghai, but his father, Hiao-tsiun Ma, loved music and chose it as his profession. Ma senior learned to play the violin and became a professor of music at Nanjing University. In 1936, troubled by the increasing cultural and political instability in China, he emigrated to Paris. Yo-yo Ma's mother, Marina, a mezzo-soprano from Hong Kong, and a former student in Hiao-tsiun Ma's music-theory class at Nanjing, moved to Paris in 1949. They were married there soon after and in 1951 had a daughter; in 1955, they had a son. In Chinese tradition, all family members from the same generation share the same written character in their names, in this case *Yo*, which means "friendship." Their daughter was named Yeou-cheng and their son Yo-yo. *Ma* means "horse."

Yo-yo Ma describes his parents as two very different people. His father was the rational, systematic, and intellectual parent; his mother the more passionate one. They even spoke two different dialects of Chinese. Hiao-tsiun instructed his children in French history, Chinese mythology, and calligraphy. Naturally, he also taught them music, using a system for teaching very young children to play by intense short practice stints rather than long hours at their instruments. Yeou-cheng learned the violin but later gave up her musical career to become a pediatrician. Yo-yo Ma selected the cello and at the age of four he amazed his teacher

by playing a Bach suite. At five, the little boy, playing both cello and piano, gave his first public recital at the University of Paris.

In 1962, the Ma family moved to New York, where Hiao-tsiun took a job at a school for musically talented children and shortly after established the Children's Orchestra of New York. Meanwhile, his son kept astounding the critics with his extraordinary talent and ended up studying with two acclaimed cellists, Leonard Rose of the internationally famous Juilliard School of Music, and Janos Scholz. In 1963, Leonard Bernstein, the composer and then conductor of the New York Philharmonic, invited Yo-yo to appear on the nationally televised *American Pageant of the Arts*, a money-raiser for the future John F. Kennedy Center for the Performing Arts in Washington, D.C. Yo-yo made his Carnegie Hall debut at nine years of age. At fifteen he performed the Saint-Saens concerto with the San Francisco Symphony. In 1968, he entered the Professional Children's School, skipping two years and graduating from high school when he was fifteen.

Enrolling in Juilliard's college division for the fall, Yo-yo Ma spent the summer at Meadowmount, a music camp in the Adirondacks. This was his first experience away from home and he went wild, missing rehearsals, leaving his cello outside in the rain, drinking, painting graffiti, and going for midnight swims. Yo-yo Ma attributes his rebellion partly to the strain of growing up with two contradictory cultures. At home, like other Chinese children, he had to obey family rules, live within a rigidly structured framework, and submerge his individuality. At school, he was free to explore his identity. At home, he spoke only Chinese and was constantly reminded

of his Chinese ancestry and traditions. "But I was also American," Yo-yo told an interviewer for the *New Yorker* magazine, "growing up with American values." Today, he is embarrassed by his teenage escapades. In America they would have been considered standard adolescent pranks; they were taken much more seriously by his Chinese parents.

Rather than focusing exclusively on his musical career, Yo-yo decided to go to college. He entered Columbia University, while continuing to study at Juilliard, and lived at home. This arrangement seemed too much like high school to him, however, and after visiting his sister at Radcliffe, he transferred to Harvard. There he kept up his musical career, while undertaking a full-time academic program, studying history, anthropology, literature, science, sociology, and math. He explains his ability to combine both academic courses and music by his fitful work habits. He worked in waves, sometimes staying up far into the night to write a paper, at other times practicing more diligently than usual if a concert was in the offing. During this period, he later admitted, his standards for both his studies and his performances were not as high as they should have been. On the other hand, he says, going to Harvard was the "best decision" he ever made because it expanded his education and his world in a way that no musical conservatory could have done.

While at Harvard, Yo-yo continued to do concerts, playing on campus as well as accepting professional engagements elsewhere. He gave solo recitals and performed in chamber music and orchestral concerts with student and faculty musicians. He formed a student trio with pianist Richard Kogan and violinist Lynn Chang. On many weekends he performed in the Boston suburbs where he often tried out new musical compositions, and for four summers he went to the Marlboro Festival in Vermont where he met the legendary cellist Pablo Casals, then in his mid-nineties. He played in the orchestra with Casals conducting and says it was "an inspiration for a lifetime." During his college years, he also made his debut in London with the Royal Philharmonic as the soloist in the "Elgar Cello Concerto." He was soon getting so many requests to perform that he realized he could make a good living as a cellist and considered dropping out of Harvard. His father exhorted him to stay and insisted that he limit the number of engagements to one a month. As a good Chinese son he obeyed. He graduated from Harvard with a B.A. in humanities in 1976 and in 1991 the university awarded him an honorary doctorate in music. Yo-yo also spent three years as an artist-in-residence at Harvard's Leverett House.

Though dedicated to his music and his career, Yo-yo had a personal life as well. The first summer at Marlboro, he renewed his acquaintance with Jill Hornor, a sophomore at Mount Holyoke, who had signed on as a festival administrator. That summer's friendship evolved into love on Yo-yo's part. But when he first worked up the courage to tell her how he felt, she told him she considered him a cherished younger brother. By the time Yo-yo en-

tered Harvard, Hornor had gone to Paris for her junior year abroad. The infatuated young man wrote her every day and ran up exorbitant bills as he burned up the transatlantic telephone wires. His unceasing efforts changed her feelings and soon his love was reciprocated. After Mount Holyoke, Jill went to graduate school at Cornell, in Ithaca, New York, studying German literature, while Yo-yo was finishing up at Harvard. In the spring of 1977, he bought a wedding ring. Then he called Jill and told her to be at her house at seven that evening but he did not tell her why. He took the next bus to Ithaca, rang her doorbell, got down on his knees and proposed. She agreed to marry him.

The year 1978 was a momentous one for Yo-yo Ma. He won the Avery Fisher Prize, one of the most prestigious in classical music. Ever since the prize had been established three years earlier it had been awarded to multiple winners. But Yo-yo seemed so far ahead of any of his competitors that the honor was accorded to him alone. Designed to give outstanding young instrumentalists the chance to perform with major orchestras, the prize included commitments to play with the New York Philharmonic and the Chamber Music Society of Lincoln Center.

On May 20, 1978, Yo-yo married Jill, his long-time love. The marriage to an American woman from New England

created strains between Yo-yo and his parents. They did not disapprove of Jill personally, but they feared that her Western upbringing would conflict with the Chinese family structure, where obedience to the wife's in-laws is part of the heritage. They also worried that the children of a Chinese-American intermarriage would drift even further from the Chinese heritage. Hiao-tsiun was particularly upset and was alienated for a while from his son. By the time the couple's children, Nicholas and Emily, were born, however, Yo-yo parents had come to appreciate Jill and accept the situation. When Yo-yo and Jill celebrated their tenth anniversary, Yo-yo's parents, then living in Taiwan part of the time, came back to the United States to join the festivities.

When Yo-yo was twenty-four he had an operation on his spine. He had been suffering from scoliosis for many years, and this condition, a curvature of the spine, was probably worsened by the position in which a cellist plays his instrument. The medical procedure was anything but routine. If certain nerves were damaged during the operation he might be unable to play. Still, he had little choice; his spine was so bent that if allowed to worsen it would press on internal organs.

For six months afterward the operation, Yo-yo was in an upper-body cast to keep his spine completely rigid. Happily, his wife brought his cello to

---

employment among high-salaried workers who were the chief support of their families.

Another explanation of the high unemployment rates in the face of rising prices emphasized the poor fit between skills and the kind of jobs available. The complex economy of the 1970s and early 1980s required highly trained people—men and women who could operate computers, perform experiments, write reports, design equipment, do market research. By the late 1970s there were some 25 million people classified as "technical, professional, managerial, and administrative" workers. This "new class" was affluent and enjoyed a low

unemployment rate. But millions of Americans, especially among minorities, lacked these skills and could find no place in the new "high-tech" economy no matter how much demand pressure consumers displayed for goods and services.

Liberals advocated major government retraining programs to teach the new technical skills. Conservatives pointed out that such programs were certain to be expensive, and because deficit spending was one source of inflationary pressure, the process might be self-defeating. Clearly the nation faced a dilemma: It could have full employment, but apparently only at the expense of more severe inflation.

the hospital and the doctors found a way to cut the cast so he could practice. During his recuperation, while the results were still uncertain, Yo-yo contemplated what he would do with his life if his musical career were terminated. One of the things he considered was social work because of his great love for people. Luckily for both him and the music world the operation was a success; his fingers were not affected and his cello playing was as accomplished as ever.

When he fully recovered, his concert career took off and soon he was playing all over the world in solo recitals, chamber music performances, and duets with his good friend, the pianist Emanuel Ax, whom he had met at Marlboro. Yo-yo Ma has been on the road almost continuously since then. In 1986 and 1987 he went to China where he spent hectic days playing concertos and meeting his father's colleagues from forty years before. He was made an honorary professor at the Shanghai Conservatory where he gave a master class. By the mid-1980s he had achieved "superstar" status, selling out concert halls for his performances and winning eight Grammy Awards. He is acclaimed internationally as a spokesman for classical music and its essential place in society.

Concertizing is only one ingredient in Yo-yo Ma's musical life. He finds it fulfilling to teach and nurture young musicians. One of his favorite haunts is Tanglewood in Lenox, Massachusetts, the summer home of the Boston Symphony Orchestra where he invariably gives one or two performances in July and August. At Tanglewood he also teaches the cello to young musicians from all over the country who compete to earn places in the Tanglewood Music Center. His performing and teaching activities at Tanglewood during the summer of 1989 were televised in a documentary seen on the Arts and Entertainment Network and BBC Television. When he travels to other cities, he is willing, if his schedule is not too hectic, to give master classes, where he does not insist that the students use his particular technical or interpretative methods. He also likes to play concerts with young, unknown soloists.

Yo-yo Ma is not just a virtuoso performer. He is also a partisan of his instrument, seeking constantly to add to the rather limited classical cello repertory, by adapting music originally meant for other instruments to the cello and by playing a great deal of twentieth-century music, including new works by recent composers. In January 1993, playing with the New York Philharmonic, he performed Oskar Moravetz's "Memorial to Martin Luther King," with its large cello part, in honor of the slain black leader's birthday. In May 1992 he presented the world premiere of Tod Machower's composition "Begin Again Again" for cello and live computer hyperinstruments. This performance involved four computers and three engineers, and Yo-yo used both an electric cello and his own eighteenth-century Italian-made instrument. He has also experimented with jazz in recent years, giving concerts in which he plays both written-out parts and his own improvisations.

Yo-yo Ma, with his sparkling dark brown eyes and expressive face, is still boyish-looking at the age of thirty-eight in spite of his frenetic schedule. He is universally liked for his openness, charm, and puckish sense of humor. He regrets the time spent on the road and away from his wife and children, but he has trouble turning down requests for concerts and engagements. He has tried very hard to make time to be at home and prevent his obligations from encroaching on his family life. In recent years, he has become more identified with his origins, studying China's history and culture and the Confucian ethic. Still, he is a man divided. As he admitted in a recent interview, "It's hard for me to say just who or what I am. I'm a person of various influences; sometimes they connect, sometimes they don't." Yet, taken together, the mixture of cultures has produced an extraordinary performer and a compassionate man.

★ THE CARTER YEARS ★

Jimmy Carter would be forced to shoulder much of the blame for the economic troubles of the late 1970s. Yet when he took office in January 1977, many people were optimistic that this ex-peanut farmer, who had come from nowhere to win the presidency, would be an effective leader. They would be disappointed.

Carter as President. Americans at first were impressed by Jimmy Carter. Though a Washington outsider, he opted for experienced people in selecting his cabinet: Cyrus Vance at the State Department, Harold Brown at the Defense Department, and Joseph Califano at the Department of Health, Education, and Welfare. His choice for treasury secretary was Michael Blumenthal, president of the Bendix Corporation. The White House inner circle, however, would be made up mostly of outsiders like Carter himself.

The Carter style at first seemed refreshingly informal. He broke with precedent by walking in his own inaugural

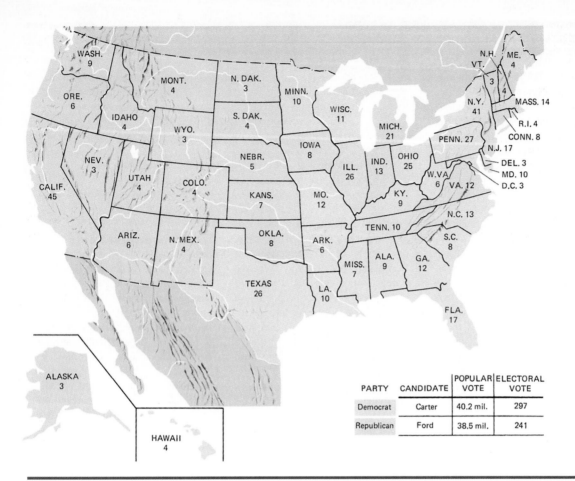

PARTY	CANDIDATE	POPULAR VOTE	ELECTORAL VOTE
Democrat	Carter	40.2 mil.	297
Republican	Ford	38.5 mil.	241

THE ELECTION OF 1976

parade with his wife, Rosalynn, and his daughter, Amy, by his side. From the White House he answered citizens' phoned-in questions on TV and wore blue jeans and old sweaters around the Oval Office. Amy went to a Washington public school, like other unpretentious residents of the District of Columbia, rather than a private school. Carter also tried to reduce the number of White House officials, and he cut back on staff limousines and television sets.

The politicians on Capitol Hill found him less pleasing. Having run against the Washington "establishment," Carter had trouble achieving a working relationship with Congress. He also experienced the congressional backlash against presidential leadership following Watergate and the abrasive years of the imperial presidency. Inexperienced in the ways of Washington, he and his staff often fumbled badly.

Carter's first mistake was to attack a congressional sacred cow by cutting off federal funding for eighteen dams and other water projects in the West. His arguments that the projects were wasteful were valid, but he had not reckoned with the importance of "pork barrel" to members of

Congress and the significance of irrigation in the West. Faced with a storm of protest, he retreated. He did little better in his early relations with key congressional leaders, failing to consult Senate Majority Leader Robert Byrd on which senators to brief on energy policy, and announcing federal appointments in House Speaker Thomas ("Tip") O'Neill's own Massachusetts district without first informing him. Eventually, Carter and his advisers improved relations with Congress, but they were never able to establish an effective partnership with those who enacted the nation's laws.

Domestic Policies . The gravest domestic policy question Jimmy Carter faced was how to end the nation's dependence on foreign oil. The challenge aroused all the president's considerable moral fervor. At one point he called the battle to make the United States oil-independent (borrowing a phrase from philosopher William James) "the moral equivalent of war."

Unfortunately, his actual recommendations to Congress in February 1977 were disproportionately modest: a federal tax on crude oil imports and on "gas-guzzling" cars. Given the president's grave tone and dire warnings, this program struck many Americans as ludicrous. Humorist Russell Baker abbreviated the "moral equivalent of war" to MEOW. Congress was similarly unimpressed and acted slowly, though eventually giving the president much of what he asked for.

In March 1979, with oil supplies once more in jeopardy because of a new Middle East crisis, and with the Three Mile Island accident raising new doubts about nuclear power, Carter again turned his full attention to the energy problem. Additional modest recommendations followed: a standby gasoline rationing plan, a program to develop synthetic fuels, and $10 billion for energy-conserving mass transit. It was a case once again of too little, too late. In the

summer, near-disaster was triggered by the turmoil in Iran. During the confusion of the Islamic fundamentalist revolution that overthrew the shah, Iranian oil production, a major source of American energy, dropped drastically. The oil-importing nations were soon bidding against one another for the reduced world supply, thereby tripping off a panic that left Americans fuming in long gas lines through June and July. By now many citizens had concluded that here, as in other areas, Carter was an ineffectual leader.

The oil crisis of 1979–1980 accelerated the inflation surge. In 1979, prices leaped 13.3 percent in a single year. In early 1980 they rose still faster, threatening to reach an astronomical 18 percent for the year if not stopped. The Federal Reserve, under its new head, Paul Volcker, raised

Jimmy and Rosalynn Carter walk to the White House from the Inauguration—happy as two larks.

interest rates to discourage spending with borrowed money. The president established a Council on Wage and Price Stability to monitor wage and price guidelines. Neither move worked at first. Interest rates were pushed to 20 percent in early 1980, but prices continued to rise. The council proved ineffective. Its orders were unenforceable and its fruitless "jawboning" only made the administration again seem feeble and incompetent.

Foreign Policy. Carter's foreign policy was not an outstanding success either. Liberals, who shared his sense that America must distance itself from aggressive Vietnam-era policies, endorsed his treaty with Panama ending exclusive American control of the Canal Zone. This agreement, they believed, was necessary to avoid a dangerous confrontation with Panamanian nationalists and to raise American stock in Latin America. Liberals also applauded his "human rights" campaign to use America's good offices to support victims of government oppression around the world. They endorsed his strong support for the new strategic arms limitations talks (SALT II) with the Soviet Union, which promised to slow the nuclear arms race.

Most conservatives saw these initiatives in a different light. The human rights policy, they said, all too often offended conservative foreign leaders who were friends of the United States and opponents of the Soviet Union. The Panama Canal treaties had weakly surrendered American rights of seventy years' standing. SALT II was a Soviet trick.

Its predecessor, SALT I, had lulled America to sleep, enabling the Soviets to catch up and then pass the United States in conventional weapons. The Soviet navy, for example, had become a global fleet able for the first time to challenge the United States in every corner of the high seas.

There was one foreign-policy area, however, namely Arab-Israeli relations, where everyone agreed that Carter deserved praise. In November 1977 Egyptian president Anwar Sadat had made an unprecedented visit to Jerusalem, the Israeli capital. For the first time the head of an Arab state had recognized the legitimacy of the Jewish nation and it looked as though peace between Egypt and Israel might be at hand. Unfortunately, the peace process soon bogged down over the thorny problem of Palestinian self-rule, and it seemed that Sadat's bold initiative would come to nothing. To break the impasse, in September 1978 Carter induced both Sadat and Israeli Prime Minister Menachem Begin to come to Camp David, the presidential hideaway in the Maryland mountains, to discuss the differences between the two countries. Carter used every means to get these two stubborn men to agree and finally succeeded in squeezing a joint peace statement from them. As a result of the Camp David accords, in March 1979 Israel and Egypt signed a peace treaty that bound the two nations to full diplomatic relations, to phased-evacuation by Israel of the Sinai Peninsula, conquered during the 1967 war, and to some form of autonomy for the Palestinians living in the West Bank and Gaza Strip. However, the treaty did not bring

Probably the high point of Carter's presidency: the hand clasp confirming the Camp David accord between Egypt's Anwar Sadat (on left) and Israel's Menachem Begin.

peace to the Middle East. None of the other Arab nations followed Egypt's lead and the Palestinian issue continued to fester. But for the first time in its history Israel was at peace with one of its Arab neighbors.

The Hostage Crisis. Whatever credit Carter earned from the Camp David accords was squandered by his handling of the hostage crisis with Iran. Iran was a distant, exotic place to most Americans in 1979, an Islamic—though not Arabic—nation located on the oil-rich Persian Gulf. It was ruled despotically by Shah Mohammed Riza Pahlevi, a close friend of America. The United States had helped the shah gain his throne in 1953 by a CIA-managed plot against his enemies, and considered him a bulwark of anti-Soviet stability in the Middle East. In January 1979 he was ousted by internal enemies who despised his repressive methods, his friendship with the West, and his attempts to modernize his conservative land. The Shah fled to Mexico, leaving behind a nation in turmoil. In October he was admitted to a New York hospital for treatment of cancer. This show of American hospitality outraged the faction now dominant

Americans became obsessed by the Iranian hostage crisis. Here grade school pupils are writing letters to the American prisoners.

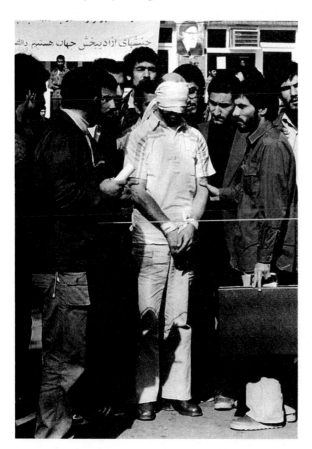

The blindfolded man is an American held hostage by the students of the Iranian Islamic Revolutionary Committee. They seem rather older than most students.

in Iran, the Islamic fundamentalists led by the ultraorthodox religious leader, the Ayatollah Ruhollah Khomeini. On November 4, 1979, a group of pro-Khomeini Iranian students, probably with the Ayatollah's approval, invaded the American Embassy in Tehran and took hostage more than sixty American citizens, mostly embassy employees.

Months of protest, negotiation, and maneuver would follow, but to no avail. Seizing the embassy of a country that one was not at war with was contrary to all civilized practice and no government could have condoned it. But America found itself dealing with a regime ruled by fanatics. The Islamic fundamentalists considered America "the Great Satan" and demanded ransom to release the hostages. The United States must surrender the shah to his enemies, apologize for supporting him in the past, and agree to turn over to the Iranian government all the assets that the shah supposedly had taken with him when he fled his homeland. If it did not, not only would the hostages be kept prisoner, but they might well be tried for espionage, and if convicted, executed.

The United States could not possibly accept such conditions and did not. The administration froze billions of dollars of Iranian assets in the United States, cut off all trade with Tehran, and appealed to the United Nations and the World Court to condemn the hostage-taking. Nothing worked. As the weeks passed Americans became obsessed with the hostage crisis. Public frustration and anger at American impotence grew and voices were soon raised demanding retaliation. Some people called for a declaration of war against Iran and a blockade of the Persian Gulf. Irate citizens attacked Iranian students attending American universities. The administration too became consumed with the hostage crisis to the neglect of other important matters. In late April 1980 the president ordered a military rescue operation from U.S. naval vessels in the Persian Gulf against the advice of Secretary of State Vance. This maneuver failed dismally and eight men died in the attempt. Vance resigned. The public's level of frustration rose to new heights.

The Cold War Resumes.   From the time Carter became president, relations between the Soviet Union and the United States had seesawed. Carter and many of his liberal advisers believed at the outset that the United States had subordinated too many other considerations to winning the Cold War. A more important destabilizing force than the

East-West conflict, they said, was the disparities between the wealthy nations of the world's northern industrial belt and the poor ones of the southern portion of the globe. In a 1977 speech at Notre Dame the president noted that "an inordinate fear of communism" had "led us to embrace any dictator who joined us in our fear." Reflecting these sunny views, the first two Carter defense budgets, already down from the Vietnam War, fell to the lowest proportion of total federal outlays since 1960. In June 1979 the president signed the SALT II agreement, further limiting the growth of U.S. and Soviet nuclear arsenals, and sent the treaty to the Senate for ratification.

Carter's optimism was not shared by everyone. By now many Americans were suspicious of the Soviet Union and détente. The Soviets, they observed, were becoming increasingly aggressive in South Yemen and, through their Cuban surrogate, in Angola in West Africa. The Soviet Union was also hiding behind détente to build up its conventional and nuclear arms to unprecedented levels. In 1976 a coalition of hard-line anti-Soviet hawks from government, business, the universities, and the intellectual community, organized the Committee on the Present Danger. In its founding manifesto the committee warned

The Electoral Vote, 1980

Carter 49
Reagan 489

that "the principle threat to our nation and the cause of human freedom" was "the Soviet drive for dominance based on an unparalleled military build-up."

All hope of further implementing détente collapsed in late December 1979 when Soviet troops and tanks poured across the border into Afghanistan, the Islamic country bordering Iran, to prevent a Soviet puppet leader from being toppled by his opponents. The Soviet invasion confirmed the hard-liners' contentious but shocked Carter. The president indignantly announced that Soviet premier Leonid Brezhnev had deceived him. He now told the American people that the United States must once more seek to contain Soviet expansionism and be prepared to defend the free flow of oil to the West from the Persian Gulf region. To implement this policy (quickly labeled "the Carter Doctrine"), he cut off sales of wheat and advanced technology to the Soviet Union, withdrew the United States team from the 1980 summer Olympics in Moscow, shelved SALT II for the foreseeable future, and asked Congress to enact legislation requiring all nineteen- and twenty-year-olds to register for the military draft.

The 1980 Election.   Despite this vigorous response, with each passing week the public came to perceive the Carter administration as feckless and impotent. Americans listened to the president's homilies about energy belt-tightening, "malaise," and international morality, and felt irritated and depressed. They watched events abroad and saw only a growing American powerlessness. The public's gloomy mood helps explain the outcome of the 1980 election.

Carter had to fight for renomination against Senator Edward Kennedy of Massachusetts. Though Kennedy had seriously damaged his reputation for honesty and courage in 1969 when he failed to save the life of a young woman aide when their car went into the water off Chapaquiddick Island, the senator had the support of the party's liberal wing. The president battled hard and ultimately won the nomination. The Republican nominee was Ronald Reagan, the sixty-nine-year-old spokesman for the new southern and western political right. The former California governor appealed to many of the same backlash voters who had supported George Wallace and Richard Nixon in 1968, with the added backing of business groups associated with the exploding industry and enterprise of Texas, southern California, the Mountain States, and the South.

Though divorced and a former actor, Reagan had been raised in an evangelical Protestant household and endorsed the conservative social agenda of the new religious right. Led by a group of preachers who had learned to make effective use of TV broadcasting, by the mid-1970s this rapidly growing segment of Protestantism had become a formidable challenge to the mainstream liberal Protestant groups. In 1979

Reverend Jerry Falwell, founder of the fundamentalist Moral Majority, speaking out for conservative positions during the 1980 presidential campaign.

Baptist minister Jerry Falwell organized the Moral Majority to bring the nation's evangelicals into the political arena. The Moral Majority endorsed abortion restriction, traditional family values, heterosexuality, tougher laws against drugs, lower taxes, school prayer, expanded defense spending, and a more aggressive anti-Communist foreign policy. They insisted that they supported pluralism and favored separation of church and state, but they pledged to defeat candidates for office opposed to their platform. Along with a cluster of secular "New Right" groups, the new religious right operated through political action committees (PACs) funded by money raised through direct mail appeals.

The Carter administration hoped for a breakthrough on the hostages to give it an electoral boost. But the Iranians toyed with the American negotiators, reinforcing the impression of administration weakness. When election day arrived the hostage crisis remained unresolved. The result was an impressive Republican victory. Reagan received 43 million popular votes to 35 million for Carter. Going down to defeat along with the president were a flock of liberal Democratic senators and representatives targeted by the New Right and the Moral Majority. Reagan would have a Republican Senate to work with and, though the House of Representatives would remain in Democratic hands, it was doubtful if it could check the powerful conservative surge.

★ CONCLUSIONS ★

It had taken twelve years, it seemed, for the conservative promise of 1968 to finally be realized. At the time, the defeat of Hubert Humphrey by Richard Nixon had appeared to be a drastic swing in the political pendulum. The voters had rejected one of its most liberal political leaders and endorsed one of its most conservative. Americans had repudiated the most powerful surge of reform in a generation and plumped for stability and order.

But those who hoped for a major swing to the right in public policy had been disappointed. Richard Nixon turned out to be a less doctrinaire man than his opponents had feared. He supported some of the environmentalists' policies, endorsed a guaranteed annual income, and ended the American quarantine of Communist China. Nixon was scarcely a liberal, and during a second full administration might have devoted more attention to the conservative agenda. But his character failings and his political limitations erupted in the form of Watergate and prevented him from achieving anything after 1972.

His successor, Gerald Ford, though also a conservative, had little prestige and standing, and he damaged whatever moral authority he might have had by pardoning the ex-president. Though in 1976 the public repudiated Ford for a more liberal man, it did not betoken an ideological shift. Carter nonetheless might have reversed the conservative current if he had been adept and likable. He was neither, and in 1980 the voters turned him out of office to try once more to get what they had failed to do in 1968. In the end it was Ronald Reagan, rather than Richard Nixon, who would launch the real conservative experiment.

★★★★★★★★ FOR FURTHER READING ★★★★★★★★

Richard Nixon. *Six Crises* (1962) Published just before Nixon's defeat in his 1962 race for the California governorship. Tells Nixon's own version of major crises in his life, including the Hiss case, the Checkers Speech, Eisenhower's heart attack, Nixon's near-catastrophic visit to Caracas, the "kitchen debate" with Khrushchev, and the 1960 presidential contest with Kennedy.

Gary Wills. *Nixon Agonistes: The Crisis of the Self-Made Man* (1970)
One of the best analyses of Richard Nixon and his place in American political history. It is also a valuable comment on the contradictions and illusions of the liberal tradition in twentieth-century American history.

Theodore White. *Breach of Faith: The Fall of Richard Nixon* (1975)
An excellent summary of Watergate by a master of political journalism who once admired Nixon.

Richard Nixon. *Memoirs* (1978)
This book illustrates the importance of looking at both sides of almost any story. Not ultimately convincing, but it does make it clear that Nixon was a fallible human being, not some inhuman monster.

Henry Kissinger. *The White House Years* (1979)
A fascinating inside report on the making of American foreign policy during Nixon's first four years, by his national security adviser at the time. Kissinger gives Nixon generally high marks as a diplomat, but also reveals this president—and himself—to be poor administrators and rather devious men.

John Osborne. *White House Watch: The Ford Years* (1977)
A moderate appreciation of the Ford administration by a liberal journalist.

Robert Shogan. *Promises to Keep: Carter's First Hundred Days* (1977)
A journalist's favorable report on the Carter administration's first three months in office. Shogan was allowed to attend cabinet meetings to write this book. A curiosity in light of the later course of the Carter administration.

Haynes Johnson. *In the Absence of Power: Governing America* (1980)
A thoughtful indictment of the Carter administration for its feebleness and lack of competence.

Studs Terkel. *Working People Talk About What They Do All Day and How They Feel About What They Do* (1974)
Terkel turned on his tape recorder and interviewed 130 people from a wide range of occupations, socioeconomic groups, and ethnic communities. Here they talk about the frustrations and gratifications of earning a living in the 1970s while maintaining their sense of individual worth.

Barry Commoner. *The Politics of Energy* (1979)
An indictment of American energy policy by a man of the political left. Commoner believes that most of the nation's energy difficulties have been caused by big-business groups greedy for profits. Central planning, he says, can solve them.

Robert B. Stobaugh and Daniel Yergin, editors. *Energy Future: Report of the Energy Project at the Harvard Business School* (1978)
The authors of the essays that make up this study *do* take the

energy crisis seriously. It is real, not manufactured. They recommend various solutions, but say that the most effective way to deal with the crisis is strict conservation of energy resources.

William Quandt. *Decade of Decision: American Policy Toward the Arab-Israeli Conflict* (1977)
The single best volume on this important subject.

Christopher Lasch. *The Culture of Narcissism: American Life in an Age of Diminishing Expectations* (1979)
A pessimistic and somewhat carping book about what has gone wrong with American culture in the 1970s. Like so many other contemporary studies of American culture and so-ciety, this book is both a diagnosis and a symptom of the problem it diagnoses.

Ralph E. Smith (ed). *The Subtle Revolution: Women at Work* (1979)
A survey of the enormous changes that have taken place in women's roles in the American economy since 1945, with special emphasis in the 1970s.

Kirkpatrick Sale. *Power Shift: The Rise of the Southern Rim and Its Challenge to the Eastern Establishment* (1975)
A good analysis of the political rise of the Sun Belt and its significance for national affairs.

31★

THE "REAGAN REVOLUTION"

What Was It?
What Did It Accomplish?

1980	Ronald Reagan elected president • Republicans gain control of Senate
1981	Beginning of Reagan era • Conservative agenda put into place • Cutbacks in domestic social programs • Huge increases for defense • Tax cuts seen as stimulus to economic growth • Deregulation of industries • Reagan fires striking air traffic controllers
1982	Budget deficits mount • Breakup of AT&T • Midterm elections see Democrats pick up seats in House while GOP retains Senate control • Contra aid a political issue
1983	Reagan continues to stress military build-up; adds new missiles in Europe • American marines sent to Lebanon • President pushes Star Wars to counter Soviet missile threat • 241 marines killed in Beirut terrorist attack • Soviets shoot down Korean airliner killing 269 • U.S.-Soviet relations worsen
1984	Reagan reelected in landslide • AIDS crisis grows ever larger
1985	Stock market continues to be bullish
1986	Space shuttle disaster • Trade imbalance worsens • U.S. jets attack Libya • Reagan-Gorbachev summit in Iceland ends on chilly note • Iran-Contra scandal breaks
1987	Congress probes Iran-Contra affair; televised hearings begin • Bork nomination to Supreme Court defeated in Senate • Stock market crash • Reagan and Gorbachev meet in Washington and sign agreement eliminating medium-range missiles from Europe • Scandals beset religious right
1988	Reagan era winds down

onald Reagan came to office as spokesman for many of the same forces and ideological groups that had supported Richard Nixon in 1968. Nixon's pragmatic moderation on domestic policy and support of détente had disappointed them. Would the new president do the same?

In his inaugural address on January 20, 1981, Reagan outlined a conservative agenda. "Government," he said, was "not the solution to our problem. Government is the problem." He would "get the government back within its means and . . . lighten our punitive tax burden." He would end the runaway inflation and get the economy moving again. His intention to break from détente was equally clear. His administration would restore America's standing in the world. Our international adversaries would find that while we craved peace we would "maintain sufficient strength to prevail if need be." Finally, in his conclusion, he tipped his hat to his new religious right constituency. "We are," he declared, "a nation under God," and he believed that "God intended for us to be free." He hoped that in future years Inauguration Day would be "declared a day of prayer."

The next eight years have sometimes been called the "Reagan Revolution," a term that implies major rightward shifts in the course the nation was taking. Was there a Reagan Revolution? Did the nation alter its political direction? Did the Reagan victory usher in marked changes in the economy, in the relations of classes and people, in America's role in the world, in cultural values?

★ THE FIRST TERM ★

The American Economy. As Reagan's inaugural address made plain, a major conservative target would be the abuses of "big government" and especially high taxes. This attitude was standard conservative doctrine. Ever since the days of the New Deal, conservative Republicans had accused the Democrats of raising taxes to pay, in part, for their spending extravagances. In the 1970s conservatives had made drastic local tax reduction a key part of their agenda. The passage in 1978 of Proposition 13 in California had marked the political right's imminent revival. The measure sharply reduced local property taxes. In one year the taxes paid by Californians fell by almost 40 percent. Proposition 13 severely reduced the ability of local communities to support social programs and education and provide needed physical facilities, but to many conservatives these consequences were more than acceptable.

The coalition behind the late seventies tax revolt was composed of varied elements. In California, and some other states, it included homeowners socked by skyrocketing property taxes as a result of soaring real estate values. These increases made many ordinary people rich on paper but without the actual income to pay their taxes. Opponents of the existing tax regime also included people caught in "bracket-creep." The roaring inflation of the late seventies, they noted, pushed their incomes up into ever higher income tax brackets without in fact giving them more actual purchasing power. One very powerful force behind the tax revolt were the rich, high earners who always opposed giving away a large part of their income to government.

Each of these groups can be considered pragmatic tax cutters; they wanted to avoid the personal burden of taxation. But there were those who were prepared to argue a broader case for tax cuts. "Libertarians" opposed all taxation because they opposed virtually all government. Many were disciples of the Austrian economist Frederick Hayek or the American economist Milton Friedman, men who preached the necessity of laissez faire in all aspects of social and economic life. Others were followers of Ayn Rand, a writer and pop philosopher whose novels and treatises glorified the lone hero fighting government or the ignorant mob. During the late 1970s the "supply-side" theories of Arthur Laffler became part of the conservative arsenal. Laffler denounced the dominant Keynesian theories that emphasized pumping up demand to achieve growth. As stagflation attested, it was not working. Instead, he said, it was necessary to stimulate output by cutting taxes drastically. Lower taxes would encourage effort and enterprise now dampened by excessive burdens on success. There was no need to worry about the resulting government deficits. As production, profits, and jobs grew the government would be able to cover its expenses even at the lower tax rates since total revenues would rise.

Through his enthusiastic disciple, the journalist Jude Wanniski, Laffler made a deep impression on several young, dynamic members of Congress including the Republicans Jack Kemp of New York and David Stockman of Michigan. In 1976 Kamp, joined by Senator William Roth of Delaware, introduced a bill for a 30 percent across-the-board income tax reduction to restore the economy and encourage growth. During the 1980 campaign Reagan had at least tentatively embraced the Kemp-Roth tax proposals. Like other "supply-siders," the candidate felt that the new economics expressed more truly than the liberals' timid talk of limits and no-growth the American spirit of enterprise and expansion. Not all Republicans agreed. George Bush, Reagan's chief opponent during the Republican nomination race, had called the Laffler theory "Voodoo economics." Among Reagan's own campaign advisers, traditional conservatives like

Arthur Burns and Milton Friedman, sworn enemies of the deficits they believed drastic tax cuts would create, expressed reservations about the Laffler theories. Not prepared to make a key issue of such a controversial view during the campaign, Reagan muted the tax cut as an issue.

As the new president took office the country did face daunting economic problems. Inflation was running at double-digit rates, the highest since the Civil War. Unemployment was growing and overall economic growth rates were lower than in previous decades. Worst of all, the United States was losing its international competitiveness. There was no way that the country could have remained the towering giant of the 1950s when the rest of the world was still struggling to regain its feet after World War II. By 1980, as we saw, Western Europe had recovered, thanks to American aid, and surpassed its prewar levels. East Asia, Korea, Taiwan, Singapore, and above all Japan had become economic dynamos. Germany and Japan, especially—our two chief enemies in the 1940s—had become more efficient than the United States in many areas of production. Whole classes of American manufactures had been replaced by foreign imports: steel, textiles, shoes, clothing, consumer electronic goods, cameras. Japan and Germany had even made drastic inroads in automobiles, once the quintessential American product.

At one time the United States had sold much of its manufactured goods abroad. By 1980 we had lost much of our overseas markets to our competitors. The United States could still count on areas of international economic excellence. American agriculture was the most productive in the world; Boeing, Lockheed, and McDonnel-Douglas still produced the world's best airplanes. As the eighties dawned the United States was ahead in computers and computer chips. Silicon Valley, south of San Francisco, was a creative powerhouse with dozens of electronic firms, headed by inspired tinkerers, thinking up ways to put the transistor and the microchip to use. Very soon IBM, the giant business machine company, and Apple, a scrappy newcomer run by two self-taught computer whizzes, would launch the personal computer revolution. Still, by the early 1980s, the United States was clearly slipping in its international economic standing relative to the upstarts in Europe and East Asia. By the opening years of the 1980s, whether one focused on the immediate problems of inflation and unemployment or on America's long-term relative decline, many people believed that the country must try new economic policies.

The Tax Cuts. Ronald Reagan began his presidency with a flourish. Just hours after his swearing-in ceremony, the Iranians accepted American terms and the embassy hostages at long last started for home. The inauguration festivities were the flashiest and costliest on record. Funded in part by the new president's rich California friends, they featured a week of extravagant champagne-and-caviar parties and the most lavish balls that anyone could remember. Nancy Reagan, a former Hollywood actress, dazzled the guests and reporters with her designer gown and opulent jewelry. Critics said that the rich were sending a signal that the United States government now was firmly in their hands and that the wealthy no longer need apologize.

Once the dust of the inaugural ceremonies had settled, the administration's first order of business was a tax-cutting bill. Prepared by David Stockman, head of the Office of Management and Budget, the proposed cuts promised to get the economy going again by unleashing enterprise and encouraging the work ethic. They were the most drastic and extensive on record. The Democrats controlled the House of Representatives by a small margin and might have defeated the measure, but after the failures of the Carter years many felt that the country had given the Republicans a mandate for change. Reagan, moreover, proved to be an effective parliamentary leader. His charm, his good humor, his rugged manliness appealed especially to southern Democrats ("Boll Weevils"), many of whom proved willing to desert their party to support the president. The clincher came when an unbalanced young man shot the president on March 30 while he was leaving a Washington hotel. Reagan's courage and good humor while recovering aroused

Some people liked her style and her fierce loyalty to "Ronnie," but others considered Nancy Reagan a vapid, meddling woman.

the admiration of the country and hastened the bill's passage through the legislative process.

The Economic Recovery Act of 1981 mandated a 25 percent cut in everyone's personal income tax over a three-year period and a sharp reduction, from a 70 to a 50 percent maximum, of the tax on "unearned" income from appreciation of real estate and other investments. It also authorized a drastic cut in corporate taxes—the "largest tax cut in the history of American business," one Reagan official described it—to stimulate investment.

Conservatives hailed the measure as a long-overdue unleashing of the nation's innovative energies. But there were deep private doubts within the administration itself. Stockman admitted in a frank 1981 magazine article that "greed" had been a key motivating factor in writing the tax bill. After he resigned as budget director, Stockman wrote a best-selling book on his administration years in which he described the White House staff as "illiterate when it came to the essential equation of policy." These were people who "never read anything," and "lived off the tube." The president himself was "a kind, gentle, and sentimental man," but he was incapable of understanding "the complexities, intricacies, and mysteries involved in the tax breaks."

Actually, according to Stockman, although the administration professed to believe the supply-side doctrines, it had a secret agenda. Many Reagan officials hoped, he said, that if the deficits following the tax cuts grew too fast, the liberals in Congress would be compelled to cut their wasteful domestic programs. Thus the threat of soaring budget deficits could be put to good use in the conservative war against the welfare state. Liberals would later claim that it was this desire to frustrate liberal programs that actually was at the heart of the administration's tax policy.

The tax cut failed to produce the quick economic stimulus its proponents had promised. But perhaps these early months were not a fair test. Toward the end of the Carter administration, Paul Volcker, head of the Federal Reserve System, had tightened the money supply and raised interest rates to take the steam out of inflation. By the time Reagan came to office the "Fed's" policies had slowed private spending and investment and produced a severe business recession on top of all the other economic problems. By December 1982, unemployment soared to 10.8 percent of the labor force; 12 million Americans were out of work. This was the largest percentage of jobless since the Great Depression. It was worse among blacks and teenagers: 20.2 percent and 24 percent, respectively.

But the "Fed's" tight money policies finally began to affect prices as well. In 1980, Carter's last year, consumer prices had risen by over 13 percent. By 1983 price rises had slowed to a little over 3 percent. Toward the end of Reagan's second term pessimists would warn that inflation was still an untamed dragon, but in fact it would never become the frightening monster of the late 1970s.

Volcker and the president would be given credit for ending the socially and economically ruinous inflation of the 1970s. Actually, many forces contributed to the advent of relative price stability. Clearly one major price deflator of the Reagan years was the end of the oil shortage. By the early 1980s conservation measures had begun to ease world petroleum demand, while at the same time total world oil output, stimulated by high prices in the 1970s, began to grow. Before long the world was awash in oil reserves. Dramatic oil price declines would not come until mid-decade, but by 1982 the decade-long oil price surge had ceased, removing a major force behind the powerful inflation thrust of the seventies.

Another important inflation-easing force was the declining bargaining power of American labor. Here, the rising unemployment rates of 1980 to 1983 were significant.

David Stockman, the Reagan administration's conservative budget adviser, apparently expressing a skeptical opinion of several liberal "entitlement" programs.

Reagan and Labor

Ronald Reagan, though at one time a trade-union leader himself, was not organized labor's closest friend. His coolness toward the trade-union movement showed itself in many ways, but one of the most dramatic was his firing of all the members of PATCO, the Professional Air Traffic Controller Organization, for striking against the government. The strike was indeed illegal, but it is hard to believe that a pro-labor president would not have shown more forbearance.

The following is a record of a press conference held August 3, 1981, in which Reagan and his attorney general announced their plans to clamp down on the striking air controllers.

The President. This morning at 7 A.M. the union representing those who man America's air traffic control facilities called a strike. This was the culmination of 7 months of negotiations between the Federal Aviation Administration and the union. At one point in these negotiations agreement was reached and signed by both sides, granting a $40 million increase in salaries and benefits. This is twice what other government employees can expect. It was granted in recognition of the difficulties inherent in the work these people perform. Now, however, the union demands are 17 times what had been agreed to—$681 million. This would impose a tax burden on their fellow citizens which is unacceptable.

I would like to thank the supervisors and controllers who are on the job today, helping to get the nation's air system operating safely. In the New York area, for example, four supervisors were scheduled to report for work, and 17 additionally volunteered. At National Airport a traffic controller told a newsperson he had resigned from the union and reported to work because, "How can I ask my kids to obey the law if I don't?" This is a great tribute to America.

Let me make one thing plain. I respect the right of workers in the private sector to strike. Indeed, as president of my own union, I led the first strike ever called by that union. I guess I'm maybe the first one to ever hold this office who is a lifetime member of an AFL–CIO union. But we cannot compare labor-management relations in the private sector with government. Government cannot close down the assembly line. It has to provide without interruption the protective services which are government's reason for being.

It was in recognition of this that the Congress passed a law forbidding strikes by government employees against the public safety. Let me read the solemn oath taken by each of these employees, a sworn affidavit, when they accepted their jobs: "I am not participating in any strike against the Government of the United States or any agency thereof, and I will not so participate while an employee of the Government of the United States or any agency thereof."

It is for this reason that I must tell those who fail to report for duty this morning they are in violation of the law, and if they do not report for work within 48 hours, they have forfeited their jobs and will be terminated.

Q. Mr. President, are you going to order any union members who violate the law to go to jail?

The President. Well, I have some people around here, and maybe I should refer that question to the Attorney General.

Q. Do you think that they should go to jail, Mr. President, anybody who violates this law?

The President. I told you what I think should be done. They're terminated.

The Attorney General. Well, as the President has said, striking under these circumstances constitutes a violation of the law, and we intend to initiate in appropriate cases criminal proceedings against those who have violated the law.

Q. How quickly will you initiate criminal proceedings, Mr. Attorney General?

The Attorney General. We will initiate those proceedings as soon as we can.

Wage earners do not threaten strikes to force wage increases from their employers when business is bad and there are thousands of unemployed ready and willing to take their jobs. In the early 1980s, with over 10 percent of the labor force jobless, wage pressures inevitably eased. Unions were compelled not only to moderate their wage demands to avoid further layoffs but they were often forced to "give back" wage and fringe benefits they had previously won for their members.

If organized labor had been a more powerful force in America during the 1980s, the wage-depressing effects of the slump might have been more limited. But organized labor was weak and on the defensive by the time Reagan took office.

Several factors explained labor's decline. During the 1950s unions had lost prestige because of Communist infiltration and connections with organized crime. They had also suffered from the changing nature of the labor force.

Unions had always been strongest among male workers and, since the 1930s, within heavy industry, especially steel, coal, and automobiles. By the 1980s the proportion of male to total workers had declined. So had the proportion of industrial workers to the total. By 1980 the coal, steel, and automobiles—the "smokestack" industries—were all in trouble owing to foreign competition and had cut back on their labor force. It is true that the service trades had simultaneously ballooned. But white-collar service workers were more resistant to union organizing than were blue-collar workers. The shift of industry to the South, the section most resistant to the trade union movement, led to further membership losses. Unions made valiant attempts to organize the new groups and, in fact, made some inroads among public employees and women. But overall they were less successful with them than with the northern male artisans and industrial workers of the past. Still, if unions did not grow, they also did not decline. Figures for union membership, as a percentage of all employees, were about the same—24 percent—in 1980 as they had been in 1960.

Then came the Reagan administration. The president's appointees to the National Labor Relations Board, the New Deal–created agency that supervised union collective-bargaining elections, slowed the process of authorizing elections and put a damper on unionization. The president also took a tough line toward work stoppages. In August 1981, when the Professional Air Traffic Controller Organization (PATCO) called an illegal strike against the government, Reagan fired all 11,000 members and refused to hire them back when they relented. PATCO went bankrupt and disbanded. PATCO was not a large organization, but clearly

the popular president had struck a powerful symbolic blow against the entire trade union movement. Between 1980 and 1984 total trade union membership dropped by over 2.7 million members. By 1988 only 17 percent of American full-time workers were members of trade unions, a 6 percentage point decline since the beginning of the decade. Only about 12 percent of workers in the private sector were unionized by 1992.

Most observers assumed that administration hostility to unions was responsible for most of this deterioration. Certainly organized labor believed so. But the downsizing of heavy industry, the need to meet the competition of new global markets, and the aging of union leadership also contributed to the process. Trade unionism in the United States would have to remake itself to counteract these powerful trends and seemed unable to do so.

Reagan and the Poor. As we have noted, the administration hoped to use the tax cut to justify cutting domestic social programs. But its opposition to the welfare state was not merely fiscal. Reagan and his advisers were passionately convinced that the welfare "entitlements" of the 1960s, many still flourishing in 1980, had only made poverty and dependency worse. As conservative social thinker Charles Murray would write in 1984, the nation's poverty programs had "tried to provide more for the poor and produced more poor instead." In 1968, 13 percent of Americans had been classified as "poor." The proportion of poor in 1980 was exactly the same: 13 percent. And all this had cost billions of dollars! How could better results be achieved—and at less expense? The Reaganites' views were also influenced by

The smiles did not last. President Reagan soon fired the striking air traffic controllers.

their class affiliations. There is no question that a substantial portion of Reagan supporters were successful middle-class people who, whatever their attitudes during the 1960s, by the 1980s had ceased to feel much sympathy with those who had been left behind in the "race of life."

Liberals denounced the proposed cuts in welfare as selfish and cruel. The president assured the public that his policies would maintain a "safety net" for the most vulnerable and disadvantaged groups in society. He would, however, get rid of the "welfare cheats" who received money, though actually unqualified under the law; he would eliminate programs that had proved ineffective; he would reduce high administrative costs. Wherever possible he would demand that the able-bodied work rather than receive handouts. Liberals were not reassured.

Spurred by the administration's goading, Congress cut back substantially on federal social programs. It reduced the food stamp program by 14 percent, the child nutrition program 28 percent, Aid to Families with Dependent Children 14 percent, Supplemental Security Income 11 percent, Low Income Energy Assistance 11 percent, financial aid for needy students 16 percent, job-training programs 37 percent, health block grants 24 percent, and many others in similar proportions. The president and his colleagues claimed that none of this seriously harmed the poor; his critics claimed that its effects were devastating.

Cutting through the rhetoric to the truth is not easy. There can be no question that the poor were hurt. One estimate suggests that between 1983 and 1985 the tax- and services-cutting policies together reduced the income of households earning less than $20,000 a year by a total of $20 billion and increased that of families making more than $80,000 by $35 billion. By 1984 the Census Bureau reported that income distribution in the United States was more unequal than at any time since 1947, when the bureau first began to collect accurate figures on the subject. By 1984 the proportion of Americans living below the official "poverty line" had grown from 13 percent in 1980 to 14.3 percent. Nor was the loss felt only by the poorest. In 1986 the "middle fifth" of income recipients, those people dead center economically, were receiving a lower proportion of total national income than at any time since 1947.

But there was another side of the coin as well. By the late 1980s unemployment had fallen below 6 percent nationally, and in some parts of the nation—the Northeast and the West Coast—it was even lower. These coastal sections were rich in universities and engineering colleges and were disproportionate beneficiaries of high-tech defense spending. The administration could also point with pride to job creation in the 1980s. At no time in the past, its friends noted, had the country created jobs for so many people in so short a period as under the Reagan "watch." Though the job market had been flooded by the "baby-boomers" born after 1945 and by women in larger numbers than ever before, it had absorbed them all.

Critics countered that not all these jobs were good ones. Far too many were unskilled, minimum-wage positions as fast food handlers, janitors, hospital aides, unskilled factory workers, bank tellers, and so forth. People with jobs such as these were forced to rely on two or more family wage earners to achieve a reasonable living standard. In many cases their parents had been able to achieve the same standard with only one. All told, critics noted, American real wages were not rising. In the past the majority of wage earners had been swept along by the surge in productivity. In the late 1970s, however, this process had ceased; many Americans could buy no more with their incomes in 1985 than in 1975. For the first time in memory, they said, adult Americans could no longer assume that their children would be better off than they were.

These criticisms were valid, but whether the administration could be blamed for them was unclear. The failure of American real wages to rise as in the past could be accounted for in several ways. Young workers were less skilled and the economy in the 1980s had to absorb an unusually large proportion of such young men and women. As their skills improved, economists argued, their pay would rise. There was also the new reality of intense foreign competition. The high factory wages of the past were gone because the products of those factories now came from low-wage countries abroad—Mexico, Taiwan, South Korea, Thailand, the Philippines. At $10 an hour or more for wages in Detroit, Pittsburgh, Cleveland, or Buffalo, American manufacturers could not compete. Their choices were limited: cut wages, shut down, or move their manufacturing processes "offshore" to some low-wage country while keeping the front office at home.

The same analysis could explain the growing gap between rich and poor. America *could* compete in those economic areas where skills, talent, and advanced education counted. That was why the entertainment business, the media professions, financial services, computer design and programming, and medicine and law all flourished. Foreigners could not do these jobs for us, or not as well as we could for ourselves; we could even do many of these jobs for them. One part of the U.S. economy, accordingly, prospered while the other slumped.

If many Americans were worse off than their parents, then, a large group of well-educated young men and women were forging well ahead of them. These "yuppies," young upwardly mobile professionals, became the social phenomenon of the decade. As depicted by the media, they were brash, materialistic, self-centered, politically and socially insensitive, and greedy. Many, it was said, used their

One of the problems of the 1980s and 1990s was that of homelessness. Experts disagreed about why there were now thousands who lived on the streets, but clearly the problem was an embarrassment to Americans.

quick riches for self-indulgence—in luxury apartments, high performance cars, imported wines and gourmet foods, class A restaurants, and illegal drugs, especially cocaine. For a time cocaine became a major "recreational drug" in yuppie circles. In some of the more prosperous cities of the Northwest and West Coast by the late 1980s whole neighborhoods catered to yuppie tastes. Food emporia carried quiche and Brie cheese; car dealers sold Mercedes and Volvos; wine merchants offered imported chablis and champagne. Writers and directors found yuppies interesting material. In 1984 Jay McInerny's *Bright Lights, Big City* depicted the trials of a young man in New York just after college who falls into the yuppie trap of "coke" and alcohol and finds it impossible to pull his life together. In Oliver Stone's movie "Wall Street," the innocent but ambitious young hero is turned into a financial buccaneer by the blandishments and example of a successful and corrupt tycoon.

Yet even if yuppies were often indifferent to the poor, poverty remained a reproach to America. Especially distressing were the homeless, a new class of deprived Americans who, by the mid-1980s, were to be found living

on the streets, under bridges, in parks and public squares, and in municipal shelters in many American cities. Critics of the administration charged that cuts in welfare and housing appropriations explained the surge in homelessness. But the problem was more complex than this. Many of the street people were single men and women afflicted with alcoholism or drug addiction. Many others were mentally ill persons who, in a previous generation, would have been admitted to state mental hospitals. These institutions, often squalid "snake pits," were now largely shut down, however, and those formerly warehoused in them, out of sight, were now blocking doorways, begging on the streets, using telephone booths and elevators as toilets, and sometimes insulting or assaulting pedestrians. Many Americans were dismayed by their plight; civil rights advocates sought to defend them against official harassment. But no one knew for sure how to solve the problem within practical limits.

But the plight of the homeless was just a part of the problem of continued poverty in a generally rich society. The existing welfare system was not very effective. The programs were necessary, perhaps, to keep people from starving, but they were obviously incapable of transforming society's unsuccessful and their children into self-supporting members of the community. Merely throwing money at poverty would never, it seemed, create confident, independent men and women capable of self-support. People will only sacrifice when they think it will lead to some positive goal. By 1981, the whole welfare "mess" seemed so intractable that it is easy to understand why most middle-class citizens tried to put it out of their minds.

Yet we must not assume that the Reagan administration was able to demolish the entire welfare state constructed since the 1930s. The administration did not get more than a portion of the domestic program cuts it proposed. Behind every "entitlement"—whether useful and economical, or ineffective and wasteful—was a powerful constituency that resisted elimination or drastic cuts. A Democratic House, and even the Republican-controlled Senate, often refused to give the president what he wanted. Despite its efforts, the administration was unable to secure the domestic budget cuts it pushed for. The feeling seemed to be: "Cut the other fellow's program; it's a waste of money. But leave mine alone." The administration's efforts to slash programs it believed expendable met fierce resistance and achieved only modest success.

None of these programs was as sacred, or as untouch-

A "Gray Panther" lady defending her income against Reagan administration efforts to economize.

able, as Social Security. As the decade progressed, it became ever clearer that the aged were no longer an underprivileged group. The income of people over age sixty-five, owing to private pension plans and Social Security payments, was now greater than average. The poor were now primarily families with young children, especially those headed by single parents. Children, in effect, were the new poor. Why continue to cosset the elderly when so many of them were well off? the critics asked. Why not limit the benefits of those over sixty-five in the name of social equity?

The Social Security system was also becoming enormously expensive and economically unsound. And yet well-organized lobbies for "senior citizens" were able to prevent most attempts to cap Social Security payments or tax Social Security income. When the president proposed revisions to hold down soaring Social Security outlays and make the system fiscally workable, the outcry from elderly voters forced him to drop the issue like a hot potato. Eventually it required a bipartisan congressional commission to add some actuarial sense to the system by increasing Social Security taxes, skipping some projected increases in payments, and mandating a gradual rise in the minimum retirement age. But before long the public was complaining that Social Security tax increases were becoming more burdensome for many than income taxes.

All told, then, the administration was forced to retain much of the welfare state it had inherited from its predecessors.

Defense Policy. An even worse budget-buster was defense appropriations. Like many conservatives, Reagan considered Jimmy Carter's foreign policies feeble and believed his predecessor had allowed the Soviet Union to leap ahead of the United States. During the 1980 presidential campaign he described a "window of vulnerability" in nuclear arms as well as deficiencies in conventional arms that had to be corrected if America was to remain strong. Reagan came to office pledged to a massive arms build-up that would increase American military power relative to the Soviet Union. Though a one-time liberal who had deplored Cold War antagonisms for a time after World War II, during the 1960s and 1970s Reagan had become intensely suspicious of the Soviets and wary of their aggressive policies around the world. At one point during his presidency he would call the Soviet Union an "evil empire," and "the focus of evil in the modern world."

In the first news conference of his administration the president attacked détente. It had been "a one-way street" that the Soviet Union had "used to pursue its own aims." Among his earliest proposals as president was a five-year, $1.7-trillion increase in defense spending to catch up with

During the 1980s Americans began to see a new economic phenomenon: Japanese-operated, Japanese-owned factories in the United States.

the Soviets. Congress scaled down the administration's military shopping list despite the determined resistance of Secretary of Defense Caspar Weinberger, but overall defense outlays leaped from $135 billion in 1980 to $210 billion in 1983 and to $231 billion in 1984. All told, the Reagan administration would engineer the largest military build-up in peacetime American history.

Budget Deficits.   The explosion in defense spending more than offset the moderate cuts in domestic programs and, combined with the giant tax cuts, produced the largest budget deficits Americans had ever experienced. The results were ironic. As Democratic critics quickly pointed out, for decades the Republicans had denounced their opponents as wild spenders who had mortgaged the nation's future to gratify their urge to throw money at problems. Now, under a Republican president, the annual deficit went from Carter's $60 billion in 1980 to over $180 billion in 1984. By the final year of his first term, Reagan had increased the national debt by an additional $650 billion, a sum almost as great as the total deficits run up by every president from Franklin Roosevelt to Jimmy Carter.

The deficits frightened many people. Some of the criticism was clearly motivated by politics. Democrats, though seldom bothered before by large government shortfalls, now warned of financial catastrophe if the deficits were not reduced. More disturbing, the deficits created uneasiness in the business community and among academic economists. Heavy government borrowing, they said, would quickly exhaust the limited supply of domestic savings and propel interest rates still higher. In fact, this did not happen. Instead, billions of dollars from abroad—especially from Japan and

Western Europe—flowed into American treasury coffers to meet the government's needs. But this process only raised other questions. Such foreign capital was volatile. It would be available only as long as American interest rates were relatively high and foreign investors had confidence in America's fiscal soundness. If interest rates fell, or if investors lost their faith in America's economic solvency, they might well pull their money out abruptly, causing a severe financial crunch. Meanwhile, Congress and the president argued bitterly over cutting expenditures, with the Democrats determined that defense outlays must be reduced, and the administration demanding domestic budget cuts. During Reagan's first term, nothing was accomplished; the national debt continued to grow.

Deregulation and the Environment.   An important part of the president's economic program was deregulation of industry. Conservatives believed the federal government should give business free rein to compete. Legal monopolies and industries tied down excessively by regulations designed to protect the public were inefficient. If America was to become more productive entrepreneurs must be unleashed. Public safety and consumer interests would be taken care of primarily by free market forces.

The process of deregulation had already begun in the Carter administration. In 1978, in the Airline Deregulation Act, Congress phased out the regulatory Civil Aeronautics Board, allowed free choice by airlines of any route they wished to fly, and permitted them to set their fares competitively. In 1980 the deregulation process was extended to truckers and, to a more limited extent, to railroads. That same year the Depository Institutions and Monetary Control

Act ended the tight rein on banks and "thrifts." Savings and Loan Associations (S&Ls) could now pay market interest rates to depositors and lend on more than just mortgages. Commercial banks too could pay depositors more to attract savings and could also enter the business of trading in stocks and bonds. In 1982, as a result of an antitrust suit initiated by the Carter administration, the courts ordered the breakup of the American Telephone and Telegraph Company, which had enjoyed a near monopoly on telephone services in many parts of the country. There would now be twenty-two local Bell Companies for local calls plus a scaled-down AT&T, which would retain its long-distance services but would have to compete with special long-distance companies. The new AT&T could also branch out into computers.

Under Reagan the hands-off policy accelerated. Reagan and his lieutenants sought to reduce the government's role in consumer protection in the interest, they said, of freeing business from unnecessary chains. The Department of Agriculture stopped printing booklets describing poor dietary habits and detailing good ones. Administration appointees allowed a dubious mixture of fat, meat scraps, gristle, and ground bone to be sold to consumers without warnings previously required. The administration cut drastically the budget of the Consumer Product Safety Commission. Under Thomas Auchter the Occupational Safety and Health Administration, federal watchdog of the workplace, was transformed from an "adversary" of business to "a cooperative regulator." Transportation secretary Drew Lewis revoked safety standards mandating automatic seat belts or airbags for automobiles by 1984.

Most controversial of all was the administration's attempt to reduce the government's role in environmental protection. Many in the administration deplored what they considered the excesses of the environmentalists. By the 1980s, they said, every project to increase the country's energy output, improve the country's roads and highways, provide new office space, lower the cost of raw materials, or exploit natural resources inevitably crashed into a wall of environmental regulation or encountered a wave of environmental lawsuits. The presence of some obscure "endangered species," like the tiny snail darter fish, could bring to a grinding halt a major dam project; the claim that a new building might cast a shadow over a park could stop a skyscraper from going up. A single drop of cancer-causing chemical could close down a reservoir or industrial plant. Every major construction scheme was invariably burdened with reams of "environmental impact" statements and other elaborate documentation that added to costs. During the early 1980s a joke went the rounds among Reaganites: How many Americans did it take to replace a light bult? Answer: Five—one to change the bulb and four to write an environmental impact statement. The administration claimed, then, that its chief concern was to lower costs and raise productivity. Its critics insisted that its anti-environmentalism was primarily a payoff to the business groups whose support it counted on. When criticized, the administration responded that its opponents were elitists who wished to preserve pristine environments that only a few could appreciate at the expense of jobs and growth that would benefit the many.

Although liberals claimed that the American voter still supported liberal causes, the public mood was undoubtedly more conservative than in the recent past. But environmental concerns still had powerful support. Many Americans remained deeply worried about water and air pollution from radioactive and chemical poisons, and they were willing to incur expense, and risk interference with private profit, to avoid exposure to these hazards.

The chief federal agency for safeguarding the public

Secretary of Interior James Watt posed against the sort of western scenery his opponents said he was determined to ruin.

health against pollution and contaminants was the Environmental Protection Agency (EPA), established under Richard Nixon in 1970 and given jurisdiction over a wide range of environmental concerns. During the Reagan administration, EPA's budget was steadily cut, falling from $5.6 billion in fiscal 1980 to $4.1 billion in fiscal 1984. Reagan's appointee as EPA head was Anne Burford, who administered a $1.4-billion "superfund" to clean up toxic waste dumpsites that dotted the nation and menaced the health of many Americans. Burford, however, was not an effective guardian of the public's health. Her sympathies seemed to lie primarily with the firms accused of pollution, and she came under attack for delaying the vast task of ridding the environment of places where chemical companies and industrial firms had disposed of dangerous substances over the years. In February 1983, Rita Lavelle, Burford's subordinate in charge of the clean-up program, resigned under fire from critics who charged that she had deliberately dragged her feet to protect various business groups from incurring the expense of paying for the clean up. The following December, she was convicted of perjury for denying knowledge of Burford's violation of waste-dumping laws. In March 1983, Burford too had resigned. Her successor was William Ruckelshaus, the first EPA administrator under Nixon. Though a conservative Republican and a former executive of Weyerhaeuser lumber company, a major raw material processor, he seemed trustworthy and won the approval of the environmentalists.

On the other hand, Reagan's secretary of the interior, James Watt, did not. A Denver lawyer, Watt was head of the Mountain States Legal Foundation, a public interest law firm financed by the conservative Colorado brewer, Joseph Coors. The foundation was a legal arm of the so-called Sagebrush Rebellion, a movement of western ranchers, mine owners, timber barons, and irrigation farmers opposed to federal control of western resources and determined to transfer public lands to state management. Under Watt the firm had initiated lawsuits challenging federal regulation of public land use for the sake of ecological balance, recreational use, and resource conservation.

The environmentalists had opposed his selection to head the Interior Department but, in the wake of the Reagan 1980 election sweep, were unable to stop it. They got what they had feared. Pleading the need to encourage economic growth, Watt authorized oil-drilling in four areas off the Carolina coast that his predecessors had declared off-limits, opened up millions of acres of federal land to prospecting and exploitation by mineral and timber companies, and proposed to sell 35 million acres of federal land to private companies. Environmental pressure groups like the Wilderness Society, the Sierra Club, the Audubon Society, and the National Wildlife Association denounced Watt, but,

despite misgivings, the president kept him. Then, in October 1983, Watt made a remark to a public gathering that managed to offend Jews, the handicapped, blacks, and women simultaneously. Reagan forced him to resign and replaced him with William Clark, a close White House adviser.

First-Term Foreign Policy. Reagan's first term coincided with a gap in the leadership of the Soviet Union. Following the death of Leonid Brezhnev in November 1982 there was a succession of short-term, interim Soviet leaders. Not until Mikhail Gorbachev, a vigorous man of fifty-four, became Communist Party Chairman in March 1985 did the United States have a secure leader to deal with.

In the interim, Soviet-American relations deteriorated. The Soviet invasion of Afghanistan and the hostage-taking episode in Tehran, as we saw, had compelled the Carter administration to assume a more aggressive stance toward America's adversaries. But to the Reaganites Carter's policies still seemed weak and irresolute. Reagan and his closest foreign-policy advisers—Secretary of State Alexander Haig, national security advisers Richard Allen and William Clark, nuclear arms negotiator Paul Nitze, and UN Ambassador Jeane Kirkpatrick—believed the Soviet Union to be the author of virtually all the turmoil and tension in the world. The USSR, they said, had used détente as a screen to vastly increase its military power and had cheated on SALT I and other arms agreements. Either directly, or through surrogates, it was responsible for upheavals in Africa, Latin America, and East Asia. The USSR and its satellites and allies were behind the wave of bombings, airplane hijackings, and hostage-taking around the world. They were the ultimate source of Arab intransigence against Israel in the Middle East. Kirkpatrick espoused the theory that "authoritarian" regimes differed fundamentally from "totalitarian" regimes. The first, widespread in the Third World, were capable of change. We should be willing to support them, human rights violations notwithstanding, if they supported us. Totalitarian societies, like the Soviet Union, however, were incapable of change; they had to be contained. Time would show that some of the conservative foreign-policy analysis was exaggerated or invalid; it would also show that some of it was correct.

Shortly after taking office, Reagan found himself forced to deal with a possible Soviet invasion of Poland. In mid-1980, Solidarity, an anti-Communist union started by rebellious Polish shipyard workers, challenged the corrupt and repressive puppet regime in Warsaw and its Soviet masters. As Reagan took up the reins of office in early 1981 it looked as if Soviet troops would march once more, as they had in Hungary, Czechoslovakia, and earlier in Poland itself, to put down the popular uprising. The Soviets avoided an invasion, but in mid-December 1981 they installed a still more repressive regime under Marshall Jeruzelski that imposed martial law and imprisoned Solidarity's leader, Lech Walesa.

Reagan was not prepared to take military action against the Soviets. Yet the president used the occasion effectively to drive home his theme of the Soviet Union as an "evil empire" and the source of the world's turmoil. During the 1981 Christmas season Reagan ordered lighted candles placed in the White House windows to attest to America's concern for the Polish people and imposed several new economic sanctions on the Soviet Union.

And Reagan took advantage of other Soviet mistakes to score points in the U.S.–Soviet international rivalry. In September 1983 a Soviet Mig fighter shot down a Korean Airlines passenger plane that had wandered off course into Soviet air space, killing 269 passengers and crew. The attack was probably an accident, but international opinion was outraged, and the administration used it as another occasion to condemn the Soviet regime.

But if much of the administration's anti-Soviet actions belonged primarily to the war of words, a real Soviet-American confrontation erupted over intermediate range nuclear missiles in Europe. Neither SALT I nor SALT II had stopped the nuclear arms race. Both sides continued to add to their nuclear delivery systems: long-range ICBMs, bombers, nuclear-carrying submarines, tactical nuclear weapons, and intermediate-range nuclear weapons. In Europe the Warsaw Pact countries and NATO confronted one another with a variety of middle-range nuclear weapons as part of the balance of terror that lay at the heart of the Cold War deterrence policy. In 1980 the Soviets upgraded their Intermediate Nuclear Force (INF) weapons with a new, better rocket. On the urging of the America's NATO ally West Germany, Carter promised to send new, upgraded American weapons to restore the balance. But his term ended before he could act, leaving the issue to his successor.

Reagan accepted the commitment to send new "cruise" and Pershing II missiles to Europe. Yet at the same time the United States continued to negotiate with the Soviets at Geneva for some sort of mutual intermediate range nuclear arms accommodation.* Months passed while the American negotiators and their Soviet counterparts sought a solution. The Russians threatened to "walk out in indignation" and hinted at still more dire, if unspecified, consequences if the United States actually deployed the new Pershing II missiles on German soil as scheduled in late 1983. Talks at Geneva on the Pershings soon reached an impasse, and it looked as if Soviet-American relations were once more reaching a crisis.

The pressure on the administration to rescind its plans to deploy the Pershings ballooned to enormous proportions in late 1982 and 1983. In Western Europe a new generation of young men and women now feared nuclear war more than the Soviet threat. Marches and rallies, many of them anti-American, erupted in many cities of America's NATO allies to protest the deployment and to demand that the arms race cease once and for all. In the United States, too, the INF crisis fed fears of nuclear holocaust. During 1983 the antiwar and nuclear disarmament movements, in eclipse since the end of the Vietnam War, revived explosively. As in Europe there were marches and rallies in major American cities protesting the arms race and demanding a "nuclear freeze." The nuclear freeze movement received wide support in Congress and among liberal religious groups, including the Conference of Catholic Bishops. Groups of dovish intellectuals proposed that the United States pledge itself to no first nuclear strike. Meanwhile public jitters were aggravated by Jonathan Schell's best-selling *The Fate of the Earth*, detailing the catastrophic effects of nuclear war. The whole "no nukes" media campaign culminated in ABC television's *The Day After*, a graphic and horrifying depiction of what a nuclear attack would do to one American midwestern community.

Convinced that it would only encourage Soviet expansionism, the administration resisted the pressure to draw back. It also upped the arms race ante. In March 1983 the president had proposed, almost as an afterthought, that the United States abandon MAD (Mutually Assured Destruction) as its sole reliance for nuclear peace. Why not try to find some high-tech *defense* against enemy missiles. Called the Strategic Defense Initiative (SDI) by its friends and Star Wars by its enemies, the proposal was profoundly unsettling. Many scientists announced that it was simply not possible technically; so why waste billions on such a science-fiction scheme? Proponents of MAD insisted that SDI would only encourage further Soviet fears and hence further Soviet militancy. There is now some evidence that the administration tried to deceive both Congress and the Soviets about SDI's practicality by faking the results of several missile interception tests. Yet among Soviet leaders, it seems clear, the Star Wars scheme came as a thunderbolt. We later found out how far behind the West the Soviet economy was. To compete with NATO, the USSR was already spending as much as 25 percent of its GNP on defense. By contrast, even with the Reagan arms build-up of the early 1980s, Americans were spending only 6 percent of their GNP. And nowhere was the Soviet economy so behind the capitalist nations as in high-tech. Star Wars now threatened

---

*At the same time, at Vienna, the Soviets and the Americans were negotiating to limit "strategic," long-range nuclear delivery systems.

This is the way an artist imagined the starwar (SDI) system would work. It is now clear that the whole Strategic Defense Initiative will never be more real than this. The Clinton administration virtually terminated the program in May 1993.

the Soviets with another giant round of arms competition with the West—and in the very area where they were furthest behind.

Despite the peace movement protests, the administration refused to relent on the Pershing deployment. In late November 1983 the Pershings were put in place on German soil. The Soviets now walked out of the ongoing arms talks, declaring that "changes in the global strategic situation" had made it "necessary for the Soviet side to review all problems under discussion." For the first time in many years the United States and the USSR would not be discussing how to contain the arms race. U.S.–Soviet relations had reached a low point, and many people around the world feared they would get still worse.

Reagan was equally aggressive in other corners of the world, although when real danger appeared, prudence often overcame his hard line. In the Middle East the president maintained close ties with Israel and was rumored to have encouraged the Israeli invasion of Lebanon in 1982. In September 1983, in the hope of pacifying that chronically chaotic country, Reagan sent American marines to Lebanon. Rather than bringing peace, the marines themselves became targets of warring Lebanese factions, several of them representing violently anti-American, pro-Iranian groups. Earlier in the year a Muslim fanatic had detonated an explosives-laden truck next to the American embassy in Beirut, killing forty-seven people, including sixteen Americans. In October 1983, soon after the marines arrived, another Muslim terrorist carried out a similar attack against the marine barracks in Beirut, killing 241 American servicemen.

In February 1984 the president decided that the marines were too exposed and removed them from the scene of the violence. Many Americans questioned whether the entire affair had not betrayed impulsiveness mixed with weakness, a disastrous combination in the conduct of international affairs. Meanwhile, ominously, the same anti-American Muslim groups in Lebanon had begun to take hostages among the Americans residing in Beirut, and the media, as well as the victims' families, began to pressure the administration to do something to recover the kidnapped men.

Reagan's foreign policy missteps did not affect his standings in the public opinion polls. Somehow, Americans considered even his failures acceptable. The president's personal charm, his relaxed manner, and his good looks sugar-coated his actions. The "great communicator" was able to convey a verbal message of no-nonsense toughness toward America's enemies that conflicted at times with his actions. He was able to seem like a "good guy" while cutting programs for the poor. A generation raised on images seemed to take his words and manner more seriously than his deeds. Exasperated opponents would dub him the "Teflon president," because nothing adverse seemed to stick to his political skin.

Nicaragua. Reagan's policies in Central America and the Caribbean were in tune with his general anti-Soviet views. The president and his advisers saw the hands of the Soviets and their Western Hemisphere surrogate, Cuba's Fidel Castro, behind much of the social and political unrest in Latin America. They feared the Marxist powers might establish another beachhead in the Americas that, like Cuba, would threaten America's interests in the Western Hemisphere. In El Salvador the administration intervened to help the conservative-to-moderate regime of Napoleon Duarte against a Marxist-led insurgency. In October 1983, American troops invaded the tiny island republic of Grenada, ostensibly to ensure the safety of several hundred American students studying for their medical degrees on the island, but actually to keep the Cubans from getting a toehold. The action satisfied the American public's yearning for redress after the inglorious Lebanon fiasco, but peace groups and a number of America's allies condemned it as unnecessary aggression.

The most inflamed point in the Americas was Nicaragua, like El Salvador, a small republic in Central America. The country was ruled by the Sandinistas, a leftist group responsible for the overthrow in 1979 of the American-supported strongman, Anastasio Somoza. Since coming to power, the Sandinistas, led by Daniel Ortega, had established a one-party political system and had governed by increasingly dogmatic and authoritarian Marxist principles. Observers disagreed over whether the Sandinistas were inherently anti-American and pro-Soviet, or whether the United States had pushed them in that direction. The administration had no doubt that the Sandinistas were allied with Castro and the Soviet Union and accused them of aiding the Salvadorean rebels and stir-ring up general anti-American discontent in Latin America.

The administration tried to topple the Sandinista regime and replace it with one more to America's liking. It authorized spying operations in the Central American republic, conducted intimidating military maneuvers along the Honduras-Nicaragua border and off the Nicaraguan coast, and began to mine Nicaraguan harbors to prevent delivery of Soviet and Cuban arms to the Sandinistas. The latter was clearly illegal, and there were loud protests both in the United States and abroad.

But the administration's chief weapon against the Nicaraguan leftists was the military force called the "Contras," made up mostly of anti-Sandinista Nicaraguan exiles, who despised Ortega and his regime as repressive and pro-Soviet. The American government provided arms, logistical support, and intelligence to the Contras, hoping that they would overthrow the Ortega government and replace it with one more democratic—and more pro-American.

Americans had mixed feelings about the civil war raging in Central America and their country's role in it. Most deplored another Marxist bridgehead in the Americas, but many feared a replay of Vietnam with the quagmire transferred to this hemisphere. In 1983, a Vietnam-shy Congress passed, over the president's protest, the Boland Amendment requiring the chief executive to consult Congress before using any more Defense Department money to supply the

His critics called him the "Teflon President," but he won the affection of many mainstream Americans.

Contras. Thereafter, Congress blew hot and cold over the Contras, at times refusing them funds of any sort, at other times restricting their use entirely to "humanitarian" aid—food, clothing, medical supplies, and the like. Frustrated by congressional anti-Contra actions, fiercely dedicated anti-Communist hardliners within the CIA and the National Security Council soon began to consider ways to evade Congress's intentions. Their schemes would soon precipitate a constitutional crisis.

Reelection. In 1982 the administration had faced, and failed, its first electoral challenge. The 1982 midterm elections found the economy still lagging badly. As a result of the anti-inflation clampdown by the Fed, unemployment was at a frightening 9.7 percent. The Republicans blamed the recession on their predecessors, but the Democrats made substantial gains in the House, though they did not regain control in the Senate.

By 1984 the economy had sprung back. There remained many soft spots especially in the old Snow Belt industrial areas and now, owing to the drop in world oil prices, in the "Oil Patch" of Texas, Oklahoma, and Louisiana as well. But the Pacific Coast, and those parts of the Northeast that had made the successful transition to computers, high-

The volatile Democratic presidential candidate Gary Hart in a pose imitative of Adlai Stevenson—though Stevenson's shoes had only one hole.

tech, and the information revolution, had surged remarkably. And although the poor were probably poorer, upper-middle-class America in most parts of the country had begun to feel flush and confident again.

As the 1984 presidential election approached the Democrats faced a popular president who could claim he had ended the decade-long inflation surge and brought renewed prosperity. Yet there was no lack of Democratic challengers. In the end, the Democratic race came down to Senator Gary Hart of Colorado and former Vice President Walter Mondale of Minnesota. Hart claimed to speak for the younger, yuppie voters who were coming of age in the 1980s. Mondale represented a more traditional New Deal, bread-and-butter sort of liberalism. To the left of both was Jesse Jackson, a black minister sprung from the civil rights movement, who sought to create a "Rainbow Coalition" of blacks, Hispanics, feminists, gays, and other minorities and social dissenters. Jackson was the first serious black presidential contender, and his candidacy had special meaning for black voters.

The Democrats slugged it out for months during the primaries, which had by now become a grueling, expensive obstacle course for presidential candidates. In the end Mondale won on the first ballot at the Democratic convention in San Francisco. The convention itself was primarily a media event. Jackson gracefully apologized for an anti-Semitic remark he had made in private; the keynote speaker, governor Mario Cuomo of New York, eloquently celebrated the Democrats' social sympathies and their ability to make one "family" of America's diverse strands. Hoping to take advantage of a "gender gap" that gave Reagan less female than male support, Mondale boldly chose a woman, Representative Geraldine Ferraro of New York, as his running mate. In a fit of rare political honesty, he also promised, if elected, to raise taxes to bring down the escalating budget deficits.

In the end the contest was no contest. By the fall the economy was booming and many Americans felt that Reagan had restored America's standing in the world. Underscoring the new pride was the American sweep at the Summer Olympics in Los Angeles in part owing to a Soviet bloc boycott. The Republican campaign slogan, "It's Morning in America," proclaimed in a rash of TV ads, proved effective. As the contest reached the home stretch, one Reagan adviser noted that he "almost felt sorry for Mondale, . . . it's like running against *America*."

But the Democrats also made some serious mistakes. The public was in no mood to think about deficits and were even less happy with talk about additional taxes. Mondale would regret his promise at the convention. Then, too, Ferraro proved a liability rather than an asset when her family finances came under fire as less than irreproachable.

Jesse Jackson's "Rainbow Coalition" never went very far, but he reinforced black pride when he became the first serious black presidential candidate.

On election day it was a Reagan landslide. The Republican ticket won every state except Minnesota, Mondale's home state, and garnered 59 percent of the popular vote. The Republicans had done well in almost every electoral sector. Despite Ferraro, a large majority of women had voted Republican; so had a majority of Catholics and many more Jews than in the past. Young and old had gone for the president. The Moral Majority, Reagan's allies on the religious right, had managed to register more voters than the Rainbow Coalition, and its success showed, especially in the South and West. There was one bit of good news for the Democrats, however. Despite the Reagan landslide, the new House of Representatives would remain under Democratic control.

★ THE SECOND FOUR YEARS ★

Few presidents have accomplished as much in their second term as in their first. By the beginning of its fifth year a successful administration has achieved most of its agenda and has depleted its energies. Besides, all its tricks have become familiar and easy to counter. In Reagan's case the problems were compounded by the 1986 midterm elections, when the Democrats regained control of the Senate, making it even more difficult for the administration to win congressional cooperation than before.

The administration's second-term problems were aggravated by the president's age and health. Reagan was already seventy when he became president, the oldest man to hold the presidential office. In addition, he had survived an assassination attempt in 1981, and by 1987 he had undergone surgery for colon cancer and an enlarged prostate. At times in his second term he seemed to be tired, distracted, and forgetful. He still read prepared speeches magnificently, but did poorly at extemporaneous press conferences where he had to think on his feet, and so avoided them. Some Americans believed he had lost his grip.

The AIDS Crisis. Troubles and conflicts would come in shoals during Reagan's second four years. In 1981 the calamity of AIDS burst on the scene when scientists discovered that a hitherto unknown agent was attacking the immune systems of thousands of victims and destroying their resistance to cancer and various infectious diseases. It soon became apparent that the afflicted were predominantly homosexual males and the disease was transmitted through infected bodily fluids including semen and blood. In 1984

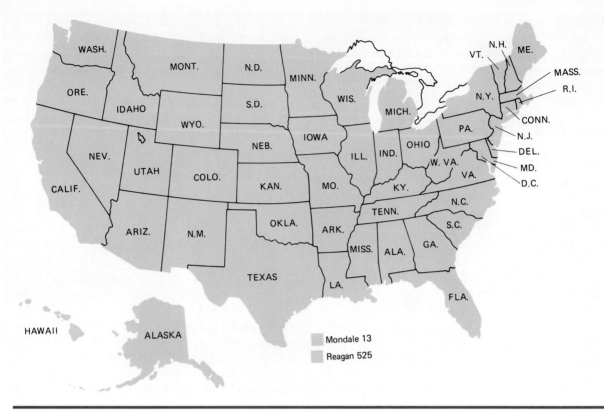

THE ELECTORAL VOTE, 1984

Mondale 13
Reagan 525

French and American scientists identified the disease-causing agent as a virus that entered the bloodstream and destroyed the body's ability to manufacture antibodies.

AIDS (acquired immunodeficiency syndrome) was not a "gay" disease as such. It also infected drug users who shared heroin needles, as well as people who had received blood transfusions before techniques were developed to screen the AIDS virus from blood donations. But even five years after the first data became available, over 70 percent of all AIDS victims remained homosexuals. Most of the rest were intravenous drug users. The great majority were adult men, though the number of women and children infected with AIDS was growing.

The disease ravaged the gay community. Until its advent, homosexuals, concentrated primarily in a few large, cosmopolitan cities like New York, San Francisco, Chicago, and Los Angeles, had developed a confidence and assertiveness beyond anything in the past. The mood fed a sexually permissive lifestyle that provided the perfect environment for the AIDS virus to flourish and spread. AIDS ran through New York's Greenwich Village, the Castro district in San Francisco, and other gay communities like the Black Death, cutting down young men in the thousands and undermining the hard-won self-confidence that gays had acquired since the late 1960s. It also produced a sharp upsurge of antigay feeling. Though the disease obviously afflicted other groups, social conservatives, including many of the Moral Majority, saw it as a sign of God's displeasure at homosexuality.

Although medical experts insisted that the disease could not be transmitted by casual contact, many people initially feared AIDS victims, however they had acquired the disease. People began to avoid contact with gays; they demanded that AIDS-infected children be kept from school. Medical personnel took to wearing masks and gloves when in the presence of AIDS patients. Some surgeons even declared they would not perform major operations on people infected with the AIDS virus. Fear of AIDS also began to affect relations between heterosexual men and women; experts claimed that all sexual contact with infected people created the risk of infection. Combined with a surge of genital herpes and other sexually transmitted diseases, the advent of AIDS took its toll of the permissive sexual revolution of the 1960s and 1970s.

The president was caught in the middle of the controversies and the anger that swirled around the AIDS scourge.

Though he owed much politically to the Moral Majority and supported conservative positions on abortion and the family, Reagan, a former Hollywood actor, was not an unworldly, provincial man. Yet he was accused by gays of resisting mobilizing the nation's medical resources against AIDS out of homophobia. The president did insist that people had "a moral obligation not to endanger others," and he endorsed mandatory testing of federal and state prisoners, patients admitted to VA hospitals, and marriage-license applicants. These suggestions fell far short of the enforced mass-testing programs demanded by a few far right advocates, but many gays and civil libertarians claimed they would place the jobs and insurance coverage of AIDS patients in jeopardy and were preliminary to an official policy of quarantine. Some even saw it as a harbinger of concentration camps for homosexuals. Never highly popular in the homosexual community, the administration probably lost whatever support it had among an emerging self-conscious social minority.

Retreat of the Religious Right. As his second term approached its end Reagan also found his support among the religious right less sustaining. The rapid growth of fundamentalist Protestant groups and their increasing self-confidence and political activism, as we have seen, had benefited Reagan and political conservatism generally. Since his election, the Moral Majority coalition and similar groups had applauded the president's pronouncements on abortion, on school prayer, on traditional family values. They had been less impressed with his actions. Reagan, some said, talked a good game but did little to implement it.

In 1987, following Justice Lewis Powell's decision to retire from the Supreme Court, the president sought to ap-

pease his supporters on the religious and political right by nominating Robert Bork to succeed Powell on the High Court. Bork, a federal appeals court justice and former law professor, had opposed the judicial activism of many of his liberal predecessors on the bench. He had also attacked the Court's recent tendency to uphold the right of privacy against state interference and to expand civil liberties protections and the scope of affirmative action. Liberals, civil libertarians, even many middle-of-the-road citizens saw Bork as an extremist, outside the conservative mainstream, and they feared having him and his views entrenched for life at the nation's judicial center. After widely watched televised hearings, the Senate rejected him.

Angry at the defeat the administration defiantly nominated another far right judge, Douglas Ginsburg. The hasty choice represented a victory for Attorney General Edwin Meese against the advice of Howard Baker and other White House moderates. Ginsburg soon confessed to having smoked marijuana while a law professor, and in a matter of days agreed to withdraw his name. The president then nominated Anthony Kennedy of Sacramento, a man closer to the center, whom the Senate finally confirmed. But the ill-conceived initial selections underscored for many social conservatives how little the administration had accomplished in actually reversing the liberal trends of the day.

By 1987 the religious right itself was in retreat, a victim of its own excesses. The chief culprit in the reverse was Jim Bakker, a fundamentalist preacher who, along with his blonde wife, Tammy Faye, had become an evangelist media star on the flourishing religious right TV network. Bakker was one of a number of fundamentalist preachers who used the electronic media effectively to disseminate their messages of good works, salvation, righteous living, and anti-

The smile on Judge Robert Bork's face did not last long. Opposed by liberals who deplored his conservative views, he was not confirmed by the Senate as Associate Supreme Court Justice.

The wildly successful TV evangelist Jim Bakker and his wife, Tammy—before the fall.

modernism. He and other "televangelists" had vast followings who responded enthusiastically to their appeals for funds "to continue the good work." The Bakkers; in addition to their TV ministry (called PTL, for "Praise the Lord") were sponsors of a large resort in Fort Mill, South Carolina, that combined the features of Disneyland, a revival camp, and a country club. There the devout, who paid a substantial sum, could spend their vacations soaking up the sun and God's word at the same time.

In March 1987 Bakker resigned as head of PTL after the media published stories that he had paid over $100,000 to a former PTL employee to keep her from revealing that he had been sexually intimate with her. Soon after, he was also accused of having made homosexual advances to several young men. In 1989 after investigation of his sales practices at Fort Hill, he was tried for fraud and sentenced to forty-five years in prison.

Bakker's associates, unwilling to see PTL dismantled, called in Jerry Falwell, the Virginia preacher who in 1979 had founded the Moral Majority, to rescue the organization. Falwell quickly uncovered serious financial irregularities in the management of PTL. He also revealed how the Bakkers had used the contributions of the faithful for their own private advantage.

The Jim and Tammy scandal hurt the evangelical movement as a whole. Many sincere followers of fundamentalist preachers became disillusioned. Contributions to TV evangelism dropped; membership growth in fundamentalist churches slowed. Falwell, discouraged by the un-Christian squabbling and infighting that had erupted over his handling of PTL, announced in late 1987 that he was abandoning political activism and would hereafter focus on his pastoral duties as minister at the Thomas Road Baptist church in Lynchburg, Virginia. In 1989 the Moral Majority officially disbanded.

The Space Shuttle.   Reagan's second term was also marred by a space shuttle disaster that highlighted the administration's fecklessness and lack of direction in its commitment to space exploration. Although January 28, 1986, was unusually cold, National Aeronautics and Space Administration (NASA) officials, following several previous postponements, authorized the space shuttle *Challenger*

The religious right's sparkplug, the Reverend Jerry Falwell—looking particularly benevolent here.

Seven brave Americans—men and women—died when the Challenger *space shuttle exploded after takeoff on a cold January day in 1986 from Cape Kennedy, Florida. The tragedy set back the American space program by more than two years.*

launch from Cape Kennedy. Shortly after takeoff the shuttle exploded in a ball of flame, killing all seven crew members including Christa McAuliffe, a Concord, New Hampshire, schoolteacher who had come along on the launch to help publicize the shuttle program among the nation's schoolchildren.

The tragedy for a time crippled the American space program. The investigation that followed showed that, to hold costs down, NASA had ignored repeated warnings that the O-ring seals on the shuttle's solid-state rockets were defective and had also authorized the launch against expert advice that icing on the rocket might create a problem. To prevent a repetition of the catastrophe, NASA stopped all shuttle launches until the fuel-seal problem was solved. It quickly became clear that the country had invested too many of its space eggs in the shuttle basket. With the space shuttle out of service for the foreseeable future, the United States was forced to turn to older rockets to launch needed civilian and military communications satellites. When these failed with dismaying frequency, many informed Americans lamented the parlous state of American technology. Meanwhile, the Europeans and the Soviets forged ahead in their satellite programs, making America seem a has-been in space. Having promised to restore America's world prestige and pride, the space policy fiasco once again made the administration look bad.

Economic Abuses. During Reagan's second term the economy's performance remained spotty. Unemployment

continued to decline, reaching 6 percent in December 1986 and dropping another percentage point by the end of the administration. The inflation rate remained low: During the first quarter of 1986 prices were rising at only 2.2 percent per year, the lowest since 1953. Most spectacular of all was the stock market boom. In 1985 the Dow Jones Index of leading industrial stocks rose by over 20 percent; in 1986 it leaped by another 15 percent; in the first half of 1987 it soared into the stratosphere.

The stock market boom in part reflected buoyant corporate profits and earnings. Clearly certain industries flourished during the decade. In 1983 IBM's personal computer reinforced the movement toward individualizing computing power already begun by Apple, a Silicon Valley firm established by two young inventors, Stephen Wozniak and Steven Jobs. By mid-decade almost every aspect of life was affected by the little box with a keyboard and a screen—the way people banked, wrote letters, kept accounts, and even spent their leisure time. Whole industries—computer magazines, computer retailers, software manufacturers, computer consultants—grew up around the new device. High-tech stocks were the engine that helped push the stock market to greater highs.

But the bull market also expressed other, less admirable, elements of the 1980s economic culture. The Reagan victory did unleash enterprise, but clearly not all was of the constructive sort. The president and his circle of advisers and allies transmitted the message that there was no need to apologize for wealth, that government was there to befriend business, not to restrain it. This attitude fueled an

The faces of America's competitors. Young Korean women producing electronic gear at Samsung Electronics near Seoul.

unashamed frenzy to get rich without the painful necessity of making a better product or providing a better service.

One aspect of this mood was the resort by men and women in the securities business to "insider trading," the use for private speculative gain of information not available to the general public. Great fortunes were made during the bull market years by such traders as Ivan Boesky using illegal means of manipulating the stock market.

Junk bonds and leveraged buyouts also expressed the new attitude. Junk bonds were securities issued by private firms that were risky to investors. To compensate, they paid high interest rates. Previously scorned by investors, they gained popularity when a young Los Angeles financier, Michael Milken, convinced the investing public that they were actually a good risk. Before long Milken's firm, Drexel, Burnham, Lambert, was selling many millions of dollars of junk bonds to private and corporate investors.

With this new source of funds other shrewd financiers, with relatively little money of their own, bought up large companies, often engaging in fierce bidding wars with their existing managers and large stockholders. The battles for control took on the dimensions of financial epics that resembled the struggles of Gould, Fisk, Vanderbilt, and other robber barons to manipulate Gilded Age corporate finance for their own ends. If successful, the "corporate raider" was seldom interested in improving the efficiency of the new firm or the quality of its product. Usually, he sold off the pieces of the firm that were profitable, often receiving more from the sales of the parts than the whole company had cost him. The remaining husk was not only deprived of its more profitable subsidiaries; it was also saddled with millions of dollars of high-interest junk-bond debt.

Defenders of the system said that it put the managers of sleepy and complacent corporations on their toes. To avoid takeovers they were forced to manage better. Even the large debt was a healthy spur to efficiency, they claimed. Critics pointed out, however, that for many years to come large American corporations would be burdened with back-breaking debt that would starve innovation, research, and product development. While the Japanese and America's other foreign competitors were building better mousetraps and selling them to customers all over the world, we were building fancier credit instruments that shifted income from one American pocket to another, but led to no net increase in the country's wealth or income.

Still another dubious aspect of business during the 1980s was the mismanagement of the nation's "thrifts," the savings and loan associations (S&Ls) that hitherto had provided much of the money for home-buyers mortgages. Until the late 1970s these institutions had been closely regulated. The interest rates they could pay depositors were kept low; their loans were confined to mortgages on private homes.

When market interest rates soared in the 1970s they ceased to be competitive in attracting savings even though the government insured the safety of these savings up to $100,000. In 1980, as we saw, Congress partially deregulated the S&Ls, allowing them to pay competitive interest rates and invest in many other things besides home mortgages. This helped. It stemmed the outflow of deposits, but caused other problems. To pay the higher rates the S&Ls required higher-paying and more liquid investments than the typical twenty-year, 10 percent home mortgage. Many bought the junk bonds that Drexel, Burnham, Lambert and its competitors were offering. Others turned to grandiose commercial projects of dubious profitability. Some simply fell into the hands of con artists who made loans to friends, family, or even disguised versions of themselves on no real security. Much of this high flying was confined to the fastest-growing sections of the country—California, the Mountain States, Texas, and Florida. When, during the mid-1980s, the economies of some of these places deflated, many S&Ls found themselves with millions of dollars of worthless IOUs and unable to pay their depositors.

The public would have been outraged at such practices in any case, but matters were made much worse by the fact that billions of dollars of S&L deposits were insured by the federal government. This meant that the American taxpayer would have to make good on the troubled thrifts' depositors' claims. By the last months of the Reagan term, a few experts close to the events warned that a crisis was building. Few took it seriously. It failed to become an issue during the 1988 campaign, but remained a ticking bomb waiting to detonate.

Deficits.   The most worrisome aspect of the economy from the mid-1980s on was America's deteriorating international position. For the previous three-quarters of a century the United States had sold floods of farm and manufactured goods abroad, far more than we bought. The trade surplus had been offset by large American exports of capital, so that the United States for many years had been the world's largest creditor nation. In 1971, for the first time since 1914, we ran a trade deficit. It was not until the 1980s, however, that this trade gap began to expand at a dangerous rate. By 1984 the American trade shortfall had reached $107 billion a year. In 1986 it had gone to $170 billion, by far the largest in our history.

No nation can continue to run trade deficits for very long unless other nations are willing to lend it money. And so it was now. By 1984, for the first time since World War I, seventy years before, the United States had become a net debtor nation, owing its creditors billions more than they owed us. By 1990, one estimate held, Americans would be paying interest to foreign lenders of over $100 billion a year. The nation's debtor status had humiliating and unsettling effects. Increasingly foreigners came to own ever larger amounts of American assets—stocks, bonds, manufacturing firms, and real estate. In 1990 Americans were

This is ENIAC, one of the first electronic computers. The power of this vast machine is greatly exceeded by the simplest desk top computer of today.

startled and chagrined when a Japanese company bought Rockefeller Center in New York, long considered an American icon. Bit by bit, worried critics said, we were selling our heritage for a mess of Sonys, Toyotas, and Nikons.

The reasons for the sweeping change in America's international position were not simple to diagnose. The quality of American manufactured products relative to their foreign competition had clearly slipped. Through the mid-1980s American industrial and university laboratories continued to lead the world in cutting-edge research. But American companies no longer seemed able to convert this research into attractive, competitively priced consumer goods. Some experts blamed the failure on the excessive focus of American business managers on short-range corporate profit and their own personal financial advantage, versus long-range company growth. Others blamed American workers: They were careless, undisciplined, and ill-educated. Still others blamed the high cost of capital. Americans were not saving; they were spending a larger proportion of their income than ever before. With little domestic saving, investment capital was higher priced here than abroad.

During the 1980s, perceptions such as these spawned a flood of self-critical analyses that pointed the finger at one aspect or another of American culture or policy: our poor educational system, especially the lower levels; our lack of pride in work and insistence on instant gratification; our excessive spending on defense, which protected American industry against the rigors of domestic competition. Toward the decade's close a minor industry of books and articles appeared proclaiming the intellectual and cultural thinness of Americans, especially the young. Alan Bloom's *The Closing of the American Mind*, though a difficult book, became a best-seller in 1987. The results of various international tests, meanwhile, showed that Americans ranked behind the citizens of almost all industrial nations in their knowledge of geography, math, science, history, art, and virtually everything else. The message was obvious: How could such a collection of primitives expect to compete with the rest of the world?

But other observers absolved Americans of much of the blame and pointed the finger at others. America's chief international rival was Japan, and Japan, many critics said, did not play fair. While the United States remained open to foreign imports, the Japanese refused to buy American goods even when they were indisputably superior to the domestic product. Japan did not act as a normal society where individuals were anxious to buy the best products at the lowest prices wherever produced. Japanese consumers saved a large part of their income and then bought only goods produced at home. Moreover, said the "Japan bash-

ers," the Japanese government, though professing to favor open markets, actually raised a multitude of phony barriers to foreign goods while at the same time dumping such Japanese products as computer microchips at below cost on foreign markets to destroy the local industry. Japan, in fact, considered international trade a form of warfare, and, said some critics, its enormous trading surplus with the United States was a kind of revenge for military defeat in 1945.

Whatever the facts, the administration placed strong pressure on the Japanese to import more American goods. They proved evasive. Agreements were reached but did not accomplish their ends. Somehow American companies could not sell their products in Japan. Japanese trade policies angered many Americans. By the end of the decade many would see Japan as a worse threat to the United States than the Soviet Union. Labor unions and business groups demanded that Congress hit back with tariffs and other restrictive legislation. And at times the government did. Washington forced the Japanese to limit the number of automobiles exported to America. But the Japanese countered this policy by upgrading their car exports to luxury models to increase their dollar volume. In March 1987 the administration imposed duties on a wide range of Japanese electronic goods in response to the dumping of microchips. In the end the Reagan administration, like its successor, would be constrained by the desire to avoid the sort of international trade war that had worsened the effects of the 1930s Great Depression. Problems with Japan were bad enough, but looming ahead was the economic union to be forged in 1992 by the industrial countries of Western Europe. Would this create another world economic powerhouse to compete with the United States?

But not only had the United States accrued enormous foreign debts in the 1980s; the American government had piled up enormous domestic debts. As we saw, the tax cuts of 1981 and after, combined with the giant defense build-up of the early eighties, had produced unparalleled annual federal deficits. These continued even after defense spending leveled off. Congress, under Democratic control, refused to cut domestic spending further; the Republican administration refused to consider raising taxes, or raising them enough. In 1985 Congress passed the Gramm-Rudman Act to force itself to cut the deficit. The law mandated specific yearly target reductions of the federal deficit under penalty of automatic meat-ax, across-the-board cuts in all federal outlays that no one wanted.

Gramm-Rudman did seem to impose some fiscal restraint. By 1988 the annual deficit was down to $155 billion from the $221 billion of 1985. Yet Americans still had reason for concern. By that year the deficit had pushed the total national debt to over $2.6 trillion, more than $10,500

Henry Cisneros

In April 1981, a tall, slender Mexican-American was elected mayor of San Antonio, Texas, with 62 percent of the vote. Henry Cisneros's election victory marked the triumph of a talented young man. It also marked the abrupt arrival on the political scene of the millions of Mexican-Americans who, until Cisneros's victory, had failed to make a major impression on American public life.

Henry Cisneros's career is the epitome of one sort of immigrant success story. His way was eased by education, by strong family standards and values, and by elite patronage. He was never confrontational. Cisneros learned that in San Antonio in the 1970s and 1980s the way to get results was by hard bargaining and compromise, not by intimidation and angry attack.

Cisneros was born in June 1947 into a middle-class Mexican-American home. His mother was the daughter of Jose Romulo Munguia—a supporter of the Mexican democratic leader Venustiano Carranza—who left his homeland for the United States in 1924 with 18 cents in his pocket and established a successful print shop on San Antonio's West Side. His father's family had roots in the original Spanish settlers of New Mexico. Though his paternal grandfather was poor and worked as a farm laborer, George Cisneros, Henry's father, managed to wrest an education for himself. After college he worked for the government as a civil servant and, following World War II military service, remained in the Army reserve, rising to the rank of full colonel.

Henry grew up in San Antonio's Prospect Hill. Four blocks away began the *barrio*, the dilapidated slums where most of the city's thousands of Chicanos lived in poverty. The Cisneros's neighborhood was an at-tractive area of tree-lined streets and substantial frame houses, many formerly occupied by San Antonio's large German population. Clearly Henry would not have to start from the lowest rung of the ladder.

The Cisneros-Munguia clan provided an ideal climate for achievement. Grandfather Munguia was a self-taught intellectual who had accumulated a large library on Mexican history and culture. He introduced his grandchildren to the pleasures of reading and encouraged them to respect their ancestral heritage. Henry's parents, George and Elvira, were ambitious for their four children, but reinforced their wishes by both precept and example. Each of the Cisneros children had prescribed household chores to perform. The family also dined together regularly and George and Elvira made the dinner table a forum for the exchange of ideas. The Cisneros dinner table debates often went on for hours after the dishes were cleared.

Henry and the other children attended good Catholic parochial schools. At Central Catholic High Henry was spotted as a bright lad and taken under the wing of Brother Martin McMurtrey, the school's outstanding teacher of English and literature. This sort of patronage would be repeated more than once in later years, and it would be an invaluable boost to Henry's career.

Drawing on his father's example, Henry at first considered a military career. When he failed to get into the Air Force Academy, however, he chose Texas A&M, at College Station, Texas. There, his lively intelligence, his good humor, and his capacity for friendship made him a big man on campus. At the close of his sophomore year he was selected sergeant-major of the Texas "Aggie" band. Success at Texas A&M by itself was a useful accomplishment for any ambitious Texan. But equally important was the patronage of Wayne Stark, director of the Aggie Memorial Student Union. Stark sought out talented young people, especially from the minority communities, and encouraged them to use their potential. With wide connections around the state, he was able to gain entry for the Mexican-American to the Houston and Dallas business community.

Henry's life changed when he was sent to a student conference on United States affairs held at West Point. The meeting was an eye-opener. For the first time Henry met undergraduates from the elite colleges and discovered how far behind he was. "I was totally outclassed," he later said. "We sat around a conference table and I never opened my mouth." After this trip east Henry surrendered all thought of a military career and decided to become an urban planner.

In January 1969, after graduation, Henry, just twenty-one, became assistant director of the Model Cities Program for San Antonio. Before the Model Cities era, San Antonio politics had been dominated by the Good Government League (GGL), a coalition of civic-minded business people and good-government reformers. The GGL represented the "Anglo" establishment, though it generally received much Mexican-American support. Model Cities, by raising Mexican-American ethnic pride, split many Mexican-Americans away from the GGL. In 1969 Pete Torres ran against the GGL slate as an independent and won election to the City Council.

The Model Cities experience was a wonderful training ground for Henry Cisneros. "Everything I know about citizen participation and the mechanics of making government work, I learned during the Model Cities years," he later declared. Model Cities also convinced him that he needed more training in administration and finance and in 1970 he, and his young bride, Mary Alice, left for Washington, D.C., where Henry enrolled in George Washington University's doctoral program in urban administration.

While pursuing his studies, Cisneros worked for the National League of Cities (NLC), a lobbying agency for American cities seeking federal grants. At the NLC offices he met a flock of big-city mayors who had come to Washington to beg Congress and the administration for favors. Before completing his degree at George Washington University, Cisneros applied and was accepted as a White House Fellow, a highly competitive internship program established by Lyndon Johnson to introduce bright young people to the problems and challenges of government.

Cisneros was assigned to Elliot Richardson, Nixon's Secretary of Health, Education, and Welfare, as a general assistant. He was singularly fortunate. Richardson was a blueblood Bostonian with high principles. He would later become the Nixon administration's "Mr. Clean," one of the few Nixon associates not tainted by Watergate. Richardson took the young couple from San Antonio under his wing and not only provided Henry with valuable political training, but also exposed him and Mary Alice to the cultural life of Washington and changed Henry's dress style to fit eastern elite standards. Richardson also helped Cisneros get financial support for two years at the Kennedy School of Government at Harvard. In 1973, Harvard granted him a master's degree in public administration.

In August 1974 Henry and his wife returned to San Antonio where Henry had a job waiting as assistant professor of environmental studies at the local branch of the University of Texas. By the time the couple returned home, the Good Government League was in a shambles, having the previous year failed to get its candidate elected mayor for the first time in twenty years. Despite its disarray, and although many Mexican-Americans no longer supported the GGL, Henry accepted the league's nomination for city councilman. Mounting a highly personal campaign, he won in a landslide and, at twenty-seven, became the youngest councilman in the city's history.

The young council member came to office at an auspicious time. The San Antonio Anglo leadership was divided between an older group of businessmen belonging to the downtown Greater Chamber of Commerce and a younger element, with roots in the suburbs, that belonged to the Northside Chamber of Commerce. The first represented the remnants of GGL power in the city; the second had little use for the decrepit GGL. The two groups also disagreed over the city's future economic growth. The Greater Chamber people were essentially contented. They did not oppose growth, but neither did they push for it very hard. Their adversaries were aggressive promoters of new shopping malls, industrial parks, and housing developments, but mostly on the city's suburban outskirts where land was cheap.

Cisneros was pro-development and pro-business, unlike Ernie Cortes, head of Communities Organized for Public Service (COPS), a grass-roots organization inspired by Saul Alinsky's Chicago-based Industrial Areas Foundation. Alinsky was the father of a community organized by neighborhood people to force concessions out of "the establishment," and COPS adopted an angry confrontational approach to the business community. As a city councilman, Cisneros often cooperated with COPS, but he believed their style was counterproductive. The Southwest Sun Belt was undergoing an explosive period of growth, and San Antonio, he believed, must grab some of it for itself. But the growth must not be confined to the new suburban areas and solely benefit the white middle class. Rather, business people who sought favors and concessions of San Antonio must promise to build their factories, stores, and offices close to minority neighborhoods so that jobs, contracts, and other boons would come to the city's black and Mexican-American population as well as the Anglo middle class.

Cisneros served three terms on the San Antonio City Council and became in those six years the hero of the city's Mexican-American population by fighting for protection of the city's water supply and for lower natural gas rates. In 1980 he decided to run for mayor when Lila Cockrell, the well-liked Anglo lady and the first woman mayor of a large American city, decided to return to private life.

His opponent was John Thomas Steen, a rich insurance executive and a member of the city's old business establishment, though himself a self-made man. Steen's supporters included the old GGL people and the downtown business community. Cisneros, of course, had his own Mexican-Americans on his side. He also won over a segment of the new suburban developers, at odds with the city's traditional business establishment. These business people were willing to accept Cisneros's vision of a community-benefits-oriented development and contributed generously to his campaign. On April 4, 1981, Henry Cisneros won handily with 62 percent of the vote, including almost half those in San Antonio's Anglo precincts.

Cisneros's election attracted wide media attention. Here was the first Mexican-American mayor of a major American city. Yet in fact the city's head did not wield great power. San Antonio had an appointed city manager who handled its routine day-to-day affairs; the elected mayor's $4,000 annual salary reflected the mayor's limited powers. The only way that Cisneros could afford the job was by continuing to teach at the university. Though he was little more than the first among equals on the City Council, he made his mark on city policy by his intelligence, moral force, public support, and his ability to establish the council's agenda.

Cisneros's administration was a resounding success. He managed to lower fuel prices for consumers, get the legislature to establish a school of engineering in San Antonio, and draw industry to the city. In some ways his most important achievement was to give the city's Mexican-American majority a sense of participation in the political process and reduce ethnic conflict. When he ran for reelection in 1983, Cisneros won an astounding 94 percent of the total vote.

Cisneros's success gave him national visibility. Here was a well-spoken, personable—and moderate—Mexican-American who demonstrated the willingness of American society to reward merit from any group. In July 1983 President Reagan selected him as a member of the National Bipartisan Commission on Central America to consider American policy in El Salvador and toward the Sandinistas of Nicaragua. Here he served as a balance wheel to the conservatives who favored a hard-line policy toward the Central American left. In the end, the commission report reflected many of the mayor's concerns for human rights violations by the far right in both countries. In a number of dissenting footnotes he also proposed a dialogue with the Marxist Sandinista group to discourage them from exporting revolution to their neighbors.

On July 4, 1984, Henry Cisneros, with his wife and two small daughters, faced the national press in front of Walter Mondale's home in St. Paul, Minnesota. Mondale had virtually won his campaign for the Democratic presidential nomination and was interviewing potential vice presidential candidates. Mondale said that Cisneros would make a "superb vice president"; he had "the ability, the strength, the values, the drive." Although at home his Hispanic background had come to seem irrelevant, the mayor himself recognized that he filled a special niche in a Mondale election strategy. When questioned by the reporters about his possible contribution to a Democratic ticket, Cisneros declared that he thought he would bring to the vice president's job important special values—values "related to our country's relationship to the south, values that relate to how people are living in the central cities of America, values that relate to the problems of those who lose by the transitioning American economy."

In the end, Mondale's choice fell on Congresswoman Geraldine Ferraro of New York, who represented another important ethnic group. Yet the candidate-hunting process had made Henry Cisneros a national figure.

Toward the end of the 1980s Cisneros's career seemed to falter. In 1989 he announced that, owing to personal and financial problems, he intended to leave office as mayor of San Antonio when his current term ended. But Cisneros was not out of the public eye. In early 1990 he joined with several long-time associates to form the Cisneros Group, a firm dedicated to managing investments for pension funds, universities, and other institutional clients. Cisneros was frank about his motives. As mayor his salary had been almost nominal; he had been forced to support his family by his writing and lecturing. Now, he told reporters, he intended to establish "an asset base sufficient not to have to depend upon fund-raising." He also continued to speak out on public issues, especially ones of interest to Texas, minorities, and San Antonio.

With Bill Clinton's election as president, Cisneros resumed his political career. In December 1992 the president-elect nominated Cisneros as secretary of housing and urban development (HUD), the federal department most directly involved in the gritty problems of the nation's cities. Early in the new administration he won easy confirmation by the Senate.

Cisneros would still be only fifty-three by the time the twenty-first century began, and his future seemed bright. In the years ahead, the demographers predicted, Latinos would become the nation's largest minority ethnic group, and they were sure to be heard from politically. As a lawyer friend said at the time of the cabinet nomination: "No one who knows Henry thinks that being HUD secretary is the last thing he is going to do."

for every man, woman, and child. The interest alone on this sum amounted to $214 billion each year. Such an interest payout deprived the private capital markets of an enormous amount of badly needed investment funds. The deficit also thwarted every proposal for additional federal programs, no matter how meritorious or cost-effective. Whether intended or not, Reaganomics had incapacitated the government, the only agency that could tackle many of the problems that faced the American people.

Yet the administration did accomplish one significant fiscal reform. In May 1986 Congress passed a major tax revision act that closed loopholes that aided the rich, phased out deductions for consumer interest charges but retained those on home mortgages, and removed many poor people from the federal income tax rolls entirely. But in compensation, the bill further lowered rates for top income earners to 28 percent. The bill was "revenue neutral": It neither raised nor lowered total tax receipts. But some critics considered it more favorable to the rich than the poor.

"Irangate". In 1986–1987 Ronald Reagan seemed to lose his Teflon coating. The event that changed his luck was a secret arms-for-hostages deal with Iran with the profits from the sale of weapons secretly shunted to the Nicaraguan Contras. Reagan himself may not have known about the "Irangate" actions undertaken by his National Security Council advisers, but if he had not himself broken the law and violated the Constitution, he had displayed a dismaying ignorance of events taking place just a few hundred feet from the Oval Office. Many critics said the Iran arms deal revealed the serious decline of the president's personal capacity.

Two motives apparently moved the chief Irangate instigators: William Casey, head of the CIA; Lt. Colonel Oliver North of the National Security Council (NSC); and his chief at the NSC, Vice Admiral John Poindexter. All three men believed the Nicaraguan Sandinistas were a dangerous threat to American interests in the hemisphere. But Congress resisted supplying the Contras with the funds they needed and for a time had cut these off entirely. The end of American aid would assure a Marxist victory in Central America, the small circle at the CIA and the NSC believed. They also believed, apparently, that they could make some sort of contact with "moderate" elements in Iran, leaders who might be induced to take a more friendly position toward the United States than the Khomeini regime.

The key to this policy was arms sales to Iran. The Iranians were desperate for military weapons to help defeat the Iraqis, with whom they had been at war since 1980. They would pay any price to get guns, missiles, and aircraft parts, and perhaps in gratitude, the Casey-North-Poindexter theory apparently went, they would adopt a more reasonable view of the United States. Making contact with the Iranians might serve several other purposes as well. The Iranians, it was clear, had influence over the Muslim fanatics who had taken Americans hostage in Lebanon, if they had not in fact sponsored them directly. President Reagan and other Americans, deluged for months with pathetic media stories about the victims' plight, had become excessively concerned about freeing them. Though for months the president had been proclaiming that the United States would never pay ransom for hostages, he apparently did not object when North, Poindexter, and others suggested that the Iranians might be induced to use their influence to get the hostages released in return for sorely needed arms.

There was an additional element in the complicated covert scheme. The profits from the deal did not have to be made public. Why not just transfer these funds to the Contras, thus getting around Congress's unwillingness to fund the "freedom fighters" struggling to overthrow the Marxist Nicaraguan regime?

The Iran-Contra deals were conceived in mid-1985 when the president authorized the then National Security Adviser, Robert McFarlane, to contact Iranian officials and offer to sell them arms. Soon after, he approved sending American missiles in Israeli possession to the Iranians, the first of several shipments. At the end of 1985 National Security Council aide Lt. Colonel North told the Israelis that he intended to use the profits from future sales to the Iranians to secretly fund the Contras.

In May 1986 North and McFarlane, the latter now a private citizen, flew to Iran to meet with Iranian "moderates" and make a deal for further arms sales in exchange for the Lebanon hostages. They quickly found that there were no real "moderates" in the Iranian government and they did not secure the release of any of the captives. In fact, shortly after their visit Muslim extremists in Lebanon took several new American hostages. Finally, on November 2, the day before a Lebanese magazine published details of the arms sales and McFarlane's visit to Teheran, the extremists released the first of a small group of kidnapped Americans.

The actual arms deals took place through intermediaries, who took a share of the profits. An uncertain portion of the remainder ended up in the coffers of the Contras where it paid for arms and supplies in the anti-Sandinista guerrilla war, though by this time Congress had relented and had agreed to resume military aid.

Most Americans were shocked when they learned of the Iran-Contra deal at the end of 1986. The public had counted on Ronald Reagan to be tough on terrorists and America's enemies generally. He had repeatedly denounced the Libyans and the Iranians and held them accountable for bombings and hostage-takings. In April 1986, after a number of airplane hijackings, airport bombings, and an attack on an American servicemen's discotheque in West Berlin that implicated the Libyans, Reagan ordered an air attack against the Libyan cities of Tripoli and Benghasi from aircraft carriers and from air bases in Britain. One of the attacks almost killed Libyan strongman Muammar Qaddafi. Over 77 percent of the American public endorsed the attacks, although they feared the volatile Qaddafi would retaliate and, in droves, canceled plans to travel in Europe and the Mediterranean during the summer of 1986.

But after this bold strike, what was the public now to make of the deal with the worst terrorists in the entire Mideast? It seemed hard to believe that the Ronald Reagan who had authorized the arms-for-hostages trade was the same man who had ordered the Libyan and Grenada attacks. The deal would come to seem especially ironic when, in late 1987, the United States and the Iranians became involved in a minor shooting war in the Persian Gulf following the administration's risky decision to place Kuwaiti oil tankers under American protection to fend off attack by the Ayatollah's forces.

Americans from all parts of the political spectrum were appalled by the Iran-Contra affair. What antiterrorist credibility did America have left now that it had made a deal with Iran to ransom hostages? And who was running American foreign policy? Congress had cut off funds for the Contras. Did the administration or, more accurately, a small cabal within the administration, have the right to ignore the nation's constitutional policy-making processes?

At first the president denied that there had been an arms-for-hostages deal. He acknowledged that the United States had sent "defensive weapons" and spare parts to Iran but refused to concede that the purpose had been to buy the hostages' freedom. Few people believed him. A week or so later Attorney General Meese admitted that profits from the arms sales had been diverted to the Contras, and soon thereafter the president announced that he had fired Oliver North and accepted the resignation of Admiral Poindexter.

Through the weeks of new revelations that followed, the president seemed confused and ill-informed about what had been done under his very nose. Chief of staff Donald Regan, to save his own reputation, soon disclosed a White House where confusion reigned and where, he said, only his own rearguard actions had prevented open scandal.

Moderates and liberals were especially dismayed. As more information surfaced, it became clear that a rogue operation, without supervision by constitutional authorities, had been mounted by quite junior officials in the government, in violation of federal law. Once again, as under Nixon, an administration had violated public trust and ridden roughshod over the Constitution. In mid-December Reagan authorized a special prosecutor, as in the Watergate affair, to investigate the Iran-Contra matter. The president also appointed a commission headed by former Republican Senator John Tower of Texas to investigate what had happened. Meanwhile, Congress established its own investigating committee to look into the affair.

In late February 1987 the Tower Commission issued a report condemning the administration's operations as "chaotic" and "amateurish." It expressed dismay at Reagan's "personal management style" and criticized him for allowing his concern for the hostages to get in the way of his good sense, but it absolved him of actual wrongdoing. The chief Tower Commission Report culprit was Donald Regan, who was blamed for not keeping the president informed of White House operations. Regan, now under heavy attack, fought to keep his job, but the First Lady, Nancy Reagan, highly protective of her husband, turned against him and helped force him out. Soon after, Howard Baker, the respected former senator from Tennessee, assumed the role of White House chief of staff. Many people, skeptical of the president's grasp, applauded the change. At least now the aging chief executive would have a skilled and savvy man to back him up.

The congressional hearings on the Iran-Contra affair began in early May 1987 with a parade of witnesses who told of the complex negotiations and intrigues that constituted the operation. The two chief witnesses were Colonel North and Admiral Poindexter, both of whom appeared under grant of partial immunity from legal prosecution. CIA director Casey could not be examined; he had died of a brain tumor, taking his knowledge of the intrigue to the grave.

During the televised hearings, Poindexter did not make a favorable impression, but the young, crisp, articulate North made a powerful case for his actions and managed to indict his critics as people of dubious patriotism. The public at first ate it up. For a week or two the nation found itself in the grip of "Ollimania," an uncritical acceptance of North, at his own word, as a patriot and a hero.

Meanwhile, the president's reputation and standing slipped badly. A December 1986 poll showed that Reagan's approval rating had dropped from 67 percent to 46 percent in one month. In late April 1987, some 65 percent of those asked by a *Washington Post*–ABC poll believed the president was not telling the truth about his role in the Iran-Contra fiasco. The Teflon, it seemed, had finally begun to wear off the country's chief executive.

Nicaragua Resolved. The polls also showed that the public remained unwilling to become deeply involved in

To millions of Americans he was a hero; to others a dangerous adventurer. Lt. Colonel Oliver North testifying to a congressional investigating committee on his role in the Iran-Contra affair.

Nicaragua. In early 1986, of those questioned by the pollsters, 62 percent opposed giving aid to the Contras. Even among those who considered themselves Reagan partisans, only 35 percent favored Contra assistance.

Yet the president and his advisers continued to seek the overthrow of Daniel Ortega and his government. Liberals, as well as activists on the left, meanwhile continued to liken Nicaragua to Vietnam and warned against becoming bogged down in another military and political swamp, this one nearer home.

Toward the end of 1987 it began to look as if a peaceful solution might emerge in Central America after all. Five Central American nations, led by president Oscar Arias-Sanchez of Costa Rica, agreed on a peace plan designed to bring the Contras and Sandinistas together, to introduce democratic practices into Nicaragua, and end the threat of superpower intervention in that country. The plan was hailed around the world as a model of local self-determination, and President Arias won the 1987 Nobel Peace Prize for his role in its conception. In the United States, most Democrats also approved of it as a way out of the Central American impasse, but the administration remained skeptical. The plan, it said, did not guarantee Soviet exclusion from Nicaragua, hold Ortega to strict enough account for fulfilling his part of the bargain, or sufficiently protect the interests of the Contras. It looked for a time as if the peace plan had stalled. Then, in late March 1988, the Sandinistas and

the Contras signed a cease-fire. In 1990 an anti-Sandinista coalition led by Violetta Chamorro won a surprise victory over the Sandinistas in a free election. It finally looked as if the Nicaragua problem would be peacefully resolved.

The Soviet Union and Arms Reduction.   During 1985 and 1986, following the arms negotiations breakdown, the United States and the Soviet Union continued to snipe at one another, mostly over spying activities. But vast changes were underway in the Soviet Union that would soon transform worldwide international relations.

The author of these changes was the new soviet leader, Mikhail Gorbachev, a reformer who sought to revive a society increasingly corrupt, rigid, and ineffectual. Back in the 1960s when Nikita Khrushchev had threatened "to bury" the West under a tide of Soviet goods, Communist economic prowess seemed a reality. But as the 1980s advanced, the USSR appeared ever more incapable of providing the consumer products its people craved and the economic strength and technological capacity it needed to compete against the industrial capitalist nations in the world arena. Gorbachev perceived the weaknesses of the Soviet system and pushed his reform policies of *glasnost* (openness) and *perestroika* (economic restructuring) to overcome them.

Gorbachev was impelled primarily by domestic concerns. But he recognized that the Soviet Union's commitment to expansionist foreign initiatives were unbearable economic burdens and must be reduced if Soviet restructuring was to succeed. Perhaps, as some observers believed, the prospect of another arms race with the United States, especially a Star Wars hightech competition, was a critical factor in his decision to contract Soviet power around the world.

The first fruit of Gorbachev's foreign policy was the resumption of U.S.–Soviet arms talks broken off in 1983. Eventually, in December 1987, Gorbachev and Reagan signed an agreement in Washington eliminating all medium-range missiles in Europe, thereby accepting the main ingredients of the American position at Geneva three years before. For the first time, a whole class of nuclear missiles would actually be eliminated. During his visit to the United States the affable, balding, Soviet leader delighted the American public. He joked and smiled and stopped his limousine on a Washington street to shake hands with pedestrians. Americans even liked his wife, Raisa, though Nancy Reagan, it seemed, did not. The trim and stylish Raisa Gorbachev was the first Kremlin "First Lady," one wag remarked, who weighed less than her husband.

"Black Monday".   In some sense the Reagan era ended with a crash on October 19, 1987, when the stock market dropped over 500 points in a few hours. This was the most

The "Evil Empire" did not look so evil this day. Gorbachev and Reagan signing the INF nuclear arms reduction treaty in the White House.

catastrophic one-day decline in the history of Wall Street. In the estimate of experts, a trillion dollars in paper wealth had been wiped out between August 25, when stocks had reached their all time Dow Jones peak of 2722, and October 20, with most of the loss on Black Monday itself.

For a time there were dire predictions that the nation, and perhaps the world, was staring another Great Depression in the face. The disaster did not happen. Stocks soon recovered and by mid-1990 had risen above their 1987 high. Nor did the nation go into an economic tailspin. Modest growth continued; unemployment remained low; price increases neither slowed nor accelerated.

And yet something significant had happened. Black Monday dissipated the cloud of cocky and arrogant economic confidence that surrounded the Reagan era. Thereafter there would be less flaunting of wealth and less facile defense of crude financial wheeling-dealing. For many high-flying yuppies the stock crash represented a whiff of mortality, and it was sobering. As the magic went out of stocks and bonds, employment in the nation's financial centers dropped. No longer would the best and the brightest of the nation's undergraduates head straight for the graduate business schools and six-figure jobs on Wall Street. In Chicago, Los Angeles, Boston, and New York, down went the prices of luxury condominiums and sales of quiche and Brie. The United States remained two unequal economic nations, but the privileged no longer exuded the assertivenss and self-confidence of the recent past. Soon after the 1987 crash the media were announcing the end of the 1980s. By the early 1990s there were even signs of revived liberal confidence.

★ CONCLUSIONS ★

Ronald Reagan and his supporters hoped to launch a "revolution," a conservative revolution. They achieved at least part of what they sought.

They wished to limit the size and scope of government, and they succeeded to a point. Domestic programs for the nonworking poor were reduced, restrained, or eliminated. Few new ones were adopted. The federal government reduced its oversight role in many areas of business activity. Federal participation in a wide range of activities was replaced by state control instead. More important, however—whether the result was intended or fortuitous—the drastic tax cuts created a problem of severe deficits that promised to tie the hands of the federal government for years to come.

Yet the conservative ideologues were never able to make the cut in activist government they really wanted. There were too many constituents for aid to dependent families, Head Start, water and air pollution controls, resource conservation, health research, and the many other functions and roles that modern government had assumed even in the United States. Federal budget outlays on existing domestic programs continued to grow, though at a slower pace.

Increased efficiency and the elimination of fraud and waste were essential parts of the Reagan program for government. Here the administration's record was a mixture of hypocrisy and inattention. Early in the next administration congressional probes revealed that the Department of Housing and Urban Development under Secretary Samuel Pierce, Jr., had squandered millions of dollars in dubious, and probably illegal, housing projects that benefited insiders rather than the poor. At the same time the S&L scandal burst on the public consciousness. Though there was plenty of blame to go around, the Reagan administration had encouraged further S&L deregulation and the slack administration of remaining restraints had occurred under Reagan appointees.

The Reaganites had promised to revive the American economy and tap new sources of economic productivity. The United States would once more become the economic locomotive that pulled the free world. And the average American, not just the rich, would benefit, for a booming economy would scatter its blessings over all. The administration could point to some economic successes. Reaganite economic policies helped break the dangerous inflationary cycle of the 1970s. During the 1980s, moreover, the economy absorbed millions of new workers entering the job market. Once past the 1982–1983 slump, the economy began a growth phase that lasted longer than any in history.

Yet the economic downside was undeniable. During the decade there was a shift of income shares from the poorest groups to the richest, with the very richest 1 percent improving their relative standing more than any other sector of the public. Administration policies alone did not explain this outcome; world economic trends were surely in part responsible as well. Still, Reaganite tax policy and deregulation encouraged the unequal result. Nor did the administration's economic policies stem America's relative international decline. Indeed, many experts believed that the massive federal budget deficits imposed severe limitations on any possibility for improving the country's competitiveness. Too much of the nation's savings, they said, was absorbed by the persistent deficits; they prevented needed federal expenditures for education, roads and bridges, research, and many other things required for the United States to catch up to its chief world rivals.

The Reaganites came to office resolved to restore respect for traditional social values. They sought to limit abortion rights and strengthen old-fashioned family structures. Their immediate success was limited. There was little that any administration in Washington could do in the short run about the drastic changes in American sexual mores and family patterns. Illegitimacy, divorce, and broken families continued to plague the nation. The conservatives' long-term impact on social values promised to be more significant, however. Through their appointments to the federal courts, Reagan and his successor probably had assured that the legal rights of women, blacks, criminal defendants, artists, and political outsiders, which had been generously expanded during the 1960s and 1970s, would in time be restricted. But at most federal court decisions affected grass-roots Americans marginally.

Reagan had come to office pledged to restoring world respect for the United States and reducing Soviet power and political influence. He left with America and its allies on the verge of an astonishing victory over their Communist adversaries. Two years into his successor's administration, the Soviet Union had ceased to be a threat to Western Europe or, for that matter, to any nation around the world. Everywhere communism was collapsing; the Cold War was over and it would be hard to refute the claim that the West had won.

Obviously the Reagan arms build-up and the stubborn resolve to deploy new nuclear weapons on NATO soil do not by themselves explain the stupefying result. The containment policy went back to the late 1940s and had been supported by half a dozen administrations. Yet it would be difficult to dismiss the influence of eighties hard-line policies in inducing Kremlin leadership to reconsider aggressive Soviet international commitments.

Was there a Reagan Revolution? Keeping in mind the normal inertia of America's political culture, its resistance to quick shifts, the term may be valid. The years 1981–1988 witnessed more rapid change than most equal intervals of the past. Inevitably, however, Americans would disagree over whether to cheer or to scoff.

******** FOR FURTHER READING ********

Ronnie Dugger. *On Reagan: The Man and His Presidency* (1983) A highly critical view of Reagan and his administration by the publisher of the *Texas Observer*, a liberal magazine. Despite the bias, it is a useful source for Reagan's first term.

Elizabeth Drew. *Campaign Journal: The Political Events of 1983–1984* (1985) Theodore White no longer writes his quadrennial histories of American presidential elections. In their absence we will have to do with Elizabeth Drew's. This volume is not as readable as White's *The Making of the President* series, but it is probably better reportage.

Charles Murray. *Losing Ground: American Social Policy, 1950–1980* (1984) Though this work deals with the years before Reagan's presidency, it expresses many of the conservative attitudes toward social policy that characterized the Reagan administration. It should be read as a document of conservative thought.

Sidney Blumenthal. *The Rise of the Counter-Establishment: From Conservative Ideology to Political Power* (1986)

A critical, liberal-oriented treatment of the conservative surge of the 1970s and 1980. Blumenthal focuses on the ideological foundations of conservativism in the 1980s and the intellectuals who created that foundation.

Thomas Ferguson and Joel Rogers. *Right Turn: The Decline of the Democrats and the Future of American Politics* (1986)

This is another critical appraisal of the Reagan administration. The authors conclude that Reaganism triumphed, not because public opinion shifted to the right, but because the Democrats collapsed politically and a new elite, composed of rich business people, manipulated the electoral process successfully to achieve their conservative ends.

Robert S. McElvaine. *The End of the Conservative Era: Liberalism After Reagan* (1987)

Placing his faith in a cycle theory of conservative-liberal swings, McElvaine believes the impetus behind the Reagan Revolution had waned by the mid-1980s. He warns the Democrats against conservative "me-tooism" in the mistaken quest for popular support.

Randy Shilts. *And the Band Played On: Politics, People, and the AIDS Epidemic* (1987)

A crack San Francisco reporter chronicles the AIDS plague, both as an unfolding human tragedy and as a story of folly and error. Shilts blames both the gay community and the government, especially the Reagan administration, for their failure to see the magnitude of the impending disaster and to act quickly to contain it.

Garry Wills. *Reagan's America* (1988)

An impressionistic, skeptical view of Ronald Reagan's life and career by a liberal scholar of the American presidency. Wills finds the key to much of Reagan's presidency in the illusory values Reagan acquired as a youth in the Midwest and as a young actor in Hollywood.

Jack W. Germond and Jules Witcover. *Wake Us When It's Over: Presidential Politics of 1984* (1985)

Germond and Witcover don't respect the way Americans now nominate and elect their presidents. This description of the 1984 election emphasizes the work of professional media and campaign advisers who package the candidates and brainwash, mislead, and deceive the voting public in the process.

David Stockman. *The Triumph of Politics: The Inside Story of the Reagan Revolution* (1986)

The Reagan budget director's account of how he sold the president and his advisers an economic policy that he himself was unsure of and how, in his estimate, it failed.

Martin Anderson. *Revolution* (1988)

A "supply-side" true-believer's view of the Reagan Revolution. Anderson believes it really was a revolution.

Donald Regan. *For the Record: From Wall Street to Washington* (1988)

Bitter at being made the scapegoat for the Iran-Contra fiasco, Reagan chief-of-staff Don Regan reveals the confusion in the White House, Nancy Reagan's influence on the president, and various astrologers' influence on her.

Peggy Noonan. *What I Saw at the Revolution* (1990)

A witty and wry account of what it was like to be a speechwriter for Ronald Reagan. By a conservative admirer.

Nancy Reagan. *My Turn: The Memoirs of Nancy Reagan* (1989)

The former First Lady gets *her* licks in in this volume—after taking it on the chin herself. Many of the critics were snide about the book, but it is not without merit.

Clyde Prestowitz. *Trading Places: How We Allowed Japan to Take the Lead* (1988)

Japan-bashing at its most convincing by a former U.S. trade official who had to negotiate with the Japanese.

Laurence Tribe. *Abortion: The Clash of Absolutes* (1990)

A sophisticated history and analysis of the abortion war by a strong pro-choice constitutional lawyer at Harvard Law School.

Kevin Phillips. *The Politics of Rich and Poor: Wealth and the American Electorate in the Reagan Aftermath* (1990)

Phillips is the conservative political analyst who helped inspire the Nixon administration's "forgotten American" strategy. He is disillusioned by Reaganomics and deplores—and probably exaggerates—its upward redistributive effect. He foresees a new populist uprising based on class resentment just down the road.

Paul Freiberger and Michael Swaine. *Fire in the Valley: The Making of the Personal Computer* (1984)

The best single-volume history of a subject so new that the ancient past is 1975. Good reading if you've got an Apple or PC.

32★

A DIFFERENT AMERICA?

Would Diversity and the Cold War's End Change America?

1988	Presidential Race. George Bush defeats Michael Dukakis
1989	Economic slump begins • Bush appoints Anthony Kennedy and Antonin Scalia to Supreme Court • Berlin Wall razed, Communism collapses in Eastern Europe
1990	Bush agrees to raise taxes • Savings and Loan defaults reach over $100 billion • Iraq invades Kuwait, U.S. sends troops to Persian Gulf
1991	Business bankruptcies reach record high • Clarence Thomas, nominee for Supreme Court, accused of sexual harassment by Anita Hill • Gulf War • American air, naval, and ground forces attack Iraq win quick victory • In USSR Boris Yeltsin replaces Mikhail Gorbachev • Soviet Union dissolved • Cold War ends
1992	Presidential election, Bill Clinton defeats George Bush • U.S. troops sent to Somalia for humanitarian reasons
1993	Clinton starts administration with rash of gaffes • Appoints an ethnically diverse set of top advisers • Seeks to legalize gays in the military • Yugoslavia falls apart and ethnic war breaks out among constituent parts • U.S. troops withdrawn from Somalia • Clinton budget, cutting growth of deficits, passed • Also National Service Plan for Youth and Family Leave Bill • Congress passes NAFTA • Administration introduces major federal health care reform bill prepared by First Lady, Hillary Rodham Clinton
1994	American military forces sent to Haiti to restore democracy • Administration health care bill not passed by Congress

Without question 1989 was a watershed in global history. In that momentous year the Cold War that had divided the world into two opposing camps for almost half a century and defined much of the internal policies of both East and West came to a sudden, astounding halt. But 1989 was not a pivot in domestic politics. At home, though a new administration under George Bush came to office, it was, in most ways, an extension of its predecessor. The domestic political shifts of the 1990s did not become fully visible until the beginning of a new Democratic administration under Bush's successor, Bill Clinton. Still, it could be argued that the mediocrity of Bush's political leadership paved the way for a political turnaround. That switch in turn would highlight forces, urges, agendas, and opinions that had previously been obscured. The nation would discover within itself deep fissures—ideological, cultural, and political—that it had seldom experienced in such acute forms before.

Would the end of the Cold War and new forces make a major difference in the lives of most Americans? Would they transform the nation? Or would the United States absorb the changes, and fundamentally remain the same as it had been since the 1960s?

The 1988 Presidential Election.   Initially hurt by the Iran-Contra affair, Ronald Reagan's reputation had recovered as he approached the end of his second term. The special Iran-Contra prosecutor continued to pursue and try the accused culprits, but the American public lost interest in the whole affair. When, finally, in early 1993, George Bush, now a lame-duck, pardoned former Secretary of Defense Caspar Weinberger of charges that he had lied to Congress about Iran-Contra, the outcry was less than deafening. The accelerated collapse of Soviet power and the winding down of the Cold War also helped restore Reagan's popularity. Many Americans concluded that his tough anti-Soviet stands and saber rattling had worked. Democrats, nevertheless, took heart. At least in 1988 they would not have to run against the "Great Communicator" again. He would soon be off to his beloved California and trouble them no more.

The 1988 presidential race brought out a small band of Democratic contenders. Only two, Gary Hart, Walter Mondale's competitor in 1984, and Jesse Jackson, the black minister who represented his party's most liberal wing, had nationwide name recognition as the prolonged nomination campaign began. In the summer of 1987 Hart virtually dared the media to investigate his private life. They did, and the *Miami Herald* caught him spending the night alone with a Miami model-actress in his Washington townhouse. He

soon dropped out of the nomination race. In the end the Democratic contest narrowed down to Jackson and the governor of Massachusetts, Michael Dukakis, a cool, cerebral technocrat who claimed to have made his state into a model of high-tech efficiency worthy of emulation by the whole nation. Jackson sought to reactivate his diverse Rainbow Coalition, but did not win a large enough proportion of the white vote in the state primaries to create a decisive lead. In the end, Dukakis won the nomination and chose Senator Lloyd Bentsen of Texas, a conservative Democrat, as his running mate.

Vice President George Bush had an early lead on the Republican side and quickly leaped ahead of his chief adversary, Senator Minority Leader Robert Dole. He won on the first ballot at New Orleans and chose a young senator from Indiana, Dan Quayle, to share the ticket.

The 1988 presidential campaign was not a credit to the American political process. Even more than in other recent political campaigns, image-making eclipsed serious issue discussion. Neither side took the electorate's intelligence very seriously and TV short bites completely dominated the race. Dukakis sought to emphasize "competence" over ideology; he would make America competitive again in the world economy. But the Democrats also harped on the fact that Quayle had ducked active military duty in Vietnam in favor of safe and comfortable National Guard service and had a feeble academic record to boot. The Republican campaign was even more negative. It showed TV clips of polluted Boston harbor to demonstrate Dukakis's weak interest in environmental controls, although federal budget cuts under Reagan were largely to blame. Even more effective was a Republican TV spot featuring a convicted black murderer, Willie Horton, who, while on furlough under a Massachusetts prison release program, had raped a white woman. The Dukakis forces cried foul; the Republicans, they said, were appealing to racial bigotry. But the spot seemed to be effective.

At first Dukakis was ahead. He seemed to many the more authentic man. Bush, the son of a former Connecticut U.S. senator, had gone to private schools and Yale University; his background was elite, old stock, Yankee Northeast. Though he claimed a he-man Texas pedigree from his years in the oil business in Houston, many voters considered him at first an overage Ivy League preppie. And his bearing, speech, and demeanor reinforced the impression. But as the weeks passed, Dukakis proved to be an awkward, wooden campaigner who struck few sparks. As the campaign progressed Bush was able to shake off the preppie image and take on some of the glow of Ronald Reagan. He also made effective use of the public's deep tax aversion.

His most memorable campaign line was: "Read my lips; no new taxes." As the race approached the home stretch with the Republican well ahead, Dukakis dropped the competence line and began to play on the unspoken resentments of many wage earners against the unequal benefits of the Reagan Revolution. The populist appeal helped, but came too late. On November 8 the Bush-Quayle ticket won forty states to ten, with a popular vote of 48.8 million to 41.8 million, and an electoral vote of 426 to 112. Dukakis had carried a small group of the most liberal states of the Northeast, the Midwest, and the Pacific Coast, but had lost everywhere else.

★ THE BUSH ADMINISTRATION ★

The Domestic Scene. As president, George Bush proved to be almost as conservative as his predecessor. During the campaign he had talked about a "kinder, gentler nation" and a "thousand points of light," phrases that suggested that compassion would replace rugged individualism as the administration watchword. And as president he made stabs at strengthening environmental safeguards, raising educational standards, and providing help for working mothers. But he did not follow through. He appointed William Riley, a friend of strict environmental regulation, as EPA administrator, but refused to support new clean air regulations that he believed would handicap economic growth and, on the advice of his conservative chief of staff, John Sununu, refused to endorse an aggressive international campaign to combat global warming. He also proposed measures to improve the nation's seriously ailing educational system but insisted that it must be done with minimal funding. In much of his domestic agenda, Bush was a captive of his own antitax promises and the Reagan legacy of enormous federal deficits. Given these constraints there was simply no money for new initiatives, even if the president had favored them.

And there was also the snowballing S&L crisis. It soon became clear that billions more would be needed to bail out thrift depositors than anyone expected. By 1990, the treasury's estimates of S&L defaults ran to well over a $100 billion; some experts said the totals would ultimately be much greater. And little of this amount would be recovered by sales of the thrifts' assets; the taxpayer would have to pay. Besides the sheer magnitude of the disaster, it soon became obvious that more than incompetence and inattention were involved. Each day brought new revelations of how federal regulators and members of Congress had abetted the S&L manipulators in exchange for favors and campaign contributions. In the summer of 1990, the president's son, Neil, became the target of conflict of interest charges involving deals made by the bankrupt Silverado Savings and Loan of Denver. Though members of both parties were implicated in the scandals, polls showed that the public blamed the Republicans more.

In mid-1990, with the federal budget deficit once more soaring and the Gramm-Rudman meat-ax about to be applied, the president finally breached the taboo on raising taxes. If the Democrats went along with a package of budget cuts he would consider measures to raise additional revenue. The statement, violating his "no new taxes" promise,

Deregulation had some unexpected consequences. None dismayed Americans more than the abuses it fostered in the savings and loan system. Here Charles Keating, Jr., president of California's failed Lincoln Savings Company, is being grilled by Senators on his use of political influence to benefit his firm. He was later convicted and sentenced to jail.

produced a sensation. Many Americans acknowledged that something had to be done about the deteriorating national infrastructure, poor schools, the destructive effects of the drug plague, and the mounting costs of health care, but few wanted to pay for these needs. Though the lowest taxed citizens of any industrial nation, they had been overwhelmed by a decade of anti-tax propaganda. Republican politicians, facing the 1990 midterm elections, backed away from the president's proposals as fast as possible. By the summer of 1990, high-level negotiations to cut budget deficits between the administration and Democratic congressional leaders had stalled over who would go first on higher taxes and benefits cuts and risk public wrath.

Still another prickly domestic problem of the first Bush months was abortion. In 1980 Bush had favored liberal abortion rights for women, but by the 1988 election he had joined his party's official pro-life position. Though the Moral Majority had disbanded and the New Right impulse had subsided, social conservatism remained a powerful force in the nation. By the 1990s it had come to focus most of its energies on reversing the 1973 Supreme Court decision in *Roe* v. *Wade*.

By decade end it was clear that the Supreme Court was the key to the pro-life campaign's success. However reluctant to reverse the court's direction too quickly, a conservative majority almost certainly would overthrow the liberal abortion rules. This expectation made each new Supreme Court nomination a battlefield between pro-life and pro-choice proponents. By 1989 the appointments of Justices Anthony Kennedy and Antonin Scalia had already tipped the balance toward the pro-life side, and in the case of *Webster* v. *Reproductive Health Services* the court decided by a five to four margin that Missouri could limit the right to abortion more strictly than allowed in *Roe* v. *Wade*. Even after *Webster* the earlier ruling still stood in cases where no state law was in place, but it seemed as if the days of *Roe* were numbered. In his *Webster* dissent Justice Harry Blackmun, author of the 1973 decision, expressed the mood of the pro-choice forces: "I fear for the future," he wrote. "The signs are evident and very ominous, and a chill wind blows."

The *Webster* decision shifted the abortion war to the states where bitter battles to modify *Roe* by state law soon broke out. The pro-choice forces won most of these and their surprising strength frightened many Republicans, who sought to distance themselves from their party's pro-life stand. But these were merely preliminary. Then, in the summer of 1990, Justice William Brennan, the Court's most liberal member, retired. Bush nominated, and the Senate confirmed, an obscure, conservative New Hampshire judge, David Souter, to succeed him. Soon after, Thurgood Marshall, the only black justice and an outstanding liberal,

joined Brennan in retirement. The overturn of *Roe* v. *Wade*—and much else the liberal Court had made law—appeared imminent.

The Clarence Thomas–Anita Hill Affair.   The Court's domination by conservatives seemed clinched when Bush nominated Judge Clarence Thomas to succeed Marshall. Thomas was an African-American but he was also a conservative, a combination that appealed to the president. Bush claimed that Thomas was the person best qualified for the job, but more than a few Americans suspected that he was chosen to assure confirmation of a conservative justice. As a black man, Thomas could not be "Borked" by the liberals who would be chary of voting against a man of his race.

But the confirmation process proved to be more than usually rocky. Thomas played it cool when asked directly by senators at the confirmation hearings in October 1991 about his views on abortion. He had not made up his mind, he said. Few believed him. His conservative positions on many issues were well known, and it seemed unlikely that he had no formed opinion on the most lively debate between conservatives and liberals. But the Bush strategy seemed to be working when, abruptly, a new issue was injected into the process. On October 11 a black woman law professor at the University of Oklahoma, Anita Hill, appeared before the Senate Judiciary Committee to declare that when she worked for Thomas on the Equal Employment Opportunity Commission eight years before he had harassed her by making sexually suggestive remarks and overtures. Now, an almost routine procedure was transformed into a televised drama that gripped the nation tightly for three days.

The confrontation pitted two blocs against each other. Hill's complaints highlighted a long simmering issue: sexual harassment in the workplace. Many women believed that it was a serious problem all too often ignored. Feminists claimed it was another example of the mistreatment of women that permeated all of American life. It was part of the same male sensibility that condoned "date-rape," pornography, and other assaults on women. On the other side were those—predominantly men—who believed the issue exaggerated, and many more men who were puzzled about what constituted sexual harassment. Few of the millions who watched the confirmation proceedings on TV were entirely comfortable with either position, and it was said by some observers that the hearings were part of a forced-draft learning process for the American public.

Thomas categorically denied the charges, often graphic. He was, he said, like black males in the past, being lynched. Most of the senators, recognizing that two of the most delicate subjects in American life—gender and race—

were involved, treated the two participants warily. But some feminists saw the all-male inquisitors as insensitive to Anita Hill's situation. During the hearings themselves a majority of Americans told the pollsters that they believed Thomas more than Hill and in the end he was confirmed. But in later months, as women reviewed the confrontation, many came to believe that Anita Hill had been right, and the feeling would strengthen feminist resolve to make women's views more politically effective. And, if nothing else, the Thomas confirmation hearings served to raise public consciousness of sexual harassment as a problem on the job, on campuses, and in other areas of private life. Revelations of sexual misconduct by public figures were soon making headlines around the country.

The Cold War Ends. If Bush seemed beleaguered at home, abroad he could glory in the fruits of his predecessors' policies. In Eastern Europe Gorbachev was quickly dismantling, or allowing to be dismantled, the Warsaw Pact and the entire political settlement that the Soviets had imposed in Eastern Europe after 1945. In 1989 popular movements in Poland, Hungary, Rumania, Bulgaria, Czechoslovakia, and the German Democratic Republic overthrew corrupt and tyrannical Communist regimes in power for over forty years and replaced them with administrations professing democracy and respect for free market economics.

The revolution in East Germany would have the most momentous consequences. No single episode of the miraculous year 1989 would match the razing of the Berlin Wall as a symbol of change. The world public watched transfixed as the wall came down and Germans on both sides of the line mingled as one people for the first time since 1945. Propelled by Chancellor Helmut Kohl of West Germany, the Communist collapse in East Germany was quickly converted into an economic merger of the two Germanies, soon followed by full political union.

Meanwhile the Soviet leader, bedeviled by a fast sinking economy, was making further cooperative arrangements with the United States. In May 1989 the United States and the Soviets agreed to reopen the START nuclear disarmament talks, and Gorbachev and Bush both proposed sub-

If no event symbolized the Cold War so vividly as the erection of the Berlin Wall, no event epitomized its end as clearly as its destruction in November 1989.

stantial cutbacks in the troops and conventional weapons deployed against the other in Europe. That same month Bush declared "it was time to move beyond containment and seek the integration of the Soviet Union into the community of nations." The collapse of the Warsaw Pact and Soviet disarmament pledges were soon followed by long convoys of tanks, artillery, and troop-carriers moving eastward from the satellites to the Soviet Union proper. By this time the Soviets had withdrawn their military forces from Afghanistan after admitting that the 1979 invasion had been an expensive blunder. They also began to reduce their support for revolutionary client regimes in Africa, Asia, the Middle East, and Latin America. Deprived of Soviet subsidies and arms, many of the left wing insurrections around the world subsided.

Even the People's Republic of China felt the effects of the freedom wind that had begun to sweep the world. Mao's successors ended the hard-line Communist micro-management of the economy, and foreign capital and technology poured into the country. The new dispensation also unleashed native Chinese entrepreneurship. China's overall output and wealth leaped but, as in other fast-developing nations in the past, the gains were partly offset by losses. Not all Chinese benefited equally; both millionaires and criminals grew in number. Corruption of government officials became widespread. Though liberalizing the economy, the aging Chinese leaders, Deng Xiaoping and Li Peng, refused to move toward a democratic, multiparty system and a free press, and among a core of students and intellectuals the mood became bitter.

On May 17, 1989, during a visit to China by Soviet premier Gorbachev, a million protesters camped out in Beijing's Tiananmen Square to demand political reform. The protesters, predominantly young men and women, announced their democratic agenda in massive posters and erected a large white plaster statue that resembled the Statue of Liberty in New York Harbor. As a measure of China's recent modernization, they were able to keep in touch with sympathetic groups around the world by videotape and fax machine. For a time the hard-line regime seemed stunned and unwilling to take bold action. Then, in early June, it ordered the army to clear the square. The brutal operation, caught on tape for the world to see, succeeded at the cost of many hundreds of lives. The military crackdown was followed by a period of repression marked by trial and conviction of many Tiananmen Square demonstrators.

Americans had almost universally cheered the eruption of the Chinese "Democracy Movement." It seemed as if the world's largest nation would finally be liberated from the Communist yoke. The crackdown produced outrage and strong demands for economic and diplomatic sanctions against the People's Republic. But in the end, caution prevailed. The Bush administration condemned the repression and called for liberalization of Chinese political life, but Bush refused to break off the profitable new economic ties with Beijing. Critics accused the administration of putting dollars before people.

China had reverted, but few doubted that the setback was temporary. And, in the Western Hemisphere, it even looked as though the Castro regime in Cuba, abandoned economically by the Soviet Union as too costly, might be forced to change soon.

Clearly, the Cold War was over and it seemed that containment had worked. The West had won! In the first flush of triumph, a foreign-policy expert, Francis Fukuyama, published an article titled "The End of History," proclaiming that the world's age-old confrontations were finally at an end. The system of liberal capitalism was now universally valued and the bases for conflict were gone.

Few Americans regretted the end of the Cold War, but it left some dissenters uncomfortable. For those on the political left it was difficult to accept the wisdom of post-1945 American foreign policy whatever the outcome. On the far right there was an equivalent discomfort. Who would serve as demon to blame the world's international evils on now that the Soviet Union had retreated? Liberals took another position. Perhaps we had overestimated the Soviet threat. Was it possible that our fears had been excessive and we had sacrificed too much of our wealth and freedom to defeat a paper tiger? A majority of Americans, probably, assumed that containment had been necessary and that its validity had been confirmed by events: The fact that when it suited the Soviet leaders the Cold War ended seemed telling.

In the early years of the 1990s there was no way of knowing who was right. The question of post-1945 American Cold War policy promised to remain the focus of debate for years to come among Americans of different temperaments and different ideological and political persuasions.

★ THE GULF WAR ★

And then, in the summer of 1990, the United States was confronted with an international crisis that abruptly deflated the euphoria over the end of the Cold War. Suddenly it became clear that the world was still an uncertain and dangerous place and that Americans could not afford to put their heads in the sand.

Iraq Invades Kuwait. During the marathon Iraq-Iran War (1980–1988) the United States had tilted toward Iraq.

Although it was the aggressor in the war and although its leader, Saddam Hussein, was a brutal tyrant who used terror and poison gas against his own people, Iraq seemed preferable to an Iran controlled by the Shiite fundamentalists who had taken American hostages a decade before. American support had helped prevent Iraqi defeat and by 1988 the two Mideast countries had arranged a cease-fire. Yet Saddam had not disarmed. Instead, with the help of the Soviet Union and enormous arms purchases from France, Germany, and the United States, he had constructed the most formidable military machine in the Mideast.

What the American government had not taken into account was that the same fierce Iraqi urge to control the oil-rich Persian Gulf region that had led to the attack on Iran had not ceased. In fact, there was a new reason for Iraqi aggression against its Gulf neighbors: its need to pay the billions in debts incurred by its ill-starred war with Iran. For months Saddam had been denouncing the rulers of the small neighboring sheikdom of Kuwait for producing too much oil, thereby keeping the price low, while simultaneously demanding border adjustments in Iraq's favor. Yet it was a complete surprise when, on August 2, 1990, Iraqi troops and tanks plunged across the border into Kuwait and seized control of the country. Soon after, Saddam announced that Kuwait would be incorporated into Iraq as its nineteenth province.

Aside from the total lawlessness of the attack, Iraq would now control a substantial portion of the world's petroleum resources and, if unchecked, would be in a position to intimidate the other major Gulf oil producers into doing his economic bidding as well.

The Iraqi invasion shocked much of world opinion. Could the international community permit naked aggression to stand unchallenged? Could it tolerate an adventurer like Saddam having a choke hold on much of the world's petroleum supply. In short order the United Nations Security Council, with powerful American support, passed a series of resolutions condemning the unprovoked aggression against Kuwait and demanding that the Iraqis withdraw from their small neighbor. To back the resolution, the UN voted to impose an embargo on all goods and supplies to Iraq and to block export of Iraqi oil to markets abroad.

The Iraqi invasion forced some difficult choices on President Bush. The UN by itself could not enforce the sanctions; it lacked military power. Clearly the United States, the world's most powerful nation, must bear the primary burden of stopping Saddam, lest his appetite grow with the eating and his example inspire other aggressors. Unpunished naked aggression would frustrate all possibility for Bush's "new world order" in the wake of the Cold War. And there was a more immediate danger. Saddam's troops in Kuwait were just over the border from Saudi Arabia, the largest petroleum producer in the world. After gobbling up Kuwait, what would stop him from conquering the fabulously rich but militarily weak Saudi kingdom, a friend of the United States in the Arab world?

Finally, there was the hazard of nuclear arms. Iraq had long sought to acquire nuclear weapons, and although Saddam's drive to make Iraq a nuclear power had been set back for years by an Israeli air attack on his nuclear facilities in 1981, he had clearly resumed the quest. Now that Saddam had revealed his aggressive policies, the nuclear issue became urgent. If he succeeded in constructing a nuclear arsenal the entire Mideast would be destabilized in ways too frightening to contemplate.

Yet U.S. intervention entailed serious risks at home and abroad. Ever since Vietnam, Americans had been wary of overseas military commitments beyond the defense of Europe through NATO. Would intervening in the Gulf produce another drawn-out, bloody war? As pessimists noted during the Gulf crisis: "Wait till the body bags start to arrive!" And if the war should prove costly, would the American people stay the course or would they demand withdrawal? Withdrawal without victory would, in turn, reinforce the post-Vietnam self-doubt that still burdened the nation and further undermine its capacity for world leadership. And what about the domestic political consequences of another inconclusive Vietnam-type war? Wouldn't the voters hold the administration responsible for such a debacle?

And there were other imponderables as well. What would be the reactions of the Arab peoples to an American intervention in the gulf? During the crisis various Western "experts" on the Mideast and Islam solemnly proclaimed that Saddam would incite a holy war against the American infidels. The United States would be depicted as a latter day crusader nation moved by hatred of Islam and by a desire to protect its client, Israel. Many skeptics also warned that any attempt to stop Saddam would ignite widespread terrorism by pro-Iraq Islamic groups. And their fears were widely shared. For the six months following the August invasion air travel, domestic and overseas, plummeted as tourists and business people shied away from exposure to terrorist attacks. Finally, there was the Soviet Union. It was still a great power and had been the major patron of the Iraqi military, helping to train the Iraqi army and supplying much of Iraq's planes and arms. Would it accept the rout of its Mideast client?

Though beset by doubts, after consulting our NATO allies and pro-American nations in the Mideast, Bush dispatched a force of 125,000 troops to Saudi Arabia to deter any move by Saddam against that Arab kingdom. Meanwhile, on the diplomatic front, Secretary of State James Baker and Defense Secretary Richard Cheney set off on whirlwind transatlantic trips to line up military, diplomatic, and financial support for the American move. They succeeded in winning the endorsement and promise of troops and financial help from Egypt, Syria, and other Arab nations, as well as from Britain, France, Italy, and several other NATO allies. Even the Soviet Union endorsed the sanctions against Iraq, though the Soviet government remained uneasy about the massive intrusion of the United States into the sensitive Mideast, and refused to send either military help or provide financial support to what Bush soon labeled Operation Desert Shield.

During the fall and early winter of 1990 thousands of troops of the anti-Iraq coalition, mostly Americans, and millions of tons of munitions, planes, and supplies were ferried to Saudi Arabia to confront the Iraqis and keep them at bay. The American troops in the Gulf reflected the new post-Vietnam army. It was all-volunteer; it included many blacks and Hispanics; and, for the first time for any American military force, it possessed a substantial proportion of women, though not in combat positions.

Meanwhile the UN embargo and the oil sanctions failed to induce the Iraqis to pull out. Instead, Saddam's army defiantly dug in along the Kuwait-Saudi border prepared to fight the kind of defensive war that had served so effectively against the Iranians. Playing to fears among the American public, Saddam thundered that his forces would turn any coalition attack into a bloodbath and might use poison gas and germ warfare. He also threatened to use the thousands of foreigners from coalition countries caught in Iraq or Kuwait when the crisis began as human shields. They would be dispersed to strategic locations where they would be injured or killed by coalition forces' bombs if Iraq were attacked. While outraging the Western nations, Saddam sought to win over the disaffected Arab masses by depicting himself as a Robin Hood who would share Gulf oil wealth with the poor and proclaiming himself a champion of the Palestinian people in their struggle against Israel. On several occasions he announced that if the coalition nations agreed to hold a Mideast conference to settle the Arab-Israeli problem, he would consider making concessions on Kuwait. The coalition considered the move little more than propaganda and, reluctant to reward Saddam's aggression by accepting "linkage" of the Kuwait and Palestinian issues, it rejected these terms.

At first Americans were sharply divided over the Gulf crisis. At one end of the opinion range was a small group who believed that intervention in the region represented a shameful instance of American imperialism and war-mongering. A much larger bloc of Americans, while deploring Iraqi aggression, favored waiting longer to see if sanctions would work. Finally, even at the outset, a substantial minority of Americans were convinced that nothing except actual force would evict Saddam from Kuwait and even if he left, if unpunished, he would remain a major threat to peace in the strategically critical region.

The administration itself initially hoped that Saddam might back down if confronted by a convincing threat. To bolster UN credibility, two days after the November Congressional elections, Bush announced that he was doubling the number of American troops in Saudi Arabia. The reinforcements would include crack military units from Germany and the army's best armored equipment. The coalition forces now could not only stop any invasion of Saudi Arabia; they could also evict Saddam's forces from Kuwait if he refused to withdraw them.

The November escalation angered the antiwar forces and Americans who favored waiting for sanctions to work. In Congress prominent Democrats, including normally hawkish Senator Sam Nunn of Georgia, head of the Armed Services Committee, protested loudly. Nunn held Senate hearings in which a parade of military and foreign policy experts warned about the dangers and uncertainties, military and diplomatic, of a ground war in the Mideast. Around the country various peace groups, inspired by the Vietnam experience, began to hold rallies and demonstrations demanding the United States disengage from the Gulf.

During the Thanksgiving holiday Bush went to Saudi Arabia to visit the troops and there concluded, apparently, that Saddam would not be intimidated; that force would actually have to be used. Soon after the president returned home, the administration prevailed on the UN Security Council to go beyond the earlier resolutions and approve the actual use of force against Saddam if his forces did not leave Kuwait by January 15, 1991.

The use-of-force resolutions gave many Americans the jitters. To calm a nervous public Bush invited the Iraqi foreign minister to Washington to discuss the crisis while promising to send Secretary Baker to Baghdad for similar discussions. At this point Saddam decided to release the foreign hostages. But, as a stalling tactic, he refused to see Baker until the very eve of the January 15 UN deadline.

On January 2 Bush concluded that the use of force could not be avoided. But before ordering an attack, he decided, he would send Baker to Geneva to meet with the Iraqi foreign minister for last-ditch negotiations. He also gave Baker a personal letter to deliver to Saddam reiterating the American position. Nothing was achieved at Geneva. Tariq Aziz, the Iraqi foreign minister, refused to budge and contemptuously declined to transmit the president's letter to his chief. This dismissive act played into Bush's hands. Until now, wary of a divisive debate, the administration had avoided asking Congress for authorization to use force, arguing that as commander-in-chief the president by himself had the power to order an attack. Many Americans considered this a risky abuse of executive power and the administration finally yielded to pressure. The insulting Iraqi gesture at Geneva helped the administration's cause. The debate over the authorization, especially in the Senate, was passionate. A majority of Democrats in both houses urged sticking longer with the economic sanctions; a few questioned the administration's motives. But enough Democrats joined Bush to give him the authority to use force in the Gulf. The issue of peace or war was now up to Saddam Hussein.

War and Victory.   Actual shooting war, called Desert Storm, began on January 16 in the early evening, eastern standard time, when, on signal from General Norman Schwartzkopf, the commander of the Gulf forces, the United States and its coalition partners launched a massive air offensive against Iraq. The targets of the initial attacks—conducted by radar-invisible stealth fighters, F-15s, low flying Tomahawk cruise missiles, and other high-tech weapons—were Iraqi command headquarters, communications centers, electric power stations, scud missile launchers, chemical weapons factories, and H-bomb development facilities. The results were spectacular. During the next few days the American public saw pictures of incredible pin-point hits on vital Iraqi facilities achieved with few if any coalition losses. A wave of euphoria and relief swept over the nation; the war, it seemed, might be won with air power alone without the need to use ground forces. Coalition troops would not have to face the "elite" Iraqi Republican Guard who, it was said, had proved deadly against the Iranians during the recent Iraq-Iran War.

Once the fighting started most public doubts fell away. A wave of patriotism swept the nation and Americans took to wearing red, white, and blue bunting and tying yellow ribbons around curbside trees to indicate support for the troops. In the Mideast, day after day coalition bombers, fighters, and missiles raced across the desert to drop their explosives on Iraqi troops, tanks, artillery, bridges, and communications facilities. Much of Iraq's water supply, sewage facilities, and electric generation plants were quickly destroyed. The coalition forces sought to avoid hitting homes, shops, and offices, but inevitably mistakes occurred and Iraqi civilians died.

The Iraqis retaliated by releasing millions of gallons of oil into the Persian Gulf to deter amphibious landings on the Kuwaiti beaches and to foul desalination plants in Saudi Arabia. The Iraqi air force showed little fight, however, and before long a large proportion of its best planes escaped to Iran where they were interned for the duration of the war. The only offensive weapons the Iraqis could wield were scud missiles, weapons of terror without military worth.

The targets of the scuds were Riyadh, the Saudi capital, and Tel Aviv, Haifa, and other Israeli cities. Israel was not a coalition nation, but Saddam believed that if he could goad the Israelis into retaliation, their response would so offend the Arab world that the hastily forged Gulf coalition would fall apart. Fortunately, powerful pressure from the United States and the loan of American-manned anti-scud Patriot missiles deterred the Israelis from counterattack. Yet the scuds were more than an annoyance. One disastrous scud attack killed twenty-eight American service troops in Riyadh. The need to take them out tied up coalition planes and troops.

The Iraqis were not good losers. When they retreated from Kuwait they set fire to the oil wells. Here we see one of the many fire-fighting experts the Kuwaiti government hired to put out the searing flames.

As the winter days passed Americans remained glued to their radios and TVs for Gulf news. The media complained that the government did not allow reporters the free movement to roam battlefield areas as in Vietnam but, rather, insisted on filtering the news and doling it out through information pools. But most Americans were impressed with the official spokespersons who briefed the reporters and the public daily. Most effective were Colin Powell, head of the Joint Chiefs of Staff, a vigorous black general who grew up in New York City, and Norman Schwartzkopf, commander-in-chief of all the Gulf forces, a cultivated West Pointer who had lived in the Mideast and fought in Vietnam. Both officers were articulate and compassionate men who did not fit the military troglodyte image associated with the commanders in Vietnam. Both became folk heros.

As his military "assets" eroded under the around-the-clock air and missile bombardment, Saddam sought to save himself by appealing to Gorbachev for diplomatic help. Though they had favored the UN sanctions, the Soviets were worried about the growing influence of the U.S. in the Mideast and were not averse to currying favor among the radical Arab leaders and masses who saw Saddam as a savior rather than villain. In mid-February, with a ground attack clearly imminent, the Soviets got the Iraqis to agree to leave Kuwait, but only with conditions that violated the UN resolutions. By this time the coalition leaders, convinced that, despite Soviet diplomatic efforts, Saddam would not give in to the coalition's demands, had chosen a date for launching a ground attack; and they were in no mood to make concessions that would enable Saddam to save his military forces and claim victory in confrontation with the United States. President Bush rejected the terms of the Soviet proposal and gave Iraq 24 hours to surrender. Saddam responded by launching another scud missile at Israel.

On February 23 at 8 P.M. eastern standard time, the coalition launched the long-awaited ground assault. General Schwartzkopf had deceived the Iraqis into believing that the coalition would attack amphibiously across the beaches from the Gulf and head-on from the south across the Saudi-Kuwaiti border. Instead the main armored units—U.S., British, and French—were sent far to the west to swing north and then east around the main Iraqi defenses cutting the entrenched Republican Guards and the bulk of Iraqi armor off from retreat north to Baghdad. Meanwhile, Saudi, Egyptian, and Kuwaiti troops, bolstered by U.S. marines, crossed into occupied Kuwait.

For a few hours the public held its breath. No one knew for sure whether the air campaign against the dug-in Iraqi forces had been successful in eroding their fighting ability. Some observers believed that the Republican Guards, at

least, would fight to the death and inflict horrendous casualties on coalition forces. And once cornered, it seemed likely that the Iraqis would use poison gas against the coalition.

The fears were misplaced. Thousands of Iraqis, waving coalition surrender leaflets, gave up without firing a shot. Where the better troops resisted they were quickly subdued. In sharp fighting south of Kuwait City the marines defeated the main Iraqi army and forced it into headlong retreat northward. The defeated Iraqis fled on foot or in surviving tanks, military trucks, and confiscated civilian cars and buses. As they retreated they were mercilessly pounded from the air by coalition planes. The planes often had to fly through clouds of black smoke from hundreds of burning oil wells that the Iraqis had ignited before they fled Kuwait.

But the fleeing Iraqis had nowhere to go in any case. The armored sweep around left end had smashed the Republican Guard in one brief, one-sided armor battle. In a day or two the vaunted Guard, as well as those Iraqis fleeing from the south, were cut off and forced into a pocket around Basra. In a hundred hours the Iraqi army had ceased to exist as a fighting unit and president Bush ordered a cease-fire.

Only 125 American soldiers had died in the fighting in the Gulf in the seven weeks of active air and ground conflict. The Iraqis, however, had suffered thousands of casualties and had lost most of their equipment. Saddam Hussein's military power had been largely destroyed. The victory was one of the most complete and total in the history of modern warfare.

★ THE ELECTION OF 1992 ★

The American people never loved George Herbert Walker Bush as they had Ronald Reagan. He was too much the aloof patrician, the over-age preppie who tried too hard to affect the common touch. Then came the Gulf War victory, and for a time Bush's popularity leaped. Not that everyone felt the war had been perfectly concluded. Some Americans believed that Bush should have ordered the coalition troops on to Baghdad, the Iraqi capital, to oust Saddam Hussein from power, a view confirmed by the Iraqi dictator's vengeful treatment, after the fighting stopped, of his own nation's Kurdish population. The Kurds had to be rescued from starvation and massacre by UN forces and relief workers. Still, the public considered the president's overall handling of the Gulf crisis resolute and effective and admired him for it. A major opinion poll in March 1991 showed that 91 percent of the American people, a truly extraordinary proportion, believed that Bush was doing a good job.

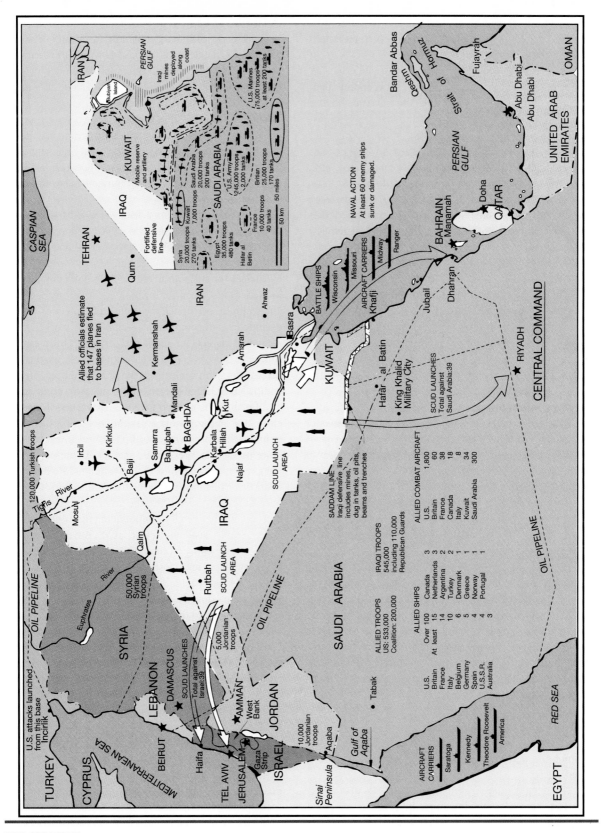

THE GULF WAR

Never did a president slide so quickly. The cause was the onset of the longest, though not the deepest, recession since the end of World War II.

The Economic Slump. The American economy had begun to slump by late 1989. By then the real estate boom, fueled by lavish credit from savings and loan associations and by the bounding public optimism of the Reagan era, had begun to flatten. Before long no one could sell or rent all those office buildings and apartments constructed during euphoric times. By 1991 housing experts were reporting vacancy rates in commercial and industrial property as high as 25 percent in some cities. Clearly, it would take years before that building excess could be worked off. Meanwhile, the giant construction industry went into a precipitous slide.

There were some benefits of the real estate slump: falling house prices and rents. But these too had a serious downside. The economic boom of the 1980s had been stoked in part by homeowners whose property values had soared for almost a decade. Owning a house worth several hundred thousand dollars made one feel unexpectedly affluent. Now, suddenly, that wealth began to vanish and along with it went consumers' high expectations.

Many Americans, moreover, were heavily in debt by 1990. They had caught the consumer fever of the Reagan era and had gone into hock for cars, boats, VCRs, home computers, second homes, and travel. During the decade the savings rate of Americans had dropped to all-time lows. Now, with dark economic clouds rolling in, consumers were having second thoughts. It was time, many felt, to bring down debt and save, not spend. In short order, the crowds in the malls began to dwindle and a flock of venerable stores, including the Macy's chain, found themselves in bankruptcy.

The end of the Cold War also contributed to the recession. Whatever future gains might come, in the short run the collapse of the Soviet threat depressed the economy. With the Soviet ogre gone, Congress slashed billions from the budget formerly spent on ships, planes, rockets, tanks, and other weapons. Simultaneously, a congressional Base Closure and Realignment Commission marked for closing military bases all over the country. Particularly hard hit on both counts were states like California, Michigan, and Connecticut where shipyards, gun factories, tank plants, and aircraft companies had flourished or where major air, naval, and army bases had been located. Many communities were devastated when the factories and bases closed.

The deregulation movement of the 1980s also contributed to the economic downturn. In the long run, perhaps, rigorous competition could be counted on to reduce prices and enhance quality, benefiting all. But in the short run it introduced an element of harsh economic instability. In the wake of airline deregulation, for example, new airlines sprouted like weeds to compete with the existing giant carriers. There was a quick boom in the market for pilots, mechanics, and flight attendants. Down came fares and for the first time millions of students and poorer Americans began to travel by air. But then came the bust. The competition for passengers soon drove major carriers like Eastern and Pan American into bankruptcy, creating severe unemployment among airline personnel. Between 1990 and 1992, most of the major airlines announced layoffs of thousands of employees.

The public's economic fears were fed by worrisome long-term trends. During the 1990s economic pundits would talk much of "globalization." The development of electronic networks for transferring money; of international exchanges for stock and commodity transactions; of free, borderless movement of technology, skilled management, and technical personnel; the decline of protective duties to exclude foreign commodities—all of these worked to create global markets for goods and services. This meant that American businesses competed with the best that the world had to offer, with bankruptcy the price of failure. Firms felt compelled to become "lean and mean" by cutting out layers of management, seeking to reduce workers' fringe benefits, and slashing wages. (It did not apparently mean reducing the compensation of top executives, whose salaries often seemed to rise despite mediocre company performance.) Many tranferred their operations to cheap-labor countries in Latin America or the Pacific Rim. Over and over, during the early 1990s the public would be dismayed with yet another headline announcing that a major firm— TWA, Sears, Eastman Kodak, IBM, American Airlines, GM—was shucking off thousands of workers, white collar as well as blue, and closing less efficient plants or abandoning less profitable routes, to remain competitive. Even workers not directly affected wondered how long they would continue to draw a paycheck.

As the months passed, the economy's figures grew ever more disquieting. Bankruptcies, individual and corporate, set a record high in 1991, a 21 percent increase over the year before. That same year General Motors, the nation's largest manufacturing company, reported a $4.45 billion loss, the largest single-year corporate loss on record. In May 1992 the jobless rate reached 7.5 percent nationally.

Fortunately, there were several buffers against the sort of collapse that had devastated the nation after 1929. Unemployment insurance, an alert and well-informed Federal Reserve bank, federal old-age pensions, and other social welfare mechanisms—all contributed to placing a floor under the economy. But still, Americans worried about the future as they had not for twenty years.

The Bush administration committed a serious political blunder by discounting the severity of the economic downturn and the worries of the voters. The recession would be short, the president said, and self-righting. The government must not do anything to worsen the federal deficit by a major public works program or a large tax-cut stimulus. Bush endorsed the Federal Reserve's interest rate cuts and pushed tax incentives to encourage business investment, but he refused to go further.

The public soon accused the president of obsession with foreign affairs and indifference to domestic problems. By late 1991 the polls revealed a precipitous drop in Bush's popularity. In November, the *New York Times*–CBS poll showed Bush's job performance rating down to 51 percent, a drop of 16 percentage points from October.

The Nomination Battles.   It was this accelerating economic descent that formed the background of the 1992 presidential campaign. By the early months of 1992 five Democrats were battling for their party's nomination: former senator Paul Tsongas of Massachusetts, former governor Jerry Brown of California, Senators Tom Harkin of Iowa and Bob Kerry of Nebraska, and Bill Clinton, governor of Arkansas. Harkin and Kerry dropped out early, leaving the other three to fight it out through most of the primaries. Jerry Brown struck many as an eccentric, and his campaign seemed increasingly quixotic. Tsongas, who had quit the Senate when he contracted cancer and was now, he claimed, fully recovered, impressed many voters as honest and aboveboard. His message that Americans would have to sacrifice to extricate the country from its malaise sounded a note of austerity that some voters admired for its honesty. The front-runner almost from the beginning, however, was William Jefferson ("Bill") Clinton, the young governor of Arkansas.

Clinton, a southerner of working-class origins, was brought up in a small Arkansas town by his mother and stepfather. A brilliant student, he took a degree in international affairs at Georgetown University and then, in 1968, won a prestigious Rhodes Scholarship to study at Oxford University in England. These were the turbulent years when many male college students, opposed to what they considered an unjust war in Vietnam, demanded American withdrawal and resisted being drafted. Bill Clinton was an antiwar protester at Oxford and managed to avoid serving in the military by some fancy maneuvering. He returned from Britain and went to Yale Law School where he met fellow student Hillary Rodham, a young woman from Illinois. In 1975 they were married.

After teaching and practicing law in Arkansas, Clinton ran for state attorney general. In 1979, at the age of thirty-three, he was elected governor of his home state. In his five terms in the statehouse he modernized and liberalized Arkansas and won plaudits from his fellow governors for his effective leadership. Clinton belonged to the Democratic Leadership Council (DLC), a group of middle-of-the-road Democrats who opposed the party's left-liberals as big spenders and isolationists. The DLC favored programs to cut federal welfare rolls, encourage family preservation, hold down deficit spending, and make the United States strong internationally. Through such policies, it believed, the Democrats could recapture the blue-collar voters they had lost to Ronald Reagan. The governor did have a political liability: He was a long-winded orator. Addressing the 1988 Democratic National Convention, he had put his audience to sleep while he droned on and on. But he was also capable of great eloquence, and in informal settings his charm was highly effective.

After the usual weary weeks of campaign slogging in Iowa, New Hampshire, and the other early primary states, Clinton pulled away from Tsongas on "Super Tuesday," the simultaneous March 10 primaries in the southern states of Florida, Louisiana, Mississippi, Oklahoma, Tennessee, and Texas. Tsongas held on until Clinton won Wisconsin and Michigan soon after, and then withdrew. Jerry Brown remained in the race as a spoiler, but after the June California primary the man from Arkansas had the requisite number of votes for nomination. At the Democratic convention in New York, he won the nomination on the first ballot and delivered a long-winded "Clinton Special" acceptance speech. He more than made up for this lapse by choosing the personable young senator from Tennessee, Albert Gore, as his running mate.

Bush, meanwhile, though the incumbent president, was fighting a surprisingly tough adversary in his own party for the nomination. Patrick Buchanan, a combative right-wing journalist and TV personality, entered the Republican primaries against Bush and attacked the president as too concerned with overseas problems and at most an *ersatz* conservative. His most effective jab was Bush's repudiation of his 1988 slogan: "Read my lips; no new taxes." Faced with a runaway federal deficit, Bush had supported the bipartisan 1990 tax bill designed to raise federal revenues by $164 billion over five years. In fact, his was a responsible position to take, given the nation's fiscal plight, but it seemed a betrayal of his no-tax promises. Still, Buchanan was not able to achieve more than one-third the vote in any of the Republican state primaries, and he won relatively few delegates.

Buchanan did establish a conservative claim on the party, however, and forced the Republican National Convention in Houston to give him a hearing. Delegates at the August convention renominated the Bush-Quayle ticket without a serious challenge, but Buchanan and his conservative followers were able to make their weight felt. In a prime-time speech, Buchanan denounced Hillary Clinton as a "radical feminist" and called the coming campaign a religious and cultural war. "The agenda Clinton and Clinton would impose on America," he proclaimed—"abortions on demand, a litmus test for the Supreme Court, homosexual rights, discrimination against religious schools, women in combat—that's change all right. But . . . it is not the change we can tolerate in a nation that we still call God's country." Moderate Republicans winced at these remarks, and to some voters they seemed strident and divisive. Many feared that the Republicans would seek to deflect attention from the economy by stirring up fierce social and cultural resentments.

The Campaign.   The 1992 presidential campaign marked the political debut of Ross Perot, a self-made Texas billionaire. One of Perot's chief assets was that he was not a politician. The public had become acutely skeptical of the professional "pols" for a flock of reasons. For one thing, they seemed incapable of governing. During the previous dozen years a Republican president and a Democratic Congress had been at logger heads, and few of the country's pressing problems had been addressed. There had also been a succession of scandals that had seriously tarnished Congress. In 1990 five United States senators were accused of using their political influence to help Charles Keating, head of the Lincoln Savings and Loan Association of California. Keating, in turn, had raised $1.5 million for the senators' reelection campaigns. The Senate had rebuked its erring members and one, Alan Cranston of California, announced he would not run for reelection. More recently, a scandal had erupted over the use of overdraft checks by House members at the House of Representatives bank. In effect, scores of members had been taking interest-free loans for themselves. The House leadership tried to bury the scandal but failed and before long a clutch of representatives were rushing to announce that they would not seek reelection. Public disenchantment with the professional politicians spurred a movement to set term limits on elected officials. By 1992 there was serious talk of a constitutional amendment to keep U.S. senators and representatives from running for reelection more than a prescribed number of times.

Perot profited from this disgust with politics-as-usual. But in fact, his political views were not easy to define. He favored fiscal restraint and deficit reduction and talked about making America competitive in the world economy, but there did not seem to be any core vision. Still, when he announced that if he could get on the ballot in all fifty states he would run for president, the response was enthusiastic. As much as a third of the American public saw Perot as a real alternative to a corrupt and ineffective party system that had failed the nation. Perhaps, they said, he could actually make the political system work again. But he also appealed to voters because he was neither Bush nor Clinton. He was the choice, it was said, of those who preferred "none of the above." Thousands flocked to his hastily established campaign offices and worked hard to get him on the ballot for November.

Unfortunately for his followers, Perot was a volatile personality. On July 16, after the Democratic convention, he abruptly announced his withdrawal from the race. Then, on October 1, having sat out much of the campaign, he decided to reenter. He later explained that Bush administration threats to injure his business and disrupt the wedding of his daughter had driven him from the contest. The excuse seemed weird and many of his followers wondered if the man was not too eccentric to trust. What kept his candidacy alive was the continuing scorn of many voters for both of the major party nominees.

The campaign was as raucous and dirty as usual. The Democrats took an early lead. Soon after the convention Clinton and Gore set off on an eight-day campaign bus tour that started in New Jersey and ended up in St. Louis. Speaking to large and small groups along the way, the Democratic candidates seemed refreshingly open and folksy. Democratic fortunes surged. Early polls showed the Clinton approval rating at 55 percent to Bush's 31 percent.

To reinvigorate their flagging campaign Republican leaders induced James Baker to quit as secretary of state and take charge. His task was formidable. Week after week the economic indicators reinforced the sense of economic crisis. On August 25 the Conference Board, a New York-based research organization, reported that its index of consumer confidence had fallen 3.2 points that month. Early in September the Census Bureau published figures showing that the number of Americans below the poverty line had reached the highest level since 1964 and that average median family income had declined for the second year in a row. Clinton promptly used the bureau's figures to blast the Bush administration.

Everyone knew that the slumping economy was the Republicans' albatross. James Carville, the Democratic campaign manager, had prepared a large sign that he prominently displayed at campaign headquarters—"It's the Economy, Stupid"—to keep the party campaign in clear focus. And generally it remained on target. To contrast with the timid Republican wait-and-see attitude toward the economy, the Democrats promised tax breaks for the middle class, deficit reduction, a more efficient health care system, and heavy investment in education and long-neglected infrastructure to increase America's international competitiveness.

To deflect the Democratic attack, Bush offered one-time economic payoffs to key constituencies. In South Dakota he announced a $1 billion federal program to subsidize wheat sales abroad. Soon after, in Texas, he promised $775 million in aid to farmers affected by recent floods. Vice President Quayle, meanwhile, told Detroit defense workers, fearful of layoffs, that the Defense Department would spend $250 million to upgrade M-1 tanks.

But outbidding the Democrats economically took second place to undermining Clinton's reputation and character. The Arkansas governor was personally vulnerable. Just before the New Hampshire primary, a former nightclub singer, Gennifer Flowers, alleged in a supermarket tabloid that she and Clinton had had a twelve-year affair during his governorship. Clinton had indeed placed Flowers on the state payroll, in what seemed like a possible payoff to a lover. Coming early, the accusations almost derailed the Clinton nomination campaign. The governor and his wife appeared together on the TV program "60 Minutes" before the New Hampshire primary to declare their love and refute the charges. The tactic worked, but many voters were left with a sense that Clinton had been less than fully candid.

The adultery charge had been largely contained by the time the presidential race itself began, but the Republicans probed other weak spots in Clinton's personal armor. George Bush—if not his running mate—was a genuine war hero. He had been a navy pilot in World War II and had been shot down by the Japanese over the Pacific. Clinton, too young for that earlier war, had been the right age for combat in Vietnam, but, as we have seen, like many college students, he did not serve. Though he denied it, the Republicans charged that Clinton had avoided induction by a dubious manipulation of the draft system. They also claimed that he had denounced the United States at anti-war rallies while at Oxford and they hinted that he had betrayed his country to the Soviets while on a student trip to Moscow in 1969.

Perot, Bush, and Clinton appeared together three times in presidential "debates." None of them made a fatal mistake, but Clinton did marginally better than the others. A *New York Times*–CBS News poll in late October showed Clinton at 40 percent, Bush 35 percent, and Perot 15 percent.

The actual results in November were not very different. Clinton took 32 states with 370 electoral votes and 43 percent of the popular vote (43.7 million). Bush won 168 electoral votes from the remaining 18 states with 38 percent of the popular vote (38 million). Perot did not carry a single state but received 19 percent of the popular vote (19.2 million).

The vote breakdown showed few surprises. The Democratic challenger carried most of the large industrial states and lost most of the South and the farm belt. He won about 40 percent of the suburban vote—almost as much as the city vote—a result that suggested how uneasy about the economy even middle-class Americans were in November 1992. But Clinton's vote proportions remained highest among Hispanics, blacks, and Jews, all traditional Democrats. He also did better among women than men and proved especially popular among both the oldest and the youngest voters.

The 103rd Congress promised to be similar to the 102nd in its party proportions. The Democrats retained majorities in both houses. And despite the scandals, the predicted purge of House and Senate incumbents did not materialize. The public, apparently, forgave their own representatives their transgressions. Still, there had been some significant nonparty changes. Four women, two from California, had been elected to the Senate, bringing the total to an unprecedented six. One of these—Carol Moseley Braun—would be the first black woman senator. The House also saw an increase in the number of women, up to 47 from the previous 28. The black and Hispanic delegations had also leaped: blacks from 25 to 38; Hispanics from 10 to 17. The new senator from Colorado would be a Native-American, the first in the Senate in sixty years. California voters had also elected the first Korean-American to Congress. Though the process was far from complete, Congress—and American political institutions generally—was clearly starting to mirror the gender and ethnicity of the country as a whole.

★ THE CLINTON ADMINISTRATION ★

Though Bill Clinton was the choice of only a minority of the electorate, the American public was initially more than willing to give the young president the benefit of the doubt. Maybe he *could* revive the economy, improve education and health care, control the burgeoning deficit, and usher in an era of international stability and justice. It did not take long before Clinton had dissipated much of this initial hope and goodwill.

Early Gaffes. The public gave mixed reviews to his choices to cabinet and subcabinet-level posts. Liberals were wary of Senator Lloyd Bentsen of Texas as treasury secretary. Many foreign-policy experts considered Warren Christopher, Clinton's nominee for secretary of state, a colorless and timid bureaucrat without leadership qualities. The president's choices for key economic posts—secretary of labor (Robert Reich) and Council of Economic Advisers head (Laura D'Andrea Tyson)—were in step with his cam-

The Ecological Credo

No issue promises to be as urgent in the years ahead as the fate of the natural environment, for it is the very foundation of human society and its preservation is essential to us all. While no one denies this proposition, many disagree about how it is to be applied. At one extreme are those who feel that we are already doing enough to protect the air, the water, the forests, the oceans, the animal world, that to attempt more would be at the expense of human living standards and comfort. At the other extreme are those inclined to place the natural world ahead of human concerns and surrender much of the modern age to a higher ecological ethic. Most Americans fall in the reasonable middle, not denying the necessity for prudent care of the world's physical foundations but believing that these must be balanced against the realities of modern life.

No public figure has been as closely identified with the ecological vision as Vice President Al Gore. In the selection below Gore presents his view of human kind's need not to forget that planet earth is not infinite and that we must treat it with great respect.

"The edifice of civilization has become astonishingly complex, but as it grows ever more elaborate, we feel increasingly distant from our roots in the earth. In one sense, civilization itself has been on a journey from its foundations in the world of nature to an ever more contrived, controlled, and manufactured world of our own imitative and sometimes arrogant design. And in my view, the price has been high. At some point during this journey we lost our feeling of connectedness to the rest of nature. We now dare to wonder: Are we so unique and powerful as to be essentially separate from the earth?

"Many of us act—and think—as if the answer is yes. It is now all too easy to regard the earth as a collection of "resources" having an intrinsic value no larger than their usefulness at the moment. Thanks in part to the scientific revolution, we organize our knowledge of the natural world into smaller and smaller segments and assume that the connections between these separate compartments aren't really important. In our fascination with the parts of nature, we forget to see the whole.

"The ecological perspective begins with a view of the whole, an understanding of how the various parts of nature interact in patterns that tend toward balance and persist over time. But this perspective cannot treat the earth as something separate from human civilization; we are part of the whole too, and looking at it ultimately means also looking at ourselves. And if we do not see that the human part of nature has an increasingly powerful influence over the whole of nature—that we are, in effect, a natural force just like the winds and the tides—then we will not be able to see how dangerously we are threatening to push the earth out of balance."*

*From Al Gore, *Earth in the Balance: Ecology and the Human Spirit* (Boston: Houghton Mifflin Company, 1992, pp. 1–2).

paign emphasis on strong government economic leadership and did not arouse much debate. More controversial to conservatives were choices that appeared to be part of a social agenda. The president, they said, seemed more interested in accommodating various minorities and outsider groups than finding the best person for the job. And his choices to head various departments in fact were often from demographic groups outside the main political stream: Mexican-Americans Henry Cisneros (HUD) and Frederico Pena (Transportation Department) Lebanese-American Donna Shalala (Health and Human Services Department); Ron Brown, Mike Espy, and Hazel O'Leary, all African-Americans, as secretaries of Commerce, Agriculture, and Energy, respectively; Roberta Achtenberg, an acknowledged gay woman, as HUD undersecretary for Fair Housing and Equal Opportunity. All told, of fourteen people nominated for cabinet positions, two were Hispanic, three were black, and three were women. And Clinton made no bones about the demographic gauge of his appointment agenda. He wanted to have a cabinet that "looked like America," he said.

Clinton's effort to find a female attorney general caused him particular difficulties. The quest for a woman head at the Justice Department was inspired apparently by the First Lady, herself a highly successful lawyer. Mrs. Clinton remained a controversial figure. Much admired by feminists and liberals, she was disliked by many conservatives and traditionalists who considered her too liberal and too devoted to her career. She had assumed a low profile during the presidential campaign, but after the election she began to play an active role in the administration's decision-making process. The First Lady's opinion clearly influenced the initial choice as attorney general of Zoe Baird, chief counsel for the Aetna Insurance Company.

A problem soon developed. Baird, the *New York Times* revealed, had employed an illegal alien from Peru to take care of her child, contrary to the immigration law. Clinton tried to save the nomination, but the bad publicity induced him to withdraw it on January 22, 1993. He next proposed federal judge Kimba Wood of New York for the Justice Department job. He changed his mind when it came out that she too had employed an illegal alien as household helper. Not until mid-March did Florida state attorney Janet Reno, his third choice, make it through to confirmation.

One appointment gaffe threatened to alienate Clinton's important black constituency. In late April the president nominated Lani Guinier, a black law professor at the University of Pennsylvania, as head of the Civil Rights Division of the Justice Department. A friend of both the Clintons, Guinier had written several articles that, critics claimed, put black empowerment and preference ahead of a colorblind political and legal system in which both races were treated alike. Conservatives branded Guinier a "quota queen," but even many moderates were made uncomfortable by her idea of minority veto power over certain legislative initiatives. The White House ignored early warnings that her confirmation would create another administration headache, but then in early June, after he had read her law journal writings, Clinton decided to withdraw the nomination.

The response was predictable. Black leaders denounced it as surrender to racism. Representative Kweisi Mfume, a Maryland Democrat who headed the Congressional Black Caucus, warned Clinton that there were "a number of bills that come through this Congress . . . that we provide the winning margin on." The conserv-

The appointment of Janet Reno as the first woman Attorney General raised great expectations among feminists. However, her reputation was tarnished by her handling of the Branch Davidian affair in Texas, where scores of followers of cult leader David Koresh died by fire when federal officers raided their compound.

atives, meanwhile, gave little credit to the president for vetoing Guinier. The initial choice seemed just another sign of White House incompetence.

By now many people had begun to question both the administration's political judgment and the president's steadfastness. Polls in late May showed that Clinton's approval rating was abysmal, the lowest for any president after the same period in office since polling began in the 1930s. At the end of the month, in a major damage-control move, Clinton appointed David Gergen, an ex-Reagan strategist, as White House adviser. Someone simply had to stop the repeated goofs.

Gergen's steadying presence may explain what many observers considered a very shrewd selection for Supreme Court justice when Byron White, a Kennedy appointee, decided to retire in mid-1993. Clinton's choice, in June, settled on Judge Ruth Bader Ginsburg of New York. Ginsburg was a liberal, but not an ideologue. She supported women's right to abortion but did not believe in judicial activism. Her nomination sailed through the Senate without serious demurer. Her appointment probably ensured the safety of *Roe* v. *Wade* for the foreseeable future. It did not, however, end the picketing outside abortion clinics and the attempts by pro-life activists to disrupt their operations. In fact, the rancor over abortion seemed to get worse. In March 1993 David Gunn, an abortion clinic doctor, was shot and killed in Pensacola, Florida, by a 37-year-old pro-life activist. Pro-choice proponents were soon warning that legal abortion was being shut down by violence and intimidation.

Gays in the Military. In the midst of the attorney general nomination fiasco, Clinton issued a series of executive orders that deeply offended conservative Americans, though they clearly pleased others. In short order the president lifted the so-called gag rule that forbade federally funded family planning clinic personnel from discussing the abortion option with clients; rescinded restrictions on using fetuses from elective abortions in federally funded medical research; and ordered Secretary Donna Shalala to review a Bush-era prohibition on the French-developed RU-486 abortion pill. In the environment area Clinton ordered the Forest Service to halt clear-cutting by loggers in the Sierra Nevada region to protect the endangered spotted owl. He also canceled the Bush-created Council on Competitiveness, an agency designed to encourage business by loosening the restrictions on environmental practices. Meanwhile, Interior Secretary Bruce Babbitt sought to raise the fees paid by ranchers, loggers, and miners for the use and exploitation of federal lands.

The most controversial executive order of all, however, related to homosexuals in the military. For many years gay men and lesbians had quietly served in the nation's armed

As you can see here, gay men and lesbian women were not shy about denouncing the discriminatory policies they experienced in the military services.

forces. No one doubted that they had made as good soldiers, sailors, or airmen as heterosexuals. But they could only serve if they hid their sexual identities. Open acknowledgment or discovery of gay preferences had been punished by dismissal from the military. Clinton had made a promise during the campaign to lift the discrimination on gays in the military if elected and had won the support of gay voters. Soon after the inauguration, he sought to follow through on his promise by executive order.

Social conservatives denounced the move as giving homosexuality moral and legal parity with heterosexuality. Many military leaders claimed that acknowledged gays would undermine the esprit de corps of military units and reduce their combat effectiveness. In Congress, the Senate Republican minority leader, Robert Dole of Kansas, and Democrat Sam Nunn of Georgia, head of the Senate Armed Services Committee, threatened to override Clinton's executive order by statute if he persisted. After much backing and filling, the president—through the good auspices of Defense Secretary Les Aspin and head of the Joint Chiefs of Staff, Colin Powell—arranged a compromise. Called "don't ask, don't tell" by the media, it provided that the military authorities would not question new recruits on their sexual orientation and would not investigate the sexual preferences of military personnel already serving. For their part, gays and lesbians would not advertise their sexual preferences and would not engage in sexual activities while on duty on pain of discharge from the service. It seemed a makeshift solution and it pleased few fully. The military

leaders remained uneasy with homosexuals in uniform, while gays felt that they had been denied full equality of treatment. Most Americans, however, polls showed, believed the agreement an acceptable solution to a difficult problem.

Foreign Affairs.   Clinton's early unsteadiness in domestic matters was matched by his waffling on foreign policy.

The Cold War's end was hailed everywhere as a boon to humanity, but it created daunting new problems. By 1993 the former Soviet Union had disappeared as a political entity. In August 1991 a cabal of old-line Communists attempted a coup against the reformer Gorbachev and for a few days the democratic world feared the return of the repressive Soviet system. Fortunately, grass-roots democratic forces, led by Boris Yeltsin, the president of the Russian Federation, rushed to Gorbachev's support and squelched the revolt. But Gorbachev himself did not long survive. Instead, Yeltsin became head of the Soviet state and pushed far beyond his temporizing predecessor. Yeltsin moved quickly to dismantle the Soviet command economy and replace it with a market economy like the West's. He abolished the Communist party and sought to establish democratic institutions including a free press and an independent judiciary. He even allowed the break-up of the Soviet Union. Soviet troops were removed from parts of the USSR not primarily Russian, allowing a flock of nationalities, including Byelorussians, Ukrainians, Armenians, Georgians, the Baltic peoples, Azerbaijanis, Kazakhstanis, and others, to create their own independent nation-states. Unfortunately, in several cases, these new nations, driven by age-old ethnic hatreds and rivalries, soon became entangled in bitter local wars that threatened the stability of large regions.

Meanwhile, the new Russian Federation, a large nation in its own right, and a nuclear power still to be reckoned with, encountered difficult problems. The Russian people lacked a democratic tradition and, faced with the turmoil of democratic change, many began to yearn for the discipline and certitude of the old Communist era. And even among those who rejected communism, many favored the anti-Western, antisecular, and repressive era of the pre-1917 czars rather than Western democracy. Nor did Yeltsin's economic reforms at first solve many problems. By 1993 more Russians were experiencing crime, corruption, and inflation than the prosperity and abundance the free marketeers had predicted. Many former Soviet subjects, and even some Westerners, were wondering whether the collapse of the Soviet Union had not been a mixed blessing.

The Clinton administration tried to bolster Yeltsin and his reform agenda. If nothing else, Russia—along with Ukraine and Kazakhstan—remained a nuclear power, and the United States feared return of a nuclear-equipped hos-

Marian Wright Edelman

Ten days before the United States Supreme Court issued *Brown v. Board of Education of Topeka*, the landmark decision outlawing school segregation, Marian Wright's father, the Reverend Arthur Wright, died. He had followed the case avidly and had spoken often about what it would mean for the future of black children in America. His last words to his daughter, whom he called "Booster" for her vivacious personality, were spoken as she rode to the hospital with him in an ambulance. "Booster," he said, "don't let anything get in the way of your education." His words gave the fourteen-year-old black girl the courage to feel that she "could be and do anything." And to this day she still strongly believes that she can change the world for the better.

Marian was born on June 6, 1939, in Bennettsville, South Carolina, where Jim Crow laws prevented black people from drinking Coke at drugstore soda fountains or playing in local parks. Arthur Wright, minister of Shiloh Baptist Church, was determined to remedy the situation. Bringing together members of the black community he built a playground, complete with a small merry-go-round and a canteen, behind his church. Blacks were forced to swim in a small creek contaminated by hospital sewage, and he hoped to install a swimming pool as well. Unfortunately, he could not raise the money to finish the project. Reverend Wright also became involved in other humane projects. Realizing that older blacks often had no place to live in South Carolina, Reverend White established a home for the aged, the first of its kind in the state, across the road from his house. His wife, Maggie Leola Bowen Wright, ran it with the help of her children who did their share of the home's cooking and cleaning. Helping others was as important a part of Marian's upbringing as her schooling.

"Service," she was taught, "is the rent we pay for living."

Named for singer Marian Anderson, Marian was the youngest of Maggie and Arthur Wright's five children. First born was sister Olive, who until recently has taught math and science in the Washington, D.C., public school system. Then came her three brothers, Arthur Jr., Harry, and Julian, who are involved in educational counseling and church activities. Gender, however, played no part in how the children were raised. Both the boys and the girls were expected to go to college and have careers: both were taught how to clean house.

Marian did exceptionally well in school. She was a drum majorette in the school band and studied piano and voice, though her first love was literature and her favorite author was Tolstoy. The only time her father did not give her chores at home was when she was reading, so she says she "read a lot." Although she wanted to go to the more cosmopolitan Fisk University in Nashville where her sister had gone, Marian's now-widowed mother convinced her to attend Spelman College, which was closer to home. Spelman, in Atlanta, founded in 1881, is the largest and most prestigious private liberal arts college for black women. In the late 1950s and early 1960s, its students, advised to wear hats and gloves when they were off campus, were required to attend chapel six days a week and were expected to obey strict laws regarding dormitory curfews. The latter, presumably, were to discourage too much involvement with the black male students at nearby Morehouse College.

Intending to enter the foreign service when she graduated from college, Marian applied for and was awarded a Merrill scholarship for a junior year abroad. She spent the first summer in

Paris at the Sorbonne and the academic year at the University of Geneva. The following summer she went to the Soviet Union on a Lisle Fellowship. She had heard that W.E.B. DuBois was living there and she hoped to meet him. He had already left for other parts by the time she arrived in Moscow, but she witnessed the celebrated "kitchen debate" between Nikita Khrushchev and Richard Nixon. The year away from home gave her an enormous amount of confidence and the feeling that she could get along anywhere in the world.

She returned to Spelman for her senior year and found the civil rights movement gathering steam. She soon got into the thick of it. She had been aware of the particular unfairness of segregation from her early childhood when a car and a truck collided near her home and the ambulance driver picked up the slightly hurt white truck driver but refused to take the severely injured black victims to the hospital. In addition, with Spelman located in Atlanta, civil rights leaders including Martin Luther King, Whitney Young, and Carl Holman were a constant presence on the campus. Marian participated in the sit-ins at the Atlanta City Hall cafeteria in 1960 along with a large group of black college students and rallied volunteers at Spelman by putting up a notice on campus reading "Young ladies who can picket, please sign below." She was one of those arrested and spent the night in jail reading C.S. Lewis's *The Screwtape Letters*, which she had brought along to the sit-in just in case.

Her night in jail, and her work cataloguing discrimination complaints at the NAACP office, changed her career plans. After graduating from Spelman, Marian had planned to go to graduate school at Georgetown University to major in Russian studies. Now she decided to go to law school. Although she was not sure she had an aptitude for the law, she believed that as an attorney she would be able to do the greatest good for the civil rights movement. She applied to Yale Law School and was accepted and awarded a John Hay Whitney Fellowship to enable her to attend. It was there that she got to know Robert Moses, a Harvard M.A. who helped found the Student Nonviolent Coordinating Committee, and who came to Yale periodically to meet with members of the Northern Student Movement. At this point he was engaged in the dangerous task of encouraging blacks in Mississippi to register to vote.

Marian went to Mississippi in 1963 during the spring break of her third year in law school to help Moses. There she discovered that there were only three black lawyers in the whole state and they were all in Jackson. When some black would-be voters were arrested in Greenwood, ninety-six miles away, there were no lawyers around to plead their case and the defendants had to spend three weeks in jail until bail money could be raised. The experience in Greenwood, Marian has said in a recent interview, convinced her to finish law school. "I hated every minute of it . . . [but I knew] I was needed in Mississippi."

When she got back to New Haven, she found that the NAACP Legal Defense and Educational Fund had established an internship program to train young lawyers to work in the South. After her graduation from Yale Law School, Marian took a year of training with the NAACP in New York, learning the subtleties of civil rights law, and then in the spring of 1964 returned to Jackson, where she opened a legal office to deal with civil rights cases. Unable to be admitted to the Mississippi bar until she fulfilled the nonresident's yearlong residence requirement, Marian arranged with the three black Jackson lawyers to sign the papers she prepared. When she was finally eligible to take the exam, she passed on her first attempt and became

the first black woman admitted to the Mississippi bar.

Marian and the three lawyers were kept very busy from the time she arrived in the state. Nineteen sixty-four was the first year of the Mississippi "summer project" in which hundreds of students, both white and black from all over the country, came to help register black voters. The white authorities were bitterly hostile and clamped down hard on the volunteers. There were many arrests, and some of the students were beaten badly by the police. There was plenty of work for civil rights lawyers. This was also the summer that civil rights workers Andrew Goodman, Michael Schwerner, and James Chaney were killed by members of the Ku Klux Klan. Marian said she had to learn basic survival techniques "like starting up your car in the morning with the door open in case there's a bomb."

She stayed in Mississippi for four years and during that time became active in the community action programs under the federal War on Poverty. Some black activists rejected cooperation with the government. She, however, believed, and still believes to this day, it is always best to work within the system. Her particular interest was in Head Start, a program administered by the Office of Economic Opportunity established under the War on Poverty Act passed by Congress in 1964. Head Start was designed to improve the life chances of poor young children by early educational enrichment as well as health services and nutrition programs. Marian worked as general counsel for the Child Development Group of Mississippi (CDGM), a volunteer organization of private civil rights activists, educators, and ministers formed after Mississippi as a state refused to apply for Head Start money. Bypassing the state authorities CDGM received $1.5 million to launch a Head Start project directly from the federal government. The organization offended powerful people in Mississippi and Washington by its insistence on de-

segregation and involvement in civil rights activities. But Marian and other friends were able to save the program. Since then, and in spite of almost yearly worries about refunding, Head Start has helped many preschool children in Mississippi.

It was in Mississippi that Marian met Peter Edelman, a Jewish lawyer from Minneapolis and the man she would marry. In 1967, Harvard Law School graduate Edelman was a legislative assistant to Senator Robert F. Kennedy, who came to the state when his Senate Subcommittee on Employment, Manpower, and Poverty held hearings in Jackson. Edelman was advised to look up Marian Wright before the subcommittee convened. They met for dinner and talked for hours into the night. Marian testified before the subcommittee and took the committee on a tour through the Delta where people were living in shacks without heat, electricity, or running water and where unbathed babies had swollen bellies from lack of food. Wright sometimes says that it was hungry children who brought her and her husband together.

In March 1968, Marian Wright moved to Washington, partly to be with Peter and partly because she felt that it would be more effective to deal with the problem of poverty on a federal level. Soon after she arrived, she became counsel to the Poor People's Campaign, which had decided to carry out its campaign to compel the nation to confront economic inequality despite the assassination in April of its leader Martin Luther King, Jr. In addition, she established the Washington Research Project, to explore issues in the public interest and to lobby congress for funds to expand services to children. In July 1968 Peter and Marian were married in the Virginia backyard of Adam Walinsky, Robert Kennedy's other leading legislative assistant. This was the first interracial marriage in the state of Virginia since its "miscegenation" laws were declared unconstitutional.

The wedding took place after Robert Kennedy was assassinated. Edelman, as well as other senior aides to Kennedy, had received a Ford Foundation grant after the senator's death to help them with their passage to other occupations. Peter and Marian used the money to travel around the world, spending time in Africa, Vietnam, India, and Prague. When they returned to Washington Peter became the associate director of the Robert F. Kennedy Memorial. Marian went back to helping poor children through the Washington Research Project, now focusing on education.

Three years later, Marian again shifted her locale, this time to Boston, when Peter accepted a job as vice president of the University of Massachusetts. Marian was named director of the Center of Law and Education at Harvard University but commuted to Washington on a weekly basis to administer the Washington Research Project. By now the Edelmans had two sons, Joshua and Jonah; another son, Ezra, was born in 1974. With the understanding that raising a biracial, interfaith family would present unusual adjustments, the boys were brought up with strong values and a deep belief in God and instructed to honor and respect the religious traditions of their father and mother. Each one was given what the family likes to refer to as a "Baptist Bar Mitzvah," with both a Baptist minister and a rabbi presiding.

The plight of needy children continued to concern Marian Edelman. Since her Mississippi Head Start days she had been formulating various plans to deal with children's problems. One factor in her choice was the recognition that people were "tired of the concerns of the sixties" but that children always aroused public attention. In 1973 she founded the nonprofit, nonpartisan Children's Defense Fund (CDF) as a spin-off from the Washington Research Project. Obtaining financing only from private individuals and foundations, she staffed the CDF and began to issue flawlessly researched reports on children's issues such as day care, health, and nutrition. Some of the early topics the CDF looked into included a survey of the treatment of institutionalized children, an inquiry on the use of children in medical experiments, and an investigation into why so many of the nation's school-aged youngsters were not actually going to school. Other issues it tackled were the foster care system, child abuse, infant mortality, children's nutrition, drug use, and homelessness.

In 1979 the Edelmans moved back to Washington D.C., where Marian became more and more engrossed in the CDF and Peter became a professor at the Georgetown University School of Law. By 1993 the CDF had a staff of over a hundred and a budget exceeding $10.5 million. In 1983 the CDF became involved in what Marian Edelman saw as an ever-growing priority: babies born out of wedlock. Besides publishing reports and press releases on this problem, the CDF began an advertising campaign aimed directly at adolescents, warning them about the consequences of having sex too early as well as sex without birth control. The CDF aimed at a pragmatic rather than a moralistic strategy. Between 1984 and 1988 it lobbied Congress to expand Medicaid services to poor children, using as a major argument that increasing children's health services actually decreased government future costs in doctor and hospital bills. The CDF had major successes in inducing Congress to expand Head Start and nutrition programs for children and also became involved in working for the passage of a child-care bill that, when enacted in 1990, was the first such measure since 1971. The Act for Better Child Care provides billions of dollars for child-care assistance for low-income working families.

The CDF's basic goals for children include: "a healthy start," through basic health care; a "head start" through quality preschool education; and a "fair start"

through economic security for families. Marian Wright Edelman makes sure that she constantly keeps the CDF in the public's mind. She lectures widely, gives frequent interviews, and writes articles and books. She has won a prestigious MacArthur Fellowship and a Rockefeller Foundation award. Her most recent book, published in 1992, is *The Measure of Our Success: A Letter to My Children and Yours*. This ninety-seven-page work, which became a best-seller in hardcover, is mostly a message about parenting, but Chapter 5 "If the Child Is Safe: A Struggle for America's Conscience and Future," implores the government, the community, and families to take concerted action on behalf of American children. Her critics have said that Edelman focuses too much on government's responsibility for children and not enough on the family's role.

One member of CDF's board of directors is Edelman's friend, Hillary Rodham Clinton, whom she has known since 1969. Marian herself is known in Washington as one of the "First Friends" of the Clintons. So far, unlike many other professional friends of the president and First Lady, she has declined to take a job with the Clinton administration and claims she is not interested in competing for the next opening on the Supreme Court or in running for elected office. She wants to stay "focused just on children" and she thinks she can be more effective working outside of government than inside. Marian Edelman, a workaholic who is just now beginning to show gray in her short curly hair, hopes that her personal future will bring a little more time for going to the movies and taking weekend trips to New York City with her husband. But it is difficult to picture her slowing down. She told an interviewer she follows the advice of Martin Luther King, Jr., who instructed his supporters to keep active. "If you can't fly, run," he said. "If you can't run walk. If you can't walk, crawl, but by all means keep moving."

THE MODERN WORLD

tile regime. The Russians in turn wanted from the United States and the West financial aid to help modernize their obsolescent industrial infrastructure. But few Americans, in a time of economic hardship at home, were willing to endorse paying out billions of American tax dollars to save a former enemy. The administration offered small amounts of financial aid, promised technical help, and sought to encourage private investment, but it was unwilling and unable to do more.

Though the future of the former Soviet Union would in the end assuredly be the bigger problem, during the administration's early months the fate of the former Yugoslavia was a more agonizing issue.

Yugoslavia, in the chaotic Balkan peninsula, had been cobbled together after World War I out of a diversity of ethnic and religious groups—Slavs, Greeks, Albanians, Catholics, Orthodox Christian, Muslims, and others. Antagonisms among these groups had been held in check by the Communist regime established in 1946 by Marshal Josip Broz Tito. After Tito's death in 1980 Yugoslavia quickly fell apart. The core, with its capital in Belgrade, remained under the control of the largest ethnic group, the Orthodox Christian Serbs. In 1992 the Slovenes declared their independence as did the Roman Catholic Croats, and the Greek-speaking Macedonians. In the midsection of the former Yugoslavia, with their capital in Sarajevo, the city where the Austrian archduke's assassination in 1914 had tripped off World War I, were the Bosnians, many of whom were Muslims, despised by the Christian Croats and Serbs alike. In 1992 the Bosnians too proclaimed their independence. The European nations and the United States recognized the independence of all the Yugoslav successor states except Macedonia to which Greece, a NATO member, fearing designs on its own territory, objected.

Coveting its territory and hostile to Muslims, neither the Serbs nor the Croats were willing to accept an independent Bosnia, at least not with its initially proclaimed expansive boundaries. Serbs and Croats soon launched a campaign to destroy the new government in Sarajevo or at least compress it into a mini-state composed almost entirely of Muslims. The Serbs, especially, employed "ethnic cleansing" terror tactics to drive the Muslim population out of regions they coveted. Serb forces raped Bosnian women, shelled open cities and towns, and threw Muslim men into brutal concentration camps where many died. The whole appalling process reeked of the Nazi Holocaust and sent a shudder through the European and American publics.

But neither the European nations nor the United States wanted to become entangled in the age-old hatreds of the Balkans and refused to do much about it. They sent food and medicine. Several European countries contributed peacekeeping troops to UN forces stationed in Bosnia.

Britain tried to broker a negotiated peace. But no country was willing to use military muscle to stop the Serbs and Croats and enforce a settlement. During the presidential campaign Clinton scolded the Bush administration for timidity and promised to use American influence and, if needed, its military power, to stop the atrocities in Bosnia. After his inauguration, however, Clinton waffled. The American government authorized airdrops of food and medicines to besieged Muslim towns and threatened to use air power to attack the Serbs. The West European nations and the United States imposed an economic embargo on Serbia. But in the end, Clinton refused to authorize the use of force until and unless the European nations, closer than the United States to the killing fields, were willing to intervene directly. They said no, and Clinton threw up his hands in frustration.

In truth, most Americans, however sympathetic to the Bosnians, recognized the danger of entanglement in the Balkan morass. Yet some observers depicted it as another sign of Clinton's weakness and indecisiveness on the foreign policy front.

Clinton was indeed inconsistent in his response to foreign provocations. During the summer of 1993 the president ordered the bombing of Saddam Hussein's intelligence facilities to stop threats to American patrol planes flying over Iraqi territory. He also despatched special force commandos to Somalia to capture warlord Mohammed Farah Aidid who was impeding the UN humanitarian efforts.

Americans did not need to look any further than Somalia to spot the dangers of foreign intervention when humanitarian considerations, rather than vital U.S. interests, were the primary concern. The Somalia difficulty was not of Clinton's making. Back in December 1992, just after his election defeat, the lame duck Bush had sent a force of U.S. marines into the East African nation to prevent mass starvation. The mission—Operation Restore Hope—was purely humanitarian, Bush said, and American troops would be back home in two or three months.

Somalia was a shell of a nation, without even the rudiments of functioning political or physical infrastructures. Central authority had collapsed and local warlords, little better than gangsters, preyed on innocent civilians. The country was also victim of severe drought, but humanitarian agencies seeking to relieve the hunger and disease were kept from doing their job by political turmoil. For months before Bush's decision, the American public had seen a flood of heart-rending TV images of starving infants, with swollen bellies, too weak to cry, and fly-covered adults reduced to bags of bones.

The American troops despatched by Bush restored order and ended the famine. Announcing that the mission had been accomplished, Bush ordered withdrawal of most

American troops. In May 1993 the UN took over the job of protecting the relief workers and medical personnel who remained in the country. Some 5,000 Americans were assigned to the UN forces.

By the summer the picture had changed. Aidid, the Somali strongman, initially cowed, began to attack the UN troops. After he had killed fifty Pakistani peacekeepers, the UN forces, including Americans, sought to capture him and destroy his power. In effect, the United States began to settle into a shooting war in a country where it had come to provide humanitarian succor. In September Aidid's forces ambushed a group of Americans under UN command and killed fifteen. The American public, having enthusiastically supported Operation Restore Hope, now screamed with pain. American troops must be brought home immediately. In Congress, Republicans, though hawkish under their own president, now sounded like isolationists. Clinton was risking American lives unnecessarily, they announced, and for a time Congress threatened to limit his power to send troops into danger areas.

To many observers, the Somali imbroglio seemed a cautionary tale that must be heeded in the future: The United States could not be the world's emergency rescue squad. Speaking before the United Nations in New York in September 1993 Clinton finally acknowledged the reality by calling for well-defined missions for the world organization and distinct plans for pull-outs when these were accomplished.

The administration could bask in one foreign-policy success during its first half year in office. Bush's secretary of state, James Baker, in the wake of the Gulf War victory, had induced the Israelis and Palestinians to open talks with one another in Madrid on the issue of Palestinian self-rule in the Israeli-occupied territories. The Palestinian delegates were all members of the Palestine Liberation Organization (PLO) led by Yasir Arafat, but Israel, considering the PLO a terrorist organization and refusing to recognize it officially, ignored their political connections. The Palestinian negotiating team members were merely private individuals from the occupied territories. In any event, the talks, which soon adjourned to Washington, dragged on for months with little progress.

By this time, however, an election in Israel had replaced the hard-line Likud party by the liberal Labor party headed by Yitzhak Rabin, a former Israeli general. Equally important, perhaps, world geopolitical circumstances had changed. The collapse of the Soviet Union had removed a major backer of intransigent Arab militancy. Arafat's support of Iraq in the Gulf War, moreover, had alienated the rich Saudis and Kuwaitis from the PLO and sharply reduced its financial support. Both the Israelis and Arafat, finally, found themselves under attack by Islamic fundamentalists

who despised both the Jewish state and the secular Arabs represented by the PLO.

Both sides, in a word, were ready to change their minds, and when the Norwegians offered to serve as go-betweens, they agreed to direct face-to-face negotiations. In a series of secret meetings in Norway, PLO leaders and the Israeli foreign minister, Shimon Peres, pieced together an interim agreement on Palestinian self-rule that included Israeli recognition of the PLO as the de facto government of the Palestinian people with internal authority over the Gaza Strip and the city of Jericho on the West Bank. Looking ahead, it promised negotiation of further increments of authority and territory to the PLO. Though they said nothing about a fully sovereign Palestinian state, the terms were ambiguous enough so that Arafat and his supporters could see it as a first step toward independence, and the Israelis could feel reassured that a hostile and vengeful independent Palestine would not become their uncomfortable neighbor in the near future. In return for its concessions, meanwhile, Israel could anticipate ending the draining *Intifada*, the Palestinian guerrilla war against Israel, and finally achieving peace with its Arab neighbors.

Though the United States was not directly involved in the Norway negotiations, it had started the peace process in Madrid, and its good offices remained vital for a successful carrying out of the agreement. Clinton seized the opportunity to place the United States behind the accord and invited both the Israelis and Arafat to Washington to sign it. On September 13, 1993, on the sun-dappled White House South Lawn, the Israeli leaders and the PLO put their signatures to the document at the table where Anwar Sadat and Menachem Begin had signed the Camp David accords. U.S. Secretary of State Warren Christopher and Russian Foreign Minister Andrei Kozyrev witnessed the agreement, a gesture that symbolized the role that reconciliation between the former Cold War adversaries had played in the outcome. The high point of the ceremony was the handshake between the long-time enemies. The crowd of distinguished guests on the lawn cheered when Arafat grasped and shook the hands of Peres and Rabin.

A very long and bumpy road lay ahead in the Middle East; many things could go wrong before peace was achieved between Israel and its Arab enemies. But the momentous first step had been taken. Though Clinton had had little to do directly with the breakthrough negotiations, the president at the ceremonies had projected the image of a statesman that partially offset his recent foreign-policy failures. Soon after the historic occasion polls showed a sharp improvement in Clinton's foreign-policy rating by the American public.

Domestic Accomplishments. By the summer of 1993 the administration finally seemed to be moving on the domestic front. On February 17 the president had delivered a televised speech to a joint session of Congress outlining his economic program. He proposed a modest short-term federal spending increase to jolt the still lagging economy into life. He also asked for increased long-term government outlays on education, job training, and research in line with Labor Secretary Robert Reich's views that the United States needed a skilled and educated labor force to compete in the globalized economy. The government, Clinton said, should also invest in the nation's dilapidated transportation system and in a high-speed national computer network to make it a leader in the information age. Clinton also took up the issue of national health care in an economic context. The rising costs to the government of the existing health care system (Medicare and Medicaid) were getting out of hand and must be contained if the country was to control its budget deficits. He would soon submit a health plan to Congress developed by a task force headed by his wife, Hillary Rodham Clinton, he announced.

But the main emphasis of the Clinton economic program was on how to control the growth of the federal debt. The immense annual federal deficits were seriously damaging the economy, most experts agreed. Federal borrowing to meet the deficits absorbed a huge mountain of private savings and so slowed the growth of domestic capital investment. Interest payments, moreover, on this vast and growing debt—already at $4 trillion—soaked up far too much of the federal budget, making any new federal programs, no matter how deserving, virtually impossible. How could the nation, for example, justify the multibillion dollar Superconductor-Supercollider for nuclear research in Texas when it had to pay billions in interest annually to foreign and domestic holders of American government IOUs?*

To keep the debt burden from getting worse Clinton proposed a series of spending cuts, especially in defense costs. But he also proposed new taxes. The largest of these would be a tax on all sources of energy (a BTU tax) that would not only raise revenue but also encourage resource conservation. There would also be new "sin" taxes on tobacco and alcoholic beverages, a hike in the income tax for high-income recipients, and an increase in the proportion of Social Security pensions of more affluent retirees subject to federal tax. All told, he said, his plan would reduce the projected increase in the deficit some $325 billion over a five-year period. Clinton concluded his address with some eloquent words: "This is nothing less than a call to arms to restore the vitality of the American dream."

"When I was a boy," he concluded, "we had a name for the belief that we should all pull together to build a better, stronger nation. We called it patriotism, and we still do."

---

*In late 1993 Congress killed the Supercollider in any event.

The public, though nervous about any tax increase, liked the speech and the plan. Overnight polls showed that 79 percent of the American public supported the president's proposals. But the favorable attitude did not last. The succession of White House missteps, including the mysterious en masse firing of the White House travel office, continued and further undermined the public's confidence in the administration. Meanwhile, the Republicans presented a remarkably united front against the budget bills when submitted to Congress. The administration proposals, they said, contained too few cuts and too many tax hikes. Mounting a filibuster in the Senate, they succeeded in eliminating virtually the whole of the president's $30 billion stimulus package. They could not stop the rest of the $1.5 trillion budget bill, however. It passed with $496 billion of new taxes, mostly on gasoline and high-income taxpayers, and almost $500 billion of spending reductions over a four-year period, including cuts in Medicare and Medicaid as well as defense. Final passage in Congress was as close as possible. A number of Democrats, facing tough reelection campaigns in the fall, and fearing the voters' deeply embedded tax aversion, defected from the administration. The budget bill finally cleared both houses in early August by a hair's breadth. In the Senate it required Vice President Gore's vote to break the tie vote.

The budget bill as passed was substantially different from the one the president had submitted. Many of the programs and outlays for making America more competitive through improved education, new research facilities, and augmented infrastructure had been discarded. What remained was primarily a deficit-reduction bill. The president's supporters insisted that reducing the growth of deficits was a key aspect of spurring productivity. By itself, it would boost future growth rates. And besides, given Clinton's limited mandate and the unsettled public mood, the bill was all that could be expected. Yet some critics faulted him for yielding too much to opponents. Once again, they said, the president had proved too willing to compromise.

By this time, however, the administration could count other victories. In early February the president signed into law a Family Leave Bill allowing employees several months of unpaid leave from their jobs to attend to young children or sick relatives. Congress had passed the same bill under Bush but could not muster the votes to overcome his veto. Soon after, Clinton signed the "Motor Voter" bill easing the complicated voter registration process in federal elections by automatically registering voters at the time they applied for auto licenses. Then, shortly after the budget victory, Congress passed, in modified form, the president's National Service Plan for Youth, a scheme to help pay education cost for thousands of young Americans who signed up to serve the elderly, the poor, the homeless, and other disadvantaged groups as part of a domestic Peace Corps.

None of these bills promised to be earthshaking in their consequences, though they were not inconsequential either. But clearly more significant was the president's victory over his opponents in the fight over the North American Free Trade Agreement (NAFTA). This agreement sought to unite into one economic unit Canada, the United States, and Mexico, a market of over 350 million consumers and producers unobstructed by tariffs or other barriers. Many Americans feared that it would accelerate the departure of factories and jobs south of the border, and several of the major industrial unions oppposed it bitterly. The treaty had been negotiated by the Bush administration, and at first Clinton seemed reluctant to support it, especially because so many Democrats were beholden to union political support. But by the fall of 1993, he had concluded that he must stand up for freer international trade generally if the United States was to compete in the global economy, and he decided to make NAFTA's passage a test of his leadership. In November, after a major administration show of political muscle, the treaty won by a narrow vote. Though the victory margin included more Republican than Democratic yeas, most observers gave Clinton an "A" for presidential leadership.

National Health Insurance. By a wide margin Clinton's most important initiative during his first year was his health insurance scheme. Drawn up by a Health Task Force headed by Hillary Clinton, it was submitted to Congress in late September 1993.

No one doubted that the country's health delivery system was in crisis and badly needed reform. Health costs as a proportion of total national product were already close to 15 percent, about $1 trillion annually. Outlays on health care in the United States were larger proportionately than any other country's. And costs were getting worse. By the year 2000 total health care costs were projected to reach almost 19 percent of GNP. This runaway process threatened to undermine the quality of life for everyone. Each dollar spent for health care came out of some other benefit or need: education, leisure, nutrition, housing, entertainment, fashion, culture, the environment, science, and everything else that made life enjoyable, comfortable, interesting, and productive. Whole sectors of the economy would inevitably contract as health care expanded. The nation, moreover, would lose its productive edge if health care costs for American firms and individuals grew more rapidly than their equivalent abroad. Already many large American companies were complaining bitterly that a large part of the cost of their product represented health care outlays for their workers.

No American first lady has been as active in public life as Hillary Rodham Clinton. A graduate of Yale Law School, she had a thriving law practice in Little Rock when her husband became president and she came with him to Washington. There, unlike any of her predecessors, she became a powerful force in White House policy-making.

But even at these bloated prices the system did not do a consistently good job. Some Americans were indeed adequately insured against illness, and many at least muddled through under the existing system. Members of private insurance plans could usually choose their own doctors and hospitals. Other insurees belonged to health maintenance organizations (HMOs), which employed a panel of salaried doctors and other medical personnel and frequently ran their own clinics and hospitals.

The millions of Americans with health insurance received competent medical attention. In fact, American doctors were among the best trained in the world; American hospitals were among the best equipped in the world. And waits for visits to specialists and for tests and medical procedures were usually short in the private sector. But there were an estimated 37 million Americans who had no health care coverage at all. Such people, usually the working poor, did without medical attention entirely or were thrown on the dubious resources of public hospitals or of private hospital emergency rooms. The public paid for these services indirectly, either through higher community taxes or through medical charges passed along to insured patients. But even the insured often could not count on health coverage to protect them adequately. Many health plans excluded preexisting conditions or serious chronic disease. Many people forfeited their coverage when they lost or left their jobs. Retirees on Medicare had to pay for their medicines, often a major cost for people living on pensions.

The Health Task Force under the First Lady held its first session on March 29, 1993. Thereafter Hillary Clinton and her staff and advisers held hearings around the country. Fearing that leaks would enable the lobbyists and the skeptics to pick apart any plan before it could be officially submitted, the task force kept its meetings and its deliberations private, a procedure that aroused criticism.

The administration finally submitted its health plan to Congress in late September 1993 in the form of a 246-page document. The scheme set off one of the most intense political debates, in Congress and out, since the 1960s.

The plan rejected national health insurance administered by the government and paid for largely by taxes. This was the system used in Canada and most of Western Europe. Many experts said that it was the cheapest since, with a "single payer" (the government), it involved less paperwork, and, in addition, enabled the government to impose cost limits on doctors, drug companies, and hospitals by simple fiat. It had serious drawbacks, however. The experience of Europe showed that it often led to long waits for non-life-threatening medical procedures and resulted in strict rationing of health care that seemed inhumane. Recent figures of national health insurance abroad also indicated that it did not even contain costs effectively. But in any case, national health insurance smacked of the "socialized medicine" that most Americans deplored and was never very seriously considered by the task force.

Instead, to hold costs down, the Clinton plan proposed managed competition. Regional health alliances would represent consumers in striking bargains with drug companies, doctors, and hospitals for the lowest costs. All citizens would be covered whether they worked for large corporations, which normally paid employees' health insurance, or for small firms, which often did not. People would not be denied health insurance for preexisting conditions or dumped from the insurance rolls because they lost their job. The plan would provide for long-term care, preventive care, payment for prescription drugs and children's eyeglasses, and some mental health and substance-abuse care. Employers and patients would pay much of the cost. This was no threat to large companies, which generally already provided such plans for their employees. It did trouble small employers who often did not. The self-employed would pay their costs themselves, but could deduct these from their income tax. The remaining funding would come from a tax on cigarettes and perhaps hard liquor, two items that contributed to poor health in the first place.

No one could be sure what the final plan would look like after it emerged from the grinder of public debate. Virtually every group with a stake in the status quo, as well as many health care reformers with different ideas and agendas, would take shots at the scheme for both sincere and selfish reasons. Doctors and hospitals feared the loss of freedom to choose treatments and procedures and to determine the prices and fees they could charge. Taxpayers feared new and higher taxes. Small-businesses owners said the costs would bankrupt them and eliminate thousands of jobs. Many of the smaller health insurers feared being squeezed out. Some experts said the Clinton plan would not hold down technology-driven cost increases. Others believed that the scheme did not mandate real competition. But almost everyone agreed that Americans could not continue as in the past; thus even Republican congressional leaders did not feel that they could afford to be tagged as obstructionists, and they presented a health reform plan of their own. With a strong consensus that the existing system was untenable, it was clear that the Clinton administration, for better or worse, was going to midwife a fundamental change in the nation's health care delivery system one way or another.

Most Americans initially favored the president's proposals. His televised presentation to Congress was agile and convincing. At one point, brandishing a pen, he declared dramatically that if any bill that came from Congress did not include universal coverage, he would veto it. But as the measure worked its way through the legislative process the public began to have doubts. In Congress conservatives attacked it as likely to expand the already excessive federal bureaucracy. Some liberals continued to prefer the single-payer scheme. Outside of Congress every group with a stake in the nation's health care system weighed in. The insurance companies, certain that they would be deprived of profits, mounted major TV advertising campaigns to convince the public that the bill was unworkable. Small business attacked it as a crippling burden that they could not afford. Physicians groups also took potshots at the administration measure. As the bill wended its way through Congress it was worn down by successive concessions of the White House and the Democratic leadership. Before long Clinton, in desperation, abandoned his dramatic pledge to veto any health bill that did not supply universal coverage. He would accept less than a hundred percent and allow full coverage to be gradually phased in.

He immediately came under fierce fire from his liberal constituency for abandoning his principles. Others, not necessarily committed to universality, said he was waffling once more. Whether the result of weak presidential leadership, public uncertainty and confusion, or the lobbying of special interests, by the time Congress adjourned in August 1994 the health care bill still had not been passed. Many observers, anticipating Democratic setbacks in the fall Congressional elections, believed it unlikely any major overhaul of the country's health care system was likely during the administration's remaining years. All told, however well intentioned, the effort to reform the health insurance of the American people had hurt the president's standing, reversing the popularity gains of the previous year.

Before Congress adjourned, however, the administration won one important victory. For years Americans had brooded over the surge of crime that made the streets of the cities dangerous places to walk even in broad daylight. In fact, crimes such burglary were down, but violent crime was up. In many cities shootouts between criminals, usually connected with drug dealing, caught the daily headlines. Innocent bystanders were often trapped in the crossfire.

In early 1994 Congress debated a major crime bill designed to ease the public's fears. Among its provisions were large federal grants to the cities to beef up their police forces, money for various inner city social and sports programs to provide counseling services and recreation to inner city youths, and further restrictions on ownership of weapons deemed dangerous in the hands of criminals. The bill came under attack from the National Rifle Association, an organization represented hunters, target shooters, and many who believed broadly defined gun ownership one of the rights guaranteed by the Constitution. It also offended Republican conservatives in Congress who deplored its pro-

visions for large scale social services. These, they said, were too reminiscent of the failed social programs of the Great Society. The administration fought for the bill but it was close. Losing in August 1994 on a procedural vote, the White House was able to rally and get the bill through just before the summer recess.

The Whitewater Affair. By mid-point in his term the Clinton record was in fact mixed. Yet the public had the decided impression that the president was not a strong leader. Friends argued that the fault was as much the public's as the president's. The American people did not know what they wanted in either foreign policy or in domestic matters and any policy proposals were certain to come under fire from all sides. Critics responded that it was the president's responsibility to guide the voters in a desirable direction; Clinton gave up too quickly. He wanted too much to be liked.

Some of the very people who attacked the president for weak leadership were working as hard as they could to undermine his ability to lead by assailing his character. Undoubtedly Clinton was less than a saint. Even after he became president various young women showed up at press conferences and on talk shows to accuse him of making sexual overtures to them while he was Governor of Arkansas. More serious were charges that the Clintons had used their powerful position in the state to advance their own financial interests. One such charge involved a remarkable gain for Hillary Clinton in a commodities market deal alleged to have involved insider information. More serious was "Whitewater," the generic term for a real estate deal by Clinton while governor to develop a tract of land for housing and recreation in the Ozarks. Critics claimed that it involved illegal relations with powerful business groups, including Savings and Loan promoters. The Clintons said that there had been nothing illegal about Whitewater; they had actually lost money on the deal.

If the president and his wife had been more forthcoming, observers said, they might have been believed. Instead, they seemed determined to cover up the details of the scheme and did every thing they could to avoid an investigation. In the end they failed. Attorney General Janet Reno, under pressure from the Republicans, finally appointed a special prosecutor to look into Whitewater. He was replaced during the summer of 1994 by one less friendly to the Clintons. In July Congress itself began hearings on the role of the Treasury Department and the White House in trying to fend off investigators. To many who watched the proceedings on TV it seemed as if the Assistant Secretary of the Treasury, Robert Altman, had bent the ethical rules if not actually broken the law in defense of the administration's reputation. He soon resigned.

The just-stranded ship in the background is the Golden Venture, a vessel used to carry illegal Chinese immigrants to the United States. Some of these desperate people are shown huddled in the foreground after the vessel went aground off New York City.

It was hard to tell how damaging Whitewater would ultimately be to the administration. More revelations were certain to come. Some believed it was Clinton's Watergate. Others assumed that it was so complicated that it bored the public and would eventually blow over. But added to the other charges it undoubtedly helped to undermine the president's moral authority and reduce his effectiveness as a leader.

★ RACE, GENDER, AND NATIONALITY ★

As the millennium's end approached, deep population changes began to alter the texture of American life. The new demographics were reflected in Clinton appointment policy; they played out even more significantly on the nation's cultural and intellectual stages.

Demographic Change. The profile of the American population was changing rapidly in the 1980s and 1990s. Birthrates were falling, health was improving, and people were living longer. As the net effect of these trends, between 1980 and 1991 the median age of the American people rose from 30 years to 33.1 and promised to go much higher in the years ahead as the baby boomers of the post-1945 era moved past middle age.

The rise in average age was certain to affect American life in profound ways. An aging population was an ailing population. Much of the soaring costs of medicine were incurred at the end of life as doctors employed heroic methods to delay death by a few weeks or months. In the years ahead, demographers predicted, the flood of people in their eighties and nineties would put intense pressure on the already overloaded health care system.

The problem encouraged new approaches to the last years of life. The "living will" movement proposed legally validating the right to reject life support systems when all hope for recovery from serious illness had passed. The euthanasia movement sought to allow people with terminal illnesses to choose suicide—to "die with dignity"—rather than linger hopelessly in pain. Living wills offended relatively few; legal suicide made many Americans uncomfortable. The activities of Dr. Jack Kervorkian, the "Suicide Doctor," in assisting seriously ill patients to end their lives, scandalized many and led the Michigan legislature to make assisted suicide a crime in 1993.

An aging population raised nonmedical problems as well. As the ratio of retired people to workers rose, the need to support them promised to be a drag on the incomes of the young and economically most productive. Many younger workers feared that the Social Security system would become bankrupt, and when they were ready to retire the money would simply not be there. In 1983, a bipartisan revision of the Social Security Act had helped make the federal pension system solvent. Social Security taxes had been raised as had the age at which future pensioners would receive full benefits. But many American workers, in their prime years, would now be paying more in old-age pension contributions than in income tax. The problem raised the specter of a generational battle between younger workers and retirees that few people welcomed.

And what about the psychology of a geriatric society? How would the country deal with a population with an increasingly foreshortened horizon? "Seniors" could not be faulted for special concern about their own immediate circumstances and the here-and-now. But that was not necessarily the best thing for the country as a whole. An aging population was a less innovative and less socially conscious population. Would America, as it grayed, become less creative and less compassionate?

Other demographic trends raised problems of adjustment as well. Overall United States birthrates had been dropping for some time. Unlike the citizens of several other advanced industrial countries, Americans still had enough babies each year to offset aggregate mortality. But these birthrates were not equal across the ethnic and racial board. Whites had birthrates of 64.7 per thousand women in 1989; blacks had birthrates of 90.4. Hispanic groups too, especially Mexican-Americans and Puerto Ricans, had higher birthrates than people of European antecedents. By themselves these differentials meant that the population of both blacks and Hispanics would inevitably increase faster than "Anglo" whites.

Immigration. The growing numbers of Euro-Americans and Afro-Americans derived mostly from natural increase. Much of the Hispanic—as well as the Asian—increase came from immigration, rather than births, however. America re-

mained a magnet for millions around the world, and during the 1980s immigration was responsible for a third of the country's net population increase. As we saw, as early as the 1970s, the major sources of immigration had switched from Europe to Latin America and Asia. By 1990 three times as many Asians as Europeans came to America, and eight times as many people from Latin America, primarily Mexico, the Caribbean, and Central America. These figures, however, described only legal immigration. Many experts held that the illegal immigration from the newer sources was at least as great. Already the differential birthrates of blacks, European whites, Asians, and Hispanics were changing the overall look of Americans. By the 1990 census almost 25 million Americans were Hispanic and they were the fastest growing group in America with increases during the 1980s of a startling 6.1 percent annually. The continuing wave of immigrants was certain to shift the racial and ethnic balance still further as time passed. In 1993 a Census Bureau report predicted that the Hispanic population of the United States would exceed the black population by the year 2010. It also projected a total population of 392 million in 2050 of which only 53 percent would be "Non-Hispanic White," while 16 percent would be black and 22.5 percent Hispanic. At that date Asians, about 3 percent in 1990, would make up 10 percent of the total population.

The magnitude of non-European immigration was in part the result of relaxed American immigration practices. The immigration law of 1986 allowed relatives of a resident to claim legal entry into the United States. Many thousands took advantage of minimal family connections. The law sought to reduce "illegals" by threatening with punishment any employer who offered work to someone without the precious "green card" attesting to lawful residence. The law was not effectively enforced, however, and did little to deter illegal entry. Virtually anyone, moreover, who set foot on American soil could claim asylum from religious or political persecution and stay in the United States if the claim was valid. With little money or personnel for the purpose, investigation of claims was slow and meanwhile the immigrant was allowed to move into the community at large. Few if any ever appeared to find out what the Immigration and Naturalization Service had determined. Still another leak in the system allowed illegal immigrants to stay if they had children born in the United States. Under the Constitution these children were American citizens; thus there was no way to deport their parents. Many immigrant couples, critics said, came to the United States and conceived children before the authorities could expel them. They then remained, courtesy of their American-born offspring.

America's chief drawing card, as in the past, was wages far higher than in less developed countries. In the Southwest and California the immigrants did construction jobs, worked as domestics, and performed farm labor of all kinds. On the East Coast they were taxi drivers, housekeepers, and restaurant workers. Many toiled long hours in sweatshops, making cheap garments like their European predecessors eighty years before. Some began small businesses—groceries, truck gardens, restaurants, laundries.

Despite low wages, long hours, and absence of benefits, they sought entry to the United States in every way possible. Among the Chinese, criminals had taken over smuggling of workers from the Asian mainland into the United States. Charging each illegal immigrant as much as $30,000, these unscrupulous entrepreneurs kept them in near slavery, toiling at menial jobs or even working as prostitutes, until they repaid their debt. This deplorable traffic was highlighted in June 1993 when a small freighter, the *Golden Venture*, carrying 300 ill-fed, sick Chinese aliens, grounded on a New York beach. Rounded up by the authorities and confined until American officials could dispose of their cases, they represented only the tip of the illegal immigration iceberg.

The loose immigration policies of the United States were thrown into still more vivid relief by the events of early 1993 in lower Manhattan. Suddenly, on February 26, 1993, a colossal explosion ripped through the lower floors of one of the twin towers of the World Trade Center, the second tallest buildings in the world. Six people died in the explosion in the underground parking garage and thousands had to be hurriedly evacuated by stairs to escape the deadly smoke. In a matter of days combined federal and local police forces discovered the culprits, a group of Muslim immigrants from North Africa and the Middle East who worshipped at mosques in Brooklyn and New Jersey under the spiritual guidance of Sheik Omar Abdel-Rahman.

A fundamentalist Egyptian cleric who despised the secular Arab government of his homeland and allegedly preached violence against the perceived enemies of Islam, including America, Sheik Rahman had been allowed to enter the United States, though his views were well documented. In the next months the FBI uncovered plots among the Sheik's other adherents to blow up the UN, plant bombs in the major tunnels and bridges connecting New York and New Jersey, and assassinate American politicians and American Jewish leaders considered unfriendly to Islamic causes. In the summer of 1993 the alleged conspirators, including Sheik Rahman himself, were indicted. Four of the defendants in the World Trade Center bombing were convicted in May 1994 and sentenced to long terms in prison.

Without doubt the feelings of native-born Americans toward the newest immigrants were, as in the past, tainted by prejudice. Arab-Americans, for example, undoubtedly suffered from anti-Muslim attitudes of Westerners, intolerance reinforced by the World Trade Center bombing; crude racism obviously played a part in biases toward people from Asia and Latin America. But the swelling immigration tide raised reasoned concerns as well. What was the net economic impact, for example, of the flood of immigrants? Did the newcomers take more from the economy in the way of free public education, medical services, and "welfare" than they contributed in taxes and needed skills? Did they displace poor, but striving, Americans from necessary entry-level jobs? The answers were not clear, but the governor of California, a state hard-hit by defense cutbacks and soaring unemployment rates, concluded that they did. The United States must tighten its immigration laws, declared Governor Pete Wilson, even if this meant repealing the existing citizenship provision of the Fourteenth Amendment.

Nor was Governor Wilson the only one concerned about the costs of uncontrolled immigration. Many black leaders complained that foreigners were undermining the wages of, and stealing jobs from, black American citizens. Some American-born Hispanic citizens also thought that the deluge from Latin America and the Caribbean hurt them economically. Middle-class white Americans seldom competed directly with foreign-born workers from latin America, but Asians were another case. Many, it seemed, were nosing out white Americans for top professional jobs and elite college admissions. At the prestigious University of California, Asians in turn complained that university officials had put a lid on admission of Asians in order to guarantee blacks, Hispanics, and whites a prescribed proportion of new freshman admissions. Asian freshman would have to have higher high school grades, better SAT scores, and a longer roster of extracurricular activities than others to get in. When criticised by Asian parents and spokespersons, the Berkeley administration noted that the university "must provide effective leadership in an increasingly multiethnic society. . . ." In effect, "diversity" took precedence over "merit."

The Struggle Over Culture. The changing proportions of the American population promised shifts in values and culture. What would these be when a majority of Americans were no longer of European ancestry? The answer was not clear but there was certain to be disagreement and rancor.

Some effects already seemed apparent. At colleges and universities around the country nonwhite students and faculty, often led by blacks, demanded curricula changes to refocus courses on the achievements, values, and history of non-European peoples. Ever since the 1960s, colleges had offered black history, Asian culture, Latin American studies, and the like. But the Western tradition continued generally to be the core of the cultural and intellectual curriculum. The new "multicultural" mood on campuses, especially the more cosmopolitan ones, sought to replace this emphasis. At Stanford, for example, the administration dropped the long-term required course, Western Culture, in 1988 in favor of a three-course sequence "Cultures, Ideas, Values," that de-emphasized the European component of the core. Time devoted to Shakespeare, the Greek dramatists, Aquinas, Freud, the classic American writers, would be reduced and Asian, Middle Eastern, Latin-American, and African authors and thinkers given the space vacated. President Donald Kennedy of Stanford announced: "We confirm that many minority issues and concerns are not the special pleadings of interest groups, but are Stanford issues—ones that engage all of us."

Curriculum revisions like Stanford's assumed the idea of a common core for all Americans to share, though a somewhat different one from the past. Some multiculturalists, however, rejected the idea of a shared tradition entirely. Americans had no truly common experience, and each component of the country's population need understand only its own cultural heritage.

The new cultural offensive on campus was directed not only at Euro-centered education. There was a parallel feminist drive to change the campus intellectual and cultural environment. If the usual curriculum gave excessive attention to Europe and its traditions, feminists declared, it was also dominated by the male view of the world.

Feminist scholarship and thought had been evolving ever since the late 1960s toward a view of culture, history, science, and politics that broke with traditional approaches to several of the disciplines. Feminist scientists claimed that "male" science ignored the intuitive nature of much knowledge; feminist literary critics denounced the exclusion of talented women and their insights from the standard literary "canon"; feminist historians noted that half the world's population had been ignored by the male-led discipline. Feminist social scientists and psychologists also sought to change basic perspectives on the nature of men and women. They distinguished "sex," a biological category, from "gender," a socially and historically "constructed" entity. The observable differences between the way men and women thought and behaved derived predominantly from the cultural environment of a particular time and place, not from physical organs and hormones.

The new perspectives of race, ethnicity, and gender were strongest in the academic world where they were particularly influential in the humanities departments. There, they appealed not just to black and female faculty and students but also to younger men and women who had been influenced by the ideological shifts of the late 1960s and 1970s. In the field of American history, a woman's perspective, an ecological perspective, and a Native American perspective were added to the previously adopted black perspective, to alter the traditional emphases. The new history of the frontier, for example, not only evened the balance be-

tween whites and Indians—that had been mostly accomplished already. It also emphasized the aggressive and insensitive quality of the "winning of the West" and helped undermine the masculine, "cowboy" mythology.

One effect of these new currents was to polarize student bodies. Observers of campus life noted that, increasingly, black and white students ate separately, partied separately, and studied separately. On some campuses, black students demanded their own residences and student centers, and university administrations often obliged. Defenders of the self-segregation tendency claimed that it was necessary to protect black students, many from inner-city backgrounds, against a hostile, predominantly white university environment. Critics said that it created resentment and encouraged the very thing it was designed to prevent.

There were also growing tensions on campus between men and women as feminists redefined "rape" and sexual harassment to include long-tolerated male practices. Some observers felt that the new concern was long overdue. For far too long men had imposed their wills on women in the guise of "boys will be boys." Men must be made to accept "no" for an answer. Traditionalists often questioned the new attitudes. The evils were exaggerated, they said. Some of the practices proscribed were inevitable parts of the "mating game" and not offenses at all. The university's attempts to protect women, some critics insisted, treated them as children. More than a few men professed to be thoroughly confused about what they could or could not do.

It is hard to say what was cause and what effect, but the new multiculturalism, feminist sensibility, and "political correctness" made some campuses acrimonious places during the early 1990s. At Dartmouth, where an off-campus, student-run, conservative paper frequently attacked "politically correct" views of the college's faculty and students, there were frequent clashes over the whole range of cultural issues. At the University of Pennsylvania nine black students, offended by a *Daily Pennsylvanian* editorial attacking affirmative action, destroyed 14,000 copies of the student newspaper. Modern campuses, one Ivy League professor remarked, had "the cultural diversity of Beirut. There are separate armed camps. The black kids don't mix with the white kids. The Asians are off by themselves. Oppression is the great status symbol."

At some campuses racial and gender tensions encouraged verbal slurs and even physical assaults. To prevent such attacks university administrations instituted "codes" of campus speech and conduct designed to prevent offending any group. Traditionalists and some civil libertarians considered these both repressive and fatuous. And at times the courts agreed. In October 1991 a U.S. District Court struck down the University of Wisconsin's speech code as a violation of First Amendment free speech rights.

The new cultural and ideological styles and tensions went beyond the universities. A gay sensibility began to alter the tone and content of the performance and visual arts. One manifestation was a flock of moving plays about the devastation wrought by AIDS on the homosexual community. There was also a growing irreverence toward mainstream "square" values and culture informed by a gay perspective. At times the influence was subtle and nuanced. At other times, however, it challenged "square" moral and aesthetic values by flaunting extreme aspects of the gay sensibility. The photographs of Robert Mapplethorpe, for example, showed men engaged in undisguised sado-masochistic homosexual acts. Even more extreme was an occasional "in your face" confrontational quality apparently designed to offend and provoke. One of the works of Andres Serrano, called "Piss Christ," was a photograph of a crucifix immersed in Serrano's own urine.

Conservative, traditional, and centrist Americans did not allow the cultural rebels' claims and positions to go un-challenged. Pat Buchanan's speech at the Republican National Convention in Houston was one attack on the perceived extremist offensive against mainstream values. Bush's secretary of education, William Bennett, noted of the Stanford curriculum change that a great university had been "brought low by the forces of ignorance, irrationality, and intimidation."

The sharpest attack on Mapplethorpe and Serrano came from North Carolina Senator Jesse Helms. Helms deplored their works themselves, but his special target was the funding they had received from the National Endowment for the Arts, a federal agency supported by tax money. Why should the American people be asked to pay for such immoral exhibitions? Over the opposition of many intellectual and artistic leaders who invoked the First Amendment right to free expression, Helms proposed in 1989 to end the federal funding of the arts and humanities entirely. Helms' objections to Mapplethorpe were not unique. Under pressure from cultural conservatives the

The explosion of violence in South Central Los Angeles following the acquittal of white police officers for a brutal attack on a black driver shocked the country. The rioters beat whites and Hispanics and destroyed property—especially white or Korean-owned stores.

Corcoran Gallery of Art in Washington cancelled a Mapplethorpe exhibit. In Cincinnati the following spring the director of the Contemporary Arts Center was indicted by a grand jury for displaying obscenity when he put on a Mapplethorp exhibit.

Helms and his sympathizers did not get their way. The Cincinnati art director was acquitted; the National Endowment for the Arts survived. But the attack of cultural conservatives clearly put a damper on public support for unconventional, nontraditional art.

Race Relations.   Academe and the intellectual and artistic worlds are rather remote from the lives of most Americans. But the widening national divisions both affected and reflected the way many Americans regarded their fellow citizens.

Race relations during the late 1980s and 1990s in many ways became more tense. Following the successes of the civil rights movement, racial reconciliation and mutual acceptance seemed to spread widely across groups, sections, and classes. The process soon reversed. Economic stagnation and retreat in the inner cities created a degree of hopelessness and frustration that fed black racial resentments. In some ghetto communities these feelings were directed not just at whites but also at Asian storekeepers who seemed prone to exploit black customers while at the same time treating them discourteously. In New York, Los Angeles, and other cities Korean grocers and black customers engaged in feuds that led to boycotts and picketing.

At the same time the late 1980s and 1990s witnessed an eruption of white racism that frightened many moderate Americans. White supremacist and anti-Semitic groups—"skinheads" and neo-Nazis—proliferated in the Northwest, Mountain States, and the South. In 1991 David Duke, former Grand Wizard of the Louisiana Ku Klux Klan, placed second in the state gubernatorial primary and, in the general election, came frighteningly close to defeating the Democratic candidate.

Serious violence would damage the nation's record of racial tolerance through the period. In 1986, in New York's Howard Beach, a group of white youths attacked some black young men whose presence in their neighborhood they resented, leading to the death of one. Anger ran high in the black community, which demanded and got a special prosecutor to push the case. Violence was narrowly averted when the jury convicted three of the youths for second-degree murder. In another New York neighborhood, where a close-knit community of orthodox Hassidic Jews lived close by a black community, the death of a young black boy in an automobile accident led to several days of racial violence aimed at Jewish residents of Crown Heights, in Brooklyn. One black youth was tried for the death during the distur-

bances of a visiting Australian Jewish scholar, but was acquitted by a predominantly black and Hispanic jury. In Miami, the shooting of two black motorcyclists in 1989 by a Hispanic policeman set off three days of riots in the black Overtown and Liberty City districts. Six people were shot, 27 stores burned, and 400 people arrested.

Los Angeles, however, was the setting of the most serious racial explosion of all. The city had never solved the problems that triggered the Watts riots of 1965. In the South-Central district of the city poverty remained as ingrained as ever; crack-cocaine had brought wholesale gang violence and murder; family disintegration and out-of-wedlock births had become the norm for thousands of residents. Relations between the community and the Los Angeles police, never very good, had worsened under police chief Daryl Gates, a man who seemed to have little respect for the city's minority population. The people of South-Central Los Angeles saw the police as brutal and racist; the police in turn saw the people of the district as criminal and hostile.

The trigger for massive community violence was the abuse by the police of black motorist Rodney King in early March 1991, after a high-speed freeway chase. The cops kicked King and beat him mercilessly with their batons for fifteen minutes. The doctors later described his major injuries as a fractured skull, broken leg, and shattered eye socket and cheekbone. The brutal attack on a single unarmed civilian was recorded by a citizen on his camcorder. Played over and over on the local and national airwaves, the tape outraged millions of Americans of all races. Faced with such vivid evidence of brutality, the authorities indicted four Los Angeles Police Department members for using excessive force.

The trial, in April 1992, was not held in Los Angeles where the jury was apt to be multiracial. Instead, it was removed to predominantly white and conservative Simi Valley. On April 29, to the amazement of many Americans who saw the evidence of guilt as cut and dried, the jury of ten whites, one Asian, and one Hispanic acquitted three of the officers completely and convicted one on a minor charge.

South-Central Los Angeles erupted within minutes in a fountain of rage and violence, which the slow-acting police at first did little to stop. White and Latino truckers and motorists were pulled from their vehicles and beaten and stomped. Hundreds of stores, offices, and shops were torched and looted, with Korean-owned businesses particular targets, though even black establishments were not spared. Latinos and others joined the riots, which spread beyond South-Central and threatened to spill over into affluent white neighborhoods. Not all the destruction was politically motivated. Many of the rioters were obviously taking advantage of the legitimate outrage to steal and destroy.

The violence spread to several other cities including San Francisco, Atlanta, Seattle, Miami, and Las Vegas. As they watched the TV images of smoke, flame, broken glass, looting, and tear gas, many Americans feared a reprise of the sixties' "Long Hot Summers." After five days, physical and emotional exhaustion, the voices of responsible community leaders, and National Guard and federal troops put a stop to the disorders. Rodney King himself appeared on TV to ask for calm. "I mean, please, we can get along here," he pleaded. "We can all get along. We've just got to." A final reckoning of the costs listed 58 lives lost and $1 billion of property damage. More than 11,900 people were arrested mostly for burglary and for receiving stolen goods, a few for beating innocent bystanders.

In the wake of the catastrophe, the presidential candidates visited Los Angeles and made promises that something would be done to improve conditions. Los Angeles replaced Police Chief Gates with a man more sensitive to the feelings of the ghetto community. In early 1993 the Justice Department indicted the acquitted police on federal charges that they had violated Rodney King's civil rights. This time the trial was held in Los Angeles itself before a less racially uniform jury, and this time the jury voted to convict two of the four officers. Black Americans by and large felt satisfied by the verdict and there was no eruption. The city and the nation heaved a sigh of relief at being spared a repetition of the earlier disaster. But in the wake of the Rodney King and similar trials, some Americans expressed concern that juries were too strongly influenced by racial loyalties and too little by the evidence.

Balkanization.   In fact, there were disturbing signs that Americans were beginning to lose their sense of common identity and define themselves primarily as part of some smaller, more cohesive, quasi-tribal group. One illustration was the startling outcome of a federal Summer of Service program established to bring young Americans together in community projects. As a preliminary, in June 1992, some 1,500 youths from all over the country gathered at a facility near San Francisco to receive training and orientation. As reported in *Newsweek* in September 1993, the group splintered almost immediately along a dozen different fault lines. In three days it had divided into black, Hispanic, Native American, and gay/lesbian/bisexual caucuses. Vegetarians complained that the organizers had ignored their diet needs. Some groups chose to exclude others from their meetings entirely.

But the signs were everywhere. Some Americans felt that the federal mandate of bilingual education aided and abetted the process. However benign in its intentions, it discouraged foreign-born children from acquiring English and perpetuated group separateness. In Milwaukee, the school board sought to establish a publicly financed high school just for black males. The curriculum would emphasize the black experience and so, it was said, raise the self-esteem of the young black men, a group who often failed in the regular schools. Critics said it was divisive and should not be paid for out of public taxes.

The multicultural trend profoundly disturbed many Americans who prized the civic unity of the past. In 1992 Arthur Schlesinger, Jr., a distinguished liberal historian, published *The Disuniting of America*, deploring the divisive effects of the new sensibility. Schlesinger lauded the discovery of ethnic and racial "roots" by Americans and credited it with giving neglected groups their proper due. But he also praised, with qualification, the assimilationist ethic of the past. Noting the growing tribalism around the world and its often murderous effects, he warned that denial of common values and sense of the past might well propel the United States along the same dangerous, discordant path as Yugoslavia, the former Soviet Union, and language-torn Canada. Americans should be wary of replacing the focus on the individual that had long been central to the country's tradition with the concept of group identity so common elsewhere in the world. "Watching ethnic conflict tear one nation after another apart, one cannot look with complacency at proposals to divide the United States into distinct and immutable ethnic and racial communities, each taught to cherish its apartness from the rest."

Yet other intellectuals praised the new trends. Ronald Takaki, an American historian of Japanese ancestry, in *A Different Mirror*, described how Americans "have been constantly redefining their identity" and lauded the retention of strong ties with ancestral cultural and intellectual roots. As if to overcome the assimilationist forces, Takaki, like other multiculturalists, emphasized the victimization through history of ethnic and nonwhite Americans by the old-stock, Anglo-Saxon elite.

★ CONCLUSIONS ★

It is difficult to reach firm conclusions about events that are still unfolding. Historians deal with the past, not the present; they need perspective. Yet it seems likely that the last years of the twentieth century will see sweeping changes in the nation's culture and values. Demographic change, racial antagonisms, feminist activism—all churning for two decades—seem to have broken through the surface in the 1990s. The America that appears to be emerging—rancorous, exasperated, bigoted—is not a pretty picture. But perhaps what Americans are observing is only a transitional stage to a more harmonious equilibrium that will incorporate the new currents without destroying the old core. If America has one unique virtue it is the ability to use the best from everywhere, and if the past is any guide it will do so again.

And not every expert accepts the predictions of cultural revolution. Some believe that the assimilation process, though spotty, is actually still very much at work. Ethnic, religious, and even racial intermarriage rates were soaring during the 1980s and 1990s. In a few generations, some observers noted, individual Americans would not even be able to identify with any one ethnic group; they will be mixtures of many different human stocks. And the differential birthrates were not likely to last as immigrants improved their living standards and became more willing to have fewer—though better clothed, sheltered, and educated—children.

Meanwhile, there was some hope that the United States might come to grips with its economic problems now that the Cold War had ended. If the Clinton budget succeeded in reducing the extent of future deficits, the United States might be able to increase its investments in human and physical capital. If the administration's health care plan cut costs and improved national health, there would be more money for other endeavors. And if Clinton made a dent in long-standing national problems he might restore the public's faith in the ability of government to influence events. Time will tell.

✸✸✸✸✸✸✸✸ FOR FURTHER READING ✸✸✸✸✸✸✸✸

Arthur M. Schlesinger, Jr. *The Disuniting of America* (1992)
A noted liberal, a founder of Americans for a Democratic Society, Schlesinger does not fault an *inclusive* American culture. He does, however, fear the damaging effects of recent tribalism on the concept of a roughly shared history and set of values among Americans. He also believes that it would be a serious error to regard Americans primarily as members of an ethnic, religious, or racial group, rather than as individuals.

Ronald Takaki. *A Different Mirror: A History of Multicultural America* (1992)
Takaki, himself a Japanese-American, celebrates the diversity of America. He emphasizes the difficulties that "ethnics" and their descendants—of European and non-European origins—have faced in a society dominated for many years by people of mostly North European ancestry. His formula for success is acceptance of continuing diversity rather than assimilation.

Robert Hughes. *The Culture of Complaint: The Fraying of America* (1992)
Hughes is a prominent Australian-born art critic and nonacademic historian who finds both the purveyors of political correctness and many of their shriller conservative critics rather foolish people. A plague on both your houses, says he.

Katherine Roiphe. *The Morning After: Fear, Sex and Feminism* (1993)
A young Ivy League graduate who condemns what she considers the excesses of feminist responses on campus to male behavior toward women. A feminist herself, she believes some of her colleagues' descriptions and prescriptions have turned back the clock to Victorian times when women were considered fragile beings, surrounded by dangers. She is daughter of the talented American novelist Ann Roiphe.

Catherine MacKinnon. *Only Words* (1993)
A leading feminist attorney insists that much of male behavior toward women is abusive and coercive. She attacks pornography, especially, as demeaning to women and calls for strict laws against it. A professor of law at the University of Michigan, MacKinnon has been influential in the drive to exclude various sorts of erotic material from protection from censorship under the First Amendment.

Dinesh D'Souza. *Illiberal Education: The Politics of Race and Sex on Campus* (1991)
A sharp indictment of "politically correct" attitudes and teachings on American campuses by a young conservative, Asian by birth, who rejects the philosophy behind affirmative action and other forms of ethnic preference. D'Souza is at least as hard on timid university administrators as on those who extract from them concessions that meet their own agendas.

APPENDIX

In Congress, July 4, 1776

The Declaration of Independence

The Unanimous Declaration of the Thirteen
United States of America

When in the Course of human events, it becomes necessary for one people to dissolve the political bands which have connected them with another, and to assume among the powers of the earth, the separate and equal station to which the Laws of Nature and of Nature's God entitle them, a decent respect to the opinions of mankind requires that they should declare the causes which impel them to the separation.

We hold these truths to be self-evident, that all men are created equal, that they are endowed by their Creator with certain unalienable Rights, that among these are Life, Liberty and the pursuit of Happiness.

That to secure these rights, Governments are instituted among Men, deriving their just powers from the consent of the governed.

That whenever any Form of Government becomes destructive of these ends, it is the Right of the People to alter or to abolish it, and to institute new Government, laying its foundation on such principles and organizing its powers in such form, as to them shall seem most likely to effect their Safety and Happiness. Prudence, indeed, will dictate that Governments long established should not be changed for light and transient causes; and accordingly all experience hath shewn, that mankind are more disposed to suffer, while evils are sufferable, than to right themselves by abolishing the forms to which they are accustomed. But when a long train of abuses and usurpations, pursuing invariably the same Object évinces a design to reduce them under absolute Despotism, it is their right, it is their duty, to throw off such Government, and to provide new Guards for their future security.

Such has been the patient sufferance of these Colonies; and such is now the necessity which constrains them to alter their former Systems of Government. The history of the present King of Great Britain is a history of repeated injuries and usurpations, all having in direct object the establishment of an absolute Tyranny over these States. To prove this, let Facts be submitted to a candid world.

He has refused his Assent to Laws, the most wholesome and necessary for the public good.

He has forbidden his Governors to pass Laws of immediate and pressing importance, unless suspended in their operation till his Assent should be obtained; and when so suspended, he has utterly neglected to attend to them.

He has refused to pass other Laws for the accommodation of large districts of people, unless those people would relinquish the right of Representation in the Legislature, a right inestimable to them and formidable to tyrants only.

He has called together legislative bodies at places unusual, uncomfortable, and distant from the depository of their public Records, for the sole purpose of fatiguing them into compliance with his measures.

He has dissolved Representative Houses repeatedly, for opposing with manly firmness his invasions on the rights of the people.

He has refused for a long time, after such dissolutions, to cause others to be elected; whereby the Legislative powers, incapable of Annihilation, have returned to the People at large for their exercise; the State remaining in the mean time exposed to all the dangers of invasion from without, and convulsions within.

He has endeavoured to prevent the population of these States; for that purpose obstructing the Laws for Naturalization of Foreigners; refusing to pass others to encourage their migrations hither, and raising the conditions of new Appropriations of Lands.

He has obstructed the Administration of Justice, by refusing his Assent to Laws for establishing Judiciary powers.

He has made judges dependent on his Will alone, for the tenure of their offices, and the amount and payment of their salaries.

He has erected a multitude of New Offices, and sent hither swarms of Officers to harass our people, and eat out their substance.

He has kept among us, in times of peace, Standing Armies without the Consent of our legislatures.

He has affected to render the Military independent of and superior to the Civil power.

He has combined with others to subject us to a jurisdiction foreign to our constitution, and unacknowledged by our laws; giving his Assent to their Acts of pretended Legislation:

For quartering large bodies of armed troops among us:

For protecting them, by a mock Trial, from punishment for any Murders which they should commit on the Inhabitants of these States:

For cutting off our Trade with all parts of the world:

For imposing Taxes on us without our Consent:

For depriving us in many cases, of the benefits of Trial by Jury:

For transporting us beyond Seas to be tried for pretended offences:

For abolishing the free System of English Laws in a neighbouring Province, establishing therein an Arbitrary government, and enlarging its Boundaries so as to render it at once an example and fit instrument for introducing the same absolute rule into these Colonies:

For taking away our Charters, abolishing our most valuable Laws, and altering fundamentally the Forms of our Governments:

For suspending our own Legislatures, and declaring themselves invested with power to legislate for us in all cases whatsoever.

He has abdicated Government here, by declaring us out of his Protection and waging War against us.

He has plundered our seas, ravaged our Coasts, burnt our towns, and destroyed the Lives of our people.

He is at this time transporting large Armies of foreign Mercenaries to compleat the works of death, desolation and tyranny, already begun with circumstances of Cruelty & perfidy scarcely paralleled in the most barbarous ages, and totally unworthy the Head of a civilized nation.

He has constrained our fellow Citizens taken Captive on the high Seas to bear Arms against their Country, to become the executioners of their friends and Brethren, or to fall themselves by their Hands.

He has excited domestic insurrections amongst us, and has endeavoured to bring on the inhabitants of our frontiers, the merciless Indian Savages, whose known rule of warfare, is an undistinguished destruction of all ages, sexes and conditions.

In every stage of these Oppressions We have Petitioned for Redress in the most humble terms: Our repeated Petitions have been answered only by repeated injury. A Prince, whose character is thus marked by every act which may define a Tyrant, is unfit to be the ruler of a free people.

Nor have We been wanting in attentions to our British brethren. We have warned them from time to time of attempts by their legislature to extend an unwarrantable jurisdiction over us. We have reminded them of the circumstances of our emigration and settlement here. We have appealed to their native justice and magnanimity, and we have conjured them by the ties of our common kindred to disavow these usurpations, which, would inevitably interrupt our connections and correspondence. They too have been deaf to the voice of justice and of consanguinity. We must, therefore, acquiesce in the necessity, which denounces our Separation, and hold them, as we hold the rest of mankind, Enemies in War, in Peace Friends.

We, therefore, the Representatives of the United States of America, in General Congress, Assembled, appealing to the Supreme Judge of the world for the rectitude of our intentions, do, in the Name, and by Authority of the good People of these Colonies, solemnly publish and declare, That these United Colonies are, and of Right ought to be Free and Independent States; that they are Absolved from all Allegiance to the British Crown, and that all political connection between them and the State of Great Britain, is and ought to be totally dissolved; and that as Free and Independent States, they have full Power to levy War, conclude Peace, contract Alliances, establish Commerce, and to do all other Acts and Things which Independent States may of right do.

And for the support of this Declaration, with a firm reliance on the protection of divine Providence, we mutually pledge to each other our Lives, our Fortunes and our sacred Honor.

JOHN HANCOCK

NEW HAMPHIRE
Josiah Bartlett
William Whipple
Matthew Thornton

MASSACHUSETTS BAY
Samuel Adams
John Adams
Robert Treat Paine
Elbridge Gerry

RHODE ISLAND
Stephen Hopkins
William Ellery

CONNECTICUT
Roger Sherman
Samuel Huntington
William Williams
Oliver Wolcott

NEW YORK
William Floyd
Philip Livingston
Francis Lewis
Lewis Morris

NEW JERSEY
Richard Stockton
John Witherspoon
Francis Hopkinson
John Hart
Abraham Clark

PENNSYLVANIA
Robert Morris
Benjamin Rush
Benjamin Franklin
John Morton
George Clymer
James Smith
George Taylor
James Wilson
George Ross

DELAWARE
Caesar Rodney
George Read
Thomas M'Kean

MARYLAND
Samuel Chase
William Paca
Thomas Stone
*Charles Carroll, of
  Carrollton*

VIRGINIA
George Wythe
Richard Henry Lee
Thomas Jefferson
Benjamin Harrison
Thomas Nelson, Jr.
Francis Lightfoot Lee
Carter Braxton

NORTH CAROLINA
William Hooper
Joseph Hewes
John Penn

SOUTH CAROLINA
Edward Rutledge
Thomas Heyward, Jr.
Thomas Lynch, Jr.
Arthur Middleton

GEORGIA
Button Gwinnett
Lyman Hall
George Walton

Resolved.   *That copies of the Declaration be sent to the several assemblies, conventions, and committees or councils of safety, and to the several commanding officers of the continental troops; that it be proclaimed in each of the United States, at the head of the army.*

The Constitution of the United States of America

We the People of the United States, in Order to form a more perfect Union, establish Justice, insure domestic Tranquility, provide for the common defence, promote the general Welfare, and secure the Blessings of Liberty to ourselves and our Posterity, do ordain and establish this Constitution for the United States of America.

ARTICLE I

Section 1. All legislative Powers herein granted shall be vested in a Congress of the United States, which shall consist of a Senate and House of Representatives.

Section 2. The House of Representatives shall be composed of Members chosen every second Year by the People of the several States, and the Electors in each State shall have the Qualifications requisite for Electors of the most numerous Branch of the State Legislature.

No Person shall be a Representative who shall not have attained to the Age of twenty-five Years, and been seven years a Citizen of the United States, and who shall not, when elected, be an Inhabitant of that State in which he shall be chosen.

Representatives and direct Taxes shall be apportioned among the several States which may be included within this Union, according to their respective Numbers. [which shall be determined by adding to the whole Number of free Persons, including those bound to Service for a Term of Years, and excluding Indians not taxed, three fifths of all other Persons.][1] The actual Enumeration shall be made within three Years after the first Meeting of the Congress of the United States, and within every subsequent Term of ten Years, in such Manner as they shall by Law direct. The Number of Representatives shall not exceed one for every thirty Thousand, but each State shall have at Least one Representative; and until such enumeration shall be made, the State of New Hampshire shall be entitled to chuse three; Massachusetts eight; Rhode Island and Providence Plantations one; Connecticut five; New York six; New Jersey four; Pennsylvania eight; Delaware one; Maryland six; Virginia ten; North Carolina five; South Carolina five; and Georgia three.

When vacancies happen in the Representation from any State, the Executive Authority thereof shall issue Writs of Election to fill such Vacancies.

The House of Representatives shall chuse their Speaker and other Officers; and shall have the sole Power of Impeachment.

Section 3. The Senate of the United States, shall be composed of two Senators from each state, [chosen by the Legislature thereof,][2] for six Years; and each Senator shall have one Vote.

Immediately after they shall be assembled in Consequence of the first Election, they shall be divided as equally as may be into three Classes. The Seats of the Senators of the first Class shall be vacated at the Expiration of the second year, of the second Class at the Expiration of the fourth Year, and of the third Class at the Expiration of the sixth Year, so that one third may be chosen every second Year; [and if Vacancies happen by Resignation, or otherwise, during the Recess of the Legislature of any State, the Executive thereof may make temporary Appointments until the next Meeting of the Legislature, which shall then fill such Vacancies.][3]

No Person shall be a Senator who shall not have attained to the Age of thirty Years, and been nine Years a Citizen of the United States, and who shall not, when elected, be an Inhabitant of that State for which he shall be chosen.

The Vice President of the United States shall be President of the Senate, but shall have no Vote, unless they be equally divided.

The Senate shall chuse their other Officers, and also a President pro tempore, in the Absence of the Vice President, or when he shall exercise the Office of President of the United States.

The Senate shall have the sole Power to try all Impeachments. When sitting for that Purpose, they shall be on Oath or Affirmation. When the President of the United States is tried, the Chief Justice shall preside: And no Person shall be convicted without the Concurrence of two thirds of the Members present.

Judgment in Cases of Impeachment shall not extend further than to removal from Office, and disqualification to hold and enjoy any Office of honor, Trust or Profit under the United States: but the Party convicted shall nevertheless be liable and subject to Indictment, Trial, Judgment and Punishment, according to Law.

Section 4. The Times, Places and Manner of holding Elections for Senators and Representatives, shall be prescribed in each State by the legislature thereof; but the Congress may at any time by Law make or alter such Regulations, except as to the Places of chusing Senators.

[The Congress shall assemble at least once in every Year, and such Meeting shall be on the first Monday in December, unless they shall by Law appoint a different Day.][4]

Section 5. Each House shall be the Judge of the Elections, Returns and Qualifications of its own Members, and a Majority of each shall constitute a Quorum to do Business; but a smaller Number may adjourn from day to day, and may be authorized to compel the Attendance of absent Members, in such Manner, and under such Penalties as each House may provide.

Each House may determine the Rules of its Proceedings, punish its Members for disorderly Behaviour, and, with the Concurrence of two thirds, expel a Member.

---

[1] Bracketed material superseded by Section 2 of the Fourteenth Amendment.
[2] Bracketed material superseded by Clause I of the Seventeenth Amendment.

[3] Bracketed material modified by Clause 2 of the Seventeenth Amendment.
[4] Bracketed material superseded by Section 2 of the Twentieth Amendment.

Each House shall keep a Journal of its Proceedings, and from time to time publish the same, excepting such Parts as may in their Judgment require Secrecy; and the Yeas and Nays of the Members of either House on any question shall, at the Desire of one fifth of those Present, be entered on the Journal.

Neither House, during the Session of Congress, shall, without the Consent of the other, adjourn for more than three days, nor to any other Place than that in which the two Houses shall be sitting.

Section 6. The Senators and Representatives shall receive a Compensation for their Services, to be ascertained by Law, and paid out of the Treasury of the United States. They shall in all Cases, except Treason, Felony and Breach of the Peace, be privileged from Arrest during their Attendance at the Session of their respective Houses, and in going to and returning from the same; and for any Speech or Debate in either House, they shall not be questioned in any other Place.

No Senator or Representative shall, during the Time for which he was elected, be appointed to any civil Office under the Authority of the United States, which shall have been created, or the Emoluments whereof shall have been encreased during such time; and no Person holding any Office under the United States, shall be a Member of either House during his Continuance in Office.

Section 7. All Bills for raising Revenue shall Originate in the House of Representatives; but the Senate may propose or concur with Amendments as on other Bills.

Every Bill which shall have passed the House of Representatives and the Senate, shall, before it become a Law, be presented to the President of the United States; If he approve he shall sign it, but if not he shall return it, with his Objections to that House in which it shall have originated, who shall enter the Objections at large on their Journal, and proceed to reconsider it. If after such Reconsideration two thirds of that House shall agree to pass the Bill, it shall be sent, together with the Objections, to the other House, by which it shall likewise be reconsidered, and if approved by two thirds of that House, it shall become a Law. But in all such Cases the Votes of both Houses shall be determined by Yeas and Nays, and the Names of the Persons voting for and against the Bill shall be entered on the Journal of each House respectively. If any Bill shall not be returned by the President within Ten Days (Sundays excepted) after it shall have been presented to him, the Same shall be a Law, in like Manner as if he had signed it, unless the Congress by their Adjournment prevents its Return, in which Case it shall not be a Law.

Every Order, Resolution, or Vote to which the Concurrence of the Senate and House of Representatives may be necessary (except on a question of Adjournment) shall be presented to the President of the United States; and before the Same shall take effect, shall be approved by him, or being disapproved by him, shall be repassed by two thirds of the Senate and House of Representatives, according to the Rules and Limitations prescribed in the Case of a Bill.

Section 8. The Congress shall have Power To lay and collect Taxes, Duties, Imposts, and Excises, to pay the Debts and provide for the common Defence and general Welfare of the United States; but all Duties, Imposts and Excises shall be uniform throughout the United States;

To borrow Money on the credit of the United States;

To regulate Commerce with foreign Nations, and among the several States, and with the Indian Tribes;

To establish an uniform Rule of Naturalization, and uniform Laws on the subject of Bankruptcies throughout the United States;

To coin Money, regulate the Value thereof, and of foreign Coin, and fix the Standard of Weights and Measures;

To provide for the Punishment of counterfeiting the Securities and current Coin of the United States:

To establish Post Offices and post Roads;

To promote the Progress of Science and useful Arts, by securing for limited Times to Authors and Inventors the exclusive Right to their respective Writings and Discoveries;

To constitute Tribunals inferior to the supreme Court;

To define and punish Piracies and Felonies committed on the high Seas, and Offences against the Law of Nations;

To declare War, grant Letters of Marque and Reprisal, and make Rules concerning Captures on Land and Water;

To raise and support Armies; but no Appropriation of Money to that Use shall be for a longer Term than two years;

To provide and maintain a Navy;

To make Rules for the Government and Regulation of the land and naval Forces;

To provide for calling forth the Militia to execute the laws of the Union, suppress Insurrections and repel Invasions;

To provide for organizing, arming, and disciplining, the Militia, and for governing such Part of them as may be employed in the Service of the United States, reserving to the States respectively, the Appointment of the Officers, and the Authority of training the Militia according to the discipline prescribed by Congress;

To exercise exclusive Legislation in all Cases whatsoever, over such District (not exceeding ten Miles square) as may, by Cession of particular States, and the Acceptance of Congress, become the Seat of the Government of the United States, and to exercise like Authority over all Places purchased by the Consent of the Legislature of the State in which the Same shall be, for the Erection of Forts, Magazines, Arsenals, dock-Yards, and other needful Buildings;—And

To make all Laws which shall be necessary and proper for carrying into Execution the foregoing Powers, and all other Powers vested by this Constitution in the Government of the United States, or in any Department or Officer thereof.

Section 9. The Migration or Importation of such Persons as any of the States now existing shall think proper to admit, shall not be prohibited by the Congress prior to the year one thousand eight hundred and eight, but a Tax or duty may be imposed on such Importation, not exceeding ten dollars for each Person.

The Privilege of the Writ of Habeas Corpus shall not be suspended, unless when in Cases of Rebellion or Invasion the public Safety may require it.

No Bill of Attainder or ex post facto Law shall be passed.

No Capitation, or other direct, Tax shall be laid, unless in Proportion to the Census or Enumeration herein before directed to be taken.[5]

No Tax or Duty shall be laid on Articles exported from any State.

No Preference shall be given by any Regulation of Commerce or Revenue to the Ports of one State over those of an-

---

[5]Modified by the Sixteenth Amendment.

other: nor shall Vessels bound to, or from, one State, be obliged to enter, clear, or pay Duties in another.

No Money shall be drawn from the Treasury, but in Consequence of Appropriations made by Law; and a regular Statement and Account of the Receipts and Expenditures of all public Money shall be published from time to time.

No Title of Nobility shall be granted by the United States: And no person holding any office of Profit or Trust under them, shall, without the Consent of the Congress, accept of any present, Emolument, Office, or Title, of any kind whatever, from any King, Prince, or foreign State.

Section 10. No State shall enter into any Treaty, Alliance, or Confederation; grant Letters of Marque and Reprisal; coin Money; emit Bills of Credit; make any Thing but gold and silver Coin a Tender in Payment of Debts; pass any Bill of Attainder, ex post facto Law, or Law impairing the Obligation of Contracts, or grant any Title of Nobility.

No State shall, without the Consent of the Congress, lay any Imposts or Duties on Imports or Exports, except what may be absolutely necessary for executing its inspection Laws: and the net Produce of all Duties and Imposts, laid by any State on Imports or Exports, shall be for the Use of the Treasury of the United States; and all such Laws shall be subject to the Revision and Control of the Congress.

No State shall, without the Consent of Congress, lay any Duty of Tonnage, keep Troops, or Ships of War in time of Peace, enter into any Agreement or Compact with another State, or with a foreign Power, or engage in War, unless actually invaded, or in such imminent Danger as will not admit of delay.

ARTICLE II

Section 1. The executive Power shall be vested in a President of the United States of America. He shall hold his Office during the Term of four Years, and, together with the Vice President, chosen for the same Term, be elected, as follows.

Each State shall appoint, in such Manner as the Legislature thereof may direct, a Number of Electors, equal to the whole Number of Senators and Representative to which the State may be entitled in the Congress: but no Senator or Representative, or Person holding an Office of Trust or Profit under the United States, shall be appointed an Elector.

[The Electors shall meet in their respective States, and vote by Ballot for two Persons, of whom one at least shall not be an Inhabitant of the same State with themselves. And they shall make a List of all the Persons voted for, and of the Number of Votes for each; which List they shall sign and certify, and transmit sealed to the Seat of the Government of the United States, directed to the President of the Senate. The President of the Senate shall, in the Presence of the Senate and House of Representatives, open all the Certificates, and the Votes shall then be counted. The Person having the greatest Number of Votes shall be the President, if such Number be a Majority of the whole Number of Electors appointed; and if there be more than one who have such Majority, and have an equal Number of Votes, then the House of Representatives shall immediately chuse by Ballot one of them for President; and if no Person have a Majority, then from the five highest on the List the said House shall in like Manner chuse the President. But in chusing the President, the Votes shall be taken by States, the Representation from each State having one Vote; A quorum for this Purpose shall consist of a Member or Members from two thirds of the States, and a Majority of all the States shall be necessary to a Choice. In every Case, after the Choice of the President, the Person having the greatest Number of Votes of the Electors shall be the Vice President. But if there should remain two or more who have equal Votes, the Senate shall chuse from them by Ballot the Vice President.][6]

The Congress may determine the Time of chusing the Electors, and the Day on which they shall give their Votes; which Day shall be the same throughout the United States.

No Person except a natural born Citizen, or a Citizen of the United States, at the time of the Adoption of this Constitution, shall be eligible to the Office of President; neither shall any Person be eligible to that Office who shall not have attained to the Age of thirty-five Years, and been fourteen Years a Resident within the United States.

[In Case of the Removal of the President from Office, or of his Death, Resignation, or Inability to discharge the Powers and Duties of the said Office, the Same shall devolve on the Vice President, and the Congress may by law provide for the Case of Removal, Death, Resignation or Inability, both of the President and Vice President, declaring what Officer shall then act as President, and such Officer shall act accordingly, until the Disability be removed, or a President shall be elected.][7]

The President shall, at stated Times, receive for his Services, a Compensation, which shall neither be increased nor diminished during the Period for which he shall have been elected, and he shall not receive within that Period any other Emolument from the United States, or any of them.

Before he enter on the Execution of his Office; he shall take the following Oath or Affirmation—"I do solemnly swear (or affirm) that I will faithfully execute the Office of President of the United States, and will to the best of my Ability, preserve, protect and defend the Constitution of the United States."

Section 2. The President shall be Commander in Chief of the Army and Navy of the United States, and of the Militia of the several States, when called into the actual Service of the United States; he may require the Opinion, in writing, of the principal Office in each of the executive Departments, upon any Subject relating to the Duties of their respective Offices, and he shall have Power to grant Reprieves and Pardons for Offences against the United States, except in Cases of Impeachment.

He shall have Power, by and with the Advice and Consent of the Senate, to make Treaties, provided two thirds of the Senators present concur; and he shall nominate, and by and with the Advice and Consent of the Senate, shall appoint Ambassadors, other public Ministers and Consuls Judges of the supreme Court, and all other Officers of the United States, whose Appointments are not herein otherwise provided for, and which shall be established by Law: but the Congress may by Law vest the Appointment of such inferior Officers, as they think proper, in the President alone, in the Courts of Law, or in the Heads of Departments.

The President shall have Power to fill up all Vacancies that may happen during the Recess of the Senate, by granting Commissions which shall expire at the End of their next Session.

Section 3. He shall from time to time give to the Congress Information of the State of the Union, and recommend to their

---

[6]Bracketed material superseded by the Twelfth Amendment.
[7]Bracketed material modified by the Twenty-fifth Amendment.

Consideration such Measures as he shall judge necessary and expedient; he may, on extraordinary Occasions, convene both Houses, or either of them, and in Case of Disagreement between them, with Respect to the Time of Adjournment, he may adjourn them to such Time as he shall think proper; he shall receive Ambassadors and other public Ministers; he shall take Care that the Laws be faithfully executed, and shall Commission all the Officers of the United States.

Section 4. The President, Vice President and all civil Officers of the United States, shall be removed from Office on Impeachment for, and Conviction of, Treason, Bribery, or other high Crimes and Misdemeanors.

ARTICLE III

Section 1. The judicial Power of the United States, shall be vested in one supreme Court, and in such inferior Courts as the Congress may from time to time ordain and establish. The Judges, both of the supreme and inferior Courts, shall hold their Offices during good Behaviour, and shall, at stated Times, receive for their Services, a Compensation, which shall not be diminished during their Continuance in Office.

Section 2. The judicial Power shall extend to all Cases, in Law and Equity, arising under this Constitution, the Laws of the United States, and Treaties made, or which shall be made, under their Authority;—to all Cases affecting Ambassadors, other public Ministers and Consuls;—to all Cases of admiralty and maritime Jurisdiction;—To Controversies to which the United States shall be a Party;—to Controversies between two or more States;—between a State and Citizens of another State;—between Citizens of different States;—between Citizens of the same State claiming Lands under Grants of different States, and between a State, or the Citizens thereof, and foreign States, Citizens or Subjects.[8]

In all Cases affecting Ambassadors, other public Ministers and Consuls, and those in which a State shall be Party, the supreme Court shall have original Jurisdiction. In all the other Cases before mentioned the supreme Court shall have appellate Jurisdiction, both as to Law and Fact, with such Exceptions, and under such Regulations as the Congress shall make.

The Trial of all Crimes, except in Cases of Impeachment, shall be by Jury; and such Trial shall be held in the State where the said Crimes shall have been committed; but when not committed within any State, the Trial shall be at such Place or Places as the Congress may by Law have directed.

Section 3. Treason against the United States, shall consist only in levying War against them, or in adhering to their Enemies, giving them Aid and Comfort. No Person shall be convicted of Treason unless on the Testimony of two Witnesses to the same overt Act, or on Confession in open Court.

The Congress shall have Power to declare the Punishment of Treason, but no Attainder of Treason shall work Corruption of Blood, or Forfeiture except during the Life of the person attainted.

ARTICLE IV

Section 1. Full Faith and Credit shall be given in each State to the public Acts, Records, and judicial Proceedings of every other State. And the Congress may by general Laws prescribe the Manner in which such Acts, Records and Proceedings shall be proved, and the Effect thereof.

Section 2. The Citizens of each State shall be entitled to all Privileges and Immunities of Citizens in the several States.

A Person charged in any State with Treason, Felony, or other Crime, who shall flee from Justice, and be found in another State, shall on Demand of the executive Authority of the State from which he fled, be delivered up, to be removed to the State having Jurisdiction of the Crime.

[No Person held to Service or Labour in one State, under the Laws thereof, escaping into another, shall, in Consequence of any Law or Regulation therein, be discharged from such Service or Labour, but shall be delivered up on Claim of the Party to whom such Service or Labour may be due.][9]

Section 3. New States may be admitted by the Congress into this Union; but no new State shall be formed or erected within the Jurisdiction of any other State; nor any State be formed by the Junction of two or more States, or Parts of States, without the Consent of the Legislatures of the States concerned as well as of the Congress.

The Congress shall have Power to dispose of and make all needful Rules and Regulations respecting the Territory or other property belonging to the United States; and nothing in this Constitution shall be so construed as to Prejudice any Claims of the United States, or of any particular State.

Section 4. The United States shall guarantee to every State in this Union a Republican Form of Government, and shall protect each of them against Invasion; and on Application of the Legislature, or of the Executive (when the Legislature cannot be convened) against domestic Violence.

ARTICLE V

The Congress, whenever two thirds of both Houses shall deem it necessary, shall propose Amendments to this Constitution, or, on the Application of the legislatures of two thirds of the several States, shall call a Convention for proposing Amendments, which, in either Case, shall be valid to all Intents and Purposes, as Part of this Constitution, when ratified by the Legislatures of three fourths of the several States, or by Conventions in three fourths thereof, as the one or the other Mode of Ratification may be proposed by the Congress; Provided that no Amendement which may be made prior to the Year One thousand eight hundred and eight shall in any Manner affect the first and fourth Clauses in the Ninth Section of the first Article; and that no State, without its Consent, shall be deprived of its equal Suffrage in the Senate.

ARTICLE VI

All Debts contracted and Engagements entered into, before the Adoption of this Constitution, shall be as valid against the United States under this Constitution, as under the Confederation.

This Constitution, and the Laws of the United States which shall be made in Pursuance thereof; and all Treaties made, or which shall be made, under the Authority of the United States, shall be the supreme Law of the Land; and the Judges in every State shall be bound thereby, any Thing

---

[8]This paragraph modified in part by the Eleventh Amendment.

[9]Bracketed material superseded by the Thirteenth Amendment.

in the Constitution or Laws of any State to the Contrary notwithstanding.

The Senators and Representatives before mentioned, and the members of the several State Legislatures, and all executive and judicial Officers, both of the United States and of the several States, shall be bound by Oath or Affirmation, to support this Constitution; but no religious Test shall ever be required as a Qualification to any Office or public Trust under the United States.

ARTICLE VII

The Ratification of the Conventions of nine States, shall be sufficient for the Establishment of this Constitution between the States so ratifying the Same.

DONE in Convention by the Unanimous Consent of the States present the Seventeenth Day of September in the Year of our Lord one thousand seven hundred and eighty seven and of the Independence of the United States of America the Twelfth. IN WITNESS whereof We have hereunto subscribed our Names.

GEORGE WASHINGTON—*President and deputy from Virginia*

NEW HAMPSHIRE	MASSACHUSETTS
John Langdon	*Nathaniel Gorham*
Nicholas Gilman	*Rufus King*
CONNECTICUT	MARYLAND
William Samuel Johnson	*James McHenry*
Roger Sherman	*Daniel of St. Thomas Jenifer*
NEW YORK	*Daniel Carroll*
Alexander Hamilton	
	VIRGINIA
NEW JERSEY	*John Blair*
William Livingston	*James Madison, Jr.*
David Brearley	
William Paterson	NORTH CAROLINA
Jonathan Dayton	*William Blount*
	Richard Dobbs Spaight
PENNSYLVANIA	*Hugh Williamson*
Benjamin Franklin	
Thomas Mifflin	SOUTH CAROLINA
Robert Morris	*John Rutledge*
George Clymer	*Charles Cotesworth Pickney*
Thomas FitzSimons	
Jared Ingersoll	*Charles Pinckney*
James Wilson	*Pierce Butler*
Gouverneur Morris	
	GEORGIA
DELAWARE	*William Few*
George Read	*Abraham Baldwin*
Gunning Bedford, Jr.	
John Dickinson	Attest: William Jackson,
Richard Bassett	*Secretary*
Jacob Broom	

THE AMENDMENTS

ARTICLES in addition to, and Amendment of the Constitution of the United States of America, proposed by Congress, and ratified by the Legislatures of the several States, pursuant to the fifth Article of the original Constitution.

ARTICLE I

[*Articles I through X, now known as the Bill of Rights, were proposed on September 25, 1789, and declared in force on December 15, 1791.*]

Congress shall make no law respecting an establishment of religion, or prohibiting the free exercise thereof; or abridging the freedom of speech, or of the press; or the right of the people peaceably to assemble, and to petition the Government for a redress of grievances.

ARTICLE II

A well regulated Militia, being necessary to the security of a free State, the right of the people to keep and bear Arms, shall not be infringed.

ARTICLE III

No Soldier shall, in time of peace be quartered in any house, without the consent of the Owner, nor in time of war, but in manner to be prescribed by law.

ARTICLE IV

The right of the people to be secure in their persons, houses, papers, and effects, against unreasonable searches and seizures, shall not be violated, and no Warrants shall issue, but upon probable cause, supported by Oath or affirmation, and particularly describing the place to be searched, and the persons or things to be seized.

ARTICLE V

No person shall be held to answer for a capital, or otherwise infamous crime, unless on a presentment or indictment of a Grand Jury, except in cases arising in the land or naval forces, or in the Militia, when in actual service in time of War or public danger; nor shall any person be subject for the same offence to be twice put in jeopardy of life or limb; nor shall be compelled in any criminal case to be a witness against himself, nor be deprived of life, liberty, or property, without due process of law; nor shall private property be taken for public use, without just compensation.

ARTICLE VI

In all criminal prosecutions, the accused shall enjoy the right to a speedy and public trial, by an impartial jury of the State and district wherein the crime shall have been committed, which district shall have been previously ascertained by law, and to be informed of the nature and cause of the accusation; to be confronted with the witnesses against him; to have compulsory process for obtaining witnesses in his favor, and to have the Assistance of Counsel for his defence.

ARTICLE VII

In Suits at common law, where the value in controversy shall exceed twenty dollars, the right of trial by jury shall be preserved, and no fact tried by a jury shall be otherwise re-examined in any Court of the United States, than according to the rules of the common law.

ARTICLE VIII

Excessive bail shall not be required, nor excessive fines imposed, nor cruel and unusual punishments inflicted.

ARTICLE IX

The enumeration in the Constitution, of certain rights, shall not be construed to deny or disparage others retained by the people.

ARTICLE X

The powers not delegated to the United States by the Constitution, nor prohibited by it to the States, are reserved to the States respectively, or to the people.

ARTICLE XI

[*Proposed March 4, 1794; declared ratified January 8, 1798*]

The Judicial power of the United States shall not be construed to extend to any suit in law or equity, commenced or prosecuted against one of the United States by Citizens of another State, or by Citizens or Subjects of any Foreign State.

ARTICLE XII

[*Proposed December 9, 1803; declared ratified September 25, 1804*]

The Electors shall meet in their respective states and vote by ballot for President and Vice-President, one of whom, at least, shall not be an inhabitant of the same state with themselves; they shall name in their ballots the person voted for as President, and in distinct ballots the person voted for as Vice-President, and they shall make distinct lists of all persons voted for as President, and of all persons voted for as Vice-President, and of the number of votes for each, which lists they shall sign and certify, and transmit sealed to the seat of the government of the United States, directed to the President of the Senate;— The President of the Senate shall, in the presence of the Senate and House of Representatives, open all the certificates and the votes shall then be counted;—The person having the greatest number of votes for President, shall be the President, if such number be a majority of the whole number of Electors appointed; and if no person have such majority, then from the persons having the highest numbers not exceeding three on the list of those voted for as President, the House of Representatives shall choose immediately, by ballot, the President. But in choosing the President, the votes shall be taken by states, the representation from each state having one vote; a quorum for this purpose shall consist of a member or members from two-thirds of the states, and a majority of all the states shall be necessary to a choice. [And if the House of Representatives shall not choose a President whenever the right of choice shall devolve upon them, before the fourth day of March next following, then the Vice-President shall act as President, as in the case of the death or other constitutional disability of the President.][10]—The person having the greatest number of votes as Vice-President, shall be the Vice-President, if such number be a majority of the whole number of Electors appointed and if no person have a majority, then from the two highest numbers on the list, the Senate shall choose the Vice-President; a quorum for the purpose shall consist of two-thirds of the whole number of Senators, and a majority of the whole number shall be necessary to a choice. But no person constitutionally ineligible to the office of President shall be eligible to that of Vice-President of the United States.

ARTICLE XIII

[*Proposed January 31, 1865; declared ratified December 18, 1865*]

Section 1. Neither slavery nor involuntary servitude, except as a punishment for crime whereof the party shall have been duly convicted, shall exist within the United States, or any place subject to their jurisdiction.

Section 2. Congress shall have power to enforce this article by appropriate legislation.

ARTICLE XIV

[*Proposed June 13, 1866; declared ratified July 28, 1868*]

Section 1. All persons born or naturalized in the United States, and subject to the jurisdiction thereof, are citizens of the United States and of the State wherein they reside. No State shall make or enforce any law which shall abridge the privileges or immunities of citizens of the United States; nor shall any State deprive any person of life, liberty, or property, without due process of law; nor deny to any person within its jurisdiction the equal protection of the laws.

Section 2. Representatives shall be apportioned among the several States according to their respective numbers, counting the whole number of persons in each State, excluding Indians not taxed. But when the right to vote at any election for the choice of electors for President and Vice President of the United States, Representatives in Congress, the Executive and Judicial officers of a State or the members of the Legislature thereof, is denied to any of the male inhabitants of such State, being twenty-one years of age, and citizens of the United States, or in any way abridged, except for participation in rebellion, or other crime, the basis of representation therein shall be reduced in the proportion which the number of such male citizens shall bear to the whole number of male citizens twenty-one years of age in such State.

Section 3. No person shall be a Senator or Representative in Congress, or elector of President and Vice President, or hold any office, civil or military, under the United States, or under any State, who, having previously taken an oath as a member of Congress, or as an officer of the United States, or as a member of any State legislature, or as an executive or judicial officer of any State, to support the Constitution of the United States, shall have engaged in insurrection or rebellion against the same, or given aid or comfort to the enemies thereof. But

---

[10]Bracketed material superseded by Section 3 of the Twentieth Amendment.

Congress may by a vote of two-thirds of each House, remove such disability.

Section 4. The validity of the public debt of the United States, authorized by law, including debts incurred for payment of pensions and bounties for services in suppressing insurrection or rebellion, shall not be questioned. But neither the United States nor any State shall assume or pay any debt or obligation incurred in aid of insurrection or rebellion against the United States, or any claim for the loss or emancipation of any slave; but all such debts, obligations and claims shall be held illegal and void.

Section 5. The Congress shall have power to enforce, by appropriate legislations, the provisions of this article.

ARTICLE XV

[*Proposed February 26, 1869; declared ratified March 30, 1870*]

Section 1. The right of citizens of the United States to vote shall not be denied or abridged by the United States or by any State on account of race, color, or previous condition of servitude.

Section 2. The Congress shall have powere to enforce this article by appropriate legislation.

ARTICLE XVI

[*Proposed July 12, 1909; declared ratified February 25, 1913*]

The Congress shall have power to lay and collect taxes on incomes, from whatever source derived, without apportionment among the several States, and without regard to any census or enumeration.

ARTICLE XVII

[*Proposed May 13, 1912; declared ratified May 31, 1913*]

The Senate of the United States shall be composed of two Senators from each State, elected by the people thereof, for six years; and each Senator shall have one vote. The electors in each State shall have the qualifications requisite for electors of the most numerous branch of the State legislatures.

When vacancies happen in the representation of any State in the Senate, the executive authority of such State shall issue writs of election to fill such vacancies: *Provided,* That the legislature of any State may empower the executive thereof to make temporary appointments until the people fill the vacancies by election as the legislature may direct.

This amendement shall not be so construed as to affect the election or term of any Senator chosen before it becomes valid as part of the Constitution.

ARTICLE XVIII

[*Proposed December 18, 1917; declared ratified January 29, 1919; repealed by the Twenty-first Amendment December 5, 1933*]

Section 1. After one year from the ratification of this article the manufacture, sale, or transportation of intoxicating liquors within, the importation thereof into, or the exportation thereof from the United States and all territory subject to the jurisdiction thereof for beverage purposes is hereby prohibited.

Section 2. The Congress and the several States shall have concurrent power to enforce this article by appropriate legislation.

Section 3. This article shall be inoperative unless it shall have been ratified as an amendment to the Constitution by the legislatures of the several States, as provided in the Constitution, within seven years from the date of the submission hereof to the States by the Congress.

ARTICLE XIX

[*Proposed June 4, 1919; declared ratified August 26, 1920*]

The right of citizens of the United States to vote shall not be denied or abridged by the United States or by any State on account of sex.

Congress shall have power to enforce this article by appropriate legislation.

ARTICLE XX

[*Proposed March 2, 1932; declared ratified February 6, 1933*]

Section 1. The terms of the President and Vice President shall end at noon on the 20th day of January, and the terms of Senators and Representatives at noon on the 3d day of January, of the years in which such terms would have ended if this article had not been ratified; and the terms of their successors shall then begin.

Section 2. The Congress shall assemble at least once in every year, and such meeting shall begin at noon on the 3d day of January, unless they shall by law appoint a different day.

Section 3. If, at the time fixed for the beginning of the term of the President, the President elect shall have died, the Vice President elect shall become President. If a President shall not have been chosen before the time fixed for the beginning of his term, or if the President elect shall have failed to qualify, then the Vice President elect shall act as President until a President shall have qualified; and the Congress may by law provide for the case wherein neither a President elect nor a Vice President elect shall have qualified, declaring who shall then act as President, or the manner in which one who is to act shall be elected, and such person shall act accordingly until a President or Vice President shall have qualified.

Section 4. The Congress may by law provide for the case of the death of any of the persons from whom the House of Representatives may choose a President whenever the right of choice shall have devolved upon them, and for the case of the death of any of the persons from whom the Senate may choose a Vice President whenever the right of choice shall have devolved upon them.

Section 5. Sections 1 and 2 shall take effect on the 15th day of October following the ratification of this article.

Section 6. This article shall be inoperative unless it shall have been ratified as an amendment to the Constitution by the legislatures of three-fourths of the several States within seven years from the date of its submission.

ARTICLE XXI

[*Proposed February 20, 1933; declared ratified December 5, 1933*]

Section 1. The eighteenth article of amendment to the Constitution of the United States is hereby repealed.

Section 2. The transportation or importation into any State, Territory, or possession of the United States for delivery or use therein of intoxicating liquors, in violation of the laws thereof, is hereby prohibited.

Section 3. This article shall be inoperative unless it shall have been ratified as an amendment to the Constitution by conventions in the several States, as provided in the Constitution, within seven years from the date of the submission hereof to the States by the Congress.

ARTICLE XXII

[*Proposed March 24, 1947; declared ratified March 1, 1951*]

Section 1. No person shall be elected to the office of the President more than twice, and no person who has held the office of President, or acted as President, for more than two years of a term to which some other person was elected President shall be elected to the office of the President more than once. But this Article shall not apply to any person holding the office of President when this Article was proposed by the Congress, and shall not prevent any person who may be holding the office of President, or acting as President, during the term within which this Article becomes operative from holding the office of President or acting as President during the remainder of such term.

Section 2. This article shall be inoperative unless it shall have been ratified as an amendment to the Constitution by the legislatures of three-fourths of the several States within seven years from the date of its submission to the States by the Congress.

ARTICLE XXIII

[*Proposed June 16, 1960; declared ratified April 3, 1961*]

Section 1. The District constituting the seat of Government of the United States shall appoint in such manner as the Congress may direct:

A number of electors of President and Vice President equal to the whole number of Senators and Representatives in Congress to which the District would be entitled if it were a State, but in no event more than the least populous state; they shall be in addition to those appointed by the States, but they shall be considered, for the purposes of the election of President and Vice President, to be electors appointed by a State; and they shall meet in the District and perform such duties as provided by the twelfth article of amendment.

Section 2. The Congress shall have power to enforce this article by appropriate legislation.

ARTICLE XXIV

[*Proposed August 27, 1962; declared ratified February 4, 1964*]

Section 1. The right of citizens of the United States to vote in any primary or other election for President or Vice President, for electors for President or Vice President, or for Senator or Representative in Congress, shall not be denied or abridged by the United States or any State by reason of failure to pay any poll tax or other tax.

Section 2. The Congress shall have power to enforce this article by appropriate legislation.

ARTICLE XXV

[*Proposed July 6, 1965; declared ratified February 23, 1967*]

Section 1. In case of removal of the President from office or of his death or resignation, the Vice President shall become President.

Section 2. Whenever there is a vacancy in the office of the Vice President, the President shall nominate a Vice President who shall take office upon confirmation by a majority vote of both Houses of Congress.

Section 3. Whenever the President transmits to the President pro tempore of the Senate and the Speaker of the House of Representatives his written declaration that he is unable to discharge the powers and duties of his office, and until he transmits to them a written declaration to the contrary, such powers and duties shall be discharged by the Vice President as Acting President.

Section 4. Whenever the Vice President and a majority of either the principal officers of the executive departments or of such other body as Congress may by law provide, transmit to the President pro tempore of the Senate and the Speaker of the House of Representatives their written declaration that the President is unable to discharge the powers and duties of his office, the Vice President shall immediately assume the powers and duties of the office as Acting President.

Thereafter, when the President transmits to the President pro tempore of the Senate and the Speaker of the House of Representatives his written declaration that no inability exists, he shall resume the powers and duties of his office unless the Vice President and a majority of either the principal officers of the executive department or of such other body as Congress may by law provide, transmit within four days to the President pro tempore of the Senate and the Speaker of the House of Representatives their written declaration that the President is unable to discharge the powers and duties of his office. Thereupon Congress shall decide the issue, assembling within forty-eight hours for that purpose if not in session. If the Congress, within twenty-one days after receipt of the latter written declaration, or, if Congress is not in session, within twenty-one days after Congress is required to assemble, determines by two-thirds vote of both Houses that the President is unable to discharge the power and duties of his office, the Vice President shall continue to discharge the same as Acting President; otherwise, the President shall resume the powers and duties of his office.

ARTICLE XXVI

[*Proposed March 23, 1971; declared ratified July 5, 1971*]

Section 1. The right of citizens of the United States, who are eighteen years of age or older, to vote shall not be denied or abridged by the United States or by any State on account of age.

Section 2. The Congress shall have power to enforce this article by appropriate legislation.

Presidential Elections

Year	Candidates Receiving More than One Percent of the Vote (Parties)	Popular Vote	Electoral Vote
1789	GEORGE WASHINGTON (No party designations)		69
	John Adams		34
	Other Candidates		35
1792	GEORGE WASHINGTON (No party designations)		132
	John Adams		77
	George Clinton		50
	Other Candidates		5
1796	JOHN ADAMS (Federalist)		71
	Thomas Jefferson (Democratic-Republican)		68
	Thomas Pinckney (Federalist)		59
	Aaron Burr (Democratic-Republican)		30
	Other Candidates		48
1800	THOMAS JEFFERSON (Democratic-Republican)		73
	Aaron Burr (Democratic-Republican)		73
	John Adams (Federalist))		65
	Charles C. Pinckney (Federalist)		64
	John Jay (Federalist)		1
1804	THOMAS JEFFERSON (Democratic-Republican)		162
	Charles C. Pinckney (Federalist)		14
1808	JAMES MADISON (Democratic-Republican)		122
	Charles C. Pinckney (Federalist)		47
	George Clinton (Democratic-Republican)		6
1812	JAMES MADISON (Democratic-Republican)		128
	De Witt Clinton (Federalist)		89
1816	JAMES MONROE (Democratic-Republican)		183
	Rufus King (Federalist)		34
1820	JAMES MONROE (Democratic-Republican)		231
	John Quincy Adams (Independent-Republican)		1
1824	JOHN QUINCY ADAMS (Democratic-Republican)	108,740	84
	Andrew Jackson (Democratic-Republican)	153,544	99
	William H. Crawford (Democratic-Republican)	46,618	41
	Henry Clay (Democratic-Republican)	47,136	37
1828	ANDREW JACKSON (Democratic)	647,286	178
	John Quincy Adams (National Republican)	508,064	83
1832	ANDREW JACKSON (Democratic)	687,502	219
	Henry Clay (National Republican)	530,189	49
	William Wirt (Anti-Masonic)		
	John Floyd (National Republican) }	33,108	7

[handwritten note next to 1824: "No Majority"]

Year	Candidates Receiving More than One Percent of the Vote (Parties)	Popular Vote	Electoral Vote
1836	MARTIN VAN BUREN (Democratic)	765,483	170
	William H. Harrison (Whig)		73
	Hugh L. White (Whig)	739,795	26
	Daniel Webster (Whig)		14
	W. P. Mangum (Anti-Jackson)		11
1840	WILLIAM H. HARRISON (Whig)	1,274,624	234
	Martin Van Buren (Democratic)	1,127,781	60
1844	JAMES K. POLK (Democratic)	1,338,464	170
	Henry Clay (Whig)	1,300,097	105
	James G. Birney (Liberty)	62,300	0
1848	ZACHARY TAYLOR (Whig)	1,360,967	163
	Lewis Cass (Democratic)	1,222,342	127
	Martin Van Buren (Free Soil)	291,263	0
1852	FRANKLIN PIERCE (Democratic)	1,601,117	254
	Winfield Scott (Whig)	1,385,453	42
	John P. Hale (Free Soil)	155,825	0
1856	JAMES BUCHANAN (Democratic)	1,832,955	174
	John C. Frémont (Republican)	1,339,932	114
	Millard Fillmore (American)	871,731	8
1860	ABRAHAM LINCOLN (Republican)	1,865,593	180
	Stephen A. Douglas (Democratic)	1,382,713	12
	John C. Breckinridge (Democratic)	848,356	72
	John Bell (Constitutional Union)	592,906	39
1864	ABRAHAM LINCOLN (Republican)	2,206,938	212
	George B. McClellan (Democratic)	1,803,787	21
1868	ULYSSES S. GRANT (Republican)	3,013,421	214
	Horatio Seymour (Democratic)	2,706,829	80
1872	ULYSSES S. GRANT (Republican)	3,596,745	286
	Horace Greeley (Democratic)	2,843,446	—*
	Other Candidates		63
1876	RUTHERFORD B. HAYES (Republican)	4,036,572	185
	Samuel J. Tilden (Democratic)	4,284,020	184
1880	JAMES A. GARFIELD (Republican)	4,453,295	214
	Winfield S. Hancock (Democratic)	4,414,082	155
	James B. Weaver (Greenback-Labor)	308,579	0
1884	GROVER CLEVELAND (Democratic)	4,879,507	219
	James G. Blaine (Republican)	4,850,293	182
	Benjamin F. Butler (Greenback-Labor)	175,370	0
	John P. St. John (Prohibition)	150,869	0
1888	BENJAMIN HARRISON (Republican)	5,447,129	233
	Grover Cleveland (Democratic)	5,537,857	168
	Clinton B. Fisk (Prohibition)	249,506	0
	Anson J. Streeter (Union Labor)	146,935	0

*Greeley died shortly after the election: the electors supporting him then divided their votes among other candidates.

Year	Candidates Receiving More than One Percent of the Vote (Parties)	Popular Vote	Electoral Vote
1892	GROVER CLEVELAND (Democratic)	5,555,426	277
	Benjamin Harrison (Republican)	5,182,690	145
	James B. Weaver (People's)	1,029,846	22
	John Bidwell (Prohibition)	264,133	0
1896	WILLIAM McKINLEY (Republican)	7,102,216	271
	William J. Bryan (Democratic)	6,492,559	176
1900	WILLIAM McKINLEY (Republican)	7,218,491	292
	William J. Bryan (Democratic; Populist)	6,356,734	155
	John C. Wooley (Prohibition)	208,914	0
1904	THEODORE ROOSEVELT (Republican)	7,628,461	336
	Alton B. Parker (Democratic)	5,084,223	140
	Eugene V. Debs (Socialist)	402,283	0
	Silas C. Swallow (Prohibition)	258,536	0
1908	WILLIAM H. TAFT (Republican)	7,675,320	321
	William J. Bryan (Democratic)	6,412,294	162
	Eugene V. Debs (Socialist)	420,793	0
	Eugene W. Chafin (Prohibition)	253,840	0
1912	WOODROW WILSON (Democratic)	6,296,547	435
	Theodore Roosevelt (Progressive)	4,118,571	88
	William H. Taft (Republican)	3,186,720	8
	Eugene V. Debs (Socialist)	900,672	0
	Eugene W. Chafin (Prohibition)	206,275	0
1916	WOODROW WILSON (Democratic)	9,127,695	277
	Charles E. Hughes (Republican)	8,533,507	254
	A. L. Benson (Socialist)	585,113	0
	J. Frank Hanly (Prohibition)	220,506	0
1920	WARREN G. HARDING (Republican)	16,143,407	404
	James M. Cox (Democratic)	9,130,328	127
	Eugene V. Debs (Socialist)	919,799	0
	P. P. Christensen (Farmer-Labor)	265,411	0
1924	CALVIN COOLIDGE (Republican)	15,718,211	382
	John W. Davis (Democratic)	8,385,283	136
	Robert M. La Follette (Progressive)	4,831,289	13
1928	HERBERT C. HOOVER (Republican)	21,391,993	444
	Alfred E. Smith (Democratic)	15,016,169	87
1932	FRANKLIN D. ROOSEVELT (Democratic)	22,809,638	472
	Herbert C. Hoover (Republican)	15,758,904	59
	Norman Thomas (Socialist)	881,954	0
1936	FRANKLIN D. ROOSEVELT (Democratic)	27,752,869	523
	Alfred M. Landon (Republican)	16,674,665	8
	William Lemke (Union)	882,479	0
1940	FRANKLIN D. ROOSEVELT (Democratic)	27,307,819	449
	Wendell L. Willkie (Republican)	22,321,018	82

Year	Candidates Receiving More than One Percent of the Vote (Parties)	Popular Vote	Electoral Vote
1944	FRANKLIN D. ROOSEVELT (Democratic)	25,606,585	432
	Thomas E. Dewey (Republican)	22,014,745	99
1948	HARRY S. TRUMAN (Democratic)	24,179,345	303
	Thomas E. Dewey (Republican)	21,991,291	189
	J. Strom Thurmond (States' Rights)	1,176,125	39
	Henry Wallace (Progressive)	1,157,326	0
1952	DWIGHT D. EISENHOWER (Republican)	33,936,234	442
	Adlai E. Stevenson (Democratic)	27,314,992	89
1956	DWIGHT D. EISENHOWER (Republican)	35,590,472	457
	Adlai E. Stevenson (Democratic)	26,022,752	73
1960	JOHN F. KENNEDY (Democratic)	34,226,731	303
	Richard M. Nixon (Republican)	34,108,157	219
1964	LYNDON B. JOHNSON (Democratic)	43,129,566	486
	Barry M. Goldwater (Republican)	27,127,188	52
1968	RICHARD M. NIXON (Republican)	31,785,480	301
	Hubert H. Humphrey (Democratic)	31,275,166	191
	George C. Wallace (American Independent)	9,906,473	46
1972	RICHARD M. NIXON (Republican)	45,631,189	521
	George S. McGovern (Democratic)	28,422,015	17
	John Schmitz (American Independent)	1,080,670	0
1976	JAMES E. CARTER, JR. (Democratic)	40,274,975	297
	Gerald R. Ford (Republican)	38,530,614	241
1980	RONALD W. REAGAN (Republican)	42,968,326	489
	James E. Carter, Jr. (Democratic)	34,731,139	49
	John B. Anderson (Independent)	5,552,349	0
1984	RONALD W. REAGAN (Republican)	53,428,357	525
	Walter F. Mondale (Democratic)	36,930,923	13
1988	GEORGE H. BUSH (Republican)	48,881,221	426
	Michael Dukakis (Democratic)	41,805,422	112
1992	WILLIAM J. B. CLINTON (Democratic)	44,908,254	370
	George H. Bush (Republican)	39,102,343	168
	H. Ross Perot (Independent)	19,741,065	—

Chief Justices of the Supreme Court

Term	Chief Justice
1789–1795	John Jay
1795	John Rutledge
1795–1799	Oliver Ellsworth
1801–1835	John Marshall
1836–1864	Roger B. Taney
1864–1873	Salmon P. Chase
1874–1888	Morrison R. Waite
1888–1910	Melville W. Fuller
1910–1921	Edward D. White
1921–1930	William H. Taft
1930–1941	Charles E. Hughes
1941–1946	Harlan F. Stone
1946–1953	Fred M. Vinson
1953–1969	Earl Warren
1969–1986	Warren E. Burger
1986–	William Rehnquist

Presidents, Vice Presidents, and Cabinet Members

President and Vice President	Secretary of State	Secretary of Treasury	Secretary of War	Secretary of Navy	Postmaster General	Attorney General	Secretary of Interior
1. George Washington (1789) John Adams (1789)	Thomas Jefferson (1789) Edmund Randolph (1794) Timothy Pickering (1795)	Alexander Hamilton (1789) Oliver Wolcott (1795)	Henry Knox (1789) Timothy Pickering (1795) James McHenry (1796)		Samuel Osgood (1789) Timothy Pickering (1791) Joseph Habersham (1795)	Edmund Randolph (1789) William Bradford (1794) Charles Lee (1795)	
2. John Adams (1797) Thomas Jefferson (1797)	Timothy Pickering (1797) John Marshall (1800)	Oliver Wolcott (1797)) Samuel Dexter (1801)	James McHenry (1797) John Marshall (1800) Samuel Dexter (1800) Roger Griswald (1801)	Benjamin Stoddert (1798)	Joseph Habersham (1797)	Charles Lee (1797) Theophilus Parsons (1801)	
3. Thomas Jefferson (1801) Aaron Burr (1801) George Clinton (1805)	James Madison (1801)	Samuel Dexter (1801) Albert Gallatin (1801)	Henry Dearborn (1801)	Benjamin Stoddert (1801) Robert Smith (1801) J. Crowninshield (1805)	Joseph Habersham (1801) Gideon Granger (1801)	Levi Lincoln (1801) Robert Smith (1805) John Breckinridge (1805) Caesar Rodney (1807)	
4. James Madison (1809) George Clinton (1809) Elbridge Gerry (1813)	Robert Smith (1809) James Monroe (1811)	Albert Gallatin (1809) George Campbell (1814) Alexander Dallas (1814) William Crawford (1816)	William Eustis (1809) John Armstrong (1813) James Monroe (1814) William Crawford (1815)	Paul Hamilton (1809) William Jones (1813) Benjamin Crowninshield (1814)	Gideon Granger (1809) Return Meigs (1814)	Caesar Rodney (1809) William Pinckney (1811) Richard Rush (1814)	
5. James Monroe (1817) Daniel D. Thompkins (1817)	John Quincy Adams (1817)	William Crawford (1817)	Isaac Shelby (1817) George Graham (1817) John C. Calhoun (1817)	Benjamin Crowninshield (1817) Smith Thompson (1818) Samuel Southard (1823)	Return Meigs (1817) John McLean (1823)	Richard Rush (1817) William Wirt (1817)	
6. John Quincy Adams (1825) John C. Calhoun (1825)	Henry Clay (1825)	Richard Rush (1825)	James Barbour (1825) Peter B. Porter (1828)	Samuel Southard (1825)	John McLean (1825)	William Wirt (1825)	
7. Andrew Jackson (1829) John C. Calhoun (1829) Martin Van Buren (1833)	Martin Van Buren (1829) Edward Livingston (1831) Louis McLane (1833) John Forsyth (1834)	Samuel Ingham (1829) Louis McLane (1831) William Duane (1833) Roger B. Taney (1833) Levi Woodbury (1834)	John H. Eaton (1829) Lewis Cass (1831) Benjamin Butler (1837)	John Branch (1829) Levi Woodbury (1831) Mahlon Dickerson (1834)	William Barry (1829) Amos Kendall (1835)	John M. Berrien (1829) Roger B. Taney (1831) Benjamin Butler (1833)	
8. Martin Van Buren (1837) Richard M. Johnson (1837)	John Forsyth (1837)	Levi Woodbury (1837)	Joel R. Poinsett (1837)	Mahlon Dickerson (1837) James K. Paulding (1838)	Amos Kendall (1837) John M. Niles (1840)	Benjamin Butler (1837) Felix Grundy (1838) Henry D. Gilpin (1840)	
9. William H. Harrison (1841) John Tyler (1841)	Daniel Webster (1841)	Thomas Ewing (1841)	John Bell (1841)	George E. Badger (1841)	Francis Granger (1841)	John J. Crittenden (1841)	

President and Vice President	Secretary of State	Secretary of Treasury	Secretary of War	Secretary of Navy	Postmaster General	Attorney General	Secretary of Interior
10. John Tyler (1841)	Daniel Webster (1841) Hugh S. Legaré (1843) Abel P. Upshur (1843) John C. Calhoun (1844)	Thomas Ewing (1841) Walter Forward (1841) John C. Spencer (1843) George M. Bibb (1844)	John Bell (1841) John McLean (1841) John C. Spencer (1841) James M. Porter (1843) William Wilkins (1844)	George E. Badger (1841) Abel P Upshur (1841) David Henshaw (1843) Thomas Gilmer (1844) John Y. Mason (1844)	Francis Granger (1841) Charles A. Wickliffe (1841)	John J. Crittenden (1841) Hugh S. Legaré (1841) John Nelson (1843)	
11. James K. Polk (1845) George M. Dallas (1845)	James Buchanan (1845)	Robert J. Walker (1845)	William L. Marcy (1845)	George Bancroft (1845) John Y. Mason (1846)	Cave Johnson (1845)	John Y. Mason (1845) Nathan Clifford (1846) Isaac Toucey (1848)	
12. Zachary Taylor (1849) Millard Fillmore (1849)	John M. Clayton (1849)	William M. Meredith (1849)	George W. Crawford (1849)	William B. Preston (1849)	Jacob Collamer (1849)	Reverdy Johnson (1849)	Thomas Ewing (1849)
13. Millard Fillmore (1850)	Daniel Webster (1850) Edward Everett (1852)	Thomas Corwin (1850)	Charles M. Conrad (1850)	William A. Graham (1850) John P Kennedy (1852)	Nathan K. Hall (1850) Sam D. Hubbard (1852)	John J. Crittenden (1850)	Thomas McKennan (1850) A. H. H. Stuart (1850)
14. Franklin Pierce (1853) William R. King (1853)	William L. Marcy (1853)	James Guthrie (1853)	Jefferson Davis (1853)	James C. Dobbin (1853)	James Campbell (1853)	Caleb Cushing (1853)	Robert McClelland (1853)
15. James Buchanan (1857) John C. Breckinridge (1857)	Lewis Cass (1857) Jeremiah S. Black (1860)	Howell Cobb (1857) Philip F. Thomas (1860) John A. Dix (1861)	John B. Floyd (1857) Joseph Holt (1861)	Isaac Toucey (1857)	Aaron V. Brown (1857) Joseph Holt (1859)	Jeremiah S. Black (1857) Edwin M. Stanton (1860)	Jacob Thompson (1857)
16. Abraham Lincoln (1861) Hannibal Hamlin (1861) Andrew Johnson (1865)	William H. Seward (1861)	Salmon P. Chase (1861) William P. Fessenden (1864) Hugh McCulloch (1865)	Simon Cameron (1861) Edwin M. Stanton (1862)	Gideon Welles (1861)	Horatio King (1861) Montgomery Blair (1861) William Dennison (1864)	Edward Bates (1861) Titian J. Coffey (1863) James Speed (1864)	Caleb B. Smith (1861) John P. Usher (1863)
17. Andrew Johnson (1865)	William H. Seward (1865)	Hugh McCulloch (1865)	Edwin M. Stanton (1865) Ulysses S. Grant (1867) Lorenzo Thomas (1868) John M. Schofield (1868)	Gideon Welles (1865)	William Dennison (1865) Alexander Randall (1866)	James Speed (1865) Henry Stanbery (1866) William M. Evarts (1868)	John P. Usher (1865) James Harlan (1865) O. H. Browning (1866)

President and Vice President	Secretary of State	Secretary of Treasury	Secretary of War	Secretary of Navy	Postmaster General	Attorney General	Secretary of Interior
18. Ulysses S. Grant (1869) Schuyler Colfax (1869) Henry Wilson (1873)	Elihu B. Washburne (1869) Hamilton Fish (1869)	George S. Boutwell (1869) William A. Richardson (1873) Benjamin H. Bristow (1874) Lot M. Morrill (1876)	John A. Rawlins (1869) William T. Sherman (1869) William W. Belknap (1869) Alphonso Taft (1876) James Cameron (1876)	Adolph E. Borie (1869) George M. Robeson (1869)	John A. J. Creswell (1869) James W. Marshall (1874) Marshall Jewell (1874) James N. Tyner (1876)	Ebenezer R. Hoar (1869) Amos T. Akerman (1870) G. H. Williams (1871) Edwards Pierrepont (1875) Alphonso Taft (1876)	Jacob D. Cox (1869) Columbus Delano (1870) Zachariah Chandler (1875)
19. Rutherford B. Hayes (1877) William A. Wheeler (1877)	William M. Evarts (1877)	John Sherman (1877)	George W. McCrary (1877) Alexander Ramsey (1879)	R. W. Thompson (1877) Nathan Golf, Jr. (1881)	David M. Key (1877) Horace Maynard (1880)	Charles Devens (1877)	Carl Schurz (1877)
20. James A. Garfield (1881) Chester A. Arthur (1881)	James G. Blaine (1881)	William Windom (1881)	Robert T. Lincoln (1881)	William H. Hunt (1881)	Thomas I. James (1881)	Wayne MacVeagh (1881)	S. I. Kirkwood (1881)
21. Chester A. Arthur (1881)	F. T. Frelinghuysen (1881)	Charles J. Folger (1881) Walter Q. Gresham (1884) Hugh McCulloch (1884)	Robert T. Lincoln (1881)	William E. Chandler (1881)	Timothy O. Howe (1881) Walter Q. Gresham (1883) Frank Hatton (1884)	B. H. Brewster (1881)	Henry M. Teller (1881)
22. Grover Cleveland (1885) T. A. Hendricks (1885)	Thomas F Bayard (1885)	Daniel Manning (1885) Charles S. Fairchild (1887)	William C. Endicott (1885)	William C. Whitney (1885)	William F Vilas (1885) Don M. Dickinson (1888)	A. H. Garland (1885)	L. Q. C. Lamar (1885) William F Vilas (1888)
23. Benjamin Harrison (1889) Levi P Morgan (1889)	James G. Blaine (1889) John W. Foster (1892)	William Windom (1889) Charles Foster (1891)	Redfield Procter (1889) Stephen B. Elkins (1891)	Benjamin F Tracy (1889)	John Wanamaker (1889)	W. H. H. Miller (1889)	Jon W. Noble (1889)
24. Grover Cleveland (1893) Adlai E. Stevenson (1893)	Walter Q. Gresham (1893) Richard Olney (1895)	John G. Carlisle (1893)	Daniel S. Lamont (1893)	Hilary A. Herbert (1893)	Wilson S. Bissel (1893) William L. Wilson (1895)	Richard Olney (1893) Judson Harmon (1895)	Hoke Smith (1893) David R. Francis (1896)
25. William McKinley (1897) Garret A. Hobart (1897) Theodore Roosevelt (1901)	John Sherman (1897) William R. Day (1897) John Hay (1898)	Lyman J. Gage (1897)	Russell A. Alger (1897) Elihu Root (1899)	John D. Long (1897)	James A. Gary (1897) Charles E. Smith (1898)	Joseph McKenna (1897) John W Griggs (1897) Philander C. Knox (1901)	Cornelius N. Bliss (1897) E. A. Hitchcock (1899)
26. Theodore Roosevelt (1901) Charles Fairbanks (1905)	John Hay (1901) Elihu Root (1905) Robert Bacon (1909)	Lyman J. Gage (1901) Leslie M. Shaw (1902) George B. Cortelyou (1907)	Elihu Root (1901) William H. Taft (1904) Luke E. Wright (1908)	John D. Long (1901) William H. Moody (1902) Paul Morton (1904) Charles J. Bonaparte (1905) V. H. Metcalf (1906) T. H. Newberry (1908)	Charles E. Smith (1901) Henry Payne (1902) Robert J. Wynne (1904) George B. Cortelyou (1905) George von L. Meyer (1907)	Philander C. Knox (1901) William H. Moody (1904) Charles J. Bonaparte (1907)	E. A. Hitchcock (1901) James R. Garfield (1907)

President and Vice President	Secretary of State	Secretary of Treasury	Secretary of War	Secretary of Navy	Postmaster General	Attorney General	Secretary of Interior
27. William H. Taft (1909) James S. Sherman (1909)	Philander C. Knox (1909)	Franklin MacVeagh (1909)	Jacob M. Dickinson (1909) Henry Stimson (1911)	George von L. Meyer (1909)	Frank H. Hitchcock (1909)	G. W. Wickersham (1909)	R. A. Ballinger (1909) Walter L. Fisher (1911)
28. Woodrow Wilson (1913) Thomas R. Marshall (1913)	William J. Bryan (1913) Robert Lansing (1915) Bainbridge Colby (1920)	William G. McAdoo (1913) Carter Glass (1918) David F. Houston (1920)	Lindley M. Garrison (1913) Newton D. Baker (1916)	Josephus Daniels (1913)	Albert S. Burleson (1913)	J. C. McReynolds (1913) T. W. Gregory (1914) A. Mitchell Palmer (1919)	Franklin K. Lane (1913) John B. Payne (1920)
29. Warren G. Harding (1921) Calvin Coolidge (1921)	Charles E. Hughes (1912)	Andrew W. Mellon (1921)	John W. Weeks (1921)	Edwin Denby (1921)	Will H. Hays (1921) Hubert Work (1922) Harry S. New (1923)	H. M. Daugherty (1921)	Albert B. Fall (1921) Hubert Work (1923)
30. Calvin Coolidge (1923) Charles G. Dawes (1925)	Charles E. Hughes (1923) Frank B. Kellogg (1925)	Andrew W. Mellon (1923)	John W. Weeks (1923) Dwight F. Davis (1925)	Edwin Denby (1923) Curtis D. Wilbur (1924)	Harry S. New (1923)	H. M. Daugherty (1923) Harlan F. Stone (1924) John G. Sargent (1925)	Hubert Work (1923) Roy O. West (1928)
31. Herbert C. Hoover (1929) Charles Curtis (1929)	Henry L. Stimson (1929)	Andrew W. Mellon (1929) Ogden L. Mills (1932)	James W. Good (1929) Patrick J. Hurley (1929)	Charles F. Adams (1929)	Walter F. Brown (1929)	W. D. Mitchell (1929)	Ray L. Wilbur (1929)
32. Franklin D. Roosevelt (1933) John Nance Garner (1933) Henry A. Wallace (1941) Harry S. Truman (1945)	Cordell Hull (1933) E. R. Stettinius, Jr. (1944)	William H. Woodin (1933) Henry Morgenthau, Jr. (1934)	George H. Dern (1933) Harry H. Woodring (1936) Henry L. Stimson (1940)	Claude A. Swanson (1933) Charles Edison (1940) Frank Knox (1940) James V. Forrestal (1944)	James A. Farley (1933) Frank C. Walker (1940)	H. S. Cummings (1933) Frank Murphy (1939) Robert Jackson (1940) Francis Biddle (1941)	Harold L. Ickes (1933)
33. Harry S. Truman (1945) Alben W. Barkley (1949)	James F. Byrnes (1945) George C. Marshall (1947) Dean G. Acheson (1949)	Fred M. Vinson (1945) John W. Snyder (1946)	Robert P. Patterson (1945) Kenneth C. Royal (1947) *Secretary of Defense* James V. Forrestal (1947) Louis A. Johnson (1949) George G. Marshall (1950) Robert A. Lovett (1951)	James V. Forrestal (1945)	R. E. Hannegan (1945) Jesse M. Donaldson (1947)	Tom C. Clark (1945) J. H. McGrath (1949) James P. McGranery (1952)	Harold L. Ickes (1945) Julis A. Krog (1946) Oscar L. Chapman (1949)
34. Dwight D. Eisenhower (1953)	John Foster Dulles (1953)	George M. Humphrey (1953)	Charles E. Wilson (1953) Neil H. McElroy (1957)		A. E. Summerfield (1953)	H. Brownell Jr. (1953)	Douglas McKay (1953)

President and Vice President	Secretary of State	Secretary of Treasury	Secretary of War	Secretary of Navy	Postmaster General	Attorney General	Secretary of Interior
Richard M. Nixon (1953)	Christian A. Herter (1959)	Robert B. Anderson (1957)	Thomas S. Gates (1959)			William P. Rogers (1957)	Fred Seaton (1950)
35. John F. Kennedy (1961) Lyndon B. Johnson (1961)	Dean Rusk (1961)	C. Douglas Dillon (1961)	Robert S. McNamara (1961)		J. Edward Day (1961) John A. Gronouski (1963)	Robert F. Kennedy (1961)	Stewart L. Udall (1961)
36. Lyndon B. Johnson (1963) Hubert H. Humphrey (1965)	Dean Rusk (1963)	C. Douglas Dillon (1963) Henry H. Fowler (1965) Joseph W. Barr (1968)	Robert S. McNamara (1963) Clark M. Clifford (1968)		John A. Gronouski (1963) Lawrence F. O'Brien (1965) W. Marvin Watson (1968)	Robert F Kennedy (1963) N. deB. Katzenbach (1965) Ramsey Clark (1967)	Stewart L. Udall (1963)
37. Richard M. Nixon (1969) Spiro T. Agnew (1969) Gerald R. Ford (1973)	William P. Rogers (1969) Henry A. Kissinger (1973)	David M. Kennedy (1969) John B. Connally (1970) George P. Schultz (1972) William E. Simon (1974)	Melvin R. Laird (1969) Elliot L. Richardson (1973) James R. Schlesinger (1973)		Winton M. Blount (1969)	John M. Mitchell (1969) Richard G. Kleindienst (1972) Elliot L. Richardson (1973) William B. Saxbe (1974)	Walter J. Hickel (1969) Rogers C. B. Morton (1971)
38. Gerald R. Ford (1974) Nelson A. Rockefeller (1974)	Henry A. Kissinger (1974)	William E. Simon (1974)	James R. Schlesinger (1974) Donald H. Rumsfeld (1975)			William B. Saxbe (1974) Edward H. Levi (1975)	Rogers C. B. Morton (1974) Stanley K. Hathaway (1975) Thomas D. Kleppe (1975)
39. James E. Carter, Jr. (1977) Walter F. Mondale (1977)	Cyrus R. Vance (1977) Edmund S. Muskie (1980)	W. Michael Blumenthal (1977) G. William Miller (1979)	Harold Brown (1977)			Griffin B. Bell (1977) Benjamin R. Civiletti (1979)	Cecil D. Andrus (1977)
40. Ronald W. Reagan (1981) George H. Bush (1981)	Alexander M. Haig, Jr. (1981) George P. Schultz (1982)	Donald T. Regan (1981)	Caspar W. Weinberger (1981)			William French Smith (1981)	James G. Watt (1981) William Clark (1983)
41. Ronald W. Reagan (1985) George H. Bash (1985)	George P. Schultz (1985)	James A. Baker III (1985)	Caspar W. Weinberger (1985)			Edwin Meese III (1985)	Donald P. Hodel (1985)
42. George H. Bush (1988) James D. Quayle III	James A. Baker III (1988)	Nicholas Brady (1988)	Richard B. Cheney (1988)			Richard L. Thornburgh (1988)	Manuel Lujan, Jr. (1988)
43. William J. B. Clinton (1993) Albert Gore, Jr. (1993)	Warren Christopher (1993)	Lloyd Bentsen (1993)	Les Aspin (1993)			Janet Reno (1993)	Bruce Babbit (1993)

984   Appendix

Writing About History

Dr. Robert Weiss

What is "history"? We employ the word constantly to refer to everything from the "history" of the world to an individual's "history." But how often do we stop to think about what the word means? The following essay addresses this question, and provides some fundamental principles for reading, researching, and writing historical reports and essays.

★ WHAT IS HISTORY? ★

History can best be defined as a record and interpretation of past events. This statement is not very complicated, yet it is not as simple as it may appear. Let us examine it more carefully.

The "record" part is straightforward. Since the purpose of history is to inform us about what happened in the past, it must include substantial data, or "facts" (a troublesome word that some social scientists avoid). Names, dates, places, and events are the essence of history. But historical writing is not a compendium of facts. It consists of facts placed in a sequence to tell a connected story. A work of history is not merely a story, however. It also must analyze what happened and *why*—that is, it must interpret the past for the reader in a useful and informative manner. It is not sufficient, for example, to state that the American Revolution began in 1775–76, and then give an account of the relevant individuals and events, such as George Washington, Thomas Jefferson, Lexington and Concord, and the Declaration of Independence. The historian must proceed to the next step: Why did the Revolution occur in 1776? Here again, historians must resort to concrete data, including the Proclamation of 1763, the Boston Massacre, the Boston Tea Party, and the Intolerable Acts. Rather than simply composing a catalog of events, however, the historian must weave the material into a well-integrated narrative that analyzes the *process* whereby the American colonies severed their political ties to the mother country. To accomplish this task, historians must make certain value judgments concerning the role and significance of these events. Which were more important, and which were less important? What was the relationship of each event to the others, and what does each tell us about the behavior of the American colonists?

To address questions like these, historians must place their material within an appropriate historical context. An account of a past event is not very instructive unless it is analyzed as a component of a larger sequence of events within a specific social, political, and economic setting. The Boston Tea Party, for example, would be analyzed in relation to such factors as British financial expenses incurred during the French and Indian War, colonial views regarding commerce and taxation, Britain's relationship with its empire, and the role of merchants in American colonial society. Only by examining such factors can we hope to understand why both sides behaved as they did.

Historical interpretation takes place on many levels. Some historians focus on the "larger forces" in history, such as the industrial revolution of the nineteenth century and the communications revolution of the twentieth century. Obviously

these developments exerted a profound effect on the way we live. The emphasis on context, however, also acknowledges the human element in history. Human beings are the actors in the historical drama, and an effective historical work attempts to explain why people behaved as they did. A history of the American Revolution, for example, would be incomplete if it documented the events leading up to American independence, but offered no insights as to *why* formerly loyal subjects of the British crown took up arms against their mother country. To understand human behavior, the historian, like the psychologist or psychiatrist, must examine the effects of "larger forces" and specific events on people as well as the ways in which the people themselves perceived these forces and events. To appreciate the American desire for independence in 1776, one must view the events of the 1700s through eighteenth-century, not twentieth-century eyes.

A note of caution should be introduced here. To understand the behavior of various groups is not necessarily to endorse it. By using the proper resources, the historian can understand such phenomena as the Reign of Terror during the French Revolution, the development of slavery in the American South, and the ascendancy of Hitler in Germany. But this claim does not imply that the historian approves of guillotines, slavery, or Nazism. Rather, it asserts the historian's responsibility to analyze all facets of history, even those that he or she finds personally reprehensible.

The preceding paragraphs indicate the "subjective" nature of the interpretive process. When historians make the transition from recording data to interpreting that data, they are imposing an order and a meaning on a set of circumstances that they usually did not experience firsthand. Moreover, historians' interpretations often differ from those of various parties who *did* experience the events. While historians' interpretations should always be based on evidence, there comes a point at which they must transcend that evidence and rely on their own insights, values, and experiences in forming conclusions. Historians collect facts, and when they feel they have mastered them, they draw conclusions as to their significance and their relationship to one another. This process is not unique to the history profession, but is characteristic of all the natural and social sciences. Like all scientists, historians must pursue the maximum feasible "objectivity" in forming their conclusions, while acknowledging the impossibility of total objectivity. Historians must be aware of their personal biases and values so they can monitor the effects of these biases on their interpretations of the past. At the same time, writers of history should never allow the fear of "subjectivity" to stifle the creative process.

★ READING HISTORY ★

An understanding of the fundamentals of historical writing will make the student of history a more discerning and selective reader. Although no two historical works are identical, most contain the same basic elements and can be approached in a similar manner by the reader. When reading a historical monograph, concentrate on the two basic issues discussed in the preceding section: facts and interpretation.

Interpretation. The first question the reader should ask is: What is the author's argument? What is his theme, his interpretation, his thesis? A theme is not the same as a topic. An author may select the Civil War as a *topic*, but he then must propose a particular theme or argument regarding some aspect of the war. (The most common, not surprisingly, is *why* the war occurred.)

Discovering the author's thesis is usually easy enough because most writers state their arguments clearly in the preface to their book. Students often make the crucial error of skimming over the preface—if they read it at all—and then moving on to the "meat" of the book. Since the preface indicates the manner in which the author has used his data to develop his arguments, students who ignore it often find themselves overwhelmed with details without understanding *what* the author is attempting to say. This error should be avoided always.

The more history you read, the more you will appreciate the diversity of opinions and approaches among historians. While each author offers a unique perspective, historical works fall into general categories, or "schools," depending on their thesis and when they were published. The study of the manner in which different historians approach their subjects is referred to as *historiography*. Every historical subject has a historiography, sometimes limited, sometimes extensive. As in the other sciences, new schools of thought supplant existing ones, offering new insights and challenging accepted theories. Below are excerpts from two monographs dealing with the American Revolution. As you read them, note the contrast in the underlying arguments.

1. "Despite its precedent-setting character, however, the American revolt is noteworthy because it made no serious interruption in the smooth flow of American development. Both in intention and in fact, the American Revolution conserved the past rather than repudiated it. And in preserving the colonial experience, the men of the first quarter century of the Republic's history set the scenery and wrote the script for the drama of American politics for years to come."*

2. "The stream of revolution, once started, could not be confined within narrow banks, but spread abroad upon the land. Many economic desires, many social aspirations were set free by the political struggle, many aspects of colonial society profoundly altered by the forces thus set loose. The relations of social classes to each other, the institution of slavery, the system of landholding, the course of business, the forms and spirit of the intellectual and religious life, all felt the transforming hand of revolution, all emerged from under it in shapes advanced many degrees nearer to those we know."†

What you have just read is nothing less than two conflicting theories of the fundamental nature of the American Revolution. Professor Jameson portrays the Revolution as a catalyst for major social, economic, and political change, while Professor Degler views it primarily as a war for independence that conserved, rather than transformed, colonial institutions. The existence of such divergent opinions makes it imperative that the reader be aware of the argument of every book and read a variety of books and articles to get different perspectives on a subject.

All historical works contain biases of some sort, but a historical bias is not in itself bad or negative. As long as history books are composed by human beings, they will reflect the perspectives of their authors. This need not diminish the quality of historical writing if historians remain faithful to the facts. Some historians, however, have such strong biases that they distort the evidence to make it fit their preconceived notions. This type of history writing (which is the exception rather than the rule) is of limited value, but when properly treated can contribute to the accumulation of knowledge by providing new insights and challenging the values—and creative abilities—of other historians.

Evidence. Once you are aware of the author's central argument, you can concentrate on his use of evidence—the "facts"—that buttress that argument. There are several types of questions that you should keep in mind as you progress through a book. What types of evidence does the author use? Is his evidence convincing? Which sources does he rely on, and what additional sources might he have consulted? One strategy you might adopt is to imagine that *you* are writing the monograph. Where would you go for information? What would you look at? Then ask yourself: Did the author consult these sources? Obviously no writer can examine *everything*. A good historical work, however, offers convincing data extracted from a comprehensive collection of materials.

As you begin to ask these questions, you will develop the skill of critical reading. Used in this sense the word *critical* does not mean reading to discern what is wrong with the narrative. Rather, it refers to analytic reading, assessing the strengths and weaknesses of the monograph, and determining whether the argument ultimately works. All historical works should be approached with a critical—but open—mind.

One important point to remember is that you need not accept or reject every aspect of a historical monograph. In fact, you most likely will accord a "mixed review" to most of the books you read. You may accept the author's argument but find his evidence inadequate, or you may be impressed by his data but draw different conclusions from it. You may find some chapters tightly argued but others unconvincing. Even if you like a particular book, almost inevitably you will have some comments, criticisms, or suggestions.

★ RESEARCHING HISTORY ★

Most history courses, especially advanced ones, require some type of research project. Research skills are vital to history, and can be developed by observing certain rules.

The first rule is to know exactly what you are researching. Every history project begins with a question or problem. Thus the first step is to select a manageable question.

---

*Carl N. Degler, *Out of Our Past*, rev. ed. (New York: Harper and Row, Harper Colophon Books, 1970), p. 73.

†J. Franklin Jameson, *The American Revolution Considered As a Social Movement* (Boston: Beacon Press, 1956), p. 9.

Remember, a question is different from a topic. You may choose the American Revolution as a topic, for example, but you then must choose some aspect of the Revolution that interests you. Obviously a project such as "Discuss the American Revolution in all its aspects" is not realistic. You may be interested in the causes of the Revolution. This is a legitimate question, but still a broad one, more appropriate for a book than a paper. You would do better to select a more specific question, such as "Was the American Revolution really a revolution?" This question poses a specific problem, which will require you to collect data and then formulate a definite argument.

Once you have chosen the question, you begin the search for information. There are several possible sources you may wish to explore. First, you might want to consult your professor, who should be familiar with the relevant literature. This approach could be productive; on the other hand, the professor may want you to develop research skills on your own. In that case, a good encyclopedia, such as the *Encyclopaedia Britannica*, will provide a brief but useful overview of a topic and will cite the works from which the information was collected. Even more valuable is an American history textbook. The bibliography section for the appropriate chapters—and, if included, a list of recommended readings—will direct you toward the appropriate literature.

The library card catalog constitutes another vital source of information. It contains three types of cards, which may be filed separately or together, but are always in alphabetical order: author, title, and subject cards. Author cards are filed according to the author's last name; title cards, according to the book's title (excluding "the"); and subject cards by major topical groupings. Obviously subject cards are the most appropriate when you are looking for sources and ideas. If you are uncertain as to *how* your particular topic is filed, choose a heading that sounds appropriate. To come back to our sample topic, possibilities include: "American Revolution"; "Revolution—United States"; "United States—History—Revolution." If you should pick the wrong heading, the catalog will usually have one card under that heading referring you to the proper subject category. If you already have compiled a list of names and/or authors, you can save much time by going directly to the author and title cards.

The following is the card for a famous work in American history. Note the diversity of information that the card contains. (See below.)

This information not only helps you to locate a book, but can indicate whether the book is relevant to your topic. Often, however, you cannot determine a book's usefulness until you have examined its table of contents and perhaps skimmed through a chapter or two.

As you search for materials, you should be aware that historical sources are divided into two general categories: primary and secondary. Primary sources are those produced by the historical characters themselves or their contemporaries: correspondence, diaries and journals, autobiographies, government publications, newspapers, and similar documents. Secondary sources include books, magazine articles, and Ph.D. dissertations written by later scholars or writers. In most cases, primary sources are more impressive, since they provide a firsthand account of the events in question. Unfortunately they are often more difficult to locate. In the case of the American Revolution, for example, much primary information does exist, including correspondence, newspapers, and government materials. While some of these materials, such as the letters of Washington and Jefferson, are available in printed form in many university libraries, other materials exist only in the original manuscripts and are confined to special libraries, state historical societies, and similar institutions. Fortunately primary materials are not required for all assignments. Consult your professor and use your own judgment to determine what types of sources are most appropriate for your project.

Once you have selected your sources, the task of note taking begins. Thorough notes are the key to successful research. When you locate a source on the library shelves, the first step is to fill out a note card listing the author, title, publisher, and publication date. You might also note the library call number, in case you need to consult the book again. Once you have recorded this information, the next step is to read the appropriate sections of the book or article, and to jot down any information that may be helpful to you on additional cards. The general rule is one idea per card. Following this procedure allows you to arrange and rearrange your notes in the course of your writing. As you are taking notes, rephrase the data in your own words. Or, if you use the author's language, be sure to put quotation marks around it to indicate it is a direct quote. Always include on your card the author, title, and the page(s) on which you found the information. This will be useful when you wish to cite the material in a footnote. Remember, if you are using a book, you need not read the entire book, but only those sec-

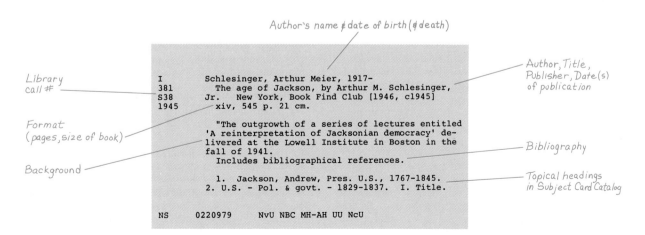

tions relevant to your topic. Magazine articles generally should be read in their entirety.

★ WRITING HISTORY ★

Once you have collected your data, you face the often difficult task of putting your ideas on paper. Composing a history essay allows for few legitimate shortcuts. By adhering to a particular set of procedures, however, you can minimize difficulties while enhancing the quality of your writing.

The first step in writing a paper is to create an outline. Although students often avoid this stage in their haste to "get started" on their project, the outline performs a critical role in the creative process. Not only does it contribute to a more logical and coherent development of ideas, but it also helps you see and eliminate many structural problems before you become engrossed in the actual writing. As a general rule, the earlier you can spot any problem, the easier it is to resolve. The outline may be as general or as specific as you wish. It serves not as an ironclad script for you to follow, but as a general framework to provide direction for the narrative. It can be modified later to accommodate ideas that occur to you as you proceed.

After you complete the outline, you should begin your paper with a clear statement of your argument. For example, if you are addressing the question of whether the American Revolution really was a revolution, you should begin by taking a clear position on the question. It is important to note that the position need *not* be a simple "yes" or "no"; it may be more complicated than that. History is seldom black and white; most often it consists of many gray areas. Whatever position you take, it should be made explicit. If you fail to do this, the effectiveness of your writing will be diminished, since your readers may not be aware of the point of your essay. A common mistake students make is to treat a paper like a mystery story, giving readers the "clues" first and supplying the "solution" at the end. This style is not conducive to good history. State your argument in the beginning so that your readers will be able to follow—and assess—your narrative.

From your introduction you should move smoothly into your narrative. It is here that you develop your argument, using your evidence in a convincing manner. The narrative should exhibit a logical sequence of ideas, not a random collection of data. While evidence is crucial, the key to successful writing is in the elaboration of evidence. Contrary to a popular slogan, the facts do not speak for themselves. Rather, the author must explain the relevance of his facts to his central argument. Few people, for example, would dispute the statement that George Washington crossed the Delaware River to surprise the Hessians at Trenton. The author, however, must explain why this event was significant to his topic. Otherwise it becomes a mere fact of passing interest, without any greater meaning.

History involves the process of change over time, and an effective narrative must illustrate this process. To do so, the narrative must connect diverse facts so that they form a cohesive story. Each sentence should follow logically from the preceding one, and lead into the next one; each paragraph should do the same. To accomplish this, you must pay particular attention to *transition*; that is, moving from one topic to a related topic. Too often students shift from one topic to another with-

out explaining the connection between the two. A historical essay that shifts immediately from Washington's crossing of the Delaware to Jefferson's authorship of the Declaration of Independence creates confusion as to the course of the narrative. A successful transition can be effected by inserting a sentence such "While some individuals fought for independence on the battlefield, others pursued it in the halls of the Continental Congress." This sentence establishes a concrete relationship between the two events.

In addition to elaborating your evidence, you must cite the sources of this evidence. Any information that is not "common knowledge" should be demarcated by a footnote. If you are uncertain as to proper footnote use and form, consult a stylistic manual such as Kate Turabian's *A Manual for Writers*. Although some footnotes can be complicated, the basic forms for books and articles are illustrated below.

For books:

Robert E. Brown, *Middle-Class Democracy and the Revolution in Massachusetts, 1691–1780* (Ithaca, N.Y.: Cornell University Press, 1955), p. 27.

Notice that the footnote includes the author, title, publisher, date, and page on which the information was found. As mentioned earlier, it is essential that you record this information when taking notes.

Articles are footnoted as follows:

Jesse Lemisch, "Jack Tar in the Streets: Merchant Seamen in the Politics of the American Revolution," *William and Mary Quarterly*, 3rd Series 25 (July, 1968): 347–381.

This footnote includes the author, title, the journal in which the article appears, and the date and edition of publication. The pages indicated are those from which the information was taken. Note that the title of the book or journal is underlined, while the title of the article is placed within quotation marks.

For an article by one author appearing in a work edited by another:

Gordon S. Wood, "Rhetoric and Reality in the American Revolution," in *Essays on the American Revolution*, ed. David L. Jacobsen (New York: Holt, Rinehart and Winston, 1970), pp. 50–52.

This form combines various elements of the previous two styles (all forms are based on Turabian's *Manual*.)

In addition to knowing *how* to footnote, you must learn *when* to footnote. All specific data that are not common knowledge, as well as all direct quotes, should be cited. Never use historians' words or ideas without giving them credit in a footnote. To do so constitutes plagiarism, which is a serious offense within the academic world. For stylistic purposes, most readers prefer one comprehensive footnote at the end of a paragraph to a footnote at the end of each individual sentence. (A single footnote may cite several sources.) In the case of a direct quote, however, a footnote must appear at the end of a sentence. If you use a series of quotations, one multiple footnote may suffice. The word *footnote* implies that the citations should appear on the bottom of the page on which the cited material appears. While this is the most convenient arrangement for the reader, it complicates the typing of the paper substantially. Therefore, most professors will accept a separate footnote section at the end of the narrative.

One final word regarding footnotes. While you must cite a source every time you take data from it, you need only give the full citation the *first* time you cite the source. After that, an abbreviated footnote form is acceptable. For example:

Brown, *Middle-Class Democracy*, p. 11.

Adopting this form can save you considerable time in the typing of your paper.

Although all individuals must develop their own style of presenting evidence, a few basic rules should be observed. Keep your language clear and succinct. Avoid wordiness and redundancies. Expressions such as "a determined, headstrong, ambitious, unyielding, persevering individual" are repetitious and stylistically unacceptable. Make sure you have command of your vocabulary; do not employ "impressive" words if you are unsure of their precise meaning. Avoid excessive quoting. Quotes are a highly effective means of illustrating ideas and attitudes, but when used excessively, they *become* the narrative, rather than highlighting the narrative. Let your characters speak for themselves, but remember that the final argument must be yours.

Learn to employ active rather than passive verbs in your writing. "Congress passed a law" reads better than "A law was passed," and is also more informative since it reveals *who* passed the law. Since history is a record of the past, it should be written in the past tense.

> Incorrect: "Hitler invad*es* Russia in June of 1941"
> Correct: "Hitler invad*ed* Russia in June of 1941."

Since you are, in a sense, telling a story, humorous anecdotes and interesting asides, when used properly, can make your narrative more readable. If your writing includes extensive quantitative (numerical) data, you might want to incorporate the information into charts or appendices to avoid interrupting the flow of your narrative.

When you have completed the actual narrative, you should summarize your argument *briefly* in your conclusion. Just as your introductory paragraph prepares your readers for your argument, your conclusion reaffirms the major ideas that you want to communicate to your readers.

After the narrative comes the bibliography, which is a list of all the sources you have used in the course of your work. Several differences distinguish a bibliography from footnotes. While the sequence of footnotes is determined by your narrative, the bibliography is arranged in alphabetical order. Most bibliographies are divided into primary and secondary sources, and subdivided into general categories, such as books, articles, newspapers, and government documents. Moreover, the bibliographic form differs slightly from that of footnotes. Examples of proper bibliographic form follow:

Brown, Robert E. *Middle-Class Democracy and the Revolution in Massachusetts, 1691–1780*. Ithaca, N.Y.: Cornell University Press, 1955.

Lemisch, Jesse. "Jack Tar in the Streets: Merchant Seamen in the Politics of the Revolutionary America." *William and Mary Quarterly*. 3rd Series 25 (July, 1968): 371–407.

Wood, Gordon S. "Rhetoric and Reality in the American Revolution." In *Essays in the American Revolution*, pp. 43–65. Edited by David L. Jacobsen. New York: Holt, Rinehart and Winston, 1970.

Although the form differs from that of footnotes, most of the information is the same. Note that in the case of articles, however, the bibliography gives the page numbers for the entire article, while the footnote gives only those pages from which information has been extracted. Note also the way the authors' last names stand out in a bibliography enabling the reader to see at a glance which sources you have used. (The bibliographic form used here comes from Turabian's manual. If you have any questions regarding the bibliography, consult Turabian or some other manual.)

The final stage in writing a paper is proofreading. Ideally, you should compose a first draft, proofread it carefully, and then rewrite the paper where necessary. If you write only one draft, make your corrections as neatly as possible. Unless otherwise instructed, papers should be typed, double-spaced.

Finally, pay strict attention to deadlines. Allot adequate time for each project, including time for typing and proofreading. If you encounter any difficulties, inform your professor immediately. Do not wait until the due date to reveal that you cannot submit your paper on time.

PHOTO CREDITS

Library of Congress. **449** Library of Congress. **450** Harper's Weekly. **451** Library of Congress. **452** The Bettmann Archives, Inc. **454** New York Historical Society.

456 The Granger Collection **458** Library of Congress. **460** National Portrait Gallery, Smithsonian Institution. **461** National Portrait Gallery, Smithsonian Institution. **463** National Portrait Gallery, Smithsonian Institution. **465** Library of Congress. **466** Culver Pictures. **470** State Historical Society of Wisconsin. **471** International Museum of Photography, George Eastman House. **472** International Museum of Photography, George Eastman House. **473** Library of Congress. **474** International Museum of Photography, George Eastman House. **476** Library of Congress. **477** Public Domain. **479** AFL-CIO. **481** Library of Congress. **485** Library of Congress.

488 The Granger Collection. **493** Library of Congress. **495** National Archives. **496** Museum of the City of New York. **499** Brooklyn Museum. **500** Library of Congress. **501** (top) Museum of the City of New York. **501** (bottom) The Sophia Smith Collection, Smith College. **503** Library of Congress. **504** Brown Brothers. **509** Culver Pictures. **510** Museum of the City of New York. **511** Museum of the City of New York.

514 Superstock. **517** National Museum of American History, Smithsonian Institution. **520** Library of Congress. **523** National Archeological Archives, Smithsonian Institution. **524** LIbrary of Congress. **525** Library of Congress. **530** The Granger Collection. **531** NYU Fales Library. **532** The Henry Ford Museum and Greenfield Village. **533** New York Public Library. **535** Library of Congress. **536** Kansas State Historical Society, Topeka. **538** South Dakota Art Museum Collection, Brookings. **539** Library of Congress. **543** Library of Congress.

546 Superstock. **550** Library of Congress. **553** (bottom) Library of Congress; **553** (top) Library of Congress. **555** Library of Congress. **559** Library of Congress. **560** Library of Congress. **562** Library of Congress. **563** Library of Congress. **565** Dewitt Collection, University Hartford. **566** JUDGE. **567** Library of Congress. **568** Dewitt Collection, University of Hartford.

572 Library of Congress. **576** Culver Pictures. **577** National Archives. **578** Library of Congress. **582** Library of Congress. **583** JUDGE. **585** (top) Culver Pictures. **585** (bottom) Library of Congress. **586** Chicago Historical Society. **588** Library of Congress. **589** Courtesy, Dartmouth College Library. **592** Library of Congress. **593** c. 1988, The Detroit Institute of Art, City of Detroit Purchase. **594** Library of Congress.

598 Bettmann. **602** Bancroft Library, University of California at Berkeley. **605** (top) c. The Art Institute of Chicago, All Rights Reserved. **605** (bottom) The Cleveland Museum of Art, Gift of Amelia Elizabeth White. **606** Walt Kuhn Papers, Archives of American

Art, Smithsonian Institution. **607** International Museum of Photography, George Eastman House. **609** Library of Congress. **610** New York Historical Society. **611** The Museum of the City of New York. **612** Brown Brothers. **614** Library of Congress. **615** MIT Historical Collections. **618** Brown Brothers. **624** Salvation Army National Communications Department.

628 The Granger Collection. **631** Carnegie Library of Pittsburgh. **633** Library of Congress. **637** Culver Pictures. **639** Chicago Historical Society. **641** State Historical Society of Wisconsin. **642** The Bettmann Archive, Inc. **643** The Schlesinger Library, Radcliff College. **645** Library of Congress. **647** New York Historical Society. **648** Brown Brothers. **649** Culver Pictures. **651** Library of Congress. **656** National Portrait Gallery, Smithsonian Institution.

660 Superstock. **663** Library of Congress. **665** The Bettmann Archive, Inc. **669** (top) Culver Pictures. **669** (bottom) The Bettmann Archive, Inc. **672** (top) UPI/Bettmann Newsphoto. **676** (top) Library of Congress. **676** (bottom) Bethlehem Steel Corporation. **677** (top) Herbert Hoover Presidential Library. **677** (bottom) National Archives. **680** Library of Congress. **681** National Archives. **684** Library of Congress.

688 Art Resource. **691** National Portrait Gallery, Smithsonian Institution. **693** Life Magazine. **694** Brown Brothers. **695** UPI/Bettmann Newsphotos. **698** Museum of the City of New York. **699** UPI/Bettmann Newsphotos. **701** Whitney Museum of American Art, New York. Gift of Edith and Milton Lowerthal in memory of Juliana Force. **703** Portrait Gallery, Smithsonian Institution. **704** (top) Charles Scribner's Sons. **704** (bottom) The Bettmann Archive, Inc. **705** National Archives. **710** Brown Brothers. **711** UPI/Bettmann Newsphotos. **712** UPI/Bettmann Newsphotos. **713** The Bettmann Archive, Inc.

716 National Museum of American Art, Washington, D.C./Art Resource (detail). **719** Philadelphia Museum of Art. **721** Culver Pictures. **722** Museum of Fine Arts, Boston. **723** The James Van der Zee Institute. **726** Whitney Museum of American Art. **728** Franklin D. Roosevelt Library, **729** Soil Conservation Service. **730** Library of Congress. **731** National Museum of American Art, Smithsonian Institution, Gift of Mr. & Mrs. Moses Soyer. **732** National Museum of American Art, Smithsonian Institution. Transfer from the U.S. Department of the Interior, Nation. **735** AP/Wide World Photos. **736** Library of Congress. **743** Museum of the City of New York. **744** Franklin D. Roosevelt Library.

748 Franklin D. Roosevelt Library. **751** Franklin D. Roosevelt Library. **754** Bildarchive Preussischer Kulturbesitz. **757** UPI/Bettmann Newsphotos. **759** Franklin D. Roosevelt Library. **762** National Archives. **763** National Archives. **764** National Archives. **765** Library of Congress. **766** Franklin D. Roosevelt Library. **768** Yivo Institute. **770** Franklin

D. Roosevelt Library. **771** The Bettmann Archives, Inc. **774** Franklin D. Roosevelt Library. **777** National Archives.

780 Lisa Quinones/Black Star. **783** National Portrait Gallery, Smithsonian Institution. **787** UPI/Bettmann Newsphotos. **790** Ralph Crane, Life Magazine, Time, Inc. **791** (top) Brown Brothers. **791** (bottom) Russell Lee, FSA, Library of Congress. **792** AP/Wide World Photos. **794** UPI/Bettmann Newsphotos. **795** AP/Wide World Photos. **799** UPI/Bettmann Newsphotos. **805** UPI/Bettmann Newsphotos. **808** UPI/Bettmann Newsphotos.

816 Arthur Ricker/Black Star. **819** Paul Schutzer, Time, Inc. **821** U.S. Air Force Photo. **823** Fred Ward/Black Star. **824** Arthur Ricker/Black Star. **826** NASA. **828** John Launois/Black Star. **829** Neal Boenzi/The New York Times. **833** Claus Meyer/Black Star. **836** AFL-CIO. **841** UPI/Bettmann Newsphotos. **844** Dick Swanson, Time-Life Picture Agency. **847** Mike Nauney/Black Star.

850 UPI/Bettmann Newsphotos. **853** UPI/Bettmann Newsphotos. **854** SYGMA. **855** Kent State University News Service. **857** Burt Ginn/Magnum Photos. **860** J.P. Laffont/SYGMA. **864** Burt Ginn/Magnum Photos. **865** City of Miami. **867** (top) Arthur Seitz/SYGMA. **867** (bottom) Democratic National Committee. **869** Marc Pokempher/Black Star. **871** Charles Gatewood. **872** Rene Burri/Magnum Photos. **874** (top) Alain Dejean/SYGMA. **875** (bottom) J.L. Atlan/SYGMA. **876** City of San Antonio-Mayor's Office. **876** Andrew Sackes/Black Star. **881** Jimmy Carter Museum and Library. **882** Jimmy Carter Museum and Library. **883** (bottom) Philippe Ledre/SYGMA. **883** (top) Arnold Zann/Black Star. **885** Pokempner/.Black Star.

888 Peter Turnley/Black Star. **891** Bill Fitzpatrick/The White House. **892** UPI/Bettmann Newsphotos. **894** Marc Pokempner/Black Star. **896** AP/Wide World Photos. **897** Paul Conklin/Montmeyer Press. **898** Franklin/SYGMA. **899** Steve Northup/Black Star. **902** Department of Defense. **903** Mary Anne Fackelman-Miner/The White House. **904** Rick Friedman/Black Star. **905** AP/Wide World Photos. **907** UPI/Bettmann Newsphotos. **908** (top) Nancy Plerce/Black Star. **908** (bottom) Courtesy Old Time Gospel Hour, Lynchburg, VA. **909** NASA. **910** AP/Wide World Photos. **911** Courtesy of Sperry Corporation. **918** Dennis Brack/Black Star. **919** Bill Fitzpatrick/The White House.

922 Bettmann. **925** Dennis Brack/Black Star. **927** Christopher Morris/Black Star. **931** Stephane Compoint/Sygma. **939** Mark Reinstein/Uniphoto. **940** Evan Agostini/Gamma Liaison. **948** Robert F. Kusel/Sygma. **951** Paul de Maria/Sygma. **955** Steve Grayson/Gamma Liaison.

INDEX

994